Development Economics

Development Economics

Debraj Ray

PRINCETON UNIVERSITY PRESS
PRINCETON, NEW JERSEY

Copyright © 1998 by Princeton University Press
Published by Princeton University Press, 41 William Street, Princeton, New Jersey 08540
In the United Kingdom: Princeton University Press, Chichester, West Sussex

Library of Congress Cataloging-in-Publication Data
Ray, Debraj.
    Development economics / Debraj Ray.
        p.   cm.
    Includes bibliographical references and index.
    ISBN 0-691-01706-9 (cl : alk. paper)
    1. Development economics. I. Title.
  HD75.R39   1998
  338.9--dc21   97-33459

This book has been composed in Palatino

Princeton University Press books are printed on acid-free paper and meet the guidelines for permanence and durability of the Committee on Production Guidelines for Book Longevity of the Council on Library Resources

http://pup.princeton.edu

Printed in the United States of America

10 9

ISBN-13: 978-0-691-01706-8 (cloth)

For my parents, Radha and Kalyan

Contents

Preface   **xv**

Chapter 1: Introduction   **3**

Chapter 2: Economic Development: Overview   **7**

2.1. Introduction   7
2.2. Income and growth   10
    2.2.1. Measurement issues 10 • 2.2.2. Historical experience 16
2.3. Income distribution in developing countries   21
2.4. The many faces of underdevelopment   25
    2.4.1. Human development 25 • 2.4.2. An index of human development 27 • 2.4.3. Per capita income and human development 29
2.5. Some structural features   33
    2.5.1. Demographic characteristics 34 • 2.5.2. Occupational and production structure 34 • 2.5.3. Rapid rural–urban migration 36 • 2.5.4. International trade 38
2.6. Summary   42
Exercises   44

Chapter 3: Economic Growth   **47**

3.1. Introduction   47
3.2. Modern economic growth: Basic features   48
3.3. Theories of economic growth   51
    3.3.1. The Harrod–Domar model 51 • 3.3.2. Beyond Harrod–Domar: Other considerations 58 • 3.3.3. The Solow model 64
3.4. Technical progress   71
3.5. Convergence?   74
    3.5.1. Introduction 74 • 3.5.2. Unconditional convergence 74 • 3.5.3. Unconditional convergence: Evidence or lack thereof 75 • 3.5.4. Unconditional convergence: A summary 80 • 3.5.5. Conditional convergence 82 • 3.5.6. Reexamining the data 84
3.6. Summary   88

Appendix   90
3.A.1. The Harrod–Domar equations 90 • 3.A.2. Production functions
and per capita magnitudes 91
Exercises   94

Chapter 4: The New Growth Theories   99

4.1. Introduction   99
4.2. Human capital and growth   100
4.3. Another look at conditional convergence   105
4.4. Technical progress again   107
4.4.1. Introduction 107 • 4.4.2. Technological progress and human
decisions 108 • 4.4.3. A model of deliberate technical progress 109 •
4.4.4. Externalities, technical progress, and growth 112 • 4.4.5. Total
factor productivity 117
4.5. Total factor productivity and the East Asian miracle   119
4.6. Summary   123
Appendix: Human capital and growth   125
Exercises   126

Chapter 5: History, Expectations, and Development   131

5.1. Introduction   131
5.2. Complementarities   132
5.2.1. Introduction: QWERTY 132 • 5.2.2. Coordination failure 136 •
5.2.3. Linkages and policy 138 • 5.2.4. History versus expectations 143
5.3. Increasing returns   147
5.3.1. Introduction 147 • 5.3.2. Increasing returns and entry into
markets 148 • 5.3.3. Increasing returns and market size: Interaction 150
5.4. Competition, multiplicity, and international trade   152
5.5. Other roles for history   155
5.5.1. Social norms 155 • 5.5.2. The status quo 156
5.6. Summary   159
Exercises   161

Chapter 6: Economic Inequality   169

6.1. Introduction   169
6.2. What is economic inequality?   170
6.2.1. The context 170 • 6.2.2. Economic inequality: Preliminary
observations 171
6.3. Measuring economic inequality   173
6.3.1. Introduction 173 • 6.3.2. Four criteria for inequality
measurement 174 • 6.3.3. The Lorenz curve 178 • 6.3.4. Complete
measures of inequality 184

6.4. Summary   192
Exercises   193

Chapter 7: Inequality and Development: Interconnections   197

7.1. Introduction   197
7.2. Inequality, income, and growth   199
7.2.1. The inverted-U hypothesis 199 • 7.2.2. Testing the inverted-U hypothesis 201 • 7.2.3. Income and inequality: Uneven and compensatory changes 209 • 7.2.4. Inequality, savings, income, and growth 211 • 7.2.5. Inequality, political redistribution, and growth 218 • 7.2.6. Inequality and growth: Evidence 220 • 7.2.7. Inequality and demand composition 223 • 7.2.8. Inequality, capital markets, and development 226 • 7.2.9. Inequality and development: Human capital 237
7.3. Summary   238
Appendix: Multiple steady states with imperfect capital markets   241
Exercises   244

Chapter 8: Poverty and Undernutrition   249

8.1. Introduction   249
8.2. Poverty: First principles   250
8.2.1. Conceptual issues 250 • 8.2.2. Poverty measures 253
8.3. Poverty: Empirical observations   256
8.3.1. Demographic features 257 • 8.3.2. Rural and urban poverty 259 • 8.3.3. Assets 259 • 8.3.4. Nutrition 261
8.4. The functional impact of poverty   267
8.4.1. Poverty, credit, and insurance 268 • 8.4.2. Poverty, nutrition, and labor markets 272 • 8.4.3. Poverty and the household 279
8.5. Summary   288
Appendix: More on poverty measures   290
Exercises   292

Chapter 9: Population Growth and Economic Development   295

9.1. Introduction   295
9.2. Population: Some basic concepts   297
9.2.1. Birth and death rates 297 • 9.2.2. Age distributions 300
9.3. From economic development to population growth   302
9.3.1. The demographic transition 302 • 9.3.2. Historical trends in developed and developing countries 303 • 9.3.3. The adjustment of birth rates 307 • 9.3.4. Is fertility too high? 318

9.4. From population growth to economic development 326
9.4.1. Some negative effects 326 • 9.4.2. Some positive effects 332
9.5. Summary 338
Exercises 340

Chapter 10: Rural and Urban 345

10.1. Overview 345
10.1.1. The structural viewpoint 345 • 10.1.2. Formal and informal urban sectors 346 • 10.1.3. Agriculture 348 • 10.1.4. The ICRISAT villages 349
10.2. Rural–urban interaction 353
10.2.1. Two fundamental resource flows 353 • 10.2.2. The Lewis model 353
10.3. Rural–urban migration 372
10.3.1. Introduction 372 • 10.3.2. The basic model 373 • 10.3.3. Floors on formal wages and the Harris–Todaro equilibrium 374 • 10.3.4. Government policy 379 • 10.3.5. Comments and extensions 386
10.4. Summary 395
Exercises 398

Chapter 11: Markets in Agriculture: An Introduction 403

11.1. Introduction 403
11.2. Some examples 404
11.3. Land, labor, capital, and credit 409
11.3.1. Land and labor 409 • 11.3.2. Capital and credit 412

Chapter 12: Land 415

12.1. Introduction 415
12.2. Ownership and tenancy 416
12.3. Land rental contracts 420
12.3.1. Contractual forms 420 • 12.3.2. Contracts and incentives 423 • 12.3.3. Risk, tenancy, and sharecropping 431 • 12.3.4. Forms of tenancy: Other considerations 436 • 12.3.5. Land contracts, eviction, and use rights 441
12.4. Land ownership 445
12.4.1. A brief history of land inequality 445 • 12.4.2. Land size and productivity: Concepts 446 • 12.4.3. Land size and productivity: Empirical evidence 453 • 12.4.4. Land sales 456 • 12.4.5. Land reform 457
12.5. Summary 462

Appendix 1: Principal–agent theory and applications   463
12.A.1. Risk, moral hazard, and the agency problem 463 •
12.A.2. Tenancy contracts revisited 466
Appendix 2: Screening and sharecropping   474
Exercises   478

Chapter 13: Labor   483

13.1. Introduction   483
13.2. Labor categories   484
13.3. A familiar model   486
13.4. Poverty, nutrition, and labor markets   489
13.4.1. The basic model 489 • 13.4.2. Nutrition, time, and casual labor
markets 499 • 13.4.3. A model of nutritional status 500
13.5. Permanent labor markets   504
13.5.1. Types of permanent labor 504 • 13.5.2. Why study permanent
labor? 505 • 13.5.3. Permanent labor: Nonmonitored tasks 507 •
13.5.4. Permanent labor: Casual tasks 515
13.6. Summary   522
Exercises   524

Chapter 14: Credit   529

14.1. Introduction   529
14.1.1. The limits to credit and insurance 529 • 14.1.2. Sources of
demand for credit 531
14.2. Rural credit markets   532
14.2.1. Who provides rural credit? 532 • 14.2.2. Some characteristics
of rural credit markets 540
14.3. Theories of informal credit markets   543
14.3.1. Lender's monopoly 543 • 14.3.2. The lender's risk
hypothesis 544 • 14.3.3. Default and fixed-capital loans 545 •
14.3.4. Default and collateral 546 • 14.3.5. Default and credit
rationing 548 • 14.3.6. Informational asymmetries and credit
rationing 553 • 14.3.7. Default and enforcement 555
14.4. Interlinked transactions   561
14.4.1. Hidden interest 563 • 14.4.2. Interlinkages and
information 564 • 14.4.3. Interlinkages and enforcement 564 •
14.4.4. Interlinkages and creation of efficient surplus 565
14.5. Alternative credit policies   572
14.5.1. Vertical formal–informal links 573 • 14.5.2. Microfinance 578
14.6. Summary   584
Exercises   586

Chapter 15: Insurance 591

15.1. Basic concepts   591
15.2. The perfect insurance model   596
    15.2.1. Theory 596 • 15.2.2. Testing the theory 597
15.3. Limits to insurance: Information   600
    15.3.1. Limited information about the final outcome 601 •
    15.3.2. Limited information about what led to the outcome 602
15.4. Limits to insurance: Enforcement   605
    15.4.1. Enforcement-based limits to perfect insurance 606 •
    15.4.2. Enforcement and imperfect insurance 608
15.5. Summary   615
Exercises   617

Chapter 16: International Trade 621

16.1. World trading patterns   621
16.2. Comparative advantage   627
16.3. Sources of comparative advantage   630
    16.3.1. Technology 630 • 16.3.2. Factor endowments 631 •
    16.3.3. Preferences 636 • 16.3.4. Economies of scale 638
16.4. Summary   643
Exercises   644

Chapter 17: Trade Policy 647

17.1. Gains from trade?   647
    17.1.1. Overall gains and distributive effects 647 • 17.1.2. Overall
    losses from trade? 650
17.2. Trade policy: Import substitution   656
    17.2.1. Basic concepts 657 • 17.2.2. More detail 660
17.3. Export promotion   676
    17.3.1. Basic concepts 677 • 17.3.2. Effect on the exchange rate 678 •
    17.3.3. The instruments of export promotion: More detail 679
17.4. The move away from import substitution   684
    17.4.1. Introduction 684 • 17.4.2. The eighties crisis   685 •
    17.4.3. Structural adjustment 690
17.5. Summary   699
Appendix: The International Monetary Fund and the World
    Bank   701
Exercises   705

Chapter 18: Multilateral Approaches to Trade Policy   711

18.1. Introduction   711
18.2. Restricted trade   714
     18.2.1. Second-best arguments for protection 714 • 18.2.2. Protectionist tendencies 715 • 18.2.3. Explaining protectionist tendencies 717
18.3. Issues in trade liberalization   725
     18.3.1. Introduction 725 • 18.3.2. Regional agreements: Basic theory 727 • 18.3.3. Regional agreements among dissimilar countries 730 • 18.3.4. Regional agreements among similar countries 735 • 18.3.5. Multilateralism and regionalism 746
18.4. Summary   753
Exercises   755

Appendix 1: Elementary Game Theory   757

A1.1. Introduction   757
A1.2. Basic concepts   757
A1.3. Nash equilibrium   759
A1.4. Games over time   767

Appendix 2: Elementary Statistical Methods   777

A2.1. Introduction   777
A2.2. Summary statistics   778
A2.3. Regression   783

References   805

Author Index   829

Subject Index   835

Preface

This book provides an introduction to *development economics*, a subject that studies the economic transformation of developing countries. My objective is to make a large literature accessible, in a unified way, to a student or interested individual who has some training in basic economic theory. It is only fair to say that I am not fully satisfied with the final product: in attempting to provide a well-structured treatment of the subject, I have had to sacrifice comprehensiveness. Nevertheless, I do believe that the book goes quite far in attaining the original objective, within the limitations created by an enormous and unwieldy literature and the constraints imposed by my own knowledge and understanding.

The primary target for this book is the senior undergraduate or masters level student with training in introductory or intermediate economic theory. I also recommend this book as background or supplementary reading for a doctoral course in development economics, along with the original articles on the subject.

Mathematical requirements are kept to a minimum, although some degree of mathematical maturity will assist understanding of the material. In particular, I have eschewed the use of calculus altogether and have attempted to present theoretical material through verbal argument, diagrams, and occasionally elementary algebra. Because the book makes some use of game-theoretic and statistical concepts, I have included two introductory appendixes on these subjects. With these appendixes in place, the book is self-contained except for occasional demands on the reader's knowledge of introductory economic theory.

I begin with an overview of developing countries (Chapter 2). I discuss major trends in per capita income, inequality, poverty, and population, and take a first look at the important structural characteristics of development. Chapters 3–5 take up the study of economic growth from several aspects.

Chapters 6–8 shift the focus to an analysis of *unevenness* in development: the possibility that the benefits of growth may not accrue equally to all. In turn, these inequalities may influence aggregate trends. This interaction is studied from many angles. Chapter 9 extends this discussion to population growth, where the relationship between demography and economics is explored in some detail.

Chapter 10 studies unevenness from the viewpoint of structural transformation: the fact that development typically involves the ongoing transfer of resources from one sector (typically agriculture) to another (typically industry and services). This chapter motivates a careful study of the agricultural sector, where a significant fraction of the citizens of developing countries, particularly the poor, live and work.

Chapters 11–15 study informal markets in detail, with particular emphasis on the rural sector. We analyze the land, labor, credit and insurance markets.

Chapter 16 introduces the study of trade and development. Chapter 17 motivates and studies the instruments of trade policy from the point of view of a single country. Finally, Chapter 18 studies multilateral and regional policies in trade.

For programs that offer a single semester course in economic development, two options are available: (1) if international economic issues can be relegated to a separate course, cover all the material up to the end of Chapter 15 (this will require some skimming of chapters, such as Chapters 4–6 and 11–15); (2) if it is desirable to cover international issues in the same course, omit much or most of the material in Chapters 11–15. A year-long course should be able to adequately cover the book, but some supplementary material may be required for international economics, as well as financial issues in development, such as inflation and monetary policy.

This book could not have been written without my students and the many classes I have taught in development economics over the years: I thank students at Boston University, at the Indian Statistical Institute, at the People's University of China in Beijing, at Stanford, and at Harvard. I would also like to thank the many people who have read and commented on earlier drafts of this book and have used them in courses they have taught, among them Jean-Marie Baland, Abhijit Banerjee, V. Bhaskar, Gautam Bose, Ira Gang, James Foster, Patrick Francois, Gabriel Fuentes, Bishnupriya Gupta, Ashok Kotwal, Dilip Mookherjee, Jonathan Morduch, James Robinson, Ann Velenchik, Bruce Wydick, and Frederic Zimmerman.

Several people have made contributions to this text. Chief among them is Parikshit Ghosh, my intrepid and thoroughly uncontrollable research assistant, whose contributions to this book are too numerous to mention. I would also like to thank Eli Berman, Gary Fields, Hsueh-Ling Huynh, Chiente Hsu, Luis-Felipe López-Calva, Anandi Mani, Ghazala Mansuri, Jonathan Morduch, and Hiranya Mukhopadhyay for input at various stages.

Much of this book was written while I was Director of the Institute for Economic Development at Boston University. I thank Margaret Chapman, Administrative Assistant to the Institute, for covering for my many administrative lapses during this period. I thank the Instituto de Análisis Económico (CSIC) in Barcelona, where this book was completed, and the Ministerio de

Educación, Government of Spain for financial support during my stay. I am very grateful to Peter Dougherty, my publisher at Princeton University Press, for his help and encouragement.

I would like to record my deep appreciation to a (smaller) set of people who have shaped the way I think about economics: Kenneth Arrow, Doug Bernheim, Bhaskar Dutta, Joan Esteban, Mukul Majumdar, Tapan Mitra, Dilip Mookherjee, Kunal Sengupta, Amartya Sen, and Rajiv Vohra.

I thank Monica Das Gupta for innumerable discussions, and words of advice and encouragement.

Finally, I owe gratitude to Angela Bhaya Soares who always wanted me to write a magnum opus but will have to be content with what she gets, to Bissera Antikarova and Farahanaaz Dastur for seeing me safely through bad times, to Nilita Vachani for creating unforeseen but happy delays, and to Jackie Bhaya for getting me started on it all.

Debraj Ray
Boston University
September 1997

Development Economics

Chapter 1

Introduction

I invite you to study what is surely the most important and perhaps the most complex of all economic issues: the economic transformation of those countries known as the developing world. A definition of "developing countries" is problematic and, after a point, irrelevant.[1] The *World Development Report* (World Bank [1996]) employs a threshold of $9,000 per capita to distinguish between what it calls high-income countries and low- and middle-income countries: according to this classification, well over 4.5 billion of the 5.6 billion people in the world today live in the developing world of "low- and middle-income countries." They earn, on average, around $1,000 per capita, a figure that is worth contrasting with the yearly earnings of the average North American or Japanese resident, which are well above $25,000. Despite the many caveats and qualifications that we later add to these numbers, the ubiquitous fact of these astonishing disparities remains.

There is economic inequality throughout the world, but much of that is, we hope, changing. This book puts together a way of thinking about both the disparities and the changes.

There are two strands of thought that run through this text. First, I move away from (although do not entirely abandon) a long-held view that the problems of all developing countries can be understood best with reference to the international environment of which they are a part.[2] According to this view, the problems of underdevelopment must first and foremost be seen in a global context. There is much that is valid in this viewpoint, but I wish to emphasize equally fundamental issues that are *internal* to the structure of developing countries. Although a sizeable section of this book addresses international aspects of development, the teacher or reader who wishes to

---

[1] The *Third World*, a group of low-income countries united by common economic characteristics and often a common history of colonialism, is just as much a political as an economic concept. Narrower economic classifications are employed by several international organizations such as the World Bank. A composite index that goes beyond per capita income is described in *Human Development Report* (United Nations Development Programme [1995]). There is substantial agreement across all these classifications.

[2] This view includes not only the notion that developing countries are somehow hindered by their exposure to the developed world, epitomized in the teachings of *dependencia* theorists, but also more mainstream concerns regarding the central role of international organizations and foreign assistance.

concentrate *exclusively* on these aspects will not find a comprehensive treatment here.

The second strand is methodological: as far as possible, I take a unified approach to the problems of development and emphasize a recent and growing literature that takes a level-headed approach to market failure and the potential for government intervention. It is not that markets are intrinsically bad or intrinsically good: the point is to understand the conditions under which they fail or function at an inefficient level and to determine if appropriate policies grounded in an understanding of these conditions can fix such inefficiencies. These conditions, I argue, can be understood best by a serious appreciation of subjects that are at the forefront of economic theory but need to permeate more thoroughly into introductory textbooks: theories of incomplete information, of incentives, and of strategic behavior. Few people would disagree that these considerations lie at the heart of many observed phenomena. However, my goal is to promote a student's understanding of such issues as a commonplace model, not as a set of exceptions to the usual textbook paradigm of perfect competition and full information.

Because I take these two strands to heart, my book differs from other textbooks on development in a number of respects. Most of these differences stem from my approach to exposition and choice of subject matter. Although I do not neglect the historical development of a line of research or inquiry, I bring to bear a completely modern analytical perspective on the subject. Here are some instances of what I mean.

(1) The story of economic underdevelopment is, in many ways, a story of how informal, imaginative institutions replace the formal constructs we are accustomed to in industrialized economies. The landlord lends to his tenant farmer, accepting labor as collateral, but a formal credit market is missing. Villagers insure each other against idiosyncratic shocks using their greater information and their ability to impose social sanctions, but a formal insurance market is missing. Institutions as diverse as tied labor, credit cooperatives, and extended families can be seen as responses to market failure of some sort, precipitated in most cases by missing information or by the inability of the legal system to swiftly and efficiently enforce contracts. This common thread in our understanding is emphasized and reemphasized throughout the book.

(2) The absence or underfunctioning of markets gives rise to two other features. One is the creation of widespread externalities. Proper classification of these externalities provides much insight into a variety of economic phenomena, which appear unconnected at first, but which (in this sense) are just the common expression of a small variety of external effects. So it is that simple concepts from game theory, such as the Prisoners' Dilemma or the coordination game, yield insights into a diverse class of development-related problems. Again, the common features of the various problems yield

a mental classification system—a way of seeing that different phenomena stem from a unified source.

(3) A fundamental implication of missing markets is that *inequality* in the distribution of income or wealth plays a central role in many development problems. It isn't that inequality has not received attention in treatises on development; it certainly has. However, what has recently begun to receive systematic analytical treatment is the *functional* role of inequality: the possibility that inequality, quite apart from being of interest in its own right, has implications for *other* yardsticks of economic performance such as the level of per capita income and its rate of growth. The emphasis on the functional role of inequality runs through the book.

(4) It is necessary to try to integrate, in an intuitive and not very abstract way, recent theoretical and empirical literature with the more standard material. This isn't done to be fashionable. I do this because I believe that much of this new work has new things to teach us. Some important models of economic growth, of income distribution and development, of coordination failures, or of incomplete information are theories that have been developed over the last decade. Work on these models continues apace. Although some of the techniques are inaccessible to a student with little formal training, I do believe that all the ideas in this literature that are worth teaching (and there are many) can be taught in an elementary way. In this sense this book coincides with existing texts on the subject: the use of mathematics is kept to a minimum (there is no calculus except in an occasional footnote).

Partly because other development texts have been around for a good while, and perhaps in part because of a different approach, this text departs significantly from existing development texts in the points cited in the preceding text and indeed in its overall methodological approach.

Combining the complementary notions of incomplete information, a weak legal structure (so far as implementation goes), and the resulting strategic and economic considerations that emerge, we begin to have some idea of what it is that makes developing countries somehow "different." Economic theorists never tire of needling their friends with questions in this regard. Why is the study of developing countries a separate subject? Why can't we just break it up into separate special cases of labor economics, international trade, money, and finance, and so on? Certainly, they have a point, but that's only one way to cut the cake. Another way to do so is to recognize that developing countries, in their different spheres of activity, display again and again these common failures of information and legal structures, and therefore generate common incentive and strategic issues that might benefit from separate, concentrated scrutiny.

This approach also serves, I feel, as an answer to a different kind of objection: that developing countries are all unique and very different, and generalizations of any kind are misleading or, at best, dangerous. Although this sort of viewpoint can be applied recursively as well *within* countries, regions, districts and villages until it becomes absurd, there is some truth to it. At the same time, while differences may be of great interest to the specialized researcher, emphasizing what's common may be the best way to get the material across to a student. Therefore I choose to highlight what's common, while trying not to lose sight of idiosyncrasies, of which there are many.

A final bias is that, in some basic sense, the book is on the *theory* of economic development. However, there is no theory without data, and the book is full of empirical studies. At the same time, I am uninterested in filling up page after page with tables of numbers unless these tables speak to the student in some informative way. So it is with case studies, of which there will be a number in the text.[3] I try to choose empirical illustrations and case studies throughout to illustrate a viewpoint on the development process, and not necessarily for their own sake.

I started off writing a textbook for undergraduates, for the course that I have loved the most in my fourteen years of teaching. I see that what emerged is a textbook, no doubt, but in the process something of myself seems to have entered into it. I see now that the true originality of this book is not so much the construction of new theory or a contribution to our empirical knowledge, but a way of thinking about development and a way of communicating those thoughts to those who are young, intelligent, caring, and impressionable. If a more hard-bitten scholar learns something as a by-product, that would be very welcome indeed.

My commitment as the author is the following: armed with some minimal background in economic theory and statistics, and a healthy dose of curiosity, sympathy, and interest, if you study this book carefully, you will come away with a provocative and interesting introduction to development economics as it is practiced today. Put another way, although this book offers (as all honest books in the social sciences do) few unambiguous answers, it will teach you how to ask the right questions.

---

[3] Case studies, which are referred to as boxes, will be set off from the text by horizontal rules.

Chapter 2

Economic Development: Overview

By the problem of economic development I mean simply the problem of accounting for the observed pattern, across countries and across time, in levels and rates of growth of per capita income. This may seem too narrow a definition, and perhaps it is, but thinking about income patterns will necessarily involve us in thinking about many other aspects of societies too, so I would suggest that we withhold judgement on the scope of this definition until we have a clearer idea of where it leads us.

—R. E. Lucas [1988]

[W]e should never lose sight of the ultimate purpose of the exercise, to treat men and women as ends, to improve the human condition, to enlarge people's choices. . . . [A] unity of interests would exist if there were rigid links between economic production (as measured by income per head) and human development (reflected by human indicators such as life expectancy or literacy, or achievements such as self-respect, not easily measured). But these two sets of indicators are not very closely related.

—P. P. Streeten [1994]

2.1. Introduction

Economic development is the primary objective of the majority of the world's nations. This truth is accepted almost without controversy. To raise the income, well-being, and economic capabilities of peoples everywhere is easily the most crucial social task facing us today. Every year, aid is disbursed, investments are undertaken, policies are framed, and elaborate plans are hatched so as to achieve this goal, or at least to step closer to it. How do we identify and keep track of the results of these efforts? What characteristics do we use to evaluate the degree of "development" a country has undergone or how "developed" or "underdeveloped" a country is at any point in time? In short, how do we measure development?

The issue is not easy to resolve. We all have intuitive notions of "development." When we speak of a developed society, we picture in our minds a society in which people are well fed and well clothed, possess access to a variety of commodities, have the luxury of some leisure and entertainment, and live in a healthy environment. We think of a society free of violent discrimination, with tolerable levels of equality, where the sick receive proper medical care and people do not have to sleep on the sidewalks. In short, most of us would insist that a *minimal* requirement for a "developed" nation is that the *physical* quality of life be high, and be so uniformly, rather than being restricted to an incongruously affluent minority.

Of course, the notion of a good society goes further. We might stress political rights and freedoms, intellectual and cultural development, stability of the family, a low crime rate, and so on. However, a high and equally accessible level of *material* well-being is probably a prerequisite for most other kinds of advancement, quite apart from being a worthy goal in itself.[1] Economists and policy makers therefore do well (and have enough to do!) by concentrating on this aspect alone.

It is, of course, tempting to suggest that the state of material well-being of a nation is captured quite accurately in its per capita gross national product (GNP): the per-head value of final goods and services produced by the people of a country over a given year. Indeed, since economic development at the national level was adopted as a conscious goal,[2] there have been long phases during which development performance was judged exclusively by the yardstick of per capita gross domestic product (GDP) growth. In the last few decades, this practice increasingly has come under fire from various quarters. The debate goes on, as the quotations at the beginning of this chapter suggest.

We must be careful here. No one in their right mind would ever suggest that economic development be identified, in a *definitional* sense, with the level or growth of per capita income. It is perhaps universally accepted that development is not just about income, although income (economic wealth, more generally) has a great deal to do with it. For instance, we noted previously that economic advancement should not be restricted to a small minority. This means, in particular, that development is also the removal of poverty and undernutrition: it is an increase in life expectancy; it is access to sanitation, clean drinking water, and health services; it is the reduction of infant mortality; it is increased access to knowledge and schooling, and lit-

---

[1] This is not to suggest at all that it is *sufficient* for every kind of social advancement.

[2] For most poor countries, this starting point was the period immediately following World War II, when many such countries, previously under colonial rule, gained independence and formed national governments.

eracy in particular. There is an entire multitude of yardsticks. Paul Streeten's thoughts, summarized in the quotation at the beginning of this chapter, capture this "multidimensionality" very well.

Far more intriguing is the sharp focus of Robert Lucas' words (see quotation). At first they appear narrow, perhaps even missing the point, whereas the more holistic scenario sketched in the foregoing paragraphs seems pretty much the way to go. In thinking this we would be wrong. Neither Lucas nor any intelligent person believes that per capita income *is* development. What's hidden in these words is actually an approach, not a definition. It is really a belief about the world, which is that *the universal features of economic development—health, life expectancy, literacy, and so on—follow in some natural way from the growth of per capita GNP*, perhaps with the passage of time. Implicit here is a belief in the power of aggregate economic forces to positively affect every other socioeconomic outcome that we want to associate with "development." This outlook may be contrasted with the view that a correlation between GNP and other desired features is not automatic, and that in many cases such connections may not be present at all. According to this view, per capita GNP fails as an adequate overall measure and must be supplemented by other indicators directly.

The debate implicit in the two quotations is not about what development *means*, on which there is possibly widespread agreement. It is really about a view of the world—about the possibility of finding a smaller set of variables that correlates well with the multifaceted process of development. Note well that, in a way, saying too much is saying too little. It may be that per capita income does not capture all aspects of development, but a weighty assertion that no small set of variables ever captures the complex nature of the development process and that there are always other considerations is not very helpful. In this sense, the view that economic development is ultimately fueled by per capita income may be taking things too far, but at least it has the virtue of attempting to reduce a larger set of issues to a smaller set, through the use of economic theory.

This book implicitly contains a reduction as well, although not all the way to per capita income alone. In part, sheer considerations of space demand such a reduction. Moreover, we have to begin *somewhere*, so we concentrate implicitly on understanding two sets of connections throughout this book. One is how average *levels* of economic attainment influence development. To be sure, this must include an analysis of the forces that, in turn, cause average levels (such as per capita GNP) to grow. The other connection is how the *distribution* of economic attainment, across the citizens of a nation or a region and across the nations of the world, influences development. The task of understanding these two broad interrelationships takes us on a long journey. In some chapters the relationships may be hidden in the details, but they are always there: levels and distribution as twin beacons to guide our inquiry.[3]

This is not to say that the basic features of development will be ignored. Studying them is our primary goal, but our approach to them lies through the two routes described in the previous paragraph.

We begin, then, with a summary of the historical experience of developing countries over the past few decades. We pay attention to per capita income, then to income distribution, and then consider other indicators of development. We then try to understand how these manifold characteristics of development correlate with the smaller set of features: income levels and distribution. This chapter ends with an overview of the structural characteristics of developing countries. We describe the occupational distribution of the population, the share of different sectors (such as agriculture and services) in national income, the composition of imports and exports, and so on.

2.2. Income and growth

2.2.1. Measurement issues

Low per capita incomes are an important feature of economic underdevelopment—perhaps *the* most important feature—and there is little doubt that the distribution of income across the world's nations is extraordinarily skewed. Per capita incomes are, of course, expressed in takas, reales, yuan, and in the many other world currencies. To facilitate comparison, each country's income (in local currency) is converted into a common currency (typically U.S. dollars) and divided by that country's population to arrive at a measure of per capita income. This conversion scheme is called the exchange rate method, because it uses the rates of exchange between the local and the common currencies to express incomes in a common unit. The *World Development Report* (see, e.g., World Bank [1996]) contains such estimates of GNP per capita by country. By this yardstick, the world produced $24 trillion of output in 1993. About 20% of this came from low- and middle-income developing countries—a pittance when we see that these countries housed 85% of the world's population at that time. Switzerland, the world's richest country under this system of measurement, enjoyed a per capita income close to 400 times that of Tanzania, the world's poorest.

---

[3] Even the double emphasis on levels and distribution might not be enough. For instance, the *Human Development Report* (United Nations Development Programme [1995]) informs us that "the purpose of development is to enlarge all human choices, not just income. The concept of human development is much broader than the conventional theories of economic development." More specifically, Sen [1983] writes: "Supplementing data on GNP per capita by income distributional information is quite inadequate to meet the challenge of development analysis." There is much truth in these warnings, which are to be put side by side with Streeten and certainly contrasted with Lucas, but I hope to convince you that an understanding of our "narrower" issues will take us quite far.

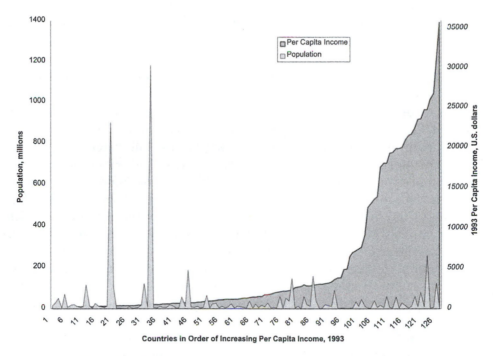

Figure 2.1. Per capita income and population for selected countries.

Figure 2.1 displays per capita income figures for selected countries. The figure contrasts per capita incomes in different countries with the populations of these countries. No comment is necessary.

The disparities are enormous, and no amount of fine-tuning in measurement methods can get rid of the stark inequalities that we live with. Nevertheless, both for a better understanding of the *degree* of international variation that we are talking about and for the sake of more reliable analysis of these figures, it is best to recognize at the outset that these measures provide biased estimates of what is actually out there.

(1) For one thing, underreporting of income is not uncommon in developing countries. Because tax collection systems are not as efficient as those prevailing in the industrialized market economies, there is a greater incentive to underreport income or output for tax purposes. The national accounts may not be comprehensive as well.[4]

In addition, the proportion of income that is actually generated for self-consumption is relatively high in developing countries. As we shall soon see, the proportion of the population living in the rural sector in developing countries is large. Many of these individuals are subsistence farmers who

_____

[4] For instance, in the case of India, Acharya et al. [1985] estimated that 18–21% of total income in 1980–81 went unrecorded in the national accounts (see also Gupta and Mehta [1981]). For related work on the "black" or "parallel" economy, see Chopra [1982] and Gupta and Gupta [1982].

grow crops that they themselves consume. Such outputs may not be reported adequately.

Although we can make educated guesses about the degree of underestimation involved, there is really very little that we can do about correcting for this problem.

(2) A far more serious issue comes from the fact that *prices* for many goods in all countries are not appropriately reflected in exchange rates. This is only natural for goods and services that are not internationally traded. Exchange rates are just prices, and the levels of these prices depends *only* on commodities (including capital) that cross international borders. The prices of nontraded goods, such as infrastructure and many services, do not affect exchange rates. What is interesting is that there is a systematic way in which these nontraded prices are related to the level of development. Because poor countries are poor, you would expect them to have relatively low prices for nontraded goods: their lower real incomes do not suffice to pull these prices up to international levels. However, this same logic suggests that a conversion of all incomes to U.S. dollars using exchange rates *underestimates* the real incomes of poorer countries. This can be corrected to some extent, and indeed in some data sets it has been. The most widely used of these is the Heston–Summers data set (see box). Recently, the World Bank started to publish income data in this revised format.

Purchasing Power Parity Measurement of Income:
The International Comparison Program

According to GDP estimates calculated on an exchange-rate basis, Asia's weight in world output fell from 7.9% in 1985 to 7.2% in 1990—and yet Asia was by far the fastest growing region during this period[5]. This same period also witnessed a sharp decline in some Asian countries' exchange rates against the dollar. Now does that tell us something about the shortcomings of GDP exchange-rate estimates? In an attempt to correct for such anomalies, two economists at the University of Pennsylvania, Alan Heston and Robert Summers, created a new data set called the Penn World Tables (PWT; also called the Heston–Summers data set). It consists of a set of national accounts for a very large set of countries dating from 1950 and its unique feature is that its entries are denominated in a set of "international" prices in a common currency. Hence, international comparisons of GDP can be made both between countries and over time.

Actually, the trouble with market exchange rates for GDP calculations is not so much that they fluctuate, but that they do not fluctuate around the "right" average price, if "right" is to be measured by purchasing power. Even if exchange rates equalize the prices of internationally traded goods over time, substantial differences remain

---

[5] See *The Economist*, May 15, 1993.

in the prices of nontraded goods and services such as housing and domestic transportation. These prices need to be corrected for as well. The most ambitious effort, to date, toward estimating the "correct" international prices is the United Nations International Comparison Program (ICP), which carried out detailed price comparisons for a set of benchmark countries every fifth year between 1970 and 1985. Apart from domestic price data, the procedure also involves the use of national accounts expenditure data. The PWT were constructed using the ICP data.

As a first step, the ICP gathers detailed data on prices of 400–700 items in each of a set of benchmark countries. The price of each item is then divided by its corresponding price in the United States, thus yielding a *relative* price. These items are then classified into one of 150 expenditure categories (110 consumption, 35 investment, and 5 government expenditure categories). By an averaging procedure, the average relative price for each category is obtained, which makes 150 relative prices (or "price parities") available for each country.

Next, national currency expenditure $p_{ij}q_{ij}$ (i.e., price times quantity for each item i in each benchmark country j) on each of the 150 categories is obtained from each country. This is used to estimate the quantities involved in national output. How is this done? Dividing the expenditure for each category by its relative price, that is, $(p_{ij}q_{ij})/(p_{ij}/p_{US})$ yields an estimate of the quantity in the category, valued at its corresponding U.S. price, $q_{ij}.p_{US}$. Note that it is possible to make international comparisons of output by simply using these quantities valued at U.S. prices. However, U.S. prices alone do not reflect the tastes of all countries, so we still have to construct international prices to evaluate these quantities.

For this, recall that we have 150 categorywise relative prices for each country. For each category, the international relative price is obtained by aggregating the relative price for this category over all benchmark countries, based on a method suggested by statistician R. C. Geary. The method is such that the international relative price obtained for any item is a specialized weighted average of the relative price of that item in all the countries in the set. Thus the international price for any item may differ from a country's domestic price. For instance, because food is cheaper in a rich country than in a poor country, the international price of food tends to be higher than its domestic price in a rich country. At the same time, the international price of investment is lower than in a rich country. The quantities obtained earlier from expenditure data are now valued at the international prices, which yields the value of national output at these prices. The *purchasing power parity* (PPP) for any country is the ratio of its domestic currency expenditures to the international price value of its output.

From the set of benchmark countries, PPPs for other countries are extrapolated using capital city price surveys conducted by other agencies. Once a complete set of PPPs is available, extrapolations are made for the value of GDP of the entire set of countries for other years between 1950 and 1988. For instance, RGDP (i.e., real GDP for other years, using 1985 international prices as the base year prices) is extrapolated on the basis of growth rates of different economies, and CGDP (calculated nominal GDP for other years at international prices in those years) is calculated using price indexes and current price national accounts data for those years.

Apart from GDP data, the PWT also offers data on selected countries' capital stocks and demographic statistics. In the revised GDP calculations based on PPP, Asia's

Eight Largest: 1993 $ billions, PPP Method

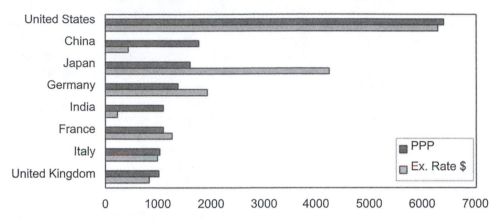

Eight Largest: 1993 $ billions, Exchange Rate Method

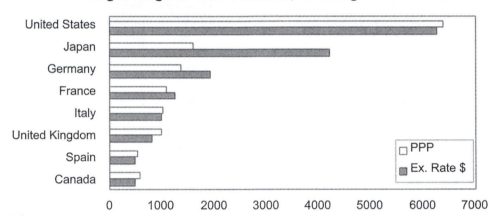

Figure 2.2. The world's eight largest economies: exchange rate and PPP calculations. Source: World Development Report (World Bank [1995]).

share in world output in 1990 jumped from 7 to 18%. China emerges as the world's third largest economy and India comes in at fifth place. The United States remains the world's largest economy.

Figure 2.2 shows how the eight largest economies change when we move from exchange rates to PPP calculations.

Although the Summers–Heston data are useful for real comparisons, remember that exchange rate-based data are the appropriate ones to use for international financial transactions and capital flows.

Briefly (see box for more details), *international prices* are constructed for an enormous basket of goods and services by averaging the prices (expressed, say, in dollars) for each such good and service over all different countries. National income for a country is then estimated by valuing its outputs at *these* international prices. In this way, what is maintained, in some average sense, is *parity* in the *purchasing power* among different countries. Thus we call such estimates PPP estimates, where PPP stands for "purchasing power parity."

PPP estimates of per capita income go some way toward reducing the astonishing disparities in the world distribution of income, but certainly not all the way. For an account of how the PPP estimates alter the distribution of world income, consult Figure 2.3.

The direction of change is quite clear and, from the foregoing discussion, only to be expected. Measured in PPP dollars, developing countries do better relative to U.S. per capita GNP, although the fractions are still small, to be sure. This situation reflects the fact that domestic prices are not captured adequately by using exchange-rate conversions, which apply correctly only to a limited set of traded goods.

(3) There are other subtle problems of measurement. GNP measurement, even when it accounts for the exchange-rate problem, uses market prices to compare apples and oranges; that is, to convert highly disparate goods into a common currency. The theoretical justification for this is that market prices

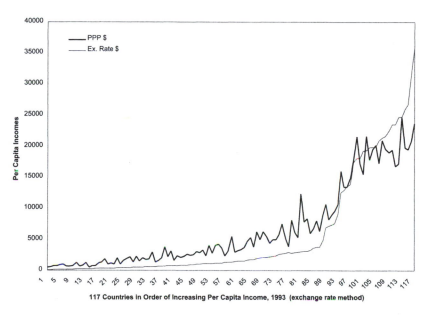

Figure 2.3. PPP versus exchange rate measures of GDP for ninety-four countries, 1993. Source: World Development Report (World Bank [1995]).

reflect people's preferences as well as relative scarcities. Therefore such prices represent the appropriate conversion scale to use. There may be several objections to this argument. Not all markets are perfectly competitive; neither are all prices fully flexible. We have monopolies, oligopolistic competition, and public sector companies[6] that sell at dictated prices. There is expenditure by the government on bureaucracy, on the military, or on space research, whose monetary value may not reflect the true value of these services to the citizens. Moreover, conventional measures of GNP ignore costs that arise from externalities—the cost of associated pollution, environmental damage, resource depletion, human suffering due to displacement caused by "development projects" such as dams and railways, and so forth. In all of these cases, prevalent prices do not capture the true marginal social value or cost of a good or a service.

All these problems can be mended, in principle, and sophisticated measures of GDP do so to a large extent. Distortions in prices can be corrected for by imputing and using appropriate "shadow prices" that capture true marginal values and costs. There is a vast literature, both theoretical and empirical, that deals with the concepts and techniques needed to calculate shadow prices for commodities. An estimated "cost of pollution" is often deducted in some of the measures of *net* GDP, at least in industrialized economies. Nevertheless, it is important to be aware of these additional problems.

With this said, let us turn to a brief account of recent historical experience.

2.2.2. Historical experience

Over the period 1960–85, the richest 5% of the world's nations averaged a per capita income that was about twenty-nine times the corresponding figure for the poorest 5%. As Parente and Prescott [1993] quite correctly observed, interstate disparities *within* the United States do not even come close to these international figures. In 1985, the richest state in the United States was Connecticut and the poorest was Mississippi, and the ratio of per capita incomes worked out at around 2!

Of course, the fact that the richest 5% of countries bear approximately the same ratio of incomes (relative to the poorest 5%) over this twenty-five year period suggests that the *entire* distribution has remained stationary. Of greatest interest, and continuing well into the nineties, is the meteoric rise of the East Asian economies: Japan, Korea, Taiwan, Singapore, Hong Kong, Thailand, Malaysia, Indonesia, and, more recently, China. Over the period 1965–90, the per capita incomes of the aforementioned eight East Asian economies

---

[6] In many countries all over the Third World, sectors that are important or require bulk investment, such as iron and steel, cement, railways, and petroleum, are often in the hands of public sector enterprises.

(excluding China) increased at an annual rate of 5.5%. Between 1980 and 1993, China's per capita income grew at an annual rate of 8.2%, which is truly phenomenal. For the entire data set of 102 countries studied by Parente and Prescott, per capita growth averaged 1.9% per year over the period 1960–85.

In contrast, much of Latin America and sub-Saharan Africa languished during the 1980s. After relatively high rates of economic expansion in the two preceding decades, growth slowed to a crawl, and in many cases there was no growth at all. Morley's [1995] study observed that in Latin America, per capita income *fell* by 11% during the 1980s, and only Chile and Colombia had a higher per capita income in 1990 than they did in 1980. It is certainly true that such figures should be treated cautiously, given the extreme problems of accurate GNP measurement in high-inflation countries, but they illustrate the situation well enough.

Similarly, much of Africa stagnated or declined during the 1980s. Countries such as Nigeria and Tanzania experienced substantial declines of per capita income, whereas countries such as Kenya and Uganda barely grew in per capita terms.

Diverse growth experiences such as these can change the face of the world in a couple of decades. One easy way to see this is to study the "doubling time" implicit in a given rate of growth; that is, the number of years it takes for income to double if it is growing at some given rate. The calculation in the footnote[7] reveals that a good approximation to the doubling time is seventy divided by the annual rate of growth expressed in percentage terms. Thus an East Asian country growing at 5% per year will *double* its per capita income every fourteen years! In contrast, a country growing at 1% per year will require seventy years. Percentage growth figures look like small numbers, but over time, they add up very fast indeed.

The diverse experiences of countries demand an explanation, but this demand is ambitious. Probably no single explanation can account for the variety of historical experience. We know that in Latin America, the so-called debt crisis (discussed more in Chapter 17) triggered enormous economic hardship. In sub-Saharan Africa, low per capita growth rates may be due, in large measure, to unstable government and consequent infrastructural breakdown, as well as to recent high rates of population increase (on this, see Chapters 3 and 9). The heady successes of East Asia are not fully understood, but a conjunction of farsighted government intervention (Chapters 17), a relatively equal domestic income distribution (Chapters 6 and 7), and a vigorous entry into international markets played an important role. As

---

[7] A dollar invested at r% per year will grow to two dollars in T years, where T solves the equation $[1+(r/100)]^T = 2$. This means that $T \ln_e[1+(r/100)] = \ln_e 2$. However, $\ln_e 2$ is approximately 0.7, whereas for small values of x, $\ln_e(1 + x)$ is approximately x. Using this in the equation gets you the result.

you may have noted from the occasional parentheses in this paragraph, we will take up these topics, and many others, in the chapters to come.

Thus it is quite possible for the world distribution of income to stay fairly constant in *relative* terms, while at the same time there is plenty of action *within* that distribution as countries climb and descend the ladder of relative economic achievement. Indeed, the few countries that we have cited as examples are no exceptions. Figure 2.4 contains the same exercise as Chart 10 in Parente and Prescott [1993]. It shows the number of countries that experienced changes in income (relative to that of the United States) of different magnitudes over the years 1960–85.

Figure 2.4 indicates two things. First, a significant fraction (well over half) of countries changed their position relative to the United States by an average of one percentage point or more *per year*, over the period 1960–85. Second, the figure also indicates that there is a rough kind of symmetry between changes upward and changes downward, which partly accounts for the fact that you don't see much movement in the world distribution taken as a whole. This observation is cause for much hope and some trepidation: the former, because it tells us that there are probably no traps to ultimate economic success, and the latter, because it seems all too easy to slip and fall in the process. Economic development is probably more like a treacherous

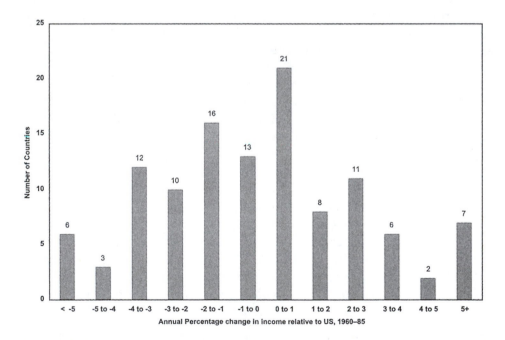

Figure 2.4. Annual percentage change in PPP income of different countries relative to U.S. levels, 1960–85. Source: Penn World Tables.

road, than a divided highway where only the privileged minority is destined to ever drive the fast lane.

This last statement must be taken with some caution. Although there appears to be no evidence that very poor countries are doomed to eternal poverty, there is some indication that low incomes are very sticky. Even though we will have much more to say about the hypothesis of ultimate convergence of all countries to a common standard of living (see Chapters 3–5), an illustration may be useful at this stage. Quah [1993] used per capita income data to construct "mobility matrices" for countries. To understand how these matrices work, let's start by converting all per capita incomes to fractions of the *world*'s per capita income. Thus, if country X has a per capita income of $1,000 and the world average is $2,000, we give country X an index of 1/2. Now let's create categories that we will put each country into. Quah used the following categories (you can certainly use others if you like): 1/4, 1/2, 1, 2, and ∞. For instance, a category with the label 2 contains all countries with indexes between 1 and 2; the category 1/4 contains all countries with indexes less than 1/4; the category ∞ contains all countries with indexes exceeding 2, and so on.

Now imagine doing this exercise for two points in time, with a view to finding out if a country transited from one category to another during this period. You will generate what we might call a *mobility matrix*. The diagram in Figure 2.5 illustrates this matrix for the twenty-three year period 1962–84, using the Summers–Heston data set. The rows and columns of the matrix are exactly the categories that we just described. Thus a cell of this matrix defines a pair of categories. What you see is a number in each of these cells.

	1/4	1/2	1	2	∞
1/4	76	12	12	0	0
1/2	52	31	10	7	0
1	9	20	46	26	0
2	0	0	24	53	24
∞	0	0	0	5	95

Figure 2.5. *The income mobility of countries, 1962–84. Source: Quah [1993].*

Look, for instance, at the entry 26 in the cell defined by the categories 1 (row) and 2 (column). This entry tells us the percentage of countries that made the transition from one category to the other over the twenty-three year period. In this example, therefore, 26% of the countries who were between half the world average and the world average in 1962 transited to being between the world average and *twice* the world average. A matrix constructed in this way gives you a fairly good sense of how much mobility there is in relative per capita GNP across nations. A matrix with very high numbers on the main diagonal, consisting of those special cells with the same row and column categories, indicates low mobility. According to such a matrix, countries that start off in a particular category have a high probability of staying right there. Conversely, a matrix that has the same numbers in *every* entry (which must be 20 in our 5×5 case, given that the numbers must sum to 100 along each row) shows an extraordinarily high rate of mobility. Regardless of the starting point in 1962, such a matrix will give you equal odds of being in any of the categories in 1984.

With these observations in mind, continue to stare at Figure 2.5. Notice that middle-income countries have far greater mobility than either the poorest or the richest countries. For instance, countries in category 1 (between half the world average and the world average) in 1962 moved away to "right" and "left": less than half of them remained where they were in 1962. In stark contrast to this, over three-quarters of the poorest countries (category 1/4) in 1962 remained where they were, and none of them went above the world average by 1984. Likewise, fully 95% of the richest countries in 1962 stayed right where they were in 1984.[8] This is interesting because it suggests that although everything is possible (in principle), a history of underdevelopment or extreme poverty puts countries at a tremendous disadvantage.

This finding may seem trite. Poverty should feed on itself and so should wealth, but on reflection you will see that this is really not so. There are certainly many reasons to think that historically low levels of income may be *advantageous* to rapid growth. New technologies are available from the more developed countries. The capital stock is low relative to labor in poor countries, so the marginal product of capital could well be high. One has, to some extent, the benefit of hindsight: it is possible to study the success stories and avoid policies that led to failures in the past. This account is not meant to suggest that the preceding empirical finding is inexplicable: it's just to say that an a priori guess does not yield straightforward answers. We will have much more to say on this topic throughout the book.

There is actually a bit more to Figure 2.5 than lack of mobility at the extremes. Look at the next-to-poorest category (those with incomes between

---

[8] Of course, our categories are quite coarse and this is not meant to suggest that there were no relative changes at all among these countries. The immobility being described is of a very broad kind, to be sure.

one-quarter and one-half of the world average in 1962). Note that 7% of these countries transited to incomes above the world average by 1984. However, over half of them *dropped* to an even lower category. Thus it is not only the lowest-income countries that might be caught in a very difficult situation. In general, at low levels of income, the overall tendency seems to be movement in the downward direction.

To summarize, then, we have the following observations.

(1) Over the period 1960–1985, the *relative* distribution of world income appears to have been quite stable. The richest 5% of the world's nations averaged a level of per capita income that was about 29 times the corresponding figure for the poorest 5%. By any standards, this disparity is staggering, and especially so when we remember that we are talking about incomes that have been corrected for purchasing power parity.

(2) The fact that the overall distribution has remained stationary does *not* mean that there has been little movement of countries within the world distribution. Of particular interest in the 1980s is the rise of the East Asian economies and the languishing of other economies, particularly those of sub-Saharan Africa and Latin America. Diverse growth experiences such as these can change the economic composition of the world in the space of a few decades. Nonetheless, a single explanation for this diversity remains elusive.

(3) The observation that several countries have changed relative positions suggests that there are no ultimate traps to development. At the same time, a history of wealth or poverty does seem to partly foretell future developments. The mobility of countries appears to be highest somewhere in the middle of the wealth distribution, whereas a history of underdevelopment or extreme poverty appears to put countries at a disadvantage.

(4) That history matters in this way is an observation that requires a careful explanation. Poor countries do seem to have some advantages. They can use, relatively free of charge, technologies that are developed by their richer counterparts. Scarce capital in these countries should display a higher rate of profit, because of the law of diminishing returns. They can learn from mistakes that their predecessors have made. In this way differences across countries should iron themselves out over the longer run. Thus the observation that history matters in maintaining persistent differences needs more of a justification than might be obvious at first glance.

2.3. Income distribution in developing countries

The international disparity of national income is only one indication that something is fundamentally askew with global development. Add to this the astonishing inequalities observable *within* each of the vast majority of developing countries. It is commonplace to see enormous wealth coexisting with great poverty, and nowhere is this more evident than on the streets of Bombay, Rio de Janeiro, Manila, Mexico City, and the other great urban conglomerates of the developing world. It isn't that such inequalities do not exist in the developed world—they certainly do—but coupled with the low average income of developing countries, these disparities result in an outcome of visible poverty and destitution.

We will have much more to say on the topic of income distribution later in this book (see especially Chapters 6 and 7). As an overview, however, it is useful to get a feel for the magnitude of the problem by looking at some data.[9] Figure 2.6 summarizes recent information on inequality for selected countries, spanning the range between poorest and richest.[10] The figure records the income share of the poorest 40% of the population as well as the income share of the richest 20% of the population. By simply eyeballing the data, you can see that the poorest 40% of the population earn, on average, around 15%—perhaps less—of overall income, whereas the richest 20% earn around half of total income. Even though there is plenty of variation around these averages (see subsequent discussion), this is a large discrepancy. Remember, moreover, that to understand how these inequalities affect the poorest people in each country, we must compound this intracountry inequality with the intercountry differences that we already discussed. The poor are twice cursed: once for living in countries that are poor on average, and then again for being on the receiving end of the high levels of inequality in those countries.

Figure 2.6 also plots tentative trends in these shares as we move from poor to rich countries. There appears to be a tendency for the share of the richest 20% to fall, rather steeply in fact, as we cross the $8,000 per capita income threshold (1993 PPP). However, there is also a distinct tendency for this share to rise early on in the income scale (mentally shut out the patch after $8,000 and look at the diagram again). The overall tendency, then, is for the share of the richest 20% to rise and then fall over the cross section of incomes represented in the diagram. The share of the poorest 40% displays the opposite relationship, although it is somewhat less pronounced. At both extremes of the income scale, the share is relatively high, and falls to a minimum around the middle (in the cluster represented by $4,000–9,000 of per capita income).

---

[9] One can imagine that the statistical problems here are even more severe than those involved in measuring per capita income. The goal is to measure the incomes earned *by different groups* in the same country and compare them, so all the measurement difficulties are compounded (except for the problem of international price comparability), because no system of overall, national accounts can be used to estimate the incomes of any one *subgroup* of the population.

[10] In particular, we omit data on Eastern Europe and the former Soviet Union, where levels of economic inequality are traditionally lower, which complicates the overall pattern.

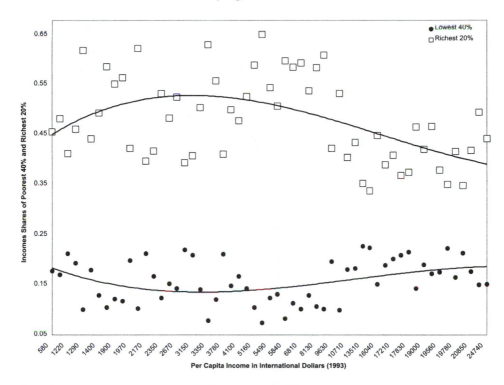

Figure 2.6. Income shares of poorest 40% and richest 20% for fifty-seven countries arranged in order of increasing per capita income (PPP). Source: World Development Report (World Bank [1995]) and Deininger and Squire [1996a].

The two trends together suggest, very tentatively indeed, that inequality might rise and then fall as we move from lower to higher incomes. This is the essence of a famous hypothesis owing to Kuznets [1955] that is known as the inverted U (referring to the shape traced by rising and then falling inequality). We will take a closer look at this relationship in Chapter 7. For now, nothing is really being said about how inequality in a single country changes over time: what we have here is a snapshot running over different countries.

South Asian countries, such as India, Bangladesh, and Sri Lanka, many African countries, such as Tanzania, Uganda, Kenya, Senegal, Nigeria, and Ghana, and a few of the poorer Latin American countries, such as El Salvador, Nicaragua, and Bolivia, populate the first stretch in this diagram. Then come the middle-income countries, with a large concentration of Latin American nations—Guatemala, Peru, Brazil, Colombia, Costa Rica, Mexico, Chile, Panama—as well as fast-growing Asian countries such as Thailand and Malaysia. At the $9,000 mark we hit countries such as Korea, Puerto Rico, Portugal, and Mauritius, and this is the approximate region in which we see a drop in the income share of the richest 20%. We then move into the rich countries, mainly European and North American, with a sprinkling of East Asian nations—Singapore, Japan, and Hong Kong—among them. Specific data on income and inequality are provided for a subsample of countries in Table 2.1.

The data presented here suggest that economic development is an inherently uneven process. At very low levels of income, average levels of living

Table 2.1. *Shares of poorest 40% and richest 20% for selected countries.*

Country	Per capita income (1993 PPP)	Share of poorest 40% (in %)	Share of richest 20% (in %)
0–3,000 PPP			
Tanzania	580	18	45
Uganda	900	17	48
India	1,220	21	41
Bangladesh	1,290	19	46
Senegal	1,650	11	59
Nicaragua	1,900	12	55
Pakistan	2,170	21	40
El Salvador	2,350	12	53
Sri Lanka	2,990	22	39
3,000–9,000 PPP			
Peru	3,220	14	50
Guatemala	3,350	8	63
Brazil	5,370	7	65
Colombia	5,490	12	54
Costa Rica	5,520	13	50
Panama	5,840	8	60
Thailand	6,260	11	59
Mexico	6,810	10	60
Malaysia	7,930	13	54
Venezuela	8,130	11	59
9,000+ PPP			
Rep. Korea	9,630	20	42
Portugal	10,710	18	40
Mauritius	12,420	18	43
Spain	13,510	23	35
United Kingdom	17,210	20	41
France	19,000	19	42
Japan	20,850	18	42
United States	24,740	15	44

Source: *World Development Report* (World Bank [1995]) and Deininger and Squire [1996a].

are very low, and so it is very difficult to squeeze the income share of the poorest 40% below a certain minimum. For such countries the income share of the rich, although high, is nowhere close to the extraordinarily high ratios observed in middle-income countries. This indicates the possibility that as economic growth proceeds, it initially benefits the richest groups in society more than proportionately. This situation is reflected in a rise in the income share of the upper quintile of the population. The share of the poorest groups tends to fall at the same time, although this does not mean that their income goes down in *absolute* terms. At higher levels of per capita income, economic gains tend to be distributed more equally—the poorest quintiles now gain in income share.

It is worth noting (and we will say this again in Chapter 7) that there is no inevitability about this process. Countries that pursue policies of broad-based access to infrastructure and resources, such as health services and education, will in all likelihood find that economic growth is distributed relatively equally among the various groups in society. Countries that neglect these features will show a greater tendency toward inequality. Indeed, matters are actually more complicated than this. These policies may in turn affect the overall rate of growth that a country can sustain. Although many of us might want to believe that equity and growth go hand in hand, this may well turn out to be not true, at least in some situations. The need to discuss this crucial interaction cannot be overemphasized.

The combination of low per capita incomes and the unequal distribution of them means that in large parts of the developing world, people might lack access to many basic services: health, sanitation, education, and so on. The collection of basic indicators that makes up the nebulous concept of progress has been termed human development, and this is what we turn to next.

2.4. The many faces of underdevelopment

2.4.1. Human development

Income is distributed unequally within all countries, and especially so in developing countries. We also noticed a fair degree of variation in inequality across countries: middle-income countries have significantly higher inequality. This variation suggests that excessive reliance on GNP per capita as a reliable indicator of overall development might well be dangerous. A relatively prosperous country may fare poorly on some of the commonsense indicators of development, such as literacy, access to drinking water, low rates of infant mortality, life expectancy, and so on. In part, this is because income is distributed unequally, but other features may be at work as well. The social and economic empowerment of women may serve to significantly reduce infant mortality and (more generally) raise the health and nutritional status of children, yet neither income nor its equal distribution across *households* fully guarantees the empowerment of women. Likewise, a country that promotes popular science and health education programs might be a welcome outlier in the health category, even though income may be low or poorly distributed. Later in this section, we will emphasize the *overall* correlation of "human development" with per capita income, but it is worthwhile to be sensitive to the outliers, because they tell a different story.

Consider the countries of Guatemala and Sri Lanka. The income and income distribution data for these two countries have been extracted from Table 2.1 and reproduced in Table 2.2.

Table 2.2 informs us that in 1993, Guatemala had per capita income that exceeded that of Sri Lanka, but the distribution of this income speaks for itself. In Guatemala, the poorest 40% of the population had access to a bit less than 8% of national income. The corresponding share for Sri Lanka is almost *three* times as large.

Now look at some of the "human development" indicators for these two countries, compiled in Table 2.3. Except for access to safe water, these indicators are very different indeed. Life expectancy is a good seven years higher in Sri Lanka. Much of this difference stems from the huge difference in the infant mortality rate, defined as the number of children (per thousand live births) who die before the age of 1. In Sri Lanka this figure is eighteen per thousand; in Guatemala it is more than two and a half times higher. Sri Lanka has an adult literacy rate of close to 90%; that of Guatemala is only 54%.

Looking at these two tables, it is hard to escape the conclusion that the highly unequal distribution of income in Guatemala is responsible, at least in part, for these differences in some natural yardsticks of development.

However, that isn't the whole story. Even a relatively equal distribution of income may not be enough. Of course, one reason for this is that per capita income is not high. For instance, however stunning the efforts of Sri Lanka are, countries such as Hong Kong do better simply because there

Table 2.2. *Shares of poorest 40% and richest 20% for Sri Lanka and Guatemala.*

Country	Per capita income (1993 PPP)	Share of poorest 40% (in %)	Share of richest 20% (in %)
Sri Lanka	2,990	22	39
Guatemala	3,350	8	63

Source: *World Development Report* (World Bank [1995]) and Deininger and Squire [1996].

Table 2.3. Indicators of "human development" for Sri Lanka and Guatemala.

Country	Life expectancy (years)	Infant mortality rate (per 1000)	Access to safe water (% of pop.)	Adult literacy rate (%)
Sri Lanka	72	18	60	89
Guatemala	65	48	62	54

Source: *Human Development Report* (United Nations Development Programme [1995]).
Note: All data are for 1992, except for access to safe water, which is the 1988–93 average.

are more resources to play with. However, what about a country such as Pakistan? The 1995 *World Development Report* lists Pakistan with a 1993 per capita GDP of $2,170. The poorest 40% of the population earn 21% of the total income. These overall figures are similar to those of Sri Lanka, but Pakistan has a life expectancy of only 62 and an infant mortality rate of ninety-one per thousand, *five* times that of Sri Lanka. The literacy rate for Pakistan was only 36% in 1992—significantly less than half that of Sri Lanka. Clearly, government policies, such as those concerning education and health, and the public demand for such policies, play significant roles.

2.4.2. An index of human development

Many of the *direct* physical symptoms of underdevelopment are easily observable and independently measurable. Undernutrition, disease, illiteracy—these are among the stark and fundamental ills that a nation would like to remove through its development efforts. For quite some time now, international agencies (like the World Bank and the United Nations) and national statistical surveys have been collecting data on the incidence of malnutrition, life expectancy at birth, infant mortality rates, literacy rates among men and women, and various other direct indicators of the health, educational, and nutritional status of different populations.

As we have seen, a country's performance in terms of income per capita might be significantly different from the story told by these basic indicators. Some countries, comfortably placed in the "middle-income" bracket, nevertheless display literacy rates that barely exceed 50%, infant mortality rates close to or exceeding one hundred deaths per thousand, and undernourishment among a significant proportion of the population. On the other hand, there are instances of countries with low and modestly growing incomes, that have shown dramatic improvements in these basic indicators. In some categories, levels comparable to those in the industrialized nations have been reached.

The United Nations Development Programme (UNDP) has published the *Human Development Report* since 1990. One objective of this *Report* is to coalesce some of the indicators that we have been discussing into a single index, which is known as the *human development index* (HDI). This is not the first index that has tried to put various socioeconomic indicators together. A forerunner is Morris' "physical quality of life index" (Morris [1979]), which created a composite index from three indicators of development: infant mortality, literacy, and life expectancy conditional on reaching the age of 1.

The HDI has three components as well. The first is life expectancy at birth (this will indirectly reflect infant and child mortality).[11] The second is a measure of educational attainment of the society. This measure is itself a composite: it takes a weighted average of adult literacy (with weight 2/3) and a combination of enrollment rates in primary, secondary and tertiary education (with weight 1/3). The last component is per capita income, which is adjusted somewhat after a threshold (around $5,000 in PPP dollars, 1992) is crossed. Less weight is given to higher incomes after this point, on the grounds that there is diminishing marginal utility to higher incomes. The HDI is calculated by defining some notion of a country's achievements in each of these three components, and then taking a simple average of the three indicators.

The creation of composites from such fundamentally different indicators as life expectancy and literacy is a bit like adding apples and oranges. It is arguable that rather than create composites, the reader should view the different indicators (as we will do presently) and then judge the overall situation for herself. The advantage of a composite index is its simplicity and, of course, its political power: in this era of sound bites, it is far easier and appears to be more "scientific" to say that country X has an "index" of 8 out of 10, rather than laboriously to detail that country's achievements (or lack of them) in five different spheres of development.[12] The HDI might *look* scientific and the formulae used to create the final average might *look* complex, but that is no reason to accept the implicit weighting scheme that it uses, because it is just as ad hoc as any other. It cannot be otherwise. Nevertheless, the HDI is one way to combine important development indicators, and for this reason it merits our attention.

The HDI creates, for each country, a final number that takes a value somewhere between 0 and 1. The number is to be (tentatively) interpreted as the "fraction of ultimate development" that has been achieved by the country in question. Because these notions of "ultimate bliss" are embodied in the HDI, it is not surprising that the indicator is relatively varied among the poorer

[11] The goal for life expectancy is taken to be 85 years, and achievement with respect to this component is measured by the narrowing of the discrepancy from this goal.

[12] Note that the use of per capita income is not immune from this criticism. After all, per capita income is also a composite index of human "welfare" and is not to be equated with it.

countries, but then flattens out sharply as we move into richer countries.[13] Thus statements made in the *Report*, such as "the HDI of industrial countries (0.916) is *only* 1.6 times higher than that of developing countries (0.570), even though their real GDP per capita (PPP\$) is 6 times higher," are meaningless.[14]

Although such comparisons of ratios simply do not make sense, the *rankings* generated by the HDI are of some interest because they illustrate how it is possible for a relatively high-income country to fare so badly in meeting basic socioeconomic goals that its HDI index falls behind that of a relatively poor country. One way to show how this happens is to present the HDI ranking for different countries as well as the rankings induced by per capita GDP. It is then possible to study the difference in the two rankings induced by these two measures. A positive difference means that the country has done better in "human development" relative to its position in the GDP rankings; a negative ranking means the opposite. What about the examples of our previous section: Sri Lanka, Guatemala, and Pakistan? The ranking approach justifies what we already saw on the basis of specific indicators. Sri Lanka has a positive rank differential of +5. Guatemala and Pakistan have negative rank differentials of -20 and -28, respectively.

2.4.3. Per capita income and human development

There is little doubt, then, that per capita income, or even the equality of its distribution, does not serve as a unilateral guarantee of success in "human development." This sentiment is captured very well in one of the views of development with which we started this chapter.

At the same time, the apparently narrow perspective of mainstream economists, with its hard-nosed focus on per capita income as a summary statistic of development, may not be too out of line. It is arguable that although taking a wider and multidimensional view of development is *conceptually* correct, per capita GDP still acts as a fairly good *proxy* for most aspects of development.[15] For instance, it can be argued that rising income

---

[13] The goal for life expectancy is taken to be 85 years, and achievement with respect to this component is measured by the narrowing of the discrepancy from this goal. Thus the life expectancy index is given by $L \equiv (l - 25)/(85 - 25)$, where l is the life expectancy in years of the country in question. The educational attainment index is $E \equiv e/100$, where e is the combined educational enrollment rate, expressed as a percentage. The adult literacy index is $A \equiv a/100$, where a is the adult literacy rate, expressed as a percentage. Finally, the income index is $Y \equiv (y - 100)/(5,448 - 100)$, where y is "adjusted income" and 5,448 is the *maximum* level to which adjusted income is permitted to climb [see the *Human Development Report* (United Nations Development Programme [1995, p. 134])]. Countries with per capita incomes of \$40,000 (1992 PPP) would be given an adjusted income of this maximum.

[14] The emphasis in the quoted sentence (from p. 19 of the *Report*) is mine. An earthquake of 8 on the Richter scale is not "only" 14% more powerful than one that measures 7 on the Richter scale.

[15] For additional information on this debate and related matters, see the contributions of Anand and Harris [1994], Aturupane, Glewwe and Isenman [1994], Desai [1991], Naqvi [1995], Srinivasan [1994], and Streeten [1994].

levels ultimately and inevitably translate into better health, nutritional, and educational standards in a population. It is, therefore, a useful exercise to see from cross-country data, how much "explanatory power" per capita GDP has over other basic indicators.

One way to go about this exercise is to collect data on per capita income as well as on some other facet of development that we might be interested in, and then connect the two by means of a *scatter diagram* (see Appendix 2). In brief, a scatter diagram allows us to eyeball possible relationships between a *dependent variable* whose variation we are seeking to explain (such as infant mortality or life expectancy) and one or more *independent variables* whose variation presumably "explains" the changes of the dependent variable. In the present situation, our independent variable is per capita income.

In this section, we chose three indicators of development that are of interest: life expectancy at birth, the infant mortality rate, and the adult literacy rate. To be sure, these indicators are not entirely independent of each other. For instance, life expectancy *includes* the possibility of dying before the age of 1, which is infant mortality. Nevertheless, these are common indicators that enter into indexes of development, such as the HDI or the physical quality of life index.

Figures 2.7–2.9 simply plot the relationship between these variables and per capita income, by looking at a cross section of countries. It is only to be expected that as we move into the range of countries with *very* high per capita income, these indicators will be at high levels as well, and they are. So as not to dwarf the entire exercise by these extremes, we leave out all countries with per capita income exceeding $9,000 PPP (1993). In principle, this makes the case *against* per capita income stronger. Variation in income here is somewhat smaller, and there is therefore much room for other policies or characteristics to affect the outcome.

Each of these diagrams has a cross-bar that is drawn at the average values of the data in that sample. For instance, the cross-bar in Figure 2.8 is located at an average per capita income of $3,500 and a literacy rate of around 72% (which are the averages for the sample). The scattered dots are the observations, of course. The idea of the diagram is to check the *correlation* between the two variables concerned (see Appendix 2). If the correlation is expected to be positive, for instance, we would expect most of the dots to lie in the northeast and southwest quadrants of the cross-bar. This is our expectation for literacy and life expectancy. For infant mortality, we expect the relationship to be negative, so the observations should lie in the northwest and southeast quadrants of the cross-bar.

By and large, the relationship between per capita income *alone* and each of these variables is strikingly strong. In each of the three cases, the great majority of the observations lie within the expected quadrants. The figures speak for themselves to express the idea that per capita income is a powerful

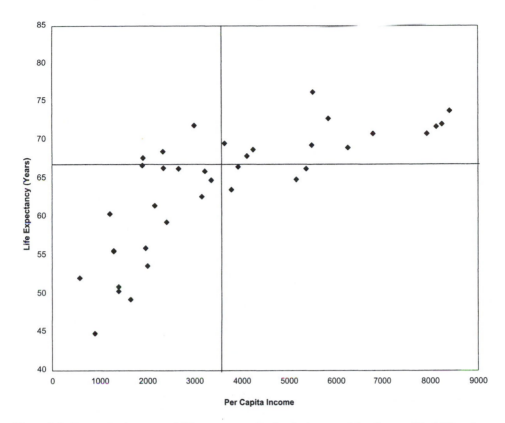

Figure 2.7. Per capita income and life expectancy for developing countries. Source: World Development Report (World Bank [1995]) and Human Development Report (United Nations Development Programme [1995]).

correlate of development, no matter how broadly we conceive of it. Thus we *must* begin, and we do so, with a study of how per capita incomes evolve in countries. This is the subject of the theory of economic growth—a topic that we take up in detail in the chapters to come.

A further point needs to be stressed. By looking at the actual *levels* of achievement in each of these indicators, rather than just the ranking across countries that they induce, I have actually made life more difficult for the argument in favor of per capita income. In an influential book, Dasgupta [1993] showed that per capita income is correlated even more highly with other indicators of development if we consider *ranks* rather than *cardinal measures*. In other words, if we rank countries according to their per capita GDP levels and then compute similar ranks based on some other index (such as adult literacy, child mortality, etc.), then we find a high degree of statistical correspondence between the two sets of ranks if the set of countries is sufficiently large and wide ranging. Because I have already carried out cardinal compar-

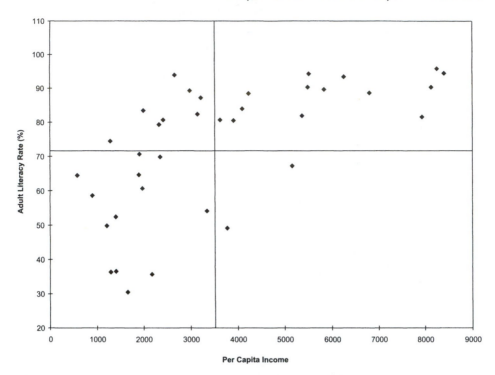

Figure 2.8. Per capita income and adult literacy rates for developing countries. Source: World Development Report (World Bank [1995]) and Human Development Report (United Nations Development Programme [1995]).

isons, I will skip a detailed discussion of these matters and simply refer you to Dasgupta's study for a more thorough reading.[16]

The point of this section is not to discredit human development, but only to show that we must not necessarily swing our opinions to the other extreme and disregard per capita income altogether. To be more emphatic, we must take per capita income very seriously, and it is in this spirit that we can appreciate the seemingly narrow quotation from Robert Lucas at the beginning of this chapter.

To complete this delicate balancing act, note finally that the relationship between per capita income and the other indicators is strong but far from perfect (otherwise the data would all lie on some smooth curve linking the two sets of variables). The imperfect nature of the relationship is just

---

[16] There are several authors who have argued that higher per-capita income is correlated with indicators of the quality of life; see, for example, Mauro [1993], Pritchett and Summers [1995], Boone [1996] and Barro [1996]. However, with country fixed effects properly accounted for in panel data, the evidence is somewhat mixed: see Easterly [1997]. Indeed, we do not claim that simple cross-country studies can settle the issue conclusively, and we certainly do not propose that income is a complete determinant for all other facets of development.

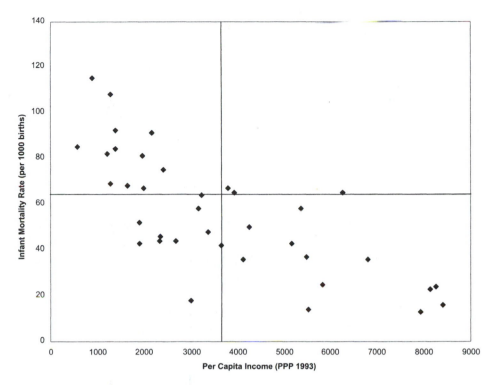

Figure 2.9. Per capita income and infant mortality rates for developing countries. Source: World Development Report (World Bank [1995]) and Human Development Report (United Nations Development Programme [1995]).

a macroreflection of what we saw earlier with countries such as Sri Lanka, Pakistan, and Guatemala. Inclusion of the *distribution* of per capita income would add to this fit, but even then matters would remain undecided: social and cultural attitudes, government policy, and the public demands for such policies, all would continue to play their role in shaping the complex shell of economic development. Thus it is only natural that we concentrate on economic growth and then move on to other pressing matters, such as the study of income distribution and the operation of various markets and institutions.

2.5. Some structural features

Our final objective in this chapter is to provide a quick idea of the structural characteristics of developing countries. We will examine these characteristics in detail later in the book.

2.5.1. Demographic characteristics

Very poor countries are characterized by both high birth rates and high death rates. As development proceeds, death rates plummet downward. Often, birth rates remain high, before they finally follow the death rates on their downward course. In the process, a gap opens up (albeit temporarily) between the birth and death rates. This leads to high population growth in developing countries. Chapter 9 discusses these issues in detail.

High population growth has two effects. It means that overall income must grow faster to keep per capita growth at reasonable levels. To be sure, the fact that population is growing helps income to grow, because there is a greater supply of productive labor. However, it is not clear who wins this seesaw contest: the larger amount of production or the larger population that makes it necessary to divide that production among more people. The negative population effect may well end up dominant, especially if the economy in question is not endowed with large quantities of capital (physical or human).

A second effect of high population growth (or high birth rates, to be precise) is that the overall population is quite young. It is easy to get an intuition for this: high birth rates mean that a proportionately larger number of children are always entering the population at any given point of time. This means that the population is heavily weighted in favor of children. This may be quite delightful, as any of us who has grown up with several brothers, sisters, and cousins knows, but it does not change the grim reality of utter economic dependence, especially for those in poverty. There are many untoward consequences of an abnormally young population, and these include poverty, child labor, and low education.

Figure 2.10 shows us how population growth rates vary with per capita income. The thin line plots annual growth rates of population for 1970–80; the thick line does the same for 1980–93. In both cases the horizontal axis records 1993 percapita income (PPP). The variation is substantial (remember: per capita income isn't everything!), but there is a clear downward trend in the growth rate, both with per capita income and over time (for the same country).

2.5.2. Occupational and production structure

Agriculture accounts for a significant fraction of production in developing countries. Indeed, given that substantial agricultural output is produced for self-consumption and so may not be picked up in the data, the proportion is probably higher than that revealed by the published numbers. For the poorest forty-five countries for which the World Bank publishes data, called the *low-income countries*, the average proportion of output from agriculture is

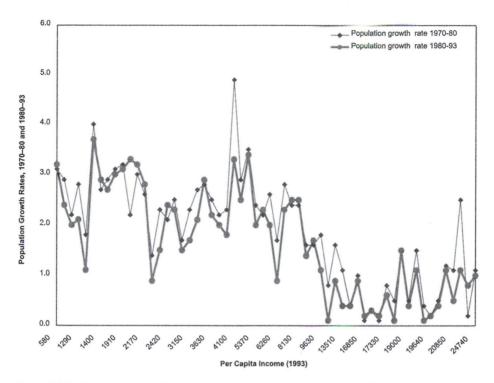

Figure 2.10. Population growth rates and per capita income. Source: World Development Report (World Bank [1995, 1996]).

close to 30%. Remember that the poorest forty-five countries include India and China and therefore a large fraction of the world's population. Data for the so-called middle-income countries, which are the next poorest sixty-three countries and include most Latin American economies, is somewhat sketchier, but the percentage probably averages around 20%. This stands in sharp contrast to the corresponding income shares accruing to agriculture in the economically developed countries: around 1–7%.

Even more striking are the shares of the labor force living in rural sectors. For the aforementioned low-income category, the share averaged 72% in 1993 and was as high as 60% for many middle-income countries. The contrast with developed countries is again apparent, where close to 80% of the labor force is urbanized. Even then, a large fraction of this nonurban population is so classified because of the "commuter effect": they are really engaged in nonagricultural activity although they live in areas classified as rural. Although a similar effect is not absent for developing countries, the percentage is probably significantly lower.

Figure 2.11 displays the share of the labor force in agriculture as we move over different countries indexed by per capita income. The downward trend

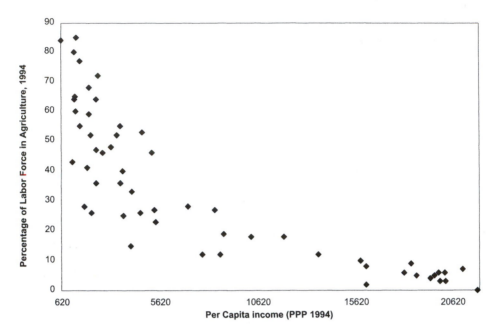

Figure 2.11. Fractions of the labor force in agriculture. Source: World Development Report (World Bank [1996]).

is unmistakable, but so are the huge shares in agriculture for both low- and middle-income countries.

Clearly, agricultural activity forms a significant part of the lives of people living in developing countries. We therefore devote a good part of this book to agricultural arrangements: the hiring of labor, the leasing of land, and the operation of credit markets. The overall numbers for production and occupational structure suggest that agriculture often has lower productivity than other economic activities. This is not surprising. In many developing countries, capital intensity in agriculture is at a bare minimum, and there is often intense pressure on the land. Add to this the fact that agriculture, especially when not protected by assured irrigation and ready availability of fertilizer and pesticides, can be a singularly risky venture. Many farmers bear enormous risks. These risks may not look very high if you count them in U.S. dollars, but they often make the difference between bare-bones subsistence (or worse) and some modicum of comfort.

2.5.3. Rapid rural–urban migration

With the above-mentioned features, it is hardly surprising that an enormous amount of labor moves from rural to urban areas. Such enormous migrations deserve careful study. They are an outcome of both the "push" from agriculture, because of extreme poverty and growing landlessness, and the perceived "pull" of the urban sector. The pulls are reinforced by a variety of factors, ranging from the comparatively high wages and worker protections offered in the organized urban sectors to the effect of the media in promoting the urban lifestyle as a desirable end in itself. The media is often misleading and so are the benefits of the organized sector, which are often accessible only to a lucky minority of workers.

Consider the rates of growth of the urban sector in developing countries. For the forty-five low-income countries covered by the World Bank, the average rate of urban population growth over the period 1980–93 was 3.9% per year. Compare this with an average rate of population growth of 2% per year for the same countries over the same period of time. Urban growth was simply double that of overall population growth for these countries. Imagine, then, the pressure on the cities of these countries. For the sixty-three countries classified as middle-income by the Bank, the urban growth rate was 2.8% per annum over the period 1980–93, to be compared with a population growth rate of 1.7% per year. Once again, we see evidence of a pressure on the urban sector that is just not captured by the overall population growth figures. On the other hand, the high-income developed countries exhibit near balance: urban populations grew at 0.8% per year, while overall population grew at 0.6% per year.

This is not to say that such migrations are somehow undesirable. Indeed, how did developed countries get to the point that they are now at? The fact of the matter, however, is that all these processes are *accelerated* in modern-day developing countries, and the speed-up imposes enormous strains.

One piece of evidence that reveals these strains is the fact that an unusually large fraction of the population in developing countries is classified as being in the tertiary or "services" sector. Before we take a look at the data, it is useful to conceptualize matters a bit. Think of what we consume as our income increases. Our first needs are for food and clothing. As we have more income to spare we switch to industrial products: radio, television, bicycles, automobiles, and the like. At a still higher level of income we begin to register a high demand for services: banking, tourism, restaurants, and travel. It is not surprising, then, that the developed countries allocate a large fraction of their nonagricultural labor force to the services sector. Countries such as Australia, the United States, the United Kingdom, Norway, and Sweden have about 70% of the total labor force in the services sector; the corresponding figures for some other developed countries such as Japan are somewhat lower. That isn't odd at all. What *is* odd is that many developing countries exhibit large fractions of the labor force in "services" as well!

Figure 2.12 illustrates the general point and Table 2.4 provides data for particular countries. Expressed as a fraction of the nonagricultural labor force, the proportion in the services sector is not at all different from what we see in developed countries. At the same time, the proportion of people

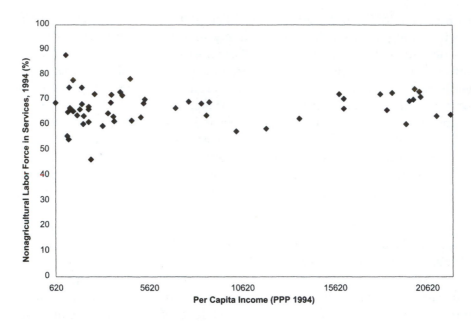

Figure 2.12. Nonagricultural labor in services. Source: World Development Report (World Bank [1996]).

in agriculture *does* vary a great deal, as we have already seen. What we are seeing, then, for developing countries, is a *classification* of a large part of the labor force into "services" simply because such services are waiting positions or fallback options for laborers lacking an industrial job. That is, the enormous services sector in developing countries is symptomatic of the development of the unorganized or *informal* sector, on which we will have more to say in Chapter 10. This sector is the home of last resort—the shelter for the millions of migrants who have made their way to the cities from the rural sector. People who shine shoes, petty retailers, and middlemen: they all get lumped under the broad rubric of services because there is no other appropriate category. It is fitting that the World Bank Tables refer to this sector as "Services, etc." The large size of this sector in developing countries is, in the main, a reflection of the inability of industry in these countries to keep up with the extraordinary pace of rural–urban migration.

2.5.4. International trade

By and large, all countries, rich and poor, are significantly involved in international trade. A quick plot of the ratio of exports and imports to GNP against per capita income, does not reveal a significant trend. There are large countries, such as India, the United States, and Mexico for which these ratios are not very high—perhaps around 10% on average. Then again, there

Table 2.4. Percentage of the non-agricultural labor force in services for selected countries.

Country	Per capita income (1994 PPP)	Nonagr. labor force in services
Tanzania	620	69
Nigeria	1,190	88
India	1,280	61
Senegal	1,580	65
Honduras	1,940	67
Ghana	2,050	68
Philippines	2,740	72
Indonesia	3,600	69
Egypt, Arab Republic	3,720	63
Ecuador	4,190	72
Botswana	5,210	63
Brazil	5,400	70
Venezuela	7,770	69
Spain	13,740	63
United Kingdom	16,150	70
Canada	19,960	74
Japan	21,140	63
United States	25880	71

Source: *World Development Report* (World Bank [1996]).

are countries such as Singapore and Hong Kong for which these ratios attain astronomical heights—well over 100%. The modal ratios of exports and imports to GNP are probably around 20%. Trade is an important component of the world economy.

The differences between developing and developed countries are more pronounced when we look at the *composition* of trade. Developing countries are often exporters of primary products. Raw materials, cash crops, and sometimes food are major export items. Textiles and light manufactured items also figure on the list. In contrast, the bulk of exports from developed countries is in the category of manufactured goods, ranging from capital goods to consumer durables. Of course, there are many exceptions to these broad generalizations, but the overall picture is broadly accurate, as Figure 2.13 shows. This figure plots the share of exports that comprise primary products against per capita income. We have followed the now-familar method of using cross-bars at the mean levels of per capita income and primary share (unweighted by population) to eyeball the degree of correlation. It is clear that, on the whole, developing countries do rely on primary product exports, whereas the opposite is true for the developed countries.

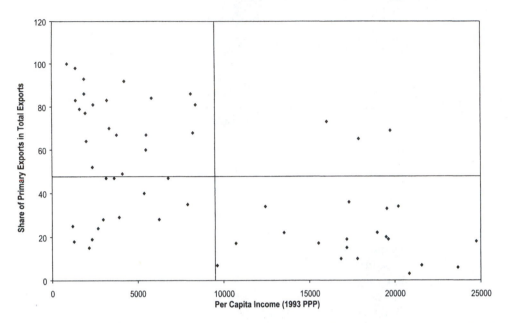

Figure 2.13. Share of primary exports in total exports. Source: World Development Report (World Bank [1995]).

Notice that there are some developing countries that have a low ratio of primary exports. Countries such as China, India, the Philippines, and Sri Lanka are among them. These countries and many of their compatriots are attempting to diversify their exports away from primary products, for reasons that we indicate subsequently and discuss at greater length later in the book. At the same time, there are developed countries that export primaries to a great degree. Australia, New Zealand, and Norway are among them.

The traditional explanation for the structure of international trade comes from the theory of *comparative advantage*, which states that countries specialize in the export of commodities in which they have a relative cost advantage in production. These cost advantages might stem from differences in technology, domestic consumption profiles, or the endowment of inputs that are particularly conducive to the production of certain commodities. We review this theory in Chapter 16. Because developing countries have a relative abundance of labor and a relative abundance of unskilled labor within the labor category, the theory indeed predicts that such countries will export commodities that intensively use unskilled labor in production. To a large extent, we can understand the aforementioned trade patterns using this theory.

At the same time, the emphasis on primary exports may be detrimental to the development of these countries for a variety of reasons. It appears that primary products are particularly subject to large fluctuations in world prices, and this creates instability in export earnings. Over the longer run,

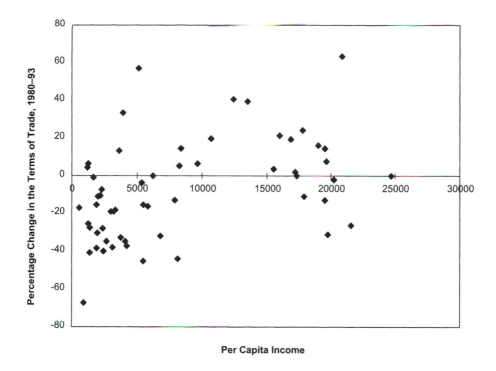

Figure 2.14. Changes in the terms of trade, 1980–93. Source: World Development Report (World Bank [1995]).

as primary products become less important in the consumption basket of people the world over, a declining price trend might be evident for such products as well.

The definite existence of such a trend is open to debate. At the same time, we can see some broad indication of it by studying how the *terms of trade* for different countries have changed over recent decades. The terms of trade for a country represent a measure of the ratio of the price of its exports to that of its imports. Thus an increase in the terms of trade augers well for the trading prospects of that country, whereas a decline suggests the opposite. Figure 2.14 plots changes in the terms of trade over the period 1980–93 against per capita income. There is some indication that the relationship is positive, which suggests that poor countries are more likely than richer ones to face a decline in their terms of trade. Primary exports may underlie such a phenomenon.

In general, then, activities that have comparative advantage today might not be well suited for export earnings tomorrow. The adjustment to a different mix of exports then becomes a major concern. Finally, technology often is assimilated through the act of production. If production and exports are

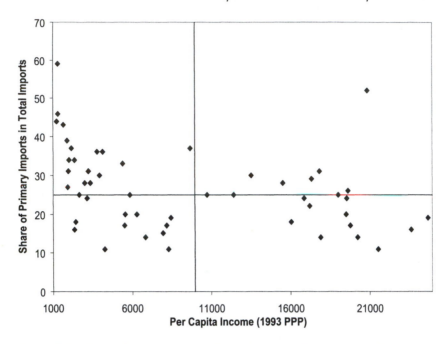

Figure 2.15. Share of primary imports in total imports. Source: World Development Report (World Bank [1995]).

largely limited to primary products , the flow of technology to developing countries may be affected. We discuss these issues in Chapter 17.

The *import* mix of developing countries is more similar to that of developed countries. Exporters of primary products often need to import primary products as well: thus India might be a major importer of oil and Mexico a major importer of cereals. Primary exports for each country are often concentrated in a handful of products, and there is no contradiction in the fact that primaries are both exported and imported. A similar argument establishes that although developed countries might export manufactured items, there is always a need for other manufactures that are in relatively short supply. Trade patterns in this aggregated form are therefore quite similar over countries, as Figure 2.15 reveals.

We summarize: developing countries are likely to have a high ratio of primary goods in their total exports, but as far as imports are concerned, there is significantly less variation.

2.6. Summary

We began with a discussion of what the term *economic development* might mean. It is a multifaceted concept, embodying not just income and its growth, but also achievements on other fronts: reductions in infant mortality, higher life expectancy, advances in literacy rates, widespread access to medical and health services, and so on. Per capita income is sometimes used as an (incomplete) indicator for overall economic development, but should not be identified conceptually with development in the broader sense.

We turned next to per capita income data for countries. Using exchange rates to convert local currencies into dollars, we obtained per capita income evaluated according to the *exchange rate method*. The disparities across countries is enormous. Some of this disparity is due to underreporting of income, but a far more serious problem arises from the fact that price levels are systematically different across countries: dollar prices for nontraded goods and services tend to be lower in developing countries. The *purchasing power parity method* attempts to correct for this by constructing international prices that are used to estimate national incomes. Cross-country disparities in per capita income are then smaller, but still large: the richest 5% of the world's nations averaged a per capita income that was about twenty-nine times the corresponding figure for the poorest 5%, over the period 1960–85.

There have been substantial changes in incomes for many countries. The meteoric rise of East Asia is a case to be noted. This case is contrasted with the fact that much of Latin America and sub-Saharan Africa languished during the 1980s. Thus, although the world distribution of income remained fairly unchanged in relative terms, there was plenty of movement within that distribution. However, there is evidence that a history of underdevelopment or extreme poverty feeds on itself. Using *mobility matrices*, we noted that middle-income countries have significantly higher mobility than either the poorest or the richest countries.

Next, we studied income distribution *within* countries. By and large, income is more unequally distributed in developing countries than in their developed counterparts, which suggests that the poor in developing countries are twice hit: once at the level of distribution across countries and then at the level of distribution within countries. Income distribution is particularly bad for middle-income countries, and most of this extreme inequality appears to be located in Latin America.

With income and income distribution out of the way, we then returned to the broader notion of development. The *Human Development Index* is the name given to a set of indicators developed by the United Nations Development Programme. It combines three indicators—life expectancy at birth, educational attainment, and per capita income—with weights to arrive at a combined index. We noted that just because an overall index is provided does not mean it should be necessarily taken seriously: the weights are, of course, quite arbitrary. Nevertheless, the overall idea of human development is a laudable attempt to conceptually go beyond per capita income as an operational measure of development.

Nevertheless, per capita income isn't a bad predictor of human development. We showed that the correlations between per capita income and other variables that describe "human development" are high, even if attention is restricted only to the subsample of developing countries.

Finally, we described some structural characteristics of developing countries. We looked at *demographic characteristics* and showed that there is a general tendency for population growth rates to decline with increased per capita income. We discussed very briefly some of the effects of population growth on per capita income. We then studied *occupational and production structure*: agricultural activity accounts for a significant fraction of occupations in developing countries. At the same time, the rates of *rural–urban migration* are very high indeed. In part, this is reflected in the observation that a large fraction of the nonrural labor force is engaged in a nebulous activity called "services." This category includes all sorts of informal activities with low setup costs, and in developing countries is a good indicator of urban overcrowding. At the end, we discussed *patterns of international trade*. Developing countries are largely exporters of *primary products*, although this pattern shows change for middle-income countries. Primary product exports can be explained using the theory of *comparative advantage*, although we note that primary product exports have intrinsic problems, such as a strong tendency for their international prices to fluctuate, which creates instability in export revenues. The import mix of developing countries is, however, more similar to that of developed countries.

Exercises

■ (1) Per capita income is a measure of purchasing power. People who live and work in developing countries often find that their incomes are meager when buying an international airline ticket, making an international phone call, sending an airmail letter to a friend who lives abroad, buying a book published by an international publisher, or importing consumer goods. They don't feel that poor when they buy vegetables at the local store, get a haircut, travel domestically by train, bus, or even by taxi, or buy a local textbook. Use these intuitive comments to understand what a traded good is and what a nontraded good is. Note that a potentially tradable good may become effectively nontraded because of import or export restrictions. Why are nontraded goods generally cheaper in poor countries? In addition, if they are cheaper, would their incomes look better (relative to the United States, say) when measured by the exchange-rate method or by the PPP method?

■ (2) McDonald's operates in various countries. It has been found that the relative price of a Big Mac is a better guide to the overall cost of living than estimates using the exchange rate. Why do you think this might be the case?

■ (3) Why do you think that European or Japanese television transmits at resolutions that are superior to those in the United States? After looking into this question, formulate a hypothesis that suggests why countries that have poor infrastructure might be more likely to leapfrog over countries with better infrastructure insofar as the installation of new infrastructure is concerned. Use telephone networks as an example.

■ (4) Make sure you understand the power of exponential growth (and of rapid exponential inflation) by doing the following exercises:

(a) How quickly will a country growing at 10% a year double its income? Quadruple its income? What about a country growing at 5% per year?

(b) Suppose a country's per capita income is currently growing at 5% per year. Then it shaves an additional percentage point off its population growth rate for the next twenty years, but overall income continues to grow at the same rate. How much richer would the country be at the end of twenty years (per capita)?

(c) Suppose that Brazil experiences inflation at 30% per month. How much is this per year? Do your calculations first without compounding (the answer then is obviously 360%). Now do it properly by compounding the inflation rate.

■ (5) Construct an imaginary mobility matrix from a sample of countries that shows *no* mobility at all. What would it look like? What would a mobility matrix with "perfect mobility" look like? What would a mobility matrix look like if poor countries grow, on average, faster than rich countries?

■ (6) Use Table 2.1 to construct what is known as a *Kuznets ratio* (named after the economist and historian Simon Kuznets): the ratio of incomes earned by the richest 20% of the population to the those earned by the poorest 40% of the population. If incomes were distributed almost equally, what value would you expect this ratio to assume? What values do you see? In the sample represented by Table 2.1, do you see a trend as we move from poor to rich countries?

■ (7) Think of various indicators of development that you would like to see in your concept of "economic development." Think about why per capita income, as measured, may or may not be a good proxy for these indicators. Find a copy of the *Human Development Report* and look at it to see how different indicators are combined to get the HDI. Do you think that the method of combination is reasonable? Can you suggest a better combination? What do you think of the idea of presenting data on each of the indicators *separately*, instead of combining them? Think of the advantages and disadvantages of such an approach.

▪ (8) A cogent example in which per capita magnitudes may be misleading if we do not have a good idea of distribution comes from the study of modern famine. Why do famines simply not make sense if we look at them from the viewpoint of worldwide per capita availability of food grain? Do they make better sense if we look at just food-grain availability per capita *in that country*? After mulling this over for a while, read the insightful book by Sen [1981].

▪ (9) (a) Why do you think population growth rates fall with development? If people consume more goods, in general, as they get richer and children are just another consumption good (a source of pleasure to their parents), then why don't people in richer countries "consume" more children?

(b) Why are countries with higher population growth rates likely to have a greater *proportion* of individuals below the age of 15?

(c) Are poorer countries more likely to be rural or is it that rural countries are more likely to be poor? Which way does the causality run, or does it run both ways?

(d) Why do you think the international price of sugar might fluctuate more than, say, that of automobiles?

Chapter 3

Economic Growth

3.1. Introduction

Of all the issues facing development economists, none is quite so compelling as the question of economic growth. In Chapter 2, we examined the historical growth of nations and found a variety of annual growth rates. It is true that all of these numbers, with very few exceptions, were in the single digits, but we also took pains to appreciate the power of exponential growth. A percentage point added to the growth rate can make the difference between stagnation and prosperity over the period of a generation. Small wonder, then, that the search for key variables in the growth process can be tempting. Indeed, until recently, and for precisely this reason, no economic analysis has fired the ambitions and hopes of more policy makers in developing countries than the theory and empirics of economic growth.

Robert Lucas, in his Marshall Lectures at the University of Cambridge, stated:

> Rates of growth of real per-capita income are . . . diverse, even over sustained periods . . . . Indian incomes will double every 50 years; Korean every 10. An Indian will, on average, be twice as well off as his grandfather; a Korean 32 times. . . .

> I do not see how one can look at figures like these without seeing them as representing *possibilities*. Is there some action a government of India could take that would lead the Indian economy to grow like Indonesia's or Egypt's? If so, *what*, exactly? If not, what is it about the "nature of India" that makes it so? The consequences for human welfare involved in questions like these are simply staggering: Once one starts to think about them, it is hard to think about anything else.

I quote Lucas at length, because he captures, more keenly than any other writer, the passion that drives the study of economic growth. We sense here the big payoff, the possibility of change with extraordinarily beneficial consequences, if one only knew the exact combination of circumstances that drives economic growth.

If only one knew . . . , but to expect that from a single theory (or even a set of theories) about an incredibly complicated economic universe would be unwise. As it turns out, though, theories of economic growth take us quite far in understanding the development process, at least at some aggregate level. This is especially so if we supplement the theories with what we know empirically. At the very least, it teaches us to ask the right *questions* in the more detailed investigations later in this book.

3.2. Modern economic growth: Basic features

Economic growth, as the title of Kuznets' [1966] pioneering book on the subject suggests, is a relatively "modern" phenomenon. Today, we greet 2% annual rates of per capita growth with approval but no great surprise. Remember, however, that throughout most of human history, appreciable growth in per capita gross domestic product (GDP) was the exception rather than the rule. In fact it is not far from the truth to say that modern economic growth was born after the Industrial Revolution in Britain.

Consider the growth rates of the world's leaders over the past four centuries. During the period 1580–1820 the Netherlands was the leading industrial nation; it experienced an average annual growth in real GDP per worker hour[1] of roughly 0.2%. The United Kingdom, leader during the approximate period 1820–90, experienced an annual growth of 1.2%. Since 1890, the United States is considered to have usurped the leader's seat, and its average growth rate during the period 1890–1989 was a (relatively) dramatic 2.2% a year. Thus GDP per worker has grown at an *accelerated pace*, especially since 1820. Clearly, by today's standards, even the fastest growing economy two centuries ago would be considered practically stagnant.

Note once again that although an annual growth rate of 2% in per capita GDP does not appear very impressive, a moment's reflection (and calculation) reveals the enormous potential that such growth carries if it is sustained. Simple calculation shows that at the 2% rate, a nation's per capita GDP doubles in 35 years—a length of time comfortably shorter than the lifespan of an individual. This means that modern economic growth enables people to enjoy vastly improved living standards compared to not only their fathers but also perhaps their older cousins!

A glance at Table 3.1 shows how economic growth has transformed the now-developed world within the space of a century. This table displays per capita real GDP (valued in 1970 U.S. dollars) for selected OECD[2] countries in the years 1870, 1913, and 1978. The 1913 and 1978 columns include, in parentheses, the ratio of per capita GDP in those years to the corresponding

---

[1] Notice that we are referring here not to growth in per capita GDP as such, but growth in GDP *per worker hour*, or labor productivity. However, data on growth strongly suggest that the former is largely driven by the latter.

[2] OECD stands for the Organization for Economic Cooperation and Development, a group of developed North American and European nations.

Table 3.1. *Per capita GDP in selected OECD countries, 1870–1978.*

Country	Per capita GDP (1970 U.S. $)					
	1870	1913		1978	
Australia	1,340	1,941	(1.4)	4,456	(3.3)
Austria	491	1,059	(1.2)	3,934	(8.0)
Belgium	939	1,469	(1.6)	4,795	(5.1)
Canada	619	1,466	(2.4)	5,210	(8.4)
Denmark	572	1,117	(2.0)	4,173	(7.3)
Finland	402	749	(1.9)	3,841	(9.6)
France	627	1,178	(1.9)	4,842	(7.7)
Germany	535	1,073	(3.7)	4,676	(8.7)
Italy	556	783	(1.4)	3,108	(5.6)
Japan	248	470	(1.9)	4,074	(16.4)
Netherlands	830	1,197	(1.4)	4,388	(5.3)
Norway	489	854	(1.7)	4,890	(10)
Sweden	416	998	(2.4)	4,628	(11.1)
Switzerland	786	1,312	(1.7)	4,487	(5.7)
United Kingdom	972	1,492	(1.5)	3,796	(3.9)
United States	774	1,815	(2.3)	5,799	(7.5)
Simple average	662	1,186	(1.8)	4,444	(6.7)

Source: Maddison [1979].

baseline (1870) figure. The numbers are stunning. On average (see the last row of the table), GDP per capita in 1913 was 1.8 times the figure for 1870; by 1978, this ratio climbed to 6.7! A nearly sevenfold increase in real per capita GDP in the space of a century cannot but transform societies completely. The developing world, which is currently going through its own transformation, will be no exception.

Indeed, in the broader sweep of historical time, the development story has only just begun. The sustained growth in the last century was not experienced the world over. In the nineteenth and twentieth centuries, only a handful of countries, mostly in Western Europe and North America, and largely represented by the list in Table 3.1, could manage the "takeoff into sustained growth," to use a well-known term coined by the economic historian W. W. Rostow. Throughout most of what is commonly known as the Third World, the growth experience only began well into this century; for many of them, probably not until the post-World War II era, when colonialism ended. Although detailed and reliable national income statistics for most of these countries were not available until only a few decades ago, the economically backward and stagnant nature of these countries is amply revealed in less quantitative historical accounts, and also by the fact that they are way behind the industrialized nations of the world today in per capita

Table 3.2. Per capita GDP in Selected Developing Countries Relative to that of the United States, 1987–94.

| Country | PPP estimates of GNP per capita (U.S. = 100) | | Approx. annual growth |
	1994	1987	1987–94
Rwanda	1.3	3.8	↓
Ethiopia	1.7	2.0	↓
India	4.9	4.4	↑
Kenya	5.7	5.1	↑
China	9.7	5.8	↑
Sri Lanka	12.2	10.7	↑
Indonesia	13.9	10.0	↑
Egypt	14.4	14.4	—
Russian Federation	17.8	30.6	↓
Turkey	18.2	20.9	↓
South Africa	19.8	23.9	↓
Colombia	20.6	19.0	↑
Brazil	20.9	24.2	↓
Poland	21.2	21.4	↓
Thailand	26.9	16.4	↓
Mexico	27.2	27.8	↓
Argentina	33.7	32.1	↑
Korea, Rep	39.9	27.3	↑
Greece	42.2	42.1	↑
Spain	53.1	50.2	↑
United Kingdom	69.4	70.2	↓
Canada	77.1	83.2	↓
France	76.0	75.9	↑
Japan	81.7	74.7	↑
Switzerland	97.2	104.5	↓

Source: *World Bank Development Report* [1996].

GDP levels. To see this, refer to Table 3.2. What this table does is record the per capita incomes of several developing countries *relative* to that of the United States, for 1987–94. It also records the movements of per capita income in these countries relative to the United States over the same period.

There is, then, plenty of catching-up to do. Moreover, there is a twist in the story that wasn't present a century ago. Then, the now-developed countries grew (although certainly not in perfect unison) in an environment uninhabited by nations of far greater economic strength. Today, the story is completely different. The developing nations not only need to grow, they *must* grow at rates that far exceed historical experience. The developed world already exists, and their access to economic resources is not only far higher than that of the developing countries, but *the power afforded by this access is on display*. The urgency of the situation is further heightened by the extraordinary flow of information in the world today. People are increasingly and more quickly aware of new products elsewhere and of changes and disparities in standards of living the world over. Exponential growth at rates of 2% may well have significant long-run effects, but they cannot match the parallel growth of human aspirations, and the increased perception of global inequalities. Perhaps no one country, or group of countries, can be blamed for the emergence of these inequalities, but they do exist, and the need for sustained growth is all the more urgent as a result.

3.3. Theories of economic growth

3.3.1. The Harrod–Domar model

In its simplest terms, economic growth is the result of abstention from *current* consumption. An economy produces a variety of commodities. The act of production generates income. The very same income is used to buy these commodities. Exactly *which* commodities are produced depends on individual preferences and the distribution of income, but as a broad first pass, the following statement is true: commodity production creates income, which creates the demand for those very same commodities.

Let's go a step further and broadly classify commodities into two groups. We may think of the first group as *consumption goods*, which are produced for the express purpose of satisfying human wants and preferences. The mangos you buy at the market, or a fountain pen, or a pair of trousers all come under this category. The second group of commodities consists of what we might call *capital goods*, which we may think of as commodities that are produced for the purpose of producing *other* commodities. A blast furnace, a conveyor belt, or a screwdriver might come under the second category.[3]

Looking around us, it is obvious that the income generated from the production of all goods is spent on *both* consumer goods and capital goods. Typically, households buy consumer goods, whereas firms buy capital goods to expand their production or to replace worn-out machinery. This generalization immediately raises a question: if all income is paid out to households, and if households spend their income on consumption goods, where does the market for capital goods come from? How does it all add up?

The answer to this question is simple, although in many senses that we ignore for now, deceptively so: households save. No doubt some borrow too,

---

[3] It should be clear from our examples that there is an intrinsic ambiguity regarding this classification. Although a mango or a blast furnace may be easily classified into its respective category, the same is not true of screwdrivers or even a fountain pen. The correct distinction is between the flows of current and future consumption, and many goods embody a little of each.

to finance current consumption, but on the whole, national savings is generally positive. All income is not spent on current consumption. By abstaining from consumption, households make available a pool of funds that firms use to buy capital goods. This is the act of *investment*. Buying power is channeled from savers to investors through banks, individual loans, governments, and stock markets. How these transfers are actually carried out is a story in itself. Later chapters will tell some of this story.

By entering a new business, by expanding a current business, or by replacing worn-out capital, investment creates a market demand for *capital goods*. These goods add to the stock of capital in the economy and endow it, in the future, with an even larger capacity for production, and so an economy grows. Note, however, that without the initial availability of savings, it would not be possible to invest and there would be no expansion. This is the simple starting point of all of the theory of economic growth.

Implicit in this story is the idea of *macroeconomic balance*. If you think of a circuit diagram with income flowing "out" of firms as they produce and income flowing back "into" firms as they sell, you can visualize savings as a leakage from the system: the demand for consumption goods alone falls short of the income that created this demand. Investors fill this gap by stepping in with their demand for capital goods. Macroeconomic balance is achieved when this investment demand is at a level that exactly counterbalances the savings leakage. This concept is summarized in Figure 3.1.

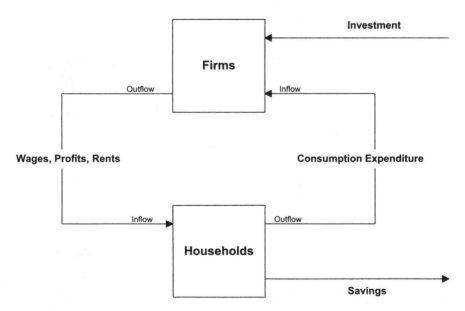

Figure 3.1. Production, consumption, savings, and investment.

Saving and Investment

The cycle of production, consumption, saving, and investment that constantly regenerates itself is as old as human civilization. In some cases, savers and investors are exactly the same individuals, using their own funds; in other cases, they are not.

Primitive man was both a saver and an investor. Time being his only resource, he "saved" time from activities related to current consumption, such as hunting, and "invested" it in making stone implements. These tools served as capital that enhanced his future production potential in hunting.

In traditional agricultural economies, the farmer is, to some extent, both a saver and an investor. For instance, she might save some grain from current output and invest it as seed for the future grain production. Alternatively, she might channel part of the proceeds from the sale of a crop into the purchase of a tractor or a pair of bullocks. In these cases, the act of saving and the act of investment are intimately connected.

In centrally planned economies, such as the former Soviet Union, and in mixed economies as well (which includes countries such as the United States, Japan, India, and South Korea), a significant part of investment is carried out by the government. Typically, the government earns revenue through taxation. Taxes are then spent by the government on various activities, which include both current consumption (such as maintaining a bureaucracy) and investment (such as building new highways).

However, in modern capitalist societies, the bulk of saving and investment generally is carried out by two distinct groups—households save and firms invest. Households save by spending less on current consumption than their current income permits. Firms invest by acquiring new technology, plants, and equipment that increase their future production capacity. Observe that the fact that households hold their savings in the form of a bank balance, shares, or bonds does not *automatically* increase the level of investment in the economy. By curtailing current consumption (i.e., saving) in this manner, they only make resources available for investment, which is the act of actually applying these current resources to the purchase of fresh capital.

Recent literature in economics has emphasized the fact that investment in education and training that raises the skills embodied in labor is no less an investment. Skills may not be tangible objects like machinery, but they contribute to increased production just as any piece of machinery does. The act of training and education may be aptly termed investment in *human capital*. It is important to note, however, that despite its enormous significance as a factor in production, investment in human capital is not normally included in the data for savings and investment. Separate estimates of such investments must be made, and in this chapter and elsewhere we will see why this is necessary.

If you understand the basic concept of macroeconomic balance, you understand the foundations of *all* models of economic growth. Economic growth is positive when investment exceeds the amount necessary to replace depreciated capital, thereby allowing the next period's cycle to recur on a larger scale. The economy expands in this case; otherwise it is stagnant or even shrinks. This is why the volume of savings and investment is an important determinant of the growth rate of an economy.

It is easy to see that our simplified concepts hide important elements of reality. For instance, we have neglected, for now, the deeper question of which factors govern the amount of savings and investment. Nevertheless, the story so far does illuminate some aspects of reality in a stark way, and therein lies its value. For now, let us see where it takes us, and then we will expand the analysis once we feel comfortable with the basics.

A little algebra at this stage will make our lives simpler. It will also enable us to include some more features with a minimum of fuss. Divide time into periods $t = 0, 1, 2, 3, \ldots$. We will keep track of dates by tagging the appropriate variable with the date. Here is standard economic notation: Y denotes total output, C denotes total consumption, and S denotes total savings. Remember that these variables are *aggregates* over the population. In particular, S nets out those who are borrowing for current consumption. Then the following equation *must* be true as a matter of accounting[4]:

$$(3.1) \qquad\qquad Y(t) = C(t) + S(t)$$

for all dates t. In words, national income is divided between consumption and savings. The other side of the coin is that the value of produced output (*also* equal to Y, please note) must be matched to goods produced for consumption plus those needed by investors; that is,

$$(3.2) \qquad\qquad Y(t) = C(t) + I(t),$$

where I denotes investment. Equations (3.1) and (3.2) are one step away from the famous macroeconomic balance equation

$$(3.3) \qquad\qquad S(t) = I(t)$$

or "savings equals investment," which you must have seen in an introductory macroeconomics course. We can use this equation to complete our basic argument. Investment augments the national capital stock K and replaces

---

[4] We assume that the economy is *closed*—that there are no net flows of resources from or to the outside world. Moreover, we ignore government taxation and expenditures. All of these extensions are easy enough to incorporate.

that part of it which is wearing out. Suppose that a fraction δ of the capital stock depreciates. Then, of course,

$$(3.4) \qquad\qquad K(t+1) = (1-\delta)K(t) + I(t),$$

which tells us how the capital stock must change over time.

Now we introduce two important concepts. The *savings rate* is just savings divided by income: $S(t)/Y(t)$ in our model. Call this s. The savings rate depends on a multitude of characteristics in the economy, which we will discuss subsequently.

Our second concept is also a ratio: the *capital–output ratio*, which we call θ. It is the amount of capital required to produce a single unit of output in the economy, and it is represented by the ratio $K(t)/Y(t)$.

Combining (3.3) and (3.4), using these new concepts, and moving terms around a bit (see the Appendix to this chapter for the easy details), we arrive at a very influential equation indeed:

$$(3.5) \qquad\qquad s/\theta = g + \delta,$$

where g is the overall rate of growth that is defined by the value $[Y(t+1) - Y(t)]/Y(t)$. This is the *Harrod–Domar* equation, named after Roy Harrod and Evsey Domar, who wrote well-known papers on the subject in 1939 and 1946, respectively.

It isn't difficult to see why the Harrod–Domar equation was influential. It has the air of a recipe. It firmly links the growth rate of the economy to two fundamental variables: the ability of the economy to save and the capital–output ratio. By pushing up the rate of savings, it would be possible to accelerate the rate of growth. Likewise, by increasing the rate at which capital produces output (a *lower* θ), growth would be enhanced. Central planning in countries such as India and the erstwhile Soviet Union was deeply influenced by the Harrod–Domar equation (see boxes).

A small amendment to the Harrod–Domar model allows us to incorporate the effects of population growth. It should be clear that as the equation currently stands, it is a statement regarding the rate of growth of *total* gross national product (GNP), not GNP per capita. To talk about per capita growth, we must net out the effects of population growth. This is easy enough to do. If population (P) grows at rate n, so that $P(t+1) = P(t)(1+n)$ for all t, we can convert our equations into per capita magnitudes. (The chapter appendix records the simple algebra involved.) Instead of (3.5), we now get

$$(3.6) \qquad\qquad s/\theta = (1+g^*)(1+n) - (1-\delta),$$

where g^* is now the rate of *per capita* growth.

This is an expression that combines some of the fundamental features underlying growth: the ability to save and invest (captured by s), the ability to convert capital into output (which depends *inversely* on θ), the rate at which capital depreciates (δ), and, last but not least, the rate of population growth (n).

Actually, equation (3.6) looks a little complicated. There is an approximation that makes quick estimates far easier. To see this, expand the right-hand side of (3.6) to get $s/\theta = g^* + n + \delta - g^*n$. Now both g^* and n are small numbers, such as 0.05 or 0.02, so their product is very small relative to the other terms and can be ignored as an approximation. This gives us the approximate equation

$$(3.7) \qquad\qquad\qquad s/\theta \simeq g^* + n + \delta,$$

which goes well with (3.5) and can be used in place of (3.6) without much loss of accuracy.

At this point, you may want to do the exercises with the Harrod–Domar model at the end of this chapter, so that you feel more comfortable with the material so far.

Growth Engineering: The Soviet Experience

The Harrod–Domar model, as we have seen, has both descriptive and prescriptive value. The growth rate depends on certain parameters and, in a free market economy, these parameters are determined by people's tastes and technology. However, in a socialist, centrally planned economy (or even in a mixed economy with a large public sector), the government may have enough instruments (such as direct control over production and allocation, strong powers of taxation and confiscation, etc.) to manipulate these parameters to influence the growth rate. Given a government's growth objectives and existing technological conditions (e.g., the capital–output ratio), the Harrod–Domar model can be used to obtain policy clues; for example, the desired rate of investment to be undertaken so as to achieve this aim.

The first controlled experiment in "growth engineering" undertaken in the world was in the former Soviet Union, after the Bolshevik Revolution in 1917. The years immediately following the Revolution were spent in a bitter struggle—between the Bolsheviks and their various enemies, particularly the White Army of the previous Czarist regime—over the control of territory and productive assets such as land, factories, and machinery. Through the decade of the 1920s, the Bolsheviks gradually extended control over most of the Soviet Union (consisting of Russia, Ukraine, and other smaller states) that encompassed almost the whole of industry, channels of trade and commerce, food-grain distribution, and currency. The time had come, therefore, to use this newly acquired control over the economic machinery to achieve

Table 3.3. *Targets and achievements of the first Soviet five Year Plan (1928–29 to 1932–33).*[a]

	1927–28 (actual)	1932–33 (plan)	1932 (actual)
National income	24.4	49.7	45.5
Gross industrial production	18.3	43.2	43.3
(a) Producers' goods	6.0	18.1	23.1
(b) Consumers' goods	12.3	25.1	20.2
Gross agricultural production	13.1	25.8	16.6

Source: Dobb [1966].
[a] All figures are in 100 million 1926–27 rubles.

the economic goals of the revolutionary Bolsheviks, the foremost among these goals being a fast pace of industrialization.[5]

Toward the end of the 1920s, the need for a coordinated approach to tackle the problem of industrialization on all fronts was strongly felt. Under the auspices of the State Economic Planning Commission (called the *Gosplan*), a series of draft plans was drawn up which culminated in the first Soviet Five Year Plan (a predecessor to many more), which covered the period from 1929 to 1933. At the level of objectives, the plan placed a strong emphasis on industrial growth. The resulting need to step up the rate of investment was reflected in the plan target of increasing it from the existing level of 19.9% of national income in 1927–28 to 33.6% by 1932–33. (Dobb [1966, p. 236]).

How did the Soviet economy perform under the first Five Year Plan? Table 3.3 shows some of the plan targets and actual achievements, and what emerges is quite impressive. Within a space of five years, real national income nearly doubled, although it stayed slightly below the plan target. Progress on the industrial front was truly spectacular: gross industrial production increased almost 2.5 times. This was mainly due to rapid expansion in the machine producing sector (where the increment was a factor of nearly 4, far in excess of even plan targets), which is understandable, given the enormous emphasis on heavy industry in order to expand Russia's meager industrial base. Note that the production of consumer goods fell way below plan targets.

An equally spectacular failure shows up in the agricultural sector, in which actual production in 1932 was barely two-thirds of the plan target and only slightly more than the 1927–28 level. The reason was probably that the Bolsheviks' control over agriculture was never as complete as that over industry: continuing strife with the *kulak* farmers (large landowners from the Czarist era) took its toll on crop production.

---

[5] On the eve of the Revolution, Russia took a back seat among European nations in extent of industrialization, despite a rich endowment of natural resources. According to the calculations of P. Bairoch, based on the per capita consumption of essential industrial inputs, namely, raw cotton, pig iron, railway services, coal, and steam power, Russia ranked last among nine major European nations in 1910, behind even Spain and Italy. See Nove [1969].

3.3.2. *Beyond Harrod–Domar: Other considerations*

The story of the Soviet experiment with growth (see box) brings home the message that investment and savings are not just aggregate objects, but themselves have important components that may need to be controlled separately. Some key sectors may need more investment than others, and these may well spark a growth spurt in other sectors. Of special importance is the balance between urban and rural sectors, or more narrowly, between agriculture and industry. The question of sectoral balance is complicated enough to merit separate inquiry, and we will return to this issue in later chapters.

Even at the level of the aggregative simplicity of the Harrod–Domar model, there remains much to understand. Take another look at the basic Harrod–Domar model, captured by equation (3.6). It tells us that *if* savings rates, capital–output ratios, population growth rates, and depreciation rates are such and such, *then* the resulting growth rate is so many percentage points. We are, of course, entitled to make such "if–then" statements and in many cases, they make good sense, but in many cases they do not. The reason they may not always be useful is that the very parameters (savings rates, capital–output ratios) that are used to predict growth rates may themselves be affected by the growth process. Put another way, such variables may not be *exogenous* to economic growth, but may be themselves be *endogenously* determined.

What we are going to do in the following sections is study, one by one, the different sources of endogeneity that may affect the workings of the simple model. Of course, the end result of putting all these forces together into one framework may be very complicated. This is why we will attain a better understanding of the various features by studying them one at a time.

The endogeneity of savings

Perhaps the most important parameter in the Harrod–Domar model is the rate of savings. Can it be treated as a parameter that can be manipulated easily by policy? That depends on how much control the policy maker has over the economy. In fact, there are several reasons to believe that the rate of savings may itself be influenced by the overall level of per capita income in the society, not to mention the *distribution* of that income among the population. We will return to this issue in more detail in Chapter 6, but let us take a first look at it now.

Imagine that you live in a society where the bare necessities of life require an expenditure of $1,000 per year. It is quite plausible that if your income is also around $1,000, you will not be saving much; indeed, it is likely that you might be borrowing to make ends meet. Thus at low levels of income, it is not surprising to encounter rates of savings that are small or even negative (although without the goodwill of your creditors or the possibility of default, negative *lifetime* savings are probably impossible). This simple observation extends to poor countries as well: economies where the majority of the citizens are close to subsistence levels of consumption are unlikely to have a high rate of savings. In such circumstances, it is unlikely that the government or policy maker can do much to raise the savings rate significantly. Growth efforts must then rely on other sources of capital accumulation, such as external credit or aid.

As the economy grows, leaving subsistence levels behind, there is increased room for savings. This does not *necessarily* mean that savings will indeed grow. Notions of "what is necessary" in a society can and do change. Thus the United States, one of the world's richest countries, also has one of the world's lowest rates of savings. However, in these situations there is more scope for affecting the rate of savings.

Issues of subsistence, while of fundamental importance in the poorest countries, are somewhat less important in richer societies (including many developing countries). Other factors come into play. One consideration is the overall distribution of income within the country, and possibly across countries as well. The existence of *some* inequality may spur savings among the middle class (and by extension, among middle-income countries as a whole) because of the desire for prestige and status in the global economy of which they are increasingly a part. Note that although such aspirations may be held by both the middle class and the poor, it is the middle class that is in a better position to pander to these ambitions (or attain them for their children) by saving high fractions of their income. As already discussed, the poor (including poor countries) cannot do so, even if they want to.

The foregoing analysis suggests that there should be some tendency for the savings rate to significantly rise as we move from very poor to middle-income levels, both *within* a country and across countries. What happens at even higher levels of income is possibly more ambiguous. On the one hand, the rich are even more capable of high savings, so that the overall rate of savings should be no lower than that of their middle-class counterparts (absolute *levels* of savings will be higher, of course, but we are interested in the ratio). Extending the argument in the previous paragraph it is possible to argue that there might be a tendency for the rate of savings to decline. Although the rich (and rich countries) can *afford* to save, the fact that they are ahead of many other individuals (or other countries) blunts their need to accumulate wealth for this purpose. Current consumption may become relatively attractive.

All these concepts necessitate an adjustment in the Harrod–Domar theory, although not a drastic one: as incomes change, the savings rate that enters into the Harrod–Domar formula (3.6) will change. This creates a tendency over time for the growth rate of a country to alter in a way that mirrors the movement of the savings rate with income. For instance, if we were to take the foregoing argument literally, the prediction is that *both* low- and high-income countries have lower growth rates than middle-income countries.

This example illustrates another feature as well. In a sense, the simple Harrod–Domar model is a *neutral* theory of economic growth. It provides no reason why growth rates systematically differ at different levels of income. There is no "feedback" from the level of per capita income to the many parameters affecting the growth process. With the amendment in this example, neutrality is lost: a pattern linking per capita income to growth rates is created. This is a feature that will reappear in this chapter.

The endogeneity of population growth

Just as the savings rate might vary with the level of per capita income, population growth rates vary too. Indeed, as Chapter 9 discusses in detail, there is an enormous body of evidence that suggests that population growth rates systematically change with the overall level of development of a society. If that is indeed so, we have another reason for the variation of per capita growth rates that is quite independent of any systematic variation in the rate of savings.

The fundamental variation of population growth rates with the level of development is known to social scientists as the *demographic transition*. This phenomenon is so important to our understanding of economic development that we have devoted Chapter 9 to its study and to discussion of closely related issues. Nevertheless, let us go through a quick version of the story for an application in the context of economic growth.

The idea is very simple. In poor countries, death rates, especially among children, are very high. The greater incidence of famine, undernutrition, and disease, as well as difficult conditions of sanitation and hygiene, all contribute to this outcome. It is not surprising, then, that birth rates are high as well. Faced with the possibility of death, families must procreate at a greater rate to reach some target number of surviving offspring. The combination of a high birth rate and a high death rate actually serves to keep the *net* population growth rate, which is the difference between birth and death rate, at a low level. With an increase in living standards, death rates start to fall. For various reasons that we shall discuss in Chapter 9, birth rates adjust relatively slowly to this transformation in death rates. This causes the population growth rate to initially shoot up. The increase is all the more dramatic if the decline in death rates is rapid. In the longer run, and with further development, birth rates begin their downward adjustment and the population growth rate falls to a low level once again. This "inverse-U" shaped behavior of the population growth rate has been noted in many different countries

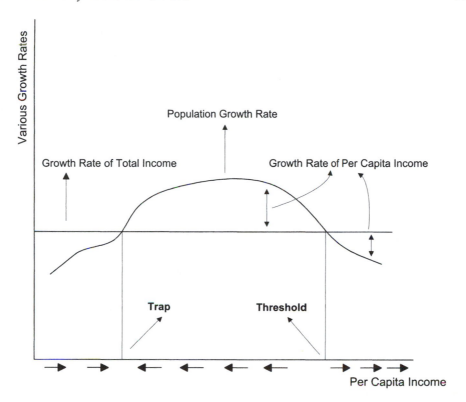

Figure 3.2. Endogenous population growth and economic growth.

and is referred to as the demographic transition . If this compressed description has raised several questions in your mind, don't worry; it should. As promised, we will return to these issues later in the book.

For now, concentrate on the implications of the demographic transition for per capita economic growth. Figure 3.2 exhibits two lines on the same graph, where the horizontal axis depicts per capita income and the vertical axis shows growth rates of various kinds. The first line is flat: it displays the overall growth rate (*not* per capita, but net of depreciation) in the Harrod–Domar model, as given by (3.5). The line is flat because we are simplifying the analysis by assuming that all parameters other than the population growth rate (including the savings rate) are unaffected by per capita income.[6]

A second curve, also marked in the diagram, shows how the rate of growth of population might vary with per capita income. In line with the demographic transition, we may think of such a curve as initially rising with per capita income and later falling. To be sure, we are simplifying a complicated story with this easy-to-digest diagram. In particular, there are several factors other than per capita income that make for "development"

---

[6] Of course, we argued in the previous section that this may not be the case, but (and I have said this before) this is a way to understand the effects of different factors one by one.

(as we have already discussed) and the rate of population growth depends on these factors as well. However, the current formulation is chosen to make a specific point, to which we now turn.

Remember from our approximate version of the Harrod–Domar equation (3.7) that the growth rate of per capita income is just the growth rate of overall income (net of depreciation) minus the rate of population growth. This is shown in Figure 3.2 as the vertical distance between the two curves at every level of per capita income. Note that under this reformulation of the Harrod–Domar model, the rate of growth of per capita income turns out to depend on the current income level. For instance, in our diagram, the rate is initially positive (up to the level of per capita income marked "Trap"), then negative (up to the level of per capita income marked "Threshold"), and then finally positive again.

If you understand this, then it is easy to see the implications for per capita economic growth. Start from a very low level of per capita income, to the left of "Trap." Then it is clear from the diagram that because the rate of growth of per capita income is positive, per capita income will rise over time; it is as if the economy moves along the horizontal axis toward the point marked "Trap." Now the meaning of the trap should become clear in this context, for if we start just *above* this critical level of per capita income, population growth will outstrip overall growth of income, and the economy will actually become *poorer* in per capita terms. The little arrows along the horizontal axis indicate the directions of movement.

Now consider the second critical level of per capita income, marked "Threshold." By the same arguments, it is easy to convince yourself that if the economy is fortunate enough to be to the right of the threshold, per capita income will increase over time, and the economy will be in a phase of sustained growth. To summarize, in the absence of some policy that pushes the economy to the right of the threshold, the economy will tend to be caught in the trap.

The little model summarized by this diagram is a caricature of reality,[7] but perhaps it is not too much of a caricature. As we saw in Chapter 2,

---

[7] There are several reasons why any model is simplistic, and we should note them if we want to use models wisely. For instance, there is no reason why the population curve should ever cut the flat line that depicts overall income growth. It is quite possible that overall income growth is good enough even for high rates of population growth. It is easy to see that in such a case, our traps and thresholds would disappear. Nevertheless, as population growth peaks, the economy will pass through a prolonged period of slow growth (instead of slowing to a complete halt), and the ideas that we discussed in this section remain just as valid, although not in equally stark form. There are other points as well. Our population growth curve neglects the notion of demographic transition as a process in time. For instance, as per capita income *declines*, is it true that population growth reverts to the levels that it had seen earlier? Our diagram assumes that the answer is literally "yes," and this is certainly an exaggeration. Modeling these time irreversibilities appropriately is certainly important, but they will not detract from the main points of what we have to say, and this is what makes a model capable of being relevant, even though it may be unrealistic.

there are several countries that have been unable to enjoy per capita growth because all the growth in overall income has been eaten up by the rapid rate of population growth. More generally, the diagram suggests that there are situations in which a *temporary* boost to certain economic parameters, perhaps through government policy, may have sustained long-run effects. This is easy enough to see with the present model, so let us talk ourselves through one such example. Imagine that the economy is just to the left of the threshold, so that it is sliding back toward the trap (because population growth exceeds income growth). In this situation, a jump in the savings rate can shift the rate of overall income growth to a level that outstrips the population growth rate, and therefore pulls the threshold down. You easily can see this diagrammatically by mentally pushing up the flat line in the diagram and seeing that the threshold moves to the left. In this case, the economy can grow. Note, moreover, that *the policy that boosts savings does not have to be a permanent one.* Once the economy crosses a certain level of per capita income, the old savings rate will suffice to keep it from sliding back, because population growth rates fall of their own accord in response to the higher standard of living.

Likewise, a strong family planning drive or the provision of incentives to have less children can pull down the population curve, again converting a seemingly hopeless situation into one that can permit long-run growth. Again, as the economy becomes rich of its own accord, population growth rates will be endogenously induced to fall, so that the once necessary policy now becomes superfluous.

The idea that temporary changes in policy can have lasting long-run effects is important. We will return to this again at several points and we will see that there are common strands shared by seemingly very different situations that permit the use of such temporary policies.

The foregoing discussion, especially the examples, illustrates a point about which we must be very aware. Factors that we treat as *exogenous* (e.g., savings) may well be influenced by the outcomes that they supposedly "cause" (e.g., income or its rate of growth). This is not to say that there is *no* causal relationship at all between savings and growth rates, but if the feedback from growth to savings is also significant, we may need to incorporate this in the theory. We told a similar story with population growth rates, which are just as capable of being endogenous.

More important than the mere recognition of endogeneity is the understanding that such features may fundamentally alter the way we think about the economy and about policy. We saw how this might happen in the case of endogenous population growth, but the most startling and influential example of all is the model that we turn to now. Developed by Solow [1956], this model has had a major impact on the way economists think about economic growth. It relies on the possible endogeneity of yet another parameter in the Harrod–Domar model: the capital–output ratio.

3.3.3. The Solow model

Introduction

Solow's twist on the Harrod–Domar story is based on the law of diminishing returns to individual factors of production. Capital and labor work together to produce output. If there is plenty of labor relative to capital, a little bit of capital will go a long way. Conversely, if there is a shortage of labor, capital-intensive methods are used at the margin and the incremental capital–output ratio rises. This is exactly in line with our previous discussion: according to the Solow thesis, the capital–output ratio θ is *endogenous*. In particular, θ might depend on the economywide relative endowments of capital and labor.[8]

The Solow equations

To understand the implications of this modification, it will help to go through a set of derivations very similar to those we used for the Harrod–Domar model. We may retain equations (3.3) (savings equal investment) and (3.4) (capital accumulation) without any difficulty. Retaining, too, the assumption that total savings $S(t)$ is a constant fraction s of total income $Y(t)$, we may combine (3.3) and (3.4) to get

(3.8) $$K(t+1) = (1 - \delta)K(t) + sY(t).$$

If we divide through by population (P_t) and assume that population grows at a constant rate, so that $P(t+1) = (1+n)P_t$, (3.8) changes to

(3.9) $$(1+n)k(t+1) = (1-\delta)k(t) + sy(t),$$

where the lowercase ks and ys represent per capita magnitudes (K/P and Y/P, respectively).

Before going on, make sure you understand the economic intuition underlying the algebra of (3.9). It is really very simple. The right-hand side has two parts, depreciated per capita capital [which is $(1-\delta)k(t)$] and current per capita savings [which is $sy(t)$]. Added together, this should give us the new per capita capital stock $k(t+1)$, except for one complication: population is growing, which exerts a downward drag on per capita capital stocks.

---

[8] This is not to deny that θ may be driven by other factors, such as the pace of technological progress. We will have much to say about this presently, but as usual, one step at a time!

This is why the left-hand side of (3.9) has the rate of growth of population (*n*) in it. Note that the larger the rate of population growth, the lower is per capita capital stock in the next period.

To complete our understanding of the Solow model, we must relate per capita output at each date to the per capita capital stock, using the *production function*. The production function, as you know, represents the technical knowledge of the economy. In this model, capital and labor work together to produce total output. With constant returns to scale, we may use the production function to relate per capita output to per capita input. (The Appendix to this chapter brings you up to date on these matters if you're feeling rusty.)

Figure 3.3 shows a typical production function with diminishing returns to per capita capital. Notice that as per capita capital increases, the output–capital ratio falls because of a relative shortage of labor. Note that output per *person* continues to rise, of course. It is just that with a relative shortage of labor, the *ratio* of output to capital used in production falls. In Figure 3.4, we use this production function to determine what the per capita capital stock must be at date $t + 1$ if the current per capita stock is k. Simply translate equation (3.9) into the diagram. To do so, multiply the output from any given capital stock by s, which gives us fresh investment, and add the result to the depreciated capital stock. The end product is the curved line in Figure 3.4, which looks very much like the production function itself (and indeed, is closely related), but has been transformed in the way we just described. Figure 3.4 also plots the left-hand side of (3.9), the straight line $(1 + n)k$

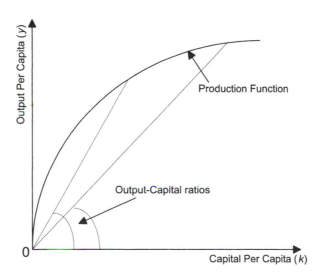

Figure 3.3. *How capital per capita produces output per capita.*

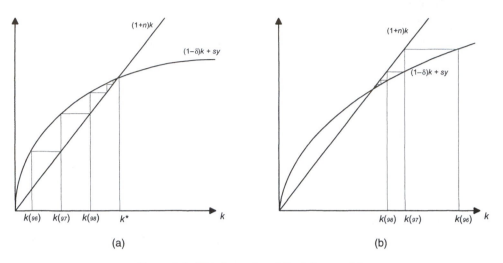

Figure 3.4. *The dynamics of the Solow model.*

as k changes. Observe that because of diminishing returns, the curved line initially lies above this straight line and then falls below.[9]

The steady state

Armed with this diagram, we can make some very strong predictions about growth rates. Figure 3.4 shows us two initial historical levels of the per capita capital stock—one "low" (Figure 3.4a) and one "high" (Figure 3.4b)—starting in the year 1996. With the low stock, the output–capital ratio is very high and so the per capita capital stock can expand quite rapidly. How do we see this in Figure 3.4? Well, we know from (3.9) that the supply of per capita capital is read off by traveling up to the point on the curved line corresponding to the initial stock $k(1996)$. However, some of this supply is eroded by population growth. To find $k(1997)$, we simply travel horizontally until the line $(1 + n)k$ is touched; the capital stock corresponding to this point is 1997's per capita capital stock. Now just repeat the process. We obtain the zigzag path in Figure 3.4a. Note that the growth of per capita capital *slows down* and that per capita capital finally settles close to k^*, which is a distinguished capital stock level where the curved and straight lines meet.

Likewise, you may trace the argument for a high initial capital stock, as in Figure 3.4b. Here, there is an *erosion* of the per capita stock as time passes, with convergence occurring over time to the *same* per capita stock, k^*, as in Figure 3.4a. The idea here is exactly the opposite of that in the previous paragraph: the output-capital ratio is low, so the rate of expansion

---

[9] If you've been following the argument particularly closely, you will see that this last statement is exactly true if we make the additional assumption that the marginal product of capital is very high when there is very little capital and diminishes to zero as the per capita capital stock becomes very high.

of aggregate capital is low. Therefore, population growth outstrips the rate of growth of capital, thus eroding the *per capita* capital stock.

We can think of k^* as a *steady-state* level of the per capita capital stock, to which the per capita capital stock, starting from *any* initial level, must converge.

In other words, growth in the Solow model loses its momentum if capital is growing too fast relative to labor, which is precisely what happens to the left of k^* in Figure 3.4a. The reason is diminishing returns to capital, which creates a downward movement in the capital–output ratio as capital is accumulated faster than labor. The lower output–capital ratio then brings down the growth of capital in line with the growth of labor. This means that the long-run capital–labor ratio must be constant (and this is captured by the ratio k^*).

However, if the per capita capital stock settles down to some "steady-state" level, then so must per capita income! Thus in this version of the Solow model, there is no long-run growth of per capita output, and *total* output grows precisely at the rate of growth of the population. In particular, the savings rate has no long-run effect on the rate of growth, in sharp contrast to the prediction of the Harrod–Domar model.

Matters seem confusing at this point. We just studied the Harrod–Domar model, where the rate of savings most certainly affected the growth rate, and now the Solow model tells us that there is no such effect, at least in the long run. Yet these confusing discrepancies melt away once we recall that the Solow model brings in a feature that the Harrod–Domar model did not possess: diminishing returns to capital, which create endogenous changes in the capital–output ratio. This is the feature that chokes off growth in the Solow model. Look again at Figure 3.4 and observe that the smaller the degree of diminishing returns, the closer is the curve in that diagram to a straight line and the longer it will take for the per capita stock of capital to settle down—k^* becomes larger. The Harrod–Domar model studies the limiting case of this process where there is no diminishing returns at all and consequently no such steady state k^*: in that case, the per capita capital stock can grow indefinitely. Therefore, whether the Solow model or the Harrod–Domar model is more relevant is ultimately an empirical question and, as we shall soon see, the jury is still out on the issue. In any case, as long as we appreciate that the different predictions are driven by different assumptions (in this case, with regard to the nature of technology), there is absolutely no reason to be confused.

How parameters affect the steady state

The rate of savings in the Solow model does not affect the long-run growth rate of per capita income (which is zero so far), but it certainly affects the long-run *level* of income. So does the rate of depreciation and the growth rate of population. All these effects work through changes in the steady-state level of capital per capita, which in turn affects the steady-state level of per capita output, which is the same as per capita income in the long run.

To see this a bit more formally, note from Figure 3.4 and our discussion so far that *were* the economy to start from the steady-state level of k^*, it would stay at k^* in every period (after all, that is what the term "steady state" means). This means that in equation (3.9), we can put $k(t) = k(t+1) = k^*$. If we use the notation y^* to denote the per capita output producible from k^*, and move terms around in (3.9) a bit, we obtain the equation that describes the steady state:

$$(3.10) \qquad \frac{k^*}{y^*} = \frac{s}{n + \delta}.$$

The effects of changes in various parameters can now be easily seen. An increase in s, the rate of savings, raises the right-hand side of the equation, necessitating an increase in the left-hand side to restore equality. This means that the new steady-state capital–output ratio must be *higher*. With diminishing returns, this can only happen if the new steady-state level of k^* (and y^*) is higher as well. We thus see that an increase in the savings rate raises the long-run level of per capita income. By exactly the same logic, check that an increase in the population growth rate or the rate of depreciation will lower the long-run level of per capita income.

To complete your understanding, make sure you understand the economics behind the algebra as well. For instance, a higher rate of depreciation means that more of national savings must go into the replacement of worn-out capital. This means that, all other things being equal, the economy accumulates a smaller net amount of per capita capital, and this lowers the steady-state level. You should similarly run through the effects of changes in the savings rate and the population growth rate.

Level effects and growth effects

The population growth rate is a parameter with an interesting double effect. As we have just seen, higher population growth *lowers* the steady-state level of per capita income, but note that *total* income must *grow* faster as well as a result! This must be the case because we know that the economy converges to a steady-state level of per capita income, which is impossible unless the long-run growth of *total* income equals the rate of growth of the population.

This double effect of population growth arises from a fundamental characteristic of labor that makes it different from any other commodity. Labor is *both* an input in production and a consumer of final goods. The former effect tends to raise total output; the latter effect tends to lower savings and

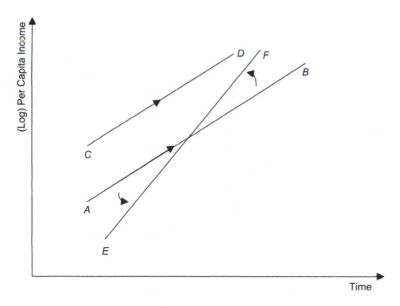

Figure 3.5. Level effects and growth effects.

investment. The first effect drives the higher rate of growth of total income; the second brings down the steady-state level of per capita income.

Therefore, apart from its intrinsic interest, population growth is noteworthy as an example of a parameter that has both a *level effect* and a *growth effect* on income. We will discuss this feature of population growth in more detail in Chapter 9.

A growth effect is an effect that changes the rate of growth of a variable, typically income or per capita income. A level effect, in contrast, leaves the rate of growth unchanged, while shifting up (or down) the entire path traced out by the variable over time. Figure 3.5 illustrates the difference between the two effects. This diagram draws growth paths of the logarithm of income over time, such as those marked by *AB*, *CD*, or *EF*. Note that with a constant rate of growth, the path of log income appears as straight lines on this diagram.[10] A path such as *CD* is distinguished from a path such as *AB* only by a change in the overall level; growth rates are the same along the two paths. On the other hand, a path such as *EF* exhibits a higher growth rate than *AB* or *CD*. Parameters that only cause "parallel" shifts, such as the move from *AB* to *CD*, are deemed to have level effects. Parameters that twist the growth path to *EF* are those with growth effects. Combinations of the two are possible as well, as we have already seen in the case of population growth and total income.

---

[10] Suppose that the growth rate of income is g, and $Y(0)$ is the starting level of income. Then $Y(t) = Y(0)(1+g)^t$ for all dates t. Taking logarithms, we see that $\ln Y(t) = \ln Y(0) + t\ln(1+g)$. This simple calculation shows us that in Figure 3.5, the intercept of a growth path on the vertical axis gives us a measure of the level, whereas the slope is a measure of the rate of growth.

As an example, let us see why savings rates only have level effects in the Solow model. Consider an increase in the savings rate. Of course, output will go up and it will stay higher. This also means that the per capita capital stock will be higher in every period after the rise in savings rates. Use Figure 3.4 to check that the steady-state capital stock per capita must go up, so that the net effect of an increase in the savings rate is to push capital and output (per head) to a higher *level*—a higher long-run level. Note that the *long-run* effect on income *growth* is nil: income will simply grow at the rate of population, just as it did before.

You may ask how it is that we move to a higher *level* of per capita income if the rate of growth is unaffected. The answer is that it is the *long-run* growth rate that is unaffected: in the short and the medium run the increase in the savings rate pushes the economy to a higher trajectory, but the effect is ultimately killed off by diminishing returns. The savings rate has a level effect only in the Solow model.

This discussion suggests that level versus growth effects is highly model-specific. For instance, in a world with constant returns to scale, the savings rate *does* have growth effects: a look at the Harrod–Domar equation confirms this.

The exercises at the end of this chapter contain further discussion of level and growth effects.

Summary so far

The Solow model studies a situation where the capital–output ratio changes with the per capita availability of capital in the economy. The change is driven by the postulate of diminishing returns, so that a higher per capita stock raises the capital–output ratio. This contrasts with the Harrod–Domar model, where the assumption of a constant capital–output ratio essentially rules out diminishing returns.

The relative validity of these two models is open to empirical scrutiny and the theoretical predictions are very different. In particular, the Solow model tells us that parameters such as the savings rate have only level effects, in contrast to the growth effects of savings in the Harrod–Domar model. Indeed, in the simple version of the Solow model studied so far (but soon to be extended), there is a steady-state level of per capita income to which the economy must converge, *irrespective of its historical starting point*. More dramatically, the Solow model infers that *regardless of the initial per capita capital stock*, two countries with similar savings rates, depreciation rates, and population growth rates will converge to similar standards of living "in the long run"! This is the hypothesis of international *convergence*, and it has led to a large literature, which we will come to in due course.

What are we to make of all this? Does the Solow model predict that there is, finally, no per capita growth? How do we ever reconcile this with the evidence of the data, which suggests ongoing growth as well as persistent disparities between rich and poor? What does the "long run" mean, anyway? In addition, why should we buy these odd implications of the Solow model, when the Harrod–Domar story is much simpler, *and* permits continuing rates of per capita growth? In any case, no two countries have the same savings and population growth rates, so why should we care about a claim of convergence that relies on such absurd assumptions?

These are all good questions, but the proper answers require a far more agnostic approach—one that does not take model building literally, but only as a pointer to interesting, often hidden aspects of economic reality.

3.4. Technical progress

Our first task in an overall assessment is to introduce technical progress into the Solow model.

Recall that the Solow model makes a strong claim. In the absence of technical progress, a country cannot sustain per capita income growth indefinitely. For this to happen, capital must grow faster than population, but in such a case, the hypothesis of diminishing returns implies that the marginal contribution of capital to output must decline, which eventually forces a decline in the growth rate of output and, therefore, of capital. This is the substance of the previous section.

The foregoing argument loses its force if there is continuing technical progress; that is, if the production function *shifts upward* over time as new knowledge is gained and applied. As long as the optimistic force of this shift outweighs the doom of diminishing returns, there is no reason why per capita growth cannot be sustained indefinitely.

Is this a reason to abandon the Solow model? Most certainly not, and for two reasons. First, think of the model as a way to organize ideas. Think of two broad sources of growth: one is through better and more advanced methods of production (technical progress) and the second is via the continued buildup of plant, machinery, and other inputs that bring increased productive power.[11] The model claims that *in the absence of the first source, the second is not enough for sustained per capita growth*. It does *not* state that growth is impossible, period. Viewed in this way, the Solow model is a pointer to studying the economics of technological progress, arguing that it is there that one must look for the ultimate sources of growth. This is not to say that such a claim is necessarily true, but it is certainly provocative and very far from being obviously wrong.

---

[11] This is not to deny that these two sources are often intimately linked: technical progress may be *embodied* in the new accumulation of capital inputs.

Second, the *method* of reasoning used in the basic Solow model can be adapted easily to include technical progress of this kind. Let's take a few moments to go through the adaptation, because the arguments are important to our understanding of the theory of growth.

A simple way to understand technical progress is to envision that such progress contributes to the efficiency, or economic productivity, of labor. Indeed, as we will see later, it is not only increased technical know-how, but other advances (such as increased and better education) that contribute to enhanced labor productivity. Thus although we concentrate here on technical progress, our approach applies equally to the increased productivity brought about by higher education, and not necessarily newer technology.

Let's begin by returning to equation (3.8), which describes the accumulation of capital and remains perfectly valid with or without technical progress. Now let's make a distinction between the working population $P(t)$ and the amount of labor in "efficiency units" [call it $L(t)$] used in production—the *effective population*, if you like. This distinction is necessary because in the extension of the model that we now consider, the productivity of the working population is constantly increasing. The simplest way to capture this increase in productivity is to postulate that

$$(3.11) \qquad\qquad L(t) = E(t)P(t),$$

where we can think of $E(t)$ as the efficiency or productivity of an individual at time t. Not only does population grow over time (at the rate of n, just as before), but we now take it that efficiency grows too at the rate of π. Thus $E(t+1) = (1+\pi)E(t)$. We equate this increase in productivity to technical progress, so we will refer to π as the rate of technical progress.

One more step and our adapted model is complete. Recall how we passed to (3.9) from (3.8) after dividing through by the working population to obtain per capita magnitudes. We do the same here, but with a twist: we divide by the *effective* population $E(t)P(t)$ to arrive at what looks like per capita capital and income, but with a difference. These are magnitudes *per efficiency unit of labor*. Let's call them $\hat{k}$ and $\hat{y}$ to distinguish them from the earlier per capita values k and y. Performing the required division, we get something that looks very much like our old equation (3.9):

$$(3.12) \qquad (1+n)(1+\pi)\hat{k}(t+1) = (1-\delta)\hat{k}(t) + s\hat{y}(t).$$

Now we simply apply the old ideas regarding production functions, just as we did before. Capital per efficiency unit of labor ($\hat{k}$) produces output per efficiency unit of labor ($\hat{y}$). As in the basic Solow model, if there is too much capital per efficiency unit, we have a shortage of (effective) labor and

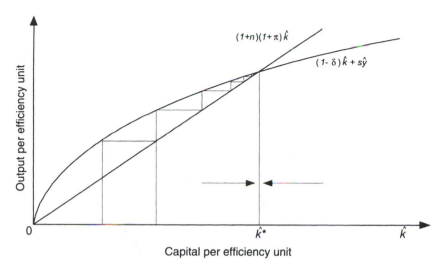

Figure 3.6. The Solow model with technical change.

the output–capital ratio tends to fall: diminishing returns to an input still applies, but this time to *efficiency* units of labor. Thus Figure 3.6 repeats, in spirit, the analysis done for equation (3.9) in Figure 3.4. *Exactly* the same logic applies to equation (3.12).

Over time, the amount of capital per effective labor may rise or fall. Observe that if it is rising, this simply means that physical capital is growing faster than the rate of population growth and technical progress *combined*. However, then diminishing returns sets in and *output* per efficiency unit rises, but not in the same proportion. By examining (3.12), it is clear that the fresh savings generated therefore *also* fail to rise proportionately, and this tones down the growth rate of capital per efficiency unit. In Figure 3.6, this discussion corresponds to the region lying left of the intersection point $\hat{k}^*$. In this region, the growth rate of total capital falls over time as capital per efficiency unit rises. Likewise, to the right of the intersection, capital per efficiency unit *falls* over time.

All roads lead, then, to the steady-state level $\hat{k}^*$. So far the analysis runs parallel to the case of no technical progress. The novelty lies in the interpretation. Note that *even though* capital per efficiency unit converges to a stationary steady state, the amount of capital per member of the working population continues to increase. Indeed, the long-run increase in per capita income takes place precisely at the rate of technical progress!

With long-run growth introduced into the model, it is now time to take a closer look at the important notion of convergence and to distinguish between several shades of the definition.

3.5. Convergence?

3.5.1. Introduction

The preceding section showed us how to modify the Solow model to include technical change. This, together with the Harrod–Domar model, concludes our first look at the theory of economic growth. We are now in a position to evaluate some fundamental implications of this framework and to apply these implications to the data.

3.5.2. Unconditional convergence

At the heart of the Solow model is the prediction of *convergence*, but the notion of convergence comes in several flavors. The strongest prediction, and therefore the one that is potentially the easiest to refute, is called *unconditional convergence*. Suppose we postulate that countries, in the long run, have no tendency to display differences in the rates of technical progress, savings, population growth, and capital depreciation. In such a case, the Solow model predicts that in *all* countries, capital per efficiency unit of labor converges to the common value $\hat{k}^*$, described in the preceding section, and this will happen irrespective of the initial state of each of these economies, as measured by their starting levels of per capita income (or equivalently, their per capita capital stock).

Does this sound trivial? After all, we are assuming that all long-run parameters are similar. Under such an assumption, how could we expect anything other than convergence? In fact, the assertion is far from obvious. What are assumed to be the same are exogenous parameters of the model, but *not* the initial level of the capital stock or per capita income. The claim of convergence is then based on the analysis that we conducted for the Solow model: its content is that in the face of similar parameters governing the evolution of the economy, *history in the sense of different initial conditions does not matter*.

Empirically, the assertion of unconditional convergence is even stronger. At the back of our minds we base such convergence on certain assumptions regarding the similarity of parameters across countries. However, there is no guarantee that these assumptions hold in reality, so if we were to find convergence, it would be a striking finding, not a trivial one.

Figure 3.7 illustrates (unconditional) convergence. As in Figure 3.5, we plot the logarithm of income against time, so that a constant rate of growth (such as that experienced in the steady state) appears as a straight line. The line AB plots the time path of (log) per capita income at the steady state, where income per efficiency unit of labor is precisely at the level generated by $\hat{k}^*$. The path CD represents a country that starts below the steady-state level per efficiency unit. According to the Solow model, this country will

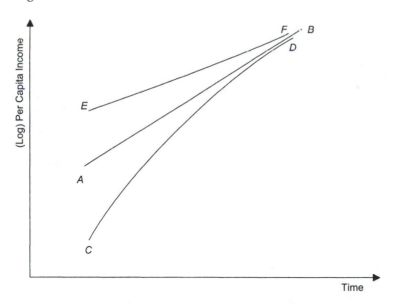

Figure 3.7. *Illustration of unconditional convergence.*

initially display a rate of growth that *exceeds* the steady-state level, and its time path of (log) per capita income will move asymptotically toward the *AB* line as shown. Over time, its growth rate will decelerate to the steady-state level. Likewise, a country that starts off above the steady state, say at *E*, will experience a *lower* rate of growth, because its time path *EF* of (log) income flattens out to converge to the line *AB* from above. At least, that is what the hypothesis has to say.

Convergence, then, is indicated by a strong negative relationship between growth rates of per capita income and the initial value of per capita income.

It is quite clear from our discussion that the hypothesis of unconditional convergence takes us out on a limb. Not only does it require the convergence of countries to their own steady states, but it asserts that these steady states are all the same! Let us see what the data have to say on this matter.

3.5.3. Unconditional convergence: Evidence or lack thereof

The first problem that arises when testing a hypothesis of this sort is the issue of time horizons. The systematic collection of data in the developing economies started only recently, and it is hard to find examples of reliable data that stretch back a century or more. There are, then, two choices: cover a small number of countries over a large period of time or cover a large number of countries over a short period of time. We will look at examples of both approaches.

A small set of countries over a long time horizon

Baumol [1986] examined the growth rates of sixteen countries that are among the richest in the world today. Thanks to the work of Maddison [1982, 1991], data on per capita income are available for these countries for the year 1870. Baumol's idea was simple but powerful: plot 1870 per capita income for these sixteen countries on the horizontal axis and plot the growth rate of per capita income over the period 1870–1979 (measured by the difference in the logs of per capita income over this time period) on the vertical axis. Now examine whether the relationship between the various observations fits the level convergence hypothesis. As we discussed in the previous section, if the hypothesis is correct, the observations should approximately lie on a downward-sloping line.

Indeed, the exercise seems to pay off very well. Although the countries in Maddison's data set had comparable per capita incomes in 1979, they had widely different levels of per capita income in 1870. It appears, then, that Baumol's finding supports the unconditional convergence hypothesis quite strongly.[12] Figure 3.8, which is taken from De Long [1988], carries out this exercise by plotting the countries with the log of 1870 income on one axis and their subsequent growth on the other. The countries, read from poorest to richest *in 1870*, are Japan, Finland, Sweden, Norway, Germany, Italy, Austria, France, Canada, Denmark, the United States, the Netherlands, Switzerland, Belgium, the United Kingdom, and Australia. The figure shows the strong negative relationship in Baumol's study that is characteristic of unconditional convergence.

Unfortunately, Baumol's study provides a classic case of a statistical pitfall. He only considered countries that are rich ex post; that is, they had similar per capita GDP levels in 1979. In 1870, with no knowledge of the future, what criteria would tell us to choose these countries ex ante to test convergence down the road? A good illustration of the statistical error is the inclusion of Japan in the sample. It is there precisely because of hindsight: Japan is rich today, but in 1870, it was probably midway in the world's hierarchy of nations arranged by per capita income. If Japan, why not Argentina or Chile or Portugal?[13]

Thus, it may be alleged that the "convergence" that Baumol found is a result only of a statistical regularity rather than any underlying tendency

[12] Baumol regressed the log difference in per capita income between 1870 and 1979 on the logarithm of 1870 per capita income and a constant. A slope coefficient of -0.995 and an R^2 of 0.88 was obtained. A slope close to -1 means that by 1979, almost all the initial gaps in per capita income had been erased.

[13] Suppose you were to look at today's successful basketball stars. They would come from a variety of backgrounds; some poor and some rich. You could say that they "converged" to success, and in fact the rags-to-riches stories that we see often in the media bolsters such unwarranted perceptions. However, from this you cannot predict that a randomly chosen sample of kids who *aspire* to be basketball players will all "converge"! Hindsight is no substitute for prediction.

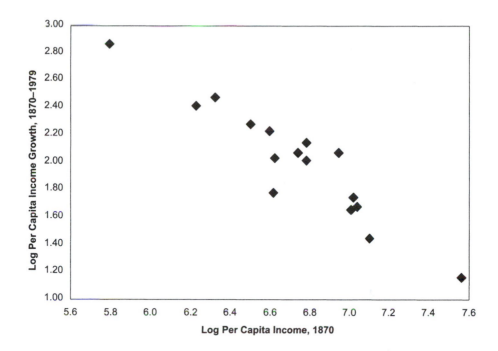

Figure 3.8. Growth and per capita income for the sixteen countries studied by Maddison.

of convergence.[14] A *true* test of convergence would have to look at a set of countries that, ex ante, seemed *likely* to converge to the high per capita GDP levels that came to characterize the richest nations several decades later.[15] It would not be fair to claim that the poor nations of Asia or Africa displayed such potential then, but a whole host of countries (many in Europe, and some in Latin America)—all of which are left out of Baumol's study—were very much in the same position as many of the countries included in Maddison's set of sixteen, in terms of income levels and economic promise (as perceived *then*). Thus Baumol's data have a "selection bias." Only those countries that are success stories were selected to study convergence. This is using wisdom after the event. Does the evidence on convergence hold up in a rigorous statistical test if we broaden the set of countries in the manner suggested in the foregoing text?

De Long (1988) addressed this question by adding, to Maddison's sixteen, seven other countries, which in 1870 had as much claim to membership in the "convergence club" as many included in Baumol's original set.

---

[14] Note that although we use this study as an illustrative warning, Baumol himself did see the problem immediately after a number of scholars pointed out the error. Our exposition relies heavily on the critique and extension of Baumol's study carried out by De Long [1988].

[15] This likelihood may be determined on the basis of the extent of their existing integration into the world economy, as well as their per capita income levels then.

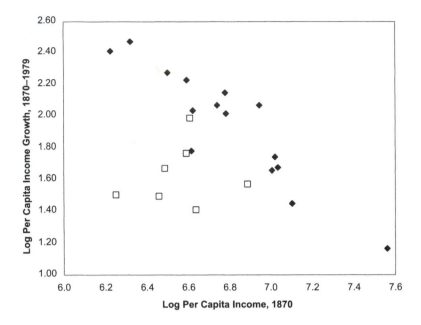

Figure 3.9. Growth and per capita income for the twenty-two countries studied by De Long. New countries are shown as squares; original countries as diamonds. Source: De Long [1988].

These additional countries are Argentina, Chile, East Germany, Ireland, New Zealand, Portugal, and Spain. Three of these countries (New Zealand, Argentina, and Chile) figure in the list of top ten recipients of British and French overseas investment (in per capita terms) as late as 1913. Investors' faith in these economies reflects a very favorable perception regarding their growth prospects at that point in time. *All* the new countries included had per capita GDP levels in 1870 higher than Finland, which was the second lowest in Baumol's sample.[16]

Figure 3.9 shows the modified pictures after De Long's countries are added and Japan is dropped from the initial sixteen. The earlier observations from Figure 3.8 appear as unlabeled dots. Now matters don't look so good for convergence, and indeed, De Long's statistical analysis confirms this gloomier story. Baumol's original regression can now be repeated on this new data set: regress the log difference in per capita income between 1870 and 1979 on the logarithm of 1870 per capita income and a constant.[17] The slope coefficient of the regression is still appreciably negative, but the

---

[16] The lowest is that of Japan and it is significantly below the rest. De Long dropped the data on Japan in his analysis, because its inclusion would necessitate the inclusion of several other countries at comparable income levels in 1870. But accurate 1870 data for such countries do not exist.

[17] For a discussion of regression and associated concepts, see Appendix 2.

"goodness-of-fit" is very bad, as indicated by the fact that the residual disturbance term is very large.

De Long also argued, and correctly so, that the 1870 data are likely to contain large measurement errors (relative to those in 1979), which make the various observations more scattered than they actually should be and makes any measurement of convergence more inflated than the case actually merits.[18] De Long repeated his regression exercise, assuming a stipulated degree of measurement error in the 1870 data and making necessary amendments to his estimation technique to allow for this, and found that the slope coefficient comes out to be very close to zero—indicating that there is very little systematic relationship between a country's growth rate and its per capita GDP, at least in the cross section of the twenty-two countries studied.

A large set of countries over a short time horizon

The second option is to include a very large set of countries to test for unconditional convergence. This approach has the advantage of "smoothing out" possible statistical irregularities in looking at a small sample. The disadvantage is that the time span of analysis must be shortened to a few decades, which is the span over which reliable data are available for a larger group of countries.

In Chapter 2, we used the Summers–Heston data set to say something about the world distribution of income over the period 1965–85. If you turn back to that chapter and reread the discussion there, it should be clear that unconditional convergence sounds like a pretty long shot. At the very least, the gap between the richest and the poorest countries does not seem to have appreciably narrowed. With per capita GDP expressed as a fraction of the U.S. level in the same year, a plot of the average for the five richest and the five poorest nations over a twenty-six year period (1960–85) displays a more or less constant relative gap between them. This is not to say that the poorest countries have not moved up in absolute terms: the average per capita income of the poor countries [expressed as a fraction of a fixed level (1985) of U.S. per capita GDP, as opposed to contemporaneous U.S. levels] shows a clear upward trend over the period. Nevertheless, the disparity in *relative* incomes (let alone that in *absolute* incomes) has stayed the same, because the poorest countries have grown at more or less the same rate as the richest.

An objection at this point is that a good sample should be broad based; that is, focused not merely on the richest and the poorest in the sample.

---

[18] Imagine that a set of families all have the same incomes in 1960 as well as in 1990. They are surveyed in both these years. However, the survey in 1960 is inaccurate, so there are errors of measurement, whereas the survey in 1990 is accurate, showing that they all have the same income. Then these families will (statistically) appear to have "converged" to the same income from different starting levels.

Indeed, we were careful to do this in Chapter 2 as well, where we noted how diverse the experiences of different countries have been over this period. We noted, moreover, that if we group countries into different clusters and then construct a mobility matrix to track their movements from one cluster to another, there is little tendency for countries to move toward a common cluster.

A similar tendency is noted from a different kind of statistical analysis. Parente and Prescott [1993] studied 102 countries over the period 1960–85. In this study, each country's per capita real GDP is expressed in relative terms: as a fraction of U.S. per capita GDP for the same year. The authors then calculated the standard deviation[19] of these values separately for each year. Whereas the convergence hypothesis says that countries move closer to each other in income levels, we expect the standard deviation of their relative incomes to fall over time. In Parente and Prescott's study, however, it actually *increased* by 18.5% over the twenty-six year period, and the increase was fairly uniform from year to year. However, there is some variation here if we look at geographical subgroupings. The standard deviation in relative incomes for Western European countries shows a clear decline. In fact this decline persists through the period 1913–85. On the other hand, the same measure applied to Asian countries displays a significant and pronounced increase, and the divergence in this region is consistent with data going all the way back to 1900.

To put the data together in yet another way, suppose that we regress average per capita growth between 1960 and 1985 on per capita GDP in 1960. Just as in the Baumol study, the tendency toward level convergence would show up in a negative relationship between these two variables,[20] but, in line with the discussion in the rest of this section, there is no clear tendency at all. Barro [1991] observed that the correlation between these two variables is only 0.09, which amounts to saying that there is no correlation at all.[21] Figure 3.10 uses the Heston–Summers data to plot per capita income in 1960 against the average annual growth rate between 1960 and 1985. The lack of a pattern in the data needs no comment.

3.5.4. Unconditional convergence: A summary

Our understanding so far has been negative, but it is useful all the same. Recall that the Harrod–Domar model, in its simplest form, predicts the "neutrality" of growth rates with respect to per capita income. Because of the as-

---

[19] The standard deviation of a set of observations is a statistical measure that indicates how closely bunched or how spread out in value the set of observations is. A higher measure of the standard deviation means a higher "spread" or dispersion around the average. See Chapter 6 and Appendix 2 for more detail.

[20] Note that in considering the entire data set, we avoid the ex post bias discussed earlier.

[21] For a definition of correlation, see Appendix 2.

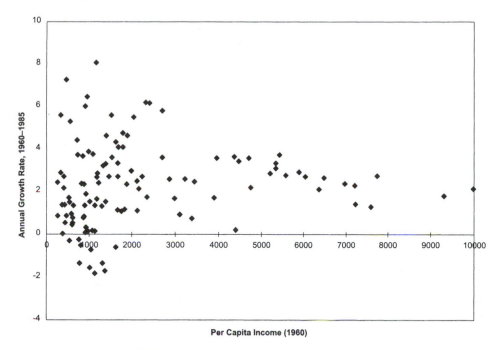

Figure 3.10. Per capita GDP (1960) against average annual growth rate, 1960–85. Source: Penn World Tables Mark II.

sumption that returns to capital are *constant*, parameters such as the savings rate have growth-rate effects, whereas per capita income plays no role to speed up or slow down the pace of growth. The Solow model, on the other hand, demotes the savings rate to a parameter that only has level effects. A too-rapid rise in per capita capital (and therefore in per capita output) is predicted to contain the seeds of its own deceleration, because the economy runs into diminishing returns to capital. Thus, provided that all the parameters of the Solow model are constant across countries, convergence across countries is an implication of that model.

This prediction of the Solow model in its simplest, strongest form appears to be clearly rejected by the data. It follows that the simple version of the Solow model is not valid, but we have learned something, because the Solow model can be treated as a benchmark from which we can explore different routes. Our task, then, is to examine several directions of reconciliation between the theory and the data, and, in so doing, to learn new ways to look at the data.

In closing this section, let us dispose of a simple objection first. We could say that the simple Harrod–Domar model was right after all. It predicts the neutrality of growth rates with respect to per capita income. By and large, that is what we seem to get, so why study the Solow model? The main rejoinder to this point of view is that the assumption of constant returns to *physical* capital alone is simplistic in a way that does not seem to fit the facts. Physical capital does need labor to operate: we are far from a world of pure automation. There is little doubt that in the absence of other inputs, or technical progress, a straightforward accumulation of machines would fail to lead to corresponding increases in output. Capital and labor do go hand in hand. Thus we may think of the Solow model as being absolutely correct in postulating diminishing returns to each input separately, but at the same time lacking in some important dimension that enriches the story and does not predict convergence.

3.5.5. *Conditional convergence*

Consider the obvious weak link in the prediction of unconditional convergence: the assumption that across all countries, the level of technical knowledge (and its change), the rate of savings, the rate of population growth, and the rate of depreciation are all the same. This notion certainly flies in the face of the facts: countries differ in many, if not all, these features. Although this has no effect on the Solow prediction that countries must converge to *their* steady states, the steady states can now be different from country to country, so that there is no need for two countries to converge to *each other*. This weaker hypothesis leads to the notion of *conditional convergence*.

To discuss this concept, we retain the assumption that knowledge flows freely across countries, so that technological know-how is the same for all countries,[22] but we allow other parameters, such as savings rates and population growth rates, to differ.

We already know that in the Solow model, these parameters only have level effects on per capita income. The growth rate of per capita income in the long run is determined entirely by the rate of technical progress, which we've assumed to be the same for all countries. This leads to the prediction of *convergence in growth rates:* although long-run per capita incomes vary from country to country, the long-run per capita growth rates of all countries are (predicted to be) the same.

Figure 3.11 illustrates convergence in growth rates. Now there is no single line that depicts the steady-state time path of (log) per capita income for all

---

[22] Of course, this assumption (like every other assumption) can be questioned as well, but not as easily as one might think. For instance, we could say that very different techniques are used in dairy farming in India and in the United States, so it must be the case that the technology is different. This argument is wrong. The assumption that technology is the same does not imply that the actual production *technique* is the same in two countries. The different techniques in dairy farming more likely are due to the different relative availabilities of labor and capital. In India, where labor is plentiful and capital is scarce, it would be absurd to adopt the capital-intensive methods of dairy farming used in the United States. This does not mean that Indians are unaware of U.S. farming methods (or vice versa). The assumptions of an identical *technology* and an identical *technique* are distinct. For a detailed analysis of technological diffusion across countries that relies on patent data, see Eaton and Kortum [1997].

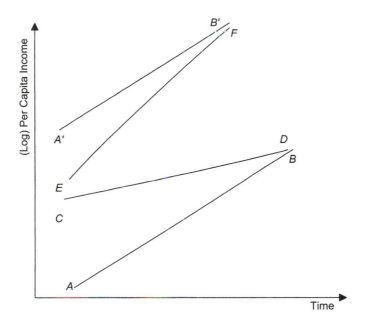

Figure 3.11. Convergence in growth rates.

countries. Instead, different countries have their own steady-state paths, as illustrated by the lines AB and $A'B'$. We've assumed, however, that *these paths are all parallel to one another*, given that the hypothesis maintains the same rate of technical progress (and therefore the same rates of steady-state growth) across all countries.

Now imagine that the country with steady-state path AB starts at a point C above the steady-state path. The Solow model predicts that over time, this country will exhibit a slower rate of growth than the steady-state path as it slopes in to its steady-state path AB. This path is given by the curve CD. Likewise, a country that starts at point E below its steady-state path $A'B'$ will exhibit a rate of growth higher than that of the steady state, with the resulting path EF converging upward to its steady-state path.

This illustrates convergence in growth rates, but at the same time raises a troubling question. In terms of a practical test that we can apply to data, what exactly is implied by this form of convergence? Recall how unconditional convergence asserted that the change in income of a country must be negatively related to its starting level of per capita income. Does growth convergence assert something similar—that poorer countries have a tendency to grow faster? The answer is no, and Figure 3.11 shows us why. The country that starts at point C is actually poorer than the country that starts at point E, but the former country actually grows *slower* than the latter. Growth rate convergence implies that a country that is *below its own steady state grows faster* than its steady-state growth rate, but to test this we have to also use the data to identify *where* these steady states are. For this reason, unconditional convergence is really an unconditional hypothesis: asserting that all the steady states are in the same place obviates the need to condition for the positions of different steady states. On the other hand, the weaker hypothesis of growth rate convergence needs to be appropriately "conditioned" on the position of steady states.

The idea of controlling for the position of steady states amounts to factoring out the effects of parameters that might differ across countries and *then* examining whether convergence occurs. Such a concept is called *conditional convergence*, because we are "conditioning" on possible intercountry differences before we examine the possibility of convergence.

The next section tells us how to begin to think about controlling for various parameters.

3.5.6. Reexamining the data

To apply notions of conditioning properly to the data, it is important to see, in some more detail, what the theory is trying to tell us.[23] To do this, we begin by solving for the steady state $\hat{k}^*$ in the Solow model with technical progress. What follows looks a little complicated. To make it easier, I'll tell you where we are heading: we are going to find a relationship between per capita income and the various parameters (such as savings rates and population growth rates) that we estimate with the data.

To solve for the steady state, use the familiar method of putting $\hat{k}(t) = \hat{k}(t+1) = \hat{k}^*$ in (3.12), which tells us that

$$(1+n)(1+\pi)\hat{k}^* = (1-\delta)\hat{k}^* + s\hat{y}^*.$$

Rearranging this equation, we see that

$$\frac{\hat{k}^*}{\hat{y}^*} = \frac{s}{(1+n)(1+\pi) - (1-\delta)},$$

and using the same approximation that we used to derive (3.7) from (3.6), we see that

(3.13)
$$\frac{\hat{k}^*}{\hat{y}^*} \simeq \frac{s}{n + \pi + \delta}.$$

To go further, we must relate output to capital input more precisely. In other words, we need to specify a production function. The most common specification is a Cobb–Douglas production function (see the Appendix to this

---

[23] The material in this section draws on the study by Mankiw, Romer, and Weil [1992] and Mankiw [1995].

chapter for more detail). If Y denotes total output, K denotes total capital, and L denotes effective labor, then

$$Y = K^\alpha L^{1-\alpha}$$

for some parameter α between 0 and 1, which (as we will soon see) measures the relative importance of capital in production. Dividing through by L, we can write the production function in "per effective labor" form,

$$\hat{y} = \hat{k}^\alpha,$$

and by moving the variables around a bit, we can write this equation in the equivalent form

$$\frac{\hat{k}}{\hat{y}} = \hat{y}^{(1-\alpha)/\alpha}.$$

Substitute this formula, evaluated at the steady state, into (3.13) to obtain

$$\hat{y}^* \simeq \left[\frac{s}{n + \pi + \delta}\right]^{\alpha/(1-\alpha)}.$$

Now express this in logarithmic form to see that

(3.14) $$\ln \hat{y}^* \simeq \frac{\alpha}{1-\alpha} \ln s - \frac{\alpha}{1-\alpha} \ln(n + \pi + \delta).$$

Finally, we rewrite $\hat{y}^*$ in per capita form, which is something that we can observe directly from the data. At the moment it is in terms of effective units of labor. Recall that $L(t) = E(t)P(t)$, where $P(t)$ is population and $E(t)$ is the productivity of an individual at time t, which grows at the rate of technical progress π. Thus $E(t+1) = (1+\pi)E(t)$, and we see that

$$\hat{y}^* = \frac{Y(t)}{P(t)E(0)(1+\pi)^t} = \frac{y(t)}{E(0)(1+\pi)^t},$$

where $y(t)$ is per capita income at date t, $E(0)$ is technical knowledge at some baseline date (say 1965 or 1985), and t is counted in terms of years elapsed from the baseline date. Taking logarithms of both sides of this equation, we see that

$$\ln \hat{y}^* = \ln y(t) - \ln E(0) - t \ln(1+\pi).$$

Substituting this expression into (3.14) and moving terms around, we obtain

(3.15) $$\ln y(t) \simeq A + \frac{\alpha}{1-\alpha} \ln s - \frac{\alpha}{1-\alpha} \ln(n + \pi + \delta),$$

where A is just the collection of terms $\ln E(0) + t \ln(1+\pi)$.

The plan now is to actually look at the data, which gives us information on the variables $y(t)$, s, and n, and then regress $y(t)$ on the parameters exactly along the lines suggested by (3.15). Observe that the intercept term A is an "unknown" from the point of view of the regression exercise; it will be estimated after the best possible fit is found to the data.

Likewise, as far as the empirical exercise goes, the coefficients on $\ln s$ as well as on $\ln(n + \pi + \delta)$ are unknowns and will be estimated by the best fit to the data. However—and this is the power of a theoretical prediction—the theory suggests that after we are done estimating the equation, the coefficients will be close in value to each other [they are *both* supposed to equal $\alpha/(1 - \alpha)$], but of opposite sign.

In fact, more can be said. Recall that α is the coefficient on capital in the production function and it mirrors the importance of capital in the production process. A rough estimate for α can found by looking at the share of capital in national income[24]; it turns out to be around one-third. Therefore, $\alpha/(1 - \alpha)$ should be around 0.5.

Therefore we enter the empirical study with the following expectations:

(1) The coefficients on the term $\ln s$ are positive and the coefficient on the term $\ln(n + \pi + \delta)$ is negative. This captures the Solow prediction that savings has a positive (level) effect on per capita income and population growth has a negative (level) effect on per capita income.

(2) The estimated coefficients have the same approximate magnitude, and this magnitude is around 0.5.

Mankiw, Romer, and Weil [1992] tested these predictions using the Heston–Summers data set. They took $\pi + \delta$ to be approximately 0.05, or around 5% per year, and used the average of investment–GDP ratios over the period 1965–85 to form an estimate of the savings rate. The variable y is given by per capita GDP in the year 1985. The resulting regression shows the following features:

(1) More than half the worldwide variation in per capita GDP in 1985 can be explained by the two variables s and n. The correlation coefficient of the regression is 0.59. This is a powerful finding indeed.

(2) As predicted by the Solow model, the coefficient of $\ln s$ is significant and positive, whereas that of $\ln(n + \pi + \delta)$ is significant and negative. In qualitative terms, as long as we do not stick to the absurd assumption of equal savings and population growth rates (and therefore the prediction of unconditional convergence), the Solow model predicts broad relationships that do show up in worldwide data. However, there is a bug:

(3) The coefficients are too large to be anywhere close to 0.5: the coefficient on savings is 1.42 and that on population is −1.97. Moreover, the

---

[24] The Appendix to this chapter points out precisely the assumptions required to apply this proxy.

coefficients are far from being of similar magnitude. Population growth rates seem to have a larger depressive effect on per capita incomes than the upward kick from savings rates.

The large coefficients observed in the data have a very important implication. Although variations in savings and population growth rates seem to yield the predicted *direction* of variations in per capita income, the discrepancies in per capita income that are actually observed across countries are too large relative to those predicted by the theory. Once again, we see the tension between two different strands of reasoning. The large observed differences in per capita incomes suggest that there is little or no diminishing returns to capital. The Harrod–Domar model seems to be a better choice in this sense. At the same time, we cannot buy the fact that there are constant returns to scale in physical capital alone. The new theories of growth that we will discuss subsequently provide a possible way to ease this tension.

To go on, then, what we have shown so far is that once we drop the assumption that all parameters are the same across countries, the Solow model does make some sense of the data. However, this leads to a different sort of problem. Even though the foregoing exercise may be perfectly satisfactory, don't we owe it to ourselves to understand just *why* savings rates and population growth rates remain systematically different across countries? Just *assuming* that this is true is not a very satisfactory explanation of what we observe. If we believe that human beings the world over are driven by a common set of economic motivations and that there is no fundamental difference in their genetic desires to save or procreate, then the differences that we do observe may be driven by their particular economic experiences, rather than result from some irreconcilable cultural or social differences. This brings us back to the question of endogeneity of these variables. A fuller theory must account for why savings propensities, as well as population growth rates, are different across countries.

A similar criticism applies to the assumed exogeneity of technical progress. If so much of the action occurs because of this parameter (and indeed, the Solow model asserts that *all* long-run growth comes from technical progress), then the question of *which* forces drive technical progress becomes highly relevant as well. In turn, this raises the question of whether technical progress costlessly diffuses to other countries, because the same economic forces that create new knowledge may have an incentive to restrain its costless dissipation. Once again, the newer theories of growth that we discuss in Chapter 4 bear on some of these issues.

So the data answers some questions, but raises new and intriguing ones as well. Nevertheless, there is no doubt that the exercise of conditioning takes us much further than the naive hypothesis of unconditional convergence. At the very least, it points the way to further questions, some of which we will take up later.

3.6. *Summary*

This chapter began our study of the theory and empirics of *economic growth*, which is defined as annual rates of change in income (total or per capita). We observed that growth rates of 2% or more per capita are a relatively modern phenomenon, systematically attained first by the United States, and only in this century. Developing economies are way behind in per capita income relative to their developed counterparts, and larger rates of per capita growth are consequently high on the priority list for such countries.

Our study of growth theory began with the fundamental notion of macroeconomic balance. Savings equals investment: absention from current consumption paves the way for increases in capital equipment. More capital creates more output. Thus two parameters are immediately relevant: the *savings rate*, which tells us how much an economy "abstains," and the *capital–output ratio*, which tells us how the resulting increase in capital translates into output. This allows us to derive an equation that relates the savings rate and the capital–output ratio to the rate of growth, which is the basic feature of the *Harrod–Domar model*. The Harrod–Domar equation can be extended to include depreciation of capital and to allow for a growing population. In the Harrod–Domar model, population growth unambiguously eats into per capita growth, because the role of labor as a factor of production is not captured adequately by a fixed capital–output ratio. This leads us to consider more seriously the possible *endogeneity* of parameters such as the savings rate, the population growth rate, and (of course) the capital–output ratio itself.

Both the savings rate and the rate of population growth vary with different levels of per capita income. This introduces the possibility that the rate of per capita growth may itself vary depending on the current level of per capita income. In extreme cases, these considerations lead to development *traps* and *thresholds*. Per capita income may be stuck (or spend very long periods of time) in traps, but there may be critical thresholds as well, beyond which sustained growth occurs. This is the first demonstration of the possibility that initial conditions may drive long-run outcomes.

The endogeneity of the capital–output ratio led us to a classical theory: the *Solow model*. In Solow's twist on the Harrod–Domar story, the capital–output ratio adjusts with the relative availability of capital and labor. This adjustment occurs because of diminishing returns to each of these inputs, and we can use *production functions* to capture such effects. To continue, if capital grows faster than the labor force, then each unit of capital has less labor to man it, so that output divided by capital falls. Thus savings fall *relative to the capital stock*, and this slows down the rate of growth of capital. Exactly the opposite happens if capital is growing too slowly relative to labor. This mechanism ensures that in the long run, capital and working population grow exactly at the same rate, and per capita growth ultimately vanishes. Capital and labor maintain a constant long-run balance that is known as the *steady-state* capital stock (per capita). We showed how different parameters affect the steady-state level of the capital stock and (thus) the steady-state level of per capita income. We drew a distinction between *level effects* and *growth effects*.

Growth dies out in the simple Solow model because there is no *technical progress*. If you think of technical progress as a steady growth in knowledge that continually increases the productivity of labor, it becomes important to distinguish between the working population and *effective labor*, which is the working population multiplied by (the changing level of) individual productivity. Thus effective labor grows as the sum of population growth and technical progress. With this amendment, the Solow arguments apply exactly as before, with all per capita magnitudes reexpressed per units of effective labor. This means, for instance, that while the long-run capital stock, *relative to effective labor*, settles down to a steady-state ratio, the capital stock per person keeps growing and it does so at the rate of technical progress. Likewise, per capita income keeps increasing in the long run precisely at the rate of technical progress.

The notion that per capita growth settles down to equal the rate of technical progress led us to the idea of *convergence*. Under an extreme version of this concept, known as *unconditional convergence*, relative income differences between countries must die away in the long run. A weaker version, called *conditional convergence*, states that controlling for possible differences in cross-country parameters, such as in the rates of savings, initially poor countries grow faster. Convergence is intimately connected to the notion of diminishing marginal productivity of capital: it is based on the idea that a poorer country has a marginal return to capital and therefore exhibits a higher rate of per capita growth.

We observed, next, that no evidence of unconditional convergence is found in the data. We examined a small set of countries over a large time horizon (a century). The problem with the original version of this analysis is that it chose countries that already were known to be rich at the end of the time period of the study (1979), but were obviously scattered at different levels of per capita income in 1870. This created an illusion of convergence. The addition of more countries eliminated the effect. We followed this with a study of a larger set of countries over a smaller time horizon. Again, unconditional convergence was not supported by the data.

Conditional convergence requires us to allow for possibly different rates of savings and population growth. In the last part of the chapter, we started to think about conditioning by deriving a regression model from the basic

Solow theory. Quite surprisingly, variations in the savings rate and the population growth alone explained over half the observed variation in per capita incomes across countries. However, the estimated magnitudes of the coefficients for savings and population are too large to be reconciled with the simple Solow model. This is a puzzle to which we return in the next chapter. We also noted that the assumption that savings rates are exogenous across countries may be too strong, and so a regression model might do better (conceptually, at least) by choosing a set of parameters that can reasonably be presumed to be independent. We return to this as well in the coming chapter.

Appendix

3.A.1. The Harrod–Domar equations

We record here the simple steps that lead to the Harrod–Domar equations (3.5) and (3.6). First, combine the equations (3.3) and (3.4) to obtain

$$K(t+1) = (1 - \delta)K(t) + S(t).$$

Now if savings is a constant fraction s of income, then $S(t) = sY(t)$ for all dates t, whereas if the capital–output ratio is θ, then $K(t) = \theta Y(t)$ for all dates t. Using these calculations in the preceding expression, we see that

(3.16) $$\theta Y(t+1) = (1 - \delta)\theta Y(t) + sY(t),$$

so that

$$\frac{Y(t+1) - Y(t)}{Y(t)} = \frac{s}{\theta} - \delta.$$

The left-hand side of this equation is just the rate of growth g, and so our derivation is complete.

What if the population is growing as well? In this case we must massage (3.16) a little bit to get it into per capita terms. Let $y(t) \equiv (Y(t))/(P(t))$ denote per capita income. Then simply by dividing both sides of (3.16) by $P(t)$, we see that

$$\theta y(t+1)\frac{P(t+1)}{P(t)} = (1 - \delta)\theta y(t) + sy(t).$$

Now dividing through by $y(t)\theta$, we see that

$$\frac{y(t+1)}{y(t)}\frac{P(t+1)}{P(t)} = (1 - \delta) + \frac{s}{\theta}.$$

We are almost there. Simply note that $(y(t+1))/(y(t)) = 1 + g^*$, where g^* is the rate of per capita growth, and that $(P(t+1))/(P(t)) = 1 + n$, where n is the rate of population growth. Substituting these expressions into the preceding equation, we get (3.6).

3.A.2. Production functions and per capita magnitudes

Production functions

A *production function* is just a simple mathematical description of how various inputs (such as capital, land, labor, and various raw materials) are combined to produce an output. The function is not meant to capture the production process in its entirety, but to imply a convenient expression of it.

Suppose that capital and labor are the only two inputs.[25] Then a mathematically abstract but useful way of writing a production function is to state that

$$(3.17) \qquad Y = F(K, P),$$

where K stands for capital and P stands for the working population in that production activity.

Cobb–Douglas production functions

What is F? It is just an abstract statement about the functional *form* (and even this sort of abstraction is useful in theory), but in many contexts, particularly for empirical studies, it needs to be given a more specific form. One form that is especially popular is the *Cobb–Douglas production function*

$$(3.18) \qquad Y = AK^\alpha P^{1-\alpha},$$

where $0 < \alpha < 1$ and A is a positive constant.

What does the Cobb–Douglas production function capture? First of all, the parameter A is a measure of the degree of technological knowledge in the economy. The larger is A, the larger is the magnitude of output for any fixed combination of K and L.

---

[25] The labor input in the production function can have different meanings, depending on the context. Sometimes, labor merely means physical man-hours supplied, or if man-hours per worker is understood to be fixed, merely the number of workers. In other contexts, when labor productivity is growing over time, the labor input in the production function usually signifies the number of *effective* labor hours supplied.

With the Cobb–Douglas function, A can also be interpreted as a measure of the productivity of labor.[26] To see this, note that (3.18) can be rewritten as

(3.19) $$Y = K^\alpha (EP)^{1-\alpha},$$

where E is just $A^{1/(1-\alpha)}$. Then EP is just the amount of *effective units* of labor used in production.

Finally, note that if factors are paid their marginal products (which will be the case if all markets are perfectly competitive), then α can be interpreted as the share of capital income in total national income, and $1 - \alpha$ can be interpreted as the corresponding share of labor income. A little calculus makes this point quickly. The marginal product of capital is given by

$$\frac{\partial Y}{\partial K} = \alpha A K^{\alpha-1} P^{1-\alpha} = \alpha \frac{Y}{K},$$

so that the share of capital income is just

$$\frac{\partial Y}{\partial K} \cdot \frac{K}{Y} = \alpha.$$

Constant returns to scale

Take another look at the Cobb–Douglas productionfunction (3.18). Suppose that we scale up both the units of capital and the units of labor in production by the *same* proportion; for instance, double the scale. Then K becomes $2K$ and L becomes $2L$. Using (3.18), it is easy to see that output increases by a factor of $2^\alpha 2^{1-\alpha} = 2$. Output doubles as well. This property of production functions (which all production functions need not necessarily possess) is called *constant returns to scale*.

More generally, constant returns to scale is characterized by the following feature: if *all* inputs are increased by a factor $\lambda > 0$, output will increase by the *same* proportion λ. You can easily check that this more general property is true of the Cobb–Douglas production function.

There is an easy way to describe constant returns to scale for *any* abstract production function F. For all $\lambda > 0$, it must be the case that

(3.20) $$\lambda F(K, L) = F(\lambda K, \lambda L).$$

---

[26] Indeed, the Cobb–Douglas function does not make a useful distinction between the productivity of labor and the productivity of capital. The interpretation in the text can be applied just as easily to capital as well as to labor.

Per capita magnitudes

Production functions with constant returns to scale have a nice property. They allow us to relate *per capita* input to *per capita* output. To see this, choose λ to be equal to $1/P$ in equation (3.20). Putting in this value, (3.20) tells us that

(3.21) $$\frac{F(K, P)}{P} = F\left(\frac{K}{P}, 1\right)$$

Using (3.17) on the left-hand side of this equation, we may conclude that

(3.22) $$Y/P = F(K/P, 1).$$

Notice that the function on the right-hand side in (3.22) is a function of the K/P ratio *alone*, and not of each of the inputs *separately*. Denote per capita levels of output and capital by y and k, respectively; in other words, $y = Y/P$ and $k = K/P$. Further, rewrite the function $F(K/P, 1)$ in more compact form as $f(k)$. Then equation (3.22) becomes

(3.23) $$y = f(k).$$

Notice that the preceding form represents production relationships between per capita levels *only*; that is, between per capita capital and per capita output.

The following facts about $f(k)$ can be proved:

(1) If $F(K, P)$ is increasing in both its arguments, then $f(k)$ is increasing in k.

(2) If $F(K, P)$ exhibits diminishing returns to each of its inputs, then $f(k)$ exhibits diminishing returns in k.

The second point is worth noting carefully. It says that if there are diminishing returns to both factors in the production function, then the *per capita* production function displays diminishing returns in per capita capital used in production. In the main text, we implicitly used constant returns to scale to arrive at the per capita description of a production function, and then used diminishing returns to each input *separately* to assert that per capita output exhibits diminishing returns with respect to per capita capital. This particular shape lay at the heart of the predictions of the Solow model.

Finally, let's see what the per capita production function looks like in the Cobb–Douglas case. Dividing both sides of (3.18) by P and denoting by lowercase letters the per capita values, you can easily check that the Cobb–Douglas function translates into the per capita form

(3.24) $$y = k^{\alpha}.$$

Check for yourself that the preceding two claims are true in this particular example.

Exercises

■ (1) A firm is set up to produce and sell cotton shirts. It buys plant and machinery for $2 million and land for $1 million, and constructs a warehouse for another $1 million. Each year, it hires 100 workers and pays each of them $2,000 per year. It buys $600,000 worth of cotton fabric to be used in making the shirts. The firm sells 100,000 shirts a year, which it prices at $10 per shirt.

(a) How much profit does the firm make on a yearly basis, if you do not count its setup investment?

(b) How much income does the firm generate every year?

(c) What is the capital–output ratio of the firm? Explain, using this example, why a capital–output ratio that exceeds 1 is perfectly compatible with profit making.

■ (2) The best way to think about the Harrod–Domar equations is to attach some numbers to them. First, let us work with the simple Harrod–Domar equation (3.5). Imagine that a country has a national savings rate of 20% and that the capital–output ratio is 4. This latter statement means that $4 of capital equipment is used, on average, to produce $1 of output. Finally, suppose that capital lives forever, so that $\delta = 0$.

(a) Let's calculate the rate of growth of overall GDP. The savings rate is 20%, so that applying (3.5), we obtain an annual growth rate of 0.05, which translates into 5% per year. Now figure out (i) what the savings rate should be to get growth rates up to 8 and 10% per year and (ii) what the capital–output ratio should be (at a savings rate of 20%) to get the growth rates up to the same 8 and 10% per year. Take a good look at these numbers. Why does the savings rate need to *rise* to raise the growth rate? Why does the capital–output ratio need to *fall*? What does a fall in the capital–output ratio mean in economic terms?

(b) A growth rate of 5% a year looks pretty good, but not once we start accounting for depreciation and population growth. What happens to the growth rate if the depreciation rate rises to 1% per year and then rises to 2%? Does this make sense? What rate of savings is needed (at a capital–output ratio of 4) to keep a growth rate of 5%, if the depreciation rate is 3%?

(c) Now introduce population growth and turn your attention to the more refined version of the Harrod–Domar equation, given by (3.6). Suppose that the savings rate is 20%, the capital–output ratio is 4, the depreciation rate is 1%, and the rate of growth of population is 2% per year. What is the rate of *per capita* income growth? Play with different rates of population growth. What rate of population growth would drive the per capita growth rate to zero? Does it make sense that higher rates of population growth, other things being equal, tend to bring down the rate of per capita income growth?

(d) Appreciate the usefulness of an equation that allows you to take a first pass at the relationship between economic variables of crucial importance. No (good) economist would suggest that these relationships are exact, but they do help you form some crude estimates as a policy maker. For instance, if you know the rates of depreciation, the capital–output ratio, and the population growth rates, you can form an estimate of how much savings is needed to push per capita income growth to some given target.

■ (3) Suppose that the country of Xanadu saves 20% of its income and has a capital–output ratio of 4.

(a) Using the Harrod–Domar model, calculate the rate of growth of total GNP in Xanadu.

(b) If population growth were 3% per year and Xanadu wanted to achieve a growth rate *per capita* of 4% per year, what would its savings rate have to be to get to this growth rate?

(c) Now go back to the case where the savings rate is 20% and the capital–output ratio is 4. Imagine, now, that the economy of Xanadu suffers violent labor strikes every year, so that whatever the capital stock is in any given year, a quarter of it goes unused because of these labor disputes. If population growth is 2% per year, calculate the rate of per capita income growth in Xanadu under this new scenario.

(d) If you were a planner in Xanadu and could costlessly choose the savings rate for that country, how would you go about making your decision? Think about the pros and cons of changing the savings rate and record your opinions here.

■ (4) (a) Suppose that as a professor in India my salary is rupees (Rs) 100,000 per year and that I get a raise of Rs 1,000 per year. Suppose that a school teacher who earns Rs 50,000 per year also gets the same raise of Rs 1,000. Convince yourself that the growth *rates* of our incomes are indeed different. Thus two countries growing at the same rate may well have a widening *absolute* income gap over time.

(b) We saw that even growth rates of per capita incomes that sound low, such as 1.5% per year, are a relatively modern phenomenon that has occurred, by and large, in the last century or so. There is an interesting way to see this that also teaches us about the power of exponential growth. Suppose that the average income of a person in a developed country is $20,000 per year (this is a bit on the high side, but no matter). Now go *back* in time by scaling this number *down* by 1.5% per year. What would the average income have been 200 years ago?

■ (5) This is an exercise to understand the Solow model. (a) The economy of Ping Pong produces its GNP using capital and labor. The labor force is growing at 2% per year. At the same time, there is "labor-augmenting" technical progress at the rate of 3% per year, so that each unit of labor is becoming more productive. How fast is the effective labor force growing?

(b) Now let's look at the production possibilities in Ping Pong. We are going to plot a graph with capital *per unit of effective labor* (k) on the horizontal axis and output *per effective unit of labor* (y) on the vertical axis. Here is a description of the "production function" that relates y to k. As long as k is between 0 and 3, output (y) is given by $y = (1/2)x$. After k crosses the level 3, an *additional* unit of k only yields one-seventh *additional* units of y. This happens until k reaches 10. After that, each additional unit of k produces only one-tenth additional units of y. (To draw this graph, you may want to measure the y axis in larger units than the k axis; otherwise, the graph is going to look way too flat.) On a graph, plot this production function. What are the capital–output ratios at $k = 2$, 6, and 12? Note that the answers you get in the case $k = 6$ and 12 are different from what happens at the margin (when you increase capital by one unit). Think about why this is happening.

(c) Now let us suppose that Ping Pong saves 20% of its output and that the capital stock is perfectly durable and does not depreciate from year to year. If you are told what $k(t)$ is, describe precisely how you would calculate $k(t+1)$. In your formula, note two things: (i) convert all percentages to fractions (e.g., $3\% = 0.03$) before inserting them into the formula and (ii) remember that the capital–output ratio *depends* on what the going value $k(t)$ is, so that you may want to use a symbol like θ for the capital–output ratio, to be replaced by the appropriate number once you know the value of $k(t)$ (as in the next question).

(d) Now, using a calculator if you need to and starting from the point $k(t) = 3$ at time t, calculate the value of $k(t + 1)$. Likewise do so if $k(t) = 10$. From these answers, can you guess in what range the long-run value of k in Ping Pong must lie?

(e) Calculate the long-run value of k in Ping Pong. (Hint: You can do this by playing with different values or, more quickly, by setting up an equation that tells you how to find this value.)

■ (6) Consider the Solow model with a production function $Y(t) = A \cdot K(t)^\alpha L(t)^{1-\alpha}$, where A is a fixed technological parameter. Explicitly solve for the *steady-state* value of the per capita capital stock and per capita income. How do these values change in response to a rise in (a) the technological parameter A, (b) the rate of saving s, (c) α, (d) δ, the depreciation rate, and (e) the population growth rate n?

■ (7) (a) Consider the Solow model. Show that savings rates and depreciation rates have only level effects on both per capita income and total income. What about the effect of population growth on per capita income?

(b) Recall the Harrod–Domar model. What kind of effect do the same parameters have on income in that model?

■ (8) *Discuss* whether the following statements are true or false.

(a) The Harrod–Domar model states that a country's per capita growth rate *depends* on its rate of savings, whereas the Solow model states that it does not.

(b) According to the Harrod–Domar model, if the capital–output ratio in a country is high, that country will grow faster.

(c) To understand if there is convergence in the world economy, we must study countries that are currently rich.

(d) Middle-income countries are more likely to change their relative position in world rankings of GNP than poor or rich countries.

(e) In the Solow model, a change in the population growth rate has no effect on the long-run rate of per capita growth.

(f) In the Solow model, output per head goes down as capital per head increases, because of diminishing returns.

■ (9) Consider the model of endogenous population growth that we summarized in Figure 3.2. Suppose that the curve describing population growth rates always lies below the line describing growth of total incomes. Explain this situation in words and describe what per capita growth rates will look like (over time) for an economy that starts from a low initial per capita income.

■ (10) Think of two reasons why a country with a lower ratio of capital to labor might grow faster than a country with a higher ratio, and two reasons why it might grow slower.

Chapter 4

The New Growth Theories

4.1. Introduction

The last chapter left us with several questions. Even though the answers to many of them are still not properly understood by economists, it is worth listing, in summary form, some of the main concerns:

(1) While the Solow model gets some of the predicted correlations correct, how do we reconcile the huge observed differences in per capita income with the more modest predictions of the model? We can exaggerate the theoretical predictions only at the cost of ascribing a constancy of economic returns to physical capital that physical capital simply does not possess.

(2) Can we be satisfied with a theory that only *assumes* differences in key parameters without *explaining* these differences? In particular, the endogeneity of these variables with respect to the very features that they seek to "explain" may be of crucial importance.

(3) Long-run per capita growth may well be driven by technical progress alone, but this does not mean that technical progress falls on societies like manna from heaven. Human beings, through their conscious actions (and some luck), determine the rate of technical progress, and if this is so, such actions should be part of an explanatory theory, and not simply black-boxed. Moreover, is it reasonable to assume that new technology, once discovered, flows easily from country to country? What are the consequences of dropping this assumption?

(4) Finally, do capital and labor, along with the smooth unimpeded flow of technical knowledge, tell the whole story of economic production? After all, if this were the case, we would observe enormous differences in the rate of return to capital between rich and poor countries (with poor countries having by far the higher return), and if we do not observe this disparity, it should be only because of an enormous flow of capital out of developed countries to developing countries. However, we observe neither massive differentials nor massive flow of capital from developing to developed countries.[1] Are

---

[1] Contrast this with the huge flows of *labor* from developing to developed countries, which is much more in line with the simplistic theory and has been (relatively) suppressed only of late because of tight restrictions on immigration.

there different *grades* of labor that enter the production function differently and affect, in turn, the rates of return to physical capital? This brings us to the study of *human capital*.

In this chapter, we take a look at several recent theories that try to make sense of some of these issues. Do not look for answers to all the questions that we have raised, because you will not find them. You will, however, see how economists go about this business and you will also learn to appreciate how simple models like the Solow model serve as fundamental building blocks for more sophisticated theories.

One general theme of the theories that we will now study is that the whole notion of convergence has been overemphasized. Factors that make for both convergence and divergence are likely to coexist. Moreover, although this gives rise to a final picture that might look "neutral," there is no reason to believe that a simplistic neutral theory like the Harrod–Domar model is correct. More complex combinations of different factors may be at work.

4.2. *Human capital and growth*

So far we have considered labor to be a single input of production, augmented, perhaps, by the pace of technical progress. A number of recent theories go beyond this simple postulate. Rich countries not only have access to a large stock of physical capital, but by investing time and money in education, it is also possible for these countries to produce a large stock of *human capital*: labor that is skilled in production, labor that can operate sophisticated machinery, labor that can create new ideas and new methods in economic activity. It is important to contrast this form of labor with unskilled labor. Developing countries are likely to have a shortage of the former and a surplus of the latter. The implications for the rate of return to physical capital may be more in line with the data, as we will see. Likewise, observed income differences across countries may become more explicable.

The basic idea is simple.[2] Augment the Solow model by permitting individuals to "save" in two distinct forms. So far all savings were translated into holdings of physical capital (or rights to the proceeds from such capital), but households can also "save" by investing in education, which raises the market value of labor that they supply in the future. Such savings may benefit the individual or household directly or we can adopt a more dynastic view in which altruistic parents invest in the education of their children. Although there are important differences in the various theories, we can neglect them for the purpose of the current exposition.

---

[2] For contributions to this literature, see, for example, Uzawa [1965], Lucas [1988], Barro [1991], and Mankiw, Romer, and Weil [1992].

In the starkest version of this theory, we consider just two inputs of production: physical capital and human capital.[3] However, this is not the same as the capital–labor model. The difference is that human capital is *deliberately* accumulated and is not just the outcome of population growth or exogenously specified technical progress. Thus suppose that

$$(4.1) \qquad y = k^{\alpha} h^{1-\alpha},$$

where h this time stands for human capital and unskilled labor has been omitted for now. Moreover, you can think of y, k, and h as aggregate or per capita magnitudes, because I am going to simplify my exposition (without losing anything of importance) by assuming that the overall population is constant. Finally, we will neglect depreciation. All of this is icing on our conceptual cake; the omissions can be put back later without changing our understanding in any fundamental way.

Now part of the output is consumed, just as before, but the remaining part of the output can be used in two ways. First, a fraction s of it is saved, permitting the accumulation of capital:

$$(4.2) \qquad k(t+1) - k(t) = sy(t).$$

Another fraction q is saved in a different way: it is used to augment the quality of human capital,[4] so that

$$(4.3) \qquad h(t+1) - h(t) = qy(t).$$

It can be shown (see the Appendix to this chapter for a demonstration) that starting from any initial configuration at date 0, call it $\{h(0), k(0)\}$, the equations (4.1), (4.2), and (4.3) cause the economy to ultimately have all its variables—y, k, and h—growing at some common rate, and this rate is determined by the savings rate s as well as the propensity to invest in human capital, as measured by q.

It is very easy to figure out what this rate is. Let r denote the ratio of human to physical capital in the long run. Divide both sides of (4.2) by $k(t)$ and use (4.1) to note that

$$\frac{k(t+1) - k(t)}{k(t)} = sr^{1-\alpha},$$

---

[3] The omission of unskilled labor is *not* an unimportant simplifying assumption. It has consequences that we note subsequently.

[4] For instance, one can think of $qy(t)$ as the quantity of physical resources spent on education and training.

which gives us the growth rate of physical capital. Likewise, divide both sides of (4.3) by $h(t)$ and use (4.1) once again to see that

$$\frac{h(t+1) - h(t)}{h(t)} = qr^{-\alpha},$$

which gives us the growth rate of human capital. Because these two growth rates are the same in the long run (so that the ratio of human to physical capital also stays constant), we must have $sr^{1-\alpha} = qr^{-\alpha}$, or simply

(4.4) $r = q/s.$

This equation makes perfect sense. The larger is the ratio of saving in human capital relative to that of physical capital, the larger is the long-run ratio of the former to the latter. We can now use this value of r to compute the long-run growth rate. Use any of the preceding growth-rate equations to do this, because all variables must grow at the same rate in the long run. For instance, the growth-rate equation for k tells us that

$$\frac{k(t+1) - k(t)}{k(t)} = sr^{1-\alpha} = s^{\alpha}q^{1-\alpha},$$

so that the long-run growth rate of all the variables, including per capita income, is given by the expression $s^{\alpha}q^{1-\alpha}$.

This simple model has several implications.

(1) First, it is perfectly possible for there to be diminishing returns to physical capital and yet for there to be no convergence in per capita income. If countries have similar savings and technological parameters, they do grow at the same rate in the long run, but there is no tendency for their per capita incomes to come together: initial relative differences will, by and large, be maintained. This concept relates to the seemingly paradoxical finding that the world seems to behave in a way that is roughly consistent with the Harrod–Domar model, even though the Harrod–Domar model, with its assumed constancy of returns to physical capital, is just not realistic. Note that *physical* capital, as measured, does not include improvements (through an equally important form of investment) in the quality of labor. However, it is quite conceivable that although there are strong diminishing returns to physical capital alone, there may be broadly constant returns to physical and human capital *combined*. This observation might go some way toward reconciling a paradox that we noted earlier: the world behaves as if output were constant returns to scale in capital, but direct observation of production processes and the share of physical capital contradict this. The mists clear if we realize that we may be talking about two different forms of capital: in the

former case, "capital" refers to a broader notion that embodies both physical and human components.

(2) There is another implication of the overall constancy of returns. Both the rate of savings and the rate of investment in human capital now have growth-rate effects once again, and not just level effects as in the Solow model. Because these decisions affect the growth rate (unlike in the Solow model), models of this kind are called *endogenous growth theories*, because the pace of growth is determined from *within* the model and is not simply attributed to exogenous technical progress. Of course, in this sense, the Harrod–Domar model is the first example of endogenous growth theory![5]

(3) Note, however, that the growth effects in item 2 are related to the constancy of returns to physical and human capital combined. If we drop this assumption by introducing a third factor of production (say unskilled labor) that grows exogenously, this effect would go away and the resulting model would look much more similar to the Solow model. That is, physical and human capital together would still exhibit diminishing returns (because of the presence of a third input). Even then, there is a twist to the present story that could explain the overly large coefficients in the Mankiw–Romer–Weil analysis of the last section. Let us pause for a while to consider the implications.

Once human capital is introduced, it is expected that the coefficients on savings rates and population growth rates will be significantly larger than those predicted by the simple Solow model. This is because an increase in savings raises national income, and in so doing provokes a greater accumulation of *both* physical and human capital, so the net predicted effect on the future is now much larger than that predicted by the accumulation of physical capital alone. Moreover, there is now a reason why the regression coefficient on population growth rates is likely to be significantly higher than the corresponding coefficient on savings rates. The reason is that savings in physical capital (which is what is counted in the data as "savings") does not account for current savings in terms of human capital (at the rate q in the model). On the other hand, an increase in the growth rate of population lowers per capita income and thereby cuts into *both* forms of savings. Thus an increase in physical savings is only an increase in one of two ways of saving, whereas an increase in the population growth rate diminishes both kinds of savings. One can therefore predict that the coefficient on population growth is likely to exceed the coefficient on physical savings, and indeed, as we have already seen, it does. Mankiw, Romer, and Weil [1992] provided a lucid description of this effect, and you can consult their paper for more details.

[5] See also von Neumann [1945–1946].

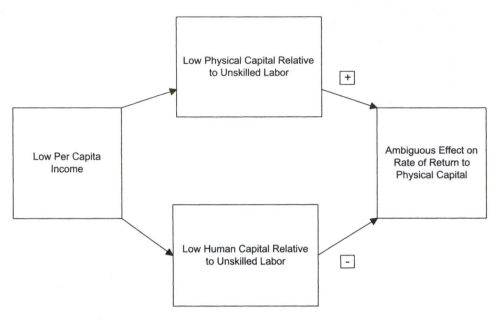

Figure 4.1. The opposing effects of skilled and unskilled labor on the return to physical capital in the endogenous growth model.

(4) The introduction of human capital also helps to explain why rates of return to physical capital may not be as high in poor countries as the simple Solow model predicts. The fact that there is a shortage of unskilled labor in rich countries tends to lower the rate of return to physical capital. However, there is also a relative abundance of skilled labor (or human capital), and this effect works in the opposite direction, driving up the rate of return. The net effect is one in which we do not expect large differences in the rate of return to physical capital. Figure 4.1 provides a diagrammatic exposition of this argument.

Moreover, the differences in the wages of unskilled labor continue to be high. This might explain the great pressures for immigration, while accounting at the same time for the less energetic movements of capital from developed to developing countries.[6] The same argument translates into the ambiguity of growth rates. Recall that in the Solow model, the per capita growth of GDP in a rich country tends to slow down because of diminish-

---

[6] At the same time, this cannot count as a fully satisfactory explanation of the small-scale migration of physical capital from developed to developing countries, because this model then also would predict that rates of return to human capital must be higher in the developing countries—an observation which is probably not borne out by the facts. Thus a complete explanation of the low observed flows must ultimately rest on other factors, such as the fear of political instability or capital confiscation in developing countries, or ignorance of local conditions. This issue ties in at a broader level with the observations of Feldstein and Horioka [1980], who suggested that capital is quite immobile internationally (even across developed countries). See, for instance, Gordon and Bovenberg [1996] and the references therein.

ing marginal returns to physical capital. However, under the endogenous growth approach, the rate of return on physical capital is buffered by an expanding stock of human capital, thus making perpetual growth possible. Indeed, there is even the possibility that rich countries grow faster than poor ones. Note that the overall growth rate in the model just discussed is given by $s^\alpha q^{1-\alpha}$. Physical savings rates on their own do not entirely determine the overall rate of growth.

(5) Sharpening the argument in item 4, we see that the model predicts no tendency toward unconditional convergence even if all parameters are exactly the same across all countries. In this case, the theory is neutral toward growth, just as the Harrod–Domar model, but there is an important difference. *Unlike* the Harrod–Domar model, the present theory still maintains the hypothesis of diminishing marginal returns *to each input separately*. Note that in the long run, the ratio of human to physical capital is a certain determinate fraction (q/s in the language of the model). This means that if a country has too low a current output relative to its endowment of human capital (perhaps because of the destruction of part of its physical capital or some historically high endowment of skilled labor), it tends to grow faster in per capita terms. Put another way, the model generates the following two predictions:

(5a) Conditional convergence after controlling for human capital. By conditioning on the level of human capital, poor countries have a tendency to grow faster.

(5b) Conditional divergence after controlling for the initial level of per capita income. By conditioning on the level of per capita income, countries with more human capital grow faster.

It is because countries that are rich have, on average, more human capital that, on the whole, the model predicts neutrality in the growth rates with respect to per capita income. Effects (5a) and (5b) tend to nullify each other. Can this be seen in the data? To some extent, it can.

4.3. Another look at conditional convergence

Recall from the study of Barro [1991] (discussed earlier) that a plot of growth rates against per capita income from the Summers–Heston data yields no evidence of unconditional convergence.[7] Barro then went on to see if this effect persisted when conditioned for the different levels of human capital in different countries. We summarize his findings here.

[7] See also the book by Barro and Sala-i-Martin [1995], which takes up these issues in greater detail.

As you might imagine, it is difficult to get a reliable and accurate measure of human capital. Literacy rates, primary and secondary school enrollments, the extent of vocational training, and the presence of research universities all count in one way or another, and it is impossible to capture all these terms in a single analysis. Using data from the United Nations, it is possible to obtain measures of school enrollment at the primary and secondary levels, and Barro used these as rough proxies for the total stock of human capital.

Now run the following regression. As the dependent variable, take the average growth in per capita real GDP over the period 1965–1985. As independent variables, include (among others) baseline per capita GDP in 1960 and the school enrollment data that we just described.[8] Recall that if we try to test *unconditional* convergence, all that will appear on the right-hand side of this regression is baseline per capita GDP. Because we are attempting to *condition* for other factors, a regression with several independent variables, not just one, is in order.[9]

The results are interesting and suggest that the model of the previous section is not completely misguided. *Conditioning* for human capital in the way just described, the coefficient on per capita GDP is negative and significant, as the Solow model and the preceding human capital model predict. Likewise, with baseline per capita GDP included, the coefficients on both the secondary and primary education variables are positive and significant. Thus, the correlations that we obtain are compatible with predictions (5a) and (5b) of the model in the previous section. The results suggest, therefore, that the unconditioned plot of growth rates on per capita GDP picks up the net effect of two factors. First, a high per capita GDP *in itself* does tend to slow down future growth rates. At the same time, higher endowments of human capital tend to speed them up. Because countries that have a high per capita GDP also tend to have high stocks of human capital, these two effects tend to cancel out when lumped together.

Of course, if high-income countries *invariably* had high stocks of human capital, it would be impossible to attribute per capita growth separately to these factors, and the regression would have no power. The same observation suggests that it may be worth looking at countries where there are "abnormal" imbalances between human and physical capital. One such example is Japan in 1960, which had a low stock of physical capital, but a relatively high stock of human capital. Its phenomenal growth in the post-World War II period is consistent with the implications of the endogenous growth theory. To a lesser extent, the same is true of Korea and Taiwan, although the inclusion of human capital still fails to account satisfactorily for the magnitudes of growth displayed by these countries.

---

[8] For details as well as a list of the other variables, see Barro [1991].

[9] Appendix 2 to this book contains a more detailed description of how a multivariate regression achieves this goal.

At the other end of the spectrum are sub-Saharan African countries, where school enrollmentrates in 1960 were typically low relative to their 1960 per capita GDP. These countries have also grown slower. Indeed, the expanded regression with human capital included does a better job of predicting their performance.

We may conclude, then, that a reasonable description of the growth process probably includes endogenous components such as the accumulation of human capital. At the very least, these extended models do a better job of fitting the data than the more simplistic specifications of Harrod–Domar and Solow.

4.4. *Technical progress again*

4.4.1. *Introduction*

It is time to return to technical progress—an important concept that we have placed so far in a black box. Recall that in the Solow model, all long-run per capita growth is driven by technical progress—the rate at which the productivity of factors of production increases. In the endogenous growth model with human capital, or indeed in the Harrod–Domar model, there are other sources of growth as well, such as savings and human capital accumulation.

Note, however, that as soon as we postulate the existence of *some* fixed factor of production, such as unskilled labor or land, and if we postulate that production is constant returns to scale in all factors taken together, sustained growth becomes difficult to explain without the existence of continued increases in the body of knowledge; that is, in the way of putting together inputs to make outputs. This observation is actually more subtle than it appears at first glance, so let us dwell on it some more.

Recall that in both models that permit endogenous growth (the Harrod–Domar and the human capital theories), we assumed that *production exhibits constant returns in all inputs that can be deliberately accumulated per capita.*[10] Without this assumption, growth ultimately dies out. The reason is simple. In the presence of a fixed factor (say population as a source of unskilled labor), diminishing returns set in if the per capita magnitude of the accumulated factors becomes too high relative to the fixed factor. A special case of this is the Solow model, where capital is the only accumulable factor, but the ideas apply more generally.

Thus constant returns permit "endogenous" growth, whereas theories that postulate diminishing returns (because of some nonaccumulable fac-

---

[10] To be more precise, the production function must exhibit nondecreasing returns in all accumulable factors, at least asymptotically as the factors of production become large in quantity.

tor of production) must ultimately rely on technical progress to generate growth.[11]

4.4.2. Technological progress and human decisions

Technical progress does not occur in a vacuum. Many years ago, such advances were the result of spontaneous insight or the lonely work of individuals. It is a characteristic of recent history that research and development is carried out by firms, who deliberately divert resources from current profits in the hope of future profits. Now R&D (research and development) is a household word, and we see that large numbers of scientists and researchers are hired by companies with the express purpose of increasing economic productivity via the creation of new production methods. More often than not, the successes are patented, thereby slowing down (though never entirely stopping) the drift of knowledge from the original innovator to competitors. In many countries, the public sector encourages research. Technical progress also occurs on the job, in the form of learning by doing. Advances in technology in some sector of the economy can trigger off advances in others or lay the groundwork for new findings elsewhere.

We can classify technical progress roughly into two categories.

(1) First, there are those gains in knowledge that are created by the *deliberate* diversion of resources from current productive activity, in the hope that they will result in profitable production in the future. These innovations may take the form of the introduction of new products for production or consumption (product innovation) or the introduction of new methods to carry out the production or distribution of an existing product (process innovation).

(2) Second, there is the transfer of technical knowledge that occurs from the innovating firm, or a core of innovating firms, to the rest of the world. This diffusion, in turn, can be of two types. The new technology can become known to "outsiders," who can then profit from it directly, or the new technology may lay the groundwork for other innovative activity, not necessarily by the individual or organization that carried out the original innovation.

These two notions of technological advancement have very different implications for behavior. We can think of the first notion as capturing those aspects of technical progress that can be *internalized* by the innovator for profit.

---

[11] To some extent, the *exact* distinction is not worth taking seriously. Even with diminishing returns, accumulable factors can drive growth rates for long periods of time, and the closer the model is to constant returns, the more persistent is the role of accumulable factors such as physical and human capital. In this sense, the model of constant returns is like a limiting case of the model with diminishing returns. At one level, it appears that there is a sharp discontinuity between the two theories, if we look at the very long run. This discontinuity disappears, however, once we realize that the smaller is the impact of diminishing returns, the more persistent is the effect of factors that are accumulated.

Without this component, we might still have our Edisons and Einsteins, but innovation, in the sense of applying scientific knowledge to the creation of more productive technologies for the sake of economic profit, would largely disappear from the face of the earth.

The second notion, that of diffusion, has more complicated implications for technical progress. Its immediate effect, of course, is to make a new innovation widely available, thereby suggesting that a faster rate of diffusion is conducive to technical progress. A second look suggests that the story is more complicated. Such transfers, or externalities, might slow down the rate of "deliberate" technical progress. Certainly, firms that lobby for the protection of intellectual property rights and the enforcement of patent laws act as if they believe that this negative effect is a necessary outcome of diffusion. Finally, there is a third, more subtle component. The process of diffusion (of knowledge) might itself spur more innovation, as technological leaders struggle to stay abreast of the competition from rivals who pick up slightly older technology.

4.4.3. *A model of deliberate technical progress*

Here is a first pass at constructing a simple model of deliberate technological progress, along the lines of Romer [1990].[12] We assume that an economy has a *given* stock of human capital, which we denote by H. Human capital may be devoted to production (of final goods) or may be employed in a research sector, which produces "knowledge."

Let us try to get at a tangible interpretation of "knowledge." To this end, suppose that production is carried out by machines and labor (including skilled labor in the form of human capital). At this stage, we could simply write down a production function as we have done so far, but instead of that it is more useful to look closely at the "machine sector."

We use what might be called a "Platonic construction." Imagine that all the machines in the world, *including those that have not yet come into being*, are arrayed in a line. Some of the machines already exist—we have blueprints for them. *Research* may be thought of as moving rightward across this line to bring more machines from the shadowy Platonic universe into existence, as the blueprints for their construction are invented ("discovered" is probably more apt in this conceptualization). Figure 4.2 illustrates this concept. All machines named from 0 up to the index $E(t)$ may be thought of as existing at date t. R&D consists of moving the boundary $E(t)$ to the right, resulting in more and more advanced states of knowledge: $E(t+1)$, $E(t+2)$, and so on.

What do these machines do? There are two ways to think about how R&D contributes to production as the E frontier is progressively shifted. One

---

[12] Shell [1967] presented one of the earliest models of this type.

Figure 4.2. Knowledge and machine variety.

interpretation is that new blueprints displace older blueprints, so that more production is carried out, and more productively, with newer machine forms. Alternatively, maybe the greater *variety* of machines available adds to productivity. In this second view, no machine is more productive than any other, but the ability to disperse production among different varieties is itself conducive to production.[13] The particular interpretation is unimportant here, although, in general, there are some differences.[14]

Imagine that once these blueprints come into being, it is easy enough to produce one unit of each existing machine by using one unit of "capital", or foregone output. This simplified description allows us to think of the *quantity of capital* as the total stock of these machines, whereas the *state of technical knowledge* is given by the joint productivity of all existing blueprints. With this interpretation in mind, it is possible to write down what is called a "reduced-form" production function:

$$(4.5) \qquad Y(t) = E(t)^{\gamma} K(t)^{\alpha} [uH]^{1-\alpha},$$

where $E(t)$ denotes the amount of technical know-how at date t, $K(t)$ is the capital stock at date t, and u is the fraction of human capital devoted to the production of final goods. Note that there is really no such thing as a homogeneous stock of capital. The term $E(t)^{\gamma} K(t)^{\alpha}$ represents the joint effect of the total stock of machines (K) as well as their productivity (proxied by E). See the problem set at the end of this chapter for an example.

In the knowledge sector, the *existing* state of knowledge, as well as the amount of human capital put to work in R&D, combine to produce new knowledge. We describe the rate of growth of knowledge by the simple equation

$$(4.6) \qquad \frac{E(t+1) - E(t)}{E(t)} = a(1-u)H,$$

where $1 - u$ is (by definition) the fraction of H devoted to the production of knowledge and a is some positive constant.

---

[13] This second interpretation, adopted by writers such as Romer [1990], Grossman and Helpman [1991], and Ciccone and Matsuyama [1996], stems originally from the consideration of product variety in *consumer* demand (see Dixit and Stiglitz [1977]). If machines are reinterpreted as commodities for final consumption and each blueprint is interpreted as a different means of satisfying the same basic want (so that the postal service, the telephone, the fax machine, and email all satisfy our need for communication), then this is technical progress as well. In Chapter 5 we return to this class of models.

[14] One important implication is for the rate of depreciation. With faster R&D under the first interpretation, we expect that existing capital goods will be discarded faster by firms.

Finally, capital grows using the familiar equation

$$(4.7) \qquad\qquad K(t+1) - K(t) = sY(t),$$

where s is the rate of savings .

This structure is very similar, at first glance, to the Solow model. Technical progress occurs at some rate given by (4.6), but the point is that the right-hand side of the equation is not exogenous. Both the *stock* of human capital in the economy, proxied by H, and its degree of utilization in R&D affect the *rate* of technical progress. Thus the stock of human capital is capable of exhibiting growth effects in some situations.[15]

In the present model, human capital has direct use in productive activity, so there is a trade-off between production "today" and a better technology "tomorrow." The allocation of human capital between the two sectors is captured by the variable u. How u is actually chosen by a society depends on a complex set of factors. A benevolent government might choose u to maximize some notion of social welfare, in an attempt to trade off the present benefits of higher production with the potential benefits of future production. However, in most economies, the choice of u is a decision made jointly by private economic actors, who seek economic gain. In such a case, our earlier discussion is relevant. The degree of appropriability of the technology through patent protection and the rate of diffusion of knowledge to outsiders become important factors. The point remains, however, that innovators must retain some rights over the expanded profits of their innovation, not as a moral prerogative, but as a practical one.

It follows that the simplest theory of technological progress must depart from the world of perfect competition, because a blueprint, once acquired, costs next to nothing to replicate. Thus perfect competition implies that freely available new knowledge is costlessly disseminated, but then new knowledge for economic profit would not be produced. It follows that theories that rely on a deliberate allocation of resources to R&D must allow *some* monopolistic power, however temporary.[16]

---

[15] This particular "growth effect" is sometimes overemphasized, but should not be taken all that literally. It all depends on the precise specification of knowledge creation, and can vary from model to model. The fact remains that there is an interaction between human capital and the pace of technical advance that is worth investigating.

[16] See, for example, Romer [1990] or Grossman and Helpman [1991]. The alternative is to assume that knowledge is publicly provided by a planner or a benevolent planner, which is the appropriate interpretation of Shell [1967], cited earlier.

4.4.4. Externalities, technical progress, and growth

Positive and negative externalities

The second model of technical progress concentrates on the "externalities" that are generated through actions of individual capital accumulation or R&D. This is our first look at externalities in this book, but it won't by any means be the last, so let us pause to understand what the term means. Suppose that an industrialist invests an enormous amount of money in building a railway line from a mining center to a large port city. The line is built to transport ore from the mines (which are presumably owned by the industrialist). There is a sleepy town near these mines, and the railway line passes through the town. Consider the following scenario.

Given that the line is present, the town is now galvanized to life, because transport to the city becomes easier, and soon the line is used to transport people and other forms of business as well as iron ore. Under some situations the industrialist could siphon off all the benefits by charging an appropriate price for travel on the line, but there are situations where this might be impossible (e.g., the government steps in and decrees that the line should be used for travel at a regulated price). In the latter case, the investment by the industrialist has generated *positive externalities* for other individuals and businesses. The term "externalities" is used to emphasize the fact that these benefits cannot be fully "internalized" by the industrialist as extra profits.

There are direct externalities, then, for those who can profitably use the railway line for their own travel and business, but there are externalities for others as well. The town now becomes a viable residential area for those who do not wish to live in the big city. People wish to commute, so they move to the town. Real estate values go up. The owners of such real estate also benefit, even though they might never use the railway. These are positive externalities as well.

Now consider another sleepy town that also lies on the line, but has no railway station so the trains thunder right by. Far from being able to enjoy the better transportation facilities, the residents of this town suffer from increased noise and air pollution because of the presence of the railway. These are *negative externalities*. Again, they are externalities because there is no market through which the industrialist (or other enthusiastic travelers) can compensate these unhappy residents for their pain.

Externalities, as we will see again and again in this book, are a pervasive feature of economic life. Later, we will see how externalities severely distort decision making away from desirable outcomes. At present, I'd just like you to observe that the acts of both R&D and capital accumulation (both physical and human) have varied and significant effects on other economic agents. At an individual level, the externalities may be negative. For instance, a new technological discovery can wipe out the economic power of an existing patent and inflict losses on the patent holder. Even at a worldwide level, there are horrendous possibilities (think of nuclear physics and some of its implications), but only an extremely pessimistic individual would argue that, on average, the externalities of capital accumulation, as well as technological progress, have not been overwhelmingly positive.

To capture this notion in a model, consider a very simple framework in which production takes place with physical capital and labor (a specification just as in the Solow model).[17] However, it is necessary to go a little bit beyond an aggregative model. Imagine, then, that the economy is populated with several firms and each firm is equipped with a production function to produce output

$$(4.8) \qquad Y(t) = E(t)K(t)^\alpha P(t)^{1-\alpha},$$

where $Y(t)$ is output, $K(t)$ is capital, and $P(t)$ is labor employed, all at date t. The term $E(t)$, just as before, stands for some measure of overall productivity, and it is a macroeconomic parameter common to *all* firms in the economy.

This is a standard growth model, but here is the twist that we focus on. We want to study the case where the productivity parameter $E(t)$ is neither exogenously specified (as in the Solow model) nor determined by deliberate R&D decisions (as in the model of the preceding section), but is *a positive externality generated by the joint capital accumulation of all firms in the economy*.[18] In this way, we capture the fact that capital accumulation by each firm might be on a selfish basis. Nevertheless, the process of accumulation might have a positive impact on all other firms in the economy, which we capture by its salutary effect on the parameter $E(t)$. Let us use the notation $K^*(t)$ to denote the average capital stock in the economy and suppose that the external productivity term is related to the average stock by the equation

$$(4.9) \qquad E(t) = aK^*(t)^\beta,$$

where a and β are positive constants. Substituting this expression into (4.8), we see that

$$(4.10) \qquad Y(t) = aK^*(t)^\beta K(t)^\alpha P(t)^{1-\alpha}.$$

We are now in a position to understand how the externality affects accumulation decisions. Suppose, first, that all the firms in the economy are owned

---

[17] The model in this section is based on Romer [1986].

[18] As usual, we neglect numerous other features for the sake of expositional simplicity. Among these is the suppression of any deliberate investments in R&D, as in the model of the last section. This allows us to see the externality issue with more clarity. In addition, we can interpret K as privately accumulated R&D, which has positive benefits to other firms. This is the interpretation favored by Romer [1986]. For a similar externality in the context of human capital, see Lucas [1988].

by a benevolent planner. The planner then has effectively internalized the externality, because she *values* the capital investment of any one of her firms on the overall productivity of her other firms. Compare this scenario to the case where the firms are all separately owned. In this situation no firm values the positive externalities that it has on other firms, because there is no way to extract these benefits in the form of larger profits.

The foregoing comparison yields the following observation: in the presence of positive externalities (or more precisely, complementarities; see subsequent text), firms tend to *underinvest* in capital accumulation relative to what is considered optimal by a benevolent planner. This is simply because the private marginal benefits from investing are less than the social marginal benefits, which is just another way of saying that there are positive externalities at the margin. This is a point that recurs in various guises throughout the book.

There is a second implication of positive externalities that is related fundamentally to the growth model: the observation that constant (or even decreasing) returns *at the level of the firm* can coexist with increasing returns *at the level of society*. Note that each individual production function is assumed to be constant returns to scale in capital and labor. On the other hand, the externalities created by accumulation of capital yield a *macroeconomic* production function that may exhibit increasing returns. The easiest way to see this is to reconsider the production function from the point of view of a benevolent planner. For simplicity, assume that all firms are identical. Then $K(t) = K^*(t)$ in (4.10) and the "social" production function is

$$Y = aK^{\alpha+\beta}P^{1-\alpha},$$

which exhibits increasing returns to scale.

Why is the presence of increasing returns important? One answer is that under such conditions, per capita economic growth is not just positive, but tends to *accelerate* over the long run. Romer [1986] is a proponent of this point of view.

Complementarities

A *particular* type of externality, which can coexist with both positive and negative effects, relates not to the *level* of utility, or monetary reward, that others experience when an action is taken, but to the *ranking* of the alternatives that they have. This is the notion of *complementarity*, which is also well illustrated by the growth model we have been discussing. Indeed, let us use this model to introduce the concept.

Imagine that an individual firm is making its decisions regarding capital accumulation. To do this, it must forecast its future productivity. Given equation (4.10), this productivity depends on the future path of *average* capital accumulation by all firms in the economy. If this path is predicted by a firm to be swiftly climbing, the firm will believe that its future productivity also will rise at a correspondingly high pace, because of the externality. Under such expectations about the future, each firm will be more willing to trade off current consumption (or profits) for future profits, and will therefore accumulate more capital.

Put another way, and more generally, the fact that a single individual takes some action increases the incentives for others to take the same (or similar) action. Thus my decision and your decision to accumulate more capital are complementary in the sense that a greater accumulation of capital on my part raises your incentive to do so as well. Note well that in the present example, this looks very much like a case of positive externalities, but it is really a different aspect of externalities that is not captured by whether they are positive or negative to begin with. For instance, one individual inflicts positive externalities on all others by driving safely, but this does not necessarily mean that others will drive more safely as well. Alternatively, in the case of the railway line, the owners of real estate who benefit are not necessarily induced to participate in any complementary activity (such as building railway lines themselves). Thus positive or negative externalities refer to the *level* of satisfaction (or reward or punishment) experienced by others as the result of your actions, whereas complementarity refers to an increased *relative* preference that others experience for choosing similar actions because you acted in a particular way. To be sure, complementarities do belong to the general class of externalities (just as positive and negative externalities do).

Let us now return to the growth model under discussion and apply this idea (there will be many more applications to come). In the language of the Solow model, think of each firm as choosing its savings "rate" s, which is the same as the rate of investment in this context. Translated appropriately, what we have just shown is that if the firm believes that the average s in the economy is high, then, using (4.9) and (4.10), so will be the projected path of its own productivity and it will choose a larger s. Figure 4.3 shows how individual firms choose s by reacting to the projected average choice of s, denoted by s_a, of all other firms.

Now we need to complete the story by recognizing that the average rate of investment s_a is not something that's exogenous, but is itself the average outcome of all individual investment choices. For instance, in the special case where all firms are identical, the equilibrium average must be one in which s_a equals s, the optimal choice of a representative firm. In the language of Figure 4.3, we see that an equilibriuminvestment rate for the economy as a whole consists of the intersections of the function that describes the choice of s with the 45° line, because these intersections represent precisely the points

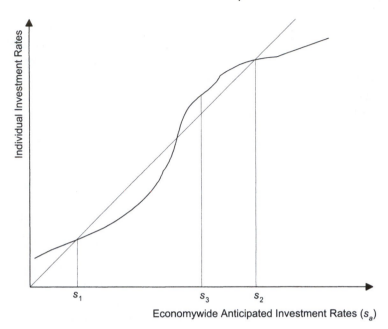

Figure 4.3. Individual investment rates (s) as a function of projected average economywide rates (s$_a$).

where expectations match actual outcomes generated by those very same expectations!

Look at two such intersections, marked s_1 and s_2. How is it that exactly the same economy can possess two different modes of equilibrium behavior? The answer is that an equilibrium is not just an equilibrium of actions; it is also an equilibrium of *beliefs*. Under s_1, all individual firms anticipate a low accumulation profile for the entire economy. This pessimistic forecast generates pessimistic actions, and the actions in turn justify the forecasts! On the other hand, s_2 is characterized by optimistic forecasts regarding accumulative behavior, and the externalities that are created as a result provoke high savings, thereby justifying the initial forecast. On the other hand, the prediction is not completely empty; it isn't being claimed that anything can happen. For instance, the investment rate s_3 cannot be a self-justifying equilibrium of beliefs and actions.

The existence of multiple equilibrium when there are complementarities is a topic that will recur at several points. Let us note one of the implications in the present context. The analysis suggests that two identical copies of the same economy might grow at different rates, depending on the historical context in which expectations were developed. This is not to say that all economies are in fact identical and that the reason they differ is *only* a matter of expectations, but different expectations, and the historical experience that shapes expectations, indeed lead to different outcomes.

4.4.5. Total factor productivity

So far we have studied technical progress from various conceptual angles. It is also important to think about how we can *measure* such progress. In this section, we introduce the concept of *total factor productivity* as a measure of technical progress and explain why an accurate measure of this concept is useful in practice.

To begin with, it is useful to go back to the simplest specification of a production function. In symbolic notation, we write this as

$$Y(t) = F(K(t), P(t), E(t)),$$

where $Y(t)$ is output at date t, $K(t)$ is capital at date t, $P(t)$ denotes the labor force at date t, and $E(t)$ is some measure of knowledge at date t. The notation $F(K, P, E)$ simply means that output is a function of all three variables.

Published data yield estimates of Y, K, and P, even though with each one there are important problems of measurement. The variable E is a more nebulous object, representing the state of knowledge, and cannot be directly measured. Hence, obtaining an estimate of E, or at least the *growth* in output attributable to E, requires a trick. To see how the argument goes, imagine first that there is no increase in E over time, so that output is essentially a function of capital and labor alone. Now let us track the growth of output.

We use the notation $\Delta X(t)$ to denote the change in some variable X over periods t and $t+1$: thus $\Delta X(t) \equiv X_{t+1} - X(t)$. It is easy to see that as a first approximation, the equation

(4.11) $$\Delta Y(t) = \text{MPK}\,\Delta K(t) + \text{MPL}\,\Delta P(t)$$

must hold, where MPK denotes the marginal product of capital and MPL denotes the marginal product of labor around the date t. The intuition behind this equation is very simple. *Because we assume for the moment that there is no technical progress*, the total increase in output between any two dates must be made up of the total increase in all inputs, weighted by their marginal contribution to total output.[19]

Now divide through by $Y(t)$ in equation (4.11), and multiply and divide by $K(t)$ and $P(t)$ in their corresponding terms to get

$$\frac{\Delta Y(t)}{Y(t)} = \frac{\text{MPK} \cdot K(t)}{Y(t)}\frac{\Delta K(t)}{K(t)} + \frac{\text{MPL} \cdot P(t)}{Y(t)}\frac{\Delta P(t)}{P(t)}.$$

[19] If you are wondering why this equation is only an approximation, simply observe that, in general, the marginal products of the capital and labor inputs "continuously" vary as the economy grows. Instead of tracking this total variation, we are simply using an average of these marginal products—hence our terminology in the text: marginal product "around the date t".

Look at the terms (MPK · $K(t))/(Y(t))$ and (MPL · $P(t))/(Y(t))$. *Under the assumptions of constant returns to scale and perfect competition*, introductory economics tells us that all factors are paid their marginal products. If this is indeed so, then MPK and MPL are simply the payments to a single unit of capital and labor, respectively. Multiplying these by the total amounts of capital and labor, and then dividing by aggregate output gives us the *share* of national income accruing to these factors of production. Therefore, if we define $\sigma_K(t) \equiv (\text{MPK} \cdot K(t))/(Y(t))$ and $\sigma_P(t) \equiv (\text{MPL} \cdot P(t))/(Y(t))$, our equation becomes

$$\frac{\Delta Y(t)}{Y(t)} = \sigma_K(t)\frac{\Delta K(t)}{K(t)} + \sigma_P(t)\frac{\Delta P(t)}{P(t)},$$

where $\sigma_K(t)$ and $\sigma_P(t)$ are the income shares of capital and labor, which are observable from the data. We now have a situation where *both* sides of the equation are observable. What if we insert the actual data and the equation does not "add up," with the left-hand side equalling the right-hand side? Well, then, our initial assumption that E is unchanged must be wrong and there must have been some technical progress (or regress). The extent of progress can then be measured by the difference between the left-hand and right-hand side of the equation. This difference is often referred to as *growth in total factor productivity* (or TFP growth). Thus TFP growth is positive when output is increasing faster than predicted by the growth of inputs, and this is a way to quantify technical progress. We summarize all this in the equation

$$(4.12) \qquad \frac{\Delta Y(t)}{Y(t)} = \sigma_K(t)\frac{\Delta K(t)}{K(t)} + \sigma_P(t)\frac{\Delta P(t)}{P(t)} + \text{TFPG}(t),$$

where TFPG(t) stands for TFP growth over the periods t and $t+1$. Note once again that *everything* in equation (4.12) except the term TFPG is measured by looking at the data; TFP growth is then calculated as the "residual" from this equation.

There are several points to note about this methodology.

(1) The concept of total factor productivity *level*, as opposed to its *growth*, is not important. The level carries no information at all, because it can be chosen arbitrarily. What matters is how the level *changes* over time, and this is what is calculated in equation (4.12).

(2) Be careful measuring increases in $P(t)$, which stands for the labor force. One standard method is simply to proxy this by the rate of population growth. Such a proxy may be all right in some cases and highly misleading in others, as we will see. The error is especially pronounced in countries where the participation rate in the labor force has significantly altered over time.

(3) The concept of an aggregate capital stock, and indeed of an aggregate labor force, may be useful in a theoretical exposition, but in practice we may need to aggregate stocks of capital that are growing at different rates. This can be done by expressing aggregate capital growth as the weighted sum of different subgroups of capital, much in the same way that we express aggregate output growth as the weighted sum of capital and labor. Concentrating, as we have already, on the importance of human capital accumulation, we can easily see how important it is to correct for changes in the *quality* of the labor force when we measure the growth of labor input. Correction can be done if we have some idea of the proportions of the population at various stages of education.[20]

(4) Finally, the methodology runs into problems if either factors of production are not paid their marginal product or if the production function is not constant returns to scale. In either of these cases, we cannot use the observed shares of a factor (such as labor) in national income to proxy for the variables σ_P or σ_K. We lose the ability to measure these variables, and once this happens, we can no longer get a handle on TFP growth.[21]

4.5. Total factor productivity and the East Asian miracle

We already mentioned the spectacular rates of economic growth enjoyed by East Asia since 1965. Over the period 1965–90, the region grew faster than any other region in the history of the world. Most of this growth was due to stellar performances by eight economies: Japan, Hong Kong, Korea, Taiwan, and Singapore in the East, and three Southeast Asian countries, Indonesia, Thailand, and Malaysia. Economists have turned to these countries for clues that might explain their success—clues that perhaps can be transplanted elsewhere with a similar effect.

One issue is understanding the *sources of growth* in these countries. Based on the many theories that we have studied, we can trace high growth to one or more of several contributing factors: among these, the most important are

---

[20] We might be tempted to include changes in the quality of the labor force, brought about through education, in the overall concept of technical progress. This is, however, conceptually wrong. With a different mix of educated labor, we are simply moving along the same production function. Of course, if the productivity of a person at the same level of education happens to change, this ought to be picked up in the TFP calculations.

[21] This is not to say that all is lost. Sometimes, adjustments are possible in the accounting, to get upper and lower bounds in the calculated rate of technical progress. For instance, if there is increasing returns to scale, we can tell the direction of the bias. With increasing returns to scale, observed factor shares *underestimate* the true productivity of factors. We therefore end up attributing too much to the residual terms, which is another way of saying that we *overestimate* the rate of technical progress.

capital accumulation, both physical and human, and the pace of technical progress.

These eight economies have taken huge strides in the accumulation of physical and human capital. Rates of savings in these countries (excluding Japan) were lower than those in Latin America in 1965, but in 1990 the excess over Latin America was nearly 20 percentage points. Investment rates are higher than average in the world economy but not remarkably so, although private investment is significantly higher. These countries are net exporters of capital, in contrast to most other developing economies. Human capital levels, by all indications, are very high relative to per capita income levels. By 1965, Hong Kong, Korea, and Singapore had already achieved universal primary education, and soon secondary enrollment rates began to climb. In 1987, Korea had a secondary education enrollment rate of 88% (up from 35% in 1965), and that of Indonesia was 46%, well above the average for countries at that level of per capita income. (Thailand was below the predicted average, however.) Real expenditures per pupil have risen significantly as well.[22]

How about growth in TFP? Did this account for a significant fraction of the phenomenal growth rates that we observe? *The East Asian Miracle*, published by the World Bank, argues that it did indeed. In fact, the study coined the phrase "productivity-based catching up" for this rapid TFP growth and pushed the notion that such growth was largely the outcome of *openness*: specifically, openness to international trade allowed the world's technological frontier to be rapidly absorbed by the East Asian economies. Thus the prescription (see World Bank [1993]):

> "Most explanations of the link between TFP growth and exports emphasize such static factors as economies of scale and capacity utilization. While these may account for an initial surge of productivity soon after the start of an export push, they are insufficient to explain continuing high TFP growth rates. Rather, the relationship between exports and productivity growth may arise from exports' role in helping economies adopt and master international best-practice technologies. High levels of labor force cognitive skills permit better firm-level adoption, adaptation, and mastery of technology. Thus, exports and human capital interact to provide a particularly rapid phase of productivity-based catching up.

Now, it is important for practical policy makers to know just what lies at the heart of the East Asian miracle. If the bulk of growth came from the accumulation of physical and human capital, then we are led to one sort of conclusion: that policies aimed at these variables can have enormous effects on growth. On the other hand, if TFP growth lies at the core of the overall growth spurt, then we are led to a set of policies that favor sectors conducive to technology assimilation. If the foregoing quotation is taken seriously, the trade sector is surely in this class. If this is the case, then countries can benefit

---

[22] This very brief account is taken from the World Bank study on East Asia (World Bank [1993]).

most from having economies that are open to trade, and a trade policy aimed at openness becomes of critical significance. Of course, no one is arguing that it's one or the other. Like most things that we have studied so far, it's probably a bit of everything. Nevertheless, some idea of the quantitative magnitudes certainly helps.

This is precisely why TFP accounting, as developed in the previous section, can be of immense use. By decomposing overall growth into several components, it helps us understand what drives growth and therefore pushes policy in the right direction.

According to the World Bank study that we have mentioned, approximately two-thirds of the observed growth in these economies can be attributed to the accumulation of physical and human capital, and primary education is the single largest contributor among these factors. The remaining growth comes from TFP growth. This is particularly held to be the case for Japan, Korea, Hong Kong, Thailand, and Taiwan. Make no mistake: the study does not argue that TFP growth is *the* dominant factor in growth, but relative to other developing economies, the contribution of productivity change appears to be very high indeed. Because of this seeming anomaly, the World Bank study devotes much thought to the sources of TFP growth. One of the main conclusions is summarized in the foregoing quotation.

Now, careful TFP accounting is needed to conclusively establish that productivity growth has indeed been high in these countries, so that we can then go on to evaluate the export argument as a basis for technological catching-up. Young [1995] does just this. His study is exemplary in that it really makes an effort to control properly for all changes in inputs of production. Recall the warnings of the previous section: it is important to properly measure input growth. This means that one has to account properly for rising participation rates, transfers of labor between agriculture and industry (if one is looking only at the nonagricultural sector of the economy, where TFP growth was supposedly concentrated), and certainly the changes in education levels as well as the rapid pace of capital accumulation. Remember that TFP growth is the *residual* after these inputs have taken their crack at explaining overall growth. Young's careful study shows that "all of the influences noted above. . . serve to chip away at the productivity performance of [Hong Kong, Singapore, South Korea, and Taiwan], drawing them from the top of Mount Olympus down to the plains of Thessaly." For the period 1966–90, it turns out that in manufacturing, productivity growth varied from a low of *negative* 1.0% in Singapore to a respectable, but not astronomically high, 3.0% in South Korea. Singapore was a particularly bad performer (as far as TFP growth goes), and the other three countries were respectable, but not strikingly above average. Tables 4.1 and 4.2 detail Young's findings and list TFP growth in several other countries for the sake of comparison.

Table 4.1. Average TFP growth, 1966–90.[a]

	Hong Kong	Singapore[b]	South Korea	Taiwan
Economy[c]	2.3	0.2	1.7	2.1
Manufacturing[b]	NA	−1.0	3.0	1.7
Other industry	NA	NA	1.9	1.4
Services	NA	NA	1.7	2.6

Source: Young [1995]. [a]NA denotes not available. [b]Years are 1970–90 for Singapore. [c]Agriculture excluded in the case of Korea and Taiwan.

Table 4.2. Comparative TFP growth in selected countries.

Country	Period	Growth	Country	Period	Growth
Canada	1960–1989	0.5	Brazil	1950–1985	1.6
France	1960–1989	1.5	Chile	1940–1985	0.8
Germany	1960–1989	1.6	Mexico	1940–1985	1.2
Italy	1960–1989	0.5	Brazil[a]	1960–1980	1.0
Japan	1960–1989	2.0	Chile[a]	1960–1980	0.7
United Kingdom	1960–1989	1.3	Mexico[a]	1940–1970	1.3
United States	1960–1989	0.4	Venezuela	1950–1970	2.6

Source: Young [1995]. [a]Manufacturing alone.

This sort of study is very useful indeed, because it tells us what to focus on. It appears that the East Asian countries have grown rapidly, but they have grown the old-fashioned way, through an extraordinary process of improvement of the labor force, as well as sustained capital accumulation. In no way does this detract from their success, but it does tell us that technological improvement may not be the most important factor. It is not that the World Bank single-mindedly focused on this issue, it is simply a question of emphasis. In the rest of this section, let us see how different factors can, and did, affect TFP growth computations in this study.

Because technical progress is the residual term in all TFP accounting, it is imperative to properly measure the inputs of production and to keep accurate track of how quickly they have grown. Recall the TFP equation from the previous section:

$$(4.13) \qquad \frac{\Delta Y(t)}{Y(t)} = \sigma_K(t)\frac{\Delta K(t)}{K(t)} + \sigma_P(t)\frac{\Delta P(t)}{P(t)} + \text{TFPG}(t).$$

The first question is, What is a good measure of $P(t)$? Certainly not population, because the labor force grew much faster than the population in the four countries that Young studied. This growth resulted from increased labor force participation. Over the period 1966–90, participation rates climbed from 38 to 49% (Hong Kong), 27 to 50% (Singapore), 27 to 36% (South Korea), and 28 to 37% (Taiwan) (Young [1995, Table I]). If we use population rather than the true labor force in (4.13), it is obvious that $P(t)$ will grow more slowly than the labor force really did. This fact tends to artificially raise the estimate of TFP growth. Correcting for this overestimation takes away a significant amount of TFP growth: 1% per year from Hong Kong, 1.2 and 1.3% per year from Korea and Taiwan, and all of 2.6% per year from Singapore. (Young [1995, p. 644]).

Next, if one is interested in TFP growth in the nonagricultural sector, and particularly in manufacturing, it is not enough to simply take into account increased participation rates in the economy as a whole. We have to account for rural–urban migration, because this means that the rate of growth of the nonagricultural labor force *exceeded* that of the overall labor force. Making this correction lowers TFP growth even further. These effects are particularly strong for South Korea and Taiwan, where agricultural employment declined rapidly as a fraction of total employment.

Finally—and this is something that we have already noted—we must include changes in physical and human capital. Physical capital is already in equation (4.13) and it should be taken care of with careful measurement. Investment to GDP ratios have climbed steeply in the East Asian countries studied by Young (with the exception of Hong Kong). This means that rates of growth in $K(t)$ exceed rates of growth of $Y(t)$ in (4.13), thereby depressing the growth in the residual (which is TFP). The educational correction enters into $P(t)$. Labor input must be weighted by educational characteristics. More educated labor is equivalent to more labor, and Young finds that this correction contributes about 1% per year to the growth of the labor force.

The lesson in this section is that factors such as those discussed must be taken into account very carefully before we pass judgment on the importance of technical progress in growth. Otherwise policy prescriptions may be substantially distorted.

4.6. Summary

We studied some of the newer theories of economic growth. We began with *human capital*, a notion of skilled labor that can be created or augmented through education or training. Thus human capital can be accumulated along with physical capital, and all labor cannot naively be regarded as a single input. With this extension in place, we see that predictions of convergence are considerably weakened: poor countries tend to have a higher marginal rate of return to physical capital because of its shortage relative to *unskilled* labor, but the very same countries also have a shortage of human capital, and this drags down the rate of return to physical capital. The net effect is ambiguous and might serve to explain why growth rates do not appear to systematically vary with per capita income.

Nevertheless, we did note that this extended model continues to predict conditional convergence: controlling for the level of human capital, poorer countries should tend to grow faster. Some support for this view is found in cross-country regressions that have growth rates as dependent variables, and (initial) per capita income as well as measures of human capital as independent variables. The estimated coefficient on per capita income is negative, whereas that on human capital is positive.

The second class of growth theories that we studied dealt with technical progress in more detail. Instead of treating technical progress as an exogenous black box, we thought of progress as stemming from two sources: *deliberate* innovation, fostered by the allocation of resources (such as physical and human capital) to R&D activity, and *diffusion* or spillovers from one firm or industry to know-how in other firms or industries. We observed, however, that some degree of patent protection is, in general, necessary for the first source of technical progress to persist. We then constructed a model of technical progress in which new blueprints come into being through deliberate acts of R&D: these innovations consume resources, but have long-run payoffs. We can think of the production function as forever shifting due to these changes in knowledge, and countries with larger stocks of human and physical capital might be able to achieve faster and more frequent shifts (because they have more resources to allocate to research). This is an alternative model that weakens convergence and does so despite the fact that the marginal returns to physical capital may be diminishing *at any one point of time*. The phenomenon of diminishing returns is countered by the steady expansion of knowledge.

We then turned to a study of spillovers, and how they lead to a pace of growth that is suboptimal from a social point of view. We began this part of the chapter by introducing the idea of *externalities* and distinguishing between *positive* and *negative* externalities. In the context of growth theory, we observed that the act of accumulation of physical capital by one firm positively affects the productivity of other firms. This is an externality of a particular kind, which we called a *complementarity*. A complementarity arises when one agent's choice of an action increases the incentive for other agents to take that same sort of action. In the growth example, my accumulation of capital might raise your productivity, which encourages you to accumulate more capital as well.

Complementarities create the possibility of *multiple equilibria*. In the context of the growth example, it is possible that the *same* economy experiences two or more conceivable paths of capital accumulation. Along one path, accumulation is slow simply because everybody expects everybody else to accumulate slowly, which leads to a perceived slow expansion in future productivity. More optimistic expectations support a path of rapid accumulation, in which productivity growth is rapid as well. How multiple equilibria might arise and how they are supported by different expectations of economic agents are topics that we take up in the next chapter.

Finally, we studied the *measurement* of technical progress. We noted why measurement is important: we can empirically account for the role played by technical change per se, rather than other factors accounting for growth, such as increased rates of savings. The idea is very simple. Using a production function and supposing that all factors are paid their marginal products, we can estimate the increase in output that "should be" due to accumulation of productive factors *alone*. If we see that output is growing even faster than the predictions made from pure accumulation, it must be because overall or *total factor productivity* (TFP) is growing. TFP growth is thus backed out as a residual, as the difference between actual growth rates of output and the growth rates of factors, weighted by their contribution to output. To apply such TFP calculations in a sensible way, we need to be careful about several things. In particular, we need to make sure that we properly account for input growth. For instance, the growth of the labor force is *not* just the growth rate of the population: participation rates as well as the educational composition of the working population might be systematically changing over time.

We applied the TFP methodology to the East Asian "miracle" of rapid growth. How much of this growth can be "explained" by technical progress? Proper TFP accounting reveals that technical progress *is* important, but not as much as was commonly supposed. Rapid rates of capital accumulation—of both the physical and human variety—appear to play a more important role in explaining the East Asian miracle.

Appendix: Human capital and growth

In this Appendix we show how to prove convergence in the model of human capital and growth, as summarized by equations (4.1), (4.2), and (4.3). Using (4.2) and (4.1), we see that

$$(4.14) \qquad \frac{k(t+1)}{k(t)} = s\frac{y(t)}{k(t)} + 1 = sr(t)^{1-\alpha} + 1,$$

whereas

$$(4.15) \qquad \frac{h(t+1)}{h(t)} = q\frac{y(t)}{h(t)} + 1 = qr(t)^{-\alpha} + 1,$$

where $r(t)$ is just the ratio of human to physical capital at date t: $r(t) \equiv (h(t))/(k(t))$.

Combining equations (4.14) and (4.15), we see that

$$\frac{r(t+1)}{r(t)} = \frac{qr(t)^{-\alpha} + 1}{sr(t)^{1-\alpha} + 1},$$

and manipulating this a bit gives us the two equivalent forms

(4.16) $\qquad r(t+1) = \dfrac{q}{s}\dfrac{1+(r(t)^\alpha/q)}{1+(r(t)^{\alpha-1}/s)} = r(t)\dfrac{(q/r(t))+r(t)^{\alpha-1}}{s+r(t)^{\alpha-1}}.$

Now we can use the two forms in (4.16) to establish the following two claims:

(1) If at any date t, we have $r(t) > q/s$, then it must be that $r(t) > r(t+1) > q/s$.

(2) If at any date t, we have $r(t) < q/s$, then it must be that $r(t) < r(t+1) < q/s$.

These two observations, coupled with the statement (see main text) that once $r(t)$ *equals* q/s it will stay right there, constitute the proof of convergence.

We will prove observation 1. The proof of observation 2 is analogous.

So imagine that at the same date, we have $r(t) > q/s$. Then it is easy to see that

$$\frac{1+(r(t)^\alpha)/q}{1+(r(t)^{\alpha-1})/s} > 1,$$

and combining this with the first equality in (4.16), we see that $r(t+1) > q/s$.

Likewise, it is easy to see that

$$\frac{q/(r(t))+r(t)^{\alpha-1}}{s+r(t)^{\alpha-1}} < 1,$$

and combining this observation with the second equality in (4.16), we conclude that $r(t) > r(t+1)$. This proves observation 1. By the preceding discussion, the proof of convergence is complete.

Exercises

▪ (1) Consider two sources of human capital accumulation—education and on-the-job training—and think about what factors might be conducive to each. In the education sphere, keep in mind the distinction between primary and higher education. Discuss what you might expect in the following societies.

(a) Societies in which individuals typically look after their ageing parents, compared to societies in which parents do not expect economic benefits from their children.

(b) Societies in which education is supplied by the free market, compared to societies in which the state is responsible for the provision of education.

(c) Societies in which a large proportion of the population is rural, and farming is typically carried out with the use of household labor.

(d) Societies in which employers cannot write long-run contracts with their employees.

(e) Societies in which individuals with high education can easily emigrate, and in which loans are often required for education.

■ (2) Think about the model of human capital and growth introduced in this chapter. One useful feature of this model is that it simultaneously explains how rates of return to physical capital as well as the wage rate for unskilled labor might be low for developing countries (see Figure 4.1 for a summary). But there is a problem with this argument.

(a) Using a Cobb-Douglas production function with three inputs instead of two, show that such a model predicts that the rate of payment to *human capital* must be higher in developing countries. Explain why this is a problem by comparing the wages of administrators, doctors, lawyers, educators etc., across developed and developing countries.

(b) Adapt the Cobb-Douglas specification in part (a) to allow for differences in technology across developed and developing countries. Now it is possible to generate situations in which the return to every input is lower in developing countries. Which input is likely to have the lowest return (in a relative sense)?

(c) Provide some arguments for systematic technological differences across developed versus developing countries. If technology blueprints are known, why can they not be instantly imitated?

■ (3) Capital might flow from rich to poor countries in one of two ways. Entrepreneurs or corporations in developed countries might set up plants and factories in developing countries: we can think of this as *direct* foreign investment. Or capital might flow in the form of loans to or holdings of stock in developing countries: this is *indirect* investment. Think about the various factors that might affect each of these types of investment.

■ (4) Suppose that production depends on three inputs: land, capital, and labor. Assume that total land is given and cannot be changed. Suppose that two countries are believed to have the same production function, population growth and savings rates, but different levels of land. Explain how you would test for conditional convergence.

■ (5) Distinguish between two forms of technical progress. One is *embodied* in the introduction of new goods or machinery. The other is *disembodied*: with exactly the same inputs, there is an improvement in methods of production. Discuss examples of each. What forces govern the diffusion of such progress (along each of these two dimensions) to developing countries?

■ (6) Suppose that new technical knowledge arrives in the developed world and later diffuses to the developing world. Countries which lag behind more in the world income hierarchy would then have access to a greater pool of new (yet unadopted) ideas. Would this allow such countries to grow faster than their more developed counterparts (who, after all, have to invest resources in creating the new knowledge)? Is this a route to convergence? Discuss.

■ (7) Patent protection yields temporary monopoly power to inventors, allowing them to earn rewards from their patenting. But patent protection also slows down the speed of technological diffusion to competitors, reducing the competitive incentive to innovate. Contrast these two effects and discuss their relative strengths as the intensity of patent protection is exogenously increased.

■ (8) Here is a way of seeing why greater input variety in production is akin to technical progress (see also Chapter 5, where this topic is taken up in more detail). Suppose that an output Y is produced by n different kinds of machines, $X_1, X_2, \ldots, X_n$. No machine is necessary in production, and there are diminishing returns to each machine, but the whole process exhibits constant returns to scale. One way of capturing this is to use the production function:

$$Y = (X_1^\alpha + X_2^\alpha + \cdots + X_n^\alpha)^{1/\alpha},$$

where α lies between zero and 1.

(a) Show that if all machine inputs are increased by some factor λ, then output also increases by the same factor. This means that there is constant returns to scale in production.

(b) Show that if there are at least two different kinds of machine inputs, then there is diminishing returns to each input.

(c) Now suppose that each machine has a new blueprint for its manufacture, but once the blueprint is known, B units of any of these machines can be produced by using one unit of "capital" (which is measured in the same units as final output). Show that if a given amount of capital K is available, it should be used to make the same quantity of each machine so as to maximize the final output from production.

(d) Show that for a given variety of machines (i.e., given n), the production function can be rewritten as a function of *aggregate* "capital" K in the form

$$Y = n^{\frac{1-\alpha}{\alpha}} BK.$$

(e) Now using this expression, show that both an increase in the productivity of machine-production and the variety of available machines is akin to technical progress. Provide intuition for why an increase in machine variety is akin to an increase in overall productivity.

■ (9) The economy of Wonderland produces magic potions using capital (K) and labor (L). Total output is growing at the rate of 5% per year. The rental rate per unit of capital is 0.1 bottles of magic potion. The physical capital–output ratio is 3:1. The stocks of capital and population are growing at the rate of 3 and 2% respectively. Assume that everybody works.

(a) If all output is paid in wages and rent, calculate the shares of capital and labor in national income.

(b) Estimate the rate of technical progress (or TFP growth) in Wonderland.

(c) Suppose that doubling the inputs results in 2.5 times the original quantity of magic potion. How does this affect your answer to part (b)?

(d) Suppose the owners of capital possess patent rights over their inventions and the rental rate reflects the monopoly price on capital rentals. How does this affect the growth-accounting approach used in the foregoing answers?

(e) Suppose that only half the labor population is engaged in production at any date. How does this affect your answer? If this proportion is increasing over time, what would happen to your estimate?

Chapter 5

History, Expectations, and Development

5.1. Introduction

In the last chapter, we studied some of the classic theories of economic growth and their implications. Some of these implications, such as the predicted positive link between investment rates and growth rates, are certainly borne out by the data. Others do not appear to be. One of the most important implications of the Solow model that is *not* supported by the data is the prediction of convergence in living standards across countries. To be sure, such unconditional convergence is not predicted by any of these models, which really embody if–then statements. Thus, for instance, the Solow model states that *if* savings rates and *if* population growth rates are the same for two countries, and *if* the rate of technical progress flows in an unimpeded way across the countries, *then* the two countries will come together, over time, in terms of per capita incomes. Such predictions were called *conditional convergence* in the previous chapter.

Now, statements regarding conditional convergence are often predicated on the similarity of parameters (such as savings rates) that we provisionally consider to be exogenous, and not on some deeper underlying characteristic, which would presumably *determine* investment rates, or the rates of technical progress, or even population growth rates in a wider framework. What if such characteristics (such as social attitudes or the expression of individual preferences) are dependent on the *history* of a country's development, or perhaps on what its citizens *expect* of their own future? This is not to say that the earlier models are wrong, but that they explain matters at one level, and that to understand more we must go deeper, by not necessarily regarding as exogenous what these models regard as exogenous.

What we seek, then (in the context of economic growth), is an explanation of just *why* investment rates are persistently different or why a given rate of savings translates into different growth rates under different circumstances. More broadly, we are interested in seeing how historical forces and expectations shape the overall economic pattern displayed by a country or region. You may not have attended numerous conferences on economic development at the time of reading this book, but I have (and you soon will). Many are the occasions when such questions are raised, and equally numerous are the occasions when the panelist or speaker weightily invokes the complex, deep role played by culture, society, and "historical forces." Indeed, the thorny issues of development are difficult, and to understand them we must understand all the complexities of society, in its many forms. On the other hand, simply *asserting* how complicated matters are does not take anybody very far (although I have often been surprised by the frequency with which such pronouncements are described as "insightful," as "going beyond the narrow boundaries of our discipline," and so on).

The fact of the matter is that people the world over are intrinsically the same: they are all human beings, with the same hopes and desires. Why do cultures and economies, born from the same intrinsic material, perform so differently? If there is a single recipe for economic success, why do all nations not converge on that recipe? This question demands an answer.

The purpose of this chapter is to discuss some issues that are important in understanding this question. We concentrate on two features that have already come up in earlier chapters: the role of *history* and the role of *expectations*.

Both our history and our expectations change the way we behave today and in the future. There are two key ideas that we shall explore to understand why this is so. Once you see how these ideas work, you will see their presence in a variety of situations and will be able to use them to understand and classify many different economic phenomena.

History and expectations interact and work through two main channels: *complementarities* and *increasing returns*. The two main sections of this chapter are divided along these channels.

5.2. Complementarities

5.2.1. Introduction: QWERTY

Look at the arrangement of keys on your computer or typewriter. The top left row begins with the familiar sequence $q, w, e, r, t, y, \ldots$. Have you ever wondered just how this particular sequence came into being? David [1985] offers a fascinating account of typewriter history, observing that the QWERTY arrangement sprang largely from a need to avoid typebar tangles. Have you ever seen one of the original typewriters? They were mechanical, of course. You hit the desired key and a long lever bearing the imprint of this key would rise up and hit the typewriter ribbon. If you hit two keys at once or two keys in very quick succession, the two levers would jam. The QWERTY key layout emerged, in part, to reduce the frequency of such jams.

In no way was it *the* best keyboard for a more idealized object, such as an electronic typewriter or a computer keyboard. Indeed, the Dvorak system, introduced in 1932, presented an alternative that repeatedly won speed-typing contests. Alternative keyboards are standard on many computers today. Why, then, despite its obvious inefficiency today, does QWERTY still rule the roost?

To understand this, it is important to realize that typing skills (until very recently) were part of the intricate network of business and industry. Typists came from typing schools and were almost exclusively hired by firms.[1] Given that all firms were hiring QWERTY-trained typists, it made little sense for any *one* of these firms to invest in, say, Dvorak-style keyboards, and train their typists accordingly; the costs involved in retraining were simply too high. This statement is perfectly compatible with the fact that if *all* firms and typing schools (by an incredible act of coordination) had adopted a different system, the efficiency gains would have been significant. We have, then, a self-fulfilling situation that is difficult for any individual to get out of, because the return to each person depends on what everybody else is doing. You simply cannot ask the question, "QWERTY or Dvorak for you?" in a vacuum. Your answer depends on how others have answered the question.

This divergence between individual cost and social gain occurs whenever a system of production, or organizational form, exhibits *externalities*, so that the cost or benefit of adopting that system by an individual depends on how many *other* individuals have adopted that system. (Externalities were already introduced in Chapter 4.) What we have here is the by now familiar special case of complementarities.

Specifically, the adoption costs of a system may be reduced by the number of existing adopters. In the case of QWERTY, the creation of typing schools and a pool of typists trained in a particular way lowered the cost of new individuals adopting that same system. However, it is perfectly possible that QWERTY has a higher cost *curve*.

Look at Figure 5.1, which plots the cost of adoption of a technology by an individual against the number of people in the economy who have already adopted that technology. The higher, inefficient cost curve belongs to QWERTY. True, the cost of adoption falls as the number of people adopting QWERTY increases. That's what complementarities are all about. However, imagine that there is another system out there (Dvorak) with a lower cost *curve*. That is, at every population size of existing users, Dvorak has a lower cost of adoption. Thus Dvorak's lower cost curve represents a competing, more efficient system.

Now here comes the role of history. Dvorak may have a better cost curve, but *QWERTY is already there by the advantage of historical precedence*, and so commands a market size of N. The new technology currently has no market share, so the comparison of cost *levels* is really between a point such as

---

[1] We are considering times that precede the growth of the market for personal typewriters.

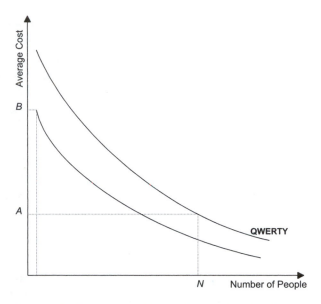

Figure 5.1. Cost curves with complementarities in adoption.

A for QWERTY and *B* for the competing system. Faced with these cost levels, a new user will adopt QWERTY and not Dvorak, and this perpetuates QWERTY's market size.

Examples of the QWERTY lock-in effect abound. At the time of writing of this book, the personal computer industry in the United States was characterized by domination of Intel, the leading chip manufacturer, together with the Microsoft operating system. Competing chips exist: an example is the RISC line of chips. Adopted by Apple in its PowerPC line or used by DEC in the Alpha chips, these chips often run at clock speeds that greatly exceed that of Intel chips. Hence it has been argued that RISC chips have a greater potential than Intel chips, but to bring this potential to life, companies must write operating systems that exploit the particular qualities of the chip. Who will write such an operating system if other companies are wary of writing software for such a system, and who will write the software for an entirely new system, if many customers are already locked in? This is another example of how history creates a lock-in effect that is difficult to get out of.[2]

Recall another example of complementarities: the endogenous growth model studied in Chapter 4, based on technological diffusion. In that model, a higher rate of capital accumulation by the economy as a whole raised

[2] Microsoft does support the Alpha with a native version of Windows NT, but companies are wary of writing other software on this platform unless there are a large number of (home) buyers using the Alpha. Conversely, the Alpha will not sell unless software is written for it. At the time of writing, it is unclear how this failure of coordination will resolve itself.

productivity for all individual firms, thus raising the rate of return at the individual level. This increases the payoff from investment, so that investment by one agent has a positive effect on investment by another. We also noted the possibility of multiple equilibria in that model. Depending on historical experience, the economy may settle at any one of these equilibria. I want you to note here that the structure of the problem is the same as that of QWERTY or the Intel–RISC example. Extract the common elements for your understanding. We will have occasion to use them later.

The fact that externalities take the particular form of a complementarity plays a crucial role in this sort of argument. When externalities are such that the cost of an action *increases* with the number of adopters, they cannot be responsible for multiple equilibria or historical lock-in. To see this, consider an alternative scenario in which there are "congestion effects." There are two alternative traffic routes, A and B, between two cities. The cost to a commuter depends on congestion on the route she is using: the more the traffic (or number of "adopters" of that route), the *higher* the adoption cost for her. This is exactly the opposite of the QWERTY example. It is easy to see that here *both* routes will be used by commuters.

Because this example is so simple, I offer a diagram to contrast it sharply with the QWERTY story. Figure 5.2 displays the total number of commuters as the line XY on the horizontal axis. We count the number of people traveling on route A from left to right and the number on route B from right to left. The cost curve of adopting route A is drawn in the usual fashion; that for route B is drawn in mirror-image form, because we are counting from

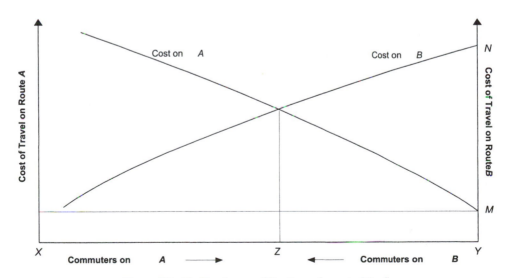

Figure 5.2. Traffic: A case of "anticomplementarities."

right to left for that route. Note that these curves are *upward sloping*, in contrast to the QWERTY example, because an increase in the number of users of a particular route inflicts negative externalities on a user by raising her cost of transportation.

Now observe that history can have no effect on the equilibrium dispersion of traffic on these routes. For instance, suppose initially that route A existed and then route B was set up. Initially no one used route B, so the cost of travel on this route is only YM (see diagram). Route A has a cost of YN, which is larger. Hence, traffic will begin to switch to the new route, which drives up its cost and brings down the cost of the old route. Ultimately, XZ commuters will use A and the rest, ZY, will use B, and transportation costs will be equalized across routes. This solution ultimately occurs regardless of whether A or B was created first.

What do we learn from this discussion? Three things: first, it is possible that, because of complementarities, there may be "multiple equilibria" in a system. After all, everybody using Dvorak would also be a stable state of affairs (provided we could somehow get there). Thus in this example, universal adoption of the QWERTY system and universal adoption of the Dvorak system represent two equilibria, which no individual can affect by some unilateral action. Second, the *particular* equilibrium in which society might find itself depends on the history of that society. For instance, QWERTY was initially popular and appropriate because of the jamming typewriters. The jamming typewriters went away, but QWERTY didn't. History and externalities combined to lock QWERTY in. Finally, we saw that externalities create possible multiple equilibria, and historical lock-in occurs *only* when externalities take the form of complementarities.[3]

5.2.2. *Coordination failure*

Pervasive complementarities might therefore lead to a situation where an economy is stuck in a "low-level equilibrium trap," while at the same time there is another, better equilibrium, if only all agents could appropriately *coordinate* their actions to reach it. This view of underdevelopment has gained some popularity.[4] Its genesis lies in a classic paper by Rosenstein-Rodan [1943], which went unnoticed by mainstream economists for many decades.

According to this view, economic underdevelopment is the outcome of a massive *coordination failure*, in which several investments do not occur simply

[3] This statement is a bit too strong. What one can show is that multiple *Pareto-comparable* equilibria can only occur when there are complementarities. Moreover, we do not assert that historical dependence and multiple equilibria must *necessarily* occur in all cases where there are complementarities.

[4] See, for example, Murphy, Shleifer, and Vishny [1989a], Matsuyama [1991], Krugman [1991a], Rodríguez-Clare [1996], Ciccone and Matsuyama [1996], and Baland and Francois [1996].

because other complementary investments are not made, and these latter investments are not forthcoming simply because the former are missing! The argument sounds circular. It is and it isn't, as we will soon see. For now, observe that this concept provides a potential explanation of why similar economies behave very differently, depending on what has happened in their history.

From Rosenstein-Rodan comes the parable of the shoe factory. Imagine a region where there is potential for investment in a number of different enterprises. Suppose, moreover, that all the output of the enterprises must be sold within the region.[5] Now suppose that a giant shoe factory is set up, which produces a million dollars worth of shoes and thus creates a million dollars of income in wages, rents, and profits. Can the enterprise survive? It can only if all the income is spent on shoes, which is absurd. The recipients of the new income will want to spend their money on a variety of objects, which includes but is certainly not limited to footwear! Thus the shoe factory on its own cannot be viable.

Now consider a different thought experiment. Imagine that enterprises are set up in the correct ratios in which people spend their money on different commodities. For instance, suppose that people spend 50% of their income on food, 30% of their income on clothing, and 20% of their income on shoes. In that case, setting up *three* enterprises in the ratio 50:30:20 would actually generate income that would come right back to these enterprises. The conjunction of the three enterprises would be *jointly* viable, in a way that each individual enterprise was not.[6]

Now here is where the issue of coordination makes an appearance. Suppose that no entrepreneur is large enough to invest in more than one enterprise. Then notice that each entrepreneur would invest *if he were to believe that the others would invest as well*, but in the absence of such optimistic beliefs, he would not do so, for the same reason that the shoe factory in isolation would not be set up. Thus we have two equilibria: one in which the region is devoid of any investment at all and another in which there is investment by all three entrepreneurs in the appropriate proportion.

Whether or not such a coordinated equilibrium would arise depends on the expectations that each entrepreneur holds about the others. To the extent that the formation of expectations is driven by past history, it may well be that a region that is historically stagnant continues to be so, whereas another region that has been historically active may continue to flourish. At

[5] This is the important assumption of *no trade*, which we discuss later.

[6] Of course, the more varied and diverse is the range of commodities on which people spend their income, the more varied and diverse the enterprises that are set up would need to be. The point should be clear from the example.

the same time, there may be nothing that is intrinsically different between the two regions.[7]

Is this situation the same as the QWERTY example? It is. Think of "investing" and "not investing" as the two options analogous to adopting QWERTY or Dvorak. Note that the gain to investing depends positively on investments made by others. Therefore, we are in the standard framework of complementarities, and viewed from this angle, the possibility of multiple equilibrium outcomes should not be at all surprising.

Coordination failure emerges from complementarities, and the situation that generates it is often known as a *coordination game*.[8] The "failure" manifests itself in the inability of a group of economic agents, whose actions are "complementary" in the sense described earlier, to achieve a "desirable" equilibrium, because of the presence of another "undesirable" equilibrium in which they are trapped. This notion of coordination is closely linked with the concept of *linkages*, to which we turn next.

5.2.3. Linkages and policy

The parable of the shoe factory is particularly compelling if many different industries are involved in coordination to a "desirable" equilibrium. Figure 5.3 provides an example of the interaction between various industries. Only a small number of industries are involved in this diagram, but you can see the point. The idea of the arrows is to suggest that one industry might facilitate the development of another by easing conditions of production in the latter industry.

Note that it is quite possible for these links to be simultaneously in two states: one in which all activity is depressed and another in which the links are active. The problem is that if all industries are simultaneously in a depressed state, it may be hard to "lift" the entire network of linkages to a more active state.

Of particular interest is the structure of the various linkages that connect different industries. Hirschman [1958] distinguished between *backward* and *forward* linkages. Thus, in Figure 5.3, the steel industry facilitates the development of other industries, such as railways, by increasing the availability of steel and/or lowering its price. This is an example of a forward linkage—one that works by affecting the ease of *supply* of another product. A forward linkage is captured in this diagram by the direction of the arrows. On the other hand, the steel industry possesses a backward linkage to the coal industry:

---

[7] This argument thus steps away from historical determinism, in the sense that it allows for initial accidental occurrences to have long-term effects that are completely different, and yet allows for sudden swings that are driven entirely by coordinated changes. We return later to the question of history versus expectations.

[8] For a description of coordination games, see Appendix 1.

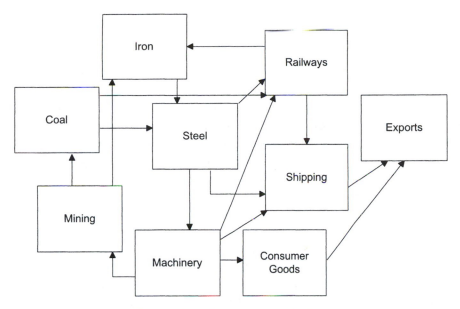

Figure 5.3. Linkages and coordination.

the expansion of the former raises the *demand* for the latter. Likewise, the shipping industry links forward to exports and backward to railways: the former because it facilitates the transportation of exports; the latter because it creates a demand for freighting of products from the interior to the ports. Typically, a backward linkage is created by reversing the direction of the arrows in Figure 5.3. If industry *A* facilitates production in industry *B*, then an expansion of industry *B* (for some other reason) will generally create an increase in demand for the product of industry *A*. Thus backward linkages are like "pulls" and forward linkages are like "pushes."

The concept of linkages is important because linkages have a bearing on policy. Suppose that an economy is in a depressed equilibrium; how would a policy be framed so as to take the economy to a better equilibrium? Rosenstein-Rodan introduced the idea of a *big push*, a policy that simultaneously creates a coordinated investment in many different sectors of the economy. Such a policy has two important features. First, it requires a massive (presumably public) investment in many different sectors of the economy at once. Second, an idea of the *quantitative* allocation of the investment across different sectors of the economy is necessary. To go back to the example of the previous section, it would be incumbent on the government or the policy maker to know the proportions of their income that consumers spend on different commodities. In the example illustrated by Figure 5.3, it would be necessary to know the correct mix of investments, otherwise there would be, say, too much investment in shipping and too little in coal.

This is a tall order on both counts. The investment is presumably immense. For most developing countries, this would require an infusion of foreign aid that is probably way too large. In post-war Europe, the Marshall Plan did provide a huge infusion of funds, and it was in the context of such possibilities, reparations in particular, that Rosenstein-Rodan made his original argument. Significantly more problematic than the size of the required investment are the informational requirements of such an exercise. It is simply not practical for the government to have the information to parcel out the investment to different sectors or for the government to have the information to run each such sector.

There is another objection to this policy that is more fundamental than either of the considerations described in the preceding text. It is that the policy does not exploit the fact that the desirable outcome *is also an equilibrium*. Put another way, if incentives are provided carefully and selectively, we can partly (though not wholely!) rely on the market to correct this coordination failure. This is where the concept of linkages acquires its importance.

Hirschman's idea was simple yet profound: instead of following the big push, which is akin to a policy of "balanced growth," follow a deliberate policy of *un*balanced growth. That is, selectively promote the development of certain key sectors in the economy, and as the linkages generated by these key sectors make their presence felt, the market will respond to the unbalanced situation by making the other investments spontaneously.

How would such key or *leading sectors* be chosen? Several considerations arise. Remember the obvious: all these considerations are predicated on the fact that the available resources of the policy maker are limited. If this were not the case, then investments could be made in all sectors without heed to opportunity cost.

(1) The *number* of linkages that a given sector possesses is certainly an important factor. Government support of music and the arts is a noble and desirable ideal indeed, but it is not the appropriate sector to push in the interests of solving an economywide coordination failure. However, even after the obvious nonstarters are removed, there remain many serious contenders. Coal or steel? Railways or highways? Heavy industry or labor-intensive enterprises? Each is a nontrivial choice, and the answers must depend on the particular configuration of the economy. In all these cases, we look for the maximum punch per buck; that is, the largest number of other sectors that will be affected as a result of the development of the chosen sector.

(2) The number of linkages is not the only concern. The *strength* of each linkage matters as well. In this regard, the character of the link, whether it is forward or backward, assumes some importance. Forward linkages are essentially facilitatory: they increase the viability of some other sector from the point of view of production, from the supply side as it were. Backward

linkages increase the demand for the product of another sector. At first sight, these factors appear to be equivalent: why does it matter whether a sector is stimulated by lowering its costs or increasing its prices, as long as there are profits to be made? In general, it does matter: from the point of view of the sector that benefits from the linkage, a backward linkage directly raises the price of its output, stimulating higher production or supply. A forward linkage reduces the price of *one* of its inputs of production, but in general there are many inputs. The overall effect is far more diffuse. At the same time, the falling price of the input might affect more than one sector in which the input is used as a factor of production. The point is that the effect is relatively small for each sector and is, therefore, less likely to tip it over the threshold into a high-investment regime. The diffuse nature of a forward linkage has informational implications as well. For sectors that do not expand by the growth of existing firms, but by the entry of new firms, backward linkages carry a sharper flow of information. If the price of leather rises as a result of expansion of the shoe industry, it is pretty clear that leather is now a more profitable venture. However, if the price of coal falls because of an expansion in its supply, there is now a whole range of possibilities, and the flow of information is accordingly more noisy and more complex.

(3) Finally, it is important to look at the "intrinsic profitability" of each sector. To be sure, this term is vague. After all, we have just argued that the profitability of a particular sector depends on investments in other sectors. It is a useful criterion, nevertheless. Suppose we find that the export sector has far more linkages than the development of highways, peso for peso. It is also rich in backward linkages, and although highway development might raise the demand for inputs that go into road making, it should be quite obvious that the main effects are in the nature of forward linkages. Is this an argument for the government to make a large-scale investment in the export sector at the expense of highways? Not necessarily, and the reason for this is that exports are more likely to be taken up by the private sector, because there are profits to be made. It is difficult (though not impossible) to turn highway construction and maintenance into a profitable venture, especially in poor countries where charging profit-making tolls might be politically or economically infeasible. In this case, *the government maximizes the chances of overcoming coordination failure by investing in the least profitable activity*, provided of course that such activities have linkages as well. Thus a leading sector need not be intrinsically profitable, but it must spur other sectors that are. This simple observation also suggests that the role of government is often to take up intrinsically unprofitable activities and cautions us to not make blanket statements such as "governments are incapable of covering their costs" without studying the sectors involved.

These considerations suggest several examples of leading sectors. Among them are heavy industry, exports, tourism, transportation, and agriculture.

At various points in this book we will examine some of these sectors: for instance, the role of agriculture in Chapter 10 and the role of exports in Chapters 17 and 18. The box in this chapter shows how heavy industry has been deliberately fostered by at least one government as a leading sector.

Heavy Industry as a Leading Sector: Early Planning in India

The Indian economy is best described as "mixed." Although most consumption goods and practically all agriculture lie in the hands of private enterprise, many capital goods and infrastructural services (e.g., heavy engineering, iron and steel, fertilizers, the railways, etc.) are produced in the public sector. Largely influenced by the Soviet experiment with planning (see the box in Chapter 3), Indian policy makers believed that heavy industry was *the* leading sector to encourage: its growth would pull up the remainder of the economy.

Until very recently, the Indian government was empowered with powerful instruments (such as the Industrial Licensing Policy[9]) that controlled the size and allocation of investment to even those sectors that were largely in private hands. The acquisition of such powers by the Indian government from the moment of birth of the Republic (in 1947) showed an unwillingness to rely purely on the market mechanism. In other words, the Indian government wanted to push certain sectors that the market, left to its own devices, might not promote.

The Planning Commission was established on 15 March 1950, under the chairmanship of the first Prime Minister of India, Jawaharlal Nehru. The first Five Year Plan covered the period 1951–52 to 1955–56. As in the Harrod–Domar theory, there was an emphasis on raising overall rates of investment. The second Five Year Plan (1955–56 to 1960–61) went a step further. One of the main architects of the plan was Professor P. C. Mahalanobis, an eminent statistician and advisor to Prime Minister Nehru.

The Mahalanobis model, which served as the foundation of the second plan, bore a close resemblance to a framework enunciated by the Soviet economist Feldman in 1928, on which Soviet planning in the 1930s was largely based. *Both models argued that to achieve rapid growth, careful attention was to be given not only to the size of investment, but also to its composition.* In particular, these models stressed the need to make substantial investments in the capital goods sector so as to expand the industrial base and remove possible future bottlenecks in machine-producing capacity. One implication of following this policy is that growth in *consumer* goods is initially low, but accelerates once the industrial base is sufficiently enlarged. This emphasis on heavy industry in India's second Five Year Plan is illustrated by the fact that 34.4% of planned investment was in the investment goods sector, compared to only 18.2% in consumer goods and 17.2% in agriculture (Hanson [1966, p. 126]).

---

[9] Investments in industry above a certain size required procurement of licenses from the Indian government. By controlling the number of licenses issued, the government aimed to control the size of various industries in accordance with its plans and policies.

During the plan period, we note that national income grew by 4% per annum on average. Given the almost stagnant nature of the Indian economy in the preceding half century or even more, this was pretty dramatic. Raj [1965] observed that "the percentage increase in national income in the last thirteen years has been higher than the percentage increase realized in India over the entire preceding half a century."[10]

Industry, given the greater share of investment it received, did much better than the nationwide average. Overall industrial production grew at an average rate of 7% per annum over the period of the first two plans. For the second plan period alone, the general index of industrial production grew by roughly 35% between 1955–56 and 1960–61, and that of machine production soared to 250% of its starting level in the meager space of five years (Hanson [1966. p. 169]). However, there were some serious shortfalls in the infrastructural sector: power production missed its target of 6.9 million kilowatts by 1.2 million, and underinvestment in railways gave rise to bottlenecks and strain toward the end of the period (Hanson [1966]).

In conclusion, although the first two Five Year Plans set India on a path of aggregative growth unprecedented in her history, the abysmally poor living conditions for the majority of the populace at the outset of the plan programs coupled with the increasing population pressure over the period hardly left any room for complacence at the beginning of the Third Plan period.

5.2.4. History versus expectations

So far we have discussed the idea of complementarities and have seen how such externalities may precipitate a coordination failure. The case of several sectors simultaneously functioning at a suboptimal level requires a policy that assists the economy to move from a suboptimal outcome to one that is more efficient. In the previous section, we considered such policies.

All of this analysis is based on the presumption that, somehow, *history* pins down the equilibrium, and makes it difficult for firms, individuals, or sectors to free themselves in a coordinated way from the low-level equilibrium trap. Yet we also asserted that if somehow the expectations of the economic agents involved could be changed, movement would occur, magically as it were, from one equilibrium to the other. What prevents expectations from changing? After all, we do observe large swings of expectations in other situations. For instance, a large component of fashion rests on the expectations of the majority that something (trousers with large holes in them, pet rocks, Amitabh Bachhan films, or certain unnameable contemporary musicians) is currently "cool," and therefore should be "experienced" so as not

---

[10] However, population growth during the period exceeded expectations and, more alarmingly, showed a rising trend, mainly due to a fall in the death rate caused by improvements in medical care. Consequently, *per capita* national income grew by only 1.8% per year, which, though still creditable, is considerably less cheerful.

to be left out. This "something" does change, and it changes often. Why do we not observe a similar ease of movement out of bad equilibria into good? Why must we fall back on Hirschman and Rosenstein-Rodan?

This is a good question, and it will come back to haunt us at different points in the book (see, for instance, Chapter 9). Let us take a first pass at addressing this question; there will be other occasions as well.

You might want to keep the following example in mind. Consider the development of an export sector, specialized in electronic components. It may be that such a sector is dependent on a steady and reliable supply of skilled engineers. There may, indeed, be good engineering schools in the country or, at the very least, opportunities to acquire such skills abroad. If such a sector were to come up, engineers would earn a very high rate of return on their training, as firms invested to take advantage of the skilled labor. The problem is how would this sector develop on its own? The externalities imposed by the *current* absence of personnel and know-how may make the costs of investing in the nascent export promotion sector very high. Thus initially the demand for skilled personnel is quite low, and the consequent rates of return to acquiring such skills might, as a result, be too limited to encourage their acquisition. Yet the same combination might well thrive if both were somehow simultaneously forthcoming. We have here another example of a familiar coordination failure.

This argument is conveniently summarized by using a simple model.[11] Figure 5.4 shows us two sectors, Old and New. In both panels Old and New, we suppose that externalities are present: the return to any one individual for participating in a sector depends positively on the number of individuals already active in that sector. These observations are captured by drawing rates-of-return lines in both panels that slope upward with the number of individuals in that sector. To complete the description, we locate the initial allocation of individuals across the two sectors (given by history). This is given by OA people in Old and OB people in New. You could think of the line segment AB as the total number of people in the economy: as the allocation of people changes, the only thing that is altered is the *position* of AB, but not its length.

Figure 5.4 is drawn to deliberately illustrate two points. First, the rate-of-return line in New is "better" than in Old: if they were to be superimposed on the same panel, the New line would lie above the Old line. Second, and in contrast to the first point, at the starting location, the *actual* rate of return in Old, r_0, exceeds the actual rate of return in New, r_N.

Note that all the examples discussed so far fit quite neatly into this framework. For instance, the return in New can be interpreted as the wages paid

---

[11] For detailed analysis of similar models, see, for example, Krugman [1991a] and Matsuyama [1991].

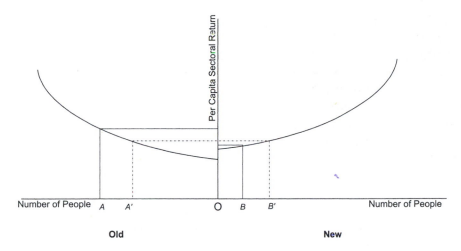

Figure 5.4. Externalities and history.

to people who decided to acquire engineering skills, *as a function of the number of individuals who already had acquired such skills.* In this interpretation, if you think of the alternative occupation as conferring no externalities, you can imagine that the rate-of-return line in Old is nearly flat, whereas the one in New slopes upward. Alternatively, think of New as typewriters with the Dvorak system or, for that matter, as alternative chip designs, whereas Old contains the QWERTY typewriters or Intel chips. The rate of return is then interpreted as the total amount of satisfaction accruing to a consumer or user, net of the cost of purchase or usage. In all these examples, it is useful to think of *OA* as a large segment, whereas *OB* is very small, perhaps zero.

Now we are ready to make this model run. Imagine that, as indicated in Figure 5.4, the rate of return in Old exceeds the corresponding rate in New. Then, as time passes, individuals will gravitate from New to Old. This describes the failure of an exciting new sector when there is not enough critical mass to keep the momentum going. Matters end with everybody in Old and nobody in New. Private markets fail to incorporate the social externality, leading to an inefficient outcome. This is precisely the substance of the foregoing examples.

Figure 5.4 also reveals that had there been sufficient critical mass, matters would have been entirely different. For instance, suppose that history initially put us at the allocation *OA'* and *OB'*, where the rates of return in the two sectors are exactly equal. Then the slightest additional tilt toward New can spark an accelerating tempo of beneficial change, as people switch over to the new technology (or the new product or a new way of life).

Now here is a different story that works entirely on the basis of expectations. Begin again in the situation where *OA* individuals are in Old and the rest, *OB*, are in New. Now imagine that for some reason *everybody* believes that *everybody else* will be in New tomorrow. Never mind where this belief came from. Simply note that *if* this belief is genuinely held by someone, he must also believe that New is the sector to be in because the return there is higher. Consequently, he will gravitate to New tomorrow. However, if everybody thinks the same way, everybody will be in New, and the seemingly absurd belief is completely justified! Thus, it seems from this argument that history plays no role at all. *Irrespective* of initial conditions, there are only two self-justifying outcomes that are possible—everyone in Old or everyone in New—and that *both* outcomes are always possible, depending only on expectations.[12]

How do we square this story with the one that we described earlier?

To address this question, it is important to recognize a serious problem with the analysis of the previous paragraph. It ignores the fact that these sectoral shifts take *time*. It *is* possible that a swarm of people gravitate from Old to New, but it does not follow that the rates of return to being in that sector *instantaneously* adjust to the new level as displayed by the diagram. Recall the example that motivated this model. A supply of skilled engineers provokes the development of the export sector, thereby raising the returns to these skills *over time*. Thus, although we believe that the diagram is accurate as a long- or even a medium-run description of returns, it cannot be a good description of what happens *immediately*.

Once we recognize this time factor, the argument begins to unravel.[13] It is no longer the case that even with the expectation that everybody else will be in New, our individual will move there just yet. He will wait until the rate of return in that sector climbs above the rate of return that he is currently getting in Old, and this will continue to be higher in the short run. If our man thinks this way, others will as well, so people will postpone the move, and this destroys the self-justifying nature of the expectation that everyone else will indeed move there tomorrow. It is possible to show quite easily that history makes a triumphant reentry: now *expectations* play no role and initial conditions once again must determine the entire outcome.

The essential point of the foregoing argument is that people will delay their decisions beyond what they expect others to do, so as to avoid the time lag that occurs in the build-up of returns. This tendency to delay a potentially costly move can trap the economy. This is precisely what occurred in the situations described by Rosenstein-Rodan and Hirschman: everybody wants everybody else to go first. There is no solution to the problem.

The delay problem also tells us why it is easier to generate a new fashion than to pull an economy out of a coordination failure. One characteristic

---

[12] There is also a third outcome in which the rates of return in the two sectors are exactly equalized, but it is possible to rule this out on the grounds of "stability."

[13] See Adserà and Ray [1997] and, in a distinct but related context, Chamley and Gale [1994].

of fashion is that the initial users might be thought of as "innovators": they don't care that they are different; indeed, they probably *like* the idea of being different. Hence, there is no cost and probably a gain to "going first." Once this happens, the followers can follow in due course. In the case of an economic coordination failure, going first means taking economic losses. Unless there are entrepreneurs who deliberately run against the economic tide, either because of overoptimism or simple arrogance, we cannot break a coordination failure in the same way as old fashions are broken. Sometimes there are such entrepreneurs.[14]

This argument also teaches us that expectations play a role when there is some advantage to going first. One such advantage comes from the costs of entry into a new sector. It may be that earlier entrants get the better jobs, for instance, because of more years of experience. Alternatively, if we take these sectors literally as two geographical regions, then it may be that congestion increases the costs of moving later, perhaps because of difficulties in finding suitable housing. In such cases, it is possible that economic agents trade off the lower *current* returns from moving now with the higher costs of moving in the future. This might spark a process of "migration" from Old to New even though Old is currently more profitable. Sustaining this migration requires the belief that others will migrate as well. In this sense, expectations might overcome history to some extent.[15]

5.3. *Increasing returns*

5.3.1. *Introduction*

A production activity displays *increasing returns to scale* if an expansion in the scale lowers the unit costs of operation. Equivalently, a proportionate increase in the variable inputs of production leads to a greater-than-proportionate increase in the output from the activity.

In theories of growth such as the Harrod–Domar or Solow models, increasing returns did not play a traditionally important role (but recall the endogenous growth models of Chapter 4). One important exception stands out in the early literature: the classic paper by Young [1928], which emphasized the role of increasing returns in development. The idea is simple, but very powerful. It has two parts to it. First, the ability to realize the gains from increasing returns depends on the size of the available market for the product. If the market is small, a profitable product may never make it into the market. Second, and more subtly, the size of the market may itself depend on the ability to exploit increasing returns, expand production, and pay out in-

---

[14] On fashion cycles, see, for example, Pesendorfer [1995]. On overoptimistic entrepreneurs, see Manove [1997].

[15] On these matters, see Matsuyama [1991] and Krugman [1991a].

come to employees. Consequently, it is possible for an economy to be caught in a low-level trap, much like the one described in the previous section, but arising from a different source.[16]

5.3.2. *Increasing returns and entry into markets*

Consider an example. Suppose that a developing country has a small domestic market for automobiles that is currently serviced by imports from well-known international auto manufacturers. Now imagine that a local man-ufacturer designs a car that is particularly suitable for domestic conditions. For instance, the design may be a highly fuel-efficient car that has a low max-imum speed. The low speed might make this car unsuitable for the German autobahn, but it is perfectly adequate for the capital city of this developing country, where traffic of all kinds is particularly dense and road conditions are not very good. Moreover, the enhanced fuel efficiency is welcome, given current balance-of-payments conditions. Let us conclude, then, that although this new model may not be the best under ideal road conditions, it is never-theless well suited to the conditions prevailing in the country.

The manufacturer is eager to start production of this new design, but soon runs into a difficulty. She realizes that the market is presently saturated with automobiles and that her only hope of expansion is to take this market away for herself. This is a challenge she is quite willing to assume, but there are other difficulties. Like many mass-production technologies, the produc-tion of automobiles involves increasing returns to scale, and she will have to sell a large quantity of cars in order to reduce production costs to profitable levels.

The situation is illustrated in Figure 5.5. On the vertical axis is unit cost of production and on the horizontal axis is the production of automobiles, with quantity adjusted for quality. Thus, because her fuel-efficient design is locally efficient by assumption, our producer has an average cost curve of production that is *uniformly* lower than the prevailing average cost of produc-tion of established manufacturers. Because of increasing returns, both these average cost curves are downward sloping in quantity sold. The problem is that the going market is currently at a point like Q, with an average cost of a. Although our producer has a lower cost *curve*, she is initially at a higher point on that cost curve, with a current production level of (near) zero and a unit cost of b, which exceeds a.

---

[16] Actually, the difference is not as great as it appears at first glance. Complementarities are like a form of increasing returns to scale, taking place at the level of society, rather than at the level of the individual producer or consumer. What we are going to argue is that history also matters if increasing returns to scale do not manifest themselves in the form of externalities, but are "internal" to the individual, firm, or organization.

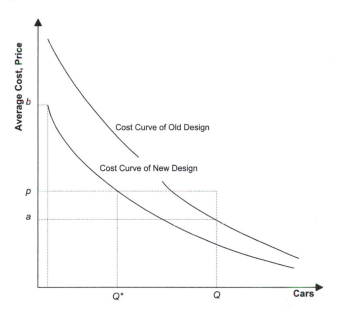

Figure 5.5. Increasing returns and history.

Now, none of this would ever be a problem if consumers *instantly* switched loyalties upon the introduction of the new technology. Our producer could sell quantity Q from day one, beating whatever market price happened to be prevailing, but is this reasonable? Perhaps not. More likely the new technology will have to filter its way into the market, with more and more people switching to the new car as they realize its merits under local conditions. Rome wasn't built in a day and neither are new products or industries. This gradual transition leads to the following dilemma: *during the transitional period where customers are progressively switching to the new product, our producer must function at a loss.* This is easy enough to see from Figure 5.5. If the going price of the rest of the industry is at p, our producer must undercut this price from day one if the transitional process is ever to get under way. Then, at least until production levels reach the point Q^*, the producer will have to contend with losses.

Losses would not be a problem if capital markets were perfect. Our producer could get a loan to cover the interim losses. However, if capital markets are imperfect or missing, she cannot gain access to such credit and the whole (socially worthwhile) project may be scuttled.[17]

What caused this problem? Three things: (1) there are increasing returns to scale in production, (2) credit markets are missing or incomplete, and (3) customers switch slowly, so that it takes time to build a new market. Note that in the absence of increasing returns to scale, the other features pose

---

[17] *Why* capital markets might be missing is a subject of discussion elsewhere (see, for instance, Chapters 7 and 14).

no problem at all. If average costs do not decrease in the level of production, then a socially efficient replacement of an older technology can always invade the market, starting if need be at small levels and building up quantities of output over time. To see this, grab a pencil and sketch the story of Figure 5.5 with the slopes of both cost curves reversed, but their relative levels maintained (i.e., keep the new technology more efficient). It is easy to see that no threshold level like Q^* is needed for the producer to break even and make a profit. Even small quantities can be sold at a profit, which increases steadily as more and more customers adopt the new product.

If we combine the notion of positive externalities at the level of society and increasing returns to scale at the level of the individual, it is possible to take the argument one step further. *If it is known, or somehow perceived, that new technologies cannot invade existing markets for one or more of these reasons, and if such technologies can be developed only at a cost, the incentives to develop them are seriously crippled.* This has far-reaching implications. It is reasonable (although the point can be argued) that technologies created in developed countries are appropriate for the conditions of those economies. However, if these technologies are already in place in developing countries, newer technologies that take advantage of the particular conditions of developing countries may be extremely difficult to engineer. The private sector alone may not do it.

5.3.3. Increasing returns and market size: Interaction

In the last section, we studied a situation where an existing market is already supplied by a rival firm. We argued that in the presence of capital market imperfections and slowly changing customer loyalties, a new firm would find it difficult to penetrate that market. The argument rested fundamentally on the presence of increasing returns. Thus, even a more efficient firm must incur losses at low levels of production and may not have the funds to withstand these losses. Hence, historical conditions dictate the course of new developments.

In making this argument, we assumed that the market was of given size. This study is what might be called a *partial equilibrium* analysis, where we saw how the market restricts entry and production, but did not worry about how the lack of production might feed back on market size. This approach is certainly the correct way to think about things if we are looking at the fortunes of a single firm, such as our innovative car producer. After all, a single firm contributes a negligible quantity to national income and to the market demand for final products.

On the other hand, this sort of analysis neglects a larger picture. If *many* activities are restricted in this fashion, the demand for these activities will be affected through a feedback mechanism. This sounds vague, so let us go immediately to a concrete economic example.[18]

The example that we consider has to do with the provision of intermediate inputs that are required in the production of final output in the economy. One feature of economic development is the creation and use of increasingly sophisticated methods of production, often characterized by their "round-aboutness." Almost any productive activity can serve as an example. Let's take construction. In developing countries, construction is a pretty labor-intensive activity. The area is cleared by hand, rubble is removed in small baskets carried by hand, cement is often mixed at the site and carried by hand, and walls are put up brick by brick. In industrialized economies, each of these tasks has been automated: cranes are used for clearing and prefabricated walls are erected at the site. Each automated instrument, in turn, is produced through a complicated activity: think about how cranes and prefabricated walls are themselves produced. Thus the final production of a house is reduced to a large series of automated steps, each of a high degree of sophistication and requiring the provision of many intermediate inputs.

These sophisticated inputs can be extremely costly to produce if they going to be sold in tiny markets. The manufacture and sale of cranes requires that there be a fairly large demand for cranes in construction, and so it is with prefabricated walls. Otherwise it is simply not worth setting up separate plants to manufacture these items. In other words, intermediate inputs are often produced under conditions of increasing returns to scale.

At the same time, the provision of intermediate inputs, and the consequent roundaboutness of production, can have very productive consequences, because production not only benefits from *scale*, it also benefits from the *variety* of inputs that are employed. To see this in concrete terms, suppose that output is produced using a constant returns to scale technology that includes as inputs intermediate goods as well as labor. If the quantity of labor as well as of all *existing* varieties of intermediate inputs is doubled, then output doubles: this is just a feature of constant returns to scale. This notion suggests that if the production budget is doubled, output doubles too. Not so, simply because a doubling of all inputs is only *one option* under a doubling of the budget. It is also possible to expand the *variety* of intermediate inputs that are used in production. The option to expand variety leads to a situation where output more than doubles: with input variety, increasing returns to scale is built in provided that the underlying production function exhibits constant returns. It follows that the productivity of the economy depends on the scale and richness of operations of the intermedi-

---

[18] Our discussion is based on Ciccone and Matsuyama [1996]. But the general formulation has been used by many others: see, for example, Dixit and Stiglitz [1977], Grossman and Helpman [1991], Romer [1990], and Rodríguez-Clare [1996].

ate goods sector. In this context, see also Chapter 4 and the problem set for that chapter.

We are now in a position to see how this leads to multiple equilibria. Suppose that the economy is "poor" and exhibits a low demand for the final product. This situation means that intermediate production cannot occur at an economically viable scale, which means that the prices of intermediate goods are high. Consequently, firms substitute away from intermediate goods to the use of raw labor. This lowers productivity because of the argument in the previous paragraph and generates low income in the economy. Low income in turn generates a low demand for the final good, and the vicious cycle is complete. The other side of the coin is a virtuous circle. High demand for the final consumption good increases the demand for intermediates, and because these intermediates are produced under conditions of increasing returns to scale, prices of intermediates fall. Falling prices encourage a further substitution away from labor to intermediates, which raises the productivity of the economy. Incomes rise as a consequence and so does demand, completing the virtuous circle.

Increasing returns is crucial for this sort of argument. It is the presence of increasing returns that permits an industry to thrive when demand (or the size of the market) is high, bringing down the prices of that industry. This has the cumulative effect of expanding production even further, which reinforces the initial effect. On the other hand, diminishing returns is essentially *ahistorical*. A large scale of production cannot lead to a higher level of productivity, so no chain of cumulative causation is possible. This rules out the possibility of multiple equilibria, some of which are unambiguously better than others.

In conclusion, note the parallel between increasing returns and complementarities. Increasing returns means that a larger scale of operations has a salubrious effect on the unit costs of that very organization. Positive externalities that take the form of a complementarity pass on that beneficial effect to other economic agents. In this sense, complementarities can be viewed as a kind of increasing returns at the level of society. Little wonder that the two have similar effects.

5.4. Competition, multiplicity, and international trade

There is an interesting alternative way to think about externalities. All externalities can be viewed as the absence of, or imperfection in, some appropriate set of markets. The entrepreneur who builds a mass transportation system in a city raises the real estate prices of locations near to the transportation system and thereby creates an externality. Here is another way of thinking about this: there is no "competitive market" in which potential real estate beneficiaries can compensate the entrepreneur for building the system. If there were such a market, the externality would be completely internalized and the system would be built if and only if it were socially beneficial.

Sometimes this way of thinking is not very useful. Think of traffic congestion on a busy street. People caught in the traffic are affected to different degrees. Imagine a competitive market system with market-determined compensation rates to be paid from one driver to another for all imaginable contingencies (one if you are on your way to a hospital to have a baby, one if you are late for a meeting, one if you are out for a relaxed drive, and so on). If such markets existed and all contingencies were immediately verifiable, then indeed all externalities would be internalized and (for instance) the streets of Calcutta would hum efficiently. However, this is the vision of markets taken to the point of absurdity.[19] The QWERTY example of externalities falls into this category, as does the Romer model of knowledge spillovers that we discussed in Chapter 4.

On the other hand, this view sometimes leads to useful insights. This is especially so when we consider the theories of coordination failure and linkages owing to Rosenstein-Rodan, Hirschman, and their followers. Recall Figure 5.3. Where, precisely, is the externality? The figure suggests, for instance, that the steel industry cannot expand because there is a limited market for products that use steel. These limited markets go from product to product, finally feeding back on the steel industry (see the figure for some of these feedback loops). The question is: How does this notion of a "limited market" transmit itself to a producer?

There is only one answer to this question. It is that the producer fears that an expansion of output will lead to a fall in the price of the commodity. This argument includes the inability to find a buyer, which is just another way of saying that extra quantities cannot be sold at any positive price. The lowered price is, of course, a positive externality for the buyer of the product, but the producer is not interested in the fortunes of the buyer.

Consider similarly a backward linkage. If a producer feels that he cannot expand production easily because the price of his *inputs* will go up, he may not carry out the expansion even though socially it may be good (the higher price conferring an externality on the supplier of the input).[20]

It is very important to understand that such answers make sense only if the market system is not competitive in the usual textbook sense: *that there is a price at which one can buy or sell unlimited quantities of a commodity.* If a producer (or a buyer) is negligible compared to the overall size of the

---

[19] One reason why it is absurd is that contingencies are *not* verifiable, so that the required system of payments cannot generally be implemented.

[20] These externalities are referred to as *pecuniary* or monetary externalities, as opposed to the "nonpecuniary" or technological externalities of congestion, QWERTY, and the like. See Scitovsky [1954] for a treatment. I am not going to emphasize this distinction too strongly, because there are conceptual difficulties in doing so.

market, her actions cannot significantly affect the price nor can her output go unsold at the prevailing market price. Thus the externalities arising from backward and forward linkages are fully internalized by the fixed price, and our previous arguments do not apply.

Thus competitive markets cannot be associated with coordination failures or with the inability to internalize backward and forward linkages. This observation continues to be true for the previous section as well. With competitive markets and price-taking behavior, the notion that the size of the market imposes a limit to efficient production simply does not hold.

We must, therefore, examine whether or not it is reasonable to drop the competitive markets hypothesis in some situations. Does it make sense to assume that a seller can sell "unlimited" quantities of some good at any given price? Perhaps it does (at least as an approximation) when the economic agents involved are small relative to the overall size of the sector. With frictionless international trade, the competitive markets hypothesis may be compelling: entrepreneurs in any one country may be "small" relative to the scale of the world economy. In that case it is impossible to sustain a coordination failure, because output always can be exported or inputs imported.[21]

We will consider international trade in detail in later chapters. For now, it is important to appreciate that the models of this section rely on limited trade in the commodities concerned. For example, if one of the sectors in Section 5.2 is infrastructure, then it is reasonable that that sector is nontraded or, at least, that the output of that sector is domestically produced or installed. In that case, the possibility of a limited market becomes real.[22] Likewise, many intermediate goods are nontraded. The entire package that comes with using an intermediate input includes producer services in training, installation, and maintenance. These are typically produced and provided domestically. The point, then, is not that the goods themselves cannot be traded—they can— but that they have to be largely produced and marketed domestically for the considerations in this chapter to be important.[23]

---

[21] One should interpret this statement with some caution. It *is* possible that there are multiple equilibria even with competitive markets. The point is that these equilibria don't have unambiguous welfare comparisons with one another. Some individuals will be worse off in one of the equilibria, while others must be better off. In contrast, the multiple equilibria of a coordination failure have a stronger property: typically, *all* individuals are better off in one of the equilibria compared to another. In other words, the equilibria can be ranked by the Pareto criterion.

[22] Thus Murphy, Shleifer and Vishny [1989] considered the example of a coordination failure generated by the provision (or lack thereof) of a railroad system. Without the railroad, industry may not be created in the interior of a country. Without the industry, there is no financial incentive to build the railroad. If railroad services could somehow be imported (which is absurd), the failure of coordination would not occur and multiple Pareto-ranked equilibria would disappear.

[23] Rodríguez-Clare [1996] provided a useful discussion of the nontradability of intermediate inputs and the role of nontradability in sustaining multiple equilibria.

5.5. Other roles for history

There are several ways in which history plays an important role in the determination of development paths. We have concentrated on two of them in this chapter. At least two other pathways are worth mentioning. We will see them later in this book as well.

5.5.1. Social norms

We carry the belief through this book that society is composed of rational individuals who seek out improvements wherever they are available. At the same time, what individuals can do is tempered by what society thinks is acceptable. Is it acceptable to make profits in a business? Is it acceptable to forsake long-standing ties with an extended family and migrate? Is it acceptable to use contraceptives? Is it acceptable for women to work? Is it acceptable to charge interest on a loan? Is it acceptable not to wait one's turn at a queue? The list goes on and on.

What is fascinating is that every society has its norms, some of which are upheld by law. At the same time, it is far from clear that only the "best" norms survive. Norms that are best in one setting, in one history, may be inimical to development in another setting. This does not mean, however, that norms will be eroded overnight. The desire for human beings to conform is immense, and as long as conformity is fundamental, norms will take their own time to change.

The way I have put these ideas forward might suggest that norms are always a hindrance and that conformity can only slow down the pace of development. Nothing could be further from the truth. Without norms of decency and appropriate social conduct, economic life would simply fall apart. We would need to police every passenger who disembarked from a taxi, lest he run off without paying the fare. There are more subtle norms as well. What about insider trading, which is forbidden by law in the United States and frowned upon in corporate society, but which is perfectly legal in Switzerland? What about the norm that requires someone in Bangladesh to care for her extended family?

Nevertheless, there are certainly situations that call for an alteration of norms, simply because the underlying environment has changed. In Chapter 9, we study how fertility reductions are slowed down by group norms that value a large number of children. Such values may have been socially useful in a society where rates of mortality were high, but they are less relevant in a society in which mortality has declined. Still, the desire for conformity permits such norms to live on.

Suppose that a region has traditionally viewed rice farming as a way of life—as a noble activity that provides the means of survival. Not only might this concept be enshrined in individual attitudes as the "correct" way to farm one's land, but it might enter into the folklore, social and cultural rituals, festivals of celebration, and, indeed, notions of how the year is divided between work and leisure. Now if there are other regions, perhaps other countries, that grow rice more efficiently and there are improved modes of transportation to bring rice to the first region, it may be that the first region is better off switching to a cash crop such as sugar or cotton. How might this change come about? Not easily, as you might imagine. The first innovator might be frowned upon by society as someone who has sold out—as someone who has taken away his land from its natural (and perhaps sacred) use. It might even be the case that he is sanctioned by the village elders. If the urge to conform is strong enough, he may not break away. Thus it is the particular *history* of this village that makes it slow to change. There is nothing in the genetic makeup of the particular residents in this village that makes it so; it is simply reverence for a norm that has outlived its time.[24]

It is important to understand that in a conceptual sense, the role played by group norms fits perfectly into the externality-based models of multiple equilibria that we studied earlier in this chapter. Adhering to the norm is often like the bad equilibrium, as in the previous story. The externality is created by the fact that as more individuals depart from the norm, it becomes easier for *other* individuals to depart from the norm as well. When people do diverse things, the desire to conform has less of a stranglehold.

5.5.2. The status quo

Finally, history plays a role because it establishes a *status quo*, and the status quo often determines whether a new policy can be undertaken. The argument that we shall now discuss has two principal features: (i) most new policies have winners and losers, even though the policies may be desirable in some overall sense, and (ii) the promise to pay compensation to the losers may not be credible or implementable. We will see in Chapter 17 how this issue creates substantial barriers to free trade.

Suppose that a policy is introduced to build a new dam that will provide controlled irrigation to an large agricultural area and provide electric power generation as well. To carry out the construction of the dam, some existing villages will have to be badly damaged or even destroyed, and several thousand people will have to be resettled. There will also be destruction of some existing cultivable land. In a nutshell, the policy will bring gains to some and

---

[24] Agricultural conservatism is not only peculiar to developing countries, although this story with its harvest festivals and village elders might suggest so. In Europe, North America, and in countries such as Japan, few sectors are protected and subsidized as much as agriculture. There are complex reasons for this, but there is little doubt that the notion of the farm as a way of life to be protected, both in the interests of tradition and self-sufficiency, has played its part in sustaining such protectionist tendencies.

losses to others, and the historical allocation of land will determine who the gainers and the losers are. When groups of people form, as they invariably will, to lobby for or against this proposal, they will align themselves with the possible losers and gainers.

This example is not drawn at random. Consider, for instance, the intense controversy over the construction of the Sardar Sarover Dam on the Narmada River in India. Building the dam (and the irrigation canals connected to it) will displace hundreds of thousands of people. Apart from the environmental issues that surround the building of the dam, the major concern is resettlement of the affected villagers and payment of adequate compensation. The major benefits involve vastly expanded provision for flood control, irrigation, and electricity. The resulting conflict over the dam has been explosive. Members of a dedicated movement—the *Narmada Bachao Andolan*[25]—have protested the construction by threatening to drown themselves in the waters of the river. Proponents of the dam include state governments in India and the World Bank, which originally provided funding.

Now look at this example from a different perspective: often it is possible simply to add up all the gains and losses involved from a certain policy. For instance, it should surely be possible to estimate the loss of land and crop output from the dam and the losses to displaced villagers, as well as the potential gains from surrounding areas to be serviced by the dam. If the gains outweigh the losses, as they certainly ought to if the dam is ever built, it should surely be possible for the gainers to compensate the losers. However, there are at least three problems with the payment of appropriate compensation.

(1) *Valuations.* It is often extremely difficult to place valuations on the various implications of a project. How does one evaluate compensation to a villager who is forced to leave his ancestral home? A particularly cynical answer might be to use the market price of his land as compensation, but this is inadequate apart from being cynical. A current market price for land that threatens to be underwater pretty soon may not be well defined, and how does one estimate the income losses to a landless laborer in that village? Likewise, it may be difficult to estimate benefits, and if one accounts for positive externalities, there is often just as much likelihood that costs as well as the benefits will be underestimated. The issue of proper valuation is compounded by strategic considerations. Opponents will claim that the benefits, however they are measured, are exaggerated and the costs are underplayed. Proponents will claim immense benefits. Cost–benefit analysis is a dangerous "science."

(2) *Gainers and Losers.* The Narmada dam is a good example of a project that has fairly well-defined sets of gainers and losers, but for many projects,

---

[25] A literal translation is Movement to Save the Narmada.

this may be a difficult proposition. Consider a move to unequivocal free trade. Will engineers in a country benefit? Will textile workers or agricultural laborers benefit? The answers to such questions are difficult and complex: they depend on how the economy does postreform, on the sectors that will succeed in the international market, and the sectors that die out. Sometimes it is possible to form fairly precise estimates of the consequences, but frequently this is very difficult. Fernandez and Rodrik [1991] argued that in the presence of such uncertainties, *a reform policy that is commonly known and agreed to be beneficial ex post may be vetoed ex ante*. Imagine submitting such a policy to a public referendum. An individual voter may know that the policy will benefit 60% of the population by $100 and hurt the remaining 40% by $100, but is he, the voter, part of the 60% or part of the 40%? He may not know the answer to *that* particular question, and if he fears the risks, may well vote against the policy.[26]

(3) *Consistency.* Points 1 and 2 are closely connected to, although conceptually distinct from, the issue of *consistency*. Many policies might be easier to implement if the gainers somehow committed to pay adequate compensation to the losers, but the problem is that even if gainers and losers can be identified, compensation may not be forthcoming after the fact. For instance, it may be impossible to tax all the potential beneficiaries of a project until *after* the project has been carried out, but once the project has been completed, we are politically (although not morally and perhaps not legally) in a new status quo, where the situation is that the project is in place. At that point, compensation may never be forthcoming. The promise of compensation may not be consistent over time.

To be sure, this issue is exacerbated by the possibility that there has been no proper accounting of gains and losses. The amount of compensation may be perennially in dispute, and so might never be paid or be paid inadequately. Likewise, the possibility that gainers and losers may be difficult to identify also weakens the implementability of a compensation scheme. (Think about the queue of potential applicants after you create a free-trade regime. Who are you going to single out for compensation?)

If compensation is perceived to be not forthcoming, inadequate, or somehow an empty promise, then the viability of a project assessed by the method of adding up all gains and losses simply loses relevance. Viability will depend on how hard the losers lobby against the project and how hard the gainers lobby to preserve the project, and simple addition of gains and losses may not account for the final outcome. In certain situations where the gainers are spatially concentrated or are more effective in lobbying for one of several reasons, certain policies may be enacted even when losses outweigh the

---

[26] The Fernandez–Rodrik argument is actually more subtle than this. We return to it later in the text (see, for instance, the problem set for Chapter 18).

gains. An example is the selective placement of a prohibitive tariff that helps business in a certain industry, but hurts all consumers in a very diffuse way. Losses might outweigh the gains, but the industry may be more successful in its lobbying efforts because the gains are so much more concentrated.

5.6. Summary

This chapter began with a question that was, in turn, generated by our previous studies. In what sense do initial conditions matter for development? Might two countries with the same potential for development be locked into two different equilibria—one "good" and one "bad"? We focused on two features: *history* and *expectations*, and argued that the two are intertwined in many ways.

We first studied *complementarities*, which are a form of externalities that "reinforce" some common action, such as the decision to adopt a new method of production or to export a particular product. We looked at typewriter keys as an example. The QWERTY arrangement was initially developed to slow down the speed of typing on mechanical typewriters, but persists to this day because of a lock-in effect. If everybody uses QWERTY, then it pays for me to learn QWERTY as well. This approach is perfectly compatible with the notion that there may a typing technology out there that is better for all concerned. Likewise, it is possible for a region to be in a depressed state: nobody invests there because no one else does, but there could just as easily be an alternative scenario in which investments are made by all. Sometimes a history of no investment, coupled with the expectation that the no-investment scenario will continue, is self-perpetuating.

The possibility that an economy, or more generally, a group of economic agents, might be caught in a "bad" equilibrium, when there is another "good" equilibrium in sight, is called a *coordination failure*. If the actions of all concerned could somehow be coordinated, the economy might be able to move to the "good" equilibrium. However, individuals act independently and may not be able to effect the switch in a coordinated way: hence the term "coordination failure." To break such coordination failures, the concept of *linkages* is important. One activity might foster appropriate conditions for another: then there is a *link* between the two activities. This isn't any different from a complementarity, but we pursue the idea in more detail. In the sphere of production, we think of *forward* and *backward* linkages. A forward linkage lowers the cost of production for another activity; for example, greater production of steel lowers the cost of shipbuilding. A backward linkage raises the demand for another activity; for example, increased steel production might raise the demand for coal. We used the notion of linkages, both forward and backward, to discuss appropriate policies to break a coordination failure.

Why does a history of coordination failure exert such a stranglehold over future developments? People seem to coordinate easily to changing fashions, so why are technologies or investments any different? Why can't expectations change overnight, if they are indeed self-fulfilling? To address this question we studied, in more detail, the question of how history and expectations interact. We showed how many coordination problems can be expressed as a *migration problem*. We considered two sectors: Old and New. The rate of return (or the wage) to living in Old is constant, but the rate of return in New varies *positively* with the number of people settled there. In a bad equilibrium, everybody lives in Old. There is another equilibrium in which everybody lives in New. The problem is that a move from one equilibrium to another requires a coordinated act of migration. We showed that if externalities manifest themselves with a lag, then the move may become increasingly difficult, if not impossible. Mavericks—individuals who are comfortable taking losses—are needed to move the economy from one situation to the other. Mavericks are easy enough to find in fashion, but when economic loss is involved, mavericks are harder to find. This is why historically determined equilibria may be very sticky.

We then turned to the role of *increasing returns* in generating multiple equilibrium outcomes. The basic idea is very simple: suppose that there are fixed costs to serving a particular market, so that average costs decline with production volume. Then if one firm is already present in the market by virtue of historical precedence, it may be difficult for a new firm to break into that market, even if it has access to a superior technology. The problem is that to exploit the superior technology, the new firm must produce in large volume. If customers do not switch instantly the firm will have to bear losses in the short or medium run, which, if capital markets are imperfect, may be impossible. Thus with increasing returns, the chronological order of arrival to a market plays a role.

We then studied how increasing returns affects the size of the market. Again, the basic idea is very simple. If increasing returns technologies cannot be used fully in an economy because of small market size, production generally will be at inefficient levels and income payments will be lower. These incomes complete a vicious circle: because incomes are low, the market size is small. We illustrated this phenomenon by studying *production roundaboutness* as a potential source of increasing returns.

We then went on to note the role of *limited competition*, and limited international trade in particular, in generating these sorts of outcomes. If all production can be sold in unlimited quantities at some going prices and there are no constraints on volume, then these coordination failures cannot occur. The possibility of international trade is a bit like perfect competition: the chances of any producer being limited by quantity considerations on the world market are that much smaller. Thus the models of this chapter rely on some degree of limited international trade.

We ended this chapter with a description of two other routes through which historical developments can influence future outcomes. The first of these is *social norms*. Norms are built around traditional activities, and in many ways they permit the smooth functioning of those activities. At the same time, social norms can hinder productive change. We began this theme here, but it will reappear in later chapters. Second, we considered the role of the *status quo* in determining the success of new policies. Suppose that a project raises total national income, but that there are gainers and losers relative to the status quo (prevailing at the time of debating the project). If *total* profits or incomes are higher, though, this shouldn't pose a problem: the gainers can simply compensate the losers. The payment of compensation is a tricky issue that is plagued with problems of incentives, information, and implementation. We discussed how and why these problems come about. We then concluded that if compensation cannot be paid, the status quo places a much greater drag on the implementation of policies that might be socially beneficial in the sense of raising overall incomes. Raising overall incomes is not enough if compensation cannot be paid: the incomes of *each* group must be enhanced by the policy. Unfortunately, few policies have such pleasing properties, and in this way, the status quo can block many routes to development.

Exercises

■ (1) Suppose that fax machines are made newly available in NeverNever-Land. Companies are deciding whether or not to install a machine. This decision partly depends on how many *other* companies are expected to install fax machines. Think of a graph that describes how many companies *will* install fax machines as a function of how many companies are *expected* to install fax machines.

(a) If there are complementarities in the adoption of fax machines, describe the shape of this graph.

(b) Now suppose that even if no companies in NeverNeverLand are expected to install fax machines, A companies will indeed do so (because of communication to the outside world). If x companies are expected to install, then an additional $(x^2)/1000$ companies (over and above the number A) will install machines. This occurs up to a maximum of one million companies (which is the total number of companies in NeverNeverLand). Plot this relationship as a graph.

(c) Think of A as the strength of contact with the outside world. Analyze the equilibrium adoption of fax machines in NeverNeverLand as A varies.

Pay attention to the possibility of multiple equilibria. For which values of A does a *unique* equilibrium exist? Provide some intuition for your answer.

■ (2) Complementarities arise in all sorts of situations. Here is a tax evasion problem. Suppose that each of N citizens in a country needs to pay a tax of T every year to the government. Each citizen may decide to pay or to evade the tax. If an evader is nabbed, the law of the country stipulates payment of a fine of amount F, where $F > T$. However, the government's vigilance is not perfect, because it has limited resources to detect evaders. Assume that out of all the people who evade taxes, the government has the capacity to catch only one, and this person is chosen randomly. Thus, if n people have decided to evade taxes, each has probability $1/n$ of being caught. In what follows, we assume that people simply calculate the expected losses from each strategy and choose the strategy with the lower expected loss.

(a) If the number of evaders is m, show that the average (expected) loss to an evader is F/m. This is to be compared with the sure loss faced by someone who complies, which is T.

(b) Why is this situation like a coordination game? Describe the complementarity created by one citizen's actions.

(c) Show that it is always an equilibrium for nobody in society to evade taxes. Is there another equilibrium as well? Find it and describe when it will exist.

■ (3) Consider a hypothetical economy in which each worker has to decide whether to acquire education and become a high-skilled worker or remain low-skilled. Education carries a cost of C. Assume that interest-free education loans are available to everybody. Let I_H and I_L denote the incomes earned by a high- and low-skilled worker respectively. These incomes are defined as $I_H = (1 + \theta)H$ and $I_L = (1 + \theta)L$, where H and L are constants ($H > L$) and θ is the fraction of the population that decides to become high skilled. This formulation captures the idea that a person's productivity is positively linked not only to his own skills, but also to that of his fellow workers. Assume that all individuals simultaneously choose whether or not to become skilled.

(a) Explain why this is like a coordination problem. What is the complementarity?

(b) Show that if $H - L < C < 2(H - L)$, there are three possible equilibria: one in which everybody acquires skills, one in which nobody does, and a third in which only a fraction of the population becomes high-skilled. Give an algebraic expression for this fraction in the last case, and argue intuitively that this equilibrium is "unstable" and is likely to give way to one of the two extreme cases.

(c) Change the preceding example slightly. Suppose the return to low-skilled occupations is now given by $I_L = (1 + \lambda\theta)L$, where λ is some constant. The return to high-skilled jobs is the same as before. Show that if the value of λ is sufficiently high, there is only one possible equilibrium.

(d) Explain why multiple equilibria arise in the first case but not in the second.

(e) Consider another variation. Incomes from different occupations are independent of the number of high-skilled people in the economy. Specifically, $I_H = H$ and $I_L = L$. However, the cost of education is variable, and is given by $C(\theta) = (1 - \theta)/\theta$ (the idea here is that it is easier to learn if there are more educated people around). Show that once again, there are three possible equilibria. Describe them.

∎ (4) Here are other examples of coordination problems. Discuss them and think of other situations which can be modeled in this way.

(a) *International debt*: Suppose that a country considers default on its international debt to a creditor country. In case of default, the creditor country can stop trade with the defaulter, even though this action may be costly for the creditor country to do. Hence, the more potential defaulting countries there are, the more difficult it becomes for the creditor country to "punish" a defaulter. Show that this situation gives rise to a coordination problem among the defaulters, and describe precisely the complementarity among borrower countries.

(b) *Investing in the stock market*: Suppose that a stock yields returns that exceed the average market rate if no one sells the stock in panic. Now imagine that for every person who panics and sells the stock, the rate of return on the stock decreases. Show why this is a coordination problem and describe the possible equilibria.

(c) *Cities*: Think of the emergence of cities as an outcome of coordination games. What would we mean by multiple equilibria in this context? Discuss this answer with respect to the concentration of certain types of industries in certain locations: for example, computer companies in Silicon Valley.

∎ (5) You are the minister of planning in a developing country with a poorly developed industrial sector. You would like to create a climate in which industrialists will invest and create economic growth. After much investigation, you realize that you are faced with the following basic problem. I'll state it with a series of examples.

Nobody wants to invest in the coal industry because there is no developed railway to demand coal nor any factory furnaces that use coal. Nobody wants to invest in railways because they are scared that nobody will want to transport products on them (there are few products to transport at present). They are also scared that there won't be any coal to run the railway. Nobody wants to develop new products whose sale requires transportation because there isn't a railway system. There is a problem similar to coal in the extraction of iron ore. There isn't a steel industry, so who would want to extract large quantities of iron? Besides, there isn't a firm that makes good extraction equipment. Talking to investors, you find that this is so because such equipment needs an extraction industry to demand their products and no such industry yet exists! Of course, potential investors in steel tell you that they can't find firms to sell them iron, and so on.

You realize that you are facing two kinds of issues. One is like a "chicken-and-egg" problem: industry *A* needs industry *B* and *vice versa*. Neither wants to get in there until the other does. The other is a problem of "linkages": there is a chain of industries, with each having "forward" linkages to the sectors that demand its output, and "backward" linkages to the sectors that produce the outputs it demands.

(a) By drawing on my examples and expanding them with others, draw charts that show these different issues.

(b) You are going to recommend that the government take on the task of operating some of these industries (there are limited funds, so the government can't do everything). What kind of industries in your chart should the government get into?

(c) "A leading sector is a particular sector of the economy that can stimulate the development of many other sectors." Using what you have learned from this problem, try to explain the characteristics of a powerful leading sector.

■ (6) Why might the presence of "overoptimistic entrepreneurs"—those who systematically overestimate the profits from pursuing new activities—help in getting rid of coordination failures? Relate this observation to relative frequent swings of coordination equilibria in the fashion industry.

■ (7) Compare the backward and forward linkages generated by (a) software exports, (b) domestic food production, (c) transportation, (d) textile exports, and (e) heavy industry.

■ (8) Consider a society where people throw garbage on the streets. A person who does so inflicts negative externalities on others: suppose that the (psychic) dollar cost to any one person is an, where $a > 0$ is a positive constant and n is the number of (other) people who throw garbage on the streets. Assume that your own act of throwing garbage on the street gives you a (psychic) dollar "convenience gain" of G (because you don't have to wait for the next trash can) and a (psychic) dollar "shame loss" of c/n, where $c > 0$

and n, again, is the number of other garbage throwers (the idea is that the shame is smaller the more the number of other garbage throwers).

(a) Show that nobody throwing garbage on the streets is always an equilibrium in this example.

(b) Show that there is a threshold population size such that if population exceeds this threshold, everybody throwing garbage on the streets is *also* an equilibrium. Why is the threshold dependent on the parameters G and c, but *independent* of a? Explain intuitively.

(c) Starting from a situation where everybody is throwing garbage on the streets, assess the chances of moving to the good equilibrium of part (a) overnight. Why do you consider such a move unlikely? Discuss this with reference to the arguments in the text.

(d) Consider a policy that imposes a fine $F > 0$ on every garbage thrower. Show that the threshold population required to support the bad equilibrium must rise with the fine.

(e) Suppose that the fine is such that the actual population falls below the threshold. In this case, discuss why the fine policy may be removed after a few years with a permanent change implemented in social norms.

■ (9) You are introducing a new vacuum cleaner design in a tropical society which works well under humid conditions. The vacuum cleaner is produced under increasing returns, so that the unit cost of production declines with the price. Discuss how the following factors affect your likelihood of success: (a) the proportion of the population who already use vacuum cleaners, (b) the per capita income of the society, (c) the market for loans, and (d) the flow of information. If vacuum cleaners are produced under decreasing returns to scale, which of these factors continue to be important?

■ (10) A country is considering the adoption of two different telephone networks. Network A is an older network. It involves initial capital expenditures of $2 million, but will pay off $120,000 per year for a lifetime of fifty years. The newer network B involves a capital expenditure of $5 million, but will pay off at the rate of $200,000 per year over a lifetime of fifty years. Assume there is no discounting of the future so that to make comparisons, the government simply adds up all costs and revenues and looks at net worth, choosing the project with the higher net worth.

(a) Which network will a government with *no* installed telephone network choose?

(b) Suppose that a government had just installed network A (before the new technology B came along). Would it now shift to network B?

(c) Explain why this example helps you understand why "leapfrogging" in infrastructure might occur.

■ (11) Suppose that diamonds can be extracted for the cost of $100 per diamond. Consumers value diamonds according to the following formula, expressed in dollar equivalent units:

$$V = 10000\sqrt{x},$$

where x is the number of diamonds extracted.

(a) Plot the total cost and value of extracting diamonds on a graph, with x, the quantity of diamonds, on one axis and total costs and values on the other.

(b) What is the socially optimal extraction level of diamonds, assuming that consumer valuations and extraction costs are given exactly the same weight? Calculate this amount and indicate the economic reasoning that leads you to this conclusion. Also show the socially optimal extraction level on the same graph that you used for part (a).

(c) Show that a monopolist producer of diamonds would produce exactly the socially optimal level of diamonds provided that he had the power to charge different prices for each diamond sold. How is the total surplus divided among the consumers and the producer?

(d) Now assume that diamonds are produced by many small producers who take the price of diamonds as given in making their extraction decisions. Assume that each producer has a very small production capacity (up to which he can extract at $100 per diamond), but that an unlimited number of producers can enter. Show that the socially optimal level will be produced once again. How is the total surplus divided among the consumers and the producers?

(e) Now return to part (c) and assume that the monopolists is *not* permitted to charge different prices for each diamond he sells, but must charge the same price for all diamonds. Now show that production will fall *below* the socially optimal level. This discrepancy can be understood by observing that the producer fails to fully internalize the marginal social gain from an additional diamond produced. Carefully verify that you indeed understand this.

(f) Show that these ideas can be used to extend and understand the discussion in the text regarding externalities and international trade.

■ (12) Suppose that people's attitudes can take three possible positions: L, M, and R, where you can think of L as leftist, R as rightist, and M as middle-of-the-road. Consider a society in which *it is known that* a fraction α are M types, and the remaining fraction $1 - \alpha$ are divided equally between L and

R, but no individual is known to be L, M, or R at first sight. Suppose that each individual gets satisfaction S from expressing his or her own true views, but feels a loss ("social disapproval") in not conforming to a middle-of-the-road position. The amount of the loss depends on the fraction α of M types: suppose that it equals the amount $\alpha/(1 - \alpha)$.

(a) Show that there is a threshold value of α such that everybody in society will express their own view if α is less than the threshold, but will all express M-views if α exceeds the threshold.

(b) What happens if we change the specification somewhat to say that the "social disapproval loss" equals $\beta/(1-\beta)$, where β is the expected fraction of people who *choose* to express M views (and not necessarily the true fraction of M types)?

(c) Indicate how you would extend the analysis to a case in which there are potential conformist urges attached to each of the views L, M, and R, and not just M.

Chapter 6

Economic Inequality

6.1. Introduction

So far we have studied countries in their entirety. Economic growth is about changes in aggregate or average incomes. This is a good measure of a country's development, but it is far from being the only one. In this chapter, we begin to study a theme that recurs throughout the book: the analysis of the *distribution* of income, or wealth, among different groups in society. Economic growth that spreads its benefits equitably among the population is always welcome; growth that is distributed unequally needs to be evaluated not simply on the basis of overall change, but on the grounds of equity.

There are two reasons to be interested in the inequality of income and wealth distribution. First, there are philosophical and ethical grounds for aversion to inequality per se. There is no reason why individuals should be treated differently in terms of their access to lifetime economic resources.[1] It is, of course, possible to argue that people make choices—good and bad decisions—over the course of their lifetime for which only they are responsible. They are poor because "they had it coming to them." In some cases this may indeed be true, but in most cases the unequal treatment begins from day one. Parental wealth and parental access to resources can start two children off on an unequal footing, and for this fact there is little ethical defense. To hold descendants responsible for the sins of their ancestors is perhaps excessive. At the same time, we run into a separate ethical dilemma. To counteract the unequal treatment of individuals from the first day of their lives, we must deprive parents of the right to bequeath their wealth to their children. There may be no way to resolve this dilemma at a philosophical level.

Nevertheless, we can work toward a society with tolerable levels of inequality in everyday life. This goal reduces the dilemma in the preceding paragraph, because it reduces the scope for drastically unequal levels of accumulation (though of course it cannot entirely eliminate the problem). We cannot speak of development without a serious consideration of the problem of inequality.

---

[1] I make this statement assuming that there is no fundamental difference, such as the presence of a handicap or ailment, in the need for two people to have access to economic resources.

Second, *even if* we are uninterested in the problem of inequality at an intrinsic level, there is still good reason to worry about it. Suppose you simply care about overall growth, but find that inequality in income and wealth somehow reduce the possibilities of overall growth (or increase it; at this stage the direction of change is unimportant). Then you will care about inequality at what might be called a *functional level*; to you, inequality will be important not for its own sake, but because it has an impact on other economic features that you do care about.

In this book, we will pay attention to both the intrinsic and the functional features of inequality. To do this, we must first learn how to think about inequality at a conceptual level. This is the issue of *measurement*, which is the subject of this chapter. In Chapter 7, we will examine, both at an empirical and theoretical level, how inequality interacts with other economic variables, such as aggregate income and the growth of aggregate income.

6.2. What is economic inequality?

6.2.1. The context

At the level of philosophy, the notion of inequality can dissolve into an endless sequence of semantic issues. Ultimately, economic inequality is the fundamental disparity that permits one individual certain material choices, while denying another individual those very same choices. From this basic starting point begins a tree with many branches. João and José might both earn the same amount of money, but João may be physically handicapped while José isn't. John is richer than James, but John lives in a country that denies him many freedoms, such as the right to vote or travel freely. Shyamali earned more than Sheila did until they were both forty; thereafter Sheila did. These simple examples suggest the obvious: economic inequality is a slippery concept and is intimately linked to concepts such as lifetimes, personal capabilities, and political freedoms.[2]

Nevertheless, this is no reason to throw up our hands and say that *no* meaningful comparisons are possible. Disparities in personal income and wealth at any point of time, narrow though they may be in relation to the broader issues of freedom and capabilities, mean *something*. This statement is even more true when studying economic disparities *within* a country, because some of the broader issues can be regarded (at least approximately so) as affecting everyone in the same way. It is in this spirit that we study income and wealth inequalities: not because they stand for *all* differences, but because they represent an important component of those differences.

---

[2] On these and related matters, read the insightful discussions in Sen [1985].

6.2.2. *Economic inequality: Preliminary observations*

With the preceding qualifications in mind, let us turn to *economic* inequality: disparities in wealth or income. In this special case, some caveats need to be mentioned, even though we may not take them fully into account in what follows.

(1) Depending on the particular context, we may be interested in the distribution of current expenditure or income *flows*, the distribution of wealth (or asset *stocks*), or even the distribution of lifetime income. You can see right away that our preoccupation with these three possibilities leads us progressively from *short-term* to *long-term* considerations. Current income tells us about inequality at any one point of time, but such inequalities may be relatively harmless, both from an ethical point of view and from the point of view of their effects on the economic system, provided the inequality is temporary. To make this point clearly, consider the following example. Imagine two societies. In the first, there are two levels of income: $2,000 per month and $3,000 per month. In the second society, there are also two levels of income, but they are more dispersed: $1,000 per month and $4,000 per month. Let us suppose that the first society is completely mobile: people enter their working life at one of the two levels of income but stay there forever. In the second society, people exchange jobs every month, switching between the low-paid job and the high-paid job. These societies are obviously unrealistic caricatures, but they suffice to make the point. The first society shows up as more equal if income is measured at any one point in time, yet in terms of average yearly income, everyone earns the same in the second society.

Thus our notions of cross-sectional inequality at any one point in time must be tempered by a consideration of *mobility*. Whether each job category is "sticky" or "fluid" has implications for the true distribution of income. Often we are unable to make these observations as carefully as we would like, because of the lack of data, but that does not mean that we should be unaware of them.

(2) It may also be of interest to know (and we will get into this later in the book) not only *how much* people earn, but *how* it is earned. This is the distinction between *functional* and *personal* income distribution. Functional distribution tells us about the returns to different factors of production, such as labor (of different skills), capital equipment of various kinds, land, and so on. As you can imagine, this is only half the story. The next step is to describe how these different factors of production are owned by the individuals in society.

Figure 6.1 illustrates this process. Reading from left to right, the first set of arrows describes how income is generated from the production process. It is generated in varied forms. Production involves labor, for which wages

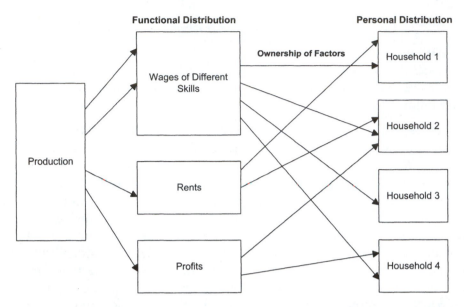

Figure 6.1. Functional and personal distribution of income.

are paid. It involves the use of land or capital equipment, for which rents are paid. It generates profits, which are paid out as well. Production also involves payments for various nonlabor inputs of production. These other inputs are in turn produced, so that in the ultimate analysis, all incomes that are generated can be classified under payments to labor of different skills, rents, and profits. The distribution of income under these various categories is the *functional distribution of income.*

The second set of arrows tells us how different categories of income are funneled to households. The direction and magnitude of these flows depend on who owns which factors of production (and how much of these factors). Households with only labor to offer (household 3 in the diagram, for instance) receive only wage income. In contrast, households that own shares in business, possess land to rent, and labor to supply (such as household 2) receive payments from all three sources. By combining the functional distribution of income with the distribution of factor ownership, we arrive at the *personal* distribution of income—a description of income flows to individuals or households, not factors of production.

You might well ask: why should we care about this two-step process? Isn't a direct knowledge of the personal distribution good enough for our analysis? The answer is that it isn't, and there are at least two good reasons for this. First, the understanding of income *sources* may well influence how we judge the outcome. Money that is received from charity or the welfare state may be viewed differently from the same amount received as income for work. Amartya Sen, in a closely related context, refers to this as the problem of "recognition" or self-esteem (see Sen [1975]):

> "Employment can be a factor in self-esteem and indeed in esteem by others. . . . If a person is forced by unemployment to take a job that he thinks is not appropriate for him, or not commensurate with his training, he may continue to feel unfulfilled and indeed may not even regard himself as employed."

Although there may not be much that we can do about this (so far as a theory of measurement goes), we should keep it in the back of our minds while we proceed to a final judgment about inequality.[3]

Second, and possibly more important, functional distribution tells us much about the relationship between inequality and other features of development, such as growth. Our understanding of how economic inequalities are created in a society necessitates that we understand both how factors are *paid* and how factors are *owned*.

The preceding discussion lays down a road map for our study of inequality. We look at economic inequalities from two angles. In this chapter, we put all sources of income into a black box and concentrate on the evaluation of income (or wealth or lifetime income) distributions. This part of the story is *normative*. All of us might like to see (other things being the same) an egalitarian society, but "egalitarian" is only a word: what does it mean when we are confronted with several alternative income distributions, which we must evaluate? How do we rank or order these distributions? This part of the chapter discusses how we measure inequality, or equivalently, how we rank alternative distributions with respect to how much inequality they embody.

With measurement issues out of the way, we proceed in Chapter 7 to a study of the economics of income distributions: how inequality evolves in society, the effects that it has on other features of economic development, such as output, employment and growth rates, and how these other features feed back in turn on income and wealth distributions. This part of the story is *positive*. Whether or not we like the notion of egalitarianism per se, inequality affects other features of development.

6.3. *Measuring economic inequality*

6.3.1. *Introduction*

If there is a great deal of disparity in the incomes of people in a society, the signs of such economic inequality are often quite visible. We probably

---

[3] Often, ingenious theories of measurement can go some way to resolve difficulties of this sort. For instance, it might matter for our measurement of literacy rate whether an literate person has access to *other* literate persons. On these matters, see Basu and Foster [1997].

know a society is very unequal when we see it. If two people are supposed to share a cake and one person has all of it, that's unequal. If they split 50–50, that's equal. We can even evaluate intermediate divisions (such as 30–70 and 40–60) with a fair amount of precision.

All that goes away, however, once we have more than two individuals and we try to rank intermediate divisions of the cake. Is it obvious how to compare a 20–30–50 division among three people with a 22–22–56 division? In such cases, and in even more complicated ones as well, it might be useful to try and "measure" inequality. This means that we develop or examine inequality indices that permit the ranking of income or wealth distributions in two different situations (countries, regions, points of time, and so on).

The question naturally arises: what are the properties that a "desirable" inequality index should satisfy? It is difficult to have complete unanimity on the subject, and there is none. If, to avoid controversy, we lay down only very weak criteria, then many inequality indices can be suggested, each consistent with the criteria, but probably giving very different results when used in actual inequality comparisons. If, on the other hand, we impose stricter criteria, then we sharply reduce the number of admissible indices, but the criteria loses wide approval.

As we will see, this problem is endemic, which is all the more reason to have a clear idea of what criteria lie behind a particular measure. Remember that by "believing" what a measure of inequality reports, you are identifying your intuitive notions of inequality with that particular measure. If you are a policy maker or an advisor, this form of identification can be useful or dangerous, depending on how well you understand the underlying criteria of measurement.

6.3.2. *Four criteria for inequality measurement*

Suppose that society is composed of n individuals.[4] We use the index i to stand for a generic individual; thus, $i = 1, 2, \ldots, n$. An *income distribution* is a description of how much income y_i is received by each individual i: $(y_1, y_2, \ldots, y_n)$.

We are interested in comparing the relative "inequality" of two income distributions. To this end, we need to capture some of our intuitive notions about inequality in the form of applicable criteria.

(1) *Anonymity principle.* From an ethical point of view, it does not matter *who* is earning the income. A situation where Debraj earns x and Rajiv earns

---

[4] In this section, we refer to "income" as the crucial variable whose inequality we wish to measure. You could replace this with wealth, lifetime income, and so on. Likewise, the recipient unit is called an individual. You could replace this by "household" or any other grouping that you might be interested in.

y should be viewed as identical (from the point of view of inequality) to one in which Debraj earns y and Rajiv earns x. Debraj may well be disgusted with this sort of change (if x happens to be larger than y), but it will be very difficult for him to persuade other people that the overall degree of inequality in his society has deteriorated because of this. Thus permutations of incomes among people should not matter for inequality judgments: this is the principle of *anonymity*. Formally, this means that we can always arrange our income distribution so that

$$y_1 \leq y_2 \leq \cdots \leq y_n,$$

which is the equivalent of arranging individuals so that they are ranked from poorest to richest.

(2) *Population principle.* Cloning the entire population (and their incomes) should not alter inequality. More formally, if we compare an income distribution over n people and another population of $2n$ people with the same income pattern repeated twice, there should be no difference in inequality among the two income distributions.[5] The population principle is a way of saying that population size does not matter: all that matters are the *proportions* of the population that earn different levels of income.

Criteria 1 and 2 permit us to view income distributions in a slightly different way. Typically, no data set is rich enough to tell us the incomes of every single individual in the country. Thus the data are often presented in the following way. There is a set of income *classes*, where each class typically is presented as a range of incomes; for example, "$100 per month or less," "$300–400," and so on.

Figure 6.2 illustrates this procedure using a hypothetical example. A population of people earn an income somewhere between zero and $1,000 in this example. The raw data are shown in the left panel of the figure. (You will almost never see data expressed like this for an actual population.) The anonymity principle tells us that we can number people in order of increasing income and no useful information is lost. The population principle tells us that it does not matter how many people there are; we may normalize everything to percentages. The right-hand panel gives us a common way to put together this information. Income classes are on the horizontal axis and the percentage of the population that falls into each income class is on the vertical axis. Neither the names of people nor the actual numbers in each income class matter.

---

[5] Warning: Cloning only one segment of the population while keeping the remainder unaltered may well affect our notions of inequality. Suppose that there are two incomes, $100 and $1,000. The population principle says that all income distributions are equally unequal provided the same percentage of people earn $100. If the *proportion* of people earning the low income changes, then inequality will, in general, be affected.

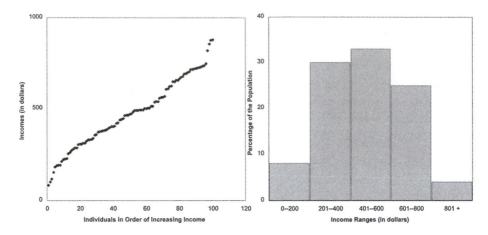

Figure 6.2. Income distribution arranged by income classes.

(3) *Relative income principle.* Just as population shares matter and the absolute values of the population itself do not, it is possible to argue that only *relative* incomes should matter and the absolute levels of these incomes should not. If one income distribution is obtained from another by scaling *everybody's* income up or down by the same percentage, then inequality should be no different across the two distributions. For instance, an income distribution over two people of ($1,000, $2,000) has the same inequality as ($2,000, $4,000), and this continues to be true if dollars are replaced by cruzeiros or yen. This is the relative income principle: it is tantamount to the assertion that income *levels*, in and of themselves, have no meaning as far as *inequality measurement* is concerned. Certainly, absolute incomes are important in our overall assessment of development, although the distinction between "absolute" and "relative" in the context of inequality measurement may not be that easy to draw.[6]

With the relative income principle in place, it is now possible to present data in a form that is even more stripped down. Both population and incomes can be expressed as shares of the total. The major advantage of this approach is that it enables us to compare income distributions for two countries that have different average income levels. Figure 6.3 shows how this is done with the very same hypothetical data that we used to generate Fig-

---

[6] Is it as easy to buy the relative income principle as the population principle? Not really. What we are after, in some sense, is the inequality of "happiness" or utility, however that may be measured. As matters stand, our presumption that inequality can be quantified at all forces us to make the assertion that the utilities of different individuals can be compared. (On the analytical framework of interpersonal comparability that is required to make systematic egalitarian judgments, see, for example, Sen [1970] and Roberts [1980].) However, the relative income principle needs more than that. It asserts that utilities are proportional to incomes. This is a strong assumption. We make it nevertheless because Chapter 8 will partially make amends by studying the effects of absolute income shortfalls below some poverty line.

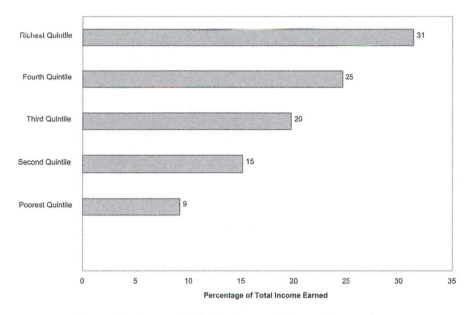

Figure 6.3. *Income distribution by population and income shares.*

ure 6.2. In Figure 6.3 we have divided the population into different equal-sized groups in order of poorest to richest. Because population size is unimportant in the measurement of inequality (by the population principle), using percentages is enough. We use quintiles (one could use deciles as well depending on the richness of the original data). For each quintile, we record the income share earned by that quintile of the population. Because people have been arrayed from poorest to richest, these income shares increase as we move from the first to the fifth quintile. The relative income principle tells us that income *shares* are all we need in the measurement of inequality.

(4) *The Dalton principle.* We are now in a position to state our final criterion for evaluating inequality. Formulated by Dalton [1920], [7] the criterion is fundamental to the construction of measures of inequality. Let $(y_1, y_2, \ldots, y_n)$ be an income distribution and consider two incomes y_i and y_j with $y_i \leq y_j$. A transfer of income from the "not richer" individual to the "not poorer" individual will be called a *regressive transfer*. The Dalton principle states that if one income distribution can be achieved from another by constructing a sequence of regressive transfers, then the former distribution must be deemed more unequal than the latter.

How far do these four criteria take us? Understanding this is the task of the next section. Before we do this, let us formally define an inequality measure. It is a rule that assigns a degree of inequality to each possible distribution of the national cake. In other words, it takes each income distribution

[7] See also Pigou [1912], after whom the principle is also called the Pigou–Dalton principle.

and assigns a value to it that can be thought of as the inequality of that distribution. A higher value of the measure signifies the presence of greater inequality. Thus an inequality index can be interpreted as a function of the form

$$I = I(y_1, y_2, \ldots, y_n)$$

defined over all conceivable distributions of income $(y_1, y_2, \ldots, y_n)$.

The requirement that the inequality measure satisfy the anonymity principle can be stated formally as follows: the function I is completely insensitive to all permutations of the income distribution $(y_1, y_2, \ldots, y_n)$ among the individuals $\{1, 2, \ldots, n\}$. Similarly, the requirement of the population principle can be translated as saying that for every distribution $(y_1, y_2, \ldots, y_n)$,

$$I(y_1, y_2, \ldots, y_n) = I(y_1, y_2, \ldots, y_n; y_1, y_2, \ldots, y_n),$$

so that cloning all members of the population and incomes has no effect. Thus by taking the lowest common multiple of the populations of any collection of income distributions, we can always regard each distribution as effectively having the same population size. The relative income principle can be incorporated by requiring that for every positive number λ,

$$I(y_1, y_2, \ldots, y_n) = I(\lambda y_1, \lambda y_2, \ldots, \lambda y_n).$$

Finally, I satisfies the Dalton transfer principle if, for every income distribution $(y_1, y_2, \ldots, y_n)$ and every transfer $\delta > 0$,

$$I(y_1, \ldots, y_i, \ldots, y_j, \ldots, y_n) < I(y_1, \ldots, y_i - \delta, \ldots, y_j + \delta, \ldots, y_n)$$

whenever $y_i \leq y_j$.

6.3.3. *The Lorenz curve*

There is a useful way to see what the four criteria of the previous section give us. Pictures often speak more than words, and in the context of inequality measurement, there is a nice diagrammatic way to depict the distribution of income in any society. The resulting graph is called the *Lorenz curve*, which is very often used in economic research and discussion; therefore, it is worthwhile to invest a little time in order to understand it.

Suppose we sort people in a population in increasing order of incomes. Figure 6.4 shows a typical Lorenz curve. On the horizontal axis, we depict *cumulative* percentages of the population arranged in increasing order of income. Thus points on that axis refer to the poorest 20% of the population,

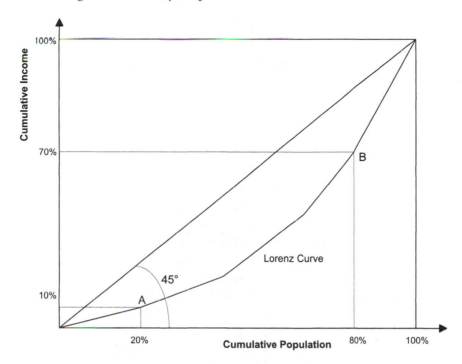

Figure 6.4. The Lorenz curve of an income distribution.

the poorest half of the population, and so on. On the vertical axis, we measure the percentage of national income accruing to any particular fraction of the population thus arranged. The point *A*, for example, corresponds to a value of 20% on the population axis and 10% on the income axis. The interpretation of this is that the poorest 20% of the population earns only 10% of overall income. Point *B*, on the other hand, corresponds to 80% on the population axis and 70% on the income axis. This point, therefore contains the information that the "poorest" 80% enjoy 70% of the national income. An equivalent way to describe this is from "above": the richest 20% have 30% of gross income for themselves. The graph that connects all these points is called the Lorenz curve.

Notice that the Lorenz curve begins and ends on the 45° line: the poorest 0% earn 0% of national income by definition and the poorest 100% is just the whole population, and so must earn 100% of the income. How would the Lorenz curve look like if everybody had the same income? Well, it would then coincide *everywhere* with the 45° line, that is, with the diagonal of the box. The poorest 10% (however selected) would then have exactly 10% of national income, whereas the richest 10% will also have the same 10%. In other words, any cumulative fraction of the population would share exactly that fraction of national wealth. Because the 45° line expresses the relationship $Y = X$, it *is* our Lorenz curve in this case. With increasing inequality, the

Lorenz curve starts to fall below the diagonal in a loop that is always bowed out to the right of the diagram; it cannot curve the other way. The slope of the curve at any point is simply the contribution of the person at that point to the cumulative share of national income. Because we have ordered individuals from poorest to richest, this "marginal contribution" cannot ever fall. This is the same as saying that the Lorenz curve can never get flatter as we move from left to right.

Thus in Figure 6.4, the "overall distance" between the 45° line and the Lorenz curve is indicative of the amount of inequality present in the society that it represents. The greater the extent of inequality, the further the Lorenz curve will be from the 45° line. Hence, even without writing down any formula for the measurement of inequality, we can obtain an intuitive idea of how much inequality there is by simply studying the Lorenz curve.

Some of the conceptual problems encountered in the measurement of inequality can also be brought out with the aid of this diagram. In Figure 6.5, the Lorenz curves of two different income distributions, marked $L(1)$ and $L(2)$, are represented. Because the second curve $L(2)$ lies entirely *below* the first one, it is natural to expect a good index to indicate greater inequality in the second case. Let's try to understand why this is so. The fact that $L(1)$ lies above $L(2)$ has the following easy interpretation: if we choose a poorest $x\%$ of the population (it does not matter what x you have in mind), then $L(1)$ always has this poorest $x\%$ earning at least as much as they do under $L(2)$. Thus regardless of which precise value of x you pick, the curve $L(1)$ is

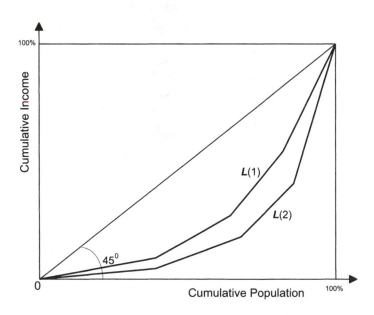

Figure 6.5. Using the Lorenz curve to make judgments.

always "biased" toward the poorest $x\%$ of the population, relative to $L(2)$. It stands to reason that $L(1)$ should be judged more equal than $L(2)$.

This criterion for inequality comparisons is known as the *Lorenz criterion*. It says that if the Lorenz curve of a distribution lies at every point to the right of the Lorenz curve of some other distribution, the former should be judged to be more unequal than the latter. Just as we required an inequality measure to be consistent with the criteria of the previous section, we require it to be consistent with this particular criterion. Thus an inequality measure I is *Lorenz-consistent* if, for every pair of income distributions $(y_1, y_2, \ldots, y_n)$ and $(z_1, z_2, \ldots, z_m)$,

$$I(y_1, y_2, \ldots, y_n) \geq I(z_1, z_2, \ldots, z_m)$$

whenever the Lorenz curve of $(y_1, y_2, \ldots, y_n)$ lies everywhere to the right of $(z_1, z_2, \ldots, z_m)$.

This is all very nice, but now confusion starts to set in. We just spent an entire section discussing four reasonable criteria for inequality comparisons and now we have introduced a fifth! Are these all independent restrictions that we have to observe? Fortunately, there is a neat connection between the four criteria of the previous section and the Lorenz criterion that we just introduced: *an inequality measure is consistent with the Lorenz criterion if and only if it is simultaneously consistent with the anonymity, population, relative income, and Dalton principles.*

This observation is very useful.[8] First, it shuts down our apparent expansion of criteria by stating that the earlier four are together exactly equivalent to the Lorenz criterion. Second, and more important, it captures our four criteria in one clean picture that gives us exactly their joint content. In this way we can summarize our verbal ethical criteria in simple graphical form.

The preceding observation is so central to our understanding of inequality that it is worth taking a minute to see why it is true. First, observe that the Lorenz curve automatically incorporates the principles of anonymity, population, and relative income, because the curve drops all information on income or population *magnitudes* and retains only information about income and population *shares*. What we need to understand is how the Dalton principle fits in. To see this, carry out a thought experiment. Pick any income distribution and transfer some resources from people, say from the fortieth population percentile, to people around the eightieth population percentile. This is a regressive transfer, and the Dalton principle says that inequality goes up as a result.

Figure 6.6 tells us what happens to the Lorenz curve. The thicker curve marks the original Lorenz curve and the thinner curve shows us the Lorenz

---

[8] For a useful discussion of the history of this result, see the survey by Foster [1985].

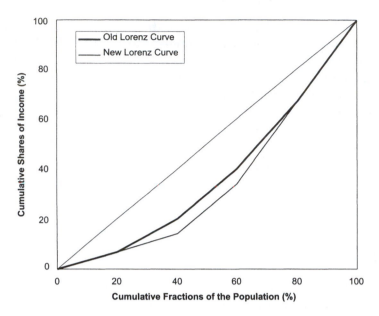

Figure 6.6. The Dalton principle and the Lorenz criterion.

curve after the transfer of resources. What about the new curve? Well, nothing was disturbed until we get close to the fortieth percentile, and then, because resources were transferred away, the share of this percentile *falls*. The new Lorenz curve therefore dips below and *to the right* of the old Lorenz curve at this point. What is more, it stays below for a while. Look at a point around the sixtieth population percentile. The income shares here are reduced as well, even though the incomes of people around this point were not tampered with. The reason for the reduction is that Lorenz curves plot *cumulative* population shares on the horizontal axis and their *cumulative* income share on the vertical axis. Because people from the fortieth percentile were "taxed" for the benefit of the eightieth percentile, the new share at the sixtieth percentile population mark (and indeed, at all percentiles between forty and eighty) must also be lower than the older share. This state of affairs persists until the eightieth percentile comes along, at which point the overall effect of the transfer vanishes. At this stage the *cumulative* shares return to exactly the level at which they were before. In other words, the Lorenz curves again coincide after this point. In summary, the new Lorenz curve is bowed to the right of the old (at least over an interval), which means that the Lorenz criterion mirrors the Dalton principle; that is, they agree.

The converse comparison is true as well: if two Lorenz curves are comparable according to the Lorenz criterion, as in the case of $L(1)$ and $L(2)$ in Figure 6.5, then it *must* be possible to construct a set of disequalizing transfers leading from $L(1)$ to $L(2)$. We leave the details to an exercise at the end of this chapter.

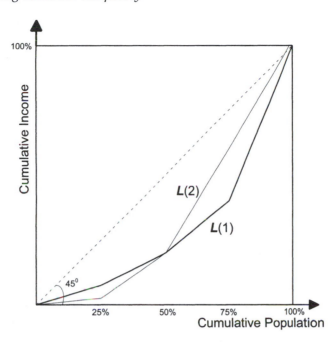

Figure 6.7. Ambiguous comparisons: A Lorenz crossing.

At this point, it looks like we are all set. We have a set of criteria that has a clear diagrammatic reformulation. It appears we can compare Lorenz curves using these criteria, so there is apparently no more need to make a fuss about inequality measurement. Unfortunately, matters are a bit more complicated. Two Lorenz curves can *cross*.

Figure 6.7 illustrates a Lorenz crossing. There are two income distributions that are represented by the Lorenz curves $L(1)$ and $L(2)$ in the diagram. Observe that neither Lorenz curve is uniformly to the right of the other. For two income distributions that relate to each other in this fashion, the Lorenz criterion does not apply. By the equivalence result discussed previously, it follows that our four principles cannot apply either, but what does it mean for these criteria "not to apply"? It means that we *cannot* go from one distribution to the other by a sequence of Dalton regressive transfers. Put another way, there must be *both* "progressive" and "regressive" transfers in going from one distribution to the other. The following example illustrates this point.

Example. Suppose that society consists of four individuals who earn incomes of 75, 125, 200, and 600. Now consider a second income distribution, given by (25, 175, 400, 400). Compare the two. We can "travel" from the first distribution to the second in the following manner. First transfer 50 from the first person to the second: this is a regressive transfer. Next transfer 200 from the fourth person to the third: this is a progressive transfer. We have arrived at the second distribution. Of course, these transfers are just a "construction" and not something that need have occurred (e.g., the two distributions may be for two different four-person societies). Try another construction. Transfer 50 from the first person to the third: This is regressive. Transfer now 150 from the fourth to the third: this is progressive. Finally, transfer 50 from the fourth to the second: this is progressive as well. Again, we arrive at the second distribution.

Hence, there are many imaginary ways to travel from the first to the second distribution, but the point is that they *all* necessarily involve at least one regressive and at least one progressive transfer. (Try it.) In other words, the four principles of the previous section are just not enough to permit a comparison. In this case we *have* to somehow weigh in our minds the "cost" of the regressive transfer(s) against the "benefit" of the progressive transfer(s). These trade-offs are almost impossible to quantify in a way so that everybody will approve.[9]

What about the Lorenz curves in the example? Sure enough, they mirror the complications of the comparison. The poorest 25% of the population earn 7.5% of the income in the first distribution and only 2.5% of the income in the second. The opposite comparison holds when we get to the poorest 75% of the population, who enjoy only 40% of the total income under the first distribution, but 60% of the income under the second distribution.

Now go back and look at Figure 6.7 once again. You can see that $L(1)$ and $L(2)$ are precisely the Lorenz curves for the two distributions in this example.

Despite these ambiguities, Lorenz curves provide a clean, visual image of the overall distribution of income in a country. Figure 6.8 provides several examples of Lorenz curves for different countries. By looking at these figures, you can get a sense of income inequalities in different parts of the world, and with a little mental superimposition of any two diagrams you can compare inequalities across two countries.

6.3.4. *Complete measures of inequality*

Lorenz curves provide a pictorial representation of the degree of inequality in a society. There are two problems with such a representation. First, policy makers and researchers are often interested in summarizing inequal-

---

[9] Shorrocks and Foster [1987] argued for a fifth principle, which they call transfer sensitivity. This principle tries to compare progressive transfers at the lower end of the income distribution with regressive transfers at the upper end, arguing that if both involve the same size transfer, then the former should be "ethically allowed" to outweigh the latter: inequality should come down under the composite transfer. This principle further broadens the scope of comparison, but is still not enough to rule out ambiguities.

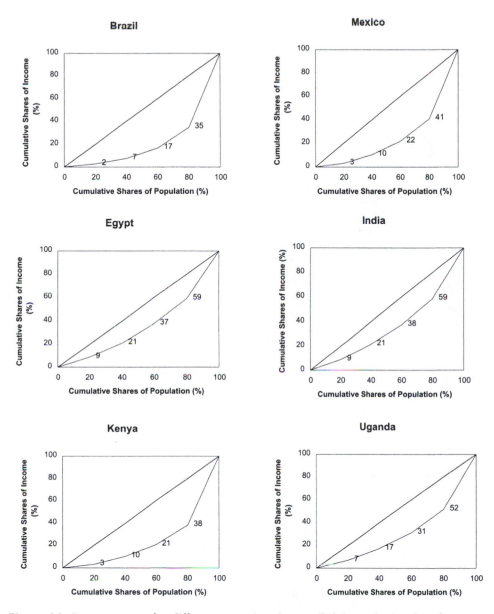

Figure 6.8. Lorenz curves for different countries. Source: Deininger–Squire data base; see Deininger and Squire [1996a].

ity by a *number*, something that is more concrete and quantifiable than a picture. Second, when Lorenz curves cross, they cannot provide useful inequality rankings. Thus an inequality measure that spits out a number for every conceivable income distribution can be thought of as a *complete ranking* of income distributions. As we will see, this completeness does not come

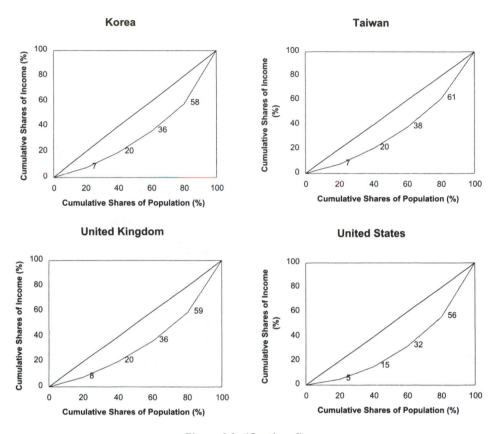

Figure 6.8. (Continued).

free of charge: it means that in some situations, inequality measures tend to disagree with one another.

We now survey some commonly used inequality measures.[10] We use the following notation. There are m distinct incomes, and in each income class j, the number of individuals earning that income is denoted by n_j. Thus the total number of people n is simply equal to $\sum_{j=1}^{m} n_j$, where the symbol $\sum_{j=1}^{m}$ henceforth denotes the *sum* over the income classes 1 through m. The *mean* μ of any income distribution is simply average income, or total income divided by the total number of people. Thus

$$\mu \equiv \frac{1}{n} \sum_{j=1}^{m} n_j y_j.$$

The following (complete) measures of inequality are often used.

---

[10] See Sen [1997] for a discussion of these and other measures, and for a comprehensive overall treatment of the subject of economic inequality.

(1) *The range.* This value is given by the difference in the incomes of the richest and the poorest individuals, divided by the mean to express it independently of the units in which income is measured. Thus the range R is given by

$$(6.1) \qquad R = \frac{1}{\mu}(y_m - y_1).$$

Quite obviously, this is a rather crude measure. It pays no attention, whatsoever, to people between the richest and the poorest on the income scale. In particular, it fails to satisfy the Dalton principle, because, for example, a small transfer from the second poorest to the second most rich individual will keep the measure unchanged. However, the range is often used as a crude, though useful, measure when detailed information on income distribution is missing.

(2) *The Kuznets ratios.* Simon Kuznets introduced these ratios in his pioneering study of income distributions in developed and developing countries. These ratios refer to the share of income owned by the poorest 20 or 40% of the population, or by the richest 10%, or more commonly to the *ratio* of the shares of income of the richest x% to the poorest y%, where x and y stand for numbers such as 10, 20, or 40. The ratios are essentially "pieces" of the Lorenz curve and, like the range, serve as a useful shorthand in situations where detailed income distribution data are missing.

(3) *The mean absolute deviation.* This is our first measure that takes advantage of the entire income distribution. The idea is simple: inequality is proportional to distance from the mean income. Therefore, simply take all income distances from the average income, add them up, and divide by total income to express the average deviation as a fraction of total income. This means that the mean absolute deviation M is defined as

$$(6.2) \qquad M = \frac{1}{\mu n} \sum_{i=j}^{m} n_j |y_j - \mu|$$

where the notation $|\cdot|$ stands for the absolute value (neglecting negative signs). Although M looks promising as a measure of inequality that takes into account the overall income distribution, it has one serious drawback: it is often insensitive to the Dalton principle. Suppose that there are two people with incomes y_j and y_k, such that y_j is below the mean income of the population and y_k is above the mean income of the population. Then a regressive income transfer from y_j to y_k certainly raises inequality as measured by M. This is obvious from the formula, because the distance of both y_j and y_k goes up and no other distance is altered, so M unambiguously rises. However, the Dalton principle is meant to apply to *all* regressive transfers, not just those from incomes below the mean to incomes above the mean. For example, take any two incomes y_j and y_k that are both above the mean, and make a transfer from the lower of the two, say y_j, to the other (higher) one. Clearly, if the transfer is small enough so that both incomes stay above the mean after the transfer, there will be no difference in the sum of the absolute difference from mean income. The mean absolute deviation will register no change in such a case, and so fails the Dalton principle. We must conclude that using as it does the entire income distribution, the mean absolute deviation has no compensatory features as a quick estimate and is therefore a bad measure of inequality.

(4) *The coefficient of variation.* One way to avoid the insensitivity of the mean absolute deviation is by giving more weight to larger deviations from the mean. A familiar statistical measure that does just this is the standard deviation (see Appendix 2), which squares all deviations from the mean. Because the square of a number rises more than proportionately to the number itself, this is effectively the same as attaching greater weight to larger deviations from the mean. The coefficient of variation (C) is just the standard deviation divided by the mean, so that only relative incomes matter. Thus

$$(6.3) \qquad\qquad C = \frac{1}{\mu}\sqrt{\sum_{j=1}^{m}\frac{n_j}{n}(y_j - \mu)^2}.$$

The measure C, it turns out, has satisfactory properties. It satisfies all four principles and so it is Lorenz-consistent. In particular, it always satisfies the Dalton transfer principle. Consider a transfer from j to k, where $y_j \leq y_k$. This implies a transfer from a smaller number [i.e., $(y_j - \mu)$] to a larger one [i.e., $(y_k - \mu)$], which increases the *square* of the larger number by more than it decreases the square of the smaller number. The net effect is that C invariably registers an increase when such a regressive transfer is made. You should check by trying out various examples that this is always the case.

(5) *The Gini coefficient.* We now come to a measure that is widely used in empirical work: the Gini coefficient. The Gini approach starts from a base that is fundamentally different from measures such as M and C. Instead of taking deviations from the mean income, it takes the difference between *all* pairs of incomes and simply totals the (absolute) differences. It is as if inequality is the sum of all pairwise comparisons of "two-person inequalities" that can conceivably be made. The Gini coefficient is normalized by dividing by population squared (because all pairs are added and there are n^2 such pairs) as well as mean income. In symbols, the Gini coefficient G is given by

$$(6.4) \qquad\qquad G = \frac{1}{2n^2\mu}\sum_{j=1}^{m}\sum_{k=1}^{m} n_j n_k |y_j - y_k|.$$

Figure 6.9. The Lorenz consistency of the Gini coefficient.

The double summation sign signifies that we first sum over all ks, holding each j constant, and then sum over all the js. This is like summing all pairs of income differences (weighted by the number of such pairs, $n_j n_k$). Notice that because each $|y_j - y_k|$ is counted twice (again as $|y_k - y_j|$), the whole expression is finally divided by 2 as well as by the population and income normalizers.

The Gini coefficient has pleasing properties. It satisfies all four principles and is therefore Lorenz-consistent, just like the coefficient of variation. Figure 6.9 shows us why the Gini coefficient is consistent with the Lorenz criterion. In this figure, we arrange everybody's incomes from lowest to highest. Now take two incomes, say y_j and y_k, with $y_j \le y_k$, and transfer some small amount[11] δ from y_j to y_k. Figure 6.9 shows us how these two incomes change. Now let us see how the Gini coefficient has altered as a result of this regressive transfer. All we have to do is see the change in those pairs in which j or k figure. Consider incomes to the left of y_j. Because y_j has come down, the difference between these incomes and y_j has narrowed by δ. This narrowing is exactly counterbalanced by the fact that y_k has gone up by the same amount, so the distance between y_k and incomes to the left of y_j has gone up by an equal amount. The same argument holds for incomes to the right of y_k: the distance between them and y_k narrows, but the distance to y_j goes up by the same amount, so all these effects cancel. This leaves us with incomes between y_j and y_k. However, the pairwise distance between these incomes and *both* y_j and y_k has gone up. So has the distance between y_j and y_k. Thus the overall effect is an increase in the Gini coefficient. This shows why the Gini coefficient is Lorenz-consistent.

There is another interesting property of the Gini coefficient that ties it very closely indeed to the Lorenz curve. Recall that the more "bowed out" the Lorenz curve, the higher is our intuitive perception of inequality. It turns out that the Gini coefficient is precisely the ratio of the *area* between the Lorenz curve and the 45° line of perfect equality, to the *area* of the triangle below the 45° line.

We have thus surveyed five indexes. Of these, the first two are very crude but nevertheless useful indicators of inequality when detailed data are unavailable. The third should not be used. Finally, both the coefficient

---

[11] We take δ small so as to preserve the ranking of individuals in ascending order of income. The argument for larger values of δ follows by breaking up the transfer into smaller pieces and applying the logic in the text.

of variation (C) and the Gini coefficient (G) appear to be perfectly satisfactory indexes, going by our four principles (or what is equivalent, Lorenz
consistency),[12] but this gives rise to a puzzle. If both C and G are satisfactory
in this sense, why use both measures? Why not just one?

This brings us back full circle to Lorenz crossings. We have just seen that
both C and G are Lorenz-consistent. This means that when Lorenz curves
can be compared, both C and G give us exactly the same ranking, because
they both agree with the Lorenz criterion. The problem arises when two
Lorenz curves cross. In that case, it is possible for the Gini coefficient and
the coefficient of variation to give contradictory rankings. This is nothing
but a reflection of the fact that our intuitive sense of inequality is essentially
incomplete. In such situations, we should probably not rely entirely on one
particular measure of inequality, but rely on a whole set of measures. It may
be a good idea to simply study the two Lorenz curves as well.

As a hypothetical example, consider two societies, each consisting of only
three persons. Let the distribution of income in the two societies be $(3, 12, 12)$
and $(4, 9, 14)$, respectively. You can easily check that for the first of our hypothetical societies, the coefficient of variation is 0.27, whereas it is 0.26 for
the second. Using C as an index, therefore, we reach the conclusion that the
first society is more unequal than the second. However, if we calculate the
Gini coefficient, the values come out to be 0.22 and 0.25, respectively. On
the basis of the latter measure, therefore, inequality seems to be higher in
the second society compared to the first.[13]

To be sure, this isn't just a hypothetical possibility. Such contradictory
movements of inequality indexes occur in real life as well. Consider, for
instance, the study by Weisskoff [1970] on inequality variations in Puerto
Rico, Argentina, and Mexico during the 1950s. Table 6.1, put together from
Weisskoff's study by Fields [1980], illustrates the ambiguities that arise.

The table is remarkable in its varied movements of inequality measures.
In each of the three countries, there is some ambiguity. In Puerto Rico, for instance, *both* the poorest 40% and the richest 5% of the population lost income

---

[12] Of course, other measures are in use as well. There is the use of *log variance* as an inequality
measure, which is just the standard deviation of the logarithm of incomes. Although it is easy
to compute and use, the log variance unfortunately disagrees with the Dalton principle in some
cases. Another measure, introduced to inequality evaluation by Henri Theil and known as the *Theil
index*, is derived from entropy theory. Although it looks bizarre at first, it turns out to be the *only*
measure that satisfies the four principles and a convenient decomposability principle that permits us
to separate overall inequality into between-group and within-group components (Foster [1983]). This
makes the Theil index uniquely useful in situations where we want to decompose inequality into
various categories, for example, inequality within and across ethnic, religious, caste, occupational, or
geographical lines.

[13] Warning: There is no connection between a value of, say, 0.25 achieved by the Gini coefficient
compared to the same number achieved by C. That's like comparing apples and oranges. All this
example is doing is contrasting different trends in the movements of these indexes as the distribution
of income changes.

Table 6.1. *Changes in inequality in Puerto Rico, Argentina, and Mexico.*

Country/date	Gini	Coeff. of variation	Income share of richest 5% (%)	Income share of poorest 40% (%)
Puerto Rico				
1953	0.415	1.152	23.4	15.5
1963	0.449↑	1.035↓	22.0↓	13.7↑
Argentina				
1953	0.412	1.612	27.2	18.1
1959	0.463↑	1.887↑	31.8↑	16.4↑
1961	0.434↓↑	1.605↓↓	29.4↓↑	17.4↓↑
Mexico				
1950	0.526	2.500	40.0	14.3
1957	0.551↑	1.652↓	37.0↓	11.3↑
1963	0.543↓↑	1.380↓↓	28.8↓↓	10.1↑↑

Source: Fields [1980]. Note: First arrow indicates a change in inequality from the previous observation; the second arrow indicates the change in inequality from two observations ago.

share, a clear sign that the Lorenz curve has crossed. This doesn't *necessarily* mean that the Gini coefficient and the coefficient of variation disagree, but they do in fact. In the case of Argentina, there is no evidence from the income shares of the richest and poorest that the Lorenz curves have crossed, but they must have, at least over the period 1953–61. Do you see why? Finally, look at Mexico for the period 1957–63. In this case, both the Gini coefficient and the coefficient of variation agree, but it's also clear from the movement of income shares that the Lorenz curves have crossed (check this). It should be abundantly clear, therefore, that unless we have a clear case where a Lorenz comparison can be made, we should consult a variety of inequality measures before making a judgment.

Clearly we have a dilemma here: the result of our comparison is sensitive to the choice of the index, but we have no clear intuitive reason to prefer one over the other. There are two ways out of this dilemma. The first, as we said before, is to examine our *notion* of inequality more closely and to come up with stricter criteria after such introspection. The result, as was pointed out, will inevitably be subjective and controversial. The second escape is to realize that human thought and ideas abound with *incomplete* orderings: everyone agrees that Shakespeare is a greater writer than the Saturday columnist in the local newspaper; however, you and I might disagree whether he is greater than Tagore or Tolstoy, and even I may not be very sure *myself*. Relative inequality, like relative literary strength, may be perfectly discernible some of the time and difficult to judge in other cases. We can learn to live with that. If a society manages to significantly increase economic fairness and humane distribution among its members, then this fact will be captured in every reasonable inequality index, and we will not have to quibble over technicalities! It pays, however, to be aware of the difficulties of measurement.

In the next chapter, we go back to economics instead of plain measurement. Our goal will be to relate inequality to other features of the development process.

6.4. *Summary*

In this chapter, we studied the measurement of *inequality* in the distribution of wealth or incomes. We argued that there are two reasons to be interested in inequality: the *intrinsic*, in which we value equality for its own sake and therefore regard inequality reduction as an objective in itself, and the *functional*, in which we study inequality to understand its impact on *other* features of the development process.

As a prelude to the study of measurement, we recognized that there were several conceptual issues. For instance, inequality in incomes may be compatible with overall equality simply because a society might display a high degree of *mobility*: movement of people from one income class to another. We also paid attention to the *functional distribution* of income as opposed to the *personal distribution* of income: *how* income is earned may have just as much social value as *how much* is earned.

With these caveats in mind, we then introduced four criteria for inequality measurement: (1) the *anonymity principle* (names do not matter), (2) the *population principle* (population size does not matter as long as the *composition* of different income classes stay the same in percentage terms), (3) the *relative income principle* (only relative incomes matter for the measurement of inequality, and not the absolute amounts involved), and (4) the *Dalton transfer principle* (if a transfer of income is made from a relatively poor to a relatively rich person, then inequality, however measured, registers an increase). It turns out that these four principles create a ranking of income distribution identical to that implied by the *Lorenz curve*, which displays how cumulative shares of income are earned by cumulatively increasing fractions of the population, arranged from poorest to richest.

However, the ranking is not complete. Sometimes two Lorenz curves cross. In such situations the four principles are not enough to make an unequivocal judgment about inequality. We argued that in this sense, our notions of inequality are fundamentally incomplete, but that forcing an additional degree of completeness by introducing more axioms may not necessarily be a good idea.

Complete measures of inequality do exist. These are measures that assign a degree of inequality (a number) to *every* conceivable income distribution, so they generate complete rankings. We studied examples of such measures that are popularly used in the literature: the *range*, the *Kuznets ratios*, the *mean absolute deviation*, the *coefficient of variation*, and the *Gini coefficient*. Of these measures, the last two are of special interest in that they agree fully with our four principles (and so agree with the Lorenz ranking). That is, whenever the Lorenz ranking states that inequality has gone up, these two measures do not disagree. However, it is possible for these measures (and others) to disagree when Lorenz curves *do* cross: we provided a numerical example of this, as well as real-life instances drawing on studies of Latin American inequality.

Thus the theory of inequality measurement serves a double role. It tells us the ethical principles that are widely accepted and that we can use to rank different distributions of income or wealth, but it also warns us that such principles are incomplete, so we should not treat the behavior of any one complete measure at face value. We may not have direct information regarding the underlying Lorenz curves, but it is a good idea to look at the behavior of more than one measure before making a provisional judgment about the direction of change in inequality (if any such judgment can be made at all).

Exercises

■ (1) Connect and contrast the following concepts: (a) inequality of current income versus inequality of lifetime income, (b) functional versus personal income distribution, (c) efficiency versus equity, (d) inequality of income versus inequality of opportunities, and (e) wage inequality versus income inequality. In each case, make sure you understand each of the concepts and how they are related to each other.

■ (2) The economy of ShortLife has two kinds of jobs, which are the only sources of income for the people. One kind of job pays $200, the other pays $100. Individuals in this economy live for two years. In each year, only half the population can manage to get the high-paying job. The other half has to be content with the low-paying one. At the end of each year, everybody is fired from existing positions, and those people assigned to the high-paying job next year are chosen randomly. This means that at any date, each person, irrespective of past earnings, has probability 1/2 of being selected for the high-paying job.

(a) Calculate the Gini coefficient based on people's incomes in any one particular period and show that it suggests a good deal of inequality. Now calculate each person's average per period *lifetime* income and compute the Gini coefficient based on *these* incomes. Does the latter measure suggest more or less inequality? Explain why.

(b) Now change the scenario somewhat. Suppose that a person holding a job of one type has probability 3/4 of having the same kind of job next year. Calculate the expected lifetime income (per year average) of a person who currently has a high-paying job, and do the same for a person with a low-paying job. Compute the Gini coefficient based on these expected per period incomes and compare it with the measure obtained in case (a). Explain the difference you observe.

(c) Generalize this idea by assuming that with probability p you hold your current job, and with probability $1 - p$ you change it. Find a formula for inequality as measured by the Gini coefficient for each p, examine how it changes with p, and explain your answer intuitively.

■ (3) Draw Lorenz curves and calculate the Gini coefficient and the coefficient of variation for the income distributions (a)–(f). In each situation, the first set of numbers represents the various incomes, whereas the second set of numbers represents the number of people earning each of these incomes:

(a) $(100, 200, 300, 400)$; $(50, 25, 75, 25)$

(b) $(200, 400, 600, 800)$; $(50, 25, 75, 25)$

(c) $(200, 400, 600, 800)$; $(100, 50, 150, 50)$

(d) $(200, 400, 600, 800)$; $(125, 25, 125, 50)$

(e) $(100, 200, 300, 400)$; $(50, 15, 95, 15)$

(f) $(100, 200, 300, 400)$, $(50, 35, 55, 35)$.

[Try to understand the implicit transfers that move you from one income distribution to the other (except for the first three, which should turn out to have the same inequality — why?).]

■ (4) What are the ethical principles that we used in our measurement of inequality? Show that these principles are exactly summarized in the concept of the Lorenz curve. Argue that if there are two income distributions for which the Lorenz curves do not cross, then the Gini coefficient and the coefficient of variation cannot disagree with each other when measuring the inequality of these two distributions.

■ (5) In a world in which there are fixed minimum needs for survival, show that an application of the relative income principle runs into problems. How would you try and modify the principle to circumvent this problem?

■ (6) Suppose that there are n people in society, arranged (without loss of generality) in increasing order of income earned. Let $x = (x_1, \ldots, x_n)$ and

$y = (y_1, \ldots, y_n)$ be two income distributions (with *total* incomes the same in the two cases).

(a) Show that the Lorenz curve for x must lie inside the Lorenz curve for y if (and only if)

$$\sum_{i=1}^{k} x_i \geq \sum_{i=1}^{k} y_i$$

for all k, with strict inequality for some k.

(b) (Extra credit.) Now suppose that the condition in part (a) does hold. Show that y can be attained from x by a sequence of regressive transfers. For details, see Fields and Fei [1978].

■ (7) The Dalton transfer principle may not be a good way to judge increases in *polarization* (for a definition, see Esteban and Ray [1994] and Wolfson [1994]). To see this, begin with a society in which incomes take all values in $100 increments between $100 and $1000, and in which an equal proportion of the population (1/10) occupies each of these classes. Show this income distribution in a diagram with incomes on the horizontal axis and population proportions on the vertical axis. Now draw another diagram with half the population at the income level $250, and another half at income level $750. Intuitively rank these two income distributions: which one has more scope for social unrest, which one might display a greater awareness of inequality, and so on.

Now show that the second distribution can be obtained by a sequence of *progressive* Dalton transfers from the first. Do you feel that your intuition is in line with the transfer principle, in this example?

■ (8) The economy of Nintendo has ten people. Three of them live in the modern sector of Nintendo and earn $2000 per month. The rest live in the traditional sector and earn only $1000 per month. One day, two new modern sector jobs open up and two people from the traditional sector move to the modern sector.

(a) Show that the Lorenz curves of the income distributions before and after must cross. Do this in two ways: (i) by graphing the Lorenz curves and (ii) by first expressing both income distributions as divisions of a cake of size 1, and then showing that the two distributions are linked by "opposing" Dalton transfers.

(b) Calculate the Gini coefficients and the coefficients of variation of the two distributions.

■ (9) Are the following statements true, false, or uncertain? In each case, back up your answer with a brief, but precise explanation.

(a) The Kuznets ratios satisfy the Dalton transfer principle.

(b) If the Lorenz curve of two situations do not cross, the Gini coefficient and the coefficient of variation cannot disagree.

(c) If a relatively poor person loses income to a relatively rich person, the mean absolute deviation *must* rise.

(d) The Lorenz curve must *necessarily* lie in the lower triangle of the diagram, bounded by the 45° line at the top and the axes at the bottom.

(e) The ethical principles of inequality measurement — anonymity, population, relative income, and transfers — are enough to compare any two income distributions in terms of relative inequality.

(f) If everybody's income increases by a constant dollar amount, inequality *must* fall.

Chapter 7

Inequality and Development: Interconnections

7.1. Introduction

In the introduction to Chapter 6, we argued that our interest in inequality can arise from two broad sources. Equality per se may be of interest to many of us, simply as a goal in itself, but even if we are not interested in the reduction or elimination of inequality as a worthy objective in itself, inequality may still be of interest for other, *functional* reasons. The presence of inequality affects the way in which an economy works and prevents (or perhaps promotes!) some other goal that we are interested in. Our objective in this chapter is to examine the interconnections between inequality and other features of economic development.

There is good reason to believe that the functional aspects of inequality are far more acute for developing countries than for their economically developed counterparts. As we have already seen, the majority of the world's population has access to very limited resources, *even if we just go by average income*. With low incomes distributed unequally, the consequences for poverty, undernutrition, and sheer waste of human life are simply unthinkable. The effects of inequality on aggregate economic performance are correspondingly stronger. Savings rates are severely affected at low levels of income; so is the capacity to do useful work. The ability to provide economic incentives is affected in more ways than one. Access to credit and finance is constrained, which reduces the efficiency of these and other markets. We will take up these topics in this chapter.

The foregoing paragraphs suggest that the connections between inequality and other aspects of development run in both causal directions. This shouldn't come as a surprise, particularly in light of our detailed discussions of endogeneity in the growth process (see Chapters 3 and 4). As long as we keep close track of the direction in which the causal story runs (and much of the time this will not be too difficult), we will be all right.

It is useful to picture in our heads the following sequence. Start with the simple story of market production and exchange that we have all been taught in our introductory economics classes. We can recapitulate this in one paragraph. Individuals hold endowments of different goods, including potential inputs, and shares in firms. Individuals can buy and sell goods and inputs, and perhaps transform inputs to outputs through the act of production. Goods are bought and sold at market prices, and these prices serve to equate the supply of and demand for every commodity. In the end, each individual can attain for herself a pattern of consumption, provided that she stays within her budget and production possibilities. Some individuals might save; others borrow.

We began this story with the assertion that *individuals hold endowments of different goods, including potential inputs.* Where do these endowments come from and what determines their distribution among persons at each point in time? This question is both meaningful and useless. It is meaningful in the sense that *given* today's distribution of endowments and today's economic interaction in the marketplace (of which we speak more presently), we generate a new distribution of endowments for tomorrow. For instance, savers add to their past stock of endowments and borrowers draw down these stocks. Young women and men acquire education and in this way, freshen or augment the endowment of human capital. Shareholders make profits or losses. Therefore, we can say something useful about inequality (or the holdings of endowments) provided we know (a) how endowments were distributed and (b) what kind of economic interaction occurred in the "previous period." In this sense today's distribution of wealth spawns, via economic interaction, tomorrow's distribution of wealth, and the process repeats itself endlessly over time and over generations. Thus economic growth and economic inequality intertwine and evolve together.

At another level, though, the question of what determines endowments is useless. We must fall back on the endowment distribution at a past date, just as we did in the previous paragraph. We simply do not have enough recorded history to go back to the beginning of time. Thus the goal is not to explain the past; it is to see how a given past influences the future, through the recursive pattern described previously. In particular, then, one question acquires special importance, and this is a question that we have already asked ourselves at the level of entire countries. Does history matter? For instance, does the operation of "free" markets ensure that *over time,* historical inequalities melt away, which permits individuals or dynasties to "converge" to some common, unchanging level of inequality? If this is indeed the case, what is the process that serves to eliminate historical advantages and disadvantages? If this is not the case, how might inequalities persist and, in doing so, what effects do they have on the economic development of a country?

This sets the stage for the theories and empirical findings that we will now discuss. These analyses take as historically *given* an initial distribution of assets, but then ask the question, Do these inequalities worsen over time or narrow? How are aggregates, such as income, employment, wealth, and growth rates affected by inequality? In turn, how do these variables affect the evolution of inequality?

7.2. Inequality, income, and growth

7.2.1. The inverted-U hypothesis

Consider, first, the empirically observed patterns that connect inequality to per capita income. We begin with the pathbreaking work of Kuznets [1955], which is the earliest attempt to correlate the presence of economic inequality with other variables such as income. Because of data limitations, Kuznets used the ratio of the income share of the richest 20% of the population to that of the poorest 60% of the population as a measure of inequality. The comparison was carried out between a small set of developing countries—India, Sri Lanka and Puerto Rico—and a small set of developed countries—the United States and the United Kingdom.

The ratios turned out to be 1.96 (India), 1.67 (Sri Lanka), and 2.33 (Puerto Rico), as opposed to the values of 1.29 (United States) and 1.25 (United Kingdom). These values are indicative of the possibility that developing countries, in general, tend to possess higher degrees of inequality than their developed counterparts. A later study by Kuznets [1963] provided further support for this possibility. In this study, data were obtained from eighteen countries; again, the sample had a mixture of developed and developing countries. The study made very clear the finding that the income shares of *upper income* groups in developed countries were significantly lower than their developing counterparts. The opposite comparison appeared to be valid for the income shares of lower income groups, although in this case the results were much less clear-cut. These findings, though sketchy, were suggestive.

Even from these narrow and somewhat impressionistic observations, it seems to be the case that economic development is fundamentally a sequential and uneven process. Instead of everybody benefiting at the same time, the process appears to pull up certain groups first and leave the other groups to catch up later. In the initial phase, inequality widens. Later, as everybody else catches up, inequality falls. This sort of reasoning (which we discuss more later) drove Oshima [1962] and Kuznets [1955, 1963] to suggest a broad hypothesis of development: that economic progress, measured by per capita income, is initially accompanied by rising inequality, but that these disparities ultimately go away as the benefits of development permeate more widely. Thus if you plot per capita income on one axis and some measure of inequality on the other, the hypothesis suggests a plot that looks like an upside-down "U": hence the name *inverted-U hypothesis*. The inverted-U hypothesis spawned a great deal of innovative and not-so-innovative thinking about the development process. An example of the former kind is described in the box on the Tunnel Effect.

The Tunnel Effect

You are driving through a two-lane tunnel, where both lanes are in the same direction and, guess what, you get caught in a serious traffic jam. No car is moving in either lane as far as you can see. You are in the left lane and your spirits are not exactly high. After a while, however, the cars in the right lane begin to move. Do you feel better or worse? It depends on how long the right lane has been moving. At first, you know that the jam has cleared further ahead and that your turn to move will come soon. Given this imminent prospect of movement, your spirits do lift considerably, even though you haven't yet moved. However, if the right lane keeps moving for long enough with no sign of things clearing up on the left lane, you soon end up frustrated and maybe just gate crash into the right lane yourself. Of course, if there are many people gate-crashing, everything will probably come to a halt anyway.

Hirschman and Rothschild [1973] used this example to discuss an apparently very different issue: the tolerance for inequality in income distribution along the path toward economic development.

It has been the experience of several developing economies that the level of inequality in the distribution of income increases over the initial phases of development. The responses to such a rise in inequality have been varied, both across economies as well as within the same economy at different points in time, and they have ranged from an enthusiastic acceptance of the growth process that accompanied the rise in inequality to violent protests against it in the form of social and political upheaval. Such differences in the tolerance for inequality may be explained with the help of the tunnel analogy.

Suppose that an individual's welfare at any point of time depends on both his present as well as expected future level of contentment (or, as a proxy, income). Although the individual generally has good information about present income, his information about future income may be far more limited.

Now consider an improvement in the economic or social position of some others around him. The individual's response to such an improvement will depend on his beliefs as to what it implies for his own prospects. If he believes such a rise in others' fortunes is indicative of brighter prospects for himself in the foreseeable future, then the improvement in their relative incomes would not make him worse off; in fact, he may be better off despite this decline in his relative income, given higher expectations about his future income. Hirschman and Rothschild described such an increase in an individual's utility (and hence a tolerance of greater inequality) resulting from an improvement in others' economic status as the *tunnel effect*.

Of course, if such an improvement in the welfare of others were to persist for a sustained period of time, without any improvement in one's own welfare, initial acceptance of the improved condition of others would soon give way to anger and frustration, as in the tunnel example. Moreover, increased inequality may not be tolerated at all if the perceived link between the growing fortunes of others and the individual's own welfare is weak or nonexistent. The greater the extent of segregation in society to begin with, the higher the possibility of this outcome. Thus sharp existing differences along racial, cultural, social, and economic lines might cause an individual to view his circumstances as fundamentally different from those of others who have attained success.

Such variations in the responses of individuals to a rise in the fortunes of others explain the differences in the tolerance of inequality, both across societies and over time. In societies with greater heterogeneity, groups of people may perceive their fortunes as being delinked, or worse, negatively correlated with those of other groups. For instance, countries such as India or Pakistan might tend to have a much lower tolerance level for inequality compared to (relatively) more homogeneous societies such as Mexico. However, even within Mexico itself, the tolerance level for inequality was much higher in the initial phases of the development process. Sustained improvement in the lives of a few at the cost of the masses led to a weakening of the tunnel effect, resulting in outbursts such as the Tlatelolco massacre in 1968, which vented the frustration of those in the "left lane."

Hirschman's tunnel effect hypothesis conveys an important lesson. If growth and equity in income distribution are considered to be the two principal objectives of the process of economic development, the development strategy has to be devised by keeping in mind the social and political context. If, given the social structure, the tunnel effect is weak (i.e., tolerance for inequality is low), a strategy of "grow first, distribute later" is unlikely to meet with success. Even with strong initial tunnel effects, the development process may be thwarted if ruling groups and policy makers are insensitive to the erosion of these effects over time.

7.2.2. Testing the inverted-U hypothesis

An inverted-U in the cross section?

A number of studies have attempted to test this hypothesis. There are two ways to do this. Ideally, we would like to track an individual country over time and note the resulting changes in inequality that occur. However, you can probably count on the fingers of one hand all the countries for which this exercise is possible, because reliable data estimates are a modern phenomenon (and are probably more doubtful than reliable even today for all but a tiny handful of countries). As a result, countries that have supposedly completed their "inverted-U" path generally lack the data on inequality to go back centuries into the past.

Given the scarcity of data for most countries and the additional feature that some kind of averaging across countries might help, a second route is to

Table 7.1. *An inverted-U in the cross section?*

Income category (1965 U.S. $)	Average Gini	Range of Gini
Less than 100	0.419	0.33–0.51
101–200	0.468	0.26–0.50
201–300	0.499	0.36–0.62
301–500	0.494	0.30–0.64
501–1000	0.438	0.38–0.58
1001–2000	0.401	0.30–0.50
2001 and higher	0.365	0.34–0.39

Source: Paukert [1973].

carry out what is called a *cross-section* study: examine variations in inequality across countries that are at different stages in the development process. Such studies have their own intrinsic limitations: countries differ widely and unless there is a systematic way to control for intercountry variation, the results must always be interpreted cautiously. At the same time, cross-sectional studies of variations in inequality have the great advantage that they mimic precisely what is difficult to do for a single country; that is, data can be obtained for (different countries at) widely different stages of development. Unless we take the view that absolutely nothing can be learned about one country from studying another country, there is perhaps something to be obtained from such an analysis.

One of the earliest examples of a cross-section analysis is that of Paukert [1973]. Fifty-six countries were classified into different income categories according to their per capita GDP in 1965, in U.S. dollars. Inequality was measured by the Gini coefficient. Table 7.1 presents some of the Paukert findings: The table reveals two things. First, there appears to be a relationship between inequality and GDP of the kind predicted by Oshima and Kuznets. At least, this is certainly the case once the data are aggregated by income category, as we have done in the second column of Table 7.1. This relationship suggests that the broad tendencies described earlier in this section do work, *on average*, across countries and over time in the development of each country. However—and this is the second feature—the variation *within* a particular category is certainly far from negligible. The third column in Table 7.1 presents the highs and lows for the Gini coefficient among countries in each category. A quick glance at this table certainly dispels the notion that the inverted-U is inevitable in the history of each country's development.[1]

---

[1] The third column does not, of course, provide a precise sense of the variation within income categories. However, a more careful analysis only strengthens our conclusions. For instance, Fields [1980, p. 69] regressed the Gini coefficient on per capita GDP (with exactly the same data set), with a squared entry on GDP as well, to capture the nonlinearities of the inverted-U. In turns out that these entries only "explain" 22% of the total variation in the Gini coefficient.

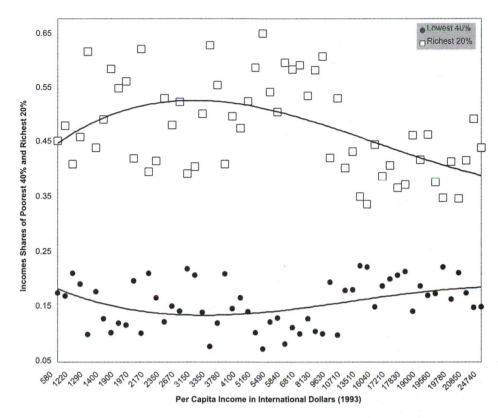

Figure 7.1. *The inverted-U hypothesis seen in the data. Source: Deininger and Squire [1996a].*

The use of a larger data set corroborates the Paukert observations. Consider, for instance, Figure 7.1 (which reproduces Figure 2.6 in Chapter 2). This diagram uses cross-sectional data[2] to show the possibility of an inverted-U. I have made no attempt to control for countries or even years for which the data are available (which we discuss more in the following text). This is a simple plot of the latest years for which country-level data on inequality are available. Note how the share of the richest 20% of the population rises and then falls as we move over countries with different per capita incomes. Exactly the opposite happens with the income share of the poorest 40% of the population. Thus at some very crude cross-sectional level, the inverted-U hypothesis has some foundation.

Cross-sectional regressions appear to support the same pattern. Consider, for instance, the study by Ahluwalia [1976], which analyzed a sample of sixty countries: forty developing, fourteen developed, and six socialist, with GNP figures measured in U.S. dollars at 1970 prices. Quite aware that summary measures of inequality might play nasty tricks (such as those discussed at

[2] For a description of this dataset, see Deininger and Squire [1996a].

Table 7.2. Test of the Kuznets inverted-U hypothesis.

Income share	Constant	y	y^2	Socialist dummy	R^2
Top 20%	−57.58 (2.11)	89.95 (4.48)	−17.56 (4.88)	−20.15 (6.83)	0.58
Middle 40%	87.03 (4.81)	−45.59 (3.43)	9.25 (3.88)	8.21 (4.20)	0.47
Lowest 20%	27.31 (4.93)	−16.97 (3.71)	3.06 (3.74)	5.54 (8.28)	0.54

Source: Ahluwalia [1976].
Note: Figures in parentheses denote t values.

the end of Chapter 6), Ahluwalia divided the population of each country in the sample into five quintiles, running from the 20% of the population with the lowest income share to the quintile with the highest income share. This way it was possible to keep track of the entire income distribution. For each quintile, Ahluwalia ran the regression

$$(7.1) \qquad s_i = A + by + cy^2 + D + \text{error},$$

where s_i is the income share of the ith quintile, y is the logarithm of per capita GNP, D is a dummy variable that takes the value 1 if the country in question is socialist, and 0 otherwise,[3] and A, b, and c are coefficients to be estimated from the regression.

Why do both y and y^2 enter into the regression? The reason is simple: by restricting the regression to include only y as an explanatory variable, it is not possible to test for the presence of a U shape, inverted or otherwise. A linear regression is incapable of allowing for directional changes. In contrast, the inclusion of the squared term permits a fit that changes direction (e.g., permits inequality to first rise and then fall as income increases). By drawing several graphs, you can convince yourself that a U shape can only occur if b and c are of different signs. For instance, if $b > 0$ and $c < 0$, then the shape that results is precisely a inverted-U. On the other hand, if $b < 0$ and $c > 0$, the graph must take the form of an "upright-U."

This tells us what to look for. Recall that the income share of the lowest quintile is *negatively* related to inequality. It follows that if the Oshima–Kuznets hypothesis is correct, the regressed curve for the lowest quintiles should take the form of an upright-U; that is, the estimated b should be negative and the estimated c should be positive. On the other hand, exactly the opposite signs should hold for the coefficients pertaining to the highest quintile. Table 7.2 summarizes the findings.

---

[3] The use of a dummy variable for socialism is based on the possibility that there might be systematic structural differences between socialist and nonsocialist countries, so inequality data from these two sets of countries should not be unconditionally pooled.

Ahluwalia's regressions get the expected results, as the summary in Table 7.2 reveals. For all quintiles but the highest, income share tends to fall initially with a rise in per capita GNP and then rises beyond a certain point. This statement is deduced from the fact that the estimated value of b is negative in all these cases, whereas that of c is positive. For the topmost quintile, the pattern is just the opposite: with rising per capita income, income share first rises and then starts to fall. In *all* cases, the regression coefficients turn out to be statistically significant (see Appendix 2 for a discussion of this concept).[4] There seems to be an inverted-U hidden in the cross section, or is there?

Words of caution

The literature on the inverted-U hypothesis resembles, to some extent, the search for the Holy Grail; that is, the search for some evidence that supports an implacable law of development.[5] There is some evidence that an inverted-U relationship is present in the cross section of the world income distribution, but there are reasons to be skeptical of these positive findings.

For one thing, the data exhibit too much variation to support some iron-clad law of economic change. We already noted this in our discussion of Paukert's [1973] study. Similar variation can be seen by simply eyeballing the data points arrayed in Figure 7.1. Per capita income alone can "explain" some, but not all and not even half, the overall observed variations in inequality from country to country. Of course, this still does not rule out the possibility that, left to itself, a country might follow the inverted-U, but there are many other differences, such as those in government policy, that get in the way. Hence, this sort of criticism rules out the *inevitability* of the inverted-U, but allows for the possibility of a bias in that direction.

Second, the inverted-U is, to some extent, an artifact of the statistical methodology that is used in inequality measurement. To see this, consider the following example adapted from Fields [1980]. Suppose that a society is composed of five individuals, who are divided between an agricultural sector and an industrial sector. Income in the agricultural sector is 100 and in the industrial sector it is 200. Initially suppose that everybody is in the agricultural sector, so that the income distribution is (100, 100, 100, 100, 100). Now suppose that development proceeds by a transfer of individuals from agriculture to industry. The income distribution will progressively see the appearance of more 200s [e.g., (100, 100, 100, 200, 200)], until everybody is in the industrial sector.

---

[4] Although each of these regressions yields its own support for the inverted-U, the "turning point" at which inequality reaches a peak and then declines varies from quintile to quintile. The richest group appears to lose income share at relatively low levels of income. On the other hand, the poorest quintile does not start to gain until a high level of per capita income is reached.

[5] Other cross-section studies include Adelman and Morris [1973], Ahluwalia, Carter, and Chenery [1979], Bacha [1979], Papanek and Kyn [1986], Bourguignon and Morrisson [1989, 1990], and Anand and Kanbur [1993a, b].

This is a caricature of development, but not a bad one. As we will see in Chapter 10, much of the growth of developing countries can indeed be captured by shifts from low-income sectors such as agriculture to relatively high-income sectors such as industry. Now, if you did the problems at the end of Chapter 6, you know that the Lorenz curves cross all the way through this sectoral shift (except right at the beginning and at the end, when there is perfect equality), so we cannot say unambiguously that inequality has gone up or down in the intermediate stages. However, calculate the Gini coefficient of the various income distributions or the coefficient of variation and you will see that it rises and then falls. Yet for "most" of this process we have Lorenz crossings.

Studies that rely on aggregate measures of inequality may simply pick up these statistical effects; as far as "real inequality" is concerned, whatever that might mean, there may be very little to say. This reasoning is why a study such as Ahluwalia's, which distinguishes between the income shares accruing to different groups, is very useful and is not subject to this particular criticism (as the Paukert study might be).

Third, a regression of the form described in equation (7.1) is not the *only* functional form that can admit an inverted-U shape. For instance, what about the alternative specification

$$(7.2) \qquad\qquad s_i = A + by + c\frac{1}{y} + D + \text{error}$$

as adopted by Anand and Kanbur [1993a] or Deininger and Squire [1996b]? This is where economic theory should play an important role: by postulating a specific model that links income to inequality, we should be able to derive a regression equation from the model itself. Unfortunately, as we will see subsequently, there are plenty of theoretical reasons to expect connections between income and inequality, and each reason precipitates a different sort of relationship. Sorting out a functional form such as (7.1) from the form in (7.2) may require a model that is far too detailed and specific to be intuitively appealing or credible, yet the choice of functional form can matter, as Anand and Kanbur [1993a, b] correctly argued.

Time series

A deeper problem with cross-sectional studies is one we have already noted: by pooling different countries and running a regression, the implicit assumption is made that *all* countries have the *same* inequality–income relationship. That is, not only are they believed to follow the same qualitative pattern (such as an inverted-U), but the same *quantitative* pattern as well: the income–inequality curve is *the same curve* for all.

This notion is hard to swallow. Countries do differ in their structural parameters and some account should be taken of this. At the same time it is unclear how much one can do. The opposite extreme is to say that every country is (a priori) completely different: one country might have one sort of curve and the other might have another, and there is no relationship between the two. This amounts to saying that all countries should be studied separately and nothing is gained by pooling the data. This is a good idea if we have huge quantities of data for each country, but we do not. Income distribution data are hard to get, and if we try to go back a century or so as well, that leaves us with very few countries indeed. For instance, Lindert and Williamson [1985] put together some of what we know regarding intertemporal inequality movements in countries over fairly long horizons. They tracked inequality movements in some European countries and in the United States using data going back into the last century and earlier. For England the upward surge in inequality during the industrial revolution is clearly visible. Other countries were picked up at a later stage (for lack of earlier data) and show steadily declining inequality. The overall availability of data is quite sparse, though.

There is middle ground here. We might agree that countries are different, but that there is still *some* connection between their inequality–income curves. For instance, amend equation (7.2) to read

$$(7.3) \qquad \text{ineq}_{it} = A_i + b_i y_{it} + c_i \frac{1}{y_{it}} + \text{error},$$

where i now stands for country and t stands for time. Now if we allow A_i, b_i, and c_i to *all* vary across countries, we essentially give up the notion of any connection at all across countries (except for the hypothesis that the relationships all have the same general functional *form*).

However, there are other ways to approach this. We might suppose, for instance, that *incremental* income affects inequality in the same way across countries, so that b_i and c_i are all the same as we vary i, but that some countries have some separate structural reason for higher or lower inequality. This is the same as saying that the curves (by country) are all *parallel* to one another, shifted this way and that by country-specific dummy variables that move the intercept term of the estimated curves.

By way of illustration and motivation, consider what might be termed the *Latin effect*. Most of the high-inequality middle-income countries are Latin American! They are richer than countries such as India, Sri Lanka, or Bangladesh, but they are poorer than Korea or Taiwan. Both sets of Asian countries have lower inequalities than their Latin American counterparts. It may be that the inverted-U is just an artificial consequence of the Latin American countries sitting in the middle: hence the "Latin effect."

Put another way, is the inverted-U that we see in the cross section driven by the observation that middle-income countries have high inequality or that middle-income countries are largely Latin American and that Latin American countries have higher inequality for other, structural reasons? There might be traditional inequities in the holdings of land, little or no implementation of minimum wage laws (often due to high inflation), and government policy that is insensitive to considerations of inequality. With large numbers, we might expect these effects to go away, but the world is not *that* big a sample when each country counts as one unit.

One sensible way to check whether this assertion makes sense is to put in a *dummy variable* for Latin American countries in the regression. The estimated coefficient on the dummy can then be interpreted as the "importance" (as far as inequality is concerned) of being Latin American per se. Ahluwalia checked this in his 1976 study. However, once we open the door to the inclusion of a Latin dummy, we might as well try out dummies for each different country in the sample.

This method gives us some flexibility to allow for structural differences across countries. At the same time, it allows us to make use of a combined data set or "panel" (which can be used to estimate the common coefficients b and c more precisely). To be sure, all this posturing is of little use unless we have data for several countries over several points of time. The data set compiled by Deininger and Squire [1996a], which we've already used in part, does have this property, as well as several others that make it attractive.[6] The data set contains an average of more than six observations per country (at different points in time). Indeed, it contains fifty-eight countries with four or more observations each.

What happens if country-specific dummies are used for the intercept terms A_i? Deininger and Squire [1996b] found that the Kuznets inverted-U hypothesis largely vanishes. The coefficients b and c in that regression are now the wrong signs for an inverted-U, and indeed, the coefficients are not significant. This suggests that structural differences across countries or regions may create the illusion of an inverted-U, when indeed there is no such relationship in reality.

When countries are examined separately, there is some evidence of a *direct* U-shaped relationship among countries with a long series of data; this is true of the United States, the United Kingdom, and India.[7] For those nine countries for which an inverted-U can be found, the findings appear to be

---

[6] The authors adopted three sets of requirements to admit different surveys into their data set: observations must be based on household surveys (rather than national accounts), on comprehensive coverage of the population, and on comprehensive coverage of income sources. See Deininger and Squire [1996a] for more details.

[7] The observation that the United Kingdom shows a "positive U" rather than an inverted one does not contradict the findings of Lindert and Williamson [1985], cited earlier. The data used in the Deininger–Squire study are all "modern": they began in the 1960s. The recent upsurge in inequality in the United States and the United Kingdom is an issue to which we briefly return when we discuss international trade policy; see Chapter 17.

extremely sensitive to the use of outlier data or recent structural changes: the authors observe that Mexico, Trinidad, and the Philippines are probably the only three countries that survive the inverted-U specification. In 80% of the sample, there is no significant relationship between inequality and income levels, at least at the 5% level (see Appendix 2).

Fields and Jakubson [1994] were the first to analyze the sort of question that Deininger and Squire take up, but their data set is somewhat more limited: there are only 35 countries, but many have several years of inequality data. With country-specific dummies for the intercept term (country fixed effects), they examined the data allowing for parallel shifts across countries in the inequality–income relationship. Their findings are very similar to those of Deininger and Squire, and cast further doubt on the existence of an inverted-U shape. In their view, if any average conclusion can be drawn, it is that inequality falls over the course of development, at least over the course of twentieth-century development (Fields [1994]).

7.2.3. Income and inequality: Uneven and compensatory changes

Types of income growth

It should be quite clear from the preceding discussion that income and inequality do not bear a simple relationship to each other. When a country experiences an increase in per capita income, the change might stem roughly from three sources. The first—and the most placid—consists of those changes that occur on an everyday basis: people accumulate wealth, acquire skills, exhibit steady gains in work productivity, and so on. Think of this as some steady sequence of 2 or 3% annual raises that you might receive at work, as well as gradual increases in your capital income stemming from the accumulation of wealth.

The second source of change is inherently uneven: some sector (such as engineering, software design, or accounting) takes off, and there is a frenetic increase in demand for individuals with these skills. The economy as a whole registers growth, of course, but this growth is highly concentrated in a relatively small number of sectors. Think of these growth spurts as the initial movements in a single lane of Hirschman's tunnel: these spurts are intrinsically inequality *creating*.

Finally, there are those changes that are "compensatory" to the second: as the growth spurt manifests itself in high incomes in some sectors, the incomes spread through the economy as demands for all sorts of other goods and services rise. Engineers buy houses, software engineers buy cars, and even accountants go on vacations. Alternatively, it may be that more and more people acquire the skills that are currently in demand, tempering the rates of return to such skills and at the same time spreading the income gains more evenly through society.

First uneven, then compensatory?

At any point in time, it is likely that some combination of all three phenomena is at work. The inverted-U would be a theoretical possibility if it is more likely that uneven changes occur at low levels of income, whereas compensatory changes occur at higher levels of income. Consider the following arguments in favor of this point of view:

(1) A basic feature of economic development is that it involves large transfers of people from relatively poor to relatively advanced sectors of the economy. In Chapter 10, we will have more to say about the "dual economy," where economically backward and progressive sectors coexist and development proceeds by the advanced sector feeding on the backward sector for resources to propel its own growth. However, it should be quite clear that economic development, viewed in this way, cannot be evenly spread across the entire population at any one point in time. Initially only a few people get access to the progressive or modern sector. This view also suggests that developed countries that have completed this transition from "old" to "new" sectors should exhibit less inequality than the developing countries that are in the middle of the transition process, where individuals are in both sectors. This argument suggests that change is first uneven and then compensatory.

(2) Technical progress initially benefits the (relatively) small industrial sector. Modern, labor-saving methods of farming in the developed countries, in contrast, are less applicable to agricultural economies that have a large number of people in the rural sector. It follows that developing countries should have higher inequality, with technical progress benefiting only a fraction of the economy: those people in the industrial sector. Again, to the extent that low incomes are connected, on average, to a smaller number of individuals in the industrial sector, technical progress is likely to have a more uneven character at low levels of income.

(3) There are other ways in which technical progress can be inequality enhancing in developing countries. It is possible to argue that technical progress is initially biased against unskilled labor and tends to drive down these wages. These skill differentials are ultimately compensated for by the growing educational status of the labor force, but this is a slower process. When it does occur, though, inequality tends to decline.

(4) Even without the biases of technical progress, industrialization itself brings enormous profits to a minority that possess the financial endowments and entrepreneurial drive to take advantage of the new opportunities that open up. It is natural to imagine that these gains ultimately find their way

to everybody, as the increased demand for labor drives up wage rates. However, the emphasis is on the word "ultimately": for many developing countries, labor is in surplus, so that wages do not rise right away, and laws that protect labor are either absent or difficult to implement.

Such changes may well create a situation in which inequality first rises and then falls in the course of development. Moreover, the particular sources of unevenness that are identified are very basic indeed. Agriculture and industry, unskilled and skilled: these dichotomous categories are likely to be affected very differently by the growth process. Thus it is not unlikely that some subset or combination of the above-mentioned factors might explain inequality differences across developing and developed countries, but to go from this observation to one that states that each country *must* travel through an inverted-U path is a leap of faith. After all, uneven (and compensatory) changes might occur not only under these situations, but in others as well. Thus it is possible for all countries to go through alternating cycles of increasing and decreasing inequality, depending on the character of its growth path at different levels of income. The complexity of, and variation in these paths (witness the recent upsurge in inequality in the United States) can leave simplistic theories such as the inverted-U hypothesis without much explanatory power at all.

7.2.4. Inequality, savings, income, and growth

Introduction

A good instance of the difficulty in making a connection between inequality and income is given by the relationship between inequality and the overall rate of savings. If you've read Chapter 3 carefully, you will see right away that this is an important question. The rate of savings affects the long-run level of per capita income and, in many cases, the rate of growth of the economy. Thus the relationship between inequality and savings creates an additional channel through which inequality interacts with income and growth in income.

The political force of the arguments presented here are also not to be taken lightly. The view that moderate or high inequalities in income distribution concentrate money in the hands of those who are willing to save, accumulate, and invest, thereby boosting the growth rate, has been used more than once to justify (or lobby for) a hands-off approach by government in matters pertaining to redistributive taxation. However, there are opposing views as well, arguing that a certain degree of redistribution can actually enhance savings and push up growth rates.

To focus our study, use the following example. Suppose that we randomly select two people from a society where assets are distributed unequally. Consider two profiles: Rohini works as a high-ranking executive in a major firm and is paid well by the standards of a developing country. Suppose that her income is $55,000 per year. Paulo, in the same country, works as a manual laborer in a construction company. His income might still be high compared to the average income in that country, but it is lower than that of Rohini: say $5,000 per year. Now carry out the following thought experiment. Invent two identical Associate Professors at the local university of the city where Rohini and Paulo live—call them Thompson and Thompson—and provide them with an income of $30,000 each. With a click of your fingers, bring Thompson and Thompson into existence and remove Rohini and Paulo from the face of the universe. What are the effects of this change on overall savings rates?

Of course Rohini and Paulo consume and save different amounts, and these in turn are different from the amounts consumed and saved by the Thompsons. With all the different incomes involved, how could we have expected otherwise? However, what about *overall* consumption and savings in the Rohini–Paulo world, as compared with the world of the Thompsons? [Of course, the fact that Rohini and Paulo (and the Thompsons) get to consume different amounts may be of normative interest in itself, but we have discussed that already and this is not what we are after in this section.] Observe that once the Thompsons come into existence, they may be consuming exactly the average of what Rohini and Paulo did, or more, or less. What criteria should we use to predict the final change?

Marginal savings rates

This discussion forces us to look a little deeper. We must study, not the *total* savings generated by various individuals, but their *marginal* savings behavior. Figure 7.2 illustrates this. The basic argument is no different from

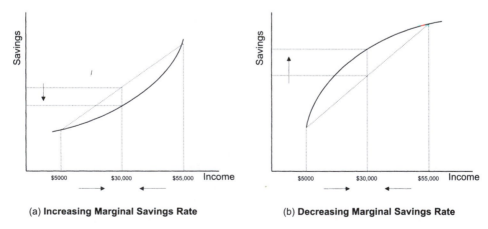

(a) **Increasing Marginal Savings Rate**   (b) **Decreasing Marginal Savings Rate**

Figure 7.2. The savings function and marginal savings behavior.

the many different examples of reasoning you have already encountered in economics courses, and there are more to come in this book. Suppose that as income increases, the marginal savings rate increases (consult Figure 7.2a). In that case, if we were to transfer a dollar of income from a poor person to a rich person, *more* of that dollar would now be saved as a result of the transfer. Exactly the opposite conclusion would obtain if less money is saved out of the marginal dollar as income increases (Figure 7.2b). Just to make sure we see this, let us apply the case of Figure 7.2b to Rohini, Paulo, and the Thompsons.

Note that the *average* savings generated by Rohini and Paulo may be found by connecting the points on the graph that represent their individual savings–income configuration, and then looking at the savings represented by the halfway point on this line. Now, the *income* represented by this halfway point is exactly $30,000, the income of each of the Thompsons. What does a Thompson save? The answer is found by reading up to the savings graph from this income point. You can see very clearly that the savings of one of the two identical Thompsons is higher than the average generated by Rohini and Paulo. The answer then is that if the income–savings relationship looks like that in Figure 7.2b, a reduction in inequality will *increase* the volume of savings in the economy. Convince yourself that this graphical technique is no different from the "marginal dollar" argument used in the previous paragraph.

Likewise, if the savings function has the shape of Figure 7.2a, a reduction in inequality depresses the savings rate in the economy. Finally, if marginal savings rates are unaffected by income, so that the savings function is a straight line, then a change in inequality has *no effect* on economywide savings at all.

The preceding arguments, by the way, constitute a good example of what economic theory has to teach us. Note that so far, we have not arrived at any simple answer regarding inequality and savings. In this sense we have learned nothing, yet we have a better idea of *what to look for* as a guidepost to the answer: the behavior of individual savings as income changes. By shifting the context of the search in this manner, we know exactly the kind of question we must ask next or (for empirical work) the sort of data that we must search for as a clue to the final answer. In this sense we *have* learned something.

We must ask, therefore, How does savings change with income? If we graph savings as a function of individual income, are we likely to get the shape of Figure 7.2a or that of Figure 7.2b? Alternatively, is the true picture more complicated than either of these?

There are several factors to be considered before we can come to a final judgment. Consider, for instance:

Subsistence needs: At the foundation of our economic lives is our need for food, clothing, and shelter. For the fortunate minority of the industrialized world, these foundations are not often a concern. For millions of individuals in developing countries, however, such considerations overwhelmingly dictate current expenditure. Although everyone would like to save for the future, for many the needs of the present prevent them from doing so. The poor may not be able to afford savings, on the average or at the margin.

Conspicuous consumption: At the other end of the spectrum are the ultra-rich in developing countries. Eager to attain the consumption levels of the rich the world over, their own consumptions are pushed to high levels. This is not to say that the ultra-rich do not themselves save, and in larger quantities than their less well-off counterparts. The point is that their *average rate* of savings may well be low and so is their propensity to save out of a marginal increase in income.

Aspirations and savings: The desire to imitate and attain the high consumption levels of the industrially developed world has often been criticized as an insult to one's "traditional" ways of life and as aping the customs of the "Western World." There is, however, nothing that is intrinsically antitraditional or Western about economic well-being, and striving for economic self-betterment is a large part of what we are all about. Note, moreover, that such economic yardsticks spring equally from invidious comparisons with one's own fellow citizens as with the standards set by industrialized economies.

For no group of people is this more true than those who are out of poverty, yet a substantial distance away from the economic comforts enjoyed by the very rich. This group includes not only our common conception of the "middle class," but perhaps people poorer than that—individuals and families whose behaviors are molded by their *aspirations* to a better economic life. More often than not, these aspirations are unselfishly long term: the people in this group are building the lives of their children and grandchildren. Such individuals typically save large fractions of their income, both on average and at the margin.

What emerges from this discussion, then, is not a clean picture, but nevertheless a provocative one for our purposes. Figure 7.3 attempts to summarize these factors in the form of a single diagram relating savings to income. It is more complicated than Figure 7.2. As individual income increases, total savings are initially zero or even negative. At some break-even point, savings turn positive and rise thereafter. In this region, the picture might locally have the shape of Figure 7.2a, because each marginal dollar of income earned is plowed to a larger and larger extent into savings. This is the income zone where economic aspirations not only matter (they surely matter for everyone), but can be pursued. Finally, as we enter regions of high income, even though *total* savings continues to rise, the *marginal* savings rate

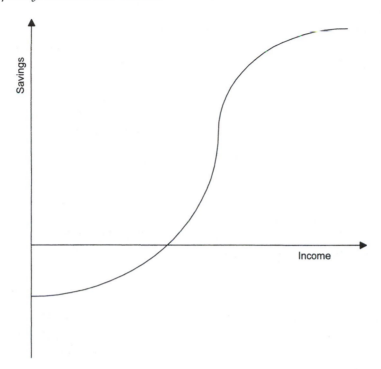

Figure 7.3. *Savings and income: a more detailed view.*

starts to decline, because the aspiration effect wears thin on the already rich. This section of the diagram looks locally like Figure 7.2b.

We may draw two implications of great importance from these observations.

Effect of inequality on savings and growth

The effect of a reduction in income inequality on the rate of savings, and therefore on the rate of growth, is likely to be complex. In an extremely poor country, redistributive policies may bring down the rate of savings and therefore the rate of growth in the medium or even long run. To see this, refer again to the initial shape of Figure 7.3 (or to Figure 7.2a). A redistribution in this region brings down the national savings rate. Without redistribution, there is a fraction of the population (however small) who possess the desire *and* the means to accumulate wealth. *With* redistribution, no person saves anything of any significance.

One is caught here in a devastating double bind. The deprivation and inequality of poor societies quite understandably provokes egalitarian policies. These very policies, however, might bring down the rate of savings and consequently the rate of growth.

What are we to make of this observation from a *normative* point of view? In the interests of growth, can we recommend inegalitarian policies? The choice is difficult, but it is all the more reason to study the alternatives more clearly! Indeed, as you work your way through this book, you will come across many other aspects of the interaction between inequality and development in poor societies, some of which necessitate hard policy choices.

For medium-income countries, the story may well be dramatically different. Redistributive policies may generate a surge of savings at the national level, because they create a large and ambitious middle class with international aspirations. This situation is captured by the later section of Figure 7.3 (or by Figure 7.2b). A redistribution in this section raises the average savings rate, because the relatively low savings rates of the poor (who can't afford to save) and the rich (who don't need to save) are transformed into the high savings of those with aspirations.

From income and savings to the evolution of inequality

Next, consider the *effect of savings behavior on the evolution of economic inequality*. Think of one isolated society and the evolution of inequality within that society or, if you like, adopt the interpretation that we are studying world inequality as a whole. As discussed previously, individuals in this society all aspire to the standards set by society in general, *but these standards, too, are evolving*. Observe, now, that depending on the initial historical conditions of economic inequality, society is perfectly capable of evolving into two very different long-run patterns. If inequality is low to begin with, these low levels of inequality may be sustainable over time. When neither the standards of living nor the underlying incomes (or wealths) are too heterogeneous, we expect a commonality of savings behavior which has the effect of keeping different economic groups in the society close together over time.[8]

On the other hand, if initial inequalities are high, they may be preserved or widened over time. The key to understanding the process is to see that for many groups in society, there is now a substantial difference between their notions of a *desired* standard of living and their *actual* standard of living. As discussed already, this has an effect on savings behavior. Imagine for simplicity that the desired standard is set by the richest groups in the society.[9] Figure 7.4 describes how savings behavior might be affected as individual income drops below the income deemed necessary to achieve the desired standard of living. The horizontal axis measures the shortfall of income from

[8] Remember, though, that we are dealing with only *one* aspect of an incredibly complicated scenario. There are many other factors that affect the evolution of economic inequality, and we will learn more about them as we progress through this book. The foregoing description is not to be taken literally, but taken only as a way to capture the effects of one (very important) set of factors.

[9] Desired standards may well be different depending on existing levels of income, but we avoid these complications here.

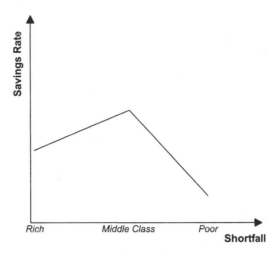

Figure 7.4. Desired standards of living, income, and
savings rates.

the desired standard; the richest, by definition, are at zero. As the shortfall increases, aspirations are created, which initially raises the rate of savings for such income groups, but this effect cannot last forever. As the shortfall continues to increase, poorer groups find that a high savings rate is simply too costly in terms of the deleterious effects on their much-needed *current* consumption, and the savings rate starts to fall again, declining in all likelihood to a level below that of the very rich.

In contrast to the standard models of economic growth described in Chapter 3, savings behavior is not only determined by income but by income and aspirations, and the latter depend on existing inequalities of income and wealth. Thus the relatively poor might find themselves in a self-sustaining low-income trap, whereas the middle class grows more rapidly than either rich or poor. Thus we might observe high mobility between rich and middle-income groups, while an insurmountable wall builds up between these groups and the poor.

This story is simplified to a large extent, but it teaches us a remarkable truth. The *very same* society may behave in completely different ways, depending on initial historical developments. Of course, this is true if history changes technology or preferences, but in this case neither has happened. In both cases we are dealing with exactly the same groups of people, whose overall preference structure is no different in the two scenarios, and nowhere in our analysis did we rely on technological differences.

The idea that historical circumstances shape the structure and course of a country's development, without recourse to explanations based on intrinsic differences (based on technology or preferences), is one that we have seen before. We will see it again, at various points in this book.

7.2.5. *Inequality, political redistribution, and growth*

In the previous section, we studied how inequality can affect growth via changes in aggregate savings. We noted that high inequalities can be harmful for growth if the middle class has a higher marginal savings rate than the either the rich or the poor.

A second connection between inequality and growth was highlighted in the work of Alesina and Rodrik [1994], Persson and Tabellini [1994], and others.[10] High economic inequality might retard economic growth by setting up political demands for redistribution. Now redistributions might take one of two broad forms. First, a policy might aim to redistribute *existing wealth* among the broader population. A good example of this is land reform. If land is held very unequally, the government may have the option to simply confiscate land from large landowners and redistribute the confiscated land among smaller peasants or landless laborers. Likewise, it is possible to have confiscatory taxes that transfer large quantities of nonland wealth to the government, which are then redistributed to the poor.

It goes without saying that the creation and implementation of such policies require extraordinary political will, as well as the availability of data on which to base such policies. Elected government officials with large land holdings are not uncommon, and even if they were uncommon, large landowners often act as vote banks, which swing the votes of an entire village or even a group of villages. In such situations, the enactment of a comprehensive land reform that would alleviate inequality becomes a very difficult proposition indeed.

Even if the political will did exist, there are the almost insuperable difficulties of implementation. To redistribute large quantities of wealth, for instance, it is necessary to know *who* has the wealth. There exist enormous quantities of wealth that are not even subject to taxes, simply because the information base required to implement such taxes is nonexistent. Even when wealth takes the form of land, which is arguably highly observable, it is difficult to implement ownership ceilings. As a large and powerful landowner, I could parcel out my holdings in the names of various members of my family, so that each parcel fell below the legally imposed ceiling.

Faced with these difficulties, most governments resort to redistributive policies that take an entirely different route: they tax *increments* to the stock of wealth, rather than the existing wealth base. Thus marginal rates of tax on high income tend to be on the high side, there are excise duties and sales taxes on the purchase of various products, and business profits are taxed as well. These taxes, *imposed as they are on the margin*, tend to bring down the rate of investment and therefore the rate of economic growth.

---

[10] See, for example, Bertola [1993], Perotti [1992], and Somanathan [1995].

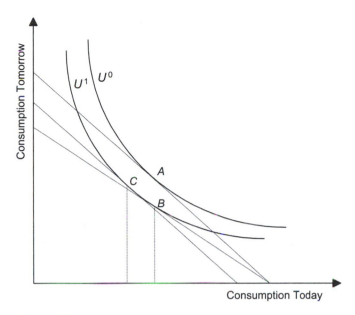

Figure 7.5. *Lump-sum taxes versus taxes on investment returns.*

Understanding why investment might be depressed with "taxes on the margin" (rather than with lump-sum taxes to redistribute existing wealth) is an exercise in elementary economic theory. Figure 7.5 depicts an individual who would like to allocate his existing wealth to consumption in two periods. Consumption "tomorrow" is achieved by (partially) desisting from consuming today and investing the released funds at a given rate of return.

Point A in Figure 7.5 depicts our person at the pre-tax level of utility (this is given by the indifference curve U^0). Now suppose that the government wishes to redistribute some of the purchasing power of this individual to other members of the society. To do this, suppose that a tax is imposed on the return to investment. This has the effect of swiveling the rate-of-return line downward, as shown in the diagram, so that our person is now at point B on indifference curve U^1.

Now consider a lump-sum tax on this individual that pulls her down to exactly the same indifference curve U^1. Of course, this means (by definition) that she will be indifferent between the two systems of taxation. However, observe that in this case, she cuts back more strongly on current consumption (compare point C to point B). Put another way, the tax on the rate of return reduces savings relative to the lump-sum tax. The reason is simple. Both lump-sum taxes and (investment) income taxes have income effects that tend to reduce consumption. However, the (investment) income tax has an additional "price effect" that tends to lower the rate of saving and investment.

In this way, high levels of inequality may retard economic growth, because such inequalities create a political demand for redistribution that can only be met by imposing taxes on *increments* to wealth, and not existing wealth. Such taxes may reduce the incentive to accumulate wealth, and therefore the rate of economic growth.

7.2.6. *Inequality and growth: Evidence*

Does initial inequality retard growth? Empirical evidence on this matter is relatively hard to come by. The villain, once again, is lack of adequate data. The use of *contemporaneous* data on inequality and growth is not very meaningful because we run into severe problems of endogeneity. After all, in the theoretical discussions so far (and in the discussions to follow), we have been careful to note that the connections, if any, can be two-way in nature. Thus we need data on *inequality* at the *start* of a relatively long time period, followed by growth figures for the subsequent period.

Then again, what is a good proxy for initial inequality? We would like to get a handle on inequalities in *wealth* or assets at the beginning of the time period, but data on these are notoriously hard to come by. One proxy for wealth inequality is the inequality of *income* at that time, but we must recognize that this is an imperfect proxy. Wealth inequalities at some date are, in a sense, the sum total of all income inequalities up to that date, and there is no reason why the last of these inequalities should adequately mirror the history of all its predecessors.

Another proxy for wealth inequality is the inequality in some (relatively) easy-to-observe asset, such as land. Data on land inequality are easier to come by, although they are plagued with problems of their own. Of these problems, the most serious is the distortion created in countries that are subject to a land reform measure through the imposition of land ceilings. In such countries land belonging to a single individual or household may be held under a variety of names, thus creating the illusion of lower inequality than there actually is. Aside from this problem, land inequality can only be a good proxy for overall inequality in wealth if agriculture is either significantly important in the economy (for the beginning of the time period under consideration), or at the very least, has been of significant importance in the recent past. Fortunately for our purposes, this is a condition that is adequately satisfied by developing countries.

Alesina and Rodrik [1994] regressed per capita income growth over the period 1960–85 on a variety of independent variables, such as initial per capita income and a measure of initial human capital. (We already encountered this sort of exercise in Chapter 4, where we discussed Barro's [1991] study). Indeed, as far as these variables are considered, Alesina and Rodrik

Table 7.3. Initial inequality and subsequent growth.

	Effect on per capita growth, 1960–85		
	Version 1	Version 2	Version 3
Constant	6.22 (4.69)	6.24 (4.63)	6.21 (4.61)
GDP60	−0.38 (3.25)	−0.39 (3.06)	−0.38 (2.95)
Prim60	2.66 (2.66)	2.62 (2.53)	2.65 (2.56)
Gini60	−3.47 (1.82)	−3.45 (1.79)	−3.47 (1.80)
LandGini	−5.23 (4.38)	−5.24 (4.32)	−5.21 (4.19)
Dem*LGini		0.12 (0.12)	
Dem			0.02 (0.05)

Source: Alesina and Rodrik [1994].
Note: Figures in parentheses denote *t* values.

used the same data as Barro. In addition, they included data on initial inequality of income and initial inequality of land.[11]

Their regression results indicated a substantial negative relationship between initial inequality and subsequent growth. Particularly strong was the influence of the Gini coefficient that represents the initial inequality in *land* holdings. Their results suggested that an increase in the land Gini coefficient by 1 standard deviation (which is only an increase of 0.16 in this case) would decrease subsequent economic growth by as much as 0.8 percentage points per year. Table 7.3 summarizes the results of some of the regressions using Gini coefficients for initial land distributions.

The independent variables are per capita income in 1960 (GDP60), primary enrollment rates in 1960 (Prim60), the Gini coefficient on income in 1960,[12] the initial Gini coefficient for land distribution (LandGini), and a dummy variable for democracy (Dem).

The first regression pools all countries for which data are available without regard to their political system. Note that the Gini coefficient for land is especially significant and negative (the Gini coefficient on initial income is less so; it is only significant at the 10% level). It is also of interest to note, in passing, that the original Barro findings continue to be upheld: initial per capita income enters negatively, whereas the human capital measure is positive.

These results are unaltered once we allow for structural differences across democratic and nondemocratic political systems. What is more, the democracy dummy is insignificant both by itself (version 3) and when interacted

[11] The income inequality data are taken from Jain [1975] and Fields [1989]. The land distribution data are drawn from Taylor and Hudson [1972].

[12] The income inequality data present some problems, because the earliest available data are for well after 1960, which creates endogeneity problems. Alesina and Rodrik corrected for this by instrumenting for initial income inequality and by running regressions for the shorter period 1970–85.

with the Gini coefficient on land (version 2). It does appear that political systems play little role in this relationship.

The Alesina–Rodrik findings are confirmed with the use of a more comprehensive data set in Deininger and Squire [1996b]. Initial land inequality is more significant than initial income inequality and stays that way even under several variations on the basic regression exercise (such as the use of regional dummies, which you recall, wrecked the Kuznets inverted-U hypothesis).[13] The insignificance of the political system also holds up under the Deininger–Squire investigation.

Viewed in this light, it is perhaps no surprise that East Asian countries such as Korea and Taiwan have some of the highest rates of investment in the world. Early land reforms in these countries placed them among the lowest in land inequalities, and surely must have promoted economic inequality overall, given the importance of agriculture in all developing countries around 1960. The Gini coefficients for land distribution in Korea and Taiwan were 0.34 and 0.31 in 1960, and these numbers are very low even by relatively moderate Asian standards. For instance, for India and the Philippines, the corresponding numbers are well over 0.5, and for Latin America, the Gini coefficient skyrockets to well above 0.8 for countries such as Brazil and Argentina.

There seems to be little doubt, then, that there is a strong and negative relationship between initial wealth inequality (as proxied by the distribution of land, anyway) and subsequent economic growth. The question is, What drives this relationship? Might it be that lower inequality encourages savings and investment, leading to higher rates of growth along the lines discussed in Section 7.2.4, or is it that the political redistribution effect is at work?

It is hard to answer these questions at the level of existing data. For instance, we might argue, as Deininger and Squire [1996b] did, that the redistribution explanation is unsupported by the regression because the democracy dummy is insignificant. After all, the political demands for redistribution should matter more in a democracy, but it is unclear whether this is necessarily the case: dictators like to remain in power just as much as democratic governments do, and they might react to high inequality with high taxes at the margin, just as a democratic government might.

Thus we must be content (for now) with the intriguing possibility that there might be a robust and negative *empirical* relationship between inequality and subsequent growth.[14] What drives this relationship is still very much an open question, but hopefully this whets our appetite to learn some more

---

[13] The problem with the Deininger–Squire regressions is that it includes investment rates as an independent variable, which has endogeneity problems. On the other hand, the Alesina–Rodrik regressions do not have regional dummies.

[14] Note that even this assertion requires more careful investigation; for instance, by using regional dummies and dropping investment from the right-hand side of the Deininger–Squire regressions.

about possible connections between inequality and development. We turn now to some other aspects of this relationship.[15]

7.2.7. Inequality and demand composition

It is a simple truth that income determines not only the *level* of consumption, but also its pattern or *composition*. Perhaps the most important example of this shifting composition is the falling share of food items in consumption as income rises. The needs for food, clothing, and shelter are fundamental and, therefore, absolutely dominant at low levels of income. As income changes, a host of new consumption possibilities open up and the budget share of these new commodities begins to rise.

At the same time, the overall pattern of expenditure in a society has implications for the distribution of income. The different products that are demanded by consumers must be produced and supplied. In general, these products set up *derived demands* for factors of production, and so influence the division of payments into wages (for unskilled and different grades of skilled labor), returns on capital equipment, rents on properties, and so on. In this way, the composition of product demand influences the functional distribution of income and (via the ownership of these factors of production) the personal distribution of income. Figure 7.6 summarizes this feedback.[16]

This feedback phenomenon leads naturally to the question of whether historical inequalities perpetuate themselves in the longer run. The answer to this question is complex, but a few suggestions emerge from the preceding discussion. As an example, imagine that there are only two inputs of production—capital and labor—and two goods that are produced—a mass consumption good and a luxury good. Suppose everyone owns the same amount of labor, but different amounts of capital. This means that some individuals (those with more capital) enjoy a larger income; the excess comes from returns to capital. Will these historically given inequalities die down over time, magnify themselves, or stay as they are?

In our example, the answer depends on demand patterns and on how these patterns translate into input demands. With a high degree of inequality to start with, the economy registers a proportionately larger demand for the luxury good. How does this translate into a derived demand for capital and labor? The answer depends on whether production of the luxury good is capital-intensive or labor-intensive (relative to the mass consumption good). If the former, then inequality begets inequality: the greater

---

[15] See also Chapter 13, where additional connections are explored in the specific context of poor economies.

[16] For a sample of the literature that studies inequality and product composition, see de Janvry and Sadoulet [1983], Murphy, Shleifer and Vishny [1989b], Baland and Ray [1991], and Mani [1997].

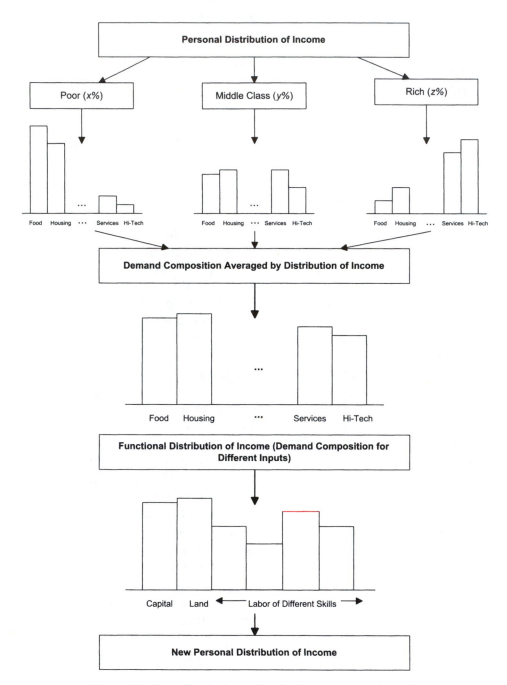

Figure 7.6. From distribution to distribution via product demand.

demand for the luxury good translates into relatively greater demand for capital, which raises the returns to capital and thereby maintains or magnifies the inequality that we started with. If the latter, then historical inequalities are self-correcting: inequality raises the demand for labor relative to capital, which leads to a reduction of inequality in the future.

As you can imagine, with many different commodities being produced and consumed, and with many different factors of production, our observations are nowhere near as clear-cut. However, a *method* suggests itself: study the commodity bundles consumed by different income groups and then see if the implied demands for factors lead to greater equality or not.

Here, as in the previous section, we see that historical differences yield the possibilities of different development experiences, *not because* of intrinsically different characteristics of a country's citizens, but because they react differently to different economic contexts. Indeed, the outcomes are not just found in persistently different economic inequalities: plenty of other things change. Each country will exhibit a marked difference in what it produces and consumes. To the extent that different commodities use capital to varying extents, there might be pronounced variations in the levels of per capita income and rates of growth as well. In particular, there is no reason to expect intercountry convergence when the dynamics of income distribution are taken into account.

Example 1. England and the United States presented an interesting contrast during the nineteenth century. Manufacturers in the United States were adept at mass production of many goods and turned out fairly sturdy versions of what, in England, was produced in high quality by skilled artisans. In the United States, the demand for such products was generated by a large middle class, which lacked the economic resources (and perhaps, also, the inclination) to generate demands for the skill-intensive, high quality, and certainly more expensive versions produced in England. The twist in the tale is that mass production also possibly ensured the existence of a large group of individuals—not so rich, not so poor—whose demands sustained mass production. In England, on the other hand, the production of skill-intensive artisan products certainly did not generate a middle class, thereby closing the circle.[17]

Example 2. As a leading example of how the internal dynamics of our process can be affected, consider the role of government. In the United States, government spending increased significantly during the two world wars and the Great Depression. Lindert and Williamson [1985] studied how the increase in government spending affected the demands for skilled vers usunskilled labor in the economy. They found that government services were

---

[17] Whether this circle was vicious or virtuous, I leave you to judge! For a discussion of product composition in England and the United States, see Rosenberg [1972] and Murphy, Shleifer, and Vishny [1989b].

significantly intensive in unskilled labor , whereas the composition of government purchases was not that different from the rest of the economy in its effects on the demand for labor skills. Indeed, an increase in the share of government employees in the labor force during this period is associated with a significant increase in equality in the United States over the same period.

These examples are related to the hypothesis of "trickle down," a phrase that has been bandied about not only in policy circles in developing countries, but in industrialized market economies such as the United States as well. The idea is simple: with enough growth and little intervention to correct income inequality, the fruits of economic development will eventually filter or trickle down to the poor, as the demands for what they (generally unskilled labor) can offer are magnified. Needless to say, this is a proposition that is far from established. As we have discussed, it is quite possible that better-off individuals in an unequal society perpetuate their own existence and relative standing. Not that this is achieved by deliberate unilateral action—individuals are generally way too small to affect the workings of the entire economy—rather, the rich might create demands for products, and therefore inputs, that only the rich can supply.

7.2.8. Inequality, capital markets, and development

The problem of collateral

We often take markets for granted. When we do our shopping at the grocery store, it is rarely the case (though it happens) that we, as consumers, take what we need and do not pay for it or that the shopkeeper takes our money and then refuses to give us what we bought. The grocery store functions because such situations are the exception rather than the rule. What makes them exceptions? One possible answer is that people are generally honest and will not cheat each other. To a large extent, this argument is correct, but it does not tell the whole story. Hidden in the background is an enormous amount of social conditioning that permits such simultaneous exchange, as well as a legal mechanism that encourages conformity to the social norm of exchange.

Social mechanisms (such as on-the-spot public disgrace) are far weaker when the acts of "buying" and "paying up" are separated in time. The perfect example of this is a loan, where money is advanced and must be repaid later. Everyday experience tells us that a potential borrower is screened much more thoroughly than a potential buyer. A borrower is typically screened for his or her ability to repay, as well as for past dealings, which signal not only ability but willingness to repay. We also know that defaults are often met by sanctions of various kinds. Nevertheless, if individuals can default on credit arrangements under the existing social and legal rules, then they well might.

This brings us to a statement of the obvious: markets cannot function unless there is a clear statement of the underlying social contract involved, *and a clear and well-defined mechanism for punishing deviations from the norm.* If I default on my credit card bill, I will be blacklisted on the computer of every credit rating organization and will not be able to use my credit card for a long time, longer than I might ever feel comfortable with. Hence I make every effort to avoid default. Likewise, a small farmer who seeks loans from a village moneylender worries about repayment because default may mean a closed door in the future. If the farmer has assets that the moneylender can make use of, there may even be collateral put up for the loan, which will be lost in the event of a default. In the same way, entire countries are "encouraged" to go on servicing past debts by the threat of sanctions on future loans or on trade relationships.

In Chapter 14, we will study such credit markets in detail. For now, the moral is very simple indeed: *what you have as collateral and the perceived extent to which you value the future relative to the present determine the degree to which you have access to the credit market.*

This moral has a striking corollary. In unequal societies, the poor may lack access to credit markets for precisely the reason that they lack collateral. To the extent that credit is necessary to (a) start a small business, (b) educate oneself or one's children, (c) buy inputs so that you can rent land and farm it, (d) smooth out consumption expenditures in a fluctuating environment, and a whole host of other things besides, the poor are shut out from (a), (b), (c), (d), and everything else that credit can nourish. (We are talking here of everyday activity, not the infrequent large loan to go to law school, or a mortgage on a house.) Note well that this shutout has *nothing* to do with the intrinsic characteristics of these individuals. They may be (and indeed are) just as honest as anyone else, but no bank or moneylender will bet money on it.

A missing or imperfect credit market for the poor is a fundamental characteristic of unequal societies. The macroeconomic implications can be quite severe, as the following simple model illustrates.[18]

An example

Imagine that I wish to become an entrepreneur and start a business. Suppose that I have personal assets worth $100,000. Unfortunately, the investment required to start up the business is $200,000. I must therefore obtain a loan. I can pledge these assets as collateral for the loan.

---

[18] The discussion that follows draws on ideas in Banerjee and Newman [1993] and Galor and Zeira [1993].

Table 7.4. Economic considerations underlying default.

Items	If I pay	If I default
Direct payment	220,000	0
Collateral loss	0	110,000
Jail	0	50,000
Seizure of profits	0	125,000
Total	220,000	285,000

Here is a description of the business. It entails setting up a small factory, which will hire fifty workers, who will be paid $5,000 each, and produce and sell widgets for a total revenue of $500,000. Imagine for simplicity that the lifetime of the business is one year. After this the loan must be repaid.

Here is a description of how the banks function. I already stated that I must put up my assets as collateral. The interest rate on the loan is 10%. If I do not repay my loan, then my assets will be seized by the bank. There is also a 50–50 chance that I will be caught, in which case I will go to jail. The expected monetary equivalent of this punishment is $50,000. In addition, my business profits for that year will be confiscated. My expected loss if this occurs is $(1/2) \times$ profits (where the 1/2 reflects the 50–50 chance of getting caught), which comes to $125,000. Of course, if I do not repay, I pocket the outstanding loan plus interest.

Faced with these pros and cons, I must decide whether or not to repay. Let us calculate the costs and benefits of repayment. Table 7.4 does this. It is easy to see that the costs of default outweigh the benefits in this example, so I will repay the loan.

What if I had only $20,000 to put up as collateral? In that case, by going through the same balance sheet as in Table 7.4, it is easy to see that the costs of default are now $197,000. This is smaller than the cost of repayment, so I will default.

This is, of course, a cartoon description of real-world calculations, but it is not a bad cartoon. For instance, we might argue that there are other costs of default, including a loss of future reputation, but there is nothing to prevent us from monetizing these costs as well and including them in the preceding calculations. Perhaps it will then be harder to default, but the qualitative message of the example is unaltered.[19]

The basic point of the example is that *credit markets might be shut down for individuals who have relatively small amounts of collateral*. This is true because

---

[19] Likewise, there are adjustments that can be made for innate honesty, in case you find this example alarmingly cynical. As described, I have not allowed for any qualms of conscience on the borrower's part, but as long as individuals are moved to *some* extent by the economic considerations described here, a variant of this example can easily be constructed to incorporate (a certain degree of) honesty.

these individuals cannot credibly convince their creditors that they will not default on their debt obligations.

Occupational choice and the credit constraint

The preceding illustration is meant to capture one way in which a missing market might influence economic outcomes; that is, by affecting the ability to freely choose occupations or investments, and thereby the evolution of inequality and output. To see how the example ties in with the broader picture, consider a very simple economy, with just three occupations: subsistence producer, industrial worker, and entrepreneur. We'll assume that neither subsistence producers nor industrial workers need any setup capital. Subsistence producers can produce some fixed amount z with their labor. An industrial worker can earn a wage w (the endogenous determination of w is a central concern in the model). An entrepreneur runs the sort of business that *hires* industrial workers, but the business requires startup capital, and this is where the credit market comes in.

In general, to be an entrepreneur, you have to qualify for a loan. Whether or not the loan is forthcoming depends on considerations exactly like those described in the preceding example. How much wealth is available for collateral? How profitable will the business be? What kind of punishments are available in the event of default? The maximum size of the loan will be limited by these factors.

Suppose that the startup cost of the business (e.g., the buying of plant and equipment) is given by the amount I. The business itself consists of hiring m industrial workers to produce an output q. The entrepreneur pays them a wage of w each. So profit is equal to $q - wm$. If the loan is repaid at interest rate r, then it is easy enough to figure out net profit: it is just $(q - wm) - (1 + r)I$.[20]

With this information in hand, we can easily figure out whether a person with some *given starting wealth* W will be granted a loan adequate enough for entrepreneurship. Suppose that you put your wealth W up as collateral. You then set up your factory and make profits. Now the time comes for you to repay $I(1 + r)$. You could try defaulting on the loan. Of course, you lose your collateral, an amount now worth $W(1 + r)$. You also face capture and punishment, but this is uncertain in a developing country (and often in developed countries too!). Let us summarize a long list of possibilities by saying that the *expected cost* of default is some fine (imprisonment, perhaps), denoted by F, and a fraction λ of the profits from your business. The fact that λ is only a fraction captures the fact that you may not be caught for

---

[20] This calculation presumes for simplicity that all individual economic occupations last only for one period. It is easy enough to extend this story by putting in many periods, but to make our main points there is no need to do so.

sure, and even if you are, it may not be possible for the lending authority to seize *all* your profits. Therefore, you *will* honor the loan if

$$I(1 + r) \leq W(1 + r) + F + \lambda\{q - mw(t)\},$$

and rearranging this, we obtain the requirement

(7.4)
$$W \geq I - \frac{F + \lambda\{q - mw(t)\}}{1 + r}.$$

The inequality (7.4) is fundamental to our understanding of the model. It tells us that banks or moneylenders will only advance loans to an individual whose initial wealth is "high enough," in the sense captured by (7.4). If initial wealth is lower, you cannot *credibly* convince the bank that you will repay your loan. *Individuals who start out with wealth lower than this critical level are, therefore, unable to be entrepreneurs whether they want to be or not.*

Note that the smaller are the values of F (the expected cost of imprisonment) and λ (the fraction of your business profits that the bank can appropriate[21]), the more stringent is the requirement of initial wealth. This makes sense. If it is very difficult to catch an offender, all that the bank has left to go on is the collateral that was put up in the first place. In the extreme case where both F and λ are zero, the credit market breaks down completely: all businesses will have to be financed from initial wealth. In terms of (7.4), the constraint reduces to $W \geq I$, but if you have that kind of wealth, you can finance your own investment.

Market conditions such as the going wage rate also determine access to the credit market. If wages are relatively low, the profits from entrepreneurship are high, and you would expect it to be easier to get a loan to go into business. Therefore, the minimum wealth threshold required to obtain a loan should decline.

This completes the description of the credit market, which is just a direct extension of our earlier example (with algebra instead of numbers).

Wealth distributions and equilibrium

Now we introduce the idea that at any date, wealth typically is unequally distributed in the economy. Think of wealth as bequests received from parents (or total assets carried over from the previous period). This distribution determines the fraction of people who have access to entrepreneurship; the remainder join the subsistence sector or become workers. These joint decisions then determine the wage rate in the economy at that date. Finally, new wealth is created from this process, we move to the next date, and the entire process repeats itself.

---

[21] This includes, of course, the probability of being caught at all.

In summary, we start with a given distribution of wealth in the economy, at time t. By figuring out how the endogenous variables in the economy (the wage rate in this case) are determined at time t, our model will track the economy into a *new* distribution of wealth at time $t + 1$. Thus we get an outcome very much like Figure 7.6, but through an entirely different channel of effects.

The starting distribution of wealth gives us the following important piece of information: for each conceivable value of the market wage rate w, it tells us the fraction of the population that is shut out of entrepreneurship. How do we get this? For each wage w, (7.4) tells us the minimum wealth level that is required to have access to credit. Using the starting distribution of wealth, we obtain the fraction of the population starting out at wealth levels lower than this required minimum. This two-step process is easily illustrated by combining the wealth distribution with the fact that minimum wealth thresholds are increasing in the wage rate; see Figure 7.7.

Note that the higher the wage rate, the higher is the fraction of the population that is shut out of entrepreneurship. This is because the minimum wealth required for access to credit goes up—something that we have already observed. These individuals must then choose between subsistence and market labor, and the choice depends on the wage rate, of course. Wages less than z, the subsistence income, will cause zero participation in the labor market. Everybody who doesn't want to be an entrepreneur will opt for subsistence production. At $w = z$, there is a jump in labor supply, because all the subsistence choices now get revised in favor of the labor market. For higher wages, the labor supply steadily increases, as more and more people get shut out of entrepreneurship and must now switch their occupational choice to labor. This process continues until we reach a high enough wage, call it $\bar{w}$, such that the profit from running a business becomes exactly the

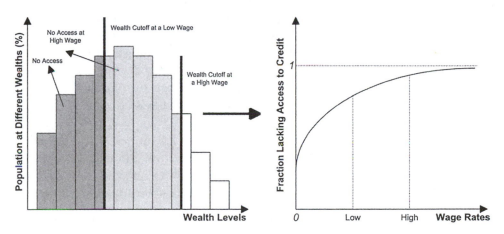

Figure 7.7. *Wage rates and fractions of people lacking access to credit.*

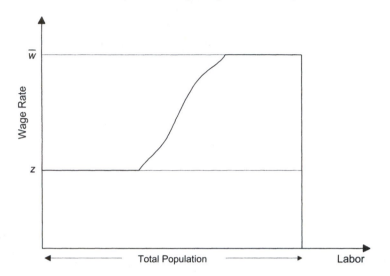

Figure 7.8. *The supply curve of labor. Note the jumps at z and at $\bar{w}$.*

same as labor income.[22] After *this* point, it should be clear that everyone, whether they can be entrepreneurs or not, will jump into the labor market. If wages exceed $\bar{w}$, labor income exceeds profit income, so no one will want to be an entrepreneur.

What emerges from this discussion, then, is a *supply curve* of labor—a description of the number of individuals who enter the labor market as the wage rate changes. Figure 7.8 summarizes the properties of this curve. It is a supply curve all right, but derived in a rather nonstandard way. Its slope, for instance, is determined by the going distribution of wealth and the way in which credit markets work! (In standard models, the slope typically mirrors labor–leisure preferences among the population.)

We now turn to the *demand* for labor. Start with a high wage that exceeds $\bar{w}$. Obviously, at such wages there is no demand for labor at all, because no one wants to be an entrepreneur. Moving down to $\bar{w}$, we see a sudden jump in the demand for labor as people now enter entrepreneurship. (This jump mirrors exactly the jump in the supply curve of labor at $\bar{w}$.) Thereafter, as the wage falls, the demand for labor steadily rises, capturing the fact that more individuals have access to the credit market with lower wages. Figure 7.9 summarizes labor demand.

We now put the two curves (Figures 7.8 and 7.9) together to determine *equilibrium wages*. The supply and demand curves for labor determine the wage level at date t. Note well just how the prevailing distribution of wealth feeds into the choice of occupations and therefore determines the shape of

[22] This critical wage $\bar{w}$ is the solution to the equation $(q - m\bar{w}) - (1 + r)I = \bar{w}$. Of course, we are assuming that the subsistence level z is less than $\bar{w}$; otherwise there would be no industrial sector in the model.

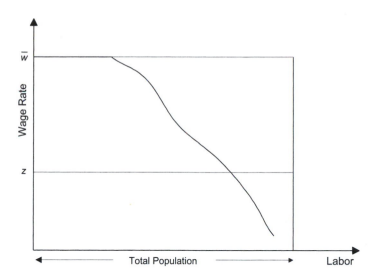

Figure 7.9. *The demand curve for labor. Note the jump at $\bar{w}$.*

these supply and demand curves, and consequently the wage rate. The three possible outcomes are described in the three panels of Figure 7.10.

The first panel, Figure 7.10a, shows what happens if the distribution of income is highly unequal (or if the economy is extremely poor), so that there are a large number of individuals with very low wealth. This situation has the effect of creating a sizable supply of labor at any wage exceeding subsistence levels, simply because there are a greater number of individuals barred from entrepreneurship. For exactly the same reason, the demand curve for labor is low, at any wage rate. The result is an intersection of the two curves at the minimum subsistence wage z. For the lucky few who are entrepreneurs, however, profits (and so income and wealth) are high.

On the other hand, if there is a great deal of equality (or if the economy is very rich), relatively few people are barred from entrepreneurship. In gen-

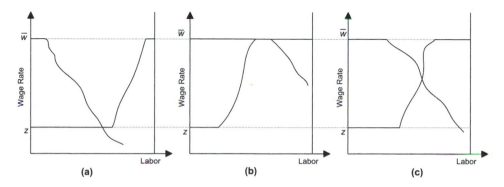

Figure 7.10. *Determination of the equilibrium wage rate.*

eral, therefore, individuals will only enter the labor market when wages are high enough to provide an attractive alternative to entrepreneurship. Consequently, the supply curve of labor shifts inward, and the demand curve shifts outward, leading to an equilibrium wage of $\bar{w}$. Note that in such a situation, everybody's *current* incomes are equalized; see Figure 7.10b.

Finally, Figure 7.10c displays an intermediate situation of moderate inequality or average wealth, where sizable numbers of people are shut out of credit markets, while another sizable fraction are not. Demand and supply curves intersect at some wage rate that lies between subsistence z and the high wage $\bar{w}$.

The inefficiency of inequality

Two features of this model are worth noticing. First, return to the high inequality case in which industrial wages are reduced to the subsistence alternative. In this situation there are some individuals in the subsistence sector. What if a fraction of these individuals could have become entrepreneurs? They would then have generated profits for themselves, which exceed the subsistence level of income to be sure, and then would have pulled more workers into the industrial sector. This scenario creates an efficiency improvement (indeed, a Pareto improvement): some section of the population can be made better off while no one else is made worse off. This is just another way to state that the market equilibrium under high inequality is inefficient: alternatives exist that can improve the lot of some individuals by hurting no one else.

Why doesn't the market permit these improvements to arise of their own accord? The reason is that the improvements require additional access to credit, and such access is barred because of the inequality in wealth. Thus we see here another functional implication of inequality: by hindering access to credit markets, it creates inefficiency in the economy as a whole. Even if we do not care about the inequality per se, the inefficiency might still matter to us.

This inefficiency is not restricted to high inequality regimes alone, although with sufficient equality it will go away. For instance, consider Figure 7.10b, in which entrepreneurial access is so easy that industrial wages rise to their maximum level. In this case, further easing of the credit market serves no function at all: the outcome is efficient to begin with. In the moderate inequality regime depicted by Figure 7.10c, inefficiency continues to persist. If some additional workers could become entrepreneurs, their incomes would rise[23] and the incomes of the remaining workers would rise as well, because of the resulting upward pressure on wages (demand rises,

---

[23] This follows from the fact that in the intermediate regime, $w < \bar{w}$. Therefore, $(q - mw) - (1 + r)I > w$.

supply falls). Again, these efficiency improvements are barred by the failure in credit markets.

If you have been following this argument closely, you might raise a natural objection at this point. Look, you might say, all these problems occur only in the here and now. *Over time*, people will save and their wealth will increase. Sooner or later everybody will be free of the credit constraint, because they will all have sufficient collateral to be entrepreneurs if they so wish. Thus after some time, everything should look like Figure 7.10b. The inefficiency you speak of is only temporary, so what is all the fuss about?

This is a good question.[24] The way to seriously address it is to think about just what constitutes the startup cost that we've so blithely blackboxed with the label I. Presumably, the startup cost of a business includes the purchase of plant and equipment—physical capital, in other words. If we go beyond the very simple model of this section, we also see a role for startup *human* capital: skilled technicians, researchers, scientists, trained managers, and so on. All of this goes into I. If we begin to think about the economy as it runs over time, surely these startup costs will change as overall wealth changes. For instance, we would expect the costs that are denominated in terms of human capital to rise along with national wealth: the wages of scientists and engineers will rise. It is even possible that the costs of *physical* capital will rise as well. Thus startup costs are endogenous in an extended view of this model and will presumably increase as wealth is accumulated. The whole question then turns on how the *ratio* of startup costs to wealth changes over time. For instance, if wealth is accumulated faster than startup costs increase, your objection would indeed be correct: the inefficiency is only an ephemeral one. If this is not the case—if startups keep pace with wealth accumulation— then these inefficiencies can persist into the indefinite future and inequality has sustained (and negative) effects on aggregate performance.[25]

Inequality begets inequality

The second feature of this model is that it captures an intrinsic tendency for inequality to beget itself. Look again at Figure 7.10a. Its outcome is generated by the fact that the majority of individuals are shut out from access to credit, so that the labor market is flooded from the supply side and is pretty tightfisted on the demand side. This market reaction goes precisely toward reinforcing the inequalities that we started with. People earning subsistence wages are unable to acquire wealth, while wealthy entrepreneurs make high

[24] Existing literature does not provide a satisfactory resolution of this problem, though it is possible to build extended models along the lines to be suggested in the text. Banerjee and Newman [1993] and Galor and Zeira [1993] both assumed that indefinite accumulation of wealth was not possible, so that the "credit trap" can persist over the long run.

[25] Thus further research on this topic will have to study the composition of startup costs and how various components are affected by the development process.

profits off the fact that labor is cheap. The next period's wealth distribution therefore tends to replicate the wealth distribution that led to this state of affairs in the first place.

Thus high inequality not only gives rise to inefficient outcomes, it tends to replicate itself, which prolongs the inefficiency. The lack of convergence (among economic agents) stems from the fact that the poor are shut out of projects (such as entrepreneurship) that yield high rates of return. Consequently, wealth disparities do not go away with time.

It is of interest to note that low inequality may *also* be self-perpetuating. Consider, for instance, the situation depicted in Figure 7.10b. In this case all economic agents earn the same, and as time passes, there is no reason for this state of affairs to change (unless rates of savings are different across individuals, but that is another matter). The Appendix to this chapter contains a very simple algebraic description of these "multiple steady states."

Pulling together the discussion in the last two paragraphs, we see here another example of possible *history dependence*. The model tells us nothing about how a history of high inequality comes about in the first place, but does suggest that a history of high inequality may persist into the indefinite future, carrying with it inefficiencies in production. The very same economy may exhibit different levels of output and investment if its history were to change to one of low initial inequality.

This history-dependent multiplicity of development paths suggests that the market system may lack a self-correcting device for large initial inequalities, especially if the credit market is constrained by the need for adequate collateral. One-time redistributive policies (such as a land reform) may well spur an economy onto a different (and faster paced) growth path. This sort of theory goes well with the empirical observations discussed earlier.

Summary

We summarize by listing the three main lessons to be learned from this model.

(1) If capital markets were perfect, an individual's wealth would not matter in deciding the amount of credit that she can obtain for consumption or investment, as long as the amount is one that she can *feasibly* pay back. In contrast, once default becomes a possibility, then what can be *feasibly* repaid may not correspond to what is *actually* repaid. In such situations the incentive to repay becomes important in determining credit allocations. To the extent that wealth matters in the ability to put up collateral, it matters in communicating the credibility of repayment and therefore in determining access to the credit market.

(2) Inequality has an effect on aggregate output. In this model, the greater the equality in wealth distribution, the greater the degree of eco-

nomic efficiency as the constraints that hinder the capital market are loosened.

(3) Finally, there is no innate tendency for inequality to disappear over the long run. A historically unequal situation perpetuates itself unless changed by government policy such as asset redistribution. This means, in particular, that two countries with exactly the same parameters of production and preferences may nevertheless not converge with each other as far as wealth distribution and output levels are concerned.

7.2.9. *Inequality and development: Human capital*

What we have discussed so far is just a fascinating sample of the many and diverse links between inequality and development. It is difficult to include a comprehensive treatment of all these connections, so we will not try. Here are a few general comments.

The previous section is of great importance because it illustrates a general principle that is of widespread applicability. *Inequality has a built-in tendency to beget inefficiency, because it does not permit people at the lower end of the wealth or income scale to fully exploit their capabilities.* In the previous section we illustrated this by the inability of a section of the population to become entrepreneurs, even though this choice would have promoted economic efficiency. However, this is only one example. For instance, in Chapter 13, we explore the theme that inequality prevents the buildup of adequate nutrition, which is certainly bad in itself, but in addition contributes to inefficiencies in work productivity. Replace nutrition by *human capital*, a more general concept which includes nutritional capital as well as skills and education, and you can begin to see a more general point.

Low levels of wealth hinder or entirely bar productive educational choices, because of the failure of the credit market. Educational loans may be difficult to obtain for reasons such as those described in Section 7.2.8. Actually, in the case of education, matters are possibly worse, because human capital cannot be seized and transferred to a creditor in the event of default. Thus human capital cannot be put up as collateral, whereas a house or business can be pledged, at least to some extent, as collateral in the event of failure to repay. It follows that the constraints on human capital loans are even more severe, dollar for dollar.

Thus the poor have to fund educational choices out of retained earnings, wealth, or abstention from currently productive work. Because they are poor, the marginal cost of doing so may be prohibitively high. (It is also true that the marginal *returns* from such investments are high, but after a point the marginal cost effect dominates.) If a wealthier person were to loan a poor person money for educational purposes, an economywide improvement in efficiency would be created. By investing money in the acquisition of human capital, the poor person can possibly earn a higher return on this money than the rich person (who has already made use of his educational opportunities to the fullest) and can therefore compensate the rich person for the opportunity cost of investment. However, this credit market is missing, because loan repayment may be difficult or impossible to enforce.

Thus high-inequality societies may be characterized by advanced institutes of education and research that rank among the best in the world. At the same time, the resources devoted to primary education may be pathetically low. There is no paradox in this, as long as we recognize the credit market failure that is at the heart of this phenomenon.

To be sure, inequalities in education feed back and reinforce the initial differences in inequality. This part of the story is also analogous to the model of the previous section. Multiple development paths can result: one characterized by high inequality, low levels of primary education, and inefficient market outcomes; the other characterized by low inequality, widespread primary education, and equalization of the rates of return to education across various groups in society, which enhances efficiency. As Loury [1981] puts it,

> . . . Early childhood investments in nutrition or preschool education are fundamentally income constrained. Nor should we expect a competitive loan market to completely eliminate the dispersion in expected rates of return to training across families. . . . Legally, poor parents will not be able to constrain their children to honor debts incurred on their behalf. Nor will the newly-matured children of wealthy families be able to attach the (human) assets of their less well-off counterparts, should the latter decide for whatever reasons not to repay their loans. (Default has been a pervasive problem with government guaranteed educational loan programs, which would not exist absent public underwriting.) . . . The absence of inter-family loans in this model reflects an important feature of reality, the allocative implications of which deserve study.

Loury was writing about the U.S. economy, and so was Okun [1975] when he judged the constrained accumulation of human capital to be "one of the most serious inefficiencies of the American economy today." Consider the same phenomenon magnified severalfold for developing countries.

7.3. Summary

In this chapter, we studied the *functional* aspects of inequality: its connections with other features of development, such as per capita income and rates of income growth.

We began with an empirical investigation of the *inverted-U hypothesis*, due to Simon Kuznets, which states that inequality rises at low levels of per capita income and then falls. Early evidence suggests that developing countries appear to have higher inequality, on average, than their developed counterparts. More detailed investigation runs into data problems. There are no sufficient data to comprehensively investigate inequality in a single country *over time*, so the majority of studies rely on analysis of inequality over a *cross section* of countries.

The first cross-section study with evidence for the inverted-U was that of Paukert. Even though his data set of fifty-six countries displayed wide variation in inequality, there appeared, on the whole, to be an inverted-U relationship over the cross section. More recent (and more comprehensive) data sets support this observation, and so (at first glance) do more formal statistical methods such as regression analysis. We discussed in this context the study of Ahluwalia, whose regressions delivered additional support for the inverted-U over a larger sample of countries than studied by Paukert.

These studies are qualified by various caveats. Cross-country variation in inequality is too much to be predicted by per capita income alone. Some measures generate inverted-U behavior even when there is ambiguity in the comparisons of underlying Lorenz curves. Finally, the exact specification of the functional form in a regression might matter.

There is a more serious objection than any of the foregoing; it stems from what we termed the *Latin effect*. What if the middle-income countries (in which inequality is highest) are mainly Latin American (which they are) and these countries exhibit high inequality simply because of structural features that are common to Latin America, but have nothing to do with their per capita income? Put another way, do different countries have their own Kuznets curves? The way to examine this is to put regional or country dummies into the regression—an approach taken by Fields and Jakubson as well as by Deininger and Squire. Of course, this approach requires several years of data for each country in the sample, a condition that is fortunately satisfied by recent data sets. When these fixed effects are allowed for, the Kuznets hypothesis fails to hold up.

The failure of the inverted-U hypothesis over the cross section (once country fixed effects are accounted for) provokes a way of thinking about income changes. We identified two sorts of changes. *Uneven changes* in income bolster the fortunes of some subgroup of people or some sector of the economy. Such changes are by their very nature inequality enhancing. In contrast, *compensatory changes* in income occur as the benefits of an initially uneven change percolate more widely through the society; such changes reduce inequality. Recasting the inverted-U hypothesis in this language is roughly equivalent to the assertion that development is like one giant uneven change followed by one giant compensatory change. *That* would create first a rise and then a fall in inequality. Although there is some support for this point of view, there is no reason for it to be an ironclad law.

We then studied several connections between inequality and income (and its growth). One is through savings. We showed that if *marginal savings* increase with income, then an increase in inequality raises savings. On the other hand, if marginal savings decreases with income, then an increase in inequality lowers national savings. We went on to discuss the possible behavior of marginal savings as a function of income. *Subsistence needs, conspicuous consumption*, and *aspirations* are all concepts that are useful in this context. We discussed the effect of inequality on savings and, consequently, growth. Conversely, we discussed the effect of savings and growth upon inequality.

We turned next to another connection between inequality and growth. High inequality might create a political demand for *redistribution*. The government might respond with a once-and-for-all redistribution of assets, but this takes political will and information regarding asset owners, so more typically the government reacts with taxes on *incremental earnings*. However, such taxes are distortionary: they reduce the incentive to accumulate wealth and therefore lower growth.

Is there evidence that inequality lowers subsequent growth, as these models suggest? This was the subject of our next inquiry. We discussed papers by Alesina and Rodrik and others that suggest that there is indeed such an empirical relationship, but its sources are unclear. Specifically, it is hard to tell from the available empirical evidence whether the effect of inequality on growth works through savings and investment, through the demands for public redistribution, or through some entirely different channel.

Encouraged by this evidence (blackboxed though it may appear), we went on to study other connections between inequality and development. We studied the relationship between inequality and the *composition of product demand*. People consume different goods (perhaps of varying technical sophistication) at different levels of income, so it must be the case that at any one point in time, the overall inequality in income distribution influences the mix of commodities that are produced and consumed in a society. The production mix, in turn, affects the demand for inputs of production, in general, and various human skills, in particular. For instance, if the rich consume highly skill-intensive goods, the existence of inequality sets up a demand for skills that reinforce such inequalities over time.

Self-perpetuating inequality can only happen if certain skills are out of bounds for the poorer people in the society. Why might this happen? After all, if credit markets are perfect, individuals should be able to borrow enough to invest in any skill they like. This paradox motivated us to study the nature of credit markets in developing societies (much more of this in Chapter 14). We saw that in the presence of potential default, loans are offered only to those people with adequate *collateral*, so that inequality has an effect in the sense that certain segments of the population are locked out of the credit market (because they have insufficient collateral). We showed that this creates an inefficiency, in the sense that certain Pareto improvements are foregone by the market. Thus inequality has a negative effect on aggregate economic performance. The greater the equality in wealth distribution, the greater the degree of economic efficiency as the constraints that hinder the capital market are loosened.

We also observed that there is no innate tendency for inequality to disappear over the long run. A historically unequal situation might perpetuate itself unless changed by government policy such as asset redistribution. This means, in particular, that two countries with exactly the same parameters of production and preferences may nevertheless not converge with each other as far as wealth distribution and output levels are concerned.

Appendix: Multiple steady states with imperfect capital markets

We complement the study of imperfect credit markets in Section 7.2.8 with a simple algebraic description of wealth accumulation. This account is only meant to be illustrative: many realistic extensions, such as the growth story sketched in the text, are possible.

Just as in the growth models of Chapter 3, we are going to track variables over time, so values like t and $t+1$ in parentheses denote dates. Thus $W(t)$ denotes a person's wealth at date t, $w(t)$ denotes the wage rate at time t, and so on.

Consider a person with initial wealth $W(t)$, who faces the choice between the three occupations described in the text. Whatever income is received from these occupations is added to her wealth (plus interest at fixed rate r), and a fixed fraction is consumed from the total. The remaining fraction becomes the *new* wealth level W_{t+1} at date $t+1$. If you like, you can just as easily think of this as being the new wealth level of the *descendant* of this individual, so that each period or date corresponds to the entire "life history" of a particular generation.

If subsistence production is chosen, then the individual produces for herself an income of z. Total assets available are then $(1+r)W(t) + z$, where, if you remember, r stands for the interest rate. If a given fraction s of this is passed on to the next date (or to the next generation), then

$$(7.5) \qquad W(t+1) = s\{(1+r)W(t) + z\}$$

is the equation that describes future starting wealth.

Alternatively, she might choose employment in the labor market for wage income, the going value of which is $w(t)$ (remember this is endogenous).

What happens in this case looks just like the subsistence option, with $w(t)$ taking the place of z. Future wealth is now given by

$$(7.6) \qquad W(t+1) = s\{(1+r)W(t) + w(t)\}.$$

Finally, she might choose to be an entrepreneur. Recall that profits in this case are given by $(q - wm) - (1+r)I$. Add this to her starting wealth. As before, a fraction s is passed on to the next generation, so the corresponding equation that describes the evolution of wealth for an *entrepreneur* is

$$(7.7) \qquad W(t+1) = s[(1+r)W(t) + (q - w(t)m) - (1+r)I].$$

Assumption 1. *Repeated subsistence cannot make someone indefinitely rich over time:* $s(1+r) < 1$.

Assumption 2. *Being an entrepreneur when wages are at subsistence levels is better than being a worker:* $(q - mz) - (1+r)I > z$.

Assumption 1 states that repeated subsistence cannot cause an indefinite rise in wealth. Look at equation (7.5) to understand just why this requires the algebraic inequality at the end of that assumption. [Hint: Reverse the inequality and see what happens to wealth over time as you repeatedly apply (7.5).]

This assumption gets us away from complicated issues that pertain to growth (recall our discussion in the text about changing startup costs.) Don't take the assumption seriously, but think of it as a tractable way to study a long-run wealth distribution (see the following text).

Assumption 2 already is implicit in the exposition of the text.

We want to study the *steady-state distributions* of wealth in this model; that is, a distribution that precisely replicates itself. Ask yourself, What is the long-run wealth of an individual (or a sequence of generations, depending on your interpretation) who earns the subsistence wage z year after year? The long-run level of "subsistence wealth" W_S will replicate itself: if $W(t) = W_S$, then $W(t+1) = W_S$ as well. Using this information in (7.5) [or (7.6), which is the same here because wages are at subsistence], we see that

$$W_S = s(1+r)W_S + sz,$$

and using this to solve for W_S tells us that

$$(7.8) \qquad W_S = \frac{sz}{1 - s(1+r)}.$$

Now, to arrive at this wealth level, we presumed two things. First, we assumed that such individuals had no access to the credit market. In the language of our model, this means that W_S cannot satisfy the minimum wealth requirement (7.4), with z substituted for w. Second, we presumed that the wages were driven down to subsistence, so that the crossing of demand and supply curves was as depicted in Figure 7.10a. This means that a sufficiently large fraction of the population must be at this subsistence level.[26]

What about the entrepreneurs? Well, they are earning profits in each period to the tune of $(q - zm) - (1 + r)I$, and we can use this to calculate their long-run wealth W_R. The procedure is exactly the same as that involved in calculating W_S, except that we use equation (7.7) this time. The calculations show that

$$(7.9) \qquad W_R = \frac{s[(q - zm) - (1 + r)I]}{1 - s(1 + r)}.$$

To make sure that this wealth level is compatible with entrepreneurship, it must be the case that, in contrast to W_S, W_R *does* satisfy the minimum wealth requirement (7.4) (with z substituted for w). By gazing at (7.4), (7.8), and (7.9), you can easily see that there is no inconsistency between the statement that W_S fails (7.4) and W_R satisfies it.

If all these conditions are met, we have generated a steady-state distribution of wealth. A fraction of the population has long-run wealth equal to W_S; the remaining fraction has long-run wealth equal to W_R. The wealth level W_S does not permit access to the credit market, whereas the wealth level W_R does. This is a high-inequality, inefficient steady state that perpetuates itself.

The same model is capable of generating an equal distribution of wealth, which is a persistent outcome as well. We now examine this possibility. To this end, imagine that wages are at level $\bar{w}$, the high level depicted in Figure 7.10b. If all workers earn these wages and all entrepreneurs pay such wages, what would long-run wealth look like?

Note that in such a scenario, there can be *no* long-run inequality, because we already noted that a wage level of $\bar{w}$ leads to the same income for both workers and entrepreneurs. By exactly the same calculations that we used to derive (7.8) and (7.9), we see that long-run wealth *for everybody* is given by

$$(7.10) \qquad W_E = \frac{s\bar{w}}{1 - s(1 + r)}.$$

Can this be a possible scenario? The answer is yes, provided that this wealth level does not prevent access to entrepreneurship. In other words, W_E must

---

[26] If you are inquisitive about exactly how large this fraction must be, look at this derivation: At the subsistence wage, the demand for labor is mn, where n is the number of people who are entrepreneurs, and the supply is $N - n$, where N is the total population. For Figure 7.10a to be applicable, the supply must exceed the demand at wage z, so that $N - n \geq mn$. This means that $n \leq N/(m + 1)$.

satisfy (7.4) (with $\bar{w}$ substituting for w). This yields an *efficient* steady-state distribution with perfect equality. Depending on initial conditions, an economy might gravitate to one steady state or the other.

Exercises

■ (1) Consider an economy of 10 people and two sectors (modern and traditional) with yearly incomes equal to $1,000 and $2,000. Suppose that all growth proceeds by moving people from the traditional to the modern sector.

(a) Plot values of the Gini coefficient and the coefficient of variation as individuals move from the traditional to the modern sector.

(b) Can you invent a Lorenz-consistent inequality measure which does *not* display the inverted-U property in this case?

■ (2) Describe what is known empirically about the relationship between the level of per capita GNP of a country and its degree of inequality. Provide at least *two* possible reasons why we might empirically observe such a relationship.

■ (3) If you had a panel data set with several year-wise observations on each country, explain how you would go about testing the inverted-U hypothesis. How would your test change (for pragmatic reasons) as the number of data points per country changed?

■ (4) Think of some sources of rapid growth that we have encountered in world history that are uneven (in that they have benefited some sectors or subpopulations, perhaps at the expense of others), and some other sources which have been even, in the sense that they are spread equally over the entire population. In this context, skip ahead in this book and read the box on Recent Changes in OECD Wages and Unemployment in Chapter 17.

■ (5) Use very short arguments to describe the following *possibilities*. You may put in a diagram and/or a simple example to illustrate your argument.

(a) Over the course of economic development, the pay ratios of skilled to unskilled labor rise and then fall.

(b) Studies of different countries over the cross section show an inverted-U relationship in inequality.

(c) An increase in inequality may lower growth rates.

(d) In economies where people have restricted access to capital markets, an increase in inequality is likely to lower equilibrium wage rates.

■ (6) Suppose that there are three individuals with three wealth levels in the economy. Denote the wealth levels by A, B, and C, and suppose that $A < B < C$.

(a) Suppose that the person with wealth level A earns an annual income of w_A, and saves a fraction s_A of it. If the rate of interest on asset holdings is r, write down a formula for this person's wealth next year.

(b) Show that if income earnings of each individual is proportional to wealth (that is, $w_B/w_A = B/A$ and $w_C/w_B = C/B$), and if the savings rate is the same across individuals, inequality of wealth next year must be the same as inequality this year, as measured by the Lorenz curve.

(c) Retain the same assumptions on income and wealth as in part (b) but now suppose that the savings rates satisfy $s_A < s_B < s_C$. Now how does the Lorenz curve for wealth next year compare with its counterpart for the current year?

(d) Carry out the same exercise as in part (c), but now assume that all wages are equal and so are savings rates.

(e) Try and understand these results intuitively as forces that change inequality over time. What features (other than the ones studied in this question) might also affect inequality in the context of this example?

■ (7) This problem tests your understanding of the effect of the income distribution on savings rates.

The economy of Sonrisa has people in three income categories: poor, middle class, and rich. The poor earn $500 per year and have to spend it all to meet their consumption needs. The middle class earn $2,000 per year, of which $1,500 is spent and the rest saved. The rich earn $10,000 per year, and consume 80% of it, saving the rest.

(a) Calculate the overall savings rate in Sonrisa if 20% of the people are poor and 50% are in the middle class.

(b) Suppose that all growth occurs by moving people from the poor category to the middle-class category. Will the savings rate rise over time or fall? Using the Harrod–Domar model and assuming that population growth is zero and all other variables are exogenous, predict whether the resulting growth rate will rise or fall over time.

(c) Outline another growth scenario where the rate of growth changes over time in a way opposite to that of (b).

(d) Understand well that this question asks you about how growth *rates* are changing. In the simple Harrod–Domar model, the growth rate is constant over time because the savings rate is presumed to be unchanging with the level of income. Do you understand why matters are different here?

▪ (8) Explain why a one-time redistribution of land is likely to have less of a negative effect on investment rather than a redistribution of income period after period (but with a similar distribution of present values of assets as the land redistribution).

▪ (9) Pooh is a country with only two occupations. You can work as a laborer or you can become an entrepreneur, who hires labor and makes profits. To become an entrepreneur, you need a loan of 20,000 pahs (a pah is the unit of currency in Pooh). With 20,000 pahs you can set up a factory that hires ten workers, each of whom you must pay an income of w pahs over the year. Together, the workers produce for you an output of 30,000 pahs. At the end of the year, you must sell your factory (for 20,000 pahs) and repay the loan. The rate of interest in Pooh is 10% per year.

(a) Suppose you were to contemplate running away instead. Imagine you would be caught, fined 5000 pah, and 20% of your business profits would be seized. You would also lose whatever collateral you put up with the bank (plus interest), but you would get to keep the 20,000 pah (plus interest that you also owe). Find a formula that describes how much collateral the bank should ask for (in pah units) before it would advance you a loan. Examine this required collateral for different levels of the wage income: $w = 1000$, 2000, and 2, 500. Does the required collateral go up or down with the wage? Explain your answer.

(b) Let's suppose that the minimum wage in Pooh is fixed by law at 500 pah. Find the collateral required to get a loan if w is at the minimum wage. Consider the following statement: "If more than x% of Pooh inhabitants are unable to put up this collateral, then some people are unable to get employment, whether as laborers or entrepreneurs." Calculate x.

▪ (10) There are two ways in which an imperfect credit market manifests itself. One is in the form of a higher interest rate; the other is in the form of a ceiling on loans. Discuss how these two phenomena may come about. In particular, why is it that a higher interest rate cannot always compensate for the possibility of default and that a credit limit needs to be set? [See Chapter 14 for more on these matters.]

▪ (11) Explain carefully why greater inequality in wealth distribution tends to shift the supply curve of labor to the right and the demand curve to the left when there are imperfect capital markets. In the process of doing this, explain how the supply and demand curves for labor depend on the wage rate, and take care to explain why the positions of these curves depend on the overall distribution of wealth.

■ (12) Using the model studied in Section 7.2.8, explain why better information regarding borrowers and their credit histories is likely to reduce the adverse effects of inequality on output.

Chapter 8

Poverty and Undernutrition

8.1. Introduction

There is no more visible characteristic of economic underdevelopment than poverty. It is also the most shocking characteristic—the outgrowth of layer upon layer of inequality. There is, first, the inequality of world income distribution. As if this were not enough, there is the inequality of income distribution within a country. The outcome, for many millions of people, is destitution, squalor, and lack of hope.

It is all too easy to provide "illustrative" examples of the development process: there are many in this book and in every textbook on economic development, but it is not easy to describe, head on, the horrors of poverty and its attendant correlates: illiteracy, undernutrition, ill health, and the utter bleakness of the future. Poverty strikes not only at the core of ongoing existence. By effectively taking away the rights of a human being to live in good health, to obtain an education, and to enjoy adequate nutrition, poverty destroys the aspirations, hopes, and enjoyment of the future as well. Poverty was a medieval scourge for a good reason: the world was generally poor then. There is little excuse for living with poverty today.

Considering that the world has generated significant growth in per capita income, its track record on poverty is pretty dismal. Over the period 1965–75, consumption per capita in developing countries grew by 32%, and then by another 26% over the period 1975–85.[1] However, by fairly conservative estimates that we will discuss subsequently, the number of poor people in the world in 1990 was over a billion (in a total of well under six billion). The figure alone is staggering.

Just as in the case of inequality, poverty is both of intrinsic and functional significance. Most people would say that the removal of poverty is a fundamental goal of economic development. Hence, the characteristics of the poor and the appropriate measure of poverty are important considerations in policies that must be sharply targeted toward the poor. However, poverty is not only of intrinsic interest: it has enormous implications for the way in

---

[1] See the *World Development Report* (World Bank [1990, Table 3.1]). The figures pertain to consumption in 1985 PPP prices.

which entire economies function. Some of these functional implications were tied up in our discussion of inequality, but there are others that are specific to poverty itself.

This chapter is divided into four parts. First, we discuss the *concept* of poverty, and—something that's obviously related—how to go about measuring it. Next, we apply some of these measures to obtain a sense of the extent of poverty in the world today. In addition to these quantitative estimates, we also describe the *correlates of poverty*: characteristics that are widely shared by poor individuals. Not only does an understanding of these characteristics help to identify the poor, but it may also serve as a focal point for policies that are geared toward ending poverty. Third, we analyze the *functional* impact of poverty. At many stages this issue links up with material in other chapters of this text, and we will point at this material to avoid repetition. Finally, we discuss policies for poverty alleviation.

8.2. Poverty: First principles

8.2.1. Conceptual issues

At the heart of all discourses on poverty is the notion of a *poverty line*: a critical threshold of income, consumption, or, more generally, *access* to goods and services below which individuals are declared to be poor. The poverty line, then, represents a minimum level of "acceptable" economic participation in a given society at a given point in time. For instance, we could collect data on minimum nutrient levels that make up an adequate diet, on the prices of foodstuffs that contain such nutrients, and on the costs of shelter and clothing, and then add up the consumption expenditures needed to obtain these basic requirements to obtain an estimate of the poverty line for a particular society. We could use the prevailing legally decreed minimum wage in a country as an estimate for the poverty line of that country. Alternatively, we could fix some other norm, say, 60% of the mean income of a country, to arrive at an estimate of its poverty line.

Nutrition-based poverty lines are not uncommon. The poverty line used in the United States is based on Orshansky's [1963, 1965] estimates, which scale by three a minimum-budget estimate for food requirements (the scaling proxies for other requirements such as rent and clothing). Indian poverty lines have traditionally been drawn by using estimates of expenditure necessary to guarantee a minimum consumption of calories. Of course, such poverty lines (and probably *all* poverty lines) should be approached with some caution and scepticism: the poorer the country, the better the nutrition-based approximation. Issues of scaling become more problematic as the average standard of living rises.

The following subsections explain some of the fundamental concerns that surround poverty measurement.

Overall expenditure or item-by-item consumption?

Should we declare a person to be poor when her *actual, observed consumption basket* falls below certain prespecified thresholds or when her *expenditure* (or overall income) falls below the minimum required to obtain these consumption standards? Certainly, we could conjure up examples where the two approaches yield different results; for instance, what are we to make of the wealthy ascetic who starves himself on an ongoing basis? At a more serious level, nutrition levels may not unambiguously rise with income.[2] For instance, canned foods may become quite popular at certain levels of income, even though their nutritive value is questionable. Thus, even through elasticities may be high with respect to changes in income, nutrient elasticities may not be correspondingly high. Income represents the *capacity* to consume, not consumption itself. Nevertheless, income- or (aggregate) expenditure-based poverty lines are far easier to use, given the scarcity of available data.

Absolute or relative?

Clearly, there is something absolute about the notion of poverty . Regardless of the society we live in, people need adequate levels of food, clothing, and shelter. Whereas it is certainly the case that there are variations in what might be considered "adequate" (shelter, in particular, might be subject to varying society-specific interpretations), nobody would deny the biological imperative of nutrition, for instance, or the near-universal norms of adequate clothing. At the same time, it is unclear that the phrase "acceptable levels of participation in society" can be given absolute meaning, independent of the contours of the society under consideration. In some societies, the ownership of a television may be deemed socially necessary for living a "full" life; in others it is not. Likewise, minimal standards of leisure, access to scientific education, ownership of private means of transportation, and so on, are all concerns that must be evaluated *relative* to the prevailing socioeconomic standards. These considerations quite naturally give rise to the need for poverty lines that share certain common components, but vary (perhaps widely) from country to country.

Note carefully that although poverty lines should (and do) incorporate relative notions of what constitutes "necessity" or "basic needs," we must still think of them as fulfilling some absolute notion of the ability to function in a society. The previous paragraph chooses our examples carefully to make this point.[3] For instance, it would be foolish to define poverty by, say, the percentage of the population earning less than half the average income of society. Such a measure confuses poverty with inequality. For instance, the

---

[2] On this, see, for example, Behrman and Deolalikar [1987] and the box on nutrition and income in South India later in this chapter.

[3] For a detailed discussion of these matters, see Sen [1983].

measure would remain completely unchanged if all incomes were scaled down by the same proportion, plunging half the population into famine!

Temporary or chronic?

As we will see, people who live in (or close to) a state of poverty, however that state is measured, often experience significant fluctuations in their income and consumption. This is especially true for the poor or near-poor in developing countries, where a large fraction of the population may depend on a quirky, weather-dependent agriculture. Expressed as fractions of their average earned income, these fluctuations are large. As Morduch [1994] pointed out, notions of "structural" or chronic poverty must therefore be complemented by a study of "temporary poverty." The latter occurs when, because of bad economic shocks (such as poor rainfall or low prices for one's production), individuals temporarily enter a poverty sample. The distinction is not just for the sake of a distinction: the policies required to combat temporary as opposed to chronic poverty may be very different.

The temporary versus chronic distinction is closely related to Friedman's [1957] famous distinction between temporary and permanent income. Income in a given year may be far from capturing the smoothed or "permanent" stream of consumption that an individual or household enjoys over time. For this reason, household or individual expenditures are often thought of as a more reliable way to assess chronic poverty.

Households or individuals?

Often household-level data on expenditure and income are all that is available. It is tempting, then, to simply express household consumption as individual averages (so that household size can be accounted for), and then apply one's favorite measure of poverty. However, this neglects an exceedingly important issue: that the allocation of expenditures *within* the house-hold are often significantly skewed. Among the potential victims are females and the elderly. There is some evidence that such discrimination grows sharper with the overall level of destitution of the household. Macroestimates of poverty should therefore be complemented by "microstudies" that study intrahousehold allocation. We will study some examples in the subsequent text.

Neglecting altogether the problems of distribution, a second set of concerns arises from the fact that larger households typically have more children. Some correction for the presence of children is desirable, because they consume somewhat less than adults. The construction of *adult equivalence scales*—conversion factors that express the consumption of children as a fraction of a representative adult—would get around this problem.[4]

Finally, there are fixed costs in setting up and running a household. Smaller households cannot spread these fixed costs over several household members. They are therefore at a disadvantage. We return to this and related issues later.

Why a poverty line, anyway?

It is possible to argue that a fixed notion of the poverty line is untenable. In part this is because of some issues raised earlier; for example, the relativity of poverty or its fluctuating nature. Even if we stick to chronic, nutrition-based measures of poverty, we *still* are unable to find some magic level of nutrition below which people abruptly go up in little puffs of smoke (in which case there would probably be no poverty to speak of, anyway). As we shall see later in this chapter, undernutrition is not the same as immediate and obvious disaster, and therefore it is more insidious. The world can indefinitely carry a stock of undernourished people, living and breeding under impaired circumstances. Although more will be said presently on such issues, it is important to realize that poverty lines are *always* approximations to a threshold that is truly fuzzy, more because the effects of sustained deprivation are often felt *at a later point in time*. There is really little to be done about this criticism except to realize that quantitative estimates of poverty lines are not to be memorized all the way down to the third decimal place and that they are basically (important) pointers to a deeper and less quantifiable concept.

8.2.2. Poverty measures

With the preceding qualifications in mind, then, we will consider a poverty line to be an expenditure threshold that is regarded as minimally necessary for "adequate" participation in economic life. People below this threshold will be said to be *poor*.

A little notation will be useful. As in Chapter 6, y denotes income (or expenditure) and subscripts $i, j, \ldots$, refer to individuals. Let's denote by p the poverty line[5] and by m the mean income of the economy.

One natural measure that comes to mind is simply to *count* the number of people below the poverty line. We might be interested in the numbers per se or in the *relative incidence* of the poor. In the latter case, divide by the total

---

[4] There are conceptual questions regarding the construction of such scales, although the existing practice of using per capita expenditure (or income) for a household can certainly be improved. For further discussion, see Deaton [1997, Section 4.3].

[5] This is taken to be denominated in the same units of currency as income or expenditure. Thus, for instance, if the poverty line is calorie-based, p represents the amount of money that is required to attain the acceptable calorie threshold.

population of the country or region under consideration. The first measure is known as the *head count*, and the latter as the *head-count ratio*, which is just head count as a fraction of population. In part because they don't place great strains on available data, these measures are widely used. In our notation, the head count (HC) is given by the number of individuals i such that $y_i < p$, whereas the head-count ratio (HCR) is just

$$(8.1) \qquad\qquad\qquad \text{HCR} = \frac{\text{HC}}{n},$$

where n is the total population.

An obvious problem with the head-count ratio is that it fails to capture the *extent* to which individual income (or expenditure) falls below the poverty line. This is related, of course, to observation 5 (Why a poverty line, anyway?) in the previous section that poverty is not a "zero–one" concept. People further below the poverty line are "poorer" than people closer to it, and the head count is insensitive to this observation. However, matters are worse than plain insensitivity: use of the head count can lead to problematic policy decisions, as the following example suggests.

Example 1: You are a planner in Ping, a poor land, where the poverty line is set at 1000 pah a year. It turns out that in Ping there are two equal-sized groups below the poverty line. One group consists of 100 individuals: they have equal earnings of 500 pah a year each. The second group also has 100 people: they earn 900 pah a year each. Of course, there are also people who are above the poverty line. You have been allocated a budget of 20,000 pah a year. You must allocate this budget among the 200 poor people.

(i) Suppose you were to forget about the poverty line. Who would you give the money to?

(ii) Now suppose that you are firmly told by the President of Ping to use this money to minimize, as far as possible, the head count. Who would you give the money to?

The point of the example is very simple. The use of the head count as a measure of poverty systematically biases policy in favor of individuals who are very close to the poverty line. Statistically, these people offer the biggest bang for the buck, because they are most easily taken above the poverty line. Yet of all the poor, they are relatively in the least need of help. A benevolent government that is perfectly secure and without fear of losing the next elections may ignore the problem and act in the best interests of the people, but most governments, like most people, are more interested in maximizing the observable and seemingly objective measures of their success.

One way to partially offset this bias, and more fundamentally take account of the extent of poverty, is to use a measure of the average income shortfall from the poverty line. An example is the *poverty gap ratio*, defined as the ratio of the average of income (or extra consumption) needed to get all poor people to the poverty line, divided by the mean income (or consumption) of the society. The reason for dividing by the average for society as a whole is that this gives us an idea of how large the gap is relative to resources that potentially may be used to close the gap. In this sense, the poverty gap ratio is not really a measure of poverty itself, but a measure of resources required to eradicate it.

In terms of our notation, the poverty gap ratio (PGR) is given by

$$\text{(8.2)} \qquad \text{PGR} = \frac{\sum_{y_i < p}(p - y_i)}{nm},$$

where m, you will recall, is mean income.

Dividing by average economywide income might give a misleading impression of poverty in highly unequal (but overall wealthy) societies with a large number of poor people. The poverty gap ratio in such societies may look pretty small, even though the plight of the poor is made no less acute by this maneuver. Therefore, a close relative of this measure, called the *income gap ratio*, is often used. This is exactly the same measure of total shortfall of the poor from the poverty line, except that we divide the shortfall by the total income required to bring all the poor people to the poverty line. This places a slightly different perspective on things. It captures more directly the acuteness of poverty, because it measures it relative to the total income needed to make that poverty go away.[6] Thus the income gap ratio (IGR) is given by the formula

$$\text{(8.3)} \qquad \text{IGR} = \frac{\sum_{y_i < p}(p - y_i)}{p\,\text{HC}},$$

where we recall that HC is just the number (head count) of the poor.

The PGR or the IGR is not susceptible to the same kind of policy distortion as the head count, as the following example shows.

Example 2: Return to the problem of Example 1. Now imagine that you are told to minimize (as far as possible) the PGR or the IGR. Does the way you now spend your money necessarily contrast with the intuitive reactions you noted in part (i) of Example 1?

It should be clear from the discussion that the PGR or IGR avoids the "bang for the buck" problem by deliberately neglecting *numbers* or *fractions*

---

[6] Of course, this measure has the *opposite* problem: by ignoring the overall wealth of the society, it tells us little about how easily the problem can be tackled, at least domestically.

of people that are below the poverty line. In a sense, PGR and IGR only capture the "per capita intensity" of poverty. The head count (or HCR), whatever its other failings, does not suffer from this problem. For this reason, it is a good idea to use measures of each type *jointly*, where possible, to evaluate the extent of poverty.

Finally, we note that *both* the head count and the poverty gap class of measures share an additional drawback relating to the fact that both these measures ignore the important issue of *relative deprivation* among the poor.[7] Relative deprivation is just another phrase for inequality *among the poor*. The new phrase is used to capture the fact that we are concerned only with the inequality among the deprived, or poor. The main concern is captured by the following example.

Example 3: Return to Example 1, where, as you will recall, there are 200 people below the poverty line; half of them have an income of 500 pah and the rest have an income of 900 pah.

(i) Suppose that each person who earns 500 pah gave 50 pah to each person who earns 900 pah. The new income levels are then 450 and 950 pah. What do you think would happen to the intensity of poverty in this new situation relative to the old? Now compute the HCR and PGR (or IGR) in both situations. Compare what the measures say with what you feel intuitively.

(ii) To make the point even more starkly, transfer 110 pah each (instead of 50 pah) between the same groups and redo the exercise.

Even if we were to take the head count and the gap-ratio measures *together*, there are other aspects of poverty that may be left out. This observation leads to more sophisticated measures of poverty that have been proposed by economists such as Sen [1976] and Foster, Greer, and Thorbecke [1984]. With better data, these more demanding measures can be easily applied. The Appendix to this chapter contains a discussion of the Foster–Greer–Thorbecke index.

8.3. Poverty: Empirical observations

We now turn to the data to get a sense of the extent of poverty and the characteristics of the poor. We begin with a universal poverty line to facilitate cross-country comparison. Be aware that this is a tricky business. We already discussed the fact that poverty has relative as well as absolute components. The choice of some "universal" poverty line creates overly high "real poverty" in some countries and too little poverty in others. To partly circumvent this problem, the *World Development Report* (World Bank [1990]),

---

[7] For a more detailed treatment of this issue, see Sen [1976].

Table 8.1. Poverty in developing countries, 1985 and 1990, using "universal" poverty lines.

	1985						1990	
	Ultrapoor (Under $275)			Poor (Under $370)			Poor	
Region	HC (millions)	HCR (%)	PGR	HC (millions)	HCR (%)	PGR	HC (millions)	HCR (%)
Sub-Saharan Africa	120	30	4.0	184	48	11.0	216	48
E. Asia	120	9	0.4	182	13	1.0	169	11
S. Asia	300	29	3.0	532	52	10.0	562	49
E. Europe	3	4	0.2	5	7	0.5	5.0	7
Mid. East/N. Africa	40	21	1.0	60	31	2.0	73	33
L. America/Caribbean	50	12	1.0	87	22	1.0	108	26
All LDCs	633	18	1	1,051	31	3.0	1,133	30

Source: *World Development Report* (World Bank [1990, 1992]).
Note: Poverty lines are at 1985 PPP prices. The 1992 report updates and changes head-count information for 1985 and provides 1990 data. The PGRs for 1985 are unaltered from the 1990 report.

which represents a landmark study on poverty in developing countries, experimented with a choice of two poverty lines: $275 and $370 per person per year, expressed in 1985 PPP prices. The range was chosen to reflect that fact that the poverty lines of some of the poorest nations fall between these two limits.[8]

Table 8.1 puts together poverty data from two *World Development Reports*. Keeping in mind that these poverty lines were chosen quite conservatively, the results are staggering, to say the least. In 1990, well over one *billion* individuals were estimated to earn less than $370 per year (or $420 per year at 1990 PPP prices). The time trend does not look very hopeful either. Except for East Asia, which experienced very high rates of growth, the absolute numbers of the poor rose significantly between 1985 and 1990. The overall percentage of people in poverty (at the $370 line) was roughly constant over this period at 30% of the population of all developing countries.

Even if we were to use the extra-conservative poverty line of $275 per year per person, we would see that in 1985, over 600 million people were poor even by these unexacting standards. The overall figures for poverty would be significantly higher were we to use country-specific poverty lines.

We now turn to the characteristics of the poor.

8.3.1. Demographic features

It is not surprising that those households whose members fall below the poverty line also tend to be large relative to the average family. For

---

[8] These are Bangladesh, Egypt, India, Indonesia, Kenya, Morocco, and Tanzania. The lower limit, $275, coincides with a poverty line used for India.

Brazil, Fishlow [1972] reported that 29% of all families had a size of six or more individuals, and over half of such families fell below the poverty line. Similarly, for Malaysia, Anand [1977] noted that the incidence of poverty rises with family size, ranging from 24% in a household of one to 46% in households with ten or more people. The *World Development Report* (World Bank [1990]) observed that in Pakistan in 1984, the poorest 10% of households had an average of 7.7 members; the corresponding national average was 6.1.

Not surprisingly, these larger, poor families often have a high ratio of dependent members, often children. In all the examples cited, the number of children per family was significantly correlated with their poverty. This is of great concern, because it suggests that the burden of poverty often falls disproportionately on the young. Given the immensely important role that childhood nutrition and education play, this is a double tragedy that overall head counts and poverty gap ratios cannot fully capture.

Clearly family size may be both a cause of poverty as well as an effect. Larger families, especially those with larger numbers of children, are likely to have lower per capita income simply because of the higher dependency ratio. To be sure, some of this dependency is eroded by institutions such as child labor, but children are not paid much. More significantly, poverty may actually feed on itself by creating the incentive to have a large number of children. Why this might be the case is a topic for Chapter 9. Suffice it to say that we speak of a correlation here, but as always, we cannot establish causality without more careful study.

There are two reasons, however, to doubt the high degree of observed correlation between household size and poverty. First, there is the problem of using per capita expenditure (or income) of the household as the relevant indicator, as most studies do. Larger households have a greater fraction of children, as we've already noted, and to the extent that children consume less than adults, the use of per capita expenditure overstates the amount of poverty. Second, some allowance should be made for the fact that larger households enjoy significant economies of scale. Once again, per capita measures generally overstate the extent of their poverty.

Correcting for these factors in a way that is conceptually satisfactory is not an easy task, but *some* allowance for adult equivalence is better than none. For instance, one could use a weight of 0.5 for children (although some variation here is also desirable, depending on age and sex). This weighting will certainly lower the estimates of poverty for large households. Correcting for increasing returns to scale—the fixed costs of setting up and running a household—has its own share of conceptual problems as well. One way out of this is to try different parametric values for returns to scale and see if "reasonable" values overturn the observed correlation between poverty and household size.[9]

It should also be noted that women are disproportionately represented as heads of poor households. The Fishlow study on Brazil cited earlier noted that there are twice as many female-headed households among the poor as among the nonpoor. This trend is widespread, being reflected in Africa, other parts of Latin America, and South and East Asia.[10] The absence of a principal male earner appears to be closely related to poverty.

For more discussion on the connections between gender bias and poverty, see the concluding section of this chapter.

8.3.2. Rural and urban poverty

Even if we take into account the differences in rural and urban cost of living, poverty in rural areas is significantly higher. Even countries with substantial advances in creating an equitable agriculture display higher rural poverty than their national averages. Table 8.2 summarizes rural–urban disparities in poverty, as well as in two major indicators of well-being, for selected countries.

8.3.3. Assets

A natural characteristic of poverty is that it is correlated with the lack of ownership of productive assets. As usual, we must be careful not to establish a one-way causal relationship between the lack of ownership of assets and poverty. Just as the paucity of assets leads to poverty, a condition of poverty leads to the sale of assets. In a word, the scarcity of assets and poverty must be viewed as closely related phenomena.

Given that poverty is so closely related with location in rural areas, it is not surprising that the bulk of the poor are found among the landless or near landless. Poverty and small-scale agriculture are especially strongly correlated in Africa: most of the poor in countries such as Botswana, Ghana,

---

[9] Anand and Morduch [1996] used the Bangladesh Household Expenditure Survey, 1988–89, to do this. Let x be aggregate household expenditure and m be household size. Then x/m is per capita household expenditure. Now introduce a scaling factor α between 0 and 1, and think of m^α as *effective* household size. Because $0 < \alpha < 1$, m^α rises slower than α, and this is a way of capturing returns to scale. The smaller the value of α, the higher the returns to scale. This procedure captures some of the adult equivalence issues as well, because it implies that the larger the household, the greater the proportion of children, and so effective household size (in adult equivalents) rises more slowly. Values of α around 0.8 or lower are sufficient to overturn the observed positive correlation between household size and poverty in the Bangladesh data. Whether this value of α represents "high" or "moderate" returns to scale requires more careful investigation, however.

[10] As Meesook [1975] and Fields [1980] observed, Thailand appears to be an exception to this rule. Social custom there provides greater assistance to women who are without a principal male earner in the household.

Table 8.2. Rural and urban poverty in the 1980s.

Region and country	Rural population (% of total population)	Rural poor (% of total poor)	Infant mortality (per 1000 live births)		Access to safe water (% of population)	
			Rural	Urban	Rural	Urban
Sub-Saharan Africa						
Côte d'Ivoire	57	86	121	70	10	30
Ghana	65	80	87	67	39	93
Kenya	80	96	59	57	21	61
Asia						
India	77	79	105	57	50	76
Indonesia	73	79	74	57	36	43
Malaysia	62	80	—	—	76	96
Philippines	60	67	55	42	54	49
Thailand	70	80	43	28	66	56
Latin America						
Guatemala	59	66	85	65	26	89
Mexico	31	37	79	29	51	79
Panama	50	59	28	22	63	100
Peru	44	52	101	54	17	73
Venezuela	15	20	—	—	80	80

Source: *World Development Report* (World Bank [1990]).

Kenya, and Nigeria are small farmers or pastoralists (*World Development Report*, World Bank [1990]). Apart from southern Africa, where the rural poor hire out their labor, the poor are largely self-employed. In contrast, in South Asia, landless labor is more widely represented among the poor. India, Pakistan, and Bangladesh all display a mix of poverty that is borne as much by landless labor as by small holders. Note, however, that after a point, the distinction between small landowners and landless laborers is blurred or meaningless: we are talking about pitifully low quantities of land in any case.

Nevertheless, it is true that there is a significant difference in poverty once we move from negligible or near-negligible holdings of land to more moderate holdings. Table 8.3 illustrates this difference.

Latin America shows the same concentration of poverty among the landless or the near landless. In Costa Rica, wage labor counts heavily among the poor, whereas Peru's poor are accounted for by small holders and herders. The poor also participate in rural nonfarm employment, largely cottage and traditional industries, the products of which are destined for home consumption or local markets.

Table 8.3. Poverty and landholding in rural Bangladesh, 1978–79.

Acres of land owned	% of total households in class	Income (taka per month)	Mean landholdings (acres)	HCR
Landless	7.1	508	0	93
0–0.5	36.1	560	0.1	93
0.5–1.0	10.5	711	0.7	84
1.0–1.5	8.9	783	1.2	78
1.5–2.5	12.1	912	2.0	68
2.5–5.0	13.8	1,163	3.5	45
5.0–7.5	5.7	1,516	6.0	23
7.5+	5.8	2,155	14.0	10
Total	100.0	865	2.1	70

Source: *World Development Report* (World Bank [1990]).

Urban poverty shows the same mix of self-employment and wage labor. Most of the poor reside in the "informal sector," which we will study in more detail in Chapter 10. Self-employment is common: as vendors, petty traders, tea-stall owners, beggars, shoe-shine boys, garbage sifters, load carriers, rickshaw pullers, roadside hawkers, and so on. Wage employment is often on a casual basis and not subject to minimum wage laws. Because of the chronic lack of assets, the vulnerability of the poor, quite apart from the low average levels of living, can be frightening.

Side by side with the scarcity of physical assets are the low levels of human capital. The most important determinant of the access to human capital is the ability to temporarily remove oneself from the labor force and use this period to acquire skills. This removal must be covered financially, through either loans or the support of close family and relatives. This kind of financial cover is the last thing one can associate with the poor and, consequently, it is far from surprising that the majority of poor have little or no human capital. Illiteracy rates are very high indeed, and among those who are not illiterate, there is little evidence of schooling beyond primary levels.

8.3.4. Nutrition

There is an intimate connection between poverty and undernutrition, especially in low-income countries. With low income, it is difficult for individuals to acquire adequate levels of food and nutrient consumption for themselves and their families. "Adequacy," as we shall see, is a loaded word, because the notion depends fundamentally on the kinds of activities in which an individual is engaged, as well as the nutritional history of that person. Nevertheless, it is not difficult to see the effects of undernutrition. In children

they are particularly severe: muscle wastage, stunting, and increased susceptibility to illness and infection. Undernutrition can also affect cognitive skills.
In adults, chronic undernutrition diminishes muscular strength, immunity to
disease, and the capacity to do productive work. In the next section, we will
see how low nutrition can feed back on a person's capacity to do work, thus
perpetuating the state of poverty in which they find themselves.

In many countries, poverty and undernutrition are closely related with
each other, because the definition of the poverty line often relies on the expenditure necessary to obtain a certain minimum food or nutrient basket
(plus some margin for nonfood items). Examples include Malaysia and India. Authors such as Lipton [1983] have argued that using a calorie-based
poverty line, or a *food adequacy standard*, is an appropriate way to measure
moderate or extreme levels of poverty in developing countries.[11] In such
examples it is not surprising that poverty and undernutrition are highly correlated. Countries such as Brazil have used measures that are not obviously
nutrition-based, but nevertheless a correlation persists between the subre-
gions or subpopulations of these countries that display the greatest degree
of poverty and the greatest degree of undernutrition. It must be mentioned,
however, that as average income rises, *poverty*, as measured by household or
per capita consumption (adjusted for the proportion of children in the household), exhibits less of a correlation with direct anthropometric measures of
undernutrition, such as measures of stunting or abnormally low weight in
children.[12]

Although the incidence of poverty and the incidence of undernutrition
may be *ordinally* related, in the sense that a poor person is more likely to
be undernourished than her richer counterpart, the relationship between *increases* in income (or expenditure) and *increases* in nutrition may or may not
be strong. Imagine that you draw a variety of different graphs to illustrate
hypothetical relationships between income earned and calories consumed.
All of these graphs may be increasing in the sense that greater income translates into more calories consumed. Thus poorer people are more likely to
be undernourished, but the flatter curves in that set of graphs suggest that
increases in income may translate (at least over some range) into a small increase in calorie consumption, whereas the steeper curves suggest a stronger
sensitivity of calorie intake to income. Thus depending on empirical findings, it is perfectly possible for the poor to be undernourished, while at the

---

[11] This is not to say that poverty should be identified with undernutrition. For one thing, persons
counted below the poverty line in any one year might be "temporarily poor" (recall our previous
discussion). For another, nutritional requirements vary from person to person, whereas the food
adequacy standard used to measure poverty is an overall average.

[12] See, for example, the exercise conducted by Glewwe and van der Gaag [1990] for Côte d'Ivoire,
using data from the 1985 Côte d'Ivoire Living Standards Survey. Côte d'Ivoire, however, did not
visibly suffer from an overall inadequacy of food supply in 1985. Children were relatively well
nourished even among the poor. This is not true of countries where the overall nutritional base is
much lower.

same time direct nutrition supplements may have a far greater impact on undernutrition than an increase in income.

There are two effects that might bear on this phenomenon, and they run in different directions. First, individuals attach significance to higher nutrition. A state of good nourishment is itself desirable, because it means greater stamina, physical and mental health, and higher resistance to illness. However, nutrition is also useful in a functional sense, as we shall soon see: it raises work capacity and, therefore, earnings ability. For both these reasons, an increase in purchasing power tends to raise nutritional status, especially if nutritional levels are low to begin with.

The second effect has to do with individual preferences for foods that taste good, or, more insidiously, foods that are well advertised and well packaged, or even worse, foods that are recognized as indicators of social and economic attainment.[13] It is easy enough in economically developed societies to downplay the strength of this effect, but in societies where food is of extreme importance in the budget, great value is assigned to the consumption of different food items, and nutrition may not be at the root of all these decisions. For example, the consumption of meat, or expensive varieties of rice, or even canned food, may be given far more social importance (as an indicator of status or wealth) than considerations of pure nutritive value warrant.[14] The desire to increase nutrition and the desire to increase food consumption for culinary pleasure or to signal social standing generally combine to create an intermediate reaction of nutrition to income.

Evidence on this issue is mixed and varies between strong and weak nutrition responses to budget changes. Overall, an increase in income has a significant effect on nutrition if nutrition is measured by the consumption of calories. However, the effect is not as strong as we might expect from a pure nutritional viewpoint.

What might we expect from such a viewpoint? The answer is best stated in terms of *elasticities*: what is the percentage change in the consumption of calories[15] when household budgets change by one percentage point? An answer of 1 means that there is an equivalent percentage change in nutrition when budgets change. Because there are subsistence minima to nutrition

---

[13] A classic application of linear programming is to the so-called *diet problem*: find the lowest-cost bundle of foods that will give you at least so many calories, so much protein, certain minima of various vitamins, and so on. The typical solutions to the diet problem offer a very low cost of attaining the required minima, but the foods will not look very appetizing.

[14] Pure *wastage* of food also may be an indicator of social standing. It is unfortunate that very often the deliberate wastage of a scarce resource is a powerful way of signaling one's social rank. Viewed from this angle, the wastage of food is no more horrific than the excessive consumption of power, wood, paper, geographical space, and many other resources in developed countries.

[15] Other nutrients are of importance as well: see the case study box on nutrition and income in South India.

levels below which it is difficult to go, this a priori notion is possibly too high. In other words, if income falls below a certain minimum, individuals may obtain their nutrition from other sources (support from relatives, for instance). As income increases, individuals presumably substitute away from these sources. Thus (and simply as a reasonable guess, no more), elasticities between 0.6 and 0.8 may be good evidence that individuals strongly adjust nutrition to income.

Is this what we observe? The answer seems to be in the negative. Estimates range between elasticities that are close to zero and those that are in the region of our a priori expectations.[16] Table 8.4 summarizes the estimates obtained in various studies; calorie elasticities are arranged in increasing order of magnitude. Of course, the idea isn't to take an average of all these findings, because the methodology and the data sets differ widely, but we can get a sense of what kind of numbers are available.

Overall, we do obtain some evidence that pure nutritional concerns do not entirely drive household decision making. However, these overall findings need to be tempered by two observations. First, there is some evidence that poorer households indeed react more strongly to changes in their budgets by purchasing more nutrients. Second, the pooling of data across the peak and lean seasons may confound the elasticity estimates. Because food supply in the peak or harvest season is more abundant, a change in the budget does not translate into significantly higher nutrient consumption. On the other hand, if food availability is low, as in the slack season, and credit markets are imperfect so that consumption cannot be fully smoothed over time (see Chapter 14), an increase in household income in the slack season is more adequately reflected in the demand for nutrition. Both these points were made by Behrman, Foster, and Rosenzweig [1994] (and by other authors as well). Behrman, Foster, and Rosenzweig use a data set from rural Pakistan, and found that a careful distinction between slack and peak seasons pays dividends. Estimated elasticities are high and significant in the slack. Moreover, they are especially high for people who are landless or near landless.

Later in this chapter, we turn to a converse relationship. What is the relationship between nutrition and the *ability* to generate income, or more broadly, on the ability to perform economically productive work?

Nutrition and Income: A Case Study from South India

How do we go about estimating a relationship between nutrition and income? Consider the demand for a basket of food items consumed by households. The statis-

[16] The survey by Behrman [1993] discusses some of these estimates.

Table 8.4. *Elasticities of calorie demand with respect to household budget, arranged in ascending order.*

Calorie elasticity[a]	Country and year	Authors
0.01	Indonesia 1978	Pitt and Rosenzweig [1985][b]
0.06	Nicaragua 1977–78	Behrman and Wolfe [1984][b]
0.07	India 1976–78	Bhargava [1991][b]
0.08	Philippines 1984–85	Bouis and Haddad [1992][c]
0.09	Philippines 1984–85	Bouis and Haddad [1992][b]
0.09	Brazil 1974–75	Strauss and Thomas [1990][c]
0.12	Bangladesh 1981–82	Pitt, Rosenzweig and Hassan [1990][c]
0.15	Indonesia 1981	Ravallion [1990][c]
0.15	Kenya 1984–87	Kenney [1989][b]
0.17	India 1976–78	Behrman and Deolalikar [1987][c]
0.20	Brazil 1974–75	Williamson-Gray [1982][b]
0.29	Pakistan 1986–87	Alderman [1989][c]
0.30	Thailand 1975–76	Trairatvorakul [1984][c]
0.33	Philippines 1984–85	Garcia and Pinstrup-Andersen [1987][c]
0.34	India 1983	Subramanian and Deaton [1996][c]
0.41	India 1983–84	Alderman [1987][c]
0.47	Indonesia 1976	Timmer and Alderman [1979][c]
0.48/0.37[d]	Gambia 1985–86	von Braun, Puetz, and Webb [1989][c]
0.51	Nepal 1982–83	Kumar and Hotchkiss [1988][b]
0.53	Brazil 1973–75	Ward and Sanders [1980][b]
0.54	Indonesia 1978	Chernichovsky and Meesook [1984][c]
0.56	Sri Lanka 1984	Edirisinghe [1987][c]
0.57	Ghana 1987–88	Alderman and Higgins [1992][c]
0.58/0.34[d]	India 1976–78	Behrman and Deolalikar [1989][b]
0.62	Sri Lanka 1980–81	Sahn [1988][c]
0.80	Bangladesh 1974–75	Pitt [1983][c]
0.86	Sierra Leone 1974–75	Strauss [1984][c]

Source: Behrman, Foster, and Rosenzweig [1994, Table 1].
[a]Calorie elasticity is estimated at the sample means.
[b]Budget was measured by household income.
[c]Budget was measured by household expenditure.
[d]The first entry pertains to the lean season, the second to the peak season when food is more abundant.

tician's choice of the basket depends on the availability of data. Average estimates of the nutrient content of each food item (its calorie, protein, calcium, and other contents) are available from nutrition data that record such information. Now suppose that household expenditure rises. Then the demand for each of these food items will change, and we can measure these changes. If we multiply all these changes by the average nutrient content (say, calories per gram or protein per liter) for each food item and add up, we obtain a measure of the change in *nutrient* consumption as expenditure changes.

This method does take into account the change in the composition of the food basket as expenditure rises, so that a shift from more to less nutritious foods can be captured as we move up the expenditure scale. The problem is that the *extent* to which such effects can be captured depends on the richness of the data describing food groupings. Often, this is inadequate. For instance, even if we had data on "rice" rather than "grain," there are substitutions between short- and long-grained varieties that cannot be picked up. With the advent of canned, processed, and packaged foods, the possibilities of substitution are endless. Another way of stating the point is that *we cannot assume that nutrient content stays constant within the food item as we move from lower to higher levels of expenditure.* Typically and unfortunately, the nutrient component seems to *fall.*

A study by Behrman and Deolalikar [1987] dramatically displays this possibility. They used the foregoing method to study six villages in two states in the semi-arid region of India, known as the ICRISAT villages.[17] For the years 1976–77 and 1977–78, special nutrition surveys were carried out and nutrient intakes were recorded for households. The nutrition surveys provided information on nine nutrients: calories, protein, calcium, iron, carotene, thiamine, riboflavin, niacin, and ascorbic acid. This suggests a *direct* approach to the problem: simply relate consumption of these nutrients to the expenditure by household.[18] Contrast this with the food basket approach, which the authors discussed as well: they considered consumption changes in six basic foods: sugar, pulses, vegetables, milk, meat, and grains. Table 8.5 summarizes some of their results. Reported in this table are the *elasticities* of expenditure on various items with respect to a change in the household budget. This is done first for the commodity groups and then on the nutrients.[19] Thus an entry of 0.57 for sugar means that *if* household expenditures were altered by 10%, the expenditure on sugar would increase by 5.7%. An elasticity of 1 means that expenditure on that item grows at the same rate as total expenditure.

We see from Table 8.5 that elasticities for food items are large and significant (the weighted average over food groups is 1.18), whereas, apart from carotene, there is no strong nutrient effect to speak of (all the estimated coefficients are insignificant at the 5% level). This raises a puzzle of some significance: Why don't poor individuals who are generally below the food adequacy standard (and the individuals in this sample were below the standard, on average) significantly respond to budget increases by increasing their nutritional intake?

We have discussed this study in some detail because it presents a counterintuitive position in a provocative way. Do not take this to mean that all subsequent studies find the same low relationship between income (or expenditure) and nutrient

---

[17] For an introduction to the ICRISAT villages, see Chapter 10.

[18] Of course, the nutrient intakes are themselves calculated with respect to a basket of food items and are therefore logically subject to the same problem. However, direct observations on 120 foods were made, and this is a very rich sample indeed, so it reduces, to a large extent, the compositional errors that we have discussed.

[19] The figures that we report are estimates that control for village and household fixed effects by the use of differencing. The overall results are similar without these controls, although the elasticity estimates for particular items, noticeably milk, do change pretty significantly. For details, see Behrman and Deolalikar [1987].

Table 8.5. Elasticities of demand for food and nutrient groups.

Food type	Elasticity	Nutrient	Elasticity
Grains	1.52*	Calories	0.37
Sugar	0.57*	Protein	0.19
Pulses	1.00	Calcium	−0.22
Vegetables	0.51*	Iron	0.30
Milk	−0.13	Carotene	2.01*
Meat	1.05*	Thiamine	0.18
		Riboflavin	0.69
		Niacin	0.21
		Ascorbic acid	1.25

Source: Behrman and Deolalikar [1987, Table 2].
Notes: An asterisk denotes that the variable was significantly affected by household expenditure (see Appendix 2 for a discussion of "significance"). The elasticities were evaluated at the sample means.

intake. There are significant variations over countries, as well as over studies done at different points in time on the same country, as the main text illustrates.

8.4. The functional impact of poverty

There is very little one can say to captures adequately the degradation, the indignity, and the dehumanization of utter economic deprivation, so I will not try. We hear often of the joys of a simple, poor life, unencumbered by materialist ambitions, rich in many ways. There is little doubt that poverty can bring out the best in human beings, in an environment where the common sharing of transient gains and losses has such immense value. On the other hand, that is no excuse for poverty, and people singing the praises of the simple, honest, loyal, trusting poor are well advised to experience a dose of poverty themselves. Economic poverty is the worst curse there is.

We move on, therefore, to arguments that *link* the incidence of poverty to mechanisms that drive its creation. It is also important to understand the informal mechanisms that spontaneously arise to cope with poverty. These mechanisms tell us something about what causes poverty, as well as the wider effects that poverty has on the economic system, and they are fundamental to the creation of appropriate policies.

The fundamental feature of poverty is that it affects the access of the poor to markets, and this change in access has repercussions for the entire economy. Practically all markets are affected: the ability to obtain credit, to sell labor, to rent land for cultivation. What we are going to discuss next are some of these effects. Of course, in a natural way, they all tie in with chapters that are devoted to a study of such markets, such as Chapters 13 and 14, so we will be brief in these matters and refer you to additional material that can be found elsewhere in this book.

8.4.1. Poverty, credit, and insurance

Credit

The market for credit naturally fails for the poor. The poor are unable to obtain loans that can be used to better their lives by allowing them to invest in a productive activity. The failure occurs for a variety of reasons.

First, the poor lack collateral that can be put up for loan repayment. Collateral is charged for two reasons. One is that the project to which the loan is being applied may *genuinely* be unsuccessful, so that the borrower is *unable* to repay the loan. Collateral is insurance against this possibility. However, this is not the principal reason by far. If projects are, *on average*, successful, then enterprising lenders realize that there are gains to be made (in an expected sense) and they fill such gaps with loans. Collateral is, more fundamentally, a means to of prevent *intentional default* on the part of the borrower.[20] The possibility of lost collateral reduces the incentive to walk away without repaying the loan. The poor lack the wherewithal to put up adequate collateral and therefore are denied loans.[21]. In Chapter 7, we discussed a model in detail that incorporates this point.

As we will see in more detail in Chapter 14, the inability of the poor to provide appropriate collateral effectively shuts them out from the formal credit market. Sometimes informal credit sources can step in to fill this gap, because they can accept collateral in forms that the formal sector cannot. The most important of these forms is labor. In increasingly mobile societies, this form of collateral is becoming rarer, because although labor services serve the first function of collateral (which is to provide a backup to the lender in the even of involuntary default), they are only of limited use in the prevention of intentional default.

Second, it can be argued that the incentives to repay for the poor are limited, independent of (and in addition to) their inability to put up collateral. To understand this, it suffices to note that each additional unit of money in hand means far more to a poor individual than to a rich individual: this is just the familiar principle of *diminishing marginal utility*. Thus when the time to repay loans comes around, the calculus of whether or not to default on

---

[20] Thus if the local pawnbroker accepts your greatgrandmother's watch, left to you as a family heirloom, as collateral for a loan, it is not so much that the watch will fetch a good price if you default on the loan. The point is that the watch is valuable *to you*, so that if you are contemplating a default in a situation where you can afford to pay, you will think twice about it.

[21] For a more complete discussion of this issue, see Banerjee and Newman [1994]

the loan is naturally twisted in favor of default. Figure 8.1 shows how this works.

In Figure 8.1, we look at two incomes, Y_p (for poor) and Y_R (for rich). Compare the two cases in a situation where the same loan L has to be repaid. Because the utility function exhibits diminishing marginal utility, it is clear that *utility loss* to the poor from repayment (given by the segment of length A in the diagram) exceeds the corresponding utility loss to the rich (given by the segment of length B).

Of course, it can be argued, in response to this observation, that the assumption of similar loan size is not sensible. Typically, the poor receive smaller loans, which destroys the easy comparability of Figure 8.1. In addition, it can be argued that we are not taking the *costs* of default into account (as we explicitly did in Chapter 5). Perhaps the stakes are higher for the poor: they have more to lose from nonrepayment, particularly in lack of future access to credit.

You could make both these points, and you would be absolutely correct in making them. The poor *do* get smaller loans, on average, and for precisely this reason. It is also possible that the poor have much more to lose from default, but this only reinforces our argument that initial poverty reduces access to the credit market. Indeed it is always in the interest of the lender to assure that loans do not permanently change the economic conditions of his borrower, so that the threat of cutting off *future* credit always has bite.

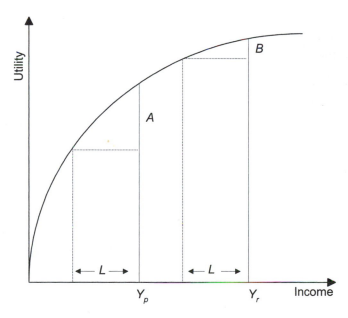

Figure 8.1. *Incentives to repay for the poor and rich: a comparison.*

We already saw in Chapter 7 that this lack of access implies a loss in national output, because productive opportunities are not being utilized by a properly functioning credit market. To the extent that lenders are unable to capture a share of the returns from these activities (because of the fear of default), they will not lend to allow individuals to exploit these opportunities.

The lack of access to credit market also affects the access of the poor to land tenancy markets. For more on this, see Chapter 12.

Insurance

On the other hand, mutual opportunities of insurance among the poor are perhaps easier to exploit. To see why this informal safety net actually works better under conditions of poverty, it is important to take a quick look at the factors that limit insurance. We take this up in much more detail in Chapter 15, on insurance.

Briefly, then, why do people insure? The reasons are fairly obvious. The future holds risks that we are unwilling to take. Our house may burn down, we may fall sick or be disabled, we may be laid off, we may run over someone in our car, and so on. To *insure* against such contingencies, we typically pay a sum of money, say every year, to an insurance company. The insurance company collects this money, and typically plays no role in your life (apart from trying to persuade you to get other things insured) until one of these bad incidents occurs, say your house burns down. In that case, the insurance company must pay the amount for which you insured your house.

Now consider what is needed for successful insurance. The first feature of all insurance is that the incident against which you are insuring must be *verifiable*, at least to some extent. You will be unable to buy insurance against the possibility that you might be in a bad mood tomorrow. It's not that it's a weird thing to insure against—people have been known to insure far stranger things—but the point is that such outcomes are not verifiable, least of all to the insurance company.

The second feature of successful insurance is that whatever you are insuring against is not subject to *moral hazard*. Moral hazard is an important economic concept that will be studied in detail in Chapters 12–14, but it is easy to convey the main idea. Suppose that I own a personal computer and insure it against damage. Now that I *am* insured, the degree of care that I take to make sure that I do not spill coffee on the keyboard may decrease, because the cost of the damage *to me* has been reduced by insurance. The point is that *there are incidents that you might want to insure against, where the probability of occurrence is influenced by your actions.* This creates a dilemma. Perfect insurance is a good idea in principle, but if it blunts the feeling of responsibility that people have for their own actions, it might make life very costly for the insurance company, or at any rate for *somebody*.[22]

To avoid moral hazard, then, companies typically retreat from the provision of complete insurance. There are deductibles if you buy a prescription drug or if you spill coffee on the computer keyboard. You typically incur some of the costs if your house is burgled, and if you buy life insurance, companies will not pay in the event of suicide, at least in the first few years of the insurance. The list of restrictions is long and varied.

In developing countries, *formal* insurance schemes are relatively rare. Indeed, on both the above-mentioned counts, there are typically severe problems. With the formal legal system at slow and fairly minimal levels, and with limited powers of verifiability, it is difficult, if not impossible, to obtain formally verifiable accounts of incidents, such as the exact degree of crop failure on someone's land holding. The same lack of information exacerbates issues of moral hazard: it is true that the crop on your land is determined by the vagaries of the weather (which is why you want insurance in the first place), but it is also the case that it can be influenced by how hard you work the land, which is very difficult for an insurance company to control. Moreover, in many cases, what is needed is nonmonetary methods of insurance. Illness in a family might necessitate the provision of care by another resident in the same village or it might require extra labor at the time of harvest. Because of these formidable problems, formal insurance is almost always missing.

We will see in Chapter 14 how these formal schemes are typically replaced by informal schemes at the level of the village community. Village members have access to far better information, and therefore can self-insure as a group in a way that no formal company can replicate.

Of course, the issues of moral hazard still remain. Perfect insurance of idiosyncratic movements in crop output may lead to the underprovision of effort by the family farm. The point is, however, that *these moral hazard problems are likely to be smaller for the poor*.

It is easy to see why. Almost by definition, the opportunity cost of labor for the poor is lower than that of richer people. The poor are more likely to be unemployed or underemployed. Even if this were not true, they are likely to earn lower wages when they are employed and, in general, the cost of their time is lower. This feature, in turn, permits them to credibly supply more effort to the task at hand (such as farming) *without* necessitating a large cutback (or "deductible") in the degree of insurance that they receive. This

---

[22] A classic example of moral hazard comes from health insurance. The United States is a leading instance of the problem. High levels of insurance create an overuse of the medical system, because patients run to their doctors on the slightest provocation and receive treatments on a scale unparalleled elsewhere in the world. Is this all for free? Of course not. Over time, insurance premiums climb to staggering heights, which creates a situation that is very costly both at the personal and the social level.

low opportunity cost of effort is helped along by the fact that their marginal utility of consumption is very high (see the discussion in the previous subsection). Therefore, even if they are participating in schemes that insure them to a high degree, they will rarely freeload on such schemes. Therefore, when the people involved are poor rather than rich, it is far easier to have informal schemes that involve a large amount of shared labor and effort, as well as transfers of money or grain, to tide over bad times.

We will see more of this kind of analysis—and some caveats as well—in Chapter 15.

8.4.2. Poverty, nutrition, and labor markets

Introduction

We already observed that, even by very conservative estimates, over a billion people worldwide were classified as poor in 1990. We also observed that a large proportion of these individuals are also significantly below adequate standards of nutrition.

The effects of undernutrition vary widely. We have already mentioned outcomes such as muscle wastage, retardation of growth, increased illness, vulnerability to infection, and the diminution of work capacity. In addition, undernourished persons are easily fatigued and exhibit marked psychological changes, manifested in mental apathy, depression, introversion, lower intellectual capacity, and lack of motivation. Life expectancy among the undernourished is low, but the undernourished do not die immediately.

In this section, we study the relationship that exists between a person's nutritional status and his capacity to do sustained work, and we study in Chapter 13 how this relationship creates a vicious cycle in the labor market: poverty leading to undernutrition, hence the inability to work, which feeds back on the incidence of poverty. Thus undernutrition plays a *functional* role apart from being of intrinsic interest. Because undernutrition affects the capacity to work, it affects the functioning of labor markets in a central way.

Energy balance

To start thinking seriously about this problem, it is useful to examine the simplest story of energy balance within the human body.[23] It has four main components.

1. *Energy input*. The periodic consumption of food is the main source of energy input to the human body. It is also the obvious point where nutrition

_____

[23] The material in this subsection draws on Dasgupta and Ray [1986, 1987, 1990], Ray and Streufert [1993], and Ray [1993].

meets economics. Access to food, in most situations, is the same as access to *income*. In the case of the poor, income chiefly represents returns to labor supply and (to a lesser extent) to nonlabor assets such as small quantities of land.

2. *Resting metabolism*. This is a *significant* proportion of the body's requirements. It represents the energy required to maintain body temperature, sustain heart and respiratory action, supply the minimum energy requirements of resting tissues, and support ionic gradients across cell membranes. For the "reference man" of the Food and Agricultural Organization (FAO), who is a European male and weighs 65 kg, this figure is around 1,700 kcal per day. Of course, the exact number varies significantly with the characteristics of the individual and the ambient environment in which he lives. An important determinant, for instance, is body mass: a higher body mass raises resting metabolism.

3. *Energy required for work*. The second significant component is energy required to carry out physical labor. The FAO's 1973 estimate, applied to their reference man, prescribed 400 kcal per day for "moderate activity." Unfortunately, as Clark and Haswell [1970, p. 11] pointed out, the FAO reference man "appears to be a European weighing 65 kg, and who spends most of his day in a manner rather ambiguously defined, but apparently not working very hard." For the poor in less developed countries, who are subject to hard labor of the most strenuous kind, this may be a somewhat conservative estimate. Although precise estimates are impossible without knowing the kind of work the individual has to perform, it is probably safe to say that the figure is significantly higher than 400 kcal per day.

Clark and Haswell's interesting book contains information on the energy requirements for various types of physical activity, culled from the work of different authors. Thus, in studies of West African agriculture, estimates of calorie consumption vary from 213 kcal per hour for carrying a log of 20 kg, to 274 kcal per hour for hoeing, to 372 kcal per hour for bush clearing, and up to 502 kcal per hour for tree felling. Of course, these are activities that are not (and cannot) be performed continuously over large stretches of time, but the European reference man with his allotment of calories for physical activity might be hard pressed to carry out any of these at minimal levels. The point, then, is clear enough. The labor of the poor is often physical labor, and physical labor requires significant amounts of energy.

4. *Storage and borrowing*. It should be quite obvious by now that, over a period of time at least, we can expects to see some form of balance between item 1, energy input, and the *sum* of the components in items 2 and 3. In the short or medium run, however, excesses or deficits can be cushioned (to some extent) by the human body. An energy deficit is met by running down stores from the body. An energy surplus is partly dissipated, partly stored.

Well-fed people in developed countries worry about the second problem (especially the possibility that energy surpluses may be stored and not dissipated). For the hundreds of millions of people that suffer undernutrition, the real problem is the first: coping with the threat of an energy deficit. A sustained deficit leads to undernutrition, and—ultimately—the breakdown of the body via illness, incapacitating debility, or death.

The point that we need to be aware of—and it is a point that we shall develop in detail in Chapter 13—is that *not only* do labor markets generate income and therefore create the principal potential source of nutrition and good health, but good nutrition in turn *affects the capacity of the body to perform tasks that generate income*. There is a cycle here, and this cycle alerts us to the possibility that in developing countries, a significant fraction of the population may be caught in a poverty trap.

To fix our ideas, ignore for the moment the possibility of borrowing or storage. Figure 8.2 shows the relationship between nutrition and the capacity to perform productive work, which we refer to as the *capacity curve*.

Observe closely the labeling of the axes in Figure 8.2. In particular, the *x* axis, which really should be "nutrition," has been labeled "income." The implicit assumption here is that all income is spent on nutrition. Nothing of substance is lost by amending this to a more realistic situation where, say, 70% of income is spent on nutrition, but as you'll see, the exposition is just easier this way. The *y* axis is labeled with the vague-sounding phrase "work capacity." How can we conceptually think about this? The idea is to think of work capacity as a measure of the total number of tasks an individual can perform during the period under review, say, the number of bushels of wheat that he can harvest during a day. The capacity curve is found by

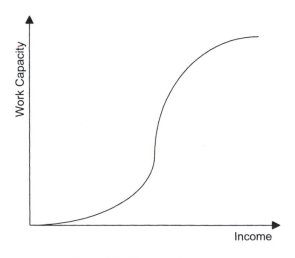

Figure 8.2. The capacity curve.

linking different nutrition (or income) points to the corresponding levels of work capacity that arc generated by the individual.

To understand the shape of the capacity curve, ask yourself what happens as we move from left to right along the x axis; that is, as we increase the amount of income (nutrition) available to the individual. Initially, most of this nutrition goes into maintaining resting metabolism, and so sustaining the basic frame of the body. In this stretch very little extra energy is left over for work (remember again that for the moment, we are ruling out the depletion of body stores of energy). So work capacity in this region is low (close to zero, if you like) *and* does not increase too quickly as nutrition levels change. Once resting metabolism is taken care of, however, there is a marked increase in work capacity, as the lion's share of additional energy input can now be funneled to work. This phase is followed by a phase of diminishing returns, as the natural limits imposed by the body's frame restrict the conversion of increasing nutrition into ever-increasing work capacity. (The curve probably even turns *downward* after a point, reflecting the usual concerns of the developed world, but we ignore that here.)

Nutrition and work capacity

The whole point of developing the biological relationship between nutrition and work capacity is to alert us to a line of thought that we will pursue in detail in Chapter 13. Although low incomes create low nutrition, *low nutrition is capable of creating low incomes*. This is the functional aspect of undernutrition: apart from being of social and ethical concern in its own right, it has an impact on the ability to earn. Thus it is not difficult to imagine a vicious circle of poverty in many low-income countries, in which low incomes are responsible for undernutrition, which in turn perpetuates those low incomes.

In Chapter 13, we take up this theme in some detail, but at this stage, it is worth thinking about how the argument may run. Several considerations come to mind.

(1) *If a low-income–undernutrition–low-income circle is possible in poor countries, why is it not possible for some groups of people in rich countries?*

This question pushes us to think about whether the vicious circle that we've described can exist in isolation, independently of whether the economy is rich or poor. The answer is that, in general, it cannot, and the reason has to do with the overall supply of labor.

A labor market is *tight* if the alternatives to working with any particular employer are relatively plentiful and attractive. Standard supply and demand theory tells us that for a labor market to be tight, there must be either a low supply relative to demand *in that market itself* or attractive opportunities in *other* labor markets.

Now, if the labor market is tight, in the sense that we have just described, the returns to work are high even though a person may have low work capacity to start with. The circle cannot be completed. These high returns, in general, permit the individual to consume adequate nutrition and hence raise his work capacity over time. The limits to which a worker's income can be pushed depend not on biological considerations, but on the opportunities available to that worker elsewhere in the labor market. If these latter considerations are salient, then a vicious circle theory based on undernutrition ceases to be valid.

The tightness of particular labor markets in particular countries is an issue that can be settled only by detailed and careful empirical work.[24]

(2) *Can't people simply borrow their way out of the vicious circle?*

This is a subtle issue that we cannot address satisfactorily until we study Chapters 13 and 14, but it is possible to provide some tentative answers. First, the credit market may simply be closed to poor individuals, for reasons that we have outlined in the preceding sections. This is especially true of consumption credit. Moneylenders are often interested in funding tangible production projects or providing working capital for such projects, and consumption loans are difficult to obtain at reasonable terms.

There is a second, more delicate answer. An economy with undernutrition traps of the kind that we are envisaging here may well be Pareto optimal! That is, there may be *no* way (in the short run) to make the undernourished poor better off without some amount of redistribution from the portion of the population with greater access to income and assets.[25] Recall from your introductory economics analysis what Pareto optimality means. It means that there is no way to rearrange endowments, production, and consumption so that all economic agents are simultaneously better off. Pareto optimality sounds very nice, and at some level it is, but it is perfectly compatible with the idea that some people are getting very few of the economic goodies. The best way to understand this is to think of dividing a cake between two people. As long as you aren't throwing any of the cake away, *any*

---

[24] Take the case of the rural labor market in India, in which the majority of India's labor force participates. There seems to be little doubt that such markets are characterized by large and persistent levels of unemployment, at least for significant fractions of the year. The evidence comes from a number of sources. For example, Krishnamurty [1988] observed from National Sample Survey data that rural unemployment rates were high *and* increasing in the 1970s, although there was significant interstate variation. Visaria [1981] and Sundaram and Tendulkar [1988] observed, moreover, that for agricultural households that were primarily engaged in the rural labor market, these rates were very high indeed. Mukherjee's thesis [1991] contains a careful review of the relevant literature and, in addition, carries out a detailed study of Palanpur village, which reinforces the foregoing findings. High unemployment is such an accepted feature for researchers studying the Indian case that theoretical analysis of labor markets is often driven by the objective of explaining and understanding this one crucial feature. The excellent survey by Drèze and Mukherjee [1991] of theories of rural labor markets illustrates this point well.

[25] This is the argument made in Dasgupta and Ray [1986].

division is Pareto optimal, including the one in which one person eats all of it.

Pareto optimality has its implications. If an economy is functioning so that its allocation of goods and services is Pareto optimal, then introducing a credit market in which people can borrow to stock up on work capacity cannot have any effect at all! The reason is that for people to lend to such a market, they must register a gain. The people who borrow presumably gain as well. People who do not participate are unaffected.[26] Then the new allocation achieved by the credit market must make some people better off and nobody worse off. This contradicts the postulate that the earlier allocation was Pareto optimal.

This argument relies on the presumption that the initial outcome is Pareto optimal. We will see more of this model in Chapter 13.

(3) *If work capacity affects future work output, won't employers wish to offer long-run contracts that take advantage of this?*

It is unclear that such contracts can be enforced unless there is some *separate* reason why workers want to stay in such contracts (there may well be, as we will see later in the book). It is unlikely that an employer will make a long-run contract with his employee *just* to extract future gains from enhanced work capacity. There is no guarantee that the employee will be around tomorrow: he may work for a different employer, perhaps in a different village; he might migrate. Under these circumstances, the employer might be extremely reluctant to engage in a nutrition-enhancing investment. Second, if a person in good health can be identified by other employers, the market will bid up the wage rate for such an employee. This means essentially that the employee will reap the entire benefit of the employer-financed investment in the form of a higher wage. If this is the case, then why undertake the investment in the first place?

The problem can be overcome if the employee binds himself to a contract that forbids him from working elsewhere in the future even though the terms elsewhere are better, but this has ethical connotations that make it unenforceable by a court of law, and rightly so, from a moral point of view.

(4) *By the way, if such long-run relationships were somehow in place for other reasons, would this have an effect on nutritional status?*

It might, but in a relationship where nutrition is used positively by the employer to build up work capacity on the part of her employee, *there must*

---

[26] The cautious reader will notice that the argument is a bit slippery here. There may be effects on relative prices that do change consumption allocations for the nonparticipants, but in the simple one-commodity model that we consider in Chapter 13, these claims are true.

be a separate factor, or set of factors, that makes the relationship inflexible in the sense that the employee is costly to replace. Consider three quick examples.

The slave economy: Slavery is perhaps the most appropriate example. Slaves were bought, and therefore each act of replacement brought with it a large outlay, apart from the daily costs involved in keeping slaves. Indeed, in the American South, slave prices rose steeply in the decades before the Civil War (Fogel and Engerman [1974, pp. 94–102]). Thus an existing slave had great value to the employer/owner. It turns out that slave diets were plentiful and varied.[27] The diet actually exceeded U.S. 1964 levels of recommended daily allowances for all the chief nutrients. Perhaps more to the point, the calorific value of the average slave diet exceeded that of all "free men" in 1879 by more than 10% (Fogel and Engerman [1974, p. 113]). In addition, the maintenance of the health of slaves was repeatedly emphasized in overseer manuals as a central objective (Fogel and Engerman [1974, p. 117]).

Industry: The effect of adequate nutrition on the productivity of workers has been emphasized repeatedly in manuals. The monograph by Keyter [1962] on South Africa, for example, contains many such references and a closing section with fifty-four recipes. This book focuses on industrial feeding, and in so doing squarely addresses the obvious reasons for feeding in the work-place: by changing the composition of wages in this manner, it forces the worker to consume a greater proportion of his wage as food.[28]

Domestic servants: This is another good example of a labor market that is likely to be inflexible. Servants are associated with characteristics acquired on the job that make them hard to replace. Not only is the loss of a servant important, but the acquisition of a new servant with minimally acceptable characteristics often results in an arduous training process. We are interested in seeing studies of this market in the Indian context; casual empiricism tells me that such studies would prove quite supportive to our thesis.[29] We re-fer the reader, instead, to an excellent monograph on the subject by McBride [1976], which cites various housekeeping manuals written for English and French housewives in the nineteenth century. Although McBride found the diet of servants to be generally parsimonious (relative to that of master and

[27] Fogel and Engerman [1974, p. 111] pointed out that among the "plantation products that slaves consumed were beef, mutton, chickens, milk, turnips, peas, squashes, sweet potatoes, apples, plums, oranges, pumpkins and peaches," in addition to corn and pork.

[28] In this context, see also Rodgers' [1975] study of some Bihar villages, though in this study the reasons for on-the-job feeding are considerably more ambiguous.

[29] Middle- and upper-class Indian households display an extremely high degree of paternalistic concern regarding the nutrition and medical care available to their servants. Such concern seems particularly out of line with the monetary wages paid to servants. Even though this paternalistic care has been molded by social custom to appear as genuine caring, there is little doubt regarding the fundamental motives behind such behavior.

mistress), more than one manual explicitly suggests means to assure servants a high level of energy. For instance, a popular French manual of the early nineteenth century recommended that servants be made to abandon the traditional Parisian practice of café au lait in the morning and substitute a breakfast of soup made from the meat left over from the previous night, so that the servant would have enough energy to work until 5 p.m. without stopping. Booth's study of life among London laborers concluded that "the quality of food given to domestic servants...is usually very good, and in all but very rare cases greatly superior to that obtainable by members of the working-class families from which servants are drawn" (Booth [1903, Vol. 8]).

8.4.3. Poverty and the household

The unequal sharing of poverty

One of the great tragedies of poverty is that the poor may not afford to share their poverty equally. Unequal sharing arises fundamentally from the fact that certain minimum amounts of nutrition, care, and economic resources have to be devoted to each person (including each child) in order for that person's life to be productive and healthy. In situations of extreme poverty, equal division of household resources might help no one, because the average amounts are far too small. The potential merit of unequal division is that it helps *some* individuals in the household to be minimally productive under extreme circumstances. This takes us right into the well-known problems of the "lifeboat ethic": a lifeboat can hold only two people and there are three individuals to save. One person must die.

The capacity curve gives us a clear idea of how the nutritional problem serves to promote unequal allocations. Figure 8.3 displays the capacity curve, marked $OAEB$. The straight line OAB is drawn from the origin so that the line segment OA equals the line segment AB. The income level corresponding to capacity B is denoted by Y^*. By construction, the income level corresponding to capacity A must be $Y^*/2$.

Now consider a household of just two persons, and suppose that their capacity curves are identical and given by the curve in Figure 8.3. Suppose that *total household income* happens to be given by Y^*. Think of two options: the household shares this income equally or one person consumes the entire income.[30] Notice that by the construction of Y^*, these two options yield exactly the same total work capacity for the household: by similar triangles, the height of B must be exactly twice that of A.

Suppose, now, that the household has an income lower than Y^*, say Y (see diagram). Equal division means that each member gets $Y/2$ and each

---

[30] Of course these two extreme options represent an exaggeration. Other intermediate divisions are obviously possible, but we neglect them for simplicity.

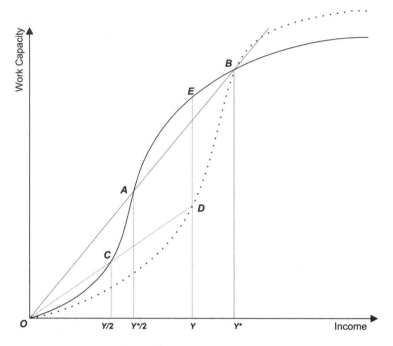

Figure 8.3. The capacity curve and unequal allocation.

person therefore has work capacity equal to the height of *C*. *Total* household capacity is therefore given by twice this height, which is just the height of the point *D*. Compare this to total household capacity if one person is al-located the entire income for consumption: it is the height of the point *E*, which is greater. It follows that at incomes below the critical threshold Y^*, *unequal consumption allocations create greater household work capacity than equal allocations.* To the extent that increased household capacity is good for future income-earning potential, we have a dilemma here.

In contrast, at household incomes above the threshold Y^*, equal division does better than unequal division. The dotted curve *ODB* was constructed from the capacity curve: it tells us what household capacity is when house-hold income is divided equally. It lies *below* the individual capacity curve until the point *B* and then rises above it.

This argument suggests why poverty is correlated with unequal alloca-tion. Note well the culprit: it is the "convex" section of the capacity curve, which captures the fact that certain minimal amounts are required as nu-tritional input before productivity gains kick in. Without this section, equal allocations would always be preferable.[31]

One reaction to this argument is that it is unrealistic: it is absurd to imagine that in the interests of maximizing household capacity, one person

---

[31] For more detailed analysis along these lines, see Mirrlees [1976] and Stiglitz [1976].

will be left to starve. This is certainly not the lesson that I want you to take away: the extremity of the result arises from the simplicity of the model. There are several reasons why the extreme unequal outcome may not come about, not the least among them being that each family member is loved and cherished. However, the situation creates a *tendency* toward unequal treatment to the extent that the income-earning potential of the household is an issue of some concern.

One common solution to the lifeboat problem is to draw lots: this has at least the virtue of being egalitarian ex ante. Drawing lots is not an entirely absurd proposition: providers of emergency care in a major disaster effectively do it all the time. However, we are talking here not about a sudden disaster, but about an ongoing process of nutritional development (so that drawing and redrawing lots on a daily or weekly basis has the same effect as equal consumption). Thus the targets of discrimination are established once and for all: certain individuals may be *systematically* denied nourishment and medical care, so that scarce resources can be better focused on some remaining subset of family members.

The receiving end

Who are the individuals who are so denied? They are typically females, both adults and children, and—the presumed harmonies of the extended family notwithstanding—the old and the infirm. Why the old should be so treated is perhaps relatively easy to understand, especially in the light of the preceding model: nutrition and medical care serve a functional role apart from being ends in themselves. They provide the foundation for income-earning capabilities in the future. The old are in less of a position to provide these capabilities. To the extent that income-earning objectives are internalized in the social dynamics of the family, the elderly will be discriminated against. That is, no *one* individual needs to make these hard decisions, but the discrimination will nevertheless manifest itself in the actions of every family member—perhaps even the elderly themselves.

Consider widows. Rahman, Foster, and Mencken [1992] studied mortality rates for widows in rural Bangladesh, and Chen and Drèze [1992] carried out a related study for several villages in northern India. The loss of a husband can be devastating in economic terms unless the widow owns assets such as land, although here too matters are complicated, because the possibility of land loss can in turn depend on widowhood (Cain [1981]). As Chen and Drèze [1992] observed, "the basic problem is not only that a widow often depends on other household members to survive, *but also that these other household members typically do not depend on her for anything essential*" (Italics added for emphasis).

Table 8.6. Age-specific death rates for widows in rural Bangladesh.

	Mortality rate (deaths per 100 person-years)				
Age group	Currently married women	All widows	Widows heading households	Widows in HH headed by sons	Widows not in HH headed by self or sons
45–54	0.89	1.36	1.68	1.15	1.63
55–59	1.78	2.06	2.21	2.13	1.23
60–64	3.10	3.83	2.42	3.86	5.84
65–69	3.81	5.56	5.20	5.15	8.27
70–79	9.43	9.99	8.63	9.88	11.67
80+	9.38	17.50	15.04	17.66	18.52
Total	**1.87**	**5.29**	**3.75**	**5.37**	**7.59**

Source: Rahman, Foster and Mencken [1992] and Chen and Drèze [1992].

Table 8.6 shows how age-specific death rates vary with widowhood in rural Bangladesh. The results are striking. Overall death rates jump by a factor of close to 3 if a woman is a widow, rather than currently married. In this group, widows who are heads of households do relatively better than the average for all widows. Widows living in households that are not headed by themselves or by one of their sons do particularly badly,[32] and the explanation for this cannot rest on the hypothesis that such households are, for some reason, intrinsically poorer than other households: there is no evidence that households with a widow have lower per capita expenditures than households without one (Drèze [1990]).

Observations such as these are not restricted to widows alone. In the context of medical care, Kochar's [1996] study of extended families in South Asia found that medical expenditures on the elderly vary systematically (and inversely) with measures of their earnings ability, which implies that the role of the household as a *production unit* looms large when nutritional or health expenditure allocations are made. This bias is reflected not only in smaller allocations of medical expenditures to elders *relative* to the expected incidence of illness in higher age groups, *but sometimes in absolute terms as well*.[33]

Once we accept the argument that intrahousehold allocation has functional as well as intrinsic motives, the phenomenon of discrimination against the elderly is easy to understand. It is somewhat more difficult to appreci-

---

[32] To be sure, the fear of being without a son for support may in turn impact on fertility decisions earlier on, and this may account in part for high fertility among groups known to discriminate against widows (see Chapter 9 for more on this).

[33] The problem is exacerbated in the presence of women and children, who accentuate the trend in allocation away from the elderly. The analysis is complicated, however, by the puzzling observation that savings are more likely to be run down for the treatment of the elderly than for young males, after controlling for the severity of the illness. Kochar's paper contains an insightful discussion of the possible causes of this seeming anomaly.

Table 8.7. Calorie intakes and requirements by sex in rural Bangladesh (1975–76).

Age (years)	Male Calorie intake	Male Calorie requirement	Female Calorie intake	Female Calorie requirement
10–12	1,989	2,600	1,780	2,350
13–15	2,239	2,753	1,919	2,224
16–19	3,049	3,040	2,110	2,066
20–39	2,962	3,122	2,437	1,988
40–49	2,866	2,831	2,272	1,870
50–59	2,702	2,554	2,193	1,771
60–69	2,569	2,270	2,088	1,574
70+	2,617	1,987	1,463	1,378

Source: Sen [1984, Table 15.3].

ate how a similar burden falls on females, both adults and children. Unless we believe that men are more fit than women for tasks of various sorts, we cannot make the case for discrimination against women on the basis of the lifeboat argument *alone*. Intrahousehold discrimination against females reflects the larger context of gender bias. Suppose, for instance, that women provide household tasks while men earn income. If household tasks are not properly monetized in the psychology of household resource allocation, then the lifeboat argument applies and we would expect to see discrimination in resource allocation against women. Likewise, even if women and men are both engaged in monetary employment, but wages to women for comparable work are lower, this will bias resources away from women.

The issue is made more complex by the question of how to measure nutritional deprivation. It may not be enough to simply observe that women receive less nutrition than men: the question is whether they receive less nutrition relative to their requirements. The evidence on this matter is not as clear-cut as you might expect. For instance, the Institute of Nutrition and Food Science (INFS) conducted a sample survey of nutritional intake by household in rural Bangladesh.[34] They also used notions of "requirement," namely, the age- and sex-specific recommendations of the FAO/WHO Expert Committee (1973). Table 8.7 summarizes some of the INFS observations on calorie intake.

The table is interesting on two counts. First, the second and fourth columns tell us that females receive systematically lower nutrition in *all* the age groups surveyed (and the age classification is pretty fine). The intake shortfall varies from a minimum of 11% (in the youngest age group) and rises to a high of 44% in the 70+ category (in line with the observations on widows made earlier).

[34] This discussion is drawn from Sen [1984, Chap. 15].

Second, and in contrast to the first observation, if the shortfall is measured relative to stated *requirements*, this discrepancy goes away. A deficit remains relative to requirements at the two youngest age groups, but there is a deficit for males as well. This raises the question of just what requirements are and how they are measured. Apart from considerations of body mass, do they presume different sets of tasks performed by men and women? In addition, how is it that the energy use of these tasks is accurately estimated without pinning down a set of tasks completely? As Sen [1984, p. 351] observed, "...there are good reasons to dispute the assumptions about the energy use of activities performed by women, which are not as 'sedentary' as calorie calculations tend to assume. Also the extra nutrition requirements of the pregnant women and lactating mothers require fuller acknowledgement." Measuring shortfalls relative to some arbitrary notion of "requirement" can be dangerously misleading.

Thus gender bias may or may not be directly manifested in consumption-requirement ratios, as far as nutrition is concerned. We may have to probe deeper. Very different sorts of allocation decisions may be at work, even those that do not have any direct opportunity costs. A female child may not be taken to a clinic when she is ill even if medical services are free. The cost of taking the child is *not* the cost of medical care, but possibly the implied cost of dowry if the child survives to maturity. A female child may not be given education or her education may be neglected simply because education of female children is not expected to pay off in larger incomes for *that* household (and it may not lower the cost of a dowry either). The box on sibling rivalry in Ghana is an example of research that looks for direct indicators such as these. Finally, sex-based differences in infant mortality may take care of a large amount of discrimination: the *survivors* may be treated relatively equally, but in looking for this we fail to count the dead.

These problems are magnified when we lack direct data on intrahousehold allocation and have to make do with indirect evidence. Deaton [1994] discussed one such method: to look at household consumption of certain "adult goods" (such as tobacco) and relate this to the proportion of girls in the household (controlling for total number of children). If there is consumption discrimination against girls, this should be reflected in an overall increase in adult consumption as the composition of children shifts in favor of females. Deaton [1989], Subramanian and Deaton [1991], Ahmad and Morduch [1993], and Rudd [1993], among others, took this interesting methodology to the data. No clear-cut findings were made, even in areas where other indicators of discrimination (such as sex ratios) were positive. Deaton [1994] observed that "it is certainly something of a puzzle that the analysis of expenditure patterns so consistently fails to show strong gender effects even when they are known to exist."

Sibling Rivalry: Evidence from Ghana

As in many other low-income economies, parents in Ghana often invest less in the human capital of their daughters than their sons. Primary school enrollments are fairly even, but by secondary school only 28% of females between age 16 and 23 attend school, whereas 42% of boys are enrolled.

A study by Garg and Morduch [1997] explored how economic constraints exacerbate gender differences in Ghana. The starting point for this study is that even if parents desire to invest a given amount in their children's human capital, they may lack the personal resources to do so, and even if expected returns are high, parents may find it difficult to borrow for such long-term investments. Children must then compete with their siblings for the resources currently available to parents. Boys have an advantage in this competition if parents perceive higher returns to this investment. If the total number of their siblings is held constant, children with fewer brothers also may get more resources than they would otherwise.

The Garg–Morduch study supports this hypothesis in the case of Ghana. For instance, the study shows that children aged 12–23 with three siblings are over 50% more likely to attend middle or secondary school when all three of their siblings are sisters than when the three are brothers. The effects are similar for boys and girls and for other sibling groups. Similar results hold for health outcomes as well. The study is consistent with the idea of "sibling rivalry" caused by parents' difficulty in borrowing to make human capital investments in their children. The study illustrates the importance of considering issues of gender within the context of markets and institutions available to households. The results suggest that improving financial systems can have important indirect benefits for the health and education of children in Ghana.

What we have learned so far is that there are dimensions along which females are discriminated against, but the obvious indicator of discrimination—nutrition—does not hold up well unless we have a precise notion of requirements. There is the additional problem that direct intrahousehold data are hard to obtain. Where they do exist—as in the Ghana study described in the box—and where data are collected on outcomes other than nutrition, such as medical care and education, there is clear evidence of discrimination against girls (see also Subramanian [1994]).

We must, therefore, seek to supplement this sort of research with indicators of differential educational attainment, direct anthropometric indicators of differential nourishment, or indicators of differential mortality and morbidity. These indicators are not without problems either,[35] but they serve as

---

[35] Kumar [1991], in his insightful study of Kerala, noted that the incidence of illness in that state of India far exceeds the national average. This is especially true of diseases such as tuberculosis. Does this prove that Kerala is the sickest state in India? It does not. Data on morbidity, or the incidence of illness, combine two features: the *actual* incidence of illness, which is not observed by the researcher,

another route to understanding the relationship between poverty and intra-household allocation.

Consider educational attainment. The *World Development Report* (World Bank [1996]) noted that for low-income countries as a whole, there were almost *twice* as many female illiterates as there were males in 1995 (the illiteracy rates were 45% for females and 24% for males). This disparity is echoed by enrollment figures: in low-income countries taken together, male enrollment in primary schools exceeded female enrollment by over 12%, and the difference exceeded 30% for secondary schools.[36] Note well that these are averages for the countries as a whole. To the extent that the relatively rich in these countries are free of the resource constraints that lead to discrimination, the corresponding figures for the poor in these countries must be more dramatic still.[37]

Consider sex ratios: estimates of female-to-male population in the developing world. In North America and Europe, the life expectancy of women is somewhat longer than for men. The roots of this difference are unclear: they may be biological, but there are also possible social and occupational factors at work. The average ratio of female-to-male population in these countries is around 1.05; that is, there are approximately 105 females for every 100 males. Figure 8.4 displays the corresponding sex ratios for many developing countries. The first panel shows the African data, the second shows the data for Asia, and the last panel shows the data for Latin America. It is evident that the problem of low female-to-male ratios is predominantly an Asian problem. The figure for Asia is peppered with data points in the range of the mid-90s, and there are several instances that are lower still.

These differences imply enormous *absolute* discrepancies. If the ratio of females to males is 93 (for every 100 males) in India, and India has approximately 440 million males (United Nations [1993]), then about 30 *million* women are unaccounted for in India *alone*.[38] Thus sex ratios around 95 or so represent *prima* facie evidence of substantial discrimination, which might

---

and its *perception* (which includes reporting the illness). Kerala, with its higher rates of education and literacy, may do very well on the latter, thus raising observed morbidity. The same ideas can be applied to the use of morbidity as a test for discrimination between boys and girls. If girls fall ill more often but the illness goes unreported, morbidity rates might look much lower for girls.

[36] These figures are for 1993.

[37] For middle-income countries these discrepancies begin to fade, at least in the aggregate terms of measurement used by the World Bank. Nevertheless, male rates of illiteracy are consistently lower than their female counterparts.

[38] This is the case if we adopt the counterfactual scenario that there "should be" 440 million males as well. There are two reasons why the number 30 million is probably an *underestimate*. First, there are also males who died in infancy or childhood because of high rates of child mortality (of course, the additional female count so implied would not all be attributable to discrimination). Second, the counterfact assumes a 1:1 parity: if the European or North American figures are taken as a benchmark, then the number of missing females would be higher still. On these and related matters, see, for example, Coale [1991], Coale and Banister [1994], Klasen [1994], and Sen [1992].

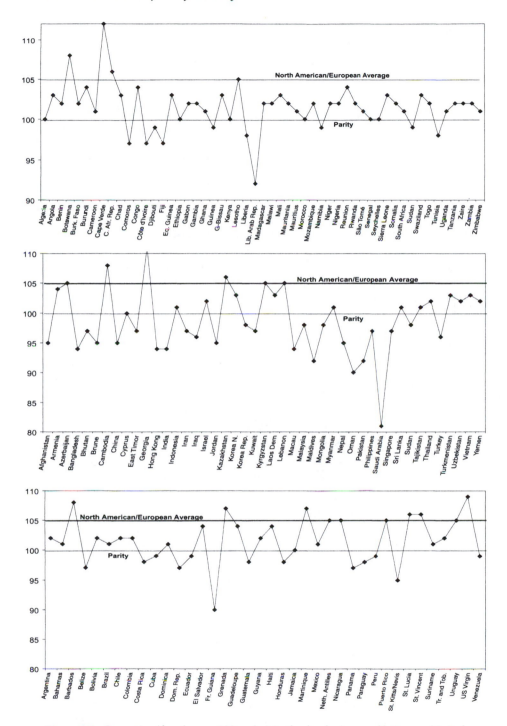

Figure 8.4. *Sex ratios (females per 100 males) in the developing world. Source: United Nations Secretariat [1996].*

include neglect in infancy or childhood (leading to death) or practices such as sex-selective abortion.

The relative absence of skewed sex ratios in Africa makes an interesting point. As we've noted before, poverty *alone* cannot be responsible for the gender biases that we do see in Asia, although poverty serves to reinforce these biases. The overall social context of discrimination also plays a role. Take, for instance, the institution of dowry. Families might react to dowry by resorting to sex-selective abortion, female infanticide, or discriminatory neglect during the infancy of a girl (which amounts to infanticide). Boys are preferred because they are a source of income and support; girls are not because they impose costs. Nevertheless, *once* a girl survives there may be less evidence of discrimination in matters of nutrition and medical care. After all, the costs, say, in terms of the potential for marriage, are only enhanced in the absence of this care. Testing for gender discrimination is therefore a complicated issue, and it may be unevenly manifested through various potential channels. There is no reason to expect that all ways and forms of discrimination will be equally in evidence.

8.5. Summary

Poverty, just like inequality, has intrinsic as well as functional aspects. We are interested in poverty in its own right, as an outcome that needs to be removed through policy, but poverty also affects other forms of economic and social functioning. It creates inefficiencies of various kinds and can exacerbate existing forms of discrimination, such as those against women.

We first studied issues of *poverty measurement*. The measurement of poverty is based on the notion of a *poverty line*, which is constructed from monetary estimates of minimum needs. We noted several problems with the concept even at this fundamental level: should income or item-by-item expenditure be used to identify the poor, are notions of the poverty line "absolute" or "relative," is poverty temporary or chronic, should we study households or individuals as the basic unit, and so on.

We then turned to well-known poverty measures: among these are the *head-count ratio*, which simply measures the fraction of the population below the poverty line. The head-count ratio is a popular measure, but it fails to adequately account for the intensity of poverty. In particular, a planner who uses the head-count ratio as a political yardstick for poverty reduction will be tempted to target the segment among the poor who are very close to the poverty line (and who are arguably not in the greatest need of help). To remedy this shortcoming, we can use measures such as the *poverty gap ratio* or the *income gap ratio*, which look at the total shortfall of poor incomes from the poverty line and express this shortfall as a fraction of national income (as in the poverty gap) or as a fraction of the total income required to bring all the poor to the poverty line (as in the income gap ratio). These measures add to the information contained in the head count, but have their own drawbacks: in particular, they are indifferent to the *relative deprivation* of the poor (see the Appendix to this chapter for more).

We then described some of the characteristics of the poor. Even going by conservative estimates, such as India's poverty line applied to the world as a whole, we see that in 1990, over 600 million people were poor. Poor households tend to be large (though there are some qualifications attached to this statement) and they are overrepresented by female heads of households. Rural areas tend to display more poverty. Poverty is highly correlated with the absence of productive asset holdings, such as holdings of land. Poverty is correlated with lack of education, and there is an intimate connection between nutrition and poverty, although nutrition levels do not seem to rise as quickly with household income as we might suppose a priori.

The fundamental implication of poverty is that the poor lack access to markets, most notably the markets for credit, insurance, land, and labor. We discussed how the absence of collateral restricts access to credit markets and how problems of moral hazard and incomplete information restrict access to insurance. We then began a study of imperfect access to the labor market (the threads of this story will be taken up again in Chapter 13). The basic idea is that poverty and undernutrition affect *work capacity*. The relationship between nutrition and work capacity can be expressed through the use of a *capacity curve*. The capacity curve creates the possibility of a low-income undernutrition *trap*. Just as low incomes are responsible for low levels of nutrition, low levels of nutrition work through the capacity curve to diminish earnings. We argued that the existence of such a trap is far more likely in countries that have low per capita incomes overall (because of labor supply effects), that it is difficult to borrow one's way out of an undernutrition trap (lack of access to credit is again relevant here, though not necessary), and that long-run contracts may not spontaneously come into play to overcome the undernutrition trap, although examples of long-run relationships that have an effect on the trap do exist.

Finally, we turned to the relationship between poverty and resource allocation *within* the household. We argued that extreme poverty promotes unequal treatment within the household, because of a "lifeboat problem": certain minima are needed for people to lead a productive life, and equal treatment may simultaneously deny everyone those minima. We showed how inflexible minima are unnecessary to derive this result by using the capacity curve to analyze an intrahousehold allocation problem. We then asked the question, Which subgroups are on the receiving end of such unequal treatment (when it occurs)? The elderly (notably widows) are among such groups. Females are generally on the receiving end as well, although this phenomenon requires more careful exploration. In particular, observations of actual nutritional treatment of *surviving* females do not reveal the same sorts of disparities as those implicit in skewed sex ratios, suggesting that much of the discrimination occurs through active neglect leading to death in infancy or perhaps practices such as sex-selective abortion. However, some other indicators of unequal treatment, such as access to education, certainly reveal more pronounced evidence of gender bias even among surviving children.

Appendix: More on poverty measures

Poverty lines suggest that there is some sort of magic threshold to poverty: people below the line are poor, whereas people above the line are not. Quite apart from the serious conceptual difficulties associated with this, there are operational problems as well. Policy makers who have an incentive to reduce poverty as measured by the head count may not cater to the poorest, but rather only to those who are easily nudged above the line. The poverty gap measure gets around this to some extent, but problems remain. Consider a natural application of the Pigou–Dalton transfer principle to the measurement of poverty:[39]

Weak Transfers Principle. *A transfer of income from any person below the poverty line to anyone less poor, while keeping the set of poor unchanged, must raise poverty.*[40]

This sounds innocuous, but as we have seen in the text, *both* the head-count ratio and the poverty gap (or the income gap) fail to satisfy this criterion. Is this just nitpicking or are there real-world phenomena that correspond to these conceptual problems? The *World Development Report* (World Bank [1990, Box 2.2]) discussed the effect of an increase in rice prices on poverty in Java, Indonesia, in 1981. Many poor households are farmers: they are net *producers* of rice, so the price hike presumably helped them, and indeed, the head-count index of poverty fell. However, this masks another phenomenon: many of the *poorest* people are not rice producers but landless laborers or farmers with other sources of income. They are net *consumers* of rice and they are adversely hit. Measures of poverty that are "transfer sensitive" could pick up this change, whereas traditional measures register a decline in poverty.

The best known measures that address the distributional underpinnings of poverty is the class proposed by Foster, Greer, and Thorbecke [1984]. The

---

[39] This is the approach to poverty pioneered by Sen [1976]. A discussion of the poverty index developed by him can be found in Foster [1984].

[40] This is called the *weak* transfers principle because it restricts consideration of transfers to those occurring between poor people. For more discussion on this matter, consult Foster [1984].

idea is very simple. Look at a variant of the poverty gap ratio in equation (8.2), given by

$$(8.4) \qquad \text{PGR}' = \frac{1}{n} \frac{\sum_{y_i < p}(p - y_i)}{p},$$

which is just the sum of all individual poverty gaps, expressed as a fraction of the poverty line, and then divided by the total number of people in the society. Distributional sensitivity is achieved by raising the poverty gaps to a power, much as we did in our discussion of the coefficient of variation as a measure of inequality. For any power α, define a class of poverty measures, called the *Foster–Greer–Thorbecke* (FGT) class, by

$$(8.5) \qquad P_\alpha = \frac{1}{n} \sum_{y_i < p} \left(\frac{p - y_i}{p} \right)^\alpha.$$

As we vary α over different values, we obtain interesting implications. First note that for $\alpha = 0$, the measure P_0 is just the head-count ratio. For $\alpha = 1$, the measure P_1 is the poverty gap ratio in (8.4). As α rises beyond 1, larger poverty gaps begin to acquire greater weight and the measure becomes increasingly sensitive to these gaps and, therefore, to questions of distribution, such as those raised by the Java price hike.

The case $\alpha = 2$ is of separate interest. With some manipulation, we can show that

$$(8.6) \qquad P_2 = \text{HCR}[\text{IGR}^2 + (1 - \text{IGR})^2 C_p^2],$$

where HCR is the head-count ratio, IGR is the income gap ratio, and C_p is just the coefficient of variation among the set of poor people (see Chapter 6 for a definition). This is a very useful way to see the FGT index for $\alpha = 2$. It tells us that when there is no inequality among the poor, poverty can be captured by some simple function of the head-count ratio and the income gap ratio alone, but the presence of inequality raises poverty. To see this, imagine that the Lorenz curve of incomes among the poor worsens, while both the head-count ratio and the income gap ratio are kept unchanged. Then, because the coefficient of variation is Lorenz-consistent, C_p will rise and the FGT index will rise as well.

There is another reason why the case $\alpha = 2$ is of interest. It marks the boundary between poverty measures that not only satisfy the transfer principle, but satisfy what one might call *transfer sensitivity*:

Principle of Transfer Sensitivity. *A given regressive transfer between two poor people must matter more if both (starting) incomes of the persons involved are reduced equally.*

It can be checked that the transfer-sensitivity principle is satisfied if and only if $\alpha > 2$. At $\alpha = 2$ the FGT index is just about insensitive to the principle.

The FGT family of poverty measures also satisfies a convenient decomposability property. Suppose we are interested in how much overall poverty in a country is contributed by various subgroups: for instance, we may be interested in looking at poverty across women and men or across various ethnic groups.[41] It would be useful if these "subgroup poverty measures," appropriately weighted by the numerical strengths of the groups, summed to the total poverty as measured by the same index. The FGT indices have this property (see Foster, Greer and Thorbecke [1984] for a more extended discussion).

Exercises

■ (1) Is poverty an absolute concept or a relative concept? There are clearly some components (such as access to food, clothing, and shelter) that we would consider necessary in any society, but there are other components that are clearly society–specific.

(a) Identify some components of "minimum needs" that you feel are specific to one society but not another.

(b) Do you think these relative components are purely social (or cultural) or are they apt to change with the per capita income of a country?

(c) Because poverty has these relative components, consider the following poverty measure: anybody who has less than half (or some predetermined fraction) of the per capita income of a society is poor. Why is this a bad approach to poverty measurement?

(d) Try and identify some basic "capabilities" that you might want any human being to have: for example, every person should be capable of obtaining adequate nutrition, every person should be capable of obtaining "adequate" housing, means of transportation, and so on. Treat the right to such capabilities as absolute. Now can you reconcile the relative and absolute notions of poverty using these absolute capabilities as a starting point? On these and related matters, read Sen [1985].

■ (2) Read the 1990 *World Bank Development Report* to see how international poverty calculations are carried out. In the light of question (1), how would you evaluate such calculations? Study the *Report* for a clear account of the characteristics of the poor and for additional material on poverty not contained in this text.

[41] See, for example, Anand [1977].

▪ (3) Evaluate the following statements by providing a brief explanation or analysis.

(a) The income gap ratio and the head count, as measures of poverty, may lead to very different uses of antipoverty resources by policy makers.

(b) World poverty shows a steadily diminishing trend all through the 1970s and 1980s.

(c) The poverty gap ratio and the income gap ratio focus attention on different aspects of the poverty problem.

(d) Both the poverty gap ratio and income gap ratio are insensitive to the inequality among the poor.

(e) The FGT indices (see Appendix) are increasingly sensitive to the income distribution among the poor, the greater is the value of α.

▪ (4) Suppose that you are comparing two economies, A and B. The FGT indices (with $\alpha = 2$) for the two countries are the same. However, the head-count and the income gap ratio are both higher for economy A than for B. What can you say about the coefficient of variation of income distribution among the poor in these two economies? What about the inequality of the *entire* income distributions in these two economies?

▪ (5) Explain why a moneylender who relies on future credit cutoffs to enforce loan repayment today will be less willing to advance loans to a poor individual for projects that guarantee future income security. Discuss the role of collateral in obtaining such loans.

▪ (6) Discuss the capacity curve and explain why the curve has an initial segment in which work capacity exhibits increasing returns with respect to nutritional input. In Chapter 13, we will discuss the implications of this in more detail, but the following exercise will provide you with some advance intuition.

Suppose that you need 8,000 units of work (in capacity units) to be performed, and you can hire all the laborers that you want. Assume that all income earned by the laborers is paid to them by you, and that all income is spent on nutrition. The capacity curve for each laborer is described as follows: for all payments up to $100, capacity is zero and then begins to rise by 2 units for every additional dollar paid. This happens until an income of $500 is paid out. Thereafter, an additional dollar paid out increases capacity by only 1.1 units, until total income paid is $1,000. At this point additional payments have no effect on work capacity.

(a) Assume that you would like to get your work done at minimum cost. Describe how many laborers you would hire to get your work done and how much you would pay each of them.

(b) Redo the exercise assuming that capacity is zero for all payments up to $275, then follows exactly the same rules for additional dollars paid as in the original problem. Interpret your answer.

■ (7) Consider the same capacity curve as in problem (6a). Suppose that a family of five members each have this capacity curve. Assume that this family has access to a source of nonlabor income, valued at $400. Assume furthermore that each unit of capacity can fetch an income of 50 cents, and that all income is spent on nutrition. We are going to examine the division of income among the family members.

(a) Show that if all nonlabor income is divided *equally* among the family members, then no one will be able to sustain any work capacity so that labor income will be zero.

(b) Find allocations of the nonlabor income that give rise to positive wage income. Compare and contrast these allocations with the equal division allocation, using various criteria (including Pareto-optimality).

Chapter 9

Population Growth and Economic Development

9.1. Introduction

The world is populated today as it has never been before. Although rates of population growth have fallen and will continue to fall, we currently add about a million people every *four* days to the world population, *net* of deaths. According to projections carried out by the United Nations, annual additions to the population are likely to remain close to the ninety million mark until the year 2015.

It took 123 years for world population to increase from one billion (1804) to two billion (1927). The next billion took 33 years. The following two billions took 14 years and 13 years, respectively. The next billion is expected to take only 11 years and will be achieved by 1998, at which time we will arrive at the staggering figure of six billion. Such is the power of exponential growth.

However, more than just exponential growth is hidden in this story. Population growth through the millennia has not proceeded at an even exponential pace. The growth rate of population has itself increased, and the trend has reversed only in the last few years. Part of our purpose in this chapter is to tell this complex and interesting story.

Yet a description of trends is not our only purpose, because this is a book about economics, not demographic statistics. We are interested primarily in how the process of development has spurred (or retarded) population growth and, more important, we want to know how population growth in turn affects economic development. As with the evolution of now-familiar variables such as per capita income and economic inequality, population and development are intertwined, and we seek to understand both strands of the relationship.

The question of how population growth affects development runs into an immediate difficulty. How do we value the lives of the people yet unborn? Is a small population living in luxury better off than a large population living under moderate circumstances? How do we compare the fact that a larger number of people are around to enjoy the "moderate circumstances" with the alternative in which luxuries are available to a smaller number, simply because the births of the rest were somehow prevented?

This is a difficult question and we do not pretend to provide an easy answer. Indeed, we simply sidestep this issue by using per capita welfare (and its distribution) as our yardstick. The implicit ethical judgment, then, is that we are "neutral" toward population: once someone is born, we include that someone as worthy of all the rights and privileges of existing humanity. At the same time, our focus on per capita welfare means that we are indifferent to the unborn and are even biased toward keeping population growth down if it affects per capita welfare adversely.

This ethical judgment is implicit in the dire warnings that we see all around us, especially in developed countries where population growth in the "Third World" appears most frightening. Population growth cannot be good. It eats into resources and into production. There is less per head to go around.

That is fair enough. We adopt the per capita perspective as well. However, this does not imply that we need be averse to population growth from a *functional* viewpoint. The existence of a population of nontrivial size may have been essential to many important advances to the world. It is unclear how much Robinson Crusoe would have accomplished on his own, even with the help of his man Friday. For one thing, there are limits to what one or two brains can think up. For another, necessity is the mother of invention, and without the pressure of population on resources, there may be no necessity and consequently no invention. Just how large population needs to be for the full realization of these salubrious effects is open to debate, but the point remains that the total quantity of available resources may itself be positively affected through population growth.

The doomsday predictions associated with population growth also have a particular slant to them. On the heels of the (perhaps defensible) feeling that population growth is unambiguously bad for humanity, there is also the observation, sometimes made with a great deal of sophistication, that unless we do something about population growth in developing countries, the world will somehow be unbalanced in favor of the peoples of these countries. That would be "unfair."

Both of these misconceptions are, to some extent, unfounded. Moreover, taken to extremes, they can be dangerous. However, clearing up misconceptions is not our main goal. These statements are corollaries of more serious questions regarding the interaction of population growth and economic development that we shall address in this chapter.

(1) What are the observed patterns of population growth across different countries and how do these patterns correlate with other features of development in these countries? Specifically, is there a close relationship between

what the now-developed countries have demographically experienced in the past and what is currently being experienced by developing countries? This will take us into a discussion of the *demographic transition*, a phenomenon you were introduced to briefly in Chapter 3.

(2) What connects these societywide patterns in population growth to the decisions made by individual households regarding fertility? What features of the social and economic environment affect these household-level decisions? In particular, how does economic development affect fertility choices?

(3) Can observed household decisions regarding the number of children be "rationalized" by the environment in which they find themselves? Alternatively, do households have more children than is good for them? This is a difficult question that we must address at two levels. The first level is what might be called the "internal level": given some economically rational level of fertility *at the level of the couple*, do couples systematically depart from this level, either because of miscalculation or because of the absence of effective contraception? The second level is "external" and comes from pondering the meaning of the italicized phrase in the previous sentence. Are there reasons to believe that a couple's decisions regarding family size have a social impact that is *not* fully internalized by them?

(4) Finally, reversing the causality from economics to demography, is it unambiguously true that population growth is harmful to the economic development of a country? What explains the interesting dichotomy between the belief that world population growth is "bad" and the belief, so widespread in developed countries, that population growth will make "them" powerful at "our" expense?

We do not pretend to have comprehensive answers to all these questions, but you will certainly find some of the issues that we discuss very provocative and worthy of further study. However, before we begin a serious discussion, it will be useful to review some basic concepts and terminology that are used by demographers. This is the task of the next section.

9.2. Population: Some basic concepts

9.2.1. Birth and death rates

To conduct a useful analysis of population and its interaction with economic development, it is necessary to understand a few basic concepts and terms. Most of what we study in this section are just definitions, and with a little patience, they are very easy to understand. These definitions set down the language in which we discuss demographic issues.

Fundamental to the study of population is the notion of *birth rates* and *death rates*. These are normally expressed as numbers per thousand of the population. Thus, if we say that the birth rate of Sri Lanka is 20 per 1,000, this means that in each year, Sri Lanka adds 20 newborn babies for every thousand members of the population. Likewise, a death rate of 14 per 1,000 means that in each year, an average of 14 people die for every 1,000 members of the population.

The *population growth rate* is the birth rate minus the death rate. Even though this works out as a number per 1,000 (6 in our example above), it is customary to express population growth rates in percentages. Thus, the population growth rate is 0.6% per annum in our example.

Table 9.1 provides us with data on birth rates, death rates, and population growth rates for selected low-income, middle-income, and high-income countries. There is a cross-sectional pattern here that we will take up in more detail when we study the demographic transition, but certain features come to mind.

First, *very* poor countries such as Malawi and Guinea-Bissau appear to have both high birth rates *and* high death rates, ranging around 50 per 1,000 for births and 20 per 1,000 for deaths. This is Group I in the table. Countries in Group II are not as poor: their death rates are much lower relative to the Group I countries, but their birth rates are still high. This isn't uniformly true of all poor countries though: some, such as India and Bangladesh (Group III), seem to have begun a fall in birth rates that is gathering momentum. Other relatively poor countries, such as China and Sri Lanka (Group IV) have already taken significant strides in this direction: both birth and death rates are low and getting lower. Group V lists some Latin American countries, where the experience is mixed: countries such as Guatemala and Nicaragua have (like the Group II countries) benefited from the drop in death rates, but the accompanying fall in birth rates has not yet occurred. Countries such as Brazil and Colombia are well into the process, as are East and much of Southeast Asia (Group VI): countries such as Korea and Thailand have very low birth and death rates (others, such as Malaysia, have not completed this process).

Table 9.1 is constructed very roughly in ascending order of per capita income. The following broad trend appears: at very low levels of per capita income, both birth and death rates are high. Indeed, this is probably an understatement: *age-specific* death rates are probably higher still (see following text). Then death rates fall. This is finally followed by a fall in the birth rates. We will see this much more clearly when we track a single country over its history.

Now for a different concept. It is worth understanding that aggregative figures such as birth rates and death rates, and especially population growth

Table 9.1. Birth and death rates (1992) and population growth rates for selected countries.

Country	Per capita income	Birth rate	Death rate	Population growth rate (%)
I.				
Mali	520	51	20	3.1
Malawi	690	51	20	3.1
Sierra Leone	750	49	25	2.4
Guinea-Bissau	840	43	21	2.2
II.				
Kenya	1,290	45	12	3.3
Nigeria	1,400	45	15	3.0
Ghana	1,970	42	12	3.0
Pakistan	2,170	41	9	3.2
III.				
India	1,220	29	10	1.9
Bangladesh	1,290	36	12	2.4
IV.				
China	2,330	18	7	1.1
Sri Lanka	2,990	21	6	1.5
V.				
Nicaragua	1,900	41	7	3.4
Peru	3,220	27	7	2.0
Guatemala	3,350	39	8	3.1
Brazil	5,370	25	8	1.7
Colombia	5,490	24	6	1.8
VI.				
Thailand	6,260	19	6	1.3
Malaysia	7,930	29	5	2.4
Republic of Korea	9,630	16	6	1.0

Source: *World Development Report* (World Bank [1995]) and *Human Development Report* (United Nations Development Programme [1995]).

rates, hide significant information about the underlying "demographic structure" of the country.

For instance, two countries with the same population growth rates may have dramatically different age structures. This is because one of the two countries (call it *A*) may have a significantly higher birth rate *and* a significantly higher death rate than the other country (*B*) (so that the two cancel out in the comparison of net population growth rates). At the same time, it is true that country *A* is adding more young people to its population than country *B*. Unless the higher death rates in country *A* are entirely concentrated among the young, which is unlikely, there will be more young people in *A* than in *B*. We might then say that country *A* has a "younger age distribution" than country *B*. As we will soon see, age distribution plays an important role in determining overall birth and death rates.

9.2.2. *Age distributions*

The age distribution of a population is given by a list of proportions of that population in different age groups. Table 9.2 gives us the age distribution of populations in different parts of the world, as of 1995. It is apparent from the table that the age distribution of developing countries is significantly younger than in their developed counterparts. I have never met a person who failed to be amazed by these figures when seeing them for the first time, and you will be too. The developing world is very young.

Just as birth rates and death rates affect age distributions, these rates are in turn affected by the age distribution prevailing at any particular moment in time. An aggregate birth rate is the outcome of the age distribution in a country, the age-specific fertility rates of women in that country, and the fraction of the population in different age groups. Similarly, the aggregate death rate is a composite that comes from age-specific death rates in a particular country, as well as the overall age distribution in that country.

These observations have important implications, as we will see. At the moment, let's pursue the more disaggregated view a bit further. An *age-specific fertility rate* is the average number of children per year born to women in a particular age group. The *total fertility rate* is found by adding up all the age-specific fertility rates over different age groups: it is the total number of children a woman is expected to have over her lifetime. In developing countries, this number can be as high as 7 or 8, and often higher. In the typical developed country, this number is 2, perhaps lower.

Of course, high total fertility rates contribute to a high birth rate, but from our discussion, it should be clear that the total fertility rate is not the *only* factor that determines the overall birth rate. In a country with a young age distribution, the birth rate can be significantly high, even if the total fertility rate is not. This is simply because the younger country has a larger percentage of the population in their reproductive years.

A parallel observation holds for death rates. Young populations are biased toward low death rates, and this is true even if age-specific death rates are high. It is worth noticing that even though most developing countries have higher death rates in each age group relative to their developed counterparts, these differences are not adequately reflected in the overall death rates, which lie far closer together. Indeed, it is perfectly possible for country *A* to have higher age-specific death rates at *every* age group than country

Table 9.2. Age distribution of the world population.

Region	Population (millions)	0–15 %	15–64 %	65+ %
World total	**5,716**	**32**	**62**	**6**
Africa	**728**	**44**	**53**	**3**
Eastern Africa	227	46	51	3
Middle Africa	82	46	51	3
Northern Africa	160	39	57	4
Southern Africa	47	37	58	5
Western Africa	210	46	51	3
Latin America	**482**	**34**	**61**	**5**
Caribbean	35.0	29	63	6
Central America	126.0	38	58	4
South America	319.0	33	62	5
Asia	**3,457**	**32**	**63**	**5**
Eastern Asia	1424	25	68	7
South-Central Asia	1381	37	59	4
Southeast Asia	484	35	61	4
Western Asia	168	38	58	4
North America	**292**	**22**	**65**	**13**
Europe	**726**	**19**	**67**	**14**
Eastern Europe	308	21	67	12
Northern Europe	93	20	65	15
Southern Europe	143	17	69	14
Western Europe	180	17	68	15
Oceania	**29**	**26**	**64**	**10**
Australia and N. Zealand	21.6	22	67	11
Melanesia	5.8	39	58	3
Micronesia	0.4	—	—	—
Polynesia	0.5	—	—	—

Source: *Demographic Yearbook* (United Nations [1995]).
Note: Individual figures may not add to total because of rounding error.

B, and yet have a lower death rate overall. This is the effect of a young age distribution at work.

Thus high rates of population growth lead to a younger population, and then on to high birth rates and low death rates. This creates an "echo effect" that keeps population growth high.

One important consequence of this observation is that population growth possesses an enormous degree of inertia. Imagine that a country that has had high population growth rates implements a policy to bring down total fertility rates. The point is that *even if this policy were to be successful, population size would probably overshoot the desired limits before settling down at an acceptable level*. The reason is simple. High population growth rates in the past lead to a young age distribution. A relatively large fraction of the population continues to be at the age where they are just about to marry and have families. Even if the total fertility rates were reduced the sheer numbers of young people would lead to a large number of births, viewed as a fraction of the *entire* population. This is the grim inertia of population growth, and more than one country has found, to their dismay, that even with the best intentions and implementation, bringing population growth to a halt is a bit like bringing an express train to an emergency stop.

9.3. From economic development to population growth

9.3.1. The demographic transition

Like economic growth, population growth is a modern phenomenon. Indeed, even if we were to know very little about the world, we could deduce this very quickly by regression in time. The world population today stands at around six billion. Let's go backward and *decrease* this number by 2% per year. This exercise would yield a population of 250,000 around 500 years ago, or a population of 10 around 1,000 years ago! This is obviously ludicrous, as the data at the beginning of this chapter indicate. This proves that population growth at around 2% per year is a phenomenon of recent vintage.

The first point to note is that the "carrying capacity" of the world was enormously different in the Stone Age than in the era of agriculture, and considerably lower than it is now. With shallow digging implements and imperfect acumen in the art of agriculture, people were confined to river basins. Starvation was common, as was early death due to a myriad of causes. The advent of agriculture changed all that, or much of that at any rate. With an increase in the carrying capacity of Mother Earth came an increase in population, but net growth was still minimal, because death rates were high and persistent. Famine continued to be commonplace, as were episodes of plague, pestilence, and war. As late as in the eighteenth century Malthus [1798] wrote of God's checks and balances to the sexual energies of women and men. A spontaneously high rate of reproduction was countered with all manner of disasters, such as regular outbreaks of plague, pestilence, and famine. So although birth rates were high, death rates were sufficiently high to keep growth rates down to a crawl. We may think of this as the *first phase* of demographic history.

A major change, however, was taking place, possibly even as Malthus was recording the grim retributions of Nature. With the advent of sanitation methods and increases in agricultural productivity, death rates began to fall around 1700, and the rise in industrial productivity sent Europe into a veritable population explosion. Table 9.3 gives you some idea of this.

The population explosion would not have taken place, of course, had birth rates simply followed death rates on their downward course without any time lag. However, this did not happen, and for two reasons. First, the very forces that caused death rates to decline also caused economic productivity to increase. For instance, the rise in agricultural productivity meant not only that there was a lower incidence of famine (thus bringing down death rates), but also that the overall carrying capacity of the economy in normal times increased. With room for a larger population, the Malthusian restraints were loosened and the urgency to bring down the birth rate therefore dissipated. Second, even if the forgoing scenario had not been the case, birth rates would probably still have been high because of the inertia that characterizes fertility choices made by households. This inertia is so important in our understanding of population trends that we will devote a fair amount of space to it in the next section. For now, we merely note that birth rates remained high even as death rates fell. This meant that population growth rates rose in this epoch, which we dub the *second phase* of demographic history.

Finally, birth rates fell as time overcame inertia, and as the population of the world rose to fill newly created carrying capacity. Population growth rates declined, until they fell to their present level in the developed world, which is around 0.7% per year. This is the *third and final phase* of demographic history.

These three phases jointly make up what is known as the *demographic transition*. Together, they paint a picture that almost all European and North American regions have seen: an increase and then a decline in the rate of population growth, changing the regime from one of high birth and death rates to one of low birth and death rates. Developing countries are going through the very same three phases, and doing so at an accelerated pace, as we will see. Almost all the countries of the world can be described as currently either in the second or the third phase of the transition.

9.3.2. *Historical trends in developed and developing countries*

It is of the *utmost* importance to understand that starting from around 1700 until well into this century, the populations of Europe and North America (most of the modern developed world) grew not only in absolute terms, but also relative to the peoples of those regions we know today as the developing world. To see this shift in population, it is useful to take a long-term view. Table 9.3 is taken from a revised estimate of the world population over the last few centuries (Carr-Saunders [1936]). We append to this table the 1995 estimates from the United Nations *Demographic Yearbook*. The results are very interesting.

Table 9.3. Geographical distribution of the world population.

	1650	*1750*	*1800*	*1850*	*1900*	*1933*	*1995*
World population (millions)	**545**	728	906	1,171	1,608	**2,057**	**5,716**
Percentages							
Europe	**18.3**	19.2	20.7	22.7	24.9	**25.2**	**12.7**
North America	**0.2**	0.1	0.7	2.3	5.1	**6.7**	**5.1**
Oceania	**0.4**	0.3	0.2	0.2	0.4	**0.5**	**0.5**
Latin America	**2.2**	1.5	2.1	2.8	3.9	**6.1**	**8.4**
Africa	**18.3**	13.1	9.9	8.1	7.4	**7.0**	**12.8**
Asia	**60.6**	65.8	66.4	63.9	58.3	**54.5**	**60.5**

Source: Carr-Saunders [1936, Fig. 8] and *Demographic Yearbook* (United Nations [1995]).

The table is constructed to emphasize the earlier centuries. Neglect the last column for the moment. What we have then is an array of population percentages running all the way from 1650 to 1933. Note the decline of Africa, in significant part due to outmigration, and the rise of North America, in large part due to immigration. At the same time, despite outmigration from Europe, her share of the world's population rose steadily over this period. Focus on the first column and the second to last column (both in boldface type) to see how the situation altered over the period 1650–1933. What we see here is the period when Europe began its demographic transition, while large parts of the present developing world still lay dormant in the first phase of demographic history.[1] In 1650, the population of Europe was about 100 million. In 1933, even allowing for emigration (which was large), it had swelled to over 500 million.

Now look at the last column of Table 9.3, which pertains to 1995. It is clear that we are in the throes of a reverse swing. Asia, which lost around six percentage points over the period 1650–1933, has returned to almost exactly the 1650 share. Africa has come back as well, but is still significantly below the 1650 share. The two gainers have been North America and Latin America. It is also instructive to add up what approximately accounts for the developing world. The population share of Asia, Africa, and Latin America combined was 81.1 in 1650. In 1933 it had dropped to 67.6. The share was 81.7 in 1995. We have come full circle.

Without this historical perspective it is easy enough to be alarmist about population expansion in developing countries. No one doubts that such expansions may be harmful, but it is certainly not the case that these countries have grown more than their "fair share." What alarms many governments in the developed world is not population growth, but *relative* population

---

[1] This description is a bit simplistic. The populations of Japan and China were also in a state of significant increase over the last half of the seventeenth century. China's expansion continued through the eighteenth century. The demographic rise of Europe is even more impressive against this moving background.

growth. A large population means greater poverty and smaller per capita access to resources, but on the international scene, it stands for greater political and economic power. The very same governments that stand for population control in the developing world are perfectly capable of pursuing pronatalist policies at home.[2]

Attitudes to Population[3]

Most individuals and governments, if polled, would agree that world population trends pose a problem. When it comes to judging trends in one's own country, however, matters are often quite different. We may deplore an action as being harmful to the interests of society, yet be tied into taking that very same action, simply because others are. Recent changes in attitudes to population, however, show a welcome transition.

At the International Conference on Population and Development, held in Cairo in September 1994, many governments clarified their stand on the population question. It was clear that many governments were actively pursuing demographic policies to limit population trends, and indeed, population growth in many developing countries has significantly declined. These outcomes are correlated with some changes in government perceptions of population growth. Although the percentage of countries that consider their rates of population growth to be too *low* has steadily declined, the number of governments that view population growth as too *high* has declined somewhat as well. Developing countries take the lead in this change of attitude. Among the developed countries, there has been little change. Indeed, an increasing number of such countries consider their rate of population growth to be too low and are concerned about declining fertility and population aging.

In Africa, we see an increasing number of countries joining the war against population: Namibia, the Sudan, and Tanzania officially inaugurated policies to reduce population growth. The Tunisian government now declares itself satisfied with the declining trend of its rate of population growth. Likewise, in Asia, more governments have declared themselves satisfied with demographic trends, although many still consider their population growth rates to be too high. China and Korea both view their current situations as satisfactory.

In contrast, in Europe, more countries are concerned with aging and population decline. Portugal and Romania now consider their population growth rates to be too low, and Croatia inaugurated a policy to promote fertility rates.

In Latin America, as in Asia, an increasing number of countries consider their population growth rates to be satisfactory. The exceptions lie in the densely populated areas of the Caribbean, and in Central America.

Little change occurred elsewhere. In North America, the United States and Canada remain satisfied with their population growth rates, as do Australia and

[2] On these and related matters, see Teitelbaum and Winter [1985].
[3] The account here relies heavily on a report of the Secretary General of the United Nations, presented to the 28th session of the Population Commission, 1995.

New Zealand in Oceania. The majority of developing countries in Oceania consider their rates of population growth to be too high (Tonga is an exception because of high rates of emigration). In Eastern Europe, four countries (Belarus, Bulgaria, Hungary, and Ukraine) consider their population growth rates to be too low. In the former Soviet Union, a majority of the governments appear to be satisfied with their current demographic regime.

At the same time, we cannot help being concerned about future trends. Look again at Table 9.3. It took Europe and North America a good 300 years to realize their population gains; it took around 50 years to lose them. If we extrapolate these trends, are we not in danger of an enormous population explosion, with a rising majority in the developing countries?

In examining this important question, we take note of a radical difference between the demographic transitions of the developed and developing worlds. The latter is being played out at a pace that is many times faster than that of the former. The second phase of demographic history in developing countries displays an intensity that is unmatched by the experiences of the now-developed world.

In developed countries, the fall in the death rate was relatively gradual, limited by the trial and error of innovation. The improved production of food, the institution of sanitation methods, and the greater understanding and control over disease yielded by medical advances all had to be discovered or invented, rather than transplanted from a pre-existing stock of knowledge.

For several reasons, including norms of late marriage in many European societies, birth rates never attained the same heights that we see in developing countries today. At the same time, birth rates fell slowly, in part due to a greater carrying capacity made possible by technical progress. Thus the second phase of demographic history was protracted, and the time span (centuries) more than compensated for the (relatively) low net growth rate. Population growth in these countries was more of a slow burn than a violent explosion, and its enormous impact was felt over centuries.

Contrast this picture with what has happened to developing countries. The decline of mortality was widespread and sudden. Antibiotics were available for a variety of illnesses; they did not have to be reinvented. The use of insecticides such as DDT provided a cheap way to bring down malaria to manageable proportions. Public health organizations began to pop up all over the developing landscape, some of them funded by international institutions such as the World Health Organization. Last, but not the least, there was widespread application of elementary methods of sanitation and hygiene. These are all blessings, because they brought to people a longer, healthier life.

The fact remains, however, that the easy and universal application of these new techniques led to a precipitous decline in death rates. The speed of decline surpassed anything experienced by Northern and Western Europeans. Everything, then, hangs on the birth rate. How quickly does it follow the death rate on its downward course? On this question hangs the future of the world's population, and certainly the economic future of many developing countries.

9.3.3. The adjustment of birth rates

Macro- and micro-inertia

The preceding story of the demographic transition relies on an enormously important feature—the well-documented failure of the birth rate to instantly chase the death rate downward. Recall from the previous section that the main impetus to the rise in population growth rates comes from the fact that death rates decline rapidly, while at the same time, birth rates hold firm. There are several reasons for this.

It is certainly true that over the past centuries, the factors that precipitated the fall in death rates were also linked with an increase in the carrying capacity of the earth. The leading example of this was a rise in agricultural productivity. This is one explanation for why birth rates did not fall (in those times). Unfortunately, this argument cannot be applied today. Many of the factors bringing down death rates in developing countries today are sanitation and health related: they do not go toward increasing carrying capacity.

We study in this section the various factors that keep the birth rate high. At the outset, it will be useful to distinguish between two forms of inertia in the birth rates: one at the level of the overall population (macro-inertia) and one at the level of the family (micro-inertia).

As discussed already, the distribution of the population by age plays an important role. The fact that both birth and death rates are initially high in a poor country makes the net population growth rate low, just as in rich countries, but there is a second implication that is quite different: the populations of the former type of countries will be very young, on average. This feature tends to keep overall birth rates high even if fertility rates are reduced at different age groups. The sheer inertia of the age distribution guarantees that young people of reproductive age continue to enter the population. One might think of this as macro-inertia—inertia at the aggregate level.

Macro-inertia is not the only form of inertia keeping birth rates high. There is also what we might call micro-inertia—inertia at the household level, perhaps in conjunction with the operation of societal norms regarding children and other socioeconomic factors. This will be our focus of attention for the rest of this section.

Fertility choice and missing markets

The angle that we explore in this section is that offspring are generally a sub-stitute for various missing institutions and markets, notably the institution of social security in old age. This absence often compels a couple to make fertility choices based on the recognition that some of their children will die. These potential deaths must be compensated for by a larger number of births.

Of course, children bring enjoyment to their parents, as they undoubt-edly do in all societies, but this is not the only reason why they are produced. On top of this "consumption-good" aspect of children is their role as an "in-vestment good"; that is, as a source of support to the family in old age, and more generally as a form of insurance. If it were possible to obtain insur-ance or old-age security from a more efficient source, these effects would go away. As we have seen already and will see on several occasions again, the fact that there is a missing market somewhere spills over into other seem-ingly disparate aspects of economic life.

To begin, then, let us get a sense of what markets are missing in this con-text. If you live and work in a developed country, you pay a good fraction of your earned income into a government fund that often goes under the name of a social security fund. When you retire, this fund pays you a retirement pension. It is necessary to contribute to this fund to receive benefits from it, although in many countries the pension is progressive (larger contribu-tors do not get back all their payments). A second source of old-age funds is an employer-subsidized retirement plan (where both you and your em-ployer makes contributions). Finally, you can save for your own retirement, not necessarily under the umbrella of any retirement plan.

Next, there are various forms of insurance that are available to you, both in your working life and in your old age. Perhaps the most important of these is medical care, but there are also other forms of insurance. Life insur-ance is among the most important of these. If you die, your spouse receives a payout from the insurance company that helps to support him or her. There is also insurance that you can buy to protect you from sudden loss of em-ployment, or from disability, or from natural disasters, or from theft. This is not the case that in developing countries: these markets are completely miss-ing. By and large, these institutions are only available to people who work in the formal sector. In the informal sector, where employment is largely casual and wages are abysmally low, there is little or no incentive to set up a re-tirement scheme between employer and employee, and even if the law says that this should happen, it is impossible to implement. Likewise, appropriate contributions to a government-run social security system are difficult, if not impossible, to assess. Large sections of the population live in rural areas or work in informal urban areas. For the same reasons of limited information, it is very difficult for an insurance company to assess the validity of claims, such as a crop failure or a sudden drop in the income of a streetside hawker. Agriculture is particularly hampered by the fact that income shocks may be highly correlated across policy holders, which necessitates large payouts for insurance companies. Of course, these correlations can be avoided by companies that operate at a national level, but such companies may lack the local expertise to collect adequate information. Therefore, insurance markets in the agricultural and urban formal sectors are often missing.

What about life insurance or personal savings? Both these avenues are somewhat more viable. With reasonable banking systems, individuals can save for their own retirement. It may be impossible to verify a crop failure, but it is certainly easier to verify death. Thus these routes to old-age support are often available.

At the same time, people often do not avail themselves of these routes. The reason why this is so has to do with low incomes. Consumption needs today are often so pressing that there is little left over to save. People therefore often hold on to assets that they might have inherited, such as land or jewelry, and sell these assets only under conditions of extreme duress. These assets form their security in old age.

Note that the more difficult it is to sell an asset for current consumption, the easier it is to save using that asset. You might respond that if it is difficult to sell that asset now, why should it be easier to sell when funds are truly needed? The answer has to do with the nature of the difficulty. Society sprouts norms around the sale of assets such as land and jewelry. It is all right to sell them under severe duress, but the sale of these assets in "normal times" might be frowned upon or regarded as a signal that the family is completely indigent. Thus the difficulty of marketing these assets is created by the emergence of social norms that protect savings in some form.

In this context, take a fresh look at children. Children are assets par excellence. They do not need to be bought, although there are costs to child rearing (see subsequent text) and they embody income-earning possibilities, both now and in the future. Because slavery is banned (and socially unacceptable anyway), it is generally not possible (though unfortunately, not impossible) to market them for cash. At the same time, when children grow up they can convert their labor power into income, both for themselves and their parents. Little wonder, then, that individuals who lack insurance and old-age security, choose to invest in the future in the form of children. This is the background against which we investigate theories of fertility choice.

Mortality and fertility

Consider the probability that a child will grow up to look after its parents. This probability is given by several factors. The child may die young; infancy is the biggest hurdle. As we know from Chapter 2, infant mortality may be close to 150 or 200 per 1,000 in several developing countries, which translates into a 15% probability of death by the end of the first year of existence. After this barrier, there are still the diseases of childhood, which are still a significant killer in many developing countries up to the age of five or so.

Third, there is the possibility that the child may not be an adequate income earner. The poorer the economy, the greater this fear.

Fourth, a child may not look after its parents in their old age. This is an interesting social factor that may cut in either direction. In societies where the norm of looking after one's parents has practically vanished or is relatively nonexistent to start with, the mental calculations that we are going to talk about may have no relevance at all for fertility decisions. For instance, economic historians such as Williamson [1985] have argued that fertility reductions in nineteenth century United Kingdom can be explained by the increasing emigration rates of adult children. If emigrees send limited remittances, this reduces the present value of children (as investment goods) considerably.

At the same time, in societies where it is accepted practice to care for one's parents, the *limited* possibility that some child might not do so may have the opposite effect on fertility: instead of lowering it, it may increase it as parents attempt to compensate for this contingency.

Finally, there is the possibility that the *parents* themselves might not anticipate being around in their old age. This is certainly a possibility in very high-mortality societies, but in general it is of second-order importance. At the stage in their lives when individuals are making their fertility decisions, they have already lived through the bulk of the (non-old-age) high-mortality phase.

Summarize the overall probability of having a given child grow up to look after you by p. This includes, then, infant and child mortality, the eventuality that the child survives but is not an adequate income earner, and the possibility that the child earns adequate income but nevertheless does not look after you. What value might p take? It is hard to tell without detailed data on each of these possibilities, but child mortality by itself might be responsible for raising p to well above 1/5. With the other factors accounted for, p may well be higher than 1/3, and the possibility that parents regard p as a one-half (or close to it) is certainly not unreasonable.

Now contrast this with the probability—call it q—that a couple finds *acceptable* as a threshold probability of receiving support from at least one child. This is a matter of attitudes toward risk and varies greatly from couple to couple. Try introspection: what probability would you find acceptable to be without any form of old-age support? If you could honestly tolerate a probability that is significantly greater than 1/10, you are an unusual person. We may therefore think of q as having values above 9/10—perhaps even as high as 95/100—certainly greater than p. The rest is a matter of simple arithmetic: how many children do you need to have—each child looking after you with probability p—so that the overall probability of having at least *one* child look after you is at least q?

This is easy to calculate (or it should be!). Suppose you have n children. Then the probability that *none* of them will look after you is $(1-p)^n$. Consequently, your rule would be to choose n—the number of your offspring—just large enough so that

(9.1) $$1 - (1-p)^n > q.$$

Let us check this out with some numbers. Say that $p = 1/2$ and $q = 9/10$. Then it is easy enough to see, using (9.1), that n must be at least 4! If you are more risk-averse than that, so that your acceptable q is 95/100, then you will need five children, and that, too, brings you barely to your acceptable threshold, as you can check by direct calculation.

Gender bias

In this context, gender bias can be immensely costly. Suppose that for some reason, a couple wishes to receive support from a son. Households will then see n as their desired number of *male* offspring. Quite simply and devastatingly, it doubles the expected number of children that the household will have.

For instance, if $p = 1/2$, if $q = 9/10$, and if the couple desire support from a male child in their offspring, then that couple will have, on average, eight children, all for the sake of ensuring *just* one son!

In many societies, the provision of old-age support is thought to be exclusively the task of male offspring. Although support (especially in nonmonetary form) from female children is just as valuable, there may be a stigma associated with receiving support from daughters as opposed to sons. This bias is, of course, a source of discrimination in favor of male children.

To be sure, this argument does not explain the rationale behind such a bias, and there may be many reasons. For instance, Cain's [1981, 1983] study of Bangladesh illustrates the importance of sons as support for widows: *the ability of widows to hold on to land depends on whether they have able-bodied sons.* This will be especially true in situations where property rights are either not well-defined or difficult to enforce by the law.

Information, income, and fertility

Let us summarize the discussion so far. Individuals choose the number of their offspring with the intention of receiving support in their old age. This support may not be forthcoming from a child for several reasons: (1) the child may die, as an infant or later in life, (2) the child may not earn enough income to support the parents, and (3) the child may break parental ties and deliberately not support its parents, even though it has the economic capability to do so. The probability of these uncertain events taken together we denoted by p.

The uncertainty described in the preceding paragraph has to be compared with the tolerance threshold of the parents, which is the minimum probability that they need old-age support, and this threshold changes with the degree of risk aversion of the parents. The degree of risk aversion, in turn, depends in part on the economic security of the parents. A higher level of security generally implies a lower degree of aversion to risk.

These factors help us to uncover, to some extent, the reasons behind a sticky fertility rate in the face of rapidly falling death rates. The first element is *information*. How is the social phenomenon of a falling death rate translated to the level of individual decision making? We have already commented on the rapidity of the decline in death rates in developing countries. For twenty-one developing countries during the period from just before World War II until 1950, the death rate dropped on average by seven per thousand population every ten years (Coale and Hoover [1958, p. 14]). For a historical demographer and indeed for any social scientist, this is a remarkable change indeed and is unparalleled in history for its rapidity. As Coale and Hoover [1958, p. 14] observed, "this rate of improvement surpasses anything from the records of areas inhabited by northern and western Europeans." Yet it would be wondrous indeed if these changes made the newspapers at the time! The fact of the matter is that individuals must often go by their own experience, by which I mean their vision of the experiences of their *parents* and the siblings and friends of their parents. It is the preceding generation that provides the only direct experience that is relevant in this context.

Thus the fall of death rates may not instantly translate into a revised estimate of mortality (see box, Three Generations).

Three Generations[4]

The village of Rampur in India was surveyed by Lewis [1952] and then resurveyed by Das Gupta [1994]. The story of Umed Singh comes from them. Umed Singh's father was Siri Chand, who was born around 1900. Epidemics of plague and cholera decimated his family, including his father and mother. Siri Chand was brought up by his uncle. As a farmer, he faced the kind of uncertainty that is difficult for us to even contemplate: consecutive crop failures, famine, the occasional bumper

---

[4] This box is based on Das Gupta [1994].

crop, the loss of *six* out of nine live births: two girls and one boy survived to adulthood. The life of the boy, Umed Singh (who was born around 1935), stands in sharp contrast to that of his father.

Umed Singh completed secondary school and became a policeman. He earned a regular salary and also received income from his land (left to him by his father). However, the uncertainties of his father's life never ceased to haunt him. He was the sole surviving son in a family that had given birth to nine children. With no objective reasoning to back his insecurity, Umed Singh worried and then worried some more. His first two children were girls. Because he wanted a boy, he insisted on having more children. He had three more children, and two of them were boys, but he continued to worry that his children would die, and this fear did not leave him until his third son was born. *All* his children survived.

As Umed Singh relived the anxieties of his father, people around him were already changing. His wife, when interviewed, felt that they should have stopped having children much earlier. So did Umed Singh's cousins and his colleagues in the police force.

Das Gupta ends the story thus: "The second generation of people who lead a secure, ordered life do not experience the anxieties left over from past insecurities. Umed Singh's oldest daughter has completed a course in teacher training and will be married shortly. She says she has no intention of childbearing in the way her mother had; three children were the maximum she would have. She is a relaxed, confident woman, who is inclined to be a little amused by her father's anxieties on behalf of his family."

Although falling death rates are central to the fertility decline, there are other factors in the construction of p that have little to do with the fall of death rates. These are the previously mentioned items (2) and (3), which may well go the other way even as death rates fall. These depend on the economic conditions of the region. The poorer the region, the greater the anticipated probability that a single child will not earn enough in adulthood to support parents; hence, the greater the incentive to have more children to compensate for this possibility. Likewise, falling death rates cannot in any way affect the social possibilities of fulfilling parental obligations. These are independent phenomena that continue to leave their mark even as death rates fall, and they might keep birth rates high.

Finally, there are the additional complications introduced by gender bias. Again, there is no guarantee that a fall in the death rates will have any impact on the degree of bias. In making this statement, we actually distinguish between two types of bias. One is what might be called observable bias; that is, measurable indicators of differential treatment of boys and girls. With development, such bias indeed lessens as resource constraints loosen. A second sort of bias has to do with the intrinsic valuation of women in society and it feeds into the perception of women as sources of old-age support. This bias actually increases with economic progress, at least to a certain extent. One important reason for the potential increase is that economic progress is associated with a decline in the importance of agriculture. To the extent that women play an important role in agriculture, they may now be perceived as relatively less capable of providing old-age support on their own. We have already seen that such biases, apart from their obvious intrinsic shamefulness, can brutally affect fertility decisions.

Hoarding versus targeting

Our discussion so far contains an implicit assumption: that parents must make their fertility decisions about later children without being able to use information about the fate of their earlier children. Is this reasonable? Again, the answer depends on just which components of p are dominant in parental psychology. For instance, if an individual worries that the child may not earn enough in adulthood to support his aging parent, this is not an outcome that lends itself to a wait-and-see strategy. By that time, it will not be possible to have a new child! If the source of the uncertainty resides in such features, all the tickets will have to be bought in advance, as it were. We may refer to this phenomenon as one of *hoarding*: children have to be stockpiled in advance, before we know which (if any) among them will provide the requisite support.

   Contrast this with a situation where infant mortality (death before the age of one) is the dominant form of uncertainty. In such a situation a wait-and-see strategy acquires greater feasibility. A couple can have a child and condition its next fertility decision on the survival of this child. The desired number of children can be attained *sequentially*; this strategy is called *targeting*. Obviously targeting generally is associated with lower fertility rates, because the total number of children do not have to be created "in advance."

   A change in the demographic regime from hoarding to targeting can lead to a drastic lowering of the fertility rate. Again, the rate at which this switch of regime occurs depends critically on the kinds of uncertainties that the couple is most concerned about. It is true, however, that a fall in the death rate can only assist in bringing about this change of regime.

The costs of children

So far we have neglected the costs of child rearing. These costs take two forms. First, there are what might be called the direct costs of children: they need to be fed, clothed, kept in good health, looked after, and schooled. Second, there are the indirect or *opportunity* costs of children that are measured by the amount of income foregone in the process of bringing up the child. Time spent at home with the child is time not spent earning income, so the opportunity cost of children is roughly proportional to the going wage rate multiplied by the number of hours spent in parenting.

In societies where this opportunity cost is low, fertility rates tend to be high. Gender bias plays a role in this as well. In many societies (including many developed countries), it is presumed that women must allocate the bulk of their time to the upbringing of children. In such societies wages for women's work are low as well. This brings down the opportunity cost of having children and keeps birth rates high.

Similarly, if there are high rates of unemployment, the opportunity costs of children comes down. Again, this can push fertility upward.

This cost–benefit approach to fertility choice is natural to economists. Becker [1960] introduced this approach to other social scientists. Often, the methodology is not very useful: simply stating that parents have children up to the point where marginal benefit equals marginal cost may be an impressive piece of jargon, but does not convey much information. To make the cost–benefit approach useful, we must either discuss benefits, or costs, or both in a way that is relevant to the situation at hand. This is what we have done so far with the notion of benefits. Instead of stating that parents derive "utility" out of children, we describe it specifically as old-age support, and this description allows us to draw the specific conclusions that we have arrived at so far. So it is with costs. We need to understand how different *kinds* of costs have different sorts of demographic implications. In the discussion that follows, we illustrate this point by considering a specific case: the effect of income improvements on fertility.

Figure 9.1 considers the preferences of a couple over the number of children it wishes to have and "other goods," denominated in terms of money. Children are on the horizontal axis; other goods are on the vertical axis. In

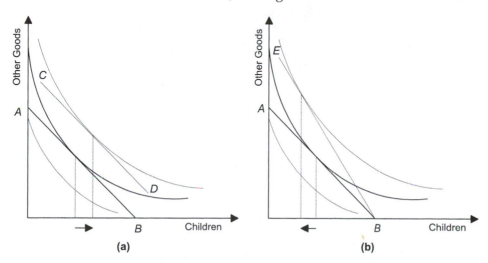

Figure 9.1. Income improvements and fertility.

what follows, we do not pay much attention to the exact form of preferences, which are represented by indifference curves in Figure 9.1. For instance, these preferences may be a reduced form of the desire for old-age support or may simply arise from the intrinsic pleasure of having children. Our focus is on the costs.

Consider, first, the total *potential* income of the couple if they were to have no children at all. Income may be wage labor or some other form of income, such as land rent. If it is the former, potential income includes all income earned by each spouse, under the scenario that they have no children to look after. This amount is represented by the height of the point *A* in Figure 9.1.

Now it should be clear that as the number of children begins to rise, the income left for "other goods" will begin to fall. It will fall for two reasons. First, there are the direct expenses of the children. Next, earned income falls as well, because one or both parents spend some time at home to look after the child. This trade-off traces out the "budget line" *AB*. With very large numbers of children, residual income available to the parents may drop to zero: this is the point *B* at which the budget line cuts the horizontal axis. Panel (a) of the figure incorporates this description.

The *slope* of the budget line (see the indicated angle in Figure 9.1) is a measure of the unit cost of having children. If income is earned, it will be the wage rate multiplied by hours foregone per child. In addition, there are the direct costs per child.

The exercise that we now conduct has to do with an increase in family income. To fix ideas, suppose first that the source of income increase is not wage income. For instance, the individual in question may be a landowner who receives all income from leasing land to tenants. Rents have gone up. In this case, the budget line will undergo a parallel shift, moving to the position *CD* [see panel (a)]. What effect does this have on fertility? Well, if children are "normal goods," the income effect must raise the demand for children, so that fertility rates go up as a result of the income increase.

Contrast this change with a change in *wage* income. In this case, the budget line will not only shift outward, it will *swivel* as well. This is because the opportunity cost of children has gone up. In Figure 9.1(b), we show this by shifting the budget line out and rotating around the point *B* at the same time, so that we have the new budget line *EB*. Potential income has gone up, but *at the same time the opportunity cost of children has gone up as well*. This creates a substitution effect away from children as well as an income effect. The substitution effect lowers fertility; the income effect raises it. The net effect is ambiguous.

Despite the ambiguity, one thing is clear from Figure 9.1: fertility certainly does not rise by as much as in the case where the income increase can be traced to "nonearned" sources. The intuition is straightforward. Wage income imposes an opportunity cost of having an extra child, whereas rental income does not. Thus wage income increases have a stronger impact on fertility reductions than rental income. This illustrates the usefulness of the cost–benefit approach, at least up to a certain point.

We can easily extend this argument to the case of gender bias. Suppose that only women look after children. Then an increase in rental income has the same effect as an increase in male wages: both lead to a parallel shift of the budget line, as in the move from *AB* to *CD*. Male wages impose no opportunity cost on childbearing if men play no part in raising children. In contrast, the swiveling of the budget line is characteristic of an increase in *female* wages. The opportunity cost of having children will go up. It follows that a society with gender bias is more likely to exhibit a reduction in fertility when female wages go up, as opposed to the case in which male wages rise. This argument was examined in a paper by Galor and Weil [1996] and by many others (see also the following box).

Women's Wages and Fertility Decline: A Study of Sweden

Over the last century or more, there has been an increase in the wages of women relative to men. This is certainly the case in currently developed countries. Along with this increase, we see a concurrent reduction of fertility. Is this clear evidence of a *causal* relationship between women's wages and fertility? It may not be. It is conceivable, for instance, that a reduction in fertility occurred for some other reason, and this reduction was associated with larger investments by women in education, which raised their wages. In this hypothetical situation, fertility and female wages are *correlated*, but no evidence of *causality* is established. What we need is *separate* evidence, quite apart from actions that may have been taken by women themselves "on the supply side," that female employment is more in demand. Then we can relate this piece of evidence to the fertility decline.

Schultz [1985] raised precisely this question and addressed it in an interesting way using Sweden as an example. In the second half of the nineteenth century, the world grain market went through a declining phase of major proportions. The exports of Swedish grain collapsed. Faced with this decline in grain demand, there was a substantial reallocation of resources in agriculture. Animal husbandry was the benefactor. Swedish exports of butter soared.

Now, dairying and the processing of milk employed a larger fraction of women than did grain farming. As a result of this reallocation, the demand for female labor went up significantly and so did the wages paid to women.

The usefulness of focusing on the butter boom is that it effectively captures a pure demand effect on female wages, rather than an effect that could have been created by supply decisions. Did fertility drop in response to the butter boom?

It did. Schultz shows that in regions where the price of butter relative to rye (the basic food grain in Sweden) is high, the ratio of female to male wages was high as well and fertility rates were lower. Indeed, following up on the link between butter prices and female wages, Schultz estimated that about a quarter of the decline in the Swedish total fertility rate from 1860 to 1910 can be explained by the rise in relative female wages. The conclusion is that "the appreciating value of women's time relative to men's played an important role in the Swedish fertility transition."

9.3.4. Is fertility too high?

So far we have tried to provide an account of why fertility rates may be high in the face of falling death rates, but "high" does not necessarily mean "suboptimal": if a family *chooses* to have a large number of children, then why should social considerations dictate anything different? There are three answers to this question.[5]

Information and uncertainty

The first answer relies on the incompleteness of *information*, which is an issue that we have already discussed. People simply may not internalize the general observation that death rates have undergone a decline, as in the example of the Rampur policeman Umed Singh (see box). In such a case, the number of children that couples have may not be socially optimal. Faced with fresh information regarding the environment that influences their fertility choices, the couple would typically revise their fertility decisions.

The second answer relies on the distinction between decisions that are made *ex ante* and their *ex post* consequences. Consider the family that wants one child, but has five, in the hope of increasing the chances of old-age support. As we have already seen, such decisions are based both on the probability of a child dying and on the degree of aversion to risk of the family. Thus it is not unlikely (and this will be true especially for poor families that are highly risk-averse) that, in fact, a large percentage of the children do survive *ex post*. Such families will have too many children and they will suffer because these children will have to be looked after and fed. The evaluation of optimality becomes problematic in this case. If a family with a large number of children is asked if they are happy with this situation, they may reply that they are not, but if asked whether they would have made exactly those fertility choices all over again (in the face of the uncertainty that shrouded

---

[5] There is a fourth as well, which is that families (especially illiterate and poor families) do not know what is best for them. In particular, they procreate without thinking or being aware of effective contraceptive methods. According to this view, an expansion in the supply of contraceptive devices and a good lecture will take care of the problem. I do not discuss this viewpoint here, but see the subsection on social norms at the end of Section 9.3.

survival), they may well say that they would have. There is no contradiction between these seemingly contradictory answers.[6]

Externalities

The third and most important answer is based on the existence of *externalities*. That is, the fertility decisions made by an individual or a couple may have implications for other members of a family or indeed for other families. To the extent that such effects are not internalized by the decision maker(s), fertility choices that are privately optimal may not be socially optimal.

As the following cases suggest, fertility-related externalities are typically *negative* (though this need not always be the case). Thus private fertility choices generally lead to overly large numbers of children.

Let us begin by studying some effects *across* families. These externalities are particularly pervasive in situations where infrastructure is provided by the government at little or no cost to users. In such cases, it is not possible for individual families to value these resources at their true social cost, because that is not the cost they (or their children) pay. This is not to say that such services should always be provided at market prices (often they represent the only way to redistribute income in an unequal society), but they do enlarge the number of situations in which an externality may be present.

Consider, for instance, the provision of free public education in an urban area. If a benevolent social planner could dictate the number of children that all families should have in that area, she would take the marginal social cost of providing educational resources into account. However, if education is provided free of charge, the *private* cost to the family typically is lower than the social cost, which therefore will not be properly internalized. It follows that the number of children that people choose to have will exceed the social optimum.

The same is true of other publicly provided services that are not valued at their true marginal cost, such as subsidized housing or health services. As I have already mentioned, these may often be the only feasible way to target the poor in a society where direct information on economic characteristics is hard to get hold of. These services have the same effect as the provision of education: they reduce private marginal costs below the social marginal costs and push fertility beyond the social optimum.

A similar set of observations applies to resources that are not properly priced, such as the environment. Such resources can be depleted even if

---

[6] Even the ex ante choices may be suboptimal, because there are missing markets. Specifically, in the absence of a missing market for insurance, in general, and old-age security, in particular, families tend to overinvest in children. If these options were provided, the number of children per poor family would surely decline. The point is, however, that the choices *are* ex ante optimal given that the markets are missing.

they are renewable: they include fisheries, groundwater, forests, soil quality, and of course the ozone layer. The main characteristic of such resources is that they are generally underpriced, so that financial incentives bias their use in the direction of overexploitation. To the extent that such underpricing reduces the cost of child rearing, fertility is biased upward.

All of these effects can be summarized in one very general framework. In Figure 9.2, we show the costs and benefits of having children (say, for a single family). For simplicity, we take the cost curve to be a straight line (so that each new child costs the same additional amount), even though there are diminishing returns to having more children. This means that the benefit function has the familiar concave shape.

Focus now on the costs. The thick straight line shows the *private* costs of an additional child and the thinner line shows the *social* costs of an additional child. The preceding discussion indicated that in many situations, the private costs may be less than the social costs. Diagrammatically, this is captured by the fact that the "social cost" line is steeper than the "private cost" line. The socially optimum number of children is found by maximizing the vertical distance between the benefit line and the social cost line. This point is found by setting marginal benefit equal to marginal social cost, which occurs at the point *A* and yields a number of children n^*. In contrast, the privately optimal number of children is found by maximizing the vertical distance

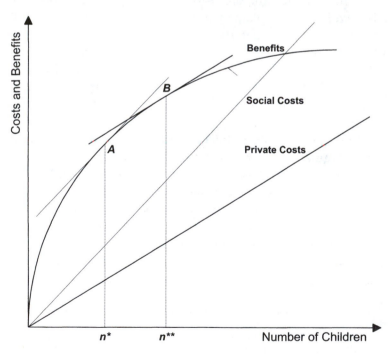

Figure 9.2. Private and social costs and fertility decisions.

between the benefit line and the private cost line. This occurs at the point B with associated number n^{**}. Note that $n^{**} > n^{*}$.

This sort of analysis summarizes all the various situations listed previously and tells us how to think about others. Here are two examples that serve as extensions of the analysis.

First, all situations may not involve a divergence between social and private costs. There may be a divergence between social and private benefits as well. Suppose that prized jobs are available for a high pay, say, $1,000 per month, but that there is a queue for such jobs. Imagine that each family sends its grown-up children to look for such jobs and that, for each child, the probability of getting the job is simply the total number of such jobs available divided by the total number of job seekers. Now having an additional child is just like buying an additional lottery ticket—like having a second shot at the prize. To the family, the probability of getting at least one job offer doubles. However, we must be careful here: the number of job seekers goes up too. This effect is minuscule at the level of the family in question, but the combined effect of *many* families buying their two lottery tickets each on *other* families is significant and negative. In the end, each family has, say, two tickets each and nobody's chances of getting the job are really increased. Worse still, that second ticket is costly: it is a child who has to be clothed and fed.

This kind of situation is easy enough to analyze in the general framework that we have set out. You can easily check that in this example there is no divergence between private and social costs, but there is a divergence between private and social *benefits*. The social benefit of an additional child is the private expected gain *plus* the losses inflicted on all other families by swelling the ranks of the job seekers by one. This is an externality.

Our second example is designed to show that externalities can occur *within* the family as well. This is especially true if there are family members in the household other than the couple making fertility decisions. Consider, for instance, a joint family: typically one in which two or more brothers pool resources to live under a common roof. I do not know if you have ever experienced the wonders of a joint family; I have friends who have. At first glance it is impossible to tell parent from aunt or uncle, because aunt and uncle participate significantly in the upbringing of children. The effect is two-way, of course: my cousins will likewise be looked after by my parents. Now this looks like a happy state of affairs (and often it is and often it isn't), but the point I wish to focus on is the observation that joint families naturally create an *intra*family externality. Knowing that one's brother and sister-in-law will bear part of the costs of child rearing lowers the private costs of having children and raises fertility!

Now something looks suspicious in this argument. There must be a "law of conservation of costs." Everybody's costs cannot be simultaneously low-

ered. For instance, the brother and sister-in-law are surely passing on some
of the costs of child rearing to *my* parents, so why does it all not cancel out,
leaving fertility decisions unaltered relative to those which would have been
made in a nuclear family? The answer is simple. It is true that my parents
are bearing part of the costs of rearing their nephews and nieces, but this is a
cost that they cannot control, because the fertility decisions regarding nieces
and nephews are being made by *someone else*. Thus these costs are fixed costs
as far as my parents are concerned, whereas the costs of their own children
that they in turn pass on are *variable*, because they make the decisions regarding their own offspring, and only the *variable* costs count in the fertility
decision. This is what Figure 9.2 implicitly teaches us. The *slopes* of the private and social costs, and not their levels, are the key determinants of fertility.
This is not easily seen in that figure, so Figure 9.3 provides an appropriate
variant. The thin line in Figure 9.3 represents the cost of one couple's children to the entire (joint) family. Because part of this cost is passed on to the
hapless brother and sister-in-law, the variable cost to the *couple* is given by
the flatter thick line passing through the origin of the diagram. Now, as we
said, the same kind of cost transfer is faced by the couple in question, which
raises their total costs, but only shifts their cost line in a parallel way (see
Figure 9.3). This shift of levels does nothing to affect their fertility choice,
which is n^{**}, above the level that is optimal for the joint family as a whole
(or for the couple had they been nuclear), which is n^*.

The same kind of argument holds if there are grandparents to look after
children. If the grandparents' costs are not fully internalized by the couple,

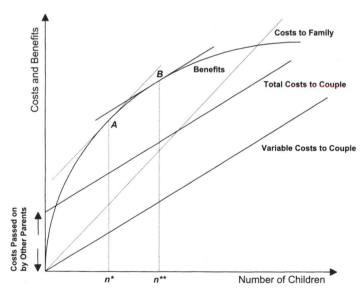

Figure 9.3. Fertility choices in joint families.

they may have too many children relative to what is optimal for *their* family, leave alone society as a whole.

Thus family structure is very important in creating externalities that lead to excessive fertility. As such structure changes from joint or extended families to nuclear families, the costs of children are more directly borne by the couple, which leads to a decline in fertility.[7]

In all the preceding cases there are negative external effects of fertility decision, so that fertility choices are typically high relative to the social optimum. There are situations in which there might be positive externalities as well, especially if the optimum for that society includes the pursuit of pronatalist policies to gain economic or military power. Such concerns may also be felt in societies in which a long history of low population growth has shifted the age distribution uncomfortably in the direction of high age groups, which places immense burdens on social security systems. To the extent that an individual family does not internalize these goals, the state may actually reward child bearing in an attempt to provide appropriate incentives. As we have already seen, such pronatalist policies are the exception rather than the rule, although they do exist.[8]

Social norms

Often, people do what other people do. The glue of conformism is what holds social relationships and societies together. Conformism assures stability and limits the need for law enforcement, and indeed it is the expression of a shared conformism that we know as culture. We have already seen a discussion of social norms in Chapter 5.

The very strength of such norms becomes a weakness when the environment of the society begins to change. Accepted, appropriate practice over many centuries may now become inappropriate, but once this happens, social practice is often slow to alter. It becomes necessary to coordinate on some *new* norm, but such coordination requires many people to move in unison. In Chapter 5, we saw how difficult this is when there are multiple equilibria involving large numbers of people, such as in technology adoption. Here read "norm" for "technology."

Norms do ultimately change and chase what is appropriate, but it may be a long time coming. Consider a poor society with high rates of infant

---

[7] It is even possible to extend this sort of argument to externalities created at the level of the couple. To the extent that men and women are disproportionately engaged in child rearing, one of the parties (typically the man) may ignore these costs and not take adequate steps to reduce fertility or the risks of pregnancy.

[8] As an interesting twist on this argument, note that pronatalist policies may themselves be self-defeating at the world level, to the extent that they inflict negative externalities on other countries. The analysis of this second layer of externalities can proceed exactly in the same way as the negative externalities discussed in the text.

mortality and intensive use of child labor in farming, as well as for old-age support. It is not surprising to find such a society celebrating the birth of many children (especially sons). Such societies develop certain attitudes toward the "appropriate" age of marriage, the role of women, the importance of contraception, the desirability of primary education, ancestor worship, and even practices such as breast-feeding. Now imagine that advances in sanitation and medicine dramatically bring down infant mortality rates. Suppose that dependence on agriculture is on the wane (or mechanization is increasing, so that child labor is less important). Suppose that institutional forms of old-age security are becoming available. Will fertility change overnight?

We have already seen that it will not, but an additional reason for this is that people still want to conform to the old practices of having and celebrating children, to early age at marriage, and so on, *simply because everyone around them is doing the same.*[9]

These conformist tendencies may be bolstered by social and religious practices such as ancestor worship, that require the continuation of every lineage, often through males. Polygyny might also keep fertility rates high, as might the social importance of community over family (which brings down the private costs of child bearing in a way that we have already described). Even property rights might play a role. For instance, if land is held communally, it might be difficult to internalize the consequent costs of fertility in terms of the fragmentation of land holdings.

Jolting such a society into a "new equilibrium" is not easy. It requires *coordinated* change. An example of such a change is one in which ancestor worship is permitted through adopted children. If everybody thinks this is acceptable, then it's acceptable. It is in this sense that programs such as family-planning programs play a very important role. Quite apart from spreading important information regarding the cost, availability and effectiveness of different methods of contraception, these programs serve as a form of *social legitimization.* Consider the family-planning experiment known as the Matlab project in Bangladesh, in which seventy "treatment villages" were served by a birth control/family-planning program in 1977, while another seventy-nine "control villages" offered no such service. Contraceptive use in the treatment villages jumped from 7 to 33% in eighteen months. By 1980, the fertility rate in the treatment villages had declined to two-thirds that of the control villages.

What does the Matlab experiment teach us? One answer is that contraception was an unknown concept. People *wanted* to have two-thirds the

---

[9] The desire for this sort of conformity can have surprising consequences. At first glance, we might think that at the margin there will be *some* movement away from accepted practice, as people trade off their desire to conform with the desire to do what is best for them, but even such marginal movements may be blocked in conformist equilibria (on this point, see Bernheim [1994]).

number of children they were having, but could not do so. Perhaps, but at face value, this is unlikely. It is far more likely that the programs sent a strong signal that a lower *desired* fertility rate is actually a good thing: it is tolerated and indeed encouraged by society at large. People responded to this by adopting contraceptive devices to lower fertility. Thus it is possible that the program served two functions simultaneously: first, contraceptives were made widely available; second, and perhaps more important, the program signaled the advent of a new social norm in which lower fertility is actually a "good thing." Thus Phillips et al. [1988] wrote of the Matlab experiment, "An intensive service program can compensate for weak or ambivalent reproductive motives and create demand for services, leading to contraceptive adoption where it might otherwise not occur."

Social norms can be altered in other ways as well. The media is immensely powerful in this regard and can "transmit" norms from one community to another. The use of television and film to suggest that small families are successful can be of great value.

Social Norms and a New Fertility Decline[10]

According to the 1994 revision of the official United Nations world population estimates and projections, a fertility transition is underway in several sub-Saharan African and South-Central Asian countries. Fertility levels have traditionally been very high in these countries.

Total fertility rates have declined in Madagascar (from 6.6 in 1980–85 to 6.1 in 1994), Rwanda (from 8.1 to 6.5), United Republic of Tanzania (from 6.7 to 5.9), Namibia (from 5.8 to 5.3), South Africa (from 4.8 to 4.1), and Mauritania (from 6.1 to 5.4). Fertility declines are also evident in Zambia, Zimbabwe, and Gambia. If we add to this list Kenya and Botswana, where evidence of a fertility decline already exists, we see the beginnings of an overall fertility decline in sub-Saharan Africa.

South-Central Asia shows continued fertility decline: fertility has fallen in Iran (6.8 to 5.0) and continues its downward course in Bangladesh (6.2 to 4.4), India (from 4.5 to 3.7), and Nepal (from 6.3 to 5.4).

As discussed in the text, a widespread change in social norms may be playing a central role. Fertility declines everywhere appear to be accompanied by a significant increase in contraceptive use. We must be careful here to not infer any sort of causal link, but the increased recourse to contraception is indicative of an accompanying social transformation. Huge jumps in contraceptive use have been seen in Kenya (up from 7% of couples in 1977–78 to 33% in 1993), Rwanda (from 10% in 1983 to 21% in 1992), Bangladesh (from 19% in 1981 to 40% in 1991), and Iran (from 36% in 1977 to 65% in 1992).

---

[10] This account summarizes material made available by the United Nations Population Division, Department for Economic and Social Information and Policy Analysis, at http://www.undp.org/popin/.

Norms regarding the age of marriage must play a role as well. In Tanzania, for example, the incidence of contraception is low (10% in 1991–92), but the average age of a woman at marriage has gone up from 19 years in 1978 to 21 years in 1988. This is also the case in countries where contraception has significantly increased.

To be sure, fertility declines are not universal in this region and do remain high in the large countries of Nigeria, Zaire, Ethiopia, and Pakistan, but going by the broader picture, change is on the way.

9.4. From population growth to economic development

Just as economic development has implications for the pace of population growth, so the latter has implications for the rate of economic development. In large part, this relationship is thought to be negative. A large population means that there is less to go around per person, so that per capita income is depressed. However, this argument is somewhat more subtle than might appear at first glance. More people not only consume more, they *produce* more as well. The net effect must depend on whether the gain in production is outweighed by the increase in consumption. In the next two subsections, we clarify how the negative argument works and then follow this argument with some qualifications that suggest possible gains from population growth.

9.4.1. Some negative effects

The Malthusian view

Beginning with Thomas Malthus, a standard view on population growth is that its effects on per capita welfare are negative. Malthus was particularly gloomy on this score. According to him, whenever wages rise above subsistence, they are eaten away in an orgy of procreation: people marry earlier and have more children, which depresses the wage to its biological minimum. Thus in the long run, the endogeneity of population keeps per capita income at some stagnant subsistence level.

This is not a completely bizarre view of human progress. It probably fit the fourteenth to the eighteenth centuries pretty well. Blips in productivity, such as those in agriculture, increased the carrying capacity of the planet, but population did rise to fill the gap. It is difficult to evaluate this scenario from a normative standpoint. Over time, it was possible to sustain human life on a larger scale, even though on a per capita scale, the Malthusian view predicted unchanged minimum subsistence. Evaluation of this prediction depends on how we compare the prospect of not being born to the prospect of living at minimum subsistence. As I already stated, we sidestep this issue to some extent and concentrate on *per capita* welfare alone. By this yardstick, the Malthusian view is neutral in its long-run view of population growth.

A central ingredient of the Malthusian argument deserves critical scrutiny. Do human beings react to economic progress by spontaneously having more children? Modern experience suggests just the opposite. Individuals do understand that having children is costly, and it is perhaps true that the costs increase with economic development, while the (economic) benefits decline. For instance, we argued in previous sections that economic development is associated with greater provision of organized old-age social security. We have seen that such institutions probably are more effective than any other in bringing down rates of fertility in developing countries. People have children for a reason, not just because it is *feasible* to have them.

Likewise, economic progress may shift societies from an extended family system to a nuclear family system. As labor force participation increases, it becomes progressively more unlikely that individuals in an extended family all find jobs in the same locality. At the same time, the insurance motives that underlie the joint family setup probably decline. With nuclear families, the costs of child rearing are internalized to a greater degree, which brings down fertility.

There are other aspects that we have discussed as well, such as an increase in female wages or reductions in infant mortality with development. All these have a moderating impact on fertility. Thus it is absurd to entertain the notion that people react to any surplus in their incomes by automatically having more children. It is true that the Malthusian theory doesn't do a bad job for fourteenth century Europe, but in poor societies it is very difficult to separate the various determinants of fertility: fertility may have been high enough (for other reasons) relative to per capita income so that the Malthusian checks and balances applied better.

So as a first pass, it may not be a bad idea to think of population growth as an exogenous variable that is driven by features other than per capita income. At any rate, in societies that are not overwhelmingly poor, it is probably the case that if population growth is endogenous, it is a *decreasing* function of per capita income,[11] and not increasing as Malthus suggested. Data such as those presented in Table 9.1 certainly support this hypothesis better than the alternative.

Using growth models

The growth models of Chapter 3 represent a good starting point in this respect. Recall the ingredients of the standard growth model: people make consumption and savings decisions. Savings are translated into investment,

---

[11] To be more precise, this is true if per capita income is a good proxy for other features of development. On these matters, see the discussion in Chapter 2.

and the capital stock of the economy grows over time. Meanwhile, the population of the economy is growing too.

We know already how to figure out the net effect of all this. The rate of savings determines, via investment, the growth rate of the capital stock. The latter determines, via the capital–output ratio, the growth rate of national income. Does all this growth translate into an increase *per person*? Not necessarily. Population is growing too, and this increase surely eats away (so far as *per capita* growth is concerned) at some of the increase in national output. In Chapter 3, we did the simple algebra that puts these features together. Our first pass at this brought us to equation (3.6), which is reproduced here:

$$(9.2) \qquad\qquad s/\theta = (1 + g^*)(1 + n) - (1 + \delta),$$

where s is the rate of savings, n is the rate of population growth, δ is the rate of depreciation of the capital stock, and g^* is the rate of growth of *per capita* income. This is the Harrod–Domar model, and the implications are crystal clear. According to this model, population growth has an unambiguously negative effect on the rate of growth. To see this, simply stare at (9.2) and note that if all parameters remain constant while the rate of population growth n increases, the per capita growth rate g^* *must* fall.

Nonetheless, we can criticize this prediction. The Harrod–Domar model, on which (9.2) is based, treats the capital–output ratio as *exogenous*, and therefore makes no allowance for the fact that an increased population raises output. After all, if the capital–output ratio is assumed to be constant, this is tantamount to assuming that an increased population has no effect on output at all. Would it not be the case that a higher rate of population growth would bring down the amount of capital needed to produce each unit of output, now that there is more labor as an input in production?

We have walked this road before; it leads us to the Solow model. In Solow's world, a *production function* relates capital and labor to the production of output. In addition, there is technical change at some constant rate. We obtained the remarkable answer in that model that *once the change in the capital–output ratio is taken into account*, the steady-state rate of growth is *independent* of the rate of savings and the rate of population growth (see our analysis in Chapter 3). All that matters for long-run growth is the rate of technological progress!

This is odd, because the Solow model now seems to tilt us to the other extreme. It suggests that population growth has no effect at all! However, this is not true: what we have shown so far is that population growth has no effect on the long-run rate of per capita income *growth*. There is a level effect, however. We briefly recall the discussion from Chapter 3.

Recall why population growth rates have no growth effect. In the Harrod–Domar model, there is an implicit assumption that labor and capital

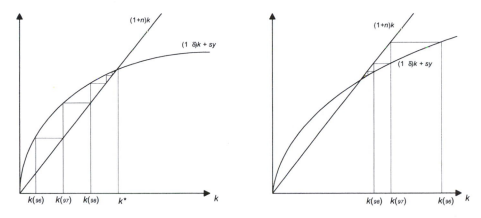

Figure 9.4. *The steady state in the Solow model.*

are not substitutable in production. Thus added population growth exerts a drag on per capita growth, while contributing nothing of substance via the production process. In the Solow model, on the other hand, population growth, while continuing to have the first effect, contributes to productive potential as the extra labor force is absorbed into productive activity through a change in the capital–labor ratio. Indeed, implicit in the Solow model is the assumption that capital and labor can be substituted for each other indefinitely, although the process of substitution may become more and more costly.[12] Because of this, population growth has no ultimate effect on the rate of growth in the Solow model.

This does *not* mean that an increase in the rate of population growth has *no* effect at all in the Solow model. It lowers the steady-state *level* of the per capita capital stock, expressed in units of capital per effective unit of labor, and in this way affects the level of per capita income, expressed again in units of effective labor. The easiest way to see this is to recall Figure 3.4, which we reproduce here as Figure 9.4.

Recall that the steady state k^*, expressed in terms of effective units of labor, is found as the intersection of two graphs. These are, respectively, the left- and right-hand sides of the equation that describes the evolution of capital stocks in the Solow model with technical progress:

$$(9.3) \qquad (1+n)(1+\pi)\hat{k}(t+1) = (1-\delta)\hat{k}(t) + s\hat{y}(t).$$

It's now easy to see that if n goes up, this "swivels" the left-hand side of (9.3) upward and brings down the steady-state level of the capital stock, expressed as a ratio of effective labor. This means that although the long-run rate of growth is unaffected by a change in the rate of population growth, the

---

[12] The cost, of course, is expressed by the marginal rate of substitution between the two inputs of production and is captured by the degree of curvature of the production isoquants.

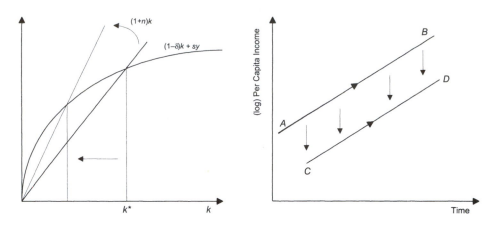

Figure 9.5. Growth rates are unaffected, but the levels shift down.

entire *trajectory* of growth is shifted downward. See Figure 9.5 for a depiction of this scenario.

Thus increased population growth has negative level effects in the standard growth models of Chapter 3. These effects are perfectly intuitive, although as we have seen, they may manifest themselves differently in different models. Population growth means that a given level of output must be divided among an increasing number of people, so that an increase in population growth rates brings down the size of the per capita cake. In the Harrod–Domar model, the effect is resoundingly negative, because population growth has no redeeming features, such as increasing the productivity of capital when more labor is available. In the Solow model, this redeeming feature is partially present. An increase in the population growth rate *both* increases the demands on the national cake and expands the ability of capital to produce the national cake. The net effect on long-run per capita growth rates is zero. Nevertheless, the level of per capita income at any given point in time is lowered.[13] This comes from the assumption in the Solow model that there are diminishing returns to every input, so that an increase in the labor intensity of production (necessitated by increased population growth) reduces the long-run per capita level of output relative to efficiency units of labor.

The growth models teach us that once the Malthusian assumption of unrestrained procreation is dropped, population growth certainly does not condemn society to everlasting subsistence. Growth in per capita income is still possible. At the same time, increased population growth does adversely affect this growth rate (as in the Harrod–Domar model), and even if it keeps the long-run growth rate unchanged, it affects the level of the trajectory (as in the Solow model).

---

[13] These last two statements are perfectly consistent, as Figure 9.5 shows.

Population and savings

There is yet another negative effect of population growth that is not considered in the growth models already presented, but is easy enough to incorporate. Faster population growth lowers the aggregate rate of savings. This happens simply because population growth eats into aggregate income. If it is true that the rich save a higher fraction of their income, savings rates may be adversely affected. More importantly, faster population growth shifts the age structure of the population toward the very young and in so doing increases the dependency ratio in families. Because children consume more than they produce, this tends to lower savings rates as well. This is one of the effects emphasized by demographers Coale and Hoover [1958] in their classic work on the subject.

The savings effect works in very much the same way as the direct population growth rate effects. In the Harrod–Domar model, it exacerbates the reduction in growth rates [allow s to fall as well in equation (9.2)]. In the Solow model, there continue to be no growth effects, but the long-run time trajectory of per capita income is shifted down.

Population, inequality, and poverty

A high rate of population growth will exacerbate the poverty problem, if the arguments in the previous section are valid. It will also worsen inequality if population growth among the poor is disproportionately larger.

Do the poor have more children? From the discussion in the previous sections of this chapter, that would appear to be the case, although the connections are not unambiguous by any means. It is more likely that the poor need children for old-age support. It is more likely that infant mortality rates are higher for the poor, so having a larger number of children to compensate is more likely to occur for the poor. We already know that this will translate into a higher expected number of *surviving* children (because risk-averse couples generally overcompensate for these risks).

It is somewhat harder to compare the relative costs of child bearing. Poor families are likely to have a higher degree of labor force participation by females, simply because additional income is of greater importance. This raises the opportunity costs of having children. However, it is also true that growth in income creates a quantity–quality trade-off in children. Richer households may want to invest proportionately greater sums in the education of their children. Consequently, the costs of an additional child (given the quality considerations) are proportionately much higher, which brings down the total number of children desired.

These considerations suggest that the poor may have higher fertility rates than the rich. To the extent that this is true, a high overall rate of population growth will have a disproportionately heavy impact on those who are already poor, or on the threshold of poverty.

Population growth and the environment

Recall the discussion on whether fertility is too high. In that discussion, one of the most important features is the underpricing of infrastructural resources. Government-provided education, health, and public transportation may all be subsidized. We also discussed why they are subsidized: it may be a second-best way to transfer resources to the poor. (Direct transfers may be infeasible because it may be impossible to credibly identify the poor.)

This observation has two corollaries. First, these resources must be consumed largely by the poor. Second, the inability of individuals to internalize the costs of these resources leads to higher fertility and consequent increased pressure on those very resources.

Under pricing arguments are not restricted to infrastructure alone. They apply to resources such as the commons (grazing land, fish stocks, groundwater) and the environment (forest cover, pollution, the ozone layer). Population growth places additional pressure on these scarce resources. Moreover, growth theory cannot be profitably applied to many of these resources: having more people around does not "produce" more forests, fish, water, or ozone. The effects are therefore stronger and more immediate.

9.4.2. Some positive effects

In the previous section, we began with the naive argument that all that population growth does is eat into available production. This is implicit in the Harrod–Domar model, for instance, but we know that population growth means a larger labor force, which contributes to additional production. Thus, at the very least, we have a tussle between the productive capabilities of a growing population and its consumption demands. The Solow model captured this well. Long-run growth of per capita income is unchanged in the Solow model because these two forces balance each other. We did note the existence of a level effect: there is more labor relative to capital on the long-run growth path. This brings down the *level* of income measured per unit of (effective) labor. This is an example of diminishing returns to labor at work. A higher ratio of labor to capital reduces its average product.

However, is that all labor is good for: production? In some broad sense, the answer is yes, but it is useful to return to a distinction between two notions of production: production using the same set of techniques, as embodied by the production function or technical know-how at any one point of time, and the production, invention, or application of *new* methods; in short, technical progress. Put another way, the pace of technical progress may be endogenous in the sense that it is affected by population size. Although we have discussed the endogeneity of technical progress before (see Chapter 4), the demographic effect on population growth merits additional attention.

The effect of population growth on technical progress can in turn be divided into two parts. First, population growth may spur technical progress out of the pressures created by high population density. This is the "demand-driven" view explored by Boserup [1981]. Second, population growth creates a larger pool of potential innovators and therefore a larger stock of ideas and innovations that can be put to economic use. This is the "supply-driven" view taken by Simon [1977] and Kuznets [1960].[14]

Population, necessity, and innovation

Necessity is the mother of invention, and population pressure has historically created necessity. Nowhere is this more true than in agriculture, where increasing populations have historically placed tremendous pressure on the supply of food. It is certainly the case that such pressure was often relieved by the Malthusian weapons of famine and disease that wiped out large sections of the population. However, it is also true that scarcity drove man to innovate, to create, or to apply methods of production that accommodated the increased population by a quantum jump in food output.

Several indicators permit us to see evidence of this even in today's world. Boserup [1981] classified countries into different grades by population density: *very sparse*, between 0 and 4 people per square kilometer; *sparse*, between 4 and 16 people per square kilometer; *medium*, between 16 and 64 persons per square kilometer; *dense*, between 64 and 256 persons per square kilometer; and *very dense*, 256 persons per square kilometer and upwards.[15]

Now consider an indicator such as irrigation. Which countries have more of it? Not surprisingly, the high-density countries do: in 1970, all the countries in Boserup's sample (of fifty-six) with more than 40% of the arable land under irrigation were dense or very dense countries, in the sense defined in the previous paragraph. Alternatively, consider the use of chemical fertilizer: it increases systematically with population density. In addition, study multi-cropping: four out of five very dense countries (in a sample of twenty-four) had more than 50% of the land devoted to multiple cropping; no other country in the sample exhibited this sort of ratio. More generally, Boserup suggested the pairing of population densities and food supply systems shown in Table 9.4 as a summary of her overall observations.

The point to be made is simple, perhaps obvious. At least in agriculture, high population densities go hand in hand with technologically more inten-

---

[14] The demand-driven story was studied in the context of a formal model by Lee [1988]. The supply-driven story was similarly explored by Kremer [1993].

[15] This scale, which is actually a coarsening of a finer division used by Boserup, is logarithmic, like the Richter scale for earthquake intensities. Each higher category used by Boserup has twice the density of the category immediately preceding it.

Table 9.4. Population densities and food supply systems.

Very sparse	→ Hunting and gathering, pastoralism, and forest fallow (one or two crops followed by a fallow period of around two decades)
Sparse and medium	→ Bush fallow (one or two crops followed by a fallow period of around one decade)
Medium	→ Short fallow (one or two crops followed by one or two years of fallow) with domestic animals
Dense	→ Annual cropping with intensive animal husbandry.
Very dense	→ Multicropping

sive forms of farming. This by itself isn't proof that such techniques were actually *invented* in high-density societies, although they almost surely were, but it does suggest that these methods, even if they were universally known, were applied more frequently in high-density societies.[16]

Agriculture is a leading example of how population growth stirs up technical progress, but it is not the only example. Here is Boserup again [1981, p. 102]:

> The increasing population density in Europe facilitated development of specialized crafts and manufactured goods. In areas of dense population, a large number of customers lived within a relatively small territory. Direct contact with customers was possible and transport costs for products could be kept at a minimum. Manufacturing industries . . . required skilled workers and traders as well as the financial services and administrative skills which were concentrated in urbanized areas. Therefore, the areas in Europe which first developed manufacturing industries were those with the highest population densities—Tuscany and the Low Countries . . . . Such concentration occurred only later in France and England.

The argument thus far is quite clear, but what is unclear is how we evaluate it. The first major problem is that much of what is attributed to population growth can also be attributed to increased per capita income. Income creates demand just as population might, and it is a combination of the two that is likely to drive innovation, or at least the sort of innovation that is motivated by the desire to make economic profit. Put another way, an increased population might correspond to a greater social need, but that need must be manifested in *economic* demand through the marketplace for innovators to respond. The income aspect of the phenomenon possibly acquires greater relative importance as basic needs (such as food) cease to pose a threat: it is

---

[16] More detailed and careful analysis of this theme must correct for the simultaneity of population and technique observations: it is possible, though unlikely, that some other set of forces (such as exogenous invention) first drove the adoption of certain methods of farming, which then increased the carrying capacity of that society. This alternative cannot be logically ruled out in the way in which Boserup presents the data.

hard to imagine how a larger population per se could spur innovations pertaining to more sophisticated products unless there is additional income to
spend on such products.

The second problem with the demand-driven story is that it predicts
some degree of cyclicity in per capita incomes: innovations raise per capita
income as production levels kick up following the innovation, but a long
hiatus should follow as population swells to bridge the newly created gap,
with per capita incomes falling once again until the pressure of resources
triggers another bout of innovation. As we shall see in the next section, this
is not the sort of long-run pattern that we observe.

Both these points are connected to the observation that population *alone*
is unlikely to be a major force on the side of demand for innovation unless
we are in a world in which the innovator is himself directly affected by the
population pressure. Early agriculture, in which the farmer and the innovator
were often the same person, is probably the only persuasive example of
such a phenomenon. Once the innovator is separated or relatively insulated
from the overall pressures of population, it takes market forces to trigger
innovative activity, and population growth by itself is not enough.

Population, diversity, and innovation

A large population is a diverse population, and the chances are higher that
someone will be lucky enough or smart enough to come up with an idea that
benefits everybody else.[17] This is the gist of the supply-driven argument. The
easiest way to appreciate this line of reasoning is to imagine that everybody
has an *independent* chance of coming up with a idea that will benefit the rest
of the human race. It is immediate how things progress in this situation:
the larger the population, the larger would be the number of people that
have useful ideas, and so the higher is the rate of technical change. There
are several senses in which we might want to qualify this statement, and we
will, but let us stick with it for now.

We combine this statement, which is about how technical progress reacts to population, with a statement about how population might respond
to technical progress. Specifically, let us suppose that population growth increases with per capita income up to a point and then falls. This is a crude
version of the demographic transition that we have already used in a different context (see Chapter 3). The left-hand panel of Figure 9.6 depicts a
typical curve that might relate per capita income to population growth.

Now let us begin the analysis by considering an initial level of per capita
income that is so low that population growth increases with per capita income. This means that we are currently on the upward-sloping segment of

---

[17] The discussion here follows Kremer [1993].

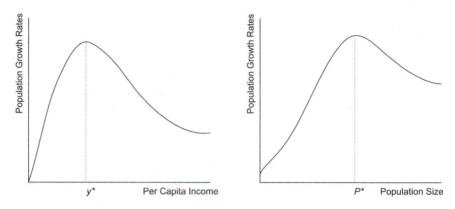

Figure 9.6. Population growth, per capita income, and population levels.

the curve in the left-hand panel of Figure 9.6. Population is growing, and it follows from our first postulate that the pace of technical progress must accelerate. Observe that per capita income *cannot* be stagnant during this phase. To prove this, suppose by way of contradiction that per capita income is unchanging. Then, after some time passes, population is higher, so that technical progress is higher. Consequently, the population growth rate now required to keep per capita income stagnant must be even higher. However, the only way to accomplish this is to increase per capita income,[18] which contradicts our supposition that per capita income was stagnant all this time.[19]

Thus as long as we are on the upward-sloping part of the curve, per capita income must rise and so must the *rate* of population growth. Thus during this phase we obtain the prediction that the population growth *rate* is increasing with the size of the population. This state of affairs continues until we reach the point at which population growth rates begin to decline in income. As long as growth rates are positive, however, the population will still grow, so that technical progress will continue to accelerate. Coupled with a diminishing pace of population growth, this implies an acceleration in the long-run rate of growth of per capita income. Thus population growth rates decline even faster. This period is therefore associated with a leveling-off and consequent decline in the rate of growth of the population. No longer will population growth rates increase with population: they should decline.

To summarize, then, if technical progress is "supply-driven" by the population, then population growth should initially be an *increasing function* of population itself, but this trend should reverse itself after some stage. The right-hand panel of Figure 9.6 puts these observations together diagrammatically: P^* is the threshold level of population that permits technical progress at a rate such that the threshold per capita income of y^* (see the left-hand

---

[18] This is because we are on the upward part of the curve in Figure 9.6.

[19] This does not rule out the possibility that there might be an initial phase in which per capita income can actually fall, but this phase must be temporary: see Kremer [1993] for a rigorous analysis.

panel) is just reached: after this point population growth rates turn down as per capita income climbs even further.

Is there any empirical truth to this assertion? Figure 9.7, which is taken from Kremer [1993], puts together various estimates of world population and the implied annual growth rates from 1 million B.C. to 1990. Observed population growth rates are plotted against the baseline values of population. Clearly for much of recorded history, population growth rates appear to be increasing with population size. The trend reversed itself only after population passed the three billion mark, which is circa 1960.

Thus the simple model of "supply-driven" innovation works surprisingly well. It does predict the same qualitative shape that we observe in the data, but we need to be careful about taking this model too literally. For instance, as set out now it also predicts that countries with large populations should exhibit a high rate of technical progress. That is, the time-series prediction passes over into a cross-section prediction, which is far more dubious, to put it mildly. However, a simple extension of the model can be used to account for this seeming discrepancy: simply allow technical progress to be a function not just of population size, but also of the per capita income of the society. After all, it takes brains coupled with economic resources to carry out useful scientific research. With this modification in place it is evident that the strong (but wrong) cross-section prediction disappears, but the time-series prediction survives unscathed. After all, if per capita income increases over time (as we argued that it will in this model), then this extension cannot overturn the qualitative features discussed earlier.

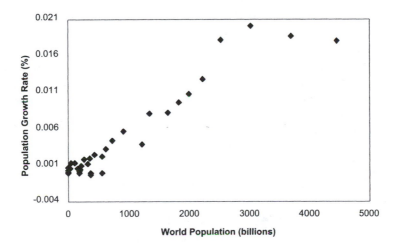

Figure 9.7. *Population growth in world history. Source: Kremer [1993, Table 1 and Fig. 1].*

9.5. Summary

In this chapter, we studied population growth and its interaction with economic development. Our goals were as follows:

1. To describe and understand the observed patterns of population growth in different countries; in particular, the phenomenon of the *demographic transition*;

2. To analyze the social and economic factors that affect fertility decisions at the level of the household;

3. To take note of possible features that create a systematic bias between levels of fertility that are *privately* optimal for the household, as opposed to those levels that are *socially* optimal; and

4. To understand the impact of population growth on economic development.

We began with terminology—the concepts of *birth rates* and *death rates*— and took a look at data on these rates for various countries. In the poorest of countries, both birth and death rates appear to be relatively high. Then death rates fall, while birth rates still remain high. Finally, countries that have higher per capita income or have made systematic efforts to control population growth exhibit birth rates that are also low. Thus population growth rates, which are just the difference between birth rates and death rates, seem to rise and then fall over the course of development.

We observed that the concept of an *age distribution* is important in this regard. Fast growing societies are also young societies, and this feature both reinforces a high birth rate (relatively large numbers of people are entering reproductive age) and keeps death rates somewhat lower than they really are in age-specific terms (because most people are young). Thus a policy that brings down the *total fertility rate* may still cause population to overshoot a desired target because of inertia.

From these various observations comes the central concept of the *demographic transition*, which is a description of three phases. In phase 1, both birth and death rates are high. In phase 2, death rates fall because of improvements in hygiene, sanitation, and medicine, but birth rates remain high. In phase 3, birth rates follow the death rate on its downward course.

The observation that birth rates remain high even as death rates fall is central to understanding the population explosion, not only in today's developing world, but historically as it has happened in Europe. Why don't birth rates decline with death rates? One answer is the *macro-inertia* of birth rates in a population that is young. In addition, there is inertia at the *micro* level as well. If the flow of current demographic information is limited, couples might instinctively use the experience of generations before them to make their decisions regarding fertility. But limited information is not the only factor that causes a slow reduction in fertility. It turns out that missing markets, notably, the missing market for old-age security, are also central to our understanding of this phenomenon. We studied the connection between the desire for old-age security, mortality, and fertility choices. Gender bias plays an important role here: to the extent that a family desires sons, this can greatly increase fertility rates. In general, these are factors that collectively shed some light on the stickiness of birth rates.

We then turned to factors that cause a systematic deviation between decisions that are privately optimal (from the point of view of the family) and decisions that are optimal from the point of view of society. Lack of information and uncertainty play a major role here, as does the presence of *externalities*, both within the household and across households. Externalities arise because there is a divergence between the social and private costs (or benefits) of having children. In this context, the role played by joint families or by externalities that are environmental or employment related are of great importance. Social norms that create a high degree of conformism to exaggerated rates of fertility are relevant as well.

Finally, we turned to an analysis of the effects of population growth on economic development. Both negative and positive effects coexist. The simplest negative effect comes from the observation that population growth eats away at a given level of resources or income, leaving less per head to go around. This sort of prediction naturally emerges from the Harrod–Domar model of economic growth, in which labor is not regarded as an essential input of production (recall that the capital–output ratio is fixed in that model). However, this observation is unduly naive, for the simple reason that an increased population means more labor input, which expands production. In the Solow model, these two effects cancel exactly as far as long-run growth rates are concerned: these rates are unaffected by the pace of population growth. However, there is a level effect: a higher rate of population growth pushes the economy onto a lower trajectory of per capita income (with the same growth rate as before). This summarizes the consensus argument that population growth is unambiguously bad for economic development.

However, there are positive arguments as well—two of them—and it is with these that we finish the chapter. One view is that population growth creates economic necessity, which forces the adoption or creation of new ideas that expand carrying capacity. This is a demand-side argument: population growth fosters spurts of development because the pressures that it creates necessitate bouts of innovation. The second view is a supply-driven argument: population growth fosters development simply because many heads are better than one. If we think of each human being as a repository of ideas then more human beings means more ideas that can be put to use for the economic benefit of mankind. Thus the rate of technical progress should increase with population size. We examine these arguments in some detail at the end of the chapter.

Exercises

■ (1) Review the concepts of birth rates, death rates, and age distributions, and the way in which these notions interact with one another. Construct an example of countries *A* and *B*, where *A* has higher death rates than *B* in *every* age category, yet has an overall lower death rate.

■ (2) Why does a young age distribution make it more difficult for a country to slow its rate of population growth? If a country suddenly drops its total fertility rate to two (which makes for a stationary long-run population), describe the path that population will take before settling at this long-run level.

■ (3) Discuss factors that have altered the carrying capacity of the planet. Explain how such increases in carrying capacity might ultimately affect fertility decisions at the level of the household.

■ (4) Explain why each country might want to take a pro-natalist stand for military or political reasons, but the combination of *all* countries taking the same pro-natalist stance may make all countries worse off relative to a neutral stance on population.

■ (5) In this chapter, we studied a model where a family wants one surviving child to provide old-age security. Let us say that the probability of any *one* child living to look after its parents in old age is 1/2 (i.e., 50–50). However, the family wants this security level to be higher, say a probability of $q > 1/2$.

(a) Describe the family's fertility choices for different values of q, by first writing down a model that captures this story, and then examining the results for different values of q.

(b) Calculate the *expected* number of surviving children for this family, under various values of q. (For a definition of "expectation" see Appendix 1.)

■ (6) Review the concepts of *targeting* and *hoarding*. Discuss the various components of the "survival probability" p (see exercise 5 as well as the discussion in the text) that will affect the relative prevalence of these two forms of reproductive behavior.

■ (7) In a world in which families use the experience of their parents in determining their own fertility behavior, discuss the role of the media (such as television) in affecting fertility.

■ (8) Why is a well-implemented ban on child labor likely to reduce fertility rates?

■ (9) Organized social security, health care, etc., will lead to a fall in fertility rates but will lead to a fall in savings rates as well. The net effect on per capita income growth rates is ambiguous. Comment.

■ (10) In the land of Oz, there are *three* inputs to production: capital, physical labor, and mental labor. Men in Oz have more physical labor power than women, but both men and women have the same amount of mental labor power.

(a) Who earns more in Oz, men or women? What do these differences depend upon?

(b) Now imagine that the technology is such that more capital raises the marginal product of mental labor faster than it raises physical labor. As the economy of Oz grows over time, its stock of physical capital is steadily increasing. How would you expect the *relative* wage of men to women to change over time? Explain.

(c) Women have one unit of labor time that they can allocate between raising children and being part of the workforce. How would this allocation be affected by the changes over time that you found in your answer to (b)? Discuss the implications for fertility levels in the population.

■ (11) Studies for many countries have shown that labor force participation by women tends to have a U-shaped pattern with respect to growth in per capita income. Explain why this contrasts with your findings in exercise 10 above. Discuss reasons why such a U-shaped curve of female labor force participation may occur. The use of income and substitution effects will help you to formulate your answer.

■ (12) Evaluate the validity of the following statements.

(a) A developing country is likely to have an overall death rate that is lower than that of a developed country.

(b) The populations of Europe and North America grew at a combined rate between 1750 and 1900 that significantly exceeded the population growth rates of developing countries at that time.

(c) If country *A* has a population growth rate that is lower than country *B*, then the average woman in country *A* has less children than her counterpart in country *B*.

(d) Birth rates may be high even when death rates may be falling.

(e) If total mortality among children remained constant, but the *incidence* of that mortality shifted from late childhood to early childhood, fertility rates should decline.

■ (13) Review the data on the demographic transitions for one developed and one less developed country. For instance, you could study the demographic transitions of England and Sri Lanka (see Gillis, Perkins, Roemer, and Snodgrass [1997, Chapter 7]) and make sure that you understand the main trends in birth rates, death rates, and net population growth rates. Think about and explain the reasons why the picture for Sri Lanka looks more "compressed" in time than the corresponding picture for England.

■ (14) You are gathering demographic data in a village. You suspect that families have a *gender bias*; that is, they have children until a certain *target number of sons* are born, but you don't have direct evidence of this. All you have is information on the sex and birth order of each child born to each family in the village. How would you use the data to test your hypothesis that there is gender bias?

■ (15) Here is more on gender bias. In many Southern Asian countries, there is evidence that the ratio of boys to girls is too high (see also Chapter 8). A ratio of 110 boys to 100 girls is not uncommon. One obvious hypothesis that springs to mind is that girls are treated badly relative to boys (or are perhaps even selectively aborted or killed), so that their mortality rates are higher. There could be much truth in these assertions. Nonetheless, it is worthwhile to investigate alternative possibilities.

(a) Begin by looking at the target rule discussed in exercise 14. Simplify the target rule using the following assumption: families have children until they have just one boy, and then they stop. Then show that on average, larger families will have more daughters.

(b) Now use the insight of part (a) to argue that in poor societies, girls might have a higher death rate than boys even if there is no discrimination.

■ (16) This is a question on joint families, externalities, and fertility choice. Suppose that Ram and Rani are the heads of a nuclear family, making their fertility decisions. For simplicity, assume away gender bias and issues of child survival. The following table details the costs and benefits (in dollars, say) of different numbers of children.

(a) Based on the information in the table, how many children would Ram and Rani have in order to maximize their net benefit?

(b) Now consider two identical nuclear families: Ram and Rani (as above), and Mohan and Mona. Ram and Mohan are brothers and the two couples form a joint family. Both couples have exactly the same costs and benefits of having children as in the table. Now suppose that 50% of the upbringing costs of each child (e.g., child care) can be passed on to the other family.

Number of children	Total benefit ($)	Additional cost
One	500	100
Two	750	100
Three	840	100
Four	890	100
Five	930	100
Six	950	100
Seven	960	100
Eight	960	100

Each couple makes independent decisions, taking only its own welfare into account. Now how many children will each couple have?

(c) Explain the reason for this seemingly paradoxical result, using the concept of externalities, and try and understand why larger families (either integrated across generations or between siblings in the same generation), will tend to have a larger number of children per couple.

■ (17) Discuss the impact of population growth on per capita income and its growth.

Chapter 10

Rural and Urban

10.1. Overview

10.1.1. The structural viewpoint

The literature on economic growth, a good part of which we studied in Chapters 3 and 4, might tempt you to view economic development (or economic growth anyway) as a process that transforms all incomes and all sectors of the economy in some harmonious and even fashion. But our study of inequality, poverty, and population growth in later chapters does alert us to the possibility of *uneven* growth—growth that first proceeds by benefiting some groups in society. The same is often true of various *sectors* of the economy. More often than not, economic development entails the rapid growth of some parts of the economy, while other parts are left behind to stagnate or even shrink. The structural transformation that inevitably accompanies change is an integral part of the development process, and to study it we must look at economies in more disaggregated form.

By far the most important structural feature of developing countries is the distinction between the rural and the urban sector. As we saw in Chapter 2, a significant fraction of the population of a typical developing country lives in the rural areas. Of this fraction, a sizable majority is connected to agriculture as a way of life. Not surprisingly, agriculture often accounts for a large share of national output as well (although the proportions are usually lower than the corresponding share of people) and almost always accounts for more than its fair share of total poverty.

Quite apart from these features intrinsic to agriculture, there is another worth emphasizing: the interconnection between agriculture and the rest of the economy, notably the industrial sector. As economic development proceeds, individuals move from rural to urban areas: agriculture acts as a supplier of labor to industry.

At the same time, labor supply isn't all that is at stake. If international trade in food grain is not an option (and it often isn't, because governments fear lack of self-sufficiency in food production), then a nonagricultural sector can come about only if agriculture produces more food than its producers need for their *own* consumption. That is, agriculture must be capable of producing a *surplus* that can be used to feed those who are engaged in non-agricultural pursuits. Thus agriculture is also a supplier of food to industry. These twin resources—food and labor—need to move in tandem if development is to proceed. We take up this point in more detail later. Before we do so, here is an overview of the nonagricultural and agricultural sectors.

10.1.2. Formal and informal urban sectors

Begin with the nonagricultural sector; that is, economic activity in urban or semi-urban areas. People who live in these areas are involved in industrial enterprises, both at the production and managerial level, and in various service sectors, such as retailing, trade, or tourism. Once we start to disaggregate our economy, it is useful to take the process a bit further, and a further division naturally suggests itself. In all developing countries, two forms of urban economic activity are apparent (although the line between them is not very finely drawn). There are firms that operate under the umbrella of accepted rules and regulations imposed by government. Often, the workers of these firms belong to a union, and collective bargaining between firms and workers is not uncommon. These firms are required to pay minimum wages and must conform to certain standards of safety, rules of compensation for workers, pension schemes, and the like. Such firms pay taxes, may receive infrastructural facilities, such as access to subsidized electricity, and may have access to foreign exchange quotas or the right to import certain inputs. Although these norms and regulations vary from country to country, the point is that such firms adhere by and large to such regulations and receive, in turn, the benefits of state economic support.

Think of these firms as the *formal sector* of the economy. The formal sector bears a close resemblance to economic activity in developed countries. Because this sector is set up in a way that permits the creation and maintenance of records, firms in the formal sector are relatively tangible entities: they can issue shares and pay out dividends, they can be audited, and they are protected by bankruptcy laws and implicit or explicit forms of insurance. To be sure, entry into the formal sector is typically costly. Perhaps only a certain minimum size of economic activity warrants the setup costs: a license may be required for operation, tax records need to be kept, pension schemes need to be set up for employees, and so on.

In contrast, the urban *informal sector* is a loose amalgam of (usually small-scale) organizations that escape the cover of many of these regulations and do not receive access to privileged facilities. The informal sector usually does not adhere to norms of minimum wages, retirement plans, or unemployment compensation. They do not pay taxes and they receive little government support. These firms or businesses are not illegal in the strict sense, but there is a shadowy penumbra within which they live, and it is often convenient for the government to look the other way. It is difficult to implement the rule that a peanut vendor pay his taxes, in part because it is impossible to ascertain how much he earns. The same goes for the hawker, the teenager who shines shoes, domestic servants, professional beggars, owners of tea stalls, rickshaw pullers, and the young boy who assists in selling bus tickets or carrying your shopping bags.

As we have seen already, an enormous fraction of the labor force comes under this classification. Setup costs are relatively low: the business or trade is usually small scale, and license fees and advance tax payments are unnecessary (although the occasional bribe may be needed).

Bolivia's Formal and Informal Sectors[1]

In 1986, Bolivia's official labor force numbered 1.6 million, which was about half of the economically active population or a quarter of the total population. The informal sector was large and the lack of proper accounting here suggests that the figure of 1.6 million is probably a significant underestimate.

In the late 1980s, nearly half of all workers were in agriculture. Industry accounted for another 20% and the rest went to services. As we noted in Chapter 2, the rapid growth of the services sector in developing countries is often an indicator that the agricultural sector is releasing labor faster than the industrial sector can soak it up. Bolivia is no exception. The services sector has grown steadily (and mainly at the expense of agriculture) since 1950. Urban workers were clustered in the cities of La Paz (40%), Santa Cruz (20%), and Cochabamba (20%). Urban incomes significantly exceeded rural incomes; the lowest incomes were in the southern highlands. Bolivia has a significant history of strong organized labor: labor unions were powerful and strong, and strikes or demonstrations are not infrequent.

Of course, most nonunionized labor was in the informal sector. This sector included nonprofessional, self-employed, unpaid family workers, domestic servants, and businesses with five or fewer employees. La Paz was the center of the informal sector, but there was also an illegal component linked to the coca industry.

The informal sector was characterized by ease of entry, the use of credit from noninstitutional sources, and nonadherence to government regulations, especially regarding the sale of smuggled goods. We can imagine, then, that the variation in informal incomes was quite high. Owners of small businesses might average an income as much as twelve times the minimum wage. In contrast, salaried workers and domestic servants made much less: typically around half the minimum wage.

Informal activities included transportation (usually unregistered buses or taxis), laundry, electrical services, black market currency transactions, money lending, family grocery stores, and the sale of food, clothing, and smuggled consumer items.

---

[1] These observations are drawn from material prepared by the Federal Research Division of the United States Library of Congress under the Country Studies/Area Handbook Program sponsored by the Department of the Army.

Industrial workers in the informal sector included seamstresses, weavers, carpenters, and butchers.

10.1.3. Agriculture

What about agriculture? In most cases agriculture is a giant informal sector in itself if we go by the preceding definition. Tax authorities have no way to observe how much output a farmer produces, and even if they do, they cannot prove it in a court of law, so agriculture often goes untaxed. Likewise, it is very difficult, if not impossible, to implement minimum wages for rural labor. Pension plans, unemployment insurance, and organized old-age security don't exist, by and large. Nonetheless, a collection of informal institutions creates substitutes for these missing sources of support, as we shall see in the chapters to come. These substitutes are necessary: people in agriculture are often very poor and they face high levels of risk. Without these informal substitutes, no city in a developing country could withstand the consequent flow of rural–urban migration that might result.

The primary occupation in agriculture is, of course, farming. The great staples, such as wheat and rice, are farmed both for self-consumption and market sales. A variety of other crops are produced, and the degree of self-consumption varies with the nature of the crop. Cash crops, such as cotton, sugar, and luxury varieties of rice, are the most market oriented and are produced largely for market sale.

Production is organized in many ways. There are family farms that farm their own land, often largely for self-consumption. There are large owner–cultivators or capitalist farms that produce crops using modern techniques and large quantities of hired labor. There are tenant farmers who lease land from other nonfarming (or partially farming) landowners and pay rents to these landowners. Finally, there are laborers who work for wages or a commission on the land of others. Laborers may be casual employees (e.g., hired just for the duration of the current harvest) or long-term permanent employees.

As we will see, the notion of risk and uncertainty is central to the concept of agricultural organization in developing countries. In more than one developing country, the state of the weather affects macroeconomic stability, the balance of payments, and even political fortunes, all because it affects the harvest. To farmers, a good harvest means a high income in a given year, but the next year could be totally different. The weather also affects the incomes of agricultural laborers, even if they do not farm their own land, because the scale of agricultural employment, is weather-dependent. Thus agricultural uncertainty is a fundamental fact of life that plays a key role in the development process.

To give you a better idea of agricultural activity in developing countries, I am going to introduce the ICRISAT sample: a well-studied set of villages in India.

10.1.4. The ICRISAT villages

Much of agriculture in the Third World is carried out in regions known as the semi-arid tropics, which are characterized by rainfall dependence (although precipitation is scanty and uncertain both in timing and volume), primitive technology and labor-intensive cultivation, poor infrastructure, and often extreme population pressure on the land. Systematic and reliable data on such regions are not widely available; most of the data collected so far (which aren't much) are erratic and often unreliable. The International Crop Research Institute for the Semi-Arid Tropics (ICRISAT) in Hyderabad, India, is a welcome exception to this rule. Since 1975, ICRISAT has put together detailed data that track the behavior and fortunes of certain representative sample households from eight villages in the Indian semi-arid tropics.[2] The volume of data now available from ICRISAT provide rich insight into the functioning of typical rural economies.[3]

Soil fertility

There are considerable differences in soil texture and quality, and hence productivity, both *within* and *across* the study villages. In Aurepalle, for example, farmers divide all village soils into five broad groups, and at the finest level of classification, they recognize twenty-one different soil categories. In contrast, consider Shirapur and Kalman, both villages in the Sholapur district of Maharashtra. Shirapur has a rich endowment of deep black soil, whereas Kalman has more upland area with shallower soils that do not retain enough moisture for good cropping in the postmonsoon season (although in this regard it does better than some other villages). The difference in land fertility across the two villages is borne out by the fact that owner-cultivated plots in Shirapur had an average plot value of Rs 29.68 per acre, whereas the corresponding figure for Kalman was Rs 17.55 (Shaban [1987]).

Rainfall and cropping patterns

Although the villages are in reasonably close proximity, rainfall patterns differ widely across them, and this is also true of a single village *across* years. Farmers react sharply to these differences: they can adopt very different crop-

---

[2] The villages are Aurepalle, Dokur (in the Mahbubnagar district of Maharashtra state), Shirapur, Kalman (in the Sholapur district of Maharashtra), Kanzara, Kinkheda (in the Akola district of Andhra Pradesh), Boriya, and Rampura.

[3] This material is largely based on Walker and Ryan [1990].

ping strategies across villages and also respond to changing climatic conditions. For example, in the villages in Mahbubnagar and Akola districts, more than 90% of the area cultivated is planted during the *kharif* or rainy season because these villages receive more copious and less variable rainfall, and are marked by shallower soils, with less moisture retention capacity.

The Sholapur villages, on the other hand, have (relatively) deep and rich soils that can hold moisture for longer periods. Rainfall is relatively low and far more erratic in terms of arrival time. Farmers in these villages, therefore, wait until the end of the monsoon and rely more heavily on *rabi* or post-monsoon season planting. Planting on dry soil at the onset of the monsoon surely would have increased the risk of crop failure in these villages, because of the uncertain arrival time of the rains.

At the same time, in Sholapur, the relative importance of monsoon and postmonsoon season cropping can vary considerably from year to year. During "normal" years of rainfall, rainy season crops account for about 40% of gross cropped area, whereas during an unusually dry season (e.g., in 1977–78), this share may drop below 10%. Sometimes, farmers also react to adverse weather conditions by altering the crop planted. An instance of this occurred in Aurepalle in 1976–77, when the southeast monsoon arrived late, and most farmers planted castor, a hardy cash crop, instead of the traditional sorghum,[4] which runs a greater risk of pest damage in case of initially scanty rainfall.

Irrigation

The uncertainty introduced by the erratic pattern of rainfall can, of course, be reduced by irrigation. However, because the farmers are poor and capital is in short supply, irrigation is not very widespread. In the late 1970s, the proportion of gross cropped area that was irrigated varied from a high of 32% in Dokur to less than 1% in Kinkheda. (The average across six villages, excluding Boriya and Rampura, was around 12% in 1975–76.)

However, thanks to increased investment by the government in agricultural infrastructure, irrigation is on the rise. In 1983–84, 20% of the land was irrigated on average in the six villages. The technology of irrigation is also changing: groundwater irrigation is becoming more popular, replacing surface irrigation from small catchment reservoirs. Furthermore, in response to rapid rural electrification, cheaper institutional credit, and technological advances in groundwater pumping, electric pump sets have rapidly replaced

[4] Sorghum is used as both food and fodder and is cultivated throughout the semi-arid tropics. Sorghum originated in the northeastern quadrant of Africa and was distributed along trade and shipping routes throughout Africa, and through the Middle East to India at least 3,000 years ago. Sorghum is now widely found in the drier areas of Africa, Asia, the Americas, and Australia. The ICRISAT home page at http://www.cgiar.org/icrisat/, from which this account is drawn, contains more on sorghum.

traditional animal-drawn and diesel-powered lifting devices. For example, in Aurepalle, agricultural wells increased by 25% from 1974 to 1984; the number was around 190 in 1984. During the same time period, electric pump sets grew in number from 75 to 136. Except in the Akola villages, joint ownership of wells is fairly common. Among the sample households, the average number of owners per well in Shirapur, Aurepalle and Kanzara were 4.8, 2.4 and 1.0 respectively.

The ownership of wells is to be contrasted with the ownership of land, which is privately owned and very intensively cultivated (for more on land ownership and operations, see Chapter 12). Public and fallow land is rare. The quantity and quality of the "village commons"—jointly owned open-access land used for animal grazing—has declined over the years, from around 20% of the total area in the study villages in the early 1950s to about 10% today.

Fertilizer use

The successful application of fertilizers requires plentiful drainage. It is not surprising, therefore, that the use of fertilizers and the availability of irrigation facilities go hand in hand. Where irrigation facilities enjoy a limited spread, the use of fertilizers is also thin. In the Mahbubnagar villages, 40% of the land is irrigated and 98% of the total volume of fertilizers used was applied to such land. Likewise in Akola, only 5% of gross cropped area had access to irrigation, but these accounted for 37% of the fertilizer usage. On the whole, the mean nutrient consumption (i.e., fertilizer use) in kilograms per hectare of gross cropped area has varied from a meager 2 in the drought-prone Sholapur villages to a somewhat healthy 25 in the better irrigated Mahbubnagar villages.

Draft power

Many important agricultural operations, such as plowing, harrowing, and tilling, require draft power. In all villages, most farmers rely on traditional animal draft power, mainly bullocks. Mechanized draft power such as that provided by tractors and harvesting machines is still out of reach for the majority of farmers, due to the large capital expenses involved. Indeed, there is an acute scarcity of draft power, even of bullocks. As in the rest of India, many households that own small amounts of land do not own bullocks. The scarcity is most pronounced in the Sholapur villages, where less than one landowning household in three owns a bullock. Sharply fluctuating fodder prices make the bullock not only an expensive but also a risky asset.

The problem of scarcity of draft animals, is somewhat mitigated if there is a well functioning market for *hiring* bullocks, but this is not the case for two reasons. First, most cropping activities must be executed within a very narrow time frame, so that all farmers across the village feel the need for bullock power more or less simultaneously: their use cannot be phased across farmers. Second, there is a fundamental incentive problem in hiring bullock power: the leasing party usually drives the animal too hard, which extracts better service, but at the cost of depleting its health and stock value (which the lessee does not internalize). The scarcity of bullocks and the incomplete market for hired bullock power drives some of the widely observed features of traditional agriculture, for example, the pattern of land-lease contracts (see Chapter 12).

Technical change

Technical change in the study villages has been most pronounced, not in the development of infrastructure or greater capital intensity of cultivation, but in the adoption of new and improved inputs, particularly seeds. High-yielding varieties (HYV) of seeds for many popular crops were introduced in India in the mid-1960s. Some of these improved varieties were adopted on a wide scale and at a remarkably fast rate in many villages, whereas others were just as quickly rejected. Among the HYVs that have enjoyed successful adoption are hybrid pearl millet[5] and modern castor varieties in Aurepalle, improved paddy varieties in Aurepalle and Dokur, and sorghum hybrids and improved upland cotton cultivars in Kanzara and Kinkheda. For these varieties, the adoption rates (proportion of farmers cultivating that crop who are using the HYV) stood at more than 70%, sometimes close to 100%.

To be sure, technical and economic problems with some of the HYVs do occur. For example, sorghum hybrids do not perform well in the red-soil Mahbubnagar villages, because they are afflicted with numerous diseases and pests. Cotton hybrids, though promising in terms of yield, require intensive plant protection, high soil fertility, and a copious supply of water for success: their adoption in the dry upland Akola villages has therefore been limited. These examples illustrate the need to mold the development and introduction of seeds to suit local conditions, as well as the need to provide complementary inputs and economic services such as irrigation and credit.

The ICRISAT villages will reappear more than once in the chapters to follow, as we study the structure of the rural sector in some detail. Not only will we look at how productive activity is carried out, we will also study the background lubricants of that activity, such as credit markets, land rental arrangements, insurance schemes, and labor contracts.

---

[5] Probably the world's hardiest crop, pearl millet is a food staple in the semi-arid tropics. Pearl millet has been used as a cereal for thousands of years in Africa and parts of the Near East, and is cultivated for both forage and grain. It is grown today in many African countries and in some Asian countries, particularly India. See ICRISAT's home page at http://www.cgiar.org/icrisat/ for more information.

Before we do that, however, it is useful to study the overall interaction between the rural and urban sectors. That is what this chapter is all about.

10.2. Rural–urban interaction

10.2.1. Two fundamental resource flows

The most important of many rural–urban interactions is the synergistic role that agriculture plays in the development of the nonagricultural sector. From agriculture comes the supply of labor to industry and the surplus of food that allows a nonagricultural labor force to survive. These are the two fundamental resource flows from agriculture, and they lie at the heart of the structural transformation that occurs in most developing countries.

There are other connections as well. Industry supplies inputs to agriculture: tractors, pump sets, chemicals of various kinds, and so on. With a large population in the rural sector, agriculture is often a major source of demand for the products of industry, which include not just durables, but final consumption goods as well. Agrarian exports can serve as the source of vital foreign exchange, which permits the import of inputs to industrial production. While these links are important, the flow of labor from agriculture to industry and the parallel flow of agricultural surplus to nurture workers in industry are often basic to the development process.[6]

10.2.2. The Lewis model

The dual economy

Lewis [1954] outlined a view of development that was based on the foregoing fundamental resource flows. This approach, which views economic development as the progressive transformation of a "traditional" sector into a "modern" sector, goes beyond the narrower picture of agriculture-to-industry transformation, but essentially builds on it. The starting point of the Lewis model is the idea of a *dual economy*.[7] In a sentence, dualism is the coexistence

[6] There are exceptions to every rule, of course. In some countries, the creation of an agricultural surplus was not fundamental to economic development. These countries relied on the export of manufactures to fund their import of food items. With international trade in food grain, it is possible in principle to have *nobody* in the agricultural sector. A country can rely entirely on imported food. Such countries do not follow the general rule that we have outlined, but why are such situations the exception rather than the rule? The answer to this question must ultimately lie with the notion of *self-sufficiency* in food: food is so basic and so much the foundation of all activity that most governments cannot bear to think of a contingency in which their nations must depend on others for this most basic of wants. Such attitudes go some way in explaining why agriculture enjoys extraordinary protection in many developed countries, such as the United States, Japan, or in the European Union.

[7] See also Nurkse [1953], Jorgenson [1961], Ranis and Fei [1961], Sen [1966], Dixit [1970], Amano [1980], and Rakshit [1982].

of "traditional" and "modern," where the words in quotes can have several shades of meaning. The traditional sector is often equated to the agricultural sector, which after all produces the traditional output of all societies. In contrast, the modern sector is the industrial sector, which produces manufactured commodities. At the same time, "traditional" can mean the use of older techniques of production that are labor-intensive and employ simple instruments. In contrast, "modern" might refer to the use of new technology, which is intensive in the use of capital. Finally, and perhaps most important at a conceptual level, "traditional" refers to traditional forms of economic *organization*, based on family as opposed to wage labor, with overall output distributed not in the form of wages and profits, but in the form of shares that accrue to each family member.[8] In contrast, "modern" describes production organized on capitalist principles, which relies on the use of wage labor and is carried out for economic profit.

At one level, these distinctions are all a bit vague. Agricultural activity can be commercial, highly capital-intensive, and employ wage labor, just like any other "modern" economic organization. The terms labor-intensive versus capital-intensive are certainly not related one for one with traditional versus modern. Similarly, it is unclear what "traditional" modes of organization mean: the form of organization may simply depend on the particular environment (the presence of uncertainty, the lack of a capital market, or limited resources). At the same time, even if we cannot furnish a perfectly logical distinction between the two concepts, they have general usefulness and help us to organize our thoughts.

Essentially, the dual economy consists of two sectors that can be characterized in a number of ways; each way has suggestive advantages, but each carries with it the possibilities of error as well. We label the two sectors "agriculture" and "industry," but recognize that these are provisional labels and subject to change when the particular issue under discussion needs a more precise description. For instance, it may be useful in some cases to view the urban informal sector as part of the "traditional" sector.

Surplus labor

Arthur Lewis proposed a framework of economic development that put the movement of labor from traditional to modern sectors on the center stage. The traditional sector, in this theory, is viewed as a supplier of labor, whereas the role of the modern sector is to soak up this supply. Why isn't all the supply immediately absorbed? The answer is that the scale of the modern sector is limited by the supply of capital. Thus capital accumulation in the modern sector becomes the engine of development. The fundamental assumption,

---

[8] On the so-called peasant mode of production, based on the notion of traditionally organized family farms, see Georgescu-Roegen [1960] and Chayanov [1991].

then, is that labor is virtually unlimited in supply, being drawn from a vast traditional sector, whereas the rate of savings and investment limits the pace of development. In this latter sense Lewis is in agreement with the Harrod–Domar view of economic growth (see Lewis [1954]):

> The central problem in the theory of economic development is to understand the process by which a community which was previously investing and saving 4 or 5 per cent of its national income or less, converts itself into an economy where voluntary saving is running at about 12 to 15 per cent of national income or more."

We have seen the Harrod–Domar theory and its many extensions in Chapters 3 and 4, and in the description of modern sector expansion due to Arthur Lewis and many other writers on the dual economy, there is very little that adds to what we have already studied. We concentrate instead on the assumption that the supply of labor is "unlimited" and on the associated problem of an adequate agricultural surplus. To understand these features, we focus on the traditional sector of the economy.

The main idea of the Lewis model is that there is a large surplus of labor in the traditional sector of the economy, that can be removed at little or no potential cost. By cost, we refer to *opportunity cost*: the loss of traditional sector output as labor supply is reduced. Figure 10.1 explains this concept in one particular context.

Figure 10.1 plots the production function on a family farm. Quantities of labor are on the horizontal axis and output is on the vertical axis. In the background is a fixed plot of land, on which this labor is applied. Because land is fixed, there are diminishing returns to the labor input. In keeping with

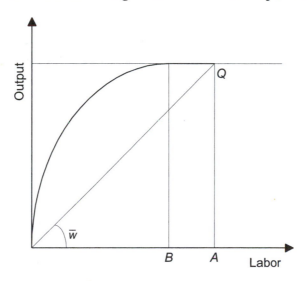

Figure 10.1. Surplus labor on the family farm.

our view that the family farm uses "traditional" techniques of production, we neglect the use of capital inputs.

The production function is drawn so that after a certain level of labor input, there is no significant effect on output. After all, there is only so much intensity at which a given plot of land can be cultivated, and after a point additional inputs of labor may have no effect at all. Thus the marginal product of labor at points such as *A* is zero or close to zero.

Now consider a reduction in the amount of labor from *A* to *B*. Because the marginal product of labor is assumed to be close to zero, total output practically stays constant when the reduction occurs. Because the family farm has so much labor relative to land, labor is in *surplus*.

When might such a situation occur? First, it might occur in economies where there is high population pressure, so that there are large numbers of people per acre of arable land. According to Lewis [1954]:

> "[This state of affairs] is obviously not true of the United Kingdom, or of Northwest Europe. It is not true either of some of the countries usually lumped together as underdeveloped; for example there is an acute shortage of male labour in some parts of Africa and of Latin America. On the other hand it is obviously the relevant assumption for the economies of Egypt, of India, or of Jamaica . . . an unlimited supply of labour may be said to exist in those countries where population is so large relatively to capital and natural resources, that there are large sectors of the economy where the marginal productivity of labour is negligible, zero, or even negative."

But the phenomenon is not just limited to agriculture. Again, Lewis [1954] puts it best:

> "Another large sector to which it applies is the whole range of casual jobs—the workers on the docks, the young men who rush forward asking to carry your bag as you appear, the jobbing gardener, and the like. These occupations usually have a multiple of the number they need, each of them earning very small sums from occasional employment; frequently their number could be halved without reducing output in this sector. Petty retail trading is also exactly of this type; it is enormously expanded in overpopulated economies. . ."

If you remember our statistical description of the proportion of the labor force in "services" (see Chapter 2), this account will strike a responsive chord.

Third, a simplistic aggregate view of population density might miss the point in many instances. Latin America has a relatively large per capita endowment of land, but at the same time land is very unequally distributed, so there are a large number of family farms in the state described by Figure 10.1. In such a case we might ask why the extra labor is not hired out to those with a surfeit of land. This is indeed possible and it does happen, but at the same time it might also be the case that the large *haciendas* use capital-intensive methods of production and do not hire labor in proportion to their size. In a word, agriculture itself may be dualistic. We will have more to say on this and related phenomena in Chapter 12.

Income sharing and surplus labor

At this stage, a natural question arises: if the marginal product of labor is close to zero, how is it that such labor is hired, unless wages themselves are close to zero as well? We all know from introductory microeconomics that an entrepreneur hires labor only to the point where marginal product equals the wage. With more labor than this, gains can be realized by cutting back on employed labor and saving on the wage bill. In other words, how can we reconcile the observation that the wage is positive (and provides for minimum subsistence at least) with the parallel observation that the marginal product is close to zero?

This brings to the forefront a second asymmetry between traditional and modern sectors. One asymmetry already was used in *production methods*. We conceived of the traditional sector as an activity intensive in labor (and in land, in the case of agriculture), but not requiring significant quantities of capital. The second asymmetry is in *organization*. A profit-maximizing firm regards wage payments to employees as a cost of production, that is subtracted from revenues in order to arrive at final profits. In contrast, a family farm values the incomes received by each of its members. For instance, the output of the farm may be shared equally among its members.[9] Thus a family farm might employ labor *beyond* the point where the marginal product equals the "wage", because the wage in this case is not really a wage at all, but the average output of the farm (which is what each member receives as compensation). In Figure 10.1, if the total labor input is A and the total output is AQ, then the average income is simply the output AQ divided by input A, which is represented by the angle marked as $\bar{w}$. Contrast this with the marginal product, which is the slope of the (almost) flat tangent to the production function at the point Q. Sharing rules of this kind shelter family members from the difficulties of finding employment elsewhere.

Income sharing is not just an agricultural phenomenon and occurs not just among families. It is not uncommon to see this in the urban informal sector as well. Thus the neighborhood store may be run by a joint family, with revenues divided among siblings. A cab driver might share his driving with a friend. The bus conductor of a crowded bus might sublease part of his ticket-collecting duties to a teen aged nephew. There are aspects of mutual insurance in these relationships that also have value. To these Lewis adds

[9] Equal sharing is only a simplifying assumption and may not hold in all situations. For instance, in Chapter 8 we studied the possibility of unequal division of output among family members in very poor family farms, because of nutritional considerations.

social prestige and charity:

> Social prestige requires people to have servants, and the grand seigneur may
> have to keep a whole army of retainers who are really little more than a burden
> upon his purse. This is found not only in domestic service, but in every sector
> of employment. Most businesses in underdeveloped countries employ a large
> number of "messengers," whose contribution is almost negligible; you see them
> sitting outside office doors, or hanging around in the courtyard. And even in the
> severest slump the agricultural or commercial employer is expected to keep his
> labour force somehow or other—it would be immoral to turn them out, for how
> would they eat, in countries where the only form of unemployment assistance is
> the charity of relatives? So it comes about that even in the sectors where people
> are working for wages, and above all the domestic sector, marginal productivity
> may be negligible or even zero.

Lewis was not alone in asserting the existence of surplus labor. Already
in the 1940s there were claims that large numbers of able-bodied people
were in surplus in the agricultural sectors of eastern and southeastern Europe and in the Soviet Union. Rosenstein-Rodan [1943] and Nurkse [1953]
were among those who held this view.[10] These writers realized that the presence of redundant labor in the agricultural sector meant that the population
surplus could be transferred out of the agricultural sector with no loss in
agricultural output. Surplus labor is, therefore, a supply of labor that, given
the preponderance of the agricultural sector in less developed economies, is
likely to be of major quantitative importance in the development process of
less developed economies. This is the classical tradition that Lewis inherited.

Surplus Labor: A Natural Experiment

Economic development with unlimited supplies of labor—Arthur Lewis's phrase
was provocative enough to instigate a flood of research on the existence of disguised
unemployment in agriculture. We have seen that disguised unemployment refers to
a situation where marginal product is less than the going wage. However, Lewis had
something stronger in mind: the possibility that "there are large sectors of the economy where the marginal productivity of labour is negligible, zero, or even negative."
Although this assertion is not strictly necessary for the Lewis framework, it suggests
the existence of a free resource in agriculture: labor.

One of the most interesting early studies on surplus labor was that of Schultz
[1964], who studied the effect of the influenza pandemic in India (1918–19). The
epidemic was sudden; the death rate reached a peak within weeks and then diminished rapidly. There were a large number of deaths. Schultz chose two years, one
before 1916–17 and one after 1919–20, when weather conditions were approximately

---

[10] See the survey by Kao, Anschel, and Eicher [1964].

equal. He then estimated the existence of surplus labor by comparing the reduction in acreage sown with the reduction in the labor force.

His findings were that, as a result of the epidemic, the agricultural population fell by 8.3% over these two years. He made the following observation [1964, p. 67]:

> The area sown in 1919–20 was, however, 10 million acres below, or 3.8% less than that of the base year 1916–17. In general, the provinces of India that had the highest death rates attributed to the epidemic also had the largest percentage decline in acreage sown to crops. It would be hard to find any support in these data for the doctrine that a part of the labor force in agriculture in India at the time of the epidemic had a marginal product of zero.

According to Schultz, therefore, surplus labor did not exist in India at the time of the epidemic.

This study is interesting in its use of a "natural experiment" to address an economic question. However, was the experiment "natural" enough? Consider the *pattern* of population decrease. Influenza epidemics attack entire households and the epidemic of 1918–19 was no exception. Thus entire plots of land were left uncultivated during this period of time. As Sen [1967] pointed out in his comment on the Schultz study, if land is not redistributed following the labor removal, it is not surprising that the sown acreage decreases. In this short span of time, this redistribution could not have taken place. Contrast this with the view implicit in the theories of Lewis and others: that is, in each family unit there is a surplus of labor. The pattern of labor removal from agriculture critically affects the fate of agrarian output.

Two extensions of the surplus labor concept.

Two extensions of the surplus labor concept are of some interest. First, note that surplus labor as defined in the previous section is purely a *technological* concept: there is simply too much labor relative to land, or more generally, too many people relative to other inputs of production, so that individuals are in surplus relative to production possibilities: remove them to other activities and output will not change because the additional labor power is of no use at all: the marginal product of labor is literally zero.

The inability of labor to add *anything* to output was criticized by several economists as an unrealistic phenomenon (see, for example, the box on the influenza epidemic in India). For instance, Viner [1957] writes:

> I find it impossible to conceive a farm of any kind on which, other factors of production being held constant in quantity, and even in form as well, it would not be possible, by known methods, to obtain some addition to the crop by using additional labor in more careful selection and planting of the seed, more intensive weeding, cultivation, thinning, and mulching, more painstaking harvesting, gleaning and cleaning of the crop.

Thus, the narrow technological concept of surplus labor may be inapplicable except in special situations. Is there a broader yet still useful specification? This raises the question of just why we are interested in the concept of surplus labor. This question can be answered from two viewpoints, each of which leads to a useful extension of the concept.

(1) *Disguised unemployment.*First of all, there is the question of efficient *allocation*. If marginal product is zero in some activity and positive in some other activity, there are efficiency gains to be had in switching resources away from the former activity to the latter. Why doesn't the market, left to its own devices, spontaneously accomplish this switch? The reason is that the zero marginal-product activity is usually characterized by a payment system that is not based (and cannot be based) on marginal product. As we saw in the previous section, it is often based on income sharing, which means that people in such activities receive the *average* product, which is surely positive (see Figure 10.1 to verify this). As long as average product in this activity is equal to marginal product in activities elsewhere, no individual would be interested in making the switch (although see the problem on family-based migration at the end of this chapter).

This line of reasoning indicates that if efficient allocation of resources is the underlying objective that motivates the concept of surplus labor, the concept is surely way too strong. It isn't necessary that the marginal product in the traditional activity be *exactly* zero. As long as the marginal product is *lower* than in activities elsewhere, there are gains to be had from a real-location of (labor) resources. If we suppose that there is a capitalist sector elsewhere that does pay according to marginal product, then the economy will exhibit a wage rate (for unskilled labor) that is a true measure of the marginal product elsewhere, and there will be efficiency gains available as long as the marginal product on the traditional activity is *less than the wage*, whether it is zero or not. This extended concept is known as *disguised unemployment*. The amount of disguised unemployment may be measured roughly by the difference between the existing labor input in the traditional activity and the labor input that sets marginal product equal to the wage.[11]

Now surplus labor may be viewed as a special case of disguised unemployment, but the generalization greatly increases the value of the narrower concept.

(2) *Surplus labor versus surplus laborers.* Our next extension takes us back to the narrower concept of surplus labor and again starts from the Viner criticism. This extension is motivated by a second possible answer to the question, Why are we interested in surplus labor? The answer is that once

---

[11] This is actually an overestimate. As labor is released from traditional activities and put to work elsewhere, the marginal product in these other activities typically falls. But as a micro estimate for one particular farm, this measure isn't a bad one.

labor is removed from agricultural pursuits, the issue of maintaining an adequate surplus of food in the economy becomes very important. Recall that in economies with limited international trade in food, an internally produced agricultural surplus is necessary if an industrial sector is to be supported.[12] After all, workers in the industrial sector demand food in the marketplace, and if such food isn't forthcoming, the resulting inflationary spiral can destroy the prospects of industrialization.[13]

So in this view, the question of *maintaining* agricultural output (or at least not letting it fall by too much) is of independent interest, quite apart from the efficiency calculus that underlies marginal product comparisons.[14]

This raises a new point. We remove *laborers*, not labor. The meaning of this cryptic sentence is that the *remaining* laborers in the traditional activity typically adjust *their* labor input once some laborers are removed (say, through rural–urban migration). If there is an increase in work effort on the part of the remaining laborers, total output may not fall even though the marginal product of labor is zero. This argument was originally made by Sen [1966] (see also Takagi [1978]).

Why would the members of a family farm raise their work hours to compensate for the departure of some of their compatriots? The answer depends on the alternative uses of labor applied to the farm. Such uses may involve leisure or working elsewhere part time. If the marginal product of such alternatives (which is exactly the marginal cost of working on the farm) rises as more and more labor is drawn away, then indeed there will not be full compensation for the lost workers, but there will be *some*. In the extreme case where the marginal cost of labor is constant, there will be full compensation for the lost workers. Even though the marginal product of labor is not zero, the farm will exhibit a surplus of *laborers*, in the sense that as laborers are removed from the farm, output will not fall.[15]

The reason for all this is very simple. Efficient resource allocation on the family farm requires that the value of marginal product of effort be equal to marginal cost. The first panel of Figure 10.2 shows how this familiar calculation yields a total labor input for the family. Now the point is just this: *if the marginal cost of family labor is constant*, then the total cost is just a straight line as shown in the figure, and total family input is determined *independently*

---

[12] I reiterate that the assumption of limited food-grain trade, although realistic, is crucial to the argument. Without it only the efficiency argument that we just examined makes any sense.

[13] For theories of development traps and inflationary spirals based on a limited surplus, see Rao [1952], Kalecki [1976], and Rakshit [1982].

[14] Of course, simply *maintaining* output isn't enough. The excess also must be released to the market for consumption by nonagricultural workers. We return to this issue after a discussion of the Lewis–Ranis–Fei model.

[15] To be sure, this cannot happen if many family members are removed, because the few that are left will have to put in immense effort to compensate and the marginal cost of such effort will surely be higher than before.

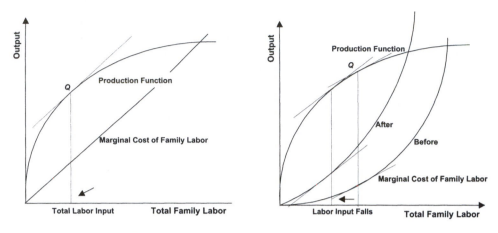

Figure 10.2. Surplus labor and surplus laborers.

of family size! This is just another way of saying that the removal of some members has no effect on total output (but note that the marginal product of labor *is* positive). The insight is that the removal of family labor has no effect on marginal cost if the marginal cost of labor for each family member is constant (and identical across members).

Of course this state of affairs is altered if marginal cost increases with effort. The second panel of Figure 10.2 shows this scenario. Then the total cost curve of the family is shifted upward as laborers are removed (provision of the same level of *family* effort as before now involves a higher marginal cost). Output will fall, but even so, the distinction between labor *effort* and the *number* of laborers is a point that is worth appreciating.

Economic development and the agricultural surplus

Armed with these forgoing concepts, we can describe the interplay between rural and urban sectors as envisaged by Lewis and later extended by Ranis and Fei [1961].

In the traditional agricultural sector there is disguised unemployment, perhaps even a core of surplus labor, and the wage rate is given by income sharing. The industrial sector is capitalistic. Economic development proceeds by the transfer of labor from agriculture to industry and *the simultaneous transfer of surplus food-grain production, which sustains that part of the labor force engaged in nonagricultural activity.*

Figure 10.3, which is based on Ranis and Fei [1961], provides a schematic description of how the labor force and the corresponding agricultural surplus is transferred in the process of development. In each panel of the diagram, the industrial labor force is read from left to right, whereas the agricultural labor force is read from right to left. Assume for simplicity that the total

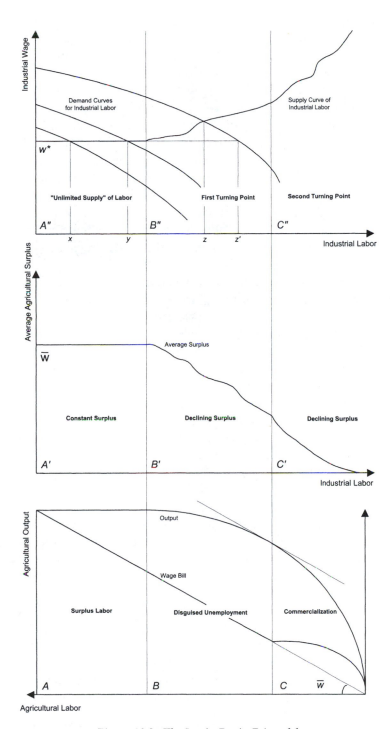

Figure 10.3. The Lewis–Ranis–Fei model.

labor force is divided between agriculture and industry. Then the width of the panels corresponds to the entire labor force in the economy.

It is best to read this figure from the bottom up. In the lowest panel, we have drawn a typical agricultural production function, except that it is drawn from right to left to reflect the way we read agricultural labor on the panels. The production function levels off just as in Figure 10.1, and there is a phase of surplus labor provided that the entire labor force is in agriculture. This is shown by the segment AB on the diagram. Moreover, if "wages" in this sector are decided by income sharing, then the average wage is just $\bar{w}$, which is proportional to the angle shown in this panel. This turns out to be the wage in the nascent industrial sector, as we will presently see. Thus the segment BC has no surplus labor, but does exhibit disguised unemployment, because the marginal product of labor in agriculture is less than the wage $\bar{w}$ for labor inputs in this segment. To the right of C, the phase of disguised unemployment ends.

What we will do in the next few paragraphs is carry out a thought experiment. Starting with a situation where the entire labor force is in agriculture, we will trace the consequences of transferring labor to the industrial sector. In particular, we will describe the minimum cost of hiring transferred labor in industry. This will give us something like a "supply curve" of labor to industry.[16] The topmost panel of Figure 10.3 shows this supply curve.

Begin with the entire labor force in agriculture. Suppose we decrease this by a small amount, so that we are still in the surplus labor phase. Then the total wage bill in agriculture falls along the diagonal straight line in the lowest panel, *provided that the wage in agriculture does not rise*. At the same time output does not fall, because we are in the surplus labor phase. An *agricultural surplus* therefore opens up; this is given by the vertical gap between the production function and the wage bill line. If we divide this surplus by the number of transferred workers, then we obtain the *average* agricultural surplus, where we are taking the average or per capita surplus amount relative to the transferred workers. It is easy to see that the average agricultural surplus in the surplus labor phase must be exactly $\bar{w}$. In the imagery of Nurkse [1953], it is as if each laborer simply moved out of agriculture with his food parcel on his back.

The average surplus is depicted in the middle panel of Figure 10.3. As discussed in the previous paragraph, the average surplus is unchanging in the surplus labor phase and is equal to $\bar{w}$. This is depicted as a horizontal line of height $\bar{w}$.

Now, observe that each transferred laborer in industry must be able to buy back his food parcel, because he is no longer employed in the agricul-

[16] It is not exactly a supply curve in the traditional sense because in its construction we account for movements in the relative price of agricultural to industrial output, as well as for changes in the agricultural wage rate induced by the transfer. See the description that follows for details.

tural sector but in industry. The minimum industrial wage required to do this is depicted in the topmost panel. Because the industrial wage is described in units of industrial goods, we must multiply $\bar{w}$ by the relative price, or the *terms of trade*, between agriculture and industry to arrive at the required minimum industrial wage. This is shown by the value w^* in the topmost panel. In the surplus labor phase, the minimum industrial wage required for compensation does not change, because the average agricultural surplus is not changing.

This creates a perfectly elastic supply of labor in the surplus labor phase, which is depicted as a horizontal line emanating from the point w^* in the topmost panel. This is the zone where it is possible to have economic development with "unlimited supplies" of labor: an expansion in the industrial sector does not drive up the wage rate.

As we now move into the phase of disguised unemployment, the average agricultural surplus begins to decline. This is because total output in the agricultural sector begins to fall, while those who are still there continue to consume the same amount per capita. This is shown by the decreasing line in the zone $B'C'$ of the middle panel.

Now what is the minimum wage in industry? Well, if the wage is still w^* as before, transferred workers will *not* be able to compensate themselves for the move, because it is physically not possible for each of them to buy $\bar{w}$ units of food. This is because the average agricultural surplus has fallen below $\bar{w}$. The immediate effect of this is that food prices start to rise: the terms of trade between rural and urban sectors begin to move against industry. To compensate for this price effect, the industrial wage must rise.

However, rising wages that cannot solve the problem. No matter how much the industrial wage rises, it is not possible for workers to buy their old food parcel back, because there simply is not enough to go around. The only way that compensation can be achieved, then, is for industrial workers to consume a mix of agricultural and industrial products, the latter compensating them for the loss of the former.

Is such compensation possible? It depends on how close the traditional wage is to minimum subsistence. The closer is $\bar{w}$ to the minimum subsistence level, the larger is the compensation required and the steeper is the increase in the required industrial wage. Conversely, the easier it is to substitute industrial consumption for agricultural consumption, the softer is the necessary increase in the compensatory industrial wage.

Ranis and Fei [1961] referred to this phase, where the supply wage of labor tilts upward, as the "first turning point."

Continue the transfer of labor until we reach the point C, where the disguised unemployment phase comes to an end. At this point, the marginal product of labor begins to exceed the traditionally given wage rate. It then becomes profitable to actively bid for labor, because the additional contribution of labor in agricultural production exceeds the cost of hiring labor. This situation means that the wage in agriculture rises. One implication is that the wage bill falls more slowly than it did before along the diagonal line of the lowest panel. It now traces the curve after C, because wages rise as the agricultural labor force decreases.

This phenomenon, which we may think of as the *commercialization of agriculture*, is associated with an even sharper decrease in the average agricultural surplus. In terms of the topmost panel, this phenomenon induces a second turning point in the industrial wage. Not only must the wage compensate for a declining agricultural surplus and a movement of the terms of trade against industry, it must now compensate workers for a higher income foregone in the agricultural sector, and this creates a still sharper upward movement in the industrial wage rate. This completes the construction of the supply curve.

We are now ready to see how the model works. The industrial sector demands labor for production. The topmost panel of Figure 10.3 shows a family of such demand curves; begin with the lowest one. This demand for labor induces a situation where the amount of industrial labor is x, hired at a wage of w^*. With industrial production, profits are realized, parts of which are plowed back as extra capital in the industrial sector. This part of the story is very similar to the Harrod–Domar and Solow paradigms. The expansion of capital means that the demand for labor rises (shift to the second demand curve in the topmost panel). Because the economy is in the surplus labor phase, this labor is forthcoming from the traditional sector with no increase in the wage, as we already discussed. Industrial employment is now at point y. However, with further investment, the demand curve for labor shifts to a point where the compensatory wage must rise. Employment rises to z. However, it would have risen even further (to point z') had the turning point not occurred. The fall in the agricultural surplus chokes off industrial employment to some extent, because it raises the costs of hiring industrial labor.

Our account is now complete. Capital accumulation in the industrial sector is the engine of growth. More capital means a greater demand for labor, which in turn induces greater rural–urban migration. As development proceeds, the terms of trade gradually turn against industry: food prices rise because a smaller number of farmers must support a greater number of nonagricultural workers. The rise in the price of food causes an increase in the industrial wage rate. The pace of development is driven by the accumulation of capital, but is limited by the ability of the economy to produce a surplus of food.

Despite all the qualifications and imperfections that we subsequently note, this is the heart of the Lewis–Ranis–Fei story: development proceeds via the *joint* transfer of labor and agricultural surplus from the "traditional" agricultural sector to the "modern" industrial sector. The ability to expand the industrial sector is determined in part by production conditions in agriculture. In particular, without the existence of a surplus in the latter sector, it is difficult to create growth in the former sector.

Policy issues

As we will see in this section, the Lewis model of economic development needs several qualifications: the details of the framework should not be taken literally, but the model helps us organize our thoughts along certain lines and throws light on different policies that can be adopted in the course of development.

(1) *Agricultural taxation.* The assumption that the wage rate in agriculture is fixed until the phase of commercialization is reached is strong. Take another look at Figure 10.3. As labor is progressively withdrawn from the agricultural sector, there is more income left for the *remaining* workers to share. Why don't they share it and raise the wage upward from $\bar{w}$? If they do, then there are two effects: (i) the agricultural surplus available to industry is reduced and (ii) the compensating wage paid to transferred workers must rise *even* in the phase of surplus labor. Even if farmers willingly market the freed surplus (if the price is right), effect (ii) remains, and the supply curve of labor to industry fails to be perfectly elastic.

This observation uncovers a problematic issue in the Lewis–Ranis–Fei theory: industry has a vested interest in taxing agriculture, because it is only through taxation that the incomes of family farmers stay low as labor is withdrawn (as shown in Figure 10.3). Indeed, the model implicitly assumes that family farms are being taxed as labor is withdrawn, thus keeping per capita income constant in agriculture and allowing the supply curve of labor to industry to remain perfectly elastic. In contrast, if taxes are not imposed, agricultural incomes will rise—surplus labor or not—and industrial wages must rise to keep migration incentives alive. The rise in industrial wages chokes off industrial profit, and this is the source of the tension between agriculture and industry.

Who would support agricultural taxation? Industrialists would: such taxation keeps agricultural incomes down and this reduces industrial wages. Industrial workers would not support such taxes, not necessarily out of solidarity for farmers, but because it would raise migration and increase the competition for jobs. Small farmers certainly oppose the policy: they are the ones who are taxed! As for large landowners, the situation is more complicated. Their response depends on the intensity of the taxation and the ease with which some of it can be evaded. Certainly they prefer no taxation to taxation, but taxation also has the effect of driving down rural wages. To the extent that large landowners are significant employers of labor, this effect may be beneficial.

Thus we see that a policy of agrarian taxation may run into severe political problems, even though it may have a beneficial effect on industrial growth. This is especially true of countries with a large fraction of the population in agriculture: the governments of such countries often draw on farmers for political support.

There is a postscript to all this. We've assumed in the preceding discussion that agricultural taxation does assist in industrial development, but this may be a shortsighted view. There are longer-term considerations. If farmers believe that greater output will be systematically taxed away, then they will lose all incentives to create, improve, or maintain productive inputs such as irrigation facilities or soil quality. There will be underinvestment in agriculture, and this underinvestment will have repercussions for the availability of *future* surplus.

The tension between a static or short-term view of agriculture as a sector to be squeezed for *current* surplus and a dynamic or long-term view of agriculture as a sector to be invested in and encouraged for the generation of *future* surplus, represents an economic issue of great importance. Walking this tightrope is no easy task and can have enormous political connotations.

Agriculture versus Industry in the New Soviet Union

Of the newly created Soviet Union of the 1920s, Dobb [1966, p. 208] wrote: "The rate at which agricultural production could expand and afford a growing supply of raw materials for industry *and foodstuffs for industrial workers* appeared as the crucial question in economic discussion in the second half of the decade: an issue upon which all other hopes and possibilities rested" (Italics added for emphasis). It wasn't that agricultural investment was nonexistent: large imports of tractors occurred in the 1920s, the majority of these going to the collective or state farms. However, the *marketed* surplus of food grain continued to be abysmally low: in 1925–26, while the total agricultural land area under cultivation was close to that of pre-war sown acreage, the surplus on the market was only around 70% of the pre-war amount. With the land reform of 1917, land was now more equally distributed and it was clear that the newly endowed peasantry were eating more and selling less.

There was no end of fretting and fuming about the problem of agriculture. Oddly enough, some intellectual hardliners centered around Trotsky in the mid-1920s continued to view "further development as only possible in the existing situation in Russia if industry were to expand at the *expense* of the peasantry"(Dobb [1966, p. 183]). This view contrasted with the relatively moderate earlier views of Lenin, who regarded agriculture as a sector to be (at least provisionally) treated as complementary to the development process, creating and retaining a *smytchka*, or bond, between the peasant and the industrial worker. In the mid-1920s the government embarked on a program of food price stabilization that limited competition among purchasers of grain and required all private traders to register with the government. State collecting organizations, which set price limits on purchases, came to occupy a larger share of the grain trade. The policy of price stabilization was successful: food prices rose only by 2% between October 1926 and March 1927, but grain purchases collapsed. Thus grain to the towns was sharply limited, as were grain exports in exchange for needed imports of industrial inputs.

In 1928, Stalin described the situation thus[17]:

> On January 1st of this year there was a deficit of 128 million poods of grain as compared with last year.... What was to be done to make up the lost ground? It was necessary first of all to strike hard at the *kulaks* (rich peasants) and the speculators.... Secondly, it was necessary to pour the maximum amount of goods into the grain regions...the measures taken were effective, and by the end of March we had collected 275 million poods of grain.... [But] from April to June we were unable to collect even 100 million poods.... Hence the second relapse into emergency measures, administrative arbitrariness, violation of revolutionary laws, raids on peasant houses, illegal searches, and so forth, which affected the political conditions of the country and created a menace to the *smytchka* between the workers and the peasants.

This was a two-edged sword: grain was wanted, but despite the intended pouring of the "maximum amount of goods into the grain regions," incentives to farmers were absolutely minimal. Short-run gains in food collection were met only with longer-run resistance. Finally, the historic decision was taken to embark on a massive state collectivization of agriculture, a story in itself. Other governments, for whom large-scale collectivization is not a desirable option, will have to solve this problem differently, but the problem *is* there all the same.

---

(2) *Agricultural pricing policy.* Agricultural taxation is not the only way to extract a food surplus. As we have seen, this policy has several problems: informational (can the government verify how much is produced or, indeed, how much land a farmer owns?), political (farmers are a powerful voting bloc), and economic (taxation creates long-run disincentives to invest in agriculture, which lowers future surplus). Food can be coaxed instead of coerced into the market by lucrative prices for output or subsidies to agricultural inputs. To be sure, a higher output price is a more costly route as far as industrial capitalists are concerned: to them, every concession to agriculture has repercussions for the industrial wage, either directly (as agrarian incomes rise) or indirectly (via a higher relative price of food).

[17] Stalin's speech was made to the Leningrad organization of the Party and is quoted in Dobb [1966].

The typical price support program consists in offering guaranteed procurement prices at which the government stands ready to buy food grain. The idea, of course, is to increase the marketed surplus of grain. At the same time, governments often are unwilling to pass on these prices to urban consumers, partly because these consumers are typically incensed by higher prices (never mind if their salaries are adjusted as a result) and partly because of the effect on the industrial wage. Thus price support programs are usually accompanied by a subsidy to urban consumers: the procured food is sold at or below market prices by the government. Of course, someone has to pay for this subsidy, and it usually comes out of the government budget.

An alternative to high procurement prices is the policy of keeping *input* prices low. Water, electricity, and fertilizer may be supplied free or at reduced prices. In India, the fertilizer subsidy *alone* accounted for an enormous chunk of the government budget: in the late 1980s, the size of the subsidy exceeded total revenues from noncorporate income taxes!

Yet another option, which has the dubious advantage of being less transparent, is to maintain an overvalued exchange rate (see Chapter 17 for much more on this). The overvaluation is kept in place by tariff or quota-based restrictions on imports. To be sure, an overvalued exchange rate serves many purposes, and this is not the place to discuss them, but one implication is that the prices of exports are kept artificially low (in terms of the domestic currency). If the country is a food exporter, this policy has the effect of discouraging food exports and shifting food sales into the domestic market. The policy has sufficient opacity about it—farmers may not be aware that the exchange rate is overvalued and reduces their export earnings—and it has the desired impact of making food available to urban consumers without a price rise.

But it is important to note that policies such as export restrictions, opaque though they may well be, do involve serious efficiency losses and can run the country into severe balance of payments problems. Moreover, if there is a sudden liberalization of the exchange rate, the opacity of the policy may just as quickly disappear and be replaced with a (now more transparent) policy of an outright ban on food exports. The Indian government has faced this dilemma in the 1990s.

Perhaps there is no way out but to endure the short-run rise in food prices, and the inherent shift in national income in favor of agriculture, with the understanding that this will be good for the entire economy in the longer run. Certainly in countries where (to begin with) there were artificial controls to selling on the market, the simple policy of allowing market-determined sales had significant effects. Contrast Russian and Chinese reforms. Russian agriculture never really recovered from the collectivization programs of the 1930s: it is a sector that neither Gorbachev nor Yeltsin seriously touched in any way. Bureaucratic collectives meant low productivity and low output, and Russians have had to import food, particularly from the rest of the Soviet bloc (in exchange for armaments and other heavy-industry products). The collapse of the Soviet bloc, the lowered demand for armaments, and the need to now pay in hard currency all led to a food shortage and high inflation.

China stands in sharp contrast. They began post-1978 reforms with agriculture. Land was given to farmers (on long leases) under the new "household responsibility system" and collective farms were disbanded. Farmers were allowed to sell on the market and market prices were unregulated. This plan actually implied two conceptual departures from earlier policy: the introduction of price incentives and the abandonment of a regional self-sufficiency-in-grain program , which had been in place since the Great Leap Forward in 1958. This policy actually required that each region plant crops for self-sufficiency, regardless of whether or not they were suited to grow those crops.

The resulting gain in agricultural productivity (and output) was impressive. In the 1970s, TFP in agriculture was 20–30% lower than in 1952, the year before collectivization. Just a few years after the reforms, TFP was back to the 1952 level and continued to grow steadily through the 1980s (Wen [1993]). Agricultural output expanded by over 40% between 1978 and 1984 (see McMillan, Whalley, and Zhu [1989]).

How much of the productivity growth can be traced to the new surge in price incentives and how much to the abandonment of the self-sufficiency policy? It appears that the former accounts for almost all of the productivity gains according to a decomposition analysis carried out by Lin and Wen [1995]. The self-sufficiency policy, macabre though it was, apparently was not the main culprit in the earlier productivity stagnation.

Thus the initial price increase promoted much of the output gains. In the longer run, this meant that China was able to avoid the problem of *continuously* rising food prices or food shortages, which in turn kept industrial wages competitive and fuelled industrial growth.

The question is whether the *initial* rise in food prices that comes from a pro-farmer pricing policy can be politically tolerated. In the case of China led by Deng Xiao Ping, the base of the Chinese Communist party was formed by the farmers (who supported the party through the Tiananmen episode).

However, there are limits to where price policy can take us unless we start from an unusually repressed base. Although Lipton's [1968] point that there is often "urban bias in rural planning" is certainly well taken, over-inflated food prices can only retard industrial development. There are other gaps to fill: as we shall see in the chapters to come, agricultural growth is often limited by access barriers to capital and credit, as well as intrinsic disincentives that arise from agrarian contracts (which occur primarily because such contracts need to play the double role of assuring *some* incentives and *some* insurance). Land reform, credit expansion, and infrastructural investment all go a long way to assuring agricultural and industrial growth. There would be no need to do this if the markets to ensure such developments functioned smoothly, but as we will see, they do not. A fuller consideration of these issues is postponed to Chapters 12–15.

10.3. Rural–urban migration

10.3.1. Introduction

The Lewis model tells us that agricultural surpluses and labor must be transferred in tandem for industrial development to begin. But as we have already noted, labor moves from one sector to another in obedience to its own wishes and objectives. To the extent that these objectives may be out of line with social goals or policies, we might have over- or undermigration to the cities. The purpose of this section is to discuss patterns of rural–urban migration.

The classic theory of rural–urban migration is based on Harris and Todaro [1970]. We start by talking about the basic theory, and then extend the framework in a number of different directions.

The main idea of the Harris–Todaro model is that the formal urban sector pays a high wage to workers and it is this high wage that creates urban unemployment (the mechanism will be examined in what follows). Many reasons might be provided for the phenomenon of an overly high urban wage. The sector may be unionized and subject to collective bargaining over wages, whereas other sectors of the economy are not remotely as organized, so that wages are more flexible in those sectors. In addition, the urban formal sector is often treated as the showcase of government policy, so that minimum wage laws, pension schemes, unemployment benefits, day care, and other facilities may be required by law. These provisions may not raise the wage directly, but amounts to the same thing, because such forms of compensation raise worker utility.

Finally, it may well be the case that firms in the urban formal sector *deliberately* pay wages that exceed levels found elsewhere so they can hire workers of the best quality and fire inferior workers after their quality is revealed. Even if there are no quality differences across workers, "supermarket" wages may still be paid if firms wish to elicit effort from their workers. The idea is that if such effort is not forthcoming, then workers are fired and returned to the informal or rural labor market. The threat of being fired induces higher effort. Of course, being fired can carry no threat if the wage package is no different from what the worker can get elsewhere; in other words, to make being fired a serious punishment, the firm must "buy the threat" by paying a higher-than-normal wage. We will see more of this sort of contract in Chapter 13.

In contrast to the high wages paid in the formal urban sector, the informal urban sector and the rural sector have low wages that fluctuate according to supply and demand considerations. There is no unionization here and government policy is difficult to implement. Moreover, if the bulk of labor is family labor (as it is in much of the urban informal businesses, as well as in rural family farms) or if the bulk of labor effort is readily monitorable (as in harvest labor), then there will be little incentive for employers in these sectors to pay higher wages as a potential threat. Even if there were such an incentive, the net effect is unlikely to dominate the huge premiums that are paid in the urban formal sector.

Migration in the Harris–Todaro model is then viewed as a response to the significant wage gap that prevails between the two sectors. Of course, not everyone can be absorbed into the formal sector at these high wages: some people are unlucky and fail to find a job, in which case they turn to the urban informal sector for some meager sustenance. Thus the migration decision is akin to leaving behind a relatively sure thing (employment as an agricultural labor or on the family farm) for the great uncertainty of employment as a formal laborer. Those who fail in this quest join the queue of the unemployed, perhaps in disguised form in the informal sector. Thus the urban informal sector (in the Harris–Todaro view) contains the failed aspirants to the formal sector dream—the lottery tickets that didn't win.

10.3.2. The basic model

We begin by assuming that there are only two sectors in the economy: a rural sector and a formal urban sector. Solely for the purpose of setting a benchmark, we assume that wages in *both* sectors are fully flexible. Later, we introduce rigidity in the urban formal wage.

Figure 10.4 captures the basic story. The width of the horizontal axis is the entire labor force in the economy. The labor force is divided between the agricultural sector, which we denote by A, and the formal urban sector, which we denote by F. The left axis of the figure records various formal wages in the urban sector, whereas the right axis records agricultural wages. The curve AB may be thought of as a demand curve for labor in the urban formal sector: like most demand curves, it is downward sloping, so that more labor can be absorbed in the sector only at a lower wage. Likewise, the curve CD captures the absorption of labor in agriculture (you can think of it as a demand curve as well, but there are other interpretations that we will discuss presently). Just as in the urban sector, more agricultural labor typically can be absorbed only at a lower wage.

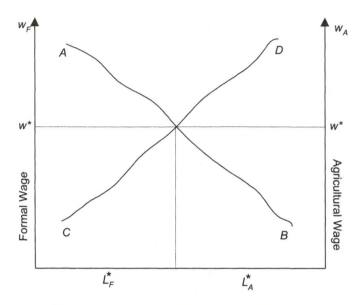

Figure 10.4. Market equilibrium with flexible wages.

It is now easy enough to combine these two "absorption curves" to analyze the equilibrium of this simple economy. To alleviate persistent migration between one sector and the other, the wages in the two sectors must be equalized.[18] This equalization occurs at the intersection of the curves AB and CD, and we can read the equilibrium wage rate and intersectoral allocation of labor from this intersection. Figure 10.4 records the equilibrium wage rate in this case as w^*, with L_A^* individuals in the agrarian sector and L_F^* individuals in the urban sector.

10.3.3. Floors on formal wages and the Harris–Todaro equilibrium

What is wrong with the preceding argument? Not much, it would appear: what we have in Figure 10.4 and the accompanying discussion is a textbook case of competitive equilibrium. The problem is that it assumes that the urban wage rate is perfectly flexible. We have already seen that this is not the case. Indeed, it is not at all unreasonable to argue that the formal urban wage is too high for market clearing to occur as described by Figure 10.4. We have provided several reasons for this. Now let us see what the implications are. In terms of our simple model, then, imagine that the wage rate in the formal sector is fixed at too high a level for market equilibrium w^* to occur. Figure 10.5 captures this situation by drawing the minimum formal wage, $\bar{w}$, at a level that lies above the intersection of the two absorption

---

[18] We neglect here the costs of migration, which can easily be incorporated into the model.

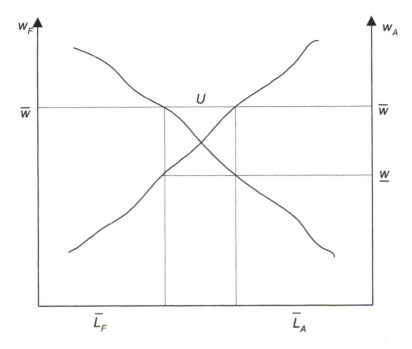

Figure 10.5. A floor on the formal wage.

curves. It follows that private-sector formal firms will hire no more than the amount $\bar{L}_F$ of labor at this wage. Where do the remainder go?

One possibility is that all the remaining individuals are employed in the agricultural sector. In that case, Figure 10.5 tells us that the wage in the agricultural sector must drop to $\underline{w}$. Now step back and look at the final outcome. In both sectors we have full employment, so that no *individual* job seeker needs to fear unemployment if she looks for a job in either sector. Nonetheless, the wages, $\bar{w}$ and $\underline{w}$, are different. This *cannot* be an equilibrium state for the economy, because with full employment in both sectors, workers will wish to migrate to the sector with the higher wage.

On the other hand, simply imposing the equality of wages across the two sectors is problematic as well. Try it. Figure 10.5 then reveals that only an amount $\bar{L}_A$ can be soaked up in the agricultural sector. If the formal and the agricultural sectors are the only two sectors in the economy, we must have a pool of unemployed people. (In the figure, U denotes the size of the resulting unemployed pool.) This cannot be an equilibrium state either. Given that agriculture has flexible wages, the unemployed workers cannot be physically located in agriculture. If they were, they would simply pour into that labor market and consequently drive the wages down. Therefore, they must be located in the urban sector. Now we have a situation in which these workers rationally migrate to the urban formal sector, even though the wages there are the same as those in agriculture *and* there is significant risk

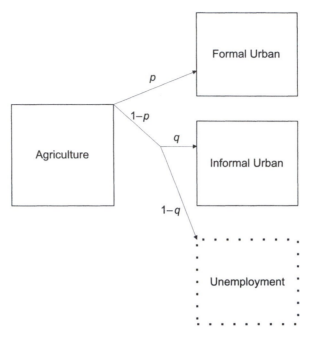

Figure 10.6. Options open to a potential migrant.

of unemployment. Under no stretch of the imagination can such a state of affairs be described as an equilibrium, even from an ex ante point of view.

Although these alternatives do not work as descriptions of the final outcome, they are suggestive of what the equilibrium might look like. The main idea is that potential migrants choose between a relatively safe (though possibly unpleasant) option, which is to stay in the agricultural sector, and the gamble of moving to the urban sector, where a high-paying formal job may or may not be attainable. In turn, the probability of getting such a job is determined by the ratio of formal job seekers to available formal jobs. Those who do not get a job might be referred to as the unemployed, but this description is not entirely accurate (and here is where the informal sector comes in). Frustrated formal job seekers may enter the informal sector, where jobs or businesses are easy enough to find but pay (relatively speaking) a pittance. Figure 10.6 schematically captures the gamble that is involved.

In this diagram, there are two sets of boxes. The left set is a single box: agriculture, with its wage w_A.[19] The right set describes the various options open in the urban sector, together with the probabilities of access. First, there is the formal sector at some high wage $\bar{w}$. The probability of obtaining such a job depends on the ratio of vacancies to job seekers. Denote this by p. Next,

[19] To be sure, this is a simplification. Agriculture may have its own variability of wages, depending on the form of the contract and the nature of employment, but for simplicity, we ignore this variability here.

there is the informal urban sector, in which our migrant can get absorbed in the event that no formal job is forthcoming. Denote the wage rate in the informal sector by w_I and assume that it is fixed regardless of the number of people in that sector.

What is needed is a calculation of the *expected value* of these two risky options. The expected value is calculated in the usual way: weigh each outcome by its probability of occurrence and add up over all outcomes. Thus the expected wage in the urban sector is neither $\bar{w}$ nor w_I, but the combination $p\bar{w} + (1 - p)w_I$. It is this *expected* wage that is compared to the wage in the agricultural sector.

In the preceding calculation, we implicitly assumed that there are only two options in the urban sector: formal or informal employment. However, once we understand how the calculation is carried out, it is easy enough to expand the urban sector to include more possibilities. For instance, it is reasonable to suppose that not everyone is guaranteed to receive even the lower income w_I in the informal sector. It may be that some individuals do not get any employment at all, so that they are "openly" unemployed. This additional option is displayed by the dotted box in Figure 10.6, with associated wages equal to zero.

How can we now compute expected values? We need to know the probability of getting an informal sector job, conditional on having been turned away from the formal sector: denote this by q. Thus after being turned away from the formal sector, the migrant manages to join the informal sector with probability q and remains openly unemployed with probability $1 - q$. The expected value of this latter set of possibilities is $qw_I + (1 - q)0 = qw_I$. Thus the overall expected wage is now $p\bar{w} + (1 - p)qw_I$.

With this small digression completed, let us return to the simpler case of just two urban outcomes: employment in the formal sector or employment in the informal sector. Suppose that we use L_I to denote informal employment. Then we can see that the ratio

$$\frac{L_F}{L_F + L_I}$$

captures the probability of getting a job in the formal sector. The number of employed people L_F tells us how many jobs there are, whereas the number $L_F + L_I$ is the measure of the total number of potential job seekers. The ratio of the two thus gives us the chances that an urban dweller will get a job in the formal or informal sector.[20]

---

[20] The careful reader will see that this statement is only correct if there is a rapid enough rate of turnover in the formal sector, so that the current level of *employment* can roughly be equated to the number of available *vacancies*. With a smaller rate of turnover, the number of vacancies is not L_F, but some number less than that, and likewise, the number of job seekers is smaller than $L_F + L_I$. The mode of analysis is very similar.

Now we can work toward the important equilibrium concept first introduced by Harris and Todaro [1970]. Migration from the rural sector may be thought of as an irreversible decision, at least for the proximate future. Because the fate of a potential migrant is not known, we must consider the *expected income* from migration and compare it with the actual income received in agriculture. Thus we may conclude that if

$$(10.1) \qquad \frac{\bar{L}_F}{\bar{L}_F + L_I}\bar{w} + \frac{L_I}{\bar{L}_F + L_I}w_I = w_A,$$

we are at an equilibrium where no person wishes to migrate from one sector to the other. This is the *Harris–Todaro equilibrium condition*.

Some remarks are in order. First, the equilibrium condition represents a situation where ex ante people are indifferent between migrating and not migrating; ex post, they will not be indifferent. The lucky subgroup who land a job in the formal sector will be very pleased that they did migrate, whereas those who seek solace in the informal sector will regret that they made the move.

Second, observe that the equilibrium concept implies a *particular* allocation of labor between the three sectors of the economy. This is because it is the allocation of labor that affects the perceived probabilities of getting a job. If it is known, for instance, that the formal sector accounts for a smaller proportion of total urban employment, individuals will think harder before they hope for a job in the formal sector. Their expected wage calculation will yield a lower wage. This prospect will lower the size of the urban labor force, but increase the size of the formal sector as a proportion of total urban employment, which in turn, feeds back on the probability of getting the formal job.

Third, the equilibrium concept in no way requires that we stick to merely *two* subsectors of the urban sector (formal and informal) or that we have only one sector in agriculture. The fundamental requirement is that *expected* wages are equalized over the two sectors for a migration equilibrium to be obtained, but these expectations may be the outcome of wages in three or more urban sectors (e.g., open unemployment may be thought of simply as another sector in which wages happen to be zero) or in several sectors in agriculture.

The Harris–Todaro equilibrium may be depicted on the sort of the diagram we have been using so far, but not with the greatest degree of clarity.[21] Recall Figure 10.5 and note that the agricultural wage of $\bar{w}$ was too high to be an equilibrium and that $\underline{w}$ was too low. It stands to reason that the equilibrium agricultural wage is somewhere between these two extremes. Note that there is no necessary relationship between this equilibrium wage and

---

[21] The main problem is that the informal sector cannot be depicted explicitly on this diagram.

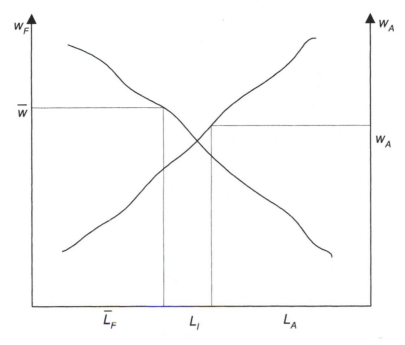

Figure 10.7. Harris–Todaro equilibrium.

the wage rate w^* that arose in the flexible market case. Figure 10.7 denotes a typical Harris–Todaro equilibrium condition.

In this figure, the equilibrium agricultural wage is given by w_A. L_A people are employed in agriculture, $\bar{L}_F$ people are in the formal urban sector, and the remainder, L_I, take refuge in the informal sector where they obtain an income of w_I. The allocation is such that (10.1) holds.

10.3.4. Government policy

The paradox of urban job creation

In this view, then, the informal sector is an outgrowth of the fact that the formal sector has wages that are too high, so that not everyone is capable of obtaining employment in this sector. At the same time, not everyone else can stay in agriculture as well, for that would make the formal sector look too attractive and induce a great deal of migration. The informal sector is a result of this migration. In the Harris–Todaro view, the informal sector acts as a necessary counterweight to the attractiveness of the formal sector and slows the pace of rural–urban migration.

To the urban observer and to the government official, however, the informal sector is an eyesore with not very pleasing properties. Unregulated economic activity in this sector is often responsible for congestion, pollution, and a high crime rate. There are several ways in we can deal with this problem, and in the rest of this section we will study some of them.

The most obvious policy that comes to mind is to somehow accelerate the rate of absorption of labor in the formal sector. Even though wages are fixed at $\bar{w}$, it is possible to generate additional demand for formal labor by offering urban businesses various setup incentives (such as tax holidays) or ongoing investment incentives (such as better treatment in the credit market). The government might itself expand the demand for formal labor by expanding the employment of public sector enterprises.

No doubt, such policies initially reduce the size of the informal sector, by simply channeling people from this sector into the greater number of formal jobs that are now available, but matters do not end there. The size of the urban sector is endogenous, and migration will rise in response to this policy. The Harris–Todaro equilibrium concept helps us to explore the nature of the final outcome, *after* fresh rural–urban migration is taken into account.

To see this, trace the effect on the Harris–Todaro equilibrium condition. Imagine that the formal labor demand curve shifts out and to the right, so that, in particular, labor demand at the wage rate $\bar{w}$ rises from $\bar{L}_F$ to $\bar{L}'_F$. In the short run, all this extra labor simply comes from the informal pool. This means that relative to the initial outcome, L_F rises and L_I falls. This raises the probability of getting a formal job. Consequently, *the expected urban wage must initially rise.*

But the initial increase cannot be fully persistent. Rural–urban migration picks up. More migrants enter the urban sector. Of course they add to the informal sector, which after its initial decline, now begins to increase once again. This phenomenon sets in motion two related forces. First, as the labor force in agriculture falls, the agricultural wage tends to rise (by how much it rises will depend on the slope or elasticity of the agricultural absorption curve). Second, as migration continues, the expected urban wage once again begins to fall (relative to the initial sharp rise). One glance at (10.1) tells you why. The fraction $L_F/(L_F + L_I)$ begins to move down as migration continues, and this brings down the probability of getting a formal job (relative to what prevailed just after the institution of the policy) and the expected urban wage drops with it.

With the agricultural wage climbing up and the expected urban wage creeping down, the two are bound to come into line once again. In the process, we have a fresh allocation of labor in the three sectors: $(\bar{L}'_F, L'_A, L'_I)$. The new allocation must satisfy the new Harris–Todaro equilibrium condition

$$(10.2) \qquad \frac{\bar{L}'_F}{\bar{L}'_F + L'_I}\bar{w} + \frac{L'_I}{\bar{L}'_F + L'_I}w_I = w'_A,$$

where w'_A denotes the new agricultural wage after the policy.

How do we compare the magnitudes in (10.1) and (10.2)? Recalling that the agricultural wage rises (or at least does not fall) after the introduction of the policy, it must be the case that the new expected wage in the urban sector exceeds the old expected wage. The only way in which this can happen in the model is if

$$\frac{\bar{L}_F'}{\bar{L}_F' + L_I'} > \frac{\bar{L}_F}{\bar{L}_F + L_I};$$

in other words, if the share of the formal sector in total urban sector employment goes up. This is a beneficial implication of the policy: the informal sector does shrink, *measured as a fraction of the total urban sector*.

However, there is another way to look at the outcome, and that is to study the resulting size of the informal sector as a fraction of the *total* labor force. Is it possible that this increases even though the assertion in the last paragraph is true? Interestingly enough, the answer is yes. Although it may be true that the informal sector shrinks as a fraction of the urban labor force, it is also true that the size of the urban labor force has expanded. If the latter effect dominates the former, the informal sector may well expand—an implication of a policy that was directly aimed at *reducing* the size of that sector!

To see this, imagine that the agricultural sector is in the surplus-labor phase of Lewis, so that the wage in the agricultural sector adjusts very little or not at all as fresh migrants move out of agriculture. In that case, the share of the informal sector in the total urban sector is practically unaltered [simply look at (10.1) and (10.2), and use the fact that w_A' is very close to w_A]. At the same time, it is certainly the case that the entire urban sector has grown from the first equilibrium to the second. This must mean that the informal sector has expanded as well.

What accounts for this seeming paradox? How is it that a policy designed to absorb people from the informal sector ends up enlarging its size? As a matter of fact, there is no paradox at all, but an observation that we see repeated in one developing country after another. Attempts to increase the demand for labor in the formal sector may enlarge the size of the informal sector, as migrants respond to the better job conditions that are available. The migration effect may dominate the initial "soak-up effect."

This observation is not limited to cases in which the demand for formal-sector labor is increased. A similar application can be carried out with regard to urban congestion, pollution, or the provision of health facilities. In each of these cases, policies aimed at directly reducing urban congestion (say, by building more roads), reducing pollution (say, by building a subway), or increasing the provision of health (say, by building new public hospitals) might all have the paradoxical effect of finally worsening these indicators. In each case, the ultimate worsening occurs because fresh migration in response to the improved conditions ends up exacerbating the very conditions that the initial policy attempted to ameliorate.[22]

Efficient allocation and migration policy

Recall for a moment the case of fully flexible wages with which we began our analysis of migration. The equilibrium there has an interesting efficiency property provided we think of the two absorption curves AB and CD (see Figure 10.4) as the competitive demand curves for labor. From elementary economic theory, we know that the competitive demand curve for labor is nothing but the value of the marginal product curve, where the price of the final output is used to compute value. In this situation, the intersection of these two curves corresponds to the case in which the values of marginal products in the two sectors are *equalized*. In all other allocations, there is a discrepancy between the two marginal products. In addition, the informal sector has a still lower value of marginal product (given by w_I), so that these allocations cannot maximize the value of total national product. The reason is simple. As long as marginal products are not equal, a small transfer of labor from the sector in which the marginal product is lower to the sector in which it is higher increases the total value of national income.

This observation should make us think twice about what it is, exactly, that government policy is trying to achieve. It is not that the informal sector, per se, is something to eliminate. Indeed, in the policies that we will now examine, getting rid of the informal sector is not the main problem at all. Getting as close to the efficient allocation of labor resources, epitomized by the crossing of the two demand curves, is what policy should be all about.

I want to reiterate that this prescription is valid only in the case where both demand curves arise through competitive profit maximization, so that they correspond to the value of marginal product. When this is not the case, it is unclear whether the intersection of the two absorption curves possesses any efficiency meaning and should somehow represent a target. However, let us ignore this qualification for now.

Consider two policies that reduce or remove the informal sector. One policy is to physically *restrict migration*. Figure 10.8 illustrates this. All individuals who do not have formal sector jobs are prevented from entering the cities. If this policy can be enforced (and this is not a trivial issue), then migration restrictions certainly get rid of the informal urban sector. The number of people in the urban sector is now just $\bar{L}_F$; the remainder, L_A^M, stay in agriculture.

Note, however, that simply getting rid of the informal sector does not ensure that we have an efficient outcome. Compare the allocation achieved

---

[22] This phenomenon is often referred to as the Todaro paradox.

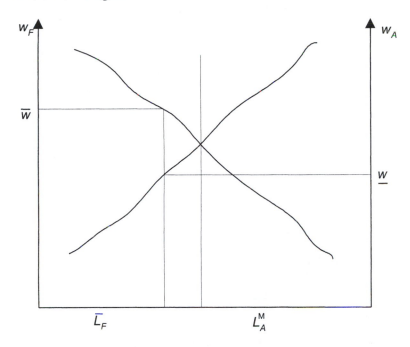

Figure 10.8. Migration restrictions.

in this way to that achieved in the case of fully flexible wages. It is clear that under a policy of migration restrictions, we have too few people in the cities relative to the efficient allocation.

The second policy is to offer a subsidy to employers in the formal sector for every unit of labor that they hire. Let us suppose that the subsidy involves financing s dollars of the formal wage for every extra labor hour that is hired by a formal-sector employer. In this case the wage that is paid by the employer is effectively $\bar{w} - s$, but the worker receives the full wage $\bar{w}$. Thus the effect is to push out the demand for labor at the formal wage $\bar{w}$, as Figure 10.9 illustrates.

Note that as the subsidy increases, formal labor demand increases. There comes a point when the formal-sector labor demand increases so much that agricultural wages are pushed up to equal $\bar{w}$, the formal-sector wage. At this point there is no urban informal sector and no incentive for anyone to migrate. This situation is illustrated in Figure 10.9, where formal employment is now at the level L_F^S and agricultural employment is at the level L_A^S under the subsidy.

I am going to return later to the issue of how the subsidy is financed and whether the subsidy can be enforced. Leaving these questions aside, we see that although the urban informal sector has been removed, there is now *too much* labor in the urban sector relative to the efficient allocation. Thus in

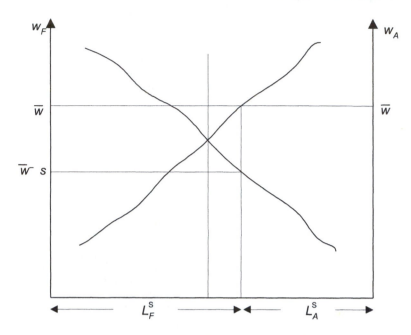

Figure 10.9. A formal-sector wage subsidy.

a way, wage subsidies achieve exactly the opposite of migration restrictions, even though both serve to eliminate the urban informal sector.

It is in this sense that we entertain a mixed policy that combines migration restrictions with wage subsidies in the formal sector. Figure 10.10 illustrates this. The subsidy is carefully chosen so that formal labor demand is hiked up to precisely the flexible equilibrium level, which is L_F^*. Note that workers still receive wage $\bar{w}$ in the formal sector, so that the flexible agricultural wage in this situation is still smaller than the formal wage if all remaining laborers stay in agriculture. Thus migration restrictions are still needed under this policy to make sure that the remaining labor (L_A^*) stays in the agricultural sector.

Are there policies that can make do without migration restrictions? The answer is that there are and, oddly enough, they involve the subsidization of employment in agriculture *even though* agriculture has perfectly flexible wages to begin with! Consider a *uniform* subsidy of s dollars per worker-hour to both agriculture and industry.[23] The first panel of Figure 10.11 shows how such a policy works, starting from a Harris–Todaro equilibrium. The demand for labor in both agriculture and the formal sector increases because the wage payouts in these sectors, *from the viewpoint of the employer*, are $\bar{w} - s$ and $w_A - s$ (instead of $\bar{w}$ and w_A). The *worker*, on the other hand, continues to compare the wages $\bar{w}$ and w_A. Because the informal sector must have shrunk, the

---

[23] Bhagwati and Srinisavan [1974] discussed the uniform subsidy that we study in this text.

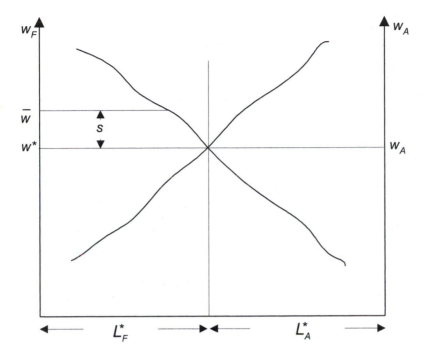

Figure 10.10. *A combination policy of migration restrictions and wage subsidies.*

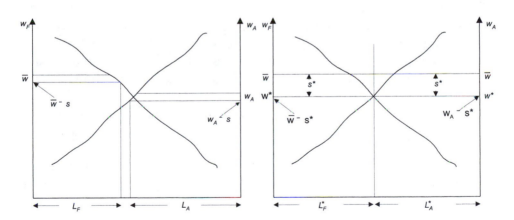

Figure 10.11. *A uniform wage subsidy.*

urban wage must have gone up (even though none of the separate wages has changed). To restore equilibrium, the agricultural wage must rise.

This process continues until the uniform subsidy reaches the level $\bar{w} - w^*$, where w^* is the old flexible-wage equilibrium. At this point, the agricultural wage must have risen to precisely $\bar{w}$ as well! This is shown in the second panel of Figure 10.11. Now there is full employment in both agriculture and the formal urban sector, there is no informal sector, *and* there is no need for migration restrictions, because the wages in the two sectors are perfectly equalized!

10.3.5. Comments and extensions

Some remarks on policy

Is there, then, a magical government policy that solves the migration problem and restores the efficient outcome without coercive restrictions on labor movement? To answer this question necessitates that we step outside the rigid confines of this simple model and examine the robustness of its predictions. Several objections may be raised. We consider them one at a time.

First, it can be argued that getting the subsidy *exactly* right might require too precise a knowledge of the parameters of the economy; specifically, the position and shape of the two absorption curves. Note that in Figure 10.11, the subsidy is chosen to be equal to $\bar{w} - w^*$. This requires that the government or planner *know* what the flexible equilibrium wage should be. This may be a tall order.

Fortunately, this criticism can be countered quite easily.[24] To see this, suppose that the subsidy was not chosen at the "correct" level s^* in the second panel of Figure 10.11, but at some point exceeding it. Then it can be seen easily that the only effect is to push up the wages *gross* of the subsidy in a uniform way, so that the net wage (paid by employers) still settles at w^* automatically. Figure 10.12 illustrates this. In this diagram, the subsidy was chosen so that it is larger than s^*. This has the effect of pushing the formal sector wage that is actually paid to workers *above* the institutional minimum $\bar{w}$. The very same thing happens in agriculture as well. It is exactly as if the greater subsidy is outweighed, dollar for dollar, by an increase in gross wage costs, so that the net effect is zero.

What this implies, then, is that the uniform subsidy does not require a precise knowledge of the parametric structure of the model. Mistakes in the size of the subsidy, as long as they do not involve too *small* a subsidy, tend to be washed out.

The second criticism is that the subsidy is not free. It has to be financed from some source. Shouldn't the costs of financing be taken into account

---

[24] On this point and its resolution, see Basu [1980].

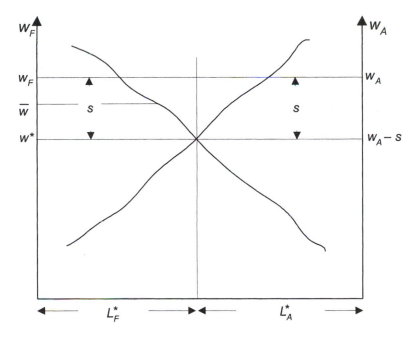

Figure 10.12. An overly generous uniform wage subsidy.

in determining the efficiency of the overall outcome? The answer is that it certainly should, but, in principle, there is a way to make the entire policy self-financing: simply impose a profits tax on firms and return the proceeds as a wage subsidy. The profit tax will form the revenue to implement the subsidy.

At first sight, this appears absurd. Note that in the end, firms would receive a net subsidy or pay a net tax. How is it that a financial policy that has no net effect on the balance sheets of firms nevertheless affects firm behavior? The answer is simple. The tax and the subsidy are conditioned on two *different* indicators of firm performance: profits and employment. If the firm does well on profits, but does not expand employment, it would pay a net tax. But the point is that it *will* want to expand employment to take advantage of the subsidy. Thus even though the two indicators cancel out when all is said and done, firm behavior can be altered substantially.

The third criticism is damaging and probably represents the single most important reason why a policy of wage subsidies is difficult, if not impossible, to implement. It is that employment figures are often very difficult to verify. Without adequate verification, it is not possible to pay a subsidy based on employment. Of course, in principle, it is perhaps possible to adequately verify that each employer is telling the truth about the number of laborers in his employ, but this would cost an immense amount of resources, which then need to be factored into an assessment of the overall efficiency of the migration policy.

Verification is a particularly serious problem in agriculture, which is an "informal sector" *par excellence*. Perhaps we could devise a scheme in which employee tax returns, for instance, are matched against their place of work, so that no fictitious employees can be invented,[25] but to do this we need a sector where tax returns are filed by all eligible employees. Such is generally not the case with agriculture, so the usual expedient of relying on alternative, complementary sources of information is not available.

We now turn to some extensions of the basic migration model.

A digression on risk and risk aversion

In this subsection, we introduce the concept of *risk aversion*. We give it plenty of importance because the concept plays a role not just here, but in the chapters that follow.

Many economic ventures and production processes are marked by substantial uncertainty regarding the final outcome. At the same time, investment decisions may need to be made well in advance of the resolution of this uncertainty. In the context of agricultural production, a farmer may have to decide how much fertilizer to use or how intensively to cultivate his land before knowing whether the weather will be favorable or adverse for a good harvest. He might even opt for the production of an entirely new crop without being sure of the return that it will bring. Similarly, in manufacturing, a firm may need to make its production decisions without knowing exactly what market conditions are going to be. For instance, when Coca Cola decided to open plants and marketing divisions in China, they made an investment commitment while being less than certain about their business prospects there. Almost all economic endeavors are marked by risk regarding the exact returns. In turn, such risk fundamentally affects the way in which people contract with one another. The migration decision is no exception, as we have already seen.

Consider a simple example to illustrate some of the issues. Suppose you are Nazim, a Turkish entrepreneur about to participate in an investment project to produce silk hats. This project is going to produce one of two possible sums of money. If your silk hats are a hit with the Turkish bourgeoisie, you are going to make a tidy profit of $10,000. If your hat factory is sabotaged, however, you will make a profit of only $2,000. Because you are a bit of a worrier, you think that there is a 50–50 chance of sabotage. Now put yourself wholeheartedly into this situation and ask yourself the following question: if the money is all that you care about, what is the *minimum* compensation for which you would be willing to surrender the rights to the proceeds of this venture? After a little bit of introspection, you may want to

---

[25] This is not to say that such a scheme is entirely foolproof.

write down a figure on a piece of paper and then think about the significance of your choice after the following discussion.

We begin by reviewing a term very popular with statisticians, called the mathematical expectation. It's something that we have already used implicitly to calculate the expected wage in the urban sector. In the preceding example, the mathematical expectation (expectation for short) of the returns to the project (before the actual outcome is known) is $\frac{1}{2}\$10,000 + \frac{1}{2}\$2,000 = \$6,000$—simply a weighted average of the various *possible* outcomes, where the weight on each outcome is the probability of its occurrence. More formally, if a project has n possible outcomes indexed by i (i.e., $i = 1, 2, \ldots, n$) and the ith outcome has a monetary value of x_i with a probability of occurrence p_i, then the expectation of the project is given by

$$(10.3) \qquad\qquad E = \sum_{i=1}^{n} p_i x_i.$$

Going back to the previous example, check whether the minimum acceptable compensation you wrote down is more or less than the expected value of the project, namely, $6,000. If you have given it a little thought and if you are psychologically similar to most people, then the amount you wrote should be less than the expected value $6,000. This is because people usually dislike risk; they prefer to have the expected value of a project *for sure* rather than go into the uncertain prospect where the return can be either more or less than that expected value with fairly even chance. Thus people will generally be willing to receive somewhat less than the expected return in guaranteed compensation, in order to give up their claim to the proceeds. This attitude is known as *risk aversion*. Of course, the more risk averse a person is, the lower will be the minimum compensation he will need to be paid. In contrast, a person who is indifferent between enjoying the uncertain returns to a project and its expected value as guaranteed compensation is said to be *risk-neutral*.

One way to capture the attitudes of individuals toward risk is to think of them as having a utility function of money.[26] The idea is that individuals act as if they are maximizing the expected value of this utility under various uncertain circumstances.

What would be the utility function of a risk-neutral person? Recall that such a person acts to maximize the expected value of her *monetary* return. This is the same as postulating that her utility function coincides with the

---

[26] Although the exposition here is unashamedly biased toward simplicity, it must be noted that the postulate of a utility function for money is a bit misleading. What the literature does is begin with preferences of individuals over various risky gambles, which is just an extension of the usual preferences in consumer theory over goods and services. The well-developed theory of decision making under uncertainty then shows that these preferences can be represented (under some conditions) by a utility function for money and the behavioral postulate that an individual acts to maximize the expected value of this utility. See Arrow [1971] for an exposition of this theory.

amount of money that she makes; in other words, that her utility function of money can be represented by a straight line. Put another way, the marginal utility of money for such a person is independent of the amount of money in her possession. From this angle, it turns out that risk aversion can be equated with the notion of a *diminishing* marginal utility of money. Figure 10.13 shows us the connection. In this diagram, the utility function is drawn so that it displays diminishing marginal utility: it is strictly concave.

Suppose that this utility function represents Nazim's preferences. The point *A* shows Nazim's utility when his profit is $2,000 and point *B* shows the utility of a profit of $10,000. How do we calculate Nazim's *expected utility* under these circumstances, assuming that the probability of each occurrence is 1/2? This is not a deep question: we calculate the expected value of utility just as we calculate the expected value of a monetary gamble or the expected number of eggs a hen might lay on any given day. We take the value *A*, multiply it by 1/2 and add it to the value *B* multiplied by 1/2 as well. There is an easy way to do this on the diagram. Simply connect the points *A* and *B* by a line and find the point *C* between the two that lies at distances proportional to the probabilities of occurrence, in this case halfway between

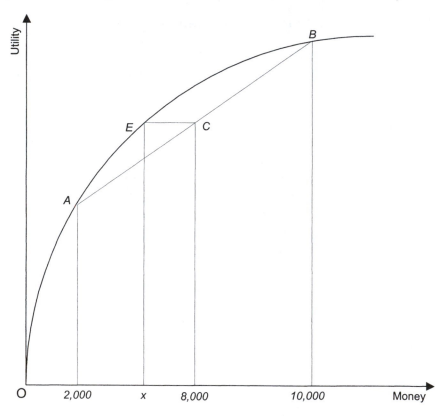

Figure 10.13. Risk aversion.

A and *B*. The (height of the) point *C* represents the expected utility of the gamble that Nazim is contemplating.

Note that if the utility function is curved in the way shown in Figure 10.13, then the point *C* must actually lie *below* the utility function. The meaning of this graphical observation is that the *expected utility of the gamble is lower than the utility of the expected value of the gamble*. This is just a way of saying that Nazim is risk-averse; he likes the gamble less than he likes receiving the expected value of the gamble for sure. This means that an amount of money smaller than the expected value will be enough to compensate him for foregoing the risky venture. To find this amount on the graph, we only need to find the sum of money whose utility equals the expected utility of the gamble. This is easy to do: simply draw a horizontal segment leftward from *C* until it meets the utility function (at *E*). The sum of money corresponding to this utility is the required amount. As we have already noted, if the utility function is shaped the way it is in Figure 10.13, this amount, marked *x* on the diagram, will fall short of the expected value. Thus this shape captures the idea of risk aversion.

With diminishing marginal utility, a dollar lost is always dearer than a dollar gained. That is why a risk-averse person faced with the prospect of gain or loss of a dollar (or any higher amount) with equal probability will be willing to pay a premium (say to an insurance agent) to avoid that risk. A risk-neutral person's utility function of money, on the other hand, can be represented by a straight line. Such a person will in fact be perfectly willing to assume the risk upon himself (if a small fee is paid to him). In a risky economy, therefore, optimal arrangements are those in which risk-neutral agents bear all the risk, while risk-averse persons settle for stable income levels, implicitly or explicitly paying the risk-averse agents premiums for bearing risk. Insurance is a straightforward example of such arrangements: an insurance company promises to cover the risk of accidental damage and loss on behalf of their clients and charges a premium in return during normal times. Many other contractual arrangements (e.g., that between firms and employees, landlords and tenants) also have a dimension of insurance to them, as we shall see in the chapters to follow.

Finally, what determines an agent's attitude toward risk? Partly, it is a matter of individual taste: some people simply tend to be more cautious than others. To a large extent, however, it is also shaped by the economic circumstances of a person. In particular, two features of the economic environment play an important role: wealth and diversification.

It is plausible to argue that wealthier people have a better ability and willingness to bear a given (absolute) amount of risk compared with relatively poor people. A given loss can be ruinous for someone living off a modest saving, whereas a millionaire would be able to shrug it off by saying you can't win 'em all. Think of Nazim's silk hats and picture Nazim as an enormously rich billionaire. In that case, it would be reasonable to expect that Nazim would evaluate this business venture at its expected value; no "risk premium" would be involved. On the other hand, if we look at this venture against a background in which Nazim's own wealth is a few thousand dollars as well, the riskiness of the venture assumes its old significance.[27]

A second crucial question is how diversified an agent's source of income is. A person who earns his income from many different sources, each subject to *independent* risks (e.g., income from a diversified portfolio of stocks) will be less sensitive to the risks at each source, because on the whole, their effects tend to cancel out. It is highly unlikely that all sources will suffer bad outcomes at once. This explains why large insurance companies can comfortably bear the risks of their clients and act as if they are risk-neutral—at any time, only a small fraction of the clientele is likely to have accidents. On the other hand, people with only one or two major sources of income (e.g., those who rely exclusively on a wage income or self-employed individuals with a single occupation or crop) are likely to be much more sensitive to the associated risks. Hence, wealth and diversification are two key factors that positively affect the ability and willingness to bear risk.

Risk aversion and migration

It is easy enough to apply the theory of risk aversion to migration decisions. Recall that the original Harris–Todaro equilibrium condition [see equation (10.1)] equated the expected wage in the urban sector to the wage in agriculture. Thus we implicitly assumed that all individuals were *risk-neutral*. The fact that their expected income might be coming from an intrinsically uncertain lottery was of no consequence to them. Expected income from a lottery is the same as a guaranteed income, as long as the two have the same value. We now see that if individuals are risk-averse, this equivalence fails to hold.

Let us try to understand what a risk-averse potential migrant would feel if the Harris–Todaro equilibrium condition (10.1) were to hold economy wide. If you have read and absorbed the discussion in the previous subsection, the answer should be very easy. The potential migrant will not migrate. The reason is that he is comparing a *certain* wage in agriculture to an *uncertain* prospect in the urban sector, both of which have the same expected

---

[27] This is often captured by assuming that individuals have *decreasing absolute risk aversion*, where the qualifier "absolute" refers to the fact that we are talking about the same gamble against the background of alternative incomes or wealth. However, matters are more complicated when we refer to a gamble whose amounts bear some given *proportion* to wealth or income. For instance, we could consider a variation on Nazim's story: he stands to gain an amount that equals his wealth if he "wins" and amount equal to that of one-fifth of his wealth if he "loses." Now we are not talking about the same gamble (as wealth changes), but about the same *relative* amount of risk. Whether relative risk aversion increases or decreases in wealth is a more subtle issue. An assumption of constant relative risk aversion is certainly not out of place.

value. However, expected value alone is not good enough for the risk-averse person. He craves insurance as well. Because the urban sector is risky, he will need an expected wage that is *strictly* higher than the wage he receives in agriculture in order to be induced to migrate. Consider Figure 10.13 once again. Note that the risky prospect has the same expected value as the safe prospect, but the expected *utility* of the risky prospect is lower.

Now let us see what effect this has on the allocation of employment across the sectors. Clearly, an economy of risk-averse individuals will exhibit *less* migration than an economy of risk-neutral agents, so in such an economy, the urban informal sector will be somewhat smaller and the agricultural sector will be somewhat larger than that predicted by the Harris–Todaro model. In this equilibrium, the expected wage in the urban sector will exceed that in the informal sector, and the extent of the difference will mirror the degree of risk aversion in the economy.

Social capital and migration

The wage in the agricultural sector is often not a full measure of the payoff to being in agriculture. The rural sector may be relatively attractive in its ability to provide forms of social support, insurance, emergency credit, and use of common property that the anonymity of the urban sector might fail to deliver.[28] The majority of these forms of support rely on two features that a traditional sector might possess in relative abundance: information and low mobility. In the chapters to follow, we will see how these two characteristics assist in the provision of various forms of support, but a quick overview is not out of place here.

Consider insurance: the provision of help in cash, kind, or services if a fellow farmer or laborer is in economic difficulties. Such difficulties may arise, for instance, if a farmer's harvest fails for some "localized" or idiosyncratic reason connected to that farmer, such as pest damage. (A generalized harvest failure means that everyone is in trouble, so the question of insuring one farmer by his compatriots is not relevant.) Now, the damage may have occurred because the farmer was willfully negligent in his application of pesticides or it may have happened because of simple carelessness or events beyond the farmer's control. This is where the role of information comes in. If people know a lot about the daily lives of their neighbors, there is a greater chance that individuals will know just *why* the damage occurred. It is very important that they know this and that the *farmer* knows that they know this, because it is only in this case that genuine insurance is possible. If bad luck cannot be separated from deliberate behavior, insurance will only create incentives for the farmer to cut back on his effort and other inputs, and

---

[28] On these matters, see Das Gupta [1987]. For a model of rural–urban migration that includes these features, see Banerjee and Newman [1997].

the system will break down. Thus information plays a role in the provision of social support.

Low mobility plays a different but equally important role. Much of the social support that we observe is predicated on some notion of *reciprocity*. I help you out today (with a loan, for instance) because I know that you will be around tomorrow to pay back the loan and perhaps help me out if I am in trouble. If this link between present and future is missing, it is very unlikely that my loan or assistance will be forthcoming in the first place. Thus low mobility justifies the expectation that true reciprocity is possible.

Low mobility serves a related function. It enables the imposition of social sanctions on a deviant. Again, consider insurance. If I have been informally participating in an insurance arrangement with my fellow farmers (where we help one another in times of trouble) and I suddenly decide not to offer any help, I can be punished by being denied insurance in the future. On the other hand, if I can just as easily migrate to another village without great personal loss, the threat of this sanction carries little punitive value, and insurance schemes will fall apart.

You can think of low mobility and high information as forms of *social capital*: they permit productivity-enhancing arrangements that would not be possible otherwise. To the extent that the urban sector lacks this social capital, the pace of rural–urban migration will be reduced, because a potential migrant will now factor in the cost of this loss. At the same time, social capital is itself eroded by the act of migration (which serves to increase mobility and lower information). Thus an initial spurt of migration from a region may balloon as social capital is thereby eroded, making it now profitable for others (and still others) to join the exodus.

Migration and family structure

Just as risk aversion, or the existence of social capital in agriculture, reduces the amount of migration compared to the benchmark Harris–Todaro model, there are other variants that predict increased migration. One particularly interesting example requires us to think about the labor absorption curve in agriculture. In the policy options discussed in the preceding text, we thought of this curve as the competitive demand curve for labor in agriculture that was induced by profit maximization, but we already know of situations where this is not the case. If agriculture is largely composed of family farms that share their income, then this curve may be regarded as the *average* product curve. To be sure, it is still downward sloping as long as there is diminishing returns to labor in agriculture.

In this case, the intersection of the two labor absorption curves has a different interpretation. If the industrial sector is capitalistic, then the labor demand curve is the marginal product curve. However, the labor absorption curve in agriculture is the average product curve, as we've already observed, and so the intersection of the two curves does *not* correspond to the point of efficient resource allocation (which is the allocation for which marginal products are equalized). The policy analysis then has to be redone with this change in mind (we omit the extension here).

I mention in passing that the same outcome is also true in cases where there is uncertainty and individuals are risk-averse, or when we take into account the presence of social capital in agriculture (as in the previous section). In each of these cases, the location of the efficient allocation must take these additional features into account.

It is interesting, however, to emphasize a somewhat different aspect of the family farm model. Suppose that potential migrants make their migration decisions in order to maximize *family income*, as opposed to individual income. Let us walk ourselves through the steps of the argument. If all family income is shared, whether earned in the rural or the urban sector, then a potential migrant who seeks to maximize family income will see the expected income in the urban sector as the gain from migration, just as before. However, the loss from migration is different. This individual's contribution to the farm, his *marginal* product, is *not* measured by his stated income on the farm, which as we've seen is equal to the average product. Because average product exceeds marginal product (consult Figure 10.1 once again), a family-income maximizer will migrate *even if expected urban income is less than the agricultural income per person*, as long as the former exceeds the marginal product on the farm. This will yield excessive migration relative to the prediction of the Harris–Todaro equation (see the problem on this subject at the end of the chapter).

10.4. Summary

This chapter contains a detailed study of *intersectoral interaction* in the development process, notably between the agricultural and industrial sectors. The basis for this study is the view that development is rarely distributed evenly across sectors; rather, it typically manifests itself in *structural transformation*—resources move out of one sector to fuel the growth of another.

By far the most important structural transformation that a developing economy goes through is the change from a predominantly rural economy to an industrial economy. This intersectoral movement is typically accompanied by a move from traditional forms to modern forms of organization: an economy in which such forms coexist is often referred to as a *dual economy*.

We began with a description of the urban sector and introduced the notions of *formal sector* and *informal sector*. We then described the basic features of the agricultural sector, and supplemented this with an introduction to the ICRISAT villages, which will reappear at several points in the book. We noted that the transformation from rural to urban is marked by two massive resource flows: the move of labor, and a parallel move of food, to support the basic needs of those individuals no longer engaged in farming. The study of balance in these resource flows is often critical to our understanding of economic development.

A theoretical framework that studies structural transformation is the *Lewis model*, which we turned to next. Development is characterized by an ongoing move of labor and resources from a "traditional sector" to a "modern sector." Ongoing capital accumulation in the modern sector provides the fuel for sustained transfers. Lewis argued that the traditional sector is characterized by *surplus labor* (a situation in which labor can be removed without loss in output). In principle, this permits, industrial development *with unlimited supplies of labor*, at least until the surplus-labor phase comes to an end.

The part of Lewis's model that deals with industrial accumulation is pretty standard, so we focused on the traditional sector. We studied, first, what surplus labor means and what forms of economic organization permit it to exist. A narrow definition of a surplus labor situation is simply one in which the physical marginal product of labor is equal to zero. However, this state of affairs cannot persist under a capitalist organization that pays a positive wage, so the concept of surplus labor naturally led to a discussion of economic organization in the traditional sector. Typically, traditional forms of organization are characterized by income sharing (or payment according to *average* product), and this allows family farms to pay positive "wages" even when the marginal product of labor is close to zero. This form of organization is of interest in itself, with or without surplus labor.

We then returned to surplus labor per se and introduced two extensions, one of which is *disguised unemployment*, a situation in which the marginal product of labor is positive but smaller than the going wage. We argued that this is just as relevant a concept as surplus labor (and a generalization of it): both concepts signal inefficiency in the intersectoral allocation of labor resources. The second extension carefully distinguished between the notions of surplus *laborers* and surplus labor.

We then integrated the traditional and the modern sectors into one interactive model. It turned out that the supply of labor to industry was perfectly elastic in the surplus-labor phase, but began to rise thereafter as the available food surplus per capita began to shrink and the *terms of trade* between agriculture and industry turned against industry. The model brings out a fundamental tension between agricultural and industrial development: industrialists like to keep agricultural prices low, because that ensures a low wage bill. On the other hand, a policy that keeps agricultural prices low has disincentive effects on agriculture and can strangle industrial development in the longer run.

This discussion led to the theme of *agricultural taxation*: how should a government that is interested in promoting industry deal with agriculture? Should it tax agriculture as much as possible, thus ensuring a large food surplus in the short to medium run, or should it invest in agriculture and look to possible long-run gains? The great debate on this subject that took place in the Soviet Union in the 1920s is still relevant today, and we discussed this briefly.

Related to agricultural taxation is the question of agricultural *pricing policy*: price support programs, subsidies to inputs such as water, electricity, and fertilizer, and (international) exchange rate policy. There is evidence from China and other countries that agricultural output reacts strongly to price incentives, and this suggests that a more liberal attitude to food prices in the short run may pay off in the longer run.

To be sure, all of these arguments rely on the premise that for economic or political reasons, free trade in food grains is problematic. Food is a special commodity: governments often desire self-sufficiency in food grains for political reasons. To the extent that an economy seeks to produce its own food supply, the considerations here are of great relevance. As economists we might *wish* that countries did not behave in this way, but pragmatic considerations of reality force us to treat the question of internal food supply as an issue of great importance.

Finally, we turned to an explicit consideration of the other resource flow involved in structural transformation: the movement of labor. We studied rural–urban migration in the framework of the *Harris–Todaro model*—a theoretical framework in which formal-sector wages have lower bounds or floors, whereas informal and agricultural wages are flexible. This thesis leads to a view of migration equilibrium in which the formal sector is characterized by an excess supply of labor, with the excess spilling over into the informal urban sector or manifesting itself in the form of open unemployment. Thus it is not wages that are equalized across sectors, but the *expectation* of wages: in the Harris–Todaro equilibrium, the average of various urban wages *weighted by the probability of employment in formal and informal sectors* is equal to the agricultural wage. This model endogenously delivers a prediction for the size of the urban informal sector and allows us to examine how different policies affect this sector. Of special interest is the so-called *Todaro paradox*, in which an expansion of formal employment leads to an enlargement of the informal sector as fresh migrants from the rural sector swarm into the urban sector response to the policy.

Policies that move the economy toward an efficient labor allocation were also considered: among them are *migration restrictions* and *wage subsidies*. Finally, we studied various extensions of the Harris–Todaro model. The extensions include a treatment of *risk aversion* (indeed, this chapter introduces this important concept which we will use later), a discussion of *social capital* in the traditional sector, and finally, the role of family structure in rural–urban migration.

Exercises

■ (1) Review the concepts of formal and informal sectors. Explain why labor might receive better treatment (in pay or conditions of work) in the formal sector. How do you think such differentials persist? Why can't informal sector workers simply enter the formal sector by offering to work on terms that undercut existing formal-sector workers?

■ (2) Describe the two fundamental resource flows that link the agricultural sector with the industrial sector. Discuss the market forces that are relevant to the magnitudes of these flows.

■ (3) Review the Lewis model of economic development. In particular, discuss the following concepts: agricultural surplus, average agricultural surplus, surplus labor, disguised unemployment, family farming, capitalist farming, and the three phases of development in the Lewis model.

■ (4) (a) Consider a family farm that is in the surplus labor phase. Now suppose that some members migrate to work elsewhere. Describe what happens to the average income of the family farm.

(b) Reconcile your observation with the assertion that the supply curve is perfectly elastic (or flat) in the surplus labor phase of development. In other words, describe when the observation in (a) is consistent with the observation in this paragraph.

■ (5) Present arguments why, all other things being the same, the industrial supply curve of labor is steeper, when the economy is closer to minimum subsistence to begin with. If food can be freely traded on the world market, do you anticipate that the supply curve will be flatter or steeper? Justify your answer.

■ (6) Taxes on industrial profits will leave less room for capital accumulation and slow down the rate of growth. Do workers already employed in the industrial sector have an incentive to lobby for such taxes, the proceeds of which are transferred to them in the form of additional benefits? Show that the answer to this question depends, among other things, on the slope of the labor supply curve to industry. Argue, in particular, that if the supply curve is horizontal (as in phase 1 of the Lewis model), the tendency for already-employed workers to vote for industrial taxation will be higher.

■ (7) Consider a labor surplus economy producing a single output, which can be consumed (as food) or invested (as capital). Labor, once employed, must be paid a fixed wage of w which is fully consumed. All surpluses from production are reinvested.

(a) Draw a diagram showing how output is distributed between consumption and reinvestment, for some chosen level of employment. Show the profit-maximizing employment level: call it L^*.

(b) Reinvested surplus raises consumption tomorrow. Suppose that a social planner cares about consumption today *and* consumption tomorrow. Show that she will always wish to choose an employment level not less than L^*.

(c) Suppose that the planner wishes to employ $\hat{L}$ units of labor, where $\hat{L} > L^*$. Carefully describe a subsidy scheme to profit maximizing employers that will make them choose this level of employment.

■ (8) Pim and her three sisters own a small farm in the agricultural sector of the land of Grim. They work equally hard, and the value of their output measured in the local currency, *nice*, is 4,000 nice, which they divide equally. The urban sector of Grim has two kinds of jobs. There are informal jobs which *anybody can get*, which pay 500 nice, and there are formal jobs which pay 1,200 nice. The probability of getting these jobs depends on the proportion of such jobs to the urban labor force, exactly as in the Harris–Todaro model.

(a) Assume that Pim compares her *own* expected returns in the two sectors and there are no costs of migration. Calculate the threshold proportion of formal jobs to urban labor force that will *just* deter Pim from migrating.

(b) The full production function on Pim's farm is given in the following table.

Number working on farm	Output (in nice)
One sister	1,500
Two sisters	2,500
Three sisters	3,300
Four sisters	4,000

Suppose that Pim and her sisters seek to maximize their *total family income*, instead of Pim simply acting to maximize her own. Assume that the threshold proportion that you derived in (a) *actually does* prevails in the urban sector. Now prove that Pim will migrate.

(c) Will any of Pim's sisters *also* wish to migrate?

(d) Provide a brief description that uses your economic intuition to contrast cases (a) and (b).

■ (9) A farm household in rural Mexico consists of five adult brothers and no other dependents. Total annual income depends on the number of brothers working on the farm through the year and is given by the following schedule:

Number of brothers	1	2	3	4	5
Total farm output (in $)	1,000	1,800	2,400	2,800	3,000

Each brother, at the beginning of the year, can decide to migrate to Mexico City, where a typical job, commensurate with his skills, pays $1,300 per annum, but the unemployment rate is as high as 50%. A person who migrates to the city cannot come back and work on the farm that year. Furthermore, all city jobs are temporary one-year appointments. Also assume, for all questions that follow, that the brothers are risk-neutral and there is no difference in the cost of living between the city and the countryside. Now consider three different scenarios.

(a) Suppose the family is completely individualistic: those brothers who work on the farm share the farm income equally among themselves. There are no remittances to or from any family member who goes to the city. Find the number of brothers who will migrate.

(b) Now suppose the family is completely altruistic: the total family income, whether from a city job or from the farm, is pooled and shared equally. How many brothers will this family send off to Mexico City to look for jobs?

(c) Here is a third possibility. Those brothers who migrate to the city become selfish and never send home any remittances, even if they are employed (maybe those in the countryside have no way to verify whether their brothers in the city have a job). However, the family sits down and makes the following arrangement: those brothers who try out their luck in the city will each be sent $200 a year from the farm income, to insure against possible joblessness (assume that this contract is always honored). Find how many brothers will decide to migrate. (Assume that if a brother is indifferent between migrating and not migrating, he does migrate.)

(d) Compare the numbers in parts (a)–(c). In light of the comparison, discuss the following assertion. "The extent of rural urban migration depends, *ceteris paribus*, on the nature and degree of altruistic links within families."

■ (10) Are the following statements true, false or uncertain? Provide a brief explanation to back up your answer.

(a) In the dual economy model, the phase of disguised unemployment must be associated with a horizontal supply curve of industrial labor.

(b) A low or moderate inequality of land holdings should slow down the pace of rural–urban migration.

(c) Migration restrictions alone lead to too many people in the informal sector.

(d) In the Harris–Todaro model, an increase in the formal sector labor demand at a fixed wage rate *must* lower the percentage of people in the informal sector, as a fraction of the urban labor force.

(e) If governments cannot tax agriculture, the supply curve of labor to industry in the Lewis model is always upward sloping.

■ (11) In the 1950s, facing massive unemployment in the cities (much of it disguised in the informal sector), the Kenyan government embarked on a "Keynesian" policy of creating new urban jobs through public investment. By many accounts, the size of the informal sector in Kenya went up instead of dropping in the months that followed. Give an economic explanation of this phenomenon, using the Harris–Todaro model.

■ (12) Carefully review the different migration policies studied in this chapter. Explain under what circumstances the flexible equilibrium allocation is the efficient allocation and how different policies situate themselves relative to the efficient allocation.

■ (13) (a) Calculate the expected values of the following lotteries: (i) 100 with probability 0.4 and 200 with probability 0.5; (ii) 100 with probability p and 200 with probability $1 - p$ (evaluate the amount as p varies between 0 and 1: does this make sense?); (iii) 100 with probability p and if this does not happen (which is the case with probability $1 - p$), then another lottery where you get 50 with probability q and 200 with probability $1 - q$; (iv) 100 with probability p, 200 with probability q, 300 with probability r, and nothing with probability $1 - p - q - r$.

(b) Suppose that you are asked to participate in a lottery where you get 1,000 with probability 0.1 and 200 otherwise. If you are risk-neutral, what is the maximum you would pay to enter the lottery? Would you be willing to pay more if you were risk-averse? Now suppose that the probability of winning is unknown. If you are risk-averse and willing to pay 600 to enter the lottery, what must be the *minimum* probability of winning 1,000?

■ (14) Suppose that two individuals A and B meet and undertake a joint project in which the returns are 1,000 with probability 0.5, and 2,000 otherwise. They are negotiating an agreement regarding the division of the returns. That is they decide on a division rule *before* the project comes to fruition and they know what the outcome is. An example is: if the outcome is 1,000, then *A* pays 20 to *B*, and *B* gets 1,200. If it is 2,000, then they split it 1,000–1,000.

Prove that if *A* is risk-averse and *B* is risk-neutral, then any efficient division rule will give the *same* amount to *A* irrespective of project outcome and *B* will bear all the risk. (Note: The division rule is efficient in the sense that no other rule exists in which *both* parties enjoy higher ex ante expected utility.)

Chapter 11

Markets in Agriculture: An Introduction

11.1. Introduction

The previous chapter described how rural and urban sectors interact in the process of development. The goal of the next few chapters is to look closely at the markets and institutions that form the rural sector and deeply influence the lives of individuals who live in developing countries. In particular, we will study the markets for land, labor, credit, and insurance. Although we emphasize rural markets, at several points the discussion will apply equally well to informal markets in the urban sector.

The study of rural organization is interesting from another perspective. Throughout this book, we stress the importance of information, incentives, and the existence of limits to contracts. These three features acquire importance in the context of missing or imperfect markets—the essential ingredient that complicates real economies. If all markets were perfect, we would only have to study supply and demand carefully, and be done with it.

An essential property of imperfect markets is that they are contagious: a market failure in some sector can lead to problems in other markets. The markets that we study in the chapters to follow are particularly interrelated, and often we discuss the lack of efficiency in one of these areas by invoking imperfections in another. This sort of reasoning will be new to some of you, because we have been brought up on a steady diet of perfect competition, and only recently has this focus started to change, at least in textbooks. (To be sure, competitive paradigm is still very useful, because it helps us to identify imperfections as departures from that paradigm.)

This short chapter serves as an introduction to the sort of world we are going to enter by providing an overview and by putting forward several examples that will fix perspectives. From the viewpoint of development economics, missing or imperfect markets represent a crucial step in our understanding of the economic problems of developing countries. They also lie at the heart of *informal institutions*, which are reactions to the market loopholes that cannot be filled because of legal, informational, or incentive constraints.

11.2. *Some examples*

The basic ideas that drive our analysis are very simple. Lack of information, the need to provide appropriate incentives, and limits to contractual enforcement create efficiency failures. Often, an unequal distribution of income or wealth exacerbates these failures. We study these in concrete situations. Consider several examples.

Information: Unobserved actions

Suppose that you are a landlord who is leasing out land to a tenant. You expect your tenant to put some minimal effort into the land. Ideally, you write this into a contract: "our agreement requires that you work ten hours a day, with a break for meals." However, such clauses are useless if, say, you are an absentee landlord who lives in the city and you cannot observe what the tenant is up to. However, you could respond, "I don't *need* to see how hard the tenant is working. I can tell just by looking at what he produces." Can you? Many factors determine output: the hardworking or lazy tenant, the rains, crop damage caused by pests, and so on. How can you be sure that low output is due to laziness rather than bad luck? Thus your contracts must be suitably limited: the incomplete market here stems from lack of observability. As we will see, this has deep implications for the efficiency of landlord–tenant relationships. The problems of unobserved action lead to what is known as *moral hazard*—the danger that an agent will take actions in his interest and not in yours—and are fundamental to the study of contracts.[1]

Information: Unobserved types

A nongovernment organization (NGO) is lending to poor farmers. Although the NGO is not necessarily driven by profits, it would like to cover its costs of lending. The problem is that some borrowers are intrinsically bad risks, but the NGO cannot spot this by looking at a borrower's face and, moreover, past records are misleading or nonexistent. What can the NGO do?

---

[1] Let's continue with the landlord–tenant example. Suppose that you can indeed observe the tenant's effort perfectly. Can you now specify effort levels in a contract? The answer is: not always. For the contract to be enforced, a third party such as a court must be able to *verify* that a claim of low effort is indeed true, and such verifiability may be impossible. This sort of imperfection limits contracts as well, and may have odd implications. One of them is that you may now want to build up long-term relationships with the tenant, using your information about past effort to design a new contract in the future with implicit rewards and punishments attached to observed performance. In contrast, the pure theory of competitive markets would be insensitive to these factors: whether you continue with a new tenant or with the old one is of no consequence in that theory.

Two possibilities are to charge an interest-rate premium on the loan or to require suitable collateral. However, high interest rates will discourage good borrowers, whom the NGO would like to reach, and will not prevent bad borrowers from defaulting (indeed, it will further encourage them to do so). Because farmers are poor, they may not be able to put up collateral. An innovative solution is to lend to groups of four or five borrowers, and cut off loans if any one member of the group defaults. If farmers know more than the NGO does regarding the characteristics of their fellow farmers, they will self-select into "safe groups." Thus group lending is a response to incomplete information.

Incentives: Conflict with insurance

The moral hazard problem outlined in the first example stems from limited information. Thus contracts have to be designed to provide appropriate incentives. For instance, if a large employer hires labor and is unable to monitor the laborer's activities, he might offer a contract that stipulates the payment of an attractive wage unless (direct or indirect) evidence accumulates regarding shirking; then the laborer will be fired. Note that "evidence" may be indirect and sometimes inaccurate; for example, the crop may be poor because of insufficient rain, not the laborer's failure to apply adequate fertilizer. It follows that contracts based on indirect evidence create uncertainty for economic agents who dislike uncertainty, and this lack of insurance constitutes an inefficiency. However, it is an inefficiency that the employer can do little about: to provide appropriate incentives he must pay different amounts for success and failure, even though these concepts may be loosely linked to the efforts of the laborer.

Incentives: Short-term contracts

The abhorrent tradition of slavery had a perversely beneficial by-product. Because employers could *own* slaves, they treated slaves as a capital good and invested in them, particularly in the spheres of nutrition and health (see Chapter 8). Contrast this with a more enlightened world in which no employer has unlimited rights over his employees: an employee can legally break a contract at any time. In consequence, employers may have little incentive to invest in their employees in the form of adequate nutrition or on-the-job training. In poor societies, this can lead to a state of affairs in which an entire population of workers is undernourished because of low wages, and this in turn feeds back on overall economic efficiency. In the end, both employers and employees may be worse off (though to be sure, this is not a call to reinstitute slavery!).

Enforcement: Limited liability

Suppose that you are a moneylender advancing a loan. You know that the loan will be used in an investment project that is risky. If it pays off, you will get your money back with interest, but if it does not, you will get nothing. Why nothing? Well, one reason may be that the borrower is poor and cannot pay out of past wealth because he has little or none. This very natural *limited liability* constraint can have sharp implications: borrowers who are thus insulated may want to overinvest in risky projects, because in effect, you bear the downside risk, not them. One outcome may be *credit rationing*, in which the standard competitive assumption that borrowers can get all the loans they want at the going rate of interest is violated. You do not raise loan levels because you are afraid of losing more if the project collapses, yet you are afraid to raise interest rates, because in this way you attract the more risky borrowers.

Enforcement: Breaking agreements

A group of poor farmers may seek to insure one another against fluctuations in their own output. Farmer *A* may transfer money to farmer *B* when *A* has a good harvest and *B* does not. If both *A* and *B* honor this scheme, then both could be better off, but how is this mutual insurance scheme to be enforced when it comes *B*'s turn to pay (after having enjoyed, say, a couple of years of transfers) and he does not? Courts of law to enforce such agreements may be nonexistent (or incapable of suitable verification). Informal insurance must then rest on an implicit nexus of social agreement, coupled with the sanction and disciplining of deviators from the agreement. Central to such a nexus is the flow of information. It must be possible to make others reliably aware of one person's "misbehavior."

   Much of what we see in these settings becomes entirely explicable once we understand that informal institutions are spontaneous creatures of the need to account for informational failures, or the need to provide adequate incentives to economic agents, or the need to make sure that contracts that cannot be enforced by law are somehow enforced by substitute arrangements. The study of informal institutions will help us resolve or at least understand some apparently puzzling observations. For instance:

Why do landlords often ask for a share of their tenant's crop instead of a fixed payment, which would save them the task of verifying and measuring output?

Why might an indebted tenant not be forced to give up his land to a landlord to whom he owes money?

Why do some moneylenders advance loans at low, even zero rates of interest?

Why are similar laborers given different contractual packages with different values?

To whet your appetite a bit more, here is an interesting example of an informal institution from West Africa.

Labor Teams and Tournaments in Rural West Africa

Incentives are fundamental to the institution of hired labor. They cut across diverse settings and echelons—from factories to farms, from the topmost managerial levels to the lower rungs of the workshop or the assembly line. Put simply, the problem is this: when ownership and labor are separated, the incentive to work hard is subdued; work tends to become lax and careless rather than energetic and creative. A multitude of labor market institutions and practices can be understood as attempts to overcome this fundamental problem of incentive and motivation of workers.

In labor-intensive agriculture, the problem is pronounced. Negligence in crucial tasks, such as tilling and planting, can cause considerable damage and slowdown, and consequently lower productivity. Underdeveloped agriculture has traditionally dealt with this problem in a number of different ways.

In rural West Africa, a unique arrangement has developed—an arrangement whose parallel can be found elsewhere only in the upper levels of corporate management, rather than in the organization of farm labor.[2] This arrangement consists of two features: the organization of laborers into teams, where payments depend on *team performance*, and the system of distributing remuneration *within* the team in accordance with *relative performance*. It is as if team members compete with each other in a tournament to take home prizes that depend on their *rank* in that tournament in terms of job performance. Workers who produce more at the end of the day rank higher and get better prizes.

Labor teams and work cooperatives, in fact, have a long historical tradition in West Africa. They are more than a century old in Central Benin, where they are referred to as *adjolou* or *donkpe*. A *donkpe* usually consists of all young men in a village, organized under a special chief (known as the *donkpegan*), working as a team in such tasks as preparing fields or building houses. Services of the group are rendered to the members' families in turn and can also be hired by outsiders for a fee. The *donkpe* also provides invaluable services in the provision of public utilities, such as the construction of roads.

Groupings of workers are not a uniquely African product, to be sure. Large armies of slaves were organized into similar "work gangs" on the farms of the southern United States before the Civil War. Members of a gang were divided into subgroups, and to each subgroup was assigned a specific task, for example, plowing, harrowing, or raking. These tasks followed a natural sequence, and thus the job done by one group built up a momentum and created a pressure on the next, leading to an intense rhythmic pace of work similar to that induced by the modern assembly

---

[2] See Houantchekon [1994], from which much of the material for this box is drawn.

line. A worker or group that performed relatively slowly would soon disrupt a chain process and would be detected, rebuked, and punished. Such specialization and interdependence possible in large work groups made the larger plantations, working with slave armies, much more productive than the smaller ones, which relied on independent, isolated workers. Fogel and Engerman, [1974] described the process as follows:

> The intensity of the pace of these gangs was maintained in three ways:
>
> First, by choosing as the ploughmen and harrowers who led off the planting operation the strongest and ablest hands.
>
> Second, by the interdependence of each type of hand on the other . . . this interdependence generated a pressure on all those who worked in the gang to keep up with the pace of the leaders.
>
> Third, by assigning drivers or foremen who exhorted the leaders, threatened the laggards, and did whatever was necessary to maintain the quality and pace of each gang's labor.

Fogel and Engerman estimated that for application of the same amount of labor, land, and capital, the average southern farm could produce 35% more output than the average northern farm, and much of the excess was attributed to the particular form of organizing labor in the South. Even among southern farms, those that relied on slave labor (the plantations which operated on a large scale and relied on worker armies were almost invariably slave farms) were 28% more productive than those that hired free labor. The utter outrage of slavery aside, this account contains important insights into the possible superiority of labor teams over more individualistic organizations, for reasons primarily related to the physical and sequential nature of the act of cultivation.

Productivity can also be enhanced through teams by means of monetary incentives. In modern day West Africa, contracts often stipulate a basic wage for team members and an output or job target. Failure to attain the target within the stipulated time frame leads to a penalty imposed on the team. The specification of a *team target* introduces an element of peer monitoring within the team: members have an incentive to prevent shirking of fellow members to avoid incurring the penalty. In this aspect, team work is similar to group lending (see the second example earlier in this chapter and our analysis of the Bangladesh Grameen Bank in Chapter 14). Sanctions within teams are illustrated by the stiff fines that most teams impose on members for absenteeism: in the ethnic group of *Kpelle* in Liberia, fines are $5 for each day of absenteeism and $2 for being late to work, whereas the daily wage rate is between 50¢ and $1.

The productivity of teams is further e nhanced through tournaments, which induce team members to compete vigorously in an attempt to outperform others and pocket the bonus. Payment of bonuses to induce greater work effort is, of course, not uncommon. However, the tournament aspect makes the foregoing scheme special, because the bonus depends not on *absolute* but on *relative* performance. The advantage of the system is that the bonus has to be paid only to one member, but the incentive that it provides to *every* worker can be quite strong.

The details of tournaments differ from one ethnic group to another. In the Liberian ethnic group *Kpelle*, the farm is divided into plots and the team is divided into groups of two. Each group is then assigned to a plot, and work on various plots starts simultaneously. The group to finish first wins the tournament. In Central Benin, on the other hand, the team works collectively and rhythmically for a major initial part of the work day, sustaining a fast pace of work through the kind of interdependence that was exploited in slave-operated farms in the antebellum South. The tournament is announced two hours before the working day ends, leading to a flurry of activity, in which the winner is decided on the basis of the number of rows cleared, cleaned, or plowed. Irrespective of specific forms, a common theme emerges: competition between members can vastly enhance overall team productivity and increase its value to employers.

11.3. Land, labor, capital, and credit

11.3.1. Land and labor

Imagine an agricultural society with several individuals who make their living in it. To put matters in the starkest way possible, suppose that agricultural production is carried out by means of only two inputs: land and labor. Very soon we will extend the story to include more inputs of production, as well as a credit market.

Now, land and labor are important assets in the economy, and different people presumably own different amounts of these assets. Just as we conceived of an income distribution (see Chapter 6), we may think of a *land distribution*, where we replace pesos of income with acres of land. Typically, the distribution of land is unequal: large plots of land are often concentrated in the hands of a few, whereas a majority of individuals have little or no land at all. Landowners with small plots are often called small holders or small farmers, whereas people with no land at all are the landless.

Similarly, there is a distribution of labor endowments. A little introspection reveals that the distribution of land holdings is likely to be far more unequal than the distribution of labor endowments. Hence, we may expect that in the absence of any sort of input market, families are left to cultivate their land with very different labor–land ratios: small holders have excessive family labor, whereas owners of huge tracts of land have to leave most of their holdings uncultivated for want of labor.

You will therefore not be surprised to learn that a market for inputs is likely to emerge under these circumstances. Either individuals with excess labor will seek employment with large landowners, or land will be leased (or sold) to small holders, or both.

The labor market will typically function with large farmers who hire the labor of those with little or no land for a wage. Under this scenario, the agricultural market clears by allocating labor from those who have little land to those who have a lot. The end result looks like a setting in which large plantations hire large amounts of labor and this labor is monitored by hired supervisors or the owner(s) of the farm.

The land (rental) market typically works with tracts of land leased from landlords to tenants in exchange for rent or perhaps a share of the crop. Under this scenario, the end result is a relatively equal *operational* distribution of land, with many tenants.

It won't be a surprise to learn that the real world displays a bit of both scenarios. In almost all agrarian societies, we can observe a fair amount of land rentals and activity in the labor market as well. However, if we've been brought up on the competitive markets diet, this might be a bit puzzling. Why do we need *both* markets to function when it seems that one is a perfect substitute for the other? Is it not the case that labor "moving" to join land for a wage is the same as land "moving" to join labor for a rent?

Indeed, you would be perfectly justified in raising this question if markets were perfectly competitive, if production exhibited constant returns to scale, and there were no uncertainty. For instance, a labor market would generate equilibrium wages to labor. What's left would be rent to the landlord. By constant returns to scale, all rents per acre must be identical across landlords.[3] Now a tenancy contract for the same level of rent must yield, as a residual, the same income as the equilibrium wage to a laborer.

Matters are different if the foregoing conditions do not hold. For instance, if there is some increasing returns to scale (over a range at least), land will be rented in large chunks and the labor market will also be needed to allocate labor to the farmers of these large tracts of land. Similarly, in the presence of uncertainty, the operation of a single market may not be able to distribute the realization of random shocks in some efficient way over the population of landowners and laborers. Consider the following example.

An insurance problem in land rentals

Suppose that you are leasing out your land to a poor tenant. He will cultivate the land and pay you a fixed rent for its use every year. Now, if the output from the land were perfectly certain, you could raise the rent until the money value of what the tenant was receiving from you (output value minus rent) was equal to whatever the tenant could get in his next best alternative. As we will see in Chapter 12, this sort of fixed rent arrangement would be efficient

---

[3] With constant returns to scale, we can use per-acre production functions. Once the wage rate is known, the marginal product of labor is determined and so is the marginal product of land, which must be the (shadow) rental rate.

under these circumstances, and although there is a cost to you (in the sense that you have to compensate the tenant for his opportunity cost), there isn't any "transaction cost" over and above this amount.

On the other hand, consider the more realistic situation where the output from the land is uncertain. If the tenant is poor and risk-averse, this uncertainty has a cost *in addition to* the opportunity cost of the tenant.[4] You will have to compensate the tenant for this cost. This can be done in many ways. For this example, it is enough to think that you will have to lower the rent that you can charge the tenant. This extra reduction, to compensate for the tenant's risk aversion, typifies a transaction cost in the rental market for land.

Possibly more important than these arguments, and a fact that will be central to our discussions, is that both land and labor markets have intrinsic incentive problems, and it is difficult to rely exclusively on any one of them. As we will see in Chapter 12, there are limitations to what can be achieved by tenancy contracts in the presence of incentive constraints. Similarly, the hiring of labor poses an incentive problem, as the following example shows.

An incentive problem in the labor market

Instead of leasing out your excess land, you decide to cultivate it yourself with the help of hired labor. Labor is available at its opportunity cost, which is just the going wage rate in the village or region. Now, if labor can be costlessly supervised, then there are no additional transaction costs and the labor contract is efficient. However, what if supervision is costly? In that case you must hire supervisors to adequately monitor labor or you must somehow provide laborers with an incentive to work. In the former case, the wages paid to supervisors (and perhaps the cost of supervising *them* as well!) are a measure of the transaction costs. In the latter case, the extra income premium paid to workers as an incentive would be the appropriate measure; more on this later.

The point of the two examples should be clear. As soon as we move away from the introductory textbook story of perfect markets, we run into transaction costs in several different markets. Whether a society exhibits a preponderance of land transactions or labor transactions therefore depends crucially on the relative magnitude of these costs.

Let us see if we can use these simple ideas to say something about the incidence of tenancy in economies with varying degrees of inequality in land holdings. Begin with the case where land is perfectly equally distributed. In

---

[4] This is an inefficiency that could have been avoided if insurance markets were perfect, so that the uncertainty, in effect, is taken away. The imperfection of insurance markets is central to this story.

such a case there should be relatively little mismatch between endowments of land and endowments of labor. Of course, different families may still have different family sizes, and this will serve as an impetus for transactions in land and labor, but on the whole, we would certainly expect the incidence of tenancy, as well as labor market activity, to be low.

This is the state of affairs in many African economies, as well as in societies where successful land reforms have occurred. Leading examples of the latter are Taiwan and Korea.

Now suppose that we conceive of greater and greater inequalities in land holdings. Picture in your mind a progressive "bowing out" of the Lorenz curve for land distribution. Now systematic discrepancies between labor endowments and land endowments will arise. These discrepancies must be resolved by an increase in labor and/or land rental market activity. Farmers with more land relative to their endowment of family labor might consider farming the extra land with the use of hired labor. Alternatively, they might want to lease out the extra land to a tenant. The chosen alternative will depend on relative transaction costs in the two markets. In many situations, it will not be worthwhile to introduce a monitoring scheme for labor (such as the hiring of supervisors) unless a large number of laborers are to be hired. It may be better to simply incur the transaction costs associated with land leasing, which do not have this element of lumpiness of fixed costs to them. Thus tenancy may rise as the inequality in land holdings becomes moderately unequal. This situation is found in the developing countries of South and Southeast Asia, as well as in some parts of Latin America.

This description is to be contrasted with situations of high inequality in land holdings, in which some farmers may hire so much labor that it pays to bear the fixed supervision costs. In such situations tenancy may be minimal or it may be *reversed*, with small landowners renting out to big landowners who are in a better position to bear the fixed costs of supervision. At any rate, very large farmers are likely to be large employers who farm their own land with the use of hired labor. There may still be a minimal amount of land under tenancy, but this is more likely to come from relatively smaller farmers. Agriculture in many Latin American countries reflects this kind of situation.

The use of land and labor markets therefore depends on the costs of market operation for each of these inputs. In the chapters that follow, we shall study these costs in greater detail.

11.3.2. Capital and credit

The argument so far has general features that both illuminate and qualify the foregoing discussion. The general idea is that markets for certain inputs spring up when there is some imbalance in the *ownership holdings* of those inputs. Thus if land is very unequally held while endowments of labor are relatively equal, we would expect institutions to emerge that equalize the actual use of these endowments. These are the land and labor markets that we will discuss in the chapters to come.

Now, our view of the rural economy as characterized by agricultural use of labor and land is overly simplistic in a number of ways. The most of important of these can be lumped under a single heading: the existence of other agricultural inputs that might determine the functioning of the market for land and labor. For instance, a critical input is animal power. Then the ownership of bullocks becomes relevant. With this mental extension, we now have three sets of inputs: land, labor, and bullock power. Typically, the ownership of these three inputs will be distributed differently among the population. The use of input markets brings the ratios of these inputs into balance with one another, so that they can be used in an efficient way for cultivation. If one of these markets fails quite dramatically, the other two will have to compensate somehow. The rental market for animal power, which functions badly if it functions at all, is particularly vulnerable. There are two main reasons for this market failure: (1) rented animals may be overworked or otherwise mistreated, because the renter has no stake in these animals as a capital good and will therefore try to maximize current services and (2) animals are often used in time-bound operations, so that everybody in a village needs bullock power at the same time. Now if the bullock market fails, the other two inputs must kick in, and so it is not surprising to find that the operational distribution of land often follows the ownership distribution of bullocks. We can use this observation to qualify the analysis of the previous section. Instead of land being leased from land-rich families to land-poor families, the opposite might happen. Families with sizable bullock holdings will be in a position to lease land *and* hire labor.

At this point yet another market must make an appearance. This is the market for credit or capital. Notice that if this market is functioning smoothly, much of the earlier discussion becomes irrelevant. Bullocks, other inputs, and indeed land should all be possible to acquire, provided that their acquisition is profitable. A perfect credit market will make the necessary funds available, and our story of markets working to bring endowments into operational line can be largely dispensed with. However, if the credit market fails, the other markets will have to adjust accordingly. For instance, without access to working capital (which entails the purchase of other inputs such as fertilizer or pesticides), a farmer may be constrained to lease out part or even all of his land *and his labor as well*. In other words, the lack of a capital market might create a situation in which land *and* labor flow from those who have no access to capital to those who do.

In this increasing complexity it is best to keep a single rule of thumb in mind: the more flexible markets will attempt to adjust for the failings of the less flexible markets, bringing the "flexible" inputs into line with the "inflexible" ones. So, for instance, in a situation of restricted credit, land and labor markets are both likely to funnel inputs in the direction of those who have access to capital equipment or bullocks. Alternatively, if some of the capital equipment (say threshers) can be easily rented, then the "equipment rental" market will be relatively active. We see then that our simplistic story with just land and labor as inputs must be greatly qualified by the functioning of the credit market.

With this overview in mind, we now turn to a study of various factor markets.

Chapter 12

Land

12.1. Introduction

As explained in Chapter 11, an economy can react to an unequal distribution of land in a variety of ways. The land market can open up, with plots rented out or sold from landowners to those with a relative abundance of labor or other inputs of production (including access to credit markets). Alternatively, the labor market can become active, with hired labor working on the larger plots of land. We have already discussed how different considerations dictate the relative levels of activity in these two markets. In this chapter, we concentrate on the market for land.

A proper functioning of the land market is very important for the overall development of the economy. If land is held unequally and many individuals fail to obtain access to it, they are likely to leave agriculture in search of a less precarious source of living. As discussed in Chapter 10, this can lead to a situation in which large numbers of migrants crowd the cities—a situation that can be politically, environmentally, and economically unpalatable.

Quite apart from political acceptability, there is the narrower question of *economic* efficiency in agriculture. Input markets such as the land market exist to bring the ratios of various inputs into line for efficient production. Do land markets serve this purpose or are they limited in their operation?

This chapter asks the following questions:

(1) How does the land rental market deal with substantial inequalities in the ownership of land? What are the main types of tenancy and how does the economic environment determine the form of the land rental contract?

(2) Are land rentals efficient? If not, which sorts of economic environments are more likely to create inefficiency?

(3) At a broader level, is inequality of ownership inefficient? Are small farms more productive than large farms?

(4) If the answer to question 3 is indeed yes, why don't we see frequent sales of land from rich to poor? What is the role of land reform?

12.2. Ownership and tenancy

Table 12.1 shows how unequal the distributions of land are in the countries of Asia and Latin America. A huge percentage of the rural population is either landless or owns very small plots of land, in contrast with a small fraction of the population who own very large quantities of land. Look at the Gini coefficients of land distribution, for example. They are very high compared to corresponding estimates of the inequality in income distributions (see Chapter 6).

Although there is substantial inequality in Asia, land inequalities in Latin America are higher by an order of magnitude. But it is also true that average landholdings are smaller in Asia and the rural population density is very much higher, which perhaps explains, to some extent, why there are limits to inequality. After all, there is some lower bound to the smallest farm size that can be profitably used in cultivation. Latin American levels of inequality in Asia would surely drive the smallest plots to sizes that are just not feasible to cultivate. In this sense, a high population density places limits on inequality.

Using somewhat more recent data, Figure 12.1 plots Lorenz curves for land inequality in two Asian countries (India and Thailand) and two Latin

Table 12.1. Ownership distribution of farms and farmland in Asia and Latin America in the early 1970s.

Country	Average operational farm size (hectares)	Percentage of farms and farmland				Gini coefficient of land concentration
		Below 5 hectares		Above 50 hectares		
		Farms	Area	Farms	Area	
Asia						
Bangladesh	1.6	90.6	67.6	n.a.	n.a.	0.42
India	2.3	88.7	46.7	0.1	3.7	0.62
Indonesia	1.1	97.9	68.7	0	13.6	0.56
Nepal	1.0	97.2	72.1	0	0.8	0.56
Philippines	3.6	84.4	47.8	0.2	13.9	
Thailand	3.7	72.3	39.4	0	0.9	0.45
Latin America						
Brazil	59.7	36.8	1.3	16.3	84.6	0.84
Costa Rica	38.1	48.9	1.9	14.5	79.7	0.82
Colombia	26.3	59.6	3.7	8.4	77.7	0.86
Peru	16.9	78.0	8.9	1.9	79.1	0.91
Uruguay	214.1	14.3	0.2	37.6	95.8	0.82
Venezuela	91.9	43.8	0.9	13.6	92.5	0.91

Source: Otsuka, Chuma, and Hayami [1992, Table 2].

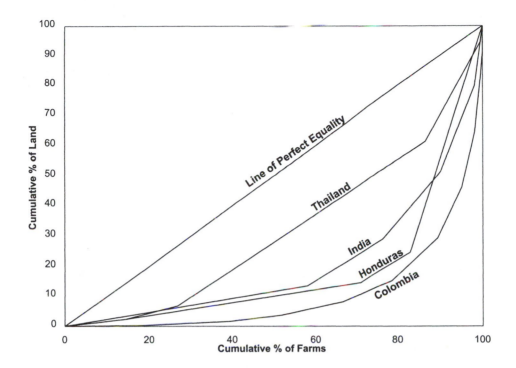

Figure 12.1. Lorenz curves for land holdings in two Asian and two Latin American countries. Source: Agricultural Censuses of Colombia [1988], Honduras [1993], India [1986], and Thailand [1988].

American countries (Honduras and Colombia). The differences in the two sets of Lorenz curves are fairly evident.

The low per capita holdings of land in Asia and the high inequality of landholdings in Latin America have a similar effect: a significant fraction of the farms are owner operated and cultivated. In Asia this fraction is particularly high, standing at around 86% (see Otsuka, Chuma, and Hayami [1992]). The Latin American fraction is lower and also includes a significant fraction of very large farms that are cultivated with the use of hired labor. Table 12.2 shows the percentage of owner-cultivated farms in different parts of the world.

The African countries are somewhat of an outlier in this respect. Much of the land is held under forms of group or communal tenure, and individual claims on such plots are weak. Thus we see that a small proportion of land is under owner cultivation simply because property rights are not well defined. The reported data are probably an understatement for all practical purposes, which reflects the ambiguity of property rights (*use* rights from plot to plot are better defined).

Table 12.2. Distribution of farms and farmland by land tenure status in the 1970 World Census of Agriculture.

	Asia	Africa	Latin America	Europe	North America	World
Countries	10	4	15	12	2	46
Farms (million)	93.3	3.5	8.6	11.9	3.1	120.4
Farm size (hectares)	2.3	0.5	46.5	7.6	161.2	10.0
Distribution of farms (%)						
Owner cultivation	85.8	5.2	60.3	67.6	63.2	79.2
Pure tenancy	5.9	1.6	17.1	9.3	12.0	7.1
Owner-cum-tenancy	8.2	6.9	6.6	23.0	24.8	10.0
Others	0.0	86.3	16.0	0.1	0.0	3.7
Distribution of farmland (%)						
Owner cultivation	84.0	9.2	80.4	58.9	36.6	61.1
Pure tenancy	5.9	3.0	6.2	12.5	11.9	9.0
Owner-cum-tenancy	10.1	29.1	5.6	28.5	51.5	27.2
Others	0.0	58.7	7.8	0.1	0.0	2.7
Percentage of share tenancy in tenanted land	84.5	0.0	16.1	12.5	31.5	36.1

Source: Otsuka, Chuma, and Hayami [1992, Table 1].

Also note that several countries provide for ownership or use rights to tenants who have worked the land for some prespecified number of years. This legal stipulation often lowers the amount of tenancy, and in the case of Asia there may be a substantial amount of informal tenancy that goes unrecorded in the data. Several countries in Latin America also uphold as a basic principle that the land belongs to those who farm it and have legalized this principle by regarding tenancy as a basis for granting use rights or ownership. This is true, for instance, in countries such as Mexico or Brazil. Such legislation has not always had a potent effect in turning land over to the tiller. Often, the reaction in Latin America has been in the direction of tenant eviction, followed by large-scale mechanized farming.

In India, for instance, the percentage of pure owner-cultivated land is almost certainly smaller than the data suggest. See the box on tenancy in the ICRISAT villages, where a higher prevalence of tenancy than that recorded in the national data is suggested. In the words of Jodha [1981]:

> ...in India, prior to independence, tenancy was largely viewed as an instrument of exploitation of the weak. Regulation of tenancy, therefore, became a key feature of post-independence India.... [Thus] efforts directed to study tenancy *per se* usually have not succeeded. Because of the great capacity of farmers to hide it, agricultural tenancy simply disappears once one starts investigating it through the usual one or two round surveys.

At the same time, the preponderance of owner–cultivators in Asian coun tries such as Korea and Taiwan is not surprising at all. These countries exhibit a relatively low degree of inequality in landholdings, so there is less need to bring land into alignment with labor.

Whereas tenancy exists all over the world, there are variations in the form of the tenancy arrangement. Latin American tenancy is largely of the *fixed-rent* variety: the tenant pays a fixed sum of money to the landlord in return for the right to cultivate the land. In contrast, Asian tenancy is characterized by a high incidence of *sharecropping*, in which the tenant yields to the landlord an agreed-upon share of the crop. Asian fractions of tenanted land under share tenancy range from around 30% (Thailand), through 50% (India) or 60% (Indonesia), all the way up to 90% in Bangladesh. In contrast, the corresponding percentages in Latin America are much lower (under 10% in countries such as Costa Rica or Uruguay and negligible in Peru, although relatively high at 50% in Colombia) (see Otsuka, Chuma, and Hayami [1992]).

Why is the form of the tenancy contract of any interest? The answer to this question must be postponed until we have examined these alternative tenancy forms in greater detail, but a preliminary observation or two is not out of line at this stage. Typically, richer tenants engage in fixed-rent tenancy, because the landlord is relieved of all risk: the rent is the same whether the crop does well or not. Thus in this sense, fixed-rent tenancy requires that the tenant be willing and able to bear the risks of agricultural production. This is generally so if the tenant has substantial wealth of his own. This is (admittedly indirect) evidence for the assertion that Latin American tenancies are held by large farmers, and perhaps even evidence for the conjecture that many tenancies flow *from* relatively poor farmers *to* relatively rich farmers.

This concept is consistent with our discussion in the previous chapter. In a country with large landholdings, agriculture may take on a highly mechanized and capitalistic form, using wage labor where labor is required. In such a regime, it may be better for smaller landowners to give up their land to large owners in exchange for a rent.

Contrast this with Asia, in which the bulk of tenancy is in the form of sharecropping. As we will see in the sections that follow, sharecropping is an arrangement that has particular value when the tenant is small and averse to risk: if a given *fraction* of output is paid as rent, then the tenant is, to some extent, insulated against output fluctuations, because he can share some of these fluctuations with his landlord. This suggests that Asian tenancy probably reflects, on the whole, land leases from relatively large landowners to relatively small landowners. However, be careful not to treat this as a general rule, even in Asia.

We will begin our study of land markets by describing tenancy contracts.

12.3. Land rental contracts

12.3.1. Contractual forms

Suppose that a landowner wishes to rent out his land to a potential
tenant. Several contractual forms are available. The simplest form of tenancy contract is what is called a *fixed-rent contract*, one in which the landlord
charges a sum of money (per year or per season) for the rental of the land
and, in turn, allows the tenant to carry out production. This sort of contract
is found wherever land rentals are observed, but by no means is it the only
form of contract that we observe, or even (depending on the region of observation) the dominant form. A second type of contract is commonly referred
to as *sharecropping*. Sharecropping comes in many flavors, but all of them
involve the sharing of the tenant's output in some preassigned proportion
between the landlord and the tenant. The proportions vary from country
to country and across regions within a country, although a 50–50 division is
commonly observed. Variations on the sharecropping contract include different proportions of division of the output depending on whether *input* costs
are also shared between the landlord and the tenant, and tied credit arrangements. The latter normally involve the advance of money by the landlord
for the tenant's purchase of output (in addition to or in lieu of cost sharing):
these "interlinked" contracts will be discussed in Chapter 14.

There is a simple but useful way to write down a class of rental contracts
that contains fixed rent and sharecropping contracts as special cases.[1] If Y
denotes agricultural output on the rented land, then write the total rent as

$$(12.1) \qquad\qquad R = \alpha Y + F.$$

If $\alpha = 0$ and $F > 0$, this is a fixed-rent contract with rent F. If $F = 0$ and α lies
between 0 and 1, then this is a sharecropping contract, where the share to the
landlord is α and the share to the tenant is $1 - \alpha$. Finally, if $\alpha = 0$ and $F < 0$,
this can be interpreted as a "pure wage contract," where the wage is simply
$w = -F$: the tenant is not a tenant at all, but a laborer on the landlord's land.
Labor contracts will be considered in Chapter 13.

Tenancy in the ICRISAT Villages

We introduced the ICRISAT study area in Chapter 10. We continue our study
here by studying land tenancy in these villages.

---

[1] See Stiglitz [1974]. The class that we describe can easily be extended to cover cost sharing in
inputs.

Landholding distributions were (and continue to be) quite skewed in all the study villages, but in most of them there is a pronounced trend toward greater equality. Households with large landholdings seem to have shed some land over the decades, whereas many formerly landless families have gained some land. In the sample, 20% of the village population consists of people who were landless in 1950, but owned plots of their own in 1982. The proportion of formerly landed families who had lost all their land by 1982 is only 4%. In sum, whereas only 62% of the population owned land in 1950, that fraction grew to 82% in 1982. It appears that such (nontenancy) land transfers mostly took place through sales rather than through land reform measures that empower long-standing tenants with ownership rights. Over the three decades, the amount of land bought and sold annually, expressed as a percentage of total land endowment for the sample households, varied between 1% for Kalman to 4% for Dokur. These are not negligible figures.

We have to be very careful in the interpretation of such data. Faced with land ceiling acts that restrict the maximum amount of land a landlord can hold, it is possible (although unlikely) that land transfers through tenancy are declared to be transfers of ownership, wherein a tenant is required to report that he owns excess-of-ceiling land when he in fact does not.[2] This suspicion received some support from an earlier study of Jodha [1981], which was based on the same survey area but on older data collected over a two year period beginning May 1975. In line with his view that tenancy is largely concealed, two years of field work were used to ascertain whether land was under tenancy or not, and "the initial concealment of tenanted plots disappeared over time." In Jodha's view, land transfers were also common during this period, but the bulk of such transfers (between 77 and 97%) were due to tenancy transactions alone.

Therefore, it is likely that the following data (although certainly vastly more indicative of widespread tenancy relative to the Indian National Census of Agriculture) still underrepresent the incidence of tenancy, or at least those forms of tenancy that involve land transfers from relatively large landowners to landless or small landowners. More circumstantial evidence indirectly supports this position, as we will see subsequently.

Agricultural tenancy is common (although not predominant relative to owner cultivation) in the ICRISAT villages. About 20% of all households sharecrop, and far less (below 5%) are fixed-rent tenants. Table 12.3 provides more detailed estimates ranging over the period 1975–82.[3]

The table lumps together all households who rent land. Some of them are "pure" tenants, but most tenants also own land of their own. For instance, "fixed-rent tenants" in the table refers to households who have *some* land under fixed-rent tenancy.

---

[2] The reason why this bias is unlikely is because land can be held in the names of various family members in an attempt to avoid the ceiling. In any case, this is somewhat different from the more commonly accepted source of bias: tenancy is underreported because of the fear of land-to-the-tiller legislation. This source typically classifies tenanted land as cultivated by the owner, whereas the possible bias that we are discussing here classifies tenanted land as land owned (and cultivated) by the tenant.

[3] The sample in each village contains households for each season in each year. Thus multiple observations (over different periods) might be accounted for by the same household.

Table 12.3. Tenancy in ICRISAT villages by household.

Villages	Households	Owners	Sharecropping tenants (%)	Fixed-rent tenants (%)	Mixed tenants (%)
Aurapalle	406	90.7	1.2	8.1	0.0
Dokur	220	82.3	15.9	0.9	0.9
Shirapur	437	69.1	30.4	0.5	0.0
Kalman	296	68.6	30.7	0.7	0.0
Kanzara	320	80.6	11.0	5.3	3.1
Kinkheda	187	85.0	14.5	0.0	0.5
Boriya	186	56.5	29.0	12.9	1.6
Rampura	216	76.4	14.8	5.6	3.2
All	2,268	76.8	18.2	4.1	1.0

Source: Shaban [1987, Table 1 (adapted)].

It is interesting to note that 80% of all tenants cultivate some land that they own (Shaban [1987]).

Clearly, the land-lease market is fairly active (even if we neglect possible under-reporting). It is also of interest to see that, overall, sharecropping is dominant as a mode of tenancy. This will yield a puzzle once we consider the Marshallian argument for the inefficiency of sharecropping (see the next section). Fifteen percent of all plots are sharecropped, whereas under two percent are in the form of fixed-rent tenancy. But there is variation across the villages. Fixed-rent tenancy is dominant in the village of Aurapalle, for instance.

Table 12.4 provides estimates of tenancy by area. The percentages of land that come under different forms of tenancy are quite similar to the corresponding percentages by household. The table brings out additional features of some interest that

Table 12.4. Tenancy in ICRISAT villages by plots.

Village	Owned			Sharecropped			Fixed rent		
	Plots (%)	Area (acre)	Value (Rs/acre)	Plots (%)	Area (acre)	Value (Rs/acre)	Plots (%)	Area (acre)	Value (Rs/acre)
Aurapalle	96.4	1.9	21.2	0.5	1.5	13.8	3.1	2.0	14.0
Dokur	84.1	1.6	42.2	14.9	2.2	40.2	1.0	1.9	40.0
Shirapur	64.5	1.6	29.7	35.5	2.5	24.9	0.0	0.2	21.3
Kalman	77.6	1.6	17.6	22.1	2.0	13.4	0.3	4.0	10.0
Kanzara	83.9	2.6	22.6	12.3	3.7	18.9	3.8	3.6	11.7
Kinkheda	92.2	3.5	15.1	7.7	2.9	10.6	0.1	2.0	10.0
Boriya	67.1	0.7	39.3	25.5	0.8	39.3	7.4	0.7	35.2
Rampura	80.7	1.0	62.8	16.1	1.2	60.7	3.1	1.4	56.2
All	80.9	1.8	29.20	17.5	2.2	27.08	1.6	1.8	27.45

Source: Shaban [1987, Table 2].

have to do with plot *sizes* and *values*.[4] Note that plot values are higher for owner-occupied plots than for tenanted plots. It is not surprising that the best quality plots are retained for owner cultivation.

Now look at plot *area* in Table 12.4. In several cases, area is significantly higher on tenanted land than on owned land. This suggests that although tenants lease land from those who are more endowed than they are, they are certainly getting fairly sizable chunks of it. Indeed, this observation also indicates that "reverse leasing"—the leasing of land from relatively small to relatively large farmers—may be present in the data.

Reverse tenancy—the apparently perverse phenomenon of *small* landowners leasing out their land to larger ones—has been observed in many places and has attracted some (but not sufficient) research attention. It is certainly not rare in the ICRISAT data. On average, in tenancy relationships, 47% of the partners came from the same farm size group, 32% of leasings were reverse (small to large farmers), and 22% of the land was leased by large farmers to smaller ones. However, in Dokur, as many as 55% of the leases were reverse. Jodha [1981] and Shaban [1991] discussed this in more detail. In any event, we should treat the high incidence of reverse leasing with some caution: as previously discussed, leases from large to small farmers may be severely underreported.

Most leases covered in the study had a brief duration—frequently not exceeding one year. About 60% of the contracts were for one cropping season only. Landlords frequently shuffle and rotate their tenants; there has been an almost total demise of traditional long-term tenancy arrangements, such as the *rehan* system in Aurepalle. This demise can be ascribed largely to land reform legislation that makes it easy for long-standing tenants to acquire ownership of the plots. Some negative effects of this development are immediately apparent: with limited tenure, the tenant loses the incentive to apply in proper amounts such inputs as manure, which is known to have residual and lasting effects (stretching beyond a year) on crop yields.

The terms of tenancy arrangements showed some variability and flexibility across the villages. In Dokur, where the use of purchased inputs is fairly high, more than 90% of the contracts stipulate 50–50 output *as well as input cost sharing*. In contrast, in Shirapur, where use of purchased inputs is much less intensive, the tenant is responsible for supplying all inputs and receives a share of 50–75% of the output. In many cases, a landlord's failure to supply his proper input share or higher cultivation costs being borne by the tenant for within-season production adjustments led to renegotiation and readjustment of the output shares. In those cases where the landlord shared in the cost of inputs, the landlord had a much greater say in the choice of the crop to be grown.

12.3.2. Contracts and incentives

There is a long tradition in economics that argues that sharecropping is essentially an inferior system to that of fixed-rent tenancy. The argument is

---

[4] Plot values, which are supposed to reflect the potential market price of the plot (per acre), are influenced most by perceptions of soil quality on that plot and whether or not the plot is irrigated.

not new and can be traced all the way back to Adam Smith. A clear statement can be found in Alfred Marshall's *Principles*. It is perhaps no coincidence that the early arguments came predominantly from English economists. At the time, fixed-rent tenancy was prevalent in England, whereas sharecropping (or *metayage*, as it was called, following the customary practice of 50–50 division) was dominant among the French.

Because Marshall is closely connected with the assertion that sharecropping is an inferior contractual system, this argument is often referred to as Marshallian inefficiency. It is based fundamentally on the *appropriate provision of incentives*.

The idea is very simple. A fixed-rent contract has the property that the tenant pays a fixed sum to the landlord no matter how much output is produced. Another way of saying the same thing is that the tenant retains 100% of any extra output that is produced. In contrast, sharecropping effectively leaves the tenant with some *fraction* of any additional output—a percentage such as 50 or 60%, depending on the exact form of the contract. Thus, *if the effort of the tenant cannot be monitored and controlled by the landlord, the tenant has an incentive to undersupply his effort*, because, under the sharecropping contract, part of the output produced by him gets siphoned off to the landlord. It would be better, instead, to extract this rent up front by charging a *fixed* payment and then leave the tenant alone.

Although this argument is pretty compelling, it is not the whole argument. If you are in a contentious mood, you could reply, "But what is so sacrosanct about the tenant keeping 100% of the extra output? Why not let him keep 110%, or even 120%, and charge an even higher rent up front? In that case the tenant would surely put in even more effort. If the move from 60 to 100% enhances efficiency, what is different about the move from 100% to 120%?"

Partly to answer this (perfectly valid) question, but mainly to introduce a line of argument that will be useful in later chapters, we need a more careful statement of the Marshallian argument.

Although the demonstration to follow is more general, it is easily described by assuming that the tenant has just one variable input of production—labor. In Figure 12.2, we plot the production function that relates output to labor applied on the rented plot of land, which is given by the curve *OA*. We also observe that labor is costly to the tenant. Labor does have other uses. For instance, part of the labor may be hired by the tenant for a wage. Even if this is not the case, the tenant could work as a laborer on somebody else's plot of land or he might have some land of his own on which he wishes to devote part of his labor. Another alternative (though this is less compelling in situations of excess labor supply) is that the tenant

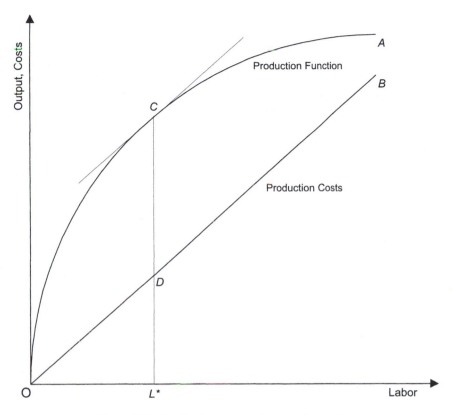

Figure 12.2. Production, cost, and economic surplus.

may simply value leisure. Whatever the reason, labor supply to the rented plot has a cost. This cost is depicted by the line OB.[5]

This depiction makes it very clear just how much economic surplus is produced by the tenancy arrangement. The surplus is precisely the difference between the value of output and the cost of producing it; that is, the vertical gap between the curve OA and the line OB. The surplus will vary, of course, with the amount of labor being applied. We are interested in the labor input level that yields the *maximum* possible economic surplus. This is the point where the vertical difference between the curves OA and OB is at a maximum. In Figure 12.2, this is attained by the labor input L^*. One characteristic of this point is that the value of the marginal product of labor, which is given by the tangent to the production function at this point, equals the unit opportunity cost of labor, given by the slope of the line OB. The surplus is given by the segment CD.

---

[5] In Figure 12.2, the production function exhibits diminishing returns to the labor input, whereas the opportunity cost of labor is depicted by a straight line. Neither of these features is necessary for the result to be described, but it makes the exposition easier.

    In the most fundamental sense, this is what lies at stake in the tenancy.
The tenant has to be compensated for his pains in farming the land. This is
why more output per se is not necessarily better, because the cost of producing that higher output is higher as well. Economic surplus is thus maximized
at some intermediate point, as shown in Figure 12.2.

    What is critical is the observation that the tenant himself has no interest
in seeking to maximize this surplus (through his choice of labor input) unless
it happens to be in his interest to do so. This is the incentive problem. Look at
Figure 12.3, which describes the effect of sharecropping on tenant incentives.
We display the original production function as the dotted line *OA*. Now
introduce a sharecropping contract, in which the tenant cedes a share of the
output to the landlord. Because the tenant receives only some fraction of
the output, the *effective return* to the tenant is the line *OE*, which is simply
the production function *OA* multiplied by a fraction (the tenant's output
share). The difference between *this* effective return and the tenant's cost *OB*
is what the tenant is interested in making as large as possible, because this
is what the tenant receives from the deal.

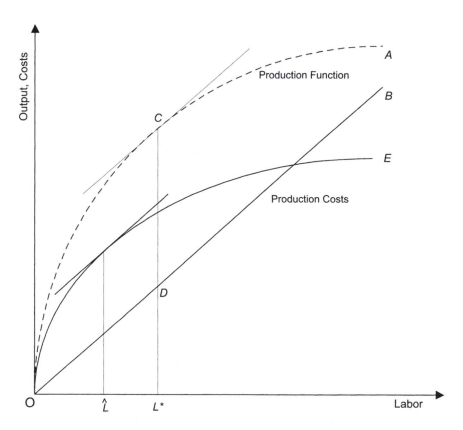

Figure 12.3. Sharecropping contracts and inefficiency.

Is this the same as maximizing economic surplus as defined earlier? The answer is no, and the reason is that the effective return to the tenant is not just a "shifted-down" form of the production function, but a "swiveling" or flattening of that function as well. Thus when the tenant maximizes his effective return (net of cost), he generally does so at a labor input $\hat{L}$ that is *smaller* than L^*, the input level that maximizes overall economic surplus. Figure 12.3 shows this clearly. Because the tenant receives only some fraction of output, *his* marginal return is smaller than the actual value of marginal product. Thus the tenant will desist from applying more labor at an earlier point: $\hat{L} < L^*$.

Compare Figure 12.3 to Figure 12.4, which shows the effects of a fixed-rent contract. The tenant's return can be depicted in this case simply by a *parallel* downward shift of the production function that is obtained by subtracting the fixed rent at every point. The result is the line $O'E$, which is just the old production function OA minus whatever the fixed rent is. The dif-

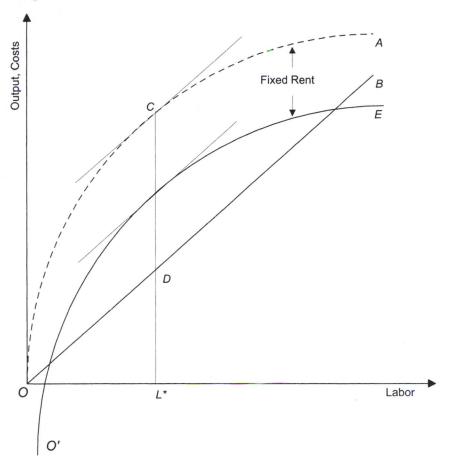

Figure 12.4. *The efficiency of fixed-rent contracts.*

ference between *this* effective return and the tenant's cost, *OB*, is what the tenant seeks to maximize through his choice of labor input.

The key observation is that this exercise is essentially identical to the maximization of economic surplus. The imposition of a fixed rent has no effect at all on tenant incentives *at the margin*, although, of course, if the fixed rent is too high he may not accept the tenancy in the first place. Figure 12.4 captures this perfectly by showing that the difference between *O'E* and *OB*, and *OA* and *OB* is maximized at the same level of labor input *L**.

Now all that is left for us to do is to see that total economic surplus must be distributed between the landlord and the tenant. If the tenant gets the same in both cases (which can always be guaranteed by adjusting the level of fixed rent to correspond to the return for the tenant under the share contract), then the landlord must be better off under a fixed-rent contract, because total economic surplus is maximized under the latter contract.[6]

With this analysis, we can easily answer why granting 100% marginal return to the tenant has special significance and why it is not optimal to offer contracts that offer higher marginal returns (such as 110 or 120%). Such contracts carry tenant input *above* the level *L** that maximizes economic surplus and, therefore, lower economic surplus as well. As we have already noted, the fact that *output* is higher does not mean that economic *surplus* is higher. Figure 12.5 captures the details of this argument. Under such a contract, the landlord presumably makes his money by charging a high fixed rent up front, so that the effective return to the tenant is initially shifted down by the amount of this rent and then rises toward the production function as the tenant is granted an amount exceeding 100% of the marginal output. All this does is goad the tenant to work even harder than the level prescribed for surplus maximization. The economic surplus is therefore reduced in this case as well. Given that the landlord gets the economic surplus net of what is passed on to the tenant, the former is better off by passing the same amount on to the tenant in the form of the pure fixed rent, as described in Figure 12.4.

To summarize then, the use of contracts other than a fixed-rent contract leads to a *distortion* of the tenant's input supply away from the efficient level. In particular, it appears that (i) sharecropping leads to undersupply of the tenant's inputs and (ii) a rational landowner trying to maximize the earnings from land lease will always prefer a suitable fixed-rent contract to any share contract.

---

[6] Diagrammatically, the landlord's return is given by the vertical difference between the production function and the effective return of the tenant. The tenant's net return, as already noted, is the effective return line minus his opportunity cost of labor. If we add these two amounts, we get the vertical distance between the production function and the opportunity cost of labor, which is precisely economic surplus.

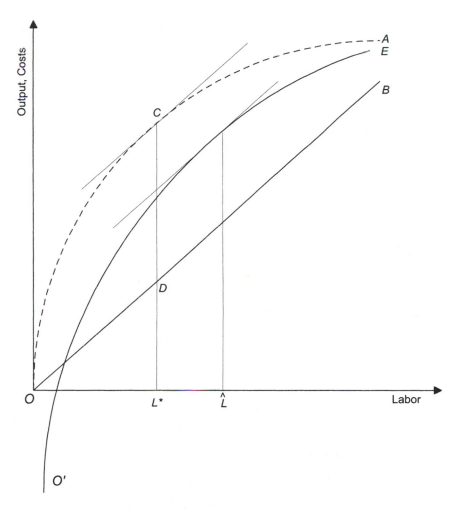

Figure 12.5. Why marginal returns to a tenant should not exceed 100%.

It is this last point that gives rise to the famous Marshallian puzzle of sharecropping. If a fixed-rent system is demonstrably superior to a sharecropping arrangement, not only from a social efficiency angle, but also from the point of view of the landlord's individual rationality, then why does sharecropping enjoy such enduring popularity in real world practice? Surely, there is more to the story than currently has been outlined.

At one level, the persistence of sharecropping seems merely a puzzle to be explained. Nothing of great importance appears to hang on it, only that contracts are in reality more diverse than theory predicts. However, this view is wrong for several reasons.

First, if we do observe sharecropping where theory tells us there should be none, then there is something wrong with the theory. At any rate, the theory needs to be augmented by a fuller description of reality. This enrichment may assist us in understanding other situations where the theory of incentives is also important. Second, and at a more practical level, if sharecropping exists despite the production losses that it appears to generate, it suggests that there are other compensating factors that necessitate such an arrangement. If these factors can be corrected by appropriate policy, the resulting inefficiencies will decline with the resulting decline in sharecropping. Third, these contractual relationships may have implications for other kinds of landlord and tenant behavior, such as the provision of credit to the tenant, the tendency to evict tenants, and the incentives to make long-run improvements on the land.[7]

Is Sharecropping Associated with Lower Yields?

The argument for the inefficiency of sharecropping relies on the assumption that the application of inputs by the tenant, such as labor, cannot be perfectly monitored and enforced by the landlord. If perfect monitoring were possible, the form of the tenancy contract would be irrelevant for our understanding of productive efficiency, because the efficient use of labor would be dictated by the landlord, irrespective of the particular choice of contract.

Can the levels of labor and other inputs chosen by the tenant be costlessly monitored and enforced by the landlord? Empirical work can shed some light on this issue. Shaban's [1987] study, using ICRISAT data, is one of the most careful contributions in this area. It is not enough to simply check whether there are differences in yield per acre across sharecropped land and other forms of land use. We must carefully control for several other factors that systematically vary with the form of tenancy (and not just the application of labor or other nonmonitored inputs). Shaban's study goes a long way toward handling these serious difficulties.[8]

The main idea (which handles quite a lot of otherwise uncontrollable variation) is to study the productivity of the *same household* that owns some land and sharecrops other land. We have already seen that the ICRISAT data is full of such "mixed" families.

At one stroke, this insight permits the researcher to control for all sorts of family-related characteristics that vary systematically across owned and sharecropped land. For instance, families that own land may have better access to working capital than families that sharecrop, in which case the productivity on owned land may be higher; this cannot be directly attributed to Marshallian inefficiency, however. Conversely, a poor sharecropper may have few alternative uses for his labor and thus may farm the land more intensively despite the disincentive effect identified by Marshall. Then productivity per acre will not be too different across owned or sharecropped land, but this does not rule out the possibility that the inefficiency is still there.

---

[7] See Singh [1989] for a survey of theories of sharecropping, which complements our observations later in this chapter.

[8] Also notable is the earlier study by Bell [1977], who first suggested the sort of methodology later extended by Shaban and others.

That's not all. It is possible that land quality varies systematically across tenanted and untenanted land. Indeed, we have already seen that this is true of the ICRISAT villages. Hence, a proper study must account for these systematic differences. The ideal tool in this respect is multiple regression (see Appendix 2): putting in several terms on the right-hand side allows us to control for the effects of these systematic differences. Shaban included plot values (see Table 12.4) as well as dummy variables for irrigation and other measures of soil quality. After all these variables are controlled for, the only remaining differences are expected to stem from the form of the tenancy contract.

The results are striking:

(1) Output and input intensities per acre are higher on the *owned* plots of a mixed sharecropper relative to the plots that he sharecrops: the average difference is 33% for output and between 19 and 55% for the major inputs.

(2) Quite a bit of this variation is due to irrigation, but certainly not all. With irrigation accounted for in the regression, output per acre is higher by 16% on owned versus sharecropped plots. Family male labor is higher by 21%, family female labor is higher by 47%, and bullock labor is higher by 17%. These differences also persist even if attention is restricted to sharecropper–owners who grow a single crop across the two types of plots.

(3) With irrigation and soil quality controlled for, there are no systematic differences between plots under fixed rent and plots under owner cultivation, just as predicted by the Marshallian theory.

These observations leave us with a vexing puzzle. If it is truly the case that sharecropping is inefficient, then why do we observe its existence? Indeed, sharecropping is the *dominant* form of tenancy in the ICRISAT villages: why do we see so much of it? Thus both theoretically and empirically, we are led to the same question, which we will now pursue in the main text.

12.3.3. Risk, tenancy, and sharecropping

Recall the discussion of risk aversion that we introduced in Chapter 10. Briefly, an individual is *risk-averse* if he prefers a certain (i.e., known or deterministic) sum of money A to a lottery with the same expected value A. Thus *the very fact* that a given amount is the expected value of some uncertain lottery is intrinsically displeasing to a risk-averse person. This is not to say that risk-averse persons cannot be compensated for taking risk. They can, but the greater the risk aversion, the greater will have to be the compensation (over and above the expected value of the lottery).

Observe that risk attitudes imply more than the ability to compare a risky gamble with an given amount of *safe* money. Two risky gambles can also be compared. As this is relevant for the issue of contractual choice in agricultural land, let us extend an example introduced when we first studied risk aversion in Chapter 10. This is the case of Nazim, the Turkish seller of hats. Recall that Nazim was considering an investment project that paid off $10,000 or $2,000, each with probability 1/2. Now compare this project, not to a safe sum of money as we originally did, but to another risky project. Suppose that Nazim compared *two* risky projects: the original project and another that pays less ($8,000) in the event of success, but pays more ($4,000) in the event of failure. Both projects cost the same to set up. Note that the projects may be compared in the following way: first, they both have the same expected value of $6,000; second, the latter project involves a lower "spread" in the returns. It makes intuitive sense that if Nazim is risk-averse, he should prefer the second project to the first. Does the utility function introduced in the previous section capture this intuition? Figure 12.6 shows that it indeed does. Both projects are shown in this figure: the first as the combination of points *A* and *B*; the second as the combination of points *A'* and *B'*. It is obvious that the expected *utility* of the second project lies above that of the first (the expected *monetary* values are, of course, the same).

We will apply this idea directly to land contracts. To do so, we will abstract entirely from the production function approach and assume that some

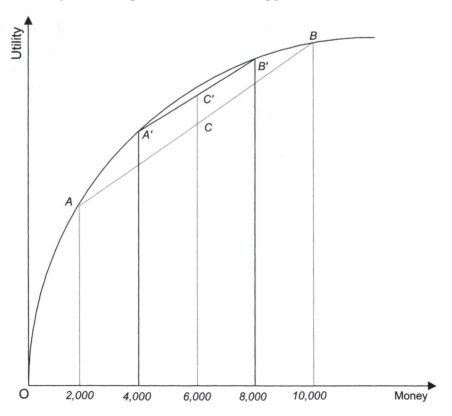

Figure 12.6. Comparison of two risky projects.

fixed amount of labor and other inputs is being applied to the tenanted land. Thus we throw out the incentive effect (discussed in the previous section) for the moment. Later, we will consider both these effects together.

Now we introduce the idea of uncertainty in agricultural production, a theme that will reappear in different contexts over the next few chapters. Even if all the inputs that a farmer can reasonably control are properly applied, the size of the harvest is still heavily dependent on Nature and will vary. For simplicity, suppose that only two levels of output are possible. We denote the values by G (for "good") and B (for "bad"). Suppose the probability that the good output will be produced is given by p.

In what follows, we consider a situation where land is leased out by a relatively wealthy landlord to a relatively poor tenant (much, if not most, of land lease is of this form). Thus it is reasonable to assume that as far as the return from this one particular plot of land is concerned, the landlord is less risk-averse than his tenant. If the landlord is wealthy, this income is just one of many sources of income, so he does not attach the same importance to it. In addition, the other sources of income may be uncorrelated with the present source, which permits diversification for the landlord. We in fact simplify by assuming that the landlord is risk-neutral, whereas the tenant is risk-averse.

First consider a fixed-rent contract in which the tenant is required to pay a rent of R to the landlord, irrespective of the fortunes of the plot. In this case, the tenant receives $G - R$ if things go well and $B - R$ otherwise. The landlord receives a sure payment of R.

Now imagine replacing this contract with a sharecropping contract, where the share is purposely chosen to provide exactly the same expected return to the landlord as before. (The reason for doing this will soon become clear.) Thus, if s is the share of the crop accruing to the landlord, then the expected return to the landlord is

$$psG + (1 - p)sB.$$

If this is equated to the landlord's return from fixed-rent tenancy, R, we see that the share of the landlord under the new contract must be given by the equation

(12.2)
$$s = \frac{R}{pG + (1 - p)B}.$$

Now observe, of course, that the expected return to the tenant is *also* the same under the two contractual modes. However, the tenant is not risk-neutral, so we still need to figure out which of the two contracts *he* prefers. Indeed, we may think of these two situations as analogous to the two projects of Nazim and draw upon the analogy. To see this, first compare tenant returns in the good state under the two contracts. With fixed rent, it is $G - R$, whereas with sharecropping, it is $(1 - s)G$. Using (12.2), we may conclude that

$$(1 - s)G - (G - R) = R - sG = R - \frac{GR}{pG + (1 - p)B} < 0,$$

by the fact that $G > B$. We may therefore conclude that the sharecropping contract *lowers* the return to the tenant in the good state. Because the share has been chosen so that expected monetary values are the same to either party under the two contracts, we may conclude that the sharecropping contract *increases* the return to the tenant under the bad state (relative to fixed rent). Now the analogy with Nazim's example should become clear: sharecropping and fixed-rent tenancy are like two projects with the same expected value, but the "spread" of returns to the tenant is narrower under sharecropping.

It follows that if the tenant is risk-averse, he should prefer the sharecropping contract over the fixed-rent contract. The landlord can play on this preference by cutting the tenant's share a bit more, but not too much, so that the tenant *still* prefers the sharecropping contract. Now the landlord, who is risk-neutral, enjoys a larger expected payoff, so he should switch from fixed rent to sharecropping.[9]

Thus sharecropping emerges as a way to share, not just the output of productive activity, but the risk that is associated with it as well. A tenant who pays fixed rent is forced to bear the entire uncertainty of production. He may be more than happy to yield some of this uncertainty to his landlord. Sharecropping accomplishes this by essentially varying the rent payable with the size of the harvest.

We have cut some corners with this explanation, and it is now time to go back and examine the missing steps. The main objection to our theory may be summarized thus: if the objective of the contract is to remove risk from the risk-averse party (tenant) to the risk-neutral party (landlord), why stop at sharecropping? It is possible to reduce tenant uncertainty even further.[10] Consider, for instance, the paying of a fixed *wage* to the tenant equal to the expected value of the tenant's return under sharecropping. A risk-averse tenant would strictly prefer the wage to the share contract, so much so that he would give up some extra income for the added insurance, which the landlord could then pocket.

[9] The reason for initially pegging the sharecropping rate to equalize expected returns to the landlord under the two forms of tenancy should now become clear. We showed that in this case, the tenant will prefer sharecropping. It follows that even if we choose a slightly higher share for the landlord, the tenant will still prefer sharecropping, so that now both parties are seen to be better off. This proves that the fixed-rent contract can be dominated by another contract. This method of proof is a familiar one in contract theory.

[10] To see this algebraically, vary the values of α and F in equation (12.1), but keep the expected value of total rent constant.

This argument suggests that in environments with large landowners and small potential tenants who are highly risk-averse, the institution of tenancy could disappear. After all, the payment of a fixed income to the tenant is tantamount to hiring him as a laborer. We have a situation where labor is effectively being hired rather than land being leased out. This may well be the case in many situations (see also our discussion in Chapter 11).

However, two considerations stand in the way of an unequivocal conclusion. First, in many situations the landlord and tenant may *both* be risk-averse, though it is probably reasonable to suppose that the latter is more so than the former. Fixed rent places all the uncertainty on the tenant, but a fixed wage places all the uncertainty on the landlord. If both parties are risk-averse, neither of these extreme contracts may be an acceptable solution. An intermediate outcome in which both individuals share risk may be preferred. Such intermediate contracts must closely resemble sharecropping, although the theory is obviously not sharp enough to predict that the share of output accruing to each individual is independent of the level of output (which is the case with sharecropping).

The second consideration that stands in the way of a wage solution is the incentive problem. Remember Marshall's argument. Just because we assumed that labor input is fixed in this section does not mean that it is so in an actual contractual situation. The lower the share afforded to the tenant, the weaker are his incentives to supply effort. In the extreme case, the hiring of wage labor is impossible unless there is a direct supervision system to ensure that the laborer is putting in the required effort. Thus we find a tension between the need to provide incentives to the tenant and the need to insure him. This combined problem fundamentally motivates our view of contracting. The landlord will offer an appropriate contract to balance incentives and insurance, but trading off some insurance necessarily implies that full efficiency isn't reached: such efficiency is incompatible with the landlord's own objectives.

We will return to this topic at various points in this text. The so-called combined problem, called the *principal–agent model*, is of such fundamental importance and widespread applicability that we devote to it Appendix 1 at the end of this chapter.

There is another objection to the risk-sharing argument for sharecropping (see Newbery [1977]. In a world where only fixed-wage and fixed-rental contracts are present, an individual agent (landlord or tenant) can control her degree of exposure to risk by merely diversifying the use of her assets and resources across fixed-rent contracts and wage contracts. Thus, landlords may lease out part of their land on a fixed-rent basis and earn secure incomes from land leased in this way. The rest can be cultivated by hired wage labor, which produces higher expected returns, but attaches the associated risk to the landlord. Similarly, a landless person may spend part of her time as employed wage labor to obtain a minimum base income and invest the rest in cultivating leased land on a fixed-rent basis, taking her chances with that venture. This kind of diversification may have the added benefit that the disincentive effects and distortions may be smaller compared to a system of full-fledged sharecropping, because fixed-rental farming at any rate ensures maximum incentives.

There are three counterobjections to this criticism. First, as we have already noted, fixed-wage contracts have their own incentive problems, so it is far from clear that a *combination* of fixed-rent contracts (which are good for incentives) and fixed-wage contracts (which are bad for incentives) must dominate sharecropping (which is middling for incentives). It all depends on how easy it is to get around the monitoring problem for hired labor. As we have observed on several occasions, this may be possible in cases where large scale hiring of labor occurs, so that it pays to hire specialized supervisory labor.

The second counterobjection is that the mixing of different contracts may be difficult to accomplish in practice. It all depends on the structure of the labor market. Some employers may demand full-time work to be carried out on their plots. This is especially of concern during the harvest season, when proper timing is of the essence. A person who finds employment during this season (and this is the season when most employment is available) may not be able to simultaneously deal with harvesting additional output on leased land.

Finally, we have neglected additional forms of uncertainty that make their appearance felt in the labor market and make the wage rate itself uncertain. Now, even if mixing is possible and even if we neglect incentive problems, it may not be possible to find a "safe asset," such as a fixed-wage contract that is lacking in all uncertainty. In such circumstances sharecropping may well dominate whatever can be achieved by mixing fixed-rent tenancy with a risky wage contract (Newbery [1977]).

12.3.4. Forms of Tenancy: Other considerations

So far we have studied the two major ingredients that affect the structure of land contracts: incentives and risk. There are several related considerations that are important as well. We discuss some of them in this section.

The double-incentive problem

Is leased land farmed only by the tenant, his or her family, and the laborers hired by them? It depends. If land is leased out by a small landowner to a large tenant or by an absentee landlord who is only interested in maintaining a secure source of rental income, the landlord usually will not be involved with the leased land in an ongoing way. Typically such leases are carried out on the basis of fixed rent, because minimal activity on the landlord's part (such as verification of tenant output) is required. Indeed, the landlord would not care whether the land is even cultivated or not, as long as the rent is paid.

On the other hand, there are situations in which the landlord is deeply involved with the crop grown on the land, the methods used for cultivation, the inputs used, and the proper maintenance and care of the leased plot. The landlord may be in a position to make suggestions, to provide managerial care, and supply inputs of production. Some of these inputs may be noncontractible, just as the tenant's labor is noncontractible because it cannot be observed or verified by the landlord.

Return to the Marshallian inefficiency of sharecropping. Ignore risk or assume that everybody is risk-neutral to display this incentive problem in its starkest form. Recall that the problem arises from the observation that if the tenant does not get to keep the entire marginal output resulting from production, he will have an incentive to undersupply effort. However, what if *both* landlord and tenant are required to apply effort, as in the discussion of the previous paragraph? Think of this as the *double incentive problem.*

If the tenant gets to keep the entire marginal output from the land, the landlord keeps none of it. (This is fixed-rent tenancy.) Of course, the tenant will then work very hard, but the landlord will have no incentive to put in effort on the leased land. Now suppose the landlord gets to keep the entire marginal output from the land, but the tenant keeps none of it. (This is the case of wage labor where the landlord is really an employer and the tenant is really an employee.) In this case, the landlord will have all the incentive to put in effort and the tenant–laborer will have none.

So we are in a double bind: the Marshallian argument applies in both directions, and we can no longer say that fixed-rent tenancy does better than sharecropping. Sharecropping may be a compromise solution in which both landlord and tenant put in some effort. Eswaran and Kotwal [1985a] study this extension.

Cost sharing of inputs

Sharecropping may be the preferred contract when input costs are shared between landlord and tenant. To see this, reconsider the Marshallian argument. Because tenant labor is noncontractible, its marginal cost is borne entirely by the tenant. However, sharecropping means that some fraction (say half) of the marginal output is taken by the landlord. Thus the tenant, instead of equating the marginal product of this labor to its marginal cost, effectively equates *half* the marginal product of his labor to its marginal cost. This means that he stops applying labor at a point when marginal product still exceeds marginal cost, so the resulting outcome is inefficient.

Suppose, however, that labor effort is indeed observable. If you have difficulty with the observability of household labor, suppose for the sake of argument that the only input in production is fertilizer and that its use is observable. In such a case the landlord could share the cost of applying fertilizer. Now consider the effect that this has on the choice of fertilizer input by the tenant. He will equate the marginal product of fertilizer *that accrues to him* to the marginal cost of fertilizer *that he pays*. Under sharecropping, the marginal product he receives is half the true marginal product, and with cost sharing thrown in, the marginal cost faced by him is halved as well. This restores efficiency, because marginal product is then equated to marginal cost.

Matters are more complicated when there are many inputs of production—some observable and some not. Then Marshallian inefficiency still applies to the inputs that are unobservable, whereas with judicious cost sharing it can be avoided for those inputs that are observable.[11] If the tenant is risk-neutral, it is still better (barring the considerations raised in the previous subsection) to lease out the land on fixed-rent tenancy, but if the tenant is risk-averse, there are advantages to sharecropping as we have seen. If several inputs are contractible and if cost sharing can be used, then the relative advantage of sharecropping is further heightened. Newbery and Stiglitz [1979] study some of these issues.

The following brief description of share contracts in the Sindh region of Pakistan illustrates some of the points of this subsection and is relevant for some of the observations made in the previous subsection as well.

───

Sharecropping in the Sindh, Pakistan

Share tenancy contracts in the Sindh are referred to as *batai*; literally, a division.[12] The landlord leases land in return for a share of the harvest; the tenant provides the labor. The costs of other inputs of cultivation—seeds, fertilizer, and pesticides, for instance—are borne by *both* landlord and tenant under a variety of cost-sharing rules. To be sure, the *crop* share and the *cost* share are closely linked. For example, a tenant who assumes sole responsibility for land preparation (i.e., provides all labor) and who has a one-half share in the cost of all other inputs gets a one-half share of the crop. This arrangement is viewed as the most common form of *batai*.

However, the 50–50 share is becoming less frequent, particularly in Sindh. The tenant's crop and cost shares vary between one-half and one-sixth, and intermediate

───

[11] These statements are somewhat loose. Marshallian inefficiency is not really defined "input by input," but by the entire complex of reactions to a particular contract. This also means that if some inputs is not contractible, the optimal cost share on the contractible inputs are not generally equal to the output share.

[12] I am grateful to Ghazala Mansuri for providing me with the material on which these observations are based.

crop shares of a one-third, one-fourth, or one-fifth are also observed. Mechanization is partly responsible for the fall in the tenant's share. Labor-intensive tasks such as land preparation and threshing, which were traditionally the sole responsibility of the tenant, are now accomplished wholly or partly with machines. Thus active landlord involvement in cultivation is present.

Multiple cropping has also increased the use of hired labor on tenanted area. The agricultural year typically consists of two seasons. In one season, a food crop (wheat or rice) is grown, and in the other, cash crops (cotton, sugar cane, and fruits) are grown. With the advent of multiple cropping, two or more crops (such as cotton and sugar cane) may need to be harvested simultaneously, while another crop (red chilies, for instance) is being planted. This situation has dramatically increased the use of hired labor on the share tenant's plot. These changes have raised the monetary costs of cultivation and reduced the tenant's role as provider of labor and draft animals. Tenants who get a one-fourth or smaller share, typically do not have draft animals and are not responsible for land preparation. The tenant's share of payments made to thresher operators and hired harvest labor are equal to his crop share.

Multiple cropping and the increasing focus on cash crops has made farming a more lucrative business. If alternative opportunities for tenants do not rise at the same rate (e.g., due to increased mechanization), a reduction in the tenant's crop share is a likely outcome. Sometimes the tenant's share differs by crop. They may get one-half or one-third of the food crop, but only one-fourth or one-fifth of the cash crop. In some cases, tenants work as agricultural wage labor in the season when the cash crop is grown and as share tenants in the season when the food crop is grown.

Limited liability and sharecropping

If a tenant is poor and his output is uncertain, then quite apart from considerations of risk aversion, there may be states of the world in which the tenant will not be *able* to pay a fixed rent. This constraint, stemming from the tenant's small wealth and the small output that he might produce, is known as *limited liability*.

Landlords who charge fixed rent will therefore know that such rent cannot always be paid. If the tenant is poor and the harvest fails, the rent will have to be forgiven or essentially advanced as a loan. However, there is no guarantee that the loan will be repaid in the future, so part or all of the rent may truly have to be forgiven.

The problem with this arrangement is that it creates an incentive for the tenant to overinvest in risky methods of production. This is because if production fails, rent is forgiven, whereas if it succeeds, the tenant gets to retain all the excess (under fixed-rent tenancy). We shall pursue this particular incentive problem in more detail in the context of credit contracts: see Chapter 14. One way to counterbalance this tendency is for the landlord to lower the rent in bad states and raise it in good states. This gives a tenant a stake in the bad outcome as well and reduces his tendency to overinvest in risky forms of farming.

Now observe that a lower rent in bad states and a higher rent in good states is akin to sharecropping. Of course, as tenants grow richer, the limited liability constraint bites less and less and then one can return to fixed-rent tenancy. This also implies that we should observe more fixed-rent tenancy if tenant wealth is higher. This observation is related to the notion of *tenancy ladders*; see Shetty [1988] and Sengupta [1997], who study the implications of limited liability for share contracts. The tendency to overinvest in risk is explored by Basu [1992].

Screening

A sharecropping contract offered along with other kinds of contracts may be a suitable screening device to obtain high-quality tenants. Suppose that a landlord is uncertain about the true ability and productivity of a prospective tenant, although the tenant himself knows precisely what his abilities are. In such a situation, it is sometimes possible to *separate* the two kinds of tenants by offering a menu of contracts.

The idea behind the argument is that high-ability tenants will prefer contracts in which they can retain a larger share of their (high) marginal product, whereas low-ability tenants would like to divide their (low) marginal product between the landlord and themselves. Now landlords would like to ferret out the high-ability tenants in a world where tenant abilities are largely unknown. By doing so, the landlord can use their higher productivity to extract more rent.[13] Note well that *all* the implicit extra surplus cannot be extracted as increased rent, because in that case no high-ability tenant will reveal himself through an appropriate choice of contract. This is where a cunningly chosen menu of contracts can make a difference.

Specifically, suppose that the landlord can ask the tenant to choose between two contracts: one in which a share of the output is offered and another in which fixed rent must be paid. It is possible, under some circumstances, to choose this menu so that the following conditions are met.

(1) A high-ability tenant will prefer the fixed-rent contract to the sharecropping contract, even though the implicit rent in the fixed-rent contract is higher. The reason is that he gets to keep his high marginal product entirely. In the sharecropping contract, he must give some of this away.

(2) A low-ability tenant will prefer the sharecropping contract to the fixed-rent contract. The fixed rent is too high relative to the extra marginal product that he would get to retain.

---

[13] However, see the subsequent remark on competition.

If these two conditions are met, then the two types of tenants will "separate" by choosing different contracts. Under this view, sharecropping is a sifting device to leave fixed-rent contracts in the hands of the most productive tenants. This screening theory also offers an explanation for the *coexistence* of sharecropping with other contractual forms.

Note that there are several problems with the screening view. First, abilities do not stay unknown *forever*: what happens once tenant abilities are revealed? After this happens there is no need to give the low-ability tenant a sharecropping contract (unless there are other considerations that we have already discussed, such as risk aversion). Thus the screening theory at best gives sharecropping an ephemeral role or a permanent role only when there is a perennial influx of fresh tenants.

Second, if a high-ability person knows that once he reveals himself, rents will be raised to squeeze the extra surplus that he generates, what incentive does he have to reveal himself in the first place? In an intertemporal context, separation is still achievable, but is a more costly proposition.

Third, and in contrast to the second point, if there is competition for different types of tenants, the role of a screening device disappears. Landlords cannot retain extra surplus from a screened tenant because the surplus will be bid away. Thus there is no incentive to screen to begin with.

Despite these problems, screening models have value for two reasons. First, they illustrate the subtle incentive problems that crop up in the choice of land contracts. Second, in more general situations in which there are multiple types of incomplete information (and not just information about tenant abilities), screening equilibria might make more sense. For this reason we provide a more formal discussion of the screening model in Appendix 2 to this chapter.

12.3.5. Land contracts, eviction, and use rights

So far, we have considered the problems of incentives and risk sharing in a static context. We have neglected the possibility that a tenancy contract may or may not be *renewed*. When nonrenewal or eviction is a possibility, the landlord acquires an additional instrument through which effort incentives are provided.

It is easy enough to see how such an option might work. Suppose that a tenant is offered a sharecropping contract for one or more of the reasons that we have already discussed. To some extent, the problem of Marshallian inefficiency might be overcome by threatening to evict the tenant in the case of poor performance.[14]

---

[14] The literature on eviction includes Singh [1983], Bardhan [1984], Dutta, Ray, and Sengupta [1989], and Banerjee and Ghatak [1996].

The possibility of eviction has several consequences. For one thing, it introduces a new form of risk for the tenant, and he will have to be compensated for this risk; otherwise he will not accept such a contract. For another, the going value of the contract must exceed the tenant's next-best opportunity; otherwise the threat of eviction has no bite. The landlord will have to examine closely whether he is willing to pay the additional compensation required to acquire the instrument of eviction.

In addition, there are other potential sources of loss for the landlord. Chief among these are activities that increase the long-run earning potential of the land, which the tenant will now be less willing to carry out. But there are gains as well. For instance, the threat of eviction can be used to ensure better performance in production, as well as to enforce loan repayment (on this, see Chapter 14).

There are two particular cases where contracts with eviction may be widely employed.

(1) *Limited liability.* Consider the limited liability contracts studied in the previous section. We have already shown that because of the need to provide appropriate incentives, such limited liability contracts often provide the tenant with a return that exceeds his opportunity cost. In such situations, the threat of removing the contract tomorrow if output is not at a satisfactory level today carries bite. Faced with such a threat, the tenant will indeed raise effort even further. Recall that poor tenants are more likely to be in a situation where the limited liability constraint is binding. It follows that the threat of eviction can be more profitably used against poor tenants.

(2) *(Nonverifiable) Information regarding tenant effort.* Suppose that the landlord can obtain some information regarding tenant efforts, but cannot write such observations into a contract because they are not verifiable in a court of law. For instance, the landlord might *know* that the tenant has spent excessive time farming his own plot of land or working elsewhere, instead of the rented plot, but cannot *prove it*. In such situations clauses such as "...and if I, the landlord, find that you have been working more than half the time on your own land instead of on the tenanted land, I reserve the right to increase my rent payments by another 10% of the crop," simply cannot be upheld. Either the tenant will take advantage of this clause or the landlord will, by claiming that the tenant has indeed cheated when he has not.

On the other hand, such nonverifiable information can be taken into account in the decision to *renew* a contract. If the tenant is no worse, intrinsically than other tenants, then the landlord will have no perverse incentive to take undue advantage of this (informal) understanding. At the same time, the tenant will be aware that it is certainly credible for the landlord to not renew the contract if he, the tenant, shirks. Thus in this case, the decision to not renew a contract can be based on information in ways that an ordinary contract *cannot* mimic. Such information is potentially valuable for contractual efficiency.

The effect of potential eviction on the welfare of the tenant needs to be examined with caution. The first sentiment regarding eviction is the usual gut reaction: if tenants can be evicted, they *must* be worse off. Like many gut reactions, this is probably correct, but there is a paradoxical counterargument that needs to be addressed first.

The argument is this: eviction can only provide additional incentives if the tenant is *strictly* better off working with the current landlord than being relieved of his current contract. This is possible if the contract package is more attractive than one in which the tenant is indifferent between working for the current landlord and seeking out alternative opportunities. Put another way, if the landlord does decide to use a contract that employs eviction as a background threat, a new tenant has to be made *better off* relative to his outside opportunities. If eviction is banned and there is an excess supply of potential tenants, a *new* tenant will not be given any more than his next best alternative. Thus it is not surprising to observe that, despite the vicissitudes and uncertainties of tenancy, tenancy is still preferable to landless labor.

This argument is correct as it stands, but it fails to adequately distinguish between *ex ante* and *ex post*. Banning eviction can greatly increase the economic welfare of *incumbent* tenants, because it changes the allocation of bargaining power between tenant and landlord. No longer can the landlord offer a contract to which the tenant can only answer "yes" or "no." Now the contract can be bilaterally bargained, because the landlord is not free to offer the plot to an alternative tenant.

That said, banning eviction may have entirely different consequences for potential tenants, such as those who are currently landless laborers. For them, fresh tenancy contracts become much harder to get, and, all other things being equal, this will reduce their welfare.

Finally, banning eviction can heighten productivity. This seems paradoxical. If productivity and efficiency can be raised, then why would the landlord not take advantage of this by not evicting tenants himself? The answer is that the productivity gain occurs *because of the transfer of bargaining power from the landlord to the tenant*, which leads to much higher income for the tenant. Remember, the landlord is not interested in maximizing productivity, but in maximizing his *own* return. These two goals are sometimes compatible, as they are in a situation of overall risk neutrality and fixed-rent tenancy, but not always.

It is important to appreciate this point a bit more carefully. To do so, we continue a line of reasoning that we introduced in our study of the risk-sharing argument for sharecropping: see Section 12.3.3. Recall that in our discussion of Marshallian inefficiency, a fixed-rent contract *both* maximized the landlord's return *and* maximized social surplus. However, as soon as we introduced the realistic features of uncertainty and risk aversion, fixed-rent tenancy represented too much of a risk for the tenant. As we have already seen, the output fluctuations for the tenant can be tempered to some extent by sharecropping, but we also noted that this gives rise to an incentive problem, which lowers productivity. We concluded that there is a fundamental trade-off between the provision of incentives and the provision of insurance, and this tension means that maximal productivity will *not*, in general, be attained.

Let's qualify that statement: maximal productivity will not, in general, be attained *unless the landlord substantially raises the tenant's share of rent*. However, the landlord has no interest in productivity per se: what does he stand to gain if the increase in productivity (and then some) is passed to the tenant? But this change *can* be achieved through effective legislation. If eviction is banned, the tenant can increase his share because of his better bargaining position.[15] At the same time, there is a potential loss in incentives because the eviction instrument cannot be applied. Which effect dominates is ultimately an empirical question. The box on Operation Barga, a program of tenancy legislation implemented in West Bengal, summarizes an empirical test of these ideas carried out by Banerjee and Ghatak [1996].

Operation Barga

The Land Reforms Act of India (1955) and its subsequent amendments stated that all sharecroppers will have *permanent* use rights on land that they lease, and, moreover, that such rights will be inheritable. Such incumbency rights could be claimed as long as sharecroppers paid the legal share of the crop to their landlords or did not leave the land uncultivated, *or unless the landlord wished to take back the land for personal cultivation.*

Loopholes such as the italicized phrase in the previous sentence have tripped up land reform legislation for decades. Landlords have routinely used the personal cultivation clause to evict tenants.

There was another major barrier. A tenant would have to formally register his status (as a tenant) with the government. But few tenants registered, faced as they were with potential intimidation from their landlords, the loss of other forms of support such as consumption credit, and the prospect of a long and arduous legal battle if they truly wanted to dispute an eviction.

The Left Front came to power in West Bengal, India, in 1977 as the ruling state government. In existing tenant laws they found possibilities to advance their agenda of agrarian reform. Even though these laws conferred only use rights and not ownership, they had potential anyway. The Left Front carried out a two-pronged attack. It took the no-cultivation clause seriously and closed off this loophole. Simultaneously,

---

[15] This is one way to interpret the point made by Mookherjee [1997].

it encouraged the registration of tenants through a much publicized program called Operation Barga (the term *barga* stands for sharecropping). The peasant organizations of ruling political parties worked along with village-level administration to encourage registration. They thwarted collusion between landlords and local officials and prevented intimidation. "Settlement camps," which were already being used by land reform officials to maintain and update land records, were actively used as tools of registration; registration certificates were issued on the spot. Over the period 1977–90, the fraction of registered sharecroppers rose from 23 to 65%.

We must be careful evaluating the direct effect of this registration scheme. During the same period of time in West Bengal, there was expansion in public and private irrigation and there was technological change as well, so we need to control for these variables. Banerjee and Ghatak [1996] showed nonetheless, that Operation Barga accounted for a significant fraction of total growth in agricultural production during this period: 36% is the figure estimated.[16]

It seems, then, that in the case of Operation Barga, the possible loss in yield due to lack of eviction threat as an instrument was far outweighed by the gain in yields accruing from a greater tenant stake in output. In the sample studied by Banerjee and Ghatak [1996], only 10% of all tenants had output shares that exceeded 50% in the pre-reform period. Post-reform, about half of all registered tenants and even a quarter of all *unregistered* tenants had shares that exceeded 50%.

12.4. Land ownership

12.4.1. A brief history of land inequality

Why the ownership of land is distributed as it is ultimately is a historical question. When population was sparse and land abundant, the issue was not so much one of the appropriate use of *land* as the appropriate use of *labor*. Thus the beginnings of modern history are marked not so much by battles for land, but struggles for the control (and ownership) of labor. This changed first in those parts of the world in which population density began to cross certain critical bounds and land became the critical factor in production. The notion of property rights slowly began to emerge, beginning with notions of community or tribal rights to tracts of land and culminating in the structure that we know today in many parts of the world: ownership rights by a single individual or family.

The path to specific property rights has seldom been smooth. Rights to land have historically been subject to challenge, largely backed by force. It was only natural that a class of overlords or rulers would emerge, who would exact tribute or rent from cultivators in return for patronage and protection. Such payments were subsequently enshrined in tradition, in social

---

[16] The direct effect is probably even higher, because sharecropping accounted for somewhat less than half of West Bengal's agricultural sector.

custom, in religious norms, and last (but not least) in the legal dictates of the state. As populations swelled the world over, these norms, regulations, and traditions were supplanted and reinforced by the power of the market. Land rents and prices rose as land became scarce relative to labor. With a cheap supply of labor, the laws that supported slavery gradually were dispensed with.

Binswanger, Deininger, and Feder [1995], in their comprehensive survey of the evolution of land relations, note that an increasing population was not the only factor that determined the skewed relationship of labor to land. Free peasants moved to the large manorial estates under measures that systematically reduced their outside options: (1) large tracts of unoccupied lands, including tracts of high quality, were assigned to members of the ruling class, thereby reducing the amount of free land available for small-scale cultivation, (2) differentially high taxes were imposed on free peasants, (3) access to markets for output was restricted by setting up marketing schemes that restricted sources of purchase, and (4) infrastructural improvements as well as various subsidies were selectively provided to farms that belonged to the ruling class. It need hardly be added that these measures necessitated a high degree of connivance between the state and the ruling class, which was not very difficult because many representatives of the state came precisely from this class.

It is not surprising, then, that the twentieth century dawned with enormous inequalities in land holdings, much of which survives unscathed as we move into the twenty-first century. This inequality gives rise to four major questions:

(1) Is such inequality compatible with productive efficiency, quite apart from the intrinsic ethical abhorrence that we may feel toward it?

(2) If there is an efficiency loss, can it be repaired through the operation of land rental markets?

(3) If land rental markets are not adequate to restore efficiency, would land sales from rich to poor spontaneously redress the balance?

(4) If neither land rental markets nor sales markets are sufficient, what is the role of land *reform*?

We have already examined the second question in detail. In the rest of this chapter, we address the remaining issues jointly.

12.4.2. Land size and productivity: Concepts

Productivity

Do small farms have higher productivity than large farms? To address this question, it is important to clarify what we mean by the term "productivity."

Consider two notions. One is *total factor productivity*: do small farms have a production *function* that lies "beyond" that of large farms? This is a hard concept to get at for two reasons. First, small and large farms do not typically use the same inputs. Thus, we need to compare the inputs in some way, presumably by multiplying by market prices, to get an overall aggregate. Second, there is the problem of valuing nonmonetized inputs such as family labor. In the following text we will have no theoretical reason to believe that small farms are more efficient in this narrow technological sense. We are after a broader notion of productivity anyway.

The second notion of productivity is "productivity in the sense of market efficiency." This is a vaguer notion, and we can roughly translate it by asking, Do small farms produce an output per acre that is closer to the "efficient market" output than large farms? However, what do we mean by market efficiency? In a world where several markets are inefficient or nonfunctional, it is unclear whether the standard rules of efficiency in *one* market promote economic efficiency overall.[17] Very tentatively, we may say that production efficiency is achieved when the values of the marginal product of all inputs equal their true marginal costs. This is the viewpoint we will use to make the subsequent theoretical arguments.[18]

This second, subtle notion is often tested very bluntly: simply ask if output per acre (perhaps correcting for land quality) on small plots exceeds those of large plots. This presumes that whenever the preceding efficiency conditions are violated, they are violated in the direction of *underapplication* of inputs. The arguments we consider in the upcoming text suggest that this may be the case, but it helps to keep the conceptual distinctions of this subsection in mind throughout.

Technology

Consider, first, the technological angle. Obviously, there are minimum sizes below which land cannot be usefully cultivated, at least for certain crops. Moreover, large plots are suitable for mechanization and cultivation with capital-intensive methods, in a way that small plots are not. Thus, from the pure technological point of view, it is reasonable to suppose that land either exhibits constant unit productivity (with all other inputs being expanded in

---

[17] The so-called theory of the second best (see Lipsey and Lancaster [1956]) states that in a world where the appropriate efficiency conditions do not hold in a number of markets, getting them to hold in any *one* market may be a bad thing. We shall see this logic applied with great vigor in the case of customs unions (see Chapter 18).

[18] All efficiency losses do not arise "at the margin." This is especially so in situations where, for instance, fixed costs of labor supervision must be incurred. In this case the *marginal* efficiency conditions may well be met, but there is nevertheless an efficiency loss arising from the supervision of labor.

proportion) beyond a certain minimum scale or displays increasing productivity once large-scale techniques of cultivation can be brought to bear.

What are the various sources of scale economies in production? First, there is the use of draft animals, which are economical only when a certain minimum size is reached. Draft animal *power* can come in divisible units if a rental market for animals exists, but for more than one reason, this market is very thin. Animals are capital goods and proper care is necessary to maintain their value over long periods of time. If they are rented out, they could be overworked or mistreated. Moreover, there is often correlation (within a village) in the use of animal power, so that an animal may be in use on the owner's land during the time that it is needed by a potential renter. Thus bullocks are typically individually owned, and the lack of a rental market creates the indivisibility.

Machinery—tractors, harvesters, threshers, pump sets—represents economies of scale on an order higher than those created by draft animals. The minimum size of land required for efficient ownership is high, but the scope for a rental market is somewhat better. Threshing can be done at any time of the year; the rental of harvesters or pump sets may be more problematic when time-bound cultivation is critical. On the whole, there should be advantages to ownership.

Thus from the narrow technological viewpoint, there seems to be little point in any debate. Large plots of land can always do just as well as smaller plots, if for no other reason than the fact that large plots can be subdivided into smaller plots and cultivated the same way small plots can. In addition, they can take advantage of any large-scale methods (such as cultivation with the use of tractors) that might be available.

Imperfect insurance markets and small-farm productivity

The insistence on technology alone misses a basic feature of cultivation: that labor plays a central role in agriculture. Both in this chapter and the chapter to follow, I have taken pains to emphasize the severe incentive problems that come with the employment of labor, either directly, or indirectly in the form of tenancy. As we will see in Chapter 13, there are often serious problems of monitoring labor, for which the employer must pay either in the form of direct supervision or indirectly in the form of contracts designed to create incentives. As for tenancy, the greater part of this chapter has been concerned with the incentive problems that arise there as well. These incentive problems would not arise if all labor were risk-neutral, for then fixed-rent tenancy could mimic ownership and distortion-free cultivation would be possible (as in Marshall's ideal) simply through the exclusive use of such rentals.

However, laborers and tenants are not risk-neutral and they do not have perfect access to credit or insurance markets (as we will see in Chapters 14 and 15). Therefore, landlords can make money by attempting to insure them against agricultural uncertainty. But In doing so, the landlords must offer contracts that fail to ensure efficiency in production. Even moderate experiments such as Operation Barga, which only confer use rights (and not ownership rights), have shown that a shift of power away from the landlord can lead to productivity gains, because of the shift in marginal output enjoyed by the tenant. Studies such as Shaban [1987], which we have also discussed, estimate the magnitude of the productivity gains that are possible simply from the extra incentive effect.

The following question arises: if there is an efficiency gain to be had, why doesn't the landlord (or employer) reap that gain by changing the contract appropriately? We have asked this question before (see the section on eviction, for instance), and the answer here is the same. If there is no limited liability (or perfect credit markets) and no uncertainty (or perfect insurance markets or risk neutrality), all efficiency gains that *can* be made, *will* indeed be made by the landlord through an appropriate choice of contract, because he can always design a contract that exhibits these gains and then remove the gains by a lump-sum tax (fixed rent) on the tenant. In a world of risk-averse or credit-constrained tenants, this isn't possible any more. Actually, to be precise, it *is* possible to offer a contract that enhances efficiency, but the landlord cannot reap the benefits of that contract without exposing the tenant to a level of risk that he will not accept. Therefore a productivity-maximizing contract will not be offered; see Mookherjee [1997].

This means that ownership of small plots that are predominantly farmed by family labor is associated with intrinsic productivity advantages that cannot be mimicked by contractual hiring of labor (unless some special conditions are met). These gains are efficiency gains in the second sense described in the previous subsection.

Imperfect labor markets and small-farm productivity

The preceding argument relied on a lack of perfect credit and insurance markets. This is why the land contract (or the labor contract) is forced to do double duty: it must provide incentives and insurance at the same time. In trying to do both, it fails to do either of them perfectly, because there are trade-offs involved. In particular, efficient incentive provision does not occur and productivity is lower on farms that are leased out or use hired labor.

A similar outcome can occur if *labor* markets are imperfect; in particular, if they display unemployment. To understand how this works, suppose first that there is full employment. Now evaluate the opportunity cost to a landowner of applying one unit of labor on the land. If this labor is *hired*, then the opportunity cost to the landowner is just the going wage rate per unit of labor,[19] but what if this is the landowner's *own* labor (or family labor)? The answer is that it's the going wage rate as well, because this is what one unit of labor *could* earn were it not to be applied on the land. In short, there is no difference in the opportunity cost of labor whether the labor is hired or is supplied internally by the family.

But the foregoing argument falls apart in a world of unemployment. For someone who hires labor, the opportunity cost of another unit of labor is still the market wage rate he needs to pay for that unit, but for family labor, the opportunity cost is *less* because there is the possibility of unemployment.

Exactly what the opportunity cost is for family labor in a climate of unemployment depends on the way in which the labor market functions. The details are unnecessary (but are given in a footnote)[20] as long as we are agreed that it must be less than the market wage. Now it is easy to see that small farms will put in more labor per acre than large farms and produce higher output per acre.

Figure 12.7 puts together these observations by drawing per-acre production functions (much the same way as we did for the Solow model in Chapter 3).[21] With a lower opportunity cost of labor (induced by the possibility of unemployment), small farms that use family labor will put in L^{**} units of labor per acre (this is the point at which marginal product equals *their* marginal cost). Large farms that hire in labor will use less units per acre (they are at L^*). Thus output per acre on small farms will tend to be higher.

Is this argument an argument for productivity gains in the sense of enhanced *market* efficiency? Here we are on slippery ground: the answer depends on the "true" marginal cost of labor. If there is unemployment in the labor market, it isn't a bad bet that the wage is too high relative to the social opportunity cost of labor. Thus a profit calculus that hinges on the market wage is likely to lead to underapplication of labor relative to the efficient level, so it appears that family farms that factor in the probability of unemployment in their opportunity cost calculations are moving closer to the efficient allocation of resources. However, a definitive answer to this inquiry must depend on a careful analysis of the particular imperfections in the labor market.

---

[19] It may be higher if there are incentive problems as in the previous subsection, but we neglect these to make our current argument as stark as possible.

[20] Here are two ways to model opportunity cost. One is that the family *knows* whether it can get a job or not. If it can, the opportunity cost is just the market wage, as in the full-employment case. If it can't, the opportunity cost is effectively zero (ignoring leisure for simplicity). On average, then, some families will have very low opportunity cost and some will have the same opportunity cost as an employer of labor. A second model is that the family does not know whether its labor can be employed elsewhere. If p is the probability of employment and w is the going wage rate, then the opportunity cost for a risk-neutral family is just the expected value, which is pw.

[21] These per-acre production functions presume constant returns to scale in land and labor (see the Appendix to Chapter 3). Again, this is a simplification. We have already acknowledged the possible gains from increasing returns and will include this in our summary. For now, we ignore it.

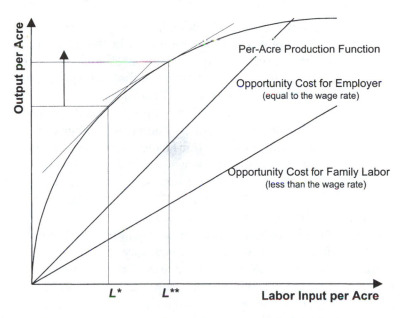

Figure 12.7. *Imperfect labor markets and small-farm productivity.*

Pooling land

It is possible to try to sidestep the productivity debate by pulling the reverse of a trick that we tried a few subsections ago: small farms must *always* win over large farms because of the incentive argument and because small landowners, if they so wish, can *pool* their land to take advantage of technological returns to scale.

This argument is problematic, however. The pooling of land recreates the incentive problem to *some* extent, although how much of it can be avoided depends on the precise source of returns to scale. For instance, suppose that the source of increasing returns is large-scale marketing. Then it is likely that the incentive problems *can* be dealt with through reform. The land can still be farmed separately and the fixed costs of setting up a marketing group can be pooled. It is not at all surprising that cooperatives whose main incentive to form was marketing have been relatively successful (the dairy cooperatives in India are a particularly visible example).[22]

On the other hand, suppose that the source of increasing returns lies at the production level (say, through the use of tractors). Then the incentive problem returns with full force: as long as *production* is joint, individual own-

---

[22] Another example of relatively successful cooperation is the sugar cooperatives of Maharashtra, India. Here, the source of increasing returns lies in crushing the sugar—a capital-intensive process in which the scope for moral hazard is minimal. The *cultivation* of sugar cane is carried out separately. For more on the role of cooperatives in rural development, see Attwood and Baviskar [1988].

ers will have a tendency to slack off. Indeed, the production activity *must* be joint if returns to scale are intrinsically embodied in the cultivation process.

A simple story that explains the incentive problem with joint farming has the same flavor as several disparate models that we have studied before. Joint production creates an *externality*. Additional effort by any one farmer leads to additional output, but the added output is *shared* among the whole team. That part of the marginal output that accrues to other members of the cooperative is an externality as far as our farmer is concerned, and unless he internalizes this through a complete sense of altruism, he will undersupply effort. To be sure, everybody else will do the same as well and productivity will be reduced below the efficient level. This is a *free-rider problem* characteristic of situations like the Prisoners' Dilemma.

We have used this sort of argument to explain the Marshallian inefficiency of sharecropping and in other contexts as well.[23] We leave the details of the argument here to an exercise at the end of the chapter.

Thus, even if you do see successful cooperatives that exploit increasing returns *outside* the cultivation sphere (such as mechanized processing or marketing), do not expect to see successful wheat or rice cooperatives. We have already seen in Chapter 10 how decollectivization in Chinese agriculture in the late 1970s brought about substantial gains in agricultural output. After collectivization in the early 1950s, TFP fell between 20 and 30% in the 1970s. In just a few years after the reforms (which essentially provided for use rights on plots), TFP was back to the precollectivization level and then continued to grow steadily through the 1980s (Wen [1993]).[24] Vietnam experienced similar gains from decollectivization (Pingali and Xuan [1992]).

Summary so far

We can summarize the observations in this section by saying that technology is at best neutral toward land size and may even favor large land sizes because of the possibility of extensive mechanization. On the other hand, with imperfect insurance markets, incentives favor the cultivation of land by owners and family labor: hired laborers and tenants typically must be given contracts that create an efficiency loss. Imperfect labor markets with unemployment heighten this proclivity by reducing the opportunity cost for family labor relative to that of hired labor. Finally, the technological gains of large farms cannot be achieved easily by small farms simply by pooling land,

---

[23] See, for instance, our analysis of fertility decisions in a joint family. The common features are brought out in Appendix 1 (Game Theory) at the end of the book.

[24] Chinese communes used the work-point system, under which output shares were determined, in part, by the ratio of work points accumulated by the individual to the total number of work points registered in the commune. To some extent, this serves to mitigate the free-rider problem because output *shares* themselves can be influenced by effort (see Sen [1964]), but this presumes that effort is *fully* observable, which is unlikely.

because that creates a free-rider problem. Hence there genuinely are two opposing sets of forces, and which effect dominates is ultimately an empirical question.

12.4.3. Land size and productivity: Empirical evidence

Available evidence suggests that the productivity gains arising from incentives (in the background of imperfect markets) do outweigh the technological returns to scale from larger plots, at least for developing countries. (Supermechanization on the order of magnitude seen in the United States and Canada is an entirely different matter altogether.) Roughly speaking, the following trend seems to be observed: the most productive farms are those that are owner-occupied and predominantly use family labor (although the very smallest farms do not unambiguously display higher productivity).[25] These are followed by large, mechanized, owner-cultivated farms that employ wage labor. There are efficiency losses with the hiring of labor, but these appear to be (partially) compensated for by mechanization. Last of all is sharecropped land, in which, as we have seen, the incentive problems arising from risk sharing are likely to be strongest. Our theories do not appear to be far off the mark.

Empirical productivity studies must be treated with a great deal of care. There is some reason to believe that small plots could be of higher quality. Good land may be more fragmented because of inheritance pressures. It may also be the case that farmers who sell off land in distress (thus becoming small holders) sell off the relatively less fertile part of their holdings. As Binswanger, Deininger, and Feder [1995] noted, there are not many studies that examine this issue (although Walker and Ryan [1990] empirically rejected the hypothesis that there is a negative correlation for size and productivity among the ICRISAT villages).

Abhijit Sen's [1981] study of a sample from West Bengal uses the value of output per acre as a measure of productivity (see preceding text for a tentative defence of this approach). Table 12.5 summarizes his findings. There appears to be clear evidence of a negative relationship between productivity and farm size among owner-cultivated farms. Among farms that have some tenanted land (under sharecropping), there is no clear trend. The very smallest farms have the lowest productivity in this case, but among the remaining classes of farms, productivity continues to decline with size. Note, however, that in every size class, productivity per acre on sharecropped land is lower than the productivity of the *same* farms under owner cultivation. Marshallian inefficiency, as in Shaban's [1987] study, is again at work. On average,

---

[25] Scale issues may really bite at very low farm sizes. Moreover, the poorest farmers may lack access to complementary inputs of production because of severe credit constraints (Binswanger, Deininger, and Feder [1995]).

Table 12.5. Rupees of output per acre by size group and tenure: West Bengal.

		Farms with some crop sharing		
Operated area (acres)	*Pure owners (Rs/acre)*	*Overall productivity (Rs/acre)*	*Productivity on owned land (Rs/acre)*	*Productivity on sharecropped land (Rs/acre)*
0–3	1313	798	867	604
3–5	1044	909	1099	709
5–8	960	842	1130	676
8–12	691 ⎫	843[a]	959[a]	604[a]
12+	624 ⎭			
All	902	851	1047	658

Source: Sen [1981: Table 7].
[a]The last two size groups have been merged because of an insufficient number of observations.

the productivity on owned land exceeds the productivity on sharecropped land by about 50%.

The inverse relationship appears at an aggregated level as well, even when the difference between owner-occupied and tenanted land is not explicitly taken into account. Tables 12.6 and 12.7, which present aggregated information for India (as a whole), northeast Brazil, the Punjab (Pakistan), and Muda (Malaysia), are taken from the work of Berry and Cline [1979]. The aggregated information supports the decreasing farm-size productivity relationship.[26] It seems that, regardless of the form of the operation, size per se plays a role. (As we have already noted, the decreasing productivity effect persists for tenants in the Sen study except at the very lowest farm sizes.) This situation suggests the possibility that labor market imperfections play a role in addition to the incentive effects, but verification of this point must await more careful empirical study.

The Berry–Cline studies also suggest that the larger the size differences, the larger the productivity differences. In northeast Brazil, the small farms are over *five* times as productive as their largest counterparts! The ratio narrows to 1.5 (which is still a sizable margin) for the relatively equal Muda River region. Thus, as Binswanger, Deininger, and Feder [1995] noted, there is some tentative support for the hypothesis that regions of greater inequality have proportionately more to gain, under an efficiency viewpoint alone, from land reform.

Rosenzweig and Binswanger [1993] emphasize another interesting aspect of the productivity–size relationship. They use the ICRISAT data set. Like the other studies, they too find that smaller farms are more productive, on

---

[26] These studies used income per acre rather than the value of output per acre. That is, all the studies subtract the cost of purchased inputs, so the effect of household labor (which we have focused on in the theoretical sections) is included in the net income calculations.

Table 12.6. Farm size and land productivity: India.

Range of farm size (acres)	Average farm size (acres)	Income per acre (rupees)
0–5	3.0	737
5–15	9.3	607
15–25	19.5	482
25+	42.6	346

Source: Berry and Cline [1979, Table A-1].

Table 12.7. Farm size and land productivity: Selected regions.

Farm size	Northeast Brazil	Punjab, Pakistan	Muda, Malaysia
Small farm (hectares)	563 (10.0–49.9)	274 (5.1–10.1)	148 (0.7–1.0)
Largest farm (hectares)	100 (500+)	100 (20+)	100 (5.7–11.3)

Notes: Largest farm productivity is normalized to 100. "Small farm" refers to second smallest size range. Source: Berry and Cline [1979].

average, than larger farms. However, they found that the advantages are systematically smaller in high-risk environments. The most powerful variable that measures this risk in their study is the variability in the date of arrival of the monsoon rains. The higher the variability in this indicator, the lower is the profitability of assets.[27] Small farms react more violently to this variable than large farms, so apart from a general decline in profitability for all wealth classes (except the richest groups), there is also a narrowing of the profit differential.

So access to credit and insurance clearly plays a role here. In particular, the greater the imperfections in these markets, the smaller the productivity differential is likely to be. It follows that land reform may have effects that outstrip the gains signaled by aggregate calculations of productivity differentials. If ownership of land also implies better access to credit, the productivity per acre of the beneficiaries may be further increased relative to the prereform values.[28]

[27] Unlike the other studies, Rosenzweig and Binswanger calculate the ratio of profits to total assets. If farming is the major occupation (which it is), this will be closely correlated with net output per acre, after subtracting production costs.

[28] The possibility that access to better credit markets might have significant effects on yields is seen in other studies as well. For instance, farm yields in Burkina Faso have been documented to be significantly affected by the availability of nonfarm income or access to credit (Reardon, Crawford and Kelley [1994] and Udry [1996]).

12.4.4. Land sales

So far, we have seen that a more equal distribution of land might result in significant productivity gains in the economy. Although there may be some loss in the exploitation of possible increasing returns, these losses appear to be more than outweighed by the incentive gains. We also have seen that tenancy contracts do not go all the way toward reaping these gains. The reason is that fixed-rent contracts are often not optimal in a second-best world. Large-scale hiring of labor, on the other hand, involves losses that arise from supervision costs.

This brings us to the issue of land *sales*. Specifically, if small landowners can buy land from rich landowners, then productivity gains can be realized. The question is, Do land markets work adequately?

All the empirical evidence that is available suggests that they do not. Land sales from relatively rich to relatively poor, while not entirely absent, are not very common either. There is some evidence for land sales by the relatively rich, perhaps to finance consumption spurts such as weddings or large investments (see, for instance, the box on ICRISAT villages earlier in this chapter or Cain [1981]), but most land sales appear to be in the form of distress sales that occur from *poor* to *rich* (see, for instance, Rosenzweig and Wolpin [1985]). These include land transfers in lieu of debt repayment (again, from relatively poor to relatively rich; see Chapter 14 for a discussion of collateral transfer).

Why are land sales markets so thin? Consider the value of land. When credit markets are imperfect, land value consists of two components. The first is the discounted sum of income streams that will emanate from working the land. The second component comes from imperfect credit markets: land can be used as collateral, and this ability has value (measured by the profitability of the additional loans that can be obtained as a result of mortgaging the land). Note that this second value would be zero if competitive credit markets prevailed and one could obtain all the loans one wanted at some going rate of interest. Under normal conditions, then, a seller will therefore want to sell the land for a price that is no less than the *sum* of these two values. Now consider what a buyer is willing to pay. If he can buy the land outright from his own funds, then he reaps both these gains as well, but if he must obtain a loan to buy the land and if he must mortgage that very piece of land for the loan, then he cannot reap the collateral value until the loan is paid off. Thus the collateral advantages of a land purchase are pushed back to a distant future when the loan has been repaid, so the buyer's *present valuation* of the land must be less than that of the seller. Thus no sale will occur; see Feder et al. [1988] and Binswanger, Deininger, and Feder [1995].

But the preceding argument has a loophole. It does not take into account the productivity gain that we discussed in the previous section. If small farmers are truly more efficient than large farmers because of the incentive problem, then the discounted sum of income streams (per acre) will be higher for small farmers than for large farmers. It remains to be seen whether the difference in this income stream outweighs the collateral value. If it does, then the absence of a land market cannot be explained with this argument.

This issue was explored by Mookherjee [1997], who showed that the foregoing argument can be rescued by explicitly studying the incentive problems that are associated with the *credit contract* that must be entered into in order to buy the land. Specifically, the optimal contract that will be designed by the lender will involve repayments to him that depend partly on the output produced by the borrower. Intuitively, a creditor effectively becomes the borrower's landlord for the period of time that the loan is outstanding. Fixed interest payments on the outstanding debt are like fixed-rent tenancy, and as we have already seen, fixed-rent tenancy is not optimal for the landlord. For the very same reason, fixed repayments are not an optimal contract for the lender. Thus the loan contract will have the same features as an optimal tenancy contract and will therefore affect productivity on the borrower's newly acquired land: specifically, it will lower productivity for exactly the same reason a tenancy contract lowers productivity. This removes the productivity advantage as long as the borrower is indebted and resurrects the collateral-based argument.[29]

12.4.5. Land reform

Putting together all that we have discussed so far, it seems that (i) productivity is higher on smaller plots than on larger plots, (ii) that these productivity gains cannot be realized by tenancy, because the tenancy contract itself erodes the productivity gain, and (iii) that land sales markets cannot adequately substitute for land tenancy markets.

To realize these gains, we are then left with the option of land transfers from rich to poor, either without adequate compensation or with full compensation paid by the government or by foreign donors, *but not entirely by the beneficiaries*. This last phrase is important. If full compensation is paid by the beneficiaries, then this is no different from a land sale, which, as we've already seen, would not have occurred spontaneously.

Unless the government wishes to spend its budget on compensating beneficiaries, or unless some enlightened foreign donor (the World Bank, perhaps!) earmarks funds especially for this purpose, it is hard to see how a

---

[29] Imperfect credit markets (and the consequent existence of a collateral value of land) are not the only factors that drive the price of land above the present discounted value of output produced from it. Speculative margins on land, especially for agricultural land that is close to an expanding city, or inflation, or government policies that discriminate in favor of large farmers all do the trick. Conversely, distress sales may be viewed as a situation in which the seller's asking price is *below* the present discounted value of the land income stream: precisely the opposite scenario. In this case land sales do become a viable proposition. Unfortunately, the seller is usually the poor farmer.

successful land reform can come about. It takes tremendous political will (resistance to powerful lobbies, in particular) to push a land reform program through. There is some possibility that large landowners will agree to *some* reform if they are faced with the credible threat of violence or forced expropriation (for a related line of reasoning, see Horowitz [1993][30]). Otherwise, major land reforms have been the product of political upheavals in society, as in Cuba, Japan, Korea, and Taiwan. Political upheaval has the advantage that large landowners are viewed as enemies, or collaborators with the previous regime, and so there is immense popular support for land reform (without the countervailing lobbies).

To be sure, there are intermediate steps that lie between government inaction and large-scale redistribution. Providing tenants with unlimited *use rights* to land is one of them. We discussed an instance of this when we studied eviction (see the box on Operation Barga). Although such reforms undoubtedly go in the right direction and can have significant effects on productivity, they fall short of reaping the full gains in an environment of imperfect credit markets. Without ownership rights, land cannot be pledged as collateral for productivity-enhancing investments. Seized land also may be redistributed as collectives, as in Mexico or Peru, but we have already remarked on the possible incentive problems associated with collective farming. Finally, land ceilings may be used to curtail ownership of large plots. Even though such ceilings are in force in many developing countries, they are easily sidestepped by holding land in several parcels under the names of friends and relatives.

We end this chapter by studying land reform movements in Korea and in Mexico. The contrasts between the two will be apparent. Our discussion leans heavily on the book by Powelson and Stock [1987].

Land Reforms: South Korea and Mexico

South Korea

Large-scale land reforms were instituted in Korea in the years following World War II. Korea was a Japanese colony before the war. The defeat of Japan and the establishment of a U.S. military government not only led to a major change in Japan's

---

[30] In the Horowitz model, land reform is viewed as a response to the possibility of destructive conflict. Landowners may agree to policies that redistribute some of their land, because the alternative is far worse for them. What is of interest is that a particular reform may generate the impetus for a further reform by altering the status quo in which agents find themselves. Thus even if there is no arrival of fresh information or any changes in the intrinsic parameters of potential conflict, land reform may appear as a continuing series of relatively small redistribution episodes, rather than one cataclysmic event. On related matters as well as for an insightful analysis of Latin American land relations, see de Janvry [1981].

international political relations, but also a radical reorientation of internal political forces that paved the way for massive redistribution of land. In contrast to many other countries, Korean land reform was not restricted to legal documents and official proclamations—it was brisk and effective.

The bedrock of the land redistribution scheme was the Land Reform Act of 1949 (amended in 1950). The Japanese, in their constant search for cheap sources of rice, had taken an active interest in Korean agriculture and acquired substantial land holdings in that country. Most of this land was transferred to former tenants at low rates: they were to pay the government 20% of their annual output for fifteen years. Thus, 240,000 hectares of Japanese-owned land were conferred upon Korean peasants. Land was also transferred from large domestic landowners to their tenants under the land-to-the-tiller scheme and the original owners were compensated. The Act stipulated that all rented land plus owned land above 3 *chongbo*[31] would be purchased by the government and sold to tenants. Landlords were compensated in government bonds worth 1.5 times the annual output on the land. Tenants, on the other hand, had to pay the government 30% of the annual yield on acquired land for five years. By 1952, 330,000 hectares were redistributed.

A major part of the transfer of land took place by direct sale from landlord to tenant. As we will now see, this does not contradict the earlier arguments in the text, because the sale price for the landlord was effectively driven below the present value of land income by the overall climate of land reform.

The government encouraged mutual arrangements in the first place, but more importantly, economic and political conditions were such as to create incentives for direct settlements and bypass official channels. By the late 1940s, tenants had acquired sufficient political clout and patronage, so much so that in many instances, that they stopped paying rent altogether, assuming *de facto* ownership. When the official reforms were initiated, the government was slow to redeem the bonds used as compensation; the market value of the bonds fell to such low levels as to make compensation worth approximately 3.5 *sok* of rice per *chongbo*. In contrast, the tenant's obligation to the government stood at around 19 *sok* per *chongbo* in the current discounted value. The substantial gap left a great deal of room for profitable private negotiation. The result was that as much as 550,000 hectares of land were transferred through direct sales. However, note that the landlord's fallback position was *not* the retention of his land: that land was going to go anyway, which is why the land market was so active.

Table 12.8 illustrates how the ownership pattern of land in the countryside was dramatically transformed by the reform in less than two decades. In 1945, 4% of the farm households held more than 3 *chongbo* of land and accounted for 26% of the cultivated acreage. In 1960, only 0.3% of households owned more than 3 *chongbo* and together they controlled just 1.2% of total acreage. One-half of the country's agricultural land had been redistributed to two-thirds of its rural population. Clearly, a greatly egalitarian distribution of land was created in South Korea, starting from a very skewed pattern of ownership that is typical to so many backward countries, within a remarkably short span of time.

---

[31] A *chongbo* is almost 1 hectare; 0.992 hectare, to be precise.

Table 12.8. Land under different occupational groups in Korea, 1947 and 1964.

	Share of land held (%)	
Category	1947	1964
Owner	16.5	71.6
Part owners	38.3	23.2
Tenants	42.1	5.2
Farm laborers	3.1	0

Source: Powelson and Stock [1987].

Its great success apart, some special features of Korean land reforms demand our attention; a few of them doubtlessly provide clues to that very success.

In many countries, attempts at land reform by the government have been thwarted by the strong lobbies of large landowners, through surreptitious manipulation of the state and bureaucratic machinery. Landlords routinely take advantage of loopholes in the law or flagrantly flout the law itself. Korean landlords had few such luxuries. Most large landowners were tainted by their cooperation with the Japanese and had therefore lost all political clout and state patronage, which led to a breakdown of traditional power relations in the countryside. Reforms were easy in such an environment.

Second, in spite of the massive transfers, the *operational* size distribution remained more or less intact. Very little land was broken up and the same farmers largely cultivated the same plots. The only difference was that erstwhile tenants assumed ownership rights on a wide scale. Consequently there was little fear of a drop in productivity in the turmoil of the transition. Finally, the land redistribution scheme was not accompanied by state intervention in other spheres of agricultural activity, such as marketing, credit, or input supplies—a feature that is rare in other countries where such reforms have been attempted. The farmer's independence was left intact, and the tenant's acquisition of land was not tied to clauses that made his reliance on the state excessive.

Apart from the egalitarian aspect of the Korean land reforms, its impact on overall agricultural productivity was no less cheerful. In the eight years immediately following the reforms, value added in agriculture grew at an annual rate of 4.0%. Over a longer horizon, agricultural output increased by 3.5% per annum from 1952 to 1971, and at 3.8% from 1971 to 1982, which amounts to an annual growth rate of 2% per capita in the latter period.

Mexico

Land reform measures in Mexico were instituted after the Revolution of 1910–17. Article 27 of the Constitution of 1917 brought all land under state ownership. However, the government reserved the right to transfer land to private citizens at its discretion. The "revolution of the south" had fought for communal farming (to form *ejidos* or communal farms), whereas the "revolution of the north" demanded small private properties. The government struck a compromise by permitting both forms, depending on local needs.

At the core of Mexico's land reform legislation, therefore, lies an essential arbitrariness, which is perhaps both a symptom and a cause of the failure of the reforms to change drastically the ownership and power structure in the countryside. Land redistribution, in practice, has proceeded at a very slow pace, spread over several decades; it occurred in short spurts during certain presidencies [notably that of Lazaro Cardenas (1934–40)], and was interspersed with long periods of inactivity. The last major expropriations took place in 1975.

Unlike South Korea, the wealthy landed class yielded substantial political clout in Mexico even in the postrevolution phase. Using their influence in government and bureaucratic circles, and taking advantage of several loopholes in the law, they were able to short-circuit the redistribution process to a considerable extent. In La Antigua, which comprises 10,000 hectares, the sugar mills and the best acreage around it were excluded from expropriation in the 1920s. Landlords often perpetrated violence on the supporters of reform: peasant leaders were murdered. In San Andrés-Tuxtla a number of commercial crops were grown, and half the acreage was devoted to cattle grazing. In the late Porfiriato, large export-oriented tobacco haciendas operated by wealthy landowners were abundant. There was intense activity of peasant leagues in these regions in the 1920s and 1930s; yet cattlemen and large owners continued to dominate, partly through the use of violence.

To the extent that redistribution actually took place, recipients were chosen not on the basis of well-defined criteria set down in the books, but on the basis of political favor mongering. In fact, land transfers (apart from the limited doses in which they were doled out) were cynically used by the ruling party as an instrument to gain a political stranglehold over the peasantry.

We may conclude that the reason behind the government's half-hearted execution of land reforms was twofold. First, reform did not yield sufficient power over the old landed aristocracy; indeed, to a large extent, the aristocracy had infiltrated the government. In addition, the government was not entirely willing to settle the land question once and for all: the issue needed to be kept alive to draw the peasants and peasant organizations into the orbit of the ruling party. Such dependence was further reinforced through the government's control over the channels of credit and input supply. These considerations were revealed in the following excerpt from an article in *The Wall Street Journal*, 14th February, 1984 (quoted in Powelson and Stock [1987]):

> "They have to come to us first if they want land," says an official with the peasant confederation. "Even if they get land, they have to come to us to get water. If they get water, they still need credits and fertilizer. The party will never lose control of the countryside."

The irregular, uncertain, and unpredictable nature of land expropriation and transfers, together with the free-rider problems caused by the formation of cooperatives with ill-defined property rights, surely undermined the productivity of Mexican agriculture and caused it to stagnate over a very long period. Table 12.9 speaks for itself.

Table 12.9. Index of Mexican agricultural output, overall and per capita.

	Agricultural output (1975 = 100)					
	1961	*1966*	*1971*	*1975*	*1979*	*1983*
Total	66	85	96	100	116	131
Per capita	106	115	108	100	103	103

Source: United Nations FAO *Production Yearbook*, 1973 and 1983; reproduced from Powelson and Stock [1987].

12.5. Summary

In this chapter, we studied land markets. We began with a study of land *rental* contracts. A landowner leases out his land to a tenant for cultivation and charges rent. The contract may be in the form of a *fixed-rent tenancy*, in which a constant sum is paid by the tenant to the landlord regardless of the output that he produces, or a *sharecropping tenancy*, in which a share of the output is relinquished by the tenant to the landlord as rent. To be sure, these are extreme forms, and we observed several variations, such as the provision of credit as part of the tenancy contract or the cost sharing of production inputs between the landlord and the tenant.

Share tenancy poses a puzzle. Economists such as Adam Smith and Alfred Marshall have argued for the superiority of fixed-rent tenancy on incentive grounds. Fixed rent allows the tenant to retain the *full* marginal product of his efforts and, therefore, does not distort the tenant's choice of inputs. In contrast, sharecropping lowers the marginal product of effort, or at least that part of it that accrues to the tenant. Thus sharecropping should be associated with lower land productivity: it should display what is known in the literature as *Marshallian inefficiency*. To be sure, this argument presumes that tenant inputs are unobservable.

Marshallian inefficiency is observed empirically. This suggests that the preponderance of sharecropping in Asia is unproductive. We studied how sharecropping, despite this inefficiency, can be an equilibrium outcome. An important driving force is the existence of uncertainty, coupled with imperfect or nonexistent mechanisms for insurance. In such situations the provision of incentives creates large uncertainties for the tenant. The tenant is willing to pay a premium for the removal (or amelioration) of this uncertainty, and we showed that the landlord has an incentive to provide such partial insurance in the land contract. Essentially, this involves sharing in the tenant's output.

There are other roles for sharecropping as well. Among them are situations in which *both* landlords and tenants participate in production (the *double-incentive* problem), in which there are restrictions (physical, legal, or social) on the tenant's ability to repay (*limited liability*), or environments in which *cost sharing* of inputs is widespread.

We ended our discussion of land rental contracts by considering the phenomenon of *eviction*. We viewed eviction as another instrument that the landlord might use to provide incentives and we discussed situations in which eviction clauses may be implicit or explicit in tenancy arrangements. Of particular interest in this context are situations in which the tenant is granted *use rights* to the land (while he does not have ownership as in a full land reform, the landlord cannot evict him). We discussed how this form of partial land reform can affect land productivity.

We then moved on to the study of land ownership, land sales, and land reform. The first important question is, Do small farms have higher productivity than large farms? We described what we mean by "productivity" in this context, and then provided some theoretical arguments and empirical evidence that bear on this question. Among the theoretical issues are (i) increasing returns to scale, (ii) the incentive problems of tenancy and large-scale farming using hired labor, and (iii) differential productivity effects resulting from unemployment in the labor market. The empirical evidence supports the contention that small farms, by and large, exhibit higher productivity.

If small farms have higher productivity, why doesn't a land *sales* market spontaneously arise to transfer land from relatively large to relatively small landholders? Unfortunately, the evidence suggests that land sales are not very common, and even where they occur, they are often in the form of distress sales from small to large landowners. We considered theoretical arguments for the absence of a land sales market.

Finally, we briefly studied *land reform*: the transfer of land from large to small landowners with or without partial compensation.

Appendix 1: Principal–agent theory and applications
12.A.1. Risk, moral hazard, and the agency problem

Hidden information and hidden action

Over the last twenty years, it has become increasingly apparent that the incompleteness and asymmetry of information between agents have a strong influence on market structures, the nature of economic transactions, and the kind of contractual arrangements people enter into. For instance, the Marshallian attack on sharecropping assumes that tenant effort is *unobserved* by the landlord, and cannot be specified. This is an example of informational incompleteness and, indeed, such incompleteness influences the choice of contract by the landlord.

Actually, two kinds of informational problems are known to have significant effects. One is the problem of *hidden information*. For example, workers may come in various levels of skills. An individual worker may know what his own level of proficiency is, but a prospective employer can only make a rough guess. Of course, the worker could communicate his knowledge, but the act of communication is itself fraught with incentive problems. For instance, each worker would like to tell the employer that he is of high quality, but how can he credibly do so? The problem in this case is to devise a contract or scheme that will accurately reveal the information of the agent. An example of this kind of problem is the screening model, introduced in the text and described more fully in Appendix 2 of this chapter.

The second problem is that of *hidden action*, often called the problem of *moral hazard*. In the hidden action problem, the benefit of a transaction to one party depends on some action taken by the other party; however, the latter may not have any incentive to take the beneficial action after a contract has been signed between the two. This is precisely the problem with a fixed-wage contract, where the action in question has to do with the choice of effort. The key element is that the action to be taken is not publicly observable, and it is difficult or impossible, therefore, to prove in a court of law that the party concerned has neglected an assigned task. A classic example is that of fire insurance. Once a building has been completely insured against accidental damage due to fire, its owner will have no incentive to install and maintain costly fire-fighting devices. Failure to do so will significantly increase the hazard of fire in the building and will reduce the company's ability to provide insurance at an affordable premium. This situation may end up hurting both parties: clients have to pay very high premiums and may not be able to purchase sufficient insurance; insurance firms, on the other hand, suffer considerable loss of business. A large part of the literature on contract theory is concerned with such problems and examines how contracts can be devised so as to provide built-in incentives that minimize the scope of morally hazardous behavior in an optimal way.

Risk and moral hazard: Interaction

We take up the hidden action or moral hazard problem here. At first sight, it appears that the problem is easy enough to solve. Simply ask for a fixed payment from the agent whose actions are difficult to monitor. Saddled with all the residual incentives, the agent will indeed choose the correct action. This is precisely the logic that underlies the Marshallian demonstration of the efficiency of fixed-rent tenancy.

However, what makes it difficult, if not impossible, to implement this sort of solution is the fact that *the provision of incentives is intimately tied to the provision of insurance*. In particular, more of one is less of the other. Consider again the debate on sharecropping versus fixed-rent tenancy. Note that to provide insurance to the tenant, the tenant's return must become more insensitive to the output produced by him. Indeed, insensitivity to outside fluctuations is what insurance is all about. Now it should be obvious that incentives to work are diluted. The two features—risk and moral hazard—interact, and resolving this interaction in a satisfactory way is the issue studied in *principal–agent models*, to which we now turn.

Principal–agent theory

There is a large class of economic models in which an economically powerful entity, called the principal, attempts to devise contractual arrangements with one or more individuals, called agents, in a way that best serves the former's interest. Examples include a firm hiring employees, a government trying to find a supplier to provide some public good like a highway, the regulation of public utilities, or a landlord–tenant relationship. The principal is supposed to have control over scarce assets or production processes that give him monopoly or quasi-monopoly power, so that he can dictate the terms of the contract or make take-it-or-leave-it offers. However, there are two constraints that must be met.

First, agents have alternative uses and opportunities for their effort and resources. To accept a contract, the agent must be compensated for the opportunity cost of his resources and time.[32] The utility a typical agent could earn by the best alternative use of his available resources is often called his "reservation utility." The principal, in devising the contract, has to take care that the agent earns at least his reservation utility from the deal (otherwise his offer will be refused). This restriction on the principal's choices is called the *participation constraint*.

Second, there is the problem of hidden action. A principal must understand that the agent will take the action most suited to his own preferences. If the action is to be altered, the terms of the contract must be suitably modified to provide the agent enough motivation to carry out the alteration. This restriction is known as the *incentive constraint*.

The optimal contract is chosen to yield the highest possible return to the principal, subject to the satisfaction of these two constraints. Let us now illustrate how this works in the context of land tenancy.

---

[32] Throughout the principal–agent literature, agents are given the freedom to refuse an offer. Therefore, slave economies and bonded labor fall outside the direct purview of this kind of analysis.

12.A.2. *Tenancy contracts revisited*

The landlord–tenant relationship beautifully illustrates the tension between risk sharing and incentives. Begin with a landlord who owns a plot of land and wishes to devise the most profitable contract for a prospective tenant/worker. Thus the landlord here is the principal and the tenant is the agent. The tenant has a reservation utility (i.e., the utility he will obtain by making the best use of his time and resources elsewhere) $\bar{U}$, which is exogenously given. The contract that the landlord offers should provide the tenant an expected utility of at least $\bar{U}$ for it to be accepted. This condition is the *participation constraint*.

Let Q denote the output obtained after cultivation. Suppose Q can take two values: "high" (H) or "low" (L). These values are realized probabilistically. The probability of the high output depends crucially on the agent's effort input. In particular, suppose that there are two levels of effort, e, to choose from: $e = 0$ or $e = 1$. When there is zero effort, the probability of high output is q. On the other hand, when the higher level of effort is provided, there is a higher probability $p\,(> q)$ of the high output being realized. However, the higher effort level involves a cost E for the tenant; hence, he will be unwilling to put in high effort unless that effort significantly affects the payment he receives from the principal. We assume, without loss of generality, that there is no cost of providing low effort.

The tenant is risk-averse. This is captured by ascribing to him a utility function of money of the form $U = U(w)$ (w being the monetary payment he receives), where $U(\cdot)$ is a strictly increasing and concave function. The concavity of $U(\cdot)$, by definition, implies the inequality

(12.3) $$\theta U(w_1) + (1 - \theta)U(w_2) < U(\theta w_1 + (1 - \theta)w_2),$$

where θ is any proper fraction and w_1 and w_2 are two different possible values of the agent's monetary income. Inequality (12.3) merely says that whenever the agent faces some uncertainty, that is, has the prospect of two unsure income levels, each with a given chance, his *expected utility* is lower than what his utility would have been if he received the expected *monetary* income *for sure*. (See the discussion in this chapter and in Chapter 10, and consult, especially, Figure 10.13.)

Overall utility is just the utility of money minus the effort cost (if any).

We assume that the principal is risk-neutral, so that his objective is to write an acceptable contract that maximizes his own expected monetary return.

For the problem to be interesting and nontrivial, we impose two conditions:

(1) We assume that the provision of high effort maximizes expected net surplus (and is hence Pareto efficient). Mathematically, this can be written as the condition

(12.4) $$pH + (1 - p)L - E > qH + (1 - q)L.$$

On rearrangement, this becomes

(12.5) $$(p - q)(H - L) > E.$$

(2) We assume that whatever the actual choice of effort, the expected net output generated is always enough to pay the agent a compensation that gives him at least his reservation utility. Given the previous assumption, all we need to specify is that there is enough surplus generated in the low-effort case. Mathematically,

(12.6) $$qH + (1 - q)L \geq \bar{w},$$

where $\bar{w}$ is the certain payment that will provide the agent exactly his reservation utility, that is,

(12.7) $$U(\bar{w}) = \bar{U}.$$

The first-best contract (efforts observed)

Suppose that the landlord can costlessly observe (and a law enforcing third party costlessly verify) the effort put in by the agent. The contracted payment to the agent can then be made conditional on the provision of a stipulated level of effort and the landlord, by prior agreement, can refuse to make any payment (or even impose a fine) if the agent fails to meet the required condition regarding effort. Thus only the participation constraint matters in this situation, not the incentive constraint.

In such a case, the optimal contract for the principal is one that asks the agent to put in $e = 1$, promising a sure payment of $\bar{w}_c$ [where $U(\bar{w}_c) = \bar{U} + E$] if and only if the tenant provides this effort. For the principal, this is preferable to asking for zero effort and paying the lower compensation $\bar{w}$ because by the preceding assumption 1, higher effort generates higher *net* expected surplus, and the principal can appropriate the whole of it if he can observe and specify the agent's level of effort.

Moreover, the optimal contract necessarily involves the same payment to the agent, irrespective of outcome, because the principal (being risk-neutral)

is better off bearing all the risk himself. A more precise argument runs as follows. Suppose the principal were to offer an acceptable contract that offered a wage w_1 in the case of high output and w_2 in the case of low output, with $w_1 \neq w_2$. First note that if this provided an expected utility any higher than $\bar{U}$, then the principal would be able to do better by reducing any one of the payments slightly. Hence, a maximizing principal will set

$$(12.8) \qquad\qquad pU(w_1) + (1 - p)U(w_2) = \bar{U}.$$

Let $\tilde{w}$ be the expected payment in the foregoing scheme, that is,

$$(12.9) \qquad\qquad \tilde{w} = pw_1 + (1 - p)w_2.$$

By the assumption that $U(\cdot)$ is a concave function, we have

$$(12.10) \qquad\qquad U(\tilde{w}) > pU(w_1) + (1 - p)U(w_2),$$

which, in conjunction with (12.8) and (12.9) implies that

$$(12.11) \qquad\qquad U(\tilde{w}) > \bar{U}.$$

Thus, if instead of making the conditional payments (w_1, w_2), the principal were to offer the fixed payment $\tilde{w}$ for sure, he would provide the agent with *more* than his reservation utility. Hence, the principal can offer a sure payment of slightly less than $\tilde{w}$ (say $\tilde{w} - \delta$), while still satisfying the participation constraint. The principal, being risk-neutral, worries only about minimizing the expected *monetary* payment to be made, and hence, clearly prefers the latter arrangement (paying $\tilde{w} - \delta$ regardless of outcome) to the former (paying w_1 or w_2, contingent on the final output). Hence the optimal contract in the full information case involves a fixed payment to the agent, just enough to cover his reservation utility. This is nothing but a labor hiring contract at a predetermined wage.

The second-best contract (efforts unobserved)

Now, let us assume, as is more realistic in most situations, that the tenant's actual supply of effort is *not* observable to the principal. What are the characteristics of the best contract the principal can design in such a scenario? Such a contract is often referred to as the "second-best" contract, to distinguish it from the previous one (i.e., the best contract under full observability of effort). We now see that the principal will want to make the payment conditional on output, paying out a high amount when the output is higher.

To begin with, suppose the best second-best contract is such that it *does* induce the agent to choose high effort. Whether it is optimal to write such a contract is something we will check later. For now, we assume that the principal is trying to design a contract that will induce the agent to choose $e - 1$, and we figure out the best possible way in which the principal can achieve this goal.

Let the contract specify a payment w_H in the case of high output and w_L when output is low. The problem is to find the values of w_H and w_L that will maximize the principal's expected return, subject to the constraints that exist. The first of these is the *incentive constraint*. If the agent is to choose a high effort voluntarily, the payment scheme must be such that his expected utility from doing so is at least as much as that from choosing a low effort. This implies the inequality

$$pU(w_H) + (1 - p)U(w_L) - E \geq qU(w_H) + (1 - q)U(w_L),$$

which, on rearrangement, becomes

(12.12) $$(p - q)[U(w_H) - U(w_L)] \geq E.$$

It is immediately obvious that because $p > q$ and $E > 0$ by assumption, we must have $w_H > w_L$ for the inequality to hold. Hence, any payment scheme that gives the agent an incentive to provide high effort must pay him more in good states (i.e., when output is high) than in bad states. The intuition is clear: the self-interested agent will care for a better outcome only if he has some personal stake in it.

The second constraint that the principal faces is the *participation constraint*. The agent's expected utility under the contract should not fall short of his reservation utility. This translates into the inequality

(12.13) $$pU(w_H) + (1 - p)U(w_L) - E \geq \bar{U}.$$

We now note the following statement.

Observation 1. *For the optimal contract, the incentive constraint (12.12) must be satisfied with equality.*

The reason is as follows. Consider any contract (inducing $e = 1$) so that (12.12) holds with *strict* inequality. Now allow the principal to make the following two adjustments. First, he reduces w_H and increases w_L by small amounts, so as to keep the expected value $pw_H + (1 - p)w_L$ the same as before. Because the incentive constraint held with inequality in the first place, it will continue to be satisfied if the size of the adjustment is small enough.

However, this adjustment raises the agent's expected utility from the contract, because it reduces the risk in his income (see Figure 12.6 and the discussion around it), while keeping its expected value the same. Therefore, given that the participation constraint (12.13) was originally satisfied, it must now be *strictly* satisfied, because the agent's expected utility has gone up.

The principal can now carry out a second adjustment to the terms of the contract: he can profitably reduce w_L by a small amount. This makes incentives (for high effort) even better and the participation constraint still holds if the reduction is small. Whereas the first adjustment gives the principal neither a gain nor a loss, because it keeps the expected payment the same, the second is clearly a gain. Hence, starting from a contract where the incentive constraint holds strictly, the principal always has a feasible way to redesign it so as to increase his expected net return. So Observation 1 must be true.

Now consider the following statement.

Observation 2. *In the optimal contract, if $w_L > 0$, then the participation constraint (12.13) must hold with equality as well.*

The proof is similar to the previous one. Suppose the participation constraint is strictly satisfied to begin with. Then lowering w_L by a small amount will still satisfy that constraint. Note also that the incentive constraint continues to be met, so it follows that the principal will certainly make this reduction if he can. The only possibility that will prevent him from doing so is that w_L may be zero to begin with, so that reducing it further would mean asking the agent to pay a penalty (rather than receive a payment) in the case of a poor harvest. Due to legal, institutional, or ethical reasons or reasons stemming from credit-market imperfections (a typical poor tenant/worker is unlikely to have much stored wealth of his own from which to pay a fine), a landlord is very unlikely to be able to exercise such an option.[33]

The preceding claims and the technique for solving the optimal values of w_H and w_L can be illustrated by a simple diagram. If we rewrite the incentive and participation constraints in the form of equalities rather than weak inequalities, we have the equations

(12.14) $$(p - q)[U(w_H) - U(w_L)] = E$$

and

(12.15) $$pU(w_H) + (1 - p)U(w_L) = \bar{U} + E.$$

By placing $U(w_H)$ and $U(w_L)$ on the Y and X axis, respectively, we can plot these two equations; see Figure 12.8. It is easy to see that equation (12.14) represents a straight line with slope 1 and intercept $E/(p - q)$ (the line AB in each panel of the figure), whereas equation (12.15) represents another straight

---

[33] The condition that the agent cannot be offered negative payments, that is, asked to pay a penalty, under any contingency, is known as a limited liability constraint; see main text. There is nothing, in principle, to prevent the landlord from imposing penalties in the event of adverse outcomes. However, in many contexts, it seems natural and realistic to impose limited liability constraints on the agent. It is not necessary, though, that the minimum payment in any contingency has to be zero. It can be any positive or negative number that seems suitable.

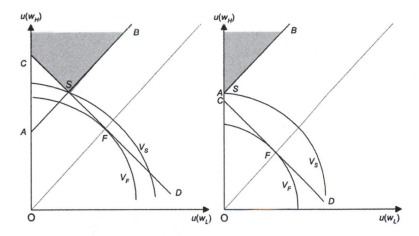

Figure 12.8. Solving for the optimal contract.

line, negatively sloped, with slope $-(1-p)/p$ and intercept $(\bar{U}+E)/p$ (drawn as the line CD in each panel of the figure). The landlord's task is to choose a pair $(w_H,\ w_L)$ or, equivalently, choose a point $(U(w_H),\ U(w_L))$ in Figure 12.8 to satisfy the two constraints. Note that all points lying above the line AB satisfy the incentive constraint, whereas those lying above CD satisfy the participation constraint. The *feasible set* of points from which the landlord can choose his contract is then given by the common region, which is marked by the shaded areas in the figure.

Next, we can draw the landlord's indifference curves. Any particular indifference curve is a locus of $(U(w_H),\ U(w_L))$ pairs that provide the same expected return to the landlord. These are downward sloping and concave, with lower indifference curves representing higher expected return for the landlord. If the landlord is to pay a higher amount in any one state, he must pay a lower amount in the other to keep his expected return the same; this explains the negative slope. If payment in one state is lowered and that in the other state is held constant, the landlord's expected return goes up because he has to make a lower expected payment; this explains why lower indifference curves signify higher expected returns. The argument for concavity is a bit more subtle and depends on the concavity of the $U(\cdot)$ function. Start at a point on an indifference curve with $U(w_H) \ge U(w_L)$. Now, say w_L is reduced somewhat and w_H is simultaneously increased so as to keep the expected payment the same. The agent now faces a risky income. Due to risk aversion, the loss in w_L is weighed more in utility terms than the corresponding gain in w_H. The larger is the (mean preserving) transfer from w_L to w_H, the smaller will be the increase in $U(w_H)$ relative to the fall in $U(w_L)$. Hence we have the concave shape of the landlord's indifference curves.[34]

---

[34] A parallel argument holds in the less relevant case where w_L initially exceeds w_H.

One further characteristic of the indifference curves is worth mentioning. At its point of intersection with the 45° line (i.e., wherever $w_H = w_L$), each indifference curve has a slope of $-(1-p)/p$. This is because such points represent complete income insurance, so that the agent is almost willing to accept a *very small* mean preserving transfer of income across good and bad states.

Going back to Figure 12.8, we have separately represented two cases. In the left-hand panel of the figure, $(\bar{U}+E)/p > E/(p-q)$, so that the intercept of CD is higher than that of AB. Clearly, the landlord, in trying to attain the lowest indifference curve, will choose the corner point S of the feasible set. This point, then, represents the second-best contract. The corresponding values on the two axes $U(w_H^*)$ and $U(w_L^*)$ give us the optimal payment scheme (w_H^*, w_L^*) from the utility function. Notice that the line AB (on which S lies) is merely an upward shift of the 45° line. Hence, in the optimal contract, it must be true that $U(w_H^*) > U(w_L^*)$, which in turn implies $w_H^* > w_L^*$. This confirms what we previously argued verbally.

The case represented in the right-hand panel is very similar to the first, only more extreme. Here, $(\bar{U}+E)/p < E/(p-q)$, so that the intercept of CD is lower than that of AB. As a result, the participation constraint is never binding: the incentive constraint exclusively determines the feasible set. The optimum point is at the corner A, which involves a payment of OA in the good state, but a zero payment in case of low output. This is an extreme example of incentives in a contract: the landlord refuses any payment at all (or makes the lowest possible payment) if performance is poor.

It is instructive to compare this with the contract given in the case of observable effort (i.e., the first-best contract). In that contract, the incentive constraint is irrelevant, so that the landlord merely chooses the lowest indifference curve without falling below the line CD (representing the participation constraint). Evidently, the best point to choose is that point on the line CD that is tangent to one of the landlord's indifference curves. Remember that CD has a slope of $-(1-p)/p$, which is the slope of the in difference curves at their point of intersection with the 45° line. Hence, tangency occurs at the point F, where CD crosses the 45° line. This point then represents the first-best contract. Being on the 45° line, this point provides the same utility $U(\tilde{w}_c)$ to the agent in either state, that is, it involves the same payment $\tilde{w}_c$ in each state. This confirms the assertion that in the case of observable effort, the optimal contract should provide full income insurance to the agent.

Furthermore, note that the indifference curve V_S passing through S is above the curve passing through F (V_F). Hence, when the tenant's effort cannot be observed, the landlord's expected return is lower than in the full information case. In other words, providing incentives for high effort is costly to the landlord.

Indeed, might the landlord be better off by not providing any incentives and simply letting the tenant choose lower effort? In the latter case, it is best for the landlord to pay $\bar{w}$ in either outcome. For the best contract with high-effort incentive to be truly optimal, it is necessary that the landlord's expected return be at least as great as what he would have obtained by not providing any incentive at all. This amounts to the condition

(12.16) $$p(H - w_H^*) + (1 - p)(L - w_L^*) \geq qH + (1 - q)L - \bar{w},$$

which on rearrangement becomes

(12.17) $$(p - q)(H - L) \geq pw_H^* + (1 - p)w_L^* - \bar{w}.$$

Note that if the increase in probability of high output with high effort $(p - q)$ and the difference in magnitude between high and low output $(H - L)$ is high enough relative to the cost of providing incentives [the right-hand side of inequality (12.17)], the landlord will prefer the high-effort contract.

Summary

In a world of perfect information the best contract that the principal can design is a contract that pays the agent a fixed wage irrespective of the outcome in production. This is good for the agent because he is made immune from any randomness in his income. It is also good for the principal because by implicitly offering income insurance to the agent (which the principal can well afford because of his own risk neutrality), he also implicitly extracts a premium from him.

Problems arise when the agent's actions and inputs are hidden, that is, when there is scope for moral hazard. If the agent is given a fixed compensation by contract, then he has a strong incentive to provide as little input as possible (because effort is costly) and then blame the poor outcome on bad weather or any other damaging exogenous factor beyond his control. To ensure that the agent puts in a good, if not efficient, amount of input, the contract has to provide him some stake in the outcome. Thus, he must be paid more when the outcome is good, but has to be penalized by reduced pay in the case of bad outcomes. This, however, introduces an element of randomness in the agent's income, because even in the case of good input supply, the outcome may be bad through sheer bad luck. Because insurance is mutually profitable, it is clear that the provision of incentives in the contract entails a corresponding loss in the form of reduced insurance. The stronger the incentives the principal would like to provide, the greater is the insurance loss. This trade-off between the insurance and incentive aspects in a contract forms the most fundamental issue in the literature on principal–agent relationships. Theoretical research attempts to identify the form of contracts that strike the optimal balance between the two aspects and tries to explain real world contractual arrangements and institutions in the process.

Appendix 2: Screening and sharecropping

This simple model illustrates how sharecropping may arise when landlords are unsure about the true ability and productivity of their tenants, and may then offer a menu of different contracts, each suitable for a specific type of agent.

Suppose there are two possible types of prospective tenants—one with high ability and the other with low. Cultivating a given plot of land, a high-ability tenant can produce an output Q_H, whereas a low-ability tenant can produce Q_L, with $Q_H > Q_L$. Other than the tenant's ability, there is no other factor affecting output. Hence, we assume away natural uncertainties and the problems of shirking or low-effort supply that lay at the core of the previous model. This is only to achieve exclusive focus on a different set of issues. Assume that the landlord does not know what the true ability of a prospective tenant is, but attaches a probability p to the event that the tenant has high ability rather than low.

Let $\bar{w}$ be the agent's reservation income (the same for both types). Any contract, to be acceptable, must provide the agent at least this much. Because risk is not an issue here, there is no need to bring in a utility function as before; the tenant will only bother about the monetary income he receives from the contract (because whatever he gets, he gets for sure).

Let us first see how much the landlord can expect to earn if he offers only a fixed-rent contract. We will then contrast this with the case where he can offer the tenant two different contracts—fixed rent and sharecropping—from which the latter is free to choose one. We will show that in the latter case, the expected return of the landlord is generally higher than that in the former.

Suppose the landlord considers offering a single fixed-rent contract. What is the maximum rent he should charge? There are two possibilities. The landlord may want the contract to be accepted no matter what the agent's type is. In this case, the fixed rent charged should be low enough to cover the reservation wage in case the tenant is *low* ability (if a low-ability tenant finds a particular contract acceptable, then so will a high ability one, because they have the same reservation wage, but the latter's productivity is higher). The landlord, to maximize his returns, will charge a rent high enough so that the agent, if his ability is low, will be indifferent between acceptance and rejection. This implies the rent to be charged is

(12.18) $R_1 = Q_L - \bar{w}.$

There is a second possibility to consider. The landlord may want to ask for the highest rent that the high-ability tenant will be willing to pay, thereby risking rejection of his offer in case the tenant has low ability. In this case, the rent charged is

(12.19) $$R_2 = Q_H - \bar{w} > R_1.$$

However, the landlord will get this rent only with probability p, because the contract will be accepted only if the tenant is of high productivity. Hence, the landlord's *expected* return from the contract is $pR_2 = p(Q_H - \bar{w})$. Clearly the landlord will choose to charge R_1 when $R_1 > pR_2$ and R_2 when $pR_2 \geq R_1$. Note the significance of the magnitude of p: the landlord will choose to ask for the lower rent R_1 when p is sufficiently low ($1-p$ is sufficiently high). This is fairly intuitive, because the landlord cannot choose to ignore a possible low-ability tenant if he thinks it highly likely that the tenant he is dealing with is actually of lower productivity. We shall assume that this is the case, that is, low-ability tenants are not so rare as to be ignored in the contract designing problem of the landlord. In other words, we assume $R_1 > pR_2$. Then the rent charged by the landlord if he offered only a fixed-rent contract would be

(12.20) $$\bar{R} = Q_L - \bar{w}.$$

Next, assume that the landlord contemplates offering two contracts and lets the agent choose one. In particular, he considers offering a contract with a fixed rent R, and another—a sharecropping contract—specifying a share $1-\alpha$ of the output to be paid to the landlord (hence, the tenant *retains* a share α of the output for himself). How should the landlord optimally choose the values of R and α, and what is the corresponding (maximized) expected return? The reason the landlord might want to offer these multiple contracts is to target each at a different type of tenant: if the *same* contract is more attractive to the tenant irrespective of his ability, then the other contract is really redundant and might as well not be offered at all. A moment's reflection shows that the fixed-rent contract is better targeted at the high-ability tenant: because he has higher productivity, he can afford to pay a higher stipulated amount while still earning at least his reservation wage. The discussion, then, naturally suggests a pair of *incentive constraints*, one for each agent. These merely say that each type of agent should get at least as much return from the contract designed for it as from any other. In the context of the present model, the incentive constraints for the high- and low-ability types, respectively, imply the inequalities

(12.21) $$Q_H - R \geq \alpha Q_H$$

and

(12.22) $\alpha Q_L \geq Q_L - R.$

In addition, there is a pair of *participation constraints*. Each type, on choosing the contract designed for it, should be able to secure at least his reservation income. This implies

(12.23) $Q_H - R \geq \bar{w}$

and

(12.24) $\alpha Q_L \geq \bar{w}.$

What is the landlord's expected return when he offers a pair of contracts denoted by (R, α)? It is a weighted average of the returns from a high-ability tenant and that from a low-ability tenant, and the weights are the respective probabilities that the tenant has one ability or the other. Mathematically,

(12.25) $V = pR + (1 - p)(1 - \alpha)Q_L,$

where V is the landlord's expected return. The landlord's aim is, therefore, to choose (R, α) in such a way as to maximize V, while satisfying the incentive and participation constraints mentioned previously.

We can simplify the problem by dropping two of the four constraints—the low-ability tenant's incentive constraint and the high-ability tenant's participation constraint [(12.22) and (12.23), respectively], and explicitly consider only the other two. Our reasoning is that as long as (12.21) and (12.24) are valid, (12.22) and (12.23) are automatically satisfied. If the share contract pays the low-ability tenant his reservation wage, then it pays even more to the high-ability tenant because he is more productive. The fact that the latter is induced to choose a fixed-rent contract instead means that the fixed-rent contract provides him at least as much, if not higher (by the incentive constraint). In other words, combining the inequalities in (12.21) and (12.24) with and the fact that $Q_H > Q_L$, we have

(12.26) $Q_H - R \geq \alpha Q_H > \alpha Q_L \geq \bar{w}.$

Hence

(12.27) $Q_H - R > \bar{w}.$

Therefore we see that (12.23) is automatically satisfied when the other constraints are and may therefore be dropped. However, it is important to note something from (12.27): under the dual contract scheme, the high-ability tenant always enjoys a "surplus," that is, some income over and above his reservation wage. This arises because of the landlord's lack of information about the tenant's true productivity and is often referred to as an "information rent." It also shows why the landlord can never naively ask the tenant about his true type and expect to get an honest answer: the tenant, even if he possesses superior ability, has an incentive to underreport his true skills so as to obtain a "softer" contract.

Why can the low-ability tenant's incentive constraint be dropped? We will argue shortly that the optimal contract has the property that the high-ability tenant is just indifferent between choosing the fixed and the share rent contract [i.e., (12.21) is valid with an equality]. If that is so, the low-ability tenant will *strictly* prefer the share contract; mathematically, you can check that when (12.21) holds with equality, (12.22) necessarily holds with strict inequality. Thus, it is enough to focus on (12.21) and (12.24) alone.

Next, we claim that when the landlord designs the contract optimally, both (12.21) and (12.24) will hold with *equality*. The reason is as follows. Suppose (12.21) holds with the "greater than" ($>$) sign. Then the landlord gains by increasing R by a small amount. The high-ability tenant continues to prefer the fixed-rent contract if the increment is low enough. The low-ability tenant, who previously preferred the share contract, now prefers it with even greater reason after the rise in rent. Both incentive constraints therefore continue to be satisfied. We have already mentioned that as long as other constraints are met, the high-ability tenant earns strictly more than the reservation wage. Hence his participation constraint continues to be met even after the small increment in rent. There is no problem with the low-ability type's participation, because the share contract has not been altered. In summary, a small increase in R is possible as long as (12.21) holds with strict inequality, so under the optimal contract equality must hold in (12.21).

Second, suppose (12.24) holds with strict inequality. Then the landlord can feasibly raise the share rate $(1 - \alpha)$ by a little bit, while still meeting all constraints. The low-ability tenant is still induced to participate as long as the rise in $1 - \alpha$ is small. The high-ability tenant continues to find the fixed-rent contract more attractive, because the share contract now pays even less than before after the rise in the share to be paid to the landlord. Hence, both relevant constraints [(12.21) and (12.24)] continue to be satisfied, and we have already argued that as long as that is true, the other two constraints can be safely ignored.

Finding the optimal pair (R, α) is now only one further step. Writing (12.21) and (12.24) in the form of equalities, we have the pair of equations

(12.28) $$(1 - \alpha)Q_H = R$$

and

(12.29) $$\alpha Q_L = \bar{w}.$$

Solving for the pair of values of α and R from the system of simultaneous equations (12.28) and (12.29), we get

(12.30) $$\alpha = \frac{\bar{w}}{Q_L}$$

and

(12.31) $$R = (Q_L - \bar{w})\frac{Q_H}{Q_L}.$$

Putting this in (12.25), we can calculate the landlord's expected earning from the best paired contract. This turns out to be

(12.32) $$V = p(Q_L - \bar{w})\frac{Q_H}{Q_L} + (1-p)\frac{(Q_L - \bar{w})}{Q_L}Q_L$$

$$= (Q_L - \bar{w})\frac{pQ_H + (1-p)Q_L}{Q_L}.$$

Given that $Q_H > Q_L$, $pQ_H + (1-p)Q_L > Q_L$. Hence

(12.33) $$\frac{pQ_H + (1-p)Q_L}{Q_L} > 1.$$

Therefore,

(12.34) $$V > Q_L - \bar{w} = \bar{R}.$$

Inequality (12.34) shows that the landlord's expected income from the paired contract (both fixed rent and sharecropping) is greater than that from the best single fixed-rent contract [compare with (12.18)], under the assumption that the probability of a tenant being of the low ability is not too low. In situations where landless tenants with sufficient diversity of skills interact with a monopolist landlord, therefore, both kinds of contractual arrangements (fixed rent and sharecropping) can be expected theoretically.

Exercises

■ (1) A farming family owns some land. Suppose that in any year the equivalent of two people are needed to farm each acre of land that they own. The following information is given to you: (i) There are six people in the family; (ii) the going annual wage per person (which each person can earn if he or she so chooses) is $1,000; (iii) each acre of land produces $3,000 worth of output (if it is farmed properly by two people, as earlier stated); (iv) the family is always free to lease out land, but the labor required to farm it must be compensated at $1,100 per person; (v) the family can always hire labor, but hired labor is useless without supervision, and to hire *one* supervisor to monitor labor (irrespective of the number of laborers that you hire), costs $2,000 per year.

(a) Calculate the rent per acre the family can hope to obtain by leasing out land.

(b) For a six-person family, what is the minimum acreage necessary for it to be optimal to lease out land? Explain your answer.

(c) Is there a threshold acreage after which the family will no longer lease out land, but hire a supervisor and employ wage labor?

Think about why you are getting these answers. To use these observations to assess the validity of the following statements: (i) a high degree of equality in land ownership means that there is a preponderance of family farms using family labor; (ii) very high inequality means that there are only family farms, or capitalist farms hiring labor; (iii) moderate levels of land inequality are often associated with tenancy.

∎ (2) (a) Generalize the setting in (1). There are ownership distributions for land, for labor, for bullocks, for access to working capital. Explain carefully how the *operational* distribution of land will relate to these various ownership distributions.

(b) As an illustration, suppose that there are just three inputs of production: land, labor, and bullock power. Assume that to produce one unit of output requires one unit of land, one unit of labor, and one unit of bullock power combined in *fixed* proportions (1:1:1). Now suppose that the entire economy has 100 units of each of these three inputs, but that each of these are distributed unequally among the population. How many input (rental) markets will need to function perfectly for efficient production to take place? Use this answer to show that the operational distribution of the inputs that do have markets must conform to the ownership distribution for the inputs that do not have markets.

∎ (3) Compare and contrast the features of agrarian structure in Latin America and Asia, paying particular attention to the problem of land ownership.

■ (4) (a) Show that in an economy with extensive possibilities for perfect crop insurance, fixed-rent tenancy must be dominant irrespective of whether potential tenants are risk-averse or risk-neutral.

(b) Show that in an economy where risk is a major factor, where tenants are risk-averse, and where the inputs of the tenant can be costlessly monitored by the landlord (and verified in court), sharecropping will be preferred to fixed-rent tenancy.

(c) In this question, why did we add the extra qualification that inputs can be verifiable? What happens if we drop this assumption? Study Appendix 1 to this chapter to find out.

■ (5) Consider a production cooperative with just two farmers. Each farmer chooses independently how much labor to supply to the cooperative. Each unit of labor is supplied at an opportunity cost of w. Output is produced by means of a standard production function (exhibiting diminishing returns), with input equal to the aggregate quantity of labor put in by the two farmers. There is no other variable input of production.

(a) Draw production and total cost as a function of labor input. Find (diagrammatically) the amount of labor input that maximizes farm surplus.

(b) Now return to the problem where labor is supplied independently. Show that if total output is divided equally among the two farmers, production will fall short of the answer in part (a).

(c) Next, suppose that farmer 1 receives a share $s > 1/2$ of the total output, while farmer 2 gets $1 - s$ (everything else is the same as before). Describe what happens to production and labor efforts as s varies between 1/2 and 1.

(d) Now change the problem by supposing that each farmer has an *increasing* marginal cost of supplying labor, instead of the constant marginal cost w. (But assume that the cost function for each farmer is the same.) Now describe how you would solve for the surplus maximizing labor inputs and total output, just as you did in part (a).

(e) Suppose you were to redo part (c) with the conditions of part (d). What difference would this make to your answer?

(f) Try to intuitively relate this exercise to the problem of Marshallian inefficiency in sharecropping.

■ (6) It is not uncommon to observe that in sharecropping contracts with cost sharing, the cost share borne by the tenant is equal to the output share accruing to him (see, for instance, the box on sharecropping in the Sindh region of Pakistan). Explain why this might be the case.

■ (7) (a) Why might tenant laws that confer permanent use rights on a tenant who has farmed a plot of land for some years have counterproductive effects on the security of a tenant?

(b) Explain why the presence of limited liability can give rise to situations in which eviction threats are used by the landlord against the tenant. Discuss the various factors that will affect tenant productivity if eviction is banned by law.

■ (8) A widely observed feature of backward agriculture is the inverse relationship between farm size and productivity; that is, larger farms tend to produce lower output per acre than smaller ones. Brief sketches of two alternative explanations for this phenomenon are provided in (a) and (b). Elaborate on these arguments, using appropriate diagrams if necessary.

(a) It has been suggested that smaller farms chiefly use family labor for cultivation, whereas larger farms rely more heavily on hired labor. Due to significant rates of unemployment in many rural labor markets, the opportunity cost of family labor may be much lower than the market wage. This may induce small farms to apply more labor per acre relative to large farms.

(b) The following sketch is an alternative "Malthusian" explanation. More fertile land, by providing an abundant source of food, causes families surviving off such land to grow very large. As children in such families become independent adults, the land tends to get fragmented, creating smaller farm sizes.

(c) Compare these two proposed explanations in terms of (i) direction of causality and (ii) policy implications with respect to redistribution.

(d) Suppose you want to test empirically which of these theories explains reality better. This is not a straightforward task, because both have the same observable implication—an inverse relationship between farm size and productivity. Suggest a way in which you can choose from the two competing hypotheses by analyzing farm data. In particular, what kind of data will you seek for the exercise? (Hint: Consider data collected from a region where major land reforms have been carried out *recently*.)

■ (9) Consider various forms of land rights: (i) communal ownership, (ii) individual use rights without ownership, and (iii) full ownership rights. Discuss how these rights affect the productivity of cultivation.

Chapter 13

Labor

13.1. Introduction

We continue here the discussion that we began in Chapter 11. Recall that in many situations, land and labor markets emerge because there is an imbalance between the ownership of various inputs of production. One such imbalance might occur in the inputs of land and labor themselves. Specifically, landholdings may be more unequally distributed than endowments of labor. In such situations a land market, or labor market, or both will have to emerge to create a balance between the *operational* holdings of land and labor.

In Chapter 12, we observed that for numerous reasons, the operation of land markets *alone* may be inadequate to create the required balance between land and labor endowments. Rental markets for land must balance the conflicting demands of providing insurance to the tenant, along with appropriate incentives for the tenant to farm the land. This is the principal–agent problem, and as we saw in the last chapter, it cannot be solved free of charge. A sacrifice of overall efficiency is entailed. We also saw that similar considerations preclude an efficient functioning of the land sales market.

Thus land markets may not be able to adequately bridge the gap between ownership and operations. A flourishing *labor* market arises, when small owners or landless individuals supply labor to large landowners who need more than just family labor to adequately carry out cultivation.

We also noted that in some situations, land and labor markets may be *complements* instead of substitutes. This is especially so with agricultural activities that are mechanized and must take place on a large scale. In this situation both land and labor are employed by those individuals with access to capital.

At the same time, labor markets do not work perfectly either, as we shall see in this chapter. Many of the problems raised in the preceding chapter find corresponding expression in labor markets. Thus, even in situations in which land and labor markets are substitutes and not complements, land markets will have some role to play. The task of this chapter, then, is to understand the market(s) for labor, the various forms that such markets assume, and the implications for the development process.

13.2. *Labor categories*

Even in a geographically contiguous region, there is no single, homogeneous labor market. We can very broadly distinguish between two types of hired labor: (1) laborers that are hired on a *casual* basis, perhaps on some daily arrangement or for some prespecified short duration (such as the harvesting period) and (2) laborers that are under some (implicit or explicit) long-term contract with their employer. As we will see, the distinction between these two categories is important, because their markets work quite differently.

Casual labor is normally hired to carry out tasks that are easily amenable to observation. Harvesting and weeding fall into this category. The tasks of long-term labor are somewhat more mixed. On large plots of land, a long-term employee may serve in a supervisory capacity, along with the owners of the farm. They might be responsible for tasks that require special care and are relatively difficult to monitor, such as the application of fertilizer and pesticides or the application of water. In addition, long-term employees might work at "standard" tasks along with their casual counterparts, participating in the harvesting process, for instance.

Common sense tells us that this division of tasks is to be expected. In a long-term relationship, an employee can be held accountable for errors or deliberate mismanagement that are only known after the passage of some time (such as the wrong application of fertilizer or pesticide). With casual employees, even those resident in the same village, this may be far more difficult. It is interesting to think about just what the source of the difficulty is. It isn't that the culprit cannot be identified just because he was a casual employee (although with large numbers of employees this might happen as well). It is that the scope for "punishing" the casual employee is much narrower. With a long-term employee, future employment may be denied or the terms of employment may be modified.

This sort of argument leads to a puzzle. Standard supply and demand models of the labor market tell us that the labor market will "clear" at a wage that mirrors accurately the opportunity cost of the worker's time: if denied employment, the worker can find employment elsewhere at the same wage, or even if the worker is unemployed, the utility of the additional leisure just compensates for the loss in wages (see following text for more details on this). In that case, the employer has no additional power over a long-term employee, because the denial of employment has no adverse consequences. This suggests that the standard model may be inappropriate for thinking about long-term relationships. Long-run contracts must involve payments that exceed the alternative expected returns from defaulting on the contract.

Our goal in this chapter, then, is to study how the casual and long-term labor markets function and to bring out some key differences between the two kinds of markets.

Labor Markets in the ICRISAT Villages

Labor Contracts

Labor markets in the ICRISAT villages are by no means homogeneous or uniform; there are vastly different kinds of arrangements that can be seen. There are two kinds of hired labor—casual labor, hired on a day-to-day and sometimes weekly basis, and permanent workers, who are on longer-term contracts that extend for months or even years. Both farm and off-farm contracts are common, the latter mostly taking the form of working in government construction projects. These projects can sometimes be hundreds of miles away, leading to the migration of workers in gangs for months, an initial loan or cash advance being a prime enticement. Daily hired labor is paid in cash in the Maharashtra villages. Only in Mahbubnagar are most of the payments in kind: mostly in paddy, sorghum, or castor. Workers engaged in harvesting and postharvesting operations are mostly remunerated on a piece-rate basis, whereas those carrying out preharvesting operations are paid daily wages.

Long-term labor contracts mostly take the form of the regular farm servant (RFS), whose main duty is usually to tend livestock and plow and cultivate fields. The contractual period varies from three to twelve months, and is often renewed. There are some permanent domestic servants, mostly women and boys. In contrast, daily laborers display a very high turnover rate. RFSs are almost exclusively in demand by wealthier landed households with plenty of acreage and their purpose is to ensure a steady supply of labor over the season. Permanent labor contracts are verbal, and before 1980, they were almost always honored. Recently, the incidence of contract violation and renegotiation is on the increase: a tightening of the labor market and favorable conditions created by the banning of bonded labor can be cited as prime reasons. The incidence of RFS contracts is on the decline.

Consistent with some of the theory to be discussed subsequently, the RFSs received significantly higher monthly wages compared to the expected earnings of daily laborers. However, they also have to work for longer hours and on harder tasks, and when this factor is taken into account, the difference in payment rates narrows considerably.

The fundamental importance of the labor market is illustrated by the fact that in the Mahbubnagar and Akola villages, hired labor constitutes 60–80% of total labor use. The contribution of men and women to total labor use is roughly the same. However, men constitute a high fraction of the family labor used on owned land, whereas women dominate the hired labor market. Of the total female labor use in the Mahbubnagar and Akola villages, 80–90% was hired.

Wages, Employment, and Participation

Average *labor force* participation rates (proportion of time spent on farming activities, whether on one's own or elsewhere) were around 42% for men and 40% for women in the six villages in 1975–76. The corresponding figures for the average *labor market* participation rates, which exclude own farm work, were around 30 and 37%, respectively.

Because there is continuous reshuffling in the daily labor market, the rate of involuntary unemployment has to be defined carefully. The following definition is

Table 13.1. Unemployment rates, ICRISAT villages, 1975–76.

	Unemployment rates (%)		
	Peak	*Slack*	*Total*
Men	12	39	19
Women	11	50	23

Source: Walker and Ryan [1990].

most appropriate: the unemployment rate is the number of days a representative daily job seeker failed to obtain a job as a proportion of the total number of days he/she tried. Table 13.1 illustrates the average unemployment rates for the villages during 1975–76:

From this table we can make two observations: (i) unemployment rates are significant, so that the opportunity cost of labor is usually well below the market wage and (ii) there is a high degree of seasonality in the demand for labor, reflected in the widely different unemployment rates for peak and slack seasons.

An interesting feature in all the villages is that in spite of widespread participation, women on the average earned significantly less than men. Tasks are usually sex specific, so that the lower wages of women could be due to either discrimination or their confinement to lower-paying tasks. Data on real wages over longer periods have shown very little upward trend: however, for the period of study, real wages did rise appreciably in most of the study villages. In Aurepalle and Shirapur, the rise was around 50% for the period 1975–84, although for Shirapur, it stood around a much more modest 11%.

13.3. *A familiar model*

It will be useful to begin with the standard supply–demand story, and then amend this for the particular features of rural markets as we go along. Figure 13.1 summarizes the usual paradigm: According to this account, the demand for labor depends, among other things, on the "going" wage (captured by w) that is paid to hired employees. It stands to reason that if the going wage falls, the demand for labor should be further stimulated (or at least not lowered), so that the resulting demand curve is downward sloping. On the other hand, the supply curve of labor is derived by a calculation of the costs and benefits of working. A higher going wage serves as better compensation for the use of labor, so this should elicit a greater supply of labor from *each* worker, as well as encourage a larger number of workers to enter the labor market. For both these reasons, it makes sense to assume that the

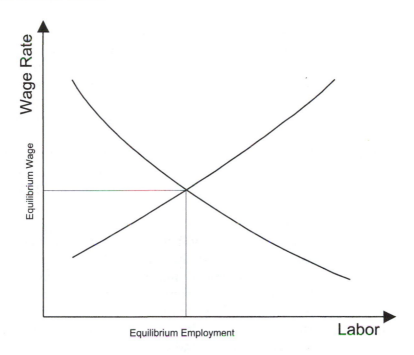

Figure 13.1. Supply of and demand for labor.

supply curve of labor is upward sloping.[1] As you know, the intersection of the supply and demand curves then gives us the *equilibrium wage*.

There are several disturbing features in this seemingly harmless description of labor markets. Observe, *first* of all, that this model does not (and in its present form, cannot) make a distinction between casual and long-term labor. It is as if different periods of time are neatly separated: what happens in tomorrow's labor market has no bearing in what occurs today and vice versa. Later, we will see why this is a bad assumption to make in some contexts.

Second, the model fails to make a useful distinction between labor *power* and *laborers*. We already know from Chapter 8 that this distinction can matter. For instance, some individuals may be excluded from the labor market because their work capacity does not permit them to participate at an adequate level.

Third, each laborer in the equilibrium of this model will be perfectly indifferent between working for his current employer and entering the labor market to search for another employer. When tasks are difficult to supervise and shirking can only be punished by termination of employment, the state

---

[1] Actually, the standard model allows for somewhat more complicated outcomes. It is possible for the supply curve of labor to "bend backward" after the wage rate exceeds a certain level. The reason for this is that a high wage (per hour) might encourage the worker to supply less hours and enjoy more leisure. In economically developed societies, this is an important case that is worth studying. We omit a discussion of this case in the context of poor societies.

of affairs described in Figure 13.1 may not persist. Put another way, the standard story assumes that all work is perfectly monitorable.

Fourth, and this follows on the preceding point, an equilibrium of the standard model in which some workers don't find jobs must leave every worker indifferent between working and not working at all. There is no such thing as *involuntary* unemployment in the model. Failure to incorporate this phenomenon leaves out a central aspect of reality.

Fifth, rural labor markets are characterized by substantial uncertainty and/or seasonality in agricultural production. At one level, this can easily be captured by the standard story. For instance, suppose that rainfall levels are uncertain and that this will affect the size of the harvest. In that case, total demand for harvesting labor will be affected as well. Collapsing this train of events, we may think of the labor demand curve as itself being uncertain; it fluctuates between the highs and lows described by the dotted lines in Figure 13.2. Of course, the corresponding equilibrium wages fluctuate as well. In Figure 13.2, the wage fluctuations lie between a band of w_H and w_L.

Now, although this account certainly captures some of aspects of uncertainty, it fails to tell the whole story. Most important, it does not illustrate the possible ways in which employees and employers cope with this uncertainty "before the fact," by writing contracts or making informal agreements that insure one party or the other from the effects of rainfall variation (in this example).

In the same way, workers may wish to smooth out seasonal fluctuations in their wage income, and employers who are willing to provide such income smoothing may be preferred by employees. The standard model is too simplistic to take these features into account.

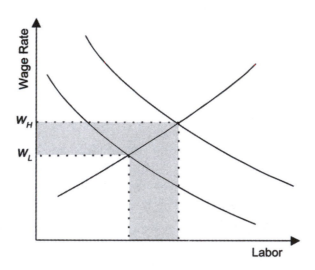

Figure 13.2. Labor market equilibrium under uncertainty.

Our goal in this chapter is to explore these variations on the standard model, in the context of rural labor markets in developing countries. We begin by taking up a theme initiated in Chapter 8: the connection between nutrition and labor markets. Initially we do not concentrate on any particular type of labor market. Subsequently, we examine the case of casual labor markets more carefully.

13.4. Poverty, nutrition, and labor markets

13.4.1. The basic model

The capacity curve

Recall the nutrition-based story of Chapter 8. In its simplest form, it introduces a relationship between nutrition and work capacity, which we call the *capacity curve*. Figure 13.3 displays a typical capacity curve.

Here is a quick summary of the discussion in Chapter 8. Because the horizontal axis of Figure 13.3 is labeled "income," our implicit assumption is that all income is converted to nutrition. Nothing of substance is lost by amending this to a more realistic situation where, say, 70% of income is spent on nutrition. The vertical axis is labeled "work capacity": think of it as a measure of the total number of tasks an individual can perform during a given period, say, the number of bushels of wheat that he can harvest during a day. The capacity curve is found by linking different nutrition (or income) points to the corresponding levels of work capacity that are generated by the individual.

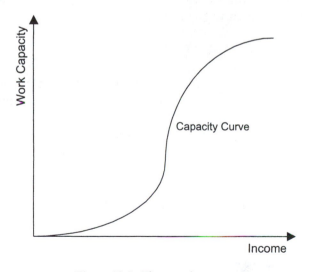

Figure 13.3. The capacity curve.

To understand the shape of the capacity curve, recall that most nutrition initially goes into maintaining the body's resting metabolism. In this stretch very little extra energy is left over for work, so work capacity in this region is close to zero and does not increase too quickly as nutrition levels change. Once resting metabolism is taken care of, however, there is a marked increase in work capacity with nutrition. Finally, there is a phase of diminishing returns, as natural bodily limits restrict the conversion of increasing nutrition into ever-increasing work capacity.

Piece rates

Thus income determines work capacity, but work capacity determines income as well. Let's try to capture this in the simplest possible way. Imagine that incomes are generated by working in a labor market where *piece rates* are paid. This is payment on the basis of tasks completed, such as 10 rupees per harvested bushel or 100 pesos per acre weeded.[2]

Piece rates have an easy pictorial representation along the same axes used for Figure 13.3. If income is paid per unit of task—say 10 rupees per bushel harvested—then we see that there is a relationship between the number of tasks that are performed (bushels harvested) and total income. Figure 13.4 draws the obvious graph that portrays this relationship. A piece rate, then, appears as a *relationship* between the number of tasks performed and the *total income* of a person.

Now we superimpose Figure 13.3 on Figure 13.4. The result is shown in Figure 13.5. Four piece rates are shown. I have called them v_1, v_2, v_3, and v_4. Thus v_1 means something like "you get paid v_1 pah for every bushel you harvest." If you have done the exercise above, you will immediately see that v_1 is larger than v_2, which in turn exceeds v_3, which is larger than v_4.

Labor supply

Now suppose that a laborer (call him Mihir) tries to obtain the *highest* possible level of income that he can possibly earn, given the constraints imposed by his capacity curve. Suppose, first, that the going piece rate is v_1. Mihir will clearly choose the point A, which yields the largest possible feasible income for him. As the piece rate drops to v_2, this maximum income falls. On the graph, Mihir now slides down to the point B, which involves less total work and lower income.

At v_3, something interesting happens. This is a piece rate that has the property that it is *just* tangent to the capacity curve along its hump. At this

[2] Obviously, not all labor can be paid this way. Some tasks are not observable, or even if they are, cannot be easily quantified or attributed unambiguously to a single individual. Thus harvesting can easily be done for piece rates. The same may not be true of sowing or application of fertilizer.

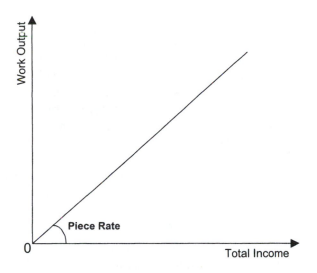

Figure 13.4. A piece rate.

piece rate Mihir can *just about* choose the point C. If the piece rate drops a little more, then the amount of work that Mihir can supply drops dramatically, jumping, as it were, from a point like C to a point like D (which is the intersection of the lowest piece rate with the capacity curve). This jump occurs precisely because the capacity curve is shaped the way it is shaped,

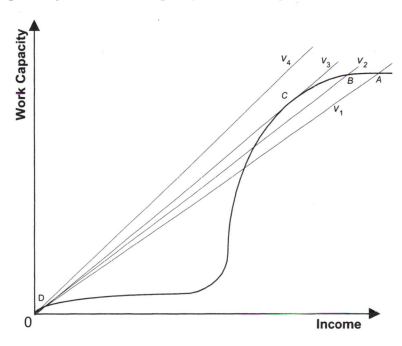

Figure 13.5. Piece rates and work effort.

with low levels of nutrition permitting only very low levels of work, and moderate to high levels creating a rapid increase in work capacity.

We can use all this information to generate a supply curve of labor, which tells us the different levels of labor power supplied at different piece rates. All we have to do is put our information on an appropriate graph, after multiplying Mihir's labor supply (at each piece rate) by the number of laborers like him in the economy. Figure 13.6 shows the transition from individual labor supply to aggregate labor supply.

The left-hand panel of Figure 13.6 shows Mihir's labor supply, by simply transplanting the information gleaned from Figure 13.5. The gap in labor supply at the piece rate v_3 captures our previous discussion that after a certain threshold wage, Mihir's labor supply must jump discontinuously. The right-hand panel effectively multiplies this individual supply curve by the number of laborers. Two things happen. First, the horizontal axis gets blown up by the number of laborers like Mihir, so you're supposed to think of these numbers as larger numbers than Mihir's labor supply, for each piece rate. Second, I've "filled up" the gap with dots; the meaning of these dots will become clear presently.

Equilibrium

To complete our description of this labor market, we introduce a demand curve for labor. This is a perfectly standard demand curve. In general, it is downward sloping to capture the fact that if labor is cheaper, employers will demand a larger quantity of it. Figure 13.7 shows the demand and supply curves on the same diagram. Two cases are of interest.

In the first case, represented by the left-hand panel of Figure 13.7, the demand curve for labor cuts the supply curve at a point that is beyond the

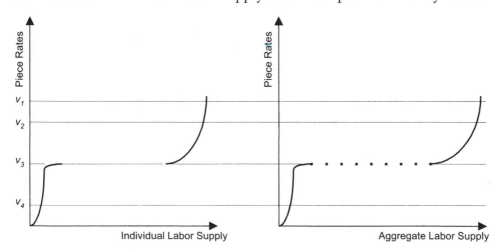

Figure 13.6. Individual and aggregate labor supply.

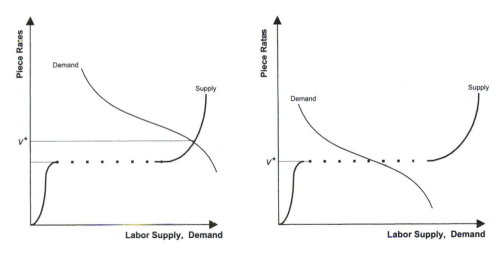

Figure 13.7. *"Equilibrium" in the labor market.*

gap in the supply curve. This case is perfectly normal: the market determines an equilibrium piece rate v^* and everybody gets to supply a "high" level of work effort, that is, a level of work effort that is somewhere on the hump of the capacity curve for each laborer.[3] The market clears in a standard fashion. This case obtains if demand is large relative to supply.

The interesting case is represented by the right-hand panel. Here *supply* is large relative to demand, so that the demand curve passes through the dotted gap in the aggregate supply curve. Now we have a problem with determining the equilibrium piece rate. If the rate is any larger than v^*, we have excess supply, which brings the piece rate down. On the other hand, for piece rates below this critical level, there is excess demand, so that wages are bid up.

However, note that a piece rate of exactly v^* can be thought of as an equilibrium, provided that we admit the idea of unemployment. Just as in Figure 13.6, we can "fill in" the gap in the aggregate supply curve by having some people work and restricting labor market access to others. This unemployment is *involuntary* in the sense that unemployed people are strictly worse off than their counterparts who are lucky to find employment. However, the piece rate cannot be bid down because no one can "credibly" supply the same amount of labor at any lower piece rate.

We see, then, that the vicious cycle is complete in this little model. Lack of labor market opportunities makes for low wages, but it is not only that wages determine work capacity: a low capacity to work feeds back on the situation by lowering access to labor markets!

---

[3] In other words, the equilibrium piece rate looks like v_1 or v_2 in Figure 13.5.

Nonlabor assets and the labor market

If you have absorbed this basic model, we can take it a step further. What we are going to do in this section is introduce the realistic possibility that people may have other sources of income. This means that, strictly speaking, it is not correct to *equate* total income with wages paid by the labor market. For instance, in rural settings, some individuals may have tiny landholdings that are leased out for cultivation. To the extent that such assets augment income possibilities, such individuals are more easily able to participate in the labor market.

This is expressed diagrammatically in Figure 13.8, which compares two individuals. The left-hand panel of this figure depicts another worker, Timir, who has access to a source of nonlabor income, of size R let us say (think of this as rent from his own landholding). Now work capacity depends on rent *plus* wages. We can easily draw this on the same kind of graph, but if the horizontal axis only involves wage income, this is done by "shifting" the capacity curve, as it were, horizontally to the left by the amount R. This is exactly what we have done in the left-hand of Figure 13.8.

The right-hand panel superimposes this diagram on the corresponding picture for Mihir, who has no sources of nonlabor income. Of course, this curve is what we have been studying all along. Note that although Mihir may be biologically just the same as Timir, his capacity curve lies to the right and below that of Timir, who enjoys some land rents.

Two piece rates are drawn, v_1 and v_2. Note first that under v_1, Mihir is only able to supply a small amount of labor, for the reasons discussed in the previous section; he is effectively excluded from the labor market. Not so Timir, who can supply labor at v_1. Even if piece rates are so high that both can supply labor (as in the case of v_2), note that Timir is still earning a larger income than Mihir. It is important to note that the larger size of Timir's income is not just because of his nonlabor assets: *he earns*

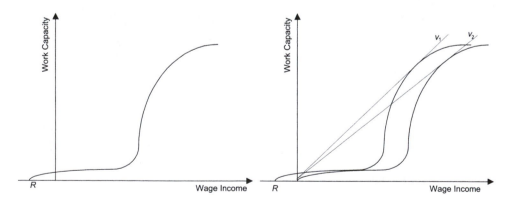

Figure 13.8. How nonlabor assets affect labor income.

higher wage income. Thus inequalities in the asset market magnify further into labor market inequalities, at least among the poor.[4] People without assets are doubly cursed. Not only do they not enjoy nonlabor income, they are at a disadvantage in the labor market relative to those who do possess assets.

Asset inequality, nonlabor income, and the labor market

Let us probe further the effects of disparate asset holdings.[5] The easiest way to think about this is to imagine that there is only one commodity produced in the economy, which is food. Food is produced using land and labor power. Now suppose that there are many individuals in this simplified economy and that each person has access to the same *capacity curve* that we described in the preceding sections. The only other asset is land. It is natural to suppose that different individuals own different quantities of land; in particular, some individuals may be completely landless. This is a rarefied world, but it is enough to provide us with some important insights that survive generalization to more realistic situations.

Observe, to begin with, that the demand curve for labor (from the previous sections) is just the sum of the demands for labor that all households have to cultivate their land.[6] To be sure, for some households (with plenty of land), their demand will exceed what they can supply on their own: these will be the employers of labor. Households with little or no land will be net suppliers of labor. Finally, those households that have approximately the land needed to absorb their own labor will be the family farms, who do not participate actively in the labor market. For the purpose of this exercise, we can think of *everyone* as participating in one giant labor market, where self-employment is treated as part of the overall market.

Now let us draw on an idea from the previous section. For each person with or without landholdings, let us keep track of the *minimum piece rate* at which he will be able to supply labor to the labor market. The left-hand panel of Figure 13.9, which essentially captures ideas from the previous section, shows the obvious: people with greater amounts of nonlabor income (rental income from land, in this case) are able to supply their labor at a lower threshold piece rate, simply because their rental income takes care of some of their nutritional needs. The right-hand of the figure plots this minimum against people arranged in increasing order of land income. People up to the index i^* are landless, so for them the minimum piece rate is unchanging. Thereafter, the minimum falls as land income increases.

---

[4] These observations do not apply to richer individuals, who are operating at higher points of the wage capacity curve, making this particular theory quite inapplicable.

[5] What follows is based on Dasgupta and Ray [1986, 1987].

[6] It is easy to see that if we assume constant returns to scale in production, the aggregate demand curve will be independent of the distribution of landholdings in the economy.

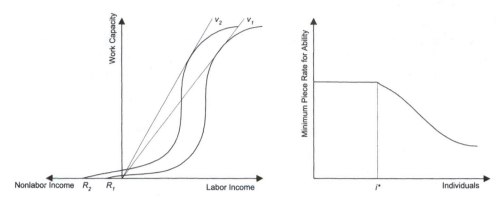

Figure 13.9. The minimum piece rate that determines ability to work.

This minimum piece rate represents the least amount for which an individual will be *able* to work on the labor market. However, there is an additional consideration. Presumably, the minimum wage at which a person will be *willing* to work rises with the amount of nonlabor income. This is because a person who has other sources of income, will value leisure more highly and will be willing to sacrifice it only for high enough compensation.

Thus two opposing forces are at work here, but we can say something reasonable about the way they interact. At very low levels of nonlabor income, people will be willing to work for anything, so that the consideration that really binds is the minimum piece rate at which they *can* work. As nonlabor income increases, this "ability-based" minimum rate falls, and at some point the willingness to work becomes the binding constraint: ability is no longer an issue.

We may therefore combine the two minimum piece rates, shown as the heavy line in Figure 13.10. The resulting U-shaped curve represents the minimum piece rate at which individuals are willing *and* able to work. Indeed, we can figure out which parts of the curve correspond to which regime. Given that individuals are arrayed in order of increasing nonlabor income, the falling portion of the curve corresponds to the zone in which ability is the operative constraint. The rising part of the curve represents the zone in which willingness is the operative constraint.

Using Figure 13.10, the supply curve of labor can be derived in a very simple yet general way. Figure 13.11 shows how this works. For each piece rate in the market, the supply of labor is given by the amounts worked by all those whose minimum piece rates lie *below* the going market wage. These are the individuals who are willing *and* able to work at the going piece rate. By varying the piece rate, we trace out a supply curve. The demand curve

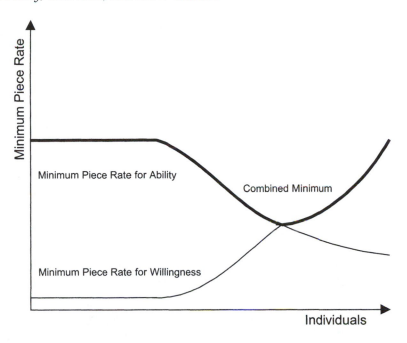

Figure 13.10. Ability and willingness: the combined effect.

is drawn just as before. The intersection of the two curves represents market equilibrium.[7]

The left-hand panel of Figure 13.11 displays one such piece rate and the segment of people who do supply labor at that piece rate, shown by the line *AB*. (The exact quantity of labor supplied will depend on the capacity curve, the size of the nonlabor incomes, as well as the going piece rate itself, in a way that we discussed in detail in the earlier sections.) People to the "left" of *A* and to the "right" of *B* are unemployed, but take a closer look and you will see that they are unemployed for very different reasons. People to the right of *B* are *able* to work, but they do not wish to. We can call them the *voluntarily unemployed* or, in keeping with the rural flavor of this model, the landed gentry. Their nonlabor incomes, derived from land rent, are too high for them to be attracted by the going piece rate. Contrast this with

---

[7] Some care must be taken here for a more precise analysis. We must account for the endogeneity of the land rental rate as well. This can be done as follows. For each "going" piece rate, use the production function to read off the labor employment that equates the marginal product of labor to that piece rate. This, in turn, determines the marginal product of land and, therefore, the rental rate corresponding to the going piece rate for labor. Multiplying the rental rate by the number of acres for each person gives us the nonlabor incomes of all persons. The minimum piece rate curve of Figure 13.10 can then be constructed, and thereafter the supply of labor at that going piece rate, along the lines for Figure 13.11. If you have followed this reasoning carefully, you will see that the curve of minimum piece rates will, in general, move around as the going piece rate is altered, because the associated rental rate on land changes. Apart from this little complication, the analysis goes through unchanged (see Dasgupta and Ray [1986, 1987] for the gorier details).

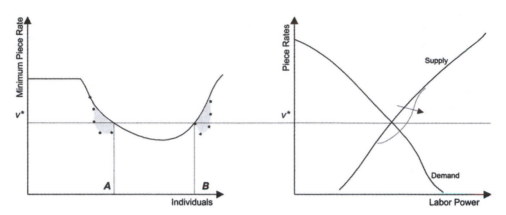

Figure 13.11. Market equilibrium.

the individuals to the left of *A*, who are unemployed not because they are
unwilling to work, but because they are *unable* to work at the going piece
rate (their resulting incomes are not high enough to reproduce the needed
work capacity). We can call them *involuntarily unemployed.*[8] Of course, you
should not take this type of unemployment completely literally. Perhaps such
individuals can work in the short run. The point is that the going wage rate
does not allow them to carry out sustained work over time without seriously
impairing their health and physical strength. For more on these matters, see
the next section.

We can use this model to analyze the effects of changes in the distribution
of wealth holdings. In the case considered here, this is tantamount to looking
at land reforms, in which land is taken away from those who have a lot
of it and given to those who have none or little of it. Certainly, such land
reforms hurt those who lose land and benefit those who gain it; that is only
to be expected. However, we can say something about what happens to *total*
output as a result. To see this, refer to Figure 13.11 once again. Suppose that
land holdings are transferred from the landed gentry just to the right of *B* to
the involuntarily unemployed just to the left of *A*.

There are two immediate effects of this transfer. First, the beneficiaries
of the reform become "more able" to work at the going market rates of remuneration. That is, their minimum piece rates come down, because their
nonlabor income has increased. Second, the losers of land become more willing to work, because their nonlabor income has decreased, so their minimum
piece rates decline as well! Thus land reform has the effect of bringing down

---

[8] We need to motivate this term with some more care. Involuntary unemployment usually refers
to the nonidentical treatment of *identical* individuals in the labor market. If we want to split hairs,
we can argue that people to the left of *A* are not identical to people *at A* (their nonlabor incomes
are different). That's true, but they are ever so slightly different, whereas the consequent impact on
their labor market performance is large. The classical notion of involuntary unemployment can be
extended to encompass this discontinuity (see Dasgupta and Ray [1986]).

the minimum piece rate for all who are directly affected by the reform. This is shown in Figure 13.11 by the dotted bulges that appear to the left of *A* and to the right of *B*.

What is the effect on labor supply? Well, at the going piece rate depicted in the diagram, labor supply must *increase*, because there are some more people who are able to work and there are more people who are willing to work. This is shown by the dotted shift of the labor supply curve in the right-hand panel of the diagram.[9] It follows that equilibrium labor use must go *up*. This, in turn, implies that total output in the economy must increase.

So a judicious land reform has the power to increase overall output in the economy. Such reforms have three effects. First, the unemployed become more attractive to employers as their nonwage income rises. Second, those among the poor who are employed are more productive to the extent that they, too, receive land. Finally, by taking away land from the landed gentry, their reservation wages are lowered, and if this effect is strong enough, this could induce them to forsake their state of voluntary unemployment and enter the labor market. For all these reasons, the number of employed labor units in the economy rises and pushes the economy to a higher output equilibrium.

I reiterate: in the presence of widespread undernutrition, land reforms may be judged desirable for their own sake. However, there is a separate, functional implication as well, and this is what I have chosen to emphasize here. There is no necessary conflict between equality-seeking moves and aggregate output in a resource-poor economy.[10]

13.4.2. Nutrition, time, and casual labor markets

Writing in 1943, Paul Rosenstein-Rodan observed that one of the fundamental features of labor markets that lack contractual structure is its neglect of possibly beneficial externalities. The example that he stressed was on-the-job training. Firms that impart on-the-job training to their workers not only contribute to their own profits, but raise the level of skills and proficiency throughout the economy.

The problem is that more often than not, firms fail to capture the *entire* benefit of their training activities. After all, workers might change jobs. This leads to an externality. On-the-job training requires substantial upfront investments in the worker, with no guarantee that the worker will be around

---

[9] The supply curve may not shift out at *every* piece rate because for some other rates the land reform may have no effect on the set of people in the labor market.

[10] It is worth noting, however, that total employment of *people* may *not* rise with a land reform, even though the total number of units of labor power employed must increase. There is a "displacement effect" at work, whereby newly productive workers are capable of displacing previously employed, less productive workers. However, as shown in Dasgupta and Ray [1987], a comprehensive land reform, involving the equalization of asset holdings, must increase output *and* employment.

to give back any of the fruits of such investments to the firm. The point is that if the *firm* has to incur such expenses, it would like to reap the gains.

Although Rosenstein-Rodan focused on training, his perceptive comments apply just as strongly to the nutritional status of workers that supply labor in a casual market, with no regulations or safeguards. Well-nourished workers are of great long-term advantage to their employers, provided that there is some way to guarantee that such workers remain in the employer's keep. In the absence of such guarantees, the collapse of nutritional status in a poor rural labor market can be comprehensive.

Nutrition is only a parable for all sorts of long-run investments that a firm could make in a worker. We have already discussed on-the-job training. Other investments that have a beneficial impact include firm-provided health insurance, as well as financing for technical training and higher education.

This is the curse of a casual labor market, and the curse is especially harsh in poor countries. To make sure that firms recoup their investments, there must be restrictions on labor movements, and these restrictions have their own costs (slavery being the extreme example). What one does about it is unclear.

13.4.3. *A model of nutritional status*

We use the nutrition parable to develop a model of person-specific investments that have effects *over time*.[11] We will extend our ideas in one important aspect: a worker's current nutritional status, and therefore his ability to carry out sustained work, depends not only on his *current* consumption of nutrients, but also on the *history* of that consumption.

Figure 13.12 tries to capture this observation by means of a single diagram. The curves marked *A* and *B* are capacity curves corresponding to distinct nutritional histories. Observe that work capacity varies with current nutrition (this is captured by the upward slope of the curve for any *given* history), but it is also affected by past nutrition (leading to distinct curves of the form *A* and *B*). At the moment we will leave unanswered the question of which history is the "better" nutritional history, or indeed why the curves might cross as they do.

Let's begin by recalling some concepts from Chapter 8 to better interpret these curves. Here is a quick summary.

The nutritional intake (assumed to be a scalar variable such as calories for simplicity) of an individual is divided between maintenance of the body and physical activity of various types. Let x_t denote the energy intake of the individual at time t, r_t denote *resting metabolic rate*, q_t denote the energy expended on physical activity, and b_t denote the energy released from (or

---

[11] This section uses and extends ideas in Ray [1993], Ray and Streufert [1993], and Bose [1997].

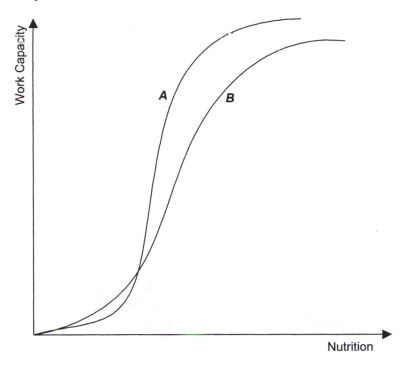

Figure 13.12. Nutritional history and the capacity curve.

stored in) the body. Then, neglecting losses due to the inefficiency of energy metabolism, we write the fundamental energy balance equation as

$$(13.1) \qquad x_t = r_t + q_t - b_t$$

for all dates t. The terms used were all introduced in Chapter 8.

There are interconnections between these variables that we now need to develop. To do this, let us introduce the notion of *nutritional status*, which is, broadly speaking, the state of an individual's physical health at any date and varies from date to date depending on the stresses he is subjected to, as well as his access to nutritional inputs. There is no need to exactly measure or quantify this concept, but for the sake of concreteness we will equate it to *body mass*, which we denote by m.[12]

The first thing to note about m is that borrowing from the body tends to lower it, whereas storage tends to increase it. We can represent this schematically as

$$(13.2) \qquad \text{given } m_t \to \text{higher } b_t \to \text{lower } m_{t+1}.$$

---

[12] Be careful to remember that we are discussing nutritional status in poor economies, so that body mass is not an inappropriate concept. For individuals in developed countries, body mass may be *inversely* related to nutritional status!

Indeed, (13.1) and (13.2) precisely represent the trade-off to an employer who hires this individual. The employer pays a wage, which the individual uses to buy nutrition x, but the employer also dictates the pace of work, which then affects q. However, the employer cannot get something for nothing. For a fixed wage, the higher he pushes the requirements of work, the greater will be the amount of borrowing from the body [inspect (13.1)] and the lower will be the next period's nutritional status [inspect (13.2)].

To go any further, we have to understand next how nutritional status (as captured by body mass) feeds back on the variables of interest such as the ability to carry out productive activity. For a given genotype, resting metabolism is related positively to body mass. Therefore, a lowering of body mass brings down resting metabolism. Is this kind of adaptation a blessing in disguise? It might be. If you look at equation (13.1) again, you will see that a lowering of r creates some extra elbow space in the energy-balance equation: the body eats up less for resting metabolism and can use this extra energy more "efficiently" for work. Call this the *resting metabolism effect*.

We must be very careful, however, to distinguish between this form of protective adaptation and the statement that such adaptation is, consequently, a *good* thing. The attendant dangers of lower nutritional status (in terms of increased susceptibility to illness, physical breakdown, disease, and death) cannot be ignored from a social point of view, no matter how efficient adaptation appears from an economic point of view.

In addition, even from an economic point of view a reduction in body mass might affect the way in which work input q is actually translated into work output. Greater physical health and strength may enable the individual to carry out tasks that an undernourished person finds difficult or impossible to do. In other words, better nutritional status may increase work capacity: call this the *capacity effect*.

Putting together the preceding two effects gives us an interesting net outcome. For a *given* amount of borrowing, the capacity curve of a person with lower nutritional status has a tendency to shift upward. This is because of the resting metabolism effect: more energy can be channeled into work. At the same time, the increased energy available for work can be used better by a better-nourished person, especially at high ranges of work output: this is the capacity effect. Thus it seems reasonable to postulate that at low work levels, the former effect dominates, so that the capacity curve shifts down with better nutritional status, whereas at higher work levels the opposite occurs. This is exactly the sort of situation depicted in Figure 13.12. We can now interpret curve B as corresponding to a better nutritional status.

Now think of things this way. If an employer can choose between creating the nutritional status given by A and that given by B, which one would he choose? One answer is that the resting metabolism effect dominates anyway, so that the employer actually *benefits* from hiring undernourished people to do his tasks for him. This is possible, but it is unlikely if the tasks involve severe manual labor. In that case the capacity effect will dominate. It is more likely that the employer would prefer to sacrifice some current output from his employee, and/or pay a higher wage (thus increasing x_t), *provided that the employee will be around tomorrow to allow him, the employer, to reap the benefits of this investment.*

The emphasized sentence in the last paragraph is precisely the problem that arises in casual labor markets. There are actually two aspects to the problem. First, because employment is casual, the employee may not physically be present for the next period. He may work for a different employer, perhaps in a different village. He might migrate. Under these circumstances, the employer would be extremely reluctant to engage in an investment when the asset might wander off at a later data. Second, if a person in good health can be identified by other employers, the market will bid up the wage rate for such an employee. This means essentially that the employee must reap the entire benefit of the employer-financed investment in the form of a higher wage. If this is the case, then why undertake the investment in the first place?

Observe that this problem can be overcome if both employer and employee were to sign a contract that requires the employee to work for the current employer in the future. This means, in particular, that the employee must forgo his right to accept alternative employment in the future. However, such contracts are often impossible to enforce at the legal level.

Thus, faced with the difficulty of appropriating the rewards of his investment, the employer may have no incentive to increase the nutritional status of his workers. He will have no incentive to pay a higher wage nor to reduce working hours. This will be especially true if the labor market is slack, a point to which we will return later.

Now comes the punch line. If our employer has the incentive to behave in this way, so has every other employer. The implication is that the casual labor market generally fails to improve the nutritional status of workers. What is of additional interest, however, is that this process generally makes employers worse off *as well*, because they have to hire workers of inferior nutritional status. This raises their labor costs even in the short run (provided that the capacity effect dominates the resting metabolism effect).

This is a classic case of a Prisoners' Dilemma. Because casual markets do not look ahead, they create nutritional externalities that everybody ends up paying for: employees through their bad nutritional status and employers through their hiring of inefficient labor.

The observation that nutritional status is degraded in the presence of casual labor markets is actually strengthened if the ability to adapt (by a decrease in resting metabolism) is heightened. The greater the resting metabolism effect, the less is the need for employers to raise wages today or to reduce work effort. When there is a surplus of labor, the casual market is likely to react to adaptive possibilities by further depressing the wage rate.

Let us summarize the discussion of this subsection. We explored the interaction between a plausible energy balance equation, fundamental to the human body, and the labor market for physical activity. This interaction is expected to be particularly pronounced in economies where labor is in surplus and wages are low. In such economies, it is a simple but basic truth that the labor market and its workings are the keys to understanding nutritional status.

Whereas the observation that the labor market is a basic determinant of nutritional status is fairly self-evident, the casual chains that lead to the final outcome require careful analysis. We show that, in a fundamental sense, a casual labor market creates a deterioration in the nutritional status of the workforce, where this status is measured by body mass (for a *fixed* genotype). In addition, this deterioration may have a negative impact on employers, who now face a pool of workers with low "baseline" nutritional status. Paradoxically enough, this low nutrition level is of the employers' own making. The situation is akin to that of a Prisoners' Dilemma.

13.5. Permanent labor markets

13.5.1. Types of permanent labor

We will use the terms "permanent laborer," "tied laborer," and "attached laborer" interchangeably to identify any laborer who commits his labor to an employer for an extended period. The period is in contrast to that for casual laborers, who are frequently hired by the day and sometimes to complete an operation lasting for a few days at best.

Think of two broad categories of attached laborers. There are those who perform special tasks that require some judgment and precision—tasks that might be difficult to monitor. Plowing, regulating the flow of irrigation water from pump sets, driving and maintaining tractors, supervision and recruitment of casual labor, and operating threshers are examples of agricultural tasks that pose monitoring problems, simply because they have an effect on the final output (or on the upkeep of machinery) that may be inseparable from a host of other effects, such as bad weather or the failure of some other complementary activity. In contrast, an activity such as weeding, harvesting, or basket weaving lends itself to natural observation, and often such tasks can be paid for on a piece-rate basis.

There are essentially three ways in which an employer can carry out nonmonitorable tasks. First, he might entrust them to *family* members, who have a spontaneous interest in the welfare of the farm. This is a good idea for small farms, but if the scale of operations is large, outsiders will have to be hired. Second, the employer might hire casual labor to carry out these tasks, but in that case direct supervision of labor becomes a necessity. Even with direct supervision, however, it is not possible to keep track of every passing moment of the laborer's activities, so a judgment of success or failure must rely on the final output. However, as I have just said, the final output is an imprecise indicator. In addition, it is often a *late* indicator. Many slack season tasks such as plowing can be judged on this yardstick only after the harvest is finally realized. By that time casual labor hired during the slack season will already have been paid. This brings us to the third option, which is to hire a subset of the labor force of the farm on a "permanent" or "attached" basis, under the implicit or explicit understanding that their employment is long term, but can be revoked if the indicators of their performance are consistently low.

In the second category of attached labor, there are no special tasks performed. Attached labor might be used to perform the tasks of casual laborers. However, what is the purpose of engaging such laborers in long-term contracts? Put another way, do long-term contracts provide some extra value to either employer or employee (or both) that short-term contracts cannot? We will see in the following text that there are situations where they indeed provide this value.

13.5.2. Why study permanent labor?

There are several reasons to be interested in studying this particular category of labor. First, recall from Chapter 10 that overmigration from rural to urban areas is a major concern in the development process. In that chapter, we studied the possible factors that create overmigration, relative to the capacity of the economy to expand its nonagricultural sector. In this context, the institution of permanent labor acts as a brake on the rapid pace of migration, much in the way that the existence of owner-occupied family farms slows down the pace of migration.

Second, the institution of permanent labor creates a variety in agricultural labor contracts that is of intrinsic interest. As we will see, those individuals who are in permanent labor contracts may be both better off and worse off than those in casual contracts, though more often the former is the case. Thus permanent or long-term jobs are often the first step in a hierarchy where individuals are constantly seeking insurance against the vagaries of a fluctuating economic environment. Thus permanent labor is more associated with fixity than with change. In contrast, casual laborers are at greater risk.

The third reason stems from the first two. The institution of permanent labor shows certain complex long-run trends as development proceeds. In many cases, the incidence of tied labor contracts falls significantly with development, thus accelerating the pace of development and lowering the level of economic security. However, there are also situations in which an expanded pace of development creates a fresh niche for permanent labor. Understanding the types of growth paths that lead to a secular decline (or increase) in permanent labor is thus of importance, because (via the preceding first factor) it tends to affect the rate of migration and because (via the preceding second factor) it tends to change the level of implicit insurance in the agrarian sector.

Secular Changes in Labor Tying in India

We make three general observations on tied labor markets in India.[13] First, the second category of labor tying that includes all kinds of tasks, not just the unmonitored ones, was dominant in the past. Second, the incidence of such attachment has undergone a steep secular decline to low current levels. Finally, there is marked regional variation in the levels of attachment in this category.

There is ample evidence in the literature on the organization of villages in social/economic anthropology that in certain Indian villages, the *entire* agricultural labor force could be partitioned into the tied labor pools of different landlords on the basis of the *jajmani* system. The following description of the system can be found in Lewis and Barnouw [1958].[14]

> Under this system each caste group within a village is expected to give certain standardized services to the families of other castes.... Each man works for a particular family or group of families with which he has hereditary ties.... The family or family head served by an individual is known as his *jajman*, while the man who performs the service is known as the *jajman's kamin* or *kam karne-wala* (literally, worker).

Another widespread form of labor tying, which is somewhat less structured and formalized, is loosely referred to as *patron–client relations* (see Beteille [1979]). Under this system, as in the *jajmani* arrangement, the employer is supposed to ensure the general well-being of the employee and, in particular, help the employee out in times of crisis such as sickness, death, or drought. In return, the laborer is expected to give maximum importance to the needs of this employer with regard to the allocation of his time. A large number of the *kamins* or clients who carried out casual tasks were paid a daily wage (in addition to their traditional payments) and were free to work for others when the *jajman* or patron did not need them.[15]

[13] The observations in this box draw on Mukherjee and Ray [1995].

[14] This description is in agreement with accounts given by Srinivas [1955, 1960], Beteille [1979], and Hopper [1957, 1965].

[15] See, e.g., Sundari [1981], Gough [1983], Breman [1974], and Hopper [1957].

Table 13.2. Secular decline in the proportion of attached laborers in Thanjavur, India.

| Village | Year | Percentage of laborers | |
		Semi-attached	Casual
Kumbapettai	1952	52	48
	1976	21	79
Kirippur	1952	74	26
	1976	20	80

Source: Gough [1983].

Hopper [1957], Lewis and Barnouw [1958], Breman [1974], Gough [1983], and Vyas [1964], as well as a number of other studies, described the secular decline of this traditional patron–client system. Table 13.2 documents proportions of tied laborers in the Indian villages surveyed by Gough in 1952 and 1976.

Apart from the secular decline in the proportion of semi-attached laborers, there is also marked regional variation in the proportion of attached laborers who carry out casual tasks. Although surveys in West Bengal (Bardhan and Rudra [1978]) and Tamil Nadu (Sundari [1981]) found significant proportions of attached laborers in fully monitored or casual tasks, contemporary surveys in other parts of India found a relative absence of such arrangements. This statement applies to the villages located in the semi-arid parts of India studied by the ICRISAT and also to studies by Chen [1991], Reddy [1985] as well as to a more recent survey of agrarian relations in Uttar Pradesh, Bihar, and Punjab by Mukherjee [1992].

13.5.3. Permanent labor: Nonmonitored tasks

In this section, we study the first kind of permanent labor. We set up the simplest model that helps us capture the basic issues involved.[16]

Production conditions

Consider a farm that carries out production with the help of different techniques that it can choose. Each technique comes with different proportions of tasks that must be monitored and tasks that can be left to casual workers. For instance, a technique of production that relies heavily on the correct and timely application of irrigation and fertilizer (as is the case with certain types of high-yielding varieties of seeds) is more likely to be intensive

---

[16] We rely on Eswaran and Kotwal [1985b] in the analysis that follows, but we use a different, simpler model. Related literature includes Bowles and Gintis [1994, 1996] and Shapiro and Stiglitz [1984].

in tasks that are hard to monitor, such as the proper regulation of irrigation water. Think of producing the same level of output with different combinations of monitored and nonmonitored tasks. Presumably the amount of physical capital that is needed changes as well from technique to technique, but for the moment we ignore this complication.

Imagine that to carry out each unit of each task requires one unit (say a man-hour) of labor. The nonmonitored tasks will be carried out by permanent laborers, and just how they are paid will be discussed in detail later. The monitored tasks will be carried out with the use of casual labor. Thus the isoquant that describes various combinations of nonmonitored tasks and monitored tasks (applied to the given plot of land) to produce a given quantity of output may as well be depicted by various combinations of permanent and casual *labor* that are required to achieve the same level of output. Denote these quantities by L_p and L_c, respectively. Figure 13.13 shows us the relevant isoquants.

Now imagine that the employer is faced with different wage rates for permanent and casual labor. (Presently we will be concerned with the determination of these wages, but ignore this for now.) Let's call these wages

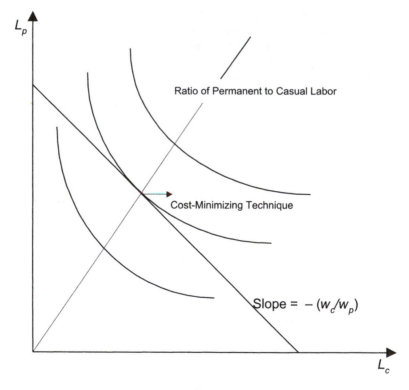

Figure 13.13. Combinations of permanent and casual labor needed for some fixed output level.

w_p and w_c respectively. Efficiency in production requires that a technique be chosen that minimizes the total cost of inputs, which is $w_p L_p + w_c L_c$, for any given choice of output. This is perfectly standard: we see that the cost line (which has a slope of $-w_c/w_p$ in Figure 13.13) must be *tangent* to the corresponding isoquant.[17]

Note that as the *ratio* of permanent to casual wages changes, employees choose different techniques of production and, therefore, different ratios of permanent to casual labor on the farm. In particular, note that as the ratio of permanent to casual wages *falls*, the cost line becomes steeper. The tangency point for cost minimization then shifts from A to A', which leads to a higher ratio of permanent to casual labor in the workforce.[18] We therefore record a simple but important observation that will be useful in what follows: *the ratio of permanent to casual labor depends inversely on the ratio of the permanent wage rate to the casual wage rate.* Note that this in itself does not tell us much, because the casual wage rate is an endogenous variable. In what follows, we uncover this endogeneity and look deeper.

Determining the permanent wage

Consider a typical employer who faces a given wage for casual labor in the market. With competitive markets, this employer can do nothing to change the casual wage. The question is, What is the minimum wage rate that he must pay a permanent laborer, so that such a laborer will have the incentive to adequately carry out nonmonitorable tasks?

The permanent wage will serve as a premium to the worker which he loses in the event that he supplies inadequate effort. The determination of this wage will therefore critically depend upon the importance that the worker attaches to *future* gains and losses. We introduce a simple and tractable story that incorporates that worker's *mental time horizon*: the extent to which the future worries him when he makes current decisions (see also Appendix 2 on game theory).

Specifically, we suppose that at each date, the worker thinks N dates into the future, and factors in the consequences of his current decisions on gains and losses in the coming N periods. The current decision is whether to put in effort or to shirk. The future consequences come from nonrenewal of the permanent contract.

---

[17] This, of course, is only the condition for *cost minimization*. Further conditions are required to pin down the correct level of output. This will depend, among other things, on the particular economic objective of the farmer, such as profit maximization, as well as the way in which the fixed input (land) restricts the production of greater levels of output.

[18] The diagrammatic argument is a bit imprecise because it assumes that the same level of output is produced when the wage ratio changes, which is generally untrue. However, even if output changes, this result will hold true as long as the isoquants are parallel to one another or, in economic jargon, are "homothetic."

These considerations motivate our focus on the following questions:

(1) What is the immediate gain to a permanent employee from shirking?

(2) How much does the employee value future losses that will be incurred following removal from the current job?

(3) How easy is it to spot (later) that the employee has indeed shirked?

(4) If the employee is relieved of his position, will other employers recognize that he is a shirker and not employ him in a prized permanent position?

The immediate gain from shirking is analogous to the gain from default. It can be most conveniently summarized by assuming that the employee exerts effort *at a cost*. This may be a psychological cost, such as the dislike of effort per se, or it may be the opportunity cost of effort (given by the remuneration from some alternative activity). Shirking is then the option to save on this opportunity cost.

To capture the second issue, we will use the idea of a worker's mental horizon as described earlier.

We provide particular specifications for questions (3) and (4). They can be easily relaxed to allow for a more general model, but to understand the essential argument there is no need to do this. We suppose that shirking can be detected at the end of the current period and that after this, the worker is laid off. Moreover, we suppose that the laid-off worker will then be denied a permanent job and must work as a casual laborer thereafter.

It is now easy to write down the equation that describes the no-shirking constraint. For this we introduce just one piece of notation from the current gain that the employee enjoys when shirking: denote this by G. Then the no-shirking constraint states simply that the gain should not outweigh the perceived loss. The employer sees no point, of course, in paying a higher permanent wage than he needs to pay to make sure that this constraint is satisfied, so that under the chosen permanent wage, the gain will just about *equal* the perceived loss:

$$G = N(w_p - w_c).$$

The right-hand side of this equation represents the perceived loss from shirking, because the worker's mental horizon is N periods into the future, and in each of these periods he will lose $w_p - w_c$ if he does shirk today. It will be useful to write this restriction by dividing through by the permanent wage:

(13.3) $$\frac{G}{w_p} = N\left(1 - \frac{w_c}{w_p}\right)$$

Thus w_p will be chosen to make sure that (13.3) holds.

Equilibrium

We may now complete the description of the model. For each conceivable casual wage, equation (13.3) will determine a permanent wage, and in this way we may derive the demand for casual and permanent labor, using the description of the production technology as summarized by the isoquants in Figure 13.13. Adding these two demands yields the demand for total labor as the casual wage changes. The demand curve for labor is summarized in Figure 13.14. If the total supply of labor is fixed at the amount $\bar{L}$, then the wage at which the total demand for labor equals $\bar{L}$ is the equilibrium of the economy.

Observe that Figure 13.14 actually conceals something about the structure of the equilibrium. Part of the total demand for labor will actually be the demand for *permanent* labor. Note by (13.3) that such labor must be paid a premium—w_p must exceed w_c—so everyone will prefer the permanent job. Indeed, individuals will offer to undercut the permanent wage (as long as their offered wage exceeds the casual wage) in order to obtain such a job. Employers, however, will reject such offers, because they know that lower wages are associated with shirking: w_p is the lowest wage at which the no-shirking constraint is satisfied. Thus identical laborers *must* be treated differentially in this equilibrium: the lucky few who get permanent jobs must be paid a

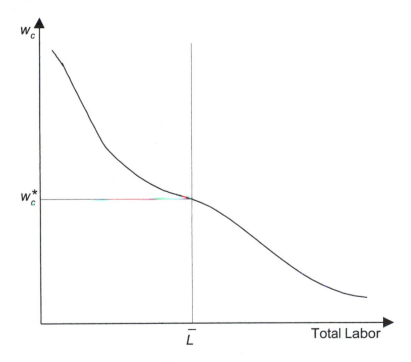

Figure 13.14. *Equilibrium in the labor market.*

premium to prevent them from shirking. The remainder will get casual jobs at the lower casual wage.

Permanent labor and economic development

We now have the ingredients at hand to investigate how the incidence of permanent labor changes with economic conditions. The main relationship that we need is given to us by equation (13.3), which describes how the permanent wage rate is chosen in response to the casual wage rate.

Suppose that the casual wage rate goes up. How will the permanent wage rate alter in response to this? The answer, as we will see, crucially depends on how the gains from shirking change. Begin by considering a situation in which the gains from shirking are unaffected by a change in the economic environment. This happens, for instance, if shirking gains are given by the monetary return from some private activity, such as the cultivation of one's own plot (and neglect of duties on the employer's plot). Algebraically, this is captured by the observation that G does not change at all. In this case, we argue that *as the casual wage rate increases, the ratio of the permanent wage to the casual wage must fall*.

To see this, simply increase the permanent wage by the same proportion as the casual wage. Then the ratio w_c/w_p will be unaffected, whereas the ratio G/w_p must fall. Thus if the no-shirking constraint (13.3) held before, the left-hand side of that condition must now be strictly smaller than the right-hand side. In other words, we have raised the permanent wage by *more* than what is necessary to ensure that shirking will not occur. This contradicts the fact that the permanent wage is chosen to minimize employer costs. A smaller permanent wage will suffice. We may therefore conclude that the permanent wage needs to be raised by a smaller percentage than the casual wage rate, and we are done.

In contrast, consider a situation in which the gains from shirking rise exactly in proportion to the casual wage rate. This occurs, for instance, if *all* shirking is done in the form of casual employment elsewhere (in this case, G simply is equal to w_c). In such a situation, the permanent wage rate must rise exactly in the same proportion as the casual wage rate. To see this, simply study the no-shirking constraint (13.3) once again. If the permanent wage is raised by any smaller proportion, then the ratio w_c/w_p registers an increase. The right-hand side of (13.3) must therefore fall. On the other hand, because G has increased in the same proportion as w_c and w_p has not, the left-hand side of the same equation must increase. However, this means that the gains from shirking now outweigh the losses, so that the new permanent wage rate must be raised higher still. This process continues until the permanent wage rate has been raised by exactly the same proportion as the casual wage rate, whereupon (13.3) holds with equality once again.

The actual situation is probably a mixture of these two extremes; that is, G rises with the casual wage rate, but not proportionately so.[19] In this intermediate situation, it is easy enough to check that the first of our two results continues to hold: the permanent wage rate rises, but not at the same rate as the casual wage rate. We may conclude that the casual wage rate and the *ratio* of permanent to casual wages are likely to be negatively correlated.

Now we can see what might happen with a change in the exogenous parameters of the model. Suppose, for instance, that there is a tightening of the labor force, so that the supply of labor $\bar{L}$ goes down. This occurs, for instance, if there is increased rural–urban migration so that rural labor becomes less plentiful. It is obvious from Figure 13.14 that this results in an increase in the equilibrium casual wage rate. By the argument just concluded, we can deduce that the ratio of permanent to casual wages falls. However, production techniques must then shift to a more intensive use of permanent labor, so that the ratio of permanent to casual employment rises. The underlying idea is very simple. As labor becomes scarcer, the *relative* premium needed to pay permanent labor falls, but, of course, the *absolute* premium might rise. This change induces a greater relative employment of permanent labor.

The same effect can be easily mimicked by an increase in the demand for labor. Suppose that there is an increase in demand for the final product, so that the derived demand for (all kinds of labor) rises. In Figure 13.14, this leads to a rightward shift in the demand for labor. With the same supply of labor as before, the equilibrium casual wage rate rises. Now *exactly* the same argument applies and the proportion of permanent labor employed in production increases.

There is, indeed, empirical evidence for this sort of change. For instance, Richards [1979] studied the incidence of permanent labor contracts in Chile. At the end of the nineteenth century, Chilean agriculture enjoyed a major boom as grain markets in Europe opened up. Richards showed that the incidence of permanent labor contracts in Chilean agriculture rose sharply.

At this point it will be useful to return to our specification of the technology of production. Note that we began with a specification of tasks that are easy to monitor and tasks that are difficult. We then proceeded to equate nonmonitorable tasks with the use of permanent labor and to equate easily monitored tasks with the use of casual labor. This interpretation allows us to say something more about the use of (this kind of) permanent labor. For in-

---

[19] Might the gains from shirking rise even faster than the increase in the casual wage rate? They might, but it is hard to think of why this might be the case. The returns from employment elsewhere cannot go up by more than the casual wage rate. The value of enjoyment of leisure time (or of self-cultivation) is unlikely to be affected by the casual wage rate, and even if it is, it is difficult to see why it would be affected *more than* proportionately. This is not to say that one simply *cannot* write down a model where G increases more than proportionately to the rise in w_c. But these possibilities can be analyzed in the same way as in the main text.

stance, suppose that there is a reduction in the cost of capital to the farmer that permits more advanced capital-intensive methods of production. To the extent that such methods are more intimately connected with nonmonitored tasks, such as the appropriate use and maintenance of delicate machinery, and to the extent that these technologies substitute away from the use of casual labor, we would expect the incidence of permanent labor to increase with a reduction in the cost of capital.

Similar effects are likely to come into play when there are exogenous shifts in agricultural technology that lead to a greater incidence of nonmonitored activities. The mechanization of agriculture is one such shift. The use of large-scale and mechanized methods of farming, such as tractors, clearly brings more complexity into production. It may be more difficult to figure out who is to blame—man or machine—if something goes wrong or, if more tasks are carried out jointly and with coordination, *which* man or machine. If this is the case, the need for long-term contracts becomes all the greater. However, it is also important to note that such mechanization, by reducing reliance on acts of God such as bad weather, may also make it easier to assign responsibilities. In that case, the incidence of permanent labor may decline. The effect of technological change on the incidence of permanent labor is a complex issue.

Our model easily allows us to incorporate these effects. Simply return to the description of the technology as captured in Figure 13.13 and extend this description a little bit by supposing that "nonmonitored tasks" are really a composite of machinery use (such as tractors and pump sets) and difficult-to-monitor labor activities (such as the proper operation of this machinery). Then "one unit" of such an input may really be viewed as an amalgam or composite of these inputs. As such its unit price is really the *sum* of permanent labor costs as well as the cost of capital.

The extended model is no more complicated than the simple model, but it allows us to make additional observations. For instance, you can check, in line with the argument made two paragraphs ago, that a reduction in the cost of capital reduces the price of this composite input and thus encourages substitution toward it, thus raising the proportion of permanent labor in production.

There are also interesting by-products of this extension. For instance, you can check that as long as the cost of capital is constant, a rise in labor demand (or a tightening of labor supply) will increase the employed percentage of permanent labor *even if* the permanent wage rises exactly in proportion to the casual wage. Thus our earlier results are, if anything, strengthened.

Now it is time to consider an important qualification to our arguments. Note that these results really pertain to the intensity of nonmonitored tasks in the technology of production and not necessarily to permanent labor per se. It is true that permanent labor contracts are needed to provide appropriate incentives in the performance of nonmonitored tasks, but is this the *only* context in which permanent labor is observed? As we have already seen, the answer is no. In fact you will recall that we explicitly distinguished between two kinds of permanent labor. So far we have only discussed one of these types. We now turn to a study of the second type.

13.5.4. Permanent labor: Casual tasks

Seasonality and income fluctuations

We take a leisurely approach to motivating the second type of permanent labor. Imagine agricultural life in a developing country. The first fact of cultivation is the existence of *seasons*. Roughly speaking, we can divide an agricultural production cycle into a *slack* season and a *peak* season. In the slack, agricultural activity is at a relative low, whereas the peak season contains the bulk of the physical activity: harvesting. Thus the demand for labor in the slack season is relatively low and spikes sharply in the peak season. This fluctuation is naturally mirrored in the behavior of spot market (casual) wages: they follow a zigzag pattern, exhibiting lows in the slack and highs in the peak season.

We can add to these observations by noting that, in addition to the natural fluctuations imposed by the presence of the seasons, there is another source of fluctuation: *uncertainty*. From the vantage point of the slack season, it is difficult to predict what the peak season wage will be, except to observe that it is likely to be higher than the slack wage. The uncertainty arises from the fact that the peak season demand for labor depends on the abundance of the harvest, and the bounty of the harvest is affected by the weather as well as a host of other factors that may be out of the control (or predictive range) of the farmer.

It is possible to temper these observations somewhat by noting that in all parts of the world, multiple cropping is on the rise. This is especially so in regions where the availability of irrigation or new varieties of seeds serves to reduce dependence on the season. To the extent that multiple cropping occurs, the spikiness of the agricultural cycle is smoothed out and seasonality plays less of a role, but the role is still prominent enough to deserve our full attention.

Fluctuation aversion

The fundamental point that we draw from seasonality is that rural wages have a built-in tendency to fluctuate, both over time and in the sense that they are only imperfectly predictable. To understand the implication of this, recall the analysis of risk aversion that we introduced in Chapter 10 and used in Chapter 12. Remember that risk aversion can be captured by postulating that an individual receives diminishing marginal utility from income. An extra $10 means more when you are earning $100 per month than when you are earning $1,000 per month. This tendency for marginal utility to diminish is connected to risk aversion in the following way: an individual would always like to transfer sums of money from his high-income state to his low-income state, because the loss of utility from a monetary reduction in the high-income state is less than the same monetary gain in a high-income state. You may want to go back to Chapter 10 and review the material on risk aversion before proceeding further.

Risk aversion is closely related to what we might call *fluctuation aversion*, a state of affairs in which an individual reacts to the prospect of a fluctuating but perhaps perfectly deterministic stream of income. In Figure 13.15, we depict a two-income stream: a wage of Rs 100 per month in the slack and Rs 200 per month in the peak. Assume for simplicity that the two seasons are of equal duration. The utility that the worker receives from Rs 100 is given by point A and the utility he gets from Rs 200 is shown by point B.

What is the *average* utility received by the worker? By our simplifying assumption that both seasons are of equal lengths, it is, of course, the average height of points A and B. This is easy enough to depict on the diagram. Simply draw the chord joining A and B and then look at the height of the

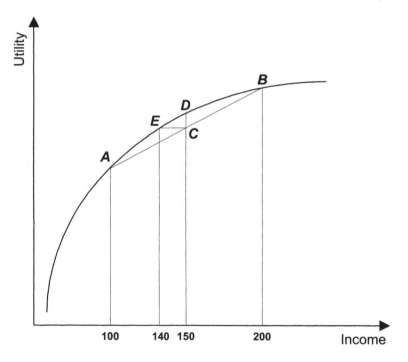

Figure 13.15. Fluctuation aversion.

midway point along this chord, marked C. This is the average utility generated by the fluctuating stream of incomes (100, 200).

Now ask a slightly different question: What is the utility received from an income stream that does not fluctuate and provides a constant flow of Rs 150 per month? This is clearly the height of point D in Figure 13.15. Notice that if the utility function displays diminishing marginal utility, the height of point D must exceed that of C. In other words, *the utility of the average income under a fluctuating stream must exceed the average utility received from that stream*. It sounds tricky, but it is actually very simple, and if you reread the section on risk aversion you should have no difficulty following this. Fluctuation-aversion and risk-aversion are closely related.[20]

Permanent contracts that smooth income

Suppose that an *employer* of labor is risk-neutral and does not mind fluctuating payments or receipts as long as they have the same average value. Suppose, furthermore, that he desires to hire labor in both slack and peak seasons. Then he can make the following speech to a prospective worker: "Imagine I pay you Rs 150 per month *throughout* the year, whether it is slack or peak. This is the average amount you are receiving anyway. Because you are fluctuation-averse, you will prefer this to a varying income stream with the same average value. Indeed, if I shade the amount a bit, say to Rs 140 per month, you should *still* prefer this to the fluctuating stream (compare points C and E in Figure 13.15). So you gain and I gain. Let's do it!"

The argument is very simple. If employers are risk-neutral and workers are risk-averse, then similar attitudes apply to fluctuations as well, and there should be scope for contractual smoothing of incomes over the slack and peak seasons. This is a form of (interseasonal) permanent labor, the second kind of permanent labor that we referred to at the beginning of this section.

The reasoning in favor of such contracts is persuasive, perhaps a bit too persuasive. Why don't we observe the entire labor force "tied" in this fashion? Casual labor should be the exception, not the rule. Indeed, as the box on labor tying in India tells us, there was a time when this was indeed the case. However, labor tying of this sort has been most definitely on the decline. The box briefly documents this trend for India, and the same is true for other countries as well as for developed regions such as Europe at earlier points in time. Today, tied labor, although present, is certainly not dominant (see, for example, Table 13.3 for the case of some Indian villages).

---

[20] The correspondence between risk-aversion and fluctuation-aversion is weaker when we extend standard expected-utility theory. A discussion of these issues is beyond the scope of this book.

Why are permanent contracts not dominant?

There are probably several reasons that we can advance (some fallacious) for the observation that labor tying of this sort is not universal.

First, our argument appears to apply only to employers who are intending to hire a particular laborer both in the slack and in the peak. If labor demand is dramatically different over the two seasons, this may not be true of all employers and all laborers. Why tie a laborer for whom you have no use in the slack? This argument is actually a bit of a red herring: if employers have no use for a laborer in the slack season, there is still scope for a contract whereby some amount is paid to that laborer in the slack, in return for a promise to work during the peak season. The laborer might then augment this payment in the slack by working elsewhere, and this would achieve the same smoothing effect.[21]

Second, seasonality itself may have declined over time, which obviates the need for the kind of permanent contract that we are discussing. The reduction in seasonality might stem from technological or infrastructural improvements (such as irrigation) that permit multiple cropping and thereby smooth out agricultural activity over the year. We have already referred to this possibility and it can play a role, but not in and of itself. As long as there is *some* seasonality, there is scope for a permanent contract of the sort described here. However, taken in conjunction with other factors that might limit the tying of labor, a reduction in seasonality may well have an effect at the margin.

Third, there might be significant uncertainty regarding the use of peak season labor. For instance, if the state of the weather is unpredictable, it may be difficult to predict, ex ante, how many laborers are going to be needed during the harvesting season. It would be silly to offer every potential employee a tied contract. This argument has merit (see Bardhan [1983]), but it still does not rule out the possibility of a large tied labor force. As an example, consider the village level studies conducted by the ICRISAT in India.[22] Fluctuations in the percentage use of hired labor over a period of ten years were measured for the three ICRISAT study villages. The gap between the highest and the lowest value is 30% for the most drought-prone village, which is Shirapur. In the other two villages, the corresponding gaps are 22 and 25%, respectively. These numbers and the argument in this paragraph (taken in isolation) suggest that the level of labor tying can climb to 70% without any risk of loss to the employer, but the level of labor tying in the ICRISAT villages is nowhere near this figure. See Table 13.3.

---

[21] See Mukherjee and Ray [1995] for more details. This paper also contains a rigorous elaboration of some of the ideas presented in this section.

[22] For more on the ICRISAT villages, see Chapter 12. For this reference, in particular, see Walker and Ryan [1990, p. 120].

Table 13.3. Proportions of tied laborers in ICRISAT villages.

Village	Type of farm	Percentage of farms employing farm servants
Aurepalle	Small/medium	13
	Large	47
Shirapur	Small/medium	6
	Large	7
Kanzara	Small/medium	0
	Large	7

Source: Pal [1993].

Fourth, consider the worker's access to credit, specifically consumption credit. Fluctuating incomes pose little or no problem if they can be smoothed by taking recourse to the credit market. Workers might be able to borrow against a high peak income in order to consume more in the slack. If this can be done at a reasonably low interest rate, then consumption is smoothed even though income is not.

This argument is sensible provided we do not go the whole way and imagine that credit markets are perfect. There are several barriers to such perfection, all of them having to do with the flow of information and the enforceability of credit contracts: we will take these issues up in Chapter 14 and in the very next argument that we consider. Thus credit markets might function to some extent to reduce the variability of consumption. Furthermore, it is possible that access to credit has improved over time, thus accounting for a decline in labor tying. Phrased in this way, an improvement in the functioning of credit markets is akin to a decline in seasonality and has largely the same effects.[23]

The previous argument tells us that a tied labor contract has close similarities to a credit contract. You can think of the extra slack season payment as a "loan" and the subsequent difference between the peak wage and the tied wage as a repayment of that loan. However, then the question of just how easy it is to repay the loan arises. Put another way, a contract that smoothes income *must* have the property that at certain times, the promised wage under the agreement must fall short of the spot wage prevailing in the casual labor market. What guarantees that a worker will not take advantage of this when the high spot wage makes its appearance?

One possibility is that in the event of such noncompliance, the worker will not be given the contract again, but this sanction is good enough only if some conditions apply. To begin with, *the contract must offer strictly more utility*

---

[23] Moreover, the argument can also be applied to permanent labor of the first type, as in Caselli [1997].

than the option of being fired. This argument is very similar to the no-shirking constraint that we derived for the case of nonmonitored permanent labor (and it will reappear when we consider credit markets). Thus permanent contracts of either type must be a strictly better deal for workers, rather than casual jobs.

But there is another condition as well: after being fired, *the worker must find it difficult to get a similar permanent job again*. Were this not the case, it really does not matter whether permanent jobs offer a utility premium over their casual counterparts. If a worker can slip back into a similar contract with great ease, then the threat of dismissal from the *current* position has little bite.

In the earlier sections of this chapter, we finessed this problem by simply assuming that a laborer fired from a permanent job would not be given another such job by *any* employer. That is, the news of the worker's infidelity would be spread far and wide by the disgruntled employer, and future access by the worker to permanent contracts would be effectively blocked. Is this a reasonable assumption? It depends. The ability to effectively transmit information regarding "deviant behavior" varies from society to society. It is plausible that in a village economy with very little mobility, in which everybody knows everybody, that such information flows freely and well. It is also possible that in an advanced society where the word-of-mouth access to information is replaced by computerized information, information also flows smoothly. If you are reading this in the United States and have ever defaulted on your credit card bill, you will know what I mean. But there are many societies now in an intermediate stage of development where mobility and migration are on the increase and in which the informational networks so characteristic of a traditional society are beginning to fall apart. As we shall see in Chapter 14, even professional moneylenders active at the village level expend considerable resources to verify the bona fides of a prospective borrower.

It is precisely in "intermediate societies" that are going through rapid change and growth, yet do not possess an advanced information technology, that it becomes very difficult to keep track of individual histories. In such societies the offers of tied contracts decrease because employers find that such contracts are increasingly difficult to enforce.

Thus the percentage of tied contracts shrinks to a point at which they can be offered without fear of breach, but why does the fact of their rarity allow easier enforceability? The answer is simple: if tied contracts are harder to come by, then those that are lucky enough to get one will not deviate from them. Even in the absence of information, it will simply be difficult to get a new contract, because there are relatively few around. It is in this sense that the increase of mobility and change in today's developing societies brings about a reduction in long-run arrangements that are largely based on trust and reciprocity.

Santiniketan's Rickshaws

Santiniketan, in the state of West Bengal, India, is a couple of hours from Calcutta and is home to a university founded by the Bengali poet Rabindranath Tagore. It is a university town, but it adjoins a busy agricultural center. It is also an increasingly popular place to own winter residences or retirement homes, and the last several years have seen an upsurge in its population.

Bicycle rickshaws are the major form of public transportation. A ride from the train station to the center of Santiniketan costs around Rs 15 (this number may have changed). But this fare rises dramatically during the Winter Festival, which attracts thousands of visitors from Calcutta and elsewhere in India. Fares of Rs 50 or more are not uncommon, because the transient tourist population dramatically increases demand relative to supply.

The permanent residents in Santiniketan understandably dislike this fare increase. Nobody appreciates the power of market forces when they work the "wrong" way. A relative of mine, who lives in Santiniketan year round did what many others like her do: she built up a long-term arrangement with a rickshawwallah. If the fare was Rs 10, she gave him 11, or perhaps she helped him out occasionally with an extra *dhoti* or an advance to buy a ceiling fan. The understanding, implicit though it was and marked with decency and goodwill on both sides, was clear: during the Winter Festival, she was not to be charged Rs 50. Here, then, is a prototypical permanent labor "contract."

Now, this sort of arrangement has been common for Santiniketan's insiders for many years. The reason why it stood the test of time was that Santiniketan's "core" population was adept at the exchange of information: a renegade rickshawwallah would not be a renegade for long: he would soon lose the constant flow of extra income during the "slack" (nonfestival) season, as the news of his bad behavior spread. But such arrangements are certainly on the decline, and personalized relationships with rickshawwallahs are giving way to more impersonal, market-based transactions.

My relative's experience with one such rickshawwallah (we'll call him Krishna) two years ago was a case in point. During the peak season of the Winter Festival, Krishna broke the deal. Instead of being (reasonably) available, he was periodically spotted ferrying tourists back and forth from the railway station. My relative was upset, but revenge was hard to extract: Santiniketan is full of new arrivals who are unknown to her, and the year after Krishna did not find it hard to enter into *another* "permanent" relationship with one of them, no doubt to be broken once the next Winter Festival rolled around.

Now at some level I sympathize with Krishna, and in his position I may have done the same. Tied "contracts" are not really contracts: they are a form of reciprocity. As mobility increases and information dries up, such reciprocity becomes increasingly harder to maintain. Krishna was only responding to the forces of the market, and like all economic agents, took full advantage of what the existing informational and economic structure had to offer, or more precisely, of what it would let him get away with. My relative will not enter into one of these contracts again and, presumably, neither will Krishna's next victim. Meanwhile (and this is the irony of it all) Krishna will be worse off and so will my relative: the lack of enforceability destroyed the possibility of making a mutually beneficial deal.

13.6. Summary

In this chapter, we studied rural labor. Like land markets, labor markets are devices of adjustment between the ownership pattern of factors and the way they are put to operational use.

We distinguished between *casual labor* and various types of *permanent labor*. Casual labor is normally hired to carry out tasks that are easily amenable to observation. The tasks of long-term labor are somewhat more mixed. On large plots of land, a long-term employee may serve in a supervisory capacity and might be responsible for tasks that require special care and are relatively difficult to monitor. In addition to these, long-term employees might work at "standard" tasks along with their casual counterparts, for instance, participating in the harvesting process.

We began with the standard supply–demand paradigm: employers demand labor, employees supply labor, and the wage adjusts to equate supply to demand. However, this story is deficient on a number of grounds: it fails to make a useful distinction between casual and permanent labor, it does not take into account individual *work capacities* and how they are affected by the labor market, it does not take into account *involuntary unemployment*, and it does not capture the *seasonality* and *uncertainty* in agricultural production. To be sure, these deficiencies are interrelated. For instance, the casual–permanent distinction is useful, in part because it represents a reaction to the seasonal nature of production in agriculture.

We moved on to these considerations. An entire section was devoted to the interrelationship between poverty, nutrition, and labor markets. There are two main building blocks: first, an individual's work capacity affects his income on the labor market and, second (and the object of our particular focus), individual income in turn affects work capacity. The first effect is captured by supposing that the market pays *piece rates* for observable tasks, so that capacity multiplied by the piece rate yields total labor income. The second effect is summarized in the *capacity curve*, which links nutrition to work capacity. We argued that a minimum threshold level of nutrition is required before a person can carry out productive work. This feature generates an individual labor supply curve that exhibits a discontinuity: at low piece rates he is unable to profitably function in the labor market, but there is a critical piece rate at which he can supply labor. In general, this piece rate depends on both the characteristics of the individual as well as his other economic endowments, such as holdings of land.

The labor market equilibrium of this model can generate involuntary unemployment, and the possibility of this outcome increases with the relative abundance of laborers to jobs.

The existence of nonlabor assets such as land can also be incorporated into the model. We showed that these alternative income-generating opportunities translate into an added advantage on the labor market: among the poor, inequality of assets magnifies further into labor market inequalities. In this sense, the labor market has a tendency to widen already existing inequalities.

The nutrition-based model of the labor market also brings out the beneficial impact of land reform. Not only does land reform lower inequalities, it also has a supply-side effect on total output, which rises.

Although it is useful, this simple model of nutrition has drawbacks. Specifically, it neglects some important *dynamic* features of the nutrition–capacity relationship. It isn't that nutrition has an immediate effect on capacity: an individual is able to "store" and "borrow" nutritional resources, and this manifests itself in intertemporal movements of a person's nutritional *status* (often captured by body mass). Hence, we extended the model to include time. In particular, employers have an incentive to build up work capacity in their employees by essentially investing in higher wages. Will they do so? The answer is negative if the labor market is casual: it may be impossible for the employer to reap the benefits of better nutrition ex post. Thus casual labor markets can be particularly harsh on undernutrition, because employers fail to internalize the long-run benefits from a well-nourished labor force. Of course, this sort of behavior degrades nutritional status in the workforce at large and can lead to a situation like the Prisoners' Dilemma, where both employers and employees are worse off.

We turned next to permanent labor (or equivalently, *attached labor* or *tied labor*). We made a distinction between permanent laborers who are employed in a supervisory capacity or carry out tasks that are hard to monitor, and permanent laborers who perform the same tasks that casual laborers perform. The two categories require different treatment. We noted that the existence of the first category relies on (1) the prevalence of large farms that do not have access to enough family labor to do the supervising and the hard-to-monitor tasks, and (2) the use of a production technology in which such tasks naturally come up (such as the care of bullocks or the maintenance and proper operation of farm equipment such as threshers or pump sets). Because such activities are hard to monitor, this sort of permanent labor must be provided with work incentives through the threat of firing (later events, such as the size of the harvest or the breakdown of farm machinery, are indicative of performance and can be used for contract renewal). For the threat to be effective, permanent workers must be paid a premium: this means that permanent jobs are prized jobs even if the people who fill such positions do not have any particular abilities. We studied a model that incorporates these effects and drew interesting conclusions about the incidence of this form of permanent labor as economywide characteristics alter.

Finally, we studied permanent laborers who are involved in casual tasks. The reason for the long-term contract in this case is implicit insurance (or consumption smoothing over the slack and peak seasons), but there is an incentive problem here. If slack wages are increased and peak wages decreased to permanent workers, then there is a tendency to breach the contract in the peak season when casual wages are higher than the contracted permanent wage. Whether the contract will be honored or not depends on (a) the size of the gain involved and (b) how easy it is for a deviant to reenter the permanent labor market at a later date. We argue that both these considerations restrict the incidence of permanent labor (of this type). To handle condition (a), only limited insurance can be provided, so that the gap between peak casual wages and the contracted wage is not too high. To handle condition (b), the economy must not have too many permanent contracts available. To be sure, if a permanent worker's deviation can be easily made known to all potential employers, the number of available permanent contracts matters less: employers will not hire the deviant anyway. It follows that less mobile economies in which the flow of information is higher tend to exhibit a larger incidence of permanent contracts. Turning this around, if development is characterized by an increase in mobility and anonymity, this type of permanent contract is likely to wither away with time.

Exercises

■ (1) Review the standard supply–demand model for the study of labor market equilibrium. Discuss some features of labor markets that require substantial extensions to, or changes in, the standard supply–demand model.

■ (2) On a graph where the total income is on the horizontal axis and the number of tasks is on the vertical axis, why does the piece rate appear as a straight line? Show that if the piece rate goes *up*, the line becomes *flatter*. What would the following contracts look like on the same graph, with the same axes?

(a) A contract that pays 10 pah a bushel for the first 20 bushels, followed by 20 pah a bushel for each additional bushel.

(b) A contract that pays a flat wage of 100 pah, plus 10 pah per bushel.

(c) A contract that pays 200 pah and *requires* you to harvest at least 20 bushels.

■ (3) In this question we review various aspects of the capacity curve.

(a) Look at the energy balance equation (13.1) that we studied. Recall that it reads as follows:

$$x_t = r_t + q_t - b_t,$$

where x is energy input, r is resting metabolism, q is energy required in work, and b is borrowing from the body.

When will borrowing be negative or positive? What do you think happens if the individual has to continue to borrow from bodily stores to meet work needs?

Let's suppose that body stores are held in the form of fat. It's well known that storage is more costly than borrowing (you need more energy to store 1 gram of fat than 1 gram of fat will release). Assuming this is true, think about which of two individuals will have a better long-run nutritional status: person A, who has a fixed energy input, or person B, who faces a fluctuating energy input with the same average intake as A? What kind of implications would this have for individuals who earn their living from casual labor markets, where employment is uncertain?

(b) Now look at the long-term implications of storage and borrowing for body mass. Let's use specific numbers for this question:

Suppose that resting metabolism needs 30 calories per day for every kilogram of body weight. Next, assume that there is only one kind of task to be done in the economy, which requires an expenditure of 1,000 calories per day. Suppose, finally, that the wage rate allows you to consume 2,500 calories per day.

Figure out the long-run body weight (in kilograms) for a person who is working under this environment. Try and describe the time path of body weight if you start from a different body weight than the long-run level.

■ (4) (a) We showed that with a large supply of labor (and with no long-term storage or borrowing effects), the equilibrium piece rate settles at the level where the line describing the piece rate is tangent to the capacity curve. Explain why this is the case.

(b) To help you understand how piece rates work in this market, begin with the situation described in the previous paragraph. Now imagine that all the laborers are given a small amount of nonlabor income. Using a diagram, show that the relationship between *wage income* and total capacity is affected as a result. Now with the same total amount of labor, try to predict what will happen to the new equilibrium piece rate. Show carefully that *it must fall*.

(c) Prove that if there is unemployment both before and after the change in nonlabor income, the *total income* (not just the labor income) of employed labor must fall as well. What gives rise to this paradoxical result?

(d) Compare the result in (c) with the observation (see text) that if there is a mix of some people with nonlabor income and some people without nonlabor income, then the individuals with nonlabor income will always do better than the individuals with no such income.

■ (5) Suppose that spot market wages fluctuate between the two values $50 and $100, each with probability 1/2. Suppose that a risk-averse worker dislikes fluctuations in income and wants to smooth out these wages. He therefore approaches a large employer, who is risk-neutral and goes by expected values. They agree on a contract (w_1, w_2), where w_1 is paid by the employer to the employee in case the spot market wage is $50, and where w_2 is paid in case the spot market wage is $100.

(a) Describe precisely the set of contracts [(w_1, w_2) pairs] that would be acceptable to the *employer*, in the sense that he would prefer to pay using such a contract rather than pay spot wages.

(b) Using part (a), argue that if the employer and the employee settle on a contract, then it must be the case that $(w_1 + w_2)/2 < 75$, and, moreover, that $w_1 > 50$ and $w_2 < 100$.

(c) Now consider an ongoing form of this contract between employer and laborer. Notice that in each period, *if* the going spot wage happens to be $100, the laborer has an incentive to break the contract and run away. Why is this? What is the laborer's short-run gain from doing so?

(d) Now we think about the long-run loss to the laborer for breaking the contract. He will surely lose future contracts with the current employer. This is a source of real loss if, in the original contract, the employer desisted from driving the laborer's compensation down to the equivalent of what he could have obtained elsewhere. Observe that this becomes more and more important if the laborer can get a permanent contract elsewhere without the current employer's knowledge. Argue that if this problem becomes very serious, then the employer will not agree to offer the permanent contract in the first place.

■ (6) Consider a second possible reason to hire permanent labor, which is to carry out tasks that cannot be easily monitored by the employer. In this case, the only punishment power that the employer might have is firing the permanent employee from the job. Consider the following information: (i) The permanent employee must be hired at a fixed wage, call it w, that is paid up front. (ii) The next best employment that a permanent employee can get is as a casual employee, say at $100 per season (neglect uncertainty and seasonality). (iii) The employee cannot be monitored, so there is always a danger that he will shirk. This cannot be found out immediately, but suppose that there is evidence of this available by the beginning of next season.

Show that the employer must always set w strictly *higher* than $100, even if there is a large potential supply of permanent workers. Discuss how the difference between w and $100 is affected by (a) alternative uses of the permanent laborer's time (shirking), (b) the likelihood of his getting another permanent laborer's job if he is fired, and (c) a change in the casual wage, currently set at $100.

■ (7) This problem explores the way in which a shortage of food might act as a constraint to industrial employment and how the situation is affected by the presence of inequality.

Suppose that an unemployed person who is not doing strenuous productive work requires 100 kilograms of wheat per year to survive. Suppose, further, that an employed low-income individual requires 200 kilograms to survive and carry out productive activity. Finally, suppose that a rich person consumes 250 kilograms of wheat per year, either directly or indirectly. And suppose that these demands are completely inelastic.

Consider an economy that produces 1 million kilograms of wheat per year and has only the three types of people discussed above. Suppose that 5,000 people live in this economy.

(a) If n (between 0 and 5,000) is the number of rich persons, find a formula for the minimum number of people in this economy that must be unemployed. Describe the way in which this number varies with n in the formula and give a verbal explanation for this variation.

(b) Suppose that the government of this country tries out a remedy of hiring unemployed people by a system of deficit financing. We already know from the calculations above that the number of unemployed people cannot be reduced beyond a certain limit. Try to describe the mechanisms that will bring the economy back to its original number of employed people.

(c) Are there *particular* government policies that might bring down the unemployment rate?

Chapter 14

Credit

14.1. Introduction

14.1.1. The limits to credit and insurance

Throughout this book, credit and insurance (or the lack thereof) play an important role. This is no accident. Many economic activities are spread out over time. The adoption of a new technology or a new crop requires investment today, with the payoffs coming in later. Even ongoing productive activity requires inputs in advance, with revenues realized at a later point in time. Finally—and this is especially true of casual labor or the self-employed—income streams may fluctuate (because of seasonality or uncertain demand conditions), and such fluctuations will be transmitted to consumption unless they are smoothed through some form of credit.

That a credit market may not function smoothly was taken as axiomatic at various points in this book. It isn't hard to see why. Two features of this market make it problematic. First, it is often very difficult to monitor exactly what is being done with a loan. A loan may be taken for an ostensibly productive reason, but may be used for other needs (such as consumption) that cannot be easily transformed into monetary repayment. Alternatively, a loan may be put into a risky productive activity that may fail to pay off. This creates the problem of "inability to repay" or *involuntary default*, at which point there is little that a lender can do to get his money back.[1]

The second problem is *voluntary* or *strategic* default, a situation in which the borrower *can* repay the loan, in principle, but simply does not find it in his interest to do so. Such a state of affairs is especially pertinent in contexts where the legal system of loan enforcement is weak. Two examples of weak enforcement come to mind. One is in the sphere of international debt (see Chapter 17). An effective international court of law does not exist, and disgruntled lenders must take recourse to punitive measures that are often limited, such as the threat to advance no further loans (which often lacks credibility) or the threat to cease trading relationships (which are subject to

---

[1] It may be possible to punish the borrower with a harsh prison term, for instance (though even here there are appropriate limits imposed by the law), and such punishments may serve to create reputation effects, but it still does not help to obtain repayment in some *given* situation.

objections from other economic actors in the lending country that gain from such trade). The second example, which we focus on here, comes from developing countries. Internal courts of law are often weak or absent, and many lenders must rely on the same sorts of punitive mechanisms as in the case of international debt, such as the threat to advance no future loans. The less effective these threats, the more they constrain the operation of credit markets in the first place.

Insurance markets, which we will study in Chapter 15, suffer from similar sorts of complications, although repayment is not the main issue. Consider crop insurance. If such insurance is provided by a large company without intimate knowledge of the insurees, it is for the insuree to assert that the harvest was bad, with no surefire way for the insurer to verify whether this was actually the case. There are, of course, some observable shocks such as weather that the company can condition its payments upon, but very often there are farm-specific, idiosyncratic shocks as well. To the extent that these shocks are difficult to observe and verify (publicly), a company-based scheme may be unable to cover the important need for crop insurance.

Indeed, even if the *outcomes* (such as farm output) can be verified, insurance is still problematic if the *inputs* cannot be verified. For instance, there is the problem that crop insurance may encourage undersupply of effort on the farm, due to the knowledge that a bad crop will be insured against.

All of these issues are exacerbated by the fact that agricultural production also exhibits a great deal of correlation across farms. Bad weather may have an entire village or group of villages clamoring for an insurance payout. Companies that can handle such payouts must be diversified over a larger area, but such diversification does not allow for microknowledge of conditions within an individual village.

It is not surprising, then, that insurance schemes in village economies are often *informal* in nature: groups of people co-insure one another under better informational conditions. As a farmer and a village resident, it may be difficult for my next-door neighbor to convince me that his crop has failed when I know about his activities on a daily basis. I may also be able to monitor his effort better, and he mine. However, such schemes, better grounded in information though they may be, can obviously not provide insurance against a correlated event (such as villagewide flooding). They also suffer from the second problem that we discussed for credit: enforceability. An individual who is in good shape this year may be that much less willing to help out someone who is not. He knows that in displaying this unwillingness, he may be locked out of future access to insurance (and he may face the disapproval of the community as well), but this may or may not be enough to deter him.

All of these arguments, as well as others made elsewhere in this book, seem to rest on the nasty presumption that human beings are out to do the best for themselves and display no altruism whatsoever. On average, these cynical presumptions may or may not be true, but this is really not the point. The main argument here is that unless there are strong reasons for each individual to participate in or conform to a particular economic institution, that institution must either adapt or die. Of course, I do not mean that there will be no unilateral acts of economic generosity otherwise. There may well be, but such acts do not form a socioeconomic institution.

14.1.2. Sources of demand for credit

In this chapter, we study credit markets. We can divide the demand for credit or capital into three parts. First, there is the capital required for new startups or a substantial expansion of existing production lines. The credit market that services these needs is called the market for *fixed capital*: capital that is poured into the purchase and organization of fixed inputs such as factories, production processes, machines, or warehouses. In contrast, there is the credit required for ongoing production activity, which occurs because of a substantial lag between the outlays required for normal production and sales receipts. Thus, merchants who buy handicrafts from poor producers advance or "put out" sums of money that are used to purchase various materials. When the product is finally produced, these credit advances are deducted from the price that the merchant pays for his wares. This market is called the market for *working capital*. Finally, there is *consumption credit*, which typically is demanded by poor individuals who are strapped for cash, either because of a sudden downturn in their production, or a sudden fall in the price of what they sell, or perhaps because of an increase in their consumption needs caused by illness, death, or festivities such as a wedding.

It is this last source of demand that also underlies the demand for insurance. The possibility of a sudden crop failure or illness can give rise to groups of individuals who band together in some form of reciprocal relationship. Certainly, such reciprocity can only be sustained over time by the *recurrent possibility* that each participant can some day be in the same unfortunate position.

Although fixed capital credit is of great importance in determining the overall growth of the economy, working capital and consumption credit are fundamental to our understanding of how an economy supports its poor and disadvantaged. In no sector is this more the case than in agriculture. The seasonality of agricultural production and the low incomes of those who live and work in the rural sector heightens the importance of working capital in production.

At the beginning of the crop cycle, the peasant faces a considerable need for working capital: money to purchase seeds, fertilizers, pesticides, and so on. These expenditures are bunched up front, and the farmer is often without sufficient funds to finance it. Hence, there is a need to borrow, with the loan repaid after the crop is harvested and sold. The repetitive taking and repayment of loans is an intrinsic feature of life, and the ease with which such loans can be taken fundamentally affects the economic productivity and well-being of millions of individuals.

When we add to seasonality the uncertainty surrounding productive activity, *consumption credit* also takes on great importance. An individual's harvest might fail, which causes immense temporary hardship that can only be alleviated through loans. Farm wages are typically lower in the lean season relative to the harvesting season, when the demand for labor is high. Moreover, there is often a high rate of unemployment in the slack season. Peasants, and landless laborers in particular, who rely on wages as a means of livelihood, find considerable fluctuations in their earnings from month to month. Credit is required for such people to smooth consumption over time to cover their needs in periods of low income by borrowing against higher expected earnings during times when the going is good.

14.2. Rural credit markets

14.2.1. Who provides rural credit?

Institutional lenders

First, there are the *formal* or institutional lenders: government banks, commercial banks, credit bureaus, and so on. Often special banks are set up, as in Thailand, the Philippines, and India, and in many other countries, to cater especially to the needs of rural production.

The main problem with formal lenders is that they often do not have personal knowledge regarding the characteristics and activities of their clientele. Often, these agencies cannot precisely monitor just how the loans are used. The problem is not just production versus consumption: for example, the fear that a loan taken ostensibly for some productive purpose may be squandered to meet the expenses of a wedding. There are other, more subtle reasons for a systematic divergence between what lenders want done with the money and what borrowers want.

To see this divergence, consider a very simple example. Imagine that loans are forthcoming at an interest rate of 10% and that there are alternative projects, each requiring a startup cost of 100,000 pesos. Suppose that the projects are arrayed in terms of their rate of return and that there are two projects with rates of return pegged at 15 and 20%. If there is no uncertainty about the projects and all projects pay off fully in the next time period, this is tantamount to saying that the projects will return gross revenues of 115,000, and 120,000 pesos, respectively.

Observe that in this case there is a perfect coincidence of interests between the bank and the borrower. The bank wants its 10% back and presumably also wants the borrower to take up the optimal project. Given that the borrower wants to make as much money as he can, there is no reason for him not take up the project with a 20% return. Everyone is happy.

Now let us change matters around a little bit. Suppose that the return to the first project is *uncertain*. Thus, keep the second project just the same as before, but suppose that the first project pays off 230,000 pesos with probability 1/2 and nothing with probability 1/2. The *expected* return is just the same as it was: if you remember from earlier chapters how to calculate this, you will see the expected revenue from the project is just $(1/2)230,000 + (1/2)0 = 115,000$.

Now think about the rankings of these projects from the viewpoints of the borrower and the lender. To do this, assume that if a project fails, the borrower cannot return any money to the lender: she simply declares bankruptcy. I will return to this assumption later. The bank would like to fund the 20% project, just as before; indeed, more than it did before, because the 20% project pays off its interest (and principal) for sure, whereas full payment happens only with probability 1/2 in the case of the 15% project.

What about the borrower's expected return? Assuming that she is risk-neutral like the bank,[2] it is $120,000 - 110,000 = 10,000$ for the safe project and $(1/2)[230,000 - 110,000] + (1/2)0 = 60,000$ for the risky project. Her expected return is *much* higher under a *riskier* project with a *lower* rate of return! She will therefore try to divert the loan to this project, and this will make the bank very unhappy.

What went wrong with the market here? What is wrong is that the borrower has *limited liability*. In this example, she pays up if all goes well, but if the project fails, she does not repay anything (she does not get anything either, but that is not the main point). In a sense, an artificial tendency for a borrower to take on too much risk is created: she benefits from the project if it goes well, but is cushioned on the downside. The bank would like to prevent this risk from being taken; often it cannot. We will come back to this scenario in more detail later. It will form the basis for theories of credit rationing.

Observe that if the borrower could somehow be made to repay the loan under every contingency, we would be back to a world that's equivalent to one of perfect certainty. The bank would not care what the borrower did with the money and the borrower would choose the project with the highest expected rate of return. However, who can repay in all (or most) contingencies? They are the relatively *rich* borrowers, who can dig into their pockets to repay even if the project goes badly. We see here, then, in particularly stark form, one important reason why banks discriminate against poor borrowers.

Thus institutional credit agencies often insist on collateral before advancing a loan. For a bank that is interested in making money, this is certainly a

---

[2] A similar example can also be constructed even if the borrower is risk-averse.

reasonable thing to do. For poor peasants, however, this usually makes formal credit an infeasible option. It is not that they lack collateral, but that their collateral is often of a very specific kind. A farmer may have a small quantity of land that he is willing to mortgage, but a bank may not find this acceptable collateral, simply because the cost of selling the land in the event of a default is too high. Likewise, a landless laborer may seek funds to cover a sudden illness in the family and pledge his labor as collateral: he will *work* off the loan. However, no bank will accept labor as collateral.

Formal Lenders in Thailand[3]

Many governments in the nascent postwar developing countries recognized the importance of their agricultural sectors, so rural policy was an integral component of government policy in general. Rural credit programs, in turn, formed a fundamental component of rural policy.

Traditionally, poor households in the countryside could obtain loans only from local village moneylenders, who charged exorbitant rates of interest. Borrowing was restricted only to cases of desperate need. The purpose of government intervention in rural credit markets was presumably twofold: the egalitarian motive of making cheap credit available to poor rural families and the motive of raising agricultural productivity and efficiency through financing the adoption of new inputs and technology on a wider scale. Thailand's experience in this area contains many insights and lessons.

In 1966, the government of Thailand founded the Bank for Agriculture and Agricultural Cooperatives (BAAC). The sole purpose of the BAAC was to lend to farm households. By 1974, the BAAC had established branches in fifty-eight of the country's seventy-one provinces. In August 1975, two years after a democratic government came to power and in an atmosphere of intense political wooing of the rural masses, the Bank of Thailand circulated a memorandum to all commercial banks. Each of them would have to lend at least 5% of its total stock of loans and advances to farm households. A bank that found it impossible to do so (perhaps because of a lack of rural networks) had to deposit the specified amount with the BAAC, which then channeled it into the agricultural sector. The required fraction was gradually increased over the next few years, until it came to rest at 11% of total deposits in 1979.

By 1975, the BAAC was already advancing 4.5 billion baht in loans. In a decade of rapid expansion, this amount increased to 23.3 billion baht in 1986. The total value of agricultural loans coming from the commercial banks also underwent a dramatic increase: according to official estimates, it stood at around 50.7 billion baht in 1986, from a starting figure of 3.9 billion in 1975.

How successful was the Thai rural credit policy? Was cheap credit channeled into every household? Were the village moneylenders weeded out and did exorbi-

---

[3] The material in this box is drawn from Siamwalla et al. [1993].

tant interest rates disappear? Unfortunately, aggregate official statistics are somewhat misleading, and detailed surveys conducted at the grassroots level reveal that, in spite of some improvements, the situation is not as rosy as anticipated.

For one thing, reports on lending by commercial banks involve a good deal of exaggeration. The central bank couldn't really monitor the lending activities of banks. "Moral suasion" formed the basis of the central bank's efforts. The commercial banks, on their part, described diverse kinds of loans as "agricultural loans," thereby stretching the meaning of the term to suit their purposes, while complying on paper with the official policy. Surveys indicate that the extent of exaggeration was around 25% and probably more.

Another problem was that commercial banks clearly made much larger loans than the BAAC: on average, the loans were *three* times as large, so that the number of households reached was relatively small (and these households were certainly the richer households).

What is astonishing is that even if we take the dramatic increase in formal lending at face value, informal loans in the late 1980s still accounted for half of total loans! The survey of Siamwalla and his associates showed clearly that the relatively poor borrowers were highly represented in the informal category. Indeed, the poorest households appeared to have had *no* access to loans, informal or otherwise: fully 42% reported no credit transactions at all during the period of the survey, and this 42% group includes the poorest households.

It is clear that the commercial banks and the BAAC lacked intimate personal knowledge of their clients' needs and characteristics. They also did not have the ability to track their borrowers closely or monitor their actions. To ensure recovery of loans, these institutions had to rely on securing proper collateral against the money lent out. It was inevitable, then, that their doors would be closed to poor farmers.

Even within the informal sector, there is a distinct tendency toward segmentation. In a national survey, over 70% of informal-sector borrowers reported that they had borrowed from only *one* lender over the past three years. Creditworthiness takes time to build: the average time of interaction with the lender concerned was close to seven years!

It is precisely the informational and monitoring advantage, stemming from these long periods of contact, that give the traditional village moneylender an edge over formal sector institutions. Such lenders mostly lend within their village or to borrowers in neighboring villages. They can (and do) use knowledge about the borrower's repayment capability or past credit record to control the size of the loan, and they ensure timely repayment by being present on the spot during the harvesting of the crop. In cases where repayment seems problematic, the village moneylender exercises a strong power by exerting social pressure or by threatening to cut off credit in future. Due to lack of information on the borrower to outsiders and the somewhat widespread practice of asking for a deposit of the borrower's land title[4] until the

---

[4] This is not the same as asking for collateral. The lender, in keeping the borrower's land title, does not acquire a legal or contractual right to seize it in case of default. Indeed, the value of the land may be too meager to cover the cost of the loan. However, the custom of asking for such a deposit ensures that the client cannot borrow from multiple sources at the same, thereby significantly reducing default motives.

loan is repaid, moneylenders have been able to create and maintain tight, secluded groups of individual client borrowers over which they wield substantial power.

Thus, the share of the informal sector in total rural credit in Thailand has dropped from the staggering 90% in 1975, but is still around a healthy 50%. However, this reduction in *share* does not reflect a decline in the total *volume* of transactions conducted in the informal market. Rapid commercialization of agriculture over the period has greatly increased the need for loans, particularly to finance working capital. Indeed, much of the loans disbursed by the formal sector are of a "flow credit" nature, that is, they are for the purposes of financing working capital in the regular production cycle. It is in unforeseen contingencies—periods of financial hardship due to disease, family crisis, or even an expensive marriage—that farmers, particularly the poorer ones, must rely on the traditional moneylender. The formal sector has functioned badly in enabling people to achieve consumption smoothing.

According to the survey done by Siamwalla et al. in the Nakhon Ratchasima province of Thailand, although 43,743 households borrowed exclusively from the formal sector, 88,145 households—about twice that number—borrowed only from the informal sector. That the latter's decision was not a matter of choice, but rather due to lack of access to the formal sector in the face of need, is reflected in the fact that there were dramatic differences in interest rates between the two sectors: the formal sector charged between 12 and 14% per annum, whereas informal sector rates were around 25% in the Central Plains, where they were lowest, and 60% or higher in other regions. The imperfect access of all borrowers to formal credit, the monitoring and information costs involved in lending without collateral, and, perhaps, the quasi-monopoly of village moneylenders over their clients explain why, in spite of massive injections of government subsidized credit into the rural economy, many poor Thai households are still subject to borrowing at exorbitant rates of interest to cover even their most pressing needs.

Informal lenders, information, and collateral

In the previous section, we discussed the problem of collateral and that some economic agents offer collateral in forms that are unacceptable to formal lenders. However, the "right" sort of *informal* moneylender may be willing to accept collateral in these forms. A large landowner who has land adjacent to that of a poor farmer may be interested in the tiny plot as collateral (indeed, perhaps more interested in the plot than in getting the loan back). An employer of rural labor will accept labor as collateral, in case the laborer–borrower fails to repay.[5]

---

[5] These assertions raise a deeper conceptual problem. The fact that some agents will accept, say, labor as collateral when others will not means that there is an imperfect market of some kind. After all, why can't the bank accept labor as a collateral and then sell this labor to a rural employer? Why can't it accept land and sell the land, if need be, to the large landowner who is interested in

It is no surprise, therefore, to find that formal banks cannot effectively reach out to poor borrowers, whereas informal moneylenders—the landlord, the shopkeeper, the trader—do a much better job.

There is another reason for the dominance of informal moneylending. Quite apart from the ability to accept collateral in exotic forms, the informal moneylender often has much better information regarding the activities and characteristics of his clientele. In the remainder of this chapter, we will have occasion to qualify this assertion a bit, but still the general point remains. A trader who advances loans for working capital often has first claim on the farmer–borrower's output; he arrives with his truck at the field on the day of the harvest. A landlord has a better chance of knowing what his tenant is doing with a loan than any commercial bank can hope to have. Thus, even in countries where government efforts to extend rural credit are strong, the informal credit sector flourishes. Take the case of India. Right after the country's political independence, in the early 1950s, a majority of rural households borrowed from the village moneylender. The *All India Rural Credit Survey*, published by the Reserve Bank of India, reveals that in 1951 only 7.2% of all borrowing was from government sources, banks, and cooperatives. By 1981, this number had jumped to 61.2% (Bell [1993]), thanks mainly to the Indian government's substantial drive to extend rural credit through official channels. Individual moneylenders by no means vanished; 24.3% of all debt was still owed to them. Similarly in Thailand, the share of the informal sector in total rural credit declined from a steep 90% in 1975 to a still influential 50% in the late 1980s (see box). On the other hand, there are countries in which most of the rural population relies almost entirely on informal-sector moneylenders. Nigeria is a case in point. A study from the late 1980s (see Udry [1994]) reveals that only 7.5% of all loans (in value) came from banks, companies, or projects. Our next box studies informal moneylenders in more detail for the Philippines.

Informal Lenders in the Philippines[6]

Like any developing country, the financial system of the Philippines has its formal and informal components. The formal financial system, under the direct supervision of the Central Bank of the Philippines, is made up of commercial banks, thrift

---

the plot? There are several answers to these questions. The resale of labor power by a bank may be indistinguishable from slavery and, therefore, it is banned by law. The resale of land may be constrained by informational problems in the proper identification of a buyer. Finally, if a bank has limited funds that it wishes to disburse to the rural sector, there is no reason to suppose that it will willingly engage in these complex credit transactions with a multitude of small individuals, rather than conclude far easier and safer deals with a relatively small number of large borrowers.

[6] This box is based on Floro and Ray [1997].

banks, rural banks, certain specialized government banks, and nonbank financial institutions such as investment houses, insurance companies, financing companies, and
securities markets. The informal sector includes relatives, friends, credit cooperatives,
rotating savings and credit associations, and the array of landlords, millers, traders,
and other agents who use financial dealings as an important subsidiary activity.

The *quantitative* importance of the informal financial sector is not precisely
known. The bulk of the financial statistics in the country reflect only the data from
formal institutions. However, there is much to be learned from various sources of
microlevel evidence provided by numerous sample credit surveys and the studies
that accompany such surveys.

The informal sector is widely diverse. At one end of the spectrum is the highly
personalized system of financial flows among relatives and friends, situated within
a scheme of reciprocity in which loan transactions do not carry interest charges.
These loans largely address day-to-day cash-flow problems to meet the consumption
and production needs of the household. Then there are cooperatives, credit unions,
rotating savings and credit associations, and other self-help organizations that are
owned and operated by their members. These alliances typically make use of pooled
funds to make loans and sometimes provide other financial services to members.
At the other end of the spectrum is the complex structure of trade and production
credit provided by input suppliers and output buyers to their client–producers. Other
examples of linked transactions, such as those between a landlord and a laborer or
tenant, are also common.

Consider a major group of informal lenders in the rural Philippines called *marketing agents*. Their prominence in the last three decades, especially in rice-growing
areas, results from rapid commercialization and intensified trading activity. Much
of the marketed rice is procured by private marketing agents consisting of paddy
traders or commission agents, rice millers, wholesalers, and retailers. These agents
usually engage in moneylending as a means to acquire claims over the produced
output and to secure the trader's share in the output (paddy rice) market. What is
therefore often involved is a cascading series of credit transactions that parallel the
distribution chain in marketing. Figure 14.1 traces a typical marketing channel and
its accompanying credit channel. Note that the various tiers of marketing activities
are not assigned to distinct agents. Traders often assume a combination of tasks.

The dominance of marketing-agent credit lies in the substantial advantage
that these agents possess in the access to information and in enforcing repayment.
Marketing-agent lenders provide loans to the vast majority of small farmers, who
are rationed out by formal financial institutions under the perception that they are
risky, noncreditworthy prospects, and they obtain very high repayment rates in the
process.

There is evidence that illustrates the considerable interaction between formal
and informal financial institutions even in the absence of government intervention.
These linkages typically take the form of a significant flow of funds between the two
sectors. Informal lenders often *borrow* from their formal counterparts; banks are an
important source of such funds.

Several studies document the flow of funds from the formal to the informal
credit sector. Geron [1989] studied 125 rural lenders operating in rice and coconut

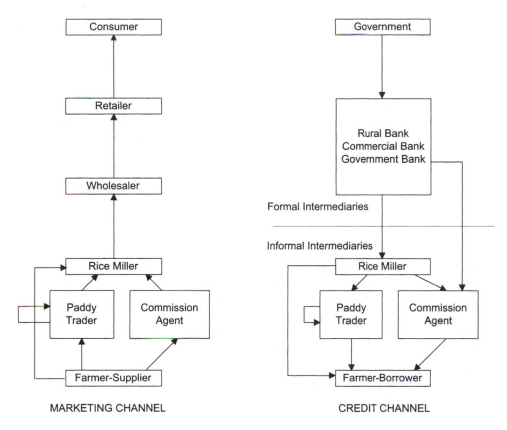

Figure 14.1. Marketing and credit channels in Philippine rice production.

producing villages. Some 70% of the respondents obtained loans from banks. Umali's [1990] survey of traders, commission agents, and rice millers involved in rice marketing in the Philippines provided further evidence of banks as important source of trader's loanable funds. Rice millers in this study borrowed as much as 80% of their funds from formal banking institutions. In Larson's [1988] study of the Philippines, 70% of the sample traders obtained 60% of their funds from formal sector banks. A 1978 TBAC informal lenders survey of 163 rural informal lenders in three Philippine provinces showed that significantly more than half of the informal lenders surveyed were savers in or borrowers from formal banks. Indeed, three informal lenders were at the same time *owners* of local banks (Agabin et al. [1988]). Eighty-four (52% of) rural informal lenders were, in particular, borrowers from the formal sector. Bank loans comprised close to half of their total operational funds. The bulk (80%) of such loans came from commercial banks.

The preceding findings are further supported by a recent comparative survey of *formal* lenders (banks) conducted by the Philippine Institute for Development Studies and the Agricultural Credit Policy Council. Their 1986 survey involved sixty-six respondent banks, including twenty-seven commercial banks, twenty-three rural banks and sixteen private development banks in eight provinces. The strength of the linkage between the formal and informal sectors seems to vary with the type of institution.

Nearly 33% of the commercial banks and development banks and 17% of the rural banks in the sample have lent to informal lenders. The percentage of total bank loans that have gone to these informal lenders ranges from 15% for rural banks to 55% for the development banks.

The predictable outcome is credit layering *across* the two sectors. A typical description is as follows. Bankers provide trade credit to rice millers and, to some extent, large traders in the agricultural sector. These clients who borrow working capital from the banks become, in effect, retailers of bank funds in the informal credit markets as they relend, either directly to small farmers or directly in the form of layered credit to other middlemen or commission agents (Agabin et al. [1988, 1989]).

14.2.2. Some characteristics of rural credit markets

If rural credit markets were perfectly competitive and smoothly functioning, there would be no need for this chapter. As in the case of any commodity, there would be a demand curve for credit and a corresponding supply curve of credit, and the intersection of the curves would determine the volume of credit and its equilibrium "price" as well, which is simply the interest rate. There would be little else to write about. Unfortunately, rural credit markets are pretty far removed from perfect competition.[7] You should already have an inkling of this from the previous section.

Informational constraints

The fundamental feature that creates imperfections in credit markets is informational constraints. We have already made this argument (and there is much more to come). To summarize the discussion so far, recall that informational gaps occur at two basic levels. First, there is lack of information regarding the *use* to which a loan will be put. Second, there is lack of information regarding the repayment decision. This deficiency includes limited knowledge of the innate characteristics of the borrower that may be relevant in such a decision, as well as limited knowledge of the defaulter's subsequent needs and activities, which place limits on his incentive to default. *All* the important features of credit markets can be understood as responses to one or the other of these informational problems.

Segmentation

A characteristic of the rural credit market is its tendency toward *segmentation*. Many credit relationships are personalized and take time to build up. Typically, a rural moneylender serves a fixed clientele, whose members he lends to on a repeated basis; he is extremely reluctant to lend outside this circle.

---

[7] For additional discussion see Besley [1995].

Most often, a moneylender's clients are from within his village or from close by, so that the moneylender has close contact with them and is well informed about their activities and whereabouts. Repeat lending—a phenomenon in which a moneylender lends funds to individuals to whom he has lent before (or has otherwise close interactions with)—is very common. To take an example, consider Aleem's [1993] intensive survey of fourteen moneylenders in the Chambar region of Pakistan. This survey showed that as many as ten moneylenders lent more than 75% of their funds to old clients—those with whom they had dealt in the past. Even among the remaining four lenders, the lowest percentage of repeat lending was reported to be 52%. You have already seen similar observations in the case of Thailand.

Interlinkage

A third feature, which may be considered an extension of the second, is the existence of what we might describe as *interlinked credit transactions*. Indeed, this is a good time to banish from your mind the image of a crafty moneylender, whose sole purpose is to lend money at exorbitant rates of interest to hapless borrowers. A majority of village moneylenders do *not* pursue usury as their sole occupation. Most of them are also wealthy landlords, shopkeepers, or traders dealing in the marketing of crops. Given a segmented market, it probably won't come as a surprise to learn that landlords tend to give credit mostly to their tenants or farm workers, whereas traders favor lending to clients from whom they also purchase grain (see the box on the Philippines). Thus segmentation often takes place along occupational lines, and the complementarity of some production relationship (tenant and landlord or farmer and trader) facilitates the credit relationship. This interlocking of markets—people who conduct their business in different markets (land, labor, credit, etc.) with the same trading partners, and indeed make the terms of transaction in one market depend on the terms and conditions in the other—is a far cry from the impersonal and independent functioning of markets that characterizes most textbook economic theory.

Interest rate variation

Segmentation has a natural corollary: informal interest rates on loans exhibit great variation, and the rates vary by geographical location, the source of funds, and the characteristics of the borrower. Sometimes the rate of interest is extraordinarily high. Aleem's survey of the Chambar region of Pakistan showed that the average annual interest rate was as high as 78.7% and involved substantial dispersion. The rate in specific cases varied from a low of 18% (which is nevertheless higher than the 12% charged by formal sector banks) to an astonishing high of 200% per annum. Siamwalla et al. reported that in most parts of Thailand, the informal-sector interest rate varied between 5 and 7% *per month*, which is dramatically higher than the 12% *per annum* charged by formal-sector banks.

However, high interest rates are not necessarily the norm in informal credit transactions. Udry's [1994] study of Nigeria (see also the box on Nigeria in Chapter 15) revealed that interest rates on loans among families were low (and dependent ex post on the financial circumstances of both borrower and lender). Low or even zero-interest loans from traders are not uncommon (Floro and Yotopoulos [1991]; Kurup [1976]). However, we will see later that the absence of interest is deceptive: given the interlinked nature of many of these transactions, interest may be hidden in other features of the overall deal (such as the price at which a trader buys output from the farmer or the implicit wage at which a laborer is required to work off an ostensibly interest-free loan).

The disparities in interest rates pose a puzzle: why aren't they smoothed out by people's attempts to make use of the arbitrage opportunities that such variations appear to present? In other words, why don't clever and enterprising agents borrow from lenders who charge comparatively lower rates and lend that money to borrowers who are paying and are prepared to pay much more? The answer has to do with segmentation and (once again) the informational variations that cause it. The personal characteristics of people matter and so does the nature or length of interaction between a borrower and a lender. The lender, before lending to a client, asks himself such questions as: Do I know him well? Is he from my village? Is he a good farmer? How much land does he possess? Does he have a pump set to irrigate his land if rainfall is scarce? The lender's decision whether or not to advance a loan and, if he does, what the terms and conditions will be, crucially depend on the answers to these questions. Thus, arbitrage opportunities may be only a mirage: the rate at which a landlord lends to client A from village X may not be the same at which he is willing to lend to client B from village Y.

Rationing

Informal credit markets are characterized by widespread *rationing*; that is, upper limits on how much a borrower receives from a lender. At first sight this appears natural: why would any moneylender advance infinite quantities of money? However, note that by rationing, we mean that *at the going rate of interest*, the borrower would like to borrow more but cannot. In this sense credit rationing is a puzzle: if the borrower would like to borrow strictly more than what he gets, there is some surplus here that the moneylender can grab by simply raising the rate of interest a wee bit more. This process should continue until the price (interest rate) is such that the borrower is borrowing just what he wants at that rate of interest. So why does rationing in this sense persist?

Note that, as a special case, rationing includes the *complete* exclusion of some potential borrowers from credit transactions with some lenders. That is, at the going terms offered by the lenders, some borrowers would like to borrow, but the lender does not lend to them. In this sense rationing is intimately connected to the notion of segmentation.

Exclusivity

Finally, many informal credit transactions are characterized by *exclusive dealings*. Moneylenders typically dislike situations in which their borrowers are borrowing from more than a single source. They insist that the borrower deal with them exclusively; that is, approach no other lender for supplementary loans. In Aleem's survey, for example, when asked whether lenders are prepared to lend to farmers who also borrow from other sources, ten of the fourteen respondents replied in the negative. This is also true of the Thai data that we've already discussed (see box). Segmentation and exclusivity together paint a picture in which it seems wrong to get an idea of overall competition in an informal credit market by simply *counting* the number of borrowers and lenders who are active. A better description is that despite the overall background of competition, *particular* dealings are often (though not always) bilateral, and informational, locational, and historical advantages often tend to confer on lenders the blessings of a "local monopoly", which they are not slow to exploit.

14.3. Theories of informal credit markets

14.3.1. Lender's monopoly

One explanation for the very high rates of interest that are sometimes observed is that the lender has exclusive monopoly power over his clients and can therefore charge a much higher price for loans than his opportunity cost (which is usually the competitive rate offered by formal-sector banks and urban credit markets). There are two problems with this line of explanation. The first is empirical. It is certainly true that the credit market is segmented, but this is not necessarily a justification for an assumption of complete monopoly. Siamwalla et al. [1993] reported in the context of Thailand that moneylenders were "thick on the ground." Aleem's 1980–81 survey of the Chambar area in Sind, Pakistan, revealed that "the often-imagined picture of a single village moneylender with monopoly power over clients in the village does not hold true in the Chambar context." Pure monopoly is not out of the question in some circumstances, but in today's rural societies, we can at best assume that lenders have "local monopoly" with limits.

The second problem is theoretical. As we will see in our subsequent discussions on interlinkage, monopoly power is *not* necessarily an explanation of high interest rates, at least of high *explicit* interest rates. From the point of view of efficient surplus generation, it is often better to pick up moneylending profits in forms other than interest. We postpone this discussion for the time being.

14.3.2. *The lender's risk hypothesis*

A somewhat more satisfactory explanation of high interest rates is provided by the *lender's risk hypothesis*. In its extreme form (see, for example, Bottomley [1975]), this hypothesis maintains that lenders earn *no* (ex ante) return on their money over and above their opportunity cost. However, as the story goes, there is substantial risk of default in rural credit markets: the borrower might default on interest payments and even part or all of the principal.

This risk comes from many sources. First, there is the risk of *involuntary* default: owing to sheer misfortune (crop failure, unemployment, disease, death, etc.), the borrower simply may not have enough money when the loan matures. Second, there is the possibility of voluntary or *strategic* default: the borrower may simply take the money and run, or stubbornly refuse to pay up. In regions where the legal machinery is not strong or functions slowly, such a possibility is not unlikely.

In the simplest version of the theory, there is an exogenous probability p of default on every dollar lent out. Competition between moneylenders drives the rural interest rate down to a point where each lender on the average earns zero expected profit (over and above the opportunity cost of funds to the lenders). Consider a typical village moneylender in this competitive market. Let L be the total amount of funds he lends out, let r be the opportunity cost of funds for every moneylender, and let i be the interest rate charged in competitive equilibrium in the informal sector. Because only a fraction p of loans will be repaid, the moneylender's expected profit is $p(1+i)L - (1+r)L$. The zero profit condition implies that this value must be zero in equilibrium, that is,

$$p(1+i)L - (1+r)L = 0,$$

which on manipulation yields

(14.1)
$$i = \frac{1+r}{p} - 1.$$

Notice that when $p = 1$, that is, when there is no default risk, we have $i = r$: informal interest rates are the same as formal-sector rates. However, for $p < 1$, we have $i > r$: the informal rate is higher to cover the risk of default. To get a sense of the magnitudes involved, take the formal-sector rate to be 10% per annum (not an unusual figure) and suppose that there is a 50–50 chance of default, that is, $p = 1/2$. You can easily calculate from equation (14.1) that i turns out to be a steep 120% per annum! Clearly, even under competition, informal-sector rates are very sensitive to the default risk.

The preceding simple story lays a finger on a very important aspect of the reality of rural credit markets—the risk of default. In sophisticated credit markets of industrialized countries, this risk is substantially lower, thanks mainly to a well-developed legal machinery that vigorously enforces contracts and because many loans are collateralized. In the absence of such devices, the possibility of default remains strong, and we are led to suspect that it is this feature that shapes some of the unique characteristics of informal credit markets that we described earlier. However, if we look at the data, the fact remains that *actual* rates of default in rural credit markets are very low indeed. Many case studies reported that although formal-sector default rates measure up to about a quarter of all loans given, in the informal sector, these rates are significantly lower. For example, Aleem [1993] estimated the rates to be below 5% in most of the cases he studied. This low estimate suggests that although *potential* default may be important, lenders manage to devise contracts and create incentives to circumvent the problem. Understanding the various ways in which lenders manipulate and lower the default risk is the key to explaining some of the main features of informal credit markets. The arguments that follow take steps in that direction.

14.3.3. *Default and fixed-capital loans*

The analysis in the earlier section is deficient in one serious respect. It assumed that the default probability is *independent* of the amount to be repaid. It is easy enough to describe situations in which this should not be the case; for instance, one of the models in Chapter 7 built exclusively on this possibility.

Larger amounts to be repaid may lead to a greater risk of default. This statement suggests that certain loans will not be given at all under *any* circumstances, irrespective of the interest rate premium, because the *premium itself affects the chances of repayment*. Likewise, large loans themselves raise the chances of default and will, therefore, not be made. What is "large" depends, of course, on the particular circumstances of the society, such as per capita wealth and the availability of alternative opportunities such as migration to another area (in the case of default).

We can extend this line of reasoning, not just to the *size* of the loan, but also to the kind of *use* to which the loan will be put. If the loan can be used by the borrower to *permanently* put himself in a situation in which he never has to borrow again, then such loans may not be forthcoming. Suppose, for instance, that a rural laborer wishes to borrow money so that he can migrate to the city and set up a small business there. Indeed, given his contacts and entrepreneurial spirit, this may be efficient from a societal viewpoint, but it would be surprising indeed if any rural moneylender advanced him such a loan. In the absence of a legal enforcement mechanism, often the only instrument that a moneylender has is the threat of not advancing loans when needed in the future. But if future loans will never be needed, then the threat has no value.

It is therefore reasonable that in the presence of strategic default, the overwhelming provision of informal loans will be for working capital or consumption purposes, rather than for fixed investments that may permanently reduce the borrower's future need for credit.

14.3.4. *Default and collateral*

The fear of default also creates a tendency to ask for collateral, whenever this is possible. Collateral may take many forms. Certain property rights may be transferred while the loan is outstanding: land may be mortgaged to the lender, and use rights to the output of that land may be in the hands of the lender as long as the loan is outstanding. Labor may be mortgaged as well, and later used, if necessary, to pay off the loan. More exotic forms of collateral are not uncommon. For instance, Kurup's [1976] study of Kerala, India, showed that ration cards (which are used to purchase subsidized food from the public distribution system) are often handed over to the lender for the duration of the loan. This is a weird special case of what is generally thought of as the mortgage of usufructuary rights. For instance, a borrower who has coconut trees on his land might mortgage the rights to the coconut output as long as his loan remains outstanding. This idea applies just as well to land that produces other crops.

Fundamentally, collateral is of two types: one in which both lender and borrower value the collateral highly, and another in which the borrower values the collateral highly, but the lender does not (the third variant is obviously not observed). From the point of view of strategic default, it is irrelevant whether the first or the second form of collateral is employed. The pawnbroker who accepts your favorite wristwatch (given to you by your grandmother) as collateral for a loan may not be particularly concerned with selling the watch if you do not repay, and may not be able to sell it for a high price either. But he knows that you attach sentimental value to that watch and hence will pay back a loan even if the rate of interest is high.

Collateral that is valuable to *both* parties has the additional advantage that it covers a lender against involuntary default as well. For these types of collateral, credit may simply be a veil for acquiring collateral, as the following simple model reveals.[8] As a by-product of this model, we obtain an alternative view of usurious interest rates.

Suppose that a small farmer is in need of a loan of size L, perhaps to tide over a family emergency. He approaches the local large landowner, who is known to lend money for such purposes. The landowner asks him to pledge land as collateral for the loan. Our farmer has a plot of land adjacent to that of the large landowner and this is what he pledges.

Now let us keep track of some of the relevant variables by introducing some notation. Let i be the interest rate charged on the loan L and let V_S (S for "small") be the (monetary) value that the small farmer places on his land. Likewise, let V_B (B for "big") be the value that the big landowner attaches to the same plot of land. Because the plot is adjacent, V_B is not a negligible value: one can certainly imagine cases in which V_B exceeds V_S. Thus we have an example here of the first kind of collateral, one which is of value to both parties.

Next, let us place a monetary value (just as we did in Chapter 7) on the loss to the farmer from default, over and above the loss of his collateral. Such losses may include the fear of not receiving future loans or even the threat of physical retribution. Summarize the money value of this loss by F.

When the time comes to return the loan, we can conceive of two possibilities:

(1) The borrower may be in a state of involuntary default: he simply does not possess the wherewithal to repay the money. In that case, he certainly loses the land, which passes into the hands of the large landowner.

(2) The borrower may contemplate willful default and take his chances with the landless labor market or even with migration to the city. The total loss to the borrower in this case is $V_S + F$, whereas the gain is that he gets to keep the principal plus interest that he owed. Thus the borrower will prefer to return the loan if

$$(14.2) \qquad\qquad L(1 + i) < V_S + F.$$

Consider, now, the lender's preferences. Does he prefer to see his loan returned or does he prefer to keep the collateral? He will prefer his money back if

$$(14.3) \qquad\qquad L(1 + i) > V_B.$$

Combining (14.2) and (14.3), we may conclude that loan repayment is in the interest of *both* parties only if

$$(14.4) \qquad\qquad V_B < V_S + F,$$

[8] The observations to follow are based on Bhaduri [1977].

which is a way of saying that the lender's valuation must not exceed the borrower's valuation by too much. In the special case where $F = 0$, so that collateral is the *only* way to force loan repayment, (14.4) says that the lender's valuation of the collateral must be less than that of the borrower.

Turn this around. Suppose that (14.4) does *not* hold, so that $V_B > V_S + F$. In this case, it follows that whenever the borrower prefers to repay the loan, the lender actually wants him not to do so! The lender would actually like the credit transaction to be an excuse to acquire the collateral (cheap). Thus collateral that is of high value to *both* lender and borrower may (paradoxically) result in credit transactions with excessive rates of default.[9]

In the present model, how might high default rates be precipitated? One way is to drive up the rate of interest so that (14.2) fails. In this case, if the borrower does not default involuntarily, the circumstances will induce him to do so willfully. The interest rate on such credit transactions will be high indeed, but the principal objective of the transaction is *not* to earn interest!

This story may be of some relevance in explaining why land inequalities rise in poor societies. Land is passed from poor to rich in lieu of unpaid debt; this much is to be expected. What the story teaches us, however, is that the debt contract may be written so as to deliberately induce these transfers.

By the way, land is only one example. Bonded labor is another. A loan may be advanced for the express purpose of ensuring a supply of cheap labor from the borrower. In this case, labor power acts as the collateral that is transferred in the end.

Finally, note that this sort of analysis works much better for consumption loans than production loans. With consumption loans (taken, say, for an illness in the family), the amount is often fixed and cannot vary with the rate of interest. With production loans, a high interest rate may be self-defeating because the borrower can scale back the amount of the loan by reducing the extent of his productive activity. This hints at a possible explanation of why interest rates may be high for some types of credit transactions but not for others. More on this topic follows later in the chapter.

14.3.5. *Default and credit rationing*

I now turn to another implication of default: the "rationing" of credit. First, a definition: *credit rationing* refers to a situation in which *at the going rate of interest in the credit transaction*, the borrower would like to borrow more money, but is not permitted to by the lender. The emphasized phrase is important. Except in very special cases, the notion of rationing makes no sense unless the "price" of the rationed commodity is specified.

---

[9] In a sense, these rates are illusory: they are provoked because the lender would like to drive the borrower into a state of default.

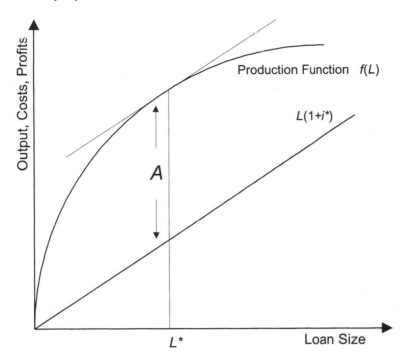

Figure 14.2. *Maximizing the rate of interest i on a loan.*

Thus if you imagine a diagram of the demand curve for loans by the borrower, credit rationing refers to all loan–interest combinations that lie to the "left" of the demand curve.

It turns out that the possibility of default is intimately tied to the existence of credit rationing, as the following simple model illustrates. Suppose that a moneylender wishes to allocate his available funds in a way that maximizes his rate of return on the funds. Imagine that there are a large number of potential farmers that he could lend to, each of whom use the loan as working capital to buy inputs for production. In Figure 14.2, we display a production function for a typical farmer that converts working capital (L) into output. The production function exhibits diminishing returns in working capital (because of other fixed inputs such as land). In the same diagram, we display the total costs to the farmer of borrowing an amount L: it is $L(1+i)$, where i is the rate of interest charged on the loan.

The moneylender would like to make this cost line as steep as possible by choosing i to be large: this is the rate of return he seeks to maximize.[10] At the same time, he cannot push the borrower too far. He does not have

[10] The careful reader will notice that the objective of maximizing i presumes that there are many lending opportunities of this kind. If this were a limited opportunity (say, there is only one such borrower), then the appropriate objective would be to maximize $L(i - r)$, where r is the opportunity cost of the moneylender's funds.

unlimited monopoly power and the farmer can always borrow from other sources *after a point*. We very simply summarize these alternatives by saying that the farmer can always have access to a net profit of A by borrowing elsewhere. Thus our moneylender cannot choose i so high that he pushes the farmer to a profit of less than A.

Figure 14.2 shows us the solution to this problem. Note that the vertical difference between the production function and the cost line (output minus loan costs) is the farmer's profit from productive activity: this difference must be kept at least as large as A. The largest interest rate i that is consonant with this requirement can be easily found. For each conceivable choice of interest rate, look at the maximal profit that the farmer can generate. This is found by setting the marginal product equal to the marginal cost $1 + i$ or, graphically, by choosing a loan so that the tangent to the production function is parallel to the cost line. The vertical difference between the production function and the cost line at this tangency point represents the maximal surplus available to the farmer at interest rate i. Thus the solution to the problem is quite simple: choose the largest interest rate i so that the farmer's (maximized) surplus does not fall short of A. The figure shows this graphically with the interest rate i^* such that the surplus is *just* A: anything higher and the farmer will go elsewhere.

Now, I want you to notice something important about the solution to the problem: at interest rate i^*, the farmer does receive his desired loan size *given that the interest rate he must pay is i^**. In other words, the solution may involve "high" or "low" rates of interest (depending on the farmer's alternatives as summarized by A), *but it will not involve credit rationing in the sense that we have defined previously*. The farmer may not be ecstatic about the interest rate he is paying on the loan, but *given* the interest rate, he is getting the desired loan size. Hence, there is no credit rationing (so far).

Now let us introduce the possibility of strategic default. Specifically, let us suppose that the farmer can willingly default on the loan. This probably means (and we will assume) that our moneylender will never lend to him again. However, the farmer can always go for his next best alternative and guarantee himself a profit of A from the next date onward.

To study the default problem, then, we have to account for the importance that the borrower attaches to *future* gains and losses. This notion influences the terms of the credit transaction that are immune to default. Thus we need a simple and tractable story that includes the borrower's *mental time horizon*: the extent to which the future concerns him when he makes current decisions. We have already used a model of this type in Chapter 13, when we discussed permanent labor contracts.

Specifically, we suppose that at each date, the farmer thinks N dates into the future and factors in the consequences of his current decisions on gains and losses in the coming N periods. We need some elementary algebra to capture the decision process. To this end, let us use the notation $f(L)$ to describe the value of the output for every loan size L. Thus $f(L)$ is simply an expression that describes the production function: as L increases, so does the value $f(L)$.

We now write down the relevant equations very quickly. The requirement that the farmer should want to participate at some interest rate i and some loan size L is just the statement that

(14.5) $$f(L) - L(1 + i) \geq A.$$

Indeed, this represented the constraint on the moneylender's choice of interest rate in the previous problem. Analogous to the considerations faced in studying land tenancy contracts (Chapter 12), we call this the *participation constraint*.

Additionally, in the presence of potential default, a fresh constraint appears. Look at what the farmer gets over his entire mental horizon of N dates. It is the amount per date, multiplied by N: $N[f(L) - L(1 + i)]$. Now what does he get if he decides to default? Well, today he will get all of $f(L)$ [because he pockets $L(1+i)$]. From tomorrow onward, he is excluded by our moneylender and so can get only A per period. Thus the total profit over the N period mental horizon is $f(L) + (N - 1)A$. For default *not* to occur, the former expression must exceed the latter; that is,

$$N[f(L) - L(1 + i)] \geq f(L) + (N - 1)A.$$

Moving this expression around, we see that

(14.6) $$f(L) - \frac{N}{N - 1}L(1 + i) \geq A.$$

Now observe that this condition looks a bit like the participation constraint (14.5), except for the term $N/(N - 1)$ that multiplies the cost line. Because this term always exceeds 1, the new restriction (14.6) is *tighter* than, and therefore effectively subsumes, the participation constraint. We call this new restriction the *no-default constraint*. Note that the shorter the mental horizon, the more difficult it is to meet the no-default constraint. For instance, if $N = 1$, so that the farmer never contemplates the future consequences of his current actions, (14.6) can never be satisfied. The farmer will always default on the loan, so no loans will be advanced.[11] On the other hand, if the farmer

---

[11] Notice that the same considerations should apply to the farmer's ability to borrow from *other* lenders, so if you are ahead of the argument, you should complain that the value of A should be affected by the farmer's mental horizon as well. We ignore this complication (though it will not make a qualitative difference in the end) and assume that these alternative contracts can always be enforced. However, see Section 14.3.7.

is very farsighted, then N is very large and the fraction $N/(N-1)$ has a value close to 1: we are then effectively back to the old problem in which only the participation constraint matters. In what follows, we are interested in situations in which N is neither too large (because that's just like the old problem) nor too small (because that will always give rise to default).

Figure 14.3 shows that the graphical study of the no-default constraint is very much like the analysis in Figure 14.2. All we do is modify the cost line by multiplying it by the factor $N/(N-1)$. Now go through the same steps as before. For each interest rate i, we need (14.6) to be met. The way to do this is to maximize the vertical difference between the production function and the *modified* cost line, and see whether this maximized difference is no less than A. To find this maximum, we must set the marginal product of the production function equal to the slope of the modified cost line, which is $N/(N-1)(1+i)$. Figure 14.3 does this by picking the loan size L so that the tangent to the production function is parallel to the modified cost line. At the interest rate i^{**}, the maximized difference *just* equals A. If the interest rate is chosen any higher, then the constraint (14.6) will fail. Thus the interest rate i^{**} and the associated loan size L^{**} represent the moneylender's optimal solution when default is possible.

Now here is the main point. Note that at the optimum credit transaction, the moneylender will advance a loan of L^{**}: the marginal product of the loan

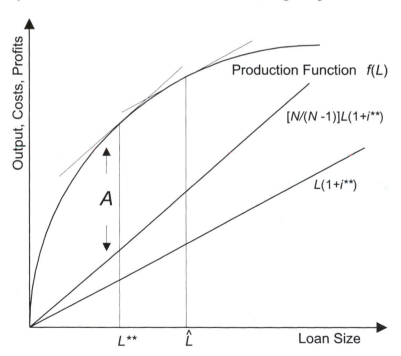

Figure 14.3. Loan contracts when default is possible.

equals $N/(N-1)(1+i^{**})$ *and not the true marginal cost of the loan as faced by the borrower,* which is $1+i^{**}$. It follows that we have credit rationing: if the borrower were asked in an interview if he would like to borrow more *at the going interest rate i^{**}*, he would answer in the affirmative. Indeed, he would like to borrow the amount $\hat{L}$ in a competitive market where all contracts can be costlessly enforced (see Figure 14.3).

Recall that when we introduced the concept of credit rationing, we asked why the moneylender would not react to such a situation by simply raising the interest rate or advancing a larger loan at the going interest rate (or some combination of the two). We can now provide an answer to this question: the fear of sparking off a default prevents such actions by the moneylender. A higher loan increases the return to a defaulter by allowing him to pocket more money. A higher interest rate increases the return as well, by allowing the defaulter to save on the repayment of more interest. The moneylender's preferred contract therefore involves credit rationing.

Credit rationing may stem from considerations other than default. In the next section, we take up this theme.

14.3.6. *Informational asymmetries and credit rationing*

Not all borrowers bear the same amount of risk. There are high-risk borrowers and there are low-risk borrowers. A diligent farmer with a significant amount of land to cultivate may be considered low risk by a lender, because the chance of crop failure and bankruptcy is low. A landless laborer in poor health is high risk. A farmer who owns a pump set or has access to assured irrigation carries lower risk than one who doesn't. Alternatively, the crop that is being grown may be more or less prone to the vagaries of the weather. Lending risk may vary significantly from borrower to borrower.

Risk may be correlated with characteristics of the borrower that are observable to the lender (such as landholdings or access to irrigation). However, it may substantially depend on other qualities that are *not* observable (perhaps farming skills or mental acumen in the face of a crisis, thriftiness, the quality of his land, and so on). When the factors that make for risk are observable, the lender can select his clients or charge appropriately higher rates for the high-risk clients. However, to the extent that clients bear different risks that cannot be discerned by the lender, an additional dimension is added to credit market transactions—the interest rate now affects the *mix* of clients that are attracted (and hence, the average probability of default). This new dimension might give rise to a situation in which at prevailing rates, some people who want to obtain loans are unable to do so; however, lenders are unwilling to capitalize on the excess demand and raise interest rates for fear that they will end up attracting too many high-risk customers.

If this last statement sounds surprising, think of the example that we discussed in Section 14.2.1. In that example, a risky project is often more attractive from the borrower's point of view, because in the event of project failure the borrower may be protected from repayment. Thus raising the interest rate may shut down the adoption of safe projects even though socially unattractive risky projects may still remain profitable from the point of view of the borrower. Following Stiglitz and Weiss [1981], we use this idea as a starting point for an explanation of credit rationing.[12]

Consider a moneylender who faces two types of potential customers: call them the *safe type* and the *risky type*. Each type of borrower needs a loan of (the same) size L to invest in some project or activity. The borrower can repay only if the investment produces sufficient returns to cover the repayment. Suppose that the safe type is always able to obtain a secure return of R ($R > L$) from his investment. On the other hand, the risky type is an uncertain prospect; he *can* obtain a higher return R' (where $R' > R$), but only with probability p. With probability $1 - p$, his investment backfires and he gets a return of 0 (for example, think of the second borrower as a farmer of a cash crop that brings in more money if the harvest is good, but is also more susceptible to weather damage).

We take it that the lender can freely set the interest rate without fear of losing his clients to competing lenders. (The same story works with competitive markets, but it's just simpler to tell it this way.) Let us suppose that the lender has enough funds to lend to just one applicant, and that there are two of them (one risky, one safe). Should he raise his interest rate until one borrower drops out? Let us see. What is the highest interest rate i for which the safe borrower wants the loan? Because his net return is given by $R - (1+i)L$, the highest acceptable rate for him is $i_1 = R/L - 1$. For the second borrower, the *expected* return is $p[R' - (1+i)L]$; hence, the maximum rate he is willing to pay is $i_2 = R'/L - 1$. Clearly, because $R' > R$, we have $i_2 > i_1$.

Let us pause for a moment to digest this. *The risky borrower is willing to pay a higher rate of interest than the safe borrower, and this interest rate is independent of his probability of success, p.* The reason is that bankruptcy yields zero, and in such a situation he defaults on the loan anyway, so his expected profits depends *only* on the success state. In this sense the risky borrower acts as if he does not care about failure.[13] Of course, the lender cares.

If the lender charges i_1 or below, both borrowers will apply for the loan. If the lender cannot tell them apart, he has to give the loan randomly to one of them, say by tossing a coin. On the other hand, if a rate slightly higher than i_1 is charged, the first borrower drops out and excess demand for the loan disappears. The lender may then go all the way up to i_2 without fear

---

[12] See also the earlier contribution of Raj [1979].

[13] This sharp description of the risky borrower's behavior is due in large part to the very simple binary specification of the project outcomes. Nevertheless, the overall insensitivity to project failure persists in more general models.

of losing the second customer. The lender's choice is then really between the two interest rates i_1 and i_2. Which should he charge?

Suppose the lender charges i_2. His expected profits are then given by

(14.7) $$\Pi_2 = p(1 + i_2)L - L.$$

On the other hand, if the lender charges i_1, he attracts each type of customer with probability $1/2$. His expected profits are then given by

(14.8) $$\Pi_1 = \tfrac{1}{2}i_1L + \tfrac{1}{2}[p(1 + i_1)L - L].$$

Under what condition will the lender be reluctant to charge the *higher* interest rate? This will happen when $\Pi_1 > \Pi_2$. Using the values of Π_1 and Π_2 from equations (14.7) and (14.8), and substituting the values of i_1 and i_2 obtained previously, we obtain the condition (which you should easily derive for yourself)

(14.9) $$p < \frac{R}{2R' - R}.$$

This condition is important! It tells us that if the high-risk type is "sufficiently" risky (remember, a lower p means a higher chance of default), then the lender will not raise his interest rate to i_2, thereby attracting the risky type. Instead, he will stick to the lower level i_1 and take the 50–50 chance of getting a safe customer. This will lead to credit rationing *in equilibrium*: out of two customers demanding a single available loan, only one will get it; the other will be disappointed. As in the previous section, the price is not raised even in the face of excess demand, but the reason is different. Raising the price would drive away the good borrower instead of the bad one, and the higher *possible* return cannot compensate for the lowered chance of repayment.

14.3.7. *Default and enforcement*

So far the possibility of default has played a crucial role in generating many of our predictions. It is now time to study the default process and its aftermath in more detail.

A good starting point is the model of Section 14.3.5. Recall the constraint (14.6), which must be met to prevent default. This constraint, you will remember, is fundamentally dependent on the mental horizon of the borrower: the number of future time periods N he worries about when making current decisions. Thus a default today, followed by $N - 1$ periods of profits A, should not be more valuable than N periods of nondefault dealings with the moneylender. This is what (14.6) captures in algebraic form.

A fundamental implication of this constraint is that the borrower's dealings with the moneylender must yield him a *greater* profit than he could get elsewhere by defaulting (otherwise he would certainly pocket the money today). An algebraic way to see this is to note that the borrower's profits are $f(L^{**}) - (1 + i^{**})L^{**}$, but using constraint (14.6), we can easily see that

$$f(L^{**}) - (1 + i^{**})L^{**} > f(L^{**}) - \frac{N}{N-1}(1 + i^{**})L^{**} = A.$$

The preceding equation also tells us that borrowers who are "patient" or have large mental horizons N can actually be given a relatively *worse* deal without fear of default. A smaller gap between the profitability of the current credit deal and that of the alternative A will be enough to make him conform: because the borrower is very patient, the threat of termination of future credit carries great bite, and hence the lender can charge stiffer rates without fear of default.

This model gives us a picture of how repayment can be ensured through dynamic threats and incentives. However, so far we have put the postdefault scenario in a black box. A defaulter must fall back on his alternative opportunities, because the current lender will no longer lend to him. Beyond this, we have said nothing about how these alternatives are arrived at.

Typically, the borrower will have access to more than one moneylender. He may therefore be tempted to default on the loan from the current lender and switch to another source when the current lender refuses to deal with him any further. Indeed, precisely this fear forced the lender to offer the borrower some premium or surplus on the loan over and above his opportunities elsewhere. Nevertheless, the existence of alternative sources of credit strengthens the incentive to default. How do lenders tackle this problem, apart from building repayment incentives into their credit transactions?

One possible answer is that a system of reputations helps to discipline borrowers. If a borrower defaults in his transactions with one lender, this may destroy his reputation in the market and mark him as a bad risk. As a result, *other* lenders may be reluctant to lend to him in the future. Clearly, this requires that information about the borrower's default action be spread throughout the lending community, so it is no surprise that a lender will eagerly make a default public, and he will certainly want to make this willingness known in advance to the borrower.

Is the rapid spread of default information a reasonable postulate for informal credit markets? It depends. In the informationally sophisticated credit markets that prevail in industrialized countries, credit histories are tracked on computer networks: a bank or credit agency can learn about a person's past offenses at the touch of a button, and the ability to learn this information quickly acts as a device to discipline the borrower. At the other extreme, consider traditional village societies with limited mobility. Community networks are very strong in these societies: everyone knows about everyone else. This may not be very pleasant if you are involved in a discreet love affair or simply don't like gossip, but these networks have social value: they act as credible sanctioning devices in situations where a computerized credit agency is missing. A violation of contractual promise against one party will not go unnoticed by others, who will limit their dealings with the offender as a result. There may even be other forms of social sanctions and censure imposed on the deviant. These threats permit acts of reciprocity and cooperation (including the granting and repayment of loans) that would not be possible otherwise.

As societies develop, mobility increases and traditional ties fall apart. Over time, informal information networks are replaced by the anonymous devices that we see in present-day industrialized societies. However, the replacement may be a long time coming. Hence, there is a large intermediate range of cases where the flow of information slows to a trickle. This is the transitional stage in which many developing countries find themselves. Indeed, it is perfectly reasonable to postulate that information flow follows a U pattern: both traditional and economically advanced societies have a lot of it, whereas societies in transition do not.

In such societies, a lender who meets a new loan applicant has few ways (or perhaps very costly ways, involving a great deal of time and a lot of painstaking enquiry) of knowing about the applicant's past pattern of behavior in credit relationships. In such a situation, a borrower has no fear of a tainted reputation due to default. What prevents the borrower from periodically defaulting and then switching sources? In addition, if this is going to be the case, why does any lender lend to him in the first place?

To be sure, such a situation is not a rarity. We have already seen that many borrowers are excluded from access to credit and that a history of borrowing is often necessary for loans. The box on informal credit markets in Pakistan underlies these trends. At the same time, informal credit markets *do* function, so we cannot fall back exclusively on the argument that credit markets must *completely* break down in the absence of information.

In the face of limited information about the past behavior of borrowers, lenders have two sorts of reactions. The first possibility is that they check out a new borrower with a great deal of wariness (see the box on Pakistan or studies such as Siamwalla et al. [1993]). The lender might expend effort and money to check the credentials of the borrower, to see that he is indeed a good risk.

The phrase "good risk" is significant. A lender wants to know whether a borrower has defaulted in the past simply because this provides a clue as to whether the borrower concerned is an *intrinsically* bad prospect. However, we must conceptually distinguish between borrowers who are intrinsic cheats and borrowers who are opportunists in the sense that the no-default constraint did not hold for them, because the terms of the credit contract did not prevent default. If only variations in the latter are true and there is no variation in the *intrinsic type* of the borrower, a lender gains no information from knowing that a borrower has defaulted in the past; he might as well devise a loan straight away that satisfies the no-default constraint. There is little to gain by checking out the past history of a borrower.

When this is the case, the credit market breaks down entirely. If lenders do not screen borrowers, then any lender who advances a loan will indeed be defaulted upon. We therefore realize that the screening efforts of a lender have enormous (positive) externalities: they prevent default on the loans of *other* lenders. However, externalities, as we well know, are not sufficient cause for someone to exert effort: he will only do so if it benefits *him*. In the present context, this means that intrinsic uncertainty about the types of borrowers, namely, the possibility that some borrowers are more default-prone than others, enables the credit market to function where otherwise it would collapse! The presence of bad types creates careful lenders, who regard past defaults as signals of intrinsically bad risks. To avoid being branded, good risks (who may be opportunists, nevertheless) *do* repay their loans.

We may therefore state the following points. First, the incentive to check out a new borrower actually enables a credit market to function by creating the fear that a default may block of access to future credit. Second, the incentive to screen a fresh borrower depends on the belief that some borrowers are intrinsically bad risks. Combining these two points, we see, paradoxically enough, that the presence of some bad types is essential for the functioning of a credit market under limited information, albeit at some reduced level.

The same is true of what we might call *testing loans*. Lenders may wish to start small and increase the loan size if borrowers return the smaller loans. These small loans serve as indirect tests of the borrower's intrinsic honesty. The point is that even honest borrowers must be subject to these initial testing phases. Taking the argument one step further, we may conclude that the presence of testing loans serves as an incentive for (honest but opportunistic) borrowers to repay, because they know that if they default, they will be subject to the slow build-up of cooperation that characterizes any new relationship, and this is costly to them.

Observe that in a sense, the market solves one kind of information failure (the lack of information on past defaults) by relying on an *additional* failure of information (lack of knowledge about intrinsic types). Because of the second failure, lenders have some incentive to screen borrowers or provide small test loans at the beginning of a relationship, and the existence of this phase acts as a deterrent to the destruction of an established relationship.[14]

---

[14] For theories that build on this idea, see Ghosh and Ray [1996, 1997], Kranton [1996], and Watson [1996].

The Cost of Information and the Credit Market: Chambar, Pakistan

As countries begin to develop and industrialize, the traditional rural structure of closely knit, isolated village communities begins to disintegrate. A great deal of mobility is created: people move from village to village, from village to town, and from town to city in response to the growing demands of commerce and trade. Access to markets in distant regions develops and people increasingly enter into transactions with strangers instead of neighbors. At the same time, the introduction of modern inputs into agriculture (e.g., fertilizers, pesticides, pump sets for irrigation, etc.) creates a surge in the need for credit and working capital.

In this environment of relative anonymity, the problem of loan recovery becomes particularly acute. Traditional community pressure can no longer be relied upon nor are there well-developed channels of information flow as in developed countries (e.g., computer networks tracking the credit histories of each individual customer, which banks and credit agencies invariably check before advancing a loan or credit line to a customer). Consequently, a farmer or worker may default on a loan from a moneylender in one town or village and approach another lender in another town for future loans, with very little risk that his past crime will be known in the new place. What prevents such aberrant behavior? How do credit markets deal with the enforcement problem in an environment of considerable mobility and borrower anonymity? A field study by Irfan Aleem of the Chambar region in the Sind district of Pakistan, provided some important clues and insights.

Chambar is a flourishing commercial region. An estimated sixty moneylenders serviced the area at the time of Aleem's study. Of these, fifteen were based in the main town of Chambar, fifteen in the three largest villages, and of the remaining thirty, a majority operated from smaller towns in the vicinity (within a radius of twenty to fifty miles). Obviously, borrowers have potential access to many different lenders and communication across all of them is weak or absent. Making borrowers repay is naturally a precarious task in such an environment.

However, the informal credit market is unusually successful in this respect: of the fourteen moneylenders interviewed by Aleem, twelve reported that less than 5% of their loans were in default.[15] This stands in sharp contrast to the average rate of default of around 30% experienced by formal sector banks and lending agencies, and is all the more remarkable in light of the fact that eleven of the fourteen lenders did not ask for any collateral at all.[16] What explains the low default rates?

It seems that limited information and the associated hazards of lending have prompted moneylenders to build up tight circles of trusted clients, and they are unwilling to lend outside the circle. It is this sharp segmentation of the market that induces most borrowers to comply with contractual terms: a defaulting borrower, who is removed from the good books of his current lender, will find it extremely difficult to find a new loan source. Thus, apparent competition between lenders and free access to multiple sources is *actually* restricted due to informational limitations,

---

[15] In the remaining two cases, the highest rate of default is 10%.

[16] Of the other three, the percentages of their total secured loans were 2, 5, and 10%.

and this restriction, in turn, helps to solve the moral hazard problems that such informational limitations give rise to.

Before taking on a new client, a moneylender usually takes various precautionary measures. It is almost always the case that the lender chooses to deal with the applicant in other markets (e.g., employing him on his farm or purchasing crops from him) for at least two seasons (i.e., for about a year) before advancing a loan, if at all. Such dealings provide some information about the loan applicant's alertness, honesty, and repayment ability. Nine out of the fourteen lenders interviewed were unwilling to give a loan without such previous interaction. Over and above this, lenders also extensively scrutinize a new client. Such scrutiny usually takes the form of traveling to the client's village and conducting interviews with his neighbors and previous business partners to assess his reliability and character. Most lenders also pursue various side businesses, such as trading in crops and retailing, so the considerable amount of time involved in information collection carries a high opportunity cost—on the order of about Rs 20[17] per day spent. It was estimated that on the average, the cost of administering the marginal loan (including the cost of initial screening and possible subsequent cost of chasing an overdue loan) was 6.54% of the loan's value.

If, after the intense screening and period of waiting, the lender agrees to advance a loan (the rejection rate for new loan applicants was around 50%), he usually begins with a small "testing loan." Most reliable information about a trading partner's characteristics can come from the experience of actually dealing with him; no number of enquiries can reveal what actual interaction will tell. Carrying out transactions with the person concerned is, therefore, the ultimate "experiment" that will reveal his characteristics. However, the experiment is risky and hence lenders exercise caution at the beginning. Only when the testing loan is duly repaid does the lender increase his trust in the client and hence increase the loan amount to match the latter's needs.

It is precisely the aforementioned factors—by-products of imperfect information—that help to discipline most borrowers. If a borrower defaults on a loan from his current lender and consequently his access to loans from the same lender is cut off, he can apply for credit from a new moneylender, but then he will have to go through a lengthy waiting period, an intense scrutiny (in the process of which the new lender's suspicion may be aroused and the application rejected), and even after that, a period of tightly rationed credit. The temporary gains from a default can be easily outweighed by these subsequent penalties.

In addition to the administration cost of loans, there are of course capital costs, which include the opportunity cost of the money lent, a premium for bad or unrecoverable debt, and interest lost on loans overdue.[18] The mean capital charge for the fourteen lenders was 38.8% for the marginal loan, whereas for the average loan, the corresponding figure was 27%.

The main reason the marginal cost is greater than the average is that most lenders had to borrow from other informal sector lenders at the margin: typically, 50% of the

[17] In 1981, the exchange rate averaged Rs 9.9 to a dollar.
[18] In a majority of such cases, interest was waived for the period of delay, for the sake of improving the chances of recovering the principal and basic interest.

lender's funds came from his own savings, 30% from institutional sources (either directly from banks, or indirectly from wholesalers, cotton mills, etc., who had access to bank loans), and the remaining 20% from other institutional lenders or clients who used him as a safe deposit (at zero interest) for surplus cash. These figures indicate that moneylenders siphon off a considerable amount of funds from the formal sector, and in this way engage in arbitrage between the highly segmented formal and informal sector markets (compare with the Philippine case). The overall rural credit market was, in its own peculiar and imperfect way, integrated.

The interest rate charged on average in the sample was 78.7% per annum. However, there was considerable variation—from a low of 18% (still higher than the 12% charged by banks) to a high of 200%. However, in light of the previous text, much of this high rate of interest can be attributed to the high information and administration costs of loans in the informal market. In fact, Aleem estimated that in most cases, the rate of interest was roughly the same as the average cost of funds, which implies that lenders made close to zero economic profits. It appears that the informal credit market in the region is most closely described by a model of "monopolistic competition" (see Hoff and Stiglitz [1997]). The ease of entry into the lending business keeps profits at zero, yet moneylenders enjoy some degree of monopoly power over their established clientele, because their superior information about the characteristics of their long-standing clients gives them an edge over competing lenders in their own market segment.

14.4. Interlinked transactions

A common feature of many loan transactions in developing countries is that credit is linked with dealings in some other market, such as the market for labor, land, or crop output. For instance, it is commonly observed that landlords are often the principal source of credit for their tenants, using their labor or even their rights to tenancy as some form of collateral. On the other hand, traders are the principal source of funds to owner–cultivators, especially those who lack access to the formal sector. Traders usually combine such credit dealings with purchase of their borrower's crop.

Interlinked contracts are formed in a variety of other ways. While loans are outstanding, the lender may have use rights to the land or other assets of the borrower, as already discussed. To the extent that the lender can directly benefit from the sorts of assets owned by the borrower, this makes credit transactions easier to enforce. However, for the direct benefit to be present, it is often necessary that the borrower and lender be engaged in similar or complementary occupations.

In one sense, interlinkage is a marriage of convenience. If a lender also has a principal occupation that ties in well with the occupation of the borrower, it may simply be convenient to carry out credit and other dealings under one umbrella contract, explicit or implicit. Thus a trader who transports rice may also advance credit to a rice-growing farmer, as well as trade in the rice produced by the farmer. According to this view of interlinkage, there isn't really any synergy between the two activities, except that they both *happen* to be carried out by the same pair of economic agents. Neither half of the deal rests tightly on the other, and in this sense there is no interlinkage.

Whatever the ultimate explanation, it does appear that in the event of coincident occupations, the interlinking moneylender has an edge over other moneylenders in credit dealings. In many parts of the developing world, the "pure moneylender" is a dying breed. Individuals engaged in moneylending most likely have a principal occupation that is not moneylending. Table 14.1 illustrates an especially detailed breakdown of borrower–lender pairs by the occupations of both individuals, from the Punjab and Sindh regions of Pakistan.

This table, taken from the work of Mansuri [1997], speaks for itself. It shows that among tenant households, landlords are an important source

Table 14.1. *Distribution of informal loans by size and tenurial status of borrowers, Punjab and Sindh, 1985.*

	Punjab			Sindh		
Borrower	Friends/ relatives	Land- lords	Traders	Friends/ relatives	Land- lords	Traders
Tenant						
Marginal	3	3	1	3	12	3
Small	6	22	5	12	62	6
Medium	5	17	5	5	13	2
Large	2	16	6	2	2	1
All tenants	16	58	17	22	89	12
Owner–tenant						
Marginal	2	2	1	—	—	—
Small	9	11	7	4	4	6
Medium	7	7	10	3	5	4
Large	9	10	13	7	1	4
All owner–tenants	27	30	32	14	10	14
Owner						
Marginal	23	2	5	7	—	8
Small	17	4	13	24	—	23
Medium	10	4	12	17	—	18
Large	7	2	21	16	—	25
All owners	57	12	51	64	1	74
Total	100	100	100	100	100	100

Source: Mansuri [1997].

of credit; indeed, they are the dominant source. The picture changes as we move to owners. In fact, study the class of owner-cum-tenants; that is, those who own some land, but lease in land besides. Loan sources are almost equally balanced between traders and landlords. Finally, those who are owner–cultivators receive their loan funding largely from traders.[19]

It is also worth noting that a small number of lenders in the study area gave cash loans at explicit interest rates. The interest rate on such loans at the time of the survey was Rs 30 on a loan of Rs 100 taken for a period of three to four months.

To be sure, this sort of association is not linked to the Indian subcontinent. Floro and Yotopoulos [1991] in their study of interlinked contracts in the Philippines distinguished between various forms of interlinkage:

> Five types of interlinkage are distinguished . . . , depending on whether the loan is tied to (1) the provision of intermediation services in relending and/or procuring output; (2) the sale of output to the lender; (3) the purchase of inputs or lease of farm equipment from the lender; (4) transfer of rights over the usufruct of the land to the lender; and (5) the provision of labor services to the lender. [Our study] indicates that the first three types are prevalent among trader–lenders, while the two last among farmer–lenders.

In this section, we explore various reasons why interlinkage is an observed mode of credit transactions.[20]

14.4.1. Hidden interest

In some societies, the explicit charging of interest is forbidden or shunned. This is the case in Islamic societies where usury is regarded as immoral and so is banned under the Shaariat law. In such situations, it is prudent to ask for interest in secondary forms and advance the loan interest-free. This prohibition may explain why usufructuary mortgage are so common in Kerala and why so many loans appear to be advanced interest-free in Islamic countries.

[19] In the Punjab or the Sindh, virtually all traders provide inputs on credit to cultivators. Traders do not require collateral and don't charge interest, but most loans are interlinked with the sale of agricultural output to the trader. In one type of contract, often referred to as *kachi bol*, the trader specifies the amount of crop required as loan repayment. Another type of contract, often referred to as *kabala*, requires the sale of a specified amount of crop to the trader at a discount below the announced support price or, in some cases, below the harvest price. Finally, some loans are given simply against a promise that the farmer will sell *all* of his crop to the trader at harvest at the going market price. Because the market price of agricultural output tends to be at its lowest level just after harvest, the compulsion to sell at harvest introduces an element of implicit interest in an interlinked contract.

[20] Interlinkages need not be linked to credit transactions alone, although they have been studied most often in this context. For an example of land–labor interlinkage, see Sadoulet's [1992] study on *inquilinaje* in Latin America.

With the need for hidden interest, interlinked contracts provide a way out. A large landowner may ask for the rights to part of the borrower's output as long as the loan is outstanding, even though the loan is recorded as interest-free. A trader may make no-interest cash advances to his suppliers, provided that the supplier agrees to sell him the crop at a discount. Even the right to use a ration card, which permits access to the public distribution system of food grain at subsidized prices, constitutes hidden charging of interest while the loan is outstanding. All these contracts may be acceptable under a law that bans *explicit* usury.

Of course, note that this explanation cannot suffice for the many situations in which charging interest is *not* banned, but widespread interlinkage is nevertheless observed.

14.4.2. Interlinkages and information

It is possible that an interlinked bargain is struck because in this way, the lender can dispense with some of the costs of keeping track of the activities of the borrower. A rice trader who makes funds available to a farmer may demand repayment in terms of the output because such repayment is easier to enforce under the *normal* routines of the trader–lender. At harvest time, the trader might arrive at the fields of his suppliers to pick up the crop for transportation. If this is something the trader has to do anyway, a useful by-product is that he gets to place first claim on the crop. Such claims are extremely powerful, because other debts are effectively pushed to a secondary position. Likewise, a laborer or tenant farmer who works on the estate of a large landowner under normal circumstances presents a relatively economical credit prospect. In the case of a default on the monetary terms of the loan, the loan can be worked off (and the implicit wages deducted as payment). These are all ways to reduce the chances of involuntary default without having to incur the *extra* costs of monitoring or tracking.

14.4.3. Interlinkages and enforcement

Interlinked relationships are sometimes useful to prevent *strategic* default as well. To see this, recall two stories with very similar features. First, think about the model of strategic default that we considered in an earlier section of this chapter. We noticed that to prevent default, the moneylender cannot drive down the borrower to his participation constraint. To avoid default, a certain surplus over the next best option had to be provided. The borrower presumably trades off the loss in this surplus at future dates with the one-time gain to be had from default.

Second, recall a very similar model from Chapter 13: the story of permanent labor carrying out nonmonitored tasks. The same general considerations applied there as well. At any date, it was possible for the permanent laborer to slack off by not putting in an appropriate level of effort, but if this deviation was detected at some point in the future, the permanent contract was removed, throwing the laborer into the casual labor market. This firing threat can only be a threat, however, if the laborer earns less on the casual market than he does with his long-term employer. Thus the permanent contract must be like an enticing carrot, which can be used as a stick in the event of noncompliance with the contract.

The simple observation that we make here is that with an interlinked relationship, a single carrot can be used as two sticks, as long as deviations cannot be carried out *simultaneously* on both fronts. Combine the two scenarios. For instance, suppose that a landlord has a tenant to whom he offers a rental contract with threat of eviction in case the output is lower than some predefined minimum. Such a contract must, for the same reasons considered in the previous stories, carry with it a certain surplus.[21] Now it is easy to see that a loan to the tenant can be supported by an "interlinked threat": if the loan is not repaid, then the *tenancy* will be removed. The surplus in the tenancy thus serves a twin role. It assures the provision of appropriate effort in the tenancy contract, while at the same time it doubles as an incentive to repay loans. In this sense, the landlord is at a distinct advantage in advancing credit to his tenant, because he has at his disposal a preexisting instrument of repayment. In contrast, a pure moneylender who lends to the same tenant must offer additional incentives for repayment *through the credit contract itself.*

14.4.4. *Interlinkages and creation of efficient surplus*

An entirely different set of reasons for interlinkage arise from its role in preventing "distortions" that lower the total surplus available to be divided between lender and borrower.[22] The mere granting of a loan at some pre-announced rate generally affects the quantity of the loan taken by the borrower. The lender may not want this, because a larger surplus is available from other loan sizes. Interlinkage is a way to counteract the distortion in loan amounts that might arise. All this might appear a bit cryptic, so let us proceed right away to some illustrations.

Loan repayment in labor

Suppose that a rural laborer, Anka, must feed herself and her family through both the slack and the peak seasons of an agricultural year. To make the exposition as simple as possible, imagine that there is no employment available in the slack season, whereas in the peak season, harvesting jobs are available

---

[21] See Dutta, Ray, and Sengupta [1989] and the references therein for examples of models of this kind.

[22] See, for example, Bardhan [1984], Basu [1987], Braverman and Srinivasan [1981], Braverman and Stiglitz [1982], and Mitra [1983].

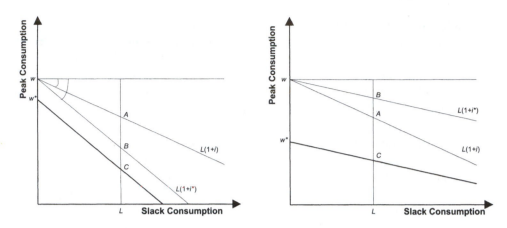

Figure 14.4. Birju's return from a contract (w^*, i^*).

that pay a wage of w. To finance her consumption in the slack season, Anka must borrow. The analysis in this section follows Bardhan [1984].

Suppose, now, that there is a large farmer, Birju, who hires harvesting labor during the peak season and also has access to funds at an opportunity cost of i per unit. In other words, i is the equivalent of the risk-free rate of return that Birju would obtain by putting these funds into the best alternative opportunity. Birju is in a position to lend money to Anka.

Because Anka is a laborer and Birju is an employer, Birju has the option to *interlink* the credit contract with a labor contract. One way to think about this is to imagine that the interlinked deal has two components: (i) the offer of a loan (to be chosen by Anka) at interest rate i^* (chosen by Birju) and (ii) the offer of a wage w^* at which Anka will pledge to supply her labor to Birju in return for the loan. A priori, w^* and i^* could be related to their counterparts w and i in a variety of different ways. In particular, w^* might be equal to w, which is just another way of stating that there is no interlinkage and that the deal in question is one of pure credit. Our task is to see how w^* and i^* are chosen.

Figure 14.4 describes the total return to Birju from a contract of the form (w^*, i^*), provided that a loan of size L is taken by Anka. The figure displays various combinations of slack and peak consumption available to Anka under the contract (w^*, i^*). The left-hand panel of the figure considers the case where $w^* < w$ and $i^* > i$. The right-hand panel looks at the case where $w^* < w$ and $i^* < i$. The former corresponds to the case where the loan is repaid with interest in both cash and labor. The latter corresponds to the case where the loan is "subsidized" in cash terms, but repayment is extracted in labor.[23] In both cases, the total return to Birju is given by the algebraic sum of the segments AB (interpretable as the interest return) and BC (inter-

---

[23] There are other possible cases as well. For example, the loan may be provided with an employment subsidy ($w^* > w$). These cases can easily be examined using a similar diagrammatic method.

pretable as the employment return). In the left-hand panel, both terms are positive. In the right-hand panel, the first term is negative whereas the second term is positive. *In both cases the net return to Birju is given by the segment AC.* Understand these diagrams well before proceeding any further.

Figure 14.5 shows Anka's method of making loan choices. Anka has preferences over slack and peak consumption. Her preferences are represented by indifference curves. What is Anka's budget line under the contract (w^*, i^*)? To find this, determine the vertical intercept w^* and then draw a line sloping downward from it that represents her trade-off between slack and peak consumption. This is precisely the line w^*C in Figure 14.4.

Anka maximizes her utility at point C, which places her on the indifference curve marked U. Note that Birju receives a profit of AC from this contract.

We have drawn this diagram assuming that the left-hand panel of Figure 14.4 is in force, but it should be clear that we can draw a similar diagram in any of the cases.

Now the question is, can Birju devise an alternative contract that places Anka on exactly the same indifference curve as before, but gives Birju a higher payoff? If he can, then we conclude that the contract depicted in Figure 14.4 *cannot* be optimal from the point of view of Birju, the lender.

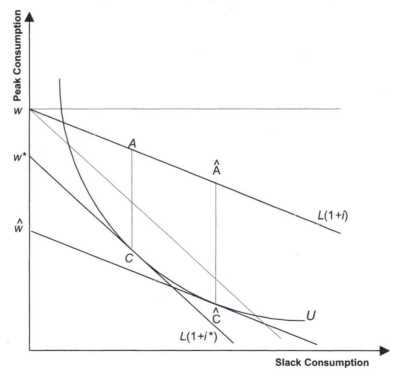

Figure 14.5. Anka's return from a contract (w^*, i^*).

There is an easy answer to this question. Study Figure 14.5, and look for the point at which the vertical difference between the indifference curve U and the line marked $L(1 + i)$ is *maximized*. This is given by the point $\hat{C}$, at which the tangent to the indifference curve is parallel to the $L(1 + i)$ line. Now, Birju could get Anka to choose this point as her consumption bundle provided he lowered the wage rate further (to $\hat{w}$), but charged exactly the same rate of interest on loans as his own opportunity cost, which is i. In that case Birju's return will be $\hat{A}\hat{C}$, *which is higher than AC*. We may therefore conclude that the contract (w^*, i^*) depicted in Figure 14.5 can be dominated by another in which Birju asks for subsidized labor services (at the wage $\hat{w}$), but provides Anka with loans at exactly the rate of interest i.

You can very easily construct a similar argument to show that the contract depicted in the right-hand panel of Figure 14.4 can be dominated by exactly the same contract $(\hat{w}, i)$.

We may conclude, then, that the dominant contract to offer is indeed an interlinked contract! No extra interest is charged on the loan; all payments are made in "labor units." There is a very simple intuition for this, and it is not unlike the Marshallian argument for fixed-rent tenancy that we saw in Chapter 12. Intrinsic in the situation is a "maximal degree of surplus" that can be generated from the credit contract. This surplus is given by the gap between the next best alternative for Anka (as captured by the indifference curve U) and the terms at which Birju can bring loans to her (as summarized by the interest rate i). It turns out that the monetary value of this surplus can be captured precisely by the vertical difference between the indifference curve U and the $L(1 + i)$ line, as shown in Figure 14.5. However, to get Anka to take a loan that will generate the full surplus, the interest rate must *not* be distorted away from i (otherwise she will choose a different consumption package such as the one represented by the point C, as distinct from $\hat{C}$). Consequently, a best contract is one that taxes her labor, which Anka treats effectively as a lump-sum tax that does not distort her loan incentives (she has to "pay the tax" anyway regardless of loan size).

Thus we have here one possible explanation for why loan repayments may be denominated in labor, even when there are no usury laws.

Loan repayment in output

We now turn to another example of possible distortions in credit contracts, stemming this time from *production* loans.[24] Our story has two players once again: Rahul, a small rice farmer, and Ayesha, a rice trader. Rahul sells his crop to Ayesha, who markets it. Rahul also needs working capital to buy the seed, fertilizer, and other inputs to grow his rice. For this he needs to borrow money. In this sense we can think of a working capital loan as an input in

---

[24] The argument that follows is based on Gangopadhyay and Sengupta [1987].

production. It isn't really: the inputs are what this loan can *buy*, but with fixed prices of these various physical inputs, we can think of production as depending on the amount of money that is available to buy these inputs.

We will depict output as physical units of rice multiplied by the market price of rice (net of costs of transportation), so now both inputs and outputs are in monetary units. Figure 14.6 describes this "production function." The horizontal axis depicts various quantities of working capital and the vertical axis shows the resulting quantities of produced output, evaluated at the market price of rice, which we'll denote by p per unit. The production function that links input and output has the usual diminishing returns shape (because of fixed inputs such as land).

Now Ayesha has access to loanable funds at an opportunity cost of i per unit (in other words, this is the rate of interest she can earn on alternative uses of these funds or the rate of interest she pays to banks for obtaining funds). In the same diagram, I have penciled in the total costs of providing different loans. For a loan size L, this is simply $L(1+i)$, just as in the previous section: it is the straight line that emanates from the origin in the graph.

Imagine for a moment that Rahul can get these loans at the very same rate of interest, or equivalently, that Ayesha owns Rahul's farm. In this imaginary combined operation, what would be the best choice of loan? This is easy enough to see: the amount of working capital should be chosen to maximize

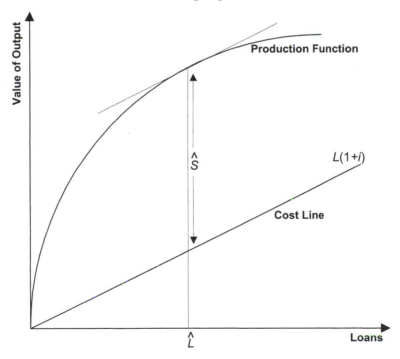

Figure 14.6. *Working capital, output, and interest.*

the value of output net of the loan cost. This amounts to finding the loan size at which the vertical distance between the production function and the cost line is maximum in Figure 14.6: this occurs at the point $\hat{L}$, where the marginal product equals precisely $1 + i$. Call the maximum profit or surplus generated in the combined business $\hat{S}$: this is shown in the diagram as well.

However, in reality, Rahul cannot get loans at this rate of interest. Unlike Ayesha, he is a small farmer and the usual informational and collateral-based constraints that we have already discussed in detail come into play. At the same time, while Ayesha does have access to these financial terms, she is a trader, not a farmer. Nevertheless, the imaginary benchmark that we have constructed in the previous paragraph is useful, because it tells us something about the maximum possible surplus that is available in the system. No loan contract can create a surplus greater than this (because all such contracts can be imitated by the combined operation). This information will be important in describing the optimal loan contract.

Returning to the story, imagine that in the absence of loans from Ayesha, Rahul can obtain some working capital loans from an informal lender and market his output through a trader. It will not be necessary to keep track of the details of this option, only the profit that Rahul can realize from it: call it A. Of course A is less than $\hat{S}$ because Rahul's loan sources aren't as good as Ayesha's. Thus A is a measure of Rahul's best alternative; Ayesha cannot push Rahul below this level of profit. Thus the *maximum* that Ayesha can hope to get from her dealings with Rahul is $\hat{S} - A$. Can Ayesha construct a contract that gets her this amount?

In a manner analogous to that in the previous section, it is possible for Ayesha to offer a contract that prescribes *both* an interest rate as well as a price at which she will buy rice from Rahul for marketing. We may therefore think of a contract as a pair of numbers (p^*, i^*), where p^* is a buying price and i^* is the rate of interest.[25] The contract is a *pure credit contract* if the price offered is no different from the market price p (which you will recall is already defined net of transportation costs and normal trader profits). Otherwise, the contract is interlinked, in the sense that credit and output transactions cannot be disentangled.

Now consider any pure credit contract. For Ayesha to make money out of such a contract, the interest rate charged must exceed the opportunity rate i, while at the same time Rahul can earn no less than A (which is his outside option). Figure 14.7 depicts one such situation. The interest rate is i^*, so that Rahul faces a cost $L(1 + i^*)$ if he takes a loan of size L. This gives rise to a cost line that is steeper than the one in Figure 14.6, but I've also

<hr>

[25] The careful reader will notice that we do not allow Ayesha to specify a loan size in the contract. This is something that Rahul chooses. In the simple version of the model that we present here, this restriction does make a difference (see Ray and Sengupta [1989]), but there are reasonable extensions of this basic framework in which our observations are completely robust.

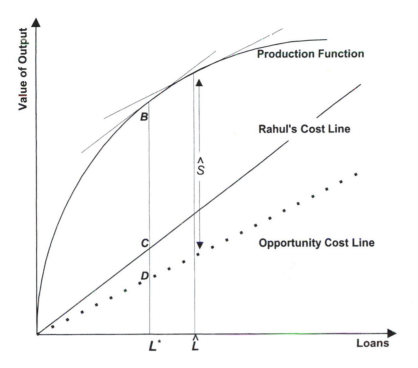

Figure 14.7. A pure credit contract.

put in that line in dotted form for comparison. Now Rahul will maximize his profits using the new cost line, and maximum profits are achieved at the point L^*, where the marginal product is equal to $1 + i^*$. It is easy to see that because marginal cost is higher than in the imaginary combined operation, the loan size chosen by Rahul must be *smaller* than $\hat{L}$. Rahul's profits are given by the vertical segment BC, whereas Ayesha's returns (over and above normal trading profit) are given by the vertical segment CD. Of course, $BC + CD$ is the *combined* surplus generated by this pure credit contract, which is simply the total vertical distance between the production function and the *opportunity* cost line $L(1 + i)$.

Note that this surplus must be less than $\hat{S}$, which by definition is the maximum vertical distance between the production function and the opportunity cost line. Thus we have shown that a pure credit contract is inefficient in the same sense as in the preceding section: it distorts Rahul's loan choice away from the surplus maximizing point. This is a starting point for our suspicion that there may be better contracts around.[26]

---

[26] This is only prima facie evidence, however: there are many situations (such as the principal–agent model that we studied in Chapter 12) in which it is impossible to attain full efficiency using *any* contract at all. Indeed, this observation lay at the heart of the inefficiency of land contracts, and motivated our discussion of land reform. In more complicated but realistic versions of the present exercise involving imperfect information, that would be the case here as well.

Can Ayesha do better than a pure credit contract? She can. Indeed, there is a contract that actually attains the maximum possible return $(\hat{S} - A)$ for Ayesha. It turns out to be an interlinked contract. The idea of such a contract is to depress *both* Rahul's marginal cost of production *and* the price he receives for his output, but to do this in equal proportion so that the *ratio* of price to marginal cost is left unchanged relative to $p/(1+i)$. This kind of move is akin to a profit tax on Rahul, which is nondistortionary in this case. Rahul will continue to choose the same loan size $\hat{L}$ as in the combined operation.

To make this a bit more formal, denote by $\hat{Q}$ the value of output in the (imaginary) combined operation. Then

$$\hat{S} = p\hat{Q} - (1+i)\hat{L}.$$

Now impose a profits tax of t per dollar on the combined operation and choose its value so that $t\hat{S} = A$. Multiplying through in the preceding equation yields

$$t\hat{S} = pt\hat{Q} - (1+i)t\hat{L}.$$

Now define a price $\hat{p} \equiv pt$, and an interest rate $\hat{i}$ such that $1 + \hat{i} = (1+i)t$. Note that $\hat{p} < p$ and $\hat{i} < i$. Offer this pair $(\hat{p}, \hat{i})$ as an interlinked contract to Rahul. Then, by construction, it is *as if* Rahul has been handed the combined operation (at Ayesha's opportunity cost of loans) and then been taxed on his profits at rate t. Now note that the tax on his profits cannot deflect his choice of loan from the efficient level $\hat{L}$. After all, if $\hat{L}$ was best in the combined operation, it must still be best now: maximizing profits must lead to the same action as maximizing t times profits.

So under this contract, Rahul makes A. He generates a total surplus of $\hat{S}$. Thus Ayesha picks up the difference: $\hat{S} - A$. She can do no better. We have shown that an interlinked contract is optimal under these particular circumstances.

Note that the interlinked contract involves *both* a low buying price as well as a low rate of interest on loans. Indeed, the rate of interest charged is below the opportunity cost of the lender!

14.5. Alternative credit policies

There has been a growing realization that the needs of rural credit cannot be adequately served with the use of large financial institutions such as commercial banks. As already discussed, the microinformation that is required for these operations precludes efficient market coverage on the part of these large organizations.

Two kinds of policies can arise in response to this observation. One is to recognize explicitly that informal lenders are much better placed to grant and recover loans from small borrowers than formal institutions are. The idea, then, is not to try to replace this form of lending, but to *encourage* it by expanding formal credit to economic agents who are likely to use these funds in informal markets. The second approach is to actually design credit organizations at the microlevel that will take advantage of local information in innovative ways. We discuss these two avenues.

14.5.1. Vertical formal–informal links

Expansion of formal credit to informal lenders

The lending of formal funds to informal markets is not a new phenomenon by any means. Large landowners or traders are in a much better position to put up collateral: from the point of view of the banks, they are good credit risks. They then use the funds to cash in on their informational advantage in informal markets. We have already seen evidence of this in our Philippine and Pakistan examples. The expansion of formal sector credit to these agents generates competition among them, and this hopefully improves the borrowing terms faced by individuals who fall outside the ambit of the formal credit system. Similarly, loans might be made to cooperative groups who are better placed to lend the funds because of social or religious ties among the members.

We can think of this policy as forging "vertical" links between the informal and the formal credit systems, rather than the more traditional policy of "horizontally" displacing one system by another.[27]

Vertical Formal–Informal Linkages: The Philippines

The Philippine government has made active attempts to incorporate the informal sector into the overall strategy of agricultural development.[28] In a sense, efforts to institutionalize the informal sector in the Philippines took place as early as the 1950s with the formation of family-run rural unit banks. Small in their capital base and in their mode of operation, the rural banks were then perceived as the stalwarts of agricultural credit delivery. Matters were not so simple, however. Von Pischke [1991] pointed out, however, that these rural bankers were "prominent local citizens who were often involved in moneylending. By becoming rural bankers they could obtain some capital from government to supplement their own. They could expand their

---

[27] For analyses of the "horizontal" scenario, see, for example, Bell [1993] and Kochar [1991].
[28] I draw here on Floro and Ray [1997].

moneylending operations by soliciting deposits." As it turned out, rural banks did not reach the majority of the small farmers.

In recent years, the focus on informal lenders has been strengthened. The government has employed a number of approaches to reach small rural borrowers in an indirect fashion. The rediscounting policies of the Central Bank have played a key role, along with fiscal policies that allocate budgetary resources and external borrowings for special credit schemes. These schemes involve the strengthening of linkages between the formal financial institutions and informal intermediaries such as traders.

However, traders are not the only type of informal intermediaries involved. In 1987, the Land Bank of the Philippines launched an aggressive wholesale lending program at below-market rates of interest to credit cooperatives, in an attempt to reach and serve small farmers (with holdings up to 5 hectares). In 1991 and 1992, respectively, 500,000 and 700,000 families received loans amounting to totals of $270 and 320 million. These amounts were disbursed to cooperatives (3,000 and 6,100 in 1991 and 1992, respectively).

Programs sponsored by the government explicitly use informal lenders as conduits of formal sector funds. In 1984, a government-sponsored program aimed at providing credit at concessionary rates to the agricultural sector by using informal lenders as intermediaries was launched. This scheme, called the National Agricultural Productivity Program (NAPP), comprised twelve specific commodity programs geared toward food self-sufficiency. Informal lender–beneficiaries included traders, millers, and input dealers. Commercial banks and rural banks participated in the program by acting as financial intermediaries between the government and the informal lenders. In addition, the government (through the National Food Authority) was also a direct lender.

Two low-cost special financing programs that are largely targeted to agricultural input suppliers are the Planters' Product Credit Scheme and the End Users/Input Suppliers Assistance Scheme. Under these arrangements, end users and input suppliers receive credit at concessionary rates of interest under the condition that they extend credits (in the form of fertilizer and pesticide credits or cash production loans) to farmers.[29]

Traders and rice millers also were utilized as credit channels under the Intensified Rice Production Program. The term "trader–millers" refers to rice trader–millers accredited by the Quedan Guarantee Fund Board who possess primary facilities such as threshers, driers, and mills. Farmers contract to supply the trader–millers with a specified volume of their produce at a buying price not lower than the government support price. Likewise, the trader–millers are required to enter into a "payment-in-kind" agreement with the National Food Authority where they deliver the milled rice equivalent of the due loan payment. This "promotion of linkages combines the strength of both sectors to supplement the resources of the informal sector." (Ghate [1992, p. 867]).

"Horizontal" competition from the informal sector therefore does not seem to be a threat to the formal institutions nor vice versa. A senior official of one of the largest commercial banks in the Philippines [in an interview with Maria Floro (May 1990)]

---

[29] Esguerra [1987] and Floro and Yotopoulos [1991] discuss this in more detail.

typifies the viewpoint of the dominant group in the formal financial sector: the commercial bankers. According to this view, informal lenders are not bank competitors. Rather, they complement the lending activities of the banking sector. According to the official,

> The informal lenders operate in a different segment of the market. The bank's market lies largely in corporate and commercial accounts which are generally fully collaterized. In fact, some of the informal lenders are, in effect, conduits of bank funds . . . . This is true with our big grain miller and trader clients who provide advances to the paddy farmers in the regular course of their business.

By allowing the traders, input suppliers, and millers to participate in the lending program, the NAPP merely formalized what was already commonplace in the informal credit market: the use of contracts that interlink credit provision with specific transactions in other markets.

Possible effects

Do these schemes intensify competition among informal lenders? I am not aware of serious empirical work that has addressed this important question. Theoretical analysis suggests, however, that the answer is likely to be mixed. Here are three reasons why.

Costs of monitoring. It is true that intensified competition per se tends to depress the interest rates in informal markets, but there are indirect effects to be considered. Among the most important of these are the fixed costs of lending: the costs of administering a loan, clearing credit histories, and then tracking the loan to make sure it is repaid. Why are these costs there in the first place? As we have seen, they must be incurred to make sure that the borrower is a good credit risk and to ensure that a loan, once taken, is repaid.

Now, if formal credit is expanded, it is likely to increase the number of active moneylenders, which increases the alternatives available to borrowers. All other things being equal, this raises the probability of a default on an existing loan (because alternative sources are more abundant). To avoid this, a lender will have to expend more resources on tracking a loan and will also have to spend more time and money to clear a borrower's credit history. If an Aleem-type world is a good depiction of reality—one in which lenders largely break even because of monopolistic competition—the increased administrative costs will *raise* the equilibrium rate of interest on a loan. Thus intensified competition can be counterproductive from the point of view of the borrowers. This is the theme explored by Hoff and Stiglitz [1998].

Collusion. It may be that lenders are engaged in collusive transactions; that is, they implicitly or explicitly agree to not invade each other's territory, thereby giving them local monopolies in their spheres of influence. For instance, two traders serving a village or a group of villages might agree to partition potential borrowers in the village into two groups, where the partition depends, perhaps, on the type of crop grown or on other characteristics that make each group relatively attractive to one of the traders. Ex post, each trader will have the incentive to invade the territory of the other (perhaps by offering a slightly better credit contract), but these invasions are kept in check by threats of a "credit war"—a temporary or permanent situation in which the traders compete ferociously with each other as punishment for the initial deviation. This is the sort of repeated game argument that reappears several times in the book [see Appendix 1 (at the end of the book) on game theory for an introduction to the subject]. Collusion is a form of farsighted interaction that is kept in place by the threat of reverting to myopic competition if the pact is broken.[30]

The probability of a strategically sustained cooperative outcome therefore depends on (1) the additional profits initially gained from undercutting one's rival, (2) the subsequent loss in terms of a reduction in profits that occurs as a result of a counterinvasion by the rival trader, and (3) the lag or detection time that elapses between the invasion and the reprisal. The probability for sustained cooperation is higher if the initial gain for invasion is small, or the subsequent loss from counter-invasion is large, or if the time lag between invasion and reprisal is long.

Now, an expansion of formal sector credit has two opposing effects: on the one hand, it tends to expand competition because each trader now has an incentive to undercut his rival. On the other hand, it tends to reinforce collusive practices by increasing the severity of credible punishments when deviations occur. The net effect depends on which of these two forces dominates.

There are actually good reasons to argue that the possibility of strategic cooperation may indeed *improve* with the credit expansion. For instance, a larger invasion of rival territory is easier to detect. Thus invasion gains will not go up as quickly as potential punishments, and this will promote strategic cooperation. Essentially, the *ratio* of invasion profits to punishment losses declines.

Other variations of the model yield similar results. For instance, consider a situation where trader 1 specializes in processing a particular crop *A*, whereas trader 2 specializes in crop *B*. Imagine a (proposed) collusive outcome whereby trader 1 (respectively 2) lends money to small borrowers specializing in the production of crop A (respectively crop B). Now trader

---

[30] Again, there is no hard evidence whether lenders actually interact in this fashion (and no evidence against it, either), but there is certainly evidence of collusion among traders in their marketing behavior: see, for example, Umali [1990].

1, say, offers a loan to a borrower specializing in crop B on the understanding that the farmer will divert some of his land to the production of crop A, which is then sold to the trader. Suppose that the production function for the farmer exhibits diminishing returns in the production of each crop (although overall it may be more suited to the production of crop B). Then the outcome will be a large gain for trader 1 if the amount of the invasion is small, but with diminishing marginal gains as the size of the intervention becomes larger.

Although the deviation gains are small, the *loss* that can be imposed on the deviating trader following a reprisal can still be substantially large. As his clients shift the pattern of crop production, this leads to a fairly small but positive marginal gain for the rival, but it still imposes large marginal losses on the incumbent trader. In this scenario, the expansion of credit lines to traders also leads to a decrease in the ratio of invasion profits to reprisal losses, leading to an increase in the chances of collusion.

The foregoing examples emphasize the importance of understanding the nature of interaction between lenders. The impact of any (credit) policy initiative on the welfare of borrowers crucially depends on the resulting effects on competition (or collusion). This line of reasoning is pursued by Floro and Ray [1997].

Differential information. Bose [1997] explores a third route. Lenders may have differential information regarding borrowers. For instance, lender A may be able to easily distinguish between good and bad credit risks, whereas lender B cannot. Then lender A essentially contaminates the pool for lender B, because he siphons off the good borrowers. Of course, if A faces a credit ceiling, he cannot siphon off *all* the good borrowers. Thus lender B faces a mix of borrowers. The mix might still be profitable enough for lender B to operate. Now an expansion of formal-sector credit will allow lender A to siphon off even more good borrowers. This might contaminate the available pool to lender B to the extent that he no longer finds it profitable to operate. The increase in A's activities may be more than offset by the shutdown in B's lending.

Here is a numerical example for the sake of concreteness. Suppose that there are 100 borrowers in the economy and each borrower seeks to borrow $1,000. The opportunity cost of funds for each lender is 10% (say this is the formal interest rate). Each lender charges 50% on informal loans.[31] Suppose that each lender has a credit limit on funds and denote this limit by x, the total number of borrowers that each lender can lend to at the rate of $1,000

---

[31] I am going to assume for simplicity that the rate of interest on informal loans is fixed or at least has a ceiling. This might occur, for instance, if no borrower will want to borrow (or will be able or willing to repay) if the interest rate crosses the ceiling. A variation with endogenous interest rates is easy to construct.

each.[32] A formal-sector expansion of credit is captured by an increase in the value of x.

Suppose that 80 of the 100 borrowers are "good" and the remaining 20 are "bad." Good borrowers will repay their loans: that is, they will return $1,500. Bad borrowers default; they return nothing. Lender A can figure out who the good borrowers are, but lender B cannot.

If the credit limit x is less than 80, lender A will use all his resources to lend to good borrowers. Assume that this is the case. Then lender B faces a population of $100 - x$, among whom $80 - x$ are good (because lender A will have made off with x good borrowers). So the expected value of a loan is given by $(80 - x)/(100 - x)1,500$, which is the probability of repayment times the full amount, plus the probability of default times zero. Lender B will therefore be willing to lend as long as

$$\frac{80 - x}{100 - x}1,500 \geq 1,100$$

where the right-hand side of this inequality is the opportunity cost of the lender. This inequality will be satisfied as long as x is no greater than 25; otherwise it will fail. This means that if x is expanded by means of a formal-sector policy to increase credit lines, both lenders A and B will expand their lending activities, but as x crosses 25, lender B will shut down altogether. Thus around this mark, formal-sector expansion will lead to a decline in informal-sector lending.

A bottom line

All this is not to say that an expansion of credit from the formal sector is bound to fail, but the simplistic expectation that such expansion will invariably lower interest rates for small borrowers may not be automatically upheld. Empirical valuation of such schemes should keep these potential pitfalls in mind.

14.5.2. Microfinance

The Grameen Bank

It is also possible for institutional lending to closely mimic and exploit some of the features of informal lending. For instance, it may be possible to design an innovative rural credit scheme in a rice-growing area in which a formal-sector institution acts both as a lender and a miller. The combined activity will permit the formal institution to accept rice output as repayment

---

[32] So the value of the credit limit is $1,000x$.

for loans. By mimicking the activities of a trader–moneylender, the formal institution may actually be able to carry out lending activities that reach small
borrowers and are profitable at the same time.

Even if such mixed institutions are difficult to put into practice, there are
ways in which the information base of a community can be put to use by a
cleverly constructed lending institution. An example of this is the Grameen
Bank of Bangladesh.[33]

In Bangladesh, as in many other developing countries, subsidized rural
credit offered by government banks laid the basis for its rural credit policy.
It didn't work. Repayment rates were low, and loans (or the forgiveness of
past loans) were often used for political reasons, undercutting the effects of
the policy.

The Grameen Bank, started in the mid-1980s by Mohammed Yunus, lends
to very poor households, and lends to *groups* of borrowers rather than individuals. A typical group consists of five borrowers, and lending to individuals within the group occurs in sequence.[34] The average loan size is around
$100. No collateral is required and the nominal rate of interest is around
20% (roughly 12% real). Over 90% of the borrowers are women. Average repayment rates are over 97% (Morduch [1997], Christen, Rhyne, and Vogel
[1994]).

Group lending and the use of information

The central feature of the Grameen Bank's lending policy is that in the event
of a default, *no group member is allowed to borrow again*. This means that
a group has to be formed very carefully by the individuals to weed out
bad borrowers who could jeopardize the creditworthiness of the group as
a whole. Observe how information is being used by the Bank even though
the Bank itself has no a priori access to it. The point is that the borrowers
themselves have the incentive to use this information to form groups, and this
induces a form of *self-selection* that no individual-based banking scheme can
mimic.[35] Consider some of the specific implications.

Positive assortative matching. Self-selection typically takes the form of
positive assortative matching (Becker [1981]), where good credit risks come

[33] Many of the observations in this section draw on Morduch [1997].

[34] In this sense the Grameen Bank also drew on the idea of Rotating Savings and Credit Associations (ROSCAS) (see Besley, Coate, and Loury [1993]), as well as credit cooperatives, from which it
indirectly drew inspiration (see Woolcock [1996]).

[35] It should be added that the Grameen Bank is just as much a social group as a bank, It requires
borrowers to observe certain codes of conduct: they make commitments to have small families,
boil their water, repair and maintain their dwellings, not make or receive dowry payments, and so
on. These social involvements make the Grameen Bank very different from an ordinary financial
institution, and may even have spillover effects on loan repayment (as with credit cooperatives in
the Philippines formed from one religious community, where Sunday prayers include pledges to
repay loans to the cooperative).

together. To be sure, both bad and good risks equally want to team up with the good risks, but if the good risks can identify other good risks, they will form a group together. Thus group formation has the property that it can drive risky types out of the market, because some of the costs of their risk-iness are borne by other borrowers instead of the bank alone. As we saw earlier in this chapter, lending to individuals has exactly the opposite effect: in the presence of limited liability, the risky types outbid the safe types (be-cause the costs of their project failures are effectively borne by the bank). Ghatak [1996] and van Tassell [1997] develop this line of argument (see also the exercises at the end of this chapter).

Peer monitoring. The argument so far assumes that borrowers are *intrin-sically* safe or risky. This is a valid assumption in many situations: group members may not be able to *control* what a fellow member does with her money, although they might still be able to predict what she is going to do (for instance, because they know her personally). In other situations, group members might be able to monitor and influence the choice of individual projects. In that case, the group will want these projects to be safe, relative to the safety levels they would choose as individual borrowers.

To see this, note once again that individual borrowing under limited liability leads to excessive risk taking, because the borrower fails to fully internalize the costs of project failure, but when borrowers congregate into groups, more of these costs are borne by fellow borrowers, who will then put pressure on one another to cut back on the level of riskiness. Thus group lending has two effects that cut in opposite directions. First, relative to indi-vidual borrowing, it *increases* the risk on any one borrower for a *given* level of project riskiness: this is a cost. Second, it creates pressures for peer mon-itoring to lower the level of project riskiness: this is a gain. Can the gain outweigh the loss and lead to a better institution overall? Stiglitz [1990] ar-gued that under some conditions, it can.

Potential drawbacks. Group lending is not without potential drawbacks. Perhaps the most serious of these occurs when one member of the group runs into genuine financial difficulties and must default. In that case it is a dominant strategy for other group members to default on their outstanding loans as well, because one member's genuine difficulties have destroyed the group's credit rating *anyway* (Besley and Coate [1995]). The Grameen Bank avoids this problem by lending *sequentially* to group members, thus mini-mizing the contagion effect of an individual default.[36]

---

[36] Sequential lending also minimizes the possibility of a coordination failure—a situation in which all the group members are solvent, but each declares default in the expectation that others will as well. The possibility of coordination failure is probably limited in small groups in which communi-cation is easy, but can lead to self-fulfilling crises in larger groups, such as cooperatives (Huppi and Feder [1990]).

The peer monitoring effects might backfire as well; that is, there may be excessive pressures to choose overly safe outcomes that are not socially optimal in terms of average profitability. For instance, a group sees as its potential loss the costs of a project failure (which is a social loss as well) *as well as* the cost of future exclusion from borrowing. The latter cost necessarily exists because the no-lending threat must be used to avoid voluntary or strategic default, but this drives a wedge between the group's calculation of private cost and the true social loss of project failure (which is thereby smaller).[37] Therefore, a group will have some tendency to be *overconservative* in its choice of projects (Banerjee, Besley, and Guinanne [1992] pursue a related line of reasoning in their study of nineteenth century German credit cooperatives).

Finally, group-based schemes may lack flexibility. This can happen in rapidly changing environments in which some group members fare much better than others. In that case, the worst-performing member slows down the group as a whole (Madajewicz [1996]; Woolcock [1996]).

Viability and performance

Viability. The Grameen Bank lends to the poor. There are limits on the interest rate that it can charge without seriously affecting repayment capacity, and loan sizes are very small. This means that each loan dollar comes with a high administrative overhead. There are costs of providing, tracking, and ensuring repayment of the loan, and these are fixed costs *per borrower*, so that small loan sizes raise these costs. In addition, as we've already seen, the Grameen Bank provides several social services as well, and despite the extraordinary commitment of its staff, these are not free.

Grameen has therefore functioned under a significant amount of subsidy, both from foreign donors as well as from the Central Bank of Bangladesh. In the period 1991–92, subsidies amounted to about twenty-two cents for every dollar lent. According to calculations carried out by Morduch [1997] for the period 1987–94, the Grameen Bank charged annual interest rates that ranged between 12 and 16.6%, but it would have had to charge borrowers between 18 and 22% to cover operating costs without any direct grants. However, there are subsidies on capital costs as well, in the form of lower-than-market interest rates on loans *to* Grameen, and these are more important than the direct grants. To cover *these* subsidies, Morduch estimated that interest rates would have to climb to 32–45%.[38]

---

[37] I have been a little cavalier with this argument. By the standard limited liability argument, the direct costs of a project failure to the group are typically smaller than the social costs (because the bank bears some of the costs). Now adding the exclusion cost means that the net comparison is ambiguous, so overconservativism is not a necessary outcome.

[38] These calculations assume that default rates do not alter as the interest rate is hiked. If one allows for this possibility, the implied interest rates are even higher, obviously.

Performance. What effect has Grameen had on the lives of people? This amounts to the empirical question, in the *absence* of the program, how much worse off would the borrowers have been? This turns out to be a very hard question to answer, precisely because Grameen has been adept at identifying good borrowers! In other words, it is not enough to look at the incomes of a borrowing household relative to the incomes of nonborrowers, even after controlling for the observable variables, such as age and education, that we (the statistical observers) can measure. The reason is that we are unable to observe characteristics such as drive, creativity, inventiveness, or entrepreneurship—traits that the borrowers themselves use when forming groups. Thus it is possible that only the more "able" borrowers have been able to access Grameen, but the incomes of such borrowers would have been relatively high even if no Grameen had existed! It follows that a regression destined to capture the effects of credit on participation will *overestimate* the positive impact of the program.

This sort of selection bias may also run the other way. Not only does Grameen look for good borrowers, it looks for poor ones: in particular, such borrowers may be poor for unobservable reasons that are not captured by the characteristics that we can measure. Now a cross-sectional regression will *underestimate* the effect of the Grameen Bank, because the incomes of those treated under the program will, on average, be lower (at least before the program). This happens because "program placement" isn't random, which is a general problem with assessment of any program that targets the underprivileged, such as setting up health services in areas with substantial undernutrition and illness, or crop extension services that are set up in areas of low know-how, or family planning programs in areas of high fertility.

One way to get around this problem is to find an *identifying variable* or *instrument*: one that affects participation in the program but does not itself affect the outcomes of participation. These are hard to find, in general. Variables that correlate with participation usually affect incomes as well, which resurrects the specter of selection bias.[39]

A potentially superior alternative is to use before–after tests on the same people. This takes care of the unobserved variation in characteristics. Of

---

[39] McKernan [1996] suggests the interesting use of the number of landowning relatives of potential borrowers as an instrument. The idea is that this will affect program participation: a person with more landowning relatives is less likely to be credit constrained. Of course, the existence of such relatives might also influence income. Moreover, variables such as these have a weak influence on participation rates. Pitt and Khandker [1995] took a different approach to get around the program placement problem. Most microfinance programs have eligibility criteria that must be met for participation in the programs. In Bangladesh, eligibility is restricted to households with less than half an acre of land. Thus noneligible households can be used to get a handle on village-level effects. Now the *additional* differences at the village level among participants can be attributed to the microfinance program. The unobservability of borrower characteristics is not an issue here, because they focus on the effects of overall program availability.

course, there may be unobserved variations over *time* that have nothing to do with the program, such as societywide economic improvements. This can be dealt with if there are *also* data on a group of people in the same locality who were not participants in the program. Unfortunately, few microfinance programs have data *both* on before–after performance and on some "control group" that did not participate.[40]

With these effects controlled for as well as possible, it appears that the effect of Grameen is around seventeen cents to the dollar (Pitt and Khandker [1995]): that is, every dollar lent serves to raise annual household expenditure by about seventeen cents. Note that this is lower than the twenty-two cents per dollar of subsidy, and we might therefore be tempted to conclude that the program is not worth it. However, in reaching this conclusion we would have to ignore the fact that Grameen is a *targeting* organization just as much as an organization for transfers: the money seems to reach the really needy and enterprising, and this would not have been possible through indiscriminate transfers of money. You might think of the five cents on the dollar as the cost of targeting, and who's to say that this isn't money well spent?

In addition, the seventeen cents impact does not include the additional earnings that are saved (note that the amounts relate to household *expenditure*, not income) nor the value of the social education that Grameen provides. It does not include the long-term acceleration in earnings that may have been made possible, and it does not capture the possible spillover effects on nonborrowing households, although there may be negative as well as positive spillovers. Thus a definitive evaluation of the Grameen Bank's success awaits further research.

Other microfinance institutions

The Grameen Bank spawned, by example, many other microfinance programs. Morduch [1997] provides a list of the many countries that have adopted finance programs based on the Grameen model: among them are several countries in Latin America, Africa and Asia, and the United States. Some of these programs have been more successful than Grameen if one goes by the narrow criteria of economic viability. For instance, the BancoSol in Bolivia lends to groups rather than individuals, just as the Grameen Bank does, but the groups are significantly richer than the clientele of Grameen. Thus average loan sizes are larger, and so are interest rates, allowing BancoSol to turn a profit. The Bank Rakyat Indonesia (BRI) lends to individuals and asks for collateral. Again, we are talking about a clientele with economic characteristics very different from those of their Bangladeshi counterparts. Thus Grameen remains a role model on two counts: because of the pioneering

---

[40] For assessments of microfinance programs using the before–after method, see, for instance, Churchill [1995] and Mosley [1996].

and innovative inroads it has made into small-scale lending and because it has reached out to very poor individuals. This last goal has understandably pulled down its viability on the very narrow yardstick of economic profit, but how does one value overall social impact? Is it valued under the broad criteria of the last section or perhaps, using the fact that so many successful microfinance programs today owe their existence to the Grameen Bank?

14.6. Summary

We studied the main features of informal credit markets. Typically credit is taken to finance ongoing production (*working capital*) or to finance shortfalls in consumption (*consumption credit*). Credit may be sought for a new venture, such as the overhead expenditures needed to switch to a new crop (*fixed capital*).

Two fundamental problems characterize credit markets: the problem of "inability to repay" (*involuntary default*) and the problem of "unwillingness to repay" (*strategic default*). In turn, both these problems are outcomes of informational imperfections. For instance, if the use of a loan cannot be monitored, it may be frittered away in consumption or in an overly risky project, leading to involuntary default. The fear that this might happen could shut down a potentially profitable credit transaction. Likewise, the absence of a legal system to honor credit transactions and a possible absence of information flow regarding defaulting borrowers might exacerbate the problem of strategic default.

We distinguished between institutional or *formal lenders*—government or commercial banks, credit bureaus, and so on—and *informal lenders*—village moneylenders, landlords, traders, and shopkeepers. Two considerations typically put formal lenders at a disadvantage relative to their informal counterparts: (1) they lack information regarding the characteristics, history, or current activities of their clients, and (2) they cannot accept collateral in some nonmonetary forms, such as labor or output. One example of the informational problem is a *limited liability* situation, in which a borrower repays if successful, but is otherwise limited by her resources to fully repay the loan. In such situations, a loan that cannot be properly monitored may be used in overly risky activities, because the borrower does not internalize the downside risk, which is borne by the bank (due to the limited liability).

We then turned to informal markets. Some characteristics of these markets are (1) *informational constraints* (which create repayment problems), (2) *segmentation* (in which lenders seem to deal with demarcated zones of borrowers), (3) *interlinkage* (in which lenders and borrowers are simultaneously transacting with each other on at least one other market, such as land or output), (4) *interest-rate variation* across borrower types, loan purpose, or spatial dimensions, (5) *credit rationing* (a borrower may wish to borrow more at the going rate of interest in the transaction, but is not permitted to), and (6) *exclusivity* (a borrower typically deals with one lender at a time).

We discussed theories that throw light on some of these characteristics. Among theories of high interest rates are those that use the notion of *lender's risk*, which create risk premiums, and theories that view credit as a veil for transferring collateral (such as land) from borrower to lender. Particular attention was placed on issues of default: in particular, we argued that the possibility of default limits the granting of fixed-capital loans that lowers the borrower's dependence on future credit, and that strategic default may create credit rationing. Credit rationing may also be the outcome of informational asymmetries: interest rates cannot be made too high because of the fear of attracting only risky borrowers who do not internalize downside risk. We studied in detail the relationship between default and information flow: societies with high mobility may lose information, thereby making it easier for a defaulting borrower to get loans elsewhere and thus shrinking the informal credit market as lenders become more wary of offering loans.

We then turned to *interlinkages*: the tying of a credit transaction to transactions in some other market, such as a land tenancy or the buying and selling of grain. Interlinkages may be a way to charge interest in hidden forms because the charging of explicit interest is banned by law or custom. Interlinked contracts may be a way to economize on the lender's cost of acquiring information about his borrower or on the cost of tracking or monitoring a loan. An interlinked contract may serve to reduce strategic default (for instance, a landlord may be well placed to lend to his tenant because he has the additional threat of removing the tenancy contract in case a loan is defaulted upon). Finally, interlinkages may be a way to maintain the "correct" relative price across a bundle of transactions, thus minimizing distortions. For instance, a high interest rate may discourage loan taking for production, but a subsidized interest rate *and* a low buying price for output may maintain the loan taking incentive while allowing a trader–lender to acquire surplus via the reduced buying price.

Our last topic covered some policy issues. Faced with the difficulties of reaching small borrowers through formal-sector credit, a government might follow the policy of expanding credit to traders and landlords in the expectation that they will pass the funds on to small borrowers and be forced by increased competition to offer better terms. We evaluated this argument and found that there are some theoretical reasons to be suspicious of this quick conclusion. The costs of loan administration and monitoring may increase with more lenders (because borrowers can more easily default on existing loans). This might *raise* interest rates instead of lower them. Expanded formal-sector credit might make it easier for informal lenders to collude (because it raises the capacity of each of them to fight a price war in the case of a deviation from strategic collusion). Additionally, an expansion of funds to lenders who can screen good borrowers easily may "contaminate" the borrower pool for other lenders, leading to a credit shutdown on their part.

Another policy response is to try to put the hidden information of local communities to work in innovative ways. The leading example of small-scale lending or *microfinance* is the Grameen Bank of Bangladesh. The Bank lends to groups of people instead of individuals. The entire group is denied future credit if one member defaults. Under such circumstances, group formation will use local information (unknown to the bank, but available to potential borrowers). Would-be members who are bad credit risks will be excluded from the group, leading spontaneously to better targeting. In addition, borrowers will have the incentive to urge each other to take on safer projects (because they now bear more of the downside risk owing to the threat of future exclusion). We discussed these and some potential drawbacks as well. Finally, we evaluated the financial viability and performance of the Grameen Bank.

Exercises

■ (1) Explain the concept of a *risk premium* in words. This example will help you understand how a risk premium may be calculated. In each of cases (a)–(d), assume that you always have the option to keep extra money in the bank at a 10% rate of interest, with no fear of losing any of this money. For each case, calculate the minimum rate of interest and, therefore, the risk premium, at which you would lend $1,000 on the informal market.

(a) With probability 1/2 the loan will be repaid with interest, and with probability 1/2 the loan will not be repaid at all.

(b) With probability 1/2 the loan will be repaid with interest, and with probability 1/2 only the principal will be repaid.

(c) With probability 1/3, the loan will be repaid with interest, with probability 1/3 only the principal will be repaid, and with probability 1/3 the loan will not be repaid at all.

(d) Just as in case (a), except that if the loan is defaulted upon, there is probability 1/2 of recovering assets from the borrower worth $500.

■ (2) If people have different costs of default, such that for each person there is a threshold repayment burden that they will always want to default upon, explain why loans above a certain size will never be offered by any lender, even with very high risk premiums built into the rate of interest. Use graphs to explain your answer.

Here is a special example that builds on the preceding general question. The following table gives default risks for various loan sizes in an informal credit market.

Loan size ($)	Loans defaulted (%)
50–99	5
100–149	10
150–199	20
200–249	25
250–300	30
>300	50

Suppose that the rate of interest in the informal sector is 18% per year and that in the formal sector (with no default) is 10% per year. Calculate the maximum loan size that will be offered in the informal-sector credit market. For what minimum rate of interest will loans in the $250–300 category be offered? (This example is more special than the general question in the first paragraph, because the default rates may also depend on the rate of interest being charged, and this is not taken into account in the example. How would you try to amend the example so that it fits the more general scenario?)

■ (3) A *risk-lover* is an individual who prefers a lottery with some expected value to a fixed amount of money with the same value. Show that with limited liability, a risk-neutral or even a risk-averse borrower may behave *as if* he is a risk-lover when considering the projects in which he would like to invest. Explain how this feature (of limited liability) drives a wedge between projects that the lender considers profitable and those that the borrower considers profitable.

■ (4) Carefully reproduce the example of a landlord lending to a laborer, where underpriced labor as well as interest can be charged as repayment for the loan. Show that the loan will be advanced at the opportunity cost of the lender, whereas all interest will be charged by underpricing labor.

■ (5) Carefully reproduce the example of a trader lending to a farmer, where output sold by the farmer to the trader at a discounted price (as well as direct interest) can be required as repayment for the loan. Show that the loan will be advanced at a rate of interest that is *below* the opportunity cost of funds for the trader, and all profits are made by the trader by buying output at a discounted price.

■ (6) Here is another way to think about output–credit interlinkage between a trader and a farmer. Recall that the borrower–farmer maximizes *his* profit. Note that (i) marginal revenue equals price times marginal product of an extra $1 of loan and that (b) marginal cost equals $1 plus the rate of interest on $1.

(a) Show that if MP is marginal product, p = price, and i is the rate of interest, then MP $= (1 + i)/p$.

(b) We argued that the optimal contractual terms must not distort the size of the loan. Show that if p^* is the price contracted by the trader and i^* is the rate of interest charged by the trader,

$$\frac{1+i}{p} = \frac{1+i^*}{p^*}.$$

■ (7) Do you expect that there will be a systematic discrepancy in interest rates between loans that are made for production purposes and loans that are given for consumption purposes? Analyze some sources of this possible discrepancy.

■ (8) An expansion of credit from formal financial institutions to large informal lenders will increase competition among such lenders and improve the terms of credit for small borrowers with no access to formal credit. Discuss.

■ (9) Consider a monopolist lender who lends to borrowers on a repeated basis. The loans are informal and are not backed up by written contracts. The lender has no way to recover a loan if the borrower chooses to default. The lender, however, threatens to cut off credit in the future to any defaulting borrower. Borrowers discount the next period's earnings by a discount factor of 0.5 (see Appendix 1 on game theory at the end of the book for a discussion of this concept).

Borrowers use the loan in cultivation. Cultivation can be done using one of two techniques. The first requires initial working capital of $100 and produces net output worth $300. The second requires $500 of working capital and yields net output of $1,000. Find the amount of loan the lender will advance to each borrower every period in order to maximize his own profits. How much is the scheduled repayment and the implicit interest rate? What are these profits? How much does the borrower earn every period from the deal?

Introduce a new factor into this scenario. Suppose the lender can keep some of the borrower's assets (like jewelry) as collateral, which he will seize in the case of default. The present value of the asset to the borrower is $300. Recalculate the optimal loan, repayment amount, implicit interest, and profits in this case. Compare the two cases and summarize the effect of collateralization on the other terms of the loan. Does it increase or decrease the welfare of the borrower and the lender?

■ (10) SelfHelp is a newly formed credit cooperative which receives partial financing from government banks. Members of SelfHelp can deposit savings with the cooperative and they can also turn to SelfHelp for a loan if they need one. If a borrower defaults on a SelfHelp loan he is punished (which is equivalent to a loss of monetary value F) and excluded from future dealings with SelfHelp. The value (to the borrower) of these future dealings is some number S. However, there is no telling whether SelfHelp will survive in the future; denote the probability of survival by p.

(a) If each member is risk-neutral, what is the *expected* value of dealing with SelfHelp in the future?

(b) If a member has an outstanding loan of L and needs to repay it (along with interest at the rate r), write down the value of his *net* gain from default.

(c) Now suppose that the probability of SelfHelp's survival depends on the percentage of borrowers who repay as well as the quantum of government assistance should a high rate of default occur. Draw a graph with the repayment rate on one axis and the survival probability on the other, and show how this graph shifts with the amount of government assistance.

(d) Use parts (b) and (c) to show that in general there can be two outcomes or equilibria for the *same* parameters: (i) there is no (voluntary or strategic) default and SelfHelp survives with little or no government assistance or (ii) there are high rates of default and SelfHelp survives with low probability despite government assistance.

(e) Show that a credible promise by the government to bail out SelfHelp in times of trouble can lead to a unique equilibrium in which all borrowers repay and little government assistance is *actually* required [scenario (i) in part (d)].

(f) Using part (b), show how the survival probability of SelfHelp can affect the size of the loans it can make to borrowers.

■ (11) A lending organization, inspired by the Grameen Bank, is attempting to provide loans to small farmers. It is lending to farmers in groups of two (say).

(a) Provide at least two reasons why a strategy of group lending may be better than a strategy of lending to individuals. Provide at least two reasons why it may be worse.

(b) A sequential lending strategy is one in which group members are given loans in some order, with the next member receiving a loan only after the earlier member has repaid. A simultaneous lending strategy is one in which all group members are given loans at the same time. In both cases, assume that default by any one member blacklists the whole group. Compare and contrast these two strategies.

Chapter 15

Insurance

15.1. Basic concepts

In this chapter, we take up the study of *insurance*. The main ideas that we seek to develop can be illustrated with an example that involves just two people.

Suppose that Asaf and Sharif are two farmers. We begin by supposing that they produce the same crop and that they use the same amounts of land and other inputs. Suppose that the harvest can take one of two values: $2,000 if all works out well and $1,000 if there is some damage to the crop. Assume that the chances of either of these events occurring is 1/2, and that this probability is the same for both Asaf and Sharif.

If Asaf and Sharif do not know each other, then they will try to do something about this uncertainty on their own. You have seen several examples by now of risk aversion and how this gives rise to the desire to smooth consumption, and we need not repeat the details here. Suffice it to say that both Asaf and Sharif would like to even out their consumption. They would like to run down their wealth a bit to make up for the shortfall when the crop is bad and stock some of the excess when the crop is good.

Using one's own wealth to smooth uncertain shocks in income is called *self-insurance*. Essentially, individuals with the wealth to do this are protecting themselves against uncertainties that they cannot control. Self-insurance can work through several channels. Stocks of cash or accumulated savings in banks can be run down (or added to) for the purpose. The same can be done with grain stocks, although holding such stocks can be costly because grain is not perfectly durable. However, this may be a preferred form of savings if rural banks are few and far between or if there are restrictions on the rapid liquidation of savings. Other assets may be run down or accumulated as well. Livestock and jewelry are two such assets, although these may be sold as a last resort. The box on self-insurance in Indian villages using bullocks will give you a flavor of how self-insurance works in practice.

Self-Insurance and Bullocks

Possibly the most important mechanism for consumption smoothing, other than market credit and intra- or interfamily lending, is the sale and purchase of assets. Farmers hold many different forms of wealth, including land, jewelry, currency, capital goods (such as pump sets), animals (such as bullocks), and stocks of food grain. It may be possible to use such assets as *buffer stocks*; that is, families accumulate stocks in periods of relative affluence and deplete these reserves to finance consumption expenditures in more difficult times. Do rural households engage in substantial buying and selling of assets for this purpose? A study by Rosenzweig and Wolpin (1993), based on the ICRISAT villages in India, suggested that for certain forms of assets, this is indeed the case.

Immobile capital—land and buildings—constitute a major part of farmers' wealth in this study, accounting for approximately 85% of total wealth. However, it is a widely observed fact that although the market for land *rentals* is very active in these regions, the asset market for land is highly inactive. Of all rural households surveyed in 1970–71 by the National Council of Applied Economic Research in India, only 1.5% undertook any kind of land sale, which suggests that this method is rarely used to finance consumption in times of need. In the non-real-estate wealth category, financial assets (stocks, bonds, etc.) have a very small share (less than 5% even for large farmers), and thus play an insignificant role. Average crop inventories held over the year accounts for about a quarter of this wealth; however, it varies a lot across harvest and nonharvest seasons, and is probably used more to smooth consumption over the year rather than across years. A sizable portion (about 19% on average) of nonland wealth is held in the form of jewelry, but the data indicate that buying and selling jewelry, too, is minimal. By far the largest component of nonland wealth is bullocks (representing 50% of the wealth for small farmers, over 33% for midsize ones, and about 27% for large farmers), and evidence is strong that farmers vary their ownership of bullocks as a primary instrument to smooth consumption.

The asset and rental markets for bullocks have exactly the opposite characteristics compared to those for land. Although there is an extremely well organized, regionally integrated market for bullocks,[1] short-term bullock leases are extremely uncommon (see Chapter 12 for further discussion). The nonexistence of the market for bullock power (as opposed to the market for bullocks) implies that there can be substantial productivity gains for a farmer who owns an animal or two; thus, from a purely productivity viewpoint, turnover in bullock ownership should be expected to be low.[2] However, a ten-year survey revealed that 86% of households were involved in at least one transaction in bullocks, indicating that many of these were probably "distress sales," motivated to meet consumption requirements.

---

[1] In India, large centralized bullock "fairs" are held in many regions at specific times of the year.

[2] Part of the potential efficiency losses arising from the absence of free flow in bullock power services is mitigated by the active rental market in land. Rosenzweig and Wolpin estimated that a farmer who did not own a bullock was 63% more likely to lease out land than a farmer who owned at least one.

A careful analysis of the data shows that this is indeed the case. Due to the presence of well integrated bullock markets, bullock prices are largely immune to village-specific production shocks, which is precisely the factor against which farmers seek insurance. This is highlighted by the fact that over 60% of bullock sales were made to buyers outside the village, with 10% going to buyers located more than 20 kilometers away.[3] The statistical results show that the probability of a bullock purchase increases significantly when income is high, and the probability of a sale decreases. Moreover, other things held constant, those people holding higher stocks of bullocks (or even pump sets) are less likely to make a purchase in the future, suggesting that on the average, just as with any other buffer stock, farmers try to maintain a target level of the asset. This pattern is strongly borne out in data on medium and small farmers. For large farmers, the fit is much weaker, suggesting that this group has much greater access to credit and other conventional instruments and does not have to rely heavily on asset sales as a means to achieve consumption targets.

Does the widespread incidence of distress sales (coupled with the absence of rental markets for draft animals) hamper efficiency and lower average agricultural output? Rosenzweig and Wolpin felt that it does. At the prevailing market prices for bullocks and other inputs, their profit function estimates show that the optimal number of bullocks owned by midsized farmers is about two. However, the average size of the bullock stock is 0.94. Through numerical simulations of their econometric model, they estimated that the provision of actuarially fair weather insurance does not increase farmer welfare substantially. The weather is only one source of risk, and farmers already have some insurance through limited credit. On the other hand, the creation of supplementary assured sources of income (say through a rural job creation policy) raises bullock stocks closer to optimal levels and thereby increases agricultural efficiency.[4]

The second major form of smoothing is taking recourse to credit. We have already discussed this in great detail and there is nothing that we need add here.

[3] This observation is unlikely to hold with much generality across countries, especially in those areas where intervillage integration is relatively small. For example, Czukas, Fafchamps, and Udry [1997] test whether livestock is used as a consumption smoothing device by households in Burkina Faso. Unlike the observations for India, the authors find that the effects of random shocks on livestock sales are indeed small, suggesting both that markets are local and that there are a fair number of alternative smoothing options.

[4] We need to be a little careful, though, in interpreting these results and drawing the conclusion that a serious "underinvestment" in bullocks exists. After all, the *aggregate* supply of bullocks must be quite inflexible at least in the short run, and can increase only to the extent that more favorable conditions lead to greater breeding. The problem is that profit and optimality calculations are performed under the *prevailing* market price for bullocks: if consumption smoothing motives are removed through the provision of alternative sources of insurance, the demand and supply conditions in this market change entirely, leading to entirely new equilibrium prices and optimality calculations. However, the mere stabilization of bullock stocks leads to some increase in output and welfare, even if the *average* size of these holdings does not increase.

What I would like to focus on here is a third source of income smoothing: that attained through mutual insurance between economic agents. As the discussion continues, you will see that this source of smoothing is, after a point, difficult to distinguish from credit, but for the moment, we postpone these complications.

To develop this idea, bring Asaf and Sharif together. We can think of four possible outcomes: (1) both Asaf and Sharif produce the good output; (2) both produce the bad output, and [(3) and (4)] one produces high while the other produces low. In the first two cases there is little that Asaf and Sharif can do to help each other; they are in identical positions. In the last two cases, they can agree to share their output equally. What this boils down to is a promise that Asaf will pay Sharif $500 when he produces high and Sharif produces low, and Sharif will pay Asaf $500 when the opposite occurs.

The following observations are to be noted. First, *if the chances of producing high output are independent across Asaf and Sharif*, elementary probability tells us that the chance of each of these four cases is 1/4. Without any consumption smoothing, Asaf's consumption in the four situations is (2,000, 1,000, 2,000, 1,000); a similar statement holds for Sharif. With the mutual insurance scheme in place, this consumption stream changes to (2,000, 1,000, 1,500, 1,500). This reflects the fact that in the first two states there is nothing to be done in the way of mutual insurance, whereas in the last two cases income is equalized. Does this provide an improvement in expected utility? It certainly does, if Asaf and Sharif are risk-averse. You can see this in exactly the same way as we did in previous chapters. Mutual insurance gives rise to a mutual gain for Asaf and Sharif.

Second, observe that *at any date*, if the high–low scenario occurs, either Asaf will have to pay Sharif or Sharif will have to pay Asaf, but not both. Mutual insurance demands that ex post, after the outcome is revealed, one party make a unilateral transfer to the other. Moreover, the slate is wiped clean after this transfer. Next year, the *same* person may be asked to pay up again. The point is that a past transfer from one person to the other does not carry a historical burden for the recipient. This is what makes a scheme of pure insurance conceptually distinct from credit. A credit scheme ties past transfers to the expected pattern of transfers in the future. An insurance scheme in its purest form does not.

Third, observe that the power of mutual insurance depends greatly on the *degree of correlation* between the outputs of Asaf and Sharif.[5] Suppose, for instance, that high or low outputs are determined entirely by the state of the weather, and not by the possibility of localized pest damage. If Asaf and Sharif are in the same village, the weather will affect them equally, and cases (3) and (4) will *never* occur. Both farmers will always be in the same position

---

[5] See Appendix 2 at the end of the book for a detailed discussion of this concept.

and no mutual insurance is possible. Weakening this extreme example a bit, if both outputs are highly positively correlated, there will be situations in which the high–low scenario occurs, but this will happen with small probability. There *are* gains to be had from mutual insurance, but the magnitude of the gains is small ex ante.

Reversing this argument, imagine a situation in which the fortunes of Asaf and Sharif are perfectly negatively correlated. It may be hard to conceive of such a situation in reality, but treat it as a benchmark for a moment. In this case, the high–low scenario will *always* occur and the gains from insurance are huge. Thus it appears that insurance groups are most likely to be formed among those people whose fortunes are as negatively correlated as possible. There is some truth to this statement, but there are also reasons to avoid such extremes (even if they exist), which we shall come to later.

The general point is that for mutual insurance to work, there must be a certain absence of positive correlation between the fortunes of the participating economic agents. This is one reason why crop insurance is difficult: agriculture does present large correlations because of the weather. Having said this, though, it is only fair to recognize that there are situations that *are* idiosyncratic across various economic agents (illness, festivities, local crop damage), and these can benefit from insurance along the lines described in the preceding text.

Finally, suppose that there are not just two people, but many replicas of Asaf and Sharif. Assume again that their fortunes are all independent. Now ask yourself what the *average* income of this large string of people will be in any given year. This problem is identical to a coin-tossing problem: toss a coin several times, and each time write down 1,000 if heads comes up and 2,000 if tails comes up. The average of this string will be close to 1,500 for a long string of tosses.[6] For exactly the same reason, the average income will be $1,500 (identify each independent coin toss with a person), provided that the number of farmers is large.

Now suppose each of these farmers follows the rule of contributing $500 to a common pot if their income is $2,000 and claiming $500 from the common pot if their income is $1,000. If the number of farmers is large enough, then it follows from the argument in the previous paragraph that in any one year, this rule is *viable*, in the sense that the surplus or deficit in the pot will be negligibly small. Again it is true that in any *one* year, a farmer will be a net contributor to or a net recipient from the common pot, but note that each farmer succeeds, in this way, in smoothing his income *completely*. In the two-farmer case, this would have been possible only if the two incomes were perfectly and negatively correlated, so that Asaf gets $2,000 whenever Sharif gets $1,000, and vice versa. However, such a state of affairs is unlikely. With

---

[6] This is what we know of in probability theory as the (strong) *law of large numbers*.

a large number of farmers, independence of fortunes is enough to get full smoothing.

It is important to note that these insurance schemes are rarely constituted in some formal way. The box (to come) on reciprocal credit–insurance arrangements in Nigeria will give you some idea of how these transactions are carried out. Underlying the transactions is some social norm of reciprocity— one that pushes you to help out a community member in need. The transfer you make might be in cash or might be in kind (such as reciprocal exchanges of labor on farming plots). As we have seen on more than one occasion in this book, social norms cannot survive for long if the economic incentives that hold such norms begin to wither away, and so despite our acceptance of reciprocity and mutual insurance as a *social* institution, we are looking for the economic underpinnings that permit such an institution to survive.

15.2. *The perfect insurance model*

15.2.1. *Theory*

The example of the previous section allows us to formulate a model of perfect insurance. Suppose that a village is populated by a large number of farmers. For simplicity, let us assume that the farmers are all identical, though this is in no way necessary at a conceptual level. For each farmer, describe his income at each date by the equation

$$(15.1) \qquad\qquad Y = A + \epsilon + \theta.$$

The income equation has three components. Think of the first (A) as each farmer's *average* income (this is a number such as $1,500 in the example of the previous section). The second component (ϵ) is a random shock that may have the same distribution across farmers, but affects each one *independently*. For instance, the crop may be eaten by animals, or destroyed by bugs, or there may be inappropriate application of water or fertilizer. The shock may represent a shortfall of income due to a sudden spike in consumption needs; for instance, a part of income may be paid off for illness (in this case think of Y as net income after such necessary expenditures). It is a local or *idiosyncratic* source of uncertainty, which might happen to every farmer but happens in an independent fashion. Finally, the third component (θ) captures all the common or *aggregate* variation in the village. This is a source of uncertainty whose realization in any year affects *all* farmers in the same way. The best way to think of this is to imagine that these are common income variations stemming from the weather (the state of the monsoon, for instance).

Because we regard A as the average income, we should think of the random terms ϵ and θ as having mean value equal to zero.

Now, a little thought will convince you that if there are a large number of farmers, all the idiosyncratic variation embodied in ϵ can be insured away in exactly the same manner as in the previous section. Farmers simply pay their realized value of ϵ into a common fund. Because ϵ is sometimes positive and sometimes negative, this amounts to saying that some farmers make positive contributions, whereas others stand to receive payouts from the common fund. This way, all the idiosyncratic variation in ϵ can be ironed out. With the insurance fund in place, a typical farmer's *insured income* is now given by

$$(15.2) \qquad \bar{Y} = A + \theta.$$

Compare (15.1) and (15.2). The income stream $\bar{Y}$ carries less risk than the original stream Y, because we have removed the idiosyncratic component. Average income is still A, of course. It follows that if farmers are risk-averse, they prefer this system of mutual insurance.

What about the aggregate shock θ? Can't we pool this in the same way? The answer is no, and the reason is that the value or realization of θ is the *same* for all the farmers in the village, so there is no insurance possible here. Neglecting self-insurance and credit for the moment, the village as a whole cannot mutually insure itself against a random event that affects everybody in the same way.

Hence it is not the case that under the perfect insurance scheme insured incomes don't fluctuate at all: they do, but the source of fluctuation is the aggregate uncertainty in the system that cannot be insured away with the use of a common pool of funds. This line of reasoning also suggests that one important determinant of mutual insurance is the relative significance of idiosyncratic to aggregate risk.

15.2.2. *Testing the theory*

The model that we described also yields a natural test for the existence of perfect insurance in a community such as an entire village. Controlling for movements in *aggregate* village consumption (which act as an indicator of aggregate uninsurable risk), fluctuations in individual household income, or, indeed, idiosyncratic shocks such as unemployment should *not* have any effect on the consumption of that household.

As we have seen on more than one occasion, regression analysis is a good tool for such a test.[7] Use the average consumption of the community and household income as independent variables. If possible, also include consumption-side shocks (such as unemployment) as independent variables. The dependent variable is household consumption. Roughly speaking, if

---

[7] See Appendix 2 at the end of the book for an introduction to regressions.

the theory of perfect insurance is right, the estimated coefficients on all the household-specific variables should be zero, and that on group average consumption should be unity. Individual consumption should track group consumption more closely than it tracks individual income.

Townsend [1993] explored this implication using three villages from the ICRISAT study, which should by now be familiar to you from repeated references in the last few chapters. Recall that the ICRISAT villages, located as they are in the semi-arid tropics of southern India, all display a high degree of risk. These risks stem primarily from crop cultivation, but spill over to labor markets, so that a landless laborer who earns wages faces a substantial amount of risk as well. The three villages studied were Aurapalle, Shirapur, and Kanzara. Household consumption data are available annually for a sample of forty households in each of these three villages for the period 1975–84. There is substantial variation in household income, and if this variation is taken as a measure of household risk, then idiosyncratic components are very much in evidence. The best way to see this is to compare the *differences* between household income and the average income of the sample, for different households. Subtracting the sample average is a bit like removing the aggregate risk. Then, if we interpret what's left as idiosyncratic risk, it is certainly the case that there is a lot of it: this residual appears to fluctuate independently across households (see Townsend [1993, Figure 1]). This means that the three ICRISAT villages present a potentially fertile case for testing the perfect insurance hypothesis.[8]

A major problem arises, however, in the construction of an appropriate regression equation. We have household-level consumption, and measures of household income. What do we use for average consumption? The answer to this question depends on whom we suspect to be the relevant group that is engaged in mutual insurance. One possibility is that the *entire* village is engaged in mutual insurance, as one group so to speak. In that case we include some measure of village average consumption. However, all we have are data from the sample!

One option is to use the sample consumption average as a proxy for the village average and hope that by the law of large numbers this gives us a good estimate of the village average. However, this runs us into another sort of problem: even if we perform the regressions household by household, if the sample is large, the *average* estimated coefficient on group consumption must be unity! This is not a sign that the perfect insurance model passes with flying colors, but just that individual consumptions in the sample must sum to the sample average (Deaton [1990]).

---

[8] At the same time, be aware that there is substantial measurement error in estimating household incomes. This sort of error invariably biases estimated coefficients on household income variables toward zero. Some of this error can be avoided by averaging the income data over households with the same crop/plot technologies, but this remains a serious issue. Measurement error can also be allowed for (to some extent) by statistical correction. See Townsend [1993, Section 6] for more details.

One way to get around this problem is to run the regression household by household (using the sample average exclusive of the household in question) and see whether *each* of the estimated coefficients on group average (and not just the average of these coefficients) is close to a value of 1. The results of this exercise are mixed.[9] Depending on the length of the time period and the choice of consumption categories in the regressions (see footnote 9), the coefficients are sometimes, but not always, close to unity. A formal statistical test of the hypothesis that the coefficients are indeed 1, is not rejected using the full set of data, but the power of this test deteriorates with other variants of the regression.[10]

The observation that the coefficients on household income are indeed close to zero is more robust and suggests that variations in household income do not significantly affect household consumption. This outcome suggests that quite a bit of smoothing is taking place, but whether it is due to insurance per se or some other form of smoothing (such as self-insurance or credit) is difficult to say.

Another way to avoid the problem of missing aggregate data on consumption is to consider *differences* between household consumption and the sample average of households. This is tantamount to subtracting group averages from both sides of the regression, equation, so that the right-hand side now contains only individual terms, such as household income of various categories, and dummy variables for sickness or unemployment. Now, to test whether group consumption moves individual consumption more than individual income does is simply a matter of whether or not the coefficients on the individual variables are zero. In contrast to the earlier regressions, these coefficients are now significantly different from zero, but their magnitudes are small.[11] For instance, the effect of household income on individual consumption seems to be no more than 14%, which is pretty small. This is like saying that a one dollar increase in contemporary household income increases consumption by no more than fourteen cents. Moreover, events such as sickness (leading to loss of work) are insignificant in the determination of household consumption.

The preceding findings suggest that although we cannot be sure that mutual insurance is at work here, there is substantial smoothing accomplished by ICRISAT households through some means or other. Informal credit markets probably account for a large chunk of this. There is separate evidence

[9] A particularly nasty problem is that data collection between the years 1982–84 dropped some consumption categories. To be sure, this has the spurious effect of making individual consumption move with household consumption. To sidestep this problem, we can use a restricted set of consumption categories throughout (such as grain consumption) or perform the regression by leaving out these last two years. The results concerning the comovement of household and group consumptions are predictably weaker.

[10] For a discussion of hypothesis testing, see Appendix 2 at the end of the book.

[11] See Appendix 2 at the end of the book for a detailed discussion of the difference between *significance* and *magnitude*.

that ICRISAT households smooth fluctuating income through credit transactions (see Cain [1981] and Walker et al. [1983]). Other mechanisms might
include grain inventories (Paxson and Chaudhuri [1994]), holdings of cash
(Lim and Townsend [1994]), and even the sale and purchase of livestock
(Rosenzweig and Wolpin [1993] and the box on self-insurance and bullocks).

Note, however, that among the growing number of empirical studies conducted on this question, the ICRISAT villages do relatively well in exhibiting
a great deal of consumption smoothing. Townsend [1995] reports on similar
regressions carried out on Thai data. The results seem to convincingly reject
the presumption of perfect risk sharing, although in other studies on Thailand, a significant degree of smoothing cannot be ruled out (Paxson [1992]
used data on Thai rice farmers to make this point). Similarly, Deaton's [1994]
study of the Côte d'Ivoire suggests that although there is comovement of
household consumption, full insurance can be convincingly rejected. Household income does significantly influence household consumption. Townsend
[1995] provides a discussion of these and other studies.

Even among the ICRISAT villages, the ability to smooth may vary significantly across households. Using a somewhat different test for insurance
than the one described here, Morduch [1995] found substantial evidence
of consumption smoothing among relatively better-off farmers, but not so
for small farmers and landless laborers (Townsend's work contains similar
observations as well). Morduch also made the point that insurance might
look good simply because households try to smooth their *income* streams so
that the remaining fluctuations can be absorbed by the available consumption smoothing mechanisms. For instance, some households may forego the
cultivation of a crop with high expected return simply because the yield
is more risky and cannot be smoothed through insurance. In this case, the
household chooses a "safer" crop and its income fluctuations are therefore
smaller and consequently easier to smooth.[12] The point is that there is a hidden cost (which is the expected value sacrificed by choosing a safer crop).
Thus, Morduch [1995, p. 108] concludes, "for less well off households in the
ICRISAT villages, production choices will be made with an eye to reducing
the likelihood that the shocks will happen in the first place."

15.3. *Limits to insurance: Information*

The general failure of the perfect insurance model to fit the facts suggests
that there are limits to the ability of households to insure one another, even if
the income shocks are idiosyncratic. Where do these limits come from? The

---

[12] The same sort of observation is true for the *way* in which a given crop is produced. Rosenzweig
and Binswanger [1993] investigated this for the ICRISAT villages; see also the earlier study by Bliss
and Stern [1982] on fertilizer choice in the northern Indian village of Palanpur.

answer is based on the same principles that informed our study of credit markets: limited information and limited enforceability.

15.3.1. Limited information about the final outcome

Think of two sorts of informational problems. One is that a person may ask for or expect transfers from his community while providing them with deliberately wrong or misleading information regarding his economic state: he might lie about the size of his harvest, he might lie about illness in the family, or, at the very least, he might be in a *position* to lie, in the sense that his community members do not have information to verify that the claimed occurrences indeed occurred.

Now this is certainly a possibility if we extravagantly expand the notion of what a community means. It is unlikely (even if speedy electronic transfers of funds were possible between villages) that a farmer in one extreme of the state of Bahia would be engaged in insurance with another unknown farmer in the other extreme of that state.[13] Even if such insurance were mutually beneficial, it is very difficult to verify the underlying circumstances on which that insurance must be based. So it's certainly true that this sort of informational barrier kicks in and precludes insurance over very large anonymous groups or spatial distance, even if such insurance could, in principle, be profitable for all concerned.

However, does this sort of informational problem occur within the village? It is hard to say, and the answer must surely vary across villages. One of the great strengths of traditional society is that they are highly endowed with *social capital*. Much of social capital is simply information flow. *A* knows if *B*'s harvest has been bad or if *B*'s father-in-law really has food poisoning. Social capital provides a fund of socially available information that permits a community to interact in ways that would not be possible in an anonymous society. Insurance is one such way, and there are others. We already discussed social capital in the context of credit in Section 14.3.7 and earlier in the context of permanent labor markets in Chapter 13. In villages where mobility is on the increase, this sort of knowledge begins to die away, reducing the scope of insurance networks. Likewise, a village that is segmented into subgroups (say, along caste lines or perhaps even along economic hierarchies such as landowners and the landless) may be unable to develop insurance schemes that cut across these lines of segmentation, simply because the flow of information is restricted. All of these theories suggest the need to extend empirical work to define more precisely what we mean by the community, and to the extent that our notion of community fails to capture these finer

---

[13] This does not prevent organized financial institutions from indirectly linking them, but that is another matter.

points (mainly because of lack of data), we might fail to capture the existence of insurance "subnetworks" simply because we are looking for one
giant network, which doesn't exist.

15.3.2. *Limited information about what led to the outcome*

The second kind of informational problem is more subtle and, as we
will see, does not altogether rule out the possibility of insurance. This is the
problem of *moral hazard*—the possibility that the occurrence of some insur-
able event can be influenced by the unobservable actions of the individual.
We've already encountered moral hazard in our discussion of land markets
(Chapter 12) and in our discussion of credit rationing (Chapter 14). Clearly,
moral hazard matters for insurance as well.

Consider mutual insurance of harvests. Everyone knows that there are
idiosyncratic shocks that can affect the state of the harvest on a particular
plot. Water, fertilizer, or pesticides may have been badly applied (inadver-
tently), or there may be damage to the crop caused by events outside the
farmer's control, or (and this is the source of the problem), the crop may be
bad because the farmer *deliberately* skimped on the use of these inputs. The
size of the harvest may be visible for all to see (so that the first informational
problem is irrelevant), but *why* the harvest is what it is requires information
of a different kind altogether. The problem, of course, is that in the presence
of full insurance, the incentive to deliberately underapply inputs is higher.

To see this in its simplest form, consider a community of a large number of identical farmers. Assume that all uncertainty is idiosyncratic. Just as
in the example of Asaf and Sharif, we suppose that there are two possible
outputs, which we denote by L (for "low") and H (for "high"). The twist in
the story is that for each of the farmers there are *two* possible probabilities of
producing the high output: call them p and q, and suppose that $p > q$. The
idea is that with greater care and better application of inputs, each farmer
can produce H with probability p, but if he underapplies inputs, the probability falls to q. Denote the extra cost of diligent effort and input use by C
(this is expressed in utility units). Finally, let u be the utility function that
describes how net outputs are translated into units of utility for each of the
farmers.

Begin by analyzing the farmer's problem without insurance. If he dili-
gently farms the land, his expected utility is $pu(H) + (1 - p)u(L)$, but he
incurs the extra cost C up front, so his *net* expected utility is given by the
expression

$$pu(H) + (1 - p)u(L) - C.$$

On the other hand if he does not apply effort, the probability of the high
output falls to q, although he saves on the extra cost, so that his expected

utility is now

$$qu(H) + (1-q)u(L).$$

Assume that in isolation, each farmer would like to put in the extra effort; that the probability gain of the high output makes it worthwhile to do so. This amounts to assuming that

(15.3) $pu(H) + (1-p)u(L) - C > qu(H) + (1-q)u(L).$

Now with insurance we can do even better. We already saw in several examples that if the farmer is risk-averse, then the utility of the expected output exceeds the expected utility of output,

$$u(pH + (1-p)L) > pu(H) + (1-p)u(L),$$

so there are clearly gains to be had from insurance. Moreover, with a large number of farmers, it is possible to set up an insurance scheme that (approximately) guarantees this for every farmer. To see how, suppose that every farmer with high output pays the sum $(1-p)(H-L)$ into a common pool, while every farmer who produces the low output receives a payout of $p(H-L)$. Do the necessary simple algebra to verify that with this scheme, each farmer gets the average value of output, $pH + (1-p)L$, *for sure*. Now all we have to do is to make sure that the scheme is feasible: that total payouts balance total receipts. To see this, note that with a large number of farmers, approximately a fraction p of them get the high output, so that the total inflow into the pool is (approximately) $p(1-p)(H-L)$. At the same time, approximately $(1-p)$ of the farmers produce the low output, so that the total outflow from the pool is $(1-p)p(H-L)$. Inflows and outflows match, so we are in business.

However, there is a flaw in this argument. We *are* in business if we can somehow guarantee that each farmer continues to put in the high level of effort. But it is not possible to do so under this insurance scheme if the extra effort cannot be verified by outside parties. If each farmer receives $pH + (1-p)L$ *regardless* of whether his output is high or low, then why incur the extra effort to raise the probability that output will be high? Thus, each farmer has an incentive to slack off under the perfect insurance scheme, and, of course, if all farmers think this way, the scheme cannot survive.

Notice that the problem is the same as that encountered in the principal–agent model. There is a trade-off between the provision of insurance and the provision of incentives. If the community wants to maintain effort at the higher level, it will have to offer incomplete insurance so that individual incentives are not destroyed. How much insurance can it safely offer?

To solve this problem, suppose that X is a farmer's net consumption when output is high and Y is his net consumption when output is low, in any insurance scheme. The requirement that the scheme be approximately viable is equivalent to the equation

(15.4) $$pX + (1 - p)Y = pH + (1 - p)L.$$

If X and Y are too close together, people will slack off. To see how close they can be, take a second look at equation (15.3), and substitute X for H and Y for L. Note that high effort will be chosen as long as

$$pu(X) + (1 - p)u(Y) - C \geq qu(X) + (1 - q)u(Y)$$

or equivalently, rearranging these terms, as long as

$$(p - q)[u(X) - u(Y)] \geq C.$$

Thus the *closest* that X and Y can get without upsetting the desired incentives is given by the equation

(15.5) $$(p - q)[u(X) - u(Y)] = C.$$

Equations (15.4) and (15.5) are two equations in two unknowns. Use them to solve for X and Y. This is the *second-best insurance scheme*—the best one can do when incentives pose a constraint.

   Note that in any solution, it must be the case that $X > Y$ [simply examine (15.5)]. This means that under the second-best scheme, *individual consumption must move with individual income*. Such a finding is consistent with the data, although to empirically test this model against others requires finer analysis.[14]

   To complete this model, consider a numerical example just to see how much insurance is restricted by these considerations. Let $H = 2,000$ and $L = 1,000$ just as in the Asaf–Sharif example. Let $p = 3/4$ and $q = 1/4$. Suppose that the utility function is given by $u(x) = \sqrt{x}$. Finally, let the additional cost of diligence assume the value 2 in utility units. Check that the condition (15.3) is comfortably satisfied, so that in isolation each farmer will indeed put in the higher level of effort. Now we solve for the second-best insurance scheme, described by the pair of numbers X and Y that solve (15.4) and (15.5). These two equations reduce to

$$\tfrac{3}{4}X + \tfrac{1}{4}Y = 1,750$$

[14] Ligon [1993] pursues this line of research.

and

$$\tfrac{1}{2}[\sqrt{X} - \sqrt{Y}] = 2.$$

Solving, we see that X is approximately \$1,832 and Y is approximately \$1,505. Thus farmers with good harvests pay out around \$170 each and farmers with bad harvests receive around \$500 each. More insurance would certainly be desirable but cannot be achieved, because the constraints on incentives would be violated.

Informational constraints pose a real problem to effective insurance. Groups with better access to the information of their members are generally in a better position to provide mutual insurance. This is also true of groups that are composed of members who feel some altruism toward one another. In this case, the incentive constraints are somewhat loosened, because each member internalizes (perhaps partially) the undesirable implications of his deviation for other group members. Hence, it will not be surprising to see that insurance arrangements between members of extended families or of the same kin group[15] are relatively common.

The flip side of this argument is that diversification possibilities within the extended family may be relatively limited. This will be the case if all members participate in a similar activity and are therefore exposed to the same set of aggregate shocks. We expect, then, that families will attempt to diversify their activities or spatial locations to lower the correlation between the incomes of family members. Rosenzweig and Stark (1989) found a tendency for marriage and kinship ties to be established across families from different geographical regions, perhaps to maximize insurance possibilities while retaining (or creating) the altruistic ties that are needed to counterbalance the absence of information. In the same spirit, Paulsen [1995] studied remittances from migrants in cities to their families in the Thai countryside.

15.4. *Limits to insurance: Enforcement*

We now turn to a different limit on insurance, that has to do with the *enforcement* of insurance arrangements.[16] Recall that mutual insurance schemes are rarely contracts that are written down in black and white and routinely backed or enforced by the law. Rather they are informal arrangements, set in the context of a social norm that encourages reciprocity and punishes deviations through social sanctions such as ostracization or public rebuke. This, too, is a form of *social* capital.

---

[15] For studies of reciprocal arrangements within kin groups, see La Ferrara [1997].

[16] For a more formal treatment of some of the issues in this section, see Coate and Ravallion [1993], Fafchamps [1996], Kletzer and Wright [1995], and Thomas and Worrall [1994].

Whether a village's endowment of social capital is enough to permit a system of mutual insurance to function is a question that can only be settled through detailed empirical work, but it is useful, anyway, to discuss the various issues that arise with the help of a simple model.

15.4.1. Enforcement-based limits to perfect insurance

Suppose, once again, that there are a large number of farmers. The simplest case is one in which all uncertainty is idiosyncratic, so let's begin with it. Assume that there are two outputs, H and L, and that the high output is produced with probability p. Because we have already discussed the moral hazard problem, we take the probability of the high output to be fixed in what follows (equivalently, effort levels are perfectly monitored).

Consider perfect insurance. We already saw what this gives each person. With a large number of farmers, each farmer receives the constant amount $pH + (1 - p)L$ regardless of what he produces. Let this "middle amount" be denoted by M. We already discussed the possibility that such a scheme can be undermined because of moral hazard, so this is not an issue we consider here.

Now picture in your mind a situation where this scheme is in place and transfers are made according to it year after year. Consider a particular year in which a particular farmer produces a high output. In that year he *could* receive a utility of $u(H)$ if he pocketed this output in its entirety, but the insurance scheme dictates that he give up some amount to the common pool, so that his utility under the scheme is really $u(M)$, which is obviously smaller. We can use this information to construct a measure of the *gain* enjoyed by a high-output individual if he decides to ignore an existing insurance arrangement and simply consume the output himself. Denoting the gain by G, we have

$$G = u(H) - u(M).$$

This is a measure of the incentive *not* to conform to the arrangement. Of course, this is only one side of the story. If the farmer deviates in this fashion, he will presumably be excluded from future access to insurance.[17] There is also the question of social sanctions, as we already discussed. All of this adds up to a future *loss* if he fails to conform today.

Just as we noticed for credit markets (Chapter 14) and (permanent) labor markets (Chapter 13), the size of the loss from future exclusion depends on

---

[17] Informational considerations are once again relevant here. Depending on how easily the news of his "crime" spreads through the community, this individual may find it more or less easy to become part of another group. We already discussed such issues in the context of credit and labor markets. They are probably less relevant in the case of insurance, involving as it does a larger group of people at a time.

the farmer's farsightedness. In each future date he loses the amount $u(M) - [pu(H) + (1-p)u(L)]$, which is just the difference between his insured utility and his stand-alone expected utility. If he has a mental horizon of N periods, the total loss is just this expression multiplied by N, the number of dates for which he thinks ahead. To this add a loss S, which is a measure of the utility damage imposed by social sanctions (such as a public scolding in the main village square). The total loss (L) from a deviation is thus given as

$$L = N\{u(M) - [pu(H) + (1-p)u(L)]\} + S.$$

Now put together the gains and losses to check if perfect insurance is indeed viable. For viability, we must have $L \geq G$, and this gives rise to the fundamental *enforcement constraint*

(15.6) $\qquad N\{u(M) - [pu(H) + (1-p)u(L)]\} + S \geq u(H) - u(M).$

This looks like an ugly equation (and it is), but it gives us some insight into the nature of the enforcement constraint.

First, look at the role of S, which is the punitive power of social sanctions. Clearly, the larger is S, the more likely it is that (15.6) holds. Second, the enforcement constraint is also more likely to hold if people value future interactions to a greater degree. This notion is reflected in a larger N. In part, a larger value of N may be interpreted as greater foresight or greater patience on the part of the farmer, but it can also be interpreted as a measure of greater faith in the durability of the scheme itself. If mutual insurance is expected to continue in the indefinite future, the loss from a single deviation is perceived to be large, and so the deviation is less likely to occur. This also brings out a "bootstrap" characteristic of such schemes (which appears in other situations as well, such as cooperative credit). The perceived instability of the insurance scheme may be self-fulfilling: N is driven down, (15.6) fails, and the scheme falls apart simply because it is expected to. Social institutions are very much like the outcomes of coordination games, and multiple equilibria are surely possible.

Third, is it the case that the greater the scope of insurance the more likely it is that the scheme will survive? This sounds pretty obvious but actually (15.6) tells us that it isn't generally true. Insurance is more beneficial when stand-alone outputs are more dispersed; in this example, when there are large differences between L and H. To be sure, this raises the perceived losses from not participating in the scheme, but it also means that more has to be contributed when the output is good [recall that the contribution is $(1-p)(H-L)$, which increases with dispersion]. This means that there is more to be gained from a deviation. The net effect can go either way.

15.4.2. *Enforcement and imperfect insurance*

What if equation (15.6) fails to hold? This means that *perfect* insurance is unattainable. We are then in a situation analogous to that discussed in the case of informational failure, where, nevertheless, some more limited form of insurance was possible. We can follow in the steps of that analysis to see what happens here. Once again, denote by X the consumption of a high-output farmer and by Y the consumption of a low-output farmer. For the scheme to be viable, the "insurance budget" must balance; this is just equation (15.4) which we reproduce here:

$$(15.7) \qquad\qquad pX + (1-p)Y = pH + (1-p)L = M.$$

Next, the enforcement constraint must be satisfied. This amounts to the statement that the gain from a deviation must not outweigh the future losses. The one-time gain is $u(H) - u(X)$. The loss is

$$N\{[pu(X) + (1-p)u(Y)] - [pu(H) + (1-p)u(L)]\} + S,$$

so the enforcement constraint may be rewritten as

$$(15.8) \qquad N\{[pu(X) + (1-p)u(Y)] - [pu(H) + (1-p)u(L)]\}$$

$$+ S \geq u(H) - u(X).$$

It will help to rewrite this in a way so that the Xs and Ys are all on one side. Transposing terms, we obtain the equivalent condition

$$(15.9) \qquad\qquad u(X) + N\{pu(X) + (1-p)u(Y)\}$$

$$\geq u(H) + N\{pu(H) + (1-p)u(L)\} - S.$$

We are after the second-best insurance scheme. We already know that everybody wants as much consumption smoothing as possible (subject to the enforcement constraint), so we are looking for the "least dispersed" values of X and Y that are compatible with both (15.7) and (15.9). There is an easy way to do this graphically. Figure 15.1 plots how the left-hand side of the enforcement constraint (15.9) changes as we alter X, starting from the perfect insurance level [which is, of course, $pH + (1-p)L$] and moving up to the no-insurance level H. Implicitly, the value of Y is altered, so that the viability condition (15.7) holds throughout this exercise. Thus Y *falls* from the perfect insurance level [also $pH + (1-p)L$] to the no-insurance level L (but this change is not explicitly carried in the diagram).

What happens to the left-hand side of (15.9)? *At the perfect insurance point* $X = pH + (1-p)L$, the value of this expression must rise. The reason

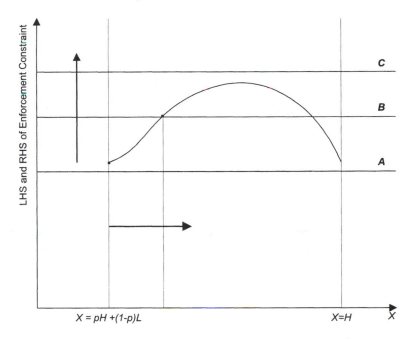

Figure 15.1. *The enforcement constraint and imperfect insurance.*

is that the term $pu(X) + (1 - p)u(Y)$ is approximately unchanging for small variations in X, at the perfect insurance point (because it attains a maximum there).[18] However, $u(X)$ increases with X, so the combined expression $u(X) + N\{pu(X) + (1 - p)u(Y)\}$ must rise with X.

What does this mean in words? It means that if we move away from the first-best insurance level, enforcement becomes easier. This is because the deviation gain falls, while the losses from future denial of insurance do not fall as fast, at least initially.

After a while, this trend reverses itself. The fall in $pu(X) + (1 - p)u(Y)$ starts to become significant for higher values of X, and ultimately this dominates the gain in $u(X)$, so the combined expression reaches a maximum and then turns down. It is possible that by this time, X has already reached the no-insurance point H so that, effectively, there is no turning down of the combined expression. Which particular case occurs depends on the parameters of the problem and is of no great significance to us, so we also put in a declining segment in Figure 15.1 for completeness.

The horizontal line in Figure 15.1 represents the right-hand side of the enforcement constraint (15.9). It is flat because it is independent of the value of X. Note that its height depends on various parameters, among them the

---

[18] This and the observations to follow can be easily verified by taking derivatives of the relevant expression with respect to X, accounting at the same time for the comovement of Y. I omit the details.

value of social sanctions. The lower the line, the greater the range of insurance schemes that satisfy the enforcement constraint.

We draw three instances of this horizontal segment. For the values represented by line *A*, perfect insurance is enforcable and there is no need to look at other schemes. Now imagine that social norms in this economy begin to wither away, so that the value of social sanctions declines. This has the effect of shifting the horizontal line *upward* to the line marked *B*. At this level, perfect insurance falls apart. The second-best insurance scheme is achieved by a higher value of *X* (and consequently a lower value of *Y*). This means that individual consumption has to move with individual income. The lower the value of social sanctions, the more will be this variability. Finally, there comes a point (shown by the line marked *C*) at which *no* insurance is possible at all.

Thus the lack of enforceability limits insurance and creates second-best insurance structures in which people must face, to some extent, the variation in their own individual fates. This model may be modified in many different ways, to yield different insights.

Self-insurance and mutual insurance

First, we can interact self-insurance or credit with mutual insurance. Following a deviation from mutual insurance, it may be possible to self-insure to some extent. This means that punishments are effectively lower, and the tendency for mutual insurance schemes to fall apart is thereby accentuated. The greater the possibilities for self-insurance, the more likely it is that mutual insurance schemes will begin to crumble. At one level this is only natural: as alternatives appear, informal substitutes can die out without much difficulty. But it is important to appreciate that the process exhibits a built-in inefficiency. The value of a deviation from mutual insurance is the *current* (high-output) return plus the future return from self-insurance. If this value is larger than the returns from mutual insurance and if there are no additional social sanctions, the mutual scheme will collapse. However, note that *at* the collapse point, the mutual scheme generates larger value than self-insurance does, provided that the power of social sanctions is small.[19] In this sense the transition is inefficient.

Correlated shocks

We also can extend the model to include aggregate (correlated) shocks to output (see Coate and Ravallion [1993]). It is easy enough to write down

---

[19] The current payoff from a deviation, if a farmer has produced the high output, is always larger than the return that any insurance scheme can provide. It follows that if *S* is small, the mutual insurance scheme fails to be enforceable at a point when it still does better than self-insurance. You may want to formally prove this by first adapting the enforcement constraint (15.6) to include a weaker self-insurance scheme following the deviation. Put $S = 0$. Now examine the point at which mutual insurance fails the enforcement constraint.

an enforcement constraint for this problem. Such a constraint has an interesting feature. If the entire economy is in an aggregate depressed state, the farmers who do *relatively* well in that state will have a greater incentive to deviate from any given mutual insurance scheme. This follows from diminishing marginal utility: when total output is lower, the value of *not* making some given contribution to an insurance fund must rise. At the same time, future expectations of gains from insurance are unchanged (if the shocks are independently distributed over time).

Consequently, it becomes more difficult to satisfy the enforcement constraint when times are bad for the economy as a whole, and so insurance weakens in such times. However, we must be careful: contrast this phenomenon with one in which there is a permanent improvement in the lot of one (or some) members of the group. Faced with a permanent improvement, they too will not contribute to mutual insurance. Thus an aggregate state of economic depression or a selective state of well-being can both contribute to the destruction of enforceable insurance opportunities.

The blurring of credit and insurance

Our third (and last) extension is much more subtle than the other two and has profound consequences for the conceptual distinction between credit and insurance. Recall that the distinguishing feature of insurance is a certain lack of regard for history. It is possible (though perhaps unlikely) that Asaf may have a bad output three years in a row, and Sharif may have enjoyed a high output for those three years. Our insurance scheme dictates that Sharif must make contributions to Asaf for those three years. Moreover, once the three years are over, the slate is wiped clean again. Thus pure insurance has a unilateral air to it: transfers do not carry an obligation to repay. Indeed, strange though it may sound, this is a necessary property of the perfect insurance scheme in the model that we described. It's not that such schemes are entirely missing in the world we live in: for instance, medical insurance has that property—but it is harder to imagine informal schemes with this property.

It turns out that the enforcement constraint throws some interesting light on this issue. It is true, as we already mentioned, that the first-best scheme has a "history-independence" property. However, what if enforcement constraints prevent implementation of the first-best scheme? This is precisely the situation that we have considered so far, yet in formulating our second-best scheme, we stuck firmly to pure insurance and did not allow past transfers to influence the future. It turns out that if we drop this requirement, we can do even better (Fafchamps [1996]; Kletzer and Wright [1995]; Thomas and Worrall [1994]).

To see this better scheme, return to the formulation of the second-best arrangement pursued in equations (15.7)–(15.9) and Figure 15.1. Recall the basic idea in this construction: high-output individuals may be reluctant to contribute to the insurance scheme because they stand to gain by keeping their entire output. They balance these gains against the losses of not being able to participate in the scheme in the future (there are also social sanctions, but we neglect these here as they are not needed to make the main point). The way we previously solved for X—the consumption of the high-output person—was by balancing these two conflicting forces in a way that was consonant with the maximum possible degree of smoothing. In doing so, we neglected another source of balance; that is, *the scheme could be designed to increase, for a high-output person, the future returns from participation in the insurance scheme*. This raises the losses from future nonparticipation and thus loosens the enforcement constraint and permits a greater degree of smoothing today.

This means that the production of high output today raises a person's share of the pie in tomorrow's scheme and likewise lowers the portion for a low-output person who receives a handout from the scheme today. However, such an adjustment doesn't affect the low-output farmer's enforcement constraint: he is *receiving* money from the system, so there is no constraint to worry about in this case.[20]

Of course, this state of affairs is not permanent: today's high-output person may be tomorrow's low-output producer, and then he will slip down a notch as far as the subsequent share in the insurance fund is concerned. Likewise, today's low-output producer may recover his "status" by producing high in the future.

The algebra of this formulation is complicated and we will not pursue the details here, but you should be able to see how the basic idea works, and—more importantly—its implications. By linking an individual's payouts in the past to current claims in the insurance scheme, the scheme ceases to be one of pure insurance and acquires some of the characteristics of credit. Your current entitlement is higher if you have paid out more in the past, which sounds, to some extent, like you are entitled to a "repayment" of some of the money that you contributed yesterday. However, this is an entitlement only *on average*. It may be that your compatriot does badly again, and then the insurance aspect of the scheme will do battle with the credit aspect: you may be "required" to forgive or roll over some of the past "debt" and even advance further "loans," so it's more complicated than pure credit. Still more interesting is the interpretation of repayment from your compatriot depending on *your* economic state today: he will be required to pay you more if your current economic state is bad, relative to when it is good.

This seemingly esoteric mixed-credit insurance scheme brings us to the frontiers of current research in this area. Is it all esoterica in reality? The

---

[20] This is true provided we are careful not to reduce his participation utility from tomorrow onward *below* the level he can attain on his own.

answer, surprisingly enough, is no: as empirical investigations unfold, we see that a great deal of informal financial interaction in developing countries is characterized by norms of both reciprocity and obligation. The former demands repeated support if circumstances require it, so it has the flavor of insurance. The latter demands some accounting of the past, so it has the flavor of credit. We end this chapter with a box that describes a pioneering empirical study in this area.

Credit as Insurance: A Case Study from Northern Nigeria

How can markets and economic institutions adapt to missing information and problems of enforcement? We have seen how these constraints can limit reciprocal transactions and force a blend of credit and insurance to develop. A study of rural credit markets in northern Nigeria by Udry [1993, 1994] provides a rich empirical illustration of institutional adaptation.

Nigeria is predominantly Islamic: over 90% of the population is Muslim. Islamic law strongly condemns the practice of charging interest for loans. Therefore, usury has always been taboo in traditional Islamic societies. Fixed repayment periods are also prohibited: "And if the debtor is in difficulty, then (there should be) postponement to a time of ease" says the *Koran*. (2: 280; quoted in Udry [1993]). At the same time, Nigerian agriculture is subject to seasonal fluctuations and random shocks (droughts, crop disease, etc.). Thus income flows are naturally highly uncertain and irregular. The need to borrow and lend in times of distress is therefore paramount. Given the stricture against charging interest, which should strongly dampen the incentive to lend, how do economic institutions deal with the problem of consumption smoothing? Is there any significant credit market alive in rural Nigeria? Udry's study, based on data collected from four randomly selected villages near the city of Zaria in the Kaduna state of northern Nigeria, shows that the answer is very much in the affirmative and that credit implicitly takes the form of interhousehold insurance against income shortfalls.

Of the 400 sample households, only 10% reported *not* having engaged in any borrowing or lending activity over the period of the survey. Indeed, 50% of households *both* borrowed and lent at various points during this interval. A noticeable feature of these loans is that they were almost always restricted within tightly knit communities, whose members knew about each other's conditions, needs, and activities. Ninety-seven percent (by value) of the 808 informal-sector loans recorded were either between residents of the same village or between relatives. Almost all such loans were remarkably informal in character: there was no written contract or witness, nor was a rate of interest or repayment date specified, implicitly or explicitly. Loans seem to be advanced purely on the basis of trust.

What is interesting about the Nigerian credit market is that the amount of money paid back depends not only on the borrower's financial situation at the time of repayment, *but also on that of the lender*. Udry's econometric analysis confirmed that the importance of the latter factor in determining the implicit rate of interest is statistically significant. This led him to conclude that the loans were not, in fact, equivalent to "equity shares" in the borrower's farm or business, but mixed devices with components of insurance and mutual risk pooling embedded in them.

It is not surprising, therefore, that the implicit realized rate of interest, calculated from loaned and repaid amounts, showed large variations; however, the median nominal monthly rate of return was about zero. Given that the monthly rate of inflation was a steep 3.7%, the average loan clearly earned a significantly negative real rate of return. This further strengthens the interpretation that the loans were really forms of mutual insurance, based on need and reciprocity. However, they were not unilateral transfers either, as a pure insurance would dictate. A transfer today carries *some* obligation to repay tomorrow.

Theory suggests that a mixed credit–insurance contract is symptomatic of enforcement problems. A household that receives a loan may decline to repay later or may repay only a meager amount. Likewise, households experiencing relative prosperity may refuse to help out their neighbors who are in need. How does the community keep default or delinquency at bay? It seems that discipline is maintained by the pressure of community opinion and the threat of censure or ostracization—instruments that can be more powerful than mere pecuniary penalties. Note, moreover, that an impersonal market, by the very fact of being *impersonal*, does not have these instruments at its disposal. What an impersonal market does share with this informal institution is another source of punishment: temporary or permanent exclusion from future participation in reciprocal transactions.

In the few cases of dispute and perceived default, a complaint is made to a community leader or village head by the lender. If, after review of the situation, the leader holds the borrower to be guilty, the punishment imposed is usually a verbal admonition and, in extreme cases, a threat to make the matter public (leading to shame and possible sanctions from the community). The latter threat is considered so severe and damaging that in his survey, Udry found not a single instance of it.

Other issues of moral hazard are likely to be secondary in the Nigerian context because of the ease of information flow. Because lending is restricted within closely knit communities, borrowers usually find it impossible to misrepresent their true financial situation or to feign crop damage, illness, or any other misfortune.

A glance at default figures in the sample is revealing. Of the 808 loans, only 47 (about 5%) were in default as perceived by the lenders themselves. Astonishingly, only three of these cases pertained to borrowers who experienced negative shocks to their income after the loan was taken. This must mean that borrowers who do not repay because of bad shocks are generally not *perceived* as having defaulted. This goes to show that it is part of the norm that the repayment burden is reduced or excused for those borrowers who run into financial trouble: proof again of the insurance aspect of these transactions.

Let's end with some observations on intervillage credit transactions. Note that a shock to income can be of two types: an *idiosyncratic* shock, which affects a single household (e.g., an illness in the family, flooding or insect damage to the family's plot, etc.), and an *aggregate* shock, which can affect an entire village or region (e.g., rainfall shortage, the flooding of a river, etc.). Because most borrowing and lending is restricted to small communities and villages, it seems that the rural credit market should be efficient in pooling risk and providing insurance against the first kind of shock, but not against the second. Udry estimated that in his sample, about half (58%) of the variation in farm yields was caused by the latter kind of shocks, so this limitation must be serious.

However, although there is practically no direct outside lending (the informational disadvantage of outsiders and the inability to charge fixed, nonstate contingent interest rates in violation of Islamic law are surely the reasons), flows of funds between villages are not entirely absent. In northern Nigeria, the Hausa tradition of long-distance trading has given rise to a network of merchants. With widespread outside connections and intimate personal knowledge of people in their own resident villages, these merchants act as pipelines for outside credit to enter the village, while still providing loans on terms that do not violate the accepted standards of the community. Intervillage insurance, though not as prevalent as intravillage arrangements, does not appear to be altogether absent.

15.5. Summary

This chapter studied *insurance*: the provision of funds to smooth out unexpected variations in income or in consumption needs. We began with an example to show how insurance can be profitable, and used this example to distinguish between *self-insurance*, which is the smoothing of consumption using one's own assets, and *mutual insurance*, which requires interaction across a number of individuals. We observed that insurance possibilities are maximal when the fortunes of individuals are *negatively correlated* (I am doing well, on average, when you are not, and vice versa). Although negative correlation may be difficult to come by in practice, a weaker condition—the *independence* of incomes—also yields considerable scope for insurance. Insurance possibilities do diminish, however, as the fortunes of individuals become more and more *positively correlated* and vanish altogether if incomes and needs move entirely in tandem across individuals. Finally, we observed that the larger the group, the greater the possibilities of mutual insurance.

We then introduced a benchmark model, which we call the *perfect insurance* scenario. In this scenario there are a large number of people who face an aggregate shock that is common to all of them (say, the weather) and the additional possibility of idiosyncratic variations in income (or consumption needs). We showed that it is optimal to pool all the idiosyncratic variation and that it will be impossible to insure against any of the aggregate variation. Hence, the solution to the perfect insurance problem yields a testable hypothesis: if the model is good, then we should see that individual (or household-level) consumption is unaffected by *individual* incomes, but it should move in perfect correlation with the aggregate consumption of the insurance group (the entire village, let us say).

We turned to regression analysis to test this implication. Use household consumption as the dependent variable and "group consumption," household income, and other household observables (such as a spell of unemployment) as independent variables. Roughly speaking, if the theory of perfect insurance is right, the estimated coefficients on all the household-specific variables should be zero and the coefficient on group average consumption should be unity. We noted several problems with this approach that largely stemmed from missing data: for instance, what do we use for group consumption when all we have are data on a sample of households? We then discussed several empirical studies. The consensus is that although the coefficient on household income is generally small (certainly way smaller than unity), we are pretty far from perfect insurance. Idiosyncratic shocks that affect household income do have a significant effect on the consumption of that household.

This conclusion motivated a study of models with *imperfect* insurance. We identified two broad factors that might impose constraints on insurance: *limited information* and *limited enforcement*.

The informational problem is one of *moral hazard*: group members may not be sure that a particular member has suffered an income loss or a consumption spike; that is, it might be difficult or impossible to verify the outcome, on which insurance transfers are predicated. At a more subtle level, it may be possible to verify the outcome, but not what led to it: did a farmer suffer a bad harvest because he was really or truly unlucky or did he apply inadequate levels of effort to cultivation? With these uncertainties, it might be foolhardy to attempt perfect insurance: there would be huge efficiency losses in production because individuals would then have the incentive to apply inadequate effort to income-generating activities. We studied the imperfect insurance problem under these constraints and described a "second-best" insurance arrangement, suitably constrained by the limited information.

One implication of this model is that individuals run into a trade-off between diversification and moral hazard. Diversified, uncorrelated incomes across group members are easiest to achieve when members are all in different occupations or they are in the same occupation, perhaps, but are geographically separated, which is hard to accomplish within a village. On the other hand, an extension of insurance schemes across villages runs straight into the moral hazard problem, because it is much harder to verify outcomes and inputs. We discussed how this trade-off can be ameliorated in practice.

The second problem has to do with enforcement. A farmer with a good harvest may be required to make a transfer to the common insurance fund. Why would he do so? One answer is that if he does not comply, he will face social sanctions from the village. He might also be excluded from future participation in the insurance scheme. Such sanctions and exclusions have costs, but they must be traded off against the benefits from retaining extra income today. This notion gives rise to another sort of constrained problem: find the best insurance scheme consistent with the requirement that all farmers will pay up when times are good. We analyzed the properties of this scheme.

There are several implications of the enforcement-constrained model. One is that increased opportunities for self-insurance tend to destroy schemes of mutual insurance, because such opportunities lower the punishment value of future exclusion. Individuals are more likely to deviate from an ongoing scheme. Likewise, the loss of social ties in the village weakens the power of social disapproval: this, too, will cause insurance schemes to fall apart.

Another implication of the enforcement-constrained model is that it generally predicts the blurring of credit and insurance. We observed that pure insurance is "history-free": the fact that I make a transfer today has no implications for what might happen tomorrow. However, when pure insurance is ruled out by problems of enforcement, a second-best compromise might be to make my future returns from the scheme positively related to transfers that I make today. The reason is that this eases the no-deviation constraint and allows for better insurance overall. The linking of future returns to current payouts can be intrepreted as a form of credit.

We ended the chapter with a discussion of rural markets in Nigeria, where this sort of mixed scheme can be seen in practice.

Exercises

■ (1) Discuss the main problems with agricultural crop insurance. Pay particular attention to the problems of correlation and information. Using these concepts, comment on the possibility of a two-tier system in which a giant insurance company makes insurance payouts to the village as a whole, while a village council decides on how to allocate the payouts to individual residents.

■ (2) Suppose that two persons, A and B, can each earn a high income (H) or a low income (L). The following table describes the probability of each of the four events. Make sure that you understand what each cell means: in particular, you should note that $q + s + 2r = 1$.

	H for A	L for A
H for B	q	r
L for B	r	s

(a) If each person expects H with probability p, and this is independent of what happens to the other person, describe q, r, and s in terms of p.

(b) Now assume that the fortunes of the two persons are correlated. Using the variables in the table, how would you capture the idea that the incomes of A and B might be *positively* correlated? Negatively correlated? How would the extremes of perfect correlation be expressed?

(c) Which of these cases do you find most conducive for mutual insurance between A and B?

■ (3) Suppose that we find that temporary income shocks (such as those due to weather fluctuations) have small effects on the consumption of a household. Then this is *prima facie* evidence that households can smooth such shocks, but the smoothing may arise from self-insurance, credit, or mutual insurance. If you have data on consumption and income for the household over several periods of time, discuss how you might use the intertemporal data to distinguish between these three sources of smoothing.

■ (4) Suppose that a household builds up stocks of assets, such as bullocks, land, jewelry, and cash. When faced with an adverse income shock in a particular year, the household will use these assets to smooth consumption. Discuss the factors that influence the choice of assets used in smoothing.

■ (5) Consider two economies: one with a high population density, so that villages are clumped together and intervillage transportation costs are low, and another in which villages are spread apart and largely isolated from one another. In which economy would you expect bullocks to be used for consumption smoothing?

■ (6) Consider two groups of risk-averse farmers. One group practices mutual insurance, but the other does not. In the questions to follow, base your arguments on the assumption that a menu of production techniques and crops are available for cultivation, and that farmers choose from this menu.

(a) If farmers can collectively choose their crops/techniques, argue that the insuring group is likely to display a higher average rate of return on its farming investments.

(b) On the other hand, argue that an existing system of insurance might dampen the *individual* incentive to adopt newly available methods or crops with a higher average rate of return.

■ (7) Quite apart from considerations of altruism, discuss why insurance among members of an extended family is more likely than insurance among a group of strangers of the same size and occupational composition.

■ (8) We have seen that moral hazard restricts the scope of insurance: if unobserved effort must be expended to produce efficient levels of output, then such effort may not be forthcoming in the presence of insurance. Review the relevant arguments in this chapter. Now, (i) discuss if poor farming groups are more or less likely to be prone to this problem than rich farming groups and (ii) show that a mixture of group credit and insurance (rather than pure insurance alone) may help avoid the moral hazard problem.

■ (9) Review the material on enforcement constraints in insurance. Why might higher mobility (of people) lead to a breakdown in mutual insurance?

Chapter 16

International Trade

16.1. World trading patterns

The post-World War II period saw an enormous expansion in world trade. At the end of the war, a historic conference in Bretton Woods, New Hampshire, paved the way for a multilateral organization: the General Agreement on Trade and Tariffs (GATT), which pledged to reduce trading barriers worldwide. In the aftermath of this new trading order and with rapid economic growth worldwide, the volume of international trade grew by orders of magnitude. World exports grew an average 7.3% per year between 1960 and 1968, and accelerated to 9.7% per year between 1968 and 1973. The year of the first oil crisis was 1973. Oil prices rose sharply as a result of coordinated reductions in oil extraction by the Organization of Petroleum Exporting Countries (OPEC) cartel. Developed countries went through a recession that was partly induced by the rising price of energy, and there was a revival of protectionist tendencies. World trade continued to expand, but at significantly lower rates: 3.3% per annum between 1973 and 1981, 2.3% between 1980 and 1985, and then 4.5% per annum between 1985 and 1990.[1]

Against this background, the performance of developing countries (during the 1970s and after) has been mixed. Table 16.1 summarizes export growth in developing countries by region. It is clear that developing countries have systematically expanded their exports. This rapid growth was partly responsible for the resurgence of protectionism; without it, growth rates may have been even faster. Of particular interest is the dramatic expansion in export volumes in Asia that has been nothing short of dramatic: the average Asian export growth rate was in double digits throughout the 1980s and exceeded the overall average for developing countries by a factor of 2.

Within Asia, the most successful export-led growth effort was that of the newly industrialized economies (NIEs): Hong Kong, Korea, Singapore, and Taiwan. Although recession in the 1970s slowed trade expansion in most parts of the world, these countries rocketed along at over 13% per annum. Their export-oriented strategies have also been adopted by other

---

[1] These figures are taken from Page [1994, Table 1.1].

Table 16.1. Annual average percentage growth of exports in developing countries.

Region	1973–82	1983–86	1987–90
All LDCs	0.2	4.7	5.7
Africa	−2.4	4.4	2.3
Asia	9.2	10.5	11.8
Europe[a]	4.3	5.1	−4.2
Middle East	−5.1	−1.1	5.4
Western Hemisphere	1.9	2.6	7.2
Sub-Saharan Africa	−1.0	1.7	1.0
Four Asian NIEs[b]	13.3	13.4	11.4

Source: *International Monetary Fund, Issues and Developments in International Trade Policy* [1992].
[a]Eastern Europe and the former Soviet Union.
[b]Hong Kong, Korea, Singapore, and Taiwan.

Asian economies—Malaysia, Indonesia, the Philippines, Thailand, and, more recently, China.

Latin American countries also saw a revival of export performance in the late 1980s and thereafter, largely stemming from their urgent need to service an enormous international debt accumulated during the 1970s (which we discuss more later). African export volumes have grown slower; in particular, sub-Saharan export performance was relatively dismal during the 1970s and 1980s.

Despite the rapid expansion of Asian exports, the long view reveals that developed countries have actually *increased* their share in the value of world trade, from around 66% in 1960 to 73% in 1991. How did this happen? In part it was because the rest of the developing world did not match Asia's performance, but in part the decline in primary product prices since the 1980s is responsible: it led to a change in relative valuations of less developed countries (LDC) and developed countries (DC) exports. Many developing countries are exporters of primary products: food, fuels, minerals, and so on. As we will see subsequently, the theory of comparative advantage explains why this pattern is to be expected (but we will note several qualifications as well). Table 16.2 provides data on the share of primaries in total exports for selected developing countries in the early 1990s. It also lists the principal exports of these countries. Figure 16.1, which reproduces Figure 2.13 from Chapter 2, shows a scatter plot of primary export ratios against the per capita income of countries for a much larger set. The tendency for primary export ratios to decline with an increased per capita income should be evident from this figure.

That said, however, it must be noted that the *composition* of exports from developing countries has significantly shifted toward manufactured exports.

Table 16.2. Export composition and principal exports for selected developing countries.

| Country | Shares (%) | | Major exports |
	Primary	Manuf.	
Ethiopia	96	4	Coffee, tea, hides & skins
Burundi	70	30	Coffee & substitutes, tea
C. African Rep.	56	44	Pearls & semiprecious stones, coffee & substitutes
Egypt	67	33	Petroleum & products, mineral fuels, textile yarn
India	25	75	Textile yarn & fabrics, industrial extractives, precious & semiprecious stones
Turkey	29	72	Fruit & nuts, clothing & accessories, iron & steel
China	19	81	Footwear, toys, textiles, metal manufactures
Indonesia	47	53	Crude petroleum, natural gas, veneers & plywood
Thailand	28	72	Rice, transistors, valves, office machines, clothing & accessories
Philippines	24	76	Transistors, valves, vegetable oils, fruits & nuts
South Korea	7	93	Footwear, synthetic fabrics, transistors & valves, ships & boats
Nicaragua	93	7	Coffee & substitutes, meat, cotton
Mexico	47	53	Crude petroleum, passenger road vehicles, vegetables
Costa Rica	67	33	Vegetables & fruits, coffee, basic manufactures
Guatemala	70	30	Coffee, sugar & honey, fruits & nuts, pharmaceutical products
Brazil	40	60	Meat & preparations, metalliferous ores, coffee
Bolivia	81	19	Natural & manufactured gas, base metal ores, tin
Colombia	60	40	Coffee, crude petroleum, coal

Source: *World Development Report* (World Bank [1995]) and the *Handbook of International Trade and Development Statistics* (United Nations [1992]).

The shift is particularly pronounced in Asia, but is a general feature for developing countries as a whole. Now, in part this may be thought of as a natural law of development. As incomes grow, items such as food are relatively less important in the consumption basket, so that all consumptions shift in favor of manufactures. There is no reason why this should not be reflected in trading patterns as well. However, there is more to it than that: the share of developed economies in manufactured exports has actually *declined*. Developing economies have more than doubled their share, from around 7% in 1970 to over 17% in 1990, whereas the share of developed economies has decreased, from around 83 to 77% over the same period.[2]

---

[2] This does not include the set of eastern European economies.

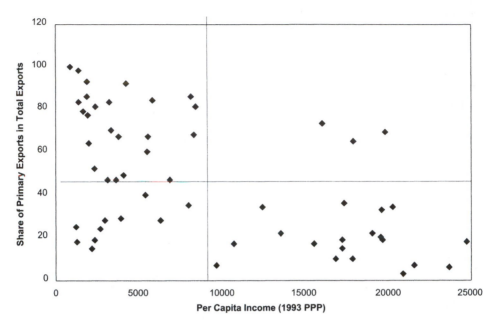

Figure 16.1. Share of primary exports in total exports. Source: World Development Report (World Bank [1995]).

Not surprisingly, the largest component of this increase came from the East Asian countries. Since the late 1980s, China has become a significant player in the OECD market for manufactures (and a Latin American shift is noticeable as well). With the exception of textiles and clothing, where trade was subject to control under various multifiber arrangements, manufactured exports grew in virtually every category.

As we will see in Chapter 17, this shift was largely the result of deliberate government policy to promote manufactured exports, either because governments feared protection against primary exports in developed countries, or because they predicted that primary product prices would inevitably decline relative to prices of manufactures, or because they felt that manufacturing was the key to technical know-how and expertise. The remarkable success of the East Asian economies has caused a policy shift in other countries as well. Many Latin American countries simplified their tariff structure and lifted quantitative restrictions on trade in the early 1990s. Significant liberalization measures are also being adopted by some African countries as well by some countries in South Asia.[3] Table 16.3 summarizes the main shifts toward manufacturing over the 1970–90 period.

However, the overall share of LDC manufacturing exports remains low: it was well below 20% at the beginning of the 1990s. This observation, along

___

[3] These include Côte d'Ivoire, Gambia, Ghana, Kenya, and Zaire in Africa, and India and Pakistan in South Asia.

Table 16.3. Trends in the share of LDC manufactured exports (percentages).

	1970	1975	1980	1985	1990
Share in world total					
All LDCs	7.0	7.4	10.0	13.3	17.1
Asia	3.7	4.7	7.2	9.5	14.1
Latin America	1.8	1.7	2.0	2.5	2.0
Africa	1.4	0.7	0.6	0.4	0.5
Share in LDC total					
Asia	52.4	62.8	71.8	71.2	82.7
Latin America	26.2	23.4	20.3	18.5	11.6
Africa	19.5	9.3	5.8	3.2	2.8

Source: Page [1994, Table 1.3].

with Figure 16.1, appears to support the following general hypothesis: LDCs export primary products and import manufactured goods, whereas developed countries import primary products and export manufactures. This is the kind of hypothesis that will be predicted by classical theories of comparative advantage (see following text).

Is this hypothesis borne out by the facts? Not entirely. It *is* true, as Figure 16.1 indicates, that LDC exports are still fairly intensive in primary products, but *import* patterns across the developed and developing world are far more similar. Figure 16.2, which reproduces Figure 2.15 from Chapter 2, shows that unlike the clear trend in the share of primary exports (as per capita income increases), there is no corresponding tendency for primary imports to rise with the level of per capita income. Table 16.4 takes this observation a step further by showing that developed countries indeed export approximately the same composition of products to other developed countries as they do to developing countries.

Indeed, despite the substantial increase in the participation of developing economies in world trade, the value of trade *within* the group of developed countries has consistently exceeded the value of trade *between* developed and developing countries. For instance, between 1980 and 1991, the value of DC exports to other DCs (as a percentage of DC exports to the world) *increased* from 71 to about 76%, whereas the value of DC exports to LDCs declined from 25 to around 21%.[4] Moreover, more than 70% of the trade within the DC bloc pertains to goods of a nonprimary nature: chemicals, machinery, equipment, and other manufactured goods.

The fact that trade among developed countries is of a very high order and that it is not in primary goods suggests that demand patterns and production technologies (and not just supply conditions) have a lot to do with trade.

---

[4] The percentage of LDC exports to DCs as a share of the value of their total exports to the world has also decreased, from around 68% in 1980 to around 60% in 1991.

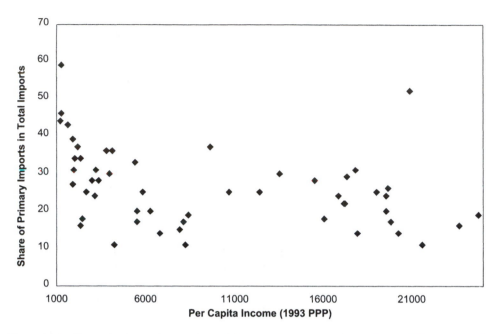

Figure 16.2. Share of primary imports in total imports. Source: World Development Report (World Bank [1995]).

Trade in similar products may be propelled by an increased demand for variety (as income increases). Similarly, trade in capital goods may be driven by greater depth and indirectness in production (on this, see Chapter 5) that creates demand for a large variety of inputs and components, not all of which are produced domestically.

Whether trade occurs in "similar" products (manufactures versus manufactures) or "dissimilar" products (manufactures versus primaries) has implications for trading patterns and free-trade arrangements that we will explore in some detail in the chapters to come.

Table 16.4. Export shares (%) by product category from developed countries to other developed and developing countries.

Product category	DCs	LDCs
Fuels, minerals, metals	8	5
Other primaries	12	11
Chemicals & related	39	35
Manufactures	41	48

Source: *International Trade Statistics Yearbook*, (United Nations [1992].)

16.2. Comparative advantage

A fundamental concept that will help us to clarify many of the issues and debates in international trade policy is the notion of *comparative advantage*. This is a concept that is simple and subtle at the same time, so it will be best to begin with an example.

Imagine there are only two countries that make up the world economy. Let's call them North (N) and South (S). In this rarefied world, only two commodities are produced: computers and rice. Both N and S are capable of producing both commodities. To make this example as stark as possible, suppose that labor is the only factor of production. Table 16.5 describes how many units of labor are required to make one computer and one sack of rice. These are the familiar input–output coefficients. To complete the description of the example, suppose that N and S are blessed with a total of 600 units of labor.

Here is what's subtle about comparative advantage, and it will be good to keep this in mind as we work our way through this example. The point is that S is more inefficient (relative to N) in the production of computers *as well as* rice, yet we are going to show that the countries will prefer to trade with each other.

Let's begin to work out the details by first drawing the production possibility frontier for each country. This is done in Figure 16.3. In this simple example, the frontiers are obviously straight lines. For instance, N can produce sixty computers if all its resources are devoted to the production of computers and it can produce forty sacks of rice if all its resources are devoted to the production of rice. By shifting labor from one of these sectors to the other, all combinations on the straight line that joins these two extremes can be produced as well. Likewise, a straight line describes the production possibilities for country S.

Now suppose that the two countries are somehow barred from trading with each other, in which case they will each have to produce all their domestic demands for rice and computers. Let us calculate the price of computers relative to that of rice in country N: it will be 10:15, which is the same as the fraction 2/3. In words, a computer in country N will cost two-thirds as much as a sack of rice. To see why this is the case, observe that if the relative price

Table 16.5. Production technologies in N and S.

Labor required	One computer	One sack of rice
In N	10	15
In S	40	20

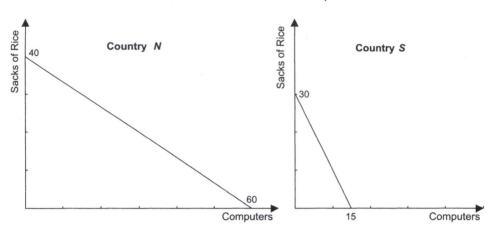

Figure 16.3. Production possibility frontiers.

were to be any *other* ratio (say 1/2), labor resources would be transferred entirely from one sector to the other. Indeed, the transfer would occur *from* the sector that is cheaper *to* the sector that is more expensive, where the words "cheaper" and "more expensive" are stated relative to the ratio 2/3. Exercises at the end of this chapter ask you to verify this sort of intuition in particular cases.

Therefore, if *both* commodities are consumed in each country (in the autarkic situation), the relative price of computers in N must be 2/3, and (by a similar calculation) this same relative price in country S must be 40:20 or 2.

Now imagine that the two countries open up to trade. What will be the outcome? Clearly, the autarkic relative prices cannot prevail in the international economy. With free trade, *one* common relative price must establish itself. There are three possibilities for the international relative price of computers to rice: (1) it may be below the autarky level 2/3 for country N; (2) it may exceed the autarkic ratio for country S, which is 2; (3) the price will lie somewhere between 2/3 and 2.

It is very easy to rule out the first and second possibilities. I will rule out the first possibility here; you can use this argument to take care of the second. Suppose that the international relative price—call it p^*—is less than 2/3. Then *nobody* in the world will produce computers! You can see this in exactly the same way that we showed that autarkic relative prices must be 2/3 and 2 (see also the exercises at the end of this chapter). However, if no one produces computers, there is no way to supply the market demand for computers. This leads to an absurd conclusion, so the first possibility can never occur in equilibrium. A mirror argument also rules out the second possibility.

This leaves us only with the third possibility: the international relative price settles somewhere between the two autarkic price ratios, and indeed, this is exactly what will happen. Figure 16.4 shows what the equilibrium

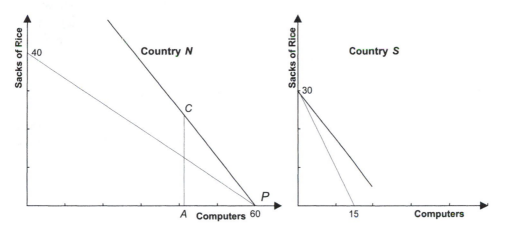

Figure 16.4. International trade.

looks like. Country N will produce only computers: this is the extreme production point marked as P. Computers in this country can now be "transformed" into rice via a better "possibility frontier" than the country had at its disposal under autarky. This is the frontier described by international trade. Because the relative *international* price of computers is less than the autarkic ratio of 2, this frontier permits higher consumption of both goods in country N than under autarky. Point C shows a typical mix of consumption. Note that this point could not have been achieved by country N under autarky, because it lies beyond the domestic production possibility frontier for that country.

The difference between the production point P and the consumption point C is made up of exports and imports. Consulting Figure 16.4, we see that country N exports AP computers and it imports AC sacks of rice.

A parallel argument holds for country S. It produces only rice and exports some of this output in exchange for computers. This is because the international relative price of computers (which, as you will see, is just the reciprocal of the international relative price of rice) is lower than its autarkic price. The end result is that country N exports computers and country S exports rice.

This simple story is based on David Ricardo's theory of comparative advantage and is often called the *Ricardian model*.[5]

There are several issues that jump out at us from this example. Let us take them one at a time.

(1) What determined the pattern of exports and imports in this example? A careful rereading should convince you that all that mattered was the

---

[5] The interested reader who wishes to pursue these matters further should consult standard textbooks in international economics (see, e.g., Caves, Frankel, and Jones [1990] or Krugman and Obstfeld [1994] and the references therein).

relative costs of producing computers and rice in each country, which determined the autarkic price ratios. The emphasis is on the word "relative." The *absolute* cost of production—actual units of labor required to produce each unit of the goods—turns out to be quite irrelevant. In particular, unless by some freak of fate the *relative* costs of production in the two countries turn out to be exactly the same, there is always scope for profitable trade by both countries. This is at the heart of the notion of comparative advantage. *Comparatively* speaking, country S is better at producing rice than country N, even though it needs 20 units of labor for the production of each sack of rice, as opposed to country N's requirement of only fifteen. Thus the qualification "comparative" in "comparative advantage."

(2) Although all this makes sense from the perspective that we adopted to study our example, it appears to make no sense at all on an individual basis. If it's cheaper to buy rice in country N, well, then, why wouldn't people buy their rice from that country and be done with it, comparative advantage or no comparative advantage? The answer is simple. The market works in our example so that rice is *not* cheaper in N, even though less labor is required for production per sack, and the market achieves this seemingly paradoxical outcome by creating different *wages* for labor in the two countries. Because labor in the technologically advanced country produces more, it must be paid a higher wage. (The two countries may have separate currencies, but the wages are still comparable once we use the exchange rate to transform one currency into the other.) The higher wage nullifies the country's advantage in the good that it has relatively less advantage in, but retains the edge for the good in which that country has a *comparative* advantage. The exercises at the end of this chapter contain further discussion of this topic.

(3) In this model, both countries are better off with trade than without it. After all, look at the consumption points in Figure 16.4. They lie beyond the autarkic frontiers, as we already observed. Because there is only one input of production—labor—these benefits must accrue evenly to everyone in the population. Therefore trade leads to gains for all. However, the generality of this finding is qualified by the assumption of a single input of production. When there are multiple inputs, different groups may benefit differently, and some groups might actually lose from trade. This is an important topic to which we will return.

16.3. Sources of comparative advantage

16.3.1. Technology

The preceding example tells us, in the broadest sense, what comparative advantage is. A country has a comparative advantage in the production of a particular commodity if it can domestically "transform" other commodities into this commodity more easily than other countries can. The fact that a country may have an absolute advantage in the production of all commodities (or none) is irrelevant in this context.

The example also highlights an important *source* of comparative advantage: a country may have a relative technological advantage in the production of some good(s). In the example, note that technical know-how is assumed to differ across countries. We assumed, in fact, that country S had a technical disadvantage in the production of both commodities. But the point is that the *relative* disadvantage of S in the production of computers was greater and this led to the particular pattern of international trade.

Technological differences form an important component of comparative advantage, but there are other determinants as well.

16.3.2. Factor endowments

One of the most important determinants of comparative advantage is the endowment of factors. Bangladesh is the world's largest exporter of jute, not so much because of some hidden technological advantage in the production of that commodity, but because of certain factors of production (land, soil of the appropriate quality, and a great abundance of labor) that make it profitable to export jute. Likewise, with or without technological advantage, South Africa would be one of the world's largest exporters of diamonds, simply because natural diamonds are found there in great abundance.

It is hardly surprising, then, that even if two countries have identical technologies in the production of various goods as well as identical preferences in the consumption of these goods, they might find it profitable to trade with each other. In the text that follows, we will go through a detailed example to illustrate this point. The model that we use is based on the work of Eli Heckscher and Bertil Ohlin and is often called the *Heckscher–Ohlin model* of trade.[6]

We'll consider a variant of the example that we used for the Ricardian model. Our fictitious countries are still N and S. This time, they produce two different goods: cars and textiles. Each of these goods is produced with capital (K) and labor (L). Assume that N is relatively well endowed with capital (or equivalently, that S is relatively well endowed with labor), and that there are no other differences between the two countries.

We will assume that the production of cars is capital intensive and that of textiles is labor intensive. We capture this idea by drawing isoquants for the production of the two goods, as in Figure 16.5. Notice that for every

---

[6] The interested reader is referred to trade textbooks such as Caves, Frankel, and Jones [1990] or Krugman and Obstfeld [1994] for further analysis.

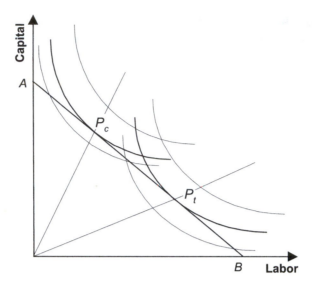

Figure 16.5. Isoquants for cars and textiles.

relative price of capital to labor, the production of cars employs a higher ratio of capital to labor than the production of textiles. Figure 16.5 displays a particular relative price of labor to capital, captured by the slope of the line *AB*. A cost-minimizing production point for cars is shown by the location P_c; a similar point for textiles is depicted by the tangency location P_t. Note that the ratio of labor to capital, as captured by the slope of the line from the origin to these points, is higher for textiles than it is for cars.

For the next few paragraphs, we will focus on the countries in autarky. Let's take *N* first. The familiar box diagram on the left-hand side of Figure 16.6 shows the efficient production configurations of cars and textiles

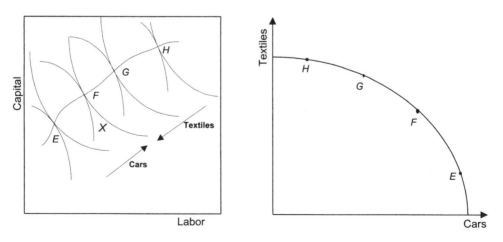

Figure 16.6. Constructing the PPF for N.

in this country. The width of the box shows the endowment of labor in N, whereas the height of the box depicts the endowment of capital. Given these two endowments, the curve $EFGH$ shows various *efficient* production combinations of cars and textiles. The combinations are efficient in the sense that none of these points can be "improved" upon by some other combination that produces *more* cars and *more* textiles *at the same time*. These are the points where the two sets of isoquants are mutually tangent to each other. Any nontangency point, such as X in Figure 16.6, can be dominated by a point such as F, where (via a judicious reallocation of factors) more of both goods can be produced.

Thus each of the points E, F, G, and H (as well as all the other combinations on the curve) corresponds to an efficient production combination of textiles and cars in N. As we move toward H from E in the figure, more cars and less textiles are produced. These points are collected together in the right-hand panel of Figure 16.6, which depicts the resulting production possibility frontier of country N.

Unlike the simple Ricardian model with just one input of production, this production possibility frontier will not, in general, be a simple straight line. It will be bowed outward to reflect the increasing difficulty of transforming one good to another (at the margin) as more and more of the latter good is produced.[7]

Now let's think about the corresponding production possibility frontier for country S. We construct this in exactly the same way as we did for country N. However, the two frontiers that we obtain (one for S, one for N) are not going to look the same, because the box that we use to construct the locus of efficient combinations for country S has different dimensions from the corresponding box for country N. Recalling that the width of the box captures labor endowment, and the height of the box represents capital endowment then the endowments of country S will be depicted by a box that's relatively fatter and relatively shorter. It follows that the production possibility frontier for country S is relatively more "stretched" in the direction of textiles, simply because labor is used more intensively in the production of textiles than in the production of cars, and labor is what S has in relative abundance (see Figure 16.7 for a comparison).

What effect does this have on the production of cars and textiles? Well, it should be clear that country S will now be able to produce relatively more

---

[7] Strictly speaking, this feature is the outcome of two factors. First, if each production function exhibits nonincreasing returns to scale, then additional equal doses of capital and labor cannot lead to increasing output at the margin. Second, the ratio of capital and labor released by reduced production of one of the goods (say cars) is inappropriate for the production of the other good (say textiles). This inappropriateness is heightened as more and more of the economy becomes dominated by car production, leaving an increasingly skewed ratio of capital to labor for textile production. A similar argument holds in the opposite direction, as we increase the production of textiles relative to cars.

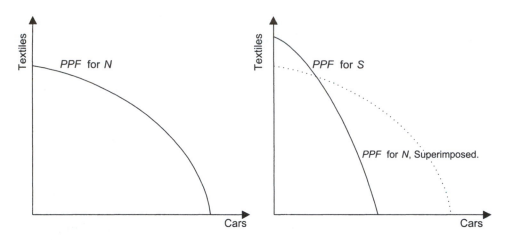

Figure 16.7. Production possibility frontiers (PPFs) in S and N.

of the labor-intensive commodity—textiles—and less of the capital-intensive commodity—cars. The producton possibility frontier of S will be another curved line, just like the frontier for country N, but it will accommodate, on the whole, a relatively greater production of textiles and a relatively smaller production of cars.

We are now all set to describe comparative advantage in this scenario. To this end, look at the two countries in autarky and suppose that they have similar preferences. In the left-hand panel Figure 16.8, we study the autarkic situation for country N. Preferences are given by the indifference curves. In the autarky equilibrium, domestic prices will be determined by the common tangency of the indifference curves with the production possibility frontier of country N.

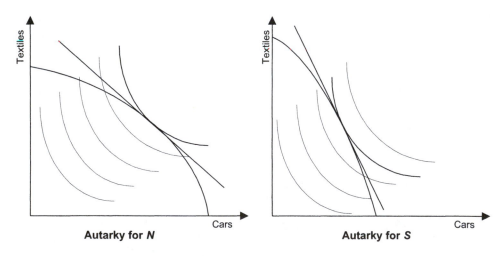

Figure 16.8. Autarkic outcomes in N and S.

Now look at the right-hand panel of Figure 16.8, where an identical construction is carried out for country S. If preferences are similar in the two countries, the two sets of indifference curves in the two panels will be the same. However, the production possibility frontiers are not. Specifically, with labor-intensive textiles on the vertical axis and capital-intensive cars on the horizontal axis, the frontier of S will look "steeper" relative to that of N. It follows that the autarkic price ratio will be "steeper" as well. In other words, the domestic price of textiles relative to that of cars will be lower than the corresponding ratio in country N. This should be no surprise. Textiles are labor-intensive and S has a relatively greater endowment of labor.

Now we can use exactly the same argument as we did for the Ricardian model. When the two countries are opened up to trade with each other, the equilibrium *international* price will settle at a level that is between the two autarkic price ratios. N will export cars and import textiles. S will export textiles and import cars. Figure 16.9 illustrates this.

Thus comparative advantage need not be the outcome solely of *technological* advantage. Even with perfect identity of technical know-how, *a country will tend to export commodities that are intensive in factors that are possessed by that country in relative abundance*. This is the essence of the Heckscher–Ohlin model of international trade.

Notice that both the Heckscher–Ohlin and Ricardian models predict plenty of trade between developed and developing countries. After all, we expect technological differences to be relatively small between countries that are in similar stages of development and possibly to be large between countries that are at different stages. The same goes with factor endowments as well. One of the main characteristics of developing countries is a low ratio of capital per person. Put in the language of the Heckscher–Ohlin theory, this

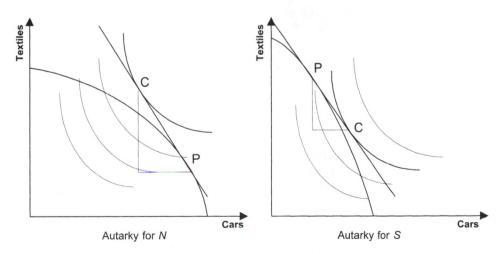

Figure 16.9. Exports and imports of S and N.

would predict relatively labor-intensive exports from the developing countries, whereas the developed countries export relatively capital-intensive commodities.[8] We may therefore conclude that these theories (at least in their simplest form) predict large volumes of trade between the developed and developing world, and relatively low volumes of trade across similar countries. As we have seen, this finding is not exactly consistent with empirical observations.

16.3.3. Preferences

Trade may also be driven by systematically varying preferences. Recall the example of the previous subsection and suppose that both countries S and N have identical technologies and factor endowments. In that case their two production possibility frontiers must be the same. Now take another look at Figure 16.8. With both production possibility frontiers identical, it appears now that domestic autarky price ratios must be identical for the two countries, so that there is no need to trade.

Not really. The argument in Figure 16.8 was based on the additional assumption that *preferences* for the two goods were similar across the two countries. This assumption may well be false in several situations. Varying conditions may indeed cause certain societies to demand high levels of certain goods: different environments (such as culinary habits, the weather, or a state of war) may be responsible. In a real sense, countries that do *not* have such high levels of demand for the particular good in question may be said to have a comparative advantage in their production.

To see this point as simply as possible, draw yourself a version of Figure 16.8 in which the production possibility frontiers of the two countries are identical. Suppose, now, that country N has a stronger relative preference for cars rather than textiles. In that case, N will exhibit indifference curves that are "tilted" in favor of cars. With the same labeling of the axes as in Figure 16.8, convince yourself that this results in a flatter set of indifference curves for country N as compared to country S. As a result, under autarky, the domestic price of cars relative to textiles in N will exceed the corresponding ratio for S. When the two countries open up to trade, N will export textiles to S and import cars, even though the conditions of production (in the sense of the overall production possibility frontiers) are identical.

The preference-based argument for trade sounds contrived at first. It appears to depend on the assumption that human beings are somehow fundamentally different across societies. As we already noticed, there are some

---

[8] Of course, it is still possible that certain specialized factor endowments may differ among similar countries. The examples of diamond mining and jute growing do not rely on the advantaged countries having any particular level of development.

situations where such differences make sense, but apart from these variations in circumstances, are there strong arguments to support systematically varying preferences?

There may well be. One of the most important differences across countries is the level of per capita income. Such differences may indeed *induce* marked differences in preferences at any point in time, although the underlying tastes may fundamentally be the same.

Here is an example. Consider your own tastes and preferences. To some extent your preferences for some goods go hand in hand with your preferences for other goods: you might wear shoes with your socks and eat butter with your toast. On the other hand, there are other goods that are clearly acquired in "stages": your first needs are for adequate food, clothing, and shelter. As you earn more and more, however, your demand for food will not rise at a corresponding pace. Other goods that you could not afford before will now come within your horizons: a bicycle, a radio, a television set, a car, and so forth, depending on your income. Put another way, your indifference curves between, say food and other goods, are not parallel to one another as you climb to higher and higher quantities of these goods. Thus, viewed at different "baseline levels," the same preference map may appear different. Hence, it's not that we view people as different across countries; it's just that they may be at different locations on the *same* preference map.

Variations in preferences may have two effects.

(1) Unlike the Heckscher–Ohlin model of international trade, which views trade as occurring between countries at different levels of development, preference variations may serve to *dampen* such trade. As an example, consider the proportion of a family budget that is spent on food. For low levels of income, it is very high indeed. As income increases, the budget share allocated to food begins to fall and keeps on falling. For precisely this reason, developing countries are likely to spend a significantly larger fraction of their national income on food. At the same time, because of the Heckscher–Ohlin theory, such countries may have a relative advantage in the *production* of food, but in this example, developing countries also tend to consume that commodity more intensively. This drags up the domestic price of food and dampens trade.

The general point that emerges is this. If richer countries prefer relatively more of the good in which they have a relative advantage in production (and the same is true of poorer countries), this will tend to dampen trade between rich and poor countries.[9] There is a parallel here with the models of inequality and development that we studied in Chapter 7. In such models, *domestic* inequalities were perpetuated if richer individuals consumed relatively more

---

[9] For an interesting argument that builds on this insight, see Markusen [1986]. See also Burenstam Linder [1961] and Copeland and Kotwal [1995].

of the goods that were produced by the factors of production that the rich themselves own in greater abundance. Isolated enclaves of rich and poor may then be the outcome. The very same effect may work here to detach groups of countries from one another: the rich countries consuming largely the products that other rich countries produce.

(2) Let us elaborate a bit more on the last point of the previous paragraph. Our argument there suggests a possible dampening of trade between the developed and developing world (relative to the volumes predicted by the simple version of the Heckscher–Ohlin theory). However, we can go a step further. There is reason to believe that trade between *similar* countries may be much larger than this version leads us to believe. To see this point, it is important to understand the preference for variety. As a country grows richer, not only does its demand for certain types of commodities grow (such as cars and computers), but there is also an increase in the demand for *varieties* of goods. Thus some individuals may prefer similarly priced Hondas to Fords, whereas others prefer the American variety. Likewise, some citizens of France may well prefer Spanish wine, whereas the opposite may be true for some Spaniards.

Preference for variety that is manifested in the overall demand pattern of a rich country may give rise to a huge volume of trade between similar rich countries. It isn't that the pattern of overall preferences is different from one country to the other; it is that *within* each country, there are individuals who prefer different varieties of some given broad commodity (such as wine or cars). Large quantities of French wine may then be sold in Spain and large quantities of Spanish wine may be sold in France. It is therefore not surprising that trade across similarly placed developed countries may be substantial, and trade across developed and developing countries may not be as large as the theories studied thus far might predict.

16.3.4. Economies of scale

The presence of increasing returns may be a major source of international trade, even if all countries have the same technology and preferences (by this last requirement we exclude even the shifts in relative commodity demands induced by a change in income, the effects of which were analyzed in the previous section). It is easy enough to see how this works by means of an example.[10]

Our example considers two goods, just as before: call them ships and aircraft. There are two countries, E and W. We will assume that each country

---

[10] The model represented by this example is part of recent literature in international trade that traces its roots to the work of Dixit and Stiglitz [1977] and Lancaster [1975] in industrial organization, and then runs through the work of economists such as Ethier [1982], Helpman [1981], Krugman [1981], and Lancaster [1980]. See also Helpman and Krugman [1989] and Krugman [1995].

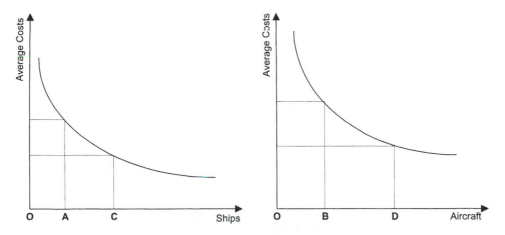

Figure 16.10. *Economies of scale in production and trade patterns.*

has *exactly* the same preference patterns for ships and aircraft, and in addition has the same technology for their production. The twist is that each of these industries will be assumed to display *economies of scale* in production; that is, we assume that the average costs of production declines with an expansion in production scale.[11]

Figure 16.10 depicts the average cost curves of both ships and aircrafts. As already indicated, these curves are downward sloping to reflect the assumption that unit costs decline with scale.

Now imagine that both countries are in a state of autarky. In that case they will have to produce their own ships and aircraft. There are limited resources to do so, of course. Although it is not necessary to do so, you could imagine here for the sake of concreteness that we are in a Ricardian world with a single factor of production—labor—being allocated between the two industries. Figure 16.10 marks out the (identical) domestic production levels in both countries. Each country produces *OA* ships and *OB* aircraft.

Now open up this scenario to trade. Note that because everything has been assumed to be identical, the relative prices of ships and aircraft must also be identical, so there appears to be no motivation for trade at all. However, a harder look at the diagram will reveal this to be a knife-edge state of affairs. If country *E*, for instance, tilts its production slightly more in favor of ships, while country *W* does the same with aircraft, it soon will be the case that *E* *appears* to have a comparative advantage in shipbuilding. This happens because the unit cost of shipbuilding will fall in country *E* relative to

[11] We have seen this before in more than one context. For instance, recall the QWERTY discussion in Chapter 5, where we assumed that a greater scale of activity reduces the individual cost of adoption of a technology.

country *W*, and this is where we use the assumption of increasing returns to scale.

Once this tilt is in place, it will magnify. Country *E* will inexorably slide toward specialization in shipbuilding, while *W* moves toward aircraft. Of course *E* does not need its excess of ships and *W* does not need its surfeit of aircraft, so *E* will export ships and *W* will export aircraft. *Thus trade may be viewed here as a way to concentrate the production of industries in some countries, to maximize the effect of increasing returns to scale.* We will return to this theme when we study regional free-trade agreements among developing countries (see Chapter 18).

The end result is that country *E* produces ships, say at the point *OC* in the left-hand panel of Figure 16.10, while country *B* produces aircraft at the point *OD* in the right-hand panel of Figure 16.10. An important point to appreciate is that *OC* typically *exceeds* twice *OA*, which represents world ship production under uncertainty, and *OD* exceeds twice *OB*, which represents world aircraft production in autarky. The reason is simple. Because both countries are able to harness the full power of increasing returns, unit costs are reduced globally, which is just another way of saying that productivity has been increased globally. This means that consumers have more income to spend on commodities, so that their total consumption must have increased relative to autarky.

Some observations are relevant here.

(1) For this model to make sense, there is no need to think of two completely different products such as ships and aircraft. One might imagine that the two goods are both *differentiated* products in the same industry (such as Boeing and Airbus). They would still be located in different countries in equilibrium, so that each country would exhibit two-way trade in the same product group. This is the phenomenon known as *interindustry trade*.

(2) Once we adopt this interpretation, it isn't hard to see how to integrate the Heckscher–Ohlin view of trade with trade in differentiated products. For instance, think of two product classes, call them *X* and *Y*, and two countries *A* and *B*. Product class *X* is capital-intensive relative to product class *Y*, and country *A* has a higher capital–labor ratio than *B*. In this case, the Heckscher–Ohlin theory tells us that country *A* will export *X* and import *Y*, and the opposite will be true for country *B*, but, in general, both countries produce *X* and *Y* (that is, complete specialization does not occur).

Now let us look a bit deeper. Imagine that each product class has several products in it, differentiated by characteristics and/or brand names. If each of these products is produced under conditions of increasing returns to scale, then although it is true that both countries *A* and *B* produce products in class *X*, it will be profitable for them to produce *different* products within each class. This happens for the same reason as the ships–aircraft example:

increasing returns is best manifested when production of each item is con-centrated in fewer locations (one location each in this special example). Thus country *A* will still be a *net* exporter of *X* products, but that will not stop it from importing other *X* products from *B*! We might think of this as the intraindustry component of trade, whereas the net trade in *X* and *Y* is the Heckscher–Ohlin component.

Note that under this interpretation, trade will continue even if both countries have the same capital–labor endowments, but there will be no Heckscher–Ohlin component: all trade will be intraindustry in this special case. At the other extreme, if the products in each class are perfectly ho-mogeneous, there will be no intraindustry trade: all trade will be of the Heckscher–Ohlin variety.

It is very easy to conceptually integrate the two views of trade into one broader framework.[12] Heckscher–Ohlin trade is a way to implicitly trade factors of production (embodied in goods), whereas trade in differentiated products under increasing returns handles the advantages of product con-centration.

(3) Are returns to scale internal to the firm, or external to the firm but somehow internal to the industry? For instance, if there are large setup costs in shipbuilding (quite apart from the variable cost in building each ship), then total average costs will decline with each ship. Now is it plausible to imagine that these economies (at the firm level) cannot be realized at the level of national demand? Perhaps. Companies such as Boeing are large suppliers of aircraft, and global demand (as opposed to restricted national demand) might well lower unit costs of production.

On the other hand, there may be returns to scale at the industry level, although each firm faces constant average and marginal costs of production. This is just the same as saying that there are positive externalities generated by each firm, that make themselves felt at the level of the industry. The fact that an engineering firm assimilates and modifies a foreign blueprint to adapt the technology to local conditions has implications not just for that firm, but for that industry as a whole. This firm has contributed to some industrywide stock of knowledge that lowers the cost to *other* firms.

Both these forms of returns to scale will be manifest in a diagram such as Figure 16.10, but they have different implications for the specific model of trade to be considered. In the first case, we need to draw on models of industry that are not based on perfect competition. There will be a few giant firms that dominate each industry, and the corresponding theory of trade will have to be modified to take account of the (perhaps limited) market power of each of these firms.

---

[12] See Krugman [1995] for a lucid exposition of this argument.

When returns are external to the firm, it is certainly logical to write down a model of trade based on perfect competition. Each firm would take international prices as given, but an expansion in production would reduce industrywise costs via the external economies thus generated. Such a story is very close to the one we told in our exposition. It illustrates the knife-edge nature of autarkic production levels (and composition) when there are increasing returns.

(4) Another explanation of trade in similar products is provided in the work of Brander [1981], where the argument is extremely spare in the sense that it relies on neither differentiated products nor increasing returns to scale nor Heckscher–Ohlin effects. Suppose that there are two identical industries in countries *A* and *B* that each produce the same homogeneous good. Under autarky, suppose that each good is produced monopolistically. Now if the two countries open up to trade, the industrialist in *A* will want to sell in market *B*, simply because monopolistic conditions of production there allow for a margin of profit for a rival. *At the same time*, his rival in country *B* will be looking to steal some of *A*'s domestic market. Thus it is possible that both industries export to the other country.[13] This creates two-way trade in the same product. Do not take the homogeneity of the product too literally: the important point is to note that monopolistic (or oligopolistic) power under autarky can give rise to trade, as firms try to erode the margins of their rivals.

(5) Observe that the preference-based story of the previous section is quite complementary to the current line of reasoning. It suggests that trade in similar products is likely to take place among similar countries. This is because preference patterns change with income, and two countries are therefore more likely to exhibit intra-industry trade when their per capita incomes are at comparable levels. The only difference is that in the preference-based story, we deliberately focused on particular types of products (so as not to have all kinds of different factors in the same model); that is, we assumed that some product varieties are almost *defined* by their country of origin: French wine is made in France, Brazilian coffee is grown in Brazil, and although Japanese cars are not necessarily made in Japan, there are aspects of their construction and setup that make them different from their American counterparts. This sort of "country identification" serves as a substitute for increasing returns, but otherwise, the two models are perfectly complementary.

(6) Finally, we note that intraindustry trade and Heckscher–Ohlin trade have very different implications for the distribution of gains from trade. This is a topic that we will take up in the two chapters to come.

[13] Brander and Krugman [1983] called this "reciprocal dumping."

16.4. Summary

This chapter begins our study of international trade. We started with a discussion of world trading patterns, and focused on developing countries. We noted that export volumes have grown rapidly the world over, and that this is also true of developing countries. Particularly noteworthy is the dramatic expansion in exports from East Asia. However, much of the trade expansion in commodity exports was eaten up by declining commodity prices in the 1980s: developed countries still account for the bulk of trade.

Developing countries largely export *primary products*: foodstuffs, fuels, and minerals, but this pattern of primary exports is undergoing rapid change, especially in Asia and Latin America. *Manufactured exports* (textiles, light machinery, toys, footwear, and some sophisticated technical products) are now a principal component of trade in several developing countries. In practically every category of items, manufactured exports have significantly increased, but there is a long way to go: in 1990, the share of manufactured exports from LDCs (as a fraction of the world total) was significantly below 20%.

Trade among developed countries has grown in relative terms, which suggests that although a significant component of trade is trade in different products among very different countries, trade in similar products is of great importance as well. This observation gets further support from the fact that developed countries import manufactures in proportions that are very similar to those of developing countries. In other words, the world picture is not one of developed countries *only* exporting manufactures and *only* importing primary products.

We then turned to *theories* of trade. We introduced the fundamental concept of *comparative advantage*. A country will export those products that it produces cheaply *relative* to other countries and import those products that are *relatively* costly to produce. In particular, if only one input (say labor) is used to produce products, then even if country A produces *every* good with less labor than country B, it will still import some goods from country B. Country B may have an "absolute disadvantage" in every product, but it will still export the products in which it has the least relative disadvantage. We discussed this important idea in detail using a simple model, known as the *Ricardian model* of trade.

The Ricardian model creates comparative advantage by positing differences in technology across countries that give rise to different costs of production. However, differences in technology, though sufficient, are not necessary. Suppose there are two factors of production: capital and labor. Suppose that good X is produced using more capital-intensive methods than good Y. Then if country A has a relative abundance of capital, it will be in a better position to produce good X, because that good uses more intensively the factor that is in relative abundance in country A. Thus differences in factor endowment, coupled with different production technologies across *goods*, create differences in comparative advantage. These issues were studied in the *Heckscher–Ohlin* model of trade. This model predicts trade across dissimilar countries and in dissimilar products: for instance, it says that labor-abundant developing countries will export labor-intensive products such as food and clothing, whereas capital-abundant developed countries will export capital-intensive products such as machinery and computers. In particular, the basic Heckscher–Ohlin model predicts the most trade across countries that are very different in their factor endowments. As we have seen, this sort of trade does happen, but it is not necessarily the dominant form of trade in the world economy.

One reason for more trade among similar countries is that preferences vary systematically with income levels. For instance, it is true that India may have a comparative advantage in rice, but rice also occupies a larger fraction of the consumption basket, because people are poorer. The net effect of this situation will be to dampen rice exports from India (relative to the simple Heckscher–Ohlin predictions). Thus systematic changes in preference patterns with incomes tend to bring down trade across dissimilar countries, provided that the same goods are demanded more even as they are produced in greater abundance, as income changes.

We then turned to a different set of reasons for trade among similar countries. Suppose that products are produced under conditions of increasing returns; then a large chunk of trade will result from the fact that it is efficient to locate each of the products in one production center. In particular, products that belong to the same product line (such as two different brands of aircraft) may be located in two different countries, and there will be trade in similar products (or *intraindustry* trade, if our classification of "industry" is broad enough, such as "aircraft"). We showed that it is possible to extend this model in a way so that it can embed Hecksher–Ohlin effects as well as the increasing returns effect within product groups. We also noted that increasing returns is not necessary for the argument. Sometimes product varieties are peculiar to countries, such as Swiss cheese or French wine. If individuals in all countries have a love of variety (or equivalently, display a diversity in tastes), trade in similar products (e.g., wine) will occur.

This sort of argument also suggests that intraindustry trade is likely to occur among countries at similar levels of development. The implications of this observation will be explored in the chapters to come.

Exercises

■ (1) Why might an increase in trade volume not correspond to an increase in hard-currency earnings? Illustrate your argument by using the example of a *devaluation*, which is a deliberate cheapening of the *exchange rate*—the rate at which domestic currency can be exchanged for foreign currency, say dollars.

(a) Why does a devaluation tend to increase the exports of a country, expressed in the local currency or in physical units?

(b) Discuss when the devaluation can raise export earnings denominated in the *foreign* currency. You can profitably use the concept of price elasticity of demand in your discussion.

▪ (2) Consider the Ricardian model of trade described in this chapter. Use Table 16.5 to answer the questions that follow.

(a) Show that if the relative price of computers to rice were any amount smaller than 2:3, country N would only produce rice. Likewise, show that country N will only produce computers if the relative price of computers to rice were to exceed 2:3.

(b) What accounts for this "knife-edge" behavior? Contrast it with the Heckscher-Ohlin model, where the production of both goods is consistent with a whole range of relative prices [see problem (4)].

(c) Now carefully redo part (a) for country S, showing that the autarkic price of computers to rice must be 2:1. Combining these two exercises, argue that if *both* goods are consumed once, the economies are opened to trade and the international relative price of computers to rice must lie between 2:3 and 2:1.

▪ (3) Here is another exercise on the Ricardian model: If less resources are used in country N to produce each of the goods, how is it that country S gets to export one of the goods? The answer is that country N must pay its factor of production (labor in our example) a higher wage.

To appreciate this point, suppose that both countries have a common currency, say dollars. Now we know that not only the *relative* international prices of the commodities must be the same, but so must be the *absolute* level of each of these prices (otherwise the country with the lower price would not have any of that product sold in it).

Now say that the equilibrium international price is $100 for both a sack of rice and a computer (so that the relative price is 1:1). Solve for the incomes of labor in the two countries, given that all sales revenues are paid out as wages. Use Table 16.5, of course. Which country has the higher wage income?

▪ (4) Understand why the Heckscher–Ohlin model does not lead to complete specialization, in contrast to the Ricardian framework. Take the car–textiles example studied in this chapter. Recall that in our example, each of these goods is produced by capital and labor, but cars use capital more intensively.

Now an increase in the relative price of cars will cause more resources to go into car production.

(a) Show that this flow of resources will cause the *ratio* of capital to wage income to rise.

(b) Which industry will be more adversely affected by the change in part (a)?

(c) Now combine the observations in parts (a) and (b) to show that textile production will still be profitable, though the total production of textiles will decline. Supplement your understanding by drawing production possibility frontiers, relative price lines, and the corresponding production points.

■ (5) If poorer people consume a greater proportion of those products which are produced using a high intensity of unskilled labor (relative to physical and human capital), show that international trade between rich and poor countries will be lower than that predicted by the Heckscher–Ohlin theory.

■ (6) Two countries, *A* and *B*, identical in all respects, each produce two goods, bread and wine, using a single input, labor. The production of each good is carried out under constant returns to scale. But a higher economy-wide production of any of the goods has positive externalities for individual production of that good: the amount of labor required to produce one unit of each good depends negatively on the *overall* production of that good in the economy. Bread and wine are demanded in equal proportions in each of the countries, irrespective of relative price.

(a) For a *given* aggregate level of production of bread and wine in the economy as a whole, sketch the production possibilities of a single producer and show that this "individual" production possibility frontier must be a straight line.

(b) Now draw the production possibility frontier for the economy as a whole. Contrast the shape of this frontier with that of the individual production possibility frontier.

(c) Show that international trade between the two countries can lead to three types of equilibria: (i) *A* produces all the bread and *B* produces all the wine, (ii) *B* produces all the bread and *A* produces all the wine, and (iii) *A* and *B* both produce both goods in exactly the same proportions. Discuss why the third equilibrium is "unstable" in the sense that a small change in the composition of production by any one country will lead the world economy progressively away from (iii). In this context, discuss how initial historical accidents can lead to the establishment of either equilibrium (i) or (ii).

Chapter 17

Trade Policy

The theory of comparative advantage appears to have a simple policy implication: there should be no such thing as trade policy or interventions to affect the directions of trade that are generated by the free market. The reason is that trade effectively expands the production possibility frontiers of each participating country. The easiest way to think about this concept is to think of trade as an alternative production activity, where quantities of some commodities (exports) are transformed into quantities of other commodities (imports). The more trade there is, the larger the number of these additional "transformation options." How can more be worse than less?

Yet the world today is riddled with all kinds of barriers to trade. Indeed, important global institutions such as the European Community (now the European Union) and the North American Free Trade Agreement would pale into insignificance were it not for the fact that they are set in a background of trade barriers all over the world. Trade barriers (of varying intensities) are still very much the norm, rather than the exception.

This brings us to two questions of fundamental importance. First, why is it that, faced with the apparently beneficial law of comparative advantage, countries seek to intervene in their patterns of trade and guide it in directions that are not spontaneously chosen by the market? Second, what are the forces that bring some groups of countries together to form mutual spheres of free trade, while maintaining or increasing trade barriers with the rest of the world?

These two questions can be classified under two headings: (1) *unilateral* policies pursued by individual countries and (2) *multilateral* policies followed by groups of countries. We take up each of these in turn. This chapter considers unilateral trade policies.

17.1. Gains from trade?

17.1.1. Overall gains and distributive effects

The classical gains-from-trade argument

A natural way to think about international trade is that it permits an expansion of the production possibility set. In the Ricardian and Heckscher–Ohlin models, we think of one good as being transformed into another in one of two ways. The transformation may be *domestic*, that is, inputs are taken away from one good and applied to the production of another (this gave us the autarkic production possibility frontier). Alternatively, the transformation may be international: one good is exported in exchange for the import of another. Thus trade may be thought of as a way to extend production possibilities. With trade in different commodities that are not locally produced, such as Spanish cava or Havana cheroots, we can also think in terms of expansion of production possibilities: new commodities can now be "produced" by the trading countries.

All of our discussions so far boil down to a single maxim: whenever the *rate* at which one commodity can be domestically transformed to another differs domestically and internationally, there is scope for gainful expansion of production. The domestic rate is captured by the slope of the production possibility frontier; the international rate is just the international relative price.

Thus it appears that trade can never be harmful to a country: it permits all that went before and then some. Note well, in addition, that the argument for the gains from trade is *independent* of whether *other* countries are following a free-trade policy themselves. This is easy enough to see if you go back to the argument of the previous paragraphs and observe that the only information we required about the rest of the world is the international relative price of different commodities, and not whether such prices were arrived at by free trade elsewhere.

The distribution of gains from trade

At the same time, it is important to keep in mind that the *potential* gains from trade should not necessarily be equated with *actual* gains to all groups concerned. Such an equation neglects the *distribution* of trading benefits within a country. This is the focus of the present section.

Let's go back to the simple Ricardian model. In that model, there is only one input of production—labor—so there is no distinction between overall gains and the distribution of those gains. If labor gains, as it surely does in that model, then everybody gains, because there is no other factor of production that loses. However, this is not the case once we admit additional factors of production, as in the Heckscher–Ohlin model.

To see what happens in the Heckscher–Ohlin model, let's return to the example with two countries, N and S, and two commodities, cars and textiles. Recall in our model that N produced cars and imported textiles, and that cars are more capital-intensive than textiles. Now imagine the process that occurs when N is opened up to trade with S, and the economy begins to produce more cars. The following sequence of events will occur:

(1) Faced with a profitable international price in car production, N will expand car production and contract textile production.

(2) To produce cars, N will demand more capital and labor. These inputs will be released by the textile industry as it contracts.

(3) However, textiles will release labor and capital (as it shrinks) in the "wrong" proportions relative to the needs of car production. This follows from the fact that car production is more capital-intensive. Specifically, textiles will release a higher proportion of labor to capital than the proportion required in the car industry.

(4) This imbalance can be remedied if car production were to become more labor-intensive and, indeed, if textile production were to become more labor-intensive as well![1] The former will aid in soaking up the excess release of labor, and the latter will help to cut down the excess release of labor.

(5) However, step [4] can happen only if individual producers face the incentives to become more labor-intensive, and this, in turn, requires that the wage rate on labor must *fall* relative to commodity prices, while the rental rate on capital must *rise* relative to commodity prices.

(6) In conclusion, owners of labor are hurt by opening up N to trade, whereas owners of capital gain.

Thus we see that the gains from trade, in the sense of an improvement for all concerned, cannot simply be inferred from the expansion of production possibilities. It is certainly true that there is an overall increase in the availability of goods and services, but we already know enough of the theory of income distribution to realize that this cannot automatically be linked to an increase in overall welfare. In our example, labor loses and capital gains.

To complete the argument, we need to know how factor endowments are held by different people in society. If every individual owns the same combination of inputs (say, capital and labor in the same proportions), then even if particular factors gain and lose, the fortunes of every individual must move together. However, if factor endowments are held in sufficiently different proportions, then some individuals will lose and others will gain.

This is not a mere theoretical curiosity. It is possible to argue, for instance, that considerations such as these lay at the heart of the debate underlying the North American Free Trade Agreement recently concluded between the

---

[1] This appears to be an impossibility: how can *all* industries become more labor-intensive at the same time? The answer is that the *mix* of industry is shifting toward the more capital-intensive sector, cars. The two effects cancel, keeping the aggregate demand for each input equal to its supply. As an example, imagine that there are two basketball teams, the Dwarfs and the Giants. Each member of the Dwarfs is shorter than each member of the Giants, so that the average height of the Giants is certainly higher than that of the Dwarfs. Now suppose the tallest member of the Dwarfs gets recruited by the Giants. In that case the average heights of both Dwarfs and Giants must come down.

United States, Canada, and Mexico, which we discuss in more detail in Chapter 18. There were fears that opening up trade with labor-intensive Mexico would lead to a lowering of U.S. wages, thus hurting U.S. labor. More generally, any factor of production that is intensively used in some commodity in the absence of trade is likely to be hurt when trade results in increased imports of that commodity. The owners of such factors or industries invariably lobby for protection.

Protectionist lobbies that create restricted trade will receive detailed examination in Chapter 18, when we examine multilateral trade policy.

17.1.2. Overall losses from trade?

Comparative advantage is a useful concept, but it is imperative to realize that it is a *static* concept—a notion that determines the advantageous exports of a country *at any one point of time*. Consider the Heckscher–Ohlin theory, for instance, which states that a country should export those products that use intensively those inputs that are present in that country in relative abundance. However, "relative abundance" is a notion that pertains to the here and now. A country that is short on physical capital and has huge quantities of unskilled labor is not condemned to always be in that position. By accumulating capital, it can reverse this situation over time. A country that has a low endowment of human capital relative to its total labor endowment can change this state of affairs by following an appropriate education policy. In turn, such a policy can alter its comparative advantage.

We can agree with the foregoing statements and yet argue that there is no need for a separate *trade* policy as such. Why not export peanuts, bananas, or coffee as long as the comparative advantage in such commodities persists? If later, through some judicious policy of capital accumulation or investment in education, a country can alter its comparative advantage, then it will have earned its right *then*, but not *now*, to export more sophisticated commodities. Meanwhile, it is best to leave the manufacture and export of "high-tech" goods to the developed world.

This is an argument worth considering in some detail, but it may be an incorrect argument all the same. Consider several aspects.

Catching up

The first point to consider is that a developing country that follows the dictates of static comparative advantage may never get into a situation where it makes the later transformation to a high-capital society. Think of primary products that we consume directly or indirectly, and are produced and exported in large quantities from the developing world. All kinds of food products are included in this description, such as bananas, tea, or coffee, as well as products that we indirectly consume as inputs in other consumption goods, such as jute. One origin of the word "primary" is that these products represent our primary needs, food being the leading example. Our first expenditures out of income are on these products.

Here is the flip side to the story. As our budget expands, the *fraction* of income that we allocate to these goods has a tendency to fall. With food items, this well-documented behavior is known as *Engel's law*, and it probably applies to other primaries as well. It follows that as world incomes grow, the demand for primaries grows as well, but possibly *not at the same rate*. This is because the growth in demand is tempered by a reduction in the budget *share* of these goods as we move away to the consumption of several other products.

The implication of all this is that there may be a tendency for the terms of trade to decline against developing countries who stay in the business of exporting manufactured products. This means that in *real* terms, the incomes of these countries do not grow as quickly as they might appear to do in the local currency.[2]

The long-run tendency for the terms of trade to turn against developing countries, even developing countries that chiefly export primary products, is in dispute, but there is little doubt that over the decade of the 1980s, there was a major crash in primary prices, and this was clearly reflected in declines in the terms of trade of developing countries, *even without focusing on those that export primary products*. See Figure 17.1 for the story over the period 1980–93.

A decline in the price of a country's exports means simply that to maintain the same rate of economic growth vis-à-vis the developed world, that country will have to save a correspondingly higher fraction of its income. This may be a tall order, and even if it is feasible to carry out, the costs are high.

Having said this, consider a counterargument. Let us agree that there has been some decline in primary prices—over the 1980s, at least. At the same time, it is the case that a reliance on current comparative advantage, other things being equal, brings in greater income *today*. Thus we have a situation where large amounts of economic revenue can be earned today, but at the cost of a future slowdown in growth rates of the very same revenue. If this is what rational individuals in the market desire, so be it. They should internalize the losses of future generations, and if they can predict these declines in the terms of trade, they should move away from such exports. Why bring in the government?

This counterargument is on shaky ground. It does imply that by comparing the welfare of future generations with the welfare of current generations, we are accepting the trade-offs chosen by the market.

---

[2] An argument that also has been advanced, usually in tandem with this one, is that primary product prices also have a tendency to fluctuate quite widely. These observations are closely connected with the work of Singer [1950] and Prebisch [1952, 1959].

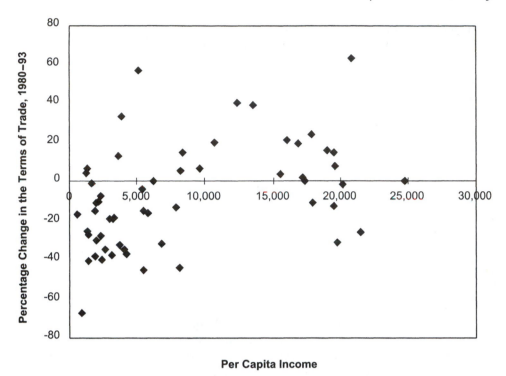

Figure 17.1. Terms of trade and per capita income, 1980–93. Source: World Development Report (World Bank [1995]).

There is no good conceptual reason, however, to accept the dictates of the market. An enlightened government may believe that future generations deserve more weight than private individuals give them through their actions. It may be that, faced with the complexities of coping with their current problems, individuals place too little weight on the long-run implications of their choices for future generations.

Mind you, this is not an argument that governments know better than individuals. It may simply be that individuals as social beings "know better" than individuals in their private sphere. In many cases, individuals as social beings empower their governments with the ability to coordinate their actions in a way that they feel is relevant for the social good, whereas at the same time they might not take the same action in isolation, in their private sphere.

Capital markets

Imagine, for the sake of argument, that the discussion of the previous paragraphs is invalid. In other words, suppose that we believe that individuals do place the "correct" weights on future generations.

Translated into the present context, this means that producers (such as farmers) in a developing country understand and correctly forecast the lack of long-term potential in exporting primary products to developed countries. They are worried either for their own sake or for the sake of future generations. Although they are currently engaged in this business, they would like to switch to another with greater growth potential. Can they?

For various reasons that we have discussed in Chapters 7 and 14, producers may not be able to find the required capital to make the transition. Faced with the absence of a smoothly functioning capital market, it is natural to expect that whatever economic activity is currently being carried out will acquire an artificial longevity, simply because radical changes are barred by the absence of a credit market. Effectively, what this does is create a bias against the future, and there is scope for trade policy in such a situation.

Positive externalities and coordination failure

Even with perfect capital markets, individual entrepreneurs may be wary of making the transition to non-primary exports simply because complementary factors are not present. We may count among such complementary factors a pool of scientists and engineers, adequate infrastructure, or a work force educated in basic skills. These are precisely the kinds of "coordination failures" that we examined in Chapter 5. No single individual can build these necessary nationwide reserves of individuals, facilities, and skills, yet the *joint* action of several individuals can. We have here, therefore, a classic case of *complementarities*. As we have seen several times, positive externalities usually bring with them multiple equilibria. In one of them, individuals remain at the status quo, with a low level of investment in the socially productive activity. In another, they move over to a new regime, reinforced by the complementary actions of one another.

Countries that export primary products can often be thought of as being stuck in the first equilibrium. The infrastructure of such countries, such as ports, the location of highways, railroads, and the allocation of power, may be intimately geared toward the export of one or two primary crops. A pool of trained scientific personnel, or simply an educated work force, may be missing. In the face of such specific facilities (and the absence of others), no individual entrepreneur will wish to initiate the grand step of socially beneficial transformation.[3]

Taking this argument a step further, consider a particularly germane example of an industry in which there may be enormous externalities to the

---

[3] The reason for this should be well known from your basic economics training. Components such as infrastructure lead to huge externalities that benefit large segments of the population. At the same time, it may be impossible to get all individuals to adequately pay for the benefits they receive. Thus these public goods usually will be undersupplied by private entrepreneurs.

rest of society: the high-technology sector. At this point, we simply do not know all the possible implications of high technology and how these implications will spill over to the rest of the economy. While the developed countries fight it out over the leading high-tech sectors—biotechnology, microelectronics, telecommunications, robotics, and the like—developing countries do not want to be far behind. A new development in biotechnology may fundamentally change the computer industry, yet no one may be sure of exactly what the change is going to be or which direction it will come from, so there cannot very well be a market to stimulate this change in advance! Remember from our earlier discussions that in the presence of markets for all contingencies, there is no such thing as an externality. Sectors (such as high technology) in which the payoffs are uncertain, not only in their values but in their incidence on other sectors, typically are lacking in many of these contingent markets, which is all the more reason why market forces alone in developing countries will possibly create underinvestment in these sectors.

High technology is only an extreme example of the externality problem. Societies that do not produce and compete in manufactures are unlikely to develop a climate or an environment in which manufacturing industries are spontaneously generated. More generally, a nation may feel the need to industrialize simply because it is accepted that in industrialization lies the key to world recognition, a greater and more decisive role in the international community, and the prestige that comes from indigenous scientific and technological discovery. These are externalities that no individual can conceivably internalize in her own actions. Of course there may be many individuals, governments, and interest groups (and certainly "scientific" economists) in developed countries who think that developing countries are best off not entering the fray, but their developing-country counterparts may not agree, and that is that.[4]

Income and wealth distribution

The arguments so far are based on the possible failure of the export sector of the economy. There are considerations that apply to the import side as well. In particular, if there are no restrictions on imports, it is obvious that the structure and composition of *imports* will depend in large part on the prevailing income distribution. Although individuals as social beings might care about the development process (captured, for instance, by the way they

---

[4] Economic arguments that emphasize the distortions that trade policy surely brings simply fail to incorporate these considerations. The fact that groups like the G-7 regularly meet and make decisions on world matters that affect all countries only adds fuel to the desire for industrialization. So does the fact that industrially powerful countries can take extreme unilateral actions (such as protective measures with or without the consent of multilateral bodies like GATT) to further their own interests. In the words of Carr [1951, p. 92] "industrialization is the sincerest tribute that ex-colonial countries can pay to the West."

vote), it is only reasonable to suppose that in their private actions they will make what they consider to be the best use of their money. Thus individuals with large incomes will demand imported cars, expensive wine and cheese, Barbie dolls, and surround sound, just as people of their incomes do in any other part of the world. This generates a large demand for consumer imports, drives up the price of foreign exchange, and makes it difficult to acquire imported inputs that may be deemed fundamentally necessary for the development process.

We might say, if this is what the market demands, what is wrong with that? Such a sentiment represents a particularly uncritical belief in the invisible hand. As we have emphasized again and again in this text, the market is very good at allocating resources, *given the existing distribution of income and wealth*, but there is no reason why the distribution itself should be treated as appropriate or "just." Thus an argument of the kind made in the previous paragraph is perfectly justifiable provided it is felt that (i) the existing distribution of income is somehow suboptimal or excessively unequal, and (ii) consequently, the market undervalues those items of greater significance from the point of view of society as a whole. In such situations we have another case for trade policy.

Large-country tariffs

A well-known argument for restricted trade comes from the theory of the "optimal tariff." Suppose that a country is "large" in the sense that the quantity of its imports of some commodity influences the international price of that commodity. Put another way, the country as a whole faces an upward-sloping supply curve for the good it imports. Then an import tariff might benefit the country. This "monopoly" argument for trade also relies on the imperfection of a market: the international market for some good is effectively not competitive, at least at the level of aggregation that the government of a single country (or group of countries). See the exercises at the end of this chapter for an illustration of this argument.

All of the foregoing topics except "Catching Up" are actually special cases of what is called the second-best theory of trade policy. If all markets are perfect, the potential gains-from-trade argument is faultless. However, some markets may be missing. For instance, imagine a world in which the market for pollution control is absent, so that industries that create pollution effectively impose an externality on others. In such a world, it is possible that opening up to trade may expand a polluting industry and lower national welfare overall. Thus the topic "Capital Markets" builds on the idea that capital markets are missing and, because of this, individual investors are unable to make ideal decisions about what to export. Likewise, the topic "Positive Externalities and Coordination Failure" is also built on a market failure: the lack of markets to reward industries for the positive technological spillovers that they generate. Similarly, the item "Income and Wealth Distribution" has a missing market as well. If the wealth or income distribution is felt to be wrong, then appropriate redistribution should be carried out using suitable lump sum taxes and transfers, which are nondistortionary. However, this depends on the ability of the government to properly identify the wealthy and the poor, which leads to severe informational and incentive problems. Indeed, this is also the reason why the potential gains from trade cannot be equated to the actual gains for all concerned. The information needed to carry out compensating transfers ex post may be limited.

17.2. Trade policy: Import substitution

We consider, then, the possible instruments available to a country that seeks to restrict or modify the pattern of its international trade in some way. This may be due in part to special interest lobbies that arise from the distributional effects of trade described earlier, or it may be that the country wishes to break free of what it considers the stranglehold of primary production (that is, it recognizes the possibility of overall losses from its current pattern of trade, as described earlier). Such countries seek to develop a new industrial base. They recognize, perhaps, that the creation of such a base will provoke the formation of a new highly skilled work force. They feel that such a work force will, in turn, yield its dividends as new industries grow to exploit the talents of these newly found endowments.

In short, the government of this country may be driven by some or all of the considerations that we discussed in the previous section. The question is, what instruments are available to it?

It is fairly evident that in the initial stages of these new developments, markets have to be captured and products sold, not simply through *existing* competitiveness (which, by definition, isn't there), but through a process of direct government intervention that creates an *artificial* competitiveness. There are several ways in which this climate of artificial competitiveness can be fostered.

For instance, many countries turn to their own domestic markets for the required target practice. After all, it is far easier to create this artificial advantage on one's home ground. In fact, the easiest way to do this is to make it more difficult for foreign firms to operate there. This is done by erecting various barriers to the importation of foreign goods and substituting for these goods by producing them domestically. Such a policy is known, therefore, as one of *import substitution*.

17.2.1. Basic concepts

The substitution of imports can take many forms, and they can run the gamut from outright bans on certain classes of imports to discriminatory treatment for domestic producers of particular goods. There are several considerations that are characteristic of an import-substitution policy.

Unequal treatment of imported goods

We already noted that import-substitution policies often are aimed at creating an atmosphere of domestic competition in some selected industries. We also saw that there may be a case (on the grounds of inappropriate income distribution) for the restriction of some consumer imports simply to provide foreign exchange for activities that are deemed to have a higher social value.

It will be no surprise, then, to see that import-substitution policies often treat imported goods differently (that is, there isn't a uniformly high wall that is raised on all imports). Some key to-be-developed sectors may receive high protection. Additionally, it is likely that *production* inputs and imported *consumer* goods will be treated quite differently. The former can often be imported under a quota at relatively low tariff rates; the latter are often banned outright or are permitted to be imported under extremely high tariff rates.

Tariffs and quotas

The actual form that domestic protection takes is often a mix of tariffs and quotas. Let us first define these concepts carefully, and then we will obtain a sense of the possibly differential impacts of these two instruments. An (ad valorem) *tariff* is a percentage that is applied to the value of an imported item, with the resulting sum of money going to the government. Thus if the tariff rate on stereo systems is 50%, and you import a stereo system worth $1,000, you will have to pay a duty of $500 to the government. What a tariff does, then, is raise the effective price of a commodity above international levels. The stereo effectively costs you $1,500. A tariff also brings in revenue to the government.

Because the effective price of the import is now higher, a tariff serves as an instrument of import substitution. Stereo manufacturers within the country perhaps incur costs of $1,400 putting together a stereo of equivalent quality. Without the tariff, they would simply go out of business. In the presence of the tariff, they can flourish in the domestic market. The potential import has been *substituted* by domestic production.

A *quota* is the stipulation of a maximum quantity on a particular good, above which no more of that good can be imported into the country. It is possible (and indeed, often happens) that a quota can be combined with a

tariff. Thus, for instance, a tariff may not be levied on imports of a good up
to some maximum limit, after which there is not an outright ban on imports
but a high tariff rate.

Tariffs and quotas typically vary from one commodity to another. For
instance, an imported input that is needed for domestic production might
be treated quite differently from one that fulfils the consumption needs of
high-income groups.

Exchange rates

A fallout of import substitution is often an exchange rate that is *overvalued*
relative to the rate that would be obtained in a world of free trade. Let's make
sure that we understand just what this means. An *exchange rate* is simply a
price at which foreign currency can be exchanged for domestic currency. For
instance, exchange rates may be expressed as the number of units of domestic
currency (peso, peseta, rupee, rupiah) needed to purchase one U.S. dollar.

Exchange rates are prices, and like all prices, considerations of demand
and supply weigh heavily in their determination. Here is the simplest story
that one can tell about exchange rates. Imagine that there are only two
currencies—the peso and the dollar—and that there are only two countries—
Mexico and the United States. Mexico imports some goods from the United
States; the United States imports some goods from Mexico. Now, we can
think of Mexico's demand for *imports* as generating an overall demand for
dollars. These are simply the dollars that will be used to pay for the imports. The greater the demand for imports, the greater the implicit demand
for dollars. On the other hand, when the United States demands imports
from Mexico, this induces a *supply* of dollars, the currency in which U.S.
consumers pay for the imports.

Note here that we could have equivalently conducted this analysis in
terms of the supply of and demand for pesos. In this two-country world, the
behavior in one currency market simply mirrors behavior in the other.

Observe that both the derived demand for dollars and the supply of
dollars depend intimately on the exchange rate. If more pesos are required in
exchange for the dollar (which is like an increase in the price of the dollar),
Mexicans will lower their demand for U.S. goods, which now seem more
expensive to them. The implicit demand for dollars will therefore decline.
As for U.S. citizens, Mexican goods will appear to be cheaper, so we can
predict a rise in the demand for Mexican goods. What this actually does to
the implied supply of dollars is uncertain, however. You can easily see two
effects at work. One is the fact that demand for Mexican goods goes up;
the other is the fact that less dollars are needed to buy the same quantity
as before. The net outcome depends on the *price elasticity of U.S. demand for*

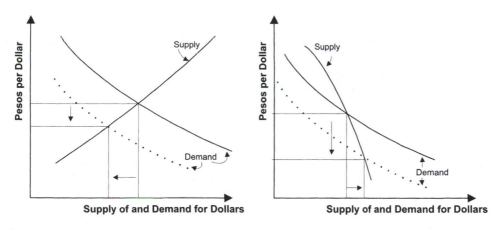

Figure 17.2. Equilibrium exchange rates.

Mexican products. Using elementary microeconomics, you should be able to deduce that if the price elasticity exceeds unity, then a decline in Mexican prices will lead to greater dollar expenditure. If the price elasticity falls short of unity, then dollar expenditure will actually fall (even though the demand for Mexican goods has indeed gone up).

Figure 17.2 combines these observations. The vertical axis represents pesos per dollar (which as we've noted is akin to the price of the dollar). The horizontal axis represents the supply of and demand for dollars. As we saw before, the demand for dollars in the international market is downward sloping. The slope of the supply function depends, as we noted, on the price elasticity of U.S. demand for Mexican products. If the slope is positive, as in the left-hand panel of Figure 17.2, then we have standard supply and demand curves that determine the equilibrium *exchange rate.* If the slope of the supply curve is negative, as in the right-hand panel, then we have a somewhat unusual demand–supply picture. Nevertheless, the equilibrium exchange rate is determined in exactly the same way in the two cases—by the intersection of the two curves.[5]

Now it is easy to see how an attempt at import substitution can affect the exchange rate. Continuing in the vein of the earlier example, suppose that Mexico imposes tariffs and/or quotas on U.S. imports. This policy has the effect of reducing the demand for imports at every exchange rate. This notion captured by a leftward shift of the demand curve for dollars to the

[5] The figure deliberately avoids a third possibility—that the supply curve is not only "perversely" sloped, but in fact so much so that it cuts the demand curve "from below." In this case the intersection of the supply and demand curves thus described is not "stable." A small movement in the exchange rate in either direction progressively leads away from the original equilibrium point, not back to it. It can be seen easily, however, that U.S. demand for Mexican imports cannot be price inelastic at *all* prices, however high. In other words, "stable" equilibria such as those considered in Figure 17.2 must always exist.

dotted lines in Figure 17.2. The equilibrium exchange rate rises or *appreciates*, in the sense that less pesos are needed to buy a dollar in the foreign
exchange market. This makes Mexican goods more expensive. If the demand
for Mexican goods is price elastic, as in the left-hand side of Figure 17.2, this
leads to a loss in dollar export revenue. The total dollar value of imports
obviously declines as well.

There is the possibility that the demand for Mexican goods is indeed
price *in*elastic. In that case, the right-hand side of Figure 17.2 applies and
the dollar value of Mexican exports climbs. However, is this case likely? We
must drop the fiction of just two countries to assess this possibility. With
most goods there are alternative countries who can step in to fill the gap, at
least with close substitutes. The larger the number of alternatives, the more
likely it is that the demand for the products of a *particular* country will be
highly sensitive to a change in price. It is reasonable, then, to assume, that
the left-hand side of Figure 17.2 does a good job capturing how exchange
rates and total dollar trade adjust in the face of import substitution.

17.2.2. More detail

Thus far, we have discussed three basic features of import substitution:
(1) different imports are likely to be treated differently, and this is especially
true of producer versus consumer goods, (2) tariffs and quotas are used in
the effort to decrease imports, and (3) import substitution most likely causes
the exchange rate to appreciate to a level that is above the market-clearing
free-trade rate. Our task now is to go over this ground in more detail.

How tariffs and quotas work

Figure 17.3 describes the effect of placing a tariff on a good. Supply and demand curves are drawn for this good, but remember, this may or may not be
a final consumption good. If it is, then the supply and demand curves have
the usual interpretation. If it is an intermediate good for use in production,
then the demand curve is to be interpreted as the derived demand for that
input.

The international price of the good is p^*. At this price, domestic supply
feeds only OA of the total demand OB. The rest, AB, is imported. Now let
us suppose that a tariff of $t\%$ is imposed. This has the effect of raising the
international price (as perceived by buyers, inclusive of the tariff) to the level
$p^*(1 + t/100)$, as shown in Figure 17.3. Total demand now falls to OD, but
domestic supply is now larger, at the level OC. It is precisely in this sense
that domestic producers are encouraged to produce the good.

Imports fall to CD. Note that with a high enough tariff, imports will
disappear altogether. This will happen for any tariff that takes prices beyond

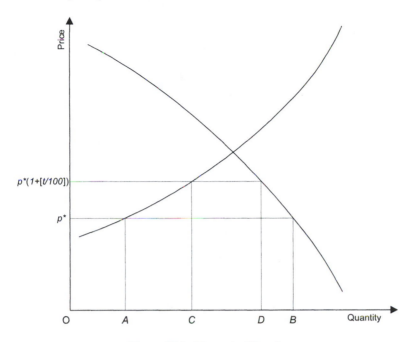

Figure 17.3. How a tariff works.

the *domestic* market-clearing price for that good. Such tariffs are referred to as *prohibitive*, for obvious reasons.

There are three immediate effects of the tariff. First, buyers lose: they pay higher prices. Second, sellers gain: they obtain higher prices. Third, the government obtains tariff revenue. We will return to a more detailed discussion of these "welfare effects" in the next topic. Before we go on to these, however, let us take a look at how quotas work.

Refer to Figure 17.4 in what follows. This diagram replicates precisely the same initial situation as Figure 17.3; that is, *OA* units are bought from domestic sources and the rest, *AB*, are imported. For the purpose of comparison with tariffs we are now going to impose a particular quota. Recall that the amount imported after the imposition of the tariff *t* was *CD* (see Figure 17.3). Let us choose precisely this quota: buyers are permitted to import up to *CD* units, duty-free; then they must buy the rest from the domestic market. To see the effect of the quota, Figure 17.4 marks off a length *EB* equal to the amount *CD*. In words, this amount of demand is a "handout" to buyers at the international price. What will the "residual demand curve" look like?

In the simplest case that we consider, the residual demand curve will slide inward by precisely the amount *EB* at every price (after all, this part of

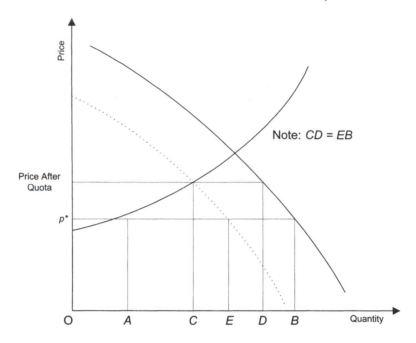

Figure 17.4. How a quota works.

the demand has already been met).[6] Now look at the equilibrium domestic price thus generated. It is just the same as $p^*(1 + t/100)$, where t is the tariff considered in the earlier case! Indeed, not only is the new domestic price the same as the old price plus tariff, the domestic production levels are the same as well and so is the amount of imports.

This observation is a simplified demonstration of the *equivalence of quotas and tariffs*. A tariff can be mimicked by a quota. Likewise, turning the preceding sequence of arguments around, a quota can be mimicked by a tariff.

However, is *everything* the same? Not really. In the first case, tariff revenues were generated and these went into the hands of the government. In the second case, the implicit revenues flow as a bonus into the hands of the buyers, who were permitted the luxury of importing a certain number of units duty-free. To check that the implied subsidy is the same, note that the total money value of the subsidy is the difference between the new domestic price and the old international price, multiplied by the amount of the quota. This is precisely $t/100$ times CD, which equals the tariff revenue of the government in the earlier case.

In the next section, we discuss the welfare effects of quotas. There we point out that the allocation of the implied revenues differs depending on

---

[6] In the upper regions of the demand curve where *total* demand was less than *EB* to start with, residual demand will, of course, fall to zero.

how the quotas were assigned. The foregoing description—that the implied subsidy flows into the hands of the buyers—is only a special situation.

In any case, we back away a little from the original claim: tariffs and quotas *are* equivalent in this example, except that they allocate purchasing power differently to the buyers and the government. In the case of tariffs, the government picks up the implied subsidy of quotas in the form of tariff revenue. Therefore, there is certainly no equivalence as far as distributional effects are concerned. However, there is an equivalent effect in terms of domestic prices, production, and import levels.[7]

If tariffs and quotas are equivalent, why do we observe both instruments in regimes of import substitution? There are two broad headings under which an answer can be provided. First, there is the question of *political power*. We already noted that tariffs and quotas place revenue in the hands of different groups. Tariff revenues accrue to government, whereas the beneficiaries of a quota reap the implied surplus. Depending on the power of business groups and their lobbies, it is possible to imagine either instrument being used, when, from the allocational point of view discussed earlier, both instruments are equivalent. For instance, if television manufacturers wished to import picture tubes (which are currently banned in an import substitution regime), would they lobby for a quota or its equivalent tariff? The answer is, of course, the quota. It is true that the beneficiaries of the quota would not be able to import beyond the quota (and in this sense the quota is more inflexible), but it is also true that in the presence of the equivalent tariff, they would not have *wanted* to import more, anyway (consult Figures 17.3 and 17.4 once again). Thus faced with a choice between the two options, television industry lobbyists may prefer the inflexibility of the quota and not have to pay a high tariff on the picture tubes that they do import.

A second reason why tariffs and quotas may be different stems from the government's *lack of complete information* regarding the economy. This requires some explanation. Let's begin by resurrecting a version of Figure 17.3, which shows the effect of a tariff on imports and domestic production. The main assumption in the illustration that follows is that the government lacks information regarding the domestic supply curve.[8]

Suppose that the goal of the government by imposing a tariff is to bring down the import of a good to a preassigned level and at the same time to en-

---

[7] The careful reader will have noticed also that we finessed this issue by asserting that after the quota, the residual demand curve moves to the left by *exactly* the amount of the quota. If the implied subsidy has an income effect on buyers (after all, it is as if they have been awarded extra income), then this might shift the total demand curve to the right. The *residual* demand curve will still be to the left of our original demand curve, but by an amount that less than offsets the quota. Thus, because the tariff revenue goes to the buyers, there may be more than just a distributional effect: domestic prices may be a bit higher than in the case of tariffs, but this is really a second-order effect; hence the fine print.

[8] The argument that follows is adapted from Weitzman [1977].

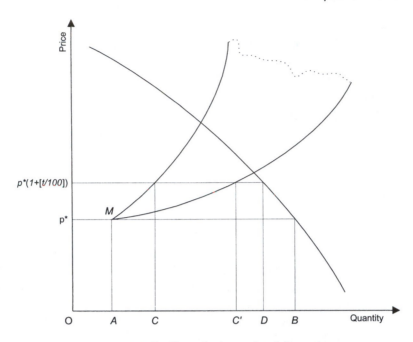

Figure 17.5. Tariffs under incomplete information.

courage domestic production. Figure 17.5 essentially reproduces Figure 17.3, but with one important difference: the domestic supply curve is now shown as a *band* emanating from the free-trade supply point, *M*. The point is that the supply curve of domestic production lies *somewhere* in this band, but by our assumption, the government has no idea where in this band it is. This has the following implication. With the given tariff, *the resulting imports could lie anywhere between the magnitudes CD and C'D*. In this sense the lack of information regarding the supply curve leads to an inability to predict the quantity of imports after the imposition of a tariff. Note that the quantity of domestic production becomes just as unpredictable, lying anywhere between the levels *OC* and *OC'*. You should note, of course, that lack of information regarding the *supply* curve was in no way crucial for this argument; lack of information regarding the demand curve would have done just as well.

We may conclude, then, that if one of the goals of the government is to control imports to some preplanned degree, a tariff may be a blunt instrument unless information regarding the economy is available in precise form. The error can be quite large. In such a situation, it may be far easier to impose a quota that directly controls the level of imports. Figure 17.6 shows how this is done.

As in Figure 17.4, the imposition of a quota of size *EB* shifts the residual demand curve to the left by precisely *EB* at every point (except at those

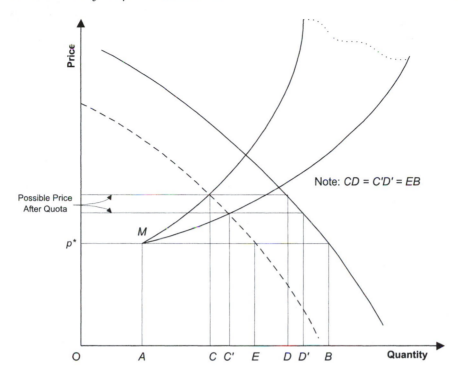

Figure 17.6. *Quotas under incomplete information.*

prices for which demand fell short of *EB*, in which case the new quantity demand is zero). Unlike the case of tariffs, there is no more uncertainty in the size of imports: it will be *EB* for sure. Now observe that we have bought our certainty at a price. We now lose control over the implicit subsidy to those producers who benefit from the quota. This could be a large or small amount, and the resulting distributional consequences can be serious enough to worry about.

Therefore, although tariffs and quotas are equivalent in a world without uncertainty (though there may still be distributional consequences), in a world with uncertainty they may have quite different effects.

We turn now to the welfare implications of trade restrictions.

Welfare effects: static and dynamic

Static welfare effects. Let's do some simple welfare accounting of the immediate effects of a tariff. Figure 17.7 reproduces Figure 17.3 (with a different focus) to enable us to do this.

In the figure, *P* represents the free-trade price and *Q* represents the domestic price with the tariff included. Recall that total domestic consumption of the good drops from *OB* to *OD*, while domestic production climbs from

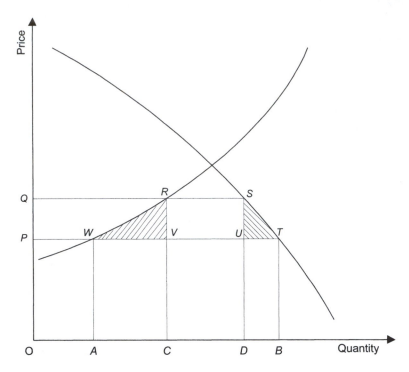

Figure 17.7. Static welfare effects of a tariff.

OA to OC. As noted in the preceding topic, domestic buyers lose. Using the simple principles of consumer surplus, we can estimate their loss with the help of Figure 17.7 as the total (irregular) area $PQST$.[9] Next, domestic producers gain. We can estimate the gain in just the same way as we estimated the loss to buyers: it is simply the increase in producer surplus. This gain is the area $PQRW$.

Suppose that we value buyers and producers equally. Then we may subtract the producers' gain from the buyers' loss. Look carefully at Figure 17.7. You will see that still leaves us with a net loss, which is the area $WRST$, but we aren't done with our accounting yet. There is also a tariff revenue that accrues to the government. This is given by the amount of imports after the tariff multiplied by the amount of the tariff. Convince yourself that the total value of revenue thus obtained is given by the area $VRSU$.

---

[9] Recall that consumer surplus at a particular price is represented by the area of the demand curve that lies above that price. Here is a rapid review in case you have forgotten. At each quantity up to the total demand at that price, the surplus accruing to the buyer is simply the difference between the price she is willing to pay and the price that she actually pays. This is nothing but the vertical distance between the demand curve and the price. "Summing up" all these vertical distances as we range over all the quantities between zero and the actual amount demanded, we obtain a measure of the total gains accruing to the consumer, which is just the area between the demand curve and the price line. Now it should be easy to check that the *loss* in consumer surplus as a result of the domestic price hike is precisely the area $PQST$, as claimed in the text.

Now compare areas $WRST$, which is the net buyer loss (after producer gains have been accounted for), and $VRSU$, which is the tariff revenue. It will be immediately apparent that the former area is larger than the latter. In fact, it is larger by the sum of the areas of the two shaded triangles WRV and UST. These are the so-called *deadweight efficiency losses* incurred in moving away from the free-market–free-trade outcome.

Our accounting is complete: buyers lose; producers gain; the government gains. With all gains and losses compared, there is still a deadweight efficiency loss.

The welfare accounting that we just carried out involves two fundamental assumptions. The first assumption is that all agents—producers, buyers, government—are given equal weight in the accounting. (This is how we added and subtracted areas in Figure 17.7.) If these agents represent identifiably different groups of individuals and we care about inequality, then such an assumption may not be the right one (we discussed this to some extent in the earlier section). For instance, the commodity may be one that is used by the richest income groups in the developing country: say laser-disc players (which may be an everyday household item by the time you read this, in which case think of some currently fanciful consumer good). If we care about inequality and there is no *direct* way to redistribute income from these groups to other (poorer) members of society, this may be a second-best way (but still a way) to do so.[10] The tariff raises producer surplus and permits producers (and their workers, and other owners of domestic inputs needed in the production of the good) to benefit. Likewise, the increased government revenues also may be channeled to programs that benefit poorer groups in society. It should be clear, however, that an *ethical* judgment regarding income distribution is needed here, as well as adequate information on how the government will use its revenues and on the identities of the producers that benefit. Thus simple welfare accounting may not be enough. There may be reasons to give more weight to producers and government, than to consumers, or there may not be any such reasons. It depends on who these groups are and it depends on the ethical judgments that we are prepared to make.

Second, our arguments hinge on the assumption that the free-trade price is *independent* of domestic policy. If the country is a large importer of a particular product, this is not the case. The analytical apparatus of this section can then be used to show that a tariff does bring in static gains for the country imposing the tariff. We leave the details of this argument to an exercise at the end of the chapter.

---

[10] The analysis of this subtle issue is overly simplistic here. A more comprehensive analysis, however, is beyond the scope of this book. See Diamond and Mirrlees [1971] and Ray and Sen [1992].

Our observations also partly bear on the issue of why protection may be unequal across different commodity groups. Some commodities, such as edible oils, may be consumed by all income groups. In this case the consumer loss may outweigh the producer gain, and rates of tariff may be quite low. Other commodities, such as steel, may be crucial for the production of many other goods. Thus even if steel is not domestically produced, it may be too costly to protect it. On the other hand, consumer goods such as laser-disc players are likely to receive high degrees of protection for the reasons mentioned previously.

Our analysis so far has concentrated on the case of tariffs. With quotas, the distributions of gains and losses is different but the method used to account for them is just the same. What we need to do is figure out who receives the implicit benefits from the quota allocation. Given the equivalence of quotas and tariffs discussed earlier, we may use Figure 17.7 to describe the various costs and benefits. Reinterpret P as the initial free-trade price, RS as the import quota, QR as domestic production, and Q as the domestic price that follows on the imposition of the quota. All costs and benefits are just as described in the case of a tariff. The only difference is that now there is no tariff revenue. Who receives the implicit amount described by the rectangle $VRSU$?

There are various possibilities, depending on the way in which quota rights are disbursed. They may be allocated to buyers by means of a lottery or a first-come–first-served basis. In such a situation, the buyers get back $VRSU$ of their loss of consumer surplus $PQST$. Quota rights may be auctioned by the government. Then competition among buyers to the rights afforded by the quotas bid up the price of quotas to precisely the amount $VRSU$. In this case, tariffs and quotas are *really* equivalent. Even though the government earns no tariff revenue, the revenue from the sale of the quota is exactly the same. Finally, the government may wish to randomly allocate quota rights (as in the first case), but a cunning bureaucrat in charge of the allocation may take bribes from buyers who wish to have the rights allocated to them. These bribes generate revenue for the bureaucrats! In this last case, we do no harm in thinking that the rectangle $VRSU$ is largely eaten up by bribery. Certainly these bribes are pocketed by the citizens of the country and if we turn a blind eye to the *distribution* of gains and losses, it makes no difference, but there may be few people who are inclined to think that way.

In conclusion, three lessons emerge. First, whether tariffs or quotas are being studied, we have learned a uniform methodology to gauge the gains and losses to various groups in society. Second, in evaluating the overall welfare gain or loss, we must *weigh* the losses or gains of the different groups, be they buyers, sellers, the government, or bureaucrats. The question of which weights to choose is fundamentally one of ethics.

Finally, observe that all we have said so far is *static*, in the sense that we are evaluating the *immediate* welfare effects of imposing a tariff. There may be important changes *over time* as well. If you go back to our discussion of the need for trade policy, you will recall that we placed much weight on this feature. Now we need to face this issue head on. Neglect of this issue is a restrictive assumption that we used in the preceding static welfare accounting.

Dynamic welfare effects and the infant-industry argument. The static argument neglects three possibilities.

Learning by doing. First, protection of an industry might encourage the learning and assimilation of new techniques of production, a process that might only be possible through actual and ongoing production on a significant scale. This may happen for two reasons. Domestic firms, encouraged by the protection afforded under the tariff, might take the opportunity to train its employees in the use of new technologies and methods.[11] In addition, the process of production, in itself, may generate a virtuous circle of learning and further efficiency in production. This phenomenon, emphasized in the work of Arrow [1962] and many others following him, is termed learning by doing.

A simple diagram will serve to contrast this essentially dynamic implication with the static analysis. Figure 17.8 extends Figure 17.3 in a fresh direction. Just as in the situation in Figure 17.3, protection is afforded to a particular sector, say telephone switchboards, by the use of a tariff. Prices rise, to start with, and domestic production of telephone switchboards is thereby stimulated. Now it is possible that the expanded scale of production will have beneficial effects on the *future* costs of production of switchboards, as well as the quality of the output. The larger scale of domestic activity induces incentives for all sorts of domestic innovations. For instance, the circuitry of a foreign switchboard may necessitate constant air conditioning to prevent the generation of excessive heat and humidity, factors that are likely to be more crucial in a tropical country than in a temperate region. Now domestic manufacturers may find it profitable to carry out adjustments to introduce a new type of switchboard that is better adapted to a hot climate. Sheer experience

---

[11] Of course, it may be (and has been) argued that such expenditures are inefficient. Why not import the goods instead and forego such training? It may be more "efficient" to do this. Such arguments may be good political material for lobbyists seeking to open up foreign markets, but it is based on weak economic theory in general. Each such decision needs to be considered on a case-by-case basis, taking into account primarily the welfare of the developing country in question. For instance, one salutary effect often ignored in simplistic economic models is possible spillovers from such investments into other sectors of the economy.

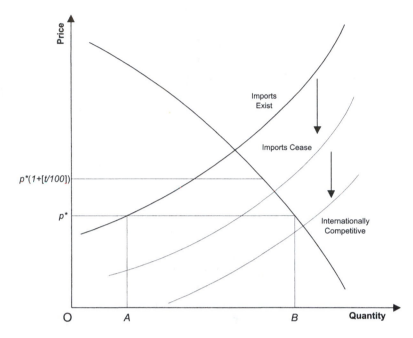

Figure 17.8. Cost reductions over time.

also brings down the costs of producing a given type of switchboard. Look at the box on Learning by Doing to get a better feel for all this.

Learning by Doing[12]

Experience (as we all know from our own experience) is a great teacher. People learn better and more efficient ways to perform a task if they have been engaged in it for a long time. Practice makes perfect, goes the popular saying. There is no reason why what is true in playing baseball or learning the piano should not also apply to more mundane production jobs. Are there significant "learning effects" in many branches of manufacturing industry? There is indeed some evidence to support this viewpoint.

The phenomenon was first observed by T. P. Wright, a U.S. aeronautical engineer, in connection with the manufacturing of airframes (airplane bodies) during the 1930s. Wright noted something quite remarkable: the extent of cost reduction achieved over time bore a more or less constant relationship to the amount of cumulative output produced to that date. In particular, each time output doubled, average cost seemed to come down by the *same* fraction of approximately 20%. This has been dubbed variously as a 20% "progress ratio" or an 80% "learning curve." In the late 1940s, extensive studies done by the Stanford Research Institute and the RAND Corporation

---

[12] This minisurvey draws on Mookherjee and Ray [1993].

revealed the existence of similar learning curves in many other related branches of manufacturing. After the Crawford–Strauss (1947) study, which found an average learning rate of 79.7% in 118 World War II airframe models, a belief in the existence of a uniform progress ratio of 20% became widespread in management circles, and production and marketing strategies were often based on this magic number.

Because the increase in productivity discussed here comes not from an improvement in machinery or creation of more capital per worker, but merely from increased labor skills arising from accumulated experience in working with the same process, it is often termed *learning by doing*. Another early and striking example of this phenomenon came from the Horndal Iron Works in Sweden, which experienced a steady increase in output per man-hour at the rate of 2% per year for 15 years, in spite of the fact that there was no new investment during this period and, hence, no radical change in the manufacturing technology. This type of productivity gain is, therefore, often termed the "Horndal effect."

Although the existence of learning by doing in many branches of manufacturing can hardly be called into question, it is doubtful whether a uniform progress ratio exists (as has been sometimes claimed) for widely different production processes. For example, Billon [1966] examined five manufacturing programs and fifty-four products with three different manufacturers, and found that progress ratios varied considerably in several dimensions: across programs, products, and firms. Alchian [1963] observed that even in the limited area of manufacturing airframes, projections and cost estimates based on the wartime data could lead to errors of up to 20–25%. A very detailed comparative study was done by Hirsch [1956], who computed twenty-two empirical progress functions for a wide variety of machine manufacturing processes. He found that in almost all cases, the progress ratio was close to a constant (i.e., a curve based on an assumed constant ratio showed a very good fit to the data). The mean progress ratio for the sample was 19.3, which seemingly comes close to confirming the folklore of a 20% rule. However, the progress ratios for the individual processes ranged between 16.5 and 24.8%, displaying a variance that is highly significant statistically. Hirsch's conclusion was "For a number of industry-wide purposes it might suffice to assume that the average progress ratio is about 19 or 20 per cent. For most firms, however, little use can be derived from using a value that has so wide a range and can lead to substantial mistakes in forecasting."

Given the widely different characteristics of various manufacturing processes, this variation is not surprising at all. If complex manufacturing processes could be broken down into simpler component processes, perhaps a more uniform progress ratio could be found for each of these components. Hirsch's study divides all manufacturing work into two classes: machine work and assembly work. The different processes described in his table constituted different mixtures of these two components. His main finding was that assembly progress ratios were much higher, with a mean of 25.6%, and showed much less variance across different products. The mean machining progress ratio was a much lower 14.1% and had a variance that was statistically significant. The lesson is clear: caution is to be exercised in basing policy prescriptions on numerically specified progress ratios. Either a context-specific estimate based on relevant data is called for or an estimate should be constructed from a vector of more basic progress ratios (in the components), which can then be combined using appropriate weights. Even then, the margin of error in forecasting may be large.

Nevertheless, strong learning-by-doing effects seem to pervade modern-day economies. The implications for industrial market structure and international trade, as well as optimal government policy in these areas, can be far reaching.

Figure 17.8 captures the net effect of these reactions by progressively shifting downward the cost curve of domestically produced switchboards.[13] This expands the supply curve of domestically produced switchboards. It is possible, indeed, that at some stage the shifted supply curve will cut the demand curve below the old international price p^*. At that point protection can be lifted with no imports. Indeed, in this case the domestic industry can be said to have attained the point of *international competitiveness*, because under current supply conditions it will even be able to export switchboards.

Spillovers. The second possibility that is neglected by the static analysis is the presence of beneficial spillovers to *other* industries. The protection afforded to an engineering industry may well create an additional demand for engineering skills and, over time, a population better equipped for engineering work in other industries. The availability of such skilled personnel may then encourage the development of these other sectors. In this context, recall the concepts of externalities and linkages that we introduced and discussed in Chapter 5. Spillovers or positive externalities serve not only to lower production costs: they encourage the acquisition of human capital, which may be a social end in itself, they provoke the provision of adequate infrastructure, and they generate new incomes. In the language developed earlier in this book, selected protection to some sectors may permit the economy to overcome coordination failures in other sectors.

Increasing Returns. A third possibility was also discussed in Chapter 5. This is the argument that there are substantial increasing returns in production in some sectors. Learning by doing may be viewed as a form of increasing returns, but there may be others, such as substantial fixed costs. In this case history matters, as we have already seen. For instance, suppose that the production of PC clones in a developing country has exactly the same cost curve as anywhere else. However, because the technology of computer manufacture was historically first accessible to developed countries, we have a chronological situation in which the market is already captured by, say, a group of multinational firms. In that case it may be difficult, if not impossible, for a rival domestic manufacturer to break into this market. It is not that

---

[13] Quality improvements such as those previously mentioned can be viewed as cost reductions in final use.

the domestic manufacturer is inefficient in the manufacture of the item. It is simply the case that, at lower scales of production, the *average* cost of production is too high for profitable activity. Figure 17.9 captures the relevant details.

In the figure, an average cost curve is depicted for the manufacture of computer hardware in a developing country. Suppose that the average cost is the same for a domestic manufacturer as well as for a foreign manufacturer. However, the foreign manufacturer is already supplying the domestic market at the level Q^f, charging a price p, incurring an average cost of production a, and making profits as shown. The domestic manufacturer may be caught in a chicken-and-egg problem here. The only way to expand production is to charge a price lower than p. However, no market will switch loyalties in a day. Therefore, the domestic manufacturer must be willing and able to bear significant losses in the transition. For instance, at the hypothetical level Q^d, the average cost of production is at b, which is above the going price p. As seen in Chapter 5, the *order* of historical entry matters here. If credit markets will not finance the intervening losses, the domestic manufacturer will not be able to enter. Again, we have a potential case for protection that is not covered by the simple static model.

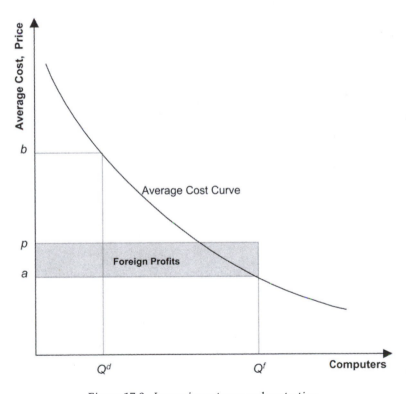

Figure 17.9. Increasing returns and protection.

The Main Problem. The infant-industry argument represents perhaps the best case for import substitution. The idea is to provide breathing space—a domestic market to increase international competitiveness. The problem is that becoming competitive is not entirely a spontaneous process, that is, something that happens without active effort and investment from industrialists themselves. In part, forces such as learning by doing have spontaneous effects, but there are also cost reductions that can be achieved only by hard restructuring of the organization, which requires effort and (often) political will.

The central question regarding the infant-industry argument has to do with the credibility of a limited promise. Protection must be limited and must expire at some deadline, *whether or not the infant has grown up.* Is this threat credible? The answer depends on the forces that a government will be subject to in the event that an industry fails to become competitive within the stipulated period of protection. Removing protection at this stage involves loss of political support, both from industrialists who enjoy the protection and perhaps from the working class as well, as workers find themselves unemployed in the resulting deluge of foreign goods. If industrialists can forecast that the government will inevitably bow to these pressures, there is absolutely no incentive for them to acquire the necessary competitiveness in the first place. Appendix 1 (at the end of the book) on game theory sets up this issue formally as a strategic model: you are encouraged to read the analysis there.

Thus the potential success of a temporary protectionist policy depends on the full credibility of its temporariness. If the policy does not work to lower costs, governments must be fully prepared (and be *seen* to be fully prepared) to abandon the policy. Only then will industry react to cut its costs. If this credibility is missing—and often it is (see Section 17.4)—temporary protection to industry degenerates into permanent protection for certain favored groups in society.

Import Substitution: Brazil

The experience of Brazil in the 1960s and 1970s illustrates many of the issues surrounding an import-substitution policy. Like India, which pursued import substitution for most of the second half of the twentieth century, Brazil's policy was driven by a fierce desire to industrialize and by the firm belief that unprotected markets would not deliver the goods spontaneously on their own accord.[14] Like India again, Brazil had an enormous domestic market. As we've seen, large countries are far more likely to pursue the import-substitution route.

[14] The brief account that follows relies heavily on Bruton [1992].

Import substitution followed a predictable sequence. The first line of attack was on consumer goods—consumer durables in particular. With easy access to import permits that cut through the tariff wall, capital goods imports remained relatively open. However, this was the easy part: after some point, the capital goods market would have to be domestically penetrated as well. Here, it was felt, was where the externalities and learning effects lay: indigenous production of capital goods was felt to be the key to the accumulation of technical know-how. The discussion that follows traces this shift.

Import substitution in Brazil dates back to the very beginning of the twentieth century, and its first wave in Brazil lasted all the way up to the mid-1960s, especially in the postwar period. Over the period 1949–64, import substitution was responsible for about a quarter of total demand growth in manufacturing, much of it in consumer goods. For the first half of this period (up to 1953), imports were strictly monitored under a licensing system that gave the imports of capital goods and agricultural equipment strong priority over consumer durables. In October 1953 a foreign exchange auction system allocated funds across different sectors: again, nearly 80% of available foreign exchange was allocated to goods favored under the licensing system. In 1957 a move toward tariffs became more pronounced: tariffs, levied differentially on different goods, were widely used. As you might expect, the cumulative effect of these protection policies was to depress imports, particularly of consumer goods. Manufactured imports as a percentage of total domestic supply fell from 14% in 1949 to 6% in the late 1960s.

From the mid-1960s until the mid-1970s, there was a brief period of outward orientation, but this was followed by a sharp return to import substitution in the second half of the 1970s. This time there was a difference: Brazil had begun the push into capital goods substitution. Imports of capital goods relative to total imports predictably showed a sharp decline during this period. Indeed, manufacturing *exports* were on the rise through the 1960s and 1970s (over the period 1965–74, the growth in manufactured exports was only second to that of Korea). Much of the export growth came from multinationals stationed in Brazil, and this was especially true of exports with some degree of technological sophistication.

Indeed, Brazil's liberal policy on foreign investment is to be contrasted with India (or Korea), and may have had reduced learning effects: the domestic spinoffs or externalities from such activities may be higher when domestic producers are in control. If we suppose that a key aim of import substitution is to achieve domestic learning and maximize externalities, it is easy to sympathize with economists who viewed this slightly schizophrenic approach (foreign investment plus inward orientation) with some disfavor.[15]

This is not to say that a policy of discouraging foreign investment is necessarily bad, but that a mix of inward orientation and foreign investment may leave a country with a combination of most of the bad effects without any of the good. The quick road to industrialization may benefit from multinational involvement, but if the gap

---

[15] As Bruton [1992] reported, TFP growth seemed to be low during this period, although this sort of aggregate data may not be sufficient to capture domestic learning at the factory level. Moreover, industries such as automobiles undoubtedly had peripheral spinoffs in the production of components even though they were dominated by foreign firms.

between what is available indigenously and the multinational frontier is very high, the spillovers may be lower. Import substitution in this sense may be like climbing a ladder rung by rung. In contrast to Brazil's shortcut approach to development, countries such as Korea chose to focus first on low-tech industries where the gap between the available local level of learning and what was required was not very substantial. This fostered local learning.

Although the Brazilian focus on foreign investment contrasts with Indian policy at that time, import substitution had one effect that was common to both countries: it created powerful domestic groups with enormous vested interests in the continuation of inward-looking policies, breeding inefficiency and lack of competitive capacity. Although both countries are considerably more outward-looking today, it has been difficult to move away from these entrenched interests. The move to outward orientation has been (relatively) easier for other countries in Latin America.

17.3. Export promotion

Many (if not most) of even the most cogent reasons for import substitution disappear for countries that have small internal markets. Such countries must fight their battles on the world market from day one. The prospects of such a war appear particularly avoidable if domestic markets are large enough to permit internal practice. Thus large countries resort more easily to import substitution. When a country is small, however, it *must* trade, and widespread import substitution is hardly an option. These countries must export successfully to the outside world.

Export promotion policies are essentially the flip side of an import substitution policy. Instead of restricting trade (by curtailing imports through tariffs and quotas), such policies generally *expand* trade beyond market-determined limits. Thus such policies are lumped together under the classification of *outward orientation*, in contrast to the gloomier, more introspective label of *inward orientation* that is used to describe import substitution policies.

There is a general tendency for governments and citizens in developed countries, as well as several international organizations, to view a regime of outward orientation as a good thing, or at any rate, as a lesser evil compared to inward orientation. A priori, it is hard to think of any objective economic basis for this sort of discrepancy in assessments. Arguments based on government-induced "distortions" under inward orientation are not enough. It is important to appreciate that *both* these departures from the market-based outcome involve substantial government intervention. It is just that the target practice necessary for unfettered competition occurs in foreign rather than domestic markets.

One possible argument is that outward orientation maintains a closer contact with technological developments in the world at large, permitting the rapid assimilation of such methods by producers in developing countries. There may be some merit to this argument, but as the studies of Alwyn Young and others have shown (see Chapter 4 for a detailed discussion), there is no hard evidence to support it. We could just as easily argue that inward orientation permits a subtler appreciation of the particular features of home markets, thus generating local technologies that are more suited to local conditions. Especially in the case of large economies, this may not be a bad argument.

Viewed from the vantage point of developed countries, what seems a more likely explanation is the fact that the outward orientation of developing countries brings more visible gains. For consumers in the developed world, there is nothing better than having a Korea, China, or India competing to bring cheap, high-quality products to their doorsteps. More goods are thus made available more cheaply. In addition, such countries often have relatively open markets for imports, and this is also a source of some satisfaction to firms in developed countries who seek to sell to such markets. In contrast, inward orientation closes out many options for foreign firms and does little (at least in the short or medium run) to provide developed countries with cheap, high-quality products.[16] From this perspective, it is hardly surprising that outward orientation earns the lion's share of kudos.

17.3.1. Basic concepts

An export promotion strategy essentially is a mirror image of an import substitution policy. In contrast to tariffs and quotas on imports, exports are subsidized in several ways. Here are some of the basic features of an export promotion policy.

Targeted nonprimary exports

Export promotion generally comprises the encouragement of various types of manufactured products that range from light manufactures, such as footwear and textiles, all the way to more sophisticated items, such as automobiles or memory modules for computers. It is rarely, if ever, the case that the export of primary products is encouraged by governments of developing countries. For one thing, most developing countries possess a comparative advantage in such products and there is nothing in particular to encourage! More to the point, countries that seek to reverse or transform the pattern of trade

---

[16] Outward orientation is not without its enemies in the developed world. Some firms and industries in developed countries will be hurt by this influx of competing products and must shift away from such products or adapt to what they would describe as "unfair competition." Charges of unfair competition include not only the role of government in promoting and subsidizing exports, but other accusations such as nonadherence to strict and supposedly universal environmental standards.

have traditionally viewed their dependence on primary exports as inimical to progress.

Reduced import duties, or import quotas for exporters

One of the main ways in which exports are promoted is by making the imported materials needed for their manufacture relatively easy to obtain. This is done by preferential duty treatment of imports that can be shown to be needed for the manufacture of items that are to be exported. Thus in an overall regime with tariffs or quotas on imports, exporters are often permitted to obtain needed imports at lower rates.

Preferential credit

An export promotion strategy often recognizes that the lack of plentiful credit can impede expansion and innovation. Therefore banks are often directed to provide credit on easier terms to those firms who export their products. These subsidies may be provided either in the form of a lower interest rate on loans or a larger loan size.

17.3.2. Effect on the exchange rate

The instruments of export promotion work very much like an import substitution policy in reverse. Note, however, that both these policies tend to overvalue the exchange rate relative to the market-clearing level. We have already seen how this works in the case of import substitution. Figure 17.10 depicts the same baseline situation as Figure 17.2. Recall that this example used two countries, Mexico and the United States. Mexico's demand for dollars is just its demand for imports (from the United States). Mexico's supply of dollars is its foreign exchange earnings from exports. The two panels in Figure 17.10 capture exactly the same two cases as those discussed for import substitution.

Observe, now, that an effective export promotion policy will create an increase in exports at each going exchange rate (pesos to dollars). What this means is that the supply curve of dollars *shifts to the right*, as depicted in Figure 17.10. It follows that the equilibrium price of dollars must fall. This is equivalent to an appreciation of the exchange rate of the peso. Take note of the qualifier "effective": for this result to hold, the policy must be able to boost dollar revenue at the going exchange rate. There may be situations in which this does not occur, at least in the short run, and then the exchange rate may depreciate. We discuss this in more detail in the next section.

Thus both import substitution and (effective) export promotion policies tend to create an appreciation in the exchange rate of the country carrying

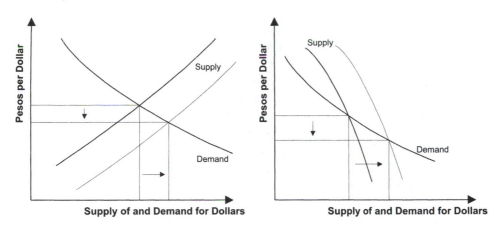

Figure 17.10. *Equilibrium exchange rates under export promotion.*

out such policies. Intuitively, this should be quite obvious. Import substitution restricts the demand for dollars, while (successful) export promotion expands the supply of dollars. Thus in both cases, there is a tendency for the equilibrium price of dollars to fall, all other things being equal.

However, the similarity ends here, because all other things are not equal. Think of a government engaged in import substitution. For such a government, an overvaluation of the exchange rate (relative to the market outcome) may be ignored or even welcome. Some sectors are protected at prohibitive levels from "unwelcome" imports, and although the appreciation of the exchange rate makes such imports appear more attractive (at market prices), these attractions can be countered by use of tariffs and quotas. In addition, those imports that are deemed necessary can be obtained at cheaper international prices (i.e., less pesos have to be forsaken per dollar to obtain such imports). The appreciation in the exchange rate harms *exports*, but governments intent on target practice in their home markets may not particularly care or bother.

Contrast this with the export-promoting government. Exports are their main concern and an appreciation of the exchange rate hurts this objective. It is therefore not surprising that export promotion often goes hand in hand with attempts to keep the exchange rate *low* by other means, such as (surprise) devaluations of the currency, followed by appropriate monetary policy.

17.3.3. *The instruments of export promotion: More detail*

The export subsidy

Let's begin by studying an export subsidy, which essentially works as the opposite number of an import tariff. Consult Figure 17.11, which depicts the domestic demand and supply curves for some product. Initially, the international price of the product is at p^*. You can read off various observations from the diagram. Domestic sales, initially, must be given by the amount OA (because any lower level of sales would be met by a higher price than the international price, and any higher level would sell only domestically at a price lower than the international price). The remaining supply at that price (all the way up to the supply curve) is exported. This is the quantity AB.

Now suppose that the government wishes to encourage the export of this commodity by introducing an ad valorem subsidy: that is, a payment of $s\%$ of the export price for every unit of the good that is exported. This shifts the *effective international* price for producers up to the level $p^*(1 + s/100)$. The effect of this shift is predictable. Production of the commodity will be stimulated as we move up the supply curve, but at the same time, domestic sales will come down. The gap between the two represents larger exports.

This is almost the end of the story, but there is an additional effect that we need to consider. Increased exports might lead to a fall in the international price of that good as greater supplies arrive on the market. Figure 7.11 incorporates this by allowing the price to fall from p^* to p^{**}, so that at the new equilibrium, the international price falls while the domestic price rises.

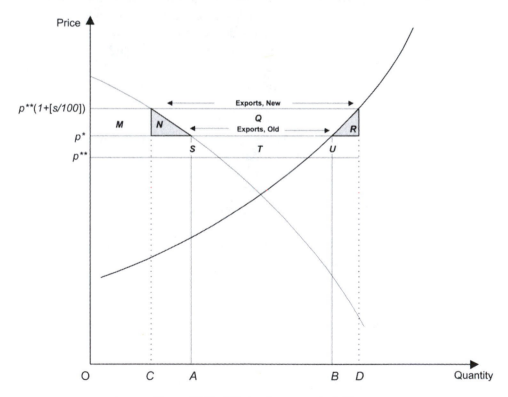

Figure 17.11. Effects of an export subsidy.

Let's pause here for a moment and incorporate this observation into our discussion on exchange rates in the preceding section. If the international price does not fall at all or falls by very little, the export subsidy will lead to an increase in export revenue at the going exchange rate. Thus the curve in that section that denotes the supply of dollars does shift to the right and, as we have already seen, this effect works toward appreciating the exchange rate. In contrast, if the international price falls significantly as a result of the export drive, revenues may even fall, and this can lead to a depreciation of the exchange rate. The former case is what we referred to in the last section as an "effective" exchange rate policy.

Whether the policy is effective or not depends, as usual, on the *elasticity of demand* for the exports of our country. If elasticity is high, then prices will not fall by much as the outside world absorbs the greater quantity of exports (perhaps at the cost of exports from some *other* country, if the products are differentiated). If elasticity is low, then the price reduction is extreme and the export subsidy policy really fails to have any impact at all in the short run.

Now, the mere fact that an export subsidy is effective, in the sense that it increases the country's revenue from exports, does not necessarily mean that it is a good thing. An evaluation depends on the gains and losses to all sorts of groups who are affected by the policy. To do this we simply follow the methodology of welfare analysis that we introduced for import substitution.

Look at domestic consumers: they paid a price of p^* and now pay a higher price as shown in the diagram. This leads to a loss in their welfare that we measure as usual by the loss in consumer surplus, which is given by the area $M + N$. Next, producers gain. By an analogous argument the gain is given by the summed areas $M + N + Q$. Third, there is the subsidy to be paid by the government, which is just total exports times the unit subsidy; that is, the total area $N + Q + R + S + T + U$.

Let us give all these three actors equal weights and add up the gains and losses. Producers and consumers together lead to the net gain Q. Squared off with the loss of the government, this accounting leaves us with a net loss, given by the sum of the areas $N + R + S + T + U$. Of these, the triangles N and R are the familiar deadweight losses, analogous to those incurred under an import substitution policy. What about the remaining bits: $S + T + U$? These have no analog in import substitution: they are losses that arise as the international price drops from p^* to p^{**}. (Observe that if there were no fall in the price, these segments would not exist.) These are gains for consumers abroad, but do not represent gains for the country under consideration.

Thus the welfare accounting in which we add the gains and losses for all concerned leads to a net (static) loss, as it must (remember that free trade maximizes production possibilities at any point in time and, therefore, national income). But just as in the case of import substitution, we must be careful to ask ourselves what adding up gains and losses means. Consider an example: suppose that the commodity is a luxury good, say cashew nuts. Suppose that in our country, cashews are consumed only by the very rich. If the income distribution is inappropriate, we might want to tax the rich and redistribute the proceeds to other members of society. However, as we have noted over and over again, such direct taxes may be ruled out on several grounds. Then you could think of the export subsidy on cashew nuts as a way to tax the rich. It creates distortions, no doubt, but there may not be a nondistortionary tax instrument available. In addition, the subsidy permits additional foreign exchange to flow into the country from the sale of what is considered to be a luxury product. Under these presumptions, we do not add gains in a straightforward way. We may need to weight these gains, and the social weight on gains by the rich may well be negative!

Of course, it may be preposterous to suggest that *all* of a country's trade policy is driven by a desire to correct the income distribution in favor of the have-nots. To be sure, export promotion policy is motivated by the same set of dynamic considerations that drive import substitution. We discussed these considerations in detail earlier, and nothing needs to be added here.

Other instruments

Other instruments of export promotion include access to credit at a rate of interest that is below market levels and preferential access to imports. Each of these is like an export subsidy, and their effects can be analyzed in similar ways. For instance, the differential rate of interest in credit ultimately must be paid for by *somebody*, and this could be the banks themselves, or the government in the form of subsidies to banks designed in part to cover such allocations, or depositors in the form of lower interest rates on savings, or even other (nonexporting) borrowers who pay a higher interest rate on *their* loans. Exporters gain in the usual way, and if there is a resulting fall in international prices of the exported good, so do international consumers. In short, the same sort of welfare analysis that we already carried out twice can be carried out ad nauseam. The analyses all lead to the same conclusions: there are gainers and there are losers, and there are little triangles of deadweight losses that are the short-term allocative losses whenever there is a departure from the free-market outcome.

At the same time, remember that these methods to evaluate the welfare effects of trade policy are limited. They presume that the present will not affect the future. As we emphasized earlier on in this chapter, much of the gains, if any, from such policies are dynamic. For instance, there may be a missing market, such as the market for capital, that prevents appropriate investments by private entrepreneurs. Directed subsidies (such as concessional credit) then may help to overcome this market failure. Alternatively, the very act of exporting to competitive markets may create positive externalities, as entrepreneurs as a group learn to compete and learn new technologies on the job rather than in the abstract.

Case Study: "Outward Orientation" in South Korea

Leaving behind a long history of colonial subjugation and sluggish growth, the Korean economy roared into economic acceleration in the early 1960s, displaying record-breaking rates of growth for the next couple of decades and more. During the first two five year plans (1962–71), the growth rate of GNP averaged 9% per year, and between 1972 and 1979, it was even higher, averaging 10% per annum. Parallel to this was an even more spectacular increase in Korean exports. During the first two five year plans, exports grew at a phenomenal 40% per annum; between 1972 and 1979, this growth rate was lower (around 28% per annum), but still remarkable.

The growth of exports was driven mainly by industrial products and heavy manufactures, not agricultural goods, minerals, or products of light industry, in which "backward" countries are supposed to have their comparative advantage. The share of heavy manufactures in merchandise exports rose from 14% in 1971 to 60% by 1984. These figures led to a popular viewpoint that Korea's growth was "export led" and was the outcome of opening up to international markets. According to the proponents of this viewpoint, the Korean boat sailed by the winds of free trade and free markets.

Not so, claimed Amsden [1989] in her book on South Korea. The architect behind the emergence of this new "Asian tiger," she argued, is a strong, interventionist state, which has willfully and abundantly provided tariff protection and subsidies, changed interest and exchange rates, managed investment, and controlled industry using both lucrative carrots and threatening sticks. Relative prices were deliberately set "wrong" to create and reap the benefits of dynamic comparative advantage, instead of letting them adjust to the "right" levels by the free play of market forces, which would have led to short-run efficiency but economic anemia in the long run. Korean development strategy has been primarily a pragmatic trial-and-error approach—with a twofold commitment to growth of exports and protected nurturing of selected infant industries.

The encouragement of exports, and manufactured exports in particular, became an active policy in the early 1960s, following unsuccessful attempts at import substitution in the 1950s. Export promotion involved the establishment of virtual free-trade regimes by the government. The incentives made available to exporters took the form of direct tax reductions, privileged access to import licenses, and preferential interest rates. Thus export promotion entailed substantial government involvement.

There was close monitoring of all export targets, virtually on a daily basis. There were strong moral and other "incentives" to meet these targets. According to Amsden, successful achievement of export targets brought rewards in the form of favored bank lending, relaxed tax surveillance, and so forth, but failure could result in penalties in the form of restricted access to domestic markets and loans.

In its promotion of manufactured exports, Korea chose first to focus on low-technology items in which the gap between the required level of skill and the skill levels available locally was not very large. This had two effects: a positive learning-by-doing experience, as well as lowered dependence on foreign expertise in the early stages of development.

Indeed, Korea's efforts at domestic target practice, using instruments familiar to import substitution, should not go unnoticed. The promotion of infant industry was an important aspect of the Korean growth strategy. In the early 1960s, targeted industries included cement, fertilizers, and petroleum refining; in the late 1960s and early 1970s, steel and petrochemicals; in the late 1970s, shipbuilding, capital and durable consumer goods, and chemicals; and, more recently, critical electronic and other component industries. Protectionist measures included preferential access to short- and long-term credit and import quotas designed to guarantee a sizable domestic market.

Add to this the deliberate encouragement and development of *chaebols* or market agents such as Daewoo, Samsung, and Hyundai, large trading companies whose activities spanned several sectors, particularly manufacturing and construction. These firms played a predominant role in strengthening Korea's export market potential and effectively were important tools for the implementation of the government's development policy. (There has been some criticism of their connections with the agents of political power.)

Overall, South Korea's choice of an export-led growth policy does seem logical given certain factors. Its limited domestic demand necessitates the exploration of other markets to sustain industrial expansion (in contrast to large countries such as Brazil or India).

Korea's outward orientation has undoubtedly brought to the economy the fruits of development. However, it would be erroneous to equate the outward orientation to a free market approach. In fact, the extent of government intervention in Korea has not been much lower than what is typically associated with a policy of import substitution.

17.4. The move away from import substitution

17.4.1. Introduction

As it turns out, many countries that pursued import substitution policies in the 1960s and 1970s did run into severe external difficulties, especially with regard to their balance of payments. Although inward-oriented policies per se were not responsible for the crises, aspects of these policies served to exacerbate the difficulties. Many countries, particularly in Latin America, have since moved away from a regime of import substitution, in tandem with other domestic policies that were instituted as part of a package of *structural adjustment*. Such adjustment programs ushered in a new role for international organizations such as the International Monetary Fund and the

World Bank. No longer were these organizations confined to prudent lending and aid: they were messengers of a new vision that countries were pushed to adopt (along with the rescue package).

Since the 1970s, the stabilization/structural adjustment package has been used in many countries. A flurry of such adjustments occurred in Latin America (and elsewhere, such as the Philippines and Turkey) in the wake of the debt crisis. Similar packages have since been applied to several African and South Asian countries. The last great giant of import substitution—India—began to move away from inward orientation in the 1990s.

This transformation in the developing world perhaps brings out the greatest practical failure of inward orientation, despite the laudable goals that often spurred such orientation. These failures have to do with the creation of entrenched domestic interests that use protection as a monopolistic (or oligopolistic) right, rather than as a temporary measure to increase competitiveness. Thus, exports are stifled by the overvaluation of exchange rates, but imports are never adequately replaced by domestic substitutes. Instead, protection acts as a wall for continued inefficiencies. This is a particularly viable proposition if the external economic environment is fortuitously good, if exports can be maintained or increased (often simply because of favorable price changes), and if the international community is willing to lend large quantities of money. This is what happened in Latin America throughout the 1970s.

What happens when the helpful external climate evaporates, as it did at the beginning of the 1980s in Latin America? The resulting crisis is very painful and can usher in sweeping economic reforms. We will study, then, the debt crisis as a prelude to structural adjustment and to a longer-run trend away from import substitution.

17.4.2. The eighties crisis

The OPEC price shocks of 1973–74 had several effects on the international economy. As expected, prices rose sharply in oil-importing countries as the energy shock made its way through the economy. However, other effects worked behind the scenes. Huge petrodollar balances were accumulated as the inflated oil revenues found their way into banks, particularly into U.S. banks. Flushed with money to lend, banks went on a lending binge through the 1970s.

Developing countries were attractive customers because they were willing to pay interest premiums: the contracted rates were about 2% in excess of interest rates on U.S. government bonds (Lindert and Morton [1989]). Countries such as Brazil responded to the oil shock by embarking on a deliberate development strategy designed to foster import substitution: foreign loans poured in to finance these investments. Mexico was an oil producer, but this only served to raise its creditworthiness in the eyes of the banks: it didn't seem to matter that Mexico had huge fiscal deficits and that its borrowings were being used to plug these deficits. Mexico's enormous public sector expansion was mirrored by Turkey, which also used its borrowings for public investment projects. In all of these countries and others, government guarantees were behind the loans, even when the loans were provided to private firms.[17] There appeared to be a widespread feeling among bankers that sovereign governments were good bets: that "countries never go bankrupt."[18]

Bankruptcy was the last thing on anyone's mind: the dollar value of exports was growing and interest rates on the debt were low. Thus existing debt could be serviced by borrowing *new* funds, and yet debt–export ratios remained steady or even fell: indeed, this was the case as long as the growth rate of exports exceeded the rate of interest on borrowings. Debt–export ratios actually *fell* for nonoil LDCs between 1973 and 1980. Even in Latin America, where the average debt burden was at its highest, debt–export ratios rose very slightly over this period.[19]

However, an extraordinary and sudden transition began at the end of the decade. With inflation running relatively high in developed countries (a second oil shock had just struck), monetary policies were tightened and interest rates went up (indeed, they had been on an upward trend throughout the 1970s). Recession worldwide also caused a drop in export earnings, largely induced by a sharp fall in export prices.[20] The pleasant formula that had kept debt–export ratios steady was no longer relevant, and the ratio began to soar, sending off warning bells. *Even then* bank lending did not falter: in the two years between 1979 and 1981 an enormous amount of money continued to flow, especially into Latin America.[21] This inertia came to an end in 1982: fresh lending by commercial banks dried up completely. A debt crisis had begun.

I say "*a* debt crisis" because this was surely not the first, although by any standards it was the largest. Countries have borrowed and defaulted (and then renegotiated) in the past: Mexico's history in these matters stretches

---

[17] Chile was an exception: most of its debt was held by the private sector, and there were no official government guarantees.

[18] These were the words of Citicorp Chairman Walter Wriston, quoted in Sachs [1989, p. 8].

[19] See, for instance, Sachs [1989, Table 1.2].

[20] Thus, there is no contradiction between a fall in export *earnings* and a continued rise in export *volume*, which, for instance, are the data you see reported in Table 16.1 (Chapter 16). As Edwards [1989] observed, the fall in export prices was so strong that despite a 30% increase in the *volume* of exports between 1980 and 1986, there was little change in export earnings during this period.

[21] Sachs [1989, Table 1.3] informs us that Argentina's net liabilities to international banks (in the reporting area of the Bank for International Settlements) grew from $5.3 to 6.3 billion, those of Brazil from $28.8 to 44.8 billion, and those of Mexico from $22.5 to 43.4 billion, all in the space of those two years!

back to the 1820s.[22] On the whole, lending to foreign governments has *not* been unprofitable even with defaults and renegotiations thrown in,[23] but it is true that lending to a certain subset of borrowers has not been profitable in the past: Chile, Mexico, and Turkey are among the members of this subset.

With very few exceptions, however, defaulting countries have not been treated too differently from their nondefaulting counterparts. The last great crisis of the 1930s led to a situation in which (almost) all developing countries were denied loans, whether or not they had repaid in the past. However, in the 1980s crisis, countries did renegotiate the debt under a mixture of concessions and threats: the larger debtors received better concessions of course, because more was at stake for the creditors.[24] Several reasons for renegotiation (as opposed to unilateral default) can be given:

(1) Countries were genuinely worried about the possibility of future bans on credit. Even when there was no historical reason to believe that defaulters would be treated any differently from nondefaulters, there was always the fear that creditors had learned their lesson and would study their history textbooks the next time around.[25]

(2) There was also the fear that other (noncredit) avenues would be closed off to defaulting borrowers. Trade credits might be suspended or banned, and there was even a possibility that trade sanctions would be imposed. Certainly, the United States wasted no time in politicizing the entire issue by stating that nonpayment amounted to a breach of normal international relations with the United States. Finally, there was the apprehension that support from international organizations such as the International Monetary Fund and the World Bank also would be withdrawn. These apprehensions were heightened when the IMF entered the renegotiation act by making concessional loans under stringent conditions that imposed policy changes on the debtor countries. Indeed, this epoch began a link between the financial support of international organizations and the enactment of particular domestic policies, which we will explore further later.

(3) Finally, there were domestic forces pushing for change. Domestic pressure all depended on the distribution of debtors *within* the borrowing

---

[22] On Mexico, see Aggarwal [1989] and, more generally, Eichengreen and Lindert [1989], Lindert and Morton [1989], and Marichal [1989].

[23] Lindert and Morton [1989] reported that lenders were promised an ex ante interest rate about 2 percentage points in excess of the "going rate" on the bonds of ten foreign governments. Ex post, with all the defaults and postponements included, the rate was still 0.42 percentage points above the going rate. Despite the wailings and moanings of creditors in the 1982 crisis, it remains to be seen whether or not they actually come out in the red at the end of it all.

[24] The moral is, if you want to be a debtor, be a *large* debtor.

[25] For theoretical analyses of the default problem, see, for example, Eaton and Gersovitz [1981], Bulow and Rogoff [1989], and the survey by Eaton and Fernandez [1995].

country and the distribution of those who stood to gain the most from future trade and normalized credit relations. If the government's ties with domestic bankers and exporters were strong, it was more willing to renegotiate the debt and pursue liberal trade policies thereafter. On the other hand, if the main political ties were with import-substituting industries or industries that depended on government contracts, the forces lobbying against change correspondingly stronger. The same was true when there were strong links with workers in protected import-substituting industries.[26]

The debt crisis quickly led to economic crisis within the debtor countries. Of course, there were massive cutbacks in investment; public sector investment in particular. Quite apart from the effects on growth, these cutbacks made the transition to export orientation (the only way to now pay for the debt) far more difficult.

A fall in investment is the outcome on one side of the balance sheet. On the flip side, existing public expenditures, including the payment of interest on the debt needed to be financed, and governments played with a combination of bond finance (which raised real rates of interest) and money creation (which raised inflation).

Higher inflation raised expectations that the government would not be able to control the currency, and there was a flight from domestic holdings of currency. Actually, this sort of capital flight was in evidence in the 1970s as well, as individuals hedged their bets. The mechanics of the capital flight have been described lucidly by Sachs [1989, p. 13]:

> The predominant mechanics of capital flight in the late 1970s and early 1980s were as follows: Suppose that the government increases transfer payments to the private economy. In order to finance these transfer payments, it borrows from the central bank. The central bank financing causes an incipient rise in the money supply as the government spends the borrowed funds. The higher money balances lead to a weakening of the exchange rate as the private sector, flush with cash, attempts to convert some of the increased transfers into foreign currency. This creates the tendency towards higher inflation.... In order to stabilize the price level, the central bank keeps the exchange rate from depreciating by selling foreign exchange in return for the domestic currency.... The central bank runs down its reserves, and the private sector increases its foreign asset holdings.

This flight of private capital was magnified by orders of magnitude as inflation took its toll. Of course it is impossible to hold the exchange rate under such conditions, and exchange rates depreciated every day. Domestically, hyperinflation meant an enormous loss of efficiency in resource allocation, substantially increased inequality, and a subsequent complete failure of relative price calculations.

---

[26] Indeed, the longer the preceding period of import substitution was, the more likely it is that entrenched interests will oppose liberalization.

A Hot Summer in Rio

As a young Indian professor visiting Rio de Janeiro in the summer of 1989–90, I cannot believe what I see (and I am referring to the economy). Indians tend to complain when annual rates of inflation cross the 10% mark, and the norms of keeping inflation low have clearly spilled over to a (relatively) tough central bank and (relatively) prudent government budgets. Here in Brazil in January, inflation is running at 40% (50%? 60%?) per *month*, and economic life looks strange indeed. My friends cannot tell me if a bottle of suntan lotion costs more than a toothbrush. Brazilians with their characteristic joy of living can take these things in stride, but there are limits.

Lower middle-class Brazilian families have invested in deep freezers. This way they can buy lots of food early in the month (milk as well) and freeze the lot before prices begin their upward climb. Wage increases are running at once a month, and as soon as I receive my first paycheck I join the crowded lines at the supermarkets to get as much of my monthly shopping done as possible. Later in the month, I'm going to run out of money (or more accurately, purchasing power).

Why would anyone keep money in the bank? Well, rates of interest are tempting—running at around 60% per month (and more as the days go by). Everybody knows that sooner or later a new stabilization policy will be introduced (with a possible levy on financial assets) and this uncertainty means that governments must pay *even* higher compensatory rates of interest to finance their expenditures, thus hastening the day of reckoning.

Of course, high nominal rates of interest mean that large firms must invest in mini-banking sectors of their own, because any delay in placing daily revenues to work means a large loss of interest. Like the deep freezers, this is another crazy allocation of resources, and the banking system is superefficient (overefficient, one might add): checks must clear almost instantaneously.

Credit cards have disappeared. For a while, a two-price system was in evidence (one if you wanted to pay cash; the other if you wanted to pay by credit card). Pretty soon this system broke down as people gave up trying to accurately forecast next month's inflation rate. Well, not being able to use credit cards is probably a gain.

As inflation accelerates, I can tell that my real salary is lower. This is not hard to figure out: if my wage is being restored (at the beginning of every month) to the same position that it was at the beginning of last month, then my average salary must be lower if inflation is higher. Perhaps a solution is to demand wage increases at more frequent intervals, but how does that help (the economy as a whole) if price hikes react endogenously to the length of the interval? I smell another Prisoners' Dilemma here and I give up.

Of course, my rent to my landlady is fixed in U.S. dollars. As the reliance on the domestic currency dies, the dollar is the only fixed point. All control over the exchange rate is obviously lost, because exchange rate depreciations on the *mercado paralelo* go hand in hand with the interest rate. The *Jornal do Brasil* fights a losing battle in its attempt to communicate market signals: it faithfully records prices of essential items from day to day. In December, potatoes were selling at prices that varied by hundreds of percentage points: all in the same city of Rio de Janeiro.

17.4.3. Structural adjustment

Summary of the problem

As the debt crisis unfolded in the 1980s, the Latin American countries were perceived to be living "beyond their means." Living "beyond one's means" took various forms, but they all stemmed from a common source: different groups in society had their own view of what their real incomes should be and how these real incomes should grow, and these views added up to far more than was actually available. High inflation was particularly good at creating inconsistent views: salary earners tended to peg their wage income aspirations at the ephemeral peak of what they received just following a wage adjustment, whereas notions of business profit were driven by the steady increase in prices that lay between two wage hikes, perhaps by the peak profit just *before* the next wage hike. Simple arithmetic confirms that these two notions of real income add up to more than the national cake.

If a government wishes to pander to these conflicting notions of real income, it must consistently run a fiscal deficit, thus clouding the sharpness of the conflict through constant or accelerating inflation.[27] Why is it that these conflicting views arise so sharply in some countries and not in others? The only answer I can provide is historical: once the tendency to run deficits and an inflationary economy sets in, it is very difficult to get rid of. This is especially the case if such deficits are financed for long periods of time through foreign borrowings. The rapid influx of foreign funds can actually permit a society to live extravagantly for a while: when the inflow dries up, the aspirations of different groups do not dry up with it, at least not instantly.

The entire problem is compounded by policies that try to keep the exchange rate overvalued, so that imports are thereby made artificially cheap. This policy, once in place, is further cemented by strong political pressures (perhaps from large industrial groups with ties to the government) to keep the exchange rate overvalued, which cheapens those imports that are permitted under quota. In addition, we have already seen that there is a feedback effect from the import substitution regime itself: it tends to further raise the exchange rate.

---

[27] This is not to say that governments deliberately create inflation to do this, but that inflation is an inevitable outcome of political weakness—the inability or unwillingness to give in to any one group at the expense of others.

An overvalued exchange rate means that export activities are effectively discriminated against. One implication of discrimination is that an economy may not be able to deal easily with a sudden balance-of-payments crisis (such as one precipitated by a termination of loans) because its exports are unable to quickly rise to the occasion. Thus a time comes when the Central Bank continues to lose foreign exchange reserves and there is little or no foreign inflow of funds to compensate. The exchange rate collapses, and there is high and accelerating inflation with all its attendant losses. A new and more austere external reality meets the internal myth that all groups in society can be kept where they were.

It is useless in these cases to blame everything on naive government mismanagement; for example, governments have no business running a deficit. The underlying problem is at once simple and profound: domestic demand is too high relative to domestic supply, because too many groups have to be given economic concessions at the same time. The government is only one of the major players in this trap of mismatched expectations. If structural adjustment is to work, there must be losers. Unfortunately, it is very difficult (within the broad market mechanism) to divide these losses in an equitable way.

Stabilization and structural adjustment

Following a crisis (and usually in coordination with organizations like the International Monetary Fund and more recently, the World Bank[28]), an *adjustment* package is imposed. The standard IMF/World Bank position in these situations is that (1) fiscal excesses, funded by money creation, lead to a balance-of-payments crisis (in the absence of a continuous injection of outside funds), (2) an overvalued exchange rate is a tax on exports and a subsidy to entrenched groups that benefit from protection and the ability to convert their gains into hard currency, and (3) all prices should reflect market supply and demand, and these include, in particular, wage rates and import prices.

A typical reform package aims to restore some fundamental notion of external balance and goes about this task by a mixture of domestic and international policies. There are two parts to the package. First, short-term measures are applied to deal with the current crisis. The crisis usually takes the form of a severe loss of foreign exchange reserves (e.g., India in 1991), but, as in the case of Latin America in the 1980s, may stem from a huge outstanding debt (Argentina, Chile, Mexico, Brazil), or (later) an extraordinarily high rate of inflation, or (as exemplified by Mexico's 1994 crisis) a speculative flight of portfolio investment. This is the policy of *stabilization*.

Stabilization. Stabilization typically involves an immediate and large devaluation to bring the domestic currency into line with international reality.

---

[28] See the Appendix at the end of this chapter for a brief description of these two organizations.

The idea is to expand exports: with a devalued currency, foreign currency export earnings will now translate into a larger quantity of domestic currency. The flip side is that the prices of nontradables must fall. In theory, this is supposed to move resources (especially capital and labor) out of the nontradables sector into exports.

Observe that a nominal devaluation, large though it may be, may have no lasting real effects if continued inflation brings domestic prices up by the amount of the inflation. For instance, imagine that we decided to call an old peso two new pesos. Under the new peso regime, we have devalued the currency to half its own value, but the "devaluation" is obviously spurious because all prices double at the same time, exactly canceling the devaluation. This absurd-sounding example can actually be mimicked by reality if a devaluation is not followed by appropriate monetary restraint. So a simultaneous attack must be made on inflation (or, if there is currently none, on the possibility of inflation).

Stopping hyperinflation in its tracks is not easy. Prices are rising by tens of percentage points every *month*, and while prices rise steadily, wages are typically adjusted in intervals, which might be yearly, semiannually (in situations of low and moderate inflation), or monthly (in a typical hyperinflationary situation). To be sure, inflation is kept alive by accommodatory money creation on the part of the government, but as we have stated more than once, this is only a symptom and not the underlying cause, which is a true mismatch of income expectations.[29]

There is enormous inertia in the process: each adjustment of price and wage is based on some presumption that the current inflationary trend will continue. In addition, as I have mentioned before, there is the psychological aspect: is a wage (or a price) adjustment felt by its recipients to be the *restoration* of status quo real income or an aggressive move to compensate in advance for future inflation? To the extent that it is the former, a policy that declares an end to all price and wage adjustments and following this up with a restrictive monetary policy (sometimes issuing a new currency as well) is likely to fail: there will always be *some* group of people who did *not* receive their "fair" adjustment when the hyperinflation was declared to be over. This group will vigorously lobby for its adjustment, but if that's granted, there is no end to the process: Other groups move in. Thus an extraordinary display of political will is involved.

The inflationary process often displays an asymmetry so obvious that we almost miss it at first. Note that labor is a commodity like any other, yet wage increases are monitored, tracked, and controlled more than any other commodity price increase. Does anyone know, for instance, if the price of vacuum

---

[29] Indeed, the end of a hyperinflationary episode is often accompanied by a temporary *increase* in the money supply, because the demand for domestic currency rises substantially just after the inflation has ended, and not feeding this demand will entail an enormous rise in interest rates.

cleaners could be adjusted only at six-month intervals? Thus a shock treatment is often accompanied by a denial of all future wage increases, but price adjustments for goods cannot be as easily controlled. Of course, if the government is firm about denying increases, this will stop the inflation, but the burden will have fallen—unfairly, many may add—on salaried employees. The more conservative the government, the more likely it is that they will be able to enforce such a policy, because they are better equipped to sacrifice equity for overall macroeconomic stability.

Other factors compound the distributional problem as well. To hold both exchange rate depreciation and reduced inflation in place, the government must avoid running a fiscal deficit. This is easier said than done. Two components of government expenditure are of particular interest. First, social spending programs are inevitably cut. This affects the poor far more than the nonpoor. Education programs are trimmed; expenditures on health and nutrition are chopped. There is typically an outburst of public opinion against the shenanigans of the government.[30]

Second, public investment projects are shelved or scrapped. To be sure, this slows down long-run capital accumulation, but there are other, shorter-term effects. As an example, think of the textbook description of how the market accomplishes a switch of resources from one industry to another. The price of good A goes up relative to the price of good B. This is exactly what happens after a devaluation, if you think of A as exports and B as non-tradables. Very well: resources must now move from B to A. However, matters aren't so simple: often A requires infrastructure, and the infrastructure is provided through public investment. "[I]ncreasing the capacity of export industries often requires both private and public investment. New export sectors generally require new investment in transport, communications and perhaps port facilities, that usually are in the domain of public investment" (Sachs [1989, p. 21]). This, along with the fall in investment elsewhere in the economy, slows down the adjustment process. The transition involves lower wages and/or rising unemployment. Like the cut in social expenditures, this phenomenon appears to widen inequality as well.

In the particular context of the debt crisis, a third component of government expenditure was relevant as well. The interest on the debt had to be paid. For many large debtor countries the government directly owed debt (as in the case where borrowings were used to finance public-sector projects). In other cases, the government was pressured to assume the debt as the private financial system gave way (Chile is a good example of this). Nobody (except for the debtor) was pushing too hard for a reduction of *this* component of

---

[30] Perhaps the most successful role played by the IMF is the one of chief ogre: governments have not hesitated to make clear that expenditure reductions have been prompted by IMF conditionality. This serves the function of taking some heat off the government.

expenditure. Indeed, in the aftermath of the debt crisis, the primary objective was *not* reform of the developing countries, but to make sure that the developing countries were in a position to repay their debts. These observations apply not only to the banks (who quite understandably cared about their own interests alone), but just as strongly to "multilateral" organizations such as the IMF that were under strong pressure to bail out the banks. A balanced view of the situation at this time must conclude that the reform packages were principally aimed at getting repayments under way, and *incidentally* effected major changes in developing countries, some of which were possibly for the better. As Lindert and Morton [1989, pp. 74–75] observed (emphasis added):

> Rescue packages involving the IMF...impose macroeconomic austerity on the debtor countries (via conditionality). Austerity is not a bad in itself,...[and] can be its own reward from the viewpoint of the adjusting nation...[but] the issue here is not the idea of conditionality, but its current marriage to repayment of private creditors. *In the 1980s, IMF conditionality has imposed macroeconomic adjustments in relation to the* debt hangover, *not just in relation to the macroeconomic* need *for austerity in the debtor country.* Some countries might be pressured too much, others too little.

To be sure, later applications of the same or similar packages were more directly motivated by a reformist agenda.

Structural adjustment. Structural adjustment is the step beyond stabilization. It involves lifting all controls that make for inward orientation and a greater reliance on market prices. Implicit is the argument that a free-market economy leads to the best state of affairs for society, or at least that redistributive policies should be pursued separately, with minimal reliance on the market mechanism.

This is not the place to reiterate points that have been repeatedly made throughout the book, but I cannot resist summarizing them once again. Markets are efficient in situations where widespread contracting is possible, in which externalities are minimal, and in which increasing returns to scale can be handled by competitive agents. We have noted also that distributional issues may justify intervention in markets when directed lump-sum taxes and transfers are ruled out by political or informational considerations. All comprehensive evaluations of a return to free markets must be conducted under this methodological umbrella.

The main elements of a structural adjustment program (SAP) are as follows:

(1) *Import liberalization.* Trade controls should be lifted. If there are quotas or other quantitative restrictions on imports, these should be replaced by tariffs. Ultimately, tariffs should be reduced or done away with altogether. As Edwards [1989], p. 180] puts it, "[R]ecently, trade liberalization has, in many

ways, become synonymous with free-market policies involving minimum or *no government intervention* at any level."

Import liberalization goes back to an old theme: the idea that unconditional free trade is the best response to world conditions, regardless of what the rest of the world is doing. As we will see in Chapter 18, the *developed* world was by no means unambiguously heading in this direction in the 1980s and the 1990s: protection was on the rise (especially in various non-tariff forms). Quite apart from the problems with unconditional free trade from a unilateral viewpoint (that we've already discussed), there are also multilateral issues regarding import liberalization that we will take up in Chapter 18.

It suffices to say at this point that the import liberalization element of a SAP is more an ideological issue; that is, it represents a direction, rather than a component that must be adopted with no exceptions. (If the latter is the case, then probably no SAP has ever been implemented.) Indeed, if we return to the debt crisis, we see that it was impossible to go in this direction in the years immediately following the debt crisis. Imports *had* to be curtailed in order to generate a trade surplus: the fall in export prices meant that an increase in export volume was like pedaling harder to stay in the same place. Thus many Latin American countries imposed *further* import restrictions even after their devaluations occurred: both tariff increases and quantitative restrictions were implemented as part of the stabilization programs. Recognizing that generating a trade surplus was the only way to service the debt, the IMF implicitly supported these steps.

(2) *"Export liberalization" or keeping the exchange rate competitive.* The second element of a SAP is to give free rein to exports by making sure that the initial devaluation that accompanies stabilization is not eroded by inflationary policies. This might require further small devaluations (a "crawl") to compensate for leftover inflation. Multiple exchange rates (where different activities such as debt repayment or imports may be supplied foreign exchange rates) are also discouraged.

It is unclear what giving free rein to exports might mean: countries such as Korea have often been touted as successful examples of export orientation; yet we have seen that government intervention to in promote exports has been of a high order. In any case, *this* is the key element of a SAP that has marked the move away from import substitution in many developing countries. Although import restrictions still exist, many countries do recognize the immense value of promoting exports and have eagerly gone along with this aspect of the policy. The move has gathered momentum as entrenched domestic interests, created by long periods of inward orientation, have slowly dwindled or shifted to a new outward-looking perspective.

The exchange rate devaluation serves another purpose as well. It *switches* expenditure away from imports (which now look more expensive) to domestic nontradables. This expenditure switch also serves to control the balance-of-payments situation. However, as we have already noted, every expenditure-switching policy can be costly, at least in the short to medium run, to the extent that resource reallocation does not take place without friction.

(3) *Fiscal and monetary discipline*. Under this heading comes a whole host of domestic policies. The autonomy of the central bank is stressed, so that fiscal deficits are not automatically approved by printing money. Fiscal deficits are frowned upon. Typically, different components of public expenditure are targeted for reduction or elimination; for instance, when India's crisis hit in 1991, there was enormous pressure from the World Bank to remove the fertilizer subsidy to agriculture and to permit agricultural exports. (The fertilizer subsidy was significantly reduced, but agricultural exports, especially exports of foodgrain, remain a contentious issue.) Likewise, Mexico's agricultural reform program of the late 1980s and early 1990s, under the auspices of a World Bank loan, aimed to remove food subsidies, to move from guaranteed prices to market prices, to abolish export controls, and to cut input subsidies.

SAPs have pushed for privatization of public-sector activities. Again, there is much to applaud and much to be cautious of. It is probably clear that the government has no business running four-star hotels for tourists and that there is a case for the privatization of airlines, but what of health care, or mass transportation, or education? A detailed evaluation of these issues, although they are of extreme importance, takes us afield of our concern with trade policy.

An example: Mexico in the 1980s

In 1982, the Mexican government announced a macroeconomic adjustment program.[31] As we have seen, Mexico was in the initial phase of its debt crisis: interest rates were high and Mexico's announced inability to service its debt had triggered an international crisis. Inflation had accelerated to an annual rate of 100% in 1982. The fiscal deficit was fully 7% of GDP. Oil accounted for over 70% of Mexico's exports, and oil prices had just begun a long downward trend. If the definition of a disaster is that several things that can possibly go wrong all go wrong at once, then disaster had struck.

An emergency program for economic reorganization, the *Programa Inmediato de Reordenación Económica* (PIRE), went into effect in December 1982. It featured drastic cuts in public expenditure, increases in the prices of goods and services provided by the public sector (including telephone, electricity, and public transportation), a devaluation of the exchange rate, strict control

---

[31] I am very grateful to Luis-Felipe López-Calva, who provided the material for this section. The discussion that follows relies on publications by Lustig [1992], Ros [1992], and Székely [1995a, b].

of wages (with centralized arrangements for wage bargaining), and credit restrictions in the banking sector. A decision to privatize state-run enterprises was announced. Trade policy was to be restructured: thus far protection had been provided to several sectors, with the use of tariffs and quotas.

Up to 1987, nothing worked. Inflation acquired a life of its own, based on expectational inertia, and by 1987 the annual rate of price increase was at 160%. With this sort of inflation the currency had to be devalued again and again, but of course inflation endogenously reacted to the devaluations. The problem was one that we have discussed in some detail: the sum total of income expectations of different groups in the society exceeded what was available. For many years, foreign borrowing had filled that gap between expectations and reality. Real income in Mexico *fell* by 0.7% over the period 1982–87 and the per capita decline was 2%. The fiscal deficit was now at 16% of GDP.

A new program, the *Pacto de Solidaridad Económica* (PSE), was announced in December 1987. This program combined the traditional or orthodox policy of fiscal and monetary austerity with so-called heterodox elements. Direct controls over prices of selected goods and services were instituted. A centralized tripartite committee was established to negotiate all changes in prices, wages, exchange rate, and tariffs among entrepreneurs, unions, and the government itself. The privatization program was accelerated and, apart from the price controls, economic activity was deregulated to a greater extent.

The policy changes that took place over the decade of the 1980s were significant indeed. In 1982, the number of state-run enterprises was 1,155; it 1990 it was 280. In 1985, Mexico joined the General Agreement on Trade and Tariffs (GATT). The percentage of goods covered by import licenses fell from 96% in that year to 19% in 1990. The maximum import tariff was reduced from 100% in 1982 to 20% in 1990, and the weighted average tariff fell from 24 to 12% during the same period.

Were there any positive results during this period? Yes, but they were mild. Annual inflation was down to around 20% in 1990 and per capita growth made a recovery in 1989 and 1990 (growing by 1.5% and 2.3% in these two years). The fiscal deficit was down to a relatively respectable 3.4% of GDP in 1990. So it's clear that the medicine worked on the system as a whole, but our theory that *some* group in society has to give must mean that there were changes in distribution. Can we identify what they are?

It isn't very hard to identify the changes. It is absolutely clear that real wages bore the brunt of the adjustment. *Real* wages in the industrial sector fell 47% in between 1982 and 1988. Indeed, this decline pretty much mirrored the erosion of the official minimum wage, which declined by 40% over

Table 17.1. Inequality in Mexico, 1984 and 1989.

	Share (%)		
	---	---	---
Year	Poorest 40%	Richest 10%	Gini coefficient
1984	14	33	0.462
1989	13	38	0.513

Source: Székely [1995a].

this period. The *share* of wages in aggregate income fell from 36 to 25.9%.[32] Incredible as it may appear, if we combine this information with the change in average real income over this period, it appears that nonwage earners continued to be *better off* during these crisis years.

Clearly, the high inflation rate during that period played a major redistributive role, as it did in all high-inflation Latin American countries. The sectoral changes that were inspired by the devaluation, as well as the reduction of import protection, had their effects as well (as discussed earlier). It is true that during 1989 and 1990, industrial wages recovered 9% (real), but that increase was not enough to offset the previous trend.

Income distribution, predictably enough, worsened over these years. Income expenditure surveys carried out by the Mexican government in 1984 and 1989 are summarized in Table 17.1, where the data confirm the significant widening of inequality over those years.

Inequality did not rise at the same pace in later years, but the trend did not reverse itself either. In 1992, the Gini coefficient stood at 0.515—marginally higher than the 1989 level.

The poverty indices are somewhat more stable. Table 17.2 provides data on the head count and poverty gap for the years 1984, 1989, and 1992.[33] Two poverty lines are used. *Extreme poverty* occurs when income is not enough to cover the cost of a basic food basket with calorie content at a minimum established by the World Health Organization. *Moderate poverty* occurs when income falls below the same basket plus an allowance for housing, clothing, education, health services, and recreation. See Székely [1995b] for the methodology used to construct these indices.

Table 17.2 tells us that the trends in poverty are not as sharp as the inequality trends, although poverty gaps for both poverty lines show an increase between 1984 and 1989. Two explanations are possible. The first is

[32] Up until a second crisis in December 1994, when a sharp devaluation provoked a flight of portfolio investment from Mexico, the minimum wage continued to fall. Between December 1987 and May 1994, the minimum wage rose by 136% (nominal), whereas the cost of the "basket of basic goods" (see subsequent discussion of poverty measure) grew by 371% (Heredia and Purcell [1995]).

[33] The FGT index (see appendix to Chapter 8) is also available and shows a trend similar to the poverty gap; I omit it here.

Table 17.2. Poverty in Mexico, 1984, 1989, and 1992.

Year	Extreme poverty		Moderate poverty	
	Head count (%)	Poverty gap (%)	Head count (%)	Poverty gap (%)
1984	10.3	3.0	29.8	10.3
1989	10.7	3.5	28.3	10.6
1992	10.8	3.2	27.8	10.2

Source: Székely [1995b].

that the adjustment programs most strongly affected salaried employees in the industrial sector—unionized workers, for instance—and these workers would not be classified below the poverty line before or after. Self-employed people in small businesses would have been affected as well. However, this explanation alone cannot be reconciled with the enormous decrease in wage rates that occurred over this period. It must also be the case that despite a drastic reduction in real wages, many households were able to avoid comparable drops in total income and per capita consumption by changing their intensity of labor-force participation. These changes might include an increase in hours worked and a search for new income-generating activities, as well as a greater fraction of family members in the work force. To be sure, these decisions might imply an increase in the dropout rates in schools and a reduction in the standards of health and nutrition at the household level, which are likely to affect the income-generating capacity of the individuals and then the income distribution in a longer-run perspective.

Recent trends in income distribution seem to mirror the old, and poverty has certainly risen since the 1994 crisis, in which a sharp devaluation provoked an enormous flight of portfolio investment from Mexico.[34] Heredia and Purcell [1995] reported that "60% of these [small and medium] enterprises, which historically employ 80% of the country's labor force, have laid off workers in 1995." The Mexican story so far seems to be one of "incomplete structural adjustment" in which the relatively poor have paid a relatively higher price for macroeconomic balance.

17.5. Summary

This chapter studied trade policies followed by individual countries. We began with a discussion of the "gains-from-trade" theorem. Trade must lead to a potential improvement for all because trade possibilities are just like production possibilities (some goods are transformed into others). Shutting down extra avenues of "production" can never be a good thing, and most of

[34] See the *Journal of International Economics* **41**, November 1996, for an analysis of the 1994 crisis.

the time it is a bad thing. This is the case for *unconditional free trade*: a policy of unrestricted trade no matter what the rest of the world is doing.

However, it is important to realize that a potential improvement in "production possibilities" may not necessarily translate into an *actual* improvement for all concerned. This is because trade affects the prices of factors of production, and factors are (in general) owned in different proportions by different groups in society. This sort of effect is most likely to occur when trade is of the Heckscher–Ohlin variety: inputs that are intensively used in the production of the imported commodity must lose value, whereas inputs that are intensively employed in the production of exportables must gain. In contrast, trade in similar commodities is more likely to lead to an *actual* Pareto improvement: there are no differential pressures on factors of production.

We continued our discussion of the gains from trade by looking at imperfect worlds: those in which market failures or market imperfections exist. In such situations, the opening up to free trade may lead to overall losses rather than gains. For instance, the exports of primary commodities may experience a long-run fall in price (the *Prebisch–Singer hypothesis*). Under these conditions a switch to manufacturing may be appropriate, but because of capital market imperfections this may not occur spontaneously. Certainly, it is better policy to address the source of the capital market imperfections, but if this is difficult for other reasons, restrictive trade policy designed to take into account *dynamic comparative advantage* may be called for. In addition, manufacturing may generate economy wide externalities that no individual industrialist internalizes, so it may be socially optimal to promote manufactures although private entrepreneurs will not automatically do so. This is the basis of export promotion policies followed by countries such as Korea.

External effects (or capital market imperfections) can also form the basis of *infant-industry arguments*: policies that restrict imports in order to nurture domestic industry.

Distributional arguments can lead to interventionist trade policy. It might be felt that the existing distribution of income or wealth is too unequal, but there is a market failure in the sense that lump-sum taxes or transfers to redistribute income are not politically or informationally feasible. In that case, a second-best response may be to ban the import of certain consumer goods. This is distortionary from a market perspective, but may be a second-best move toward social equity.

Thus the free-trade theorem is correct, but with two qualifications: (1) the gains may be unequally distributed, so that actual improvements do not occur to all, and (2) other missing markets might create valid counterarguments to free trade.

We then turned to trade policies. We discussed policies of *import substitution*: the use of tariffs and quotas to restrict imports (perhaps differentially across commodities), their effects on exchange rates, and their welfare effects from the narrow market-distortion viewpoint. These distortion losses must be compared with the possible gains discussed previously. We also discussed the infant-industry argument for protection. We then studied *export promotion* policies: export subsidies, directed credit, and their welfare effects.

There has been a general trend toward outward orientation: export promotion rather than import substitution (at least in the developing world). We took up this topic and argued that the goals of some import substitution policies may be laudable, but the policies themselves have the effect of creating entrenched domestic groups with strong vested interests in protection. To the extent that these special interest groups can successfully lobby the government to maintain their positions of privilege, this can be detrimental for the economy as a whole.

Countries can run for decades under these distortions, until some dramatic event causes a shakedown. An example of this is the *debt crisis* that many countries, particularly the countries of Latin America, experienced in the early 1980s. Enormous fiscal deficits were financed by inflows of loans from foreign banks through the 1970s. When interest rates rose in the 1980s, many countries ran into difficulties with debt service, and in the resulting panic, the supply of loans dried up altogether. Nonetheless, the debt had to be serviced and this meant a turnaround in the balance of payments: many countries, pushed along with conditional loans from the IMF and the World Bank, adopted a policy of outward orientation. Two policies that bear on trade issues are relevant in this context: *stabilization* and *structural adjustment*. Stabilization refers to the application of emergency measures to staunch an immediate balance-of-payments crisis and perhaps halt galloping inflation. Structural adjustment refers to a package of longer-run policies: trade liberalization in both exports and imports, proper management of the exchange rate, control of the fiscal deficit, and appropriate monetary policy consistent with achieving these outcomes. We discussed these policies at the very end of the chapter.

Appendix: The International Monetary Fund and the World Bank

After World War II (July 1944), the leaders of England and the United States convened a conference at Bretton Woods, New Hampshire. There plans were developed for three institutions that would shape the world economy for the next fifty years. These were the *International Monetary Fund* (IMF), the *World Bank*, and the *General Agreement on Trade and Tariffs* (GATT). Our objective here is to provide a brief overview of the functioning of the first two institutions; GATT will be taken up in Chapter 18.[35]

The IMF was established with the following objectives as stated in the Articles of Agreement[36]:

(1) To promote exchange rate stability, to maintain orderly exchange arrangements among members, and to avoid competitive exchange-rate devaluations.

(2) To assist in the establishment of a multilateral system of payments for current transactions between members, thus aiding the elimination of foreign exchange restrictions that might hamper the growth of world trade.

(3) To instill confidence in member nations by making the Fund's resources available to them under adequate safeguards, thus providing them with an opportunity to make adjustments in their balance of payments without resorting to measures that might be inimical to world development.

Also founded at Bretton Woods was the International Bank for Reconstruction and Development, perhaps better known as the *World Bank*, with the following main objectives[37]:

(1) To assist in the reconstruction and long-run development of member nations by encouraging capital investment in productive economic activity.[38]

(2) To promote private foreign investment by means of guarantees or participations in loans and other investments made by private investors; and when private capital is not available on reasonable terms, to supplement private investment by providing, on suitable conditions, finance for productive purposes out of the Bank's own capital or funds raised by the Bank.

(3) To promote the growth of international trade and the maintenance of equilibrium in balance of payments by encouraging international investment for the development of the productive resources of member nations.

It is clear from this description that the Fund was intended to be the center of the postwar international monetary system. Its objectives were primarily to *stabilize* short-run fluctuations and to tide countries over severe but temporary liquidity constraints. In contrast, the Bank was entrusted with tasks pertaining to the longer run: reconstruction and development. In this

---

[35] I thank Hiranya Mukhopadhyay for making available an extensive set of notes, on which this appendix is based.

[36] On the Articles of Agreement, see *The First Ten Years of the International Monetary Fund*, IMF, Washington, DC, August 24, 1956.

[37] On these objectives, consult Article I of the Articles of Agreement, *First Annual Meeting of the Board of Governors of the International Bank for Reconstruction and Development*, Washington, DC, September 27, 1946.

[38] This included the reconstruction of economies destroyed or disrupted by war, as well as the encouragement of the development of productive facilities in less developed countries.

context, observe that the Articles of Agreement of the IMF do not include the encouragement of long-run growth as an objective, whereas those of the Bank most certainly do.

More recently, however, these distinctions have begun to blur somewhat. With the introduction of *structural adjustment loans* by the Bank in 1980 (on which more presently), stipulations were introduced requiring any developing country in balance-of-payments difficulties to approach the Fund first for stabilization. Only then would the Bank consider longer-term finance. This blending of Fund and Bank in an overall financing package has been reinforced by the Fund's increased focus on issues of growth. For instance, moneys disbursed under a "structural adjustment facility" (in place since 1986) serve the dual objectives of strengthening the balance-of-payments situation and fostering growth as well.[39]

Loan packages offered by the World Bank are usually based on a philosophy of supply-side reforms. Thus it was traditionally the Bank's primary concern to extend "project loans" (for roads, irrigation, etc.) to developing countries. However, this emphasis has changed somewhat over the years, in line with the blurring of Bank–Fund distinctions mentioned already, and is seen clearly in the appearance of the first structural adjustment loans (SALs) in 1980 (see Mosley, Harrigan, and Toye [1991]). The importance of these SALs increased enormously with the outbreak of the debt crisis in the early 1980s.

This form of "program-based" lending, unlike the earlier form of project lending, was provided as general support for a balance-of-payments deficit and to facilitate imports that might increase or restore economic growth. Initially, as with the IMF, a structural adjustment loan was extended mainly for short-term stabilization. However, subsequent SALs focused on adjustments for different sectors of the economy. Tax reforms, the restructuring of public expenditure, measures to increase the efficiency or to support the privatization of state-owned enterprises, trade reforms, financialmarket reforms, and other sectoral reforms all come under the purview of these loans, and the loans are often conditioned on perceived success in attaining these various objectives (see Corbo, Fischer, and Webb [1992]). These reforms or structural adjustments are perceived as necessary to turn the success of a short-term stabilization program (financed either by IMF, the Bank, or both) into a permanent one and to ensure the revival of growth in a sustainable way.

This brings us to the concept of *conditionality*—a word that has gained increased recognition in international lending circles. "Conditionality" refers

[39] On the various types of arrangements offered by the IMF, see Polak [1991]. Although many facilities do pertain to short-term difficulties faced by borrower countries (in line with the original charter of the IMF), both the structural adjustment facilities and the *conditioning* of short-term loans on the adoption of government policies with long-run consequences reflect the changing nature of the Fund since the 1980s.

to the requirements that the International Monetary Fund and the World Bank increasingly impose on a member country that wishes to borrow money from them. The presumed objective of conditionality is to ensure that the member country benefits from the loans, there being some presumption that the country is not entirely capable of carrying out tough reforms without tough conditions. Following the debt crisis, there is also the desire to ensure that borrowing countries do not have difficulties repaying the loans in the future. In short, conditionality demands that a member country that uses international resources pursue a set of policies that are "appropriate" to its current economic situation.

It turns out that the Bank's practices with respect to conditionality differ considerably from those of the Fund. Fund conditionality stipulates a limited number of monitorable performance criteria (e.g., fiscal deficit to GDP ratio, growth of money supply, etc.). If, at the end of specified period, all such performance criteria are met, the member's access to the next tranche is ensured. The Bank's conditions are many (averaging fifty to sixty per SAL in recent years). Many of the stipulations are couched in general terms and leave room for interpretation (for example, "adequate" reforms in the area of trade). Thus the release of a second tranche is subject to intense negotiations and individual judgment.[40] Needless to say, these conditions vary from country to country.[41]

Note explicitly that what the Bank or the IMF considers appropriate policy may not be regarded in the same light by the borrowing country. In part, this difference of opinion may arise from a difference in political ideology. It is no secret that the distributional consequences of policies often play second fiddle to what are considered to be the large efficiency gains imposed by the disciplining forces of the market. Thus conditionality packages often impose restrictions on wage increases (to reduce inflationary pressure) or fiscal discipline by requiring cutbacks in government expenditure. To the extent that wage increases or government expenditure on public infrastructure are regarded as socially or politically progressive, such conditions are regarded with a great deal of suspicion, especially by the citizens of the developing countries on which these conditions are imposed.

At the same time, it is also the case that conditionality may prevent successful lobbying by industrial or rich agricultural interest groups that need no special mollycoddling, but who nevertheless receive special treatment because of their political and economic clout. For instance, the system of industrial licensing often acts as a means to assure lucrative deals to powerful business interests. To the extent that conditionality is directed against

---

[40] On these matters, see, for example, Polak [1994].

[41] A major instrument for these purposes is the *letter of intent*. This letter describes the policy actions that the member country has taken or intends to take in the future. This is normally accompanied by a "policy framework paper" in which the government informs the Fund and the Bank of its broad policy outlines for the coming three years.

such regressive licensing arrangements, it may be a good thing. In addition, whereas the availability of additional financing can induce governments to postpone urgently needed reforms, conditionality acts as a counterbalance to this tendency.

In short, just because the Bank or Fund imposes certain conditions for financing, as economists we need not accept these conditions as appropriate. It is important, often, to look at these conditions from the point of view of the country itself, and not just from the point of view of international lenders or funding agencies.

Exercises

■ (1) By drawing production possibility frontiers and international price lines, show that trade can be viewed as just another method of production, where exports serve as "inputs" and imports are "outputs." In so doing, show that the opportunity to trade always represents a potential Pareto improvement.

■ (2) (a) Show that if all individuals in a country have the same holdings of all factors of production (and the same shareholdings in all companies), and if there are no externalities, the opportunity to trade must lead to an unambiguous Pareto improvement in that country. In this sense, lobbying for trade barriers must come from the uneven distribution of factor endowments across people.

(b) Provide an example in which there are externalities and the opening-up to trade makes all individuals worse off, even in this completely symmetric world.

■ (3) Suppose that we divide commodities into two groups: food and non-food.

(a) Draw indifference curves that reflect the fact that preferences for food grow relatively weaker as we increase consumption of both commodities. Now introduce a budget constraint (income and fixed prices) and chalk out the consumption points as income varies. On a separate diagram, describe how food consumption varies with income for fixed market prices.

(b) Use this diagram to argue that if relative prices of food to nonfood are fixed, the growth of food consumption in the world economy will be slower than the growth of total income, Use this observation to argue that exporters of food will find export revenues growing more slowly than world income. This is the essence of the declining terms-of-trade argument for primary products.

(c) Use these arguments to provide a partial explanation for why farmers in developed countries demand (and obtain) high levels of economic support from the government.

■ (4) Review the arguments for trade policy in this chapter, paying particular attention to (i) externalities (ii) distributional issues and (iii) capital market imperfections. Show that these arguments all rely on some sort of market failure.

■ (5) Discuss circumstances under which tariffs and quotas have equivalent effects, and circumstances under which they do not. Pay particular attention to (i) issues of tariff revenue, (ii) the possibility of black markets or bribes in the allocation of quotas, and (iii) the lack of information that the policymaker may have about the economy.

■ (6) Suppose that domestic producers in a developing country are able to produce cement at a unit cost of $5 per kilogram, up to a capacity limit of ten million kilograms a year. The world price of cement is $1.50 per kilogram. Suppose that there are two categories of cement *users*: industrial construction companies, who are willing to pay up to $10 per kilogram, and demand five million kilograms a year; and household construction companies, who are willing to pay up to $2 per kilogram, and demand 25 million kilograms a year.

(a) Describe the market outcome when the country can freely export and import cement.

(b) Suppose that the government needs to balance its budget and for this purpose needs to raise revenues of $20 million a year by levying either a tariff on cement imports or an excise tax on the domestic production of cement. Can this be achieved by a tariff alone? By a sales tax alone?

(c) Is there a combined tax–tariff policy that will succeed in ensuring survival of the domestic cement industry, as well as in raising the required revenues? What criteria would you use to attack or defend such a policy?

■ (7) Here is the large-country argument for an optimal tariff. Recall the welfare analysis conducted for tariffs in this chapter. We will use this methodology in the exercise that follows.

(a) For simplicity, suppose that a good is fully imported, so that there are no domestic producers of it. On a diagram, draw the domestic demand curve and the foreign supply curve of the good to this country, and show the free trade equilibrium. Mark off the equilibrium price (p^*) and the equilibrium quantity (q^*) of the good. Shade the amount of consumer and producer surpluses generated by the equilibrium.

(b) Now draw another diagram which displays a tariff at rate t on the good. Show the new equilibrium price and quantity. Note that consumer surplus has declined and so has producer surplus. But now there is positive tariff revenue. Shade all the areas corresponding to these three magnitudes, and note that their *sum* is less than the sum of producer and consumer surplus in part (a). You have just shown, graphically, that the sum of producer and consumer surplus, and tariff revenue, is maximized at the free trade point, where tariff revenues are zero.

(c) Show (by drawing a third diagram) that if the supply curve is horizontal, a zero tariff also maximizes the sum of consumer surplus and tariff revenue *alone*. Interpret this result as stating that for a country which is unable to influence the price of its imports, the optimal tariff is zero.

(d) Now return to the general case of part (b). Focus, as in part (c), on the sum of consumer surplus and tariff revenues. (Foreign producer surplus will be neglected by the domestic government.) We will show that this sum is maximized at a strictly positive tariff. Follow these steps.

First, expand the problem to include import *subsidies* (which are simply negative tariffs). Show, just as in part (a), that the sum of consumer surplus, tariff revenues, *and* foreign producer surplus is still maximized when the tariff (or subsidy) is set equal to zero. Draw a diagram (with tariffs/subsidies on one axis and the sum of surpluses on the other) that relates this total surplus to the tariff. By our observation, this curve should look inverted-U shaped with its peak attained when tariffs equal zero.

Second, show that if the supply curve is upward-sloping, foreign producer surplus consistently increases as tariffs are lowered to zero and continues to increase with import subsidies. Draw this curve on the same diagram.

Finally, note that the government's objective is tantamount to maximizing the vertical difference between these two sets of curves. Show that this maximum point *must* be attained at a strictly positive tariff.

The only exception to this rule, as noted in part (b), is when the supply curve is perfectly flat, so that producer surplus is zero irrespective of tariff or subsidy.

■ (8) Suppose that the government follows a policy of infant-industry protection, allowing the domestic production of automobiles in an economy sheltered by tariffs on car imports.

(a) Discuss the critical features of a policy that aims to generate efficiency and international competitiveness in the car industry. Pay particular attention to the termination date of the policy.

(b) Now examine the government's incentives to remove the protectionist policy *if* the car industry does not make any progress. Explain why these incentives are crucial to the success of the original policy. Discuss different factors that might bear on these incentives (see the game theory appendix for more a more formal description of these issues).

■ (9) It may be optimal for a country to restrict the exports of some commodity for which it is a principal exporter. Examine this statement. In particular, address the question of why individual exporters do not spontaneously impose export restrictions on themselves even if it is optimal for them to do so as a group.

■ (10) The liberalization of agricultural exports is a major issue in India. Higher exports for farmers will mean greater revenues and higher prices for them. Why might the government be opposed to such a policy?

■ (11) Developed countries argue for the protection of intellectual property rights in developing countries, so that new technological advances can be protected by means of patents. They argue that such protection will enhance technical progress (because the fruits of such progress can be appropriated by the innovators, creating greater incentives for R&D). Why might developing countries not provide such protection?

■ (12) "Governments never go bankrupt. So lending to them is a wise idea. They can always repay." Using the concepts of involuntary and strategic default (see Chapter 14), examine this statement carefully.

■ (13) Suppose that there is a single lender and a single borrower, and there is no legal mechanism to enforce loan repayment. A borrower can costlessly keep any amount borrowed, but the lender can then decide not to lend to the borrower in the future. By studying the theory of repeated games discussed in Appendix 1 and by drawing on ideas in Chapter 14, construct a story of how active loan and repayment transactions can be conducted in this credit market.

■ (14) Countries that have a high international debt face what is called the *debt overhang*. The prospect of having to service a large debt from investment returns discourages investment. In such situations, some amount of debt forgiveness can help. To see this, consider the following example:

A country needs to make $2 billion of service payments on its debt. To do so, its government can attempt to raise additional resources, say by extra taxation or reduced expenditures, in order to make investments of $10 billion dollars. Only an investment with a net return of 10% or more (to the government) will be undertaken. These investments pay off $2.5 billion dollars in additional revenue: a 25% return.

(a) Show that if debt service payments have to be made from the returns, these investments will not be undertaken.

(b) Show that a certain amount of forgiveness (or postponement) of the debt service will make both the government and the creditors better off. Calculate the minimum amount of forgiveness that's necessary.

(c) Suppose a whole range of investments (at different levels) are available. Creditors might forgive some of the debt in order to induce these investments (as above) or might participate more actively in the investments themselves, asking for a fixed percentage of the returns as debt service. That is, debt is converted into equity. Compare these two options. Ideas from the theory of land tenancy (see Chapter 12) may be relevant here.

■ (15) "Conditionality" refers to the specification of certain policies that a government must follow in order to receive loans or assistance from international organizations such as the International Monetary Fund or the World Bank. Here is an example to illustrate one useful aspect of conditionality.

A loan of $10 billion is to be given to a government. Just as in the previous question, the loan may be used in investments, and the government will undertake investments if they pay off at least 10%, but not otherwise. Suppose that the ongoing debt service is $2 billion (and that debt service can only be done if these investments are made). The organization making the loan is happy with a 3% return (especially if the loan helps to service the debt).

(a) Show that if the loan is made without any conditions, it will not be used in investments but consumed, and therefore that the loan will not be made in the first place. In contrast, show that an appropriate commitment from the government in return for the loan will make the international organization, the borrowing government, and the private creditors all better off.

(b) Modify this example to create a case in which *both* conditionality and some debt forgiveness is required to create a satisfactory solution.

Chapter 18

Multilateral Approaches to Trade Policy

18.1. Introduction

With much of the world riddled with trade barriers of all kinds, it is not surprising that groups of countries have attempted to get together to promote freer trade among themselves. Such promotion may be of varying degrees. In the mildest case, group members agree to reduce or eliminate tariff or other impediments to imports that are purchased from other countries in the group. In addition, the group might coordinate to set common tariff barriers to imports from the rest of the world. Taking matters a step further still, these policies of free (or at least freer) trade might be supplanted by an agreement to permit unrestricted flows of capital and labor across the member countries.

We begin this chapter by studying protectionist tendencies: theories that describe why we are in a barrier-riddled world in the first place. We then move on to partial liberalizations of trade in the form of customs unions.

Analyzing this class of issues requires a somewhat peculiar contextual framework. As economists, we often situate ourselves in the basic structure of an unfettered market economy and analyze movements *away* from "free-market" outcomes as reactions to certain types of economic failures: imperfect information, incomplete enforcement of contracts, equity issues, and so on. The study of movements *toward* free (or freer) trade requires us to situate ourselves in a mental status quo in which trade barriers (restricted markets, more generally) are the starting point and free trade is a possible end. We must run our mental model backwards.

A brief description of the international context may be useful at this point. A significant number of the trade agreements and multilateral tariff reductions that have taken place since World War II fall under the shadow of the General Agreement on Trade and Tariffs (GATT), which is a complex multilateral system of rules and norms aimed at reducing trade barriers among countries on some coordinated, multilateral basis. The last of eight rounds of GATT negotiations, which took place in Uruguay, called for the creation of the World Trade Organization, a nascent organization that replaces GATT, and has much the same objectives in mind. It is unclear just how much GATT actively achieved. It isn't that tariff reductions the world over have not taken place. Starting with the first round of GATT talks in Geneva (1947), world tariffs have been reduced from an average rate of 40% in 1947 to around 4% in 1994 (Staiger [1995]), which is an enormous achievement. However, there are two obstacles to declaring this accomplishment a GATT success: first, along with the reduction in baseline tariffs the list of exceptions, special cases, reactions to "unfair" circumstances, and various forms of special (nontariff) protection has grown, and second, it is difficult to estimate how much of this progress would have been made anyway, with or without some organization like GATT in the background.

Nonetheless, GATT probably played a central role as an explicit coordination mechanism that permitted countries to negotiate or renegotiate trade agreements. It also played a role in the flip side of agreements: that is, as a framework to assess appropriate retaliations (either unilateral or on a multilateral basis) in case agreements were not complied with. Note that this flip side is of paramount importance: unlike the laws that govern breaches of contract domestically, there is little or nothing the international community can do to *legally* punish the governments of entire countries. Thus all agreements must, in a sense, be self-enforcing, and coordination of the enforcement mechanism can result in more ambitious and rewarding agreements. Finally, the psychological impact of GATT as an *obligation* cannot be understated. To the extent that a country wished to appear to be a responsible and sensitive citizen of the world community of nations, GATT provided a focus around which such responsibilities and sensibilities could be visibly expressed.

This brings us to a major question to be studied in this chapter. If GATT, or more generally, multilateral agreements, act as a coordination device for achieving mutually beneficial trade outcomes, this must be because there are serious grounds for such failure of coordination in the first place. The unilateral actions and reactions of a single country (the subject of Chapter 17) tell only a part of the story. The fact that country A places a tariff on the product of country B often ignites responses by country B that perhaps would not have been forthcoming in the absence of the initial move by country A. Thus the United States might consider a punitive levy on Japanese car imports in the face of perceived injustices perpetrated by Japan on exports by the United States to that country. Alternatively, faced with stiff tariffs on textile exports to the European Union (EU), a developing country might react by placing limits on EU trade with that country.

One interpretation of this situation is that trade wars are similar to the bad equilibrium of some *coordination game* [see Chapter 5 and Appendix 1 (at the end of the book) for extended discussions]. That is, both free trade and restricted trade are equilibria of the game. Under this view, multilateral organizations serve as a coordination device to attain the "good" free-trade equilibrium of the coordination game.

Alternatively, trade is perhaps more akin to a Prisoners' Dilemma than a coordination game; tariff barriers are the *only* equilibrium outcome in a static context. In this case, the role of an international organization such as GATT must be viewed differently: to try to maintain a cooperative outcome with low or nonexistent trade barriers as the equilibrium of some *repeated* interaction [see Appendix 1 (at the end of the book) for a description of repeated games]. Not only must the cooperative outcome be specified (which is enough if the problem is only one of coordination failure), but there must be a clear set of guidelines under which deviations from the cooperative outcome are punished. There is probably a grain of truth to both interpretations.

GATT also has generated several *regional agreements*, perhaps not deliberately, but as a reaction to its *most-favored-nation* (MFN) principle. The principle, enshrined in Article I of the GATT charter, states that the exports of no two member countries may be treated differently: in particular, a trade concession made to one country must be simultaneously extended to all other countries. As you might imagine, several exceptions and loopholes accompany the MFN principle. Among these is the "regional clause" (Article XXIV): groups of countries that wish to forge their own trading agreements may do so without extending these privileges to other countries (as normally would be required by MFN), provided that they form substantial free-trade zones within their blocs. This made the formation of regional trade agreements very attractive under some circumstances, because they permitted the maintenance of a common tariff wall without substantially running counter to the original spirit of GATT.

An outstanding example of this kind of far-reaching agreement is found in the formation of the European Common Market [later called the European Economic Community (EC) and more recently, the European Union (EU)] under the Treaty of Rome in 1957. With several bouts of expansion to attain its present membership of fifteen European nations, the European Union of today has pursued all the aforementioned free-trade goals and, in addition, has worked toward common social and economic policies, such as coordinated immigration and monetary policies, as well as toward a certain degree of political integration. A less ambitious arrangement is the more recent North American Free Trade Agreement (NAFTA), which permits trade in commodities across the member states of Canada, Mexico, and the United States, but stops well short of admitting the unrestricted flow of labor across the three countries.

The preceding two examples are interesting from another viewpoint as well. The EU represents an example of several *developed* economies (albeit at somewhat varying levels of per capita income and overall development) attempting to set up a community of free exchange of goods and factors. In contrast, NAFTA represents the coming together of countries at widely different stages in the development process. Although both examples share the common feature of being multilaterally negotiated regional agreements, they are different indeed from this new perspective. A central concern addressed in this chapter is whether regional agreements across countries at *similar* levels of development are more likely to occur (or succeed) than agreements across countries with different levels of development.

We end with a discussion of regionalism and whether it promotes truly multilateral free trade in the long run.

18.2. Restricted trade

18.2.1. Second-best arguments for protection

What forces drive protectionist tendencies? In Chapter 17 we discussed a number of factors, particularly relevant for developing countries, that *might* make a certain degree of prudent protection acceptable. Our arguments there hinged on two broad pillars: (1) that the social optimum is somehow different from the market optimum realized by free international trade and that some degree of protection (even if it is distortionary in the classical sense) might serve to move the economy closer to the socially desired outcome; (2) that failures in other markets (such as the market for credit) might be compensated by corrective trade policy. As an example of the first effect, consider an unequal distribution of income or wealth that spurs the demand for consumer goods, paid for by scarce foreign exchange earnings from exports. Consumer goods imports may then be taxed in the form of a tariff or a quota. As an example of the second effect, suppose that credit constraints prevent exporters of primary goods from moving into manufactures, even though the prices of primaries are unstable or declining. This might drive a wedge between "static" and "dynamic" comparative advantage.

Similarly, the infant-industry argument discussed in Chapter 17 relies on missing markets (for capital or for the internalization of spillovers). For instance, if the net present value of learning by doing is positive, there is no reason why a private producer cannot carry out this activity, provided that capital markets are perfect. To be sure, the perfection argument strains the imagination here, because there will be long periods when losses will need to be systematically financed as the infant struggles to grow up.

These arguments for restricted trade need to be treated with a great deal of caution. They can be misused by interest groups and can be misunderstood by economists. We reiterate, as we did in Chapter 17, that if there are no market failures, then the argument for free trade is faultless. Moreover, even if there are market failures, a direct policy intervention in those markets may be better (though such policy interventions may be very difficult to carry out). For instance, the income distribution argument for restricted trade presupposes that *other* means of transferring income from rich to poor are limited. However, the possibilities of making direct progress along those avenues should be thoroughly explored before trade policy is used as a second-best device.

In a world with complete markets (or with policies directly aimed at those markets that are imperfect), it is difficult to make the case against free trade. Indeed, as we already noted, world trade is just like a production technology that (except in degenerate special cases) always will be profitable to use: closing this option can only hurt and not help. Hence, the classical theory of trade policy, evolving from the writings of David Ricardo and John Stuart Mill, has a simple and direct prescription: engage in *unilateral* free trade. Never mind if your trading partners are free traders or protectionist.

18.2.2. *Protectionist tendencies*

In sharp contrast to this prescription, we see substantial protectionist tendencies in the world today. Although developing countries engage in protection, ostensibly for one or more of the aforementioned reasons, many developed countries directly or indirectly set up protective walls as well.

Several countries have set up, in groups, their own trading arrangements, and these arrangements permit them (under an article in the GATT charter) to continue to place tariffs and other barriers on imports from other parts of the world; see subsequent text for an extended discussion. As we already noted, the average level of tariffs has declined over the past decade. However, the fall in tariffs has been accompanied by increments in various forms of "special protection": voluntary export restrictions, voluntary import expansions, "orderly market arrangements," the use of antidumping or countervailing duties over and beyond any reasonable notion of an appropriate reaction to unfair trade practices, and an increased use of unilateral punishments by countries such as the United States.[1]

These nontariff trade barriers (NTBs, as they are called) have been on the increase since the 1970s, even as baseline tariffs were on the decline. As the economic domination once wielded by the United States began to fade, protectionist sentiments took off: the incredible successes of many newly emerging trading nations were viewed with a great deal of suspicion. Surely, underhanded practices allowed these countries to export as nimbly as they

---

[1] For instance, the United States subjects China to an annual review to determine whether its most-favored-nation status should be continued or revoked. Factors that lie beyond economic considerations appear to play a role in these reviews, such as whether China has made "progress" on "human rights", as defined by the United States government. Although countries such as China are difficult to bully on these matters—a U.S. move to deny MFN status was vigorously countered by lobbies with economic interests in China (including U.S. business!)—this sort of unilateral practice can be (mis)used successfully in many other cases.

did. Surely all sorts of environmental "laws" were being broken in the process. It seemed only fair to retaliate. As Bhagwati notes, the parallel between the U.S. support for free trade at a time of unquestioned economic hegemony followed by its disgruntled move toward regional agreements and protectionist sympathies, and Great Britain's similar espousal of free trade in the nineteenth century (after the repeal of the Corn Laws) and its later protectionist backlash, is nothing short of "dramatic" (Bhagwati [1990, p. 65]).

Countervailing duties and antidumping provisions—measures laid down under GATT as acceptable retaliations in the event of unfair trade practices—began to be "captured" and converted into standard instruments of protection. In the 1980s, the United States was by far the leader in imposing "countervailing duties," and other countries (including the EC) began to routinely entertain allegations of antidumping. In 1987, Messerlin[2] wrote: "First, the EC [antidumping] procedure is now far from being marginal: it involves hundreds of cases, concerns all the important trade partners of the Community and shows increasingly restrictive outcomes. Second, there is a clear tendency for this GATT-honored procedure to generate outcomes embarrassing to GATT principles: harassment, discrimination between trade partners, nontariff barriers are intrinsic to this procedure."

As Bhagwati [1990, p. 52] noted (see also Prusa [1992]), antidumping procedures can have a protective effect on trade *even if* the allegations are thrown out of court. A petitioner can easily "tie up his successful foreign rivals in expensive defensive actions in national processes which are not exactly models of impartiality and fairness. The filing of [such] complaints has a protective impact thanks to the increase in the uncertainty and cost of foreign trade." But quite apart from the potential effects of such actions, it seems that nontariff barriers have played an important role in restricting imports: Trefler [1993] observed that NTBs in U.S. manufacturing in 1983 reduced manufacturing imports by as much as 24%.

As Krugman points out, there is a seeming paradox in all of this: if free trade is the best unilateral reaction to any contingency, why do we see so much protection, and why do we need the GATT or its successor, the World Trade Organization? In his words (Krugman [1997, p. 113]):

> The compelling economic case for universal free trade carries hardly any weight among people who really matter. If we nonetheless have a fairly liberal world trading system, it is only because countries have been persuaded to open their markets in return for comparable market-opening on the part of their trading partners. Never mind that the "concessions" trade negotiators are so proud of wresting from other nations are almost always actions these nations should have taken in their own interest anyway; in practice, countries seem willing to do themselves good only if others promise to do the same.

---

[2] Messerlin [1987, p. 21], quoted in Bhagwati [1990].

18.2.3. Explaining protectionist tendencies

This brings us to the task of *explaining* why the world is as it is; why, in apparent utter ignorance of good sound economic theory, most countries seem to favor protection rather than unhampered trade: why "an increase in exports—no matter how expensive to produce in terms of other opportunities foregone—is a victory, and an increase in imports—no matter how many resources it releases for other uses—is a defeat" (Krugman [1997, p. 114]).

Protection as a Prisoners' Dilemma

One possibility is that—like the arguments made for protection in Section 18.2.1 and in Chapter 17—some amount of protection for every country is indeed a "best response": free trade is *not* the unilaterally best policy in some ambient second-best world. Of course, such a reaction undoubtedly hurts the *other* country: the move to protection in our country reduces trading possibilities for another. However, the argument does not end there: it is also the case that the other country (perhaps for similar reasons) would like to impose protection as well, and this hurts our country. The resulting structure is very much like a Prisoners' Dilemma [see the Appendix 1 (at the end of the book) on game theory]: if one country "cooperates" by having a free-trade regime, the other country "defects" by imposing protection. The resulting equilibrium of the game is where *both* countries impose protection.

Can both countries be worse off relative to free trade, as in the Prisoners' Dilemma in which the mutual defection outcome (here read protection) is dominated by the cooperative outcome (read free trade)? They surely can if the negative externalities created by protection outweigh the gains to the country that is doing the protecting (see, for example, Staiger [1995]). The observation that the *combination* of several countries, each rationally engaged in maximizing its own welfare, can lead to a situation in which all these countries are worse off was first made by Tibor Scitovsky. Scitovsky actually conjectured something stronger, which may also be true under certain circumstances: the optimum degree of protection chosen may vary *positively* with the levels of protection chosen by other countries. The outcome of such a situation would look like an escalating tariff war (Scitovsky [1942, p. 377]):

> When tariff walls have been erected all around, those who started the process will find some of their initial advantage gone; but they are also likely to find that they can improve their position by raising tariffs further, even if they initially made full use of their monopolistic position. As tariff walls rise, conferences on international trade may be called to arrest the process, which is obviously harmful to all concerned.

Figure 18.1 illustrates the possibility of a tariff war. In this diagram, two countries choose their levels of protection: none, medium, or high. Payoffs to each country are given in parentheses for each cell that represents a combination of actions.

Note that when one country chooses no protection, the best response of the other country is to choose a moderate but not high level of protection. This situation changes when one country chooses a moderate level of protection: the other then wishes to go even further. The arrows show the step-like nature of responses in this example: they lead the world economy from the free-trade payoffs of $(100, 100)$ down to a high-tariff regime in which payoffs are $(40, 40)$, yet by the inexorable logic of the Prisoners' Dilemma, each country is making rational decisions to further its own self-interest. In Section 18.3.5, we explicitly study a special case of this argument in a slightly different context.

Scitovsky foresaw the emergence of GATT and its consequent importance. If free trade were truly *the* equilibrium in some interactive game across nations, then there would be no need for an international organization such as GATT or the World Trade Organization to oversee trade.

Interest groups

Protectionist tendencies can build up in a country despite the fact that there are overall production gains to be made in trading. In Chapter 17, we observed that even when the gains-from-trade theorem is true (as it is in the

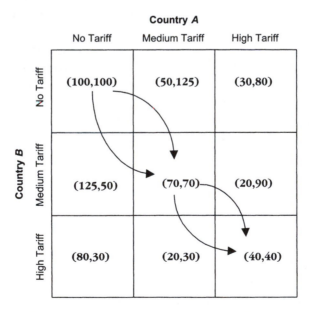

Figure 18.1. Beggar-thy-neighbor tariff escalations.

presence of complete markets), the theorem is only a statement about *overall* gains. In many situations, especially in those where trade stems from significant differences in factor endowment, international exchange brings gains and losses to different groups. In general, factors that are used intensively in the production of import-competing goods lose income, while factors that are used intensively in exportables gain. Moreover, controlling for income effects, all individuals must gain from trade as consumers.

Thus the gains from trade must be distributed correctly if the gains are to be felt by all. In principle, this can be done. Trade does expand production possibilities in the aggregate, so the overall resources available to society must have gone up. This means, in effect, that the gainers must gain *more* than the losers. To some degree, this is like comparing apples and oranges: how do we compare the increase in happiness of one group to the loss of happiness of another? However, there is a little more to it than that: there is actually more purchasing power floating around than there was before trade. Some of that purchasing power could be transferred from the gainers to the losers to compensate the losers for their loss relative to the no-trade world, and the gainers would *still* be better off.

However, the foregoing statement is a statement only "in principle." *If* swift and accurate compensation could be paid, a move from no trade (or partial trade, even) to free trade would create an improvement for all. The emphasis is on the word "if": in practice, compensation may be difficult to calculate, the gainers may be difficult to identify, and so might be the losers. Thus compensation may be an impossibility for all practical purposes and, hence, free trade continues to have ambiguous connotations for welfare. We are in the world of the "second-best," in which lump-sum taxes and transfers are not possible, and policy analysis in this context is much harder (see, for example, Feenstra and Lewis [1991] for a model in the context of trade policy). Even if it were socially appropriate to ignore the distributive aspects, the lobbies with vested interests that seek to affect the direction and intensity of international exchange would not be eliminated.

Now let's think about the interest groups that might form. Consumers surely gain from unrestricted imports: prices are lower. However, consumers are a large, nebulous group and they are difficult to organize. On the other hand, specific industries that are likely to be hurt by trade mobilize themselves relatively easily and lobby harder for protection.

Pareto [1927], foreshadowing the later influential work of Olson [1965], observed[3]:

> In order to explain how those who champion protection make themselves heard so easily, it is necessary to add a consideration that applies to social movements generally.... If a certain measure A is the case of the loss of one franc to each

---

[3] Pareto [1927, p. 379], quoted in Bhagwati [1990].

of a thousand persons, and of a thousand franc gain to one individual, the latter will expend a great deal of energy, whereas the former will resist weakly; and it is likely that, in the end, the person who is attempting to secure the thousand francs via *A* will be successful.

A protectionist measure provides large benefits to a small number of people, and causes a very great number of consumers a slight loss. This circumstance makes it easier to put a protection measure into practice.

Affected groups will invariably lobby government to further their own interests.[4] The government may acquiesce by offering them an implicit subsidy in one form or another. In the context of international trade, groups that are likely to be hurt by international trade often demand this subsidy in the form of a protective tariff or a quota (or, in a variant of more recent vintage, they might demand that other countries toughen their labor laws or environmental standards before they are allowed to export, which is just a plea for protection dressed up in ethically pleasing pronouncements).

At this point we run into a problem. The Pareto–Olson argument certainly tells us why diffuse groups (such as consumers) with relatively low gains per capita might not lobby very hard for free trade, but there is a step missing: we cannot conclude from this that lobbying invariably will be in the direction of trade *restrictions*. Why wouldn't potential *exporters* lobby to open up new markets? Indeed, governments such as those of the United States have actually courted (domestic) export interests in an attempt to garner countervailing force against the protectionist camp, and it can be argued that in many countries (such as Korea and Japan), export interests have been actively promoted. Nevertheless, history tells us that the most successful trade lobbies are protectionist, which is an interesting bias that is certainly not explained by Pareto's observations.

Rodrik [1995] pointed out that there is little in the economics literature that actually explores this bias. Most models either assume that protectionist groups are the lobbyists or yield predictions that suggest that export subsidies are just as likely (a priori) as tariffs. One possibility is that potential exporters may be just as diffuse a group as consumers. Only *after* a market is opened abroad or an export subsidy is offered will exporters "come into being": existing producers will be joined by new ones. So export interests form more of a *potential* group than an *actual* group, and many would-be exporters may be engaged in other occupations. Thus it may be much harder to organize an export lobby. In contrast, the "import competers" already

---

[4] In the theory of international trade, these considerations have been emphasized in the work of writers such as Krueger [1974], Bhagwati [1980, 1982], Feenstra and Bhagwati [1982], Findlay and Wellisz [1984], Mayer [1984], Hillman [1989], Magee, Brock, and Young [1989], and Grossman and Helpman [1994].

exist; they will protect their interests fiercely and even seek to advance them.[5]

This sort of reasoning does not completely solve the puzzle, but does push it back one step further. The foregoing argument *assumes* that the status quo situation is one with protection, and then states that protectionist tendencies are unlikely to be completely counterbalanced by export lobbies. How did the situation get to be protectionist in the first place? Rodrik [1995] made the interesting argument that even if lobbyists from both groups are symmetric, tariffs may represent a more enticing prospect than export subsidies, because tariffs bring in additional government revenue (whereas an export subsidy has to be financed). Thus protectionist policies may have an edge in influencing the government.[6] Although these are interesting speculations, there is much work to be done in this area.

Our broad conclusion from this discussion is that much of protectionist policy may be attributed to the existence of well-organized interest groups that would be damaged by opening up to free trade.

Protection as a coordination game

How likely is it that the government will give in to interest groups that lobby for protection? One answer is that if the governments of *other* countries appear not to give in to *their* interest groups, this will increase pressure on the government in question not to do so either. At the same time, the observation that governments the world over are caving in to political lobbies will probably make it easier for any one government to do the same.

What is at stake here is a game as well, but a more complicated one. It is a game in which governments interact through their trade policies, but in the process they interact with lobbyists as well. Because the value of being a strong government might depend on how many other strong governments there are, this suggests a view of the world as a *coordination game*: an offer of free trade may be met by a correspondingly open response, but in which a protective attitude might spark off a similar reaction.

Contrast the preceding argument with our earlier view of trade interaction as a Prisoners' Dilemma. According to that view, free trade is not a (one-shot) equilibrium of the interactive "game" played across countries. In the current view, free trade is *an* equilibrium, but constantly subject to the

---

[5] Fernandez and Rodrik [1991] explored another interesting aspect of this "status quo" bias. If it is known that a reform will benefit a majority of people, but it is not known just *which* individuals comprise the set of beneficiaries, the reform may stall (see the exercises at the end of this chapter for more discussion of the Fernandez–Rodrik model).

[6] Rodrik [1995] notes that over the period 1870–1914, tariff revenues in the United States provided more than 50% of total government revenue, and this fraction exceeded 90% before the Civil War. Developing countries in which income taxes contribute a small fraction of total government revenue are in much the same situation today, and customs duties serve as an irresistible source of revenue.

danger that there are *other* equilibria as well. We came across this sort of interaction before in an entirely different context (see Chapter 5 as well as Appendix 1 at the end of the book).

Figure 18.2, which is analogous to Figure 18.1, describes another illustrative example with exactly the same strategies as before (no, moderate, and high tariffs). As we've already noted, the interaction of this section is more complex and a representation of it as a game played between two governments is simplistic; nevertheless some relevant aspects of the situation are communicated. The *numbers* in the matrix of Figure 18.2 represent the government's own "direct" payoffs from any particular configuration. I have chosen the numbers to deliberately negate the Prisoners' Dilemma effect studied earlier. With only these payoffs to worry about, free trade is the only equilibrium.

Now look at the algebraic numbers (A, A'), (B, B'), and (C, C'). These are additional payoffs accruing to the government from listening to its protective lobbies. Payoffs A and A' result when the other government is adhering to free trade. If these payoffs are small simply because the government is dealing in an overall atmosphere of free trade and therefore finds it embarrassing or inconvenient to respond to lobbies, then the best response to free trade is free trade as well. The numbers B and B' are going to be larger: with the other government imposing moderate trade restraints, it becomes more "acceptable" for our government to feed our lobbies as well. Again, if the government's desire to maintain some international parity is strong,

		Country A	
	No Tariff	Medium Tariff	High Tariff
No Tariff	(100,100)	(50, 80+A)	(30, 50+A')
Medium Tariff	(80+A, 50)	(40+B, 40+B)	(25+C, 30+B')
High Tariff	(50+A',30)	(30+B', 25+C)	(20+C', 20+C')

Country B

Figure 18.2. Interest groups: protection as a coordination game.

then B (the payoff corresponding to a moderate response) is high whereas B' (the payoff corresponding to the "hawk response") still may be low. Finally, if the other government is highly protective, then the internal demands for protection may be very strong and so may be the government's willingness to accede to them, so that C' is high. You easily can see that this gives rise to the possibility of three equilibria, in which the international community behaves in quite different ways. If there are a large number of countries involved (instead of just two), it may be difficult to negotiate one's way out of the low-cooperation "equilibrium traps."

In the next section, I am going to argue that these two views go well with the notion of GATT, both as a device for coordination as well as an attempt to maintain cooperative outcomes by means of appropriate punishments.

The role of a multilateral organization

There is very little a multilateral organization such as GATT or the World Trade Organization can do except to create and to maintain the incentives for freer trade across countries. In particular, the international *legal* structure of these matters is highly problematic. It is difficult to see, for instance, how countries or groups of countries can be stopped from pursuing policies in their own self-interest, at least up to a point. International policing can perhaps stop one country from wreaking unprovoked war upon another through the use of punitive economic sanctions or military action, but we know that even such gross violations go unpunished unless (i) the countries involved are small relative to the superpowers and (ii) it is in the interest of other countries to punish the deviant (lamentably often, it is not).

Thus it is best to see multilateralism as a way to clarify a *method* of international negotiation by setting down procedures that (a) assist in coordination of policies across countries, (b) provide for some limited (incentive-compatible) sanctions in the event of a deviation from the agreed-upon policy, and (c) increase the visibility of a potential deviant by making deviations transparent (in the light of the existing procedures).

Consider the view of protection as a Prisoners' Dilemma. In Appendix 1 (at the end of the book), we see how it is possible to sustain the cooperative outcome as the equilibrium of a *repeated* interaction. The idea is very simple: countries may agree to honor free trade as long as other countries in the agreement do so. Of course, at each stage of this agreement there are incentives to deviate by imposing protection (because we assumed that the situation is one of a Prisoners' Dilemma). However, deviations will be met by suitable punishments in later periods. The fear of these punishments may be strong enough to maintain cooperation, provided that the countries are farsighted enough.

Thus, as Dam [1970], Staiger [1995], and others observed, the best guarantee that an agreement will be honored is that all parties consider adherence to the agreement to be in their own interest. This is because courts and jails are of limited relevance in an international situation. In particular, GATT must indeed include and embrace the notion of *retaliation*: "...retaliation, subject to established procedures and kept within prescribed bounds, is made the heart of the GATT system" (Dam [1970, p. 81]).

This double-edged system can be very hard to run. The ultimate objective is to work toward free trade, so retaliations and fights are antithetical to this idea, but without the possibility of such retaliation, there may be no free trade at all. As Staiger pointed out, "GATT dispute settlement procedures seem to acknowledge the essential role of retaliatory threats in preventing unilateral deviations from the agreements but at the same time display an aversion to actually allowing those threats to be carried out" (Staiger [1995, p. 1501]). Of course, this is a major concern that the new World Trade Organization will have to cope with.

When free trade is not a best response against free trade (as in Figure 18.1), multilateral systems can fail for this very reason. The entire list of contingencies under which the use of a retaliatory tariff, or an antidumping procedure, or a punitive duty is almost impossible to enumerate. Thus the use of such procedures may be aggressively and unilaterally coopted to serve as instruments for maintaining a protectionist agenda and not for fighting deviations from free-trade. We have already remarked on the rapid growth of NTBs worldwide. Similarly, GATT permitted under Article XXIV the creation of regional free-trade zones, in the sense that such zones did not have to lower protection against nonmembers of the zone, provided that the countries in question "substantially" eliminate trade barriers among themselves. But once a word like "substantially" is on the books, a lot can be done with it. Moreover, the time period for elimination of trade barriers is open: the European Union—the most successful of these regional arrangements—has been at it now for forty years. These regional agreements are often accompanied by high tariff (and nontariff) walls to the rest of the world. We return to this topic later.

We can only hope, then, that in the long run the view of free trade as a coordination game and not as a Prisoners' Dilemma turns out to be the right one. Enlightened government can surely make it so. As Bhagwati [1993, p. 45] writes, United States Trade Representative William Brock "was known to have offered a [Free Trade Agreement] to Egypt (along with the one to Israel) and to the ASEAN countries; indeed, he would have offered it to the moon and Mars if only life had been discovered there with a government in place to negotiate with." Brock's willingness to negotiate a free trade agreement to any government interested in talking about it suggests some baseline commitment to free trade provided that other governments were committed to it as well. I have used the resulting increase in any one government's ability to deal with domestic political pressure as only one example of how a coordination game can be generated; there are clearly others. An international system along the lines of GATT can help as well. It is likely that an explicit setting-out of procedure—the creation of a *transparent* system that's somehow perceived to be impartial—generates in governments an additional sense of obligation: a need to honor arrangements made in this way.[7]

18.3. Issues in trade liberalization

18.3.1. Introduction

So far, we have studied the possible causes of a fractured world trading system. We have argued that—Adam Smith, David Ricardo, and John Stuart Mill notwithstanding—the world is riddled with pressures for protection. Although some of these pressures may be justified in the context of market failures elsewhere (and we do not deny the importance of these considerations), other forces stem from well-organized interest groups that seek protection as a means to further their own economic interest, and that do more harm than good to society as a whole.

The GATT measures have fostered, or at least enabled, a surge in multilateral tariff reductions over the last five decades. We've also noted that such reductions have been accompanied by a proliferation of various NTBs: "special" cases that have become the rule rather than the exception and have slowed down or stalled the move to free trade. But one feature that stands out is the mushrooming of free-trade arrangements in regions all around the world. There are examples of such arrangements within clusters of developed countries (north–north), clusters of developing countries (south–south), and across developed and developing countries (north–south).

This move toward regionalism has been encouraged, in a sense, by the principle of multilateralism enshrined in the GATT charter: the most-favored-nation (MFN) principle, which declares that trade concessions made to any country must be automatically extended to all other member countries as well.[8] However, many countries that wish to sign preferential arrangements with one another, perhaps as much for political as for economic reasons, do not wish to see such arrangements automatically extended to all other countries by virtue of the MFN clause. So it was that Article XXIV of GATT was used, and repeatedly so: MFN need not be observed if some subset of

---

[7] See Jackson [1989], Hudec [1990], Kovenock and Thursby [1992], and Staiger [1995].

[8] Irwin [1993] traced back the origins of the MFN principle to the Anglo-French commercial treaty of 1860, in which Britain adopted the position of making its tariff reductions to France available to all her trading partners. France adopted a weaker version of this principle, and there were favorable echo effects throughout Europe until World War I put an end to all that in 1914.

countries wished to set up a free-trade zone by "substantially" eliminating all trade barriers among themselves. The seeds of regionalism were contained in this clause.

Two waves of regionalism followed. The first was in the 1960s: following on the heels of the EC set up under the Treaty of Rome (1957) came many such arrangements in the developing world. The United States, then a dominant power and a strong proponent of multilateralism, looked the other way (except for the formation of the EC which it backed, largely for political reasons). This wave of regionalism died out in the 1970s: "south–south" arrangements, in particular, did not seem to make much headway.

The second wave was a 1980s phenomenon and seems to be here to stay. The main difference this time around is the reversal of the U.S. stand on regionalism: free-trade agreements were negotiated with Israel and with Canada, and more recently Mexico was brought in as a partner in the U.S.– Canada combine under the auspices of NAFTA. The European Union gathered steam, with Greece, Portugal, and Spain entering the community, and more recently Finland, Sweden, and Austria. Likewise, Central America has revived its Central American Common Market (CACM), the Association for South East Asian Nations (ASEAN) has also been regenerated, and South America is weighing in with MERCOSUR. A more concentrated view of the future, with the United States, Canada, and their southern partners forming one zone, Japan and Asia forming another, and the EU (together with Eastern Europe) forming a third bloc, is not off the cards. Whether this regionalism will ultimately lead to true multilateral free trade is a hard question.

The revival of regionalism raises deep and important questions. The most central of these is that regionalism involves *partial trade liberalizations*, an opening of trade to some partners but not to others. Such openings have the salubrious impact of expanding trade among the partners, but they also have the effect of *diverting* trade from other, more efficient *non*partners to partners. Hence, there may be efficiency losses involved in a partial move to free trade, and there is no contradiction between this point of view and the assertion that global free trade is an improvement nonetheless. We begin this section by examining the concepts of *trade creation* and *trade diversion*, ideas which we owe to the insights of Viner [1950].

The second question about regionalism is whether it is most viable in situations where the resulting distributional effects are minimal. This will force us to think once again of interest groups: for instance, does it pay organized labor in the United States to support NAFTA? Our argument here is that despite the example of NAFTA, regional arrangements across countries with very different levels of per capita income are likely to falter. The distributional effects are too strong, and elaborate systems of compensation may need to be devised. On the other hand, countries at a similar level of development, that produce similar products, and conduct trade in differentiated varieties of the same products, are far more likely to benefit in some balanced way from trade. In the jargon of economic theory, trade among similar countries with a depth of product variety is more likely to lead to an *actual* Pareto improvement rather than a *potential* Pareto improvement.

The depth of trade in similar products depends not only on *comparable* levels of development, it depends on the level itself. A higher level of per capita income implies greater product variety both among consumption goods and among inputs of production. Both of these make for Pareto-improving trades. On the other hand, poorer countries with similar factor endowments may not have much to trade; their options lie more with the outside world. One possible exception is the case of import-substituting industrialization, in which explicit agreement on industry sharing permits developing country partners to reap some of the benefits of large markets while still maintaining a protective wall. However, this sort of integration scheme is often contentious and unstable. Unilateral trade liberalization, rather than regional agreements, might be the only real possibility open to developing countries.

Finally, there is the question of whether regionalism can be viewed as another road to global free trade. Can we hope that the formation of trading blocs will later lead to (piecewise) consolidation, culminating in free trade at the very end of it all?

18.3.2. Regional agreements: Basic theory

Trade creation and trade diversion

We introduce two fundamental concepts: *trade creation* and *trade diversion*. Both are outcomes of a multilateral tariff reduction, but the second concept, as we will see, is special: it comes into play only when some but not all of the world's countries are involved in the tariff reduction.

The following example is taken from Lipsey [1960]. Suppose that three countries, *A*, *B* and *C*, produce a commodity, say apples. We list the domestic price of apples, all in the same currency (say rupees per kilo), in Table 18.1. Suppose that country *A* is initially in a situation where it levies a tariff of 100% on imports of apples. In that case, all production of apples is domestic at the price of Rs 35 per kilo. If country *A* forms a customs union with either of countries *B* or *C* (by preferentially lowering tariffs to one of these countries), it will be able to import apples at a lower price and be better off. This is a case of *trade creation*.

Now change the initial scenario. Suppose that instead of a 100% tariff to start with, country *A* initially was in a situation where the tariff on apples

Table 18.1. *Prices of Apples in A, B, and C.*

Country	A	B	C
Price of apples	35	26	20

was 50%. In this case, it is easy to see that apples would still be imported into country *A*—from country *C*, but not from country *B*. Now suppose that *A* enters into a free-trade agreement with country *B*, dropping tariff barriers altogether, but retaining the 50% tariff on the nonmember country *C*. In this case, consumers will switch to country *B* for apple imports at Rs 26 per kilo (as opposed to the now costlier source of country *C*, which carries a consumer price tag of Rs 30, including the tariff). We now have a case of *trade diversion*, and it is clear that country *A* might be *worse off* as a result.

Examine this example more carefully. At first sight it appears that country *A* cannot be worse off by introducing the free-trade agreement. After all, consumers were paying Rs 30 per kilo (inclusive of tariff) before the agreement and now they are paying only Rs 26. However, this argument is fallacious because it fails to account for tariff revenue. It is true that before the agreement, the price was Rs 30 per kilo to consumers, but the country also gained Rs 10 per kilo in tariff revenue. Thus the *net* price being paid by the country "as a whole" was really Rs 20 per kilo—the true opportunity cost of imports from country *C*.[9] Now the cost is Rs 26 per kilo, so the *partial*—and I stress the word "partial"—reduction in tariffs between country *A* and country *B* comes at a price. The reduction represents a move from a relatively more efficient allocation of resources to a relatively less efficient one.

Of course, this example was chosen for its stark simplicity and is not meant to be a realistic description of trade in apples, but it does illustrate the basic point well: the formation of a free-trade area generally involves elements of (healthy) trade creation and elements of (possibly unhealthy) trade diversion from an efficient trading partner outside the free-trade bloc. The net effects on welfare are, in principle, ambiguous.[10]

---

[9] Note that we are neglecting here the distributive aspects of the situation. We are "adding up" gains and losses over different groups, in this case, consumers and the government, and this may or may not be advisable depending on how tariff revenues are spent. However, this simplification is useful to highlight the concept of trade diversion, so we will stick to it.

[10] The analysis of *partial* movements toward efficiency in an imperfect world is fraught with complications. It may be that the removal of a distortion in the presence of *other* distortions can make things worse. The case of trade diversion that occurs when country *A* lifts the tariff on *B* (but not on *C*) is an example of this. General pronouncements in this area, known as the *theory of the second best*, are hard to come by: see Viner [1950] and Lipsey and Lancaster [1956] for the original insights.

Note that this example has nothing to do with the possible dangers of free trade that we outlined in Chapter 17. For instance, we are not concerned here with the fate of apple growers in country A (the distributional question). The observation simply is that a *partial* move to free trade may be harmful from the point of view of overall welfare. Thus the example shows that even though global free trade may be optimal for the world as a whole (neglecting the questions raised in Chapter 17), an incomplete move toward free trade may not increase welfare "along the way." The reason: freer trade between a subset of countries may cause consumers to shift from a more efficient supplier (who still faces a tariff barrier) to a less efficient one (who is a member of the free-trade group), thereby worsening the allocation of resources.

Effects on nonmembers

So much for the effects of trade liberalization *among* countries who are involved in the multilateral process (countries A and B in this example). What about countries (such as C) who are excluded from the process? Notice that in the case of the prohibitive tariff of 100%, country C had nothing to do with country A before the formation of the trading bloc and certainly nothing to do with it after, so the formation of a regional trading agreement between A and B leaves country C unaffected. However, this is not the case if the initial situation involved trade with C. Formation of the trading bloc then excludes country C, which makes that country worse off. Although, as we have seen, the resulting trade diversion effect is bad for country A as well, there may be other aspects of the trade liberalization between A and B that make it worthwhile (overall) to those countries.

The negative effect on country C may be further heightened if the formation of a trading bloc between A and B is accompanied by increased tariffs (or trade barriers) on countries (such as C) that are outside the trading bloc. In this case, even if countries B and C are not competing in their exports to A, C may be worse off because its other exports to A (or B) might be choked off.

Thus regional trading arrangements may impose negative externalities on countries that lie outside the purview of those arrangements. Even though these externalities are partially mirrored in the form of an unwanted trade-diversion effect within the trading bloc, they may be overwhelmed by the positive effects that the package deal of a regional agreement might have for the member countries.

Note, then, that the formation of a regional trading bloc *may* or *may not* be a good thing for members of the bloc, depending on whether the trade creation effects outweigh the trade diversion effects. Nonetheless, the effect on *non*members is more unidirectional: either nonmembers are not affected (if initial barriers were so prohibitively strong that there was no trade with the region to begin with) or they are negatively affected.

This is not to say that it is impossible for a subset of countries to form themselves into a free-trade zone in such a way that (i) they are better off and (ii) countries outside the subset are just as well off as before. Indeed, the analysis of Kemp and Wan [1976] showed that such a method always exists, provided the members suitably overhaul the entire external tariff structure after the formation of the union. However, just because such an arrangement is *possible* does not mean that such an arrangement will actually come about. If a subset of GATT members wish to form a regional trading bloc or a customs union, they will do so in the way that maximizes *their* political and economic interests. Unless these interests (especially the political ones) are broad enough to internalize the possibly deleterious effects on outside parties, there is no reason to suppose that the Kemp–Wan rearrangement will necessarily come about.

18.3.3. Regional agreements among dissimilar countries

A paradox

Examples of successful free-trade agreements between countries at vastly dissimilar levels of economic development are *not* common. A leading example, to be discussed below, is the North American Free Trade Agreement. Earlier (and on a relatively minor scale), the issue of development differences did arise when Spain, Portugal, and Greece entered the EU, but the vast majority of regional agreements have taken place among countries at *relatively* similar levels of economic development. Indeed, the only parts of the world where dissimilar integration is a serious possibility is East Asia, where Japan could serve as the enormous hub around which the Asian economy might integrate, and Eastern Europe, where long-run ties with the present European Union are being explored. It is unlikely that in the foreseeable future, Africa will combine with the EU, and somewhat less unlikely, but still unlikely, that South America will become part of an extended NAFTA.

At one level, the paucity of north–south arrangements is paradoxical. The classical models of international trade teach us that the opportunities for trade are paramount when there are enormous differences in factor endowments (and/or technology). Surely, there is much to be gained when the south exports an entirely distinct set of products to the north and vice versa?

Interest groups again

One way to confront this paradox is to note, as we have several times before, that although trade brings substantial gains, these gains are not distributed evenly among all sectors of the population. Indeed, the Heckscher–Ohlin model teaches us that the gains from trade *cannot* accrue to all unless explicit compensation is paid ex post: factors of production that are intensive in the production of the imported good must lose and owners of those factors must be worse off.

For instance, in the Heckscher–Ohlin world, a developing country with a comparative advantage in products that are intensive in less-skilled labor should see substantial gains to such labor once trade begins. In contrast, its developed counterpart will be flooded with labor-intensive products, forcing it to cut back on the employment of less-skilled labor, thus reducing wages.

Of course, less-skilled labor can make investments in acquiring other skills, and it is possible to argue that over time the necessary adjustments can be made. However, the adjustments are often slow and painful, and in situations where a market for educational and training loans is weak or absent, the process can be painful enough to have political consequences. For instance, since the end of the 1970s, countries such as the United States and the United Kingdom have seen substantial increases in the ratio of wages paid to skilled versus less-skilled workers. Just *why* this has occurred is open to debate (see box), but international trade and "the invasion of the Third World" have certainly been regarded as villains in the popular press and in political circles. Even in scholarly research, where the rhetoric is kept down to tolerable levels, trade with developing countries is one of the likely suspects along with others, such as labor-displacing technological progress.[11] Hence, do not be surprised if you see organized labor (such as auto workers) siding with protectionist interests in developed countries.

Recent Changes in OECD Wages and Unemployment[12]

Over the past two decades the labor market outcomes of less-skilled workers undoubtedly worsened in OECD countries. Over the 1980s, less-skilled workers in the OECD countries suffered declines in relative wages, increased unemployment, and sometimes both. In the United States the real wages of young men with twelve or fewer years of education fell by 26% between 1979 and 1993. Between 1979 and 1992 the average unemployment rate in European OECD countries increased from 5.4

---

[11] It also may be the case that such technical progress has been an endogenous reaction to trade competition from labor-intensive developing countries. In this case, it is more difficult to separate the competing explanations.

[12] I thank Eli Berman for notes on which this box is based.

to 9.9%, and most of the unemployment was concentrated among unskilled workers. In the same period, relative wages of less-skilled workers declined slightly in several OECD countries and sharply in others.

Interest groups and political parties in these countries have not been slow to point the accusing finger at international trade. Indeed, there is some a priori rationale for such an accusation. The Heckscher–Ohlin model does suggest that as labor-intensive imports flood in from the developing countries, the wages of unskilled labor in developed countries should fall, both because of direct competition and, more indirectly, as production composition in the developed world moves away from activities that are intensive in unskilled labor.

A more balanced compendium of explanations includes the following factors:

(1) *Skill-biased technological change.* Microprocessors and other machinery and new methods of production increase the ratio of skilled to unskilled workers demanded (at fixed wages). The main evidence in favor of this is increased proportions of skilled workers employed within firms despite the increase in relative wages of skilled labor (see Berman, Bound, and Griliches [1994]).

(2) *Institutional changes.* There is some evidence of a decline in union power that protects less-skilled workers: for instance, some OECD countries experienced reductions in union representation. There is also concern regarding the decline in the quality of elementary and high school education. Some countries display evidence of declining test scores. For variations on this theme, see Somanathan [1997]. To be sure, this explanation cannot be comprehensive: the decreased demand for the less-skilled occurred simultaneously in countries that experienced very different institutional changes.

(3) *Increased demand for skill-intensive products.* A third possibility is that demand patterns have changed. There may have been an increased demand for more sophisticated products, perhaps because they are luxury goods (so they are bought more intensively as income increases) or perhaps because of an increase in quality. There is some evidence of a shift in consumption toward more skill-intensive products, but the changes in the demand for skills due to interindustry shifts in output appear small.

(4) *International trade.* Yes, there may be Heckscher–Ohlin trade effects at work. The increased exports of countries abundant in less skilled labor will lower demand for the less-skilled in the developed world. Certainly, there has been increased trade between developed and developing countries, and this explanation cannot be ruled out, but the same criticism that applied to item 3 applies here as well: the changes in the demand for skills due to interindustry shifts in output are small.

Distributive concerns such as these make it *extremely* difficult to negotiate free-trade agreements between developed and developing countries. True enough, some of the greatest *potential* gains from trade are found precisely in such negotiations, because the extreme differences in endowments of capital and labor, both skilled and unskilled, make for exciting possibilities of mutually beneficial trade. The problem is that the exciting possibilities are perceived to translate into actual effects that are *unequally distributed*.[13]

The existence of lobbies to protect the interests of those who would be hurt by free trade, *even though trade may be potentially beneficial to all*, is probably the single most important reason for the relative paucity of free-trade arrangements between developed and developing countries.

The North American Free Trade Agreement

Of the three countries currently involved in the North American Free Trade Agreement (NAFTA), the United States and Canada have had a trade treaty in place since 1988.[14] It was therefore the inclusion of Mexico in the deal that generated an enormous amount of debate. Many economists welcomed the inclusion, essentially basing their approval on the potential gains that such trade might bring. Opponents stoked another fire, emphasizing the dangers of job loss for American workers.

The volume of trade between the United States and Mexico has always been large and has been growing. In 1971, the United States provided 61.4% of Mexico's imports and took in 61.6% of its exports. By 1989, these figures had grown to 70.4 and 70.0%, respectively. Likewise, Mexico has long been the third largest buyer of American products, so it is not surprising that over the decades, the total volume of U.S. exports has come to be closely linked with the performance of the Mexican economy. In the 1970s, fluctuations in Mexican GDP brought about equiproportionate fluctuations in U.S. exports; by the 1980s, the amplitude of the induced fluctuations on American exports had increased even further. Thus, in 1986, as Mexican GDP declined 25.4%, U.S. exports plummeted by 45.4%. In light of such interdependence, it is not surprising that American policymakers looked for ways to stabilize the Mexican economy and keep it in good health. In the changed mood of American attitudes to multilateral negotiations, a regional free-trade agreement was considered an important step.

---

[13] This raises the possibility of *compensation*, which is something that we've already discussed. How do we calculate the gains and losses from trade and how are we to credibly identify the gainers and the losers? The first problem has to do with accurately predicting the counterfactual scenario that would occur if the desired free-trade negotiations were *not* to come to fruition, something which is probably impossible to do in the abstract. Even if we could do this, we would run into the second problem of *implementing* the compensation scheme; that is, of identifying the losers in an impartial way (for you can rest assured that all and sundry will join the loser's queue). In some situations, it may indeed be difficult for people *themselves* to know whether they will be losers or gainers from the proposed change. For further development of this point of view, see Fernandez and Rodrik [1991].

[14] I rely for this brief account on Aguilar [1993] and Whalley [1993], among other sources.

On the Mexican side, various developments pushed the government of this once "protectionist" country toward much greater openness. Mexico, with its substantial oil reserves, rode the tide of the oil price boom in the early 1970s, taking huge loans by using its reserves as collateral. However, after oil prices topped out, the country ran into debt servicing problems, which led to a spurt of "liberalizing" reforms. In 1986, Mexico joined the GATT and reduced its tariffs from an average of 100% to around 20%, far below the GATT stipulated ceiling of 50%. From this viewpoint, NAFTA represented the continuation of an ongoing trend. There was also the safe-haven argument: to some extent, Mexico could hope to be free of unilateral punitive measures from a giant trading partner.[15]

NAFTA stipulated a phased reduction and ultimate elimination of tariffs between the member countries on almost all fronts, and unrestricted investment opportunities. For example, Mexican tariffs on American cars were reduced from 20 to 10% immediately after the treaty, and all tariffs and export quotas were scheduled to be completely eliminated in ten years. Import restrictions on buses and trucks were scheduled to be eliminated in five years. Similarly in textiles, NAFTA eliminated barriers on 20% of trade immediately and specified the scuttling of barriers on another 65% over the next six years. The treaty also paved the way for U.S. banks and security firms to establish wholly owned subsidiaries in Mexico by the year 2000, provided immediate access to trade and investment for most petrochemicals, and full access for American firms to the Mexican insurance market. All these measures are expected to create a considerable increase in the volume of exports for both countries and a surge in North American investment in Mexico.

One of the strongest oppositions to NAFTA came from North American labor lobbies. Concern was voiced that due to elimination of tariff barriers between the two countries, many North American companies would shift their production units to Mexico to take advantage of lower wages. This, it was argued, would lead to large scale job flight from the United States, aggravating already existing problems of unemployment and stagnating real wages for blue-collar workers. This fear was captured with memorable crudeness in Ross Perot's description of U.S. jobs disappearing with a "giant sucking sound."

It isn't that such tendencies aren't already evident: U.S. companies with foreign affiliates in Mexico increased employment from 1977 to 1989 by 146,000 workers (39.4%) at the same time that employment in foreign operations of U.S. companies worldwide declined by 8%. In particular, manufacturers in the electronics and auto industries have shifted a large part of

---

[15] Small countries such as Mexico have traditionally been the strongest supporters of multilateral notions such as the MFN principle. The reasons should be obvious: they benefit from trade deals concluded between larger countries and they are relatively insulated from unilateral punitive actions. Nevertheless, these countries have also sought out safe havens such as NAFTA, fearing that today's regionalism will not protect them from protectionist actions.

their operations to Mexico; all three big automakers had set up auto or truck assembly plants in that country by 1989.

Supporters of NAFTA contend that such "cry wolf" complaints are unfounded. They argue that job flights had already started on a massive scale to other low wage countries like Taiwan and Singapore, by both American and non-American companies. Access to low wage labor in Mexico is crucial, they argue, to maintain the competitiveness and market share of American companies in world markets, and may in the long run preserve more jobs than it will lose. You can almost see Heckscher–Ohlin at work.

A distinct concern that been voiced is that importers from other countries, who face high tariff walls in the United States, may enter North American markets through the Mexican backdoor, taking advantage of lower tariff rates there and the open border created by NAFTA. To safeguard against this possibility, NAFTA built in strong "country of origin" clauses. Thus, for goods to be exempt from duty, a substantial part of them have to manufactured in one of the countries falling under the purview of the treaty. For example, cars must have 62.5% North American content to qualify for duty-free trade under NAFTA. This illustrates that in spite of freeing up trade locally, NAFTA does nothing to relax protectionist tendencies on a wider scale. Trade diversion, rather than trade creation, may be at work here.[16]

Who gains with NAFTA? Mexico has, perhaps, the safe haven that it hoped for, but the price hasn't been low. The exclusionary arrangements under NAFTA, for instance, in the sphere of car production, may not bode well for Mexico: trade diversions are part of the NAFTA package. In the absence of GATT-like safeguards that limit the extent of protectionism that can follow a regional free-trade agreement, these trends can be expected to continue as other developed countries extract their pound of flesh for providing little safe havens to their developing counterparts.

18.3.4. Regional agreements among similar countries

Agreements between countries at a similar level of development may be relatively easier to generate. We divide our discussion into separate consideration of north–north and south–south arrangements.

North–north agreements: Theory

Developed countries may be in a position to open trade among themselves without running afoul of the Heckscher–Ohlin model. That is, much of their trade may be in similar products that are differentiated, perhaps by brand,

---

[16] This does not fall exactly under the definition of trade diversion, which refers to an inefficient diversion of trade even as the same tariffs are maintained with nonmembers, but it is a broader and even more insidious form of diversion, in that exclusionary requirements are *raising* the protectionist wall surrounding NAFTA even as the walls within come down.

and do not use factors of production in drastically different proportions. Thus the main effect of a free-trade agreement may be to expand markets for the countries involved, without a serious rearrangement of factor prices. This is a situation where trade brings *actual*, as opposed to potential, Pareto improvements.

Consider the following example. Suppose that the country of Blanco only produces white wine, whereas the country of Tinto produces only red wine. Imagine that both countries currently place prohibitive tariffs on wine imports, so that Blanco's citizens are condemned to drink only white wine and Tinto's citizens are doomed to consume only red wine. Of course, both countries have people who like red and white wine, and many who would drink both. For simplicity, suppose that lovers of white and red wine are equal in number and distributed in equal amounts over the two countries.

Now imagine that negotiations are afoot to free up trade between Blanco and Tinto. Free trade would lead to a state of affairs in which Blanco continues to produce white wine, but now exports half of it to Tinto. Likewise, Tinto produces red wine and exports half its output to Blanco.

It's hard to think of who might object to the free-trade proposal. Tinto producers will be delighted: instead of having to push half their wine production down the grudging throats of white wine lovers, they can export this half to those who appreciate it. For the same reason, Blanco producers will be delighted as well.

What about consumers? Lovers of red wine in Blanco will be pleased and so will their white wine counterparts in Tinto. It remains to examine those who continue to buy their wine domestically. There is a little ambiguity here. If wine production in both countries can be expanded at constant marginal cost, then the new market opportunities will translate into greater production, and wine prices will be unaffected. In this case, consumers have no cause to complain. However, it is possible that the greater demand for both types of wine will raise wine prices, but will they raise wine prices *relative* to the increased income of consumers, who you must remember are also *producers* of the more lucrative wines? We need a more complicated model to judge this, but you can see easily that the final effect will depend on which particular input (labor, land, vineyards) is in short supply and on how the ownership of this input is distributed among the citizens of the country. If all inputs are owned equally, then higher wine prices simply return as incomes and there literally will be no objection to the free-trade agreement.

Notice the contrast between this view of trade and a situation of trade that rests on different input intensities in production. In such situations, we already have seen that there are well-defined groups of gainers and losers. The losers will protest, even if trade is beneficial overall, and potentially gainful agreements can be blocked. In the Blanco–Tinto example, the gains from trade accrue to all concerned and, therefore, permit a smoother passage to free trade.

In ending this section, we qualify the similar-products theory. It is not necessarily the case that whenever similar products are produced, there will be no restraints at all to opening up trade. One situation in which trade freedoms may be lobbied against is the case of monopolistic production in the absence of free trade. In this situation, trade serves the virtuous function of reducing monopoly power: the threat of imports acts as a disciplining force on monopolists who make super-profits in protected regimes. Such monopolistic interests, if they are powerful in the government, will block free-trade arrangements. However, even if we grant this possibility, the strength of the resulting protest cannot equal the indignant, self-righteous outcries over Heckscher–Ohlin-type losses. That the labor and sweat of hardworking citizens in developed countries may be demeaned by the cheap invasion from the underdeveloped world has a sense of tragedy to it that the loss of monopolistic rents can never hope to equal. As for the developing countries, well, that's just too bad: tragedy often begins and ends at home.

The European Union

The European Union, which was born under the Treaty of Rome, March 25, 1957, consisted initially of Belgium, France, West Germany, Italy, the Netherlands, and Luxembourg.[17] The principles set out under that treaty went far beyond those for a free-trade area (no impediments to intracommunity trade) or a customs union (a common external tariff wall): they called for the establishment of a common market in goods *and* in factors of production, and monetary union. In addition, they sought "a high degree of convergence of economic performance, a high level of employment and of social protection, the raising of the standard of living and quality of life, and economic and social cohesion and solidarity among Member States."

The United Kingdom, Ireland, and Denmark then joined the community, and they were followed by the southern European countries of Greece, Portugal, and Spain. Further additions in the 1990s were Finland, Austria, and Sweden, bringing the total to fifteen member nations.

The enlargement of the EU to include Portugal, Greece, and Spain certainly had a north–south flavor to it. Even with the relatively minor differences that Spain, Portugal, and Greece presented (relative to the incumbent members of the original EU), incorporation of these "southern" countries presented cause for some debate. These were distinctly poorer countries. Political motives were fortunately in favor of incorporation: they were newly created democracies and the EU wanted them to stay that way. Indeed, a

---

[17] For this brief account, I rely on Flam [1992], the *Economist* [1988], and several miscellaneous sources, including the web page of the European Union at http://europa.eu.int/.

large amount of EU resources were directed to the southern countries for infrastructural purposes.

The EU had abolished mutual tariffs as far back as 1968, but the continuation of a plethora of regulations and standards impeded trade within the community. A much more ambitious scheme was launched to dismantle all remaining trade barriers and achieve more complete economic integration. The chief goal of European integration remained the creation of a single, seamless market, within which "four freedoms" would be enshrined: the free flow of goods, services, labor, and capital. The agenda, commonly referred to as "1992" (after its target year of implementation), was set out in a White Paper in 1985 that listed 300 concrete measures (later reduced to 279) to be taken. In these proposals, four types of nontariff barriers were targeted for elimination:

(1) *Fiscal barriers*, such as taxes and subsidies in agricultural trade, and the practice of discriminatory taxation—domestic firms being taxed at lower rates by many member countries.

(2) *Quantitative restrictions*, such as quotas, mainly on agricultural goods and steel, and on the share of foreign firms in the market for road and air transport services.

(3) *Market access restrictions* on other member countries: many of these applied to public procurement, especially water, energy, telecommunications equipment, transportation services, and construction, but a few also applied to private banking and insurance, road and air transportation, some professions, and direct investment.

(4) *Real costs* incurred in trade between community countries, arising out of the current need to check goods at the border, both for taxation purposes as well as to uphold national health regulations and trade policies against nonmember countries. Such costs consist of the cost of bureaucracy and paperwork, delays at the border, and the cost of adjustment arising out of different technical regulations on product packaging, marketing, and so forth among member countries.

By the end of 1993, European integration was far from complete, as illustrated by the enormous price differences across countries for certain commodities. For example, prices of pharmaceutical products differed by a factor of 10 or more between countries with price controls (Greece, Portugal, and Spain) and those without (e.g., Denmark, Germany, and Netherlands), telecommunications equipment could differ in price by 40%, and car prices by 93% for the same model. Car prices were substantially higher in some member states due to their relatively high levels of automobile taxes and import quotas on cars from Japan.

This illustrates some of the subtle problems of establishing a common market in practice—going beyond draft proposals and White Papers. Relaxation of border restrictions on commodity flows should be accompanied by harmonization of internal duties and taxes, the adoption of uniform policies toward nonmember countries, similar health and packaging regulations *within* the community, and so on. In the absence of such harmonization, either trade barriers will remain or arbitrage will lead to business and revenue flight from highly taxed, more restrictive countries. Proposals have been floated to create tax bands, within which member countries have to restrict their rates of commodity taxation. However, countries differ in their responses to such proposals: France, with its long stretch of land border, is a vocal supporter; Britain, which enjoys its privileged seclusion as an island nation (which gives it the cushion of high transport costs and low arbitrage opportunities) has shown only a lukewarm response to such policies.[18]

What about the external face shown by the EU to the rest of the world? It is true that *tariff* barriers to the rest of the world have shown a steady decline, but there has been a proliferation of nontariff barriers, as we mentioned earlier in this chapter. Between 1966 and 1986, the coverage of nontariff barriers increased by many orders of magnitude: from 10 to 56% (which was around the U.S. level at that time).[19] Restrictions against Far East producers have been commonplace.[20] Even though EU members have been each others' lowest-cost suppliers for many commodities (Baldwin and Venables [1995]), no effort seems to have been spared to make this set of goods as large as possible through the use of various barriers.

Of particular interest is the Common Agricultural Policy (CAP) of the EU, which parallels the desires of many other developed countries (such as the United States, Japan, and Switzerland) to protect their agricultural sectors, come what may. Agriculture is strongly subsidized within the EU, and large external tariffs ensure that imports are minimal.

[18] As another example, attitudes to environmental regulation varied widely and were closely tied to economic interests. Germany, Denmark, and the Netherlands favored strict Community standards. Automobile emissions and recycling were among the hot issues. The poorer southern members were unwilling to have domestic industry bear the higher costs, and they certainly did not favor national standards on the environment, because this would restrict southern exports within the community. France and Italy sought laxer standards on auto emissions to protect the interests of their domestic producers, and in this they were assisted by the weakness of their environmental lobbies. Denmark sought strict standards on bottle recycling; of course, this would make it much more difficult to export bottled beverages to Denmark. That the EU has made progress on these many issues, but not without enormous effort, is both a tribute to them and a lesson to other future communities.

[19] See Winters [1993, p. 207]. "Coverage" refers to the percentage of EU imports subject to one or more nontariff barriers.

[20] Consider Jagdish Bhagwati's amusing aside on "a sentiment that was beautifully expressed by Signor Agnelli of Fiat: 'The single market must first offer an advantage to European companies. This is a message that we must insist on without hesitation.' It is, of course, fine for Signor Agnelli to express such sentiments: after all, Fiat has run for years, not on gas, but on [voluntary export restrictions] against the Japanese. But should economists also embrace such sentiments?" (Bhagwati [1993, pp. 39–40]).

The supply of products such as cereals, milk, and beef soon far exceeded demand. Rather than slash returns to agriculturalists (as the market would dictate) price-support programs continued into the 1990s. Direct quotas were used to restrict production of such items as milk and sugar. Compensation was also offered to farmers who withdrew land from cultivation. The agricultural reform of mid-1992 continued these provisions, although price supports are being replaced by more quotas and direct income subsidies. One sometimes wonders whether the undernutrition and hunger that is so characteristic of developing countries is a story of another planet, because the two scenarios appear to be so brutally unconnected.

In 1992, the Maastricht Treaty went much further, calling for the formation of a single European *Union*. With this treaty, the community bootstrapped itself to new heights, endeavoring "to promote economic and social progress which is balanced and sustainable, in particular through the creation of an area without internal frontiers, through the strengthening of economic and social cohesion and through the establishment of economic and monetary union, ultimately including a single currency in accordance with the provisions of this Treaty." The story of the European Union is being written today.

In spite of much commonality of interest and outlook and a cultural affinity for each other, differences do remain. For instance, the newly elected government in France has somewhat different views on economic policy compared to Germany: these (and many other considerations) will surely generate some interesting debate on the road to European union.

South–south agreements: Theory

The foregoing arguments and observations require both similarity in per capita income, so that the products demanded are similar (and therefore not likely to vary much in factor composition), *and* a certain depth in consumption or input variety. Developing countries may satisfy the first criterion, but fail the second. To caricature the situation a bit, if two developing countries both produce potatoes, there may be little of mutual value to exchange.

Thus south–south agreements, many and frequent though they may have been, have never represented a large fraction of trade (compared to the amount of trading the very same countries conduct with the rest of the world). Such agreements also attempted to promote, at least until recently, a particular end. Quite apart from the needs of political solidarity that may have brought developing countries together, there was also the need to exploit markets on a larger scale than that permitted by import-substituting industrialization.

We can illustrate this situation using a model very similar to one used in Chapter 16. Imagine that two developing countries, *A* and *B*, are engaged in inward-looking industrialization and that they wish to produce several products domestically. Think of two such products: cars and steel. Both require large setup costs and both might benefit from large markets (the average cost of production is decreasing in market size). The problem is that neither of these products are currently being produced under competitive international conditions: they are being protected, for one or another of the reasons discussed in Chapter 17.

Now suppose that *A* and *B* enter into a free-trade agreement. The idea is to *pool* their markets so that each of these industries will have access to a larger base of customers. In this way, *individual* import substitution is converted into *joint* import substitution. Will this measure be successful? Perhaps: if one of the two industries locates in *A* and the other industry obediently locates in *B*, then both countries will be delighted with the bargain.[21]

The point is that there is no necessary reason to expect such harmony. This is especially so if one of the countries involved in the agreement is larger (or better endowed with infrastructure or has a larger local pool of skilled workers) than the other: a flight of large-scale industry from the relatively poorer country to the relatively richer country might ensue. Regional inequalities may magnify instead of narrow.

The need for similarity between countries is only underlined by considerations such as these. The more similar the participating countries, the greater the likelihood that locational choices for industry will be evenly distributed among them. However, increasing returns converts similarity into a knife-edged proposition: a small chance difference may magnify over time.

This isn't a new point. Economists such as Myrdal [1957], Hirschman [1958], Henderson [1988], and Krugman [1991b] have studied the process of *agglomeration*—a chain of activities in which each additional link in the chain heightens the prospects for a fresh link to be forged. We studied these processes in great detail in Chapter 5. *Locational* choices have this very flavor: a good climate for industry may encourage further locational choices in the same place by fresh industry, making further influx still more attractive and so on.[22]

The question is, if such locational spirals are at work, what can the partners in the free-trade zone do about it? One possibility is to actually constrain such locational choices; that is, to farm out industries to different countries in the deal. This is very difficult to do and requires an enormous amount of

---

[21] See, for instance, the study by Pearson and Ingram [1980] on the effects of forming a hypothetical customs union between Ghana and Côte d'Ivoire. They argued that gains could be realized by closing down duplicate factories and increasing output in those that remained. Of course, the main problem is whether the union will be of *mutual* advantage, as we discuss in the main text.

[22] These concerns have not gone unnoticed in north–north arrangements such as the EU. Quah [1994] found that there has been some widening of regional inequalities in some countries of the EU. As we have already observed, a significant fraction of the EU budget is devoted to fighting these regional inequalities.

policy intervention (which is one of the things that one presumably wants to avoid in the first place by creating a free-trade zone). In addition, an elaborate compensation scheme may need to be worked out, so that *potential* gains in the aggregate can be translated into *actual* gains for all.

The other possibility is to allow freedom of locational choice, but to hope that the overall benefits of freer trade within the zone will outweigh the regional inequalities that are created in the process. This possibility depends crucially on the trade-creation aspects of the agreement, quite apart from the locational choice problem. The greater the scope for trade, especially in similar (but differentiated) products, the more likely it is that Pareto improvements will result. Taking this to the extreme, if there is great depth in product variety, the locational issues may be largely overwhelmed by the positive aspects of new trade creation: this is probably the case with the EU. It is very unlikely that developing countries can pass this test, if for no reason other than the fact that product variety is an increasing function of the average level of development.

To summarize, then, south–south trade is generally low, because a lot of their trade (but not with one another) is of the Heckscher–Ohlin variety (product variety is low among developing countries). Regional agreements may permit efficient locational choices of industry among the partners, but regional imbalances may develop as a process of cumulative causation sucks industry away from the relatively peripheral partners to the relatively more central, industrially advanced partners. Transfer schemes to compensate for these flows are generally very difficult to construct: among other things, a precise forecast of the possible agglomeration effects is called for.

Examples of south–south arrangements

So it's not surprising that among the myriad regional agreements proposed before 1990 among developing countries (especially during the 1960s), only five arrangements have the modest virtue of displaying a share of intraregional exports (as a fraction of the total exports of the region) in excess of 4%, sustained all the way up to 1990 (de Melo and Panagariya [1993a]).[23] We briefly discuss these arrangements here (and some other related ones).

The Association of South East Asian Nations (ASEAN), founded in 1967, is the oldest such grouping in East Asia. It comprises Brunei, Indonesia, Malaysia, the Philippines, Singapore, and Thailand. This arrangement really started as a preferential trade zone, but new initiatives are afoot to convert the bloc into a free-trade zone. ASEAN did boost trade among its members: exports within the region, which were around 4.4% of total regional exports in 1960, jumped to over 20% in 1970 and have stayed at around 18%. (For

---

[23] The volume edited by de Melo and Panagariya [1993b] provides an excellent survey of the main issues surrounding regional integration.

purposes of comparison, intra-EU exports were over 60% of their total exports in 1990.)

With the EU as a powerful regional grouping, there has been a strengthening of interest in Asian regional organizations as a counterpoint to regionalism elsewhere. In 1991, President Mahathir of Malaysia proposed the formation of an East Asian Economic Group (EAEG), consisting of Japan, the East Asian Newly Industrializing Countries (NICs) China, and the ASEAN countries. The United States, busy with its own NAFTA, opposed this grouping, with support from Australia and New Zealand. The first reaction was to change the name to the East Asian Economic *Caucus* (EAEC), to dispel concerns that a closed bloc was being formed. It appears now that the Asia Pacific Economic Cooperation (APEC) group, consisting of the EAEC as well as the United States, Australia, New Zealand, and Canada, will be the primary forum for multilateral discussion. Of course, all of this is quite far from any sort of widespread free-trade area in the region, something that will probably need Japan's active encouragement.[24]

Three of the five agreements that pass the 4% test of de Melo and Panagariya [1993a] are located in Latin America: the Andean Pact, the Latin American Free Trade Agreement (1960) (later replaced by the Latin American Integration Association under the Montevideo Treaty of 1980), and the Central American Common Market (1960).[25] Of these, the Central American Common Market (CACM), formed by Costa Rica, El Salvador, Guatemala, Honduras, and Nicaragua, did display a striking increase in interregional trade. The intraregional export share rose from 7% in 1960 to around 25% in 1970 and later, but the debt crisis of the 1980s changed all that, with quantitative import restrictions among the members pulling this share back down to around 15%.[26]

CACM functioned more like a customs union than any of the other groupings. It did implement tariff reductions across the board and converged on a common external tariff. A central objective of CACM was to maintain its overall inward orientation, but counterbalance the small markets of its members by encouraging region-based industrialization in an overall climate of import substitution. However, it was very hard to maintain this, perhaps for the very reasons that we cited in the previous section. Political differences among the CACM added to the complexities of the situation, and in the 1980s the CACM turned more into a forum for regional peace. The year 1990 saw

[24] Japan has (publicly) opposed the formation of regional trading blocs. Like its predecessors, the United States and the United Kingdom, Japan as a dominant economic power seems to be currently committed to the multilateral route. Political considerations (a desire to avoid the resurrection of fears regarding Japanese dominance in the region) may play just as important a role as economic ones.

[25] Much of the account that follows relies on Nogués and Quintanilla [1993].

[26] Because hard-currency exports revenue was the main mode of debt service and repayment, intraregional exports understandably suffered much more than exports elsewhere.

a renewal in the context of a more liberalized trading regime within these economies, but recent debate has yet to produce a consensus on issues such as foreign investment, intellectual property rights, and telecommunications.

The Andean Pact, signed in 1969 by Bolivia, Chile, Colombia, Ecuador, Peru, and Venezuela had an explicit agenda to promote of balanced regional industrialization. Import substitution at the regional level was at the heart of the pact, as in so many of the agreements signed during the 1960s.[27] Thus the planning of industrial allocations was an essential part of the pact, and the scheme of regulations proposed was comprehensive and complex.

The Andean Pact only passed the 4% test around 1990. The share of intra-regional exports had hovered around 3.7% since 1975, although in all fairness the 1960 base was a much lower 0.7%. The complexity and stringency of the regulations, as well as the problem of dividing regionwide benefits in some equitable fashion, led to much dispute. In 1976 Chile withdrew from the Andean Pact because it wished to pursue a far more ambitious program of unilateral trade reform. Other unilateral Latin American reforms soon followed, beginning with Bolivia and Mexico in the 1980s.

Like the CACM, the Andean Pact was revived in a more liberal trading atmosphere. The Act of La Paz (1990) created a free-trade zone between Bolivia, Ecuador, and Venezuela. Ecuador and Peru followed with the Act of Barahona in 1991. There were several differences between the countries, especially in their degree of outward orientation, and these had to be accommodated in the renewals.

The Latin American Free Trade Area (LAFTA) represented the main (and the earliest) Latin American grouping: the signatories were Argentina, Bolivia, Brazil, Chile, Colombia, Ecuador, Mexico, Paraguay, Peru, Uruguay, and Venezuela. Again, regional shares of trade were relatively low, first climbing steadily from 7.9% (1960) to 13.7% (1980), and then plunging to a low of 8.3% as the debt crisis took hold. LAFTA was replaced by the Latin American Integration Association (LAIA) under the Montevideo Treaty of 1980, mainly to increase the flexibility of partial agreements.

This sort of regional integration really went nowhere, because the overall atmosphere in Latin America was one of import substitution, and this spilled over into many of the intraregional (cross-national) impediments to industrial activity and trade. More recent proposals for regional integration were put forward in an atmosphere that is far more open to external trade. The debt crisis, oddly enough, is partly responsible for this, because the need to expand exports to meet debt payments contributed to the increased degree of openness.

---

[27] Economic thinking at that time centered around the writings of economists such as Raúl Prebisch, whose views on the long-term behavior of primary export prices we have already encountered (see Chapter 17). Sheltered industrialization was felt to be the appropriate path to economic progress, and regional agreements were naturally designed around this theme.

Among the recent developments, the one to watch is MERCOSUR. Exactly one year after NAFTA, on January 1, 1995, Argentina, Brazil, Paraguay, and Uruguay signed a major free-trade agreement; Chile and Bolivia joined more recently. MERCOSUR countries do have similar per capita incomes (except for Paraguay and Bolivia), so this is a plus. There is also evidence of accelerating intraregional trade between the member countries, and the trend can be expected to continue under MERCOSUR: total trade among Argentina, Brazil, Paraguay, and Uruguay grew from under $3 billion in the late 1980s to over $12 billion in 1994.

A declared objective of MERCOSUR is to incorporate all Latin American countries by early next century and then move on to join hands with NAFTA. If the American region ultimately forms its own free-trade area, this is likely to be the origin of it all.

The last of the five south–south arrangements that passed the 4% test is a West African grouping: the Economic Community of Western African States (ECOWAS).[28] ECOWAS was founded in 1975 and brought together all the sixteen nations of West Africa.[29] It was large and diversified, but product diversification did not amount to much: extractive industry and agricultural exports were the main activities. It is hard to imagine, given the theory that we have already set out, that much would come out of ECOWAS, and not much did. Extreme political instability in many of the member states added to the disarray. ECOWAS probably made it into the 4% list because of falling oil prices over the 1980s, which brought down Nigeria's export figures to the rest of the world by a huge amount. This decline would artificially raise the intraregional share.

Subsets of ECOWAS have attempted to form customs unions as well: among these is the Communauté Economique de l'Afrique de l'Ouest (CEAO), which had seven members, headed by the relatively industrialized Côte d'Ivoire and Senegal. Differences in the degree of development necessitated the establishment of a Community Development Fund to compensate members for the loss of tariff revenues, while special attempts were made to locate industry in the poorest regions. CEAO did have an impact on intraregional trade, but the old Latin American story can be seen here (and for ECOWAS more generally): an overall climate of import substitution impeded the development of intraregional trade as well.

Elsewhere in Africa, the Treaty of Brazzaville (1973) created the Customs and Economic Union of Central Africa (UDEAC). Cameroon, the Central African Republic, Chad, Congo, Gabon, and Equatorial Guinea were the members.[30] A later revision of the treaty pushed back the establishment of a

---

[28] The account that follows is based on Foroutan [1993].

[29] The countries were Benin, Burkina Faso, Cape Verde, Côte d'Ivoire, Gambia, Ghana, Guinea, Guinea Bissau, Mali, Mauritania, Niger, Nigeria, Liberia, Senegal, Sierra Leone, and Togo.

[30] Equatorial Guinea acceded to the union in 1985.

common external tariff and created a complex system for intraunion trade: tariffs on such trade did exist and varied with the commodity as well as the countries participating in the trade. As in the CEAO, economic differences across the member countries were strong (but not strong enough for Heckscher–Ohlin trade): Cameroon, Congo, and Gabon were significantly richer than the other three members. Similar disparities marked the unsuccessful grouping of Burundi, Rwanda, and Zaire, another Central African initiative. East and Southern Africa have also been home to a variety of groupings, but the emergence of a new South Africa will likely change several of these.

It is worth reiterating that south–south arrangements for very poor states, such as those in sub-Saharan Africa, can only benefit from an expansion in the market size for various industries, but given the economic diversity in the groupings the chances of industrial relocation are very high. These arrangements are either restricted a priori, which leaves very little to be done by the region (the increasing returns impetus for regional arrangements is effectively nullified), or a complex compensation system has to be worked out. To their credit, several of these groups do contain special clauses that directly aim at promoting the industrial development of their poorest members, but the formulas involved are complicated and the various inflows and outflows to the common funds have been a source of constant controversy, which is only to be expected.

18.3.5. Multilateralism and regionalism

Roads to global free trade

The arguments in the previous section inexorably lead to an important and difficult question: is (tolerance of) regionalism an alternative to globally coordinated multilateralism? That is, can the fostering of regional agreements eventually lead to free trade for all? This question is not easy to answer. Regionalism is based on a *reciprocal freeing of trade* between partners (and incidentally, such reciprocity is often easier when the distributive aspects of a move toward free trade is kept to a minimum), but these reciprocal moves invariably involve negative effects on nonmembers. These effects may not be internalized, which leads to a splintered world economy dotted with trading blocs. In the world of the second best, where trade diversion is just as much a possibility as trade creation, there is no telling if the relatively easy path of quick regional agreements is preferable to the rockier but possibly further-reaching route of globally coordinated changes.

As we have already seen, the founders of GATT, persuaded by the United States, embraced multilateralism: the most-favored-nation principle required that a trading concession made by one country to another should extend automatically to *all* member countries of GATT. The idea, then, is to maintain *relative* efficiency calculations in an imperfect world: if country C is more efficient than country B in the export of a particular good when a 50% tariff is in effect on imports from both those countries, country C will continue to be more efficient when a 25% tariff is applied, *provided* that it is applied uniformly to both countries.

However, the MFN was not an unconditional concept: Article XXIV of GATT allowed for the formation of regional trading agreements within a subset of GATT countries, as long as such agreements went all the way to a "substantial" elimination of trade barriers. The reason for the inclusion of this clause was probably the feeling that *unrestrained* free trade among some countries (even if they were a small subset of the world's nations) was somehow special and that it would ultimately assist the drive to true multilateralism on a global scale.

Bhagwati [1993, p. 45], in a lucid and informative essay, speculated somewhat tongue-in-cheek on how this might happen:

> One possibility is to encourage, not discourage, Japan to line up the Asian countries (all the way to the Indian subcontinent) into an AFTA, with the U.S. lining up the South Americans into the NAFTA, on a schedule, say, of 10 years. Then Japan and the United States, the two "hubs," would meet and coalesce into a larger FTA at that point, finally negotiating with the European Community and its associate countries to arrive at the Grand Finale of multilateral free trade for all...

Some simple theory

How does one think about these issues? There is an immense variety of considerations that complicate the analysis: countries surely differ in size, income, and ability to gain from trade, and there are a variety of political pressures for protection (and for export subsidies as well) that cannot be ignored in a comprehensive treatment. However, theory must begin somewhere, and it will be useful to sketch an extremely simple model that brings out some of the essential features of the situation at hand.[31]

Imagine, then, that there are a large number of countries, each specialized in the production of a *single* good.[32] Indeed, we will take this caricature a step further and suppose that each country is endowed with a fixed amount of a single good (equally owned by its citizens), which it can consume or export. Thus, we may use the same label to denote countries as well as goods.

We assume that individuals in the countries are all alike: they like to consume all the goods, although the proportions in which such goods enter their consumption basket will, of course, depend on relative prices.

---

[31] I am grateful to Hsueh-Ling Huynh for useful discussions on the subject matter of this section. I draw liberally on our joint observations.

[32] The basic structure that we use here is due to Krugman [1991c].

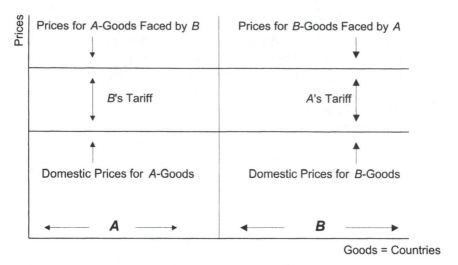

Figure 18.3. Trading blocs: the symmetric case.

With free trade among all countries, prices will settle at their international levels. To make our later points as starkly as possible, suppose that all preferences across goods are perfectly symmetric (given some choice of units for each good) and all countries have the same quantitative endowment (measured in these units) of their unique goods. Then under free trade, all equilibrium prices will look the same and each individual in each country will enjoy exactly the same level of welfare: the "free-trade level of welfare." They will also consume the same basket of goods, regardless of citizenship.[33] Note that by the free-trade theorem, *there can be no other allocation of goods that is Pareto-improving, in the sense that some individuals are better off under the new allocation, while everybody else is just as well off.*[34]

Now let's use this model to study regional free-trade blocs. Imagine, then, that the world is divided into two *equal-sized* free-trade regions, *A* and *B*. Figure 18.3 shows this graphically. The horizontal axis contains all labeling of goods (and countries). The first half of this segment is one free-trade area (*A*); the second half is another (*B*). Now observe that region *A* as a whole has some monopoly power over the goods it buys from region *B* (and vice versa), so by the large-country argument for protection (see Chapter 17 and the exercises there), they will both erect tariff walls on each other's products. We take it that tariff revenues are distributed equally to all citizens of the bloc.

Figure 18.3 depicts the outcome. Citizens of *A* face, in equilibrium, a common price for each of the *A* goods and a common price for each of the

---

[33] Indeed, in this model, they will consume equal quantities of every good.

[34] The theorem applies here because all markets are perfect and there are no externalities: I have deliberately removed the possibilities of losses from trade (as discussed in Chapter 17) so as to examine the situation in its most basic form.

B goods, but these two prices are no longer the same: *B*'s prices will now appear *higher* to citizens of *A* because of the tariff. Exactly the same thing happens from *B*'s point of view. The result is trade diversion (relative to the free-trade outcome): because prices for nonbloc goods are higher, individuals within each bloc consume more of the bloc goods and less of the nonbloc goods.

The final outcome is one in which all individuals in all countries obtain the same welfare. (This follows from our simplifying assumption that preferences are symmetric and from our consideration of equal-sized trading blocs, so that the tariffs are symmetrically imposed.) However, their consumption of *goods* is different (depending on which bloc they reside in). By the free-trade theorem, the welfare of each individual in each bloc must be lower relative to global free trade.[35]

You may well ask, if welfare is lower, why impose these tariffs in the first place? Couldn't the blocs just keep away from imposing the tariffs? The outcome would then be just like free trade and everybody would be happier. This is a good question and we must study it at two levels. First, assume that the two blocs are *already* in place. Suppose that one of the blocs refrains from imposing a tariff. Then the best response of the other bloc is to impose a tariff (because of the optimal tariff argument—see Chapter 17). The tariff revenues (which are redistributed to the citizens of the bloc countries) more than make up for the ensuing distortion in prices. This is *precisely* an illustration of the Prisoners' Dilemma studied by Scitovsky (see the example in Figure 18.1 and Section 18.2.3). To be sure, the other bloc will react in similar fashion. The end result is the Prisoners' Dilemma at work: *both* blocs are worse off relative to free trade.

But your question raises a second-level issue: why were the blocs formed *at all*, if everyone concerned knew that their formation would lead to a tariff war in which all citizens would be worse off relative to global free trade? Indeed, there is no reason for the two blocs to form of their own accord if they could predict the consequences of their formation.

The same logic applies to the formation of every *equal-sized* arrangement of blocs: welfare levels must be lower relative to free trade as the Prisoners' Dilemma of protection sets in. This does *not* mean, however, that welfare levels continue to monotonically decline as we include more and more blocs, because as the number of blocs increases further, two things happen: (i) the trade-diversion effect becomes smaller (most consumption for each bloc is from outside that bloc) and (ii) the optimum tariff falls as well as each bloc loses monopoly power. The resulting pattern is complicated but appears to be broadly U-shaped: an increase in the number of (equal-sized) blocs first

---

[35] Note well that we are using here the fact that welfare levels are equal *across* all agents to derive this result as an application of the free-trade theorem.

lowers and then increases welfare. These observations are borne out in the work of Krugman [1991c].[36]

The foregoing observations are interesting, but they *still* do not address the basic question: why do these blocs exist in the first place if all they do is generate outcomes that are inferior to global free trade? Multilateral negotiation across blocs should ultimately eliminate all of them, much in the anecdotal way described by Bhagwati in the preceding section.

However, an implicit assumption has crept in here. Just because the model has been constructed in a symmetric fashion does not mean that its *equilibrium outcomes* will be symmetric as well. Bloc formation is an *endogenous* outcome, and there is no reason to expect that symmetric blocs will form in equilibrium.[37]

To illustrate the differences that asymmetry can bring, suppose that the world is divided not into two trading blocs, but that there is only *one* free-trade bloc—say *A* in Figure 18.3—while the remaining countries (our erstwhile *B*) are all independent actors. In this situation, no country outside bloc *A* will find it profitable to impose a tariff, because its monopoly power is vanishingly small: it is only one of many countries on the international scene. Thus the "unilateral" version of the free trade theorem holds for these countries: free trade is a best response no matter what the rest of the world is doing.

This yields *exactly* the same situation that we discussed a few paragraphs ago: it is as if bloc *B* (which now isn't a bloc at all) had decided not to impose a tariff on *A*. We saw there that the best response for *A* was indeed to impose a tariff of its own. In the case discussed earlier this is what sparked off the Prisoners' Dilemma. Now matters end right at this stage. *A* imposes a tariff on the rest of the world, but the rest of the world sticks to free trade.

Now observe that under this equilibrium the welfare of *A*'s citizens *must* exceed that under global free trade! After all, *A* could have chosen a zero tariff, which would have given its citizens the global free-trade outcome, but did not. Ergo, *A* must be better off than under free trade.[38] Needless to say, *everybody* cannot be better off because of the free-trade theorem, so the citizens of the rest of the world must be worse off.

Thus the asymmetry of trading blocs generates very new considerations. If there is one trading bloc and the rest of the world is unorganized, the trading bloc must be better off relative to global free trade. This follows as

---

[36] Krugman [1993] noted, further, that effect (ii) need not necessarily be invoked in creating the U-shaped pattern; the trade diversion effects summarized in (i) will do. It is also of some interest that world welfare appears to be minimized at three blocs: this observation comes from numerically simulating the foregoing model for different parametric values.

[37] The observation that coalition formation may not involve symmetric coalitions even if the background situation is symmetric is beginning to emerge in more recent theories of coalition formation; see, for example, Bloch [1995, 1996], Ray and Vohra [1997a, b], and Yi [1996].

[38] For an elaboration of this point, see Saxonhouse [1993].

a simple corollary of the Prisoners' Dilemma argument: all we need to show is that under some monopolistic power, the optimal tariff is positive (the details of this argument are contained in an exercise in Chapter 17).

Several observations are relevant here. First, the result is true *independent* of the size of the trading bloc, but it requires the rest of the world to be "unorganized." Second, to go to free trade *directly* from this point requires that the rest of the world perennially make transfers to the ex-trading bloc *A*. Bloc *A* will not accept anything less, because free trade gives it *less* than what it can extract out of the current situation. Such transfers may be politically impossible (or impossible to honor ex post), leading to a persistently fragmented situation. If *A* is unsure of receiving these transfers, it will not relinquish its historically given advantage by bringing down its tariff walls.

Our third point is the most subtle and, in a way, the most interesting. Given the observation of the preceding paragraph, it follows that the only way to move to global free trade from this point is first, for the nonmembers of *A* to form their *own* trading bloc, induce the situation earlier studied in Figure 18.3, and *then* pave the way for a global free-trade agreement without transfers. Is this a possibility?

It depends. If the situation is as previously described, it surely is. The formation of *B will* drive down *A*'s per capita welfare below the global free-trade level and raise the welfare of *B*'s citizens in the bargain. The push toward global free trade can be made at that point. But this argument assumes that in the event *B* forms a bloc, we are back in the symmetric situation of two equal-sized blocs, which we already analyzed. Matters may be more complicated still. Figure 18.4 looks at an asymmetric instance of the two-bloc model. Here *A* is larger than *B*. It is possible to show that, because *A* has the

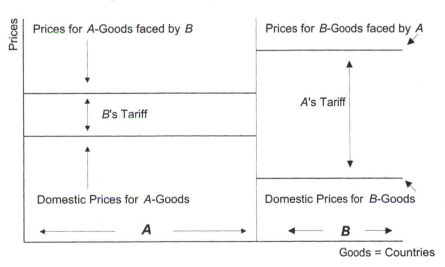

Figure 18.4. Trading blocs: the asymmetric case.

larger monopoly power, A will impose a higher tariff on B than B will on A. This is shown graphically in Figure 18.4.

What can we now say about equilibrium welfare in blocs A and B? It is easy enough to see that the welfare of citizens in A must exceed the welfare of citizens in B, but are *both* welfares below that of the global free-trade level? If they are, a final move to free trade cannot be blocked. On the other hand, if there is a situation in which A does enjoy welfare levels that exceed those under global free trade, the move to free trade may be significantly endangered. This situation could be interpreted by saying that *even if* the members of B can organize themselves into one trading bloc, they cannot pull down the per capita welfare of A below the free-trade level and, therefore, cannot bully or cajole A into opening up.[39]

Note several features of this approach. First, there are advantages to being the first in the "trading game": free-trade zones that form earlier in time and then erect a common tariff wall are in a position of some strength in subsequent negotiations. Second, we have not discussed the *choice* of the initial zone A. We know that if it is too small, in the sense that it accounts for too low a fraction of world trade, then countervailing zones can be set up, and ultimately we can expect a global free-trade proposal to be on the table.[40] Thus the members of a free-trade zone that has historical advantages would be foolish to stay too small: a certain minimal strength of numbers is necessary for subsequent bargaining. Third, if there *is* some configuration under which A cannot be pushed below free-trade welfare levels (even if B fully forms), then the prediction might be that regionalism will never give way to fully multilateral trade: trading blocs may be a stable outcome.[41]

Finally, we see that there is no presumption that the global optimality of free trade will be enough to bring it about in practice. Countries impose externalities on one another (as they do in our simple model of tariffs), and there is no reason to anticipate that they will internalize these effects, whether out of altruism or political expediency.

The *normative* goal of movement toward unconditional free trade (even if we do accept that goal as the right one) cannot be equated with the *actual* moves and countermoves that occur as nations or subgroups of nations act in their own best interests. In the words of Bhagwati [1993, p. 46]:

---

[39] I note again that this outcome depends on the unfeasibility of making persistent transfers or "side payments" from citizens of B to citizens of A after the free-trade agreement is concluded. An international system to honor such transfers may simply not be viable, for several reasons.

[40] In our simple model, if the size of A is less than half the world population, it will ultimately give way to free trade. Do not take this fraction literally though, because it depends on a very special model.

[41] The exploration of this point is simple enough in the present model, but it is important and its robustness needs to be examined along several dimensions. This exercise is beyond the scope of our book.

> The question of regionalism is...both a difficult and a delicate one. Only time will tell whether the revival of regionalism since the 1980s will have been a sanguine and benign development or a malign force that will serve to undermine the widely-shared objective of free trade for all. My judgement is that the revival of regionalism is unfortunate. But, given its political appeal and its likely spread, I believe that it is important to contain and shape it...so that it becomes maximally useful and minimally damaging....

Equilibria need not be *optimal*: individuals, groups, and countries do not always succeed in fully internalizing the effects of their interaction. The role of policy is to create conditions under which internalization can be heightened. Perhaps this is the central message of the whole book.

18.4. Summary

This chapter studied *multilateral trade policies*. The starting point was the fact that (free-trade theorems notwithstanding) we live in a protectionist world. In such a climate, organizations such as the General Agreement on Trade and Tariffs have worked to lower trade barriers in a multilateral way, coordinating the actions of different countries in the process. At the same time, some groups of countries (such as the EU) have both gone beyond GATT (by negotiating free-trade agreements among themselves) and set it back (by raising or maintaining import barriers to the rest of the world). Waves of regionalism have coexisted with the multilateral approach.

We began by studying the phenomenon of restricted trade. First, there are all the second-best arguments advanced in Chapter 17: trade interventions may be justified in the presence of other market failures. There is also the argument that countries that are large buyers of some products can actually gain by imposing tariffs on those products, but more often than not, the restrictions on trade have emerged from groups or lobbies that stand to lose from trade. Aware that compensation schemes to convert potential gains into actual Pareto improvements for all are often infeasible on political or informational grounds, these groups push for protectionist policies. In this climate, the fact that *other* countries are being protectionist can add fuel to the fire.

This sort of argument brings out two aspects of trade equilibria. They might represent Prisoners' Dilemmas and lead invariably to tariff wars: that is, countries might have a tendency to be protectionist no matter what their counterparts do and in the process collectively shoot themselves in the foot. Alternatively, trade interactions might more closely resemble *games of coordination*, in which a no-protection equilibrium coexists with a protectionist equilibrium. We interpreted the role of GATT (or any multilateral organization designed to promote free trade) in these two contexts.

We then turned to a detailed study of *regional trade agreements*. We introduced the classical concepts of *trade creation* and *trade diversion*, and argued that these concepts are useful for our understanding of free-trade zones. We also discussed the external effects of a free-trade agreement; that is, the effects on countries that are not party to the agreement.

We studied various types of regional agreements. It would seem, according to Heckscher–Ohlin, that the greatest gains from trade would come by integrating a developing country with a developed one: conditions of production are so different across the countries that there should be plenty of gains from freeing trade across them. However, we do not see many agreements across countries with different levels of development (NAFTA is an exception) and we invoke political pressure groups as an explanation. Distributional effects are strongest when dissimilar countries are involved and political lobbies to thwart integration are then likely to be strong as well.

Next, we studied free-trade agreements among *similar* countries. We argued here that if countries are at a similar level of development and are also rich enough so that there is large product variety in consumption or production, the gains from trade are likely to be equally distributed over different groups, thus reducing political pressure. Even then, the road to integration is far from smooth, as a study of the European Union indicates. Matters are worse when countries are similar, but poor. In this case, the possible gains from trade are very low, because product variety is not high. However, there is one important avenue of gain, which stems from the fact that many such countries are import substitutors. Their access to markets is therefore low and regional agreements can expand markets, allowing them to take some advantage of returns to scale while still maintaining a protective barrier vis-à-vis developed countries. The problem with this is that some countries are invariably better off than others and there is an overwhelming tendency for the bulk of industry to locate in these countries. Thus the gains from integration are very unevenly divided across *countries*, which leads to all kinds of friction. It is possible to control industrial locations and/or design elaborate compensation schemes, and these have indeed been tried, but the complexities of the situation are usually too high to make any one mechanism foolproof. Therefore south–south integration has not been too successful, although a recent and more hopeful wave of integration seems to be on its way.

We ended this chapter by studying the question of regionalism versus multilateralism. Is (tolerance of) regionalism an alternative to globally coordinated multilateralism? Might the fostering of regional agreements eventually lead to free trade for all? We constructed a simple model that serves to illustrate the main issues involved.

Exercises

■ (1) The "gains-from-trade" theorem tells us that *irrespective* of what other countries do, free trade is the best policy for any country. Yet countries routinely threaten to pursue restrictive trading practices if their trading partners do so as well. Reconcile these two observations using the arguments in the text.

■ (2) If the status quo is restricted trade, a liberalization policy may not have popular support even if it will benefit a majority of the population and even if the monetary value of the gains outweigh the losses. One reason for this is that it may be hard, ex ante, for an individual to predict whether she will be among the set of losers or gainers. Even though the gainers outnumber the losers, a risk-averse person might vote "no" on a liberalization proposal. You should be easily able to model this possibility using the notion of risk aversion developed in the text.

However, as Fernandez and Rodrik [1991] observed, a liberalization policy of this sort can be blocked by voters even if they are risk-*neutral*. To see this, consider the following example. A country has 100 people. Suppose a policy will enrich 60 people by $100 each, while it will hurt 40 people by $80 each. A number of gainers, x, already *know* that they will be gainers, and everybody else knows this fact as well. The remaining people have no idea whether they will be gainers or losers, and simply assume that they will be chosen randomly to be among the $60 - x$ remaining gainers.

If majority voting is used to determine the fate of the policy, describe what happens as x varies between 0 and 60. Provide a clear verbal intuition for your answer.

■ (3) Critically review the general arguments that suggest that increased trade between similar countries is more likely to lead to actual rather than potential Pareto improvements, while the opposite is true for new trade between countries with dissimilar factor endowments. Explicitly list the qualifications that are needed for such arguments to be valid.

■ (4) Consider the Blanco–Tinto example studied in Section 18.3.4. Describe a case where some individuals in Blanco might object to a free-trade agreement and show that this case must depend critically on the assumption that factor inputs are held unequally by different citizens. Note that even in this case, the only objection comes from the higher wine price, which is typically small, because it is distributed over the entire body of consumers. This is very different from input-side effects, as in the Heckscher–Ohlin model, which are concentrated on particular groups of people.

■ (5) Why might developing countries with a poorly developed system of income taxes be reluctant to have free trade?

■ (6) Why might environmentalists and trade protectionists form political alliances in developed countries?

■ (7) Consider the following parable. There are five individuals. They can form into groups of different sizes. A group of size 1 gets a total income of $100; of size 2, $250; of size 3, $600; of size 4, $750; and of size 5, $900.

(a) Which collection of groupings maximizes "world income" in this world of five people?

(b) If all group income must be divided equally among group members, which grouping would you expect to arise under spontaneous group formation?

(c) Explain why the answers to (a) and (b) are different. Can you tell an alternative story that attains world income maximization if people are allowed to propose unequal divisions of group income? What additional assumptions on group formation would be required for this alternative story to work?

(d) Can you use this parable to throw light on regional groupings in international trade?

Appendix 1

Elementary Game Theory

A1.1. Introduction

The theory of games is a useful way to capture interactions across individuals when each individual's actions have effects on the utilities or monetary returns of other agents. The purpose of this appendix is to provide you with an introduction to game theory as we use it in this book. The emphasis is on the concepts that are useful in a study of development. In particular, this chapter no way substitutes for a comprehensive introduction to game theory, for which you will have to consult specialized texts.[1]

A1.2. Basic concepts

The simplest way to describe a strategic situation or a game is also possibly the most abstract, so a little patience is needed to get through this part if you want to properly understand what follows. Suppose that there is a set I of individuals, sometimes called *agents* or *players*. Let's give them names by referring to each player by his/her index in the set I. Thus player i will refer to a player with the index i. Subsequently, we shall often subscript various objects with indices such as $1, 2, i$, or j, to remind ourselves that they "belong to" players $1, 2, i, j, \ldots$.

For each player i, there is a set of *strategies*. A typical strategy from this set may be denoted s_i. A *strategy profile* is a list of strategies $(s_1, s_2, \ldots, s_n)$, one for each player. To shorten our notation, let us refer to a typical strategy profile by the boldface letter **s**.

Given any strategy profile **s**, each player i receives a payoff u_i, which may depend on the entire vector of strategies within that profile. To emphasize this dependency, we sometimes refer to u_i as $u_i(\mathbf{s})$, to stress the fact that u_i is a *function* of **s**, for every player i.

Believe it or not, we are done with our description of a game! Of course, what we have so far looks deceptively simple. There are many varieties of games that fit into this framework, and soon we will see some of them.

---

[1] See Binmore [1992], Gibbons [1992], and Osborne and Rubinstein [1994] for excellent introductions to the subject.

Before that, let us take some time to understand the various concepts that we have introduced so far.

First, a strategy can mean many things, and it may or may not be describable as a single number. A strategy may stand for a simple action or a list of actions dependent on various contingencies. Second, a payoff may mean several things. It could mean the satisfaction or utility of an individual; it may stand for the monetary reward she receives; it could stand for the expected value of monetary reward or utility in an uncertain situation. Here are some examples to illustrate these matters.

Fertility decisions

Two couples live in a joint family, and each is deciding how many children to have. There is a cost of bringing up children if they are your own. Moreover, because the family is joint, the children of other couples also impose a cost (in terms of occasional child care) upon you. Suppose that the cost of bringing up your own child is c per child, and the cost imposed by the children of the other couple is d per child. (Think of this as an unavoidable cost of joint family life.) There are also benefits to having children, but to make things simple assume that each couple derives benefits only from its own children. Assume that the total benefit of having n children of your own is $A(n)$. Let's suppose that no couple can have more than N children.

(1) Here the "individuals" or "players" are couples. Describe the strategy set for each couple and the payoff from each strategy profile.

(2) Describe the special case that would arise if each couple was living completely isolated from the others. How would you describe the new payoff functions?

Adopting a new technology

In a country there are two computer systems available, A and B. Each person may adopt one of systems A or B. The cost of adoption is given by c for either system. However, the payoff from adoption of a system depends positively on the number of people who adopt that system as well. If n is this number, then the payoff is some function $f(n)$.

(3) Describe this situation as a game.

In the examples discussed so far, a strategy is a simple action, such as the decision to have x children or adopt a particular technology. In many cases, a strategy is a description of an action under various contingencies. Here are two examples to make this point.

Protecting an industry

A monopolistic industry is protected by a tariff. It must decide whether or not to cut costs and become internationally competitive. After this decision is made, the government observes whether the industry has cut costs or not, and then decides whether or not to remove the tariff that protects the industry. Following these actions, certain payoffs are received by both government and industry. Later we will describe these payoffs in more detail. For now, I would like to describe the strategy sets.

There are two "players": the industry and the government. The strategy set of the industry is simple enough: it consists of two options, "cut costs" or "do not cut costs." At first glance, a similar description appears to be the case for the government as well: "keep the tariff" or "remove the tariff." However, this is not true, and the reason it is not true is because the government gets to observe the move of the industry *before* making its decision. Thus in the description of the government's strategy we must allow for the possibility that the government's choice can depend on what it observed. It follows that the government really has *four* strategies, not two! These are (i) remove the tariff regardless of what the industry does, (ii) keep the tariff regardless of what the industry does, (iii) keep the tariff if the industry cuts costs and remove it otherwise, and (iv) remove the tariff if the industry cuts costs and keep it otherwise. As hinted at before, a strategy (for the government) here is not a simple action but a series of "conditional rules," depending on what it observes.

Landlord–tenant relationship

A landlord leases out land to a tenant. The tenant chooses labor L and produces an output Y according to a production function $Y = F(L)$. Labor costs him w per unit. The landlord chooses a contract for the tenant, which is a scheme dividing up the produced output. The scheme consists of simply an output *share* a and a fixed payment F. The interpretation is that the tenant keeps a share a of the output and makes a fixed payment F to the landlord for the right to farm the land. Let $c = (a, F)$ be the shorthand notation for the *contract* thus offered. After the contract is offered, the tenant chooses the amount of labor to devote to the land.

(4) Describe the strategies available to landlord and tenant, and the payoffs that arise from them.

A1.3. Nash equilibrium

The fundamental concept of an "equilibrium" in a game comes from the work of John Nash. The concept, known as a Nash equilibrium, can be described as follows. Imagine a strategy profile that has the property that *no* individual can do better by choosing an alternative strategy, assuming that all other players are choosing the strategy described in the strategy profile. Understand well that this property must *simultaneously* apply to all the players at the *same* strategy profile. Then such a strategy profile is called a *Nash equilibrium*.

It's best to illustrate the concept of a Nash equilibrium through the use of examples.

The Prisoners' Dilemma

This is our first instance of a game in which we will be able to fit many of our development examples. Two prisoners have committed a crime, for which they are being interrogated by the police. Each prisoner has two options: he can *cooperate* with his fellow prisoner and refuse to divulge any evidence or he can *defect* into the waiting clutches of the police and reveal all. Thus the strategy set of each prisoner consists of two strategies: cooperate or defect.

Let us suppose that if both prisoners cooperate, then no evidence can be brought against them, so that they go scot free to enjoy their booty, which is worth, say, ten units to each of them. On the other hand, if both defect, then they are put away for a while, after which they are paroled. Let us say the payoff from this situation is worth five units to each of them. It remains to describe the situation in which one cooperates, but the other squeals. In this case the latter turns state's evidence and in return is pardoned with minimal punishment. He also gets to enjoy the booty while the other languishes in jail, and this is worth, say, fifteen units to the squealer. The cooperator is put away as an unrepentant character who never confessed to his crimes, and this gives him, say, zero units. The payoffs can be summarized in the form of the following *matrix*, which is a common device in game theory:

	Cooperate	Defect
Cooperate	10, 10	0, 15
Defect	15, 0	5, 5

It is very easy to see that there is only *one* Nash equilibrium in this game; that is, only one strategy combination that has the property that each player is doing the best he can, given the actions of the other player. This is the combination in which *both prisoners defect*. Look at any other strategy combination. If it involves both players cooperating, one player would want to turn witness for the state and defect. On the other hand, if it is an asymmetric combination, then the prisoner left out in the cold would also want to defect (getting five is better than getting zero). So (defect, defect) is the unique

Nash equilibrium of this game. This is curious, to say the least, but we can observe various real-life situations that correspond, roughly speaking, to the Prisoners' Dilemma.

Fertility again. Let us look again at the foregoing fertility example. I am going to try to convince you that this has the essential feature of the Prisoners' Dilemma; namely, that the two couples might depart from an outcome that maximizes their joint utility. See also Chapter 9 where this and other related problems are discussed.

   It will be useful to work with a specific numerical example. Suppose that $N = 2$, so that each couple can have no more than two children. Now suppose that cost of bringing up each of your own children is $200, whereas the cost imposed by the other couple's children is $100 per child. Specify the benefit function as follows: the first child is valued at $350, whereas the second child is valued at $250. Thus $A(1) = 350$, whereas $A(2) = 600$. Assume that these data apply equally well to the other couple. Now we may represent the net payoff (benefit minus cost) to each couple in the following matrix, where the options "one" and "two" should be self-explanatory:

	One	Two
One	50, 50	−50, 100
Two	100, −50	0, 0

   Make sure you understand these entries (as you should if you solved the previous exercises). For instance, the strategy pair (one, two) means that the first couple has one child while the second couple has two. The first couple thus gets a benefit of 350, but then incurs a cost of 200 for its own child, and a total cost of 200 for the two children of the other couple. The net return is thus −50. The couple with two children receives benefits of 600, and although they incur costs of 400 for their two children and an indirect cost of 100 from the other couple's child, they receive a net payoff of 100.

   The relationship with the Prisoners' Dilemma should now be very clear indeed. Having one child each is the cooperative policy. However, if each couple fails to internalize the cost that it imposes on the other couple as a consequence of its fertility choice, then both couples may end up having two children each, with a payoff of zero.

The Commons. Suppose that groundwater is used for irrigation in a village. Overuse of groundwater can reduce the level of the water table, making it more costly for all farmers to extract water. This is the typical problem of the commons: groundwater is a common property resource, and the costs of using it may not be fully internalized. A simple example can be provided to make the point. Suppose that water can be extracted at two levels—*high* and *low*—and that there are two farmers. The revenue (from crop production) for each farmer increases with the use of groundwater: say it is $2,000 if the high level is applied and $1,000 if the low level is applied. The cost of extraction depends on whether the *other* farmer's use is high or low. Suppose that the extraction cost for each farmer is $500 for low and $1,300 for high, but that an additional fixed cost of $500 is incurred if the other farmer is extracting high (deeper wells will have to be dug because the other farmer's action reduces groundwater levels). A table very similar to the fertility matrix represents this situation:

	Low	High
Low	500, 500	0, 700
High	700, 0	200, 200

Again, make sure you understand the various entries. Now verify that the situation indeed corresponds to a Prisoners' Dilemma and that both farmers will extract high, even though both extracting low would have been a preferred outcome.

These are only two of many, many examples that one could be put forward. Environmental issues such as cross-border pollution or deforestation can be addressed in this way. For instance, countries might impose taxes on polluting firms insofar as their own citizens are affected by pollution, but they might fail to internalize the effects of pollution on the citizens of other countries. This may create overpollution.

In the same vein, but in an entirely different context, several industrial groups might lobby for protective tariffs so that they can have access to domestic markets. Of course, each group includes shareholders who are consumers of other products and would not like to see tariffs slapped on these other goods. Thus they do not internalize the effects of their lobbying actions on other interest groups. A Prisoners' Dilemma-like situation may well result.

Production cooperatives represent yet another example. A group of farmers working in a team have an incentive to undersupply effort, because they do not internalize the full marginal product of additional effort (additional output is divided among all farmers). The Nash equilibrium of this game is typically worse for all relative to the fully cooperative outcome.

Congestion on unregulated highways, the overuse of publicly provided (or insured) health facilities, littering, low voter turnout—the list of potential Prisoners' Dilemmas is extensive and varied.

Coordination game

Here is a game with a somewhat different flavor. We can call it the Tourists' Dilemma. Two friends are touring the Indian city of Mumbai (a large city in western India that once went by a more familiar name) and they have managed to lose each other. They have made no plans to handle this kind of emergency, but each suspects that the other will go to a familiar "tourist" location in the hope that her friend will think the same way. Indeed, the friend *does* think the same way, but the problem is that there are two possible locations (well, there are many, but let's just say there are two): Chowpatti Beach and the Apollo Bunder. If they go to different places they will understandably be very unhappy, but if they go to the same place all will be well. Indeed, Chowpatti is a better option because they can eat excellent *bhelpuri* there together. We may represent all this by saying that each friend gets a payoff of 0 if they go to different places, a payoff of 1 if they meet at the Apollo Bunder, and a payoff of 2 if they meet at Chowpatti (and eat good *bhelpuri* in the bargain). Here is the relevant matrix:

	Chowpatti	Apollo
Chowpatti	2, 2	0, 0
Apollo	0, 0	1, 1

Now it is easy enough to see that there are two Nash equilibria of this game.[2] In one equilibrium, both end up in Chowpatti. In the other, both end up at the Apollo Bunder. It all depends on what each expects the other to do.[3]

The Tourists' Dilemma creates what we might call a problem of coordination. It would be best for both to meet at Chowpatti, but if communication is somewhat limited, it is hard to see how this outcome might be guaranteed. The expectations that each holds regarding the other's course of action will crucially determine the final decision that each tourist takes.

Like the Prisoners' Dilemma, examples of coordination problems recur through this textbook.

QWERTY

As we have seen in Chapter 5, QWERTY refers to the keyboard system that we are all familiar with. It is known to be an inefficient system, which originally was designed to slow down the speed of typing on mechanical typewriters. The problem, however, is that the benefits of using QWERTY are not defined in isolation; they depend on how many other people are using

---

[2] More precisely, there are two Nash equilibria in pure strategies: we will not consider randomized strategies here.

[3] There is also the problem of *miscoordination*, in which beliefs about each other's actions are not commonly held by both players. These are important issues, but somewhat less relevant for the real-life examples that we consider.

the same system. Thus even if a better system is available, people may not switch to it if they feel that other individuals are using the old system. The same argument can be applied to a variety of technologies and systems: operating software for computers, television networks, the side of the road we drive on (though enforced by law, a coordinated system would surely have arisen spontaneously), and notions of what's fashionable.

The easiest way to represent any of these problems as a Tourists' Dilemma is to choose a two-player version. For instance, if two people who share computing resources can use Macintoshes or PCs, then these choices can be identified with Chowpatti or Apollo Bunder in the preceding example.

(5) Construct a table with the same features as the coordination game, because the choice of the same type of computer permits greater sharing of resources. One coordinated choice may yield a higher payoff than the other: depending on your preferences, you may want to give this honor to the strategy pair (PC, PC) or the strategy pair (Mac, Mac).

Social norms. Coordination games arise somewhat less transparently in social situations. Consider the social custom of having lavish weddings for one's sons and daughters, which (in my opinion) is reprehensible in any society but particularly in developing countries. The reason is not that people do not have the right to spend their money in any way they like—they do—but that such expenditures ultimately constitute a social norm to which the less wealthy feel constrained to adhere. Thus the "shame" attached to *not* having a lavish wedding may be higher when the going tradition is to have them. Such traditions, in turn, are created by many other people behaving in the same fashion. However, there is another equilibrium in which the social norm of lavish weddings is nonexistent (and such activities may even be frowned upon). You should be able to use this information to construct a simple two-person game with the same features as the Tourists' Dilemma and show that there are two Nash equilibria of this game.

As we noted several times in the book, social norms act as coordination devices in a variety of situations: such norms surround fertility decisions, the choice of which crops to grow, the behavior of motorists, cultural attitudes to dress and acceptable conduct, and so on. What is interesting is that social norms often have the power to turn situations that are intrinsically Prisoners' Dilemmas into coordination games, by imposing psychological costs of deviating from the cooperative outcome. There are many examples of this: consider, for instance, the practice of standing in queues (and respecting the first-come–first-served rule). With issues of social disapproval ignored, the selfishly rational way to deal with a queue is to violate it. Thus we have here a Prisoners' Dilemma: the cooperative queue would be disrupted systematically until no one respects queues anymore: this is the free-for-all equilibrium with low payoffs to everybody concerned. Indeed, several societies unhappily reside in an equilibrium where no queues are formed; the resulting chaos has to be experienced to be believed.

Societies that prevent this mayhem inevitably do so by erecting social norms around the formation of queues. What is the function of such a norm? It is that an individual who is seen not to conform to the norm will be publicly castigated or at least viewed with a great deal of disfavor by everybody else. This imposes psychological costs on disrupting a queue and effectively turns the cooperative outcome into a Nash equilibrium. To be sure, the other (chaotic) equilibrium is still lurking in the background: in this sense we have a coordination game with multiple equilibria.[4]

(6) Consider the following table:

	Choice A	Choice B
Choice A	10, 10	$0, 15 - x$
Choice B	$15 - x, 0$	5, 5

Show that for some range of values of x, this is a Prisoners' Dilemma, whereas for other ranges it is a Tourists' Dilemma. Provide a possible interpretation of the value of x by relating this problem to the preceding discussion of social norms.

Limited enforcement. Another class of situations in which coordination games make an appearance is one in which powers of enforcement, say, by the police or by the government, are limited. Riots with looting, such as those that occurred in Los Angeles some years ago, are an example. Many people would not loot a shop simply because retribution would be swift and sure: it is not difficult for the police to catch a solitary individual who breaks a store window and walks out carrying, say, a large leather armchair, but in an environment where hundreds or thousands of others are engaged in the same activity, it is very difficult for the police to do *anything* except perhaps engage in random arrests up to their capacity. If the capacity is small relative to the number of people involved in looting, then the probability that any one looter will be caught is very low. Thus episodes of widespread looting have a tendency to be self-reinforcing.

Corrupt practices (such as taking bribes or tax evasion) are subject to the same sort of considerations. Often, the police or tax auditors have the power to clamp down on a limited number of such cases (which may be chosen randomly). If the probability of being investigated is high, the incentives to

---

[4] There are situations in which the need of the hour is so great that social norms break down, at least temporarily, under the pressure. It is unlikely that people would queue to leave a burning building (though it has been known to happen), and on more mundane occasions when airlines offer "free seating" rather than preassigned seats, the normal orderliness of the queue quickly evaporates.

cheat the system are obviously reduced, but the probability itself depends on the number of individuals who need to be investigated.

(7) Consider a society of only two individuals. They can fake tax returns, but faked tax returns look suspicious and go into a potential audit pool. However, the government has limited capacity to audit and randomly chooses one person from this pool (if nonempty) to audit. Individuals seek to maximize their expected payoffs. Construct a table in which there are two equilibria: one in which no one fakes her return and the other in which both fake their returns.

Chapter 5 outlines a whole set of situations in which there are multiple equilibria. These are all akin to coordination games. You are encouraged to reread that discussion with this sort of model in mind.

Games, externalities, and policy

It should be appreciated that the Prisoners' Dilemma and the coordination game both represent *classes* of situations that recur in various forms in economic life, and certainly in questions of development. This is what we have tried to illustrate using a number of examples. Observe that both these games are fundamentally interesting because they exhibit *externalities*: what one player does in the game affects the payoff to the other player, and this can jeopardize the possibility of achieving a mutually satisfactory outcome. If neither player had an effect on the other, we could regard them as two isolated units and each could blissfully go about his or her business without any outside interference. Thus externalities are what makes a game a game.

However, the two classes of games represented by the Prisoners' Dilemma and the coordination game have somewhat different features. In the former class, a player wishes to defect even if his partner wishes to cooperate: this precipitates a situation in which cooperation becomes difficult to sustain as an equilibrium. In the latter case, a player will cooperate if his partner wishes to cooperate and not do so otherwise: this precipitates two equilibria (or multiple equilibria in a more general context). Thus the games are fundamentally different, and economic situations that conform to one class or the other are to be treated very differently in terms of policy.

In a situation that represents a Prisoners' Dilemma, a policy must be *persistent*, in the sense that it must constantly control and counterbalance the incentives of individuals to depart from cooperative outcomes. Thus in the example of pollution, a system of taxes on output might mimic the social costs that the polluter imposes on others, and so reduce output to more cooperative levels, but the tax system has to be maintained: as soon as it is removed, polluters will return to their old ways.

In contrast, policies associated with the coordination game can be *temporary*, in the sense that only transitory incentives need to be provided to break the situation free of the bad equilibrium. It isn't that such incentives are easy to provide: we have seen already that in situations where a large number of individuals are locked into an undesirable equilibrium, an enormous act of coordination is required. Sometimes such coordination is achieved by setting *standards*, as with the use of certain technologies or computer systems, forcing a large group to make the switch to a desired equilibrium. Sometimes punishments or fines are imposed for individuals carrying out the actions of the unwanted equilibrium. The point is that once the new equilibrium is established, the fines or the specification of standards can be removed without matters necessarily reverting to their old ways.

A1.4. Games over time

In situations such as the one described in the previous section, the agents in the game move *simultaneously*, or essentially simultaneously, which is to say that each player makes his move in ignorance of what the other player does. There are several cases, however, where a game is played over a period of time, in which one or more players take actions, followed by the actions of other players (or perhaps the same players) after the previous round of actions has been observed. Such games have an element of sequentiality to them. The purpose of this section is to discuss some features peculiar to these games.

Credibility and subgame perfection

At the heart of games with sequential moves is the notion of *credibility*. Formalized properly, it leads to a refinement of the Nash equilibrium concept, in the sense that "credible equilibria" are a subset of the Nash equilibria of the game.

The idea of credibility can easily be seen from the following simple two-player game of entry into an industry. Firm 1 is a potential entrant. It moves first, choosing to be "in" or "out". If it chooses out, then the game ends and the payoffs are 0 to firm 1 and 2 to firm 2. If it comes in, firm 2 has the choice to "accommodate" firm 1, which yields payoffs of 1 each to the firms, or "fight" firm 1, which is costly for both firms 1 and 2: the payoffs are -1 and 0, respectively. Figure A1.1 summarizes the situation.

Now consider the strategy pair in which firm 1 chooses out, while firm 2 chooses the strategy fight if firm 1 chooses in (remember, a strategy for the second firm is a *conditional* statement, because it gets to see what firm 1 does and can condition on this action). This is a Nash equilibrium, because *given* that firm 1 is choosing out the strategy of firm 2 is a best response, it will never have to move anyway. Additionally, given that firm 2 is threatening to fight, firm 1's best response is to stay out. Thus the two strategies are mutual best responses and the definition of a Nash equilibrium is satisfied.

There is something unattractive about the preceding outcome, or at any rate something that is incredible about firm 2's threat to fight. What if firm 1 were to test this threat by entering? Would firm 2 fight? The answer is that it would not: fighting yields a payoff of 0, whereas accommodation yields a payoff of 1. The only credible course of action for firm 2 is to accommodate the entry, and if firm 1 knows this, it will enter. Thus the concept of a Nash equilibrium is insufficient, in the sense that it fails to rule out "equilibria" that lack credibility.

This motivates a refinement of the Nash equilibrium concept that is very intuitive and easy to describe. Look at Figure A1.1 once again. It looks like a tree. In this example the tree is very simple—there are only two nodes—but we could imagine 1 moving, and then 2, and then perhaps player 3, or even players 1 or 2 once again, and even so, further moves are possible and so on. In this case we would have a tree with many nodes. Think of a minigame or a *subgame* emanating from each and every one of these nodes, which is the game that would occur if, for some reason, the players were to arrive at those nodes. (For instance, in our example, there is only one subgame, which is precipitated if firm 1, whether by accident or by design, were to move in.)

Credibility simply says that all strategies must be best responses to the other strategies, *not only for the original game*, but starting from *any* subgame. Put another way, the strategies should be Nash equilibria for every subgame. Such strategy combinations are said to represent a *subgame perfect Nash equilibrium*.

To see how this works in our example, return to the strategy pair under consideration. Clearly, the pair does not induce a best response on the (only) subgame of that example, so this strategy pair is not subgame perfect. There is another strategy pair that does satisfy the requirement: it is the combination (in, accommodate if in). This strategy pair is made up of mutual best responses in both subgames and is therefore subgame perfect. An

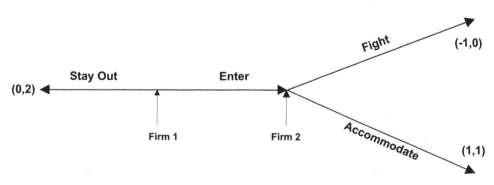

Figure A1.1. Credibility: an illustration.

important example of subgame perfection comes from the theory of infant industry perfection, a topic that we discussed in Chapter 17.

Protecting an Industry. A monopolistic industry is protected by a tariff. It must decide whether or not to cut costs and become internationally competitive. After this decision is made, the government observes whether the industry has cut costs or not, and then decides whether or not to remove the tariff that protects the industry.

To analyze this model, I am going to put in more information. There are four regimes to be considered: (1) a free-trade regime in which the industry has cut costs and is competitive on the world market, (2) a protected regime with low costs, in which protection is unnecessary for the industry's survival (3) a free-trade regime with high industry cost, in which the industry is not competitive and the product is imported, and (4) a protected regime with high costs, in which the industry is shielded from international competition and supplies the domestic market.

Figure A1.2 describes the situation in the form of a *game tree*. Suppose that there is an initial move by the government (not shown in the tree) in which protection has been granted to the industry for some period of time. During this period, the industry must decide whether or not to lower its costs or to maintain them at the currently high uncompetitive level. After the industry makes its decision, the government must decide whether or not to withdraw protection. After the government makes its decision, one of the

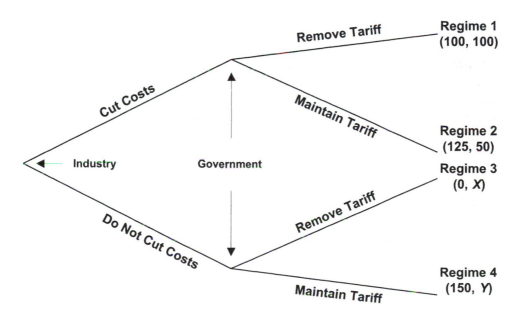

Figure A1.2. The protection game.

four regimes described previously comes into being (see Figure A1.2, which attaches regimes to the various terminal nodes of the tree).

Each regime is associated with *payoffs* to the players in the game: the industry and the government. These are shown in parentheses: the first entry represents the payoff to the industry and the second entry represents the payoff to the government. Let's examine the payoffs to the industry first.

What the industry would like best is to not cut its costs (this presumably involves some expenditure of resources, as well as the firing of lazy managers who have a vested interest in being there) *and* retain full protection. This is a case of having one's cake and eating it too, and this option yields 150. Of course, it would hate not having cut costs only to be left unprotected, and we have given this option the lowest payoff of 0. Cutting costs and staying protected is the next best alternative, at 125. Finally, cutting costs and becoming competitive with no protection (the regime 1 case) comes in at 100, well below the pampered option of staying inefficient and unproductive.

What about the government's preferences? Clearly, regime 1 is preferred (by the government) to regimes 2, 3, and 4. In regime 1, the industry is fully competitive and free trade brings benefits to consumers without harmful side effects. In regime 2, the industry has no need for protection and, although industrialists may prefer this, the government knows the industry will survive with or without protection and will withdraw protection. Thus we assign government payoffs of 100 to regime 1 and 50 to regime 2. However, it is unclear whether the government prefers regime 3 to regime 4 or vice versa. Both regimes have high costs. Regime 4 yields protectionist profits to the domestic producer, whereas regime 3 essentially gets rid of him. It is not hard to guess which regime he would prefer or lobby for. On the other hand, regime 3 is preferred to regime 4 by all consumers or users of the product: they obtain it cheaper from the world market. The government's final preference over these two regimes will be an amalgam of these two sets of conflicting interests. I have labeled the payoffs as X and Y: although they are both less than 100 as discussed previously, their relative magnitudes are crucial to the success or failure of a protectionist policy designed to lower costs, as we will see below.

Now let us proceed to an analysis of the model. Observe that the industry's strategy is simply an action: "cut costs" or "do not cut costs." The government's strategy is more complex: it is a conditional statement describing how it will react to each of these two actions. An example of a strategy *pair* is (cut costs, remove tariff whether industry cuts costs or not). Note that this strategy pair is *always* a Nash equilibrium, independent of the values of X and Y, because given that the government adopts the strategy of removing the tariff regardless of the industry's actions, the industry faces a payoff of 100 if it cuts costs and 0 if it does not (use Figure A1.2 and move along the tree). Hence, it will cut costs, and given that the industry adopts the strategy cut costs, the government does find it worthwhile to remove the tariff.

Is this strategy credible or subgame perfect? We have already seen that to answer this question, we must examine all possible subgames. It remains to examine the subgame in which the industry does not cut costs. In this subgame, the government's strategy of removing the tariff is credible if $X > Y$. That is, consumer interests must play a larger role than producer interests in determining government policy. The industry will know that if it does not perform, the government can credibly punish it: it is in the interest of the government ex post to do so.

What if $Y > X$? In this case, producer interests, or perhaps the interests of workers who are hired by the industry, loom larger in the calculus of the government. This destroys the credibility of the remove tariff regardless strategy, because in the relevant subgame, it does not constitute a best response. Can the government now get the infant industry to cut costs and grow up? It cannot.

(8) Prove that if $Y > X$, the *only* subgame perfect Nash equilibrium of this game is one in which the government chooses the strategy remove tariff if cut costs, maintain tariff otherwise, and the industry does not cut costs.

This example, together with subgame perfection, teaches us that the ability of a player (in this case, the government) to achieve some objection may depend on her preferences over *other* alternatives, neither of which is necessarily the alternative that the player finally wants to achieve.

Contracts

Principal–agent models represent a good example of sequential games in which one party, known as the principal, moves first by offering a contract to another party, the agent. It is assumed for this class of models that the contract can be enforced. The agent then reacts to the contract by choosing an action that cannot be monitored or prespecified. The choice of the action typically is influenced by the form of the contract.

Various examples in the text come under this heading. Consider, for instance, the provision of credit. The principal here is the lender, who offers a credit contract that dictates loan terms (such as the rate of interest for loans of different sizes). The agent (the borrower) then chooses some loan size. The choice of loan size obviously depends on the contract.

Alternatively, consider a land rental contract, an example that we've already encountered in this appendix. A landlord leases out land to a tenant. The landlord chooses a contract for the tenant, which is a scheme for dividing up the produced output. This is typically a function that specifies how various levels of output are allocated between landlord and tenant. *After* the contract is offered, the tenant chooses the amount of labor to devote to the land.

In the text, we have repeatedly (though implicitly) used the concept of subgame perfect equilibrium to analyze contracts. For instance, consider a land rental contract. The tenant can adopt the following strategy: "unless some *particular* contract is offered, I will choose effort level equal to zero." If the landlord believes this strategy, he will be forced to offer the particular contract that the tenant is after. However, this strategy combination lacks subgame perfection: if the tenant were faced with a contract for which he is threatening to put in zero effort, typically he would do nothing of the sort. He would put in the level of effort that is optimal for him, *given* the contract. Thus the correct way to solve these games is for the principal to put himself in the agent's shoes and compute the optimal level of action for each contract. Finally, with this information in mind, the principal should choose the best possible contract.

This motivates the general structure of a principal–agent model with unobserved agent actions. In somewhat abstract form, imagine that the agent can choose from some set of actions A, which cannot be prespecified by the principal. Final output is a function of the action chosen and may be influenced by stochastic shocks as well. Thus write

$$(A1.1) \qquad\qquad Y = F(a, \theta),$$

where Y is the value of output, a is the action chosen by the agent, and θ is the realization of some random shock (such as rainfall).

A *contract* is just the strategy chosen by the principal: it is a function $R(Y)$ that describes the reward to the agent for every output level Y. The agent then chooses some action a from the set A. If he has a utility function $u(a, R)$ that depends on the action and his reward, his objective is to

$$(A1.2) \qquad\qquad \text{maximize the expected value of } u(a, R)$$

by choosing a, where $R = R(Y)$ and Y is given by (A1.1).

The principal knows that the agent will behave in the way specified by (A1.1) for every contract that he might offer, so if the principal's utility function is given by v, his problem is to choose a *contract*, that is, a function $R(Y)$, to

$$(A1.3) \qquad\qquad \text{maximize the expected value of } v(Y - R(Y)),$$

where Y is determined by (A1.1), and a is determined by the solution to the agent's problem (A1.2). This is what we called the *incentive constraint* in several contexts (see especially the Appendix at the end of Chapter 12).

There may be other limitations on the choice of contract. The principal may need to ensure that the agent receives a certain minimum utility from the contract, otherwise the agent will not participate. This is the *participation constraint*. It is included by further constraining the maximization problem (A1.3) to require that the agent's utility, as given by the solution to (A1.2), be at least as great as some preassigned value, which is typically the agent's valuation of his next best option.

A special case of the principal–agent problem is solved in the Appendix at the end of Chapter 12.

(9) Recall the landlord–tenant example introduced previously, and also consult the Appendix at the end of Chapter 12. Show that this is a special case of a principal–agent problem and try to provide an algebraic solution for the optimal land rental contract when the agent is assumed to be risk-neutral.

Repeated games

Another class of intertemporal games that appears more than once in this book is the class of *repeated games*. A repeated game is easy enough to describe in general terms. Suppose that a set of players is involved in a game (you may choose any of the games that we have discussed so far). Now imagine that this game is played over and over again by the same set of players: it is *repeated*. Think of this as a giant game in itself. True, the individual games that comprise the giant game are not linked: nothing that you do in any of the minigames influences what the set of players can *feasibly* achieve in other minigames. Nevertheless, the very fact that the players are involved in the same relationship in the future can be used to influence current play.

To see how this works consider two players engaged in repeated play of the Prisoners' Dilemma. For ready reference we reproduce here the table that makes up a typical Prisoners' Dilemma:

	Cooperate	Defect
Cooperate	10, 10	0, 15
Defect	15, 0	5, 5

Now we need to introduce the concept of a *mental horizon*—the notion of some degree of farsightedness on the part of each player. It is absurd to imagine that at any date, each player cares only about her payoff *at that date*. It is more realistic to suppose that she also worries about her *future* payoffs. She may care *less* about payoffs that are far into the future, but the fact remains that she does care. The easiest way to do this is to suppose that a player cares about N periods (including the current one) at every point of time. Thus if $N = 1$, she is myopic and cares only about today's returns. The larger N gets, the larger is the player's mental horizon.

Digression on discounting. The preceding formulation is my shorthand for mental horizons in this book. It is easy but a bit nonstandard,[5] so for completeness I will include the standard formulation (which is only a bit more complicated and can be used in exactly the same way). Mental horizons also can be studied by supposing that each player places some weight on the future, but the weights decline geometrically further into the future. This formulation has two advantages that compensate for its added complexity. First, future concerns do not disappear all of a sudden, as in the previous paragraph: they become weaker and weaker as the future grows more distant. Second, the utility valuation across two neighboring periods in the future is independent of where you are today. To see this more clearly, let us formally complete the construction: introduce a *discount factor* δ, where $0 < \delta < 1$, that trades off tomorrow's payoff for that of today. Then a payoff t periods from now is weighted by δ^t. Thus the relative weight across any pair of neighboring dates is always δ.

Whatever the exact formulation of mental horizons, we can use the idea to explore how cooperation can be supported in repeated games by the implicit threat of retreating to noncooperation. To see this, first observe that repeated play of the (defect, defect) outcome, irrespective of past history, is a subgame perfect equilibrium of the repeated game. To see why, note that one player's strategy is always to confess regardless of how players behaved in the past; then it will be in the interest of the other player to do precisely the same.

Now the idea is to use this equilibrium to try to construct *another* equilibrium of the repeated game, which is also subgame perfect. To do this, consider the following strategy: each player cooperates at all subgames that have been reached following a history of total cooperation. In *any* other subgame, play defect. This proposed equilibrium clearly satisfies the subgame perfection property for any subgame in which total cooperation has *not* occurred in the past, because of the discussion in the previous paragraph. It only remains to check whether the mutual best response property is satisfied along the cooperative subgames (which is the relatively hard part).

Suppose that we are at such a subgame, and a player entertains the possibility of deviation by playing defect. We know from our description of strategies that this will entail the play of (defect, defect) forever after. With a mental horizon of N periods, the following calculation is relevant (see the

---

[5] It is also not a good model for situations that are more complex than the ones studied in this book, because the formulation suffers from issues of time consistency.

payoff matrix in the table preceding):

if defect, get a total of $15 + 5(N - 1)$;

if cooperate, get a total of $10N$.

In other words, defection today entails a temporary gain followed by retribution as the other player switches actions according to her given strategy. Cooperation ensures the $(10, 10)$ payoff every period. Thus the player will cooperate if $15 + 5(N-1) \le 10N$ or, equivalently, if $N \ge 2$. This means that (in this example) if each player cares at least about tomorrow as well as today, cooperation is possible in the repeated game even though it is not possible in the "stage game." Of course, the requirement on N will vary with the payoff matrix of the game.

With the discounting version, it is similarly possible to obtain a measure of the minimal degree of farsightedness required. This is left for you to do in the following exercise:

(10) Show that cooperation forever can be sustained in the repeated Prisoners' Dilemma with discounting if the discount factor is at least as large as 0.5.

Repeated games make an appearance at several points in this text. Models of permanent labor contracts in Chapter 13, credit contracts with default in Chapter 14, and insurance arrangements in Chapter 15 are examples.

Appendix 2

Elementary Statistical Methods

A2.1. Introduction

Economists, and other scientists as well, are often interested in understanding the relationship between two or more variables. For instance, an agricultural scientist might want to know how variations in annual rainfall affect crop output, a social worker might wonder whether school dropout rates have anything to do with crime rates in cities, and an economist might want to test the hunch that higher income levels, or perhaps a diminished population of storks, tend to make for smaller-sized families. An important statistical technique that allows the exploration of possible interrelationships between variables is called *regression analysis*. This book contains several instances of such analysis.

Let us suppose that we want to investigate the relationship between two variables x and y. For instance, x might be annual rainfall measured in inches and y annual crop output, say, metric tons of wheat. Our first task is to collect the data: we will need a number of *joint observations* of (x, y) values; usually, the more the merrier. Observations may be collected at various levels of detail: countries, regions, groups, individuals, and so on. In the rainfall example we might have observations from several regions or states of one or more countries, and several observations (at different points of time) for each region.

Observations collected at the same point in time but across different units (regions, countries, individuals) form a *cross-sectional* data set. Observations collected for the same unit but over different points in time form a *time series*. Mixed observations (both across units and across time) form a *panel*.

The general rule, of course, is that more data are preferred to less, but the problem is that detailed and appropriate data are often unavailable. Understandably enough, this problem is more acute for developing countries. For instance, we would love to test the Kuznets inverted-U hypothesis (see Chapter 7) with a long time series for a given country, but this kind of detail is available only for a few countries. Hence, we need to be aware of the pitfalls of limited data, and must attempt to correct for these limitations in the best way possible. In a sense, this is what statistical analysis is all about.

For example, in trying to estimate the effect of rainfall on crop output, cross-section data on rainfall and output *alone* probably will be inappropriate because there can be important (unobserved) differences that might obscure the "pure" effect of rainfall on agricultural productivity, or, worse still, the measured effect might be systematically biased because we have neglected to include some other variable that may be systematically correlated with rainfall and have its own effect on crop productivity. The following exercise provides an example.

(1) Regions with low rainfall may have invested in irrigation. If the irrigation data are not included in our analysis, explain why the measured effect of rainfall will be systematically biased *downward*.

In other situations, a pure time series may be problematic. Suppose that we are interested in knowing how household income affects family size. Again, if all the data we have pertain to household income and family size, our estimates might be confounded by changes in other variables over time: the spread of education, the availability of better birth-control methods, and so on. Some of these variables may be completely uncorrelated with income changes, but others may be correlated and might bias our estimates.

(2) Suppose that income per se has no effect on fertility choices, but education does. If we lack data on education, show that observations on income and fertility may suggest a positive relationship between the two, when in fact there is none (*ceteris paribus*).

Thus much of regression analysis is concerned with the careful estimation of bilateral relationships, while making all attempts to control for other variables that may also affect that relationship.

A2.2. Summary statistics

Before embarking on a detailed discussion of the relationship between variables x and y, let's identify some *summary features* of these variables. Suppose we have n pairs of observations: represent them as (x_1, y_1), $(x_2, y_2), \ldots, (x_n, y_n)$.

The mean

The *average* of these observations is often important, and this is typically measured by the *arithmetic mean*. It is the sum of all observations of the relevant variable divided by the total number of observations (we have n observations of each variable in the foregoing general description). The arithmetic means $\bar{x}$ and $\bar{y}$ of x and y, respectively, are mathematically represented as

$$(A2.1) \qquad \bar{x} = \frac{1}{n} \sum_{i=1}^{n} x_i = \frac{x_1 + x_2 + \cdots + x_n}{n},$$

$$(A2.2) \qquad \bar{y} = \frac{1}{n} \sum_{i=1}^{n} y_i = \frac{y_1 + y_2 + \cdots + y_n}{n}.$$

The summation symbol ($\sum$) is a shorthand description of the summation, or adding up, operation. The notation x_i denotes the ith observation of variable x, where i takes up values from 1 through n, as indicated by numbers below and above the summation. Therefore, $\sum_{i=1}^{n}$ denotes the sum of all x_is; that is, x_1 through x_n.

The variance

The mean is not the only relevant summary of the observations of a variable. We would also like to know whether the different observations lie more or less close to the mean (i.e., whether they are bunched closely to one another) or far from it (i.e., whether they are widely dispersed). One way to do this is to somehow add up all the differences of the observations from the mean. Note that *all* differences count, whether positive or negative. There is a commonly accepted measure of dispersion in statistics, which is the *variance* (or its close cousins, the standard deviation and the coefficient of variation).

The variance puts positive and negative differences from the mean on the same footing by *squaring* these differences: thus all negative signs vanish. Squaring has another property as well: it attaches proportionately greater weight to larger deviations from the mean: a difference of 2 counts as 4 as far as the variance is concerned, whereas a difference of 5 counts as 25. Mathematically, the variance is given by the formula

$$(A2.3) \qquad V = \frac{1}{n} \sum_{i=1}^{n} (x_i - \bar{x})^2,$$

which is interpreted as the average value of all (squared) deviations from the mean.[1] The variance is often presented in the following equivalent form of a *standard deviation*, which makes the units comparable to those in which the variable originally was measured:

$$(A2.4) \qquad \sigma = \sqrt{V}.$$

---

[1] There is a slight distinction between the variance and the *sample* variance that we ignore here, but see subsequent text.

Notice that it is important to take the *average* of the squared differences from the mean, and not just their sum. This is because even if individual differences are small (so that there is little "dispersion" in the data actually), the aggregate of such differences can be large simply because we have a large number of observations, and we don't want that. This kind of reasoning also suggests that the variance (or standard deviation) should be expressed as a *ratio* of the mean: if not, an innocent change in the units of measurement can affect the measure of dispersion. This gives rise to the *coefficient of variation*:

(A2.5) $$C = \frac{\sigma}{\bar{x}}.$$

Correlation

So far we have discussed summary statistics about a *single* variable. However, our main goal is to understand whether two (or more) variables move together: whether they *covary*. To understand the notion of covariance, consider the familiar example of two farmers who produce the same crop in two different parts of a country. The output of either farmer can take on only two values: H (high) and L (low). H occurs with probability p, where p is the chance of having adequate rainfall and is the same across the two farmers.

Now carry out the thought experiment of moving the farmers closer and closer together, initially starting out at two well-separated locations in the country in which they live. Because the initial locations are far apart, the probability of good rainfall in one location is "independent" of outcomes in the other location. Put another way, the knowledge that one farmer has suffered L tells us nothing about what might have happened to the other farmer. As we move the two farmers closer and closer together, their fortunes become more closely linked: if one farmer produces H, you can guess with greater and greater degrees of certainty that the other farmer has produced H as well. At the very end of this thought experiment, when the two farmers are neighbors, their outputs will covary perfectly (if rainfall is the only source of uncertainty, which we've assumed).

Note three things about this example. First, if we just focus on any *one* of the farmers, nothing changes. The probability that he produces H is p all along. The behavior of the *individual* random variables (output in this case) tells us nothing about how they might be correlated. In this sense, notions such as the mean and the variance do not tell us anything about *joint* movements of the variables x and y.

Second, the fact that two variables covary (as they do in the example here when the farmers live close to each other) tells us nothing about the direction of *causation* from one of the variables to the other, or indeed if there is a causal link between the two at all. In our example, an H for one farmer does not in any way *cause* an H for the other, even if the two outputs are perfectly correlated. It's just that there is some *third* variable (in this case, the state of the monsoon) that is a common driver for the two outputs. Therefore our notions of causality must, in some sense, be formed by common sense observations of which variable is likely to be exogenous and which is likely to be endogenous. For instance, if we took as our two variables (i) the state of the monsoon and (ii) the crop output of a single farmer, then a positive correlation between these two variables is more likely to be indicative of causality: it is highly unlikely that the output of a single farmer will influence the state of the weather.

Third, two variables may covary *negatively* as well as positively.

(3) Consider the chances of a student scoring the highest grade in mathematics in her class. Suppose the chances are given by the probability p. If two equally able students are drawn at random and their chances are examined, then show that their chances are independent if the two are in different classes, whereas they covary negatively if they are in the same class. Note that the negative covariance is perfect if each class has only two students.

A measure of observed correlation between two variables x and y is given by the *covariance*. If we have a sample of n pairs of observations (x_1, y_1), $(x_2, y_2), \ldots, (x_n, y_n)$, then the covariance[2] is given by

$$(A2.6) \qquad \mathrm{cov}_{xy} \equiv \frac{1}{n} \sum_{i=1}^{n} (x_i - \bar{x})(y_i - \bar{y}).$$

Note how this captures comovements. If, when y_i exceeds its mean, x_i exceeds its mean as well, then the covariance will be positive, but if the fact that y_i exceeds its mean has no bearing (on average) on the behavior of x_i, the covariance will be zero.[3] Similarly, if x_i tends to fall short of its mean when y_i exceeds $\bar{y}$, the covariance will be negative.

The covariance has the same problem as the variance, in that the number obtained is not free of units of measurement. To remedy this we express the covariance as a fraction of the product of standard deviations of the two variables. This yields the *coefficient of correlation*, which we denote by

$$(A2.7) \qquad R = \frac{\mathrm{cov}_{xy}}{\sigma_x \sigma_y}.$$

---

[2] Just as in the case of the sample variance, there is a slight distinction between the *sample* covariance and the covariance that we ignore here.

[3] To see this a bit more formally, note that if y_i has "no bearing" on the behavior of x_i in the sample, this just means that the distribution of x values around the mean $\bar{x}$ will look the same whether we look at the whole sample or whether we look at the subsample restricted to one particular observation of y. Restricting ourselves to the latter, we see that $\sum_i (x_i - \bar{x})(\hat{y} - \bar{y}) \simeq 0$ for each subsample of pairs (x_i, y_i) such that y_i equals some fixed value $\hat{y}$. Adding over all such subsamples (by changing the value of $\hat{y}$), we see that the covariance must be zero.

Clearly R is also positive (or negative) when the two variables comove positively (or negatively). Sometimes R^2 is reported instead of R when we do not wish to focus on the direction of the association, but only its strength (squaring removes the negative sign).

The reason for dividing by the product of the standard deviations is only in part to obtain a units-free number (dividing, for instance, by the product of the means would have achieved this goal as well). The *particular* normalization we choose has the virtue of placing R between -1 and $+1$. These extremes signify maximal correlation, whereas 0 signals lack of correlation between the two random variables. Although we omit the proof of this assertion, it can be found in any standard statistics textbook (see, for instance, Hoel [1984, pp. 385–386]).

It is important, however, to note that R or R^2 is not just a measure of association between two random variables, but a measure of a very special sort of association: one that is *linear*. Indeed, R^2 takes on its maximum value of 1 when the relationship between x and y can be expressed in the form $y_i = A + bx_i$ for all i, for some constants A and b. However, the true relationship between x and y may not be linear (though it may be very strong). For instance, a greater consumption of calories leads to an increase in work capacity over some range (see Chapter 8), but after a point the relationship between calorie consumption and work capacity turns negative (as obesity sets in). Thus the true relationship involves a zone of positive association and another zone of negative association. At the same time, if you have a large range of calorie-capacity observations and mindlessly calculate the correlation coefficient between these two variables, it may not be very high, simply because the correlation coefficient cancels out these two conflicting zones of association. The lack of a high correlation does not mean that there is *no* relationship at all: it just means that we are applying our concepts in the wrong way. The choice of a specification of the true underlying relationship is part of the economist's art, and although statistical methods can be indicative of the direction in which to go, an underlying *theory* is essential. We will consider more of this in the next section.

(4) Generate an imaginary set of calorie-capacity observations using the relationship $y = A + bx - cx^2$ (here x stands for calories consumed and y stands for work capacity). What signs would you use for the constants A, b, and c? For given constants, where do the zones of positive and negative associations lie? Now use this relationship to generate a set of observations and calculate the correlation coefficient between x and y. What would happen if you restricted your observations to only those from the zone of positive association?

A2.3. Regression

Introduction

Suppose that we are interested in the form of the relationship between variables x and y, and not just in the existence of a correlation. Suppose we have some reason to believe that x (say rainfall) has some causal effect on y (say wheat output). Among other things, we would like to know the *marginal* impact of x on y: by how much does an increase in x appear to affect y? This is the general question behind *regression analysis*.

Why are we interested in such an exercise? First, we can use regressions to *test* a proposed theory or to play off one theory against another. For example, the Solow model tells us that the per capita incomes of countries "converge," which suggests that if x is initial per capita income and y is subsequent rate of growth of per capita income, an increase in x has a *negative* effect on y. A competing theory might argue that higher per capita income enables the exploitation of investment activities with higher rates of return: this theory would have the opposite prediction. A regression using available data might throw light on the (relative) validity of these theories.

The second way in which a regression can be helpful is in *forecasting*. If, on the basis of available data, x and y seem to follow a close linear relationship and if we are prepared to believe that they will continue to do so in the future (which is possibly a strong assumption), then the regression equation can be useful for forecasting purposes. For example, if we know what the value of x is going to be in the coming months or years, then we can "predict" the value of y by applying the calculated regression formula. Very often, x is merely time or a variable that has or may be expected to have a stable time trend itself, so that its value in the near future is known to us with a fair degree of certainty. Variable x can also be a government policy parameter (like taxes), so that if a change in its value is seen to be forthcoming (or at least entertained), then the regression equation can be used to predict the impact of this policy change on the variable y.

Preliminary eyeballing: The use of scatter diagrams

Often, a careful look at the data with the naked eye will tell us more than all kinds of statistical measures. A *scatter plot* allows us to do just this. First, we decide (on the basis of our experience and/or theory) which variable is to be "causal" and which is to be the variable that's affected by the movements of the "causal variable." Following convention, we let x stand for the causal or *independent variable* and y stand for the *dependent variable* (the nomenclature itself tells us that we, as econometricians, suspect a particular direction of causation and have used this already to classify the variables).

Next, we construct a diagram in which the independent variable is put on the horizontal axis and the dependent variable occupies the vertical axis. On this diagram we record our sample observations. The resulting plot of observations is called a scatter diagram or scatter plot. Our first (and critically important) statistical technique is: stare hard at the scatter plot.

As an illustration, Figure A2.1 reproduces Figure 2.7 from Chapter 2. The independent variable is per capita income and the dependent variable is life expectancy. The observation pairs are from different countries: the data form a cross section.

To facilitate our visual examination, the figure draws in the means of each of the two variables in the form of a pair of cross lines. Note how most of the data lie in the first and third quadrants created by the cross lines. This suggests that when per capita income exceeds its mean value, life expectancy tends to exceed *its* mean value as well, which is just a way of noting that the coefficient of correlation is likely to be positive.

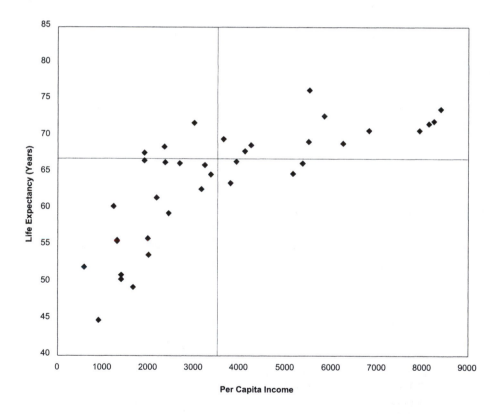

Figure A2.1. Scatter diagram of observations of per capita income and life expectancy in different countries. Source: World Development Report (World Bank [1995]) and Human Development Report (United Nations Development Programme [1995]).

After this preliminary step, it is a good idea to get a sense of the overall relationship. Is a straight line the best fit? In the example studied here, this is unlikely to be the case. The reason is that life expectancy is difficult to push beyond 80 or so (for medical reasons), whereas the jumps from 50 to 60 and from 60 to 70 can be made more rapidly. This suggests that the true relationship is more a curve than a straight line, with the curve flattening out as we move into higher ranges of per capita income. This sort of relationship seems to be broadly supported by the scatter diagram. The mathematical form of the regression should be constructed with this in mind.

Finally come two conceptually important issues. Remember that our goal is to understand if x has a strong impact on y. However, what does the word "strong" mean exactly? Figure A2.2 illustrates the problem. In both panels of this diagram we have relationships that are most likely linear. In the first panel, we have a scatter plot between x and y where the fit is remarkably good: the plots closely hug some straight line, but at the same time the slope of the line is flat. In the second panel the scatter is much more pronounced, but the slope of the "best fitted line" seems to be high. (You will appreciate the difference better if you look at the scale in which the vertical axes are drawn in the two panels: the scale is much more compressed in the second panel.)

Thus "strong" has two meanings in this context. A relationship may be estimable in a precise fashion: in the first panel, even though the effect of x on y is not large, the data tell us that this statement can be made quite precisely. The second meaning is that the effect of x on y is large. As Figure A2.2 shows, this statement is quite compatible with the observation that a precise estimate of the relationship itself is not to be had.

Note that the correlation coefficient captures the notion of "strength" in its first sense (at least when the underlying relationship is linear). It does not matter what the slope is: if the data fit perfectly on a straight line, the correlation coefficient will always equal unity.

(5) Suppose that observations on (x, y) pairs are generated directly from the equation $y = A + bx$, where A and b are constants. Assuming that $b \neq 0$ and that there are at least two observations, show that $R^2 = 1$ *irrespective* of the value of b, the slope.

The basics of regression

Suppose we feel that the relationship between x and y can be well described by a straight line. Thus we suggest a (linear) equation of the form

$$(A2.8) \qquad\qquad y = A + bx,$$

where A and b are (as yet unspecified) constants. This equation describes a *possible* relationship: it says that y assumes a value of A when $x = 0$, and

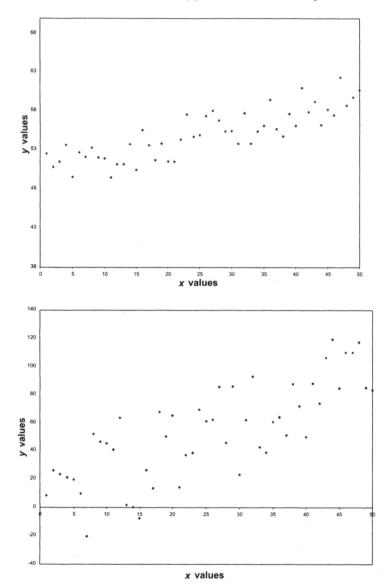

Figure A2.2. Notions of a "strong" relationship.

its value increases (or decreases) by an amount b for each additional unit increase (or decrease) in the value of x.

In graphical terms, (A2.8) describes a straight line in the (x, y) plane. Of course, if we vary the values of A and b, we will alter both the position and the slope of this straight line. Look at and compare the two panels in Figures A2.3. In both panels, the numerous dotted points represent the same scatter diagram—a plot of several pairs of joint observations of x and y. On the other hand, the two straight lines in the two panels represent two

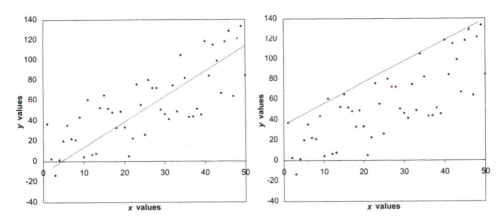

Figure A2.3. Fitting a line to a scatter.

different attempts to give a stylized picture of the relationship between x and y. In the left-hand panel, the actual data points are all more or less close to the line drawn. In the right-hand panel, however, many of the data points are quite far off. Obviously, the straight line in the left-hand panel is a better "representation" of the data than its counterpart in the right-hand panel. In other words, it "fits" the data better. Given a set of observations, therefore, our task is to find the straight line that is the "best fit" to the data; it amounts to the same thing as finding the "best" values of A and b in equation (A2.8). However, an infinite number of straight lines can be drawn on a plane, and it is impossible to judge the relative merits of *all* of them merely through visual inspection (as we did for the relatively easy task of selecting among the lines in Figure A2.3!). What precise criterion is to be used to find the proper numerical values of A and b?

Notice that for a line to be a "good fit," we require that the actual data points be not very far away from the line. For every observation x_i of the variable x, the corresponding value of y as obtained from the *stylized relationship* summarized in the given line is $(A + bx_i)$. However, the *actual*, or *observed*, value of y when $x = x_i$ is y_i. Hence, if we use the line $y = A + bx$ as a description (or a forecasting device), then for the ith observation, we have an "error" equal to $(y_i - A - bx_i)$. We would like to choose a line so as to keep such errors as low as possible, on the average. Because large errors of opposite signs may cancel each other out, it is appropriate to look at the *squares* of the various error terms. It is therefore standard statistical practice to choose the values of A and b in such a way as to make the *sum of the squared errors* as low as possible. This method of "fitting" a straight line to given data is known as the *ordinary least squares* (OLS) method. The (linear) equation thus obtained is called the (linear) *regression equation*.

An outline of the OLS procedure follows. We have collected n pairs of observations on x and y. A typical pair is denoted by (x_i, y_i). If we fit the line $y = A + bx$ to the observations, the value y_i will differ from the *predicted* value $A + bx_i$ by a margin that is the *error* in the fit at that observation pair. Under this interpretation, we may think of

(A2.9) $$y_i = A + bx_i + \epsilon_i,$$

where ϵ_i represents all kinds of random disturbances that influence y_i other than x_i. The coefficients A and b are the unknown parameters that we would like to estimate. Given any estimate $\hat{A}$ and $\hat{b}$ of A and b, we see that the *predicted value* of y_i is

$$\hat{y}_i = \hat{A} + \hat{b}x_i,$$

whereas the *prediction error* of y_i is just

$$e_i = \hat{y}_i - y_i.$$

The *sum of squared errors* (SSE, sometimes also called residual sum of squares) is therefore given by

$$\text{SSE} = \sum_{i=1}^{n} e_i^2.$$

The OLS estimates of A and b are defined as the particular values $\hat{A}$ and $\hat{b}$ of A and b that minimize the SSE for the sample data. We omit the details of the derivation, but note that the OLS estimates are given by the formulas:

(A2.10) $$\hat{b} \equiv \frac{(1/n)\sum_{i=1}^{n}(x_i - \bar{x})(y_i - \bar{y})}{(1/n)\sum_{i=1}^{n}(x_i - \bar{x})^2} = \frac{\text{cov}_{xy}}{\sigma_x^2}$$

and

(A2.11) $$\hat{A} \equiv \bar{y} - \hat{b}\bar{x}.$$

(6) If you know a bit of calculus it is very easy to derive $\hat{A}$ and $\hat{b}$ on your own. Set things up as follows: using equation (A2.9), note that the minimization of SSE is equivalent to the problem

$$\text{minimize}_{A, b} \sum_{i=1}^{n}(A + bx_i - y_i)^2.$$

Now take derivatives of this expression with respect to A and b and set the derivatives equal to zero (these are the first-order conditions). Solve the linear equations in the first-order conditions to get (A2.10) and (A2.11).

The optimally chosen value $\hat{b}$ is called the *regression coefficient*. It tells us about the *strength* of the influence of x on y; a high value of $\hat{b}$ implies that a small change in x can bring about a large change in y; a low value of $\hat{b}$ implies just the opposite.

It isn't hard to interpret the particular formula that describes $\hat{b}$. The numerator is just the covariance between x and y. The denominator is the variance of x. The regression coefficient is the fraction of "covariation" relative to the extent to which x itself varies. If there is a lot of covariance even as x varies very little, we could say that x has a large influence on y.

All said and done, however, even the *best* fitted straight line may not be a good fit. For one thing, the OLS procedure always gives you *some* answer, even when there is no relationship to write home about: you could regress Coca-Cola consumption in China on the number of red shirts sold in Denmark, and you'd still get an answer from the OLS estimates. More seriously, a systematic relationship may indeed exist but it may not be a linear one (as in our examples on nutrition and work capacity or per capita income and life expectancy). The estimated values of $\hat{A}$ and $\hat{b}$ tell us nothing about whether the overall fit is a good one. In this context, our previous discussion regarding the two notions of "strength" in a relationship is very much relevant. Finally, it is possible (and is almost always the case) that there are other explanatory variables that have been left out of the regression. The more such variables we find, the more likely it is that the fit of the regression will be improved (more on this later). This last case is the most benign and can still be informative.

The overall explanatory power of the linear regression is best summarized by our familiar friend, the correlation coefficient. As we already noted, it is quite possible for the correlation coefficient to be low even if the estimated value of b is large (and vice versa). Here is another way to see the same thing: use equations (A2.7) and (A2.10) to see that

$$R = \frac{\text{cov}_{xy}}{\sigma_x \sigma_y} = \frac{\text{cov}_{xy}}{\sigma_x^2} \frac{\sigma_x}{\sigma_y} = \hat{b} \frac{\sigma_x}{\sigma_y},$$

so that even if $\hat{b}$ is large, R (or R^2) might be low if the variance of y is very large relative to that of x. What does this mean? It means that there is a large proportion of variation in y itself that cannot be properly explained by looking *only* at variations in x. As we noted previously, this could happen for one (or a combination) of several reasons. At the same time, it is also possible that b is low, but the correlation coefficient of the regression is high: this happens if the overall variation in y is very low relative to the variation of x. The preceding equation brings out these possibilities clearly.

When we look at a fitted regression equation, therefore, the first thing we should ask is the value of R (or R^2). A low value may lead us to have little faith in the regression in the first place, although it is possible that regressions with low R^2 still can provide us with useful information, provided that the parameter b is estimated "precisely enough" (see subsequent text). This is especially the case in situations where the correlation coefficient is low, not because there has been some fundamental error of specification, but because there are simply too many explanatory variables for any one of them to have a lot of power.

Multivariate regression

The last remark in the preceding paragraph, as well as exercises (1) and (2), motivate the study of *multivariate regression*. It is most often the case that the movements of some dependent variable can never be adequately explained by one independent variable alone. Several variables need to be included on the right-hand side of the regression equation simply to bring down the quantity of inexplicable randomness on the part of the dependent variable. However, there is another, more immediate need for including additional independent variables: some of these variables may be systematically cor-related with one or more of the independent variables that we've already used *and* with the dependent variable as well, so that the exclusion of such variables attributes a compound effect to the independent variable already included.

To use the example of convergence from the theory of economic growth, note that the Solow model predicts that countries with lower initial levels of per capita income will grow faster. However, this statement is only valid *ceteris paribus*, and in most cases the ceteris will not be paribus. Thus higher per capita incomes may permit the accumulation of larger stocks of human capital, which by themselves generate faster rates of growth. A regression that includes only per capita income as an independent variable will generate a coefficient on per capita income that includes both the "direct" effect of per capita income (the Solow prediction) *and* the "indirect" effect via human capital. In this example, the two effects work in opposite directions, and the net effect may be to (apparently) show that per capita income has no effect on growth. Putting human capital as an additional variable into the regression equation helps to separate the two effects (see Chapters 3 and 4 for more detailed discussion).

The general problem is easily stated. Let y be the independent variable and let $x^1, \ldots, x^k$ be a collection of dependent variables. Then our task is to estimate a linear equation of the form

(A2.12)
$$y = A + b_1 x^1 + b_2 x^2 + \cdots + b_k x^k,$$

where the constants $(A, b_1, \ldots, b_k)$ are to be determined.

The rest of the story is a natural extension of the OLS method used in the case of a single independent variable. It is harder now to form an intuitive picture of what is going on (because scatter plots work with some difficulty with two independent variables and cannot be drawn for three or more independent variables), but the main idea is the same: we look for the "best" hyperplane that fits the multidimensional scatter of observations. Just as before, we may define the predicted value $\hat{y}_i$ for any collection $(A, b_1, \ldots, b_k)$ and any observation i as

(A2.13) $$\hat{y}_i \equiv A + b_1 x_i^1 + b_2 x_i^2 + \cdots + b_k x_i^k$$

and the prediction error e_i as

(A2.14) $$e_i \equiv y_i - \hat{y}_i.$$

Now we carry out exactly the same exercise as before: choose $(A, b_1, \ldots, b_k)$ to minimize the sum of the squares of the prediction errors $\sum_i^n e_i^2$. These yield natural extensions of the formulas (A2.10) and (A2.11).

Make sure that you understand just what these estimated coefficients mean. For instance, coefficient b_1 tells us the effect on y of a change in x^1 when all other values of $(x^2, \ldots, x^k)$ *are held constant*. This does *not* mean that the change in x^1 will have no effect on the other values of x^2. They may, in some situations, but the fact remains that b^1 is a measure of the "pure" direct effect of x^1, freed of the "contaminating" influences of the other independent variables. The "correct" regression equation, therefore, should tell us the nature of the influence of x on y, when the influence of "other factors" has been accounted for.

It remains to specify an analog of the correlation coefficient in a multiple regression exercise. This is some measure of how the dependent variable is correlated with the entire *set* of independent variables. There is an easy way to do this which nicely generalizes the single independent variable case: simply take as a measure the correlation coefficient between y and the *predicted* values $\hat{y}$ that arise from the regression. After all, the predicted values are a measure of the *joint* explanatory power of all the independent variables, taken together.[4]

---

[4] Actually, a slight variation of this measure, called the *adjusted correlation coefficient*, is used. The adjustment is employed to allow for the fact that the inclusion of *any* additional independent variables can never lower the correlation coefficient and sometimes may increase it without really contributing to explanatory power. Thus a correction is applied to the correlation coefficient, the size of the correction depending (among other things) on the number of independent or explanatory variables included in the regression. It is possible for the adjusted R^2 to decline when more independent variables are added.

(7) Verify that the correlation coefficient proposed for the multiple regression indeed generalizes the case of a single independent variable by proving that the correlation coefficient between two variables x and y is the same as the correlation coefficient between $A + bx$ and y for any constants (A, b) with $b \neq 0$.

There are two special cases of a multivariate regression that deserve some attention.

Nonlinear regressions. A multivariate regression can be used to handle situations in which the true underlying relationship is perceived to be nonlinear, either because of commonsense considerations or more sophisticated theoretical reasoning. Examples include the relationship between per capita income and life expectancy, discussed earlier in this appendix and in Chapter 2, and the Kuznets inverted-U hypothesis studied in Chapter 7.

A first step to deal with this situation is to include *both* x and x^2 as independent variables on the right-hand side of the equation. Thus, even if there really is a single independent variable, the model behaves as if there were two: the variable and its square.

What is the advantage of including the squared term? It allows different zones of positive and negative association between x and y. However, because the squared term only permits a quadratic equation to estimated, this method cannot handle more than one switch in the direction of association. But the general method easily suggests itself: include further higher powers of x if you wish to handle more complicated switches in behavior. Nonetheless, few theoretical models in economics generate such complicated behavior, unless they also happen to generate negative results of the sort "anything can happen."

(8) What kind of specification would you use to generate a regression equation for the scatter plot in Figure A2.1? Eyeball the plot and describe what values you would expect the different coefficients to have.

Some forms of nonlinearity can be converted into a linear estimation equation with very simple mathematical manipulation. For instance, suppose that we are interested in estimating the coefficients of the Cobb–Douglas production function

(A2.15) $Y = AK^\alpha L^\beta$

by using data on output (Y), capital (K), and labor (L). Clearly running a linear regression on these variables will get us nowhere, because the functional form that we are trying to estimate is inherently nonlinear. However, taking logarithms on both sides of (A2.15) will help here:

(A2.16) $\ln Y = \ln A + \alpha \ln K + \beta \ln L.$

Equation (A2.16) is a linear form that can be estimated using OLS. Convert the given data to logarithmic form to estimate the coefficients $\ln A$, α, and β. For an application of this method, see Chapter 3.

Dummy variables. Often, an additional variable takes the form of a *dummy*; that is, a variable that only takes on binary values typically represented by the numbers 0 and 1. For instance, we might wish to test the hypothesis that females earn less than males in similar jobs. We would need then to estimate a wage equation that includes several independent variables, such as age and education. Of special importance would be the dummy variable that takes the value of 0 if the worker is female and the value 1 if the worker is male. The discrimination hypothesis then states that controlling for other variables such as education and age, the coefficient on this dummy variable should be positive.

The coefficient on the dummy can be interpreted as the additional income that a worker receives simply by virtue of being male. There may be other effects as well—for instance, it is possible that a male may *also* receive more education and that education has its independent effect on wage earnings—but this will not be picked up by the dummy variable provided that education is also included in the regression equation, and indeed it should not. Whether the benefits of being male are chiefly manifested *through* factors such as better access to education and *not* directly through the labor market is something that we would like to explicitly analyze, and we don't want to lump all these effects under one general heading.

A standard way to include a dummy is through the *additive* form

$$(A2.17) \qquad y = A + bx + cD + \text{ error terms,}$$

where x is a vector of independent variables, (A, b, c) are constants to be determined (say by OLS), and D is a dummy variable that takes the value 1 in the case of a certain occurrence and 0 otherwise. For instance, D might be a country dummy that takes the value 1 if the country is Latin American and 0 otherwise (see the study of the inverted-U hypothesis in Chapter 7).

You might ask, What is the advantage of including a dummy variable when we can simply take the data apart for each of the classifications that the dummy is supposed to represent? For instance, if the data are in the form of a panel containing inequality data for some countries that are Latin American and others that are not, then why not simply create two subsets of data from this panel and run separate regressions? Indeed, we could do this, but the point is that the dummy variable approach imposes much more structure on the problem—structure often driven by theoretical considerations. Return to the wage discrimination example. We might have theoretical reasons to suppose that changes in education or age have the same effects on male and female wages *at the margin*, whereas the gender effect simply raises the wages for men (relative to women) by the same amount (or by the same percentage) at every level of education or age. This is tantamount to the assertion that the gender effect only resides in the *intercept term A* and not in the regression coefficient (or the vector of regression coefficients) represented by b.[5] Take another look at equation (A2.17). It effectively specifies the intercept term as $A + cD$ and retains the same value of b whether or not the dummy takes the value 0 or 1.

Thus the advantage of the dummy variable approach is that it allows us to tweak only those parameters that we consider theoretically affected by the dummy. This allows us to pool the data for greater statistical power. Moreover, we can (if we wish) allow the dummy to affect some of the regression coefficients by simply *interacting* the dummy with the relevant variables. For instance, suppose we believe that the wage discrimination effect grows smaller with age. Then our specification might read as follows:

$$\text{wage } = A + b_1 \text{ educ } + b_2 \text{ age } + b_3 D \text{ age } + cD + \text{ error,}$$

where the variables are self-explanatory (perhaps expressed in logarithmic terms) and D is the gender dummy. Note that the dummy has been entered in two places: first as a familiar additive shift and second to explore the idea that greater age reduces the size of the shift.

(9) What sign would you expect b_3 to have? How would you explore the conjecture that gender bias is unaffected by age, but is more pronounced for higher education levels?

Additive dummies are often referred to as *fixed effects* because they capture some shift of the regression equation that is presumably intrinsic to the characteristic captured by the dummy. Thus regressions that incorporate country, village, or time fixed effects are simply those that include the corresponding dummy variables in their specification.

Bias and significance

Apart from questions of overall fit, there is the issue of whether the estimated coefficient $\hat{b}$ can be trusted: is it far off the mark from "the truth"?

I have put the phrase "the truth" in quotes because it needs some explanation. Think of a large (potentially infinite) set of (x, y) observations that we *might* have access to: what we have in our hands is really a subset or a *sample* of these observations. Now there is some "true" relationship between

[5] In the wage discrimination example, this assertion pertains to the case in which the wage is supposed to be shifted upward by a constant *absolute* amount because of the gender term. If the shift is proportional, we need a different specification. If all effects are multiplicative, we can take the logarithmic route discussed for nonlinear estimation [see equations (A2.15) and (A2.16)].

the variables x and y, but this does not mean that our *particular* sample allows us to divine what this true relationship is. Our sample allows us to construct estimates $\hat{A}$ and $\hat{b}$ of the true relationship that we believe to be "out there," but these estimates generally would be different if we used another sample from this large "mother set" of observations. To continue the rainfall example, as our mother set of observations, think of all the rainfall that has ever occurred in history (and all that will occur) and the accompanying levels of crop output. We do not have access to this entire set: just as an example, perhaps we have all years of rainfall and crop output for alternate years between 1970 and 1997. We use this information to estimate the "true" relationship that is hidden in the mother set of observations. However, another sample of observations (say the other alternate years) may give us a somewhat different estimate.

This point of view teaches us that our estimates are *themselves* random variables in some broader sense. One aim of statistics is to develop a notion of how precise or *significant* our estimates are; that is, how confident can we be that our estimated value of $\hat{b}$ is close to the true b? A somewhat different twist on this problem is obtained by rephrasing the question a bit: *using* the estimated value $\hat{b}$ and the other data of the problem, how sure can we be that the *true* value of b is significantly different from 0, or from 1, or lies within or outside some prespecified range of values? With this twist the estimators only act as stepping stones to the true nature of things (which we can never be completely sure of because we lack all the data). We can only say things about the true relationship with some *probability*: the value of the exercise then centers on how close the probability is to 1.

Bias. Following up on the previous discussion, we may think of an OLS estimator as a *function* of the sample observations $\{(x_1, y_1), \ldots, (x_n, y_n)\}$, where you can think of each x observation as multidimensional if you like. Let's give this list of observations a name: call it z. Thus z comes from some mother set of observations, and different draws (or equivalently, different data collection exercises) give rise to different z's, all from the same mother set. Thus an OLS estimator (say of the regression coefficient b) can be thought of as a function that yields, for *every* z, an estimate $\beta(z) \equiv \hat{b}$ of the regression coefficients.

Now we can think of the average or the *expected value* of $\beta(z)$ as z ranges over all conceivable samples. Is this average the "true" value b? If it is, we say that the estimator is *unbiased*. That's just a way of saying that we can expect our estimate, on average, to be clustered around the true value that we are after. An attractive feature of the OLS estimators is that they are indeed unbiased in this sense.

Here are further details to support this observation. Let us restrict ourselves (for simplicity) to the case of a single independent variable. Suppose that in our minds, the truth is given by the model

(A2.18) $$y_i = A + bx_i + \epsilon_i,$$

where the x_is may or may not be random variables (it doesn't matter for what I'm going to talk about) and the "noise terms" ϵ_i all come as independent draws from a single distribution that itself is independent of the x values. Because ϵ is pure noise, we take it that the mean of this distribution is 0. The parameters A and b are what we are after.

Recall that our *estimate* $\hat{b}$ of b is given by the formula

$$\hat{b} = \frac{\sum_{i=1}^n (x_i - \bar{x})(y_i - \bar{y})}{\sum_{i=1}^n (x_i - \bar{x})^2},$$

where $\bar{x}$ and $\bar{y}$, you will recall, are the sample means of the x and y observations, respectively. It follows that

$$\hat{b} = \frac{\sum_{i=1}^n (x_i - \bar{x})y_i}{\sum_{i=1}^n (x_i - \bar{x})^2} + \frac{\sum_{i=1}^n (x_i - \bar{x})\bar{y}}{\sum_{i=1}^n (x_i - \bar{x})^2}$$

$$= \frac{\sum_{i=1}^n (x_i - \bar{x})y_i}{\sum_{i=1}^n (x_i - \bar{x})^2}$$

$$\equiv \sum_{i=1}^n \lambda_i y_i,$$

where the second equality follows from the fact that $\sum_{i=1}^n (x_i - \bar{x}) = 0$ and the third equality comes from letting $\lambda_i \equiv (x_i - \bar{x})/(\sum_{i=1}^n (x_i - \bar{x})^2)$. Consequently,

(A2.19) $$\hat{b} = \sum_{i=1}^n \lambda_i (A + bx_i + \epsilon_i) = b + \sum_{i=1}^n \lambda_i \epsilon_i,$$

where in deriving this equation, we have used the observations that $\sum_{i=1}^n \lambda_i = 0$ and $\sum_{i=1}^n \lambda_i x_i = \sum_{i=1}^n \lambda_i (x_i - \bar{x}) = 1$.

Now, for given observations of the x variables, I am going to take expectations over the noise terms ϵ_i. From equation (A2.19), this tells us that

$$E(\hat{b}) = b + \sum_{i=1}^n \lambda_i E(\epsilon_i) = b,$$

because the noise terms all have mean 0. This proves that the OLS estimate of b is unbiased. A similar argument applies to the estimate of the intercept term A.

Significance. The lack of bias in the OLS estimates of *A* and *b* tell us that, on average, we are not making a systematic error in our estimation of the true values of *A* and *b*. However, this does not mean that in any particular exercise, we are *at* the true value of these coefficients or even close. Figure A2.4 illustrates this concept by reiterating that any estimate is a random variable and, in general, has a distribution of possible values around its mean. What we showed in the previous section is that the *mean* is indeed the true value that we are seeking, but as the figure shows, there will be some *dispersion* around the mean. All we see is the *estimated* value $\hat{b}$, but because we do not know where the distribution in Figure A2.4 is centered, we do not know whether this estimated value is bang on the truth or is far away (or greater or less) than it. We need some probabilistic assessment of this.

What follows is a little more technical, so I will start by giving you a simple, intuitive idea of how we go about the process. Suppose that we are interested in knowing whether the *true* value of *b* is positive. (For instance, we may want to know whether rainfall truly influences crop output, whether education influences wages, or whether the stork population in a country influences the number of babies born there.) Thus we regress *y* on *x* and form an OLS estimate $\hat{b}$ of *b*.

Now suppose for the sake of argument that the true *b* is really 0. Even so, it rarely is the case that the *estimated* value $\hat{b}$ comes out to be exactly 0, because relationships that need to be estimated by statistical analysis of this sort are rarely *exact*—there are always tiny unknown outside influences, ever so minute and intractable disturbances, or simply measurement errors in variables, that tend to make the relationship between two variables somewhat fuzzy and blurred. Thus, actual farm output, although strongly dependent

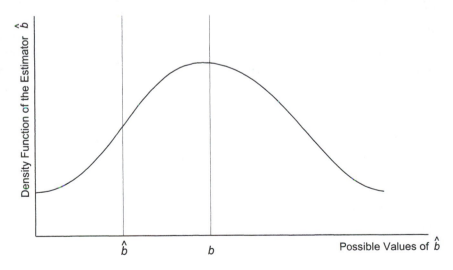

Figure A2.4. Dispersion of the OLS estimator around the true value of b.

on rainfall, also may vary slightly in response to other influences that in truth do not have any serious effect. For these reasons, we cannot be sure that a positive estimate guarantees that the true coefficient is really positive.

The art and science of drawing statistical inferences lies in discovering true and strong "structural relationships" in data that have been contaminated by the influences of these minor factors, which statisticians (partly to vent their frustration, perhaps!) refer to as "noise."

To summarize, then, the estimated coefficient of a particular "explanatory variable" may be nonzero, even if there is no real influence of that variable on y. Alternatively, it may be that in truth the relationship *is* a positive one, but does a positive *estimate* really clinch the issue?

Statisticians go about this task by specifying a provisional or *null hypothesis*. For instance, they may start by hypothesizing that the "true" value of the regression coefficient in question *is* nonpositive and then try to calculate how likely it is that the estimated value from any sample *can* turn out to be what it *does* turn out to be merely due to the effect of noise. If this probability is seen to be very low, then there exists strong reason to "reject" the null hypothesis that was assumed to start with, that is, the hypothesis that the "true" coefficient is not positive. In the case of such rejection, the opposite conclusion has to be embraced: that the independent variable in question indeed has a nonnegligible positive influence on the variable y. In this latter case, the estimated coefficient is said to be significantly different from zero or simply "statistically significant."

Note that there are two tasks to be carried out here. First, our calculation of the aforementioned probability surely depends on our belief about the strength and nature of noise in the data at hand. We need to estimate this: we do so by looking at the size of the "residuals," that is, the deviations of predicted values of y (predicted from the OLS regression equation) from actual values. This gives us some idea of the dispersion or variance in the distribution of $\hat{b}$. If this distribution is very closely clustered around the truth and if our estimate is also positive, it is very likely that the truth is positive as well. On the other hand, if this dispersion is very high, then we may not be very sure (unless the estimate itself is very large and positive).

Thus it is important to *combine* both the estimated value of the coefficient and the estimated strength of the noise to form a test of the null hypothesis. Under some statistical assumptions, this combination leads to what is called a t statistic, and we decide whether the coefficient is "significantly positive", "significantly negative" or "significantly different from zero" by embracing the opposite postulate as the null hypothesis and examining whether the value of the t statistic provides us with sufficient grounds to reject this hypothesis.

For instance, under the null hypothesis of a 0 "true" coefficient, higher values of the t statistic are more unlikely. Hence, the higher is the computed value of the t, the less plausible the null hypothesis will be. Usually, a cutoff point is decided beforehand, and if the value of t turns out to be any higher than that, the null hypothesis is rejected and the coefficient in question is pronounced to be statistically significant. Hence, in any technical report on a regression run by a researcher, it is standard practice to report the respective t values in brackets, right below the estimated coefficients, so that readers may judge the statistical significance of those coefficients.[6]

The second element of subjectivity lies in deciding beforehand *how* unlikely is "too unlikely" for a null hypothesis to be rejected. It is common practice to work with a 5% probability, that is, the null hypothesis is rejected if, under its assumption, there is less than a 5% probability that the t value takes the value it actually does in the given sample. Such a test is then called a test with "5% level of significance." Tests with 1 and 10% levels of significance are also not uncommon.

The remaining sections go into these matters in more detail.

Standard errors. Following the foregoing discussion, our first task is to determine how dispersed the distribution of the OLS estimator is. This isn't difficult, at least up to a point. We can use equation (A2.19) to calculate the variance of $\hat{b}$ for a fixed set of x observations. First rewrite (A2.19) as

$$\hat{b} - b = \sum_{i=1}^{n} \lambda_i \epsilon_i,$$

and then note that

$$(A2.20) \quad \text{variance of } \hat{b} = E(\hat{b} - b)^2 = \sigma^2 \sum_{i=1}^{n} \lambda_i^2 = \frac{\sigma^2}{\sum_{i=1}^{n}(x_i - \bar{x})^2},$$

where σ is the common variance of the (independent) error terms. It is similarly easy to show that

$$(A2.21) \quad \text{variance of } \hat{A} = \frac{\sigma^2 \sum_{i=1}^{n} x_i^2}{n \sum_{i=1}^{n}(x_i - \bar{x})^2}.$$

This is good information, but it's incomplete. In particular, we don't know what the unknown variance σ^2 is, and so we have to approximate it somehow. One way to do this is to use the *observed* variation in the estimated error terms e_i, which you'll recall are just the differences between the observed y_is

---

[6] Observe that the general philosophy reflected here is one of "not guilty, unless proven otherwise." For instance, in testing if a coefficient is significantly different from 0, the initial presumption is that the variable in question has no effect on the explained variable (x), but that presumption is later dropped if it seems too unlikely in the light of the available evidence.

and the predicted $\hat{y}_i$s. It turns out that an unbiased predictor of the variance σ^2 is given by the estimator

(A2.22)
$$\hat{\sigma}^2 \equiv \sum_{i=1}^{n} \frac{e_i^2}{n-2}.$$

An intuitive reason (somewhat unsatisfactory) for dividing by $n-2$ rather than by n is that two parameters must be estimated to compute the error terms: A and b. For instance, when computing the sample variance of a variable, it is typical to divide by $n-1$ because one parameter (the sample mean) must be estimated to compute the sample variance. This changes the degrees of freedom in the sums of squares that define $\hat{\sigma}^2$. Mathematically, it is easy to check by taking expectations that this particular division (by $n-2$) does indeed give us an unbiased estimate.

We now substitute equation (A2.22) in equations (A2.20) and (A2.21) to come up with estimates of the dispersion in $\hat{b}$ and $\hat{A}$. These are known as the *standard errors* (SE) of the estimates:

(A2.23)
$$\text{SE}(\hat{b}) = \sqrt{\frac{\hat{\sigma}^2}{\sum_{i=1}^{n}(x_i - \overline{x})^2}},$$

(A2.24)
$$\text{SE}\left(\hat{A}\right) = \sqrt{\frac{\hat{\sigma}^2 \sum_{i=1}^{n} x_i^2}{n \sum_{i=1}^{n}(x_i - \overline{x})^2}}.$$

Sometimes, regression results report these standard errors in parentheses below each of the estimated coefficients. If these errors are small relative to the size of the coefficients, we can have more faith in the qualitative predictions yielded by our estimates. For instance, if the estimated $\hat{b}$ is large and positive, while at the same time the standard error of $\hat{b}$ is small, it is very likely that the true value of $\hat{b}$ is also positive. With some more assumptions we can go further, as the next section shows.

The t distribution. There is a very special distribution called the t distribution. It looks a bit like a normal distribution (though it is flatter). It has mean 0, and its variance is determined by a parameter called its *degrees of freedom*. The t distribution is well known in statistical software programs and in older statistics texts that actually tabulate its properties. For instance, with 20 degrees of freedom, it is well known that the probability that a random variable t will exceed the value 2.086 is precisely 0.025, that it will exceed 1.725 is 0.05, and that its *absolute* value will exceed 1.725 is therefore 0.10. The t distribution plays a beautiful and critical role in the testing of hypotheses.

To see how this works, we need one assumption and one theorem.

Assumption. The errors ϵ_i of our regression model follow the well-known normal distribution.

There are theoretical arguments that justify this assumption, but it is an assumption all the same.

Theorem. If the errors are normally distributed, then the random variable

$$\frac{\hat{b} - b}{\text{SE}(\hat{b})}$$

must follow a t distribution with $n - 2$ degrees of freedom, where n is the sample size.

Hypothesis testing. The preceding theorem allows us to test various hypotheses, such as whether a regression coefficient is "significantly" positive, "significantly" negative, or just plain "significantly" different from 0.

For instance, we may be investigating whether school dropout rates have anything to do with crime rates in cities. Assume we already have regressed crime rates on dropout rates and have obtained an estimate of b. We want to know whether $\hat{b}$ is "significantly" different from 0. Alternatively, we can regress consumption on income and try to determine whether a one peso increase in income will lead to a one peso increase in consumption: the value of b we then have in mind is 1. We must form a *hypothesis* and then test it. To *test* a hypothesis means to make a decision to either *reject* or *fail to reject* the hypothesis that the population parameter b equals a particular value.

Now we are in a probabilistic world and anything can happen. We might reject the hypothesis when it is in fact true or we might fail to reject it when it is false. As researchers, we wish to limit these possibilities to a minimum, and this will determine the "power" of the test.

It is customary to limit false rejections: we want to be conservative in that we do not want to reject a hypothesis when it is actually true. Thus when we do reject the hypothesis, we want to be very confident that the hypothesis is indeed false.

The flip side of this approach is that a *failure* to reject does not mean too much: in particular, it does *not* mean that we have "accepted" the hypothesis. Indeed, it is often possible that both a hypothesis and its converse may stand (statistically) unrejected.

The proportion of samples in which false rejection occurs is called the *level of significance* of the test, usually denoted α. It is common practice to work with a 5% probability, that is, the null hypothesis is rejected if, under its assumption, there is less than a 5% probability that we have rejected the hypothesis when it was indeed true. Such a test is then called a test with "5% level of significance." Tests with 1 and 10% levels of significance are also not uncommon.

Now we will see how the t distribution plays a role in all this. For example, you are investigating whether school dropout rates have anything to do with crime rates in cities. Say you have thirty pairs of observations. You have used OLS to estimate b. If the errors are normal, you know from the foregoing theorem that the variable

$$\frac{\hat{b} - b}{\mathrm{SE}(\hat{b})}$$

has a t distribution with $n - 2$ degrees of freedom. Because your sample size is thirty, you have 28 degrees of freedom.

First, form the *null hypothesis*. Let us say that we choose as the null hypothesis $b = 0$: dropout rates have no influence on crime rates.

Second, form the *alternative hypothesis*. This is the hypothesis that dropout rates have a positive effect on crime rates. We also could have chosen as our alternative the weaker alternative that they have *some* effect, positive or negative.

Third, choose your level of significance. Say you are willing to take a one-in-twenty chance that you reject the null when in fact it is true; that is, $\alpha = 0.05$.

Fourth, look up the value t^* of the t distribution such that the probability that t exceeds t^* is no greater than 0.05. For 28 degrees of freedom, this is the value 1.701. The area to the right of this is called the *critical region* for the test. Generally speaking, it is the region in which the null hypothesis will be rejected in favor of the alternative.[7]

Finally, calculate what is called the *test statistic*: the value of the ratio $\hat{b}/(\mathrm{SE}(\hat{b}))$. (The numerator is $\hat{b}$ because we are working under the null hypothesis that $b = 0$.) Suppose that this statistic is 2. Because the theorem tells us that this test statistic follows a t distribution with 28 degrees of freedom, *we see that the chances that this statistic could have acquired the high value of 2 when the hypothesized value of b is 0 is lower than* 0.05. We would then *reject* the null hypothesis that school dropout rates have no influence on crime rates in the city.

Here is a quick summary of the general method.

(1) Specify your null hypothesis, alternative hypothesis, and the significance level α.

(2) Find the critical region using the t distribution with the appropriate degrees of freedom.

(3) Using the sample data, compute the value of the test statistic.

---

[7] The critical region depends on what our alternative hypothesis is. In our case we use the alternative that dropout rates have a *positive* effect on crime, so the critical region will be to the right of the threshold 1.701 (this will become clearer in the final step of the exercise).

(4) Check whether or not the calculated test statistic falls in the critical region.

(5) Reject the null hypothesis if the test statistic falls in the critical region. Do not reject the null if the test statistic does not fall in the critical region.

Confidence intervals. Another way to check significance is to offer the reader a *confidence interval* for your estimate; that is, provide an interval of values around your estimate with the following interpretation: the *true* value of b will lie in this constructed interval for more than a predetermined percentage of samples. This predetermined percentage (chosen by the researcher) is analogous to the level of significance in hypothesis testing and is known as the *confidence level*. Indeed, the confidence level is often denoted by $1 - \alpha$, where α is the associated level of significance. Thus confidence levels (expressed as percentages) are usually taken to be 90, 95, or 99%.

Note well that our estimator $\hat{b}$ is a random variable, so the confidence interval is random as well: it will vary from sample to sample. In contrast, the true value of b is some fixed (but unknown) number. The probabilistic statement in the previous paragraph thus refers to the chances that this randomly varying interval will contain the true value within it, and *not* to the chances of some randomly varying parameter lying within some fixed interval.

More formally, a confidence interval for a parameter b, given the estimator $\hat{b}$, is a range $I = [\hat{b} - \hat{\beta}, \hat{b} + \hat{\beta}]$ computed from the sample data so that I contains the true value b in a high enough percentage of samples (where "high enough" is given by the prechosen confidence level). In other words, choose $\hat{\beta}$ so that

(A2.25)
$$\text{probability } (|\hat{b} - b| < \hat{\beta}) = 1 - \alpha,$$

where $|\cdot|$ denotes absolute value and $1 - \alpha$ denotes the confidence level.

To find $\hat{\beta}$ we need to have an idea of how the random variable $\hat{b} - b$ is distributed. This is where the t distribution makes a reappearance. Simply divide both sides of the inequality in (A2.25) by the standard error of $\hat{b}$. Then the left-hand side is a random variable t that has a t distribution with $n - 2$ degrees of freedom. Thus (A2.25) is equivalent to the requirement

(A2.26)
$$\text{probability } \left(|t| < \frac{\hat{\beta}}{\text{SE}(\hat{b})} \right) = 1 - \alpha.$$

Using tables of the t distribution, we can find the critical value $t^*(\alpha, n-2)$ that makes this inequality true. In other words, set

$$\hat{\beta} = t^*_{\alpha, n-2} \times \text{SE}(\hat{b}),$$

where $P(|t| < t^*_{\alpha,\,n-2}) \equiv 1-\alpha$. This leads to the much more familiar expression for a confidence interval for the parameter b:

$$I = \left[\hat{b} - t^*_{\alpha,\,n-2} \times \mathrm{SE}(\hat{b}),\ \hat{b} + t^*_{\alpha,\,n-2} \times \mathrm{SE}(\hat{b})\right].$$

In summary, we construct a confidence interval for the parameter b in our linear regression model by using the following four steps:

(1) Choose your confidence level $1 - \alpha$: 90, 95, or even 99%.

(2) Look up the value $t^*_{\alpha,\,n-2}$ using tables of the t distribution or let your computer do it for you. For example, if your sample size is 120, the values $t^*_{\alpha,\,118}$ are 1.289, 1.654, and 2.358 for the 90, 95, and 99% confidence levels, respectively.

(3) Compute the estimate $\hat{\beta}$ and its estimated standard error $\mathrm{SE}(\hat{b})$.

(4) Calculate $\hat{\beta} = t^*_{\alpha,\,n-2} \times \mathrm{SE}(\hat{b})$ and finally $\hat{b} \pm \hat{\beta}$.

References

References

Acharya, S. et al. (1985). "Aspects of the Black Economy in India." National Institute of Public Finance and Policy, New Delhi.

Adelman, I., and C. T. Morris (1973). *Economic Growth and Social Equity in Developing Countries*. Stanford, CA: Stanford University Press.

Adelman, I., and S. Robinson (1989). "Income Distribution and Development," in H. Chenery and T. N. Srinivasan (eds.), *Handbook of Development Economics*, Vol. 1. Amsterdam: Elsevier Science, North Holland.

Adserà, A., and D. Ray (1997). "History and Coordination Failure." Mimeograph, Universidad Autónoma de Barcelona.

Agabin, M. et al. (1988). "A Review of Policies Impinging on the Informal Credit Markets in the Philippines." Working Paper 88-12, Philippine Institute for Development Studies, Makati, Philippines.

Agabin, M. et al. (1989). "Integrative Report on the Informal Credit Market in the Philippines." Working Paper 89-10, Philippine Institute for Development Studies, Makati, Philippines.

Aggarwal, V. (1989). "Interpreting the History of Mexico's External Debt Crisis," in B. Eichengreen and P. H. Lindert (eds.), *The International Debt Crisis in Historical Perspective*. Cambridge, MA: MIT Press.

Aguilar, L. (1993). "NAFTA: A Review of the Issues," *Economic Perspectives* (Federal Reserve Bank of Chicago) **17**, 12–20.

Ahluwalia, M. (1974). "Dimensions of the Problem," in H. B. Chenery et al. (eds.), *Redistribution with Growth*. London: Oxford University Press.

Ahluwalia, M. (1976). "Inequality, Poverty and Development," *Journal of Development Economics* **6**, 307–342.

Ahluwalia, M., N. G. Carter, and H. Chenery (1979). "Growth and Poverty in Developing Countries," *Journal of Development Economics* **6**, 299–341.

Ahmad, A., and J. Morduch (1993). "Identifying Sex Bias in the Allocation of Household Resources: Evidence from Linked Households Surveys from Bangladesh." Harvard Institute of Economic Research Discussion Paper.

Alchian, A. (1963). "Reliability of Progress Curves in Airframe Production," *Econometrica* **31**, 679–693.

Alderman, H. (1987). "Cooperative Dairy Development in Karnataka, India: An Assessment." Research Report 64, IFPRI, Washington, DC.

Alderman, H. (1989). "The Impact of Changes in Income and Schooling on the Demand for Food Quantity and Quality in Rural Pakistan." Mimeograph, IFPRI, Washington DC.

Alderman, H., and P. Higgins (1992). "Food and Nutritional Adequacy in Ghana." Mimeograph, Cornell Food and Nutrition Policy Program.

Aleem, I. (1993). "Imperfect Information, Screening, and the Costs of Informal Lending: A Study of a Rural Credit Market in Pakistan," K. Hoff, A. Braverman and J. Stiglitz (eds.), *The Economics of Rural Organization: Theory, Practice and Policy*, chap. 7. London: Oxford University Press (for the World Bank).

Alesina, A., and D. Rodrik (1994). "Distributive Politics and Economic Growth," *Quarterly Journal of Economics* **108**, 465–490.

Amano, M. (1980). "A Neoclassical Model of the Dual Economy with Capital Accumulation in Agriculture," *Review of Economic Studies* **47**, 933–944.

Amsden, A. H. (1989). *Asia's Next Giant: South Korea and Late Industrialization*. New York: Oxford University Press.

Anand, S. (1977). "Aspects of Poverty in Malaysia," *Review of Income and Wealth* **23**, 1–16.

Anand, S., and C. Harris (1994). "Choosing a Welfare Indicator," *American Economic Review* **84**, 226–231.

Anand, S., and R. Kanbur (1993a). "The Kuznets Process and the Inequality–Development Relationship," *Journal of Development Economics* **40**, 25–52.

Anand, S., and R. Kanbur (1993b). "Inequality and Development: A Critique," *Journal of Development Economics* **41**, 19–43.

Anand, S., and J. Morduch (1996). "Poverty and the 'Population Problem'." Mimeograph, Oxford University and Harvard University.

Arrow, K. J. (1962). "The Economic Implications of Learning by Doing," *Review of Economic Studies* **80**, 155–173.

Arrow, K. J. (1971). "Exposition of the Theory of Choice under Uncertainty," in C. B. McGuire and R. Radner (eds.), *Decision and Organization*. Amsterdam: North-Holland.

Attwood, D. W., and B. S. Baviskar, eds. (1988). *Who Shares? Co-operatives and Rural Development*. London: Oxford University Press.

Aturupane, H., P. Glewwe, and P. Isenman (1994). "Poverty, Human Development, and Growth: An Emerging Consensus?," *American Economic Review* **84**, 244–249.

Bacha, E. L. (1979). "Notes on the Brazilian Experience with Minidevaluations, 1968–1976," *Journal of Development Economics* **6**, 463–481.

Baland, J.-M., and P. Francois (1996). "Innovation, Monopolies and the Poverty Trap," *Journal of Development Economics* **49**, 151–178.

Baland, J.-M., and D. Ray (1991). "Why Does Asset Inequality Affect Unemployment? A Study of the Demand Composition Problem," *Journal of Development Economics* **35**, 69–92.

Baldwin, R., and A. Venables (1995). "Regional Economic Integration," in G. M. Grossman and K. Rogoff (eds.), *Handbook of International Economics*, Vol. 3, Amsterdam: Elsevier Science, North Holland.

Banerjee, A. V., and M. Ghatak (1996). "Operation Barga: A Study in the Economics of Tenancy Reform." Mimeograph, Department of Economics, University of Chicago.

Banerjee, A. V., and A. Newman (1993). "Occupational Choice and the Process of Development," *Journal of Political Economy* **101**, 274–298.

Banerjee, A. V., and A. Newman (1994). "Poverty, Incentives, and Development," *American Economic Review* **84**, 211–215.

Banerjee, A. V., and A. Newman (1997). "A Dual-Economy Model of Migration and Development." Mimeograph, Department of Economics, Massachusetts Institute of Technology, forthcoming, *Review of Economic Studies*.

Banerjee, A. V., T. J. Besley, and T. Guinanne (1992). "Thy Neighbor's Keeper: The Design of a Credit Cooperative with Theory and a Test," *Quarterly Journal of Economics* **84**, 491–515.

Bardhan, P. K. (1983). "Labor Tying in a Poor Agrarian Economy," *Quarterly Journal of Economics* **98**, 501–514.

Bardhan, P. K. (1984). *Land, Labor and Rural Poverty: Essays in Development Economics*. London/New York: Oxford University Press/Columbia University Press.

Bardhan, P. K., and A. Rudra (1978). "Interlinkage of Land, Labour and Credit Relations: An Analysis of Village Survey Data in East India," *Economic and Political Weekly* **13**, Annual Number, February.

Barro, R. (1991). "Economic Growth in a Cross-Section of Countries," *Quarterly Journal of Economics* **106**, 407–444.

Barro, R. (1996). "Democracy and Growth," *Journal of Economic Growth* **1**, 1–27.

Barro, R. J., and X. Sala-i-Martin (1995). *Economic Growth*. New York: McGraw-Hill.

Basu, K. (1980). "Optimal Policies in Dual Economies," *Quarterly Journal of Economics* **95**, 187–196.

Basu, K. (1987). "Disneyland Monopoly, Interlinkage and Usurious Interest Rates," *Journal of Public Economics* **34**, 1–17.

Basu, K. (1992). "Limited Liability and the Existence of Share Tenancy," *Journal of Development Economics* **38**, 203–220.

Basu, K., and J. E. Foster (1997). "On Measuring Literacy." Mimeograph, Department of Economics, Cornell University.

Baumol, W. J. (1986). "Productivity Growth, Convergence, and Welfare: What the Long-run Data Show," *American Economic Review* **76**, 1072–1085.

Becker, G. S. (1960). "An Economic Analysis of Fertility," in A. J. Coale (ed.), *Demographic and Economic Change in Developed Countries*. Princeton, NJ: Princeton University Press.

Becker, G. S. (1981). *A Treatise on the Family*. Cambridge, MA: Harvard University Press.

Behrman, J. R. (1993). "Household Behavior and Micronutrients: What We Know and What We Don't Know." Mimeograph, Department of Economics, University of Pennsylvania.

Behrman, J. R., and A. Deolalikar (1987). "Will Developing Country Nutrition Improve with Income? A Case Study for Rural South India," *Journal of Political Economy* **95**, 108–138.

Behrman, J. R., and A. Deolalikar (1989). "Seasonal Demands for Nutrient Intakes and Health Status in Rural South India," in D. E. Sahn (ed.), *Causes and Implications of Seasonal Variability in Household Food Security*. Baltimore, MD: John Hopkins Press.

Behrman, J. R., and B. L. Wolfe (1984). "A More General Approach to Fertility Determination in a Developing Country: The Importance of Biological Supply Considerations, Endogenous Tastes and Unperceived Jointness," *Economica* **51**, 319–39.

Behrman, J. R., A. Foster, and M. R. Rosenzweig (1994). "Stages of Agricultural Production and the Calorie-Income Relationship." Mimeograph, Department of Economics, University of Pennsylvania, Philadelphia.

Bell, C. (1977). "Alternative Theories of Sharecropping: Some Tests Using Evidence from Northeast India," *Journal of Development Studies* **13**, 317–346.

Bell, C. (1993). "Interactions between Institutional and Informal Credit Agencies in Rural India," in K. Hoff, A. Braverman, and J. Stiglitz (eds.), *The Economics of Rural Organization: Theory, Practice and Policy*. London: Oxford University Press.

Berman, E., J. Bound, and Z. Griliches (1994). "Changes in the Demand for Skilled Labor within U. S. Manufacturing: Evidence from the Annual Survey of Manufactures," *Quarterly Journal of Economics* **109**, 367–397.

Bernheim, B. D. (1994). "A Theory of Conformity," *Journal of Political Economy* **102**, 841–877.

Berry, R. A., and W. R. Cline (1979). *Agrarian Structure and Productivity in Developing Countries.* Geneva: International Labour Organization.

Bertola, G. (1993). "Factor Shares and Savings in Endogenous Growth," *American Economic Review* **83**, 1184–1198.

Besley, T. J. (1995). "Savings, Credit and Insurance," in J. Behrman and T. N. Srinivasan (eds.). *Handbook of Development Economics*, Vol. 3A, Handbooks in Economics, vol. 9. Amsterdam: Elsevier Science, North Holland.

Besley, T. J., and S. Coate (1995). "Group Lending, Repayment Incentives, and Social Collateral," *Journal of Development Economics* **46**, 1–18.

Besley, T. J., S. Coate, and G. C. Loury (1993). "The Economics of Rotating Savings and Credit Associations," *American Economic Review* **83**, 792–810.

Beteille, A. (1979). "The Indian Village: Past and Present," in E. J. Hobsbawm, W. Kula, A. Mitra, K. N. Raj and I. Sachs (eds.), *Peasants in History: Essays in Honour of Daniel Thorner.* London: Oxford University Press (for Sameeskha Trust, Delhi).

Bhaduri, A. (1977). "On the Formation of Usurious Interest Rates in Backward Agriculture," *Cambridge Journal of Economics* **1**, 341–352.

Bhagwati, J. N. (1980). "Lobbying and Welfare," *Journal of Public Economics* **14**, 355–363.

Bhagwati, J. N. (1982). "Directly-Unproductive, Profit-Seeking Activities," *Journal of Political Economy* **90**, 988-1002.

Bhagwati, J. N. (1990). *Protectionism.* Cambridge, MA: MIT Press.

Bhagwati, J. N. (1993). "Regionalism and Multilateralism: An Overview," in J. de Melo and A. Panagariya (eds.), *New Dimensions in Regional Integration.* Cambridge, UK: Cambridge University Press.

Bhagwati, J. N., and T. N. Srinivasan (1974). "On Reanalyzing the Harris-Todaro Model: Policy Rankings in the Case of Sector-Specific Sticky Wages," *American Economic Review* **64**, 502–508.

Bhargava, A. (1991). "Estimating Short and Long Run Income Elasticities of Foods and Nutrients for Rural South India," *Journal of the Royal Statistical Society Series A* **154**, 157–174.

Billon, S. (1966). "Industrial Learning Curves and Forecasting Production Requirements," *Management International Review* **6**, 65–96.

Binmore, K. (1992). *Fun and Games.* Lexington, MA: D. C. Heath.

Binswanger, H., K. Deininger, and G. Feder (1995). "Power, Distortions, Revolt and Reform in Agricultural Land Relations." in J. Behrman and T. N. Srinivasan (eds.). *Handbook of Development Economics*, Vol. 3B, Handbooks in Economics, vol. 9. Amsterdam: Elsevier Science, North Holland.

Bliss, C., and N. Stern (1978a). "Productivity, Wages and Nutrition, Part I: The Theory," *Journal of Development Economics* **5**, 331–362.

Bliss, C., and N. Stern (1978b). "Productivity, Wages and Nutrition, Part II: Some Observations," *Journal of Development Economics* **5**, 363–398.

Bliss, C., and N. Stern (1982). *Palanpur: The Economy of an Indian Village.* London: Oxford University Press.

Bloch, F. (1995). "Endogenous Structures of Association in Oligopolies," *Rand Journal of Economics* **26**, 537–556.

Bloch, F. (1996). "Sequential Formation of Coalitions in Games with Externalities and Fixed Payoff Division," *Games and Economic Behavior* **14**, 90–123.

Boone, P. (1996). "Political and Gender Oppression as a Cause of Poverty." Mimeograph, Department of Economics, London School of Economics.

Booth, C. (1903). *Life and Labour of the People in London*. Revised edition published 1969, New York: A. M. Kelley.

Bose, G. (1997). "Nutritional Efficiency Wages: Equilibrium, Comparative Statics, and Policy Implications." Mimeograph, Department of Economics, American University in Cairo, forthcoming, *Journal of Development Economics*.

Bose, P. (1997). "Formal–Informal Sector Interaction in Rural Credit Markets." Mimeograph, Department of Economics, University of Memphis.

Boserup, E. (1981). *Population and Technological Change: A Study of Long-Run Trends*. Chicago: University of Chicago Press.

Bottomley, A. (1975). "Interest Rate Determination in Underdeveloped Rural Areas," *American Journal of Agricultural Economics* **57**, 279–291.

Bouis, H. E., and L. J. Haddad (1992). "Are Estimates of Calorie–Income Elasticities Too High? A Recalibration of the Plausible Range," *Journal of Development Economics* **39**, 333–364.

Bourguignon, F., and C. Morrisson (1989). *External Trade and Income Distribution*. Paris: Development Centre Studies, OECD.

Bourguignon, F., and C. Morrisson (1990). "Income Distribution, Development and Foreign Trade: A Cross-Sectional Analysis," *European Economic Review* **34**, 1113–1132.

Bowles, S., and H. Gintis (1994). "Credit Market Imperfections and the Incidence of Worker Owned Firms," *Metroeconomica* **45**, 209–223.

Bowles, S., and H. Gintis (1996). "Asset Based Redistribution: Improving the Trade-Off between Allocative Gains and Dynamic Inefficiency Losses," MacArthur Economics Initiative Working Paper, University of California, Berkeley.

Brander, J. A. (1981). "Intra-Industry Trade in Identical Commodities," *Journal of International Economics* **11**, 1–14.

Brander, J. A., and P. Krugman (1981). "A 'Reciprocal Dumping' Model of International Trade," *Journal of International Economics* **15**, 313–321.

Braverman, A., and T. N. Srinivasan (1981). "Credit and Sharecropping in Agrarian Societies," *Journal of Development Economics* **9**, 289–312.

Braverman, A., and J. Stiglitz (1982). "Sharecropping and the Interlinking of Agrarian Markets," *American Economic Review* **72**, 695–715.

Breman, J. (1974). *Patronage and Exploitation*. Delhi: Manohar Publishers.

Bruton, H. (1992). "Import Substitution," in H. Chenery and T. N. Srinivasan (eds.), *Handbook of Development Economics*, Vol. 2, Amsterdam: Elsevier Science, North Holland.

Bulow, J., and K. Rogoff (1989). "Sovereign Debt: Is to Forgive to Forget?" *American Economic Review* **79**, 43–50.

Burenstam Linder, S. (1961). *An Essay on Trade and Transformation*. New York: Wiley.

Cain, M. (1981). "Risk and Insurance: Perspectives on Fertility and Agrarian Change in India and Bangladesh," *Population and Development Review* **7**, 435–474.

Cain, M. (1983). "Fertility as an Adjustment to Risk," *Population and Development Review* **9**, 688–702.

Carr, E. H. (1951). *The New Society*. Boston: Beacon.

Carr-Saunders, A. M. (1936). *World Population: Past Growth and Present Trends*. Oxford: Clarendon Press.

Caselli, F. (1997). "Rural Labor and Credit Markets." Mimeograph, Department of Economics, Harvard University, forthcoming, *Journal of Development Economics*.

Caves, R. E., J. A. Frankel, and R. W. Jones (1990). *World Trade and Payments: An Introduction*, 5th ed. Glenview, Ill. and London: Scott, Foresman/Little, Brown Higher Education,

Chamley, C., and D. Gale (1994). "Information Revelation and Strategic Delay in a Model of Investment," *Econometrica* **62**, 1065–1085.

Chayanov, A. V. (1991). *The Theory of Peasant Cooperatives*. Athens, OH: Ohio State University Press.

Chen, M. (1991). *Coping with Seasonality and Drought*. New Delhi: Sage Publications.

Chen, M., and J. P. Drèze (1992). "Widows and Well-Being in Rural North India," Working Paper 40, Development Research Programme, London School of Economics.

Chenery, H. B., and N. G. Carter (1973). "Foreign Assistance and Development Performance, 1960–1970," *American Economic Review* **63**, 459–468.

Chenery, H. B., and M. Syrquin (1975). *Patterns of Development, 1950–1970*. London: Oxford University Press.

Chernichovsky, D., and O. Meesook (1984). "Patterns of Food Consumption and Nutrition in Indonesia," Working Paper 670, World Bank, Washington, DC.

Cheung, S. (1969). *The Theory of Share Tenancy*. Chicago: University of Chicago Press.

Chopra, O. P. (1982). "Unaccounted Income: Some Estimates, " *Economic and Political Weekly*, April 24.

Christen, R. P., E. Rhyne, and R. Vogel (1994). "Maximizing the Outreach of Microenterprise Finance: The Emerging Lessons of Successful Programs," International Management and Communications Corporation Paper, Washington, D. C.

Churchill, C. F. (1995). "The Impact of Credit on Informal Sector Enterprises in South Africa: A Study of Get Ahead Foundation's Stokvel Lending Programme." M. A. Dissertation, Clark University.

Ciccone, A., and K. Matsuyama (1996). "Start-up Costs and Pecuniary Externalities as Barriers to Economic Development," *Journal of Development Economics* **49**, 33–59.

Clark, C., and M. Haswell (1970). *The Economics of Subsistence Agriculture*. New York: St. Martin's Press.

Coale, A. J. (1991). "Excess Female Mortality and the Balance of the Sexes in the Population: An Estimate of the Number of 'Missing Females'," *Population and Development Review* **17**, 517–523.

Coale, A. J., and J. Banister (1994). "Five Decades of Missing Females in China," *Demography* **31**, 459–479.

Coale, A. J., and E. M. Hoover (1958). *Population Growth and Economic Development in Low-Income Countries: A Case Study of India's Prospects*. Princeton, NJ: Princeton University Press.

Coate, S., and M. Ravallion (1993). "Reciprocity Without Commitment: Characterization and Performance of Informal Insurance Arrangements," *Journal of Development Economics* **40**, 1–24.

Copeland, B., and A. Kotwal (1995). "Product Quality and the Theory of Comparative Advantage," *European Economic Review* **40**, 1745–1760.

Corbo, V., S. Fischer, and S. Webb (1992). *Adjustment Lending Revisited: Policies to Restore Growth*. Washington, DC: The World Bank.

Crawford, J., and E. Strauss (1947). *Crawford–Strauss Study*. Dayton, OH: Air Material Command.

Czukas, K., M. Fafchamps, and C. Udry (1997). "Drought and Saving in West Africa: Are Livestock a Buffer Stock?" Mimeograph, Department of Economics, Stanford University, forthcoming, *Journal of Development Economics*.

Dalton, H. (1920). "The Measurement of the Inequality of Incomes," *Economic Journal* **30**, 348–361.

Dam, K. W. (1970). *The GATT: Law and International Economic Organization*. Chicago: University of Chicago Press.

Das Gupta, M. (1987). "Informal Security Mechanisms and Population Retention in Rural India," *Economic Development and Cultural Change* **36**, 101–120.

Das Gupta, M. (1994). "What Motivates Fertility Decline?: A Case Study from Punjab, India," in B. Egero and M. Hammarskjold (eds.), *Understanding Reproductive Change*. Lund, Sweden: Lund University Press.

Dasgupta, P. (1993). *An Inquiry into Well-Being and Destitution*. Oxford: Clarendon Press.

Dasgupta, P., and D. Ray (1986). "Inequality as a Determinant of Malnutrition and Unemployment: Theory," *Economic Journal* **96**, 1011–1034.

Dasgupta, P., and D. Ray (1987). "Inequality as a Determinant of Malnutrition and Unemployment: Policy," *Economic Journal* **97**, 177–188.

Dasgupta, P., and D. Ray (1990). "Adapting to Undernourishment: The Biological Evidence and its Implications," in J. P. Drèze and A. K. Sen (eds.), *The Political Economy of Hunger*, Vol. 1. Oxford: Clarendon Press.

David, P. A. (1985). "Clio and the Economics of QWERTY," *American Economic Review* **75**, 332–337.

Deaton, A. (1989). "Looking for Boy–Girl Discrimination in Household Expenditure Data," *World Bank Economic Review* **3**, 183–210.

Deaton, A. (1990). "On Risk, Insurance, and Intra-Village Smoothing." Mimeograph, Department of Economics, Princeton University.

Deaton, A. (1997). *The Analysis of Household Surveys: A Microeconometric Approach to Development Policy*. Baltimore, MD: Johns Hopkins Press (for the World Bank).

Deininger, K., and L. Squire (1996a). "A New Data Set Measuring Income Inequality," *World Bank Economic Review* **10**, 565–591.

Deininger, K., and L. Squire (1996b). "New Ways of Looking at Old Issues: Inequality and Growth." Mimeograph, The World Bank.

de Janvry, A. (1981). *The Agrarian Question and Reformism in Latin America*. Baltimore, MD: Johns Hopkins Press.

de Janvry, A., and E. Sadoulet (1983). "Social Articulation as a Condition for Equitable Growth," *Journal of Development Economics* **13**, 275–303.

De Long, B. (1988). "Productivity Growth, Convergence and Welfare: Comment," *American Economic Review* **78**, 1138–1154.

de Melo, J., and A. Panagariya (1993a). "Introduction," in J. de Melo and A. Panagariya (eds.), *New Dimensions in Regional Integration*. Cambridge, UK: Cambridge University Press.

de Melo, J., and A. Panagariya, eds. (1993b). *New Dimensions in Regional Integration*. Cambridge, UK: Cambridge University Press,

Desai, M. (1991). "Human Development: Concepts and Measurement," *European Economic Review* **35**, 350–357.

Diamond, P. A., and J. A. Mirrlees (1971). "Optimal Taxation and Public Production: I. Production Efficiency," *American Economic Review* **61**, 8–27.

Dixit, A. (1970). "Growth Patterns in a Dual Economy," *Oxford Economic Papers* **22**, 229–234.

Dixit, A. K., and J. E. Stiglitz (1977). "Monopolistic Competition and Optimum Product Diversity," *American Economic Review* **67**, 297–308.

Dobb, M. (1966). *Soviet Economic Development Since 1917.* 6th ed. London: Routledge and Kegan Paul Ltd.

Drèze, J. P. (1990). "Widows in Rural India," Working Paper no. 26, Development Research Programme, London School of Economics.

Drèze, J. P., and A. Mukherjee (1991). "Labour Contracts in Rural India: Theory and Evidence," in S. Chakravarty (ed.), *The Balance between Industry and Agriculture in Economic Development; 3. Manpower and Transfers.* New York: Macmillan (in association with the International Economic Association).

Dutta, B., D. Ray, and K. Sengupta (1989). "Contracts with Eviction in Infinitely Repeated Principal Agent Relationships," in P. Bardhan (ed.), *The Economic Theory of Agrarian Institutions.* Oxford: Clarendon Press.

Easterly, W. (1997). "Life During Growth." Mimeograph, World Bank.

Eaton, J., and R. Fernandez (1995). "Sovereign Debt," in G. M. Grossman and K. Rogoff (eds.), *Handbook of International Economics,* Vol. 3, Amsterdam: Elsevier Science, North Holland.

Eaton, J., and M. Gersovitz (1981). "Debt with Potential Repudiation: Theoretical and Empirical Analysis," *Review of Economic Studies* **48**, 289–309.

Eaton, J., and S. Kortum (1997). "International Technology Diffusion: Theory and Facts." Mimeograph, Department of Economics, Boston University.

The Economist (1988). "Europe's Internal Market." July 9.

Edirisinghe, N. (1987). "The Food Stamp Scheme in Sri Lanka: Costs, Benefits and Options for Modification," IFPRI, Washington, DC.

Edwards, S. (1989). "Structural Adjustment Policies in Highly Indebted Countries," in J. D. Sachs (ed.), *Developing Country Debt and Economic Performance.* Chicago, IL: University of Chicago Press.

Eichengreen, B., and P. H. Lindert, eds. (1989). *The International Debt Crisis in Historical Perspective.* Cambridge, MA: MIT Press.

Esguerra, E. (1987). "Can the Informal Lenders be Co-Opted into Government Credit Programs?" Working Paper Series no. 87-03, Philippine Institute for Development Studies, Makati, Philippines.

Esteban, J., and D. Ray (1994). "On the Measurement of Polarization," *Econometrica* **62**, 819–853.

Eswaran, M., and A. Kotwal (1985a). "A Theory of Two-Tiered Labour Markets in Agrarian Economies," *American Economic Review* **75**, 162–177.

Eswaran, M., and A. Kotwal (1985b). "A Theory of Contractual Structure in Agriculture," *American Economic Review* **75**, 352–367.

Ethier, W. (1982). "National and International Returns to Scale in the Modern Theory of International Trade," *American Economic Review* **72**, 389–405.

Fafchamps, M. (1994). "Risk Sharing, Quasi-Credit, and the Enforcement of Informal Contracts." Mimeograph, Department of Economics, Stanford University.

Feder, G., T. Onchan, Y. Chamlamwong, and C. Hongladoran (1988). *Land Policies and Farm Productivity in Thailand.* Baltimore, MD: Johns Hopkins University Press.

Feenstra, R. C., and J. Bhagwati (1982). "Tariff Seeking and the Efficient Tariff," in J. N. Bhagwati (ed.), *Import Competition and Response.* Chicago, IL: University of Chicago Press.

Feenstra, R. C., and T. R. Lewis (1991). "Distributing the Gains from Trade with Incomplete Information," *Economics and Politics* **3**, 21–39.

Feldstein, M., and C. Horioka (1980). "Domestic Saving and International Capital Flows," *Economic Journal* **90**, 314–329.

Fernandez, R., and D. Rodrik (1991). "Resistance to Reform: Status Quo Bias in the Presence of Individual-Specific Uncertainty," *American Economic Review* **81**, 1146–1155.

Fields, G. S. (1980). *Poverty, Inequality and Development.* London: Cambridge University Press.

Fields, G. S. (1989). "A Compendium of Data on Inequality and Poverty for the Developing World." Mimeograph, School of Industrial and Labor Relations, Cornell University.

Fields, G. S. (1994). "The Kuznets Curve: A Good Idea But...." Mimeograph, School of Industrial and Labor Relations, Cornell University.

Fields, G. S., and J. C. H. Fei (1978). "On Inequality Comparisons," *Econometrica* **46**, 303–16.

Fields, G. S., and G. H. Jakubson (1994). "New Evidence on the Kuznets Curve." Mimeograph, Department of Economics, Cornell University.

Findlay, R., and S. Wellisz (1984). "Protection and Rent-Seeking in Developing Countries," in D. C. Colander (ed.), *Neoclassical Political Economy: The Analysis of Rent-Seeking and DUP Activities.* New York: Harper and Row.

Fishlow, A. (1972). "Brazilian Size Distribution of Income, " *American Economic Review* **62**, 391–402.

Flam, H. (1992). "Product Markets and 1992: Full Integration, Large Gains?," *Journal of Economic Perspectives* **6**, 7–30.

Floro, M. S., and D. Ray (1997). "Vertical Links between Formal and Informal Financial Institutions," *Review of Development Economics* **1**, 34–56.

Floro, M. S., and P. Yotopoulos (1991). *Informal Credit Markets and the New Institutional Economics: The Case of Philippine Agriculture.* Boulder, CO: Westview Press.

Fogel, R., and S. Engerman (1974). *Time on the Cross: The Economics of American Negro Slavery.* Boston, MA: Little, Brown and Co.

Foroutan, F. (1993). "Regional Integration in Sub-Saharan Africa: Past Experience and Future Prospects," in J. de Melo and A. Panagariya (eds.), *New Dimensions in Regional Integration.* Cambridge, UK: Cambridge University Press.

Foster, J. E. (1983). "An Axiomatic Characterization of the Theil Measure of Income Inequality," *Journal of Economic Theory* **31**, 105–121.

Foster, J. E. (1984). "On Economic Poverty: A Survey of Aggregate Measures," in R. L. Basmann and G. F. Rhodes, Jr. (eds.) *Advances in Econometrics* **3**, 215–251.

Foster, J. E. (1985). "Inequality Measurement," in H. P. Young (ed.) *Proceedings of Symposia in Applied Mathematics* **33**, 31–68.

Foster, J. E., J. Greer, and E. Thorbecke (1984). "A Class of Decomposable Poverty Measures," *Econometrica* **52**, 761–766.

Friedman, M. (1957). *A Theory of the Consumption Function.* Princeton, NJ: Princeton University Press.

Galor, O., and D. Weil (1996). "The Gender Gap, Fertility, and Growth," *American Economic Review* **86**, 374–387.

Galor, O., and J. Zeira (1993). "Income Distribution and Macroeconomics," *Review of Economic Studies* **60**, 35–52.

Gangopadhyay, S., and K. Sengupta (1987). "Small Farmers, Moneylending, and Trading Activity," *Oxford Economic Papers* **39**, 333–342.

Garcia, M., and P. Pinstrup-Andersen (1987). "The Pilot Food Price Subsidy Scheme in the Philippines: Impact on Income, Food Consumption, and Nutritional Status." IFPRI, Washington, DC.

Garg, A., and J. Morduch (1997). "Sibling Rivalry." Mimeograph, Department of Economics, Harvard University.

Georgescu-Roegen, N. (1960). "Economic Theory and Agrarian Economics," *Oxford Economic Papers* **12**, 1–40.

Geron, P. (1989). "Microeconomic Behavior of Agents in a Credit-Oriented Market in an Agricultural Setting." Ph.D. Dissertation, University of the Philippines, Diliman, Quezon City.

Ghatak, M. (1996). "Group Lending Contracts and the Peer Selection Effect." Mimeograph, Department of Economics, University of Chicago.

Ghate, P. B. (1992). "Interaction between the Formal and Informal Sectors: The Asian Experience," *World Development* **20**, 859–872.

Ghosh, P., and D. Ray (1996). "Cooperation in Community Interaction Without Information Flows," *Review of Economic Studies* **63**, 491–519.

Ghosh, P., and D. Ray (1997). "Information and Repeated Interaction: Application to Informal Credit Markets." Mimeograph, Department of Economics, Texas A&M University.

Gibbons, R. (1992). *A Primer in Game Theory.* New York, NY: Harvester Wheatsheaf.

Gillis, M., D. Perkins, M. Roemer, and D. Snodgrass (1997). *Economics of Development,* 5th Edition. New York: Norton.

Glewwe, P., and J. van der Gaag (1990). "Identifying the Poor in Developing Countries: Do Different Definitions Matter?," *World Development* **18**, 803–814.

Gordon, R. H., and A. L. Bovenberg (1996). "Why Is Capital so Mobile Internationally? Possible Explanations and Implications for Capital Income Taxation," *American Economic Review* **86**, 1057–1075.

Gough, K. (1983). "Agricultural Labor in Thanjavur," in J. Mencher (ed.), *Social Anthropology of Peasantry.* Madras: Somaiya Publishers Private Ltd.

Grossman, G. M., and E. Helpman (1991). *Innovation and Growth in the Global Economy.* Cambridge, MA: MIT Press.

Grossman, G. M., and E. Helpman (1994). "Protection for Sale," *American Economic Review* **84**, 833–850.

Gupta, P., and S. Gupta (1982). "Estimates of the Unreported Economy in India," *Economic and Political Weekly*, Jan. 16.

Gupta, S., and R. Mehta (1981). "An Estimate of Underreported National Income," *Journal of Income and Wealth* **5**.

Hanson, A. H. (1966). *The Process of Planning: A Study of India's Five-Year Plans,* 1950-1964. London: Oxford University Press.

Harris, J., and M. Todaro (1970). "Migration, Unemployment and Development: A Two-Sector Analysis," *American Economic Review* **40**, 126–142.

Helpman, E. (1981). "International Trade in the Presence of Product Differentiation, Economies of Scale and Monopolistic Competition: A Chamberlin–Heckscher–Ohlin Approach," *Journal of International Economics* **11**, 305–340.

Helpman, E., and P. Krugman (1985). *Trade Policy and Market Structure*. Cambridge, MA: MIT Press.

Henderson, V. (1988). *Urban Development: Theory, Fact, and Illusion*. London: Oxford University Press.

Heredia, C., and M. Purcell (1995). "Structural Adjustment in Mexico: The Root of the Crisis." Mimeograph, Equipo Pueblo.

Hillman, A. (1989). *The Political Economy of Protection*. Reading, UK: Harwood Academic Publishers.

Hirsch, W. Z. (1956). "Firm Progress Ratios," *Econometrica* **24**, 136–144.

Hirschman, A. O. (1958). *The Strategy of Economic Development*. New Haven, CT: Yale University Press.

Hirschman, A. O., and M. Rothschild (1973). "The Changing Tolerance for Income Inequality in the Course of Economic Development; With a Mathematical Appendix," *Quarterly Journal of Economics* **87**, 544–566.

Hoel, P. G. (1984). *Introduction to Mathematical Statistics*, 5th ed. New York: Wiley.

Hoff, K., and J. Stiglitz (1993). "Imperfect Information in Rural Credit Markets: Puzzles and Policy Perspectives," *World Bank Economic Review* **4**, 235–250. Reprinted in K. Hoff, A. Braverman, and J. Stiglitz, eds., *The Economics of Rural Organization: Theory, Practice and Policy*, Chap. 2. London: Oxford University Press (for the World Bank).

Hoff, K., and J. Stiglitz (1998). "Moneylenders and Bankers: Price-Increasing Subsidies in a Monopolistically Competitive Market," *Journal of Development Economics* **55**, 485–518.

Hopper, W. D. (1957). "The Economic Organization of a Village in North Central India." Ph.D. Dissertation, Cornell University.

Hopper, W. D. (1965). "Allocation Efficiency in a Traditional Indian Agriculture," *Journal of Farm Economics* **47**, 611–624.

Horowitz, A. W. (1993). "Time Paths of Land Reform: A Theoretical Model of Reform Dynamics," *American Economic Review* **83**, 1003–1010.

Houantchekon, L. (1994). "Tournaments and Optimal Contracts for Teams in Rural West Africa." Mimeograph, Department of Economics, Northwestern University.

Hudec, R. E. (1990). "Dispute Settlement," in J. Schott (ed.), *Completing the Uruguay Round*. Washington, DC: Institute for International Economics.

Huppi, M., and G. Feder (1990). "The Role of Groups and Credit Cooperatives in Rural Lending," *World Bank Research Observer* **5**, 187–204.

International Monetary Fund (1992). *Issues and Developments in International Trade Policy*. World Economic and Financial Surveys Series. Prepared by a Staff Team led by M. Kelly and A. K. McGuirk.

Irwin, D. (1993). "Multilateral and Bilateral Trade Policies in the World Trading System: An Historical Perspective," in J. de Melo and A. Panagariya (eds.), *New Dimensions in Regional Integration*, pp. 90–119. Cambridge, UK: Cambridge University Press.

Jackson, J. (1989). *The World Trading System*. Cambridge, MA: MIT Press.

Jain, S. (1975). "Size Distribution of Income: A Compilation of Data." Mimeograph, The World Bank.

Jodha, N. S. (1981). "Agricultural Tenancy: Fresh Evidence from Dryland Areas in India," *Economic and Political Weekly*, Annual Number, A118–A128.

Jorgenson, D. (1961). "The Development of a Dual Economy," *Economic Journal* **71**, 309–334.

Kalecki, M. (1976). *Essays on Developing Economies*. Hassocks, UK/Atlantic Highlands, NJ: Harvester Press/Humanities Press.

Kao, C., K. Anschel, and C. Eicher (1964). "Disguised Unemployment in Agriculture—A Survey," in C. Eicher and L. Witt (eds.), *Agriculture in Economic Development*. New York: McGraw-Hill.

Kemp, M., and H. Y. Wan (1976). "An Elementary Proposition Concerning the Formation of Customs Unions," *Journal of International Economics* **6**, 95–97.

Kenney, E. (1989). "The Effects of Sugarcane Production on Food Security, Health, and Nutrition in Kenya: A Longitudinal Analysis." IFPRI, Washington, DC.

Keyter, C. (1962). "Industrial Feeding of African Workers." Monograph, South African Institute of Race Relations.

Klasen, S. (1994). "Missing Women Reconsidered," *World Development* **22**(7), 1061–1071.

Kletzer, K., and B. Wright (1995). "Sovereign Debt as Intertemporal Barter." Mimeograph, University of California, Santa Cruz.

Kochar, A. (1991). "An Empirical Investigation of Rationing Constraints in Rural Credit Markets in India." Ph. D. Dissertation, University of Chicago.

Kochar, A. (1996). "Do Declining Economic Contributions Lower Household Medical Expenditures on the Elderly in Developing Economies? Empirical Evidence from Rural Pakistan." Mimeograph, Department of Economics, Stanford University.

Kovenock, D., and M. Thursby (1992). "GATT, Dispute Settlement, and Cooperation," *Economics and Politics* **4**, 151–170.

Kranton, R. (1996). "The Formation of Cooperative Relationships," *Journal of Law, Economics, and Organization* **12**, 214–233.

Kremer, M. (1993). "Population Growth and Technological Change: One Million B.C. to 1990," *Quarterly Journal of Economics* **108**, 681–716.

Krishnamurty, J. (1988). "Unemployment in India: The Broad Magnitudes and Characteristics," in T. N. Srinivasan and P. K. Bardhan (eds.), *Rural Poverty in South Asia*. New York: Columbia University Press.

Krueger, A. O. (1974). "The Political Economy of the Rent-Seeking Society," *American Economic Review* **64**, 291–303.

Krugman, P. (1981). "Scale Economies, Product Differentiation, and the Pattern of Trade," *American Economic Review* **70**, 950–959.

Krugman, P. (1991a). "History versus Expectations," *Quarterly Journal of Economics* **106**, 651–667.

Krugman, P. (1991b). "Increasing Returns and Economic Geography," *Journal of Political Economy* **99**, 483–499.

Krugman, P. (1991c). "Is Bilateralism Bad?," in E. Helpman and A. Razin (eds.), *International Trade and Trade Policy*. Cambridge, MA: MIT Press.

Krugman, P. (1993). "Regionalism versus Multilateralism: Analytical Notes," in J. de Melo and A. Panagariya (eds.), *New Dimensions in Regional Integration*. pp. 58–79. Cambridge, UK: Cambridge University Press.

Krugman, P. (1995). "Increasing Returns, Imperfect Competition and the Positive Theory of International Trade," in G. M. Grossman and K. Rogoff (eds.), *Handbook of International Economics*, Vol. 3, pp. 1243–1277. Amsterdam: Elsevier Science.

Krugman, P. (1997). "What Should Trade Negotiators Negotiate About?," *Journal of Economic Literature* **35**, 113–120.

Krugman, P., and M. Obstfeld (1994). *International Economics: Theory and Policy*, 3rd ed. New York: Harper Collins.

Kumar, B. G. (1991). "Quality of Life and Morbidity: A Reexamination of Some Paradoxes from Kerala." Mimeograph, Centre for Development Studies, Trivandrum.

Kumar, S. K., and D. Hotchkiss (1988). "Consequences of Deforestation for Women's Time Allocation, Agricultural Production, and Nutrition in Hill Areas of Nepal." IFPRI, Washington, DC.

Kurup, T. V. N. (1976). "Price of Rural Credit: An Empirical Analysis of Kerala," *Economic and Political Weekly* **11**, July 3.

Kuznets, S. (1955). "Economic Growth and Income Inequality, " *American Economic Review* **45**, 1–28.

Kuznets, S. (1960). "Population Change and Aggregate Output," in *Demographic and Economic Change in Developed Countries*. National Bureau of Economic Research Special Conference Series, Princeton: Princeton University Press.

Kuznets, S. (1963). "Quantitative Aspects of the Economic Growth of Nations: VIII. Distribution of Income by Size," *Economic Development and Cultural Change* **12**, 1–80.

Kuznets, S. (1966). *Modern Economic Growth*. New Haven, CT: Yale University Press.

La Ferrara, E. (1997). "Ethnicity and Reciprocity: An Analysis of Credit Transactions in Ghana." Mimeograph, Department of Economics, Harvard University.

Lancaster, K. (1975). "Socially Optimal Product Differentiation," *American Economic Review* **65**, 567–585.

Lancaster, K. (1980). "Intra-Industry Trade under Perfect Monopolistic Competition," *Journal of International Economics* **10**, 151–175.

Langoni, C. (1972). "Distribuição da Renda e Desenvolvimento Econômico do Brasil," *Estudos Econômicos* October, 5–88.

Larson, D. (1988). "Market and Credit Linkages: The Case of Corn Traders in the Southern Philippines." Paper prepared for Citibank/ABT Associates on a Rural Financial Services Project for USAID, Manila.

Lee, R. (1988), "Induced Population Growth and Induced Technical Progress: Their Interaction in the Accelerating Stage," *Mathematical Population Studies* **1**, 265–288.

Leibenstein, H. (1957). *Economic Backwardness and Economic Growth*. New York: Wiley.

Lewis, O. (1958). *Village Life in Northern India*. New York: Random House.

Lewis, O., and V. Barnouw (1958). *Village Life in Northern India*. Urbana, IL: University of Illinois Press.

Lewis, W. A. (1954). "Economic Development with Unlimited Supplies of Labor," *The Manchester School of Economic and Social Studies* **22**, 139–191. Reprinted in A. N. Agarwala and S. P. Singh, eds., *The Economics of Underdevelopment*. Bombay: Oxford University Press, 1958.

Ligon, E. (1993). "Optimal Consumption Risk Sharing: Theory and Measurement in Rural India." Ph.D. Dissertation, University of Chicago.

Lim, Y., and R. Townsend (1994). "Currency, Transaction Patterns, and Consumption Smoothing: Theory and Measurement in ICRISAT Villages." Mimeograph, Department of Economics, University of Chicago.

Lin, J. Y., and G. J. Wen (1995). "China's Regional Grain Self-Sufficiency Policy and its Effect on Land Productivity," *Journal of Comparative Economics* **21**, 187–206.

Lindert, P. H., and P. J. Morton (1989). "How Sovereign Debt has Worked," in J. D. Sachs (ed.), *Developing Country Debt and Economic Performance*, pp. 39–106. Chicago: University of Chicago Press.

Lindert, P. H., and J. G. Williamson (1985). "Growth, Equality, and History," *Explorations in Economic History* **22**, 341–377.

Lipsey, R. (1960). "The Theory of Customs Unions: A General Survey," *Economic Journal* **70**, 496–513.

Lipsey, R., and K. Lancaster (1956). "The General Theory of Second-Best," *Review of Economic Studies* **24**, 11–32, reprinted in M. Ricketts (ed.). *Neoclassical Microeconomics*, Vol. 2, Schools of Thought in Economics Series, no. 3. Aldershot, UK./Brookfield, VT: Elgar/Gower, 1988.

Lipton, M. (1968). "Urban Bias in Rural Planning," in P. Streeten and M. Lipton (eds.). "The Crisis of Indian Planning: Economic Planning in the 1960s." London: Oxford University Press.

Lipton, M. (1983). "Poverty, Undernourishment and Hunger," Staff Working Paper 597, The World Bank.

Loury, G. C. (1981). "Intergenerational Transfers and the Distribution of Earnings," *Econometrica* **49**, 843–867.

Lucas, R. E. (1988). "On the Mechanics of Economic Development," *Journal of Monetary Economics* **22**, 3–42.

Lustig, N. (1992). *Mexico: The Remaking of an Economy*. Washington, DC: The Brookings Institution.

Madajewicz, M. (1996). "The Market for Small Loans." Mimeograph, Department of Economics, Harvard University.

Maddison, A. (1979). "Per Capita Output in the Long Run," *Kyklos* **32**, 412–429.

Maddison, A. (1982). *Phases of Capitalist Development*. London: Oxford University Press.

Maddison, A. (1991). *Dynamic Forces in Capitalist Development: A Long-Run Comparative View*, Oxford, New York: Oxford University Press.

Magee, S. P., W. A. Brock, and L. Young (1989). *Black Hole Tariffs and Endogenous Policy Theory*. Cambridge, UK: Cambridge University Press.

Malthus, T. (1798). *An Essay on the Principle of Population as it Affects the Future Improvement of Society*. London: J. Johnson.

Mani, A. (1997). "Income Distribution and the Demand Constraint." Mimeograph, Department of Economics, Boston University.

Mankiw, N. G. (1995). "The Growth of Nations," *Brookings Papers on Economic Activity* 0(1), 275–310.

Mankiw, N. G., P. Romer, and D. Weil (1992). "A Contribution to the Empirics of Economic Growth," *Quarterly Journal of Economics* **107**, 407–438.

Manning, P. (1982). *Slavery, Colonialism and Economic Growth in Dahomey, 1640–1960*. Cambridge, UK: Cambridge University Press.

Manove, M. (1997). "Entrepreneurs, Optimism and the Competitive Edge." Mimeograph, Department of Economics, Boston University.

Mansuri, G. (1997). "Credit Layering in Rural Financial Markets: Theory and Evidence from Pakistan." Ph.D. Dissertation, Boston University.

Marichal, C. (1989). *A Century of Debt Crises in Latin America: From Independence to the Great Depression, 1820–1930*. Princeton, NJ: Princeton University Press.

Markusen, J. (1986). "Explaining the Volume of Trade: An Eclectic Approach," *American Economic Review* **76**, 1002–1011.

Matsuyama, K. (1991). "Increasing Returns, Industrialization, and Indeterminacy of Equilibrium," *Quarterly Journal of Economics* **106**, 617–650.

Mauro, P. (1995). "Corruption and Growth," *Quarterly Journal of Economics* **110**, 681–712.

Mayer, W. (1984). "Endogenous Tariff Formation," *American Economic Review* **74**, 970–985.

McBride, T. (1976). *The Domestic Revolution: The Modernization of Household Service in England and France, 1820–1920*. New York: Holmes and Meier.

McKernan, S-M. (1996). "The Impact of Micro-Credit Programs on Self-Employment Profits: Do Non-Credit Program Aspects Matter?" Mimeograph, Brown University.

McMillan, J., J. Whalley, and L. Zhu (1989). "The Impact of China's Economic Reforms on Agricultural Productivity Growth," *Journal of Political Economy* **97**, 781–807.

Meesook, O. A. (1975). "Income Inequality in Thailand, 1962/1963 and 1968/1969," in *Income Distribution, Employment and Economic Development in Southeast and East Asia*. Proceedings of a Seminar sponsored jointly by the Japan Economic Research Center and the Council for Asian Manpower Studies, pp. 345–388.

Messerlin, P. A. (1987). "The Long Term Evolution of the EC Anti-Dumping Law: Some Lessons for the New AD Laws in LDCs." Mimeograph, World Bank.

Mirrlees, J. (1976). "A Pure Theory of Underdeveloped Economies," in L. Reynolds (ed.), *Agriculture in Development Theory*. New Haven, CT: Yale University Press.

Mitra, P. (1983). "A Theory of Interlinked Rural Transactions," *Journal of Public Economics* **20**, 167–191.

Mookherjee, D. (1997). "Informational Rents and Property Rights in Land," in J. Roemer (ed.), *Property Rights, Incentives and Welfare*. New York: Macmillan Press.

Mookherjee, D., and D. Ray (1993). "Learning-by-Doing and Industrial Market Structure: An Overview." in B. Dutta, S. Gangopadhyay, D. Mookherjee, and D. Ray (eds.), *Theoretical Issues in Development Economics*. London: Oxford University Press.

Morduch, J. (1994). "Poverty and Vulnerability," *American Economic Review* **84**, 221–225.

Morduch, J. (1995). "Income Smoothing and Consumption Smoothing," *Journal of Economic Perspectives* **9**, 103–114.

Morduch, J. (1997). "The Microfinance Revolution." Mimeograph, Department of Economics, Harvard University.

Morley, S. A. (1995). *Poverty and Income Inequality in Latin America during the 1980s*. Baltimore, MD: Johns Hopkins Press.

Morris, D. M. (1979). *Measuring the Condition of the World's Poor: The Physical Quality of Life Index*. Elmsford, NY: Pergamon Press (for the Overseas Development Council).

Mosley, P. (1996). "Indonesia: BKK, KURK, and the BRI Unit Desa Institutions," in D. Hulme and P. Mosley (eds.), *Finance Against Poverty, Vol. II: Country Case Studies*, pp. 228–315. London: Routledge.

Mosley, P., J. Harrigan, and J. Toye (1991). *Aid and Power: The World Bank and Policy Based Lending*. Vol. I, London: Routledge.

Mukherjee, A. (1991). "Rural Labour Markets and Seasonality: A Theoretical and Empirical Analysis." Ph. D. Dissertation, Indian Statistical Institute, New Delhi.

Mukherjee, A., and D. Ray (1992). "Wages and Involuntary Unemployment in the Slack Season of a Village Economy," *Journal of Development Economics* **37**, 227–264.

Mukherjee, A., and D. Ray (1995). "Labor Tying," *Journal of Development Economics* **47**, 207–239.

Mukherjee, P. (1992). "Report of Study on Sociological Constraints on Rural Labor." Mimeograph, Indian Statistical Institute, New Delhi.

Murphy, K., A. Shleifer, and R. Vishny (1989a). "Industrialization and the Big Push," *Journal of Political Economy* **97**, 1003–1026.

Murphy, K., A. Shleifer, and R. Vishny (1989b). "Income Distribution, Market Size, and Industrialization," *Quarterly Journal of Economics* **104**, 537–64.

Myrdal, G. (1957). *Economic Theory and Underdeveloped Regions*. London: Duckworth.

Naqvi, S. N. H. (1995). "The Nature of Economic Development," *World Development* **23**, 543–556.

Newbery, D. M. G. (1977). "Risk-Sharing, Sharecropping, and Uncertain Labour Markets," *Review of Economic Studies* **44**, 585–594.

Newbery, D. M. G., and J. Stiglitz (1979). "Sharecropping, Risk-Sharing, and the Importance of Imperfect Information," in J. A. Roumasset, J. M. Boussard, and I. Singh (eds.), *Risk, Uncertainty and Agricultural Development*. Chap. 17. New York: Agricultural Development Council.

Nogués, J. J., and R. Quintanilla (1993). "Latin America's Integration and the Multilateral Trading System," in J. de Melo and A. Panagariya (eds.), *New Dimensions in Regional Integration*. pp. 278–313. Cambridge, UK: Cambridge University Press.

Nove, A. (1969). *An Economic History of the U. S. S. R.*. London: Allen Lane.

Nurkse, R. (1953). *Problems of Capital Formation in Underdeveloped Countries*. New York: Oxford University Press.

Okun, A. M. (1975). *Equality and Efficiency: The Big Tradeoff*. Washington, DC: Brookings Institution.

Olson, M. (1965). *The Logic of Collective Action: Public Goods and the Theory of Groups*. Cambridge, MA: Harvard University Press.

Orshansky, M. (1963). "Children of the Poor," *Social Security Bulletin* **26**, 3–5.

Orshansky, M. (1965). "Counting the Poor: Another Look at the Poverty Profile," *Social Security Bulletin* **28**, 3–29.

Osborne, M. J., and A. Rubinstein (1994). *A Course in Game Theory*. Cambridge, MA: MIT Press.

Oshima, H. T. (1962). "The International Comparison of Size Distribution of Family Incomes with Special Reference to Asia," *Review of Economics and Statistics* **54**, 439–445.

Otsuka, K., H. Chuma, and Y. Hayami (1992). "Land and Labor Contracts in Agrarian Economies," *Journal of Economic Literature* **30**, 1965–2018.

Page, S. (1994). *How Developing Countries Trade*. London: Routledge.

Pal, S. (1993). "Determinants of the Choice of Regular Contracts in Indian Agriculture," Mimeograph, St. John's College, Cambridge, England.

Papanek, G. F., and O. Kyn (1986). "The Effect on Income Distribution of Development, the Growth Rate and Economic Strategy," *Journal of Development Economics* **23**, 55–65.

Parente, S. L., and E. C. Prescott (1993). "Changes in the Wealth of Nations," *Federal Reserve Bank of Minneapolis Quarterly Review* **17**, 3–16.

Pareto, V. (1927). *Manual of Political Economy*. New York: A. M. Kelley.

Paukert, F. (1973). "Income Distribution at Different Levels of Development: A Survey of Evidence," *International Labour Review* **108**, 97–125.

Paulsen, A. (1995). "Insurance Motives for Migration: Evidence from Thailand." Mimeograph, Woodrow Wilson School, Princeton University.

Paxson, C. (1992). "Using Weather Variability to Estimate the Response of Savings to Transitory Income in Thailand," *American Economic Review* **82**, 15–33.

Paxson, C., and C. Chaudhuri (1994). "Consumption Smoothing and Income Seasonality in Rural India." Mimeograph, Princeton University.

Pearson, S. R., and W. D. Ingram (1980). "Economies of Scale, Domestic Divergences, and Potential Gains from Economic Integration in Ghana and the Ivory Coast," *Journal of Political Economy* **88**, 994–1008.

Perotti, R. (1992). "Income Distribution, Politics, and Growth," *American Economic Review* **82**, 311–316.

Persson, T., and G. Tabellini (1994). "Is Inequality Harmful for Growth?," *American Economic Review* **84**, 600–621.

Pesendorfer, W. (1995). "Design Innovation and Fashion Cycles," *American Economic Review* **85**, 771–792.

Phillips, J., R. Simmons, M. Koenig, and J. Chakraborty (1988). "Determinants of Reproductive Change in a Traditional Society: Evidence from Matlab, Bangladesh," *Studies in Family Planning* **19**, 313–334.

Pigou, A. C. (1912). *Wealth and Welfare*. London: Macmillan.

Pingali, P. L., and V. T. Xuan (1992). "Vietnam: Decollectivization and Rice Productivity Growth," *Economic Development and Cultural Change* **40**, 697–718.

Pitt, M. M. (1983). "Food Preference and Nutrition in Rural Bangladesh," *Review of Economics and Statistics* **65**, 105–114.

Pitt, M. M., and S. R. Khandker (1995). "The Impact of Group-Based Credit Programs on Poor Households in Bangladesh: Does the Gender of Participants Matter?" Mimeograph, Brown University.

Pitt, M. M., and M. R. Rosenzweig (1985). "Health and Nutrient Consumption across and within Farm Households," *Review of Economics and Statistics* **67**, 212–223.

Pitt, M. M., M. R. Rosenzweig, and M. N. Hassan (1990). "Productivity, Health, and Inequality in the Intrahousehold Distribution of Food in Low-Income Countries," *American Economic Review* **80**, 139–156.

Polak, J. J. (1991). "The Changing Nature of IMF Conditionality," *Essays in International Finance*, Vol. 184. Princeton, NJ: Princeton University.

Polak, J. J. (1994). "The World Bank and the International Monetary Fund: A Changing Relationship," *Brookings Occasional Papers*. Washington, DC: Brookings Institution.

Powelson, J. P., and R. Stock (1987). *The Peasant Betrayed: Agriculture and Land Reform in the Third World*. Boston, MA: Oelgeschlager, Gunn and Hain.

Prebisch, R. (1952). "Problemas Teóricos y Prácticos del Crecimiento Económico." United Nations Economic Commission for Latin America.

Prebisch, R. (1959). "Commercial Policies in Underdeveloped Countries," *American Economic Review* **49** (Papers and Proceedings), 252–273.

Pritchett, L., and L. Summers (1995). "Wealthier is Healthier," *Journal of Human Resources* **31**, 841–868.

Prusa, T. (1992). "Why Are so Many Antidumping Petitions Withdrawn?," *Journal of International Economics* **33**, 1–20.

Quah, D. (1993). "Empirical Cross-Section Dynamics in Economic Growth," *European Economic Review* **37**, 426–434.

Quah, D. (1994). "Convergence across Europe." Mimeograph, London School of Economics.

Rahman, O., A. Foster, and J. Mencken (1992). "Older Widow Mortality in Rural Bangladesh," *Social Science and Medicine* **34**, 89–96.

Raj, K. N. (1965). *Indian Economic Growth: Performance and Prospects.* Delhi: Allied Publishers.

Raj, K. N. (1979). "Keynesian Economics and Agrarian Economics," in C. H. H. Rao and P. C. Joshi (eds.), *Reflections on Economic Development and Social Change: Essays in Honour of V.K.R.V. Rao.* Bombay: Allied Publishers.

Rakshit, M. K. (1982). *The Labour-Surplus Economy: A Neo-Keynesian Approach.* Delhi: Macmillan.

Ranis, G., and J. Fei (1961). "A Theory of Economic Development," *American Economic Review* **51**, 533–565.

Rao, V. K. R. V. (1952). "Investment, Income and the Multiplier in an Underdeveloped Economy," reprinted in A. N. Agarwala and S. P. Singh (eds.). *The Economics of Underdevelopment.* Bombay: Oxford University Press, 1958.

Ravallion, M. (1990). "Income Effects on Undernutrition," *Economic Development and Cultural Change* **38**, 489–515.

Ray, D. (1993). "Labor Markets, Adaptive Mechanisms and Nutritional Status," in P. Bardhan et al. (eds.), *Essays in Honour of K. N. Raj.* London: Oxford University Press.

Ray, D., and A. Sen (1992). "On the Economic Theory of Quantity Controls," in K. Basu and P. Nayak (eds.), *Economic Theory and Development.* New Delhi: Oxford University Press.

Ray, D., and K. Sengupta (1989). "Interlinkages and the Pattern of Competition," in P. Bardhan (ed.), *The Economic Theory of Agrarian Institutions.* Clarendon Press, Oxford.

Ray, D., and P. Streufert (1993). "Dynamic Equilibria with Unemployment due to Undernourishment," *Economic Theory* **3**, 61–85.

Ray, D., and R. Vohra (1997a). "Equilibrium Binding Agreements," *Journal of Economic Theory* **73**, 30–78.

Ray, D., and R. Vohra (1997b). "A Theory of Endogenous Coalition Structure." Mimeograph, Department of Economics, Boston University.

Reardon, T., E. Crawford, and V. Kelley (1994). "Links Between Nonfarm Income and Farm Investment in African Households: Adding the Capital Market Perspective," *American Journal of Agricultural Economics* **76**, 1172–1176.

Reddy, C. R. (1985). "Rural Labor Market in Varhad: A Case Study of Agricultural Laborers in Rain-Fed Agriculture in India." REPRP 75, WEP, International Labour Organization.

Richards, A. (1979). "The Political Economy of Gutswirtschaft: A Comparative Analysis of East Elbian Germany, Egypt, and Chile," *Comparative Studies in Society and History* **21**, 483–518.

Roberts, K. W. S. (1980). "Interpersonal Comparability and Social Choice Theory," *Review of Economic Studies* **47**, 421-439.

Rodgers, G. (1975). "Nutritionally Based Wage Determination in the Low-Income Labour Market," *Oxford Economic Papers* **27**, 61–81.

Rodríguez-Clare, A. (1996). "The Division of Labor and Economic Development," *Journal of Development Economics* **49**, 3–32.

Rodrik, D. (1995). "Political Economy of Trade Policy," in G. M. Grossman and K. Rogoff (eds.), *Handbook of International Economics*, Vol. 3, pp. 1457–1494. Amsterdam: Elsevier Science, North Holland.

Romer, P. (1986). "Increasing Returns and Long-Run Growth," *Journal of Political Economy* **92**, 1002–1037.

Romer, P. (1990). "Endogenous Technological Change," *Journal of Political Economy* **98**, S71–S101.

Ros, J. (1992). "Ajuste Macroeconómico, Reformas Estructurales y Crecimiento en México." Mimeograph, University of Notre Dame.

Rosenberg, N. (1972). "Factors Affecting the Diffusion of Technology," *Explorations in Economic History* **10**, 3–33.

Rosenstein-Rodan, P. (1943). "Problems of Industrialization of Eastern and Southeastern Europe," *Economic Journal* **53**, 202–211, reprinted in A. N. Agarwala and S. P. Singh (eds.) *The Economics of Underdevelopment*. Bombay: Oxford University Press, 1958.

Rosenzweig, M. R., and H. Binswanger (1993). "Wealth, Weather Risk and the Composition and Profitability of Agricultural Investments," *Economic Journal* **103**, 56–78.

Rosenzweig, M. R., and O. Stark (1989). "Consumption Smoothing, Migration and Marriage: Evidence from Rural India," *Journal of Political Economy* **97**, 905–926.

Rosenzweig, M. R., and K. I. Wolpin (1985). "Specific Experience, Household Structure, and Intergenerational Transfers: Farm Family Land and Labor Arrangements in Developing Countries," *Quarterly Journal of Economics* **100**, 961–987.

Rosenzweig, M. R., and K. I. Wolpin (1993). "Credit Market Constraints, Consumption Smoothing, and the Accumulation of Durable Production Assets in Low-Income Countries: Investment in Bullocks in India," *Journal of Political Economy* **101**, 223–244.

Rudd, J. (1993). "Boy-Girl Discrimination in Taiwan: Evidence from Expenditure Data." Mimeograph, Department of Economics, Princeton University.

Sachs, J. (1989). "Introduction," in J. D. Sachs (ed.), *Developing Country Debt and Economic Performance*, pp. 1–35. Chicago, IL: University of Chicago Press.

Sadoulet, E. (1992). "Labor–Service Tenancy Contracts in a Latin American Context," *American Economic Review* **82**, 1031–1042.

Sahn, D. (1988). "The Effect of Price and Income Changes on Food-Energy Intake in Sri Lanka," *Economic Development and Cultural Change* **36**, 315–340.

Saxonhouse, G. (1993). "Trading Blocs and East Asia," in J. de Melo and A. Panagariya (eds.), *New Dimensions in Regional Integration*, pp. 388–416. Cambridge, UK: Cambridge University Press.

Schultz, T. P. (1985). "Changing World Prices, Women's Wages, and the Fertility Transition in Sweden, 1860–1910," *Journal of Political Economy* **93**, 1126–1154.

Schultz, T. W. (1964). *Transforming Traditional Agriculture*. New Haven, CT: Yale University Press.

Scitovsky, T. (1942). "A Reconsideration of the Theory of Tariffs," *Review of Economic Studies* **9**, 89–110.

Scitovsky, T. (1954). "Two Concepts of External Economies," *Journal of Political Economy* **62**, 143–151.

Sen, A. (1981). "Market Failure and Control of Labour Power: Towards an Explanation of 'Structure' and Change in Indian Agriculture: Part 1," *Cambridge Journal of Economics* **5**, 201–228.

Sen, A. K. (1964). "Labour Allocation in a Cooperative Enterprise," *Review of Economic Studies* **33**, 361–371.

Sen, A. K. (1966). "Peasants and Dualism With or Without Surplus Labor," *Journal of Political Economy* **74**, 425–450.

Sen, A. K. (1967). "Surplus Labour in India: A Critique of Schultz's Statistical Test," *Economic Journal* **77**, 154–161.

Sen, A. K. (1970). "Interpersonal Aggregation and Partial Comparability," *Econometrica* **38**, 393–409.

Sen, A. K. (1973). *On Economic Inequality*. Oxford: Clarendon Press.

Sen, A. K. (1975). *Employment, Technology and Development*. Oxford: Clarendon Press.

Sen, A. K. (1976). "Poverty: An Ordinal Approach to Measurement," *Econometrica* **44**, 219–231.

Sen, A. K. (1981a). "Ingredients of Famine Analysis: Availability and Entitlements," *Quarterly Journal of Economics* **96**, 433–464.

Sen, A. K. (1981b). *Poverty and Famines: An Essay on Entitlement and Deprivation*. Oxford: Clarendon Press.

Sen, A. K. (1983). "Development: Which Way Now?," *Economic Journal* **93**, 742–762.

Sen, A. K. (1984). *Resources, Values and Development*. Cambridge, MA: Harvard University Press.

Sen, A. K. (1985). *Commodities and Capabilities*. Amsterdam: North-Holland.

Sen, A. K. (1992). "Missing Women," *British Medical Journal* **304**.

Sengupta, K. (1997). "Limited Liability, Moral Hazard and Share Tenancy," *Journal of Development Economics* **52**, 393–407.

Shaban, R. A. (1987). "Testing between Competing Models of Sharecropping," *Journal of Political Economy* **95**, 893–920.

Shapiro, C., and J. Stiglitz (1984). Equilibrium Unemployment as a Worker Discipline Device, *American Economic Review* **74**, 433–444.

Shell, K. (1967). "A Model of Inventive Activity and Capital Accumulation," in K. Shell (ed.), *Essays on the Theory of Optimal Growth*. Cambridge, MA: MIT Press.

Shetty, S. (1988). "Limited Liability, Wealth Differences, and the Tenancy Ladder in Agrarian Economies," *Journal of Development Economics* **29**, 1–22.

Shorrocks, A. F., and J. E. Foster (1987). "Transfer Sensitive Inequality Measures," *Review of Economic Studies* **54**, 485–497.

Siamwalla, A., C. Pinthong, N. Poapongsakorn, P. Satsanguan, P. Nettayarak, W. Mingmaneenakin, and Y. Tubpun (1993). "The Thai Rural Credit System and Elements of a Theory: Public Subsidies, Private Information, and Segmented Markets," in K. Hoff, A. Braverman, and J. Stiglitz (eds.), *The Economics of Rural Organization: Theory, Practice and Policy*. London: Oxford University Press (for the World Bank).

Simon, J. (1977). *The Economics of Population Growth*. Princeton: Princeton University Press.

Singer, H. (1950). "The Distribution of Gains Between Investing and Borrowing Countries," *American Economic Review* **49** (Papers and Proceedings), 251–273.

Singh, N. (1983). "The Possibility of Nonrenewal of a Contract as an Incentive Device in Principal–Agent Models." Working Paper 117 (Economics), University of California at Santa Cruz.

Solow, R. (1956). "A Contribution to the Theory of Economic Growth," *Quarterly Journal of Economics* **70**, 65–94.

Somanathan, E. (1995). "The Hindu Equilibrium and the American Dream." Mimeograph, Emory University.

Somanathan, R. (1997). "School Heterogeneity, Human Capital Accumulation, and Standards." Mimeograph, Emory University, forthcoming, *Journal of Public Economics.*

Srinivas, M. N. (1955). "The Social System of a Mysore Village," in M. Mariott (ed.), *Village India.* Chicago, IL: University of Chicago Press.

Srinivas, M. N. (1960). *India's Villages.* New York: Asia Publishing House.

Srinivasan, T. N. (1994). "Human Development: A New Paradigm or Reinvention of the Wheel?," *American Economic Review* **84**, 238–243.

Staiger, R. (1995). "International Rules and Institutions for Trade Policy," in G. M. Grossman and K. Rogoff (eds.), *Handbook of International Economics*, Vol. 3, pp. 1495–1551. Amsterdam: Elsevier Science, North Holland.

Stiglitz, J. (1974). "Incentives and Risks in Sharecropping," *Review of Economic Studies* **41**, 219–255.

Stiglitz, J. (1976). The Efficiency Wage Hypothesis, Surplus Labour and the Distribution of Income in L.D.C.'s, *Oxford Economic Papers* **28**, 185–207.

Stiglitz, J. (1990). "Peer Monitoring and Credit Markets," *World Bank Economic Review* **4**, 351–366.

Stiglitz, J., and A. Weiss (1981). "Credit Rationing in Markets with Imperfect Information," *American Economic Review* **71**, 393–410.

Strauss, J. (1984). "Joint Determination of Food Consumption and Product in Rural Sierra Leone: Estimates of a Household–Firm Model," *Journal of Development Economics* **29**, 157–184.

Strauss, J., and D. Thomas (1990). "The Shape of the Calorie-Expenditure Curve." Discussion Paper, Yale Economic Growth Center, Yale University.

Streeten, P. P. (1994). "Human Development: Means and Ends," *American Economic Review* **84**, 232–237.

Subramanian, S. (1994). "Gender Discrimination in Intra-Household Allocation in India." Mimeograph, Department of Economics, Cornell University.

Subramanian, S., and A. Deaton (1991). "Gender Effects in Indian Consumption Patterns," *Sarvekshana* **14**, 1–12.

Subramanian, S., and A. Deaton (1996). "The Demand for Food and Calories," *Journal of Political Economy* **104**, 133–162.

Sundaram, K., and S. Tendulkar (1988). Toward an Explanation of Interregional Variations in Poverty and Unemployment in Rural India, in T. N. Srinivasan and P. Bardhan (eds.), *Rural Poverty in South Asia.* New York: Columbia University Press.

Sundari, T. K. (1981). "Caste and the Rural Society: Report of a Field Study in Chingleput District." Mimeograph, Centre for Development Studies, Trivandrum.

Székely, M. (1995a). "Aspectos de la Desigualdad en México," *El Trimestre Económico* **62**, 201–243.

Székely, M. (1995b). "Economic Liberalization, Poverty and Income Distribution in Mexico." Mimeograph, Department of Economics, El Colegio de México.

Takagi, Y. (1978). "Surplus Labor and Disguised Unemployment," *Oxford Economic Papers* **30**, 447–457.

Taylor, C. L., and M. C. Hudson (1972). *World Handbook of Political and Social Indicators.* New Haven, CT: Yale University Press.

Teitelbaum, M. S., and J. M. Winter (1985). *The Fear of Population Decline.* Orlando: Academic Press.

Thomas, J., and T. Worrall (1994). "Informal Insurance Arrangements in Village Economies." Mimeograph, Department of Economics, University of Warwick.

Timmer, C. P., and H. Alderman (1979). "Estimating Consumption Parameters for Food Policy Analysis," *American Journal of Agricultural Economics* **61**, 982–987.

Townsend, R. (1993). "Risk and Insurance in Village India, " *Econometrica* **62**, 539–591.

Townsend, R. (1995). "Consumption Insurance: An Evaluation of Risk-Bearing Systems in Low-Income Economies," *Journal of Economic Perspectives* **9**, 83–102.

Trairatvorakul, P. (1984). "The Effect on Income Distribution and Nutrition of Alternative Rice Price Policies in Thailand." IFPRI, Washington, DC.

Trefler, D. (1993). "Trade Liberalization and the Theory of Endogenous Protection: An Econometric Study of U. S. Import Policy," *Journal of Political Economy* **101**, 138–160.

Udry, C. (1993). "Credit Markets in Northern Nigeria: Credit as Insurance in a Rural Economy," in K. Hoff, A. Braverman and J. Stiglitz (eds.), *The Economics of Rural Organization: Theory, Practice and Policy.* London: Oxford University Press (for the World Bank).

Udry, C. (1994). "Risk and Insurance in a Rural Credit Market: An Empirical Investigation in Northern Nigeria," *Review of Economic Studies* **61**(3), 495–526.

Udry, C. (1996). "Efficiency and Market Structure: Testing for Profit Maximization in African Agriculture." Mimeograph, Department of Economics, Northwestern University.

Umali, D. (1990). "The Structure and Price Performance of the Philippine Rice Marketing System." Ph.D. Dissertation, Stanford University.

United Nations (1993). *Demographic Yearbook.* New York: United Nations.

United Nations (1995). *Demographic Yearbook.* New York: United Nations.

United Nations Conference on Trade and Development (1992). *Handbook of International Trade and Development Statistics.* New York: United Nations.

United Nations Department of Economic and Social Development (1992). *International Trade Statistics Yearbook.* New York: United Nations.

United Nations Development Programme (1995). *Human Development Report.* New York: Oxford University Press.

United Nations Secretariat (1996). *Women's Indicators and Statistics Database (Wistat).* Version 3, CD-ROM, Sales No. E.95.XVII.6, Statistics Division.

Uzawa, H. (1965). "Optimum Technical Change in an Aggregative Model of Economic Growth," *International Economic Review* **6**, 18–31.

van Tassell, E. (1997). "Group Lending under Incomplete Information." Mimeograph, Department of Economics, University of California, Riverside.

Viner, J. (1950). *The Customs Union Issue.* New York: Carnegie Endowment for International Peace.

Viner, J. (1957). "Some Reflections on the Concept of Disguised Unemployment," *Indian Journal of Economics* **38**, 17–23.

Visaria, P. (1981). "Poverty and Unemployment in India: An Analysis of Recent Evidence, *World Development* **9**, 277–300.

von Braun, J., D. Puetz, and P. Webb (1989). "Irrigation Technology and Commercialization of Rice in the Gambia: Effect on Income and Nutrition," IFPRI, Washington, DC.

von Neumann, J. (1945–46). "A Model of General Economic Equilibrium," *Review of Economic Studies* **33**, 1–9.

Von Pischke, J. D. (1991). "Finance at the Frontier: Debt Capacity and the Role of Credit in the Private Economy," EDI Development Studies, The World Bank, Washington, DC.

Vyas, V. S., ed. (1964). "Agricultural Labor in Four Indian Villages." Studies in Rural Problems 3, Vallabh Vidyanagar AERC, Sardar Patel University.

Walker, T. S., and J. G. Ryan (1990). *Village and Household Economies in India's Semi-Arid Tropics.* Baltimore: Johns Hopkins Press.

Walker, T. S., R. P. Singh, and N. S. Jodha (1983). "Dimensions of Farm-Level Diversification in the Semi-Arid Tropics of Rural South Asia." Economic Progress Report, ICRISAT.

Ward, J. O., and J. H. Sanders (1980). "Nutritional Determinants and Migration in the Brazilian Northeast: A Case Study of Rural and Urban Areas," *Economic Development and Cultural Change* **29**, 141–163.

Watson, J. (1996). "Building a Relationship." Mimeograph, Department of Economics, University of California, San Diego.

Weisskoff, R. (1970). "Income Distribution and Economic Growth in Puerto Rico, Argentina, and Mexico," *Review of Income and Wealth* **16**, 303–332.

Weitzman, M. L. (1977). "Prices vs. Quantities," *Review of Economic Studies* **41**, 477–491.

Wen, G. J. (1993). "Total Factor Productivity Change in China's Farming Sector: 1952–1989," *Economic Development and Cultural Change* **42**, 1–41.

Whalley, J. (1993). "Regional Trade Arrangements in North America: CUSTA and NAFTA," in J. de Melo and A. Panagariya (eds.), *New Dimensions in Regional Integration*, pp. 352–382. Cambridge, UK: Cambridge University Press.

Williamson, J. G. (1985). "Did Rising Emigration Cause Fertility to Decline in 19th Century Rural England? Child Costs, Old-Age Pensions and Child Default." Discussion Paper 1172, Harvard Institute for Economic Research, Harvard University.

Williamson, J. G. (1988). "Migration and Urbanization," in H. Chenery and T. N. Srinivasan (eds.), *Handbook of Development Economics*, Vol. 1, Amsterdam: Elsevier Science, North-Holland.

Williamson-Gray, C. (1982). "Food Consumption Parameters for Brazil and their Application to Food Policy," Research Report 32, International Food Policy Research Institute, Washington, DC.

Winters, L. A. (1993). "The European Community: A Case of Successful Integration?" in J. de Melo and A. Panagariya (eds.), *New Dimensions in Regional Integration*, pp. 202–228. Cambridge, UK Cambridge University Press.

Wolfson, M. C. (1994). "When Inequalities Diverge," *American Economic Review* **84** (Papers and Proceedings), 353–358.

Woolcock, M. (1996). "Banking with the Poor in Developing Economies: Lessons from the 'People's Banks' in the Late Nineteenth and Late Twentieth Centuries." Mimeograph, Department of Sociology, Brown University.

World Bank (1990). *World Development Report: Poverty.* London: Oxford University Press.

World Bank (1993). *The East Asian Miracle.* London: Oxford University Press.

World Bank (1995). *World Development Report: Workers in an Integrating World.* London: Oxford University Press.

World Bank (1996). *World Development Report: From Plan to Market.* London: Oxford University Press.

Wright, T. (1936). "Factors Affecting the Cost of Airplanes," *Journal of Aeronautical Sciences* **3**, 122–128.

Yi, S-S. (1996). "Endogenous Formation of Customs Unions under Imperfect Competition: Open Regionalism is Good," *Journal of International Economics* **41**, 153–177.

Young, A. (1995). "The Tyranny of Numbers: Confronting the Statistical Realities of the East Asian Growth Experience," *Quarterly Journal of Economics* **110**, 641–680.

Young, A. A. (1928). "Increasing Returns and Economic Progress," *Economic Journal* **38**, 527–542.

Zeldes, S. (1989). "Consumption and Liquidity Constraints: An Empirical Investigation," *Journal of Political Economy* **97**, 305–346.

Indices

Author Index

Acharya, S., 11
Adelman, I., 205
Adserà, A., 146
Agabin, M., 539, 540
Aggarwal, V., 687
Aguilar, L., 733
Ahluwalia, M., 203–206, 208, 239
Ahmad, A., 284
Alchian, A., 671
Alderman, H., 265
Aleem, I., 541, 543, 545, 559, 561
Alesina, A., 218, 220–222, 240
Amano, M., 353
Amsden, A. H., 683
Anand, S., 29, 205, 206, 258, 259, 292
Anschel, K., 358
Arrow, K. J., xvii, 389, 669
Attwood, D. W., 451
Aturupane, H., 29

Bacha, E. L., 205
Baland, J.-M., xvi, 136, 223
Baldwin, R., 739
Banerjee, A. V., xvi, 227, 235, 268, 393, 441, 444, 445, 581
Banister, J., 286
Bardhan, P. K., 441, 507, 518, 565
Barnouw, V., 506, 507
Barro, R. J., 32, 80, 100, 105, 106, 220, 221
Basu, K., 173, 386, 440, 565
Baumol, W. J., 76–78, 80
Baviskar, B. S., 451
Becker, G. S., 315, 579
Behrman, J. R., 251, 264–267
Bell, C., 430, 537, 573
Berman, E., xvi, 731, 732
Bernheim, B. D., xvii, 324
Berry, R. A., 454, 455
Bertola, G., 218
Besley, T. J., 579–581
Beteille, A., 506
Bhaduri, A., 547
Bhagwati, J. N., 384, 716, 719, 720, 724, 739, 747, 752
Bhargava, A., 265
Bhaskar, V., xvi

Billon, S., 671
Binmore, K., 757
Binswanger, H., 446, 453–456, 600
Bliss, C., 600
Bloch, F., 750
Boone, P., 32
Booth, C., 279
Bose, G., xvi, 500
Bose, P., 577
Boserup, E., 333, 334
Bottomley, A., 544
Bouis, H. E., 265
Bound, J., 732
Bourguignon, F., 205
Bovenberg, A. L., 104
Bowles, S., 507
Brander, J. A., 642
Braverman, A., 565
Breman, J., 506, 507
Brock, W. A., 720
Bruton, H., 674, 675
Bulow, J., 687
Burenstam Linder, S., 637

Cain, M., 281, 311, 456, 600
Carr, E. H., 654
Carr-Saunders, A. M., 303, 304
Carter, N. G., 205
Caselli, F., 519
Caves, R. E., 629, 631
Chakraborty, J., 325
Chamlamwong, Y., 456
Chamley, C., 146
Chaudhuri, C., 600
Chayanov, A. V., 354
Chen, M., 281, 282, 507
Chenery, H. B., 205
Chernichovsky, D., 265
Cheung, S., 810
Chopra, O. P., 11
Christen, R. P., 579
Chuma, H., 416–419
Churchill, C. F., 583
Ciccone, A., 110, 136, 151
Clark, C., 273
Cline, W. R., 454, 455

Coale, A. J., 286, 312, 331
Coate, S., 579, 580, 605, 610
Copeland, B., 637
Corbo, V., 703
Crawford, E., 455
Crawford, J., 671
Czukas, K., 593

Dalton, H., 177
Dam, K. W., 724
Das Gupta, M., xvii, 312, 313, 393
Dasgupta, P., 32, 272, 276, 495, 497–499
David, P. A., 132
de Janvry, A., 223, 458
De Long, B., 76–79
de Melo, J., 742, 743
Deaton, A., 253, 265, 284, 598, 600
Deininger, K., 23, 24, 26, 185, 203, 206, 208, 209, 222, 239, 446, 453, 454, 456
Deolalikar, A., 251, 265–267
Desai, M., 29
Diamond, P. A., 667
Dixit, A. K., 110, 151, 353, 638
Dobb, M., 57, 368, 369
Domar, E., 55
Drèze, J. P., 276, 281, 282
Dutta, B., xvii, 441, 565

Easterly, W., 32
Eaton, J., 82, 687
Edirisinghe, N., 265
Edwards, S., 694
Eichengreen, B., 687
Eicher, C., 358
Engerman, S., 278, 408
Esguerra, E., 574
Esteban, J., xvii, 195
Eswaran, M., 437, 507
Ethier, W., 638

Fafchamps, M., 593, 605, 611
Feder, G., 446, 453, 454, 456, 580
Feenstra, R. C., 719, 720
Fei, J. C. H., 195, 353, 361–363, 365, 366
Feldstein, M., 104
Fernandez, R., 158, 687, 721, 733, 755
Fields, G. S., xvi, 190, 191, 195, 202, 205, 209, 221, 239, 259
Findlay, R., 720
Fischer, S., 703
Fishlow, A., 258
Flam, H., 737
Floro, M. S., 537, 542, 563, 573, 574, 577
Fogel, R., 278, 408
Foroutan, F., 745
Foster, A., 264, 281, 282

Foster, J. E., xvi, 173, 181, 184, 190, 256, 265, 290, 292
Francois, P., xvi, 136
Frankel, J. A., 629, 631
Friedman, M., 252
Fuentes, G., xvi

Gale, D., 146
Galor, O., 227, 235, 317
Gang, I., xvi
Gangopadhyay, S., 568
Garcia, M., 265
Garg, A., 285
Geary, R. C., 13
Georgescu-Roegen, N., 354
Geron, P., 538
Gersovitz, M., 687
Ghatak, M., 441, 444, 445, 580
Ghate, P. B., 574
Ghosh, P., xvi, 558
Gibbons, R., 757
Gillis, M., 342
Gintis, H., 507
Glewwe, P., 29, 262
Gordon, R. H., 104
Gough, K., 506, 507
Greer, J., 256, 292
Griliches, Z., 732
Grossman, G. M., 110, 111, 151
Guinanne, T., 581
Gupta, B., xvi
Gupta, P., 11
Gupta, S., 11

Haddad, L. J., 265
Hanson, A. H., 142, 143
Harrigan, J., 703
Harris, C., 29
Harris, J., 372, 373, 378–380
Harrod, R., 55
Hassan, M. N., 265
Haswell, M., 273
Hayami, Y., 416–419
Heckscher, E., 631
Helpman, E., 110, 111, 151, 638
Henderson, V., 741
Heredia, C., 698, 699
Heston, A., 12
Higgins, P., 265
Hillman, A., 720
Hirsch, W. Z., 671
Hirschman, A. O., 138, 144, 146, 153, 200, 741
Hoel, P. G., 782
Hoff, K., 561, 575
Hongladoran, C., 456
Hoover, E. M., 312, 331

Hopper, N. D., 506
Hopper, W. D., 506, 507
Horioka, C., 104
Horowitz, A. W., 458
Hotchkiss, D., 265
Houantchekon, L., 407
Hsu, C., xvi
Hudec, R. E., 725
Hudson, M. C., 221
Huppi, M., 580
Huynh, H.-L., xvi, 747

Ingram, W. D., 741
Irwin, D., 725
Isenman, P., 29

Jackson, J., 725
Jain, S., 221
Jakubson, G. H., 209, 239
Jodha, N. S., 418, 421, 423, 600
Jones, R. W., 629, 631
Jorgenson, D., 353

Kalecki, M., 361
Kanbur, R., 205, 206
Kao, C., 358
Kelley, V., 455
Kemp, M., 730
Kenney, E., 265
Keyter, C., 278
Khandker, S. R., 582, 583
Klasen, S., 286
Kletzer, K., 605, 611
Kochar, A., 282, 573
Koenig, M., 325
Kortum, S., 82
Kotwal, A., xvi, 437, 507, 637
Kovenock, D., 725
Kranton, R., 558
Kremer, M., 333, 335–337
Krishnamurty, J., 276
Krueger, A. O., 720
Krugman, P., 136, 144, 147, 629, 631, 638, 641,
    642, 716, 717, 741, 747, 750
Kumar, B. G., 285
Kumar, S. K., 265
Kurup, T. V. N., 542, 546
Kuznets, S., 23, 45, 187, 199, 202, 238, 333, 777
Kyn, O., 205

La Ferrara, E., 605
Lancaster, K., 447, 638, 728
Langoni, C., 817
Larson, D., 539
Lee, R., 333
Leibenstein, H., 817

Lewis, O., 312, 506, 507
Lewis, T. R., 719
Lewis, W. A., 353, 355–358, 361–363, 366
Ligon, E., 604
Lim, Y., 600
Lin, J. Y., 371
Lindert, P. H., 207, 208, 225, 685, 687, 694
Lipsey, R., 447, 727, 728
Lipton, M., 262, 371
López-Calva, L.-F., xvi, 696
Loury, G. C., 238, 579
Lucas, R. E., 7, 9, 10, 32, 47, 100, 113
Lustig, N., 696

Madajewicz, M., 581
Maddison, A., 76, 77
Magee, S. P., 720
Mahalanobis, P. C., 142
Majumdar, M., xvii
Malthus, T., 302
Mani, A., xvi, 223
Mankiw, N. G., 84, 86, 100, 103
Manove, M., 147
Mansuri, G., xvi, 438, 562
Marichal, C., 687
Markusen, J., 637
Matsuyama, K., 110, 136, 144, 147, 151
Mauro, P., 32
Mayer, W., 720
McBride, T., 278
McKernan, S-M., 582
McMillan, J., 371
Meesook, O. A., 259, 265
Mehta, R., 11
Mencken, J., 281, 282
Messerlin, P. A., 716
Mill, J. S., 715, 725
Mingmaneenakin, W., 534, 543, 557
Mirrlees, J. A., 280, 667
Mitra, P., 565
Mitra, T., xvii
Mookherjee, D., xvi, xvii, 444, 449, 457, 670
Morduch, J., xvi, 259, 284, 285, 579, 581, 583, 600
Morley, S. A., 17
Morris, C. T., 205
Morris, D. M., 28
Morrisson, C., 205
Morton, P. J., 685, 687, 694
Mosley, P., 583, 703
Mukherjee, A., 276, 506, 518
Mukherjee, P., 507
Mukhopadhyay, H., xvi, 702
Murphy, K., 136, 154, 223, 225
Myrdal, G., 741

Naqvi, S. N. H., 29
Nash, J., 759
Nettayarak, P., 534, 543, 557
Newbery, D. M. G., 435, 436, 438
Newman, A., 227, 235, 268, 393
Nogués, J. J., 743
Nove, A., 57
Nurkse, R., 353, 358, 364

Obstfeld, M., 629, 631
Ohlin, B., 631
Okun, A. M., 238
Olson, M., 719, 720
Onchan, T., 456
Orshansky, M., 250
Osborne, M. J., 757
Oshima, H. T., 199, 202
Otsuka, K., 416–419

Page, S., 621, 625
Pal, S., 519
Panagariya, A., 742, 743
Papanek, G. F., 205
Parente, S. L., 16, 18, 80
Pareto, V., 467, 719, 720
Paukert, F., 202, 205, 206, 239
Paulsen, A., 605
Paxson, C., 600
Pearson, S. R., 741
Perkins, D., 342
Perotti, R., 218
Persson, T., 218
Pesendorfer, W., 147
Phillips, J., 325
Pigou, A. C., 177
Pingali, P. L., 452
Pinstrup-Andersen, P., 265
Pinthong, C., 534, 543, 557
Pitt, M. M., 265, 582, 583
Poapongsakorn, N., 534, 543, 557
Polak, J. J., 703, 704
Powelson, J. P., 458, 460–462
Prebisch, R., 651
Prescott, E. C., 16, 18, 80
Pritchett, L., 32
Prusa, T., 716
Puetz, D., 265
Purcell, M., 698, 699

Quah, D., 19, 741
Quintanilla, R., 743

Rahman, O., 281, 282
Raj, K. N., 143, 554
Rakshit, M. K., 353, 361
Ranis, G., 353, 361–363, 365, 366
Rao, V. K. R. V., 361

Ravallion, M., 265, 605, 610
Ray, D., 146, 195, 223, 272, 276, 441, 495,
    497–500, 506, 518, 537, 558, 565, 570, 573,
    577, 667, 670, 750
Reardon, T., 455
Reddy, C. R., 507
Rhyne, E., 579
Ricardo, D., 715, 725
Richards, A., 513
Roberts, K. W. S., 176
Robinson, J., xvi
Robinson, S., 205
Rodgers, G., 278
Rodríguez-Clare, A., 136, 151, 154
Rodrik, D., 158, 218, 220–222, 240, 720, 721, 733,
    755
Roemer, M., 342
Rogoff, K., 687
Romer, P., 84, 86, 100, 103, 109–111, 113, 114, 151
Ros, J., 696
Rosenberg, N., 225
Rosenstein-Rodan, P., 136, 137, 140, 144, 146,
    153, 358, 499, 500
Rosenzweig, M. R., 264, 265, 454–456, 592, 600,
    605
Rostow, W. W., 49
Rothschild, M., 200
Rubinstein, A., 757
Rudd, J., 284
Rudra, A., 507
Ryan, J. G., 349, 453, 486, 518

Sachs, J., 686, 688, 693
Sadoulet, E., 223, 563
Sahn, D., 265
Sala-i-Martin, X., 105
Sanders, J. H., 265
Satsanguan, P., 534, 543, 557
Saxonhouse, G., 750
Schultz, T. P., 317, 318
Schultz, T. W., 358, 359
Scitovsky, T., 153, 717, 718
Sen, A., 453, 454
Sen, A. K., xvii, 10, 46, 170, 173, 176, 186, 251,
    256, 283, 284, 286, 290, 292, 353, 359, 361,
    452, 667
Sengupta, K., xvii, 440, 441, 565, 568, 570
Shaban, R. A., 349, 422, 423, 430, 449, 453
Shapiro, C., 507
Shell, K., 109, 111
Shetty, S., 440
Shleifer, A., 136, 154, 223, 225
Shorrocks, A. F., 184
Siamwalla, A., 534, 543, 557
Simmons, R., 325
Simon, J., 333
Singer, H., 651

Singh, N., 430, 441
Singh, R. P., 600
Smith, A., 725
Snodgrass, D., 342
Solow, R., 63
Somanathan, E., 218
Somanathan, R., 732
Squire, L., 23, 24, 26, 185, 203, 206, 208, 209, 222, 239
Srinivas, M. N., 506
Srinivasan, T. N., 29, 384, 565
Staiger, R., 712, 717, 724, 725
Stark, O., 605
Stern, N., 600
Stiglitz, J. E., 110, 151, 280, 420, 438, 507, 554, 561, 565, 575, 580, 638
Stock, R., 458, 460–462
Strauss, E., 671
Strauss, J., 265
Streeten, P. P., 7, 9, 29
Streufert, P., 272, 500
Subramanian, S., 265, 284, 285
Summers, L., 32
Summers, R., 12
Sundaram, K., 276
Sundari, T. K., 506, 507
Syrquin, M., 205
Székely, M., 696, 698, 699

Tabellini, G., 218
Takagi, Y., 361
Taylor, C. L., 221
Teitelbaum, M. S., 305
Tendulkar, S., 276
Theil, H., 190
Thomas, D., 265
Thomas, J., 605, 611
Thorbecke, E., 256, 292
Thursby, M., 725
Timmer, C. P., 265
Todaro, M., 372, 373, 378–380
Townsend, R., 598, 600
Toye, J., 703
Trairatvorakul, P., 265
Trefler, D., 716
Tubpun, Y., 534, 543, 557

Udry, C., 455, 537, 542, 593, 613, 615
Umali, D., 539, 576
Uzawa, H., 100

van der Gaag, J., 262
van Tassell, E., 580
Velenchik, A., xvi
Venables, A., 739
Viner, J., 359, 360, 726, 728
Visaria, P., 276
Vishny, R., 136, 154, 223, 225
Vogel, R., 579
Vohra, R., xvii, 750
von Braun, J., 265
von Neumann, J., 103
Von Pischke, J. D., 573
Vyas, V. S., 507

Walker, T. S., 349, 453, 486, 518, 600
Wan, H. Y., 730
Ward, J. O., 265
Watson, J., 558
Webb, P., 265
Webb, S., 703
Weil, D., 84, 86, 100, 103, 317
Weiss, A., 554
Weisskoff, R., 190
Weitzman, M. L., 663
Wellisz, S., 720
Wen, G. J., 452
Whalley, J., 371, 733
Williamson, J. G., 207, 208, 225, 310
Williamson-Gray, C., 265
Winter, J. M., 305
Winters, L. A., 739
Wolfe, B. L., 265
Wolfson, M. C., 195
Wolpin, K. I., 456, 592, 600
Woolcock, M., 579, 581
Worrall, T., 605, 611
Wright, B., 605, 611
Wright, T. P., 670
Wydick, B., xvi

Xuan, V. T., 452

Yi, S-S., 750
Yotopoulos, P., 542, 563, 574
Young, A., 121–123
Young, A. A., 147
Young, L., 720

Zeira, J., 227, 235
Zhu, L., 371
Zimmerman, F., xvi

Subject Index

Adult equivalence scales, 252
Age bias, 281
Agency problem, 463–465
Agglomeration, 741
Agricultural surplus, 361, 362, 364, 365, 367, 372
    average, 364
Agriculture, 34, 35, 259, 333, 334, 345, 346,
    348–354, 364, 366, 367, 370, 373, 380, 384,
    407, 409, 514, 515
    collectivization, 369
    commercialization of, 366
    cropping patterns, 349, 350
    draft power, 351
    economic efficiency, 415
    fertilizer use, 351
    irrigation, 350
    markets, 403–414
    output, 361
    pricing policy, 369
    productivity, 303, 307
    rainfall, 349, 350
    seasonal fluctuations, 488
    soil fertility, 349
    taxation, 367–369
Andean Pact, 743, 744
Anonymity principle, 174, 175, 178, 181
Aspirations, 216, 217
    and savings, 214
Assets, 227, 259, 309
    market, 495
    productive, 259
    stocks, 171

Balance, macroeconomic, 52, 54
Balance of payments, 370, 696, 703
Bias, age, see Age Bias
Bias, gender, see Gender bias
Bias, selection, see Selection bias
Birth rate, 33, 34, 60, 297–303, 306, 307, 313

Calorie elasticities, 264
Capacity curve, 274, 279, 489–491, 495, 502
Capital, 54, 55, 64, 68, 72–74, 81, 85, 91, 92, 99,
    110, 111, 114, 117–119, 171, 172, 223, 225,
    229, 330
    accumulation, 64, 101, 115, 121, 122, 366
    agriculture, 36

cost of, 514
and credit, 412–414
fixed, 531
growth, 88
human, 53, 100–107, 109, 110, 112, 120, 121,
    123, 125, 198, 220, 235, 237, 238, 261, 285
marginal product of, 117
nutritional, 237
per capita, 93
physical, 100–102, 106, 112, 120, 121, 123, 125,
    235
social, 393, 394, 601
working, 531, 537, 568–570
Capital accumulation, 59, 112, 113, 120, 134, 650,
    693
    human, 107
Capital goods, 39, 51, 52
Capital growth, aggregate, 119
Capital market, 149, 354
    and development, 226–237
    and inequality, 226–237
Capital stock, 64–67, 70, 74, 88, 89, 110, 113, 328,
    329
    aggregate, 119
Capital–labor ratio, 67, 329
Capital–output ratio, 55, 56, 58, 64–68, 70, 73,
    88, 90, 328
Carrying capacity, 302, 303, 307
Case studies
    Agriculture versus Industry in the New
        Soviet Union, 368, 369
    Attitudes to Population, 305, 306
    Bolivia's Formal and Informal Sectors, 347,
        348
    Cost of Information and the Credit Market:
        Chambar, Pakistan, The, 559–561
    Credit as Insurance: A Case Study from
        Northern Nigeria, 613–615
    Formal Lenders in Thailand, 534–536
    Growth Engineering: The Soviet Experience,
        56, 57
    Heavy Industry as a Leading Sector: Early
        Planning in India, 142, 143
    Hot Summer in Rio, A, 689, 690
    Import Substitution: Brazil, 674–676

Informal Lenders in the Philippines, 537–540

Is Sharecropping Associated with Lower Yields, 430, 431

Labor Markets in the ICRISAT Villages, 485, 486

Labor Teams and Tournaments in Rural West Africa, 407–409

Land Reforms: South Korea and Mexico, 458–462

Learning by Doing, 670–672

Nutrition and Income: A Case Study from South India, 264–267

Operation Barga, 444, 445

Outward Orientation in South Korea, 683, 684

Purchasing Power Parity Measurement of Income, 12–14

Recent Changes in OECD Wages and Unemployment, 731, 732

Santiniketan's Rickshaws, 521, 522

Saving and Investment, 53

Secular Changes in Labor Tying in India, 506, 507

Self-Insurance and Bullocks, 592, 593

Sharecropping in the Sindh, Pakistan, 438, 439

Sibling Rivalry: Evidence from Ghana, 285

Social Norms and a New Fertility Decline, 325, 326

Surplus Labor: A Natural Experiment, 358, 359

Tenancy in the ICRISAT Villages, 420–423

Three Generations, 312, 313

Tunnel Effect, The, 200, 201

Vertical Formal–Informal Linkages: The Philippines, 573–575

Women's Wages and Fertility Decline: A Study of Sweden, 317, 318

Cash crops, 348

Central American Common Market, 743, 744

Children
    conservation of costs, 321–323
    costs of, 315, 327, 331
    costs of rearing, 314
    direct costs, 314, 316
    opportunity cost, 314–317
    social cost, 319–321

Coefficient of variation, 189–191, 206

Collateral, 226–230, 235, 237, 268, 533, 534, 536, 537, 546–548

Collectivization, 371, 452, 458

Communal farms, 460

Communauté Economique de l'Afrique de l'Ouest, 745, 746

Comparative advantage, 40, 630
    dynamic, 714
    economies of scale, 638–642
    factor endowments, 631–636

    sources, 630–642
    static, 714
    technology, 630, 631

Compensation
    market-determined rate, 153
    minimum, 388, 389

Competition, 152–154
    perfect, 111

Complementarity, 114–116, 132–136, 152

Conditionality, 703, 704

Conformism, 323–326; *see also* Social norms

Congestion effect, 135

Consumer durables, 39

Consumer surplus, 666

Consumption, 54, 59, 115, 219, 227, 280, 327, 328, 332, 345, 519
    agricultural, 365
    autarkic, 628, 629
    average, 255
    composition, 223
    conspicuous, 214
    domestic, 665
    group, 598
    household, 284
    household-level, 598
    individual, 598
    industrial, 365
    item-by-item, 251
    level, 223
    mean, 255
    overall expenditure, 251
    per capita, 249, 262

Consumption basket, 623

Consumption goods, 51, 223

Consumption smoothing, 591, 592

Contraception, 324–327

Contract, 404
    fixed-wage, 435, 436
    interlinked, *see* Credit, interlinked transactions
    limited liability, 442
    long-run, 277
    long-term, 514
    nonrenewal of, 509
    nonverifiable information, 442
    optimal, 467–470
    paired, 478
    permanent, 517–522
    renewal of, 442
    short-term, 405
    tied, 518, 520

Contractual enforcement, limits, 404

Convergence, 70, 74–87
    conditional, 82–84, 89, 105–107, 131
    unconditional, 74, 75, 80, 83, 89, 105, 106

Convergence hypothesis, 80

Coordination, 139
  equilibrium, 137, 138
  failure, 136, 138, 140, 147, 154, 655
Coordination games, 138, 607, 712, 721–723
  limited enforcement, 765, 766
  social norms, 764, 765
  tourists' dilemma, 762, 763
Correlation, *see* Statistical methods
Correlation coefficient, *see* Statistical methods
Cost–benefit analysis, 157
Credit, 227
  access to, 231, 234, 235, 243, 519
  alternative policies, 572–584
  as insurance, 612–615
  and capital, 409–414
  collateral, 533
  consumption, 276, 531, 532
  cooperatives, 537, 538
  demand, 531, 532
  efficient surplus, 565
  formal–informal links, 573–578
  hidden, 563
  interest on, 563, 564
  interest-free, 563, 564
  interlinkages and, 565
  interlinkages and enforcement, 564, 565
  interlinkages and information, 564
  interlinked transactions, 541, 561–572
  involuntary default, 529
  layering, 540
  limited liability, 533
  limits, 529–531
  production, 568
  rate of return, 533
  repayment, 533
  repayment in labor, 565–568
  repayment in output, 568–572
  risk, 533, 566, 580
  rural, 537
  screening, 558
  strategic default, 529
  voluntary default, 529
Credit associations, 538
Credit contract, 457
  pure, 570, 572
Credit market, 227–230, 232, 234, 235, 237, 238,
    242, 268, 269, 276, 285, 413, 529, 531
  access, 270
  exclusivity, 543
  formal, 268
  imperfect, 241
  informal, 268, 536–561
  informal, lender's monopoly, 543, 544
  informal, lender's risk, 544
  informational constraints, 540
  interest rate, 541, 542

  interlinkage, 541, 544, 561–563, 565, 584
  mobility and, 268
  rationing, 542, 543
  rural, 532–543
  rural characteristics of, 540–543
  segmentation, 540, 541
Credit rating, 227
Credit rationing, 406, 548–555
  and informational asymmetrics, 553
Credit smoothing, 593
Credit unions, 538
Customs and economic union of Central Africa,
    745

Dalton transfer
  progressive, 183
  regressive, 183
Dalton transfer principle, 177, 178, 181, 182, 187
Death rate, 33, 60, 297–303, 306, 307, 312, 313
  age-specific, 282, 298, 300
Debt crisis, 693, 694, 696
  1980s, 685–690
  Latin America, 17
Debt–export ratio, 686
Default, 226, 227, 229, 237, 545–561
  costs and benefits, 228
  and enforcement, 555–561
  expected cost, 229
  intentional, 268
  involuntary, 544, 547, 548
  no-default constraint, 551
  participation constraint, 551
  risk, 545
  strategic, 544, 564
  voluntary, 544, 547
Demand, 139, 152
  consumption, 52
  derived, 223
  economic, 334, 335
  elasticity, 681
  factors, 225
  input, 223
  market, 52
  pattern, 223
  product, 223
Demand curve, 664
  residual, 661
Demographic history, 302–304, 306, 326, 327
Demographic structure, 299
Demographic transition, 60, 61, 302, 303, 306,
    307, 335
Depreciation, rate, 82
Deprivation
  relative, 256
  sustained, 253
Devaluation, 692, 695

Developing countries, definition, 3
Development, 28
    economic, 7–9, 18, 24, 151, 249, 295
    human, 25–29, 32
Diminishing marginal utility, 390
    principle of, 268
Diminishing returns, 67, 70, 71, 73, 81, 89, 93,
        102, 105, 107, 569
    to labor, 332
Discrimination, 281
    against children, 281–283
    against elderly, 281–283
    against females, 281–283, 285, 288
    against women, 313, 314
Disease, 27
Disguised unemployment, 360, 362, 364, 365
Distribution
    functional, 173
    personal, 172, 192, 223
Divergence, conditional, 105
Domestic servants, 278
Domestic supply curve, 663
Double-incentive problem, 436, 437
Doubling time, 17
Dual economy, 210, 353, 354
Dummy variable
    country-specific, 207–209
    democracy, 221, 222

East Asian miracle, 119–123
EC, *see* European Economic Community
Economic Community of Western African
        States, 745
Economic development, 249
Economic expansion, 17
Economic growth, *see* Growth
Economic surplus, 427
    maximization of, 428
Economy
    dual, 210, 353, 354
    formal urban sector, 346–348
    informal urban sector, 346–348
    rural, 345–398
    sectors of, 345
    urban, 345–398
Education, 28, 34, 100, 106, 119–121, 123, 210,
        237, 238, 258, 284, 286, 319
    school enrollment rates, 107
Efficiency losses, deadweight, 667
Employment, *see* Unemployment
    wage, 261
Endowments, distribution of, 198
Energy balance, 272–275
    energy required for work, 273
    input, 272
    resting metabolism, 273
    storage and borrowing, 273

Energy deficit, 273
Energy surplus, 273
Engel's law, 651
Entrepreneurship, 229–236, 242, 243
Equilibrium, 116, 140, 143
    multiple, 116, 135, 136, 152
    of beliefs, 116
    trap, 136, 143, 723
Equilibrium investment rate, 115
EU, *see* European Union, *see also* European
        Economic Community and European
        Common Market
European Common Market, 713
European Economic Community, 713, 716, 726
European Union, 713, 726, 730, 737–740; *see also*
        European Common Market and European
        Economic Community
    Common Agricultural Policy, 739
Eviction, 441–445
    banning, 443
Exchange rate, 12, 14, 15, 678
    competitive, 695
    depreciation, 693
    devaluation, 695
    equilibrium, 659, 660
    method, 10
Expectations, 116
Expenditure, household versus individual, 252
Exponential growth, 295
Export promotion
    access to credit, 682
    basic concepts, 677
    directed subsidies, 682
    exchange rates, 678, 679, 681
    export subsidy, 679–682
    import quotas for exporters, 678
    instruments, 679–684
    positive externalities, 682
    preferential credit, 678
    primary products, 651, 653
    reduced import duties, 678
    targeted nonprimary exports, 677
Exports, 39, 622
    composition, 622–626
    primary, 40, 41
    promotion, 676–684
    voluntary restrictions, 715
Externality, 133–135, 152–154
    negative, 112, 113, 115
    positive, 112–115, 150

Factor endowments, *see* Comparative advantage
    capital, 633
Factor(s) of production, 118
Families, joint, 321–323
Family-planning programs, 324–327

Farms
  owner-cultivated, 417, 419, 453
  owner-occupied, 453, 505
Fertility, 297, 303, 309–314, 316, 317, 319, 320,
    322–324
  age-specific, 300
  cost–benefit, 315, 317, 320, 321, 331
  hoarding versus targeting, 314
  missing markets, 308
  rate, 301, 315, 318, 324, 325, 331
  total, 300
Fertilizer, 333
Financial market, reforms, 703
Five Year Plan
  India, 142, 143
  Soviet Union, 57
Fixed-rent tenancy, 433, 434, 436, 438, 440, 441;
    see also Tenancy
Fixed-wage contract, *see* Contract
Fluctuation aversion, 515–517
Food adequacy standard, 262
Food supply, 333, 334
Foster–Greer–Thorbecke index, 291, 292
Free-market, 667
  economy, 694
Free-rider problem, 452
Free-trade, 626, 664, 665, 667
  agreements, 732, 736, 737, 741
Free-trade bloc, 750
Free-trade zone, 730, 741, 742, 744, 752

Gains-from-trade theorem, 718, 719
Game theory
  adopting a new technology, 758
  basic concepts, 757–759
  contracts, 771–773
  credibility, 767–771
  discounting, 774
  externalities and policy, 766, 767
  fertility decision, 758
  landlord–tenant relationship, 759
  protecting an industry, 759
  repeated games, 773
  strategies, 757
  subgame perfection, 768–771
  and time, 767–775
Game tree, 769
GATT, *see* General Agreement on Trade and
    Tariffs
GDP, *see* Gross domestic product
Gender bias, 283, 284, 286, 287, 311, 313, 314,
    317
General Agreement on Trade and Tariffs, 621,
    697, 711–713, 716, 723–725, 734, 747
  regional clause, 713
Gini coefficient, 188–191, 202, 206, 221

GNP, *see* Gross national product
Goodness-of-fit, 79
Goods
  capital, 39, 51, 52
  nontraded, 12, 13
  traded, 12
Gosplan, 57
Great Leap Forward, 371
Gross domestic product, 8, 13, 29, 48, 77–79, 86,
    697
  per capita, 104, 106, 202
Gross national product, 8–10, 16, 17, 20, 38, 203,
    204
  per capita, 205
  total, 55
Group lending
  peer monitoring, 580
  positive assortative matching, 579, 580
  potential drawbacks, 580, 581
Growth, 87
  capital, aggregate, 119
  economic, 25, 31, 47, 54, 61–64, 88, 211, 217,
    218
  endogenous, 107
  and income, 10–21
  and inequality, 218
  per capita, 17, 55, 63, 71, 89, 99, 106, 328, 330
  population, 33, 34, 37, 55, 60–63, 65, 68, 71, 72,
    82, 84, 86, 88, 103
  steady state rate, 83
  sustained, 49, 107
  urban, 36, 37
Growth effect, 69
Growth engineering, 56
Growth model, 114, 327
Growth rate, 56, 67, 69, 81–83, 102–106, 131, 211,
    215, 225, 336
Growth theory, endogenous, 103

Harris–Todaro equilibrium, 378–380, 384, 392
Harris–Todaro model, 372, 373, 379, 393, 394
  equilibrium, 374–379
Harrod–Domar equations, 90
Harrod–Domar model, 51–64, 80, 81, 87, 88, 102,
    103, 105, 107, 328, 330–332, 355
HC, *see* Head count
HCR, *see* Head-count ratio
HDI, *see* Human development index
Head count, 254, 255
Head-count index, 290
Head-count ratio, 254, 256, 291
Heckscher–Ohlin model, 631, 635, 637, 640, 642,
    648, 731, 732
Heston–Summers data set, 12, 80, 86
High-yielding varieties, 352

History
    social norms, 155, 156
    the status quo, 156–159
History versus expectations, 143, 144, 146, 147
Hoarding, 314
Household, female-headed, 259, 282
Household size, and poverty, 258
Human development index, 28–30
Human Development Report, 28
Hyperinflation, 692
Hypothesis
    alternative hypothesis, 802
    null hypothesis, 798, 799, 801, 802
    testing, 75, 599, 800, 801, 803

ICP, *see* International Comparison Program
ICRISAT, 349–352
ICRISAT villages, 266, 418, 420–423, 430, 431,
    453, 454, 518, 592, 598–600
IGR, *see* Income gap ratio
Illiteracy, 261
    rates, 286
Immigration, 104, 304
Imperfect markets, 403
Import substitution, 656–676
    basic concepts, 657
    exchange rates, 658–660
    individual, 741
    inward orientation, 676, 685, 695
    joint, 741
    main problem, 674
    move away, 684–699
    outward orientation, 676, 683, 684, 695
    protection, 698
    returns to scale, 672, 673
    spillovers, 672
    tariffs and quotas, 657, 658, 660–665
    unequal treatment of imported goods, 657
Imports, 41
    structure and composition, 654
    voluntary expansions, 715
Incentives, 404, 405, 451, 465, 472, 473, 475
    constraint, 475, 477
    hidden action, 463–465
    hidden information, 463, 464, 586
    moral hazard, 270, 271, 404, 463–465, 602
Income, 68, 69, 72, 213, 216, 316, 317
    average, 255
    categories, 172
    changes, 18
    classes, 175
    distribution, 10–22, 26, 32, 169–174, 176–178,
        183, 187, 189, 190, 204, 205, 207, 211, 223,
        225, 249, 416, 654, 655
    distribution, complete ranking of, 185
    distribution, mean, 186

    earned, 316
    functional, 171
    functional, distribution of, 172
    high, 3, 206
    household versus individual, 252
    inequality, 220, 221
    labor, 232
    land, 495
    low, 3, 19, 20, 206, 275
    magnitudes, 181
    mean, 255
    middle, 3, 20, 25
    nonlabor, 496–498
    per capita, 10, 11, 15–17, 19, 25, 26, 28–32, 34,
        38, 39, 41, 50, 58, 60–62, 68, 70, 73, 74, 76,
        78, 80–84, 86–88, 99, 102, 103, 105, 120, 199,
        203, 205, 209, 211, 220, 221, 225, 258, 298,
        328, 332, 334–337
    permanent, 252
    personal, 171
    relative, 176, 177, 181
    sampling, 79
    share, 22, 23, 25, 118, 182, 191, 199, 204
    sources, 172
    temporary, 252
    total, 69
    underreporting, 11
    wage, 241
Income and growth, 10–21
Income gap ratio, 255, 256, 291
Income growth
    compensatory, 209, 210
    even, 209
    per capita, 220, 331
    uneven, 209, 210
Income inequality, 220, 221
    effect on the rate of growth, 215
    effect on the rate of savings, 215
Income maximization, family, 395
Income–savings curve, *see* Savings–income
    curve
Income sharing, 357
Income smoothing, 517–519, 591, 594
Income–inequality curve, 206
Income-earning potential, 280, 281, 309
Indifference curve, 471, 472
Industrial feeding, 278
Industrial productivity, 303
Industrialization, 210
Industry, 354, 362
Inequality, 25
    asset, 220
    and demand composition, 223–226
    and development, 237, 238
    economic, 170, 216

functional, 197
and growth, 218, 220–223
historical, 198
income, 217, 222
land, 220, 222
measurement of, 173–192, 206
wealth, 217, 220, 222
Inequality index, 174, 178, 190, 192
Inequality measure
coefficient of variation, 187
Gini coefficient, 188
Kuznets ratios, 187
mean absolute deviation, 187
range, 187
Inequality–income
curve, 207
relationship, 206, 209
Infant mortality, 26–28, 30, 284, 310, 314, 331
Inflation, 17, 692, 693
Informal sector, 37, 261
Information
incomplete, 4, 5, 289, 318, 405, 441
lack of complete, 663
transmission, 520, 556–561, 601
Innovation, 333–335
supply-driven, 337
Input–output coefficient, 627
Inputs
per capita, 93
variety, 151
Institutions, informal, 348, 403, 406, 407, 614
Insurance, 270–272, 308, 309, 391, 464, 465
access, 606
aggregate shocks, 610
basic concepts, 591–596
correlated shocks, 610
crop, 530, 595
demand, 531, 532
disability, 308
enforcement, 605–610
enforcement constraint, 607, 611
formal, 271
idiosyncratic shock, 595–597, 600
imperfect, 608–610
informal, 271, 530
in land rentals, 410, 411
life, 308, 309
limits to, 529–531, 600–605
medical, 308
mixed-credit, 612
mutual, 406, 594, 595, 602, 605–607, 610, 611
nonmonetary, 271
perfect, 606–610
perfect, model, 596–600
and productivity, 448, 449
pure, 594

second-best, 604, 608, 610
self-, 591–593, 610
Interest, hidden, *see* Credit
International Comparison Program, 13
International Crop Research Institute for the
Semi-Arid Tropics, *see* ICRISAT and
ICRISAT villages
International Monetary Fund, 701–705
Inverted-U
curve, 207
hypothesis, 23, 199–206, 208, 211
hypothesis, cross-section study, 201–206
Investment, 52, 54, 56, 65, 86, 112, 114, 115, 135,
140, 141, 219, 222, 229, 230, 238, 328, 355
allocation, 139
complementary, 137
coordinated, 139
human capital, 103
rate of return, 554–556
rates, 120, 131, 218
savings and, 53
Investment–gross domestic product ratio, 86
Irrigation, 333

Labor, 36, 37, 40, 64, 65, 68, 72, 73, 82, 85, 88, 89,
91, 92, 114, 117, 118, 121, 122, 152, 171, 211,
223, 225, 229, 231–233, 273, 316, 329, 330,
355, 361, 362, 364, 366, 368, 405, 424, 425,
448, 483
bonded, 548
casual, 484–487, 500, 503, 508–514, 517, 519
demand, 232, 366, 511, 513, 514, 518
demand curve, 234, 382, 394, 492, 495, 496
and economic development, 512–515
effective, 89
effective units, 85
efficiency unit, 72–74
formal-sector, 383
grades, 100
landless, 260
long-term, 484–487, 504–522
long-term permanent, 348
marginal product of, 117
no-shirking constraint, 510–512, 520
opportunity cost, 450
permanent, 504–522
quality, 102
rural, 348, 513
seasonal, 518
seasonal, demand, 515
skilled, 100, 104
skilled versus unskilled, 225, 226
supply, 275, 345, 490–492, 499, 511, 513
supply and demand, 484, 486–489, 492, 493,
495

supply curve, 234, 367, 492, 496
tied, 506, 517–520
unskilled, 100, 101, 104, 107
wage, 260
Labor contract, permanent, 513, 521; *see also*
Contract
Labor force, 332
nonagricultural, 353
quality, 119
Labor market, 241, 272, 483, 486, 487, 495
demand, 235
equilibrium, 492, 493, 497, 499, 511, 512
incentives, 411
nonlabor assets, 494, 495
and nutrition, 489–504
permanent, 504–522
and poverty, 489–504
and productivity, 449, 450
supply, 235
Labor resources, allocation, 382, 383
Labor teams, 408, 409
productivity, 408
Labor–land ratio, 409, 445, 446
Labor–leisure preferences, 232
Land, 172
ceilings, 220
communal tenure, 417
contracts, 441–445
distribution, 221, 409, 412, 415
distribution, operational, 140
holding, 260
inequality, 221
and labor, 409, 410
leases, 419
market, 415
owner-occupied, 423
ownership, 416–419, 445–462
pooling, 451, 452
redistribution, 458–461
reform, 218, 220, 457–462, 498, 499
sales, 456, 457
size and productivity, 446–455
tenancy, 270, 416–419
Landholding, 421
Land–labor ratio, 411, 412, 483
Land-lease market, 415, 422
Landlessness, 421
Landlord–tenant relationship, 404
principal–agent theory, 465
tenancy contracts, 466–474
Land-to-the-tiller scheme, 459
Latin American Free Trade Agreement, 743, 744
Latin American Integration Association, 743, 744
Latin effect, 207
Learning by doing, 669–672

Lender's monopoly, *see* Credit markets, informal
Lender's risk hypothesis, *see* Credit markets,
informal
Lenders, *see* Credit and Credit markets
informal, 536–541
institutional, 532–536
Level effect, 69
Lewis model, 353–372
Lewis–Ranis–Fei model, 366, 367
Life expectancy, 26–28, 30
Lifeboat problem, 279, 281, 283
Limited liability, 406; *see also* Contract
and sharecropping, 439, 440
Linkage
backward, 138–141, 153, 154
forward, 138–141, 154
number of, 140
and policy, 138
strength of, 140
Literacy, 27, 28, 30, 106
Loan, 227, 229, 268, 269; *see also* Credit
ability to repay, 226
fixed-capital, 545, 546
repayment, 228
sanctions, 226, 227
size limitation, 229, 230
structural adjustment, 703
willingness to repay, 226
Loan enforcement, 529, 530
Loan repayment, *see* Default
Lock-in effect, 134–136
Lorenz
consistency, 181, 188, 189
criterion, 181–183
crossings, 190, 206
curve, 178–184, 189–191, 206
Luxury good, 223

Macroeconomic balance equation, 52, 54
Mahalanobis model, 142
Malthusian theory, 326, 327, 330
Marginal cost, of labor, 361, 362
Marginal product, 119, 395, 440
of labor, 356, 359–362, 365, 382, 425
Marginal return, 428
Marginal utility, diminishing, 268, 390
Market, 4
capital, 149, 226–237, 354
input, 413
labor, 413
land, 413
limited, 153
missing, 5, 714
Market conditions, 230
Market demand, 628

Market efficiency, 450
Market equilibrium, 234
Market failure, 413, 714
   approach, 4
Marketing agents, 538
Marshall Plan, 140
Maximal productivity, 444
Measurement errors, 79
Mechanization, 447, 453, 514
Mental time horizon, 509, 510, 550, 551, 555,
   556, 607, 773, 774
MERCOSUR, 745
MFN, *see* Most favored nation
Micro-inertia, 307
Microfinance, 578–584
   institutions, 583, 584
   performance, 582, 583
   viability, 581
Migration, 505, 520
   restrictions, 382–384, 386
   rural–urban, 36–38
Missing markets, 403
Mobility, 171, 520, 521, 557
   matrix, 19, 20
Moneylender, *see* Lenders, informal, 536
Moral hazard, 270, 271, 404, 463–465, 602
Mortality, 309–312, 324
   decline, 306
Most favored nation, 713
   principle, 713, 725, 746, 747
MPK, *see* Capital, marginal product of
MPL, *see* Labor, marginal product of
Multicropping, 333, 515, 518
Multilateralism, *see* Trade, multilateralism
Multiplicity, 152

NAFTA, *see* North American Free Trade
   Agreement
Nash equilibrium, 759–765, 767, 768, 770, 771
No-default constraint, 551, 552, 558; *see also*
   Default
No-shirking constraint, 510–512, 520
Nonmonitored tasks, 507–515
North American Free Trade Agreement, 713,
   714, 726, 730, 733–735
NTB, *see* Trade, nontariff barriers
Nutrient consumption, 265, 278
Nutrients, 265, 266
   levels, 251
   minimum, 250
Nutrition, 237, 249–251, 253, 258, 261–267, 274,
   489, 500
   and labor markets, 272
   and productivity, 278
   supplements, 263
   and work capacity, 275–279

Nutritional status, 272
   a model, 500–504
   capacity effect, 502, 503
   resting metabolism effect, 502, 503
Nutritive value, 263

Occupational choice, 232
   credit constraint, 229
OECD, *see* Organization for Economic
   Cooperation and Development
Old-age security, 308–311, 313–316, 318, 324,
   327, 331
On-the-job training, 499, 500
OPEC, *see* Organization of Petroleum Exporting
   Countries
Operation Barga, 444, 445, 449, 458
Opportunity cost, 355
   of labor, 425
Ordinary least squares, 787–789
Organization for Economic Cooperation and
   Development, 48
Organization of Petroleum Exporting Countries,
   621
Oshima–Kuznets hypothesis, 202, 204
Outmigration, 304
Output, 81, 85, 92, 117
   per capita, 65, 93
Ownership holdings, 412
Ownership rights, 421

Pareto improvement, 727
Pareto optimality, 276
Participation constraint, 476, 477
Patent, 108, 109, 111
Patron–client system, 506, 507
Penn World Tables, 12
Perfect competition, 118, 641
PGR, *see* Poverty gap ratio, 255
Piece rate, 490, 497
   minimum, 495, 496, 498, 499
Pigou–Dalton transfer principle, 290
Political systems, 221
Polygyny, 324
Population
   age distribution, 300
   cumulative shares, 182
   demand, 335
   density, 333
   effective, 72
   female-to-male ratio, 286
   growth, 33, 37, 55, 60–63, 65, 68, 71, 72, 82, 84,
   86–88, 103, 295–340
   growth, rates, 131
Population growth
   demographic effect, 333
   patterns, 296

Population growth rate, 298
  age structure, 299, 300
Population principle, 175, 178, 181
Poverty, 20, 249–292, 331
  absolute, 251
  chronic, 252
  concept of, 250
  correlates, 250
  functional impact of, 250, 267–288
  and household size, 258
  and the household, 279–288
  measure of, 253–256
  policies for alleviation, 250
  relative, 251
  rural, 259
  temporary, 252
  unequal sharing of, 279–281
  urban, 259
Poverty gap ratio, 255, 256, 290
Poverty line, 250, 251, 253, 254, 262, 291
  calorie-based, 262
  country-specific, 257
  universal, 256
Poverty measure, bias, 254
PPF, *see* Production possibility frontier
PPP, *see* Purchasing power parity
Price
  autarkic relative, 628, 629
  distortions, 16
  international, 12, 13, 15
  international relative, 628, 629
  market, 15
  ratio, autarkic, 628
  relative, 13
Price elasticity, 658, 659
Price support, 370
Principal–agent model, 435, 771–773
Principal–agent theory, 463–474, 483
  incentive constraint, 465, 469
  participation constraint, 465, 466, 469
Prisoners' Dilemma, 452, 713, 717–721, 749–751,
    760–762, 773
  common resources, 761
  fertility, 761
Privatization, 697, 703
Product curve
  average, 394, 395
  marginal, 394
Production, 110, 111, 329, 332, 451
  absolute cost, 630
  autarkic, 642
  capital–labor ratio, 632, 641
  cost of, 357, 641
  economic, 99
  economies of scale, 639

efficient, 632
  factors of, 107, 171
  inputs, 122
  levels, 639
  returns to scale, 640–642
  scale, 639
  structure, 34
Production function, 65, 71, 85, 88, 91, 93, 109,
    110, 117, 119, 328, 356, 364, 424, 425, 427,
    428, 432, 447, 569, 571
  Cobb–Douglas, 84, 91–93
  per capita, 93
Production methods, 357
  capital-intensive, 514
Production possibility frontier, 633–636, 647
Productivity, 110, 113–115, 121, 152, 443
  agricultural, 303, 307
  forecast, 114
  individual, 72
  and insurance markets, 448, 449
  and labor markets, 449, 450
  and land size, 415, 446–455
  market efficiency, 447
  nonmonetized input, 447
  and technology, 447, 448
Products, 41
  marginal, 118
  primary, 38–41
Profit, 111, 115, 236
  business, 228, 230, 231
  net, 229
Profit maximization, 382, 394
Profitability, intrinsic, 141
Property rights, 445
Protectionism, *see* Trade, protectionism
  second-best arguments, 714, 715
Purchasing power, 219
  parity, 12, 13, 15, 257
PWT, *see* Penn World Tables

Quality of life, index, 28, 30
Quotas, 657–659, 668, 676, 714, 740
  protective, 720
  and tariffs, equivalence of, 662

R&D, *see* Research and development
Ranking, 114
Ranks, 31
Rate of return, 135, 144, 145, 219
  physical capital, 105
Real estate, values, 112
Redistribution, 211, 215, 216, 236
  political, 218–220, 222
Reference man, 273
Regionalism, *see* Trade, regionalism

Regression, 78, 90, 204, 205, 208, 221, 599
  cross-sectional, 203
  equation, 787
  linear, 204
Regression analysis, 783–804; *see also* Statistical
    methods
  bias, 795, 796
  coefficient regression, 789
  covariance, 789
  dummy variable, 793, 794
  multivariate, 790–794
  multivariate, nonlinear, 792, 793
  ordinary least squares, 787–789
  prediction error, 788
  significance, 794–804
  significance, confidence intervals, 803, 804
  significance, hypothesis testing, 801–803
  significance, null hypothesis, 798, 799, 802
  significance, standard errors, 799, 800
  significance, t-distribution, 800, 801
  sum of squared errors, 787, 788
Regressive transfer, 177, 181
Relative deprivation, 256
Relative income principle, 176, 178
Rental market, 483
Research and development, 108–113
Resources
  allocation, 450
  depletion, 320, 332
  environmental, 332
  infrastructural, 332
  transfer of, 181, 182
Retirement plan, employer-subsidized, 308
Returns to capital, 81, 225
Returns to scale, 114, 118, 258
  and market size, 150–152
  constant, 92, 107
  increasing, 147
  increasing, and entry into markets, 148–150
  technological, 451
Reverse leasing, 423
Ricardian model, 629, 635
Risk, 36, 270, 348, 442, 443, 448, 449, 463–467,
    557, 594, 598, 603
  high, 553–555
  low, 553–555
  nonobservable, 553
  observable, 553
Risk aversion, 388–393, 395, 431–437, 516
Risk sharing, 443
Rural–urban interaction, 353
Rural–urban migration, 36–38, 123, 348, 361,
    366, 372–395, 513

SAL, *see* Structural adjustment loan
Sales, market-determined, 370

Sampling income
  absolute, 79
  per capita, 79
  relative, 79
Sanctions, 226
  on future loans, 227
  on trade relationships, 227
  social, 605–607, 610, 612
Savings, 52, 54, 59, 61, 63, 86, 100, 102, 103, 213,
    219, 222, 309, 327, 328, 331, 355
  aggregate, 218
  and aspirations, 214
  average, 213
  endogeneity, 58
  investment and, 53
  levels, 59
  rate of, 55, 58, 67, 70, 84, 86, 88, 103, 105, 111,
    115, 131, 211, 215–217
  savings rate, marginal, 212–215, 218
  savings rate, national, 215
  total, 214
Savings–income curve, 213, 214
Scatter diagram, 30; *see also* Statistical methods
Scatter plot, *see* Statistical methods, scatter
  diagrams
Screening, and sharecropping, 474–478
Seasonality, 515, 516, 518, 519, 531
Sector, leading, 140–142
Selection bias, 77
Self-consumption, 348
Self-employment, 260, 261, 495
Self-insurance, 271
Self-sufficiency-in-grain program, 371
Semi-attached labor, 507
Sharecropper–owner, 431
Sharecropping, 419–421, 423, 424, 426, 429, 430,
    433, 434, 436–438, 440, 441, 453
  and screening, 474–478
Shares, population, 181
Sibling rivalry, 285
Slavery, 278, 407–409
Soak-up effect, 381
Social contract, 227
Social legitimization, 324
Social mechanisms, 226
Social norms, 155, 156, 323–326
Social security, 308, 309
Socioeconomic standards, 251
Solow model, 64–71, 74, 81–84, 86, 89–99, 100,
    104, 107, 115, 131, 328–332
Stabilization, 691–694, 703
Standard deviation, 80; *see also* Statistical
  methods
Standard of living, 19, 216

Startup cost
  of a business, 235
  ratio to wealth changes over time, 235
Statistical methods
  arithmetic mean, 778
  coefficient of correlation, 781
  correlation, 780–782
  covariance, 780–782
  cross-sectional data, 777, 778
  random variables, 780–782
  regression analysis, 777, 783–804
  scatter diagrams, 783–785
  standard deviation, 779, 780
  time series, 777, 778
  variance, 779, 780
Steady state, 66–70, 73, 82, 83, 85, 89
  distribution, 242
  distribution of wealth, 243
  growth, 328
  multiple with imperfect capital markets,
    241–244
Structural adjustment, 684, 685, 690, 691,
    694–696
  loan, 703
Structural adjustment program
  an example, 696–699
  export liberalization, 695, 696
  fiscal and monetary discipline, 696
  import liberalization, 694, 695
Subsidy, 663
  fertilizer, 370, 696
  wage, 383, 384, 386, 387
  wage, implementation, 387
Subsistence, 59
  needs, 213
  wealth, 242
Sum of squared errors, 787, 788
Summers–Heston data set, 14, 19, 79, 105
Supply, 138, 152
  economic, 335
Supply and demand, 198, 275, 658–660, 691
Supply and demand curves, 233, 234, 243
Supply curve
  domestic, 663
  labor, 232
Surplus labor, 354–360, 365, 366, 381
  versus surplus laborers, 360, 361

Targeting, 314
Tariff, 657–659, 668, 676, 714, 715, 718, 721, 738,
    749
  import, 655
  large-country, 655, 656
  multilateral reduction of, 727–730
  prohibitive, 729
  protective, 720

Tariff war, 718, 749
Tax, 222, 656, 694
  business, 218
  confiscatory, 218
  excise, 218
  increment, 218
  investment income, 219
  lump-sum, 219, 449
  marginal rates, 218
  profit, 387, 572
  redistributive, 211
  reforms, 703
  sales, 218
Technical knowledge, 99, 110
Technical progress, 71–73, 84, 85, 87, 89, 100,
    103, 107–119, 122, 131, 210, 306, 328, 329,
    332–336, 352, 354
  cross-section prediction, 337
  gains in knowledge, 108
  rate, 82, 83, 99, 111
  supply driven, 336
  time-series prediction, 337
  transfer of knowledge, 108
Technology
  cost, 133
  and productivity, 447, 448
  progress, 514, 520
Tenancy, 411, 412, 418, 448
  cost sharing of inputs, 437–439
  double-incentive problem, 436, 437
  fixed-rent, 423, 424, 474–478
  incentives, 423–431
  informal, 418
  limited liability, 439
  long-term, 423
  screening, 440, 441
  terms of, 423
Tenancy contract, 466–474
  credit-cum-tenancy, 420–445
  first-best, 467, 468, 472
  fixed-rent, 419–445
  second-best, 468–474
  share, 419–445
Terms of trade, 40
TFP, *see* Total factor productivity
Third World, 3, 296
Time series, 206; *see also* Statistical methods
Time-bound operations, 413
Total income, 494
Total factor productivity, 117–123, 371, 447, 452
  growth in, 118
  level, 118
Trade, 121
  barriers, 621
  capital goods, 626
  capital markets, 652, 653

catching up, 650–652
coordination failure, 653, 654
creation, 726–729, 746
distribution of gains, 648–650
diversion, 726–729, 746
free, 711, 712, 714–718, 721–725, 728, 729, 746, 748, 752
free-trade bloc, 748
free-trade theorem, 748–750
free-trade zones, 724
global free, 750
income and wealth distribution, 654, 655
increasing returns, 652, 653
interindustry, 640
international, 38, 40, 41, 152, 154, 656
international, increasing returns, 638
international comparative advantage, 627–630
international free, 714
international patterns, 621–626
intra-industry, 642
liberalization, 729
lobby, 720, 722
multilateralism, 723–725
nontariff barriers to, 715, 716, 725
overall losses, 650–656
positive externalities, 653, 654
preference-based, 636–638, 642
preferences, 636–638
protectionism, 714–725
reforms, 703
regionalism, 726
restricted, 714–725
sanctions, 227
terms of, 40
Trade agreements
  multilateral, 712
  unilateral, 712
Trade policy, 121
  corrective, 714
  distributive effects, 647–650
  gains, 647
  gains-from-trade, 647–649
  import substitution, 656–676
  liberalization, partial, 726
  liberalization issues, 725–753
  multilateralism, 746–753
  north–north agreements, 735–740
  north–south agreements, *see* Trade policy, regional agreements among dissimilar countries
  regional agreements, 727–746
  regional agreements among dissimilar countries, 730–735
  regional agreements among similar countries, 735–746
  regionalism, 746–753

south–south agreements, 740–746
  welfare effects, 682
  welfare effects, static and dynamic, 665–670
Trading bloc, 729, 746
  regional, 730
Transfers, 656, 694
  regressive, 187, 189
Transfer-sensitivity principle, 291
Trickle down hypothesis, 226
Tunnel effect, 200, 201, 209

Uncertainty, 515
Underdevelopment, 3, 4, 20, 25–33
Undernutrition, 27, 60, 249–292, 499, 502; *see also* Nutrition
  anthropometric measures of, 262
  chronic, 262
  effects of, 272
Unemployment, 376
  disguised, 360, 362, 364, 365
  involuntary, 488, 493, 498
  rate, 276, 400, 486, 731
  voluntary, 497
Unionization, 372, 373
Use rights, 417, 418, 441–445, 449, 458
Usufructuary mortgage, 563
Usufructuary rights, 546
Utility, 466, 469, 472, 517, 519, 602, 606, 607
  expected, 390
  marginal, 517
Utility function, 389–391, 432

Variance, *see* Statistical methods

Wage
  agricultural, 380, 381, 384
  casual, 511–513
  equilibrium, 232, 487
  formal, 384
  formal-sector, 383
  minimum, 250
  minimum industrial, 365
  permanent, 509, 510, 512, 513
  reservation, 477
  urban, 380
Wage labor, 435
Wage rate, 211, 231–234, 315, 316, 365, 366, 377, 450
  equilibrium, 374
Wages, 210, 242, 317, 357, 360, 364, 372, 373, 486, 494, 508, 511
  casual, 509
  gross, 386
  industrial, 367
  women's, and fertility, 316–318

Weak transfers principle, 290
Wealth
    distribution and equilibrium, 230–234
    distribution of, 169–174, 198, 242
    evolution of, 242
    level, 243

Widowhood, 282, 283
Work capacity, 272, 273, 275, 489, 494, 500
    and nutrition, 275–279
World Bank, 701–705
World trade, *see* Trade, international
World Trade Organization, 716, 723, 724

Debraj Ray is Professor of Economics at Boston University.